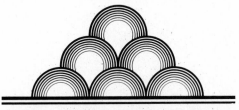

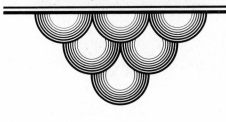

THE ROLLING STONE
RECORD GUIDE

THE

RollingStone ®

RECORD

GUIDE

**Reviews and ratings of
almost 10,000 currently available
rock, pop, soul, country, blues,
jazz, and gospel albums**

**Edited by Dave Marsh
with John Swenson**

RollingStone.

A Random House / Rolling Stone Press Book

All rights reserved under International and Pan-American Copyright
Conventions. Published in the United States by Random House,
Inc., New York, and simultaneously in Canada by Random House of
Canada Limited, Toronto.

Library of Congress Cataloging in Publication Data
Marsh, Dave.
The Rolling stone record guide.
1. Music, Popular (Songs, etc.) — Discography.   2. Sound record-
ings — Reviews.   I. Swenson, John, joint author.
II. Rolling stone.   III. Title.
ML156.4.P6M37   789.9′136′4   79-4757
ISBN 0-394-41096-3
ISBN 0-394-73535-8 pbk.

Manufactured in the United States of America
First Edition

Acknowledgments

This has been, in the best sense, a collaborative creation. We are especially indebted to several writers who contributed their expertise in helping determine which artists should be included: Bob Blumenthal, with his encyclopedic perspective on jazz; Ira Mayer, who did a similarly massive job with folk music; Chet Flippo and Martha Hume for their country music insights; Joe McEwen, who provided the special comprehensive soul music knowledge of a true Philly kid; and Kit Rachlis, who outlined the blues section. Kit was also a valuable compatriot in setting up the initial systems that made the project work as smoothly as it did, and in doing some of the early assigning and editing.

Malu Halasa and Susanne Weil did pinpoint research jobs. Barry Singer did some research and such a wide variety of other jobs that it is hard to think of him as a college intern; we would have been lost without his aid. To the other interns and research assistants, William Oei, Jeri Simon, Andy Clark, Seth Flagsberg and Ken

Gormley, we also extend our gratitude.

The staff at WKCR, the Columbia University radio station, and at J&R Music Stores in New York allowed us access to their jazz material, which proved an indispensable aid. Several dozen record company publicists made available several thousand records and a good deal of other information. From time to time, they must have been certain that this book was mythical. We probably didn't thank them in sufficient profusion then and would like to do so now.

Jann Wenner, Sarah Lazin at Rolling Stone Press, Susan Bolotin, and most of all, Rob Cowley at Random House each grasped the concept of the *Record Guide* and encouraged us in doing a good rather than a speedy job. Rob, particularly, sped us through the production process with as much finesse as any editors could have asked. His insights into some of the more arcane byways of American music were also helpful, even if we didn't always act sufficiently appreciative.

Contents

Introduction

In rock's twenty-five-year existence, hundreds of books have attempted to define or at least circumscribe the music or some part of the experience of hearing it. But until now rock has lacked a basic reference work keyed to the central unit of consumption: the LP. The oldies guides list singles, and their ratings tend to reflect market value (that is, price) rather than aesthetics, scarcity rather than intrinsic worth. But whether it's on a blue Chess label or a more recent orange one, Chuck Berry's "Maybellene" has a worth that transcends its cost. In that sense, the best creations of rock artists are genuinely priceless, and the worst genuinely worthless. This book tries to sort them out, ignoring neither the guilty nor the innocent but standing them side by side, as they coexist on record shelves everywhere.

We haven't tried to codify rock. For one thing, the form is too new and, in the strictest sense, undefined to allow that. On the other hand, a good deal of what we have had to say is merely a repetition of what's conventionally understood: we aren't the people to tell you the Beatles were uncreative. We hope we can say that we have uncovered a certain number of unsuspected gems, and we have certainly been compelled to deflate the (critical or public) reputations of certain previously overestimated performers. In the main, we've probably been overgenerous, which is not necessarily a fault. This book is, after all, designed at least as much for the general reader as for the rock cultist. (For those who get too lost, though, there is a glossary to guide you through our reviews, and a bibliography to direct you to some of the better volumes on the subject.)

The Rolling Stone Record Guide is unprecedented for a reason. Compiling a comprehensive critical guide to such a volatile area is virtually impossible. When we first began to compile this book, in late 1976, the task seemed straightforward enough. By the time the job is finished, though, about one-third of the entries will represent artistic entities who did not exist when we began. Rock groups break up, reform and spin off solo performers more quickly than the somewhat ponderous processes of print can digest them. Those interested in up-to-the-minute evaluations are better off in the pages of *Rolling Stone* itself, which reviews about 500 records yearly—something like 15 percent of the U.S. record industry's annual output. The *Record Guide* is intended for those who would rather probe the music's past, those who don't stop in the front of the record store, where the new releases are kept, but keep on going to the back, where American musical history is stored.

In order to make the *Record Guide* workable, certain guidelines were necessarily established. We focused on records released in the United States, and more specifically, upon those that are in print—that is, records that could conceivably be ordered by your local record merchant, however unlikely it may be that the store would automatically have them in stock. We chose to do LPs rather than singles because LPs have a longer shelf life, and because most people orient their buying to albums (and tapes).

We've also limited ourselves to music that is rock, is associated with rock, has influenced rock or has been influenced by rock. That is quite enough, of course, since it inevitably impinges upon other areas: blues, jazz, gospel, mainstream pop itself. But we haven't attempted to create a survey that's as comprehensive in terms of jazz recordings, for instance, as for modern rock and pop. This is a task for someone else, and it needs to be done, if only so the uninformed can have a guide to what to hear. It is shocking that there is not a book like this for the jazz listener, or the blues newcomer.

Naturally, we violated every one of our rules when it served our purpose to do so. The most difficult problem was what's in print. Records are deleted from company catalogues almost as quickly as they're conceived—often too hastily in both cases. At most large companies, if an album doesn't sell a certain minimun number of copies—say, 5,000—in a calendar year, it is dropped. This means that the early work of Aretha Franklin or Smokey Robinson is available only in anthologies or bowdlerized budget editions, a situation less than ideal from a critical viewpoint. One of the things that creating the *Record Guide* constantly brought home to us was how cavalierly corporations treat music. With the increasing concentration of record-industry power in the hands of corporate conglomerates, with all their cost efficiency and bureaucracy, little hope can be extended for a change in such policies. Sad to say, rhythm & blues fans may someday be forced to pirate or bootleg Wilson Pickett's vintage work, just as jazz and classical fans now do with rare works of the past.

A related problem is what happens when a record company itself enters an area of uncertain ownership. At this writing, the Chess Records catalogue is in severe disrepair because it has changed ownership several times in the Seventies. The catalogue's current owner, All Platinum, began a promising reissue program in 1977 (when the material was first acquired), but that program has now fallen by the wayside. Similarly, Fantasy has done little with the vast collection of Stax treasures it now controls; it would be delightful to see reissues of the quality of Fantasy's Prestige and Milestone jazz and folk sets created for the Stax R&B material.

Our basic reference guide for determining what was available was *Phonolog*, that massive yellow ring-bound volume with which habitues of record stores are probably already familiar. *Phonolog* lists thousands of records, cross-referenced by artist, song title and LP title, updated thrice weekly (thus the ring binder). It is weak on small, less commercially oriented labels, and we supplemented its information with the monthly *Schwann Records & Tape Guide*, and where possible with the label catalogues themselves. Still, it is often some time between the deletion of an album and its official demise in any of these sources; the result was that a number of

entries were written concerning artists whose entire body of work (usually no more than two or three LPs) was cut out. Those reviews appear in this volume, both as a guide to what is likely to be turning up in bargain bins in the near future, and with an eye to the future. When a revised edition of the *Record Guide* is published, it will list all cutouts. At the very least, the phrase "now deleted" at the bottom of a review here indicates what might be turning up for $1.98 at Woolworth's.

Where only a portion of an artist's work is deleted, we have not listed that portion (although reference may be made to the cutouts in the text). This is an odd circumstance—it may mean that the work of a minor or a genuinely awful performer is more fully catalogued here than the work of a master. But given the editors' hope that the *Record Guide* will be of some value as a shopping aid, it seems the best compromise.

Imported records are listed only where essential—i.e., where the body of a major artist's work is ill represented in the U.S. issues, as is the case with Buddy Holly's. Once again, future editions of the *Record Guide* ought to supply more complete import editions, particularly as the upward spiral of American record prices makes import LPs more competitive.

We chose to organize the book by artist, since that is the best way in which to see work in its perspective; the alternative suggestion was to order it chronologically, but that is confusing (what year does one date an anthology?). The listings are similarly in alphabetical order, and undated, since the text provides enough temporal reference points to give the sense of an album's era. Immediacy is central to rock, but the *Record Guide* is concerned with how and why the best of it lasts.

Establishing criteria for including performers was as perplexing as any other problem we faced. Obviously it would be fatuous to ignore the Bee Gees, sectarian not to include Billy Joel, even though these are not "rock" performers in the critical sense of the term. We took it as our job to survey most Seventies pop, all rhythm & blues, a good deal of black pop and a limited amount of country music. The reason why we chose less country than black pop is simple: when C&W strays from its roots, it is more likely to drift toward **MOR**, while the interchange between rock and black popular forms is constant—Funkadelic owes a great deal to Sixties progressive rock, while modern rock borrows heavily (still) from innovations in black pop recording techniques (including disco). We also attempted to incorporate most pop artists who reflected a specific rock influence—not Ferrante and Teicher's Beatle interpretations but surely Barbra Streisand's recordings with rock-based rhythm sections. Also, we wanted mainstream pop performers who had some sort of influence on rock and R&B performers: Frank Sinatra as the teen idol most nearly antedating Elvis Presley, Nat "King" Cole for his influence upon Ray Charles and other R&B singers.

There are also supplemental sections on jazz, R&B and gospel, as well as a section of reviews of anthologies and soundtracks. It is worthwhile to emphasize once more that these do not attempt to be as comprehensive as the pop/rock listings; any reasonably well informed jazz buff could recite a truckload of omissions. Jazz performers, like blues and gospel ones, were chosen for their influence upon rock and R&B, or because they showed that influence, in the case of some more recent artists. A few—King Oliver, Jelly Roll Morton, Louis Armstrong, Duke Ellington and Count Basie, among others—were included because their influence upon *all* American music makes it impossible to ignore them in any survey. Again, there is a need for a comprehensive jazz survey, and it is the editors' hope that the limitations of the *Record Guide* supplement will spur someone qualified to do the job.

Given these restrictions, the present volume is comprehensive in terms of artists listed through about mid-1978, with the addition of a few significant debuts released a bit later than that (e.g., the Cars). The records within each artist listing are comprehensive through late 1978; we have been able to add a few of the more important early 1979 releases as well. We, too, wish that a more up-to-date volume was possible, but there's *Rolling Stone* itself for that. We had to stop somewhere or be trapped like Sisyphus. But since *The Rolling Stone Record Guide* is intended as a permanent reference work, the editors are already contemplating the arduous task of compiling future editions. Toward that end, we'd appreciate interested readers sending us their complaints, comments, notifications of omission and any additional relevant oddments to Rolling Stone Press, 745 Fifth Avenue, New York, N.Y. 10022. We'll attempt to incorporate as many of them as possible next time.

To the extent that the *Record Guide* has precedents, they are Robert Christgau's monthly "Consumer Guide" column in the *Village Voice*, which lists twenty albums by letter grade (A to F), and Leonard Maltin's *TV Movies*, which uses a star ranking system similar to our own to evaluate several thousand films that are likely to turn up on the airwaves. From Maltin, we took the notion of a comprehensive guidebook; from Christgau, the concept of the consumer guide as the most pungent, pithy (and acerbic) form of criticism.

But what we learned while putting the *Record Guide* together was of even greater value. Writing about performers as diverse as Roscoe Holcomb, Elvis Presley and the Sex Pistols ought to be confusing, but for us, it was extraordinarily enlightening, not only because there were connections we'd previously missed, great moments that lay dormant in our minds and new music to discover and evaluate, but also because, as we progressed, the whole of popular music began to seem a seamless web. There is a certain strength in hearing Ronnie Lane sing rock as modern as today in accents as old as the British Isles, or listening to Ry Cooder merge all sorts of North American music into an individual style; piecing together the disparate elements that comprise the *Record Guide*, we got to know a fragment of the joy that such men must feel in their creations. In his monumental *Mystery Train: Images of America in Rock 'n' Roll Music*, Greil Marcus has done an extensive study of such linkages—for example, between Sly Stone's "Thank You for Talkin' to Me Africa" and "Staggolee," a story as old as the folk blues.

We experienced such shocks of recognition over and over again, whether in finding Al Green quoting country blues in a disco number or simply by discovering that General Johnson, a contemporary black writer/performer, was the man who wrote and sang the Showmen's great anthem "It Will Stand." In the end, after all the months of winnowing and verifying, it is Johnson's words that stick with us, and we hope, with you:

Don't nickname it
You might as well claim it . . .
It'll be here forever and ever
Ain't gonna fade, never no never.

Dave Marsh
February 26, 1979

Ratings

★ ★ ★ ★ ★

**Indispensable: a record that must be included in
any comprehensive collection.**

★ ★ ★ ★

**Excellent: a record of substantial merit, though flawed
in some essential way.**

★ ★ ★

**Good: a record of average worth, but one that might possess considerable
appeal for fans of a particular style.**

★ ★

**Mediocre: records that are artistically insubstantial,
though not truly wretched.**

★

**Poor: records in which even technical competence is at question,
or which are remarkably ill-conceived.**

■

**Worthless: records that need never (or should never) have been created.
Reserved for the most bathetic bathwater.**

The illustrations are the covers of five-star albums.

Reviewers

EDITORS

Dave Marsh (D.M.) was a founding editor of *Creem*, a music critic at *Newsday* and an editor at the *Real Paper* in Boston before joining *Rolling Stone* as an associate editor in 1975. Marsh writes the "American Grandstand" column, which appears monthly in *Rolling Stone*. He is also the author of a book on Bruce Springsteen.

John Swenson (J.S.) grew up a Who fanatic in Brooklyn and began writing about his mania while in college. He became records editor at *Crawdaddy* in the mid-Seventies, and since then has been performing similar functions for *Circus Weekly* while writing books about the Who, the Beatles and Kiss. Swenson is a frequent contributor to *Rolling Stone*.

CONTRIBUTORS

Billy Altman (B.A.) founded the first magazine called *Punk* in 1973. He is currently records review editor of *Creem*.

Bob Blumenthal (B.B.) is an attorney in Massachusetts who writes copiously about jazz for both *Rolling Stone* and the *Boston Phoenix*.

Georgia Christgau (G.C.) is a copy editor at the *Village Voice*, where she also contributes articles on music.

Jean Charles Costa (J.C.C.) is a guitarist who was editor of the defunct music publication *Gig*.

Chet Flippo (C.F.) is a *Rolling Stone* associate editor with a master's degree in journalism which he received at the University of Texas for writing a thesis on the rock press. Flippo is currently working on a definitive biography of Hank Williams.

Russell Gersten (R.G.) has been writing about soul music for more than a decade. He also works in special education in the Pacific Northwest.

Mikal Gilmore (M.G.) is *Rolling Stone*'s Los Angeles bureau chief.

Alan E. Goodman (A.E.G.) is a former disc jockey and reviewer for *Crawdaddy* who now works for Columbia Records.

Peter Herbst (P.H.) is a senior editor of *Rolling Stone* and former music editor of the *Boston Phoenix*.

Stephen Holden (S.H.) is the author of *Triple Platinum*, a novel about the record industry, and a frequent contributor to *Rolling Stone* and the *Village Voice*.

Martha Hume (M.H.) writes a weekly music column for the *New York Daily News* and is a former editor of *Country Music*.

Gary Kenton (G.K.) is a former editor of *Fusion* and *Creem*.

Bruce Malamut (B.M.) is a music reviewer for the *Village Voice*, *Crawdaddy* and *Circus Weekly*.

Greil Marcus (G.M.), the author of *Mystery Train: Images of America in Rock 'n' Roll Music*, writes a monthly music column for *New West* and a book column for *Rolling Stone*, where he is an associate editor.

Ira Mayer (I.M.) is pop music critic of the *New York Post*.

Joe McEwen (J.Mc.) was once known to Boston radio listeners as the disc jockey Mr. C. He has written under both names for the *Boston Phoenix*, *Real Paper*, *Village Voice* and *Rolling Stone*. McEwen is currently an A&R man at Columbia Records.

David McGee (D.Mc.) writes the "New York, New York" column for *Record World*.

John Milward (J.B.M.) is a reviewer for the *Chicago Reader* and *Rolling Stone*. Milward was also music critic for the *Chicago Daily News* before that paper's demise.

Teri Morris (T.M.), American editor of *ZigZag* and a contributing editor of *Bomp* magazine in Los Angeles, lives on a cattle ranch in California.

John Morthland (J.Mo.), a former editor of *Rolling Stone*, the *Real Paper*, *Country Music* and *Creem*, contributes frequently to these and a variety of other publications.

Paul Nelson (P.N.) founded the *Little Sandy Review*, edited *Circus Weekly* when it was still called *Hullabaloo*, and currently is an associate editor in charge of *Rolling Stone*'s record reviews.

Alan Niester (A.N.) is a high school teacher in Toronto who writes for a variety of American and Canadian magazines.

Rob Patterson (R.P.) writes a column for the Newspaper Enterprise Association and has written for *Circus Weekly* and *Gig*.

Kit Rachlis (K.R.) is music editor of the *Boston Phoenix* and has written for *Rolling Stone*, the *Village Voice* and the late *New Times*.

Wayne Robins (W.R.) is a former editor of *Creem* who is pop music critic at *Newsday*.

Frank Rose (F.R.), a contributor to the *Village Voice* and *Rolling Stone*, is currently at work on a book about styles of masculinity.

Michael Rozek (M.R.) has written for *Rolling Stone*, *Down Beat*, *High Fidelity* and the *Village Voice*. He is currently a copywriter for Arista Records.

Fred Schruers (F.S.) is a contributing editor of *Rolling Stone*. He's also contributed to the *New York Daily News*, *Black Sports* and a number of other magazines.

Tom Smucker (T.S.) works for the New York Telephone Company.

Ariel Swartley (A.S.) is a contributor to the *Boston Phoenix*, *Rolling Stone*, the *Village Voice* and other publications.

Ken Tucker (K.T.) is rock music critic for the *Los Angeles Herald Examiner*.

Charley Walters (C.W.) manages a record store on Nantucket Island, where he lives year-round.

Record Companies

A&M
ABC
Abkco
Accent (**Ac.**)
Accent/GNP (**Ac./GNP**)
Adelphi (**Adel.**)
Advance (**Adv.**)
Advent
Advent Corporation
  (**Advent Corp.**)
AECO
Aerospace (**Aero.**)
Afka
Aircheck (**Air.**)
All Ears (**All E.**)
All Platinum (**All Pl.**)
Alligator (**Alli.**)
Alshire (**Alsh.**)
Alston (**Als.**)
Althia (**Alt.**)
Amherst (**Amh.**)
Amin
Anchor
Andrew's Music (**Andr.**)
Angel
Anthem (**Anth.**)
Antilles (**Ant.**)
Apon
Apple
Archives of Folk and Jazz
  Music (**Arc. Folk**)
Archive of Piano Music
  (**Arc. Piano**)
Arctic
Argo
Arhoolie (**Arhoo.**)
Ariola (**Ario.**)
Ariola-America (**Ario.-
  Amer.**)
Arion
Arista (**Ari.**)
Arista/Freedom
  (**Ari./Free**)
Arista/GRP

Arista/Novus (**Ari./No.**)
Aristocrat (**Arist.**)
Art
Artist Direct (**Art.-Dir.**)
Ashbourne (**Ashb.**)
Ashtree (**Ash.**)
ASI
Aspekte
Asylum (**Asy.**)
Atco
At-Home
Atlantic (**Atl.**)
Audio Fidelity (**Audio
  Fi.**)
Audio Masterworks
  (**Audio M.**)
Audiophile (**Audiop.**)
Audio Rarities
Aural Explorer (**Aural**)
Avaklan
Avant
Avant-Garde (**Av.**)
A.V.I.
Avid
Avoca

Backbeat (**Back.**)
Bang
Banjar
Barclay (**Bar.**)
Bareback (**Bare.**)
Barnaby (**Barn.**)
Bay
Bean
Bearsville (**Bears.**)
Bee Hive (**Bee**)
BEEP
Bert & I
Beserkley (**Beserk.**)
Bet-Car
Bethany
Bethlehem (**Beth.**)
Big Sound
Big Tree (**Big**)

Bija
Biograph (**Bio.**)
Billingsgate (**Bill.**)
Birch
Birthright (**Birthr.**)
Biscuit City (**Bisc.**)
Bizarre (**Biz.**)
Blackbird (**Black.**)
Black Lion (**Black L.**)
Black Saint (**Black S.**)
Blank
Blarney Castle (**Blar.**)
Blind Pig (**Blind**)
Bluebird (**Blueb.**)
Blue Canyon (**Blue C.**)
Blue Goose (**Blue G.**)
Blue Labor
Blue Note (**Blue N.**)
Blues Classics (**Blues Cl.**)
Blue Sky (**Blue S.**)
Blue Thumb (**Blue Th.**)
Bomp
Bornand
Boston Brass (**Boston B.**)
Briar
Brunswick (**Bruns.**)
Buckboard (**Buck.**)
Buddah (**Bud.**)
Bullfrog (**Bull.**)
Butterfly (**Butter.**)

Cadence (**Cad.**)
Cadet
Cadet Concept (**Cadet C.**)
Caedmon (**Caed.**)
Calla
Calliope (**Calli.**)
Cambridge (**Cam.**)
Camden (**Camd.**)
Canaan
Candide (**Can.**)
Canto Libre (**Canto L.**)
Canyon
Capitol (**Cap.**)

Capitol/Pickwick
  (Cap./Pick.)
Capitol/Sovereign
  (Cap./Sov.)
Capricorn (Capri.)
Cardinal
Caribou (Cari.)
Carousel
Casablanca (Casa.)
Cash
Casino (Ca.)
Cassandra (Cass.)
Cat
Catalyst (Cata.)
Caytronics (Cay.)
Chalfont (Chal.)
Chaloff (Cha.)
Checker (Check.)
Chelsea (Chel.)
Chess
Chiaroscuro (Chi.)
Chimneyville (Chim.)
Chi-Sound (Chi-S.)
Chi-Town (Chi-T.)
Chocolate City (Choc.)
Choice
Churchill
Chrysalis (Chrys.)
Chrysalis/Warner
  Brothers (Chrys./War.)
CIME
Citadel (Cit.)
Claridge (Clar.)
Classic Jazz (Class.)
CMC
CMH
CMS
CMS/Oryx
CMS/Summit
  (CMS/Sum.)
Colonial (Colo.)
Columbia (Col.)
Columbia Special
  Products (CSP)
Communications Archives
  (Comm. Arc.)
Concept
Concept/Sonet
Concert-Disc (Con.-Disc)
Concord Jazz (Concord
  J.)
Contemporary (Contem.)
Contrast
Coral (Cor.)
Coronet (Coro.)
Corral
Cotillion (Coti.)
Counterpoint/Esoteric
  (Count.)
County (Coun.)

Cracker Barrel (Crack.)
Cream
Creative Sound (Cre.)
Creative World (Cre. W.)
Credo
Crescendo (Cres.)
Crossover (Cross.)
CRI (Composers
  Recordings, Inc.)
Crystal (Crys.)
CSP
CTI
Curtom (Cur.)

Dakar
Dana
Dark Horse (Dark)
Day Spring (Day.)
Decca
De-Lite
Delmark (Del.)
Delos
Deram
Desmar
Desto
Devi
Dharma
Different Drummer (Dif.)
Dionn
Disc
Discovery
Discreet (Discr.)
Discus
Dixieland Jubilee (DJ)
DJM
Dobre
Dolton
Dooto (Doo.)
Doré
Dot
Douglas International
  (Douglas)
Dream
DRG
Duke
Dunhill (Dun.)
Dyer-Bennett
Dyno

Earl
Eb-Sko
ECM/Polydor
  (ECM/Poly.)
ECM/Warner Brothers
  (ECM/War.)
Electrola (Elect.)
Elektra (Elek.)
Emanem (Eman.)
EmArcy (Em.)
Ember

Embryo (Emb.)
End
EMI America (EMI)
Entr'acte (Entr.)
Epic
Era (Eastman-Rochester
  Archives)
Erato
ESP Disk (ESP)
Eterna
Eubie Blake Music
  (EBM)
Euphoria (Euph.)
Event
Everest (Ev.)
Everyman
Excello (Ex.)
Exodus (Exo.)
Expériences Anonymes
  (EA)

F&W
Famous Charisma
  (Famous)
Famous Door (Fam.
  Door)
Fantasy (Fan.)
Fantasy/WMOT
  (Fan./WMOT)
Fiesta
Finnadar (Fin.)
First Amendment (First)
First American (First
  Am.)
First Artists (First Ar.)
Flashlight (Flash)
Flying Crow
Flying Dutchman (Fly.)
Flying Fish (Fly. Fish)
Flying High
Folk-Legacy (Folk-Leg.)
Folklyric
Folkways (Folk.)
Fona
Fontana (Fon.)
Fredonia (Fredo.)
Free Spirit (Free)
Fretless (Fret.)
Futura
Future

Galaxy (Gal.)
Gamble (Gam.)
Gateway (Gate)
Gee
Gemigo
Gemini Hall (Gemini)
Genesis (Gen.)
GHB
Glades

Glendale
GNP Crescendo (GNP)
Gold Mind (Gold)
Golden Age
Golden Crest (GC)
Golden Crest/N.E.
  Conservatory
  (GC/NEC)
Good News (Good N.)
Good Time Jazz (Good
  T.)
Gordy (Gor.)
GP
GP/Beller
Granite (Gran.)
Grapevine (Grape.)
Grass Mountain (Grass)
Grateful Dead (Grate.)
Great Northwest (Great
  N.)
Grecophon (Grec.)
Greedy
Green Linnet (Green)
Grenadilla
Groove Merchant
  (G.M.)
GRT
Grunt
Gryphon (Gry.)
GSC
GTO
Guitar Player Records
  (Guitar)
Guitar World (Guit.)
Gull
Gusto

H&L
Halcyon (Hal.)
Hall of Fame (Hall)
Harlequin (Harl.)
Harmony Music (Har.
  Music)
Harvest (Harv.)
Herwin (Her.)
Hi (Cream) (Hi)
Hickory (Hick.)
Historical (Hist.)
Hitsville (Hits.)
HNH
Horizon (Hori.)
Hula

IAI
Image
IMI
Imperial (Imper.)
Improv
Impulse (Imp.)
Increase (Inc.)

India Navigation (India
  Navig.)
Indian House (Indian)
Inner City (Inner)
Invictus (Inv.)
IPA/Desmar
IPS
IRM
Iron Horse (Iron)
Island (Is.)
Ivory World (Ivory)

J&J
Jamie
Janus
Jay Jay (Jay)
Jazz Classics (Jazz Cl.)
Jazzology (Jazzo.)
Jazz Trip (Jazz T.)
Jazzz
JCOA
Jet
Jewel
JRC
Ju-Pair (Ju)

Kalbala
Kaleidoscope (Kal.)
Kama Sutra (Kam. S.)
Kanawha (Kan.)
Karate (Kar.)
Kayvette (Kayv.)
KBK
Kent
Kenwood (Ken.)
Kicking Mule (Kick.)
King
King Bluegrass (King B.)
Kirshner (Kir.)
Klavier (Kla.)
Kot'ai
Kudu

Labor
Laff
Lamb & Lion (Lamb)
Land o' Jazz (Lan.)
Laurel
Laurel/Protone
  (Laurel/Pro.)
Laurie (Laur.)
Lava Mountain (Lava)
Legacy (Leg.)
LeJoint (LeJ.)
Leviathan (Lev.)
Liberty (Lib.)
Libra
Lifesong (Lifes.)
Light
Limelight (Lime.)

Little David (Li. Dav.)
Little Star (Lit. Star)
Loma
London (Lon.)
London/Decca
  (Lon./Dec.)
Lone Star (Lone)
Los Angeles (Los)
Louisianne
Louisville (Lou.)
LS
Lush

Mace
Mach
Mainstream (Main.)
Major
Malaco (Mal.)
Mamlish (Maml.)
Mango
Manhattan (Manh.)
Mankind (Mank.)
Manticore (Mant.)
Mark
Mark (Creative)
  (Mark/Cre.)
Mark 56
Marlin (Mar.)
Mary
Master Jazz (Mas. J.)
MC
MCA
Media
Melodeon (Melo.)
Melodyland (Melod.)
Memphis (Memp.)
Mercury (Mer.)
MFP
MGM
Midland (Mid.)
Midsong International
  (Mid. Int.)
Milagro
Milestone (Mile.)
Mill City (Mill)
Millennium (Millen.)
Mirror
MirroSound (Mirro.)
Mondo
Monitor (Mon.)
Monmouth-Evergreen
  (Mon.-Ev.)
Monterey (Monte.)
Monument (Monu.)
Morrhythm (Morr.)
Motown (Mo.)
Mountain Railroad
  (Mount.)
Movie Star (Movie)
Mowest (Mow.)

Muse
Mushroom (**Mush.**)
Music Is Medicine (**Music Is**)
Musicor (**Musi.**)
Myrrh

Nashboro (**Nashb.**)
Natural Resources (**Nat.**)
Nemperor (**Nemp.**)
Nessa
New Orleans
New Song (**New S.**)
New World (**New W.**)
Newpax
Nines
No Holds Barred (**No H.**)
Nonesuch (**None.**)

Oasis
Oblivion
Ode
Odyssey (**Odys.**)
Old Timey
Old Town (**Old T.**)
Olivia
Olle
Olympic (University of Washington) (**Olym.**)
Omnisound (**Omni.**)
Onyx
Opus One (**Op. One**)
Original Jazz Library (**Orig. Jazz**)
Original Sound (**Orig. Sound**)
Orion
Outrageous (**Outra.**)
Outstanding (**Out.**)
Ovation (**Ova.**)
Oyster (**Oy.**)

Pablo
Pablo Live (**Pablo L.**)
Pacific (**Pacif.**)
Pacific Jazz (**Pac. J.**)
Painted Smiles (**Paint.**)
Pandora (**Pand.**)
Parachute (**Parach.**)
Paradise
Paragon
Paramount (**Para.**)
Parrot (**Par.**)
Passport (**Pass.**)
Pathways of Sound (**Pathways**)
Paula
Pausa
PBR International (**PBR**)
Peacock (**Pea.**)

Pearl
Pelican (**Pel.**)
People (**Peo.**)
Peters International (**Peters**)
Pfeiffer (**Pfeif.**)
Phantom
Philadelphia International (**Phil.**)
Philips (**Phi.**)
Phil.-L.A. of Soul (**Phil.-L.A.**)
Philly Groove (**Philly**)
Philo
Phoenix
Piccadilly (**Picca.**)
Pickwick (**Pick.**)
Piedmont (**Pied.**)
Pine Tree (**Pine**)
Pip
Planet
Plantation (**Plant.**)
Playboy (**Play.**)
Pleiades (**Plei.**)
PM
Polydor (**Poly.**)
Portrait (**Por.**)
Poseidon (**Pos.**)
Potato (**Pota.**)
Powerpak (**Power.**)
Prestige (**Prest.**)
Private Stock (**Priv.**)
Prodigal (**Prod.**)
Progressive (**Prog.**)
Project 3 (**Proj.**)
Protone (**Prot.**)
P.T.
Puritan (**Puri.**)
Pyramid (**Pyr.**)

QCA
Quadrum (**Qua.**)
Quality (**Qual.**)
Quark
Quintessence (**Quin.**)

Radio Archives (**Radio**)
RAHMP
Ranwood (**Ran.**)
Rare Earth (**Rare**)
Ravenna (**Rav.**)
RCA
Realgood (**Realg.**)
Rebecca
Rebel
Recall
Redwood (New York) (**Redd.**)
Rego
Renaissance (**Ren.**)

Reprise (**Rep.**)
Request
Re/Se
Revelation (**Rev.**)
R.G.B.
Richmond (**Rich.**)
Ridge Runner (**Ridge**)
Riverboat (**River.**)
Riverside (**Riv.**)
Roadshow (**Road.**)
Roast
Rocket (**R.**)
Rocking Horse (**Rocking**)
Rolling Stone (**Rol.**)
Ronn
Roper
Roulette (**Rou.**)
Round
Rounder (**Roun.**)
Roxbury (**Rox.**)
RSO

Sackville (**Sack.**)
Sacred
Salsoul (**Sals.**)
Salvation (**Salv.**)
Sanskrit (**Sans.**)
Savoy
Scala
Scotti Brothers (**Scotti**)
SeaBreeze (**Sea.**)
Seed
SEP International (**SEP**)
Serenus (**Ser.**)
1750 Arch
SFM (Society for Forgotten Music)
Shadybrook (**Shady.**)
Shanachie (**Shan.**)
SHE
Sheba
Shelter (**Shel.**)
Sierra
Silk Purse (**Silk**)
Sine Qua Non (**Sine**)
Sire
Sire/ABC
Skandisk
Skyline
Skylite (**Sky.**)
Smash
Smithsonian
Solar
Solid Rock (**Solid R.**)
Solid Smoke (**Solid S.**)
Solid State (**Solid St.**)
Somnath
Song Bird (**Song**)
Sono
Soul

Soul City (**Soul C.**)
Soul Power (**Soul P.**)
Soul Train (**Soul T.**)
Sound Bird (**Sound B.**)
Sound, Inc.
Sound Stage Seven
  (**Sound S.**)
Sountrak (**Sountr.**)
Southland (**So.**)
Southwind (**Southw.**)
Specialty (**Spec.**)
Spector
Spindizzy (**Spin.**)
Spivey
Spokane
Spoken Arts (**Sp. Arts**)
Spoken Word (**Sp. Word**)
Spotlite (**Spot.**)
Spring
Springboard (**Sp.**)
SSS
Standard (**Stan.**)
Stang
Stanyan (**Sta.**)
Starday (**Star.**)
Stash
State
Stax
Stiff
Stinson (**Stin.**)
Stony Plain (**Stony**)
Strata-East
Strawberry (**Straw.**)
Studio 7
Sun
Sunbeam (**Sunb.**)
Sunnyvale (**Sunny.**)
Surfside (**Surf.**)
Survival
Swan Song (**Swan**)
Sweet Jane (**Sweet J.**)
Symposium (**Symp.**)

T-Neck
Tablight (**Tabli.**)
Tabu
Tabu/Columbia
  (**Tabu/Col.**)

Takoma (**Tak.**)
Tamla (**Tam.**)
Tattoo
Taz-Jaz (**Taz.**)
Telarc
Testament (**Test.**)
Texas Re-Cord Company
  (**Tex.**)
Thimble
Threshold (**Thresh.**)
Tifton (**Tif.**)
Timeless (**Timel.**)
Titanic
TK
Tom 'n' Jerry (**Tom**)
Tomato (**Toma.**)
Tortoise International
  (**Tort.**)
Totem
Tower
TownHall (**Town.**)
Toy
Tradition (**Trad.**)
Trash
Triangle (**Tri.**)
Tribe
Trip
Trix
True North (**True**)
Tru-Gems
Truluv
TSOP
Tulip
Turbo
Turnabout (**Turn.**)
20th Century-Fox (**20th
  Cent.**)
Ty-Ca

UBRES
UK
Unicorn (**Uni.**)
Unit Core
United Artists (**U.
  Artists**)
Unlimited Gold (**Unli.**)
Up Front (**Up. Fr.**)
Utopia (**Ut.**)

Vanguard (**Van.**)
Vanguard Twofers (**Van.
  T.**)
Vegas
Vertigo (**Vert.**)
Verve
Vesper (**Ves.**)
Vetco
Vibration (**Vibr.**)
Virgin
Virgo
Vocalion (**Voc.**)
Voyager (**Voya.**)

Waikiki
Wand
Warner Brothers (**War.**)
Waterfall
Waterhouse (**Waterh.**)
Watt
Westbound (**Westb.**)
Western Hemisphere
  (**Western**)
West 54
Whitfield (**Whit.**)
Who's Who in Jazz
  (**Who's**)
WIM
Windsong (**Wind.**)
Wing and a Prayer
  (**Wing**)
Wizard (**Wiz.**)
WK
WMOT
Wonderland (**Won.**)
Wooden Nickel (**Wood.**)
Word
World Jazz (**World**)
World Library of Sacred
  Music (**WLSM**)

Xanadu (**Xan.**)

Yazoo

Zodiac
Zim
Zap

ROCK, SOUL, COUNTRY AND POP

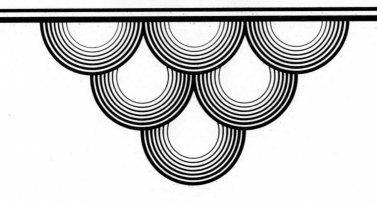

AALON
★★ Cream City / Ari. 4127
Conceptual discos set in Cream City, the futurist urban landscape where Steven Baine's Electric Train plays every Saturday night at the Jungle Desire, earth's hottest disco. The weird mixture of electronic R&B drone music and rock disco used to carry out this story is attention-grabbing, but doesn't sustain interest. "Lonely Princess" and "Jungle Desire" are the points. — J.S.

ABBA
★★ Abba / Atl. 18146
★★ Arrival / Atl. 18207
★★★ Greatest Hits / Atl. 18189
★★ The Album / Atl. 19164
★★ Waterloo / Atl. 18101
This Swedish quartet (two women, two men) is an international phenomenon; their sound—a compendium of white American pop hooks welded to mesmerizing synthesizers and the permanently anxious lead singing of the women—is pleasant and forgettable. In their conscious conquest of Everywhere, they are determined not to offend: a fixed cheeriness pervades, and thus Abba is best taken in small doses—i.e., their singles. Given this every-song-a-smiley-smash approach, the *Greatest Hits* is of the highest quality, even if it is prone to induce both sleep and cavities. — K.T.

AC/DC
■ **High Voltage / Atco 36-142**
■ **Let There Be Rock / Atco 36-151**
■ **Powerage / Atl. 19180**
AC/DC is an Australian hard-rock band whose main purpose on earth apparently is to offend anyone within sight or earshot. They succeed on both counts. — B.A.

ACE
★★ Five-a-Side / Anchor 2001
★ No Strings / Anchor 2020
★ Time for Another / Anchor 2013
This five-man English band competently reprised basic American rock, including soul. *Five-a-Side* contains their only hit, "How Long." — S.H.

JOHNNY ACE
★★★★ Johnny Ace Memorial Album / Duke 71
Johnny Ace achieved legendary status as much for the way he died—losing a game of Russian roulette on Christmas Eve 1954—as for the series of plaintive (slightly off-key) soul ballads he recorded in 1952-54, including "Pledging My Love" and "Never Let Me Go." These are the core of this endearing and historically important collection. — K.G.

ACE SPECTRUM
★ Just Like in the Movies / Atl. 18185
Ace Spectrum is a faceless New York soul group, produced by Tony Silvester and Spectrum member Ed Zant, capable of making well-crafted but eminently forgettable albums. Only one of the group's three albums remains in print, and it is the weakest. — J.MC.

DAVID ACKLES
★★ Five and Dime / Col. KC-32466
Ackles practiced a piano-based "art song" before the advent of "cabaret." His best work is on three out-of-print Elektra albums, notably *American Gothic.* More popular in England than in the United States, Ackles' work is quiet, intelligent and often pretentiously earnest. (Now deleted.) — S.H.

BARBARA ACKLIN
★★★ I Call It Trouble / Bruns. 754187
★★★ I Did It / Bruns. 754166
★★★ Love Makes a Woman / Bruns.
754137
★★★ Seven Days of Night / Bruns. 754148
★★★ Someone Else's Arms / Bruns.
754156

Acklin has been a journeyman soul singer since the late Sixties, and although her only Top Twenty pop success came in 1968 (with "Love Makes a Woman," which made No. 15), she turns in fine, light R&B performances on each of these records, in a groove established (and probably handled better, if not more pleasantly) by some of the lighter Motown singers—Mary Wells, for example. — D.M.

ROY ACUFF
★★ Best of Roy Acuff / Cap. SM-1870
★★★★ Greatest Hits / Col. CS-1034E
★★ Roy Acuff's Greatest Hits, Vol. 1 /
Elek. 9E-302
★★ Roy Acuff Sings Hank Williams /
Hickory S-134

Though he never had as many hits as his reputation might suggest, Acuff is a crucial figure in country music. He came to prominence as the star of the Grand Ole Opry in the late Thirties and early Forties, when the western influence was beginning to permeate country music. Acuff remained strictly traditional: his Smoky Mountain Boys were a classic mountain string band, and his rough singing style conveyed an unmistakable debt to the church. The Columbia album contains the songs that made his career ("Night Train to Memphis," "The Great Speckled Bird," "Fire Ball Mail," "Wabash Cannonball" and the scarifying "Were You There When They Crucified My Lord." It is absolutely essential to any country album collection. Later, more modern versions of many of these songs appear on the Capitol and Elektra albums, which are no substitute for the real thing. — J.MO.

ARTHUR ADAMS
★ Home Brew / Fan. 9479
■ Midnight Serenade / Fan. 9523

Adequate, uninspired funk guitarist. *Home Brew*'s star is for the all-star sidemen, who include some of the best names in soul sessionmen: legendary Motown bassist James Jamerson, guitarist Dennis Coffey and New Orleans drummer Earl Palmer. All have played better elsewhere; they're not present on *Midnight*. — D.M.

JAY BOY ADAMS
★★ Fork / Atl. 19195
★★ Jay Boy Adams / Atl. 18221

Countryish rock singer brought to you by the people who promoted ZZ Top. Adams lacks what might be called vigor—Top fans would say something cruder—though his singing is pretty enough. — D.M.

JOHNNY ADAMS
★ After All the Good Is Gone / Ario.
SW–50036
★★★ Heart and Soul / SSS Int'l. 5
★★ Stand by Me / Chel. 525

Heart and Soul is an interesting album of varied Sixties soul with heavy country and blues influences. Though Adams is from New Orleans, the record bears none of that city's distinctive musical flourishes. Notable songs include "Reconsider Me," "Losing Battle" and "I Won't Cry." Succeeding records unsuccessfully attempt to update the style. — J.MC.

ADDRISI BROTHERS
★ Addrisi Brothers / Bud. 5694

Slick, processed disco sung by this songwriting duo and produced and recorded in Nashville by country session master Norbert Putnam. Will 1977 be remembered as the year of cracker disco? Probably not. — J.S.

AEROSMITH
★★ Aerosmith (Featuring "Dream On") /
Col. PC-32005
★★★ Draw the Line / Col. JC-34865
★★ Get Your Wings / Col. JC-32847
★★ Live Bootleg / Col. PC-2-35564
★★★ Rocks / Col. CJ-34165
★★★ Toys in the Attic / Col. PC-33479

Each generation of rock fans needs its own heroes, and those who came of age in the mid-1970s chose Aerosmith, a selection that at first seemed based more on looks than sound. Lead vocalist Steven Tyler, with his puffy, pouty lips and salacious eyes, had the manner of his lookalike, Mick Jagger, but none of Jagger's command of song or movement. And lead guitarist Joe Perry's role seemed initially a game but limited version of Keith Richards'. But by its third album, *Toys in the Attic*, Aerosmith had defined its own hard-rock style, and *Rocks* perfected it.

Unfortunately, the band remains erratic in its composing. One doesn't get even half an album of hard-rock gems like "Sweet Emotion" or "Back in the Saddle." *Live Bootleg* is marred by uninspired performances, but a *Best of Aerosmith* would be as solid a selection of mid-1970s hard rock as anyone could hope for. — W.R.

A FOOT IN COLDWATER
★★★ **A Foot in Coldwater or All Around Us / Elek. 7E-1025**
A popular Canadian band whose style mixes Deep Purple rock with the Procol Harum structures. This compiles their best work, including "Make Me Do Anything You Want," arguably the best pop song ever to come out of Canada. (Now deleted.) — A.N.

FRANKLIN AJAYE
★ **Comedian / A&M 4405**
★ **Don't Smoke Dope, Fry Your Hair / Li. Dav. 1011**
★ **I'm a Comedian, Seriously / A&M 3642**
Mix two parts Jimmy Walker and one part David Brenner. Add stale material (ingredients: high school, being black, getting stoned). Simmer for three albums. Yields: Zilch. — K.T.

JAN AKKERMAN
★★★★ **Profile / Sire SAS 7407**
★★★ **Tabernakel / Atco 7032**
Akkerman is best known as the guitarist of Focus, the Dutch rock group. His hard, aggressively agile and imaginative guitar paced *Profile*'s first side through muscular, often frenetic jazz-rock jams, usually with only bass and drums backing. Side two included capable, unaccompanied classical guitar and lute pieces, among more straightforward electric rock playing. *Tabernakel* featured medieval and original classically oriented works, most with Akkerman alone on lute, the others with a rock rhythm section and a well-integrated and arranged orchestra. — C.W.

JAN AKKERMAN AND KAZ LUX
★★★ **Eli / Atl. 18210**
Good, crisp and eclectic guitar from Akkerman, pedestrian and somewhat exaggerated soul belting from Lux. Spare but firm hard rock mostly, guitars in front; strong beat, occasional jazz or classical tinge; original material. — C.W.

KAREN ALEXANDER
★ **Isn't It Always Love / Asy. 7E1040**
★ **Voyager / Asy. 6E-130**
Carefully produced pop albums replete with tasteful strings, mood congas, and staccato be-bop fabrications. Unfortunately Alexander's voice shows real daring only on the ballads. Her own material (almost the whole album) is undistinguished. — G.C.

WILLIE ALEXANDER AND THE BOOM BOOM BAND
★ **Meanwhile . . . Back in the States / MCA 3052**
★ **Willie Alexander and the Boom Boom Band / MCA-2323**
Barely competent funk from an old-timer on the Boston R&B scene; Alexander was associated with the city's late-Seventies New Wave resurgence, but by the time he got to the recording studio, he was already over the hill. Hold out for Mink DeVille instead. — D.M.

PETER ALLEN
★★ **Continental American / A&M 3643**
★★★ **It's Time for Peter Allen / A&M 3706**
★★★ **Taught by Experts / A&M 4584**
The prince of New York cabaret music, Allen is the latest model Noël Coward sophisticate. His well-crafted pop songs run from the frankly campy to the frankly romantic. On *Experts*, the deco-disco "I Go to Rio" and the nostalgic "Six-Thirty Sunday Morning" bring New York cabaret sensibility to its artistic peak. — S.H.

WOODY ALLEN
★★★ **The Night Club Years 1964-1968 / U. Artists 9968**
In the mid-Sixties, Allen's stand-up style— a nervous but traditional barrage of one-liners—was counterrevolutionary: his comedic mentors were Bob Hope and Groucho Marx, not Lenny Bruce and Nichols and May, the improvisationary deities of the period. However, Allen's subject matter and point of view was anarchic: he approached the world as if everyone were in analysis for having failed to score with the ideal woman (a stacked philosophy major). *The Night Club Years* catches him at his most tensely self-assured. — K.T.

ALLMAN AND WOMAN
■ **Two the Hard Way / War. K-3120**
It's hard to imagine a more inappropriate combination than Gregg Allman and Cher. This record may as well be a copy of the latest scandal-sheet gossip about Hollywood's odd couple as an attempt at music. It's the bottom of the barrel after a long fall for Gregg, and more of the same for Cher. — J.S.

ALLMAN BROTHERS BAND

★★★★★ **Allman Brothers Band at Fillmore East** / Capri. 2CX4-0131
★★★ **Beginnings** / Capri. 2CX-0123
★★ **Brothers and Sisters** / Capri. 0111
★★★★ **Eat a Peach** / Capri. 2C4-0102
★★★ **Idlewild South** / Capri. 0197
★★★ **The Allman Brothers Band** / Capri. 0196
★★★ **The Road Goes On Forever** / Capri. 2CP-0164
★ **Win, Lose or Draw** / Capri. 0156
■ **Wipe the Window, Check the Oil, Dollar Gas** / Capri. 0177

Listening to the Allman Brothers Band's first two flawed but engaging albums (repackaged as *Beginnings* and also available separately), one senses a relentless search for grandeur within a singular style of blues-rock fusion that also encompassed elements of classical and country music. Fired by Duane Allman's stinging, inventive lead and slide guitar work and by a rhythm section that pumped ferociously, the Allmans snapped up the grail on a superb live set, *At Fillmore East.* Remarkably, with three of seven cuts clocking in at 19:06, 12:46 and 22:40, there are no wasted notes, no pointless jams, no half-realized vocals—everything counts, from Duane's forceful opening slide guitar statement on "Statesboro Blues" through the fading first notes of "Mountain Jam" on side four.

More than half of the band's next album, *Eat a Peach,* is culled from the Fillmore East date, including the two-sided "Mountain Jam," which abounds in breathtaking musical interplay, particularly between Dickey Betts and Duane Allman. Three songs recorded after Duane's death find the band still riding a creative peak. "Little Martha," a guitar-dobro duet by Betts and Allman, closes the album and can be considered a symbolic passing of the mantle that marks the beginning of the end for the band. Betts, with a lyrical but softer touch than Duane, was ill-suited to front a band. *Brothers and Sisters,* although it contains Betts' "Ramblin' Man" (a hit single), is flabby. The songs lack punch, even with Gregg Allman's penetrating vocals, and there is no dynamic musicianship to pull the material out of the realm of the ordinary. *Win, Lose or Draw* is but further proof of the band's decline. Again, Gregg shines—on the title cut and on an update of Muddy Waters' "Can't Lose What You Never Had"—but his are the only notable performances. *The Road Goes On Forever* is a two-record set billed as "their greatest performances." *Comme çi, comme ça. Wipe the Windows, Check the Oil, Dollar Gas* is an album of live material culled from the band's appearances after Duane's death. — D.MC.

DUANE ALLMAN

★★★★ **An Anthology** / Capri. 2CP-0108
★★★★ **Anthology, Vol. 2** / Capri. 2CP-0139

Four discs that prove inconclusively that Allman's vision extended far beyond his groundbreaking feats with the Allman Brothers Band. In his Hourglass recordings (as well as in some tracks cut in 1969 with an unnamed band that included the Allman Brothers' bassist, Berry Oakley), one hears the tentative beginnings of the Allman Brothers' distinctive style. Allman's genius asserted itself at other times too. Here some of his finest moments as a sessionman are catalogued, including "Layla," Wilson Pickett's powerhouse rendition of "Hey Jude" and King Curtis' "The Weight." These anthologies are of more than historical interest: they are enjoyable and instructive as well. — D.MC.

GREGG ALLMAN

★★★★ **Laid Back** / Capri. 0116
★★ **Playin' Up a Storm** / Capri. 0181
★★ **The Gregg Allman Tour** / Capri. 2C-0141

Laid Back effectively recaptures much of the glory of the early Allman Brothers albums, although that group's exuberance is replaced here by a captivating sort of moroseness. At any rate, Allman turns in one superb vocal after another in his world-weary style ("Midnight Rider" and "These Days" are evocative in the extreme) and is aided by no-nonsense musicianship and some nifty arrangements.

If only the tour album were worthy of such praise. But after a fast start it disintegrates musically. An inappropriate twenty-four-piece orchestra and two spineless performances by Cowboy don't help matters. *Playin'* is also slack. — D.MC.

ALPHA BAND
★★★ **Spark in the Dark / Ari. 4145**
★★★ **Statue Makers of Hollywood / Ari. 4179**
★★★ **The Alpha Band / Ari. 4102**
J. Henry Burnett, David Mansfield and Steven Soles formed the Alpha Band during their stint as sidemen with Bob Dylan's Rolling Thunder Revue tour, and *The Alpha Band* and *Spark in the Dark* show a decided Dylan/Roger McGuinn influence, especially in Burnett's oblique lyrics and his singing. *Spark,* more slickly produced and featuring a serviceable session cameo from Ringo Starr, gets a slight edge in a close fit. *Statue Makers* might have been even better, except for its religious pretensions. — J.S.

ALQUIN
★★ **Nobody Can Wait Forever / RCA APL1-1061**
This Dutch group made its 1975 album at Dave Edmunds' Rockfield Studios in Wales, but it sounds less like Edmunds' nostalgic evocations of rock & roll than like Roxy Music. Nice guitar/sax interplay, but no songwriting or singing to speak of. For progressive fanatics only. (Now deleted.) — D.M.

SHIRLEY ALSTON
★★★ **Lady Rose / Straw. STW 6004**
★ **Shirley Alston Sings Shirelles Greatest Hits / Straw. STW 6006**
As lead singer of the Shirelles, Shirley Alston is remembered for the string of late-Fifties/early-Sixties classics ("Will You Still Love Me Tomorrow," "Dedicated to the One I Love," "Baby It's You," "Mama Said," "Soldier Boy," "Everybody Loves a Lover," "Foolish Little Girl") that made the Shirelles one of the most popular girl groups. Alston's 1977 solo album, *Lady Rose,* sets her in a quieter context to great effect, with several excellent songs written by Billy Vera, who also plays guitar and leads the backup band on the record. Her album of Shirelles remakes, however, doesn't fare nearly as well—in fact it's hard to understand why she would choose to butcher such tender moments from her past. (Now deleted.) — J.S.

AMAZING BLONDEL
★★★ **Mulgrave Street/Inspiration / DJM 701-2**
Engaging traditional English folk band that specializes in well-played acoustic jigs and ballads. This late-Seventies collection is the most recent release, but the out-of-print Blondel albums on Island (*England, Evensong, Blondel* and *Fantasia Lindum)* are well worth searching for in cutout bins. (Now deleted.) — J.S.

AMAZING RHYTHM ACES
★★ **Burning the Ballroom Down / ABC 1063**
★★★ **Stacked Deck / ABC D-913**
★★★ **Too Stuffed to Jump / ABC D-940**
★★★ **Toucan Do It, Too / ABC 1005**
Old-timey, bluegrass, Nashville steel, swing and R&B come together in the Aces' music, appropriately enough, since they're a Memphis band. If their eclecticism is sometimes disconcerting, their spirit is usually sufficient to carry listeners along. Traditionalists will be pleased with *Stacked Deck,* which renders such classics as "Life's Railway to Heaven" with stylish authenticity and presents original tunes that remain faithful to the conventions of blues and country music. *Too Stuffed to Jump* has a more contemporary sound (and cleaner production), but the Aces' passionate respect for their sources is no longer in evidence and the result is rather flat. Subsequent albums remain so. — A.S.

AMBOY DUKES
★★★ **Call of the Wild / Discr. DS 2181**
★★ **Journeys / Migrations / Main. 801**
★★ **Survival of the Fittest / Poly. 4035**
★★ **Tooth, Fang and Claw / Discr. DS 2203**
More than any other band of the late Sixties (save perhaps the Electric Prunes), the Amboy Dukes provided posterity with a working definition of the term "acid rock." Their albums, psychedelicized from covers (the original *Journey to the Center of the Mind* proudly displayed roughly fifty pot-smoking apparati) to song titles ("Why Is a Carrot More Orange Than an Orange," "The Inexhaustible Quest for the Cosmic Cabbage") to music ("Cabbage" is a two-part, ten-minute opus featuring an excerpt from Bartók's second string quartet interspersed with strains of atonal jazz and a one-minute Beach Boy parody), stand as testament to either just how far some people will go to make a buck or just how crazed rock music became during the more

frenzied moments of the last decade. Like a Veg-a-Matic, the Amboy Dukes diced and sliced every kind of imaginable music genre until the group succumbed. The various early Amboy Duke aggregations were anchored by guitarist Ted Nugent, from whose warped brain most of this music stemmed.

The early Seventies found the Amboy Dukes changing their approach—Nugent bringing his man-of-the-loincloth philosophy more to the forefront and the Dukes sounding more like a heavy-metal hard-rock band than a gang of potential burn-outs. *Call of the Wild* is the best of the later LPs, filled with ferocious instrumentals that bring to mind sweet images of rhinoceroses stampeding on a rainy, wind-swept day. — B.A.

AMBROSIA
★★★ **Ambrosia / 20th Cent. 434**
★★ **Somewhere I've Never Travelled / 20th Century 510**
This band's 1975 debut album featured two outstanding songs, a Kurt Vonnegut takeoff called "Nice, Nice, Very Nice" and "Holdin' On to Yesterday," a catchy ballad that eventually became a minor hit. Otherwise, though, Ambrosia gets bogged down in a tedious rehash of art-rock ideas apparently inspired by bands like Yes. (Now deleted.) — J.S.

AMERICA
★ **America / War. B-2576**
■ **America Live / War. K-3136**
★ **Harbor / War. BK-3017**
★ **Hat Trick / War. B-2728**
■ **Hearts / War. BS4-2852**
★ **Hideaway / War. 2932**
★★ **History: America's Greatest Hits / War. K-3110**

★ **Holiday / War. W4-2808**
★ **Homecoming / War. B-2655**
America is a triple play of mellow California folkies noted for: production by George Martin; the hit singles "Horse with No Name," "Tin Man," "Sister Golden Hair" and "Ventura Highway"; and having all their album titles since their debut start with the letter H, a *Sesame Street*-level conceit perfectly appropriate to the group's weightiness. They represent the senescence of the once-vibrant West Coast folk scene, and they sell a lot of records. Eventually they will have one called *Hawaii. History* is a greatest-hits set. — J.S.

AMERICAN FLYER
★★ **American Flyer / U. Artists LA650G**
★ **Spirit of a Woman / U. Artists LA720-G**
Middleweight supergroup consisting of former members of Pure Prairie League, Blood, Sweat and Tears, Blues Project, Velvet Underground and Blues Magoos. Less a group than a moneymaking scheme, Flyer released an elegant 1976 debut album produced by George Martin, showcasing fair-to-good material by all four members (Craig Fuller, Steve Katz, Doug Yule, and Eric Kaz), but they broke up after their second record. — S.H.

AMERICAN GYPSY
★★★ **American Gypsy / Chess CH60034**
Weird. American soul group, recorded in Holland by a Dutch producer. There are some interesting hard-rock touches, but nothing terribly distinctive either rhythmically or melodically. And beyond rhythm and melody, this sort of music has nothing to offer. (Now deleted.) — D.M.

AMERICAN TEARS
★ **Branded Bad / Col. KC-33038**
★★ **Powerhouse / Col. PC-34676**
★★★ **Tear Gas / Col. PC-33847**
Branded Bad is a decent but standard hard-rock debut. *Tear Gas* showcases the intelligently energetic songwriting and keyboard work of Mark Mangold. The first side is excellent, the second side ambitious but pretentious. Mangold's adventurousness keeps the trio promising. *Powerhouse,* however, showed little development. — K.T.

BILL AMESBURY
★★ **Can You Feel It / Cap. ST-11528**
Basically an all-purpose pop composer, Bill Amesbury has an adequate voice for his elaborate productions. A master at

adopting a wide assortment of genres, from disco to C&W to Lou Reed-like episodes, into tightly constructed pop singles with a baroque finish. As an instance of homogenization. *Can You Feel It* is pleasant but not very exciting. (Now deleted.) — B.T.

ERIC ANDERSEN
★ **A Country Dream** / Van. 6540
★★ **Be True to You** / Ari. 4033
★★★★ **Blue River** / Col. C-31062
★★★ **'Bout Changes and Things** / Van. 79206
★★★ **'Bout Changes and Things, Take 2** / Van. 79236
★★ **More Hits from Tin Can Alley** / Van. 79271
★★ **Sweet Surprise** / Ari. 4075
★★★ **The Best of Eric Andersen** / Van VSD 7/8
★★ **The Best Songs** / Ari. 4128
★★ **Today Is the Highway** / Van. 79167

Eric Andersen was the first "new Dylan." The most self-consciously sexual of the Greenwich Village folksingers, he conveyed in his early work a romanticism that owed much to the Everly Brothers' innocence and effervescence. His career, however, was always undermined by bad luck and poor judgment. His response to Dylan's going electric was to re-record his best and most popular early album *('Bout Changes and Things)* with a three-piece band *('Bout Changes and Things, Take 2)* and to coat his next with florid production *(More Hits from Tin Can Alley)*. Following the collapse of the folk scene, he pursued one fad after another: C&W *(A Country Dream)* and *Sgt. Pepper* orchestration (his out-of-print Warners albums). In 1971 he switched labels for the second time and produced his best work *(Blue River)*, which balanced pop and traditional modes and faith and fatalism. After a two-year absence, caused in part by the loss of the masters for his follow-up album, Andersen moved to Arista, where he has produced two albums *(Be True to You* and *Sweet Surprise)*. Despite the occasional brilliance of his writing—Andersen finally seems to recognize the limits of his romanticism—both are crippled by Tom Sellers' horrific production. Of the two best-of collections, the Vanguard contains the earlier material and is therefore preferable, but the Arista included several cuts from *Blue River,* arguably one of the most underrated albums by a singer/songwriter in the Seventies. — K.R.

AL ANDERSON
★★★ **Al Anderson** / Van. 79324
This 1972 solo album was made by Anderson right after he joined NRBQ from the Wildweeds, and features NRBQ drummer Tom Staley, piano player Terry Adams and trombonist Donn Adams. Anderson sings and plays guitar on a variety of light-spirited country-blues tunes and downtempo R&B numbers. — J.S.

JON ANDERSON
★★ **Olias of Sunhillow** / Atl. 18180
This is a true solo album—Anderson wrote it all and played all the instrumentals. But its texture is a result of multiple overlays, not virtuoso performances. Except for a few typical vocal flights in the Yes vein, *Olias* is a bore. — A.N.

ANGELO
■ **Angelo** / Fan. 9507
■ **Midnight Prowl** / Fan. 9554
Actually, the guy who made these singer/songwriter LPs is fairly smart. I wouldn't put my last name on this maudlin, ineptly "poetic" drivel either. — D.M.

ANGLO-SAXON BROWN
★ **Songs for Evolution** / Atl. 18192
Bad disco music meets mediocre cabaret jazz singing. — D.M.

THE ANIMALS
★★★ **Before We Were So Rudely Interrupted** / Jet JT-LA790-H
★★ **Best of Eric Burdon and the Animals, Vol. 2** / MGM SE-4454
★★★★ **Best of the Animals** / Abkco 4426
★★ **Best of the Animals** / Sp. 4025
★★ **Night Time Is the Right Time** / Sp. 4065

★ **The Greatest Hits of Eric Burdon and the Animals / MGM SE-4602**
The Animals were the only English act to approach soul and blues with the single-minded devotion of the Rolling Stones, at least in the early years (circa 1965). Led by singer Burdon, keyboard player Allan Price and bassist Chas Chandler (later, Jimi Hendrix and Slade's manager), the group was as resourceful and imaginative as any English Invasion band, and wittier than most—check "Story of Bo Diddley" on the Abkco set; a brief, amazing history of rock and roll.

The group's catalogue is in unfortunate disrepair; the originals were all on MGM and well worth seeking out. Nevertheless, most of the hits are contained on the Abkco album, including the classics "House of the Rising Sun," "I'm Crying," "We've Gotta Get Out of This Place," an anthem, and "It's My Life," a statement of purpose. The blues influence of John Lee Hooker and Bo Diddley's R&B are predominant. The LP also contains two of the key songs on the MGM *Best of*: "When I Was Young" and "A Girl Named Sandoz." But the MGM sets present a far different band—a more or less psychedelic one, which had hits with "San Francisco Nights," "Monterey" and "Sky Pilot," at the height of the Haight-Ashbury fad. The latter are included on the MGM *Greatest Hits*. While they are, in a way, great fun as memorabilia, they are surely no more than that.

The Springboard sets contain material recorded before the group hooked up with an American label. *Night Time* has them backing Sonny Boy Williamson. The principal item of importance on *Best of* is a powerhouse version of Chuck Berry's "Almost Grown," one of the group's few guitar-dominated rockers. Both are to be preferred over the MGM collections, despite Springboard's shoddy packaging.

Before is a surprisingly successful 1977 reunion one-shot, with the original group, again dominated by Price and Burdon, turning in fine, hard-nosed blues performances — D.M.

PAUL ANKA
★ **Anka / U. Artists LA314-G**
★ **Essential Paul Anka / Bud. BDS 2-5667**
■ **Feelings / U. Artists LA367-G**
■ **Live / Barn. 4008**
■ **My Way / Camd. ACL-0616**
★★ **Paul Anka Gold / Sire 3704**
★ **Paul Anka Sings His Favorites / RCA ANL1-1584**
★ **Remember Diana / RCA ANL1-0896**
★ **She's a Lady / RCA ANL1-1054**
■ **Songs I Wish I'd Written / RCA ANL1-2482**
■ **The Music Man / U. Artists LA746-H**
■ **The Painter / U. Artists LA653-G**
★ **This Is Paul Anka / Bud. BDS 5622**
■ **Times of Your Life / U. Artists LA569-G**
★ **Vintage Years 1957-1961 / Sire K-6043**
Unctuous Fifties pop singer/writer, scored in Sixties by writing "My Way" for Sinatra, in the Seventies with "Having My Baby." Useless to the end; get Neil Sedaka instead. — D.M.

AORTA
★ **Aorta / Col. CS-9785**
Rock's only venture into internal medicine—chest x-ray on the front cover, full-color disembodied heart on the inside and such song titles as "Heart Attack," "Catalyptic" and "It's Your Main Vein." Too bad the band sounds like a lounge act accidentally booked into a 1969 be-in. (Now deleted.) — B.A.

APHRODITE'S CHILD
★ **666 / Vert. 2-500**
Pompous and pointless early-Seventies Greek rock concept album masterminded by keyboardist Vangelis. Not an omen. — J.S.

APRIL WINE
★★ **April Wine Live at the El Macambo / Lon. PS-699**
★★ **The Whole World's Going Crazy / Lon. PS-675**
April Wine is a Montreal-based band that has issued numerous albums in Canada. Those albums portray the group as a delightful high-school punk outfit dealing in crass, hard-driving two- and three-minute singles. Their late-Seventies work, chronicled here, is characterized by a few good ballads repeated too many times and an unnecessary dependence on guitarist/vocalist Myles Goodwyn. — A.N.

AQUARIAN DREAM
★★ **Norman Connors Presents Aquarian Dream / Bud. 5672**
Norman Connors produced this album in 1976, around the time of his biggest commercial successes. It is somewhat more open, and the singing is much freer within the disco idiom, than the albums under his own name. — D.M.

AREA CODE 615
★★★ **Area Code 615 / Poly. 24-4002**
★★ **Trip in the Country / Poly. 24-4025**
Area Code 615 (the area code for Nashville) was a group formed by ten of Nashville's best studio musicians. These two albums, made in the late Sixties and early Seventies, are not interesting only in the light of country music history; they represent rock music's mostly unsuccessful influence on country.

Nonetheless, Charlie McCoy, Kenny Buttrey, Buddy Spicher, Mac Gayden, Weldon Myrick, David Briggs, Norbert Putnam, Elliot Mazer, Wayne Moss and Bobby Thompson are very fine musicians. Their arrangements—many of them improvisational—of such songs as "Hey Jude," "Lil' Maggie," "Just Like a Woman" and "I've Been Loving You Too Long" on *Area Code 615* make the country compositions sound as if they were written to rock and vice versa. The use of steel and harp leads on a song such as "Hey Jude" is just one example of the unorthodox approach that a country sideman can bring to a pop song. There is perhaps no better cover of that particular song anywhere.

Trip in the Country, with a liner note saying "Ding Dong the Code Is Dead?" is less successful. Here, the repertory is almost all rockified country. There are good moments, but Area Code 615 did it better the other way around. All of the group's members are now back at work playing sessions in and around Nashville. (Now deleted.) — M.H.

JOSE "CHEPITO" AREAS
★★★★ **Jose "Chepito" Areas / Col. KC-33062**
Excellent 1974 debut album from the ex-Santana percussionist, with session backing by Willie Colon (congas), Martin Fierro (tenor sax), and Santana stalwarts Tom Coster and Richard Kermode (keyboards), Doug Rauch (bass), Gregg Errico (drums) and Neal Schon (guitar). The band lays out in fine style on music at once more jazzlike and salsa rooted than the Santana band. — J.S.

ARGENT
★★★ **All Together Now / Epic E-31556**
★★★ **Anthology / Epic PE-33955**
★★★ **Argent / Epic 26525**
★ **Circus / Epic PE-33422**
★★ **Counterpoint / U. Artists LA560-G**
★ **Encore / Epic PEG-33079**
★★ **In Deep / Epic 32195**
★ **Nexus / Epic KE-32573**
★★★ **Ring of Hands / Epic E-30128**
Formed in 1970 by ex-Zombies lead singer/keyboardist Rod Argent, this band leaned heavily on its leader's talents. The first few albums show Argent in good form, especially on "Liar," "Schoolgirl" and "Dance in the Smoke" from the first album. Guitarist Russ Ballard provided the behind-the-scenes direction, writing much of the band's material, including two of its hits, "God Gave Rock and Roll to You" and "It's Only Money." Rod Argent wrote the band's biggest hit, "Hold Your Head Up." But Argent never really developed a strong identity, and since Ballard left the band in 1974 it hasn't been the same. — J.S.

ARIZONA
★★ **Arizona / RCA LPL1-5123**
Things get strange out in the desert: this 1976 record features an ensemble trying everything from Latin rhythms to Crosby, Stills and Nash harmonies. Unrealized, but interesting curiosity. — D.M.

ARMAGEDDON
★★★ **Armageddon / A&M 4513**
The late Keith Relf never sang better, not even with the Yardbirds, but the real show here is guitarist Martin Pugh: sharp chords, manic solos and refreshing acoustic textures—reminiscent of, alas, the Yardbirds. Solid drumming from Bobby Caldwell. Raw and powerful, though occasionally long-winded. — C.W.

JOAN ARMATRADING
★★ **Back to the Night / A&M 4525**
★★★★ **Joan Armatrading / A&M 4588**
★★★ **Show Some Emotion / A&M 4663**
★★ **To the Limit / A&M 4732**
★★ **Whatever's for Us / A&M 4382**
Joan Armatrading sets confessional lyrics that are neither fuddled nor sappy (surprise) to near-danceable acoustic funk, and the result is an album that's at once intimate and stylish. Armatrading's songs are personal without being self-indulgently revealing. They are built around dialogue and incident, and the observations on male-female relationships they contain are those of a survivor rather than a victim. Actually, it may be her voice, deep and flexible, that makes even abject statements sound self-respecting. Glyn John's guitar-based production is refreshingly simple, but Armatrading could have benefited from fuller arrangements. Of the earlier albums,

Whatever's for Us is the most appealing. Warm, enthusiastic, amateurish, it features Armatrading on piano as well as guitar. But both albums offer only intimations of her current direction, which *To the Limit* and *Emotion* confirm but can't extend. — A.S.

ARROGANCE
★★ **Rumors** / Van. VSD 79369
Pedestrian mid-Seventies folk rock. — D.M.

ARTFUL DODGER
★★★★ **Artful Dodger** / Col. PC-33811
★★ **Babes on Broadway** / Col. PC-34846
★★★ **Honor among Thieves** / Col. PC-34273
Debut album offers hard-driving music—the buoyant lyricism of Sixties pop meets the instrumental punch of Seventies hard rock—mated with fervently delivered straightforward lyrics reflecting the confusion, the exultation and the naiveté of youth. "Wayside," "Think Think," "Follow Me" and "Silver and Gold" are superior songs. *Honor Among Thieves* is a tentative but important step toward a tough, lean contemporary sound. Original songs—particularly "Scream," "Dandelion" and "Keep Me Happy"—show increasing sophistication of writers Billy Paliselli, Gary Herrewig and Gary Cox. Only major error is a static remake of "Keep A-Knockin'." *Babes,* however, belied the band's early energy; desperate for an audience, Dodger resorted to formula. — D.MC.

ARTHUR HURLEY AND GOTTLIEB
★ **Sunlight Shinin** / A&M 4503
Bad Crosby, Stills and Nash imitators. And if you think that the group's name smacks of a law firm, you also ought to know that the A&M album was produced by Stephen Hartley Dorff. Hats off to the clowns who thought they could put this one over on the public. — D.M.

ARTISTICS
★★★ **Articulate Artistics** / Bruns. 754139
★★★ **I Want You to Make My Life Over** / Bruns. 754168
★★★★ **I'm Gonna Miss You** / Bruns. 754123
★★★ **Look Out** / Bruns. 754195
★★★ **What Happened** / Bruns. 754153
The Artistics, on the R&B charts fairly frequently from 1965 into the early Seventies, were specialists in Motown-era soul, with one lead singer who sounded a bit like David Ruffin, another who resembled Smokey Robinson. Their only two singles to make the pop charts, "I'm Gonna Miss You" and "Girl I Need You," from '66 and '67, are both included on *I'm Gonna Miss You.* — D.M.

ASHFORD AND SIMPSON
★★★ **Come As You Are** / War. B-2858
★★ **Gimme Something Real** / War. B-2739
★ **I Wanna Be Selfish** / War. B-2789
★★ **Keep It Comin'** / Tam. T7-351
★★ **Send It** / War. B-3088
★★ **So So Satisfied** / War. 2992
Nick Ashford and Valerie Simpson wrote or produced most of the famous Marvin Gaye-Tammi Terrell hits of the late Sixties, such as "Ain't No Mountain High Enough" and "You're All I Need to Get By." In 1973 they decided to start singing duets themselves.

So far their career has hardly equaled Marvin and Tammi's. Their five albums—six counting *Keep It Comin',* the recent collection of Valerie's early solo work—are as irritating as they are interesting. Each album has one or two excellent moments, but none has the power of their Motown work.

It's tempting to blame Ashford, whose voice is horrible and whose lyrics are oversentimental. Yet their decision to make ridiculously ultraromantic albums has been their saving grace; they've resisted current trends in soul and disco, never descending to formulas. At their best—"I Had a Love," "Somebody Told a Lie," "Anywhere"—lyrics, music and voices blend together, and one does have a sense of two people struggling to express their feelings through music. — R.G.

ASLEEP AT THE WHEEL
★★★ **Asleep at the Wheel** / Epic KE-33097
★★★ **Collision Course** / Cap. SW-11726
★★★ **Comin' Right at Ya** / U. Artists LA038-F
★★★ **Fathers and Sons** / Epic BG-33782
★★★ **Texas Gold** / Cap. ST-11441
★★★★ **The Wheel** / Cap. ST-11620
★★★ **Wheelin' and Dealin'** / Cap. ST-11546
Asleep at the Wheel was possibly the greatest of the Seventies country rockers, because they leaned so intelligently toward the most interesting elements of country, especially Western Swing, as developed by Bob Wills. The group is a large one, and features horns as well as the usual country rhythm section complete with pedal steel.

Their rather checkered career, which has seen some country audience acceptance but total apathy on the part of rock fans, began with the United Artists album, moved through a brief sojourn at Epic, and finally found a more or less substantial home at Capitol, which is also where they've made their best records. *Texas Gold* and *The Wheel* score highest because principal vocalists Chris O'Connell and Ernest Tubb-soundalike Ray Benson have better material to work with. Western Swing is hillbilly music's answer to jazz (Charlie Parker allegedly admired Wills) and in songs like "Let Me Go Home Whiskey" *(Gold)*, "Miles and Miles of Texas" *(Wheelin')* and "My Baby Thinks She's a Train" *(The Wheel)*, Asleep lives up to all elements of the tradition. — D.M.

THE ASSOCIATION
★★ **The Association's Greatest Hits / War. 1707**
The pleasing ephemerality of songs like "Windy" and "Cherish" is made banal when you have to put it on the turntable rather than allow it to hit you on the radio. The Association was a prime Sixties AM radio group—leave them there in bliss. — K.T.

ASYLUM CHOIR
★★★ **Asylum Choir II / Shel. 52010**
★★ **Look Inside the Asylum Choir / Smash SRS-67107**
Asylum Choir combined the talents of two L.A. session types—Leon Russell and Marc Benno—who were trying to find a niche for their individual talents in the late-Sixties rock boom. Their first album, complete with a toilet-roll cover, falls victim to the psychedelic excesses of the time. By contrast, the second shows them moving toward their eventual solo careers— Benno working in an attractive if ultimately lightweight blues vein, and Russell developing the tumbling piano-based style that would seem so novel on his debut solo album. — J.B.M.

CHET ATKINS
★★★ **A Legendary Performer / RCA CPL1-2503**
★ **Alone / RCA APL1-0159**
★ **American Salute / RCA LSC-3277**
★★ **Best of Chet Atkins and Friends / RCA APL1-1985**
★★★★ **Chester and Lester / RCA APL1-1167**
★ **Chester, Floyd, and Boots / Camd. 2523**
★ **Chester, Floyd, and Danny / RCA APL1-2311**
★ **Chet Atkins Goes to the Movies / RCA APL1-0845**
★★ **Chet Atkins in Concert / Camd. CPL-2-1014**
★ **Chet Atkins Picks on the Beatles / RCA ANL1-2002**
★ **Chet Atkins Picks on the Pops / RCA LSC-3104**
★ **Chet Atkins Picks the Best / RCA ANL1-0981**
★ **Chet Atkins Picks the Hits / RCA LSP-4754**
★ **Country Pickin' / Camd. X-9006**
★ **Finger Pickin' Good / Camd. 2600**
★ **For the Good Times / RCA LSP-4464**
★ **Me and Chet / RCA ANL1-2167**
★ **Me and Jerry / RCA LSP-4396**
★ **Me and My Guitar / RCA APL1-2405**
★★ **Now and Then / RCA VPSX-6079**
★★★ **The Atkins-Travis Traveling Show / RCA APL1-0479**
★★★★ **The Night Atlanta Burned (The Atkins String Company) / RCA APL1-1233**
★ **This Is Chet Atkins / RCA VPS-6030**
Despite the fact that Chet Atkins is one of the most influential guitarists of the past thirty years, he has issued more dross than anyone in Nashville. A good general rule for the record buyer is to avoid any record with a title like "Chet Atkins Picks the Hits/Beatles/Rolling Stones/Minnie Pearl." Similarly, avoid titles like "Chet Atkins Goes to the Movies/Paris/ Memphis/Cuba." Only fanatical guitar students and Chet Atkins' best friends will be interested in such records. All of these records consist of Chet Atkins, his guitar and long orchestral dubs in renditions of standard songs from the year or Hollywood or the Beatles and so forth.

That said, there are three Chet Atkins albums that show the man for the virtuoso musician that he is.

The Night Atlanta Burned, by the Atkins String Company, is a beautiful recording. The idea for the album comes indirectly from John D. Loudermilk, who ran across a fragmentary composition for a mandolin orchestra that had survived the destruction of Atlanta during the Civil War. Atkins and Loudermilk came up with the idea of putting together a country chamber ensemble. Lisa Silver plays violin and viola, Atkins plays guitar, Johnny Gimble adds mandolin and Paul Yandell plays acoustic rhythm guitar.

The Night Atlanta Burned is a successful

musical experiment that should be repeated. Atkins' guitar, usually a diffident instrument, is inspired. The addition of violin, mandolin and viola give the music a texture that is lacking on any of Atkins' other albums. This record should be as well received by classical music fans as it has been by country music adherents.

Chester and Lester, a collaboration between Atkins and Les Paul, is not as experimental as it is improvisational and spontaneous. Paul's uninhibited nature provides a nice foil for the imperturbable Atkins both musically and in the brief conversations inserted between the songs. There is a sense of fun in this album, which is as close to jazz as Chet Atkins ever will come.

The Atkins-Travis Traveling Show pairs Atkins with Merle Travis, his mentor. It would be interesting to know why this album does not succeed as well as *Chester and Lester.* Both guitars are great, but I suspect that, even though they are a little different, Atkins' and Travis' styles are just too close to allow for the musical serendipity that happened with Les Paul. The between-songs patter is not as good, and the songs themselves are mostly country standards. While *The Night Atlanta Burned* and *Chester and Lester* are records that surpass the country label, *The Atkins-Travis Traveling Show* will be of interest only to country music scholars.

An overview of Chet Atkins' work suggests that Atkins works best only when challenged, and that the challenges must come from outside the field of country music. Ironically, rock musicians who learned the Atkins style seem to have seen the possibilities of his music before Atkins himself did. — M.H.

ATLANTA DISCO BAND
★ **Bad Luck / Ario. 50004**
As the name suggests, this is along the lines of crossing the Allman Brothers with a disco session band. You take it from there. — J.S.

ATLANTA RHYTHM SECTION
★★★★★ **A Rock and Roll Alternative / Poly. 1-6080**
★★★ **Atlanta Rhythm Section / MCA 2-4114**
★★★★ **Champagne Jam / Poly. 6134**
★★★ **Dog Days / Poly. 6041**
★★★★ **Red Tape / Poly. 6060**
★★★★ **Third Annual Pipe Dream / Poly. 6027**

The Atlanta Rhythm Section was formed in 1970 as a songwriter's cooperative. The group pooled the talents of two late-Sixties Atlanta bands, the Classics IV (producer Buddy Buie and guitarist J. R. Cobb) and the Candymen (drummer Robert Nix and keyboardist Dean Daugherty), with two young session players, guitarist Barry Bailey and bassist Paul Goddard.

The band put together a studio, used itself as the house band and slowly recorded two records in between bread-and-butter sessions backing up singers and recording television soundtracks. The two albums, *Atlanta Rhythm Section* and *Back Up Against the Wall,* are now reissued as a double set on MCA. *Atlanta Rhythm Section* used Rodney Justo as lead singer and was fairly inconsequential except for the fine "Another Man's Woman." On *Back Up Against the Wall* Ronnie Hammond replaced Justo as lead singer, and several tracks—the title song, "Cold Turkey Tennessee," Joe South's "Redneck" and Randall Bramblett's "Superman"—demonstrated tremendous potential.

Eventually the band's songwriting talent began to pay off. *Third Annual Pipe Dream,* the most representative early session, produced two excellent regional hits, "Doraville" and "Angel." Producer Buie had kept the ARS in tight check until that album, but after the hits, the band became more oriented to live performances and its sound changed.

Dog Days suffered from the transition as Buie's production sweetening worked against the live feel of the basic tracks. Buie changed his production strategy, and the next album, *Red Tape,* was much closer to the band's live sound, especially on the longer remake of "Another Man's Woman," highlighted by Goddard's remarkable bass solo. *A Rock and Roll Alternative* finally defined the band's recording on hard-rock tracks like "Sky High" and ballads like "So in to You." "So in to You" became a substantial nationwide hit in 1977 and finally put the group over the top after years of struggling to make ends meet. — J.S.

ATOMIC ROOSTER
★ **Atomic Rooster IV / Elek. 75074**
★ **Death Walks Behind You / Elek. 74094**
Faceless early-Seventies English hard-rock act churned out pedestrian pseudo-boogie with an occasional pause for *la grande ballade.* The best track here is keyboardist Vincent Crane's solo instrumental,

"Moods" (on *IV*), which brings to mind Vince Guaraldi on an off day. — B.A.

ATTITUDES
★★ **Attitudes / Dark SP-22008**
★★ **Good News / Dark 3021**
The predictable safeness of studio musicians, but with a certain flair. The four—Danny Kootch, Jim Keltner, Paul Stallworth and David Foster—are least slick on the more spirited selections. A disco feel is employed though not exploited, but the female backing singers are an unnecessary intrusion. *Good News* is more varied but adds only glossy pop-soul. — C.W.

AUDIENCE
■ **Lunch / Elek. 75026**
★★ **The House on the Hill / Elek. 74100**
Gus Dudgeon's echoey production of Audience's debut, *The House on the Hill,* bolstered the British groups weak instrumental palette. So they shake some complacent lunacy out of the title cut, "I Put a Spell on You," and "Jackdaw." Under careful handling, Howard Werth's voice pairs well with Keith Gemmell's ubiquitous, gruff sax. Much of their overall strategy was later to find success in some Roxy Music and David Bowie.

However, as a rock band Audience never rose above thin gruel, and its degeneration came quickly, on *Lunch,* where Werth trades his gothic atmospherics for a dabble in Americana. Flat-footed meandering results. — B.T.

BRIAN AUGER
★★★ **A Better Land / RCA LSP-4540**
★★★ **Befour / RCA LSP-4372**
★★ **Closer to It / RCA AFL1-0140**
★★ **Encore / War. K-3153**
★★ **Happiness Heartaches / War. B-2981**

★★ **Live Oblivion, Vol. 1 / RCA ANL1-2481**
★ **Live Oblivion, Vol. 2 / RCA CPL2-1230**
★★ **Oblivion Express / RCA AFL1-4462**
★★★ **Reinforcements / RCA AFL1-1210**
★★ **Second Wind / RCA AFL1-4703**
★★★ **Straight Ahead / RCA AFL1-0454**
★★ **The Best of Brian Auger / RCA AFL1-2249**
This veteran keyboard player whose heart belongs to Jimmy Smith has used rock to gain a fair amount of popularity twice—once as backup to Julie Driscoll's vocals, later with Oblivion Express. Much of his work has been reissued on budget labels, and as a result, his recording history can be confusing. The Driscoll material is by now deleted; *Befour* appeared immediately after her departure. *Oblivion Express, Land* and *Wind* mark the inauguration of Oblivion Express, including a future Average White Band member, the late Robbie McIntosh, on drums. Here the sound is closer to English progressive rock in structure—both before and after the sound is jazzier, with *Befour* including some good cops from Traffic and Herbie Hancock. *Closer* and *Straight* have some Wes Montgomery and Marvin Gaye and had fair luck on the charts (jazz and R&B as well as pop). Auger's riffing organ dominates every facet. Both the *Live* LPs are redundant, while *Reinforcements* is a standout because he again deserts jazz for pop, this time in the Average White Band-Stevie Wonder mold. — A.N.

MIKE AULDRIDGE
★★ **Blues and Bluegrass / Tak. 1041**
★★★ **Dobro / Tak. / Devi 1033**
★★ **Mike Auldridge / Fly. Fish 029**
Auldridge is a sophisticated dobro player who has recorded and performed with the Country Gentlemen and Seldom Scene bluegrass groups. He is surrounded on each of these discs with stellar lineups ranging from Linda Ronstadt to David Bromberg, Vassar Clements to Lowell George. The effect can be numbing when all fingers are flying at once, but on the debut *Dobro* in particular, the hot-licks effects are kept to a minimum and taste abounds. — I.M.

AUTOMATIC MAN
★★★ **Automatic Man / Is. LPS 9397**
★★★ **Visitors / Is. ILPS 9429**
Imaginative heavy metal paced by Bayeté's vocals and effortless keyboards, and ex-Santana member Michael Shrieve's deft

drumming (on the first album only). The debut's successful combination of Hendrix, synthesizers, R&B and hard rock gives way to jazz rock and mainstream soul on *Visitors.* — C.W.

AVALANCHE
★★★ Avalanche / ABC 1000
Medium-strength Australian rock band led by vocalist Adrian Campbell released a U.S. debut album in 1977 featuring their three hits, "Wizard of Love," "Sweet Baby Brown Eyes" and "Landslide," but were unable to duplicate their homeland success here. Good writing, strong performance, but ultimately nothing substantial. — J.S.

FRANKIE AVALON
■ 16 Greatest Hits / Trip TOP-16-21
Perhaps some of the most patronizing music ever made is gathered here. Far from being a phony successor of the golden age of Fifties rock 'n' roll, Avalon was a decadent descendant of older pop singers like Frank Sinatra and Tony Bennett. The pseudo-swing of "Swingin' on a Rainbow" is closer to the awesome vapidity of Avalon's usual Christmas-chimes-and-drip-dry-orchestra sound than is the pseudo-rock of "Two Fools." It makes sense that Nashville first started to exert a strong pull on the mass audience around the time "Venus" was popular. — B.T.

AVERAGE WHITE BAND
★★★★★ AWB / Atl. QD 7308
★★ Benny and Us / Atl. 19105
★★ Cut the Cake / Atl. 18140
★ Person to Person / Atl. 2-1002
★★★ Put It Where You Want It / MCA 475
★★ Soul Searching / Atl. 18179
★★ Warmer Communications / Atl. 19162
At first the Average White Band seemed little more than a gimmick with an ironic moniker. They played black music so convincingly that even blacks bought it. But the debut LP, *Put It Where You Want It,* also suggested considerable songwriting facility, and AWB's energy, especially the rhythmic drive of bassist Alan Gorrie and drummer Robbie McIntosh, was far more propulsive than what slavish imitators could hope to generate.

The Average White Band, you see, had a leg up on white American bands who wanted to play black—as Scots they were British colonials, so they understood cultural oppression. For AWB, black music

spoke a language to be internalized, not aped.

The second album, *AWB,* proved to be the one classic the band had in them. Nine of the ten tunes were memorably melodic and bristled with hooks. The singing of Alan Gorrie and Hamish Stuart, gracefully mixed to the fore by producer Arif Mardin, brimmed over with an authoritative enthusiasm.

Unfortunately, this glorious success was not to be repeated. *Cut the Cake* and *Soul Searching,* both given to disco and modal monotony, suggested that with Robbie McIntosh's accidental-overdose death in September 1974, something in the group died as well. — P.H.

DAVID AXELROD
■ Strange Ladies / MCA 2283
David Axelrod is the kind of performer to whom those who hate rock like to point as an example of the music's increasing "sophistication." In fact, his music indicates its increasing vitiation. Axelrod has made album versions of Handel's *Messiah* and William Blake's poetry, all as a justification for trying to cash in on rock's "seriousness." He is in fact a purveyor of the most hackneyed jazz and classical concepts, transferred with technical facility and emotional vacuity to post-*Sgt. Pepper* LPs. Big fucking deal. — D.M.

HOYT AXTON
★★★ Fearless / A&M 4571
★★ Free Sailin' / MCA 2319
★★ Less Than the Song / A&M 4376
★★★ Life Machine / A&M 3604
★ My Griffin Is Gone / Col. C-33103
★★★ Road Songs / A&M 4669
★★★ Snowblind Friend / MCA 2263
★★★ Southbound / A&M 4510
Hoyt ("The Pusher") Axton is an anomaly: a starry-eyed cynic, a hayseed wearing city shoes. Despite his backwoods sensibility (and he comes on as shaggy and sly as a honey bear), Axton is a shrewd songwriter who's been writing other people's hits for years ("Greenback Dollar" for the Kingston Trio, "Joy to the World" for Three Dog Night). Nevertheless, there are startling gaps in Axton's sophistication. Like a square who never recovered from the summer of love, he can be positively hokey (cf. "Pet Parade" on *Life Machine).* But if he sometimes out-Nashville's Nashville with his brand of barefoot slick, he's learned country music's most important lesson: simplicity. Based on precise observation

and compact melodies, the best of Axton's songs ("The Devil" on *Fearless*; "Lion in the Winter" and "Pride of Man" on *Southbound*; "Boney Fingers" and "When the Morning Comes" on *Life Machine*) achieve the timeless resonance of an Appalachian hymn.

There is no definitive Axton album; the good songs are sandwiched among the flops and filler. *Life Machine* is probably his most consistent effort; *My Griffin Is Gone*, a psychedelic relic, the most dispensable. But even the failures are listenable, and the harmonies that blend his deep, sweet, lazy voice with those of country-accented sopranos like Linda Ronstadt's are perfect. — A.S.

KEVIN AYERS
★★★ **Yes We Have No Mañanas / So Get Your Mañanas Today / ABC 1021**
Despite his earlier, playful idiosyncrasies (available now only by import), *Mañanas* was fairly straightforward and catchy (if predictable) rock; somewhat soft but never airy keyboard/guitar arrangements modestly supported Ayers' agreeably casual vocals. Good production and English studio backing, especially Ollie Halsall's guitar. — C.W.

AYERS ROCK
★★ **Beyond / A&M 4565**
★★★ **Big Red Rock / A&M 4523**
Australia's answer to jazz-rock fusion, provincial enough to cover Joe Zawinul's "Boogie Woogie Waltz" without adding much to the Weather Report version, presumptuous enough to sing and even include a string section on *Beyond*. No relation to Roy Ayers, or even Kevin Ayers. (Now deleted.) — J.S.

AZTEC TWO-STEP
★★ **Adjoining Suites / RCA AFL1-2453**
★★★ **Aztec Two-Step / Elek. 75031**
★★ **Second Step / RCA AFL1-1161**
★★ **Two's Company / RCA AFL1-1497**
Rex Fowler and Neal Shulman have pleasant, callow voices and harmonize relentlessly, if not imaginatively. Their debut LP, primarily acoustic folk rock, is still their best—"The Persecution and Restoration of Dean Moriarty (On the Road)," despite its melodic banality, was a sort of underground hit in the early Seventies. On the RCA albums, they attempt a more eclectic approach, with mixed effect. Generally, their voices are too pallid to compete with instrumental energy, and their ensemble sound is listenable but trite. — P.H.

BABE RUTH
★★ **First Base / Harv. SW-11151**
★ **Kid's Stuff / Harv. ST-11515**
★★★ **Stealin' Home / Harv. ST-11451**
Formed in 1973, Babe Ruth featured Jenny
Haan, a powerful vocalist in the Julie
Driscoll-Lydia Pense mold, and multi-instrumentalist Alan Shacklock. Within their
records can be found everything from Ital-
ian-western movie themes to rehashed soul
and Frank Zappa, not to mention disco
and all-out rock. Shacklock left after *Babe
Ruth,* the group's third and best (but deleted) album, because of commercial strike-
out; Haan followed after the fourth, *Stealin'
Home.* Supporting cast carried on with hokey baseball clichés. Their best music came
from giving Haan free reign—"Dancer"
from *Babe Ruth* sounds like the result of a
hot jam between Steve Marriott and Driscoll. — A.N.

BABY
★ **Where Did All the Money Go? / Chel.
CHL 517**
Not here, that's for sure. — J.S.

THE BABYS
★ **Broken Heart / Chrys. 1150**
★ **Head First / Chrys. 1195**
★ **The Babys / Chrys. 1129**
The folks who brought you Jethro Tull
tried to sell these wimps as the new Rasp-
berries (more or less) in 1977 and 1978.
Few were buying, perhaps because the
group was too inept to even become super-
ficial. — D.M.

BURT BACHARACH
■ **Burt Bacharach's Greatest Hits / A&M
3661**
■ **Futures / A&M 4622**
■ **Living Together / A&M 3527**
■ **Make It Easy on Yourself / A&M 4188**

■ **Reach Out / A&M 4131**
Although he was, with Hal David, perhaps
the best Tin Pan Alley-style writer of the
Sixties, Bacharach is no performer—his
voice is more affecting on TV commercials.
The proof of his talent is in the recordings
of Dionne Warwick and Gene Pitney, not
here. — D.M.

BACHELORS
★★★ **Presenting the Bachelors / Lon.
PS-353**
Irish traditional vocal group scored hits in
the early Sixties with "Marie" and
"Diane." (Now deleted.) — J.S.

RANDY BACHMAN
★★ **Survivor / Poly. I-6141**
What Bachman has survived, one sup-
poses, is being guitarist in the two most
successful Canadian rock bands of the past
ten years, Guess Who and Bachman-
Turner Overdrive. Unfortunately, those
were also two of the dullest groups ever to
score hit singles consistently, and Bachman's no bargain on his own either. So
Survivor? Big deal. Like John Garfield said,
"Everybody dies." — D.M.

BACHMAN-TURNER OVERDRIVE
★★ **Bachman-Turner Overdrive / Mer.
SRM-1-673**
★★★ **Bachman-Turner Overdrive 2 / Mer.
SRM-1-696**
★★★ **Best of Bachman-Turner Overdrive /
Mer. SRM-1-1101**
★★ **Freeways / Mer. SRM-1-3700**
★★ **Not Fragile / Mer. SRM-1-1004**
★ **Street Action / Mer. SRM-1-3713**
Bachman-Turner Overdrive, organized by
the former lead guitarist of the Guess Who,
Randy Bachman, enjoyed a brief heyday
from 1973 to 1976 as a pop alternative to
heavy metal. Tougher and raunchier than

the Guess Who's singles, their two biggest hits came in 1974. "Takin' Care of Business" was a brawny rocker without much subtlety, but "You Ain't Seen Nothin' Yet," which made No. 1 in the fall of '74, was a direct steal from the Who, and an imaginative one. But that seemed to exhaust Bachman's imagination—everything before and since is simply sluggish.

Best of contains both of the above hits, plus the group's only other Top Twenty hit, "Roll On Down the Highway," the followup to "You Ain't Seen." *Bachman-Turner Overdrive 2* contains "Takin' Care of Business," but the group's best album is probably *Not Fragile,* which has the other songs mentioned above. — D.M.

BACK STREET CRAWLER
★★★ The Band Plays On / Atco 36-125
Back Street Crawler featured the blues-based, anguished guitar of the late Paul Kossoff, who earlier played with Free. In fact, this quintet resembles Free in its solemn minor chords, throaty vocals (Terry Wilson-Slesser) and stubborn beat. Crawler is among the few groups that balance hard and soft styles. — C.W.

BAD COMPANY
★★★★ Bad Company / Swan 8501
★★ Burnin' Sky / Swan 8500
★★★ Run with the Pack / Swan 8503
★★★ Straight Shooter / Swan 8502
This state-of-the-art mid-Seventies hard-rock band began as an apotheosis of supergroups, combining lead singer Paul Rodgers and drummer Simon Kirke from Free, guitarist Mick Ralphs from Mott the Hoople and bassist Boz Burrell from King Crimson. On the strength of the solid first album, a modest hit in "Can't Get Enough," and the instant celebrity of Paul Rodgers' smooth but powerful vocal punch, the band has carved out a solid niche for itself on the arena concert circuit. The workmanlike but unflashy stolidness of the group's playing, which is virtually interchangeable on all the records, makes it at once effective and uninteresting, and while Bad Company has lived up to its commercial promise, the band must be viewed as an aesthetic failure for its inability to do anything more than exploit the hard-rock form. Rodgers' voice provides the transcendence, but the rest of the band just never leaves the ground. — J.S.

JOAN BAEZ
★★ Any Day Now / Van. 79306-7
★★★★ Ballad Book / Van. VSD-41/42
■ Baptism / Van. 79275
★ Best of / A&M 4668
★★ Blessed Are / Van. 6570-1
★ Blowin' Away / Por. PR 34697
■ Carry It On / Van. 79313
■ Come from the Shadows / A&M 4339
★★ Contemporary Ballad Book / Van. VSD 49/50
★★ David's Album / Van. 79308
■ Diamonds and Rust / A&M 4527
★★★ Farewell, Angelina / Van. 79200
★★★ First Ten Years / Van. 6560-61
★ From Every Stage / A&M 3704
★ Gracias a la Vida (Here's to Life) / A&M 3614
★ Gulf Winds / A&M 4603
★★ Hits/Greatest & Others / Van. 79332
★★★★ In Concert, Part One / Van. 2122
★★★★ In Concert, Part Two / Van. 2123
★ Joan / Van. 79240
★★★★ Joan Baez / Van. 2077
★★★★ Joan Baez / Van. 2097
★★★ Joan Baez / Van. 79160
★★★ Lovesong Album / Van. 79/80
★★★ Noel / Van. 79230
★★ One Day at a Time / Van. 79310
★ Where Are You Now, My Son / A&M 4390

Joan Baez was one of the two most influential performers of the early-Sixties folk movement—the other was the group Peter, Paul and Mary, and like them, Baez was essentially a popularizer. She played the pacifist radical—committed to civil rights, peace marches and traditional ballad singing—perfectly, partly because she so much looked the part. And when the young Bob Dylan emerged from Minnesota in 1961, it was only natural that they hooked up together. The most highly rated albums above—the first two records called *Joan Baez,* the *Ballad Book,* and both volumes of *In Concert*—all feature her on traditional material, since they were recorded before the contemporary, topical songwriters emerged in Dylan's wake.

When Dylan, Eric Andersen, Richard Farina, Phil Ochs and others made their appearance, Baez was useful for the exposure she gave their songs; her soprano was far too perfect and emotionally remote to interpret them successfully, however. In consequence, the albums where she attempted to mix contemporary and traditional material are more successful than later records where she tried to do exclusively contemporary songs. *Any Day Now,* a two-record collection of Dylan material, highlights her problem: she makes the songs of the Sixties' greatest writer seem as humorless and stodgy as the poem she reads on *Baptism.*

Perhaps Baez's most salutary quality was her political commitment; for years, she refused to pay taxes because of the Vietnam War, and she consistently supported leftist causes, often at considerable personal and professional expense. But her approach to political music is so sanctimonious it's nearly unbearable, and her few attempts at wholly political album-making have been her most disastrous recordings: *Carry It On,* featuring her ex-husband David Harris, who did time as a war resister, and *Gracias a la Vida,* a smug attempt to educate the masses politically, are the most obnoxious.

In the Seventies, Baez's career has been more unfocused than ever. The folk boom long over, unable to communicate effectively whatever she may feel about the currently fashionable singer/songwriter material left for her to sing, she has retreated on two recent albums, *Diamonds and Rust* and *Gulf Winds,* to writing her own songs. *Come from the Shadows* included the egregious "To Bobby," a panting attempt to exhume interest in her long-lapsed affair with Dylan (which may or may not have helped her become part of the 1976 Rolling Thunder Revue), while "Time Rag" on her most recent LP, *Blowin' Away,* took a slap at the popular press, always the last refuge of the artistically benighted. — D.M.

GINGER BAKER
★ **Eleven Sides of Baker / Sire SA-7532**
This 1977 album finds the former drumming star of Cream at an all-time creative low, playing out his role as rhythm king in front of a none-too-efficient group. Baker's abilities as a leader are questionable at best, but the out-of-print *Air Force* album, featuring Wings' Denny Laine and released after Baker split from Cream, still presents him at his best. (Now deleted.) — J.S.

BAKER-GURVITZ ARMY
★★ **Elysian Encounter / Atco SD 36-123**
★★ **Hearts on Fire / Atco SD 36-137**
Amazing, the way former Cream drummer Ginger Baker managed to convince not just one, but two different record companies that there would be a market for a band based around a little-known, flashy, but transparently derivative guitarist whose reputation hinged on one British Top Twenty single (Adrian Gurvitz of Gun with "Race with the Devil" respectively)

and a wired but aging jazz drummer who brought new meaning to the word tedium. It's not without good reason that Janus deleted its only BGA attempt. As of this writing it is unknown whether the Atco concern has seen the light. — A.N.

LAVERN BAKER
★★ **Let Me Belong to You / Bruns. 754160**
Baker's recordings of a pair of great novelty hits, "Jim Dandy" and "Tweedle Dee," for Atlantic in the mid-Fifties, have obscured her greater talent for more mature R&B singing. Until recently, this was well documented on an Atlantic anthology, *LaVern Baker—Her Greatest Recordings,* but in keeping with that company's slipshod lack of respect for its own heritage, the LP is deleted. The Brunswick collection is inferior, leaving a fine singer tragically unrepresented by her best work. — D.M.

BALCONES FAULT
★★ **It's All Balcones Fault / Cream 1004**
This wacky Texas Dixieland jazz *cum* lounge band runs through its weird assortment of Big Band comedy routines, rock & roll, Afro-Cuban jazz and Tex-Mex ranchero music with engaging if unsettling aplomb. The slickness that enables them to handle this odd assortment of arrangements deftly is also what ultimately keeps them from being believable. — J.S.

LONG JOHN BALDRY
★★ **Good to Be Alive / Casa. 7012**
Baldry's distinctive gravel-toned voice has made him a mainstay of the British blues scene since his early-Sixties stint with Steampacket, a group that also featured Rod Stewart. Beyond the voice, though, Baldry's importance as a leader or interpreter is marginal. This collection is characteristically tepid. — J.S.

RUSS BALLARD
★★ **At the Third Stroke / Epic JE-35035**
★★★ **Winning / Epic PE-34093**
Former Argent lead singer remains an interesting progressive pop singer even without the excellent material he had to work with in his former band. Unfortunately, singers without good material and arrangements aren't much fun to hear. — D.M.

BALLIN' JACK
★ **Ballin' Jack / Col. C-30344**
Flaccid jazz-rock played by competent instrumentalists who sound like a musicians union pickup group. — J.S.

BANCO
★ ★ **Banco / Mant. MA6-505-S1**
This 1975 Italian art-rock band's attempt to
re-create themes derived from Italian neo-
realist cinema (on side one) and arias from
their national operatic tradition (on side
two) in the mode of rock is problematic in
the extreme. But its high spirits and command of Pink Floyd–type orchestration
make Banco interesting, at least. (Now deleted.) — B.T.

THE BAND
★ ★ ★ **Anthology / Cap. SKBO-11856**
★ ★ **Cahoots / Cap. SMAS-651**
★ ★ ★ ★ **Islands / Cap. So-11602**
★ ★ ★ **Moondog Matinee / Cap. 11214**
★ ★ ★ ★ ★ **Music from Big Pink / Cap.
SKAO-2955**
★ ★ ★ **Northern Lights—Southern Cross /
Cap. ST-11440**
★ ★ ★ ★ ★ **Rock of Ages / Cap.
SABB-11045**
★ ★ ★ **Stage Fright / Cap. SW-425**
★ ★ ★ ★ ★ **The Band / Cap. STAO-132**
★ ★ ★ **The Best of the Band / Cap.
ST-11553**
The Band is a curious group that has never
quite lived up to its reputation as *the* clas-
sic American rock band of the early Seven-
ties, a reputation mostly acquired as back-
ing band for the electric Bob Dylan during
the late Sixties.

Music from Big Pink, their debut album,
sported a cover painting by Bob Dylan and
had a profound musical impact when released in mid-1968. The two-keyboard approach was quickly picked up by a number
of bands, most notably Procol Harum, but
what was really unmatchable was the intensity of the group's performances, its incredible vocalizing, which involved key

changes in voice that seemed to operate on
the members' instincts as much as on writing or arranging, and the remarkable depth
of the songwriting. Lead guitarist Robbie
Robertson was not then the exclusive
writer; Richard Manuel's contributions to
the writing, including his collaborations
with Bob Dylan, were nearly as important.
Robertson's "The Weight" was the best
song, trailed closely by "Chest Fever,"
"Long Black Veil," "Lonesome Suzie" and
"I Shall Be Released."

The Band had been performing together—originally as the backup for Ronnie Hawkins (whose sole remaining Roulette album features Robertson's incredible
playing on "Who Do You Love") in their
native Canada, later in Arkansas as Levon
(Helm, the drummer and only American)
and the Hawks and finally with Dylan. On
The Band, one of the greatest and most
profound rock & roll albums ever made,
this experience—of coming to America, of
being Canadian, of the deep and sometimes
exhilaratingly frightening experiences
they'd shared—all came home. Songs like
"Across the Great Divide," "The Night
They Drove Old Dixie Down," "Jemima
Surrender," "Look Out Cleveland" and
many more define the late Sixties and early
Seventies for thousands of listeners. *The
Band* is as close to a perfect statement of
purpose as any rock group has ever come.

The Band, however, did not produce a
hit single, and somehow has never quite
lived up to its incredible implications.
Stage Fright, which followed, had fine moments, most notably on the title song,
"Time to Kill," and "The Shape I'm In."
But it retrenched into a kind of conservatism inherent in the perfectionism of the
first two albums, but transcended there by
a feeling of release and freedom at finally
standing on their own. More problemati-
cally, Robertson, who began to write all of
the group's original material with the second LP (a practice that continued until
1975's *Northern Lights*), simply didn't turn
out enough good material for a classic album. But if *Stage Fright* was a disappointment, *Cahoots* (1971) was a catastrophe.
Robertson completely outstripped himself
here—with the exception of "Life Is a Carnival" and Dylan's "When I Paint My
Masterpiece," there simply isn't a good
song on the record. The Band may have
been rock masters, but they had to have
some kind of material to work with.

What followed was retrenchment and
confusion. *Rock of Ages* (1972), the live al-

bum, managed to capture most of the group's best material, and incorporated some delightful horn arrangements (by Allen Toussaint), but contained nothing new—even the two new songs, "Get Up Jake" and Marvin Gaye's "Don't Do It"—had been part of the group's repertory for years. *Moondog Matinee* (1973) was a misguided oldies album, with obvious and trite selections, redeemed mostly by pianist/vocalist Richard Manuel's singing on "The Great Pretender."

Northern Lights—Southern Cross (1975) turned a corner, but it was a strange one. By now, the group's records, except for the first, were beginning to seem interchangeable. *Northern Lights* added another element—the kind of bizarre organ and synthesizer fills Garth Hudson had been experimenting with onstage for several years. While it contained no truly outstanding songs, it at least made some interesting instrumental innovations. *Islands* (1976) repreated the process, with Hudson taking an even larger role, though the material still left much to be desired. Surprisingly, however, at this crucial juncture, the group decided it had had enough and decided to disband. *The Best of the Band* followed at Christmas-time of 1976; the only other project the members were expected to engage in collectively was a live LP from their final concert held at Thanksgiving of '76 in San Francisco. (A film, *The Last Waltz,* was also made of that show by director Martin Scorsese, and the soundtrack is now available on Warner Bros. 3WS-3146.)

Singer/bassist Rick Danko and drummer Levon Helm moved immediately into outside projects, Danko on his own, Helm with the RCO All-Stars. Robertson, Manuel, and Hudson kept to themselves, announcing no plans, though Robertson continued to insist the Band would continue to record together. All that's known is that this group had provided some of the highlights of rock & roll for nearly a decade; what kept it from completely realizing its potential or continuing as an active musical force will undoubtedly remain a mystery.   — D.M.

BANDIT
★ **Bandit / Ari. 4113**
Mediocre Seventies hard rock.   — J.S.

MOE BANDY
★★★★ **Best of Moe Bandy / Col. KC-34715**

★★★ **Cowboys Ain't Supposed to Cry / Col. KC-34874**
★★ **Hank Williams, You Wrote My Life / Col. KC-34091**
★★ **Here I Am Drunk Again / Col. KC-34285**
★★★ **I'm Sorry for You, My Friend / Col. KC-34443**
★★ **Soft Lights and Hard Country Music / Col. KC-35288**
Bandy was a country-music anachronism when he surfaced in 1974. He sang pure Texas honky-tonk, previously believed to be an extinct form. Honky-tonk is gutbucket C&W—drinking and cheating songs utilizing a fiddle instead of a violin section, a high harmony voice instead of vocal choirs, and a more prominent rhythm. Bandy made a few bows toward modern Nashville, but his albums are mostly models of light production that his sharp, stinging voice cuts through dramatically. *I Just Started Hatin' Cheatin' Songs Today* (GRC GA-10005) and *Bandy the Rodeo Clown* (GRC GA-10016), his two best albums, have been available only in the bargain bins since GRC folded. However, the hit singles from his three GRC albums are included on Columbia's great *Best of* package.

His weakest effort is the first Columbia album (*Hank Williams*), which despite the title song contains his one foray into schmaltz. *Drunk Again* is only a slight improvement, but *Sorry* is much more in the old GRC groove. Since honky-tonk is, after all, a limited form, his albums tend to sound samey to the uninitiated; in that case, *Best of* is most wholeheartedly recommended.   — J.MO.

ROSE BANKS
★★★ **Rose / Mo. M7-845**
Rose Banks is Sly Stone's sister, but her solo album is more conservative than might be anticipated and includes mild funk (a cover of Sly's "I Get High on You" for one), ballads and even a straightahead remake of the Elgins' "Darling Baby."   — J.MC.

BARCLAY JAMES HARVEST
★ **Gone to Earth / MCA 2302**
★ **Octoberon / MCA 2234**
★ **Time-Honoured Ghosts / Poly. 6517**
Absolutely numbing British rock, of no discernible genre and even less importance. All the right moves, none of the necessary imagination or execution.   — D.M.

NICKEY BARCLAY
★ **Diamond in a Junkyard / Ario. ST-5006**
Though Barclay's simple tunes were sympathetically supported by the jagged edges of Fanny, the all-female rock band with which she won her spurs, her subsequent solo album was truly disappointing. The largely ordinary songs here do not benefit noticeably from stylish production and genuinely superior musicianship, nor can her own pleasant voice add the spark this album sorely needs. — T.M.

BOBBY BARE
★★★ **Bare / Col. KC-35314**
★★★ **Bobby Bare Sings "Lullabys, Legends and Lies" / RCA CPL2-0290**
★★ **Country Boy and Country Girl / RCA AHL1-1244**
★★ **Cowboys and Daddys / RCA AHL1-1222**
★★★ **500 Miles Away from Home / Camd. ACL-7003**
★★ **I'm a Long Way from Home / Camd. S-2465**
★★★ **Me and McDill / RCA AHL1-2179**
★ **Memphis, Tennessee / Camd. ACL1-0150**
★★ **Paper Roses / Camd. ACL1-0533**
★★ **Singin' in the Kitchen / RCA AHL1-0700**
★★★ **Sleeper Wherever I Fall / Col. KC-35645**
★★★ **Sunday Mornin' Comin' Down / RCA ANL1-0560**
★★★★ **The Winner and Other Losers / RCA AHL1-1786**
★★★ **This Is Bobby Bare / RCA VPS-6090**
Bare's career began as "Bill Parsons," who had the No. 2 hit in the country in 1958 with "All-American Boy," a takeoff on Elvis going into the army. As Bobby Bare he was, throughout the Sixties, a staple minor-league country attraction, although he did not dent the pop charts again until 1974 with "Daddy What If."

When Bare is at his best, on the albums rated with three stars above, he sticks to a basically western, macho stance and some of the most hard-edged music in country. On stuff like "Paper Roses," he's just silly. *Me and McDill* and *The Winner and Other Losers,* released in the mid-Seventies, attempted to redefine his image in terms of the outlaw cult developing around Waylon Jennings, Willie Nelson and Tompall Glaser. The move was not entirely successful, but it did play into Bare's strengths: a stronger rhythmic and dynamic sense than

most country artists and an ability to project an adequately but not overbearingly tough male image. — D.M.

BAR-KAYS
★★ **Flying High on Your Love / Mer. SRM-1181**
★★ **Money Talks / Stax 4106**
★★ **Too Hot to Stop / Mer. SRM-1-1099**
Since their rebirth (all but two of the original Bar-Kays went down in the same 1967 plane crash that killed Otis Redding), the Bar-Kays have been a band in search of an identity. *Too Hot,* their first album in years, is unashamedly derivative Ohio Players funk, and *Flying High* and *Money Talks* continued the process. The real thing isn't so great either. — J.MC.

BARNSTORM
★★★★ **Barnstorm / Dun. 50130**
Guitarist Joe Walsh reportedly quit the James Gang because he was less interested in carrying a power trio with his soloing than in adding keyboards to the band and experimenting with a more layered sound. *Barnstorm,* Walsh's blueprint for an ideal band, involves piano, organ and guitar interlacing through a spectacular, languorous progression without sacrificing rock intensity, and may well turn out to be his only representative album. — J.S.

BARRABAS
★ **Barrabas / Atco 36-110**
★★ **Heart of the City / Atco 36-118**
★ **Watch Out / Atco 36-136**
Poor man's Mandrill, busier and less focused. — D.M.

SYD BARRETT
★★★ **The Madcap Laughs / Harv. SABB-11314**
A pleasantly ragged, informal, even primitive two-record offering from the former Pink Floyd guitarist. Deliberately basic instrumentation: Barrett strums an acoustic guitar, with occasional embellishment from David Gilmour and Richard Wright. Quite unlike the standard Floyd extravaganza, Barrett is by turns sentimental, playful or downright careless. — C.W.

ROBBIE BASHO
★★ **Voice of the Eagle / Van. 79321**
★★ **Zarthus / Van. 79339**
Basho's approach adapted John Fahey's acoustic guitar wizardry to play even further with Eastern modal concepts, but never quite got off the ground as the psyche-

delic/mystical folk music it was meant to be. — D.M.

BATDORF AND RODNEY
★ **Batdorf and Rodney / Asy. 5056**
★ **Life Is You / Ari. 4041**
★ **Off the Shelf / Atl. 8298**
This duo's three albums blend the styles of Seals and Crofts and Crosby, Stills and Nash into slick television music. After they split up, Batdorf put together the group Silver. — S.H.

DAVID BATTEAU
★ **Happy in Hollywood / A&M 4576**
A confused songwriter looking for a context to hang his hat on. Producer Ken Scott assembled an able-bodied collection of session players to help Batteau flesh out this 1976 debut record, and that faceless backup is the most interesting aspect of this generally empty enterprise. (Now deleted.) — J.S.

BAY CITY ROLLERS
★ **Bay City Rollers / Ari. 4049**
★ **Dedication / Ari. 4093**
★ **Greatest Hits / Ari. 4158**
★ **It's a Game / Ari. 7004**
★ **Rock 'n' Roll Love Letter / Ari. 4071**
Trivial, sugary, pre-teenage pop product—some watered-down oldies, but mainly original material. *Bay City Rollers* emphasized the group's clean, passionless vocal harmonies, and toned down their simplistic, anonymous, almost incidental instrumentation. *Rock 'n' Roll Love Letter* showed a slight maturing but otherwise stuck to their proven formula; *Dedication,* produced by the ordinarily estimable Jimmy Ienner, was a mere continuation. *It's a Game,* Harry Maslin producing, featured dull studio professionalism and orchestration, and

made more of a relaxed MOR pitch—it still lacked originality, energy and conviction. *Greatest Hits* assembled their numerous commercial successes, most notably "Saturday Night." — C.W.

BAZUKA
★★★ **Bazuka / A&M 3406**
Produced, composed and arranged by Tony Camillo, this sprightly disco one-shot features (predictably) the assembled cast of New York session all-stars. The 1975 hit was "Dynomite." (Now deleted.) — J.S.

B.C.G. (BOB CREWE GENERATION)
★★ **Motivation / Elek. 7E-1103**
★ **Street Talk / Elek. 7E-1083**
Crewe is one of rock's stranger figures: he first emerged as a member of the Rays (their hit was "Silhouettes") and became most successful in the early Sixties as a producer of classic records by Mitch Ryder and the Detroit Wheels and Frankie Valli and the Four Seasons. Those productions were all frankly evocative of Phil Spector.

Later he turned to disco, scoring a success with Disco Tex and the Sex-o-lettes, a breakthrough for the notorious talk-show rocker Monte Rock III. *Street Talk* continues the disco groove, but *Motivation* is a different matter, a vocal album produced by Jerry Wexler and Barry Beckett. Wexler is perhaps the greatest of the rock vocal producers, and Crewe's voice isn't bad, but nothing can completely redeem the self-penned material. — D.M.

THE BEACH BOYS
★★★★★ **All Summer Long/California Girls / Cap. STBB-500**
★★ **Beach Boys' Christmas Album / Cap. SM-2164**
★★ **Beach Boys' Concert / Cap. SM-2198**
★★★ **Best of the Beach Boys / Cap. DT-2545**
★★★ **Best of the Beach Boys, Vol. 2 / Cap. DT-2706**
★★★★ **Dance Dance Dance/Fun Fun Fun / Cap. STBB-701**
★★★★★ **Endless Summer / Cap. SVBB-11307**
★★★ **Little Deuce Coupe / Cap. SM-1998**
★★★★ **Spirit of America / Cap. SVBB-11384**
★★★ **Stack O' Tracks / EMI EST 24009**
★★★ **Surfer Girl / Cap. SM-1981**
★★★ **Surfin' U.S.A. / Cap. SM-1890**
★★ **The Beach Boys / Sp. 4021**
The Beach Boys burst out of Southern California in 1962-63 with a teen-oriented

sound that predicted much of what would come later with the invasion of the British rock acts following the Beatles. Led by composer/singer/bassist Brian Wilson (with his two brothers—Dennis and Carl—and a cousin, Mike Love), the basic sound, as expressed in such songs as "Surfin' U.S.A.," "Little Deuce Coupe," "Fun, Fun, Fun" and "Surfin' Safari," was built around Chuck Berry's guitar sound, Eddie Cochran's antiphonal rockabilly, and group vocal harmonies. The lyric themes were perfect encapsulations of middle-class suburban lifestyles, in the best sense: surfing, driving and just fooling around amounted to miniaturized acts of self-assertion, building an identity completely separate from that of adults. This inkling of rebellion was never more than implicit, though, one of the major differences between this group and the British acts that followed.

Brian Wilson's ballad style could be breathtaking. "Don't Worry Baby" used a drag race as a sexual metaphor; "Surfer Girl" was pure maudlin ode; "In My Room" a definition of wonderful rich-kid self-pity. These are great songs, and "Don't Worry Baby" alone would make Wilson and the Beach Boys major figures in rock history. While their harmony arrangements were never as soulful as those of the best R&B groups at Atlantic and Motown, nor as inventive as the Beatles', the Beach Boys helped shaped a generation of pop taste—their influence can be heard in groups as diverse as America and the Who.

Toward the middle of the Sixties, Brian Wilson became fascinated with the production style of Phil Spector. *All Summer Long* was a concept album in the Spector spirit, a celebration of liberty from school and work—it contains "I Get Around," the group's best fast song, and "Wendy," a classic ballad. *California Girls* was most explicit in its emulation of Spector and the coterie of producers associated with him in New York and L.A. (notably Shadow Morton)—it includes a pretty takeoff on the Crystals' "Then He Kissed Me" and the Ad-Libs' "Boy from New York City," both rewritten for gender purposes.

Capitol's repackaging efforts on this music have been rather formless. *Surfer Girl, Surfin' U.S.A.* and *Little Deuce Coupe* are available cheaply and separately, with a couple of minor songs deleted. *All Summer Long* and *California Girls* make a great double package (at the price of one record), but the deletions hurt worse: there was little fluff on the originals. Similarly, *Dance*

Dance Dance/Fun Fun Fun (originally titled *Beach Boys Today!* for the former, *Shut Down, Volume 2,* for the latter). The anthologies are uneven: the Springboard is nearly worthless, a jumble of hits; the late-Sixties *Greatest Hits* is adequate, but the selection is both skimpy and obvious. *Endless Summer,* released in 1974 and an immediate hit that spurred a long-lasting revival, covers all of the group's best and best-known songs; as a result, *Spirit of America,* the 1975 followup, is a bit thin, though still more than worthwhile. *Stack O' Tracks* is an oddity: instrumental tracks only from a variety of the group's best-known songs—perfect for aspiring vocalists.

The Beach Boys were essentially a studio group, as all of their concert recordings confirm. *Concert* may very well be the best of these, but that says little. The *Christmas Album* is notable only for the hit single, "Little Saint Nick," and some of the most nasal carols ever put on wax.

★★ **Beach Boys' '69 / Cap. ST-11584**
★★★ **Friends/Smiley Smile / Rep. 2MS-2167**
★★★ **Pet Sounds / Rep. 2197 (also available with** *Carl and the Passions—So Tough* **/ Rep. 2-2083)**
★★★ **Surf's Up / Rep. 6453**
★★★ **20/20/Wild Honey / Rep. 2MS-2166**
As the Sixties waned, and with the advent of mass freak-out not only in California but all over America and Europe, Brian Wilson lost touch; his real talent was for expressing simple, everyday joys, not the mystical gobbledygook then in fashion. But the decade (and drugs also) began to have its effect on him, and as a consequence, on the group, which has never been much more than a front for his personality.

Pet Sounds was the band's first commercial failure, mostly because Wilson was attempting to create the sort of pastiche the Beatles popularized with *Sgt. Pepper* before there was a market for it. The music is strong but spotty; if Wilson was ready for experimentation, it is unlikely that the other Beach Boys understood his portent. *Wild Honey* is similarly confused: the title track is a R&B-flavored smash, just the sort of thing one would have bet the Beach Boys couldn't do well. But the rest is too cute or too strained. *20/20* and *Friends* are basically collections of singles, some of which were moderate hits, most of which weren't. They were released because Wilson had bigger game in mind: a total production-conceptual masterpiece, tentatively called *Smiley Smile*.

For various reasons often chronicled elsewhere (see especially *The Rolling Stone Illustrated History of Rock & Roll*), the album was not released until the mid-Seventies, when its innovations seemed rather tepid and its focus altogether misdirected. But Wilson's mystique, particularly among critics, grew larger as the group's releases diminished—*Smiley Smile* was gonna be a perfect record, one was assured again and again. People kept saying it even through the excerpts released on *Surf's Up* were much less forceful than the simple early rock hits. It was an exercise in myth-making almost unparalleled in show business. Wilson became a Major Artist by making music no one ever heard. That the results are so trivial is a bit amusing, a bit revolting.

★ **Carl and the Passions—So Tough / Pet Sounds / Rep. 2-2083**
★★ **15 Big Ones / Rep. 2251**
★★★ **Good Vibrations—Best of the Beach Boys / Rep. K-2280**
★★ **Holland / Rep. MS-2118**
★ **M.I.U. / Rep. K-2258**
★★ **Sunflower / Rep. 6382**
★★ **The Beach Boys in Concert / Rep. 2RS-6484**
★★★ **The Beach Boys Love You / Rep. K-2258**

The Beach Boys re-formed Brother Records, distributed by Reprise, in 1970, leaving Capitol after buying back some of their early records (those released on Reprise and reviewed above). But by the time they came to Reprise, most of their best work was behind them; Mike Love had replaced Wilson almost completely as lead singer, and with age, his nasality lost most of its charm. Wilson was wiped out—he barely makes his presence felt on *Sunflower, Hol-*

land or *Carl and the Passions,* though each of the latter two contains a class effort: "Sail on Sailor" and "Marcella." Nonetheless, because of a wave of Sixties nostalgia, the group was a continuing concert draw, and *Endless Summer* helped spur sales of the Capitol albums (the live *'69* was another cash-in attempt, released in 1976 after European release some years earlier). But it was only Wilson's vaunted comeback with *15 Big Ones* in 1976 that spurred the group back into record-chart contention again; the fact that the record is strained and lifeless, a documentary look at a worm on a hook, bothered the group's revived cult not at all. Similarly, *Love You,* released in early 1977, was acclaimed a masterpiece. Yet though the compositions were somewhat stronger, it was clear that Wilson's voice was shot. Alive in the marketplace though they may have been, it was clear that the Beach Boys had ceased to be an artistic force at all.   — D.M.

THE BEATLES / Early Period
★★★★ **A Hard Day's Night / U. Artists 6366**
★★★★ **Beatles VI / Cap. ST-2358**
★★★★ **Beatles '65 / Cap. ST-2228**
★★★★★ **Live at the Hollywood Bowl / Cap. SMAS-11638**
★★★ **Live at the Star Club in Hamburg, Germany 1962 / Atl. SD2-7001**
★★★★★ **Meet the Beatles! / Cap. ST-2047**
★★★★★ **Something New / Cap. ST-2108**
★★★★★ **The Beatles' Second Album / Cap. ST-2080**
★★ **The Beatles' Story / Cap. STBO-2222**
★★★★★ **The Early Beatles / Cap. ST-2309**

The Beatles, as everyone must know, were one of the three most influential rock forces in the Sixties (along with the Rolling Stones and Bob Dylan). But they (or at least John, Paul and George) began playing together in the late Fifties as contemporaries of Buddy Holly and Chuck Berry. Their first two albums, *Meet the Beatles, The Beatles' Second* and a collection of their 1964 singles, *The Early Beatles,* released in 1965, reflect their proximity to rock & roll's beginnings. The vocal harmonies borrow from the Everly Brothers, the instrumental sound is rockabilly *cum* English skiffle band, and forward thrust predominates over melody.

Yet the Beatles were clearly different. They wrote their own material, and somehow avoided the deadening effects of rock

& roll formulas: they employed chord patterns hitherto unknown to rock and underpinned them with thickened guitar chordings and a pounding bass that had a harmonic as well as a rhythmic function. Young people were beginning to sense the power of their incipient culture, and that enthusiasm, so different from the giddy naiveté of earlier rockers, was what gave even the Beatles' renditions of Fifties tunes and Motown staples a unique freshness and power.

But the Beatles were more than just an embodiment of the Sixties *Zeitgeist.* They were leaders, a historical force, because they were capable of, for a period of years, ceaseless change. With *Something New* and *A Hard Day's Night* (both of which contain "I'll Cry Instead," "Tell Me Why," "And I Love Her" and "If I Fell"), the Beatles suddenly had become rock's most prolific writers of gorgeous pop melodies. They had also begun the eclecticism (hear the classical guitar sound on "And I Love Her") that became one of their trademarks.

Beatles '65 and *Beatles VI* continued the trend to melodicism. But more importantly, these LPs pioneered a new brand of rock: guitars were often distorted by feedback ("I Feel Fine," "She's a Woman"), the number of moving instrumental parts was increased (the bass guitar especially becoming a contrapuntal device) and new kinds of hard-rock rhythm (sometimes several different rhythms in one tune) were employed.

One should never underestimate the quality of the Beatles' early recorded work. The notion of continual growth implies progress, but the Beatles' development suggests an organic rather than an industrial model: like a hardy plant, the Beatles continually renewed themselves. They never, until the very end, recorded anything mediocre. From "I Want to Hold Your Hand" to "Eight Days a Week," songs that bracket this early period, they wrote dozens of classic pop tunes. And though their style was always changing, the Beatles' sound was consistently unique and important.

THE BEATLES / Middle Period
★★★★★ Help! / Cap. SMAS-2386
★★★★★ Revolver / Cap. SW-2576
★★★★★ Rubber Soul / Cap. SW-2442
★★★★★ Yesterday . . . and Today / Cap. ST-2553

There is no way to gauge accurately the impact these four brilliant LPs had on rock. Released in the space of a year, each dramatically expanded the form's possibilities, each had a distinctive sound (and look—*Rubber Soul* and *Revolver* are remembered for their psychedelically inspired covers as well as their music) and each was an event whose proportions helped to create a self-conscious rock community.

Help! displayed Dylan-influenced lyrics (the folky "You've Got to Hide Your Love Away," powered by John Lennon's throaty vocal and Dylanesque pronunciations, and the confessional title cut); a new guitar sound, the ephemeral one of "I Need You"; the tricky rhythm changes of "Ticket to Ride"; and a breathtaking songwriting maturity.

Rubber Soul is perhaps the Beatles' greatest album. The songs ("I've Just Seen a Face," "Norwegian Wood," "Michelle" and "In My Life" for openers) are classically melodic. The arrangements are incredibly various: the sitar in "Norwegian Wood"; the contrapuntal vocals of "You Won't See Me"; the instrumental keynote to "In My Life"; the Greek feel to the refrain of "Girl."

Revolver was remarkable because, though the Beatles were burning with a desire to get new messages across, the music survives the heavy intentions. Some of the Eastern ("Love You To") and acid-induced ("Tomorrow Never Knows") influences seem dated now; but the Beatles, conscious of their abilities but not yet self-conscious, are still making the most exciting music of their career.

Yesterday . . . and Today, actually a collection of British and American singles, is still one of the Beatles' most delightful LPs. The guitar support on "Dr. Robert" and "And Your Bird Can Sing" is incredibly active; and "Yesterday," "Day Tripper" and "I'm Only Sleeping" are some of the group's finest songs.

THE BEATLES / Late Period
★★★★★ Abbey Road / Cap. SO-383
★★★★★ Hey Jude / Cap. SW-385
★★ Let It Be / Apple AR-34001
★★★★ Magical Mystery Tour / Cap. SMAL-2835
★★★★ Sgt. Pepper's Lonely Hearts Club Band / Cap. SMAS-2653
★★★★★ The Beatles / Cap. SWBO-101
★★ Yellow Submarine / Cap. SW-153

With *Sgt. Pepper,* the Beatles entered their Mannerist period. Given the enormous amount of attention the world paid them, it's not surprising that the Beatles became self-conscious. Yet Mannerism implies not only self-consciousness but also a diminution of creative energy, a baroque attention to detail, a kind of effeteness: all of those descriptions apply to the work of this era.

Sgt. Pepper may well be the best-known pop album of all time. Its release was greeted with an effusion of paeans citing it as a bridge between pop and art. But *Sgt. Pepper* was really a thickly detailed, somewhat stiff collection of generally less-than-great Beatles tunes vaguely molded into a whole. It was not, as many speculated, a concept album, but rather an ornately produced and speciously unified pop work.

The trend toward cute self-consciousness continued with *Magical Mystery Tour.* Each of the Beatles had now assumed a fixed identity: George ("Blue Jay Way") was the heavy mystic; Paul the lighthearted romantic; Ringo the buffoon (since he was the most limited and easy to pigeonhole, Ringo had early established his persona in *A Hard Day's Night*); and John was the acid-head. Since the Beatles' entire success had depended on their phenomenal cohesion, such individualism didn't bode well. (One must add that this album contained, in addition to the avant-garde "I Am the Walrus," the ear-opening singles "Penny Lane," "All You Need Is Love" and "Strawberry Fields Forever.")

The Beatles, often called the "White Album," was the least integrated of all the Beatles LPs to this point. Still, it is two records' worth of great lyric and instrumental moments. There's the beautiful guitar solo in "While My Guitar Gently Weeps," the acoustic guitar accompaniment to the lovely "Mother Nature's Son," the hard guitar distortion in "Revolution." And the words to "Happiness Is a Warm Gun" (a work of surrealism in miniature to rival the best of Dylan) are worth the price of admission.

Hey Jude is a collection of late Beatles singles—the title cut, "Lady Madonna," "Rain," "The Ballad of John and Yoko," "Paperback Writer" and so forth. The last song is arguably the Beatles' most complex and astonishing single ever.

Let It Be, though it has the powerful title cut, is the most distressingly mediocre Beatles album. The songs generally lack focus, intensity, enthusiasm, originality—the Beatles' hallmarks.

It seems best to consider *Abbey Road* the Beatles' swan song. It's often said to be Paul's album, and perhaps the unified sec-

ond side is. Still, it's a great achievement. That second side is an operetta with no "concept" other than melodic and instrumental cohesion. The individual songs are brief dreams, making no great linear sense, but as they flow together in one long fantasy, a rough shape emerges. One remembers snatches of melody, the great guitar fills and solos (which spawned a whole school of guitar accompaniment in the Seventies), the harmonic swells. The second side of *Abbey Road* is perhaps the most purely musical work the Beatles ever created, and in its own way it stands with their best.

THE BEATLES / Collections
★★★ **Love Songs / Cap. SKBL-11711**
★★★★ **Rock 'N' Roll Music / Cap. SKBO-11537**
★★★★★ **The Beatles/1962-1966 / Cap. SEBX-11842**
★★★★★ **The Beatles/1967-1970 / Cap. SEBX-11843**

The Beatles/1962-1966 and *1967-70* are decent enough compilations—there are lots of fine songs, selected in a straight-ahead fashion. But you're always better off with any single Beatles LP—each works by itself quite well. Collections obviously fail to capture the spirit of any of the individual albums.

The *Rock 'N' Roll Music* and *Love Songs* aggregations, though, do nothing good for the group or the listener. The Beatles masterfully blended fast and slow, soft and loud. Here all you hear is one dimension. If you must have a collection, get one of the last two entries. — P.H.

BEAVER AND KRAUSE
★★★ **In a Wild Sanctuary / War. 1850**
This Beaver/Krause album makes all the mock orchestral European rock extrava-

ganzas sound like McDonald's commercials. Paul Beaver and Bernard Krause had extensive production and sidemen credentials before becoming electronic music adepts, and their synthesis of musical styles is enough to give eclecticism a good name. *In a Wild Sanctuary* leans more toward the cosmic white-noise end of synthesizer programming, but the deleted *Gandharva* is more awesome—on one side they kick out some jams with help from guitarist Mike Bloomfield, while the flip is an atmospheric set recorded in San Francisco's Grace Cathedral with Bud Shank on alto sax and flute and Gerry Mulligan on baritone. — J.S.

BEAVERTEETH
★★ **Beaverteeth / RCA APL1-2076**
★ **Dam It / RCA AFL1-2574**
Southern rock band's most distinguished move is a version of Carl Perkins' "Dixie Fried," on *Beaverteeth.* — D.M.

BE-BOP DELUXE
★★ **Axe Victim / Harv. SM-11689**
★★★ **Drastic Plastic / Harv. SW-11750**
★★ **Futurama / Harv. ST-11432**
★★★★ **Live in the Air Age / Harv. SKB-11666**
★★★★ **Modern Music / Harv. ST-11575**
★★★ **Sunburst Finish / Harv. ST-11478**
★★★★ **The Best of . . . and the Rest of Be-Bop Deluxe / Harv. SKBO 11870**
Be-Bop Deluxe's first two albums suffer from a misguided emphasis on Bill Nelson's flamboyant guitar style (Hendrix-derived glissandi with simmering sustains), with the often beautiful melodies and lyric fantasies taking a back seat to cluttered tempo changes and pointless gimmickry. The 1975 *Sunburst Finish,* Be-Bop's first American success (albeit a modest one), works better, although Nelson's split role continues to diffuse the band's impact. With *Modern Music* he concentrated on coalescing his melodic strengths with the band's instrumental personality. The upshot, musically, is their most balanced and durable LP, and lyrically, an intriguing merger of Nelson's previous fantasy obsessions with a jarring quest for secular redemption (or at least escape). *Live in the Air Age* is everything you'd expect from this band in concert, while *Best of* is just that. Be-Bop fans should also seek out Nelson's solo effort, *Northern Dream* (JEM LAF 2182). — M.G.

THE BECKIES
★★ **The Beckies / Sire 7519**
Led by Michael Brown (composer of the Left Banke's 1966 hit "Walk Away Renee"), the Beckies offer a hard-driving pop sound featuring vocalist Scott Trusty, who sings high when he means it and sounds like Bryan Ferry when he doesn't. — G.C.

JEFF BECK
★★★ **Beck, Bogert and Appice / Epic KE-32140**
★★ **Beck-Ola / Epic BXN-26478**
★★★★ **Blow by Blow / Epic PE-33409**
★ **Jeff Beck Group / Epic PE-31331**
★★★★ **Jeff Beck Group/Rough and Ready / Epic PE-30973**
■ **Live / Epic PE-34433**
★★★★ **Truth / Epic PE-26413**
★★★ **Truth/Beck-Ola / Epic BG-33779**
★★ **Wired / Epic PE-33849**
Although universally acknowledged as one of rock's premier and most influential guitarists, Jeff Beck has had problems as a solo artist and group leader. He is adept at conceiving and outfitting bands to use as vehicles for his immense talents, but apparently gets impatient, bored and/or angry with other musicians quickly—no single Jeff Beck Group has lasted for more than two albums. *Truth* and *Beck-Ola,* recorded in the late Sixties with Rod Stewart, Ron Wood (on bass) and Nicky Hopkins, both show flashes of brilliance ("I Ain't Superstitious," "You Shook Me" on the former, "Plynth," "Rice Pudding" on the latter), but Beck dominates so much he leaves the band in the dust. Stewart suffers the most; his style, not yet fully developed, is simply no match for Beck's frenetic lashings.

The next Jeff Beck Group (featuring Bob Tench, vocals; Max Middleton, keyboards; and Cozy Powell, drums) fares well at first. With a fairly anonymous band posing no threats to the infamous Beck ego, he relaxes a bit and plays (rather than toys) with the other musicians. Middleton brings some jazz texturing to the music, and Beck, picking up the cue, records some beautiful tracks, especially the long and introspective "Raynes Park Blues," on *Jeff Beck Group.* And "Situation" reveals that he has lost none of his ferocity. The promise doesn't last long, though; *Jeff Beck Group,* produced all too calmly by Steve Cropper, is easily the laziest, dullest LP in Beck's catalogue.

Apparently Beck was already planning a new band with Vanilla Fudge/Cactus veterans Tim Bogert and Carmine Appice. *Beck, Bogert and Appice* returns Beck to the field of hard rock with a vengeance. A power trio to end all power trios, *B, B and*

A wears its excesses proudly. They fracture Stevie Wonder's "Superstition," coyly croon Curtis Mayfield's "I'm So Proud" and beat Grand Funk at their own game with "Why Should I Care" and "Livin' Alone."

After the stormy demise of B, B and A, Beck changed course once again, and under George Martin's production recorded *Blow by Blow,* an all-instrumental album (no more vocalists to worry about) that shows off Beck's consummate abilities as a guitarist as never before. All styles served here, from rock to funk to jazz, and its success has led Beck into jazz-rock circles. *Wired,* with Jan Hammer on keyboards, is Beck meeting the jazz-rock fusion forces. His playing is as terse and intelligent as on *Blow by Blow,* and Hammer's accompaniment shows unusual restraint. The live Beck/Hammer album, however, marks the nadir of this talented artist's career, as excess meets excess. — B.A.

CAPTAIN BEEFHEART AND HIS MAGIC BAND
★★★★ Clear Spot / Rep. 2115
★★★ Shiny Beast (Bat Chain Puller) / War. K-3256
★★★★ The Spotlight Kid / Rep. 2050
★★★★★ Trout Mask Replica / Rep. 2027
Trout Mask is a staggering double album about three steps beyond some combination of delta blues and free jazz. Astonishingly advanced rhythmically, it also sports superb guitar work and some of the most spontaneous sax blowing (by Beefheart) ever recorded. His voice (range: four and a half octaves) sounds like a wild animal. His lyrics are often humorous, rambling discourses on the relationship between man and nature. The whole album has a wonderful childlike feeling about it.

In *Spotlight Kid* and *Clear Spot,* Beefheart attempted to hone this basic style down to something closer to the mainstream—but not much closer. *Spotlight Kid* 's guitar solos, especially, are more conventional and prominent. The lyrics aren't quite as personal, and Beefheart's blues leanings are more explicit. *Clear Spot* is quite similar; it even has one delightful soul song ("Too Much Time") that sounds like it could have been a hit single. The 1978 LP, *Shiny Beast,* was an encouraging return. — J.M.

THE BEE GEES
★★★★ Bee Gees Gold, Vol. 1 / RSO 1-3006
★★ Children of the World / RSO 1-3003

★★ Here at Last / RSO 2-3901
★★★★ Main Course / RSO 1-3024
★ Odessa / RSO 1-3007
★★★ Spirits Having Flown / RSO 3041
Except for a one-disc condensation of the two-disc *Odessa,* all of the Bee Gees' Sixties albums—made when they were an Australian version of the lightest aspects of the Beatles—are out of print. *Gold,* however, does a fine job of condensing the group's hits, from "New York Mining Disaster 1941" to really mushy stuff like "How Can You Mend a Broken Heart."

In the middle Seventies, just as their vogue seemed played out, the Bee Gees began to incorporate R&B into their lavish pop repertoire, and the result has made them a major, if not dominant, factor in the marketplace. *Main Course,* containing the hits "Jive Talkin'," "Nights on Broadway," and "Fanny," established a pop disco sound much indebted to Arif Mardin's towering productions, and the others followed suit. But the group's biggest hits came with the release of the soundtrack from *Saturday Night Fever* in 1978; the Bee Gees are now a household word, epitomizing the elaborate craftsmanship of late-Seventies pop, the cultural transference between black and white music that has occurred in the past few years, and the emotional vapidity dominating popular taste of late. *Spirits* (1979) was more pop than disco, ducking the issue, but containing what may be the best nondisco hit they have made, "Tragedy." — S.H./O.M.

BEERS FAMILY
★★ Golden Skein / Bio. 12045
★ Seasons of Peace / Bio. C-12033E
The late Bob Beers and his wife, Evelyne, spawned a family of musical traditions, and spread that music by way of the annual Fox Hollow Festival in upstate New York. The festival has served as a gathering of numerous folk and folk-based musicians, all of whom camp out and frequently jam throughout the night. Many of the songs associated with the Beers—"Dumbarton's Drums," "Seasons of Peace"—have entered the contemporary folk repertoire. Neither of these sets is well recorded, but *Golden Skein* offers a slightly more accessible song selection. — I.M.

BEGINNING OF THE END
★★★ Beginning of the End / Atco 4403
One-hit pop R&B wonders whose one hit—"Funky Nassau"—was worth the wait. — J.S.

ARCHIE BELL AND THE DRELLS
★★★ **Dance Your Troubles Away** / Phil. PZ-33844
★★★ **Hard Not to Like It** / Phil. PZ-34855
★★ **Where Will You Go, When the Party's Over** / Phil. PZ-34323

The Drells' first Philly soul efforts (for Atlantic in the late Sixties) were quintessential Kenneth Gamble and Leon Huff productions: trashy, slick and raunchy, epitomized by "Tighten Up." By the mid-Seventies, however, disco had changed the prerequisites for dance songs, and most of these songs weigh in at four minutes plus, often too much for comfort. Still, Bunny Sigler's "I Could Dance All Night," from *Dance Your Troubles Away,* harks back to the old sound, and "Let's Groove" is rocking nouveau boogie. The other albums echo the previous successes more and more faintly, unfortunately. — J.MC./D.M.

MAGGIE BELL
★★★ **Suicide Sal** / Swan 8412
Bell can really drive a song, but she relies more on grit than inspiration. On *Suicide Sal,* she's backed by Led Zeppelin's Jimmy Page, among others. A good time is had by all, and Bell's soul mannerisms are convincing in this rock setting. — A.S.

WILLIAM BELL
★★★ **Coming Back for More** / Mer. SRM-1-1146
★★★ **It's Time You Took Another Listen** / Mer. SRM-1-1193

Bell was a minor mainstay of Stax Records' Memphis soul complex during the Sixties, where he clicked with such numbers as "You Don't Miss Your Water," a wonderful soul variant of the country standard "Private Number," in duet with Judy Clay, and more obscure songs, such as "I Forgot to Be Your Lover," "Everybody Loves a Winner" and a tribute to Otis Redding, "The King Is Gone." Perhaps now that Fantasy owns the Stax catalogue, they'll release a greatest-hits collection.

That's made more likely by his late-Seventies resurgence. These are modernized Stax albums, and the hit Bell garnered from *Coming,* "Tryin' to Love Two," was one of the few recent hits (it made the charts in 1976) that could have passed for one of the songs from the classic Memphis soul era. — D.M.

THE BELLAMY BROTHERS
■ **Beautiful Friends** / War. K-3176
■ **Plain and Fancy** / War. B-3034
★ **The Bellamy Brothers Featuring "Let Your Love Flow"** / War. B-2941

The guileless exuberance of "Let Your Love Flow," a 1976 hit, is belied by the rest of these LPs, which exemplify some of the worst tendencies of contemporary pop rock: slick, gauzy harmonies overlaid on a bed of chewing-gum rhythm. Pop without the snap and crackle, in other words. — D.M.

JESSE BELVIN
★★★ **Yesterdays** / RCA 1-0966
An urbane stylist, Jesse Belvin was a black Fifties singer whose style combined equal parts of Nat "King" Cole, Johnny Ace, and Sam Cooke. His best-known records were drenched with violins, plagued by heavy white choral background singers and featured some of the most prominent jazz musicians of the day. The antithesis of R&B and rock & roll, the music on *Yesterdays,* an anthology that includes previously unreleased material, is soulful but polite. (Now deleted.) — J.MC.

JORGE BEN
★★★ **Samba Nova** / Is. 9361
★★ **Tropical** / Is. 9390
Brazilian Jorge Ben's *Samba Nova* is much closer to the street music of *Black Orpheus* than to the more familiar superclub whisperings of bossa nova. Ben, a seductive acoustic guitarist and sweet-voiced singer (but with a nice rough edge), leads a mostly percussion band through a fine set of songs aided by a touch of orchestration and several crisp, sirenic backup singers. *Nova* presents Ben very well to the North American audience.

Tropical, however, is a disappointing foray into a disco/soul revisionism of Ben's samba for which his voice and writing is totally ill suited. The album features heavy electric versions of such Ben standards as "Mas Que Nada" and several ballads so poorly arranged that Ben sometimes sounds like Cat Stevens singing in Portuguese. Only "Taj Mahal" and "My Lady" retain Ben's typical rude rhythmic energy. — B.T.

MARC BENNO
★★★ **Ambush** / A&M 4364
★★★ **Marc Benno** / A&M 4273
★★★ **Minnows** / A&M 4303
Benno's records are early examples of what was to become the L.A. style—polished studio expertise. Various musicians set the

tone for each of the albums: Booker T. Jones' chunky piano and Ry Cooder's bottleneck guitar help to create the easy-rocking intimacy of the debut. The full slate of studio musicians and the fuller production of David Anderle gave *Minnows* a slightly pop feel. *Ambush,* which utilized a pruned-down band with few additions, put Benno in a tougher setting that worked to his advantage.

While the three albums demonstrate Benno's lightweight talents (pleasant voice, smooth guitar style), they create a paradox—while there is nothing to detract from his work, there's also precious little to recommend it. — J.B.M.

BENNY AND THE JETS
★ Elton John Songbook / RCA
ANL1-0836

The inevitable MOR ripoff from Elton's hit of the same name. — J.S.

BROOK BENTON
★ Brook Benton Sings a Love Story /
RCA AFL1-1044
★★★ Brook Benton Today / Coti. 9018
★★★★ Golden Hits / Mer. 60607
★★★ The Two of Us (with Dinah Washington) / Mer. 60244
★★ This Is Brook Benton / All Pl. 3015

Nothing brings back the late Fifties like the sound of a blues riff delivered by 1001 strings. It was Benton's own idea to combine gospel intensity with lush pop arrangements, and the Mercury sides from the Fifties have more to offer than nostalgia. His singing is both smooth and smoky, and he's never lost the crisp delivery he learned in his early days with the Golden Gate Quartet. On *The Two of Us,* the duets themselves are fine, but the solo tunes are neither artist's best work. *Golden Hits,* in contrast, is a classic. From rock to ballads to blues, Benton never drops his easy elegance, yet the swirling strings don't obscure his emotional intensity.

The RCA album is a remastered hash of outtakes; the Cotillion is from the period that produced Benton's last big hit, "Rainy Night in Georgia"; the All Platinum set is Benton today, not at the height of his powers but still good enough to make a disco version of "My Funny Valentine" credible. — A.S.

CHUCK BERRY
★★ Chuck Berry / Chess 60032
★★ Chuck Berry (Greatest Hits) / Arc.
Folk 321

★★★★ Chuck Berry's Golden Decade /
Chess 1514
★★★★ Chuck Berry's Golden Decade,
Vol. 2 / Chess 60023
★★★ Chuck Berry's Golden Decade, Vol.
3 / Chess 60028
★ Chuck Berry's Golden Hits / Mer. 61103
★★★★ Chuck Berry's Greatest Hits /
Chess 1485E
★★★★ More Chuck Berry / Chess 1465E
★★ On Stage / Chess 1480E
★★ The London Chuck Berry Sessions /
Chess 60020

Chuck Berry is to rock what Louis Armstrong was to jazz. He established *the* basic mode of expression on the genre's key instrument, the guitar—an approach that shaped almost everything that was played after his rise. As a writer, his influence was hardly less great. The sagas of teenage hard luck and romance, the devoted pursuit of a half-comic, half-demonic American dream which he set down in "Maybellene," "Johnny B. Goode," "Back in the U.S.A." and a dozen others paint an America as big, brilliant, and personal as anyone's.

The most striking characteristic of Berry's style when it first appeared, with "Maybellene" in 1955, was the fast, ringing tone of his electric guitar. Although he recorded in Chicago, in close proximity to such masters of urban blues as Howlin' Wolf and Muddy Waters, he effected a drastic change in their twelve-bar style, speeding it up, simplifying it by merging it with the basic thirty-two-bar pop-song format. Berry himself listed Louis Jordan and country & western as important sources. This basic guitar sound was simple enough to move any number of teenagers to copy it—everyone from Lonnie Mack to the Beach Boys, and in England, the Rolling Stones, the Beatles, the Animals and more—but was in fact almost endlessly adaptable, as anyone who has ever heard "Brown Sugar" can attest.

Chuck Berry's Golden Decade, at least the first two volumes, tells most of the story: "Nadine," "Brown Eyed Handsome Man," "Memphis," "Almost Grown," "Reelin' and Rockin'," "Sweet Little Sixteen," "Promised Land," "Let It Rock," "Carol," "You Never Can Tell" and a half-dozen others are at the heart of the rock repertoire. Most of these were not hits when first released—only four of Berry's records made the Top Ten from 1956 to 1960—but they have become familiar to almost every rock listener because so many bands use them to supplement their performances.

This alone would make them essential to an understanding of the music. But Berry was as frequently inspired as any rock performer of his generation, ranking with Elvis Presley and perhaps Little Richard at the very pinnacle of the genre. The emotions are more often bright and lively than dark and brooding, something else that set him off from the bluesmen, but this can conceal the deadly ironic eye of songs like "School Days" or "Roll over Beethoven" or the deeply moving saga of Little Marie in "Memphis" and its sequel, "Little Marie."

Greatest Hits and *More* (a mid-Sixties singles collection—its original title was *Twist*—which has somehow survived the Chess cutout policy) merely reiterate volumes 1 and 2 of *Golden Decade.* Volume 3 is without any hits, and in fact is filled out with much of Berry's always mediocre blues playing. It is still worth hearing, even in the abysmal fake stereo that robs all this material of much of its punch—if possible, listen in mono. (Unfortunately, none of these records are available in that format.)

The Mercury and Archive of Folk and Jazz collections are from a brief, disastrous fling at the former label during the mid-Sixties. The song titles are the same, but that's about all. *On Stage* is only a mediocre live set—unfortunate, because Berry was a great, duckwalking showman in concert—and does *not* contain "Surfin' U.S.A.," no matter what the liner says.

London Sessions gave Berry his last hit (and first No. 1) in 1972 with the bathroom-risqué "My Ding-a-Ling," apart from which it is exceptional only for its sloppiness. The Chess *Chuck Berry* is the most recent Berry, released in 1975, and seems designed mostly to showcase the singing of his daughter, Ingrid Berry Gibson. One song, "Deuce," comes close to the inspired ribaldry of the early ones, and "Hi Heel Sneakers" is the only one of the classic covers that is up to snuff. Apart from that you would be better off searching out such deleted albums as *Back Home* (containing the memorable "Tulane") or the magnificent *St. Louis to Liverpool,* one of the greatest rock & roll records ever made. — D.M.

MIKE BERRY
★★★★ **Rock's in My Head / Sire 7524**
Berry is an oldies fetishist, but a superb one. He scored in England in 1961 with "Tribute to Buddy Holly," included here, then disappeared until 1975 when he cut

this LP, which consists mostly of Fifties hits like "Peggy Sue," "Hey Baby," "That'll Be the Day" and "Don't Be Cruel," changed from the originals only by reversing the tempos. A very devoted if idiosyncratic work. — D.M.

KAREN BETH
★ **New Moon Rising / Bud. 5631**
Producer John Simon tried hard with this 1975 Woodstock hippie, but couldn't come up with anything that even vaguely threatened Joni Mitchell. — D.M.

DICKEY BETTS
★★ **Atlanta's Burning Down / Ari. 4168**
★★ **Dickey Betts and Great Southern / Ari. 4123**
★★ **Highway Call / Capri. 0123**
Launch the sucker and see if she floats. What could have been promise renewed turns out to be promises, promises. Rather than break new ground, Betts exhumes some of his moldiest clichés and struggles in vain to sound like he's interested in them. For the diehard. — D.MC.

BIDDU ORCHESTRA
★★ **Biddu Orchestra / Epic PE-33903**
★★★ **Eastern Man / Epic PE-34723**
★★★ **Rain Forest / Epic PE-34230**
Heavily arranged, glibly orchestrated disco project. You need a good sound system and an auditorium to appreciate this stuff, though. — J.S.

BIG BROTHER AND THE HOLDING COMPANY
★★★★ **Cheap Thrills / Col. PC-9700**
The definitive late-Sixties acid-rock album, notable for sloppy, overlong cuts, inspired, amateurish playing, thoroughly distorted electric lead guitar playing from Sam Andrews, and the galvanic vocals of the era's most beloved and charismatic performer, Janis Joplin. You had to be there, but if you weren't, listening to this is about as close as you can come. — J.S.

BILL AND TAFFY
■ **Aces / RCA CPL1-0605**
This pair couldn't seem to make up its mind whether to be a fourteenth-rate version of James Taylor and Carly Simon or an updated, more pop-oriented version of Simon and Garfunkel. In any case, they cover the Chantels' "Maybe." If rock & roll were religion, this album would be melted at the stake for that alone. (Now deleted.) — D.M.

BILLION DOLLAR BABIES
★★ **Battle Axe / Poly. 1-6100**
Members of Alice Cooper's original group make 1977 comeback attempt. Unfortunately, they needed his singing almost as badly as he currently misses their playing. — D.M.

ELVIN BISHOP
★★★ **Hometown Boy Makes Good / Capri. 0176** ·
★★★ **Juke Joint Jump / Capri. 0151**
★★★★ **Raisin' Hell / Capri. 2CP-0185**
★★ **Rock My Soul / Epic KE-31563**
★★★★ **Struttin' My Stuff / Capri. 0165**
★★★ **The Best of Elvin Bishop: Crabshaw Rising / Epic PE-33693**
Elvin Bishop was one of the guitarists in the original Paul Butterfield Blues Band—at first paired with Michael Bloomfield and later on his own. Bishop quickly developed the humorous, countrified persona Pig Boy Crabshaw, who was equal parts the hick Tulsa kid Bishop might have been when he joined the Butterfield band, and the laconic, blues-playing sharpie that he certainly was by the time he left.

In 1970, Bishop left Butterfield for a solo recording deal with Bill Graham's Fillmore label (the material that now appears on the Epic albums). The three albums he cut for Graham were loose, funky R&B, ranging from covers of Fifties R&B tunes like "Feel It" and "So Fine" to jams with Santana's percussionists. There was also a self-effacing C&W stream of humor in the music—typified by such songs as "Hogbottom," "Stealin' Watermelons," and "Party Till the Cows Come Home." Somehow it never quite jelled. The Epic *Best of* is a representative anthology of the period; *Rock My Soul* is the third and weakest album of the series.

Bishop moved to Capricorn Records in 1974, with a new band that played similarly funky material, in a bit more relaxed (and confident) fashion. The first couple of albums, the deleted *Let It Flow* and *Juke Joint Jump,* faltered mostly because of the weakness of Bishop's lead vocals; *Struttin' My Stuff,* which added singer Mickey Thomas, produced one of the best hit singles of 1976, "Fooled Around and Fell in Love." While the focus of the group's sound remained Bishop's blues-based guitar in interplay with Phil Aaberg's keyboards and Johnny Vernazza's second guitar, the emergence of Thomas gave Bishop a flexibility he had previously lacked—the version of "My Girl" here, while it can

hardly said to be in the same league as the original, was at least more ambitious than the boogie purveyed by other groups with similar roots.

The quality of the sequel, *Hometown Boy Makes Good,* suffered partly because the quality of the material fell off, partly because it was hard to determine whether Thomas or Bishop was in charge. But *Raisin' Hell,* a live album, reasserted Bishop's control. What might have been a simple boogie blues set, no less numbing than an evening with Charlie Daniels, was redeemed by Bishop's self-effacing humor (which reemerged now that his marketability had been demonstrated) and the simple, fine playing of the group. *Raisin' Hell* is fun in a way that very little white blues of the Seventies is, a kind of joyous celebration of collective spirit. — D.M.

STEPHEN BISHOP
★★★ **Bish / ABC 1082**
★★★ **Careless / ABC D-954**
In 1977, when his debut LP was released, Bishop seemed no more than a whining but listenable post-James Taylor songwriter with a particularly (face it) unpleasant mug. But by the time 1978's *Bish* appeared, it was clear—on the basis of appearances on *Saturday Night Live* and in *Animal House*—that a good deal of what seemed too precious about Bishop was actually satire of a very subtle order. That doesn't make singles like "On and On" and "Save It for a Rainy Day" much more pleasant as radio hits—the approximation of the typical singer/songwriter's maudlin self-pity is too close for comfort. But at least it makes you smile while you push the buttons. — D.M.

BILL BLACK COMBO
★ **Award Winners / Hi 6005**
★ **Bill Black Combo / Zodiac 5006**
★ **Bill Black Combo Goes Big Band / Hi 32020**
★ **Bill Black Combo Plays the Blues / Hi 32015**
★ **Bill Black Combo Plays Tunes by Chuck Berry / Hi 32017**
★★ **Greatest Hits / Hi 32012**
★★ **Greatest Hits, Vol. 2 / Hi 32078**
★ **It's Honky-Tonk Time / Hi 32104**
★ **Memphis, Tennessee / Hi 8004**
★ **More Solid and Raunchy / Hi 32023**
★ **Saxy Jazz / Hi 32002**
★ **Solid and Country / Hi 32088**
★ **Solid and Raunchy / Hi 32003**
★ **Untouchable Sound / Hi 32009**

★ **World's Greatest Honky-Tonk Band /
Hi 32093**
"Redneck MOR" was a good description
of the Bill Black Combo. Black was the
bass player in the first Elvis Presley band
at Sun Records, and his combo turned out
raunchy saxophone-dominated instrumentals for twenty years, even after he died.
It's all interchangeable, characteristically
hard-edged (after all, they're a Memphis
band) and ultimately forgettable. — J.S.

BLACK BLOOD
★★ **Black Blood / Main. 416**
★ **Blood Brother, Blood Sister / Chrys.
1144**
Eccentric black rhythm group had minor
1975 R&B hit, "A.I.E. (A Mwana)," for
Mainstream. — D.M.

BLACKBYRDS
★ **Action / Fan. 9535**
★★ **City Life / Fan. 9490**
★★★★ **Flying Start / Fan. 9472**
★★★★ **The Blackbyrds / Fan. 9444**
★ **Unfinished Business / Fan. 9518**
Originally Donald Byrd's backing band,
the Blackbyrds stepped out into the light in
the early Seventies as a jazz-funk fusion
group with something of their own to say.
At least at first, the rhythmic bottom was
solid and danceable, the vocals were appropriately spare, and the instrumentation—particularly the horn charts—was
melodically adventurous and fulfilling. *The
Blackbyrds* was their debut, and *Flying
Start* represents a creative, if not a commercial, peak. But after the success of
Flying Start, the Blackbyrds began to see
themselves as a disco attraction rather than
as a progressive R&B act, and *City Life* exhibited a dispiriting reliance on recycled
riff-hooks and an embarrassing bent for
hollow social and psycho-cybernetic commentary. *Unfinished Business* and *Action*
simply continue the decline into self-parody. — M.G.

BLACKFOOT
★★★ **Flyin' High / Epic PE-34378**
★★★ **No Reservations / Is. 9326**
High-energy Southern hard rock circa 1975
produced by Jimmy Johnson in Muscle
Shoals and led by guitarist Rickey Medlock, son of bluegrass musician and songwriter Shorty Medlock. Two members of
Blackfoot played in the band that would
later become Lynyrd Skynyrd, and the
sound here is similar, if less
pointed. — J.S.

J.D. BLACKFOOT
★★★ **Song of the Crazy Horse / Fan. 9468**
★★★ **Southbound and Gone / Fan. 9487**
The American-born, New Zealand-based
Blackfoot built his 1975 debut LP, *Song,*
around its over-eighteen-minute-long title
track, inspired by *Bury My Heart at
Wounded Knee,* then followed it up with a
better-than-average Southern rock rec-
ord. — J.S.

BLACK IVORY
★ **Black Ivory / Bud. 5658**
★★ **Feel It / Bud. 5644**
Pedestrian soul group had a variety of
R&B chartmakers in the early Seventies
for the minor Today and Kwanza labels,
but since signing with Buddah, only "Will
We Ever Come Together" (*Feel It*) has
clicked. — D.M.

BLACKMORE'S RAINBOW
★ **Long Live Rock 'N' Roll / Poly.
1-6143**
★★ **Ritchie Blackmore's Rainbow / Poly.
6049**
★ **Rainbow Rising / Oy. 1601**
A token mood piece or two notwithstanding, Blackmore's Rainbow pushes "classic"
heavy metal with a singular lack of imagination. The better cuts on these albums resemble each other uncomfortably: you can
count on the vocal shriek to peak hysteri-
cally and former Deep Purple guitarist
Ritchie Blackmore to take one too many
guitar solos trying to perk up the limp,
melody-starved songs. The range of textures featured makes the first album wear
much better than its successors, which
have a few relatively strong hard-rock
tunes but are still made ludicrous at every
turn by the papier-mâché nastiness of their
overblown lyrics. — T.M.

BLACK OAK ARKANSAS
★ Balls of Fire / MCA 2199
★ Best of Black Oak Arkansas / Atco 36-150
★ Black Oak Arkansas / Atco 33-354
★ I'd Rather Be Sailing / Capri. 0207
★ Live, Mutha / Atco 36-128
★ Race with the Devil / Capri. 0191
★ Raunch 'N' Roll / Atco SD-7019
★ Ten-Year Overnight Success / MCA 2224
★ X-Rated / MCA 2155

Mindless gutbucket boogie hooked around the mealy-voiced antics of lead singer Jim Dandy Mangrum. Black Oak's distinguishing characteristic is that the band has three guitarists who collectively don't even add up to one good one. The pits of hard-rock senescence. — J.S.

BLACK SABBATH
★ Black Sabbath / War. 1871
★ Black Sabbath, Vol. 4 / War. B-2602
★ Master of Reality / War. B-2562
★ Never Say Die / War. K-3186
★★ Paranoid / War. K-3104
★ Sabbath, Bloody Sabbath / War. B-2695
★ Sabotage / War. B-2822
★ Technical Ecstasy / War. B-2969
★ We Sold Our Soul for Rock 'n' Roll / War. B-2923

These would-be English Kings of Heavy Metal are eternally foiled by their stupidity and intractability. In the early Seventies their murky drone was all the more appealing for its cynicism—the philosophy that everything is shit, and a flirtation with pre-*Exorcist* demonic possession. Time has passed them by; their recent stuff is a quaint bore. Their high point was *Paranoid,* a better example of their goofy malevolence than the *We Sold Our Souls* anthology, and cheaper. — K.T.

BLACK SATIN
★★ Black Satin / Bud. 5654
Group featuring lead singer Fred Parris had minor 1975 R&B hit with "Everybody Stand and Clap Your Hands (for the Entertainer)"; also cut "In the Still of the Night" and a Barry White song, which about covers it. — D.M.

BLACKSMOKE
★★ Blacksmoke / Choc. 2001
Eight-piece disco band had minor '76 chartmaker, "Your Love has Got Me Screamin'." (Now deleted.) — D.M.

OTIS BLACKWELL
★★★ These Are My Songs / Inner 1032
Author of several important Fifties tunes, including "Don't Be Cruel" and "All Shook Up" for Elvis, bears a remarkable vocal resemblance to Presley. The cover and liner notes would like to have you believe that this means Blackwell is the greater artist, which is silly. On the other hand, he is an interesting eccentric; although the band lets him down on occasion, this is worth hearing. — D.M.

NORMAN BLAKE
★ Fields of November / Fly. Fish 004
★★ Home in Sulphur Springs / Roun. 0012
★ Live at McCabe's / Tak. 1052
★★★ Whiskey before Breakfast / Roun. 0063

Blake is a superb guitarist capable of the flashiest, fastest picking this side of Doc Watson. A Nashville staple, his duets with close friend/dobroist Tut Taylor and guitarist Charlie Collins can be awe-inspiring. (*Home* and *Whiskey* are both duo albums, the former with Taylor, the latter with Collins.) Blake's backup work with, and influence on, John Hartford, Kris Kristofferson and Joan Baez, however, is also estimable.

Unfortunately, when Blake is recording as leader (and on Taylor's Rounder LP), he takes on the additional role of vocalist, a "talent" of his that is considerably less than adequate.

The natural sound quality on the two Rounder sets, though, makes them particularly appealing. *Fields of November* is a generally uninspired performance, and the live disc doesn't justify itself in ambiance or technical levels. — I.M.

RONEE BLAKLEY
■ Welcome / War. 2890
This album, released in 1975, represents an early foray by Los Angeles into main-

stream country music. Although the attempt later succeeded in the form of L.A. takeovers of performers like Dolly Parton and Crystal Gayle, it fails here.

Blakley is a singer/songwriter in the California folk tradition. This album represents an attempt to capitalize on her starring role in Robert Altman's film *Nashville,* but the production, while tasteful, lacks heart; the compositions (all Blakley originals) lack authenticity.   — M.H.

BOBBY "BLUE" BLAND
★★★★ **Ain't Nothin' You Can Do / Duke X-78**
★ **B.B. King and Bobby Bland/Together for the First Time . . . Live / Imp. 9317**
★★ **Bobby Bland and B.B. King/Together Again . . . Live / ABC ASD-9317**
★★★★ **Call on Me / Duke X-77**
★★ **Come Fly with Me / ABC 1075**
★★ **Dreamer / ABC DSX-50169**
★★ **Get On Down with Bobby Bland / ABC 895**
★★★ **His California Album / ABC DSX-50163**
★★★ **Introspective of the Early Years / Duke D-92**
★★ **Reflections in Blue / ABC 1018**
★★★ **Spotlighting the Man / Duke X-89**
★★★★★ **The Best of Bobby Bland / Duke X-84**
★★★★★ **The Best of Bobby Bland, Vol. 2 / Duke X-86**
★★★ **The Soul of the Man / Duke X-79**
★★★ **Touch of the Blues / Duke X-88**
★★★★★ **Two Steps from the Blues / Duke X-74**

The black Sinatra? Assuredly the smoothest of the hard R&B singers. Listening to Bland, one might also think that the evolution of rhythm & blues had been arrested when Ray Charles left Atlantic. The difference between them is that what Bland learned from gospel was purely technical, rather than the emotiveness Charles acquired. Bland's art, unique among bluesmen, is one of containment. His style is uncluttered, usually relying only on simple rhythm tracks with a touch of sax and brass backing, although some of his guitarists, notably Mel Brown, have been amazing.

Bland has recorded since the late Fifties, and thankfully, almost everything he has done is in print. Nearly every one of the Duke albums is a treasure, with exquisite moments: the power of Bland's voice, the delicacy of his phrasing, the sweep of what he does with songs as superficially ordi-

nary as "Call on Me" or "It's My Life, Baby." Indeed, several of his hits are standards—"I Pity the Fool" and "Farther up the Road," particularly—although they usually seem overwrought in other hands.

The *Best of* collections provide an excellent overview of his chart hits (mostly the black charts, of course), while *Introspective* sticks closer to twelve-bar, and generally more obscure, blues, to achieve a more limited end. *Two Steps* includes, in addition to the classic title track, one of the most heart-rending soul ballads ever recorded, "Lead Me On," perhaps the definitive recording of blues crooning. *Call on Me* and *Ain't Nothin' You Can Do* are the kind of records Ray Charles might have made if pop hadn't dominated his career.

Like Charles, Bland began brilliantly when he went to ABC (not by choice—Duke was sold). *California Album* and *Dreamer* have some of his most sophisticated music. But on the latter, a kind of erosion begins to set in. *Get On Down* attempts to repeat Charles' success with country songs in a blues context and mostly fails. It is charitable to describe the sessions with B.B. King as mistakes—Bland retains most of his energy and skill, King does not. The results are embarrassing for both, particularly since Bland was once B.B.'s valet.

There *are* treasures here. Given record company cutout policies, it might be wise to invest immediately. No telling how long this stuff will remain available. Bland's stature among collectors is already high—how he has missed attracting the young white audience King did is mysterious—and should these recordings be deleted, copies will become very valuable.   — D.M.

BLIND FAITH
★★★ **Blind Faith / RSO 1-3016**
This forcibly created supergroup was meant to be the rage of 1969, because it included Eric Clapton and Ginger Baker from Cream, Steve Winwood from Traffic and the then-unknown Rick Grech from Family. Two problems intervened: first, businessmen had engineered the situation from the outside, trying to cash in on reputations, and without regard to musical compatability. Second, the volatility of the performers ensured a one-album life span. It was a disappointment then, of course, but it looks a bit better now, highlighted by Clapton and Winwood's work on "Presence of the Lord" and a nice, gentle version of Buddy Holly's "Well All Right." In

its day, the relatively racy cover caused rack jobbers to ban it. Today, no one flinches, but then no one manufactures supergroups any more, either. — D.M.

RORY BLOCK
★★★ **Intoxication / Chrys. 1157**
Only available album by interesting, though rarely inspired, white blues singer. Block knows what to do with her material conceptually but she hasn't quite the heart to make her a major talent. Still, one of the worthier alternatives to the dread Ronstadt-clone syndrome. — D.M.

BLODWYN PIG
★★★★ **Ahead Rings Out / A&M 4210**
An early offshoot of the original Jethro Tull, this 1969 LP centers on guitarist Mick Abrahams and demon saxist Jack Lancaster. A spinoff of Tull's original hard-rock style, this sophisticated bruiser wears its age well. It was followed by a derivative effort, *Getting to This* (deleted), before the group disbanded. — A.N.

BLONDIE
★★★ **Blondie / Chrys. 1166**
★★★ **Parallel Lines / Chrys. 1165**
★★★ **Plastic Letters / Chrys. 1166**
Punk rock's answer to Linda Ronstadt? Blondie's Deborah Harry does for Patti Smith what Alice Cooper did for Iggy Pop: swipes a minor good idea and beats it to death. But the band can play, in a sort of revivified British Invasion style. — D.M.

BLOODROCK
■ **Bloodrock 2 / Cap. ST-491**
■ **Bloodrock 3 / Cap. SM-765**
■ **Bloodrock 'n' Roll / Cap. SM-11417**
■ **Live / Cap. SVBB-11038**
■ **U.S.A. / Cap. SM-645**
Capitol's stablemate to Grand Funk Railroad, Bloodrock codified the nadir of early-Seventies heavy metal, added horns and became even worse. The absolute bottom of the barrel. — J.S.

BLOODSTONE
★★★ **Do You Wanna Do a Thing? / Lon. 671**
★★★ **I Need Time / Lon. 647**
★★★★ **Natural High / Lon. 620**
★★★ **Riddle of the Sphinx / Lon. 654**
★★★★ **Train Ride to Hollywood / Lon. 665**
★★★ **Unreal / Lon. 634**
Bloodstone was one of the first black rock bands, influenced as heavily by Jimi Hen-

drix and Sly Stone in its good-humored approach as by soul harmony vocal groups. Its first hit, "Natural High," went to the Top Ten in 1973, presaging a string of R&B hits with mild pop appeal, although only "Outside Woman" (from *Unreal*) saw it in the Top Forty again. With *Unreal,* the group even tackled the sort of Fifties oldies ("Searchin'," "So Fine") that had previously been the exclusive province of white rock groups, a project brought to fruition on the group's best album, *Train Ride to Hollywood,* the soundtrack to its underrated, witty, self-financed 1975 movie. On *Train Ride,* Bloodstone performed material as diverse as "As Time Goes By" and "Toot Toot Tootsie" along with "Sh-Boom" and "Yakety Yak," and made it all fit in with the modern originals. An anthology of the band's best work is long overdue. — D.M.

BLOOD, SWEAT AND TEARS
★★★ **Blood, Sweat and Tears / Col. PC-9720**
★ **Brand New Day / ABC 1015**
★★★★★ **Child Is Father to the Man / Col. PC-9619**
★★★ **Greatest Hits / Col. PC-31170**
★ **Mirror Image / Col. KC-32929**
★★ **More Than Ever / Col. PC-34233**
★★ **New Blood / Col. KC-31780**
★★ **New City / Col. PC-33484**
★ **No Sweat / Col. C-32180**
It's easy to forget that Blood, Sweat and Tears began as an Al Kooper project in 1968, as part of a move toward bigger, not necessarily jazzier, rock sounds. *Child,* the only album made under Kooper's direction, is important not only because its jazz and art-song aspects expanded the scope of rock for both audience and musicians but also because it was one of the most perfectly listenable pop albums of its era. The performances are impeccable, and the song selection (numbers by Tim Buckley, Harry Nilsson, Randy Newman, Gerry Goffin and Carole King are included) is nearly perfect.

Blood, Sweat and Tears represents the pinnacle of the group's commercial success: Kooper out, vocalist David Clayton-Thomas (an acquired taste at best) in, and the group took over AM, FM and MOR playlists simultaneously by sticking to rockified Big Band jazz. But Clayton-Thomas left soon after and successive replacements were a constant headache; the band sounds more listless with each new album. Clayton-Thomas, his solo career a bust, returned for *New City, More Than Ever,* and *Brand New Day*; it helped, but not much. — A.N.

MICHAEL BLOOMFIELD
★★★ **Analine / Tak. 1059**
★★★ **If You Love These Blues, Play 'Em As You Please / Guitar 3002**
★★★ **Triumvirate / Col. C-32172**
Following his memorable stints with the Butterfield Blues Band and the Electric Flag, Mike Bloomfield embarked on a solo career plagued by erratic follow-through. The two solo efforts remaining in print—the Super Sessions are listed under Al Kooper—represent the cream of his solo career. *Triumvirate* utilizes the funky blues voice of John Paul Hammond and Dr. John's keyboards to good effect, putting Bloomfield's guitar in the kind of group context where it works best. The result is a good solid blues album from a talented trio of journeymen. *If You Love These Blues* is meant as a blues guitar primer, with Bloomfield effectively evoking the styles of the form's masters. If his scholarly presentation seems silly—the last track features him saying thanks to enough guitarists to choke a horse—his fluid interpretations of various blues styles stand up to repeated listening. — J.B.M.

BLUE ASH
★★ **Front Page News / Play. PZ-34918**
Blue Ash made a fresh, innocent Beatles-influenced album in the early Seventies, which garnered the Youngstown quartet critical acclaim and no sales. By the time this followup was released in 1978, the innocence was gone and the boys just seemed to be grinding it out. — D.M.

DAVID BLUE
★ **Com'n Back for More / Asy. 7E-1043**
★ **Cupid's Arrow / Asy. 7E-1077**
★ **Stories / Asy. 5052**
Of all the Dylan imitators of the folk-rock Sixties, David Blue was distinctly the most outrageous, because his emulation was most complete. Fortunately or not, all of those albums (for Elektra) have been deleted. Unfortunately, for sure, in the Seventies series of discs he has made for Asylum, Blue's obsession with Dylan had dwindled, and he is now just another scraggly-voiced singer/songwriter. — D.M.

BLUE MAGIC
★★★ **Blue Magic / Atco 7038**
★★★ **Magic of the Blue / Atco 36-103**
★★★ **Message from the Magic / Atco 38-104**
★★★ **Mystic Dragons / Atco 36-140**
★★★ **Thirteen Blue Magic Lane / Atco 36-120**
One of the more successful groups from the Philadelphia sophisticated soul axis, Blue Magic crossed over after strong disco response and the popularity of its 1974 single, "Sideshow." The band follows the Philly formula perfectly—Norman Harris produces, MFSB is the backup band. — J.S.

BLUE OYSTER CULT
★★★★ **Agents of Fortune / Col. PC-34164**
★★★★ **Blue Oyster Cult / Col. PC-31063**
★★ **On Your Feet or on Your Knees / Col. PG-33371**
★★★ **Secret Treaties / Col. PC-32858**
★★ **Some Enchanted Evening / Col. JC-35563**
★★★★ **Spectres / Col. JC-35019**
★★★ **Tyranny and Mutation / Col. KC-32107**
When BOC made its LP debut in '72, critics raved about its arcane and sinister lyrics, but Eric Bloom's vocals were barely audible, much less intelligible. What really made it magnetic was the hook-laden music with its parade of Buck Dharma's multilayered guitars and the Cult's reputation as a neo-fascist, vampirish New York band that would sooner suck your blood than take your money. The first three albums occasionally go off the deep end trying to preserve the claims to maniacal metalism, but when they stick, their sensation is nothing short of sexual.

On Your Feet or on Your Knees fails as an attempt to transfer the Cult's wondrously assaultive stage antics to vinyl, but not without a neck-snapping riff or two. Better to wait for a video disc. *Agents of Fortune* represents BOC's most diversified offering, from Allen Lanier's doo-wop tango, "True Confessions," to the classic Cult relic, "(Don't Fear) the Reaper," a Top Ten single. Patti Smith co-wrote two songs, "Debbie Denise" and "Revenge of Vera Gemini," and has a watery, Ronnie Spector-like guest vocal on the latter. A new direction for the Cult, explored further on *Spectres,* featuring the bone-chilling anthems "I Love the Night" and "Death Valley Nights." But *Some Enchanted Evening* was a premature live set that indicated BOC might be running out of ideas. — M.G.

THE BLUE RIDGE RANGERS
★★★ **The Blue Ridge Rangers / Fan. 9415**
When *The Blue Ridge Rangers* was released
in 1973, it seemed like a parenthesis in
John Fogerty's career—a clearing of the air
after the collapse of Creedence Clearwater,
a taking stock of past debts (in this case, to
C&W and gospel) and future prospects (a
rich and prolific solo career, one presumed). That parenthesis, however, has
lasted more than five years (including his
second solo LP, *John Fogerty*) and what
originally seemed like an aside has become
the topic sentence in Fogerty's post-Creedence career. Fogerty is the Blue Ridge
Rangers—its drummer, bass player, fiddler,
backup chorus, horn section and more. It's
a solo album with a vengeance—a one-
man virtuoso act, a slap across rock's collective will, the product of obsessive perfectionism. Too much of the album sounds
mechanical (particularly the drumming),
too much of it is plodding (Fogerty's song
choices are imaginatively obscure, but often dull), but when it catches fire ("I Ain't
Never," "Hearts of Stone," "She Thinks I
Still Care"), *Blue Ridge Rangers* no longer
seems like a retreat from rock & roll, but a
reinvestment in its mythic past. For that
it's worth it. — K.R.

BLUE SKY BOYS
★★★ **The Blue Sky Boys / Blueb.**
  AXM2-5525
From 1936 (when they made their first recordings) until 1951, some of the most authentic American music around came from
two North Carolina brothers. Bill Bolick,
who played mandolin, and his guitarist
brother Earl produced some of the finest
country harmony singing ever heard. Much
of their material was traditional British and
American ballads, often very religious
ones.
  By the time they retired in 1951, after
making 124 recordings, country music's audience had changed and there was no
longer a great demand for the mournful
mountain ballads. Now Bill works as a
postal inspector in North Carolina and
Earl is an employee of Lockheed Aircraft
in Georgia. — C.F.

BLUE SWEDE
■ **Hooked on a Feeling / EMI ST11286**
The title track, a ridiculous interpretation
of the B.J. Thomas/Lloyd Price hit, defies
categorization. If I didn't know better, I'd
swear the whole thing was an ethnic joke
concocted by Norwegians. — J.S.

COLIN BLUNSTONE
★★★ **Journey / Epic KE-32962**
★★★ **Never Even Thought / RCA**
  BXL1-2903
★★★★ **One Year / Epic E-30974**
The original voice of the Zombies. Each of
these Seventies albums is characterized by
sweet (almost sickeningly so if you're in
the wrong mood) songs with catchy, ador-
able melodies sung in Blunstone's breathy
near-soprano voice. None of them has the
intensity of the great Zombie singles, but
they're not meant to. — A.N.

BOA
★ **Schizoid / Wood. BWL1-0790**
Laughably bad 1975 album from a band
trying hard to play hard rock and make
Important Statements, failing miserably on
both counts. — J.S.

DOCK BOGGS
★★★ **Dock Boggs Interviews / Folk. 35458**
★★★ **Dock Boggs, Vol. 2 / Folk. 32392**
★★★ **Dock Boggs, Vol. 3 / Folk. 33903**
Traditional Virginia mountain musician—
banjo and voice—who recorded in 1927
and 1928, then returned to work in the
mines until rediscovered by Mike Seeger in
1963. These recordings (oddly, *Volume 1* is
no longer available) chronicle his knowledge of the area's music and social lore—
the interviews conducted by Seeger are fascinating, displaying some evidence of what
mountain music must have been like before it was popularized by Jimmie Rodgers
and the Carter Family and broadcast out
of the area. Because Boggs is a rough-
edged, unsophisticated singer and the instrumentation is minimal, he may be hard
for rock-oriented listeners to listen to, but
anyone with an interest in American music
would do well to hear him. — D.M.

HAMILTON BOHANNON
★★★ Dance Your Ass Off / Dakar 76919
★★★ Insides Out / Dakar 76916
★★★ Keep on Dancin' / Dakar 76910
★★★ Mighty Bohannon / Dakar 76917
★★★ On My Way / Mer. RSM-1-3710
★★ Phase II / Mer. RSM-1-1159
★★★ Stop and Go / Dakar 76903
★★★ Summertime Groove / Mer. SRM-1-3728

Former Motown drummer Bohannon was one of the first to perceive the tremendous possibilities of disco for percussionists. He did it to death, stomping out a whole series of big-foot beat, highlighted by the 1975 hit, "Foot-Stompin' Music," and an array of similar black Sandy Nelson titles—"Disco Stomp," "Bohannon's Beat (Pts. 1 & 2)," etc. — D.M.

GORDON BOK
★★★ Bay of Fundy / Folk-Leg. 54
★★ Peter Kagan and the Wind / Folk-Leg. 44

A Maine fisherman, sailor and folklorist, the majority of Bok's traditional and original songs and tales are concerned with the sea. "Peter Kagan," a magnificent fable, is based on tales of the seal-folk. "Bay of Fundy" is probably his best-known composition. Bok's association with the Hudson River Restoration sloop, *Clearwater,* brought him to new audiences via such shipmates as Pete Seeger and Don McLean. *Bay of Fundy,* with Ann Mayo Muir singing harmonies, is a more appropriate introduction, though the fifteen-minute story of "Peter Kagan" will no doubt enter traditional sea lore. — I.M.

TOMMY BOLIN
★★★ Private Eyes / Col. C-34329
★★★ Teaser / Nemp. 436

Bolin's solo albums prove how well rounded this much-traveled, much-troubled guitarist was. *Teaser*'s variety of material might indicate a lack of personality, but Bolin's enthusiasm suggests that his inclinations were simply freed by his solo opportunities, after stints in Zephyr, James Gang and Deep Purple. Predictably, *Private Eyes* was less eclectic: his guitar playing defined the mood without dominating needlessly. Despite natural limitations, his intense feel for groove made his vocals at least convincing on both records. His untimely death in 1976 cut off the career of one of the decade's more promising rock instrumentalists. — T.M.

MICHAEL BOLOTIN
★ Every Day of My Life / RCA APL1-1550
★★ Michael Bolotin / RCA APL1-0992

Sounding like Joe Cocker on the first of these, Bolotin can be powerful but just as forced. His songwriting, however, is soulful, as is his backup: Wayne Perkins, Wilbur Bascomb and Dave Sanborn. *Every Day of My Life* gets away from Cocker, but doesn't do much else. Save Billy Elworthy's raw guitar, the playing is very ordinary. Both records suffer from the singer's poor cover versions. (Now deleted.) — C.W.

ANGELO BOND
★★★★ Bondage / ABC 889
★★ Free Spirit / ABC D-944

For a moment in 1975, with *Bondage,* Angelo Bond seemed about to become the single-handed salvation of falsetto soul singing. But this did not pan out. — D.M.

BONEY M.
★ Love for Sale / Atl. 19145
★★ Nightflight to Venus / Sire K-6062
★ Take the Heat Off Me / Atco 36-143

Although they were in the forefront of the European pop-disco movement, Boney M. managed to squander every advantage, often through sheer tastelessness and genuinely wretched excess. The Sire album's attraction, such as it is, is the near-hit single "Rivers of Babylon," which does to reggae what some listeners might like to do to the group: drowns it. — D.M.

KARLA BONOFF
★★★ Karla Bonoff / Col. PC-34672

Karla Bonoff came to prominence when her friend Linda Ronstadt chose three of her best songs ("If He's Ever Near,"

"Someone to Lay Down Beside Me" and "Lose Again") for inclusion on 1976's *Hasten Down the Wind*. And on her 1977 debut LP, Bonoff pleasantly surprised almost everyone by doing warm, even versions of her own songs. Those three songs, plus a rendition of "Home" that stood on its own, proved Bonoff's self-sufficiency. Her admixture of country lamentation with urban neurosis was apt for the times, and she was quickly established as a mass-audience heartthrob with both intelligence and accessibility. — F.S.

THE BONZO DOG BAND
★★★★ Beast of the Bonzos / U. Artists 5517
★★★ Gorilla / Imper. 12370
★★ Keynsham / Imper. 12457
★★★★★ The History of the Bonzos / U. Artists LA321-H

When the Bonzo Dog Band first appeared in 1967, it was immediately taken to heart by the handful of critics, humorists and cultists who remain its only fans. Who had time for an absurdist horn band that sang about Mickey and Minnie Mouse's offspring or did a gurgling version of "I Left My Heart in San Francisco"? *Gorilla* was a spotty but innovative beginning—the group hit its peak on the now-deleted *Urban Spaceman* and *Tadpoles,* then adopted a more straightforward rock approach for *Keynsham,* which was problematic: the comedy suffered, and the music was pretty forgettable.

After *Keynsham,* the group split—Neil Innes and Viv Stanshall attempted to reform with the (deleted) *Let's Make Up and Be Friendly,* but without success—leaving us with the two anthologies as a legacy. *Beast* is a fine sampler, but *History* is indispensable for anyone who wants to understand such later comedic developments as *Monty Python's Flying Circus* and *Saturday Night Live.* — M.G.

BOOKER T. AND PRISCILLA
★ Chronicles / A&M 4413
★ Evergreen / Epic 33143

After the MGs broke up in 1972, Booker T. Jones, their organist, moved to California, where he recorded tepid country-flavored duets with his wife, Priscilla Coolidge, and a solo LP of no discernible direction. — J.MC.

BOOKER T. AND THE MGS
★★★★ The Best of Booker T. and the MGs / Atl. 8202

★ Universal Language / Asy. 7E-1093

A quartet consisting of organist Booker T. Jones, guitarist Steve Cropper, bassist Duck Dunn, and drummer Al Jackson, the MGs set the style for soul backup and instrumental groups of the Sixties. As accompanists on a multitude of Stax hits, they were impeccable in their taste and restraint, remarkable for their simplicity. As a solo unit, their instrumentals (the best known of which is "Green Onions") stuck closely to simple melodic statement, incorporating a tightly structured rhythm approach, Cropper's thick, fuzzy chording, and Jones' organ embellishments.

The group went its separate ways in 1972—Dunn and Jackson continued as Memphis session players, most notably for Al Green; Jones dueted with Priscilla Coolidge, his wife and sister of Rita Coolidge; Cropper went into production—but reunited for an abortive 1976 LP on Asylum, shortly after Jackson's unfortunate murder. — J.MC.

THE BOOMTOWN RATS
★★★ A Tonic for the Troops / Col. JC-35750
★★★★ Boomtown Rats / Merc. SRM1-1188

One of the better contributions of the English pub-to-punk rock scene was this (actually Irish) band's debut album, *Boomtown Rats.* Singer/writer Bob Geldof really was more in the mainstream tradition of Graham Parker, Phil Lynott and Bruce Springsteen, but when he avoids sentimentality, as he does on side two, this is one of the sparkling records of recent British rock.

Unfortunately, the 1979 followup, *A Tonic for the Troops,* finds Geldof turning into a formula writer and rampant poseur—Alice Cooper for the alienated and angry. The album's best moments are drawn from the first album (after Mercury lost the group, the Rats apparently regained the rights to their material), and with the exception of "She's So Modern" there isn't anything here that couldn't be done by any of a couple dozen other bands that slavishly worship at the altar of the Rolling Stones. Not the answer to "Whatever happened to Them?" — D.M.

DEBBY BOONE
★ You Light up My Life / War. B-3118

The title song, the best-selling single in Warner Bros. history, paces a hastily assembled group of songs from Pat Boone's daughter. Outtakes from the Boone sisters are used as filler. Second-generation schlock and roll. — F.S.

PAT BOONE
★★★ **Sixteen Great Performances** / ABC 4006
★★ **Texas Woman** / Hits. 6-405
★ **The Lord's Prayer and Other Great Hymns** / Dot 25582

Pat Boone is probably among the top five of soulless performers. But for those who were white, middle class, American, 'twixt twelve and twenty during the Fifties and *not* rebellious, the man has a certain archetypal heaviness that can't be denied. For what it is, his collection of golden oldies is pretty damn good. It's docked one star, however, for containing a couple of ringers that weren't hits and one, "Speedy Gonzales," that was racist even if it was a hit. Make that Thirteen Great Performances. The religious album is best ignored; Boone and his family have done much better work on the small gospel labels.

Texas Woman succeeds with its stew of right-wing politics, personalized Christian music and countryish L.A. middle-of-the-road. Whether anyone wants such a stew remains to be seen, but fans of American paradoxes should note that Mr. White Bucks is now recording on Motown's country label. — T.S.

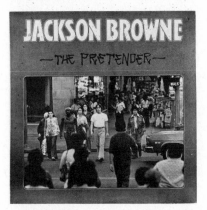

KEN BOOTHE
★★★ **Live Good** / U. Artists LA801-H

MOR reggae singer. Not bad, but not up to the best of the genre, though extremely popular in certain Jamaican circles. — D.M.

BOOTSY'S RUBBER BAND
★★★★ **Ahh . . . the Name Is Bootsy, Baby!** / War. 2972

★★★★ **Bootsy: Player of the Year** / War. K-3093
★★★ **Stretchin' Out in Bootsy's Rubber Band** / War. B-2920

It's like living inside some Ralph Bakshi cartoon—an intergalactic street world inhabited by everything from pimps to Martians. And it sounds like Hawkwind cloned with Sly all transmuted through *Bitches Brew.*

Ask William Collins, a.k.a. Bootsy, why he split Parliament/Funkadelic to form his own brand of New Age Funk and he'll tell you—the kids made him do it. The little ones who turn on without drugs—they're called "geepies," wee folk who defected from the P/Funk camp to enroll in Bootsy's psychoticbumpschool. Actually, when Collins' Hendrix-like charisma and amazingly elastic space bass started garnering too much attention in P/Funk, George Clinton decided to add another act to the P/Funk roster to be led by Bootsy Collins. Pre-Funkadelic, Bootsy was James Brown's bassist in the incomparable JB's, along with the formidable hornmen Maceo Parker and Fred Wesley. When Collins announced his solo move, they signed aboard. Wesley's Rubber Band charts are some of the most imaginative and subtle funk you'll ever behold—his and Parker's oblique maneuvers weaving in and around the rhythm section's eternal pump are no less than hypnotic.

And Bootsy's into Stars, so his specially equipped bass—a Lamborghini amongst Chevettes—was custom-built into the shape of Winky Dink. He's also into nursery rhymes, so on the second album his hound-dog rock comes packaged in the form of tunes like "The Pinocchio Theory." The track swings so hard *it hurts.* "Rubber Duckie" introduces Collins' vision of a Robin Hood who "steals from the rich and gives to poor little ole me!" It's all sorta zany, you can dance to it and . . . I'm sure you get the point. Without it, you just ain't with it. — B.M.

BOOTY PEOPLE
★★ **Booty People** / ABC 998

Disco group had minor Bicentennial R&B stomper "Spirit of 76." — D.M.

BOSTON
★★★ **Boston** / Epic JE-34188
★★★ **Don't Look Back** / Epic FE-35050

Described as a cross between Led Zeppelin and Yes, Boston's not nearly that gruesome. Most of its harmonic sense comes from L.A., which balances out all the heaviness, and guitarist/writer Tom Scholz uses his special-effects guitar tastefully. *Boston* could use more consistent songwriting, though that didn't stop the 1977 debut from selling 6 million copies. It did, however, prevent the lackluster *Don't Look Back* from qualifying as anything but a failure. Boston has a terrific formula, which it executes competently, but without inspiration, it may never amount to much. — J.MO.

BOTTOM LINE
★ **Crazy Dancin' / Greedy 1001**
If you're interested in tunes like "Disco Dobro," then this is for you. Otherwise you might as well watch *Hee Haw* outtakes. — J.S.

DAVID BOWIE
★ **Images 1966-1967 / Lon. BP-628/9**
★★ **Space Oddity / RCA AFL1-4813**
★★ **The Man Who Sold the World / RCA AFL1-4816**
The thin white duke changes musical styles like clothes, seeing rock more as an external pose than as internal combustion. Bowie is a pop actor who conceived of his incarnations—pseudo-Dylan, ultragloss decorocker, soul brother—with a forethought that precluded losing himself in his fantasy. He could always move on to another role, or perhaps films; for David Bowie, rock was the ultimate mass-communications transformer.

Images, Bowie's first recorded work, reflects both an interest in show music and an overripe Dylan fixation. And while the music had a certain cabaret charm, it lacked the distinction to provoke more than a passing response. *Space Oddity* contained the first seeds of his rocker metamorphosis, as his music grew more electric in tone and his lyrics began establishing a cogent persona. With Mick Ronson joining on guitar and a highly polished production sound, *The Man Who Sold the World* stands as his first break toward mass appeal—as the music now boasted a steely-hard rock sound with a decidedly peculiar man at the helm.
★★★★ **Aladdin Sane / RCA AFL1-4852**
★ **David Live / RCA CPL2-0771**
★★★ **Diamond Dogs / RCA AFL1-0576**
★★★ **Hunky Dory / RCA AFL1-4623**
★★ **Pin-Ups / RCA AFL1-0291**
★★★★ **The Rise and Fall of Ziggy Stardust and the Spiders from Mars / RCA AFL1-4702**

Bowie solidified his commercial appeal with metallic, ultrasmooth hard rock and an image that cleaned up the decadent aura of the Velvet Underground and sold it to teenage America like processed cheese.

Hunky Dory boasted Bowie's first successful American single, "Changes." Already a star in England, Bowie attacked the American market with presumption—to become a star, he reasoned, you must act like one. *Ziggy Stardust* was part of this pose—using the sixteen-track studio as a palette, he constructed dense hard rock that punched like a velvet boxing glove. "Suffragette City" came on like a tornado of guitars, with ultraclean sound that embodied the "mellow-thighed chick" of the lyrics. It worked, although it took his audience some time to realize that he indeed was the cracked actor, and that the "Rock 'n' Roll Suicide" that ended *Ziggy* was just another pose.

Aladdin Sane, perhaps Bowie's most satisfying album, contained both the hard rock of *Ziggy* and a more ambitious approach to the cabaret leanings of his early work. The title song was among his best ever as his cinematic wartime visions drifted like a mushroom cloud over Mike Garson's alternatingly smooth and disjointed piano. The rockers—particularly "Watch That Man" and "The Jean Genie"—again displayed his ability to transform other styles into his own (the Stones in this case), while ballads like "Lady Grinning Soul" were performed with a bombastic approach that was as surreal as it was effective.

Diamond Dogs initiated a long holding pattern for Bowie; the stark originality of his original pose became more predictable and the standouts—"Rebel Rebel" and the title tune—simply recalled the Stones rather than building off their base. It became clear that Bowie could chose his image, but his chosen visage could similarly limit his impact. *David Live,* a double set, failed largely because Bowie's live show depends as much on visuals as music. Similarly, *Pin-Ups,* a collection of Bowie's interpretations of mid-Sixties British rock classics, failed because with few exceptions he never strove to redefine or challenge the originals.
★★★★ **Changes One / RCA AFL1-1732**
★★★ **Station to Station / RCA AFL1-1327**
★★ **Young Americans / RCA AFL1-0998**
David Bowie was always a commercial animal, so it wasn't surprising when he set out to become a blue-eyed soulster. *Young*

Americans captured the sound, but Bowie's personality was given little chance to enliven the rote nature of the music. Bowie never displayed much passion, which in itself was part of his act, but when combined with slick soul music, his charade was deadly. *Station to Station* reunited Bowie with a powerful guitarist, Earl Slick, who has since gone solo. The tough rhythm chording on the album's hit single, "Golden Years," is indicative of the improvement.

Changes One is a greatest-hits package concentrating on the hard rock that brought Bowie a mass audience. Released as Bowie flashed across the screen as *The Man Who Fell to Earth,* it seemed to end the first phase of Bowie's assault on our culture. A pop personality and now a film star, Bowie had gained both, like the character in the film who came to earth from another planet with knowledge beyond that of mere mortals. Bowie's intelligent calculations have brought him this far, and it is that aura of detached creation that has made him one of pop's most intriguing personalities.

★★★★ **"Heroes"** / RCA AFL1-2522
★★★ **Low** / RCA CPL1-2030
Characteristically claiming that only now was the real David Bowie revealing himself, these two albums found Bowie collaborating with Eno, and not coincidentally, the records have the spacy sense of music and poetics of Eno's *Another Green World.* *"Heroes"* is the more successful of the two, with Bowie's new-found confidence in his new style making *Low* sound comparatively timid. "Heroes" itself was quite simply the best tune Bowie had cut in years, with the mechanical drone of the synthesized disco beat perfectly complementing the foreboding lyrics of two lovers meeting by the Berlin Wall. Bowie is himself in a similar position by placing his ego in the shadow of the technologically informed music that is his latest passion. But don't expect him to disappear—Bowie's longevity has always been based on his ability to put the slip on his shadow. — J.B.M.

BOXER
★★★★ **Absolutely** / Epic PE-34812
★★ **Below the Belt** / Virgin PZ-34115
Mike Patto's raspy vocals and Ollie Halsall's hard, lean guitar lines lead this able but unexceptional quartet's debut, *Below.* Patto can be quite convincing, and the group does know how to rock, but much of

this sounds tired. But *Absolutely,* with Halsall gone and veteran keyboardist Chris Stainton added, is far more individual and unrestrained. — C.W.

BILL BOYD AND HIS COWBOY RAMBLERS
★★ **Bill Boyd's Cowboy Ramblers** / Blueb. AXM2-5503
A fine example of the journeyman pro in Western Swing. Boyd's groups were always small (string instruments and sometimes piano, never horns), and performed creditably, though seldom spectacularly. For Western Swing diehards only. — J.MO.

THE BOYS OF THE LOUGH
★★ **The Boys of the Lough** / Philo 1026
★★★ **The Piper's Broken Finger** / Philo 1042
Like the Chieftains, the Boys of the Lough are purveyors of Scottish and Irish traditional music, though some would argue that the Boys' style is a bit less formal (or polished) than the Chieftains'. The reels, jigs, and ballads, however, led by fiddler extraordinaire Aly Bain, are really a live music whose bright textures are difficult to capture on record. *The Boys of the Lough* was recorded live, and the sound is muted and distant throughout. *The Piper's Broken Finger,* a studio effort, is more successful, and probably the best paced of the group's LPs. — I.M.

RANDALL BRAMBLETT
★★★ **Light of the Night** / Poly. 6064
★★★★ **That Other Mile** / Poly. 6045
Bramblett is a singer/songwriter/instrumentalist of no small promise, one of the most sought-after Southern session players (he's featured in Gregg Allman's touring band) and probably the most urbane Southern songwriter this side of Randy Newman. Both albums are classics of the Seventies Southern rock renaissance. Bramblett has since joined Sea Level. — J.S.

BONNIE BRAMLETT
★★ **It's Time** / Capri. 0148
★★★ **Lady's Choice** / Capri. 0169
★★ **Memories** / Capri. 0199
Without the tambourine-beating hoopla that she produced with former husband Delaney, Bonnie Bramlett has had difficulty establishing an image of her own. An energetic if not unusually emotive singer, Bramlett has stayed with the blues cum gospel style that defined Delaney and Bon-

nie. *It's Time* found her working in a "live" studio atmosphere with Capricorn regulars supplemented by singers and a horn section. The result was a smooth but ultimately sterile record. Her second album featured support by the Muscle Shoals regulars (including the horns) with Capricorn supplements, and given the strong roster of recent soul standards, it's a solidly superior effort. Paired with various Capricorn crooners—Jimmy Hall, Dobie Gray, Gregg Allman—there is plenty of energy if precious little creative inspiration. — J.B.M.

DELANEY BRAMLETT

★ **Delaney Bramlett and Friends—Class Reunion / Prod. P7-10017**
The former leader of Delaney and Bonnie and Friends found himself in such straits in 1977 that he wound up making this pathetic and soul-shriven album for Motown's "rock" label. At least Bonnie, his ex-wife, gets sympathetic production at Capricorn. — D.M.

OSCAR BRAND

★★ **Bawdy Hootenanny / Audio Fi. 6121**
★★ **Bawdy Sea Shanties / Audio Fi. 5884**
★★ **Bawdy Songs and Backroom Ballads / Audio Fi. 5847**
★★ **Bawdy Songs Goes to College / Audio Fi. 5952**
★★ **Bawdy Western Songs / Audio Fi. 5920**
★★★ **Best of Oscar Brand / Trad. 2053**
★ **Brand X / Rou. 42060**
★★ **Concert at Town Hall / Folk. 2428**
★★ **Laughing America / Trad. 1014**
★★★ **Oscar Brand and Jean Ritchie / Arc. Folk 207**
★★★ **Pie in the Sky / Trad. 1022**
★★ **Rollicking Sea Shanties / Audio Fi. 5966**
★★ **Sing Along Bawdy Songs / Audio Fi. 5971**
★★ **Singing Holidays / Caed. 1505**
★ **Wild Blue Yonder / Elek. 7168**
Oscar Brand came out of the same Forties radical left folk scene that produced Pete Seeger and Woody Guthrie, and made Leadbelly and the Weavers famous. Because his politics were closer to the mainstream, however, he was able to survive the blacklists of the McCarthy Fifties much more successfully. Like Seeger, his nearest leftist counterpart, Brand was obsessed with the folk tradition. But ideology never interfered with what he wanted to do musically. This is not altogether salutary—

in fact, it trivializes much of what later made the early folkies important to the post-Dylan generation—but it can often be more listenable and almost always is less preachy.

Brand's real reputation was made with the series of *Bawdy Songs* LPs he made for Audio Fidelity in the late Fifties and early Sixties. These were not the sorts of songs that could find their way into schoolbooks, and the always-puritanical American left never boasted much about this part of the American working-class heritage either. Today, though, after twenty years of increasingly explicit sexual reference in mainstream pop music, Brand's bawdy songs seem dated and fairly tame. How you gonna keep 'em down on the farm after they've heard "Foxy Lady"?

And Brand's other albums of traditional music simply reveal his limits as a vocalist. Far better interpretations of almost all the nonbawdy material are available from a variety of sources, particularly singers like Woody Guthrie and Ramblin' Jack Elliott. To hear Brand best, pick up the Tradition *Best of* or the album he made for that label with the neglected Appalachian ballad singer Jean Ritchie. — D.M.

BRAND X

★★★ **Live Stock / Pass. 9824**
★★★ **Masques / Pass. 9829**
★★★ **Moroccan Roll / Pass. 98022**
Progressive English band, masterminded by Genesis drummer Phil Collins (he seems more interested here), toys also with jazz fusion. Obtuse but effective. — D.M.

BRASS CONSTRUCTION

★★★★ **Brass Construction / U. Artists LA 545-G**
★★ **II / U. Artists LA677-G**
★★ **III / U. Artists LA775-H**
★★ **IV / U. Artists LA916-H**
Their first album (1975) includes the hit "Movin' " and five other one-word titles of disco length and style. Their music is accented by misconstrued images of urban origin. *II* is something of a departure; the vocals are more upfront, standardized in the jive/Ohio Players fashion. *III* and *IV* continue in this vein. And speaking of fashion, Brass Construction is one of the few black groups who made it big in 1975 without listing the astrological signs of its band members. — G.C.

BRAVE BELT

★★ **Brave Belt / Rep. 2210**

Also released as *Bachman-Turner-Bachman,* this is what Randy Bachman and friends did between the Guess Who and Bachman-Turner Overdrive. Less edifying than either. (Now deleted.) — D.M.

BREAD
★★★★ **Baby I'm-a Want You / Elek. 75015**
★ **Bread / Elek. 74044**
★★★★ **Guitar Man / Elek. 75047**
★★ **Lost without Your Love / Elek. 7E-1094**
★★★ **Manna / Elek. 74086**
★ **On the Water / Elek. 74076**
★★★★ **The Best of Bread / Elek. 75076**
★★★★ **The Best of Bread, Vol. 2 / Elek. 7E-1005**

Especially in its later days, Bread was downright inspirational. Sparkling lyricism, lush melodicism, immaculate production dynamism, foolproof vocal harmonies (with soul, no less) and a nearly unchallenged hit-single-writing capacity. The two *Best of* collections contain twenty-four mellifluously rocking jewels. *Volume 2* recaptures the glory of three classic albums cut in Bread's 1969–1973 heyday, *Baby I'm-a Want You, Manna* and *Guitar Man.* It's pop, but transcendent pop. David Gates and James Griffin went on to solo fame before reuniting in 1976 to cut *Lost . . . Love,* but it was a depressingly slouch offering, especially considering the brilliance of Gates' recent solos. — B.M.

BREWER AND SHIPLEY
★★★ **Best of Brewer and Shipley / Kam. S. 2-2613**
★★ **Brewer and Shipley down in L.A. / A&M 4154**
★★★ **Rural Space / Kam. S. 2058**
★★★ **Shake off the Demon / Kam. S. 2039**
★★★ **Tarkio / Kam. S. 2024**
★★★ **Weeds / Kam. S. 2016**

Early-Seventies fame achieved by this post-folk-rock duo ("Yankee Lady," "Tarkio Road," "One Toke over the Line," "Witchi-Tai-To") created the line of demarcation between Simon and Garfunkel imitators (they may have been the best) and Brewer and Shipley imitators (who are an insufferable legion led by Seals and Crofts). — J.S.

BRIAN AND BRENDA
★★ **Supersonic Lover / R. 2291**
★★ **Word Called Love / R. 2181**

This pair recorded for Elton John's record label, and their version of pop-soul is just about as forced and plastic as his. If you really like this kind of thing, try Marilyn McCoo and Billy Davis Jr. Or Dionne Warwick, who surpasses all duos on her own. — D.M.

DEE DEE BRIDGEWATER
★★ **Dee Dee Bridgewater / Atl. 18188**
★★ **Just Family / Elek. 6E-119**

Dee Dee Bridgewater combines silky, precise articulation with a stirring dynamic range (comparable to Streisand's but with a greater flair for jazz phrasing). She measures every vibrato, every blue note, every scream to full effect. Her sassy swagger on the rockers is commensurate with her near operatic control over the ballads. A pleasant neo-disco debut, more cause for hope than a promise fulfilled. — M.G.

BRIGATI
★ **Lost in the Wilderness / Elek. 7E-1074**

If you were a fan of Eddie Brigati's steamy, ripping Rascals vocals, this is a maddening record. Eddie and David Brigati enlist some impressive New York sessionmen for such questionable fare as a hep disco version of "Groovin' " and a Philly-soul-Muzak-disco version of "You Send Me." A song called "Lost in the Wilderness (How 'Bout a Harlem in Your Life)" is the lyrical ploy to match their musical pandering to a black audience the Rascals once *earned.* — F.S.

BRINSLEY SCHWARZ
★★★★ **Brinsley Schwarz / Cap. SWBC-11869**

Brinsley Schwarz was the best of the British pub-rock bands, and a seminal influence on what later became the British New Wave: lead guitarist Schwarz now backs up Graham Parker as part of the Rumour, while writer/bassist Nick Lowe, who has produced Parker and Elvis Costello, is a sidekick of Dave Edmunds and a performer of some merit on his own.

The two-record set *Brinsley Schwartz* is a compilation of the first two of the group's albums. The debut LP is listless funk, without the verve of the followup (originally titled *Despite It All*), which is perhaps the best country-influenced rock LP ever made. "Country Girl" has the charm and fake innocence that make Lowe's solo albums so appealing, the recording is bright and the singing is grand. On its own, *Despite It All* would be worth five stars; together, these two records are surely worth five bucks. — D.M.

JOHNNY BRISTOL
★ **Bristol's Creme / Atl. 18197**
Bristol is a former Motown producer who
did some of Gladys Knight's best records
there. On his own, he has had a couple of
hits, most notably "Hang on in There
Baby," a 1974 disco smash for MGM. But
his specialty is a kind of post-feminism seduction, encouraging women to improve
themselves flat on their backs. To which
one can only respond: "Get
fucked." — D.M.

JAIME BROCKETT
★ **Remember the Wind and the Rain / Cap.
ST-678**
This album moves as fast as a snail on the
nod. Recommended for people who really
like contemporary talking blues, meaning-
ful pauses and dulcimer solos. — A.S.

DAVID BROMBERG
★ **Bandit in a Bathing Suit / Fan. 9555**
★★ **Best: Out of the Blues / Col. C-34467**
■ **David Bromberg / Col. C-31104**
★ **Demon in Disguise / Col. C-31753**
★★ **How Late'll Ya Play 'Til? / Fan. 79007**
★ **Midnight on the Water / Col. PC-33397**
★ **Reckless Abandon / Fan. 9540**
★★ **Wanted/Dead or Alive / Col.
KC-32717**
David Bromberg has the reputation of
being an amusing performer, but most of
his albums feature live recordings, which
only shows that humorous asides and
good-time jams seldom survive on vinyl.
Bromberg's singing is terrible. When he
tries to sound tough, his voice squeaks like
an adolescent in the church choir; otherwise it simply grates. But his later efforts
(on Fantasy) prove that singing wasn't his
only problem.
In fact, though the fast-pickin' folkie-
with-a-croak earned his reputation as a
session guitarist, his solo albums demonstrate that when he loses his speed, little
else remains. Bromberg delivers seven-min-
ute cuts based on one lick, gets the notes
right but seldom the spirit, and has no style
of his own. Perhaps his worst sin is that he
makes blues and bluegrass sound
alike. — A.S.

ALBERT BROOKS
★★★ **A Star Is Bought / Asy. 7E-1035**
Brooks' comedy is distinguished by its
awareness of the pop industry of which he
is a part. As with all comedy albums, the
routines don't bear much repetition, but *A
Star Is Bought* is an ambitious project,
based on the premise (correct) that records

sell by virtue of radio airplay. The adaptable Brooks constructs comedy for any
conceivable programming philosophy, from
MOR to talk radio. The strategy recalls a
quip, on an earlier LP, that while disc
jockeys are by their very nature obnoxious,
the one playing his record might well be a
swell guy. — J.B.M.

DIANNE BROOKS
★★ **Back Stairs of My Life / War. MS
2244**
Back Stairs of My Life is a sharp-focus affair divided into a "fast" and a "slow" side.
Brooks, a black gospel-soul singer in the
mold of Aretha Franklin, is more at home
among the ballads, but the fast material
glides nicely in the hands of a studio band
led by guitarists Amos Garrett and Wah
Wah Watson and keyboardists Bill Payne
and William D. Smith. Still, it never quite
catches fire. — B.T.

ELKIE BROOKS
★★ **Rich Man's Woman / A&M 4554**
★★ **Shooting Star / A&M 4695**
★★ **Two Days Away / A&M 4631**
The smoky, seductive singer from Vinegar
Joe composes well and picks some good
covers, but too often is lost in mediocre
material and backup. Her bluesy wailing
doesn't always mix well with pop-directed
rock. — C.W.

THE BROTHERS JOHNSON
★★ **Blam!! / A&M SP-4714**
★★ **Look Out for #1 / A&M SP-4567**
★★ **Right on Time / A&M SP-4644**
Mediocre pop-funk, Seventies family style;
lots of hit singles in 1978-79, but nothing
to write home about yet. — D.M.

BROTHER TO BROTHER
★★★ **Let Your Mind Be Free / Turbo
7015**
★★ **Shades in Creation / Turbo 7018**
Soul group had a hit a few summers ago
with Gil Scott-Heron's "The Bottle" (not
included on this album), but they haven't
made very much noise since
then. — A.E.G.

ARTHUR BROWN
★★ **Kingdom Come (Import) / Track GUD
2003/4**
★★★★ **The Crazy World of Arthur Brown
(Import) / Track/Atlantic 613 005**
This weird British singer scored on an off-
the-wall 1968 hit with *The Crazy World of
Arthur Brown,* a hit single, "Fire," and a
band that included drummer Carl Palmer

and that later became Atomic Rooster.
Brown was as notorious for his wild, phan-
tom-of-the-opera screams as for his habit
of performing with painted face and wearing a flaming helmet that made him look as
if his hair was on fire. Once his theatrics
had been picked up by Alice Cooper,
Brown switched to avant-garde British
electronic music with his new band, Kingdom Come, using an automatic drum machine and generally making some pretty
bent music. A one-of-a-kind original,
"Fire" still presents him at peak
form. — J.S.

CHARLES BROWN
★★★ **Driftin' Blues / Main. 368**
The urban blues singer's only in-print al-
bum treads a thin line between inspiration
and kitsch. At his worst, Brown delivers
routine interpretations of "The Days of
Wine and Roses" and "More"; at his best,
he offers the hard-edged desperation of
"Driftin' " and a hilarious interpretation of
"Go Away Little Girl." — D.MC.

JAMES BROWN
★★ **Everybody's Doin' the Hustle / Poly.
6054**
★★ **Get Up Offa That Thing / Poly. 6071**
★★★ **Hell / Poly. 2-9001**
★ **Hot / Poly. 6059**
★★★ **Hot Pants / Poly. 4054**
★★ **Jam / 1980s / Poly. 1-6140**
★★ **Mutha's Nature / Poly. 1-6111**
★★★ **Payback / Poly. 2-3007**
★★★ **Revolution of the Mind / Poly.
25-3003**
★ **Sex Machine Today / Poly. 6042**
★★★★★ **Soul Classics, Vol. 1 / Poly. 5401**
★★★ **Take a Look at Those Cakes / Poly.
1-6181**
★★★ **There It Is / Poly. 5028**
James Brown has never been the subject of
a well-documented greatest-hits collection,
and with the disappearance of King Rec-
ords (and every James Brown album
through 1970), *Soul Classics* is just about
all that remains of his greatest period. For
a guy whose prime stretched over fifteen
years, the selection on *Soul Classics* is haphazard to say the least. The packaging is
utterly devoid of dates, notes or enticing
photos from the old days, and aesthetically
it's hard to acknowledge "Super Bad" or
"Make It Funky Pt. 3" as quintessential
JB. Still, how can you argue with "Papa's
Got a Brand New Bag," "It's a Man's,
Man's, Man's World" and "Cold Sweat"?
Sadly, Brown's remaining work traces
the decline of both his voice and his creative powers. By the time James Brown
reached Polydor, he had virtually done
away with any sense of lyric coherence in
his songs; words became secondary to
sound. For a while it worked. His early
hits on the label were a combination of
verbal, stream-of-consciousness cacophony,
and sizzling instrumental riffs. Gradually
Brown's efforts became caught up in their
own hypnotizing monotony. He finally ran
out of rhythmic ideas and by the time the
disco phenomenon exploded, James Brown
was reduced to recycling past hits under
new names. Sometimes he didn't even
bother to change that much ("Sex Machine
Today"). The bottom was reached when he
recorded a song on the *Sex Machine Today*
album complaining that others were ripping him off and then a few months later
released "Hot," a photocopy of David
Bowie's "Fame." — J.MC.

JOHN LEE AND GERRY BROWN
★★ **Mango Sunrise / Blue N.
LA 541-G**
No Caribbean accents here, despite the title. Mostly it's a mixture of heavy-rock guitar around electric piano jazz clichés, with
Lee concentrating on bass and ARP synthesizer and Brown on drums. Guest appearances by guitarists Wah Wah Watson
and Philip Catherine help, but not half
enough. (Now deleted.) — D.M.

KEISA BROWN
★★★ **Keisa Brown . . . Live / Lit. Star
1001**
Keisa Brown is a hot-blooded vocalist who
begs comparison with Etta James and Tina
Turner in their prime. Though some of the
originals fall flat, a medley of Sixties soul
standards and a talking blues recall the
classic "live" Turner and James sets of the
early Sixties. — J.MC.

MAXINE BROWN
★★ **Maxine Brown's Greatest Hits / Wand 684**
Early Sixties New York pop soul, rather after the model of Motown's Mary Wells, but with less force. A string of hits from '61 to '65 included "Funny," "All in My Mind," "Oh No, Not My Baby" and "If You Gotta Make a Fool of Somebody." The latter two have become semistandards. (Now deleted.) — D.M.

MEL BROWN
★★★ **Big Foot Country Girl / Imp. 9249**
★★★ **Impulsively / Imp. 9266**
Brown earned his reputation during the Sixties as the tough, hot blues guitarist in Bobby Bland's band, which made him just about the hottest blues and R&B guitarist in the country. On his own, he's still terrific on blues and funk material, but when he tries to stretch out toward rock or jazz idioms, he's no more impressive than the legions of other Wes Montgomery or Eric Clapton impressionists. — D.M.

OSCAR BROWN JR.
★ **Between Heaven and Hell / Col. CS-8574**
★ **Fresh / Atl. 18106**
★ **Movin' On / Atl. 1629**
Jive, histrionic funk-jazz singer with pretension to "social relevance." — D.M.

SHIRLEY BROWN
★★★ **Shirley Brown / Ari. 4129**
On her 1977 solo album, Shirley Brown's magnificent voice overcomes unskilled and unsympathetic production. "A Mighty Good Feeling" and "Givin' Up" (and the single "Blessed Is the Woman") are the stand-outs here. Her out-of-print debut for Stax, *Woman to Woman,* shows what the

right production (by the late Al Jackson) can do for her on an Aretha Franklin-inspired set. — J.S.

STANKY BROWN GROUP
★ **Stanky Brown Group / Sire K-6053**
Pre–New Wave Seventies New York City area rock band, more notable for its ability to get a recording contract than for its ability to do anything with it. — D.M.

TONI BROWN AND TERRY GARTHWAITE
★★★★ **Cross-Country / Cap. ST-11137**
This remarkable little one-shot stands as a kind of high point for this singer/songwriter team. Recorded in 1972 in between sessions with their regular group, Joy of Cooking, the album is a country-rock session produced by Wayne Moss and featuring Vassar Clements (fiddle), Charlie McCoy (harmonica), Dennis Linde (bass), Bill Aikins (piano), Kenny Malone (drums), Russ Hicks (steel guitar) and Jim Colvard (guitar). Brown and Garthwaite wrote some of their best material for this date, particularly "I Want to Be the One," "As I Watch the Wind" and "I Don't Want to Live Here." (Now deleted.) — J.S.

JACKSON BROWNE
★★★★ **For Everyman / Asy. 5067**
★★★★ **Jackson Browne / Asy. 5051**
★★★★ **Late for the Sky / Asy. 7E-1017**
★★★★★ **Running on Empty / Asy. 6E-113A**
★★★★★ **The Pretender / Asy. 6E-107**
Jackson Browne is the most accomplished lyricist of the Seventies. His miniaturist landscapes of life in the nether end of the century, as seen from the emotional and geographic climate of Southern California, provide rock's surest touchstone with the mood of the recent era; they have been instrumental in creating the Eagles–Linda Ronstadt axis of California singer/songwriter rock.
Browne's first three albums are highlighted by a preponderance of excellent songwriting. One thinks particularly of the *Jackson Browne*'s "Song for Adam," "Rock Me on the Water" and "Doctor My Eyes," his only hit single; of *For Everyman*'s momentous title track, "Ready or Not" and "These Days"; and of *Late for the Sky*'s brilliant philosophical depiction of death, "For a Dancer," as well as that album's "Fountain of Sorrow," "The Road and the Sky" and "Before the Deluge."

The themes—family, fate, death, honor, despair, with romance and the road providing the natural backdrop for all of it—are continuous and overlapping, from album to album and song to song. Browne's perspective has been described as apocalyptic, but it's really something else: a sweet-tempered survey of the doom around him, in which society at large and every smaller unit within it is finally dwarfed by the individual—sometimes an outlaw, sometimes a more common person—who stands, in the end, alone and if not triumphant, at least alive. There is great balance in his world view (if swinging from extreme to extreme can eventually constitute balance), and certainly more than the expected share of hope and humility.

If anything mars this first trio of LPs, it is Browne's occasional lapses as a performer. His singing is erratic, sometimes moving, sometimes almost callow; the arrangements range from tightly focused, almost traditional folk purity (in the melodies, and in David Lindley's guitar and violin accompaniment) to simply messy. But in the 1976 album, *The Pretender,* Browne found a perfect forum for all of his concerns, and the music came to its full flower at last. The melodies were brilliant, the songs deeply moving and perfectly constructed—"Here Come Those Tears Again" and "The Fuse" were the first successful out-and-out rock & roll he'd ever recorded—and the record's concept held together from start to finish. Indeed, moving from the opening song, "The Fuse," to the closing one, "The Pretender," led one nowhere except on the great circuitous route of life itself.

Running on Empty, released in late 1977, was the most ambitious live album project ever attempted. The performances came from everywhere—onstage, from the group's touring bus and its motel rooms, even from backstage—and the songs did the same: Browne rerecorded none of his previous repertoire and contributed only a couple of originals, supplementing them with songs written by members of his backup band like Danny Kortchmar, a tune written by his road manager, and the old Maurice Williams and the Zodiacs' hit, "Stay," which closed the set perfectly. (Both "Stay" and the rocking title song were hit singles.) It was a departure, but a fitting one. This was one outlaw who had found a society that could accept him, and from the present vantage point, the future looks bright indeed.   — D.M.

BROWNSVILLE STATION
★★ **Brownsville Station / Priv. 2026**
Detroit-based rockers began as an oldies group, and a very good one, releasing an album on Warner Bros. in the late Sixties; then to Big Tree for several more modern pop-rock affairs in the early to middle Seventies, which saw them grab their biggest hit, "Smokin' in the Boys' Room," in 1974. This 1977 LP is their most recent, but lacks the spark of the early stuff.   — D.M.

JACK BRUCE BAND
★★★ **How's Tricks / RSO 1-3021**
Melodic but hard and forceful guitar/keyboards/bass/drums quartet. Occasional jazzy interludes from electric piano. Bruce's bass is expectedly nimble and well-fitting, but his polished vocals at times become overwrought. Good drumming from Simon Phillips.   — C.W.

LENNY BRUCE
★ **"I Am Not a Nut, Elect Me!" / Fan. 7007**
★ **Interviews of Our Times / Fan. 7001**
★ **Lenny Bruce—American / Fan. 7011**
★★ **Live at the Curran Theatre / Fan. 34201**
★ **Thank You Masked Man / Fan. 7017**
★★★ **The Best of Lenny Bruce / Fan. 7012**
★★★ **The Real Lenny Bruce / Fan. 79003**
★ **The Sick Humor of Lenny Bruce / Fan. 7003**
★ **What I Was Arrested For / Casa. 7013**
Bruce was always a fascinating talker, but if you're looking for laughs, the Presence of Modern Comedy is not the man to seek out. *The Best of Lenny Bruce* contains his finest early material, and is sporadically hilarious; *Live at the Curran* is a mesmerizing monologue about his arrests, but as a three-record set may strike you as a lot to shell out for interesting rambling. *The Real Lenny Bruce,* a two-record set, contains his best, funniest routine, "Comic at the Palladium," a twenty-minute dissection of seedy show biz in both America and England, and compared with the rest of his recorded work, it seems to come out of nowhere: as acidly hysterical as his myth claims, and totally without embarrassing self-pity and intellectual pretensions. In general, Bruce tried to break down the structure of a stand-up monologue, allowing for new thoughts, new emphases, new accidents with every performance, but just wasn't imaginative or intelligent enough to feed his gabby gift with new premises from which to wing it. So often he just babbles

until he provokes an inadvertent giggle. Simplistic moralism and lame dialect humor sinks half of this album list. And while Bruce may have made the frankness of, say, Richard Pryor possible, greater artists like Richard Pryor have made Bruce's recorded work seem tame, churlish, and even sentimental. — K.T.

BRUSH ARBOR
★ Page One / Monu. MC-6637
★ Straight / Monu. MG-7613
Essentially nondescript country-rock band covering a range of bad material like Buzz Cason's "Emmylou" and the original composition "God Is Good, God Is Love," which features the immortal line "God don't grade on the curve." — J.S.

B.T. EXPRESS
★★ Energy to Burn / Col. PC-34178
★★ Function at the Junction / Col. 34702
★★ Non-Stop / Road. 41001
★★ Shout / Col. JC-35078
As formulaic as the most assembly-line vocal group production, the music of B.T. Express is the prototype for a slew of faceless bar bands who have assumed disco and funk prominence. The songs are mindlessly simple and differ little from album to album. Their first hit, "Do It ('Til You're Satisfied)" (on their now deleted Scepter album), provides the model: a repetitive vocal chant, lots of mid-range hand clapping to punctuate the beat (the bottom is all but removed from the mix), and a simple horn riff to give the barest hint of melody. If you've heard one, you've heard them all. — J.MC.

ROY BUCHANAN
★★ A Street Called Straight / Atl. 18170
★ In the Beginning / Poly. 6035
★★ Live Stock / Poly. 6048
★★ Loading Zone / Atl. 8219
★ Roy Buchanan / Poly. 5033
★ Second Album / Poly. 5046
★ That's What I'm Here For / Poly. 6020
★★ You're Not Alone / Atl. 19170
Roy Buchanan's career attests to the power both of suggestion and of the guitar in rock. He is, in a sense, the perfect example of why the best players aren't necessarily the best artists. As a technician, he has long been a legend, burning out electric solos with a trebly tone and high-volume sustain that produced distortion effects not unlike Beck's or Hendrix's. Lauded by other guitar players for his technique, in 1972 he suddenly found himself with a national

audience. But Buchanan lacks the imaginative presence to do anything with either his technique or his base of listeners.

Part of this is due to the bands with which he has usually worked: decent veterans of the Maryland bars where Buchanan made his reputation, they moved *too* easily from country to rock to blues. Because they lacked a proper vocalist—Buchanan sings in a talking monotone that deserves never to have been recorded—the guitar had to carry the whole load. And while Buchanan's howling leads could elicit nods of appreciation from guitar aficionados, they couldn't supply a sufficient musical context.

The Atlantic albums, in which Buchanan is working with better-equipped professionals—Arif Mardin among others—give him a better showcase. Although a good deal of what's on them is still self-indulgent, the smoother backgrounds at least put it in relatively tasteful relief. — J.B.M.

BUCKINGHAM NICKS
★★ Buckingham Nicks / Poly. 5058
Pleasant, albeit middleweight Los Angeles folk rock. Stevie Nicks and Lindsay Buckingham present narcotic voice and guitar respectively, although only "Crystal" gives a hint of what would galvanize when they joined Fleetwood Mac and made two of the best-selling LPs of the Seventies. — J.B.M.

THE BUCKINGHAMS
★★★ Greatest Hits / Col. CS-9812
★★ Made in Chicago / Col. KG-33333
The Buckinghams, Chicago's answer to the British Invasion and producer James William Guercio's first hit machine, encapsulated a number of influences (straight pop, R&B and progressive rock). *Made in Chicago* is a bloated two-record set that includes all their Columbia hits, while *Greatest Hits* is a more concise collection that has the distinct advantage of boasting their original organ-powered smash, "Kind of a Drag." In their heavily arranged approach, the Buckinghams predated the brass-pop sound of Chicago (also produced by Guercio) with a lighter pop consciousness that could produce indulgent dreck ("Foreign Policy") as well as sublime pop fluff— "Don't You Care," "Hey Baby (They're Playing Our Song)." — J.B.M.

LORD BUCKLEY
★★★ The Best of Lord Buckley / Elek. 74047

Buckley was a white Fifties hipster who told stories in the manner and argot of a black Fifties hipster. His repertoire was vast: the story of Christ, Gandhi, the Gettysburg Address—all retold in a guttural blur of brilliant slang. Buckley's not so much funny (though he's sporadically paralyzing) as fascinating and insightful. — K.T.

TIM BUCKLEY
★★★ **Goodbye and Hello** / Elek. 74028

This is the late Tim Buckley's 1967 masterpiece, and in fact his only commercially successful album in the United States. His second record, it epitomizes the dense songwriting and elaborate production accorded the first wave of singer/songwriters in that period. The album's theme, also typical, is announced in the very long and very Dylan-influenced title song as the conflict between the "death and war" generation and the "life and love" generation that Buckley celebrates with a solipsist's abandon. Blood, Sweat and Tears was only one of several groups who covered songs from *Goodbye and Hello,* and it was promptly predicted that Buckley would soon become our new major songwriter.

That never happened, because in the many deleted albums after *Goodbye and Hello,* Buckley futilely sought a jazz-folk fusion, and in the process virtually abandoned regular songwriting completely. His writing became progressively sparser and his vocals increasingly eccentric in expression. From *Happy/Sad* through *Starsailor* made with the horn section of the original Mothers of Invention, Buckley was almost totally forgotten in the world of Cat Stevens and James Taylor.

Late in his failed career, however, Buckley made one burning, madly erotic rock album, *Greetings from L.A.* (Warner Bros.). Curiously, this is the Buckley album his fans outside the United States have kept in print, while outside the United States *Goodbye and Hello* is out of print along with all the others. *Greetings* is probably the best album Buckley recorded, and it is certainly the best album to remember him by, for it was made by a beaten man still capable of desperate ecstasies. — B.T.

BUDGIE
★ **Bandolier** / A&M 4618
★ **If I Were Brittania I'd Waive the Rules** / A&M 4593
★ **Impeckable** / A&M 4675
★ **In for the Kill** / MCA 429

Working in the now-traditional power trio format, this band suffers from a startling paucity of original ideas, riffs or songs. Their sound is thin, their music hackneyed and repetitive, and the fact that they've endured this long is a tribute to blind optimism. — A.N.

NORTON BUFFALO
★★★ **Desert Horizon** / Cap. SW 11847
★★★ **Lovin' in the Valley of the Moon** / Cap. ST-11625

Steve Miller's harmonica player turns out to be a surprisingly capable performer on his own, with a mixture of blues and country rock and occasional dabblings with electronic effects. — D.M.

BUFFALO SPRINGFIELD
★★★ **Buffalo Springfield** / Atco 200
★★★★★ **Buffalo Springfield** / Atco 2-806
★★★★★ **Buffalo Springfield Again** / Atco 226
★★★ **Last Time Around** / Atco 256
★★★ **Retrospective** / Atco 38-105

Along with the Byrds, the Buffalo Springfield defined an eclectic country-rock style during the mid-Sixties that remains current and has been widely influential. Formed by a couple of itinerant folkies, Stephen Stills and Richie Furay, led by the macabre singer/songwriter/lead guitarist Neil Young, and anchored by ex-Dillards drummer Dewey Martin (bassists Bruce Palmer, then later Jim Messina rounded out the group), the Springfield made two brilliantly eccentric records before tearing themselves apart. The first, *Buffalo Springfield,* showcased Stills' and Young's tremendous songwriting talent (Stills' "For What It's Worth" became the band's only major hit single) and Furay's distinctively countryish lead singing.

Their second, *Buffalo Springfield Again,* is the definitive album, with both Young and Stills at the top of their songwriting game, some weird and brilliant production assistance from Jack Nitzsche, and the meanest playing they got on record. The frenetic, eerily prophetic self-analysis in Young's "Mr. Soul" and "Broken Arrow" characterized his mystical songwriting, while Stills' "Rock & Roll Woman" and "Bluebird" are the finest songs he's ever written.

For all practical purposes the group no longer existed by *Last Time Around.* Except for Young's kiss-off, "On the Way Home," Stills' pretty "Uno Mundo" and Richie Furay's breathtaking country song "Kind

Woman," the material doesn't match the band's prime output. They went their separate ways, Stills to Crosby, Stills and Nash; Young to a solo career with Crazy Horse, then later as part of Crosby, Stills, Nash and Young; Furay to Poco; and Jim Messina to Loggins and Messina.

For a group with such a short life span, the Springfield's influence becomes even more astounding. Their music has filtered relentlessly down into the work of the Eagles, Jackson Browne and countless others, a distinctly American rock style that has become the West Coast standard. Though *Again* is the definitive recording, the two-record anthology (2-806) is the best collection, highlighting pertinent material from all three records with the emphasis on the second album, including the original nine-minute version of "Bluebird," complete with the extended jam that had been edited out of the song as it appeared on *Again.* — J.S.

JIMMY BUFFETT
★★★ A-1-A / Dun. D-50183
★★★ A White Sport Coat and a Pink
  Crustacean / Dun. X-50150
★★★★ Changes in Latitudes, Changes in
  Attitudes / ABC 990
★ Havana Daydreamin' / ABC D-914
★★ Live / 2-ABC 1108
★★ Living and Dying in 3/4 Time / Dun.
  D-50132
★★ Son of a Son of a Sailor / ABC
  1046

Buffett is a protean figure—an inconsistent but occasionally great songwriter, leader of an ersatz country-rock group called the Coral Reefer Band. His songwriting is his strong suit. *Crustacean* featured a couple of crazed hippie anthems, "The Great Filling Station Holdup" and "Peanut Butter Conspiracy," and the pensive ode, "Death of an Unpopular Poet." On the ensuing records, Buffett has a bad habit of indulging in overly camp material and too many woozy booze tunes, but there are bright moments on each album. High points are "This Hotel Room," "Kick It in Second Wind," and the title track from *Havana Daydreamin'*, "Door #3," "Stories We Could Tell" and "Pirate Looks at Forty" from *A-1-A,* and the hit single off *Changes* that turned him from a cult figure to a pop star, "Margaritaville." — J.S.

SANDY BULL
★★★ Demolition Derby / Van. 6578
★★ E Pluribus Unum / Van. 6513

★★★ Essential / Van. 59/60
★★ Fantasias for Guitar and Banjo / Van.
  79119
★★ Inventions / Van. 79191

From the pristine string fantasias of his first (1963) album through the time when his drug habit interrupted his progress in 1972, Sandy Bull made spellbinding music. A near prodigy on guitar and banjo at seventeen, he became a student of jazz as well as Indian and Arabic music. This eclectic streak resulted in "Blend," a twenty-two-minute side on *Fantasias for Guitar and Banjo.* On his second album, 1965's *Inventions,* he cut "Blend II," again working with veteran jazz drummer Billy Higgins.

He also played electric and acoustic takes of Gavotte No. 2 from Bach's Suite No. 5, and an instrumental version of Chuck Berry's "Memphis, Tennessee." Influenced by Pop Staples' gospel guitar work, he split his six-string Fender electric's signal between four kinds of amplification on *E Pluribus Unum:* "Electric Blend" and "No Deposit, No Return Blues" are a smack freak's workouts for 1970 acid eaters. His last recording, 1972's *Demolition Derby,* is a scary mix of Latin juking ("Gotta Be Juicy") and country warbling ("Tennessee Waltz" and Floyd Cramer's "Last Date"). *The Essential Sandy Bull* compilation covers the terrain, but *Demolition Derby* is a haunting promise from a career that may yet be revived. — F.S.

BULLDOG
★ Smasher / Bud. 5600
Ex-Rascals Gene Cornish (guitar) and Dino Danelli (drums) couldn't rescue this now-defunct foursome's anonymous hard rock. Nothing really wrong, but precious little on target. (Now deleted.) — C.W.

CINDY BULLENS
★★ **Desire Wire** / U. Artists LA933-H
Bullens would like to come on as an authentic female hard rocker. Maybe she is, but her debut album seems a bit forced, and it is hard not to recall, in that light, that she was a featured performer in the ultimate antirock abomination, *Grease.* — D.M.

VERNON BURCH
★★★ **When I Get Back Home** / Col. PC-34701
On his deleted 1975 debut album (United Artists), Vernon Burch astounded people with his vocal similarity to Stevie Wonder. Burch mastered Wonder's touch, phrasing and general mood on songs like "Ain't Gonna Tell Nobody." He also played lead guitar, which had been his main bread-and-butter gig with the reformed Bar-Kays, and his guitar work was as derivative (in the Stax/Volt psychedelic mode made popular by Isaac Hayes circa *Hot Buttered Soul*) as his singing. The Columbia album moves him closer to a disco style and adds an Al Green touch to the Wonder influence. At some point Burch is liable to develop into a major talent if he can stop leaning so heavily on his influences. (Now deleted.) — J.S.

ERIC BURDON AND WAR
★★ **Love Is All Around** / ABC ABCD 988
War helped make Burdon's last great single, "Spill the Wine," but MGM has deleted their first LP—*Eric Burdon Declares War*—which is one of his best. *Love* is funky fooling around from the same era (1969-70, mostly) and ranks with Burdon's silliest—"A Day in the Life" as a blues song is foolish indeed. War has gone on to become one of the Seventies' most interesting and influential black bands. (Now deleted.) — D.M.

ERIC BURDON BAND
▪ **Ring of Fire** / Cap. ST-11359
▪ **Stop** / Cap. SMAS-11426
It wasn't uncommon for the early Burdon to cross the border from emotional involvement to hysteria. Generally, he was saved by the excellence of his bands, War and the Animals. By 1974, when he made these records, he couldn't have cleared customs—even when recycling some of his old hits, the band is so clumsy, Burdon so overextended, that nothing works. (Now deleted.) — D.M.

SOLOMON BURKE
★ **Back to My Roots** / Chess 19002
★ **Music to Make Love By** / Chess 60042
★★★★★ **The Best of Solomon Burke** / Atl. 8109
Unlike other soul stars of the Sixties, who sang their music with unflagging intensity—often to the point of hysteria—Solomon Burke was the master of control. The music on *The Best of Solomon Burke* is majestic and dignified, yet as powerful as the most volatile recorded performances of Wilson Pickett. But Burke's restraint was only part of his genius. He was also a most convincing storyteller, as well as a shameless eclectic, capable of absorbing a range of idioms and influences in his singing and songwriting. When Solomon said in the intro to "Everybody Needs Somebody to Love," "There's a song I sing, and I believe if everybody was to sing this song it would save the whole world," I believed him. So, it seems did Mick Jagger: Burke has proven to be one of Jagger's biggest influences as a vocalist.

Solomon Burke needed a producer's touch in the studio. His self-productions have often been embarrassing. A Barry White imitation on *Music to Make Love By* provided a temporary commercial respite, but the hopefully titled *Back to My Roots* proved to be the nadir of his career. — J.MC.

DORSEY BURNETTE
★ **Things I Treasure** / Calli. 7006
Brother of late Johnny Burnette, Dorsey was never quite as fine a rocker in the first place, and by the time of this Seventies LP, had gone the way of all ex-rockabillies: to bland C&W. (Now deleted.) — D.M.

JOHNNY BURNETTE AND THE ROCK AND ROLL TRIO
★★★★ **Tear It Up** / Solid S. 3001
Excellent sampler of the late rockabilly artist's 1956 and 1957 recordings, with excellent liner notes and pristine monaural sound. Includes his seminal "Train Kept A-Rollin'," plus the remarkable "Rock Therapy," but not his pop hits, even "You're Sixteen." — D.M.

BURNING SPEAR
★★★ **Dry and Heavy** / Mango 9431
★★★★★ **Marcus Garvey** / Is. 9377
★★★★ **Garvey's Ghost** / Is. 9382
★★★ **Live** / Isl. 9513
★★★★ **Man in the Hills** / Is. 9412
Reggae is political music by definition, and Burning Spear is the genre's most stridently political group—their first album and its best-selling title track are named for the back-to-Africa leader of the Twenties who gave Rastafarianism its cultural impetus.

Garvey is a great reggae album, and *Garvey's Ghost,* which is that album's instrumental tracks, is one of the landmarks of the reggae offshoot called "dub," which involves releasing just such instrumental tracks, and heightening them for even more intensity. But despite the group's great sense of groove and the sporadic brilliance of vocalist Winston Rodney, after *Man in the Hills,* the music has grown colder, less approachable. Even the live album, which might have been as formidable as Rodney's stage presence, peters out in playing that is virtually directionless. — D.M.

KATE BUSH
★★ **The Kick Inside** / Harv. SW-11761
English thrush who created a storm in certain critical quarters in late 1978. Not exactly New Wave, not exactly art-rock. Sort of like the consequences of mating Patti Smith with a Hoover vacuum cleaner. — D.M.

DAVID BUSKIN
★ **David Buskin** / Epic 31233
East Coast acoustic singer/songwriter. Lightweight reflective songs crooned in pleasant voice. (Now deleted.) — S.H.

JERRY BUTLER
★★★ **All-Time Jerry Butler Hits** / Trip 8011
★★ **It All Comes Out in My Song** / Mo. M7-892
★★★ **Just Beautiful** / Kent 536
★★ **Love's on the Menu** / Mo. M7-850
★★★ **Nothing Says I Love You** / Phila. 35510
★★★ **Sixteen Greatest Hits** / Trip TOP-16-45
★★ **Starring Betty Everett** / Trad. 2073
★ **Suite for the Single Girl** / Mo. M7-878
★★★★★ **The Best of Jerry Butler** / Mer. 61281
★★ **Thelma and Jerry** / Mo. M7-887
Butler began his singing career in a church choir in Chicago that also included Curtis Mayfield and Sam Gooder; together they were the original Impressions, although after Butler's "For Your Precious Love," a beautiful, big-voiced soul ballad, became a national hit in 1958, he left the group to go solo with Vee-Jay Records, while Mayfield took the Impressions in other directions. The Trip, Kent and Tradition LPs feature his Vee-Jay work, which also included "He Will Break Your Heart," with Betty Everett; "Giving Up on Love"; and an unfortunate amount of straight pop material like "Moon River."

But Butler's most brilliant music was made when he teamed with Philadelphia producers Kenneth Gamble and Leon Huff for a series of late-Sixties singles. The hits "Only the Strong Survive," "Never Give You Up," "Lost," "What's the Use of Breaking Up," "Moody Woman" and "Hey Western Union Man" resulted, and they are an apex of the era's record-making, with an appeal that stretches across pop and soul boundaries. Butler's voice was the first vehicle Gamble and Huff found for their orchestral funk ideas, and it remains the most expressive. It is reserved but emotional—the two excellent but deleted albums he made with Gamble and Huff for Mercury were called *Ice on Ice* and *The Iceman Cometh*—with a nice trick of moving from verse to verse in guttural drags. (The lyrics, particularly "Only the Strong Survive," were far ahead of their time, and easily the best Gamble and Huff have written.)

Unfortunately, Butler has not been able to keep pace with the changes in black pop taste; the series of albums he's made for Motown are strained, unable to find a satisfactory compromise between his crooning naturalness and the rhythm attack of modern disco production. The duet album with Thelma Houston, which attempts to recapture the spirit of his duets with Everett, is perhaps the best of them, but all are disappointing. — D.M.

JOAN CAROL BUTLER
★★★ **Joan Carol Butler** / Cap. ST-11476
A competent purveyor of down-home love songs, Joan Butler can be good when she's not cloying. The backing by the Muscle Shoals rhythm section emphasizes Butler's similarity to Fleetwood Mac's Christine McVie. (Now deleted.) — J.S.

PAUL BUTTERFIELD
★★★★ **East-West** / Elek. 7315
★★★ **Golden Butter/The Best of the Paul Butterfield Blues Band** / Elek. 7E-2005
★★★ **In My Own Dream** / Elek. 74025
★★★ **It All Comes Back** / Bears. 2170
★★★ **Paul Butterfield/Better Days** / Bears. 2119
★ **Put It in Your Ear** / Bears. 6960
★★ **The Butterfield Blues Band/Live** / Elek. 7E-2001
★★★ **The Paul Butterfield Blues Band** / Elek. 7294
★★★★ **The Resurrection of Pigboy Crabshaw** / Elek. 74015

It would be easy to see Paul Butterfield purely in historical terms—he was, after all, the American musician most responsible for introducing urban blues to rock audiences—but that would overlook the music, which holds up surprisingly well. Perhaps none of it equals the bluesmen he emulated, but little of it is shoddy, either. Butterfield was a popularizer, but an authentic one, who gave credit where credit was due (Little Walter, Muddy Waters, Howlin' Wolf) and rejected imitation as strongly as he did bastardization. His first album, *The Paul Butterfield Blues Band* (1965), seemed more imprisoned by blues than freed by it, but on the second, *East-West,* he cut traditional ties without losing track of them, shifting sources from Allen Toussaint's R&B to Cannonball Adderley's jazz. The album's centerpiece, however, was its title song, a thirteen-minute instrumental track whose lengthy and brilliant guitar passages (by Mike Bloomfield and Elvin Bishop) did as much as anything to establish the mystique and heroism of modern rock guitarists.

As his band continued to change personnel (Bloomfield left to form Electric Flag after *East-West*), Butterfield expanded into R&B (*The Resurrection of Pigboy Crabshaw* and *In My Own Dream*) and began to use a full horn section. If most of Butterfield's albums now seem a bit second-hand, it is in part because he was too humble a performer to conquer his sources. Unlike Van Morrison, for instance, Butterfield always conceived of blues as a tradition, not as a sensibility. Even after he disbanded the Blues Band and formed Better Days (a crack rock & roll unit that included such players as Amos Garrett and Geoff Muldaur) he never projected himself, never conveyed a sense of who he was or what he wanted to say. While both the albums recorded with his early Seventies group, Better Days (the debut album *Butterfield/ Better Days* and *It All Comes Back),* boast a formal imagination, they lack a personal one. His last record, a collaboration with former King Records' producer Henry Glover, collapses altogether. An experiment in modern R&B, *Put It in Your Ear* buries Butterfield in a mountain of effects and he seems completely lost—a final metaphor for a rich but narrow career. — K.R.

TUCKY BUZZARD
★★ **All Right on the Night** / Pass. 97001
★★ **Buzzard** / Pass. 98001
Tucky Buzzard is a blues-rock band principally of interest because of its producer, Rolling Stone Bill Wyman. They try very hard to sound (without much success) like an American blues-boogie band powered by Rolling Stone turbos. — A.N.

THE BYRDS
★★★★★ **Mr. Tambourine Man** / Col. CS-9172
★★★★★ **Turn! Turn! Turn!** / Col. CS-9254
(Jim McGuinn, guitar; Gene Clark, tambourine; David Crosby, guitar; Chris Hillman, bass; Michael Clarke, drums)

The unmistakable sound of the Byrds—trebly electric twelve-string guitar, rock bottom bass and soaring vocal harmonies—marked the rise to prominence of West Coast folk rock. Intelligence, sensitivity and self-consciousness are reflected in the first two (mid-Sixties) Byrds albums, which neatly blend traditional folk ("He Was a Friend of Mine," "Satisfied Mind," "Turn! Turn! Turn!"), new folk (a myriad of Dylan tunes) and thoughtful, original pop (Clark's "I'll Feel a Whole Lot Better," "The World Turns All around Her"). They even have a sense of humor—*Tambourine Man* closes with that big hit from *Dr. Strangelove,* "We'll Meet Again," and *Turn!* drags Stephen Foster's "Oh! Susannah!" out of the cellar, tongue firmly in cheek.
★★★★★ **Byrds' Greatest Hits** / Col. PC-9516

★★★★ **Fifth Dimension** / Col. CS-9349
★★★★ **The Notorious Byrd Brothers** /
Col. CS-9575
★★★★★ **Younger Than Yesterday** / Col.
CS-9442

Gene Clark's departure before the recording of *Fifth Dimension* tosses chief songwriting burdens on McGuinn and Crosby, and they fare more than adequately under the pressure. The group begins to experiment both lyrically and instrumentally, using the mysteries of space as exploratory grounds. "Eight Miles High," with its atonal, chaotic lead guitar (influenced by both John Coltrane and Indian ragas), ushers in psychedelia a year ahead of schedule. Roots are still revered, though, through lovely readings of traditional songs "John Riley" and "Wild Mountain Thyme." *Younger Than Yesterday,* with the last two Byrds hits, the ironic "So You Want To Be a Rock 'n' Roll Star" and the bittersweet cover of Dylan's "My Back Pages," again breaks new ground, as Hillman, a former bluegrass mandolinist, writes and sings lead on four songs, two of which ("Girl With No Name," "Time Between") are bona-fide country tunes. A *Greatest Hits* package was then released; Columbia correctly sensed that the era of Byrd hit singles was ending. Crosby drops out in the middle of recording sessions for *Notorious Byrd Brothers,* yet the band (McGuinn changes his first name to Roger at this time), using the production breakthrough that *Sgt. Pepper* made possible, keeps right on going. And they remain the Byrds, as exemplified by their transformation of Carole King's "Goin' Back," with its simple but emotional twelve-string solo.
★★★★★ **Sweetheart of the Rodeo** / Col.
CS-9670

(Roger McGuinn, guitar and banjo; Gram Parsons, guitar; Chris Hillman, bass and mandolin; Kevin Kelley, drums)

With a revamped lineup, the Byrds plunge into country music, achieving a delicate balance similar to their first two albums. Parsons, who dominates the record, pens the two originals ("Hickory Wind," "One Hundred Years from Now"), both gems. Songs by Dylan, Woody Guthrie, the Louvin Brothers and Merle Travis

are all treated masterfully. Guest musicians include John Hartford and Clarence White, flatpicker extraordinaire.
★★★ **Dr. Byrds & Mr. Hyde** / Col.
CS-9755
★★★ **Untitled** / Col. G-30127

(Roger McGuinn, guitar; Clarence White, guitar; Gene Parsons, drums; John York, bass [*Dr. Byrds*]; Skip Battin, bass)

McGuinn's ambivalence about turning the group into a country band leads to Parsons' and Hillman's departure to form the Flying Burrito Brothers. The new Byrds do some country, but they also can rock out. White brings a new dimension to Byrds guitar, most evident on "King Apathy III" and Dylan's "This Wheel's on Fire." The new band is promising, and their next effort, *Easy Rider* (available as a cutout), is a masterpiece. Battin replaces York for *Untitled,* a double set with one studio and one live LP. The live set works, with updated versions of Byrds oldies, but the studio side, save McGuinn's "Chestnut Mare" and White's rendition of Little Feat's "Truck Stop Girl," is mostly filler. Battin simply cannot write Byrd songs.
★★ **Best of the Byrds/Greatest Hits, Vol.
2** / Col. C-31795
★★★★ **Preflyte** / Col. KC-32183

The second *Greatest Hits* package, released just prior to the Byrds' final breakup in '72, is a hodgepodge of songs from the band's entire career with little to recommend it. *Preflyte* is a posthumous release of the original group's demo tape and illuminates the beauty of the initial conception. Nine of the eleven tracks hadn't been previously released, and most of them, especially "You Showed Me" and "You Won't Have to Cry" are first-rate. (The original band did re-form for one record, *Byrds* [Asylum, available as a cutout], in '73, but time had finally taken its toll, and it's an embarrassing disappointment.) — B.A.

DAVID BYRON

■ **Take No Prisoners** / Mer. SRM-1-1074
Histrionic ex-Uriah Heep singer may be the most irritating front man of Seventies rock, and his solo debut does nothing to alter that judgment. Definitely *not* a Byronic hero. — J.S.

BRIAN CADD
★ White on White / Cap. ST-11573
Inept Seventies singer/songwriter. — J.S.

CAFE JACQUES
★★★★ Round the Back / Col. JC-35294
Excellent British studio band whose dense
rhythmic mix and melodic keyboard tex-
tures recall Traffic's lyricism and Little
Feat's syncopation. — J.S.

JOHN CAGE
★★★ Electronics and Percussion / Col.
　MS 7139
★★★ HPSCHD / None. H-71224
★★★★★ Indeterminacy / Folk. FT 3704
★★★★ Variations II / Col. MS 7051
★★★★ Variations IV / Ev. 3132
Modern classical minimalist John Cage influenced Frank Zappa, Todd Rundgren,
Brian Eno and the other tape nuts of rock,
but his importance is also felt by dancers,
filmmakers and artists all over the world.
His concept of Zen-like total harmony—
not just in the music, when it exists, but in
the roles of composition, performance,
arena and participants—shifted the moment of creation, demystified it and
brought it into the concert hall. His pieces
can seem heavily manufactured, yet primordial. And with the freedom he gives to
his musicians (they do not improvise, as
jazz musicians do, but follow his scores at
will), he always makes sure some certain
somethings happen. Each performance is
caught in time, impossible to predict, for
the audience or for Cage.
　Indeterminacy is ninety stories read by
Cage, each told within the space of a minute, and none having anything to do with
the next. They are inadvertently punctuated by tape, piano and radio provided by
David Tudor, and become points of reference on a map of magic and invention.

　Variations IV, a live recording, mixes
tapes, sound effects, recorded stories, audience noise, records and live mikes. All
were controlled by Cage and Tudor (except, of course, the audience) from two
separate rooms.
　Tudor was at the amplified piano for
Variations II, which uses a score of super-
imposed geometric drawings to create mea-
surable "values" translated in the performance. *Electronics and Percussion,* five
realizations by Max Neuhaus, includes one
piece by Cage, "Fontana Mix." The Neuhaus version mixes feedback from contact
mikes resting on percussion instruments in
front of loudspeakers. Years before Hendrix, this was revolutionary, but maybe not
so interesting.
　You join the fun on *HPSCHD,* by Cage
and Lejaren Hiller, a piece for harpsi-
chords and computer-generated sound
tapes. Each copy comes with its own
computer-printout "score" for modulating
volume, treble, bass and channels. "Good
luck," Cage says in his notes to the
work. — A.E.G.

J. J. CALE
★★★ Naturally . . . J. J. Cale / Shel.
　52009
★★ Okie / Shel. 52015
★★★ Really, J. J. Cale / Shel. 52015
★★ Troubadour / Shel. 52002
J.J. Cale's music is like a softly repeated
blues mantra; its appeal lies in his attractively smoky voice and rolling guitar style,
its weakness his compositional repetition.
The songs rarely strike out with a melody
of their own, but rather become instrumental and vocal meditations around a few basic chords. For this reason, *Naturally* remains his best album, since it put this style
in a fresh setting. *Really* incorporates a bit
of country into the mix—Vassar Clements

and Josh Graves participate—and the Muscle Shoals studio band is effectively featured on "Lies." Country and bits of harder guitar rock cropped up on Cale's last two albums, but the effect is still that of a simple song taken at a loping pace. While it can be attractive as such, it rarely pushes either Cale's voice or his guitar to levels that truly involve the listener. — J.B.M.

JOHN CALE

★★ Church of Anthrax [with Terry Riley] / Col. 64259 (Import)
★★★ Fear / Is. 9301 (Import)
★★★ Guts / Is. 9459 (Import)
★★ Helen of Troy / Is. 9350 (Import)
★★★★ Paris 1919 / Rep. MS-2131 (Import)
★★★ Slow Dazzle / Is. 9317 (Import)
★★★ Vintage Violence / Col. CS-1037

John Cale, a founding member of the Velvet Underground, is a classically trained musician who studied in Europe with classical avant-gardist La Monte Young. Arriving in New York in the early Sixties, he saw rock as the ripest and most amenable form open to the avant-garde.

Vintage Violence was Cale's first solo album (he left the Velvets after the 1968 *White Light/White Heat* LP), and melodically it's a comparatively light collection, the songs loosely constructed around a central cast of losers, lovers and ghosts. The playfulness of the music belies the often morose lyrical content and offsets Cale's flat-effect vocal style.

Church of Anthrax is a collaborative effort with avant-garde classical composer Terry Riley, and is closer to jazz than anything else. Riley (on keyboards and sax) and Cale (on guitar, viola and keyboards) spiraled off into lengthy, feverish modal excercises, harbinger of experiments Brian Eno, among others, would pursue in the mid-Seventies. (A later classical attempt, *The Academy in Peril,* is completely out of print.)

John Cale didn't make a record again until 1973, this time for Reprise with Richie Hayward and Lowell George of Little Feat in supportive roles. The result, *Paris 1919,* was his towering achievement, a gentle, introspective collection, similar in tenor to *Vintage Violence.* The following year found Cale on a new label, Island. *Fear* sported a tougher, more deranged rock sound than anything since his work with the Velvets. "Fear Is a Man's Best Friend" and "Gun" are wild, frightening

insights about brutality, far more cathartic than Lou Reed's similar recordings. Cale filled his quota of lovely, folk-based melodies as well.

Slow Dazzle soon followed, and included a paean to Brian Wilson, a perverse remake of "Heartbreak Hotel" and the by now familiar amalgam of jagged, dissonant rockers and soothing, deceptive "ballads." Some critics dubbed Cale the new Jim Morrison, but those who'd been listening all along knew better.

In late 1975, Cale released his third album in less than a year, *Helen of Troy,* an assembly of grim obituaries for the living, bitter recollections, and predatory rock. It included "I Keep a Close Watch," a spitting version of "Pablo Picasso" (a track Cale had originally produced for the Modern Lovers in 1970), and a surprisingly subdued rendition of Jimmy Reed's "Baby What You Want Me to Do?" *Helen* was Cale's equivalent of Neil Young's scarifying *Tonight's the Night.* Island never even bothered to release it in the United States and promptly deleted *Slow Dazzle* and *Fear.* But they have released an excellent anthology of his work for the label, *Guts.*

In addition to his solo career, Cale has produced and/or worked extensively with the following artists: The Velvet Underground, Lou Reed, Iggy Pop and the Stooges, Nico, Terry Riley, Eno, Phil Manzanera, Kevin Ayers, Jonathan Richman and the Modern Lovers and Patti Smith. — M.G.

CALICO

★★★ Calico / U. Artists LA454-G
★★ Calico, Vol. 2 / U. Artists LA659-G

Pleasant if uneventful country rock produced in Nashville in 1975 and 1976. The first album gets a slight edge on the strength of the songwriting. (Now deleted.) — J.S.

RANDY CALIFORNIA
★ **Kapt. Kopter and His (Fabulous) Twirly Birds / Epic E-31755**
Postpsychedelic dysfunction (circa 1977) from a talented guitarist who is continually becoming lost in the sauce of his own peculiar indulgences. A variety of generes—from metallic soul ("I Don't Want Nobody") to Hendrix-influenced riff frenzy ("Downer")—are mangled here, and the covers are preposterous: the Beatles' "Rain" is transformed into a vengeful monsoon, for instance. Even the reunions of Spirit, California's original group, were less outrageous than this. — B.A.

TERRY CALLIER
★★★ **Fire On Ice / Elek. 6E-143**
★★★★ **I Just Can't Help Myself / Cadet 50041**
★★★ **Occasional Rain / Cadet 50007**
★★★★ **What Color Is Love / Cadet 50019**
Terry Callier came to minor prominence in Jerry Butler's Chicago songwriters' workshop as a songwriter for Butler, The Dells and other Chicago soul acts. But as a solo artist singing his own songs, Callier does not sing in a traditional soul form. Though a gospel chorus, an occasional saxophone, and strings are often featured on his records, Callier's music combines folk and blues elements. He strums an acoustic guitar while he sings and at times he's reminiscent of Richie Havens, though Callier's a superior vocalist and writer. The violins may tip his music into MOR territory but, as on both *What Color Is Love* and *I Just Can't Help Myself*, Terry Callier is capable of imaginative presentations. Charles Stepney produced all three. The Elektra set continues Callier's style in a more relaxed setting. — J.MC.

CAMEL
★ **Mirage / Janus 7009**
★ **Moonmadness / Janus 7024**
■ **The Snow Goose / Janus 7016**
If a group that would make an art-rock "opera" out of a saccharine children's epic like "The Snow Goose" seems like your kind of rock & roll, you're welcome to this low-rent Moody Blues. — D.M.

G. C. CAMERON
★ **G. C. Cameron / Mo. 855**
★★ **Love Songs and Other Tragedies / Mo. 819**
★★ **Rich Love, Poor Love / Mo. M7-891**
★ **You're What's Missing in My Life / Mo. M7-880**
G. C. Cameron was the lead singer on the Spinners' "It's a Shame"; after four solo albums the song remains the highlight of his career. Cameron's tenor is capable of near-perfect imitations of a range of singers from Smokey Robinson to Curtis Mayfield. The problem is that he seems to have no style of his own, a dilemma compounded by the slipshod method by which his albums are assembled. (*Love Songs* alone features eight different producers, including Stevie Wonder and Willie Hutch.) His best moment as a solo artist: the poignant "It's So Hard to Say Goodbye to Yesterday," the theme from the movie *Cooley High* (included on *G. C. Cameron*). — J.MC.

GLEN CAMPBELL
★★ **Arkansas / Cap. SM-11407**
★★ **Basic / Cap. SW-11722**
★★ **Bloodline / Cap. SM-11821**
★★ **By the Time I Get to Phoenix / Cap. ST-2851**
★★ **Galveston / Cap. ST-210**
★★★ **Glen Campbell's Greatest Hits / Cap. SW-752**
★★ **I Knew Jesus (Before He Was a Star) / Cap. SW-11185**
★ **"Live" / Cap. STBO-268**
★★ **Rhinestone Cowboy / Cap. SW-11430**
★★ **Southern Nights / Cap. SO-11601**
★ **That Christmas Feeling / Cap. SM-2978**
★★★ **The Best of Glen Campbell / Cap. ST-11577**
★★ **The Last Time I Saw Her / Cap. SM-733**
★★ **Try a Little Kindness / Cap. SM-389**
★★ **Wichita Lineman / Cap. SM-103**
In album after album, Campbell's true grit triumphs over schlock production and the necessity to cover a broad country-pop base. Campbell has long shown astute song selection, his association with Jimmy Webb ("By the Time I Get to Phoenix," "Wichita Lineman," "Galveston") having been particularly fruitful. For all but the devoted, either of the anthologies should suffice, *The Best of* being preferable because it contains the classic country boy's dream of making it in the city, "Rhinestone Cowboy," in addition to the Webb songs and "Gentle on My Mind." — S.H.

CANNED HEAT
★★ **Boogie with Hooker and Heat / Sp. TSX-3501**
★ **Canned Heat / Sp. 4026**

This group of blues aficionados (leader Bob "The Bear" Hite had a legendarily deep record collection) backed into a recording career in 1966, defined a certain wine-slugging festival spirit, then did a fast fade by the turn of the decade. Masterful guitarist and bumblebee-voiced singer Al Wilson died in 1970—the last stroke for the group.

The weak *Canned Heat* contains four warmed-over boogie numbers; each of these, except for "Bullfrog Blues," is found in John Lee Hooker's superior versions on *Boogie with Hooker and Heat.* But Hooker doesn't really seethe in their reverent company, so the two-record set is only pleasant. A dandy United Artists cutout (*The Very Best of Canned Heat*) is worth a search; it contains their epochal '68 hits "On the Road Again" and "Going up the Country," plus stompers like "Let's Work Together." — F.S.

JIM CAPALDI
★★★ Daughter of the Night / RSO 1-3037
★★★★ Short Cut Draw Blood / Is. 9336
Ex-drummer of Traffic is a more-than-credible rock singer, particularly on the oldie, "Love Hurts" and the brief originals that comprise the rest of side one of *Short Cut.* Side two, four more extended compositions, has some of the tone and much of the blandness of Traffic. *Daughter* is idiosyncratic but worthwhile. — D.M.

THE CAPTAIN AND TENNILLE
★ Come in from the Rain / A&M 4700
★★ Love Will Keep Us Together / A&M 4552
★ Por Amor Vivremos / A&M 4561
★ Song of Joy / A&M 4570
★ The Captain and Tennille's Greatest Hits / A&M 4667
One good hit, "Love Will Keep Us Together," written and performed better by Neil Sedaka; smiley, mechanical pop for the rest. The Captain (Daryl Dragon) has been a Beach Boys sideman; Toni Tennille looks like a toothpaste-commercial reject, and acts the part. As sanctimonious as they are banal. — K.T.

CARAVAN
★ Better by Far / Ari. AB 4134
★★ Caravan and the New Symphonia / Lon. PS-650
★★★ For Girls Who Grow Plump in the Night / Lon. XPS-637
★★★ If I Could Do It All Over Again / Lon. PS-582
★★★ In the Land of Grey and Pink / Lon. PS-593
★★★★ Waterloo Lily / Lon. XPS-615
There are passages on *Waterloo Lily* and *For Girls* that careen with big-band swinging presence reminiscent of Gil Evans. Caravan has that rare ability to play orchestrated rock that *rocks.* At the group's most symphonic, Caravan's odes to joy can be downright chilling. As for harmonies, it's *Wild Honey* perfection personified.

Caravan materialized out of the Early Canterbury Underground (England's unrealized answer to our 1968 mythology of the Haight), which also spawned Kevin Ayers, Pink Floyd and Soft Machine; Caravan's Pye Hastings (guitar) and David Sinclair (keyboards) were in Wildflower, which became Soft Machine.

As romantic as they are futuristic, Caravan's strong suit is the ability to sing sailing harmonies over complex-yet-linear musical settings while avoiding the Yes/Genesis overpomp trap. — B.M.

GEORGE CARLIN
★ An Evening with Wally Londo / Li. Dav. 1008
★★★★ Class Clown / Li. Dav. 1004
★ FM and AM / Li. Dav. 7214
★ Indecent Exposure / Li. Dav. 1076
★★★ Occupation: Foole / Li. Dav. 1005
★★ On the Road / Li. Dav. 1075
★ Original George Carlin / ERA 600
★ Toledo Windowbox / Li. Dav. 1005
Carlin was an imaginative if traditional stand-up comic (as recorded on the forgettable Era album) till he got high and freaked out in the early Seventies. He then evolved a more personal style (autobiography replaced characters and dialects), with an emphasis on druggy jokes and a willfully naive viewpoint. His high point is *Class Clown,* a wonderfully vulgar and accurate remembrance of high school and the Catholic church, leavened by Lenny Bruce moralism (a profound and bad influence). Carlin remains obsessed with dope, though, and his approach is already embarrassingly dated. — K.T.

CARL CARLTON
★★ Everlasting Love / ABC D-857
★★ I Wanna Be with You / ABC D-910
★★★ You Can't Stop a Man in Love / Back. X-71
Sometimes we forget that Stevie Wonder was a major Motown artist back in the Sixties; big enough, in fact, to spawn a host of

imitators. Among the most prominent was fellow Motor City singer Little Carl Carlton, who occasionally evinced a real adolescent charm: witness "I Won't Let That Chump Break Your Heart" and "Competition Ain't Nothing," both included on *You Can't Stop a Man in Love.* Though Carlton's voice never matured, he was rescued from a Detroit assembly line by the freak Top Forty success of "Everlasting Love," in 1974. But the rebirth was short-lived. Carlton proved to be too harsh and limited a singer even for a producer as streetwise as Bunny Sigler, and *I Wanna Be with You* is one of Sigler's less eventful productions. — J.MC.

CARMEN
■ **Fandangos in Space / Dun. DP-50l92**
David Bowie–produced flamenco rock band is purely for the birds. — J.S.

ERIC CARMEN
★ **Boats against the Current / Ari. 4124**
★ **Change of Heart / Ari. 4184**
★★ **Eric Carmen / Ari. AQ-4057**
A strong, intelligent pop-ballad singer, *Eric Carmen* was his solo debut after leaving the Raspberries in 1975. But one couldn't help feeling he was more convincing as a rocker in his original band, despite the two hits ("Never Gonna Fall in Love Again" and "All by Myself"). *Boats* sank in a sea of corny syrup. *Change* was more of the same. — D.M.

KIM CARNES
★ **Kim Carnes / A&M 4548**
★★ **Sailin' / A&M 4606**
L.A. singer/writer sings white country soul à la Dusty Springfield and Jackie DeShannon but with a more impersonal Hollywood gloss. *Sailin'* has the distinction of a classic Jerry Wexler coproduction and contains the 1976 American Song Festival winner, "Love Comes from Unexpected Places," which Carnes co-wrote with husband Dave Ellingson. — S.H.

THE CARPENTERS
★ **Carpenters / A&M 3502**
★ **Christmas Portrait / A&M 4726**
★ **Close to You / A&M 4271**
★★ **Horizon / A&M 4530**
★ **Kind of Hush / A&M 4581**
★ **Now and Then / A&M 3519**
★ **Passage / A&M 4703**
★★★ **Singles 1969-1973 / A&M 3601**
★ **Song for You / A&M 3511**
★ **Ticket to Ride / A&M 4205**

This brother-sister duo from New Haven epitomizes early-Seventies MOR. By the release of *Horizon,* Karen Carpenter's contralto had acquired ripe overtones while remaining serenely inexpressive. *Singles,* a greatest-hits collection, says it all. Bubbly and bland. — S.H.

PETE CARR
★★★ **Not a Word on It / Big BT 85918**
★★★ **Multiple Flash / Big 76009**
The precision and understatement of Muscle Shoals, with a debt to the Allmans and a taste of jazz. Guitarist Carr is a superb, subtle technician, reminiscent of Roy Buchanan and Jeff Beck. Chips off the latter's *Blow by Blow* perhaps, but no bad ones. — C.W.

KEITH CARRADINE
★ **I'm Easy / Asy. 7E-1066**
■ **Lost and Found / Asy. 6E-114**
Moody-voiced son of actor John Carradine scored with the title track from *I'm Easy* in Robert Altman's 1976 film, *Nashville.* Its machismo sentiments and croaked vocal are unfortunately echoed throughout that album. And yet *Lost and Found* had even less to recommend it. — D.M.

THE CARS
★★★★ **The Cars / Elek. 6E-135**
Shrewd, witty Boston area band whose 1978 debut album gets better and better with repeated listenings. Influences range from Beatlesque song structures to mid-Sixties, punk-rock elements. The playing is competent, the songs catchy and hook-ridden, the production (Roy Thomas Baker) superbly calculated. "Just What I Needed" and "My Best Friend's Girl" became minor hits on the strength of some of the most efficient harmony vocal arrangements since the Beatles. — J.S.

CARLENE CARTER
★★★ **Carlene Carter / War. K-3204**
The latest member of the Carter family of country music fame to record. Carlene's debut (produced by Brinsley Schwarz and Rumour pianist Bob Andrews) marks her as one of the best of the women country rock performers. — J.S.

CLARENCE CARTER
★★ **A Heart Full of Song / ABC 943**
★★★ **Loneliness and Temptation / ABC D-896**
Blind singer/guitarist Clarence Carter's best work has inevitably been produced by

Muscle Shoals entrepreneur Rick Hall. Unfortunately, all of the records they made for Atlantic, which include Carter's biggest hit, "Slip Away," are cut out. So is their final album, 1973's *Sixty Minutes With,* which successfully blended influences as diverse as the Doobie Brothers and C&W with Carter's own down-home *oeuvre.*

Both *Loneliness and Temptation* and *A Heart Full of Song* were self-produced and recorded in Atlanta. Clarence Carter's country-bumpkin persona continually straddles the line between successful melodrama and farce. Without Hall's direction, the uptempo tracks fall flat (often they're rehashes of "Slip Away"), and the lyrics fall just this side of soap-opera mawkishness. — J.MC.

THE CARTER FAMILY

★★★ Best of the Carter Family / Col. CS-9119
★★ Country's First Family / Col. KC-34266
★★ Fifty Years of Country Music / Camd. ADL2-0782
★★★★★ Happiest Days of All / Camd. ACL1-0501
★★★★★ Lonesome Pine Special / Camd. 2473
★★★★ 'Mid the Green Fields of Virginia / RCA ANL1-1107
★★★★★ More Golden Gems from the Original Carter Family / Camd. 2554
A3My Old Cottage Home / Camd. ACL1-0047
★★★★ Smoky Mountain Ballads / Camd. ACL-7022
★★★ The Carter Family Album / Lib. 7230
★★★★★ The Original and Great Carter Family / Camd. 586
★ Three Generations / Col. KC-33084
★★ World's Favorite Hymns / Col. 32246

The Carter Family, with Jimmie Rodgers (The Singing Brakeman), virtually invented country music as we now know it. First emerging from the Virginia-Tennessee border country in 1927, the same region and era that produced Rodgers, the Carters' effect on the development of both American country and folk music was immediately pervasive. This trio of singers from the Blue Ridge region—A.P., Maybelle and Sara—established country and folk's basic close-harmony singing style, and a great many of the songs that both traditions share. (Woody Guthrie often borrowed Carter melodies for his songs; his "It Takes a Worried Man" is a direct rewrite of their scarifying "Worried Man Blues," for in-

stance.) More recently, Maybelle (Sara's cousin and A.P.'s sister-in-law), now known as Mother Maybelle, had a heavy influence on the city folk revival of the early Sixties through her appearances at folk festivals and the like. Maybelle's flat-picking guitar style was also enormously influential on the development of both country and folk. The Carters' best-known material includes "My Clinch Mountain Home," "Worried Man Blues," "Keep on the Sunny Side," "Bury Me Beneath the Weeping Willow," "Foggy Mountain Top," "Can the Circle Be Unbroken" and "Wildwood Flower."

The family's second generation, alternatively known as the Carter Sisters, is more inclined toward standard Nashville pop country, with a particularly sanctimonious evangelical religious bent. (June Carter, one of the Carter Sisters, later married Johnny Cash.)

The Carters recorded for many labels; the best of what remains catalogued is contained on the sides currently released on Camden, RCA's budget label. The Columbia material often features the Carter Sisters, and is consequently rated lower. A ten-disc retrospective on RCA, currently available only in Japan, is long overdue for U.S. release. — C.F.

VALERIE CARTER

★★★★ Just a Stone's Throw Away / Col. PC-34155
★★★ Wild Child / Col. VC-35084

Impressive debut album by California interpretive singer who brings to the genre more funkiness and rock spirit than anyone since Bonnie Raitt. Highlight is a remake of "Ooh Child." Star-studded cast, production by a variety of heavies, including Little Feat's Lowell George and Earth, Wind and Fire's Maurice White. *Wild Child,* the follow-up, was less successful. — D.M.

JOHNNY CASH

★★★ Johnny Cash and Jerry Lee Lewis Sing Hank Williams / Sun 125
★★★★★ Johnny Cash: The Legend / Sun 2-118
★★ Johnny Cash: The Man, the World, His Music / Sun 126
★ Original Golden Hits, Vol. 1 / Sun 100
★ Original Golden Hits, Vol. 2 / Sun 101
★★★ Original Golden Hits, Vol. 3 / Sun 127
★★ Showtime / Sun 106
★★ Story Songs of the Trains and Rivers / Sun 104

★ **The Rough-Cut King of Country Music /
Sun 122**
★ **The Singing Story Teller / Sun 115**
In 1955, when twenty-three-year-old
Johnny Cash signed with Sun Records,
only Hank Williams had managed to break
through the restrictions of "hillbilly music"
to sell country records to a pop audience.
Cash did it with his first single, "I Walk
the Line," and kept on for six Sun LPs and
several extended-play 45s. Thus the rockabilly Cash was an influential figure in the
blues-country fusion that led to rock &
roll.

Rock fans will be most interested in the
Sun records, available through reissues
packaged by Shelby Singleton. Of the ten
albums listed above, however, only three
are of more than passing interest. *Johnny
Cash: The Legend,* a two-record set incorporating the first two *Golden Hits* LPs, is
the one Johnny Cash record to own. With
the late Luther Perkins on guitar, Marshall
Grant on bass, and possibly either Jerry
Lee Lewis or Charlie Rich on piano, this
is the only Cash backup band worth mentioning. The album contains most of his
classics—"Folsom Prison Blues," "Hey
Porter," "Cry, Cry, Cry," "Ballad of a
Teenage Queen," "I Walk the Line," "Get
Rhythm," "Big River" and the great "Luther's Boogie." The arrangements are clear
and simple; the production is crisp. *Original Golden Hits, Volume 3* will just about
complete the Cash Sun collection; it contains "The Wreck of the Old 97," "Rock
Island Line" and "Katy Too." Production
here is uneven, and arrangements are more
elaborate (backup vocals, more instruments).

Cash's lifelong preoccupation with
American history, folklore, freedom and
confinement are abundantly evident on
these two albums. It is significant to note,
also, that Cash's pop tunes were generally
written by Jack Clement or Cash; but all
the folk tunes were written by Cash.

Aside from the *Hank Williams* set (which
is more notable for the Jerry Lee Lewis
sides), most of the rest of these LPs are ex-
pendable, some because they are repeti-
tious of the material on the two collections
above, some because of weak material.
★ ★ ★ **Blood, Sweat and Tears / Col.
CS-8730**
★ ★ **Everybody Loves a Nut / Col.
CS-9292**
★ ★ **Greatest Hits, Vol. 1 / Col. CS-9478**
★ **Hymns by Johnny Cash / Col.
CS-8125**

★ **Hymns from the Heart / Col. CS-8522**
★ ★ **I Walk the Line / Col. CS-8990**
★ ★ **Johnny Cash Sings the Ballads of the
True West / Col. C2S-838**
★ **Mean as Hell! / Col. CS-9246**
★ ★ ★ **Orange Blossom Special / Col.
CS-9109**
★ ★ ★ **Ride This Train / Col. CS-8255**
★ ★ ★ **Ring of Fire / Col. CS-8853**
★ **The World of Johnny Cash / Col. CG-29**
Here is Johnny Cash, the folk singer.
While many of the songs are interesting
and Cash's narratives show painstaking re-
search, the series is flawed because it's
stronger on folklore than music. "Ring of
Fire" is almost the only Cash song from
this period that has survived.

Ride This Train is a particularly ambitious project, in which Cash as narrator assumes the role of American Everyman,
taking the listener to coalminers and lum-
berjacks, cowboys and outlaws—including
John Wesley Harding. This is one of the
first pop concept albums, and, one suspects, the beginning of the Johnny Cash/
Bob Dylan mutual admiration society.
Cash's recitation of American place names
(particularly Indian ones) and "Lorraine of
Pontchartrain," an original song, are the
stand-outs. The problem is that the album
contains too much talking—every song is
prefaced by a windy narrative.

Blood, Sweat and Tears, a similar concept, works better because its scope is nar-
rower: specifically, the legend of John
Henry, more generally, the American
workingman. "Tell Him I'm Gone" and
"Another Man Done Gone" are beautiful
country blues songs, and "Busted," the
Harlan Howard classic, made its first appearance here. *Ballads of the True West,* a
third concept album, is marred by its tendency to sound like a high school history
lesson—a fault shared to a lesser degree by
the other two.

Orange Blossom Special is the most musically satisfying album of this series. In addition to the ever-popular title song, the album includes three Dylan songs—"It Ain't
Me Babe," "Don't Think Twice" and
"Mama, You Been on My Mind"—plus
the country classics "Long Black Veil" and
"Wildwood Flower." The problem is that
Dylan sings Dylan better than Cash.

I Walk the Line and *Ring of Fire* are collections from Sun, and the material is superior to the
Ring of Fire, which includes the title song
and "I Still Miss Someone." *Greatest Hits*
and *The World of* are also collections from

this period, which culminated in the Cash/ Dylan duet on *Nashville Skyline*; *Greatest Hits* is superior.

★★ **Any Old Wind That Blows** / Col. KC-32091

★★ **Five Feet High and Rising** / Col. C-32951

★★ **His Greatest Hits, Vol. 2** / Col. KC-30887

★★ **Johnny Cash and His Woman (with June Carter Cash)** / Col. KC-32443

★★★★★ **Johnny Cash at Folsom Prison** / Col. CS-9639

★★★ **Johnny Cash at Folsom Prison and San Quentin** / Col. CG-33639

★★★ **Johnny Cash at San Quentin** / Col. CS-9827

★★ **Johnny Cash Sings Precious Memories** / Col. C-33087

★★ **Look at Them Beans** / Col. KC-33814

★★★ **One Piece at a Time** / Col. KC-34193

★★★ **Man in Black** / Col. C-30550

★★ **Ragged Old Flag** / Col. KC-32917

★ **Sunday Morning Coming Down** / Col. C-32240

★ **The Gospel Road** / Col. CG-32253

★ **The Holy Land** / Col. KCS-9726

★★ **The Junkie and the Juicehead Minus Me** / Col. KC-33086

★★ **The Last Gunfighter Ballad** / Col. KC-34314

★★★★ **The Rambler** / Col. KC-34833

These albums, representing Cash's output for the past ten years, contain some of his best work since Sun and some of the most embarrassing. At times Cash is antiestablishment, at others as conventional as Hubert Humphrey. Sometimes he is both on the same record.

Folsom Prison is Cash's best album since he left Sun. Musically, it's lively, committed and exciting. There isn't a bad song here, but among the best are "Folsom Prison Blues"—better than on Sun—"Cocaine Blues," "25 Minutes to Go," "Jackson," "Give My Love to Rose" and "Send a Picture of Mother." In addition, *Folsom Prison* comes as close to being a documentary about prison life as one can come without a camera. Rather than being about history, this album *is* history.

San Quentin (recorded at a performance in that prison), is also live and lively. Although it misses a bit of *Folsom*'s vitality, *San Quentin* contains the hit, "A Boy Named Sue." Columbia followed up with the two-record set which combines both prison albums.

Man in Black is the first of Cash's weird albums. It contains "Singin' in Viet Nam Talkin' Blues," done Bob Dylan style, a song about Johnny's trip to Vietnam; intentionally or not, it's an antiwar song. But this album has another song, "The Preacher Said, 'Jesus Said,' " a duet with Reverend Billy Graham. Then there's "Man in Black," Cash's famous declaration of mourning for the world.

Holy Land is like a home slide show of Cash's trip to Israel, replete with lots of talking and lots of religion; it contains "Daddy Sang Bass." *The Gospel Road* is a more sophisticated version of *Holy Land,* the soundtrack to Cash's movie about the life of Jesus. More talking; not much music. *Precious Memories* is a fine collection of country hymns.

Several of these albums are collections of country songs—*Any Old Wind That Blows* (mostly mediocre); a duet with June Carter Cash on *Johnny Cash and His Woman* (simpler and better); *The Junkie and the Juicehead Minus Me* (strange, strange, strange) and *Everybody Loves a Nut.* All are corny country curiosities that are eventually nerve-racking. Or collections of older Cash material recycled: *Sunday Morning Coming Down,* the second *Greatest Hits* LP, *Five Feet High and Rising* (one of the best).

One Piece at a Time made some sense out of this jumble. The title song, the story of an auto worker who steals a Cadillac from a factory over the course of several years, is actually funny. "Committed to Parkview," a song about commitment to a mental institution, rings true; and "Mountain Lady," a song about Mother Maybelle Carter (a seminal country influence and Johnny's mother-in-law) is beautiful.

The Last Gunfighter Ballad backslides with outlaw imagery but is saved by the incredible "Far Side Banks of Jordan." *The Rambler,* on the other hand, harks back to *Ride This Train,* but isn't pedantic. Rather than narrated prefaces, a story in the form of a dialogue weaves through the record and the songs are logically linked. There are several stand-out numbers here, including "Lady," "After the Ball," "No Earthly Good," "My Cowboy's Last Ride," and "Calilou." — M.H.

TERRY CASHMAN
★★ **Terry Cashman** / Lifes. PZ-34999
Cashman is best known for producing with Tommy West, Jim Croce. This solo debut (1976) does nothing to change that. — D.M.

CASINO
■ Casino / MCA 2191
Absolutely despicable rock band attempts a mid-Seventies (1976) revision of some Mott the Hoople ideas. (Now deleted.) — J.S.

BUZZ CASON
★ Buzz / DJM 8
Dumb country singer whose most notorious song, a groupie's tribute to Emmylou Harris, was covered badly by Brush Arbor. — J.S.

DAVID CASSIDY
★ Home Is Where the Heart Is / RCA APL1-1309
As a teenage TV rage, Cassidy spewed out mewly crap. This solo LP (his second) attempts to float above that image, but it's strictly a lead zeppelin. — K.T.

SHAUN CASSIDY
★★ Born Late / War. K-3126
★ Shaun Cassidy / War. B-3067
★★ Under Wraps / War. K-3222
David Cassidy's younger brother follows a familiar pattern—hit TV show (*The Hardy Boys*) yields pop hits, most notably "Da Doo Ron Ron," from the first album, and "Hey Deanie," from *Born Late*. The former, like all of Cassidy's oldies covers, is horrid; the latter and some of the originals on *Born Late* (particularly "Teen Dream") are first-rate pop rock, not quite as good as the Raspberries, but in contention. *Under Wraps* made no noticeable progress. The best teen idol of the decade, if that's progress. — D.M.

CASTON AND MAJORS
■ Caston and Majors / Mo. M6-814-51
This 1974 set of insufferable pseudo-operatic drivel proves that even the best

Motown session players can't save a bad concept from sounding like one. At least not this time. (Now deleted.) — J.S.

JIMMY CASTOR BUNCH
★ Butt of Course / Atco 18124
★ E-Man Groovin' / Atco 18186
★ Maximum Stimulation / Atco SD 19111
★ Supersound / Atco 18150
★ The Everything Man / Atco SD 7305
Castor made a name for himself with the 1966 Latin pop hit "Hey, Leroy, Your Mama's Callin' You." He resurfaced in 1972 with the heavy-metal funk vamp "Troglodyte," on RCA. His albums for Atco are banal attempts to parlay his latter-day funk success into the Seventies disco market. These records are failures—the only single to get chart action during this period was the wretched "The Bertha Butt Boogie Part 2," a ribald sequal to "Troglodyte." — J.S.

CATE BROTHERS
★★★ Cate Brothers / Asy. 7E-1050
★★ Cate Brothers Band / Asy. 7E-1116
★★ In One Eye and out the Other / Asy. 7E-1080
Pulsating Memphis-style blue-eyed soul produced by Steve Cropper. Brother Ernie and Earl Cate perform original material in the tradition of Sam and Dave. Their first album, *Cate Brothers,* contains their best songs, "Time for Us" and the hit, "Union Man." — S.H.

CATES SISTERS
★★ Cates Sisters / Capri. 1003
Post-Allmans Capricorn singer/songwriter duo departs from the label's Southern rock formula without noticeably improving on the concept. — J.S.

CATS
★ Love in Your Eyes / Fan. 9449
Bad mid-Seventies rock band. — D.M.

STEVE CAUTHEN
★ Local Hoedown / Bare. 534
Cauthen may have won six million dollars in one year riding thoroughbred race horses, but he's never going to make his living as a country music singer. — J.S.

FELIX CAVALIERE
★★★★ Destiny / Bears. 6958
★★ Felix Cavaliere / Bears. 6955
Cavaliere, the guiding light of the Rascals, had his first solo effort (1974) hopelessly mangled by Todd Rundgren's kitchen-sink

production. Layers of excessive keyboards and guitars remove the focus from Cavaliere's voice and straightforward compositions. *Destiny,* produced by Cavaliere himself, is a delight. High-spirited, with a host of veteran New York session players all cutting loose, Cavaliere recaptures some of his old magic. Leading the way are the funky "Flip Flop" and "Try to Believe," and "I Can Remember," a truly beautiful ballad. (Now deleted.) — B.A.

CECILIO & KAPONO
■ **Cecilio & Kapono / Col. PC-32928**
■ **Elua / Col. PC-33689**
■ **Night Music / Col. PC-34300**
Hawaii Five-O meets Brewer and Shipley. Nice shirts. — J.S.

CERRONE
★ **Cerrone's Paradise / Coti. 9917**
★ **Golden Touch / Coti. 5208**
★★ **Love in C Minor / Coti. 9913**
★ **Supernature / Coti. 5202**
The last and most dreadful word in late Seventies European disco production. "Love in C Minor" was the hit. — J.S.

CHAIRMEN OF THE BOARD
★★★ **Skin I'm In / Inv. KZ 32526**
Originally second-rate Four Tops imitators, Chairmen of the Board bowed out with a crazy album that explored the eccentric sides of Sly Stone and Stevie Wonder. Most of the songs were written by lead singer General Johnson (who left to pursue a solo career) and include two killer cuts taken at a frantic blitz: "Finder's Keepers" and "Everybody Party All Night." — J.MC.

CHAKACHAS
★ **Chakachas / H&L 11005**
Group's only hit, "Jungle Fever," a 1972 boogie stomper, is not included here. — D.M.

CATHY CHAMBERLAIN
★★★ **Rag 'N' Roll Revue / War. B-3032**
Engaging record of updated swing band music featuring Chamberlain's vocals. — J.S.

CHAMBERS BROTHERS
★ **A New Time, A New Day / Col. CG-33642**
★★ **Best of the Chambers Brothers / Fan. 24718**
★ **Love, Peace and Happiness / Col. CG-20**
■ **The Chambers Brothers' Greatest Hits / Col. 30871**
★ **The Time Has Come / Col. CS-9522**
When the Chambers Brothers switched in the late Sixties from being a "gospel family" (as represented on the Fantasy LP) to a funk and soul outfit (picking up white drummer Brian Keenan), they served as forerunners of black bands with large white audiences. Avoiding the soul studio systems of Motown, Stax or Philadelphia, they chose to psychedelicize their gospel sound. That is, they played crude, guitar-based rock and sang sloppy, spirited group vocals over the drone. The result was "Time Has Come Today," a lengthy hit in 1968.

The Chambers Brothers never evolved far from this primordial formula; they neither rocked nor, once they gave up gospel, brought their sound back home. The only really listenable tracks they produced are the smoother tunes like "People Get Ready" and sections of their "suite," "Love, Peace and Happiness," where the instinctive cohesion of the Brothers' vocals is given a chance.

Time Has Come is now a mere historical curio, *Love, Peace and Happiness* only a document (half of it is live), and the *Greatest Hits* package is of no use whatsoever. — B.T.

CHAMPION
★★ **Champion / Epic JE-35438**
Yet another unfocused late-Seventies hard-rock band. Pass. — J.S.

GENE CHANDLER
★ **Get Down / 20th Cen. 578**
★★★★ **The Girl Don't Care / Bruns. 54124**
★ **The Two Sides of Gene Chandler / Bruns. 754149**
★★ **There Was a Time / Bruns. 754131**
Like so many Chicago soul stars of the Sixties, Gene Chandler was almost entirely a creation of the songwriting and production skills of Curtis Mayfield. Under Mayfield's direction, Chandler's mid-Sixties persona was one of vulnerability. Chandler drenched Mayfield's songs with a believable desperation, like a man on the edge, phrasing each line with an exaggerated deliberateness. Chandler was able to step outside the melancholy on "Good Times," a finger-popping, Saturday-night high-school classic. The three Mayfield/Chandler songs on *The Girl Don't Care* marked the end of their collaboration, but producer Carl Davis was able to effectively duplicate May-

field's approach for a time. Unfortunately Davis was not able to maintain his grip on the singer's style, and Chandler's career—overburdened by standards and uncomfortable attempts at uptempo dance material—quickly declined. — J.MC.

CHANTER SISTERS
★★ **First Flight** / Poly. PD 1 6075
Disco, but not overly mechanical; these two Britons sing with power and control. The production and musicians work well, but the material (Bowie, "Hound Dog") often doesn't fit. (Now deleted.) — C.W.

HARRY CHAPIN
★ **Dance Band on the Titanic** / Elek. 9E-301
★★ **Greatest Stories—Live** / Elek. 7E-2009
★★ **Heads and Tales** / Elek. 75023
★ **Living Room Suite** / Elek. 6E-142
★ **On the Road to Kingdom Come** / Elek. 7E-1082
★ **Portrait Gallery** / Elek. 7E-1041
★ **Short Stories** / Elek. 75065
★ **Sniper and Other Live Songs** / Elek. 75042
★ **Verities and Balderdash** / Elek. 1012
Singer/songwriter with avid cult devised short-story song format combining moral fables and melodramas. *Heads and Tales* contains Chapin's first hit, the archetypal ballad, "Taxi." The centerpiece of *Sniper* is a tasteless Freudian interpretation of the Texas tower murders. *Verities* contains Chapin's biggest hit and best song, "Cats in the Cradle," co-written with his wife. *Greatest Stories—Live* is a live greatest-hits album that shows Chapin's febrile entertaining style. Despite fine craftsmanship, all of Chapin's work tends to be as emotionally overwrought as it is simplistically preachy. — S.H.

CHARISMA
★ **Beasts and Friends** / Rou. 42054
★ **Charisma** / Rou. 42037
A totally-out-of-it record company's attempt to keep up with the times in rock & roll. — D.M.

RAY CHARLES
★★★ **Come Live with Me** / Cross. 9000
★★★★ **Genius of Ray Charles** / Atl. 1312
★★★ **Love and Peace** / Atco 19199
★★ **My Kind of Jazz, Part 3** / Cross. 9007
★★ **Ray Charles** / Ev. 244
★★ **Ray Charles, Vol. 2** / Ev. 292
★★★★★ **Ray Charles Live** / Atl. 2-503
★★★ **Renaissance** / Cross. 9005
★★★ **Soul Brother (with Milt Jackson)** / Atl. 1279
★★★ **Soul Meeting (with Milt Jackson)** / Atl. 1360
★★★★ **The Great Ray Charles** / Atl. 1259
★★★★★ **The Greatest Ray Charles** / Atl. 8054
★★★★ **True to Life** / Atl. 19142
Ray Charles helped change the face of American popular music. Born in Georgia, blind since age six, he began recording in Los Angeles in the late Forties, as an acolyte of Nat "King" Cole. These records, now available on the two Everest LPs, are impressive mostly for their mastery of another man's form.

When he came to Atlantic and producers Jerry Wexler and Ahmet Ertegun, Charles changed his style. Although he still made jazz records, he also aimed for the rock and R&B market. His great breakthrough was to add elements of gospel music to both his singing and piano playing. The result was a series of hits, including "I Gotta Woman," "What'd I Say" and "Hallelujah I Love Her So," which were enormously popular as well as fundamentally influential. Twenty years later, they still sound startlingly fresh.

As great a blues and jazz singer and player as he was, Charles never shied away from pop. Even at Atlantic, he experimented with country & western and Big Band. But when he left Atlantic for ABC-Paramount in 1959, Charles headed straight for the middle of the road, almost deserting his R&B and jazz following. Several of his hits there, particularly "Let's Go Get Stoned," "Your Cheating Heart" and "Hit the Road Jack," retain the spirit of the early music, but most of what he did as a pure pop singer was an unfortunate waste of his immense talent.

The ABC period is now completely unrepresented; when Charles left the company (where he later recorded for his own label, Tangerine), he took possession of his own recordings, and those of the Ray Charles Singers, one of the best vocal choruses of that era. They have never been reissued. (Charles' work at his new company, Crossover, was uneven at best, though the pop-oriented *Renaissance* has flashes of the old wit.)

Atlantic's cutout policies are inexplicable. For example, "Hallelujah I Love Her So" is unavailable except as a single. So is "I Believe to My Soul," which Bob Dylan used as the melody for his "Ballad of a Thin Man." At the very least, the four-volume Atlantic *Ray Charles Story* is essential, if it can be turned up as a cutout. What's here is marvelous—the recordings with Jackson are merely middling jazz, but that may be true only to pop-oriented ears—yet it's a shame we can't have the rest. As a consequence of this disorganized recording availability, Charles has grievously been overlooked—perhaps his successful return to Atlantic with 1977's *True to Life* will rectify that. — D.M.

CHARLIE
★ Fantasy Girls / Col. PC-34081
★ Lines / Janus 7036
★★★ No Second Chance / Janus 7032
The guitars flash, and Terry Thomas can write and sing with some ability, but there's little variation or originality in the quartet's debut for Columbia. *No Second Chance*, however, relied less on guitars than keyboards, and the arrangements were more than jams. — C.W.

CHARLIE AND THE PEP BOYS
★★ Daddy's Girl / A&M SP 4563
The Stones have had few imitators more blatant than Charlie and the Pep Boys and few more engaging. Nils Lofgren produced this band of Washington, D.C., would-be punks, then stole their guitarist. (Now deleted.) — M.G.

CHASE
■ Chase / Epic BG-33737
■ Ennea / Epic E-31097
■ Pure Music / Epic KE-32572
Flee. — D.M.

SAM CHATMON
★★ The Mississippi Sheik / Blue G. 2006
Chatmon emerged a soloist from the black string bands of the Twenties and Thirties,

was a nonprofessional contributor to the Chicago blues sound (both B.B. and Albert King covered his "Cross Cut Saw Blues"), then returned to the professional rounds in the Sixties. His is a simple, steady guitar style complemented by rich vocalizations of traditional and original blues. — I.M.

CHEAP TRICK
★★★ Cheap Trick / Epic PE-34400
★★★★ Heaven Tonight / Epic JE-35312
★★★★ In Color / Epic PE-34884
★★★★★ Live at Budokan / Epic JE-35795
A heavy-metal highlight of the late Seventies, this Chicago quartet was also the least likely *looking* combo of the day: vocalist Robin Zander and bassist Tom Petersson were rock-star slim and blown-dry, but guitarist/songwriter Rick Neilsen was a ringer for Huntz Hall of the Bowery Boys and drummer Bun E. Carlos looked like an overweight war criminal on the lam.

The debut album (self-titled) was produced by Jack Douglas (Aerosmith), and only a hint of the band's power and Neilsen's compositional flair came through. But Tom Werman, who produced the second and third records, understood them perfectly: his settings and the clarity with which the songs were recorded have some of the edge Glyn Johns gives the Who. Neilsen's songs were ridiculous arabesques designed to set off his astonishing guitar work—which does power-chorded tricks in an individual yet mainstream rock style—and the group's ability to execute perfect Beatlesque harmonies behind Zander. The tone was always light and often wryly humorous: it's hard to say what "Big Eyes" or "Clock Strikes Ten" from *In Color* are about, but "Surrender," from *Heaven,* is a gem: Neilsen's parents wig out behind their own advice to him and make out on the couch while listening to Kiss records. If that isn't your idea of surrender, you've wandered into the wrong book by mistake. *Budokan* is a live set that surpasses the studio records. — D.M.

CHUBBY CHECKER
★ Chubby Checker's Greatest Hits / Abkco 4219
A former chicken plucker with a stage name clownishly aped from Fats Domino, Checker was a below-average R&B singer who hooked on to Hank Ballard's "The Twist," which subsequently became the hottest dance craze of the past twenty years. Checker even did instructional spots

on television—"Just pretend you're grinding out cigarette butts with each foot." For nostalgia buffs and cultural historians only. — J.S.

CHEECH AND CHONG
★★ Big Bambu / War. K-3251
★ Cheech and Chong / War. K-3250
★ Cheech and Chong's Wedding Album / War. K-3253
★ Los Cochinos / War. K-3252
★ Sleeping Beauty / War. K-3254

The Rise and Fall of Drug Humor—mostly its fall. Good mimics but strictly miniaturists of a boring, dated subculture. Abundant vulgarity that is extremely amusing to sixth-graders. — K.T.

CLIFTON CHENIER
★ Black Snake Blues / Arhoo. 1038
★★★★★ Bogalusa Boogie / Arhoo. 1076
★★ Bon Ton Roulet / Arhoo. 1031
★★ Live / Arhoo. 1059
★★★ Louisiana Blues and Zydeco / Arhoo. 1024
★★ Out West / Arhoo. 1072
★★★ New Orleans / Cres. 2119
★★★ Red Hot Louisiana Band / Arhoo. 1078

Chenier is an accordionist. Born in Opelousas, Louisiana, in 1925, he is the best-known exponent of zydeco—a dance music composed of traditional French, Acadian (popularly known as Cajun), and rhythm & blues elements. Chenier and his band—including brother Cleveland on rub board, a variant of the washboard—play everything from waltzes to two-steps to twelve-bar blues to local pop hits.

Obviously this is a very rhythmic music, though as *Bogalusa Boogie* in particular reveals, it is also a good showcase for a strong soloist—for instance, Chenier's imaginative accordion or John Hart's tenor sax. "Bogalusa Boogie" is also the best-recorded and most naturally mixed of these sets.

The lyrics are frequently in French, but it doesn't matter much, for this isn't really music for listening in a strict sense. And although zydeco's popularity is largely regional, it has influenced a variety of nationally known artists such as Doug Kershaw, Elvin Bishop, Ry Cooder and Taj Mahal, although none perform it as purely as Chenier.

Bogalusa Boogie, as stated, is Chenier's strongest LP to date, but if the sound is at all appealing—the accordion has been unduly maligned by Mel Bey and Lawrence

Welk—you're likely to want to hear the entire catalogue.

One cautionary note: the Steve Miller listed in the liner credits of *Out West* is not the same Steve Miller of "The Joker" or "Fly Like an Eagle" fame; the Elvin Bishop on that LP, however, is indeed the "Travellin' Shoes" man. — I.M.

CHER
★ Cher / U. Artists UXS-88
★ Cher / U. Artists UXS-94
★ Cher Sings the Hits / Sp. 4029
★ Cher's Greatest Hits / Sp. 4028

Cher's recordings, most of them packed into a surprisingly large number of compilation albums, fall roughly into three phases, marked by different arranger-producers.

The first phase coincides with the last days of the short recording career of Sonny and Cher. When Sonny and Cher's lounge act, called Caesar and Cleo, became the prototypical "hippie couple" act, Sonny and Cher, Bono readjusted Phil Spector's echoed, dense Wall of Sound studio style to fit his songs into the then-current folk-rock style. But to call the resulting hybrid of Spector's Wall of Sound and Bono's own ideas of the "protest song" (i.e.,"I Got You Babe" and "The Beat Goes On") garish is to miss the point. Sonny and Cher, and later Cher alone, always cultivated an exuberant vulgarity in order to disarm Sixties songwriting—especially the songs derived from Dylan—to push it into a more comfortably sentimental direction. The commercial wisdom of this strategy was demonstrated with Cher's version of Dylan's "All I Really Want to Do" (on *Cher*), which beat the Byrds' version on the charts.

The more lasting advantage of Sonny

Bono's studio style, however, is that it allowed Cher to *talk* her way through the dozen or so folk-rock songs that she could never have sung and that fill out the spaces between her major hits on these now-unlistenable compilation albums: "You'd Better Sit Down Kids," "Bang Bang" and so on. After Bono retired from the records entirely, succeeding producers merely replicated the formula over and over again.

★ Cher / MCA 2020
★ Cher/Greatest Hits / MCA 2127
★★★ Cherished / War. S-3046

Cher's second phase, intended to supplement her new TV career, was supervised by producer Snuff Garret. Garret's principal intention (assignment?) was to turn Cher into the sophisticated pop singer her weekly TV show required. It didn't work. While an album like the deleted *Half Breed* consists largely of puffy ballads and Cher bulling her coarse way through them, the title cut and "Gypsies, Tramps and Thieves" from the same period were the only hits. They offer the older, talking Cher against what are merely modified versions of Bono's original Spectorish conception. Neither custom-written ballads nor cover versions of "Alfie" and "The Impossible Dream" could dislodge Cher's original, increasingly ridiculous recording persona. In fact, it was only further deepened by Cher's TV personality (a mixture of fashion vamp, ethnic outsider and frail sentimentalist), and it found a new, but unexploited, vehicle in songs about adultery ("I Saw a Man and He Danced with His Wife") and about sexual education/exploitation ("Carousel Man").

★★ I'd Rather Believe in You / War. B-2898
■ Stars / War. B-2850
★ Take Me Home / Casa. 7133

The third phase of Cher's record making represents the first time she found a coherent musical context. Working with keyboardist producer Michael Omartian and producer Steve Barri, *I'd Rather Believe in You* situates her in the by-now-standardized L.A. studio sound. Medium tempo, piano-based tunes, heavy use of backup singers, rock band setups and lots of orchestral sweetening gives Cher's limited vocal range the appearance of style. The album is a transparently obvious message to Gregg Allman, but it also shows Allman that Cher can be his equal as an artistic partner, if he wants her. Interestingly, this is the only Cher album that is anything but vulgar. Cher's straightforwardness of feel-

ing (not to mention the wit she can bring to an argument with a male) remakes the songs as vehicles for her own highly assertive personality. *Take Me Home* puts her in a disco setting. That she has advanced as a singer only a little in all this time doesn't seem to matter much. Recording has been only one of several means of conveying her curiously ambiguous and suggestive public presence.   — B.T.

CHIC
★★★ C'est Chic / Atco 19209
★★★ Chic / Atco 19153

One of the most popular and probably one of the best disco groups, Chic manages to combine disco's unadventurous musical values with the conservatism of classic pop R&B. "Dance, Dance, Dance" and "Le Freak" are the big hits.   — J.S.

CHICAGO
★★★ Chicago Transit Authority / Col. PG-8
★★ Chicago II / Col. PG-24
★★ Chicago III / Col. C2-30110
★ Chicago IV—Live at Carnegie Hall / Col. K4X-30865
★★ Chicago V / Col. PC-31002
★★ Chicago VI / Col. PC-32400
★★ Chicago VII / Col. C2-32810
★★ Chicago VIII / Col. PC-33100
★★★ Chicago IX—Greatest Hits / Col. PC-33900
★ Chicago X / Col. PC-34200
★ Chicago XI / Col. JC-34860
★★★ Hot Streets / Col. FC-35512

The point of Chicago Transit Authority's debut album was that a big rock band had managed to play with some funk. But succeeding installments, as producer James William Guercio took more and more control, were about as imaginative as the group's album titles. Now and then, though, the group would come up with a pleasant hit single (1974's "Wishing You Were Here," a collaboration with the Beach Boys, is the best example), which makes *IX* worth looking into. The bizarre death of guitarist Terry Kath (he shot himself while toying with a pistol) forced the group to add session guitarist/vocalist Donnie Dacus for *Hot Streets,* which clicked behind the hit single "Alive Again."   — D.M.

CHICKEN SHACK
★ Imagination Lady / Deram 18063

This now-defunct British blues outfit's best moments were inspired by lead singer/keyboardist Christine Perfect before she left to join Fleetwood Mac (as Christine McVie). Their only album left in print is a hackneyed collection of heavy blues jams recorded after Perfect's departure. — J.S.

THE CHIEFTAINS
★★ **Bonaparte's Retreat / Is. 9432**
★★ **The Chieftains 1 / Is. 9364**
★★★★ **The Chieftains 2 / Is. 9365**
★★★ **The Chieftains 3 / Is. 9379**
★★ **The Chieftains 4 / Is. 9380**
★★★ **The Chieftains 5 / Is. 9334**
★★★ **The Chieftains 7 / Col. JC-35612**
While the Chieftains' music is not strictly traditional—they play harmony passages and compose some tunes themselves—it does have a clarity and authenticity that has made them the best-known source of Irish folk music. The band's chief virtuosos—fiddler Sean Keane and composer/piper/tin whistler Paddy Maloney—weave their instruments through a beautifully spare mix that includes a goatskin drum, bagpipes, concert flute, wire-strung harp, concertina, bones and an occasional oboe or hammer dulcimer.

Moloney and three others of the band's seven members came out of Sean O'Raida's folk orchestra in the late Fifties and made *Chieftains 1* in 1962. That record promised much, but it was five years before the band members forsook their day jobs long enough to join with fiddler Keane to make the landmark *Chieftains 2*. While both records contain jigs, reels, hornpipes and polkas, the slow airs seem to ache with the beauty of the stories underlying them.

By the release of *Chieftains 4* in 1973, Moloney had begun to compose an occasional tune, and this rich recording contains an air that became "The Love Theme from *Barry Lyndon* (Women of Ireland)." Perhaps more striking is the grimly martial "The Battle of Aughrim" or Keane's fiddle workout on a reel called "The Bucks of Oranmore." *Chieftains 5* (1976) is assured and lyrical, but their recent *Bonaparte's Retreat* is seen by purists as a tricked-up commercial effort that leaves the band at a crucial crossroads. — F.S.

THE CHIFFONS
★★★★ **Everything You Always Wanted to Hear by the Chiffons But Couldn't Get / Laur. 4001**
★★ **Sweet Talkin' Guy / Laur. 2036**
The Chiffons were one of the greatest of the early-Sixties girl groups (as well as one

of the few not produced by Phil Spector). Their hits were in the jive-talking, street-swaggering style of the time and included the mesmerizing "One Fine Day," "He's So Fine" and "Sweet Talkin' Guy" among others. But they hardly had enough to sustain twenty tracks, as even the best of this pair of LPs tries to do, and their remaining nonanthology album is a simple period piece—the title hit and some throwaway junk. You ought to own this music, but not in this form, unless you don't have a 45 spindle. — D.M.

THE CHI-LITES
★★★ **Give It Away / Bruns. 754152**
★★★★★ **Give More Power to the People / Bruns. 7541**
★★★★ **Greatest Hits/Chi-Lites / Bruns. 754184**
★★★★ **Greatest Hits, Vol. 2 / Bruns. 754208**
★★ **Half a Love / Bruns. 754204**
★★★★ **Happy Being Alone / Mer. SRM-1-1118**
★★★ **Letter to Myself / Bruns. 754118**
★★★★ **Lonely Man / Bruns. 754179**
★★★ **The Fantastic Chi-Lites / Mer. SRM-1-1147**
★★★ **Toby / Bruns. 754200**
The Chi-Lites were among the leaders of a group soul renaissance—termed "neoclassical" by Vince Aletti—that took place at the beginning of the Seventies. The group's early records hardly distinguished them from the glut of others in the field who looked to the early Temptations for inspiration. But gradually a distinct, and for soul music, unique persona began to emerge. Headed by lead singer/songwriter/producer Eugene Record, the Chi-Lites' stark portrait of excessive male vulnerability was unlike that of even the Moments and Delfonics, two other groups who exercised melancholy with great effect. Record highlighted his thin tenor with the most plaintive production gimmicks: a forlorn harmonica on "Oh Girl," windstorms on "Coldest Days of My Life." While this type of pathos was occasionally overwrought, often it was quite dramatic and effective, and *Power to the People* is a surprisingly first-rate mixture of soul-music populism and quiet desperation. After *Lonely,* the Chi-Lites lost their bass singer, and subsequent records found a retreat from starkness into simple prettiness. In 1976, Eugene Record left and the Chi-Lites were forced to regroup. Produced by longtime member Marshall Thompson, the re-

formed Chi-Lites debut, *Happy Being Lonely,* contains a crop of very good songs, mostly in the old vein, in a wide variety of delicate, nondisco harmonic settings.   — J.MC.

CHILLIWACK
★★ **All over You** / A&M 4375
★★★★ **Dreams, Dreams, Dreams** / Mush. 5006
★★ **Lights From the Valley** / Mush. 5011
At their best, Chilliwack was the finest Canadian rock band, outrocking B.T.O. and outwriting Burton Cummings. But a lack of consistency kept it from international success, and only these two albums remain in print. The A&M is one of the least successful, because it's the least diverse, though it does have "Ground Hog," a Canadian hit. *Dreams* is toned down from the band's usual hard rock, with bright melodies and harmonies—their best yet.   — A.N.

CHOCOLATE MILK
★★ **Chocolate Milk** / RCA APL1-1399
★★ **Comin'** / RCA APL1-1830
★★ **We're All in This Together** / RCA APL1-2331
This Allen Toussaint/Marshall Sehorn production unsuccessfully attempts to coin a New Orleans funk-disco compromise. The results are wooden, interesting only for the horn arrangements.   — J.S.

CHOICE FOUR
★★ **Choice Four** / RCA APL1-0913
★★★ **On Top of Clear** / RCA APL1-1400
Moderately hot disco band produced by Van McCoy features some strong ensemble vocals over the standard nonstop dance fare. They reach a high point on *On Top of Clear* (1976) with "Hey, What's That Dance You're Doing."   — J.S.

CHORDETTES
★★ **All the Very Best of the Chordettes** / Barn. 4003
Unimaginative white vocal group, patterned after classic R&B harmonizers, had two Top Ten hits in the Fifties: "Born to Be with You," in 1956, and "Lollipop," in 1958. Buy something by the Drifters instead.   — D.M.

KEITH CHRISTMAS
★★ **Brighter Day** / Mant. MA6-503-S1
Undistinguished yet interesting songwriter fails in this 1975 solo attempt despite an all-star British session cast including Mel Collins, Ian Wallace, Alan Spenner and Neil Hubbard, plus production by Greg Lake and Pete Sinfield. One good song, "Robin Head," and some great horn arrangements save it.   — J.S.

GAVIN CHRISTOPHER
★ **Gavin Christopher** / Is. 9398
Christopher has penned some hits ("Once You Get Started," "Fool's Paradise") for Rufus, and he gets backup support here from the Tower of Power horn section, but it's not enough to make this worth buying.   — J.S.

CIRCUS MAXIMUS
★★★ **Circus Maximus** / Van. 79260
★★ **Neverland Revisited** / Van. 79274
Circus Maximus was New York's answer to San Francisco's psychedelic boom, combining Country Joe's tacky Farfisa organ sound with the fuzzy social leanings of the Airplane. Predictably, most of its music sounds absurdly dated, though a few melodies linger. The best one, "Wind," was contained on the debut album, *Circus Maximus.* An out-of-character, jazzy piece dominated by piano and an irresistible chorus, the song is still a progressive FM staple. Mostly though, the most interesting thing about the band is that Jerry Jeff Walker was a member. I mean, can you imagine Jerry Jeff in a band that called itself "the circus of the mind, theatred in a tent of imagination"?   — J.B.M.

CITY BOY
★★ **Book Early** / Mer. SRM-1-3737
★★ **City Boy** / Mer. SRM-1-1098
★★ **Dinner at the Ritz** / Mer. SRM-1-1121
★★★ **Young Men Gone West** / Mer. SRM-1-1182
Similar to though not as clever as 10cc's work, *City Boy* thrived on bright harmonies, gay melodies, crisp guitars and mischievous humor—energetic, though the arrangements lacked spice. *Dinner at the Ritz* relied less on 10cc but still lacked individuality. The scoring improved but the compositions lagged; blurry engineering worsened matters. *Young Men Gone West* provided the group's finest, liveliest playing and writing, and made tentative steps toward a unique style.   — C.W.

CITY LIGHTS
★ **Silent Dancing** / Sire SASD 7512
The first but not the best of the mid-Seventies New York New Wave bands to make

a record, City Lights play flashy guitar-and-synthesizer rock. They probably owe more to latter-day Blue Oyster Cult than anyone else, but this debut album suffers in comparison; they try too hard to sound more accomplished than they are. (Now deleted.) — G.C.

CLANCY BROTHERS AND TOMMY MAKEM
★★ **Freedom's Sons / Col. CS-9336**
★ **Home Boys Home / Col. CS-9608**
★★★ **In Person at Carnegie Hall / Col. CS-8750**
★★ **The Best of the Clancy Brothers and Tommy Makem / Trad. 2050**
CLANCY BROTHERS WITH LOU KILLEN
★★★ **Greatest Hits / Van. VSD 53/54**
Not one of these sets gives the Clancys their due. Irish tradition is boisterous and sentimental, openly revolutionary and mightily respectful of the past. "The Rising of the Moon," "Jug of Punch," "The Patriot Game," "Red-Haired Mary" and "The Leaving of Liverpool" are familiar because the Clancys have made them so at festivals and concerts since the early Sixties. But the rousing spirit of their music, even on the live *Freedom's Sons* (recorded in Dublin on the occasion of the fiftieth anniversary of the uprising of 1916) doesn't make the transition to disc vibrantly enough.

Other Tradition and Stinson recordings are theoretically still available, and the entire Columbia catalogue remains in print. The Vanguard "twofer," however, is the most recently recorded (June 1973) and finds the group in strong voice and with a good sampling of the overall repertoire. The *Carnegie Hall* LP is also representative, featuring "Patriot Game" (not on the Vanguard release), a twelve-minute children's medley, and Tom Clancy's reading of W. B. Yeats' "O'Driscoll (The Host of the Air)." — I.M.

ERIC CLAPTON
★★★ **Backless / RSO 1-3039**
★★★ **Eric Clapton / Poly. 1-3008**
★★★★ **461 Ocean Boulevard / RSO 1-3023**
★★★ **No Reason to Cry / RSO 1-3004**
★★★ **Slowhand / RSO 1-3030**
★★ **There's One in Every Crowd / RSO SO-4806**
With the exception of his brief stint as Derek with the Dominos, Eric Clapton's solo career often seemed as much a reac-

tion against his past as an extension of it. Between proclamations of "Clapton is God" and the superstar guitarist persona that he invented with Cream, Clapton was often at odds with his fan's expectations. Predictably, his surroundings often defined the forms his music took.

Coming off the road with Delaney and Bonnie, Clapton's first solo record was influenced by their tambourine-shaking sound while displaying a stronger voice and songwriting talent than had earlier been apparent. This super-session aggregation centered around what was to be come the Dominos.

Following *Layla* and his heroin nightmares, Clapton returned in more subdued tones with *461 Ocean Boulevard*, which featured his pop hit of the Wailers' "I Shot the Sheriff" as well as a first-class shuffling blues in Elmore James' "I Can't Hold Out." While dominated by quieter tunes, the album contained more spirit than the lackluster followup *No Reason to Cry*, where Clapton's gentle touch revealed a soft middle.

The super-session shenanigans of *No Reason to Cry* put together a predictably tasty menu that'll leave you hungry in an hour. The heavyweights—Dylan and members of the Band—brought along their minor songs, while Clapton was left holding the bag. Pleasant, but somewhat disorienting, it pictured Clapton still looking for an appropriate niche.

Wisely he retrenched on *Slowhand* and created an album with something of the homey ambiance of *461 Ocean Boulevard*, though without tunes to match that album's highlights. But the record's relaxed feel, along with Clapton's inclination to let his guitar do a little more of the talking, puts him back in solid journeyman terrain. *Backless* continued this trend. He might not be God, but he's not dead yet. — J.B.M.

GENE CLARK
★★★ **Collector's Series: Early L.A. Sessions / Col. KC 31123**
★ **Two Sides to Every Story / RSO 1-3011**
★★ **White Light / A&M 4292**
Although he has been making records on and off since leaving the Byrds after their second album, it's hard to avoid the fact that Clark's contributions to that band remain the best things he's ever done. The Columbia album, done not long after his split from the Byrds, had a Byrds-ish feel when originally released, but it was re-

mixed when reissued and suffers terribly because of that. It now sounds like a bland country-rock album. Actually, for the best of Clark's post-Byrds work, one should seek out either of the Dillard and Clark Expedition LPs on A&M (both now out of print). — B.A.

GUY CLARK
★★ Guy Clark / War. K-3241
★★★★ Old No. 1 / RCA AHL1-1303
★★ Texas Cookin' / RCA AHL1-1944

Perhaps the best songwriter to come out of the Austin, Texas, progressive country scene. Influenced a great deal by Townes Van Zandt, Clark has a superb sense for the dramatic flourish and the keen detail. There's a modesty to his songs that allows his romantic ballads to balance hard-edged toughness with wry sentimentality, which is more evident on his first album, *Old No. 1,* than on his second and third. — K.R.

ALLAN CLARKE
★ I Wasn't Born Yesterday / Atl. 19175
★★ I've Got Time / Asy. 73-1056

When Allan Clarke left the Hollies, he entered the sphere of anonymity. His first solo album for Asylum finds him interpreting a variety of fashionable writers, from Bruce Springsteen to Gavin Sutherland, without challenging the originals. On the second, the material isn't that good. On both, you keep waiting for those Hollies harmonies, but they never arrive. — J.B.M.

THE CLASH
★★★ Give 'Em Enough Rope / Epic JE 35543
★★★★ The Clash / CBS 82000 (British Import)

The most political of the British punk bands, the Clash was also one of the best, ranking just beneath the Sex Pistols in terms of energy and impact. Unfortunately, this is a band whose metier is the single—there is nothing on either of these albums half as good as either "White Man in Hammersmith Palais" or "Complete Control." The first album (*The Clash*)—yet to be released in America, though CBS keeps promising—featured some outstanding songs, including "Remote Control," "Career Opportunities" and a bang-up version of the reggae hit, "Police and Thieves." The second *Enough Rope,* was made with Blue Oyster Cult producer Sandy Pearlman at the helm, and though it is probably as good as any attempt can be at rationalizing the sound of a punk band, it lacks the flair of the first. That almost proves disastrous, because flair is the heart of punk. Allegedly these guys have great lyrics, but they only send them to rock critics, so you'll never know—lead singer Joe Strummer makes Andy Capp sound like a BBC announcer. — D.M.

MERRY CLAYTON
★ Celebration / Ode X-77008
★ Gimme Shelter / Ode 77001
★ Merry Clayton / Ode 77012
★ Keep Your Eye on the Sparrow / Ode 77030

Merry Clayton's career has auspicious beginnings: she sang backup on the Rolling Stones' "Gimme Shelter" and fit in with that band as no singer ever had. But none of her solo LPs lives up to that promise. *Merry Clayton,* the best of them, is the only one that suggests the strength of her initial efforts as a backup vocalist. (Carole King arranged some of its material, and appears as keyboardist.) (Now deleted.) — G.C.

PAUL CLAYTON
★★★ American Folk Tales and Songs / Trad. 1011
★★ Foc'sle Songs and Shanties / Folk. 2429
★★ Whaling and Sailing Songs / Trad. 1005
★★ Whaling Songs and Ballads / Stin. 69

The late singer of traditional folk music was heavily influential in the pre-Dylan Sixties folk revival. — D.M.

DAVID CLAYTON-THOMAS
★ Clayton / ABC 1104

Ex-Blood, Sweat and Tears lead singer's only in-print solo album. Nothing to recommend. — J.S.

CLEAN LIVING
★ Clean Living / Van. VSD 79318
★ Meadowmuffin / Van. VSD 79334

Truth in packaging: squeaky folkie wholesomeness, even if they sing a lot about, and look as if they do a lot of, beer drinking. — K.T.

VASSAR CLEMENTS
★★★ Hillbilly Jazz / Fly. Fish 101
★★★ Superbow / Mer. SRM-1-1058
★★★ Vassar Clements / Mer. SRM-1-1022
★★★ Vassar Clements Band / MCA 2270
★★★ Vassar Clements: The Bluegrass Sessions / Fly. Fish 038

Clements is probably Nashville's best-known contemporary fiddler. These albums suffer somewhat from that typical side-man's bane: the inability (or refusal) to take over the sessions. Otherwise, they are quite different, though of about equal quality. *Vassar Clements* is the most varied and contains a couple of modern, experimental cuts. *Superbow* is mostly country boogie and Western Swing, and is the most cohesive. The musicianship is technically excellent, but none of these albums really catches fire. — J.MO.

JIMMY CLIFF
★★ **Follow My Mind / Rep. 2218**
★★ **Give Thanx / War. K-3240**
★★★ **In Concert: The Best of Jimmy Cliff / Rep. MS-2256**
★★★ **Jimmy Cliff/Unlimited / Rep. MS-2147**
★ **Music Maker / Rep. 2188**
★★ **Reggae Spectacular / A&M 3529**
★★ **Struggling Man / Is. 9235**
★★★★ **The Harder They Come / Mango 9202**
★★★★ **Wonderful World, Beautiful People / A&M 4251**

Jimmy Cliff's 1972 performance as Outlaw Ivan in a film called *The Harder They Come* almost single-handedly turned Jamaica and reggae into hippie-chic. (His singing on the album of the same name is inspired.) But— and this is the unfortunate contradiction that has plagued his recording career—he has since been rapped as a musical and cultural sell-out.

Some of the criticisms might be deflected if more people realized that Cliff is not a Rastafarian but a Muslim, and that his musical roots are just as much in R&B (e.g., Dee Clark) as reggae. Still, Cliff must account for the kind of musical schizophrenia that led him to record his 1975 *Follow My Mind* by cutting rhythm tracks in Jamaica,

then heading to L.A. for extensive overdubs.

Cliff's first album, *Wonderful World, Beautiful People,* is mostly composed of songs he wrote in London between 1965 and 1968. It is a gritty, insistent record, full of songs he would later fall back on, particularly "Vietnam," his statement of anger about the war. A 1972 A&M compilation called *Reggae Spectacular,* with Cliff on nine of twenty-two cuts, duplicates several of its cuts (including a version of Cat Stevens' "Wild World").

Unlimited, made in Kingston in 1973, is probably Cliff's most fervently political record. (Politically, Cliff is a true Muslim, emphasizing black cultural expression above all else.) On cuts like "Oh Jamaica" and "Under the Sun, Moon and Stars," lilting choral parts and a moving resignedness in the lyrics help lift Cliff's strong singing over poppish overdubs and easy calypso beats.

But *Struggling Man,* a 1974 Island compilation, was tepid; *Music Maker,* cut in New York that same year, was overproduced (full of prissy singing and vapid lyrics). *Follow My Mind,* despite its confused assembly, showed a strengthened vocal attack.

Cliff's version of "No Woman, No Cry" didn't stand up next to author Bob Marley's. Cliff's cover of "Dear Mother," a tune written by his talented collaborator, Joe Higgs, is good, but "Look at the Mountains" is an even better example of Cliff's recurring themes—family, God and country—twining through a homemade folk song.

In Concert: The Best of Jimmy Cliff is a 1976 release that had Cliff fronting an honest reggae band. His renewed passion and the interplay with an enthusiastic (console-boosted?) audience on songs like "Vietnam" keeps things bubbling. But almost every song dates back to 1972 or earlier—a worrisome indication that Cliff's formidable gifts have been sitting in limbo for several years now. — F.S.

LINDA CLIFFORD
★ **If My Friends Could See Me Now / Cur. 5021**
★ **Linda / Cur. 5016**

What, pray tell, is the point of Curtom recording mediocre black pop singers if label-owner Curtis Mayfield isn't even going to produce them? — D.M.

CLIMAX BLUES BAND
★★ **A Lot of Bottle / Sire K-6004**

★★★ **Climax Chicago Blues Band Plays On** / Sire K-6033
★★★ **FM Live** / Sire 2X5-6013
★★★ **Shine On** / Sire K-6056
★★★★ **Stamp Album** / Sire 6016
★★★ **Tightly Knit** / Sire 6008
The basic sound is jazz-rock-blues, and it has changed only in minor ways since Climax formed in 1968. The early records are blues dominated (as is *FM Live*), but on recent LPs Colin Cooper's reeds begin to assume parity with the guitars. — A.N.

GEORGE CLINTON
★★★★ **The George Clinton Band Arrives** / ABC 831
This is *not* the same George Clinton who masterminds Parliament-Funkadelic. The George Clinton here is white and principally a songwriter. This album, released in 1974, anticipated the pop-soul explosion spearheaded by the Bee Gees and Hall and Oates. Clinton has a liquid-smooth falsetto, and only some MOR-styled horn arrangements keep this from being a genre classic. (Now deleted.) — J.MC.

CLOVER
★★★ **Clover** / Mer. SRM-1-1169
★★★ **Love on the Wire** / Mer. SRM-1-3708
Solid San Francisco-area rock group later moved to England, where it earned its spurs backing up Elvis Costello on his first LP. — D.M.

THE COASTERS
★ **16 Greatest Hits** / Trip TOP-16-7
★★★★ **The Coasters' Greatest Hits** / Atco 111
★★★★ **Their Greatest Recordings: The Coasters' Early Years** / Atco 371
The funniest group in rock & roll history. In the Fifties, Jerry Leiber and Mike Stoller wrote a series of mini-situation comedies—"Charlie Brown," "Yakety Yak," "Little Egypt"—that defined the lighter side of the teenage dilemma. The Coasters were their vehicle, and a fine one, also capable of a fine, straight R&B harmony number like "Smokey Joe's Cafe."
   The classic era is well represented by the Atcos, though each contains a couple of important songs not on the other. (Barrett "Dr. Demento" Hansen's liner notes probably give a slight nod to the *Greatest Recordings*.) The Trip is much later—a reformed version of the group that Leiber-Stoller produced in the Seventies. The versions of the classics are inept, the new material mostly vulgar. — D.M.

ODIA COATES
■ **Odia Coates** / U. Artists UA-LA228-G
Any black singer whose first album carries an endorsement from Paul Anka is interesting, if only as a convincing argument against natural rhythm. — D.M.

EDDIE COCHRAN
★★★★ **Legendary Master Eddie Cochran** / U. Artists 9959
Though he had such hits as "Summertime Blues" and "Sittin' in the Balcony," Eddie Cochran was not one of the major commercial stars of the late Fifties. Yet his early brand of hard rock cum country and blues has proven a surprisingly durable amalgam and he has influenced the Who, among others. Cochran's manly baritone and his dueling guitars (a primeval use of overdubbing) are full of the kind of humor and power that characterizes the best rockabilly. — P.H.

WAYNE COCHRAN
★★★ **Old King Gold** / King 16001
★★★ **Wayne Cochran** / Chess 1519
Cochran and his band, the C.C. Riders, had considerable influence on the development of Southern white soul; they pioneered the kind of Big Band funk that Blood, Sweat and Tears would later make popular, though Cochran and the Riders demonstrated more authenticity and sincerity. The Chess album is seeded with classics of the "Hoochie Coochie Man"/"Little Bitty Pretty One" order marred only by the Riders' greatest limitation: Cochran's voice, a blend of Mitch Ryder and No. 3 gauge sandpaper, but without the expressiveness of either. A grand screecher in a mold made more famous by Edgar Winter, the Cochran record to look for remains *Cochran*, a deleted 1972 Epic release. — D.M.

BRUCE COCKBURN
★★★ **Circles in the Stream** / True 9475
★★★ **Further Adventures of Bruce Cockburn** / Is. 9528
★★★ **In the Falling Dark** / True 9463
Canadian singer/songwriter on this album manages to couple Jackson Browne, Gordon Lightfoot and light jazz. Not a bad trick, and the songs are good. — D.M.

JOE COCKER
★★★★★ **Joe Cocker!** / A&M 4224
★★★★ **Mad Dogs and Englishmen** / A&M 6002
★★★★ **With a Little Help from My Friends** / A&M 4182

Joe Cocker first emerged in 1969 as a novelty; an English Ray Charles soundalike singing a somewhat hysterical version of the Beatles' "With a Little Help from My Friends." The debut album (*Friends*) is in that spirit—not quite serious, but Cocker wails, ignoring the girl choruses and patronizing accompanists. The second album, *Joe Cocker!*, has the Cocker trademarks—a nose for good material, a mix of ballads and straight-ahead rockers that show both his fragility and barroom growl—in spades. The sidemen are adept but occasionally lumbering, but who cares when you've got "Delta Lady," "She Came in through the Bathroom Window" and "Hitchcock Railway." *Mad Dogs,* cut on the 1970 tour led by Leon Russell, captures the frenzy of one of rock's most exciting shows. Although it's preferred by some to *Joe Cocker!,* the insistent raucousness can be grating—it probably was to Cocker, who didn't make another record until a couple of years later.

★★★ **I Can Stand a Little Rain** / A&M 3633
★★ **Jamaica Say You Will** / A&M 4529
★★ **Joe Cocker** / A&M 4368
★★★★ **Joe Cocker's Greatest Hits** / A&M 4670
★★★ **Luxury You Can Afford** / Asy. 6E-145
★★★ **Stingray** / A&M 4574

Cocker's reemergence was stumbling. On *I Can Stand* and *Joe Cocker,* he sounded a little unsure. The slick production on the former and original material on the latter didn't help either. *Jamaica* and *Stingray* suffer from an excess of mediocre material, although the latter shows signs of renewal, particularly because of the support Cocker gets from the agile pop-soul band, Stuff, and his material, which is better than average and includes Dylan-Levy's "Catfish." — P.H.

PHIL CODY
★ **Phil Cody** / Rep. MS-2232

MOR album by sometime Neil Sedaka collaborator. Plush and empty. (Now deleted.) — S.H.

DAVID ALLAN COE
★★★ **David Allan Coe Rides Again** / Col. PC-34310
★★ **Family Album** / Col. KC-35306
★★★ **Longhaired Redneck** / Col. KC-33916
★★ **Mysterious Rhinestone Cowboy** / Col. KC-32942
★★★ **Once Upon a Rhyme** / Col. KC-33085

★★★ **Penitentiary Blues** / SSS 9
★★ **Tattoo** / Col. KC-34780
★★★ **Texas Moon** / Plant. 507

Coe's debut, a collection of prison songs, is country-flavored white blues, so there's a certain sameness to the music, and some of the lyrics are overly derivative. Still, it's full of fine harp work, and some stinging bottleneck guitar.

It's with the Columbia albums that a personal sound and stance evolves: the music is country with a beat, often heavily orchestrated with strings and background voices. He likes parody and seethes with a braggadocio that becomes increasingly overbearing. *Cowboy* is the weakest group of songs, and is mostly expendable. *Rhyme* has strong, imaginative material, and Coe's melodic sense is by now fully developed. *Longhaired Redneck* features a couple of his best songs, but here his braggadocio has turned into a distasteful (and potentially dangerous) megalomania that undercuts the whole album. The effect continues through the later records. — J.MO.

DENNIS COFFEY
★★ **Back Home** / Westb. 300
★★ **Sweet Taste of Sin** / Westb. 6105

Longtime Motown session guitarist Coffey hit in 1971 with the instrumental "Scorpio." That's not included here, nor is much else of any consequence. — D.M.

LEONARD COHEN
★★★ **Best of Leonard Cohen** / Col. PC-34077
★ **Death of a Ladies' Man** / War. B-3125
★★★★ **Leonard Cohen** / Col. CS-9533
★★★ **New Skin for the Old Ceremony** / Col. C-33167
★★★★ **Songs from a Room** / Col. CS-9767
★★★ **Songs of Love and Hate** / Col. PC-30103

Cohen is best known as Canada's poet laureate of outrage and existential despair; his novel, *Beautiful Losers,* was a Sixties classic. He is not much of a singer, but a couple of his songs, notably "Suzanne" (from *Leonard Cohen,* 1968) and "Bird on a Wire" (*Songs from a Room,* 1969), have been widely covered and occasionally have made a chart success. Although often overwrought in a pop context, his lyrics are invariably fascinating for lovers of terminal depression and morbid imagery, and his Columbia albums are well worth seeking for aficionados of gloom.

Unfortunately, when he made the switch to Warner Bros. in 1977, after a recording hiatus of a couple of years, he worked with former genius producer Phil Spector, who managed to botch the best set of lyrics that Cohen had written since his debut album by recording them with completely irrelevant musical arrangements. Nonetheless, the record might be worth searching out, if only because of its fascinatingly elliptical attack on feminist values, "Death of a Ladies' Man." — D.M.

MICHAEL COHEN
★ Everybody's Gotta Be Someplace / RCA
  ANLI-2682
★ Some of Us Had to Live / Folk. 8583
★ What Did You Expect / Folk. 8582
Troubadour with a singing/writing style like Leonard Cohen's but much cruder. — S.H.

STEPHEN COHN
★★ Stephen Cohn / Mo. M789V1
Quirky singer/songwriter scores often on this 1973 debut. Cohn's songs are thoughtful, humorous and hook-laden; his backup is expert and sympathetic. The high point here is "American Cheese." (Now deleted.) — J.S.

COLD BLOOD
★ First Taste of Sin / War. MS-2074
★★ Thriller! / War. MS-2130
Lydia Pense and Cold Blood seemed to aim at two markets: people who thought Chicago's horns played jazz and those who sought another Janis Joplin. Though her voice possessed the necessary silks and growls, Pense lacked the presence to do much with it. Her singing wasn't stiff, but it was lifeless. Next to the horn work, though, she sounded positively inspired. *Sin* recalled Chicago at its worst. *Thriller!* was the band's most successful album; the instrumentalists had some space and Pense showed more emotion than on previous outings. Their interpretation of the Band's "Sleeping," however, epitomized all that was lacking in Cold Blood—plodding and completely overarranged, the song was bled of the intimacy of the original. — J.B.M.

NATALIE COLE
★★★★ Inseparable / Cap. ST-11429
★★★ Natalie / Cap. ST-11517
★★★ Thankful / Cap. SW-11708
★★★ Unpredictable / Cap. SD-11600
With her debut album, *Inseparable,* Natalie Cole proved herself a first-class stylist who borrowed heavily from two diverse

sources: Aretha Franklin and Chaka Khan. Marvin Yancy and Chuck Jackson wrote and produced, showing an admirable ear for restraint and conciseness. Cole is molded into a variety of soul and pop styles: bar-band funk, gospel-soul and torchy ballads. The highlight: the triumphant, midtempo "This Will Be." *Natalie* aimed at a similar standard, but this and later LPs were attempts at glossy, Las Vegas versatility and left one with a feeling that Cole was unable to develop a personal style. — J.MC.

NAT "KING" COLE
★ A Blossom Fell / Cap. DF-505
★ A Mis Amigos / Cap. SW-1220
★★ Capitol Jazz Classics, Vol. 8 / Cap.
  M-11033
★ Cole Español / Cap. SM-1031
★★ Love Is Here to Stay / Cap.
  SWAK-11355
★★★★ Love Is the Thing / Cap. SM-824
★ More Cole Español / Cap. SM-1749
★ My Fair Lady / Cap. SM-2117
★ Nat "King" Cole Live at the Sands /
  Cap. SM-2434
★★ Nat "King" Cole Sings George Shearing Plays / Cap. SM-1675
★ Ramblin' Rose / Cap. ST-1793
★★ The Best of Nat "King" Cole / Cap.
  SKAO-2944
★ The Christmas Song / Cap. SM-1967
★★ The King Cole Trio / Jazz T. 5811
★★★ The Nat "King" Cole Story, Vol. 1 /
  Cap. SW-1926
★★ The Nat "King" Cole Story, Vol. 2 /
  Cap. SW-1927
★★ Unforgettable / Cap. SM-357
★ Walkin' My Baby Back Home / Cap.
  STBB-503
This Earl Hines–influenced pianist-turned-crooner became the first black male singer to gain total pop mainstream acceptance and his own TV show in the early Fifties. Cole specialized in romantic ballads; his most consistent album, *Love Is the Thing* (1957), with luscious Gordon Jenkins arrangements is still a delightful dream and smooch record. An excellent technician but a bland interpreter, Cole was always indiscriminate in his choice of material. About half of the Cole in print is singles anthologies, and many of the songs are laughably trite. In the Sixties, Cole made the mistake of rerecording his early hits—"Nature Boy," "Mona Lisa," "Too Young" et al.— with arrangements that duplicated the originals. But these remakes, which comprise the bulk of the anthologies, capture

little of the magic of the originals. For by the Sixties, Cole's voice had lost its smoothness and could evoke no longer these songs' innocent romanticism. — S.H.

JUDY COLLINS/Folk Singer
★★ A Maid of Constant Sorrow / Elek. 7209
★★★ Golden Apples of the Sun / Elek. 7222

On her first two albums, the classically trained vocalist, her voice in a lower range than that of later years, attempts Anglo-American folk chestnuts like "Wild Mountain Thyme" and "John Riley." *A Maid* is rather stiff; *Golden Apples* is more passionate—in fact, it's one of Collins' more stirring LPs. If you enjoy troubadour traditionalists, this should be your cup of Red Zinger.

JUDY COLLINS/Art Singer
★★ Judy Collins #3 / Elek. 7243
★★★★ Fifth Album / Elek. 7300
★★★★ In My Life / Elek. 74027
★★★ Recollections / Elek. 74055
★★★★★ Who Knows Where the Time Goes / Elek. 74033
★★★ Wildflowers / Elek. 74012

With *#3*, Collins began to perform the work of the contemporary songwriters—with the help of arranger Jim (later Roger) McGuinn, a couple of years before he formed the Byrds. Collins at first treated contemporary songs gingerly, as if they were precious, fragile artifacts. But with *Fifth Album* she hit her stride. Her taste was nearly unerring (as "Pack Up Your Sorrows," "Tomorrow Is a Long Time," "Thirsty Boots" and "Early Morning Rain" attest), and the singing is both compassionate and dignified. *Wildflowers* and *In My Life* find Collins and arranger/producer Joshua Rifkin turning to a kind of contemporary art song, although the material ranges from Joni Mitchell's "Both Sides Now" (on the former) to declamatory readings of "Marat/Sade" and the Brecht-Weill-Blitzstein number, "Pirate Jenny," on *In My Life*, her most political and theatrical LP. The classically inflected arrangements are often self-conscious; the material, including songs by Randy Newman and Leonard Cohen, triumphs.

Who Knows is her master album, however. The songs are wonderfully varied, from her own "My Father," to Ian Tyson's "Someday Soon," Leonard Cohen's brooding "Bird on the Wire," and most of all Robin Williamson's "First Boy I Loved";

the singing is perfectly suited to the material; and the all-star accompanists are loose and deft. *Recollections* serves as a premature greatest-hits collection, rendering *#3* and *Concert* extraneous, but it is not as worthwhile as *Fifth Album*.

JUDY COLLINS/Pop Singer
★★ Bread and Roses / Elek. 7E-1076
★ Hard Times for Lovers / Elek. 6E-171
★ Judith / Elek. EQ-1032
★★ Living / Elek. 75014
★★★ So Early in the Spring / Elek. 8E-6002
★★★ True Stories and Other Dreams / Elek. 75053
★★ Whales and Nightingales / Elek. 75010

With these albums, Collins became—through a slow process, but inexorably—an MOR pop singer, taking even the best material too slowly and sweetly. She is sometimes political, often ponderous, but the period is finally defined by Arif Mardin's lush production and the coolness of her crooning on *Bread and Roses*. *True Stories* is redeemed by a couple of good songs, and a brief reprise of her former measured elegance: the best of a bad lot. — P.H.

SHIRLEY COLLINS AND THE ALBION COUNTRY BAND
★★★★ No Roses / Ant. 7017

Collins sings traditional British Isles folk music, accompanied by acoustic and electric instruments. The "Band" is actually an all-star lineup of twenty-five British folk-rock players, gathered and coproduced by Ashley Hutchings. The atmosphere and emotion of the old receive tasteful framing with the energy of rock. (Now deleted.) — C.W.

COLOSSEUM
★★ Daughter of Time / Dun. X-50101
★★★★ Those Who Are About to Die Salute You / Dun. 50062

Colosseum was one of the first successful British blues-rock bands to turn directly to jazz. The core of the group—drummer John Hiseman, tenor/soprano saxophonist Dick Heckstall-Smith and bassist Tony Reeves—was formed immediately after recording together on John Mayall's landmark *Bare Wires* album. Hiseman and Heckstall-Smith had also worked with Graham Bond and were well-schooled jazz musicians. Colosseum was augmented by organist David Greenslade and guitarist/vocalist James Litherland. Their 1969 debut, *Those Who Are About to Die Salute*

You, stands as a high point in the peculiarly British synthesis of jazz, rock, R&B and classical elements. The extended track on side two, "Valentyne Sweet," demonstrates a conceptual link between John Coltrane and Procol Harum.

Unfortunately, subsequent Colosseum ventures, including *Daughter of Time,* fail to live up to the promise of their first record. — J.S.

COLOSSEUM II
★★★ **Electric Savage / MCA 2294**
★★★ **Wardance / MCA 2310**
Colosseum-founder/drummer John Hiseman assembled this band in late 1976 around guitarist Gary Moore, bassist John Mole and multikeyboardist Don Airey. This fiery set, released in 1977, presents the band in fine form on a number of jazz-rock-fusion instrumentals in a style similar to Jeff Beck's landmark *Blow by Blow* album. — J.S.

JESSI COLTER
★★★ **I'm Jessi Colter / Cap. ST-11363**
★★★ **Jessi / Cap. ST-11477**
★★★ **Diamond in the Rough / Cap. ST-11543**
★★★ **Mirriam / Cap. ST-11583**
Jessi Colter's first three albums present her as a tough-voiced, country-rock singer, something like Linda Ronstadt. The stance was easier to maintain as Waylon Jennings' wife—Jessi was even included in RCA's *Outlaws* anthology with Jennings and Willie Nelson. All of her records were coproduced by Jennings and featured his guitar playing as well as instrumental contributions from his backing band, the Waylors.

Colter writes all her own songs, some of which, like "Who Walks through Your Memory (Billy Jo)" and "The Hand That Rocks the Cradle," are very good. She scored a hit single with "I'm Not Lisa," a ballad from *I'm Jessi Colter.*

Mirriam is a complete departure from Colter's country rock image, a pristine, deadly sincere near-gospel album dedicated to her mother and rife with songs about God. Her singing is much starker here and the overall effect, though different, is as striking as her other material. Jennings once again supplies instrumental support and a backup vocal appearance with Roy Orbison on "I Belong to Him." — J.S.

CHI COLTRANE
★ **Chi Coltrane / Col. KC-31275**
No, this is not the daughter of Alice Coltrane and Eugene Record. Actually, Chi Coltrane sounds like Carly Simon after an attack of soul. "Thunder and Lightning," Coltrane's one departure from the "sensitive" song, was a fluky one-shot hit in 1972. *That* must be the reason this album's still in the catalogue. — A.S.

JEFFREY COMANOR
★★★ **A Rumor in His Own Time / Epic PE 34080**
Although Comanor weighs in at the light-to-welter end of the California-mellow scale, his singing and some of his songs reveal an adolescent eagerness unusual for the land of laid back. For the rest—their lack of substance is balanced by pleasing melodies and tasteful, Eagles-style production. (Now deleted.) — A.S.

COMMANDER CODY
★★ **Flying Dreams / Ari. 4183**
★★ **Midnight Man / Ari. AB 4125**
This solo album by George Frayne, the Commander himself, minus the Lost Planet Airmen, maintains the group's sense of fun but misses its musical adventurousness. For boogie-woogie stalwarts only. — D.M.

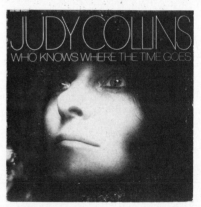

COMMANDER CODY AND HIS LOST PLANET AIRMEN
★★★ **Country Casanova / Para. 6054**
★★★ **Hot Licks, Cold Steel and Trucker's Favorites / Para. 6031**
★★★★ **Live from Deep in the Heart of Texas / Para. 1017**
★★★ **Lost in the Ozone / Para. 6017**
Hot Licks features classic old and new truck-driving songs, including the epic yarn "Mama Hated Diesels." There's also the typically tongue-in-cheek country ballad, "Kentucky Hills of Tennessee," and a

lively "Diggy Diggy Low." Billy Kirchen gets off on some state-of-the-art modern rockabilly guitar on the two Little Richard songs. The live album captures the Cody crew in their natural habitat—before a well-oiled crowd—and the band responds with some exemplary beer-drinking music in a variety of styles, all done with abundant good spirits. *Lost* reflects their uncertainty in the studio, but contains several of their trademark tunes—"Seeds and Stems (Again)," "Lost in the Ozone" and "Hot Rod Lincoln." *Casanova* swings a little more than on previous albums. But the selection of material is beginning to seem like a formula. All four of these sound like the work of a band that enjoys playing, whatever its technical shortcomings.

★★ **Commander Cody and His Lost Planet Airmen / War. BS-2847**
★ **Tales from the Ozone / War. BS-2883**
★★ **We've Got a Live One Here! / War. 2LS-2939**

For the group's first Warner's LP, producer John Boylan attempts to slow down the tempo, standardize the material, smooth off the rough edges and generally strip Cody of all the human elements that made the group stand out. He nearly succeeded, but a little personality crept through anyhow. It took producer Hoyt Axton (on *Tales*) to reduce the group to what could be any faceless, would-be L.A. country-rock band playing retreads and ready-mades. By *Live One,* the group has clearly given up. Though they lean heavily on their earlier, more inspirational material, the band's performance is perfunctory, its humor forced, and little is left but the raggedness, which has no charm by itself. — J.MO.

COMMODORES
★★★ **Caught in the Act / Mo. M7-820**
★★★ **Commodores / Mo. M7-884**
★★★ **Commodores Live / Mo. M9-894**
★★★★ **Greatest Hits / Mo. M7-912**
★★★★ **Machine Gun / Mo. M7-798**
★★★ **Movin' On / Mo. M7-848**
★★★ **Natural High / Mo. M7-902**

The Commodores took black rock to a kind of plateau in the late Seventies. They began in 1975 as a fairly nondescript but essentially powerful post-Sly revue act, but as the guitars and percussion stepped forward more boldly, they began to seem more like black music's answer to heavy metal. This came home most forcefully with *Machine Gun,* although succeeding records would be more popular. — D.M.

CON-FUNK-SHUN
★ **Con-Funk-Shun / Mer. SRM-1-1120**
★ **Loveshine / Mer. SRM-1-3725**
★ **Secrets / Mer. SRM-1-1180**
Boogie by the pound. — D.M.

BILL CONNORS
★★★ **Theme to the Guardian / ECM/ Poly. 1057**

Bill Connors' searing, pinpoint guitar playing in the original, heavily arranged, electric version of Return to Forever helped define a jazz-rock-fusion guitar style. Fans of his intense delivery will be surprised at this subdued, classically influenced record of acoustic guitar solos. Connors' compositional sense and shrewdly calculated, multiple-overdub technique suits the pristine recording style employed by ECM's Manfred Eicher. — J.S.

NORMAN CONNORS
★★ **Best of Norman Connors / Bud. 5716**
★ **Dance of Magic / Bud. 5674**
★ **Dark of Light / Bud. 5675**
★ **Love from the Sun / Bud. 5132**
★ **Romantic Journey / Bud. 5682**
★★ **Saturday Night Special / Bud. 5643**
★ **Slew Foot / Bud. 5611**
★★ **This Is Your Life / Ari. 4177**
★★ **You Are My Starship / Bud. 5655**

Since the advent of Sly Stone and Jimi Hendrix, black popular-music taste has expanded to encompass a kind of middling jazz that borrows ideas and sometimes songs from the post-Coltrane innovators, but adapts them for purposes of seduction and/or boogie. What was once transcendent has now become shallow, and Connors is a principal exponent of this lack of depth—he's gathered a couple of pop hits ("You Are My Starship" is the most notable), and seems to record as often as possible. All of these records were made since 1972. Their most significant contribution was the introduction of the talented bassist and vocalist Michael Henderson. — D.M.

RY COODER
★★★★ Boomer's Story / Rep. 2117
★★★★ Chicken Skin Music / Rep. 2254
★★★★ Into the Purple Valley / Rep. MS-2052
★★★ Jazz / War. K-3197
★★★★★ Paradise and Lunch / Rep. 2179
★★★ Ry Cooder / Rep. 6402
★★★ Show Time / War. B-3059

Cooder's albums bring forgotten songs to life and reclaim vanishing traditions. If that sounds more like a Smithsonian project than rock & roll, it's worth mentioning that Cooder has played with the Rolling Stones, recorded songs by Burt Bacharach and Bobby Womack, and knows the value of brilliant drum tracks and impassioned guitar solos as well as any rocker. *Paradise and Lunch* is his masterpiece. From the Salvation Army-style cornet on "Jesus on the Mainline" to the gospel quartet that answers him on "Married Man's a Fool," the inspired arrangements are arguably perfect. Upbeat, bristling with tricky syncopation and his own dazzling guitar (especially "Tattler"), the album makes traditional music contemporary and turns modern songs (like "Mexican Divorce") into classics. *Chicken Skin Music* is an equally polished, less lively production. It bogs down among the Hawaiian instrumentals but comes to life again with snappy street-corner harmonies and lilting Bolero rhythms. The arrangements on *Into the Purple Valley* and *Boomer's Story* are not as dramatic as those on Cooder's recent albums: they use fewer voices and the instrumentation is more conventional. Still, "Teardrops Will Fall" (on the former) and the magnificent slide-guitar rendition of "Dark End of the Street" (*Boomer's Story*) are worthy of his later work. And like all Cooder's albums, these discover and preserve songs that are delights in themselves. Cooder's first album is no different in that respect, featuring songs like "Alimony" and "Goin' to Brownsville," although their presentation is primitive compared to *Paradise and Lunch.* — A.S.

PETER COOK AND DUDLEY MOORE
★★ Beyond the Fringe / Cap. SW-1792
★ Derek and Clive (Live) / Is. ILPS 9434
★ Good Evening / Is. 9298

Cook and Moore were part of Britain's pre-Beatles comedy renaissance. *Beyond the Fringe* and *Good Evening* are Broadway soundtracks. While *Fringe* is helped considerably by the real brains, Jonathan Miller and Allen Bennett, both albums consist of brittle, dotty sketches without bite: one-listen affairs. *Derek and Clive* is *all* bite: an extended impersonation of the British working class. The slang is lost on us, and the unremitting obscenity is unequaled in its inaccuracy and humorlessness—at least, to American ears. — K.T.

SAM COOKE
★★★★ Ain't That Good News / Spec. 2115
★★ Sam Cooke at the Copa / RCA ANL1-2658
★★★ Sam Cooke Sings the Billie Holiday Story / Up Fr. 160
★★★ Sixteen Greatest Hits / Trip TOP 16-2
★★★★ That's Heaven to Me / Spec. 2146
★★★★★ The Best of Sam Cooke / RCA LSP-2625
★★★ The Golden Sound of Sam Cooke / Trip 8030
★★★★★ The Gospel Soul of Sam Cooke / Spec. 2116
★★★★ The Gospel Soul of Sam Cooke, Vol. 2 / Spec. 2128
★★★★ This is Sam Cooke / RCA VPS-6027
★★★★ Two Sides of Sam Cooke / Spec. 2119
★★★ You Send Me / Camd. ACL1-0445

Sam Cooke was not only one of the great founders of modern soul music, he was also one of the premier black gospel singers of his era. The Specialty discs here, recorded in the early Fifties (some while Cooke was still a teenager) are among the best records he ever made, and contain all the elements of the style that, applied to secular material, made him a pop giant before his tragic murder in 1964.

Cooke's best-known songs are, of course, his pop hits—"You Send Me," "Having a Party," "A Change Is Gonna Come," "Another Saturday Night," "Bring It on Home to Me" and "Twistin' the Night Away"—which are well-represented on the RCA *Best of.* Cooke's style—a soaring tenor that could capture both the exultingly joyful and the painfully tragic aspects of a song—is one of the most influential in modern music: Rod Stewart, among many others, would be lost without him. Unfortunately, his voice was often applied to rather trivial material—a problem that plagues the *Copa* set, of course, but also the *Best of* collection. There simply wasn't any reason for

Cooke to sing excerpts from "Porgy and Bess," rendered meaningless by continued trivialization over the years, when he could break hearts with a song like the great "A Change Is Gonna Come," his first posthumous release and one that ranks with Martin Luther King's best speeches as a verbal encapsulation of the changes black perspective underwent in the Sixties. — D.M.

RITA COOLIDGE
★★ Anytime . . . Anywhere / A&M 4616
★ Fall into Spring / A&M 3627
■ Full Moon / A&M 4403
★ It's Only Love / A&M 4531
★ Love Me Again / A&M 4699
★ Nice Feelin' / A&M 4325
★★★ Rita Coolidge / A&M 4291
★ The Lady's Not for Sale / A&M 4370

Rita Coolidge has released about one album per year since she began recording in 1971 (including a couple of duet attempts with her husband, Kris Kristofferson). But this former backup singer (for Delaney and Bonnie and Joe Cocker) has never matched her session work. The closest she's come, in a commercial sense, was with *Anytime . . . Anywhere,* which spawned her 1977 Top Ten hit, "(Your Love Has Lifted Me) Higher and Higher," a reworking of the Jackie Wilson standard that owed most of its punch to Booker T. Jones' production. (Jones is Coolidge's brother-in-law.) *Love Me Again,* the followup, lacks even that much charm; Coolidge simply hasn't the subtlety to pull off the interpretive role required of her on albums of nonoriginal material, although *Rita Coolidge,* with its blend of rock and R&B, comes closest to succeeding. — G.C.

MICHAEL COONEY
★★ The Cheese Stands Alone / Folk-Leg. 35

Cooney is a storehouse of songs and lore from a variety of American traditions and an interpreter of selected folk-based writers—i.e., Malvina Reynolds and John Prine. This doesn't sport a winning personality, but a sense of breadth is there. — I.M.

ALICE COOPER
★ Alice Cooper Goes to Hell / War. B-2896
★★★★★ Alice Cooper's Greatest Hits / War. K-3107
★★ Billion Dollar Babies / War. BS-2685
★★ Easy Action / War. 1845
★ From the Inside / War. K-3263
★★★ Killer / War. B-2567

■ Lace and Whiskey / War. BK-3027
★★★★ Love It to Death / War. 1883
★ Muscle of Love / War. BS-2748
★★ Pretties for You / War. 1840
★★★ School's Out / War. B-2623
★★ The Alice Cooper Show / War. K-3138
★★★ Welcome to My Nightmare / Atco 19157

Alice Cooper started out as just another bunch of weirdos who caught Frank Zappa's attention. The Zappa-influenced first album, *Pretties for You,* featured the band members in ludicrous drag, a humorous reproduction of the Mothers of Invention pose on *Absolutely Free.* Like many other Detroit bands of the early Seventies, Alice Cooper played high-energy hard rock, crudely at first, but the band improved fast and cut a great record on its third try, *Love It to Death.* That record included "I'm Eighteen," the first of a string of excellent hit singles. Although it never made another album as consistent as *Love It to Death,* the band's singles formula sharpened, producing two classics: "School's Out" and "Elected." The name Alice Cooper originally applied to the whole group but was assumed eventually by the lead singer, who dispensed with the other members and went Hollywood, teaming up with producer Bob Ezrin and guitarists Steve Hunter and Dick Wagner for *Welcome to My Nightmare,* which was his last gasp as a rocker. Now he's a *Tonight Show* guest and a hack L.A. entertainer, and the albums sound accordingly empty. — J.S.

DON COOPER
★ Ballad of C.P. Jones / Rou. 42056
★ Bless the Children / Rou. 42046
★ Don Cooper / Rou. 42044
★ What You Feel Is How You Grow / Rou. 3009

In the Seventies, every record company had to have one lightweight country-folkish singer/songwriter to record stuff like "Something in the Way She Moves," and Roulette's was Cooper. — D.M.

BILL COSBY
★ Bill / MCA MC2-8005
★ Bill Cosby Is a Very Funny Fellow Right! / War. WS-1518
★ Bill's Best Friend / Cap. ST-11731
★ Fat Albert / MCA 333
★ For Adults Only / MCA 553
★ "I Started Out as a Child" / War. 1567
★ Inside the Mind of Bill Cosby / MCA 554
★ Is Not Himself These Days / Cap. ST-11530

★ It's True! It's True! / War. 1770
★★ More of the Best of Bill Cosby / War. 1836
★ Revenge / War. 1691
★★★ The Best of Bill Cosby / War. 1798
★★★★ To Russell, My Brother, Whom I Slept With / War. 1734
★ 200 M.P.H. / War. 1757
★ "When I Was a Kid" / MCA 169
★ Why Is There Air? / War. 1606
★★ Wonderfulness / War. 1634

Along with Lenny Bruce and Woody Allen, Bill Cosby has had the greatest influence on American comedy in the past twenty years. His tightly constructed routines contained no formal "jokes": the humor was in his multitude of voices and elastic faces, and the inviting universality of the tales of his childhood in Philadelphia. Where Bruce and Allen appealed almost exclusively to a white, urban, college-educated audience, Cosby, at the height of his nightclub and recording career (about 1968–1971), was probably the best-known and loved comedian in the country. When he emerged in the late Sixties, part of his attraction lay in the fact that he was a friendly, apolitical black person. His extraordinary ability to evoke common childhood experiences—their pleasures and anguish—transcended race and, because of Cosby's pervasive presence on television, records and stage, is a vastly underestimated contribution to the acceptance of black culture and attitudes by the white middle class. However, his other material, especially that having to do with marriage, is seriously marred by a sexism all the more insidious for its gentle guilelessness. The kid routines remain his best stuff, with the side-long "To Russell, My Brother, Whom I Slept With" a marvelous work that says as much about an American childhood as Henry Roth's *Call It Sleep.* *For Adults Only* is only mildly racy, but is his worst in its nasty view of marriage as one long nag. Recently Cosby is either barren of sufficient material to fashion solid routines and stories, or desirous of breaking away from the monologue set piece. In either case, he has taken to uneven improvisation and slapstick pantomime onstage. He makes infrequent, arch and amusingly arrogant talk-show appearances (the arrogance is partially justified: he *is* a genius) and wry parodies of popular black music, the latter collected on the most recent album. This cannot last long; Cosby is certainly capable of anything and is not to be counted out. — K.T.

ELVIS COSTELLO

★★★★ Armed Forces / Col. JC-35709
★★★★ My Aim Is True / Col. JC-35037
★★★★ This Year's Model / Col. JC-35331

He looked like Buddy Holly after drinking a can of STP Oil Treatment, but this Elvis (who appeared shortly before the original died) is actually one of the better results of Britain's 1976–78 New Wave explosion. "Less Than Zero," his attack on British right-wing leader Oswald Mosely, was the most explicit song on the first album, which also featured a near hit in the ballad, "Alison." *This Year's Model* went farther, even attacking radio (with "Radio, Radio"), his one hope of ever reaching a sizable audience. *Armed Forces* is both Costello's most political LP and, oddly, his most listenable. Eventually, this man for all seasons will probably record a concept LP called *Too Late the Misanthrope* and be done with it.

In fact, Costello is a burning (if limited) guitarist and singer whose preoccupation with the dregs of life is fascinating. When he sings, on *This Year's Model,* that he sometimes feels almost like a human being, the line cuts both ways. His coldness is the only drawback—otherwise, charming might be an appropriate adjective for his songs' verve and sting.   — D.M.

ELIZABETH COTTEN

★★★ Elizabeth Cotten, Vol. 2: Shake Sugaree / Folk. 31003
★★★ Folksongs and Instrumentals with Guitar / Folk. 3526

Anyone who has learned three-finger guitar picking has probably played "Freight Train," a song Cotten composed when very young and which was later popularized by Peter, Paul and Mary. That tune and "Shake Sugaree" are the most commonly associated with her. She plays guitar and banjo left-handed, although strung as usual. She is that rare folk artist for whom the distinction between professional and traditional musician is meaningless. Both albums display her blues and ragtime-based style well.   — I.M.

COTTONWOOD SOUTH

★ Cottonwood South / Col. KC-33009

A directionless set, flirting weakly with both hard rock and MOR, unimaginatively produced by Paul Rothchild. Three of the seven members do nothing but sing, and they do have their moments, but the playing is as plain as it is spare. (Now deleted.)   — C.W.

COULSON, DEAN, McGUINNESS, FLINT
★★★★ Lo and Behold / Sire SAS 7405
A collection of Bob Dylan songs, many of them extremely obscure ("Sign on the Cross," "Odds and Ends"), produced by Dylan's favorite interpreter, Manfred Mann, and excellently performed (by a group originally known as McGuinness-Flint). (Now deleted.) — D.M.

COUNTRY GAZETTE
★★ A Traitor in Our Midst / U. Artists 5596
★★★ Live / Ant. AN-7014
★★ Out to Lunch / Fly. Fish 027
Country Gazette consisted primarily of L.A. musicians who were key figures in the early-Sixties folk revival, then moved into folk rock and later became stalwarts in the floating crap game of early Seventies country rock. Several had also worked with more traditional bluegrass groups such as Flatt & Scruggs' Foggy Mountain Boys or Bill Monroe's Bluegrass Boys. Though the most tradition-oriented of all the L.A. country rockers, they were not bluegrass purists. The problem was that while the group was full of exceptional pickers (especially fiddler Byron Berline and banjo player Alan Munde), the singing was usually barely acceptable. They also did bluegrass arrangements of some fairly dubious pop material (would you believe "Honky Cat"?). The live album is superior to the two studio efforts, if only because the songs are generally more congruous and there is more emphasis on instrumentals. — J.MO.

THE COUNTRY GENTLEMEN
★★ Bringing Mary Home / Rebel 1478
★★ Joe's Last Train / Rebel 1559
★★ Live at Roanoake / Zap 101
★★ New Look—New Sound / Rebel 1490
★★ Play It Like It Is / Rebel 1486
★★ Remembrances and Forecasts / Van. 79349
★★ Songs of the Pioneers / Pine M. 248
★★ Sound Off / Rebel 150l
★★ The Award Winning Country Gentlemen / Rebel 1506
★★ The Country Gentlemen / Van. 79331
★★★ The Country Gentlemen, Vol. 1 / Folk. 2409
★★★ The Country Gentlemen, Vol. 2 / Folk. 2410
★★★ The Country Gentlemen, Vol. 3 / Folk. 2411
★★★ The Country Gentlemen, Vol. 4 / Folk. 31031

★★★ The Gospel Album / Rebel 1497
★★ The Traveller / Rebel 1481
★★ Yesterday and Today, Vol. 1 / Rebel 1521
★★ Yesterday and Today, Vol. 2 / Rebel 1627
★★ Yesterday and Today, Vol. 3 / Rebel 1535
★★ Young Fisherwoman / Rebel 1494
Longtime bluegrass-circuit favorites, the Country Gentlemen play with an impressive, if clinical, efficiency. Known especially for on-the-mark triple harmonies and consistently high-quality live performances, the Gentlemen have always flirted with the periphery of the rock/pop audience without ever truly capturing it. The definitive works are on Folkways, though any of the Rebel/Zap LPs might be equally appealing to the initiated, and *The Gospel Album* is especially notable for its vocal tapestries. — R.P.

COUNTRY JOE AND THE FISH
★★ C.J. Fish / Van. 6555
★★★★ Electric Music for the Mind and Body / Van. 79244
★★★★ Feel Like I'm Fixin' to Die / Van. 79266
★★★ Greatest Hits / Van. 6545
★★ Here We Are Again / Van. 79299
★ Reunion / Fan. 9530
★★★ The Life and Times of Country Joe and the Fish / Van. VSD-27/28
★★ Together / Van. 79277
It would have been nearly impossible in 1967 to find people who considered themselves card-carrying freaks without a well-worn copy of the first Country Joe and the Fish album. In many ways, *Electric Music for the Mind and Body* captured the essence of a mind-expanded counterculture lifestyle: the songs deal with the three main topics of the day: dope ("Flying High"), sex ("Not So Sweet Martha Lorraine") and politics ("Super Bird"). It's an infectious blend of blues, ragaish guitar-dominated rock and good old good time music. And coming from the wilds of Berkeley, the Fish added an often sardonic sense of humor to their energetic and politically aware music; the title track of *Feel Like I'm Fixin' to Die* is a romping mock celebration of death in Vietnam set to the tune of the old rag classic, "Muskrat Ramble." The album also shows Country Joe McDonald's growth as a balladeer, with the haunting "Janis" (written for Joplin) and the mystical "Who Am I." Though a bit more subdued than the debut LP, it's a worthy

successor, demonstrating the band's maturity and willingness to explore different approaches and genres.

With *Together,* unfortunately, much of the energy and resourcefulness of the band seems dissipated. Other than the sublimely ridiculous "Rock and Soul Music" and the classic "Good Guys/Bad Guys Cheer," *Together* most assuredly isn't. McDonald's contributions are slim, leaving guitarist Barry Melton and drummer Chicken Hirsch to carry the songwriting burden, which they just weren't equipped to do. The last two albums, with keyboard player David Cohen, bassist Bruce Barthol and Hirsch all departed, are rather undistinguished, though *C.J. Fish* does feature one great song, "Rockin' Round the World," in which McDonald pulls off one of the best Mose Allison imitations ever attempted. Not surprisingly, both best-of collections lean heavily on the first two albums. The late Seventies *Reunion* is a sad, faint echo of the early material. — B.A.

DAVID COURTNEY
★ David Courtney's First Day / U. Artists LA553-G

String-fed, idea-starved pop, with schizophrenic casualness and pretension. (Now deleted.) — K.T.

LOU COURTNEY
★★★ Buffalo Smoke / RCA APL1-1696

Late-Seventies heavy funk, with a quasijazz feel and disco overtones. — J.S.

DON COVAY
★ Travelin' in Heavy Traffic / Phil. PZ 33958

A promising marriage between Don Covay and the Sound of Philadelphia resulted in a near-disastrous set. Covay, once one of

soul's most righteous storytellers, is clearly floundering in his attempt at coming to grips with black pop music in the Seventies. His body of work on Atlantic though, available only on cutouts, is remarkably personal—the Sixties soul man as a rough and rugged individualist. — J.MC.

COWBOY
★ Cowboy / Capri. CP 0127
★★ Why Quit When You're Losing / Capri. 2CX-0121

Two albums full of splendid playing diluted by soulless vocals and so-so material. A prime example of good backup musicians overstepping their talent. — D.MC.

CRACKIN'
★ Crackin' / War. S-3123
★ Makings of a Dream / War. 2989

Pedestrian but large funk band has one previous album for Warners, one for Polydor, both deleted; all four are forgettable. — D.M.

CRACK THE SKY
★★★ Animal Notes / Lifes. 6005
★★ Crack the Sky / Lifes. 6000
★ Safety in Numbers / Lifes. JZ-35041

Reminiscent of Steely Dan, with sinuous melodies, multiguitar arrangements and cheerfully perverse lyrics—"Surf City (Here Come the Sharks)"—but they are not mere imitators. Writer/lead singer John Palumbo has more interesting ideas than he has songs for. The resultant tunes are suggestive but very choppy, trying for several effects at once. Palumbo is particularly good at creating menacing modal harmonies (i.e., "Ice" on *Crack the Sky*). *Animal Notes* is a more focused, articulate album, although Palumbo's fondness for epic, orchestral arrangements and couch-confessional lyrics persists. Unfortunately, Palumbo left before the release of *Safety,* leaving the band floundering. — A.S.

FLOYD CRAMER
★ Almost Persuaded / Camd. 2508
★★ Best of Floyd Cramer / RCA LSP 2888
★ Date with Floyd Cramer / Camd. X-9016
★ Floyd Cramer and the Keyboard Kick Band / RCA HL1-2278
★ Floyd Cramer Country / RCA APD1-1541
★ Floyd Cramer Country Hall of Fame / RCA ANL1-2344
★ Floyd Cramer in Concert / RCA APD1-0661

★ Floyd Cramer Plays the Big Hits /
  Camd. ADL2-0128
★ Good Old Country Gospel / RCA
  AHL1-4778
★★ Last Date / RCA AHL1-2350
★ Piano Masterpieces / RCA APD1-0893
★ Sounds of Sunday / RCA AHL1-4500
★ This Is Floyd Cramer / RCA VPS-6031
★ Wishing You a Merry Christmas / RCA
  ANL1-1952
Nashville's leading country-pop session
pianist made only one decent record on his
own, "Last Date," which made Top Ten
on the pop charts in 1960. ("On the Re-
bound" and "San Antonio Rose," not
nearly so imaginative, also made the Top
Ten in 1961.) Cramer's tours with Chet Atkins and Boots Randolph were where he
gained his chief notoriety, but all in all, his
playing is a prime example of the worst
that happens when country goes to the
city. — C.F.

CRAWLER
★★★ Crawler / Epic PE 34900
★★ Snake, Rattle and Roll / Epic
  JE-35482
Back Street Crawler's continuation was
more bluesy hard rock using Claptonesque
guitar (Geoff Whitehorn) but less subtly
crafted keyboards from Rabbit. Close but
inferior to the Paul Kossoff-led original
group. — C.W.

CRAZY HORSE
★ At Crooked Lake / Epic KE 31710
★ Crazy Moon / RCA AFL1-3054
A good if unspectacular California rock &
roll band, Crazy Horse got the break it
needed backing Neil Young on *Everybody
Knows This Is Nowhere.* The group went on
to record several albums, the best of which,
Crazy Horse, is unavailable despite the inclusion of the classic "Downtown" and the
presence of Ry Cooder, Nils Lofgren and
Jack Nitzche. After guitarist Danny Whitten died, the Crazy Horse rhythm section
kept going without him and recorded the
sappy *At Crooked Lake,* but Neil Young
didn't forget his friend and eulogized Whitten with his weirdest and in some ways
most powerful album, *Tonight's the Night.*
Crazy Moon was a miserable 1979 comeback attempt. — J.S.

PAPA JOHN CREACH
★ Cat and the Fiddle / DJM 11
★★ Filthy / Grunt 1009
★ I'm the Fiddle Man / Bud. 5649
★ Inphasion / DJM 18

★★ Papa John Creach / Grunt BXL1-1003
★★ Playing My Fiddle For You / Grunt
  BFLI-0418
■ Rock Father / Bud. 5660
This hoary fiddler was resurrected by the
Jefferson Airplane toward the end of its career; the Grunt albums were part of the
Airplane's solo deal with RCA/Grunt. The
first was made while Creach was still in
the band, and features the usual cameos
from members of the Airplane clan. The
other two Grunt records, recorded with an
anonymous backup group called Zulu, and
the subsequent Buddah records show
Creach's thinness, both conceptually and
musically. His only dramatic move is the
hokey glissando that is repeated endlessly
over the course of these albums. — J.S.

CREAM
★★★★ Disraeli Gears / RSO 1-3010
■ Early Cream / Spri. 4037
★★★★ Fresh Cream / RSO 1-3009
★★★ Goodbye / RSO 1-3013
★★ Live Cream / RSO 1-3014
★★ Live Cream, Vol. 2 / RSO 1-3015
★★★ Wheels of Fire / RSO 2-3802
Cream was the pioneer of the power trio:
guitar, bass and drums playing loud,
largely improvised blues-based rock. Its influence was and still is enormous, even ten
years after the group disbanded. Probably
best remembered for concert work, guitarist Eric Clapton, bassist Jack Bruce and
drummer Ginger Baker were actually most
successful in the studio, where they could
ignore the limitations of a trio.
  Fresh Cream introduced their styles: Eric
Clapton's distorted, alternately smooth and
biting guitar, sporting vibrato, quickness
and a thorough knowledge of B. B. King;
Jack Bruce's thick-punching bass guitar,
his strong tenor voice, but oddly inferior
harmonica; and Ginger Baker's overpowering, technically awesome drums, complete
with twin basses. The electrified country
blues were excellent, but the original material was little more than a vehicle for virtuosity. Clapton was especially brilliant on
his solos, as was Baker during his "Toad."
Nevertheless, the guitarist overdubbed
himself throughout, making up for the lack
of another instrument.
  Disraeli Gears switched producers (Robert Stigwood to Felix Pappalardi, with
whom they stayed), resulting in more rock
and less blues, "Sunshine of Your Love"
(their first pop hit) being a prominent example. Bruce's collaboration with myth-
inspired lyricist Pete Brown became more

pronounced. It was a workable change, even considering Clapton's curious restraint during the record.

The two-record *Wheels of Fire* epitomized Cream's schizophrenia. It demonstrated increasingly varied and sophisticated studio work—Pappalardi's hand became more evident and accomplished; playing on many cuts, he amounted to a fourth member—and more acoustic instrumentation (cellos and bells even), but the firm electric blues base was still apparent on several cuts where Clapton let loose and played some of his most exotic solos.

In the studio Cream realized that everyone needn't go full tilt at once to show the group's considerable talents—a marked contrast to the album's live sides. The disciplined and comparatively brief "Crossroads" worked, but the other live numbers were too long and too wild. The formula was easy and deceptively limiting: start off simply, explode into a lengthy free-for-all, and end as begun. The brilliant moment occasionally surfaced, but self-indulgence was the general rule.

Goodbye had three more live cuts, and three from the studio, one from each player: all of the latter sounded less and less like Cream. Bruce's song, relying primarily on keyboards, recalled early Traffic, and Baker's was an equally tuneful rhythmic exercise. But the highlight was the Clapton-George Harrison collaboration, "Badge," with the Beatle handling rhythm guitar. A catchy rocker, Clapton gave it one of his most stunningly pretty solos.

Live and *Live, Volume 2* reiterated earlier misjudgments. (*Live* included one obscure studio cut.) *The Best, Rock Sensation* and the double *Heavy* LP (now deleted) remain excellent compilations. — C.W.

CREATIVE SOURCE
★ **Consider the Source / Poly. PD-1-6065**
Middling black pop trio. — D.M.

CREEDENCE CLEARWATER REVIVAL
★★★★ **Bayou Country / Fan. 8387**
★★★★★ **Chronicle / Fan. CCR-2**
★★★★ **Cosmo's Factory / Fan. 8402**
★★★ **Creedence Clearwater Revival / Fan. 8382**
★★★ **Creedence Gold / Fan. 9418**
★★★★★ **Green River / Fan. 8393**
★ **Live in Europe / Fan. CCR-1**
★★★ **Mardi Gras / Fan. 9404**
★★★ **More Creedence Gold / Fan. 9430**
★★★ **Pendulum / Fan. 8410**

★★★★★ **Willy and the Poor Boys / Fan. 8397**
Creedence Clearwater Revival was probably the greatest American singles band, one of the hardest-rocking American groups of any genre, and almost the only exponent of working-class sensibility in American rock & roll—particularly California rock & roll—after the advent of Haight-Ashbury and before the rise of punk.

Led by guitarist/vocalist/writer John Fogerty, the group simply pumped out classic rock singles, one after another, in much the same rockabilly spirit as Elvis Presley and Jerry Lee Lewis, adding some touches of New Orleans R&B and other relatively antediluvian sources. On its first album (*CCR*), the band attempted to stretch out, as was then the fashion, but though the approach garnered a hit with "Suzie Q," an extended version of the Dale Hawkins classic, Creedence didn't really hit its stride until Fogerty tightened up some three-minute songs. Then began the flood: "Bad Moon Rising," "Born on the Bayou," "Commotion," "Down on the Corner," "Green River," "Have You Ever Seen the Rain," "I Heard It Through the Grapevine" (an extended song that worked), "Proud Mary," "Travelin' Band" and "Who'll Stop the Rain." All of this occurred between 1968 and 1973, when the group fell apart.

Perhaps best of all were "Lodi," the story of a working rocker's depression at being stuck in another out-of-the-way gin mill and his determination to beat everyone, and "Fortunate Son," a stab at the privileged that only kids from the wrong side of the ultra-hip San Francisco area could have felt so sharply. (Creedence arose from roughly the same town as the psychedelic bands, but came from much poorer families.) And after a time, Fogerty burned to prove that he was as much an artist as anyone in the Grateful Dead—he apparently did not know that he was already more—and the group tried to stretch out, to make nominally "progressive" music. Not all of this was unsuccessful, by any means—"I Heard It Through the Grapevine" is more intense than any six minutes of Grateful Dead music on record—but still, his métier was the single. Eventually, the group tried to achieve a communal balance, the other members of the quartet contributing songs to the final studio record, *Mardi Gras,* a noble but disappointing affair. Since then, it's all been repackages, except for the lamentable *Live in Europe.*

Chronicle is a fine singles anthology, but *Green River* and *Willy and the Poor Boys* are great rock records in their own right. — D.M.

JIM CROCE

★★ **Faces I've Been** / Lifes. 900
★★★ **I Got a Name** / Lifes. 35009
★★★ **Life and Times** / Lifes. JZ-35008
★★★★ **Time in a Bottle—Jim Croce's Greatest Love Songs** / Lifes. JZ-35000
★★★ **You Don't Mess Around with Jim** / Lifes. JZ-34993

In the middle of a popular craze for in-flated, neurotic songwriters like Cat Stevens and James Taylor, Jim Croce's "Don't Mess Around with Jim," a brag, came as a refreshing intrusion. When followed by songs like "Time in a Bottle," "I Got a Name," "Operator" and "I'll Have to Say I Love You in a Song," it became apparent that Croce's modest, craftsman's sensibility could communicate certain feelings even better than the "sensitive" outpourings of the wounded-soul school.

Croce's singles fit in well both on AM and FM radio. Perfectly at ease with highly standardized pop-folk song forms, Croce's tactful melodies and subtly driven acoustic guitar arrangements carry his carefully crafted lyrics through clever hooks into surprisingly moving music. His accomplishments might have matured into something more imposing had he not died in a 1974 plane crash.

Croce's first album, *You Don't Mess Around with Jim,* set his permanent pattern: several gemlike love songs, two story tunes, a dollop of nostalgia and a few pleasant throwaways. The Cashman/West production formula had fully stabilized by *Life and Times,* Croce's second LP, and never varied during his short recording career. While strings and other sweetenings nudged Croce's songs into perfect commerciality, the singer himself usually sounds casually unfinished.

Simultaneously with *Life and Times,* Croce's nostalgic side began to take over and he started to produce strikingly impersonal experiments in the craft of sentiment. It fits him well. Aside from a rare embellishment in a fade-out chorus, Croce's voice was as musically laconic as it was restlessly verbal. So, while forever mawkish in his writing, the restraint of his style just manages to hover over a slough of complete sentimentality.

On *I Got a Name* there is a slight modulation into a tone of urgency, particularly with songs like "Lover's Cross," and it is probably his most emotional whole album. But the anthology of love songs, *Time in a Bottle,* contains his best moments overall. — B.T.

DAVID CROSBY

★ **If I Could Only Remember My Name** / Atl. 7203

Interesting only as Crosby's first and only solo attempt. Otherwise a wash-out. — S.H.

CROSBY AND NASH

★★ **Crosby and Nash** / Atl. 7220
★★★ **Live** / ABC 1042
★ **Whistling Down the Wire** / ABC D-956
★★★ **Wind on the Water** / ABC D-902

These two usually function better together than separately. *Crosby and Nash* contains Nash's best acoustic ballad, the Dylanesque "Southbound Train." The surprisingly rocking *Wind on the Water* was recorded with a fine touring band, and mixes political themes with intimations of old age and death. But what seemed like a creative renascence was only a one-shot. *Whistling Down the Wire* is at once smug, elitist and dull. The live album is notable mainly for featuring session stalwarts Danny Kortchmar, David Lindley, Russ Kunkel, Tim Drummond and Craig Doerge at their onstage best. — S.H.

CROSBY, STILLS AND NASH

★★ **Crosby, Stills and Nash** / Atl. 8229
★★ **CSN** / Atl. 19104

Limpid "adult bubblegum" rockers and ballads of numbingly ersatz sensitivity. The music is slick and efficient, if soulless. The vocal harmonies that were supposed to be the trio's forte are so static when played at anything near a loud volume that they actually feel like needle pricks on the brain. The trio's 1977 reunion (*CSN*) suffers from the same problems. — J.MO.

CROSBY, STILLS, NASH AND YOUNG

★★★ **Déjà Vu** / Atl. 19118
★★ **Four Way Street** / Atl. 2-902
★★★ **So Far** / Atl. 18100

The addition of Neil Young for *Déjà Vu* brought a quantum leap in songwriting ability. Young's chunky guitar and brooding vocals also picked things up a little. But there is still something hollow about this music. The aptly titled live LP (half acoustic, half electric) *Four Way Street* reveals a disturbing narcissism as each member does his solo numbers, though it does offer a few new songs and a couple minutes of electric guitar duelling between Stills and Young. But most of it is sloppy, out-of-tune versions of songs already available in superior studio takes. *So Far* is a best-of collection that is questionably programed, but still offers a reasonable overview. — J.MO.

ALVIN CROW AND THE PLEASANT VALLEY BOYS
★★★ Alvin Crow / Poly. 1–6124
★★★★ High Riding / Poly. 1–6102
Fiddler Crow heads one of the most worthy units to come out of Austin, a western swing group that plays the music spiritedly and also has the chops and imagination to extend it into something more appropriate for this era. Swing is their base, but they also dip into rockabilly, hokum and Buddy Holly-type pop on a few songs. The fusion of traditional and modern sound is natural and fluid, the songwriting generally first class. — J.MO.

CROWN HEIGHTS AFFAIR
★★ Crown Heights Affair / RCA AN–2660
★★ Do It, Do It Your Way / De-Lite 9502
★★★ Foxy Lady / De-Lite 2021
★ Saturday Night Disco / De-Lite DSR–9508
Uninspired black octet managed to hit a couple of times during the mid-Seventies disco era, first with "Dreaming a Dream" in '75, then with "Foxy Lady" in '76. Both are contained on *Foxy Lady.* — D.M.

R. CRUMB AND HIS CHEAP SUIT SERENADERS
★★ Number Two / Blue G. 2019
Artist R. Crumb, well-known for inventing Mr. Natural, Angelfood McSpade and other such endearing comics figures, actually thinks he's a 1930s bandleader. He doesn't do badly with his little quartet here, doing nice ragtimes. Especially endearing is Robert Armstrong's performance on saw. This album gives the word "charming" new credence. — C.F.

CRUSADERS
★★★★ Best of the Crusaders / Blue Th. SY–6027
★★★ Best of the Crusaders / Mo. M5–796
★★★★ Chain Reaction / Blue Th. D–6022
★★★★ Crusaders 1 / Blue Th. 6001
★★★ Free As the Wind / Blue Th. 6029
★★★ Images / Blue Th. 6030

★★★★ Second Crusade / Blue Th. 7000
★★★ Southern Comfort / Blue Th. SY–9002
★★ Those Southern Knights / Blue Th. 6024
★★★ Unsung Heroes / Blue Th. 6007
These guys lay out the funkiest groove west of Rampart Street in New Orleans. Twenty years ago they were a knife-edged Texas R&B band sweating it out nightly in the bars where their kind of music lives its life. After making their Sixties migration to L.A. for survival, they switched to playing straight jazz under the name Jazz Crusaders. None of this material remains in print, but the Motown package gives the best remaining account of what they sounded like then. The quartet consided of tenor sax player Wilton Felder, trombonist Wayne Henderson, Stix Hooper on drums and blues doctor Joe Sample on piano. Their rough-hewn yet virtuosic mix of precipitous soloing over rock-hard rhythm structures made them a particularly engaging jazz band.

It didn't take all that much for them to switch over to pure funk. All they really did was tighten up and simplify their arrangements, occasionally add a session bassist and sign up L.A. session guitarist extraordinaire Larry Carlton. The move was a success both commercially and aesthetically—hit singles like "Put It Where You Want It" gave them a mass audience, and they've become some of the most sought-after session players on the West Coast. Their own records are consistently fine, the best grease in the area. — J.S.

CRYER AND FORD
★★ Cryer and Ford / RCA APL1–1235
★★ You Know My Music / RCA AFL1–2146
Pedestrian post-Joni Mitchell singer/songwriter duo, who never quite moved past their inspiration's "Both Sides Now" period. — D.M.

BURTON CUMMINGS
★★★ Burton Cummings / Por. PR–34261
★★★ Dream of a Child / Por. JR–35481
★★★ My Own Way to Rock / Por. PR–34698
As strategist for the Guess Who and pop poet laureate of Canada, Cummings feigned the Las Vegas crooner when he wasn't doing his Jim Morrison bit. So his solo debut, *Burton Cummings,* is an MOR crusade produced by Richard the Lionhearted Perry and led into battle under

Cummings' histrionic anthem, "Stand Tall." The apparent enemy is Guess Who-nemesis Randy Bachman, whose "You Ain't Seen Nothing Yet" gets the suave treatment, right down to Cummings' vocal parody of the guitar solo. The second, *My Own Way to Rock,* has fewer highlights but less garish filigree. — J.S.

GINO CUNICO
★ Gino Cunico / Ari. 4117
★ Gino Cunico / Kam. S. 2601
Bad mid-Seventies MOR, produced by Vini Poncia, who did the same for Ringo Starr, among others. — D.M.

CURTIS BROS.
★★★ The Curtis Bros. / Poly. PD-1-6076
Competent California rock in the Buffalo Springfield/Eagles tradition. — D.M.

KING CURTIS
★★★ The Best of King Curtis / Prest. 7709
★★★ The Best of King Curtis/One More Time / Prest. 7775
In the Fifties, King Curtis was an emerging star as a session saxophonist. His honking, dirty solo on the Coasters' "Yakety Yak" was the trademark of his early style, as well as providing a definitive rock & roll performance. These two albums mark the best of his early sessions as a featured soloist. At the time, Curtis' tone, a lowdown, guttural growl, was very much in the mold of the then-popular Willis "Gatortail" Jackson. With sidemen like Brother Jack McDuff, Billy Butler and Eric Gale, King Curtis works his way through R&B standards like "Honky Tonk," "Fever" and "The Hucklebuck." The twist novelties are cloying, but a smoky reading of "Harlem Nocturne" is a stand-out.
★★★ Jazz Groove / Prest. 24033
★★★ King Soul / Prest. 7789
★★★ Soul Meeting / Prest. 7833
As leader of a session that included jazz notables like Nat Adderley, Wynton Kelly and Paul Chambers, King Curtis didn't venture far from the brawling saxophone style he brought to R&B sessions. *Soul Meeting* and *King Soul* were combined in the reissue, *Jazz Groove.* And though King was not out of his league playing blues and bop with such a formidable lineup, he proves to be a jazz frontman of only marginal interest.
★★★★ Live at the Fillmore West / Atco 359
★★★★ The Best of King Curtis / Atco 266

But if King Curtis was merely a competent jazz musician, he was a master at a simpler form. By the mid-Sixties, Curtis had few peers as a soul saxophonist and bandleader. His tone had broadened, and though the rough, muscular edges were still very much in evidence, he displayed an increased lyrical sense that sparkled on the wafting, self-composed "Soul Serenade" and ballads like "Something On Your Mind" and "You've Lost That Lovin' Feelin'."

The Fillmore album shows King Curtis as a fully matured R&B master, fronting an awesome, powerhouse band that included stalwarts Cornell Dupree, Bernard Purdy and Gerald Jemmott. Though at times one wishes for more judicious material ("Mr. Bojangles"?), there's no arguing with the performance. Curtis and the band simply erupt on potboilers "Memphis Soul Stew" and "Them Changes." It was the supreme soul band of its time. — J.MC.

LITTLE JOE CURTIS
★★ Soul / Als. 5082
The Miami disco version of soul—that is, more reliance is placed on rhythm grooves than on singers, who are usually just about as average and anonymous as this. — D.M.

CURVED AIR
★★★ Air Conditioning / War. WS 1903
★★ Phantasmagoria / War. B-2628
★★ Second Album / War. WB-1951
One of the more naive and less successful British art-rock bands to appear at the end of the Sixties, Curved Air was at its best, which was seldom, when duplicating by-then-standard ideas from Jefferson Airplane and It's a Beautiful Day. Even then, however, lead singer Sonja Kristina's deep alto never wandered far from the stiffer conventions of art song, while the band's dominant instrumentalist, violinist Darryl Way, brought to his overly long solos the barren romanticism of a classically trained technician. The group's first album *Air Conditioning* is sometimes interesting (for the eccentricity and edginess of multi-instrumentalist Francis Monkman), but by the time of the *Second Album,* a year later, the edges had been filed off and the group became a vehicle for Kristina, rather like Renaissance is for Annie Haslam. *Phantasmagoria* completed this process, the sure sign being the garbled instrumental set pieces that bracket the tedium of the fantasy suites, songs and recitations. — B.T.

PATTI DAHLSTROM
★ **Livin' It Thru / 20th Cent. T–521**
★ **The Way I Am / 20th Cent. T–421**
★★ **Your Place or Mine / 20th Cent. T–461**
Dahlstrom sings harsh and low with a country accent that might seem sexy. But don't be fooled by her album covers. Her love songs, featured on the first two LPs, *The Way* and *Your Place,* are more often tuneless bits of muddled philosophy than the breezy come-on her titles and pictures promise. Still, Dahlstrom's own songs are better than those she covers, such as "He Was a Writer." That tune and her own "(Sex) Without Love," which is sung with a chorus of heavy breathing, make *Livin' It Thru* her worst album to date. (Now deleted.) — A.S.

DICK DALE AND THE DEL-TONES
★ **Coast to Coast / Ac. 5033**
★★ **Greatest Hits / Cres. 2095**
Pre-Beach Boys "King of the Surf Guitar." The Crescendo LP collects such songs as "Misirlou" and "Let's Go Trippin'," which were heavily influential on the early Beach Boys (who covered both of these); the Accent LP is of much later vintage and includes trashy pop like "They Call the Wind Maria." Both are pretty forgettable, unless you still wear baggies and call the new kid in school a ho-dad. — D.M.

DALTON AND DUBARRI
■ **Dalton and Dubarri / Col. KC–32542**
■ **Good Head / Col. KC–33052**
■ **Success and Failure / ABC D-964**
This singer/songwriter duo leads a bar band of studio musicians through the gamut of Southern California styles. They try so hard they occasionally become sublimely funny. Statement of purpose: *Dalton*

and Dubarri's "Countrified City Band." — J.S.

ROGER DALTREY
★★★ **Daltrey / MCA 2349**
★★★ **One of the Boys / MCA 2271**
★ **Ride a Rock Horse / MCA 2147**
Lead singer of the Who. *Daltrey,* produced and written by ancient British pop star Adam Faith and young newcomer David Courtney, uses the Who vocalist's limited voice to excellent advantage. "Giving It All Away," a minor hit, is as good a song as Daltrey has ever done. *Rock Horse,* produced and mostly written by Russ Ballard, makes a variety of errors, primarily in material selection. *One of the Boys* is nearly as hard-rocking as a Who LP; it contains a fine version of Andy Pratt's "Avenging Annie." — D.M.

DANCER
★ **Dancer / A&M SP 4585**
More slick, saccharine L.A. pop-rock. Pretty faces, boring sound. (Now deleted.) — D.M.

BARBARA DANE
★★★ **Barbara Dane and the Chambers Brothers / Folk. 2468**
★★ **Barbara Dane Sings the Blues / Folk. 2471**
Dane was a staple on UAW picket lines, in civil-rights marches and at antiwar rallies, her musical approach being: "The more serious the content, the more appealing the form should be." The intermingling of politics and music is a major concern of her own Paredon label, best exemplified here as the Chambers Brothers join her for a cappella renditions of "Go Tell It on the Mountain" and "Freedom Is a Constant Struggle," among other civil-rights anthems. The blues set is heartfelt, the kind

of work that opened the way for Bonnie Raitt. — I.M.

CHARLIE DANIELS BAND
★★ **Charlie Daniels / Cap. ST-11414**
★★★ **Uneasy Rider / Epic E-34369**
The first phase of Charlie Daniels' solo career finds him grasping for his own identity as one of the first Southern rockers to follow in the wake of the Allman Brothers. That group's influence on him is transparent, though Daniels has a penchant for novelty songs ("Uneasy Rider" was even a freak hit) that the Allmans never displayed. The Capitol LP is both his most eclectic and least self-conscious effort. *Uneasy,* a reissue of one of his early LPs for Kama Sutra, has more consistently focused performances; even the two long guitar jams almost sustain themselves.
★★★ **Fire on the Mountain / Epic PE-34365**
★★ **High Lonesome / Epic PE-34377**
★★★ **Midnight Wind / Epic PE-34970**
★★ **Night Rider / Epic PE-34402**
★★ **Saddle Tramp / Epic PE-34150**
★★ **Te John, Grease and Wolfman / Epic JE-34665**
★★ **Whiskey / Epic PE-34664**
Here, a more distinctive Daniels Band sound emerges. *Saddle Tramp* shows him moving toward Western Swing (but with his own, much harder, arrangements) and country boogie-woogie. *Fire* is even more Western-oriented; the fiddle is finally as prominent as the guitar and the country-boy persona is more pronounced. *Fire* also contains the Daniels' rallying cry, "The South's Gonna Do It." The album represents Daniels' best effort in this phase, but it's already tipping his hand toward the extended Southern boogie, which he usually does to death. On suceeding albums he comes close to doing just that, despite more economical songwriting; also, his Southern pride is sounding more like trendy, empty-headed chauvinism. Some of his good-old-boyisms could embarrass even Billy Carter. — J.MO.

RICK DANKO
★★★★ **Rick Danko / Ari. 4141**
The first solo outing from the Band's bassist and co-lead singer is a moving and surprisingly fine record that approximates the ambiance of the Band's best moments without complacency or nostalgia. Danko's vulnerable vocal persona was the perfect expression of the plaintive emotion characteristic of much of Robbie Robertson's

writing, and he makes the transition to fronting his own record without faltering. Despite the fact that Danko contributed little in the way of songwriting to his old group (though he did cowrite the classic "This Wheel's on Fire" with Bob Dylan), his songs for this record are tremendous. Several tunes ("Brainwash," "Java Blues," "Sip the Wine") could well have been recorded by the Band.

The instrumental support, led by cameos from his former group mates, is also superb. Robertson handles lead guitar on "Java Blues," Richard Manuel electric piano on "Shake It," Levon Helm adds harmony vocals on "Once upon a Time" and Garth Hudson plays accordion on "New Mexico." Guest appearances by Eric Clapton and Ronnie Wood and extensive collaboration on horn charts and guitar from Doug Sahm flesh out the impressive list of sidemen. — J.S.

DAP SUGAR WILLY
■ **From North Philly (Live) / Phil. PZ-34122**
■ **The Ghost of Davy Crockett / Laff 167**
Least funny black comic alive. (Now deleted.) — K.T.

BOBBY DARIN
★★ **Bobby Darin 1936–1973 / Mo. M5-813**
★★★ **The Bobby Darin Story / Atco 131**
Bobby Darin's first record, "Splish Splash" (1958), was the first white hit for Atlantic Records. Produced by Ahmet Ertegun, Darin's record helped touch off the Italian-American rock 'n' roll craze of the late Fifties, and his influence can be heard on Dion, Fabian, Frankie Avalon and even the young Rascals. Aside from "Dream Lover," a mopey ballad, and the finger-popping "Mack the Knife," however, Darin never quite lived up to the potential of his talent. He went to Hollywood and Vegas, tried folk-rock in the late Sixties and came up with a nice hit in "If I Were a Carpenter." He then went straight pop once more at Motown in the early part of this decade. He died of a heart ailment in 1973, unrealized but also unrecognized for what he did accomplish. The Atco sides are pretty fine records, and hold some pleasant surprises for those who haven't heard them. — D.M.

DARLING AND STREET
★ **The Possible Dream / Van. VSD 79363**
Erik Darling, a one-time member of the Weavers and Rooftop Singers and an itin-

erant banjo and guitar ace, teams up here for forgettable pop-folk mishmash. *Darling* is better than this, though it's hard to find supportive evidence on records. (Now deleted.) — T.S.

BETTY DAVIS

★★★ **Nasty Gal** / Is. ILPS 9329
Almost as if she were a black Marlene Dietrich, Betty Davis defines herself by unusual sexual posturing. On *Nasty Gal* she growls and snarls, taunts lovers, reveals bedroom secrets and challenges the familiar roles of female vocalists. The insistent funk tracks may become wearying, but the songs never fail to titillate. — J.MC.

MAC DAVIS

- **All the Love in the World** / Col. PC-32927
- **Baby Don't Get Hooked on Me** / Col. PC-31770
- **Burning Thing** / Col. PC-33551
- **Forever Lovers** / Col. PC-34105
- **I Believe in Music** / Col. PC-30926
- **Mac Davis** / Col. C-32206
- **Mac Davis** / Sp. 4024
- **Song Painter** / Col. CS-9969
- **Stop and Smell the Roses** / Col. PC-32582
- **Thunder in the Afternoon** / Col. PC-34313

Singer/songwriter Davis has done more to set back the cause of popular music in the Seventies than any other single figure. His execrable pop-morality pseudo-country hits, "I Believe in Music" and "Stop and Smell the Roses," encouraged a wholesale run to sententious Muzak that makes movie director Robert Altman's vision of Nashville's self-righteousness and pomposity look like humility. His one legitimate claim to rock foot-notoriety was writing "In the Ghetto" for Elvis. — J.S.

PAUL DAVIS

★ **Little Bit of Paul Davis** / Bang 223
★★ **Paul Davis** / Bang 226
★★★ **Paul Davis** / Bang 410
★★★★ **Ride 'Em Cowboy** / Bang 401
★★★ **Southern Tracks and Fantasies** / Bang 405

Davis is a Southern singer/songwriter of some talent who began recording in the early Seventies as a neo-folkie. *Little Bit* and *Paul Davis* (Bang 226) featured original songs of love and social protest, and while his sentiments were all too often saccharine and his instrumental backing plain, his singing showed definite promise. His popu-

larity in Atlanta and the small-label ethics at Bang enabled Davis to continue recording. He found his stride with a 1974 release, *Ride 'Em Cowboy.* The ambiance here leaned more toward country-rock, with some fine songwriting (the title track, "You're Not Just a Rose," "Midnight Woman," "Bronco Rider" and "Make Her My Baby"), and excellent instrumental backing from guitarists Barry Baily and Auburn Burrell, steel guitarist Charlie Owen, drummer Roy Yeager and bassists Tom Robb and Chris Ethridge. The 1976 *Southern Tracks and Fantasies* was slickly contemporary pop, well produced and featuring some fine instrumental backing from the Muscle Shoals crew (drummer Roger Hawkins, keyboardist Barry Beckett and guitarist Jimmy Johnson). But Davis' searching-for-a-hit songwriting here is too formularized, which makes the album ultimately disappointing. — J.S.

TYRONE DAVIS

★★★ **Home Wrecker** / Dakar 76915
★★ **I Can't Go This Way** / Col. JC-35304
★★★ **It's All in the Game** / Dakar 76909
★★ **Let's Be Closer Together** / Col. PC-34654
★★ **Love and Touch** / Col. PC-34268
★★★ **Tyrone Davis** / Dakar 76904
★★★★ **Tyrone Davis' Greatest Hits** / Dakar 76902

As a modishly romantic Seventies soul singer at Dakar, Davis used his big, Joe Simon-like voice on a variety of ballads to turn in some refreshingly moody hits, all of which fit into a single stylistic pattern set by "Turn Back the Hands of Time," the first and best. His *Greatest Hits* album is great make-out music, more sincere and less erect than Barry White's mumbles. At Columbia, he was pushed into modern rhythm patterns, subordinated to the backing tracks, and generally got washed out. — D.M.

JIM DAWSON

★ **Elephants in the Rain** / RCA APL1-0993
- **Songman** / Kam. S. 2035
- **The Essential Jim Dawson** / Kam. S. 2-2616
- **You'll Never Be Lonely with Me** / Kam. S. 2049

Dawson is a hell of a sincere guy, but that's not going to rescue his songs from the realm of the truly terrible. At their liveliest, his voice and guitar sound like James Taylor in a coma, but his lyrics . . . By all means miss Dawson's tender rhapsodies on British horticultural skills ("In an English Garden") and his lubricious apologia for fallen women ("Stephanie") on the *Essential* album (a.k.a. *The Disposable Jim Dawson*). The contemporary arrangements on *Elephants* boost that LP to the barely listenable category, but the songs remain the same—yecch. — A.S.

STU DAYE
★★★ **Free Parking / Col. PC-33936**
A debut album by a rock & roller at heart, including a cover of Paul Simon's "The Boxer." The rest is original material with better than average lyrics. — G.C.

THE DCA EXPERIENCE
★★★ **Bicentennial Gold / Priv. PS 2009**
That's right—a disco record of patriotic songs. Coproducer Tony Bongiovi and his band of merrily hard-working disco all-stars prove that the genre has become the best new medium for novelty records. You can hear their version of "Yankee Doodle Dandy" at New York Yankee home games. (Now deleted.) — J.S.

THE DEADLY NIGHTSHADE
★★ **F & W / RCA BPL1-1370**
★★ **The Deadly Nightshade / RCA BPL1-0955**
The Deadly Nightshade's first record (*Deadly Nightshade*), released in 1975, would have gone unnoticed if the band had not been made up of three vaguely feminist women. Basically folk musicians, Helen Hooke, Anne Bowen and Pamela Brandt write their own material; Bowen adds an electric bass line to the banjo- and rhythm-guitar-based compositions. The group's best song, "Nose Job," is its only successful stab at synthesizing music, politics and humor, which seems to be the goal. The second album (*F & W*) contains a curious commercial bid, a disco version of "Mary Hartman, Mary Hartman," two oldies covers and an extremely confusing Bicentennial ballad as sung by a black slave, "Ain't I a Woman," which asks why a female slave isn't treated in the conventionally oppressed manner that upper-class women are granted. — G.C.

DEAF SCHOOL
★★★ **Don't Stop the World/Second Honeymoon / War. 2LS-3011**
Competent avant-punk band, which provided a sort of bridge between the pretensions of Roxy Music and the pretensions of the Sex Pistols. A mere late-Seventies con-

versation piece, more useful to the curious than the committed. — D.M.

JAMES DEAN
★★★ **James Dean / War. B-2843**
Unaccountably spotty presentation of film and dialogue from the great Fifties-rebel-role-model's three films. For some reason, producer Russ Titelman chose to emphasize *Giant,* while shortchanging material from the two better films, *Rebel without a Cause* and *East of Eden.* An interesting document of one of the great pre-rock & roll stars, but not the one that Dean deserves. — P.N.

PETER DEAN
★★ **Four or Five Times / Bud. 5613**
Fifty-ish jazz singer, notable mostly because he covers James Taylor's "Don't Let Me Be Lonely Tonight" and uses Taylor's wife (and Dean's cousin), Carly Simon, as a backing singer on both the title track and "So the Bluebirds and the Blackbirds Got Together." — D.M.

DEARDORFF AND JOSEPH
■ **Deardorff and Joseph / Ari. 4092**
Singer/songwriter duo, who share management and the Bahai faith with Seals and Crofts, were notable mostly because Danny Deardorff was a paraplegic who had to be carried onstage. Great suffering has not, in this case, produced great art. — D.M.

CHRIS DE BURGH
■ **Far Beyond These Castle Walls / A&M SP 4516**
■ **Spanish Train and Other Stories / A&M SP 4508**
Chris de Burgh is a troubadour who has adopted and expanded the early Bee Gees' most insipid mistakes while incarnating all of Donovan's medieval fantasies. He even lives in a crumbling castle whence he issued *Far Beyond These Castle Walls,* which has no less than four tracks with spoken verses.
Apparently having read Borges, de Burgh comes back stronger with *Spanish Train and Other Stories.* Tighter piano/string arrangements make it sound almost like the Cat Stevens score to Ingmar Bergman's first rock musical. — B.T.

BERT DE COTEAUX
■ **Bert de Coteaux Plays a Stevie Wonder Songbook / RCA ANL1-0923**
Stiff instrumental versions of Wonder's hits, under the direction of noted disco

arranger/producer de Coteaux. (Now deleted.) — s.h.

KIKI DEE
★★ I've Got the Music in Me / R.
BXL1-3042
★★ Kiki Dee / R. BXL1-225
★★ Loving and Free / R. BXL1-3040
★★ Stay With Me / R. BXL1-3011
These albums yield one fine single, "I've Got the Music in Me," and hardly anything else. The problem? Dee is a coward when it comes time to reach for the deeper emotions inherent in the material. Some scintillating pop arrangements are wasted as a result, much as her single with Elton John, "Don't Go Breaking My Heart," also spent time and talent frivolously. — d.mc.

DEEP PURPLE
★★ Burn / War. PR-2995
★★ Come Taste the Band / War. B-2895
★★ Deep Purple and the Royal Philharmonic / War. BS-1860
★★★ Deep Purple in Rock / War. 1877
★★★ Fireball / War. 2564
★★★★ Machine Head / War. BS4-2607
★★ Made in Europe / War. B-2995
★★★★ Made in Japan / War. SWS-2701
★★★ Purple Passages / War. 2LS-2644
★★ Stormbringer / War. PR4-2832
★★★ When We Rock, We Rock and When We Roll, We Roll / War. K-3223
★★★ Who Do We Think We Are! / War. B-2678
The Deep Purple catalogue gives one, besides an often painful headache, a fairly clear picture of the disjointed meanderings of the hard-rock trail from the demise of the Yardbirds to the first stirrings of punk rock. *Purple Passages,* a compilation of selections from the band's first three albums, established its capability of drawing buckets of inspiration from any of the musical streams running into the main current of 1968 rock. Led by guitarist Ritchie Blackmore and keyboard player Jon Lord, Deep Purple used flashes of psychedelia, classical touches and (perhaps most significantly in trying to understand the band's longevity and rather surprising consistency) plenty of bar-band, kick-out-the-stools consciousness.

Prone to self-indulgence, early Deep Purple plunged headlong into anything and everything that struck its fancy, making even their most glaring failures (most notably Jon Lord's out-of-print *Concerto for Group and Orchestra*) almost excusable.

The departures of original vocalists Rod Evans and bassist Nic Simper and the entrance of Ian Gillan and bassist Roger Glover proved to be the turning point for the band. *Deep Purple in Rock,* the fourth album, was a hodgepodge of power chords and psychedelic noodling, but with 1971's *Fireball,* the group began upping the wattage and leaving the thinking to art-rockers. Blackmore, always a respected guitarist but until then never more than the sum of his influences, began to pull feverish and original solos out of nowhere, as he and Lord began to serve as counterpoints to each other. *Machine Head* (1972) was a crowning achievement, with "Highway Star," "Smoke on the Water" and the mind-melting "Space Truckin' " leading the way through two sides of mania that left one not only battered but begging for more. *Made in Japan,* a double live recording originally released only in Japan, was hastily released in the United States soon afterward as Deep Purple began to challenge Led Zeppelin for the sonic-overload throne.

The glory period was short-lived, however. *Who Do We Think We Are!* sported only one real gem, "Woman from Tokyo," and within two years, both Gillan and Blackmore had bowed out because of internal squabbling. Lord carried on with singer David Coverdale and American guitarist Tommy Bolin, but as the Seventies entered middle age, metalloid bombardments on the eardrums were no longer the favorite pastime of the maturing audience that had been Purple's. The band died an almost unnoticed death in '76, and *Made in Europe,* recorded in '75 and released posthumously, with Blackmore on guitar, displays only the echoes of the power that once was Deep Purple. *When We Rock* is a greatest-hits selection. — b.a.

RICK DEES
★ Original Disco Duck / RSO 1-3017
"Disco Duck," a hit in the summer of '76, gave disco what it deserved while at the same time pointing out the genre's utility for novelty singles. Imagine Donald Duck singing Barry White songs and you'll get the idea. — j.s.

SAM DEES
★★★ The Show Must Go On / Atl. 18134
Sam Dees is a more than creditable songwriter, but his singing lacks distinction. His only album is professional, if none too varied, centering mostly on similarly constructed soul ballads. "Claim Jumping" is

the best, a hard-hitting Southern funk song modeled after early Johnnie Taylor hits. (Now deleted.) — J.MC.

DÉJÀ VU
■ **Get It Up for Love / Cap. ST-11604**
This gruesome Toronto band is the brain-child of Skip Prokop, founding member and self-proclaimed *auteur* of Déjà Vu's immediate stylistic predecessor, Light-house. Although unburdened by a horn section, much less a string quartet, as was Lighthouse, Déjà Vu suffers fatally from the same problem: the band's components have yet to be introduced to each other. Consisting of an industrial-weight instru-mental unit fronted by three singers intend-ing to be the new Three Dog Night, Déjà Vu flounders on inane material ground into hash by heavy-metal R&B. The sing-ers, never less than shrill, often sound like they are being emasculated. (Now de-leted.) — B.T.

DELANEY AND BONNIE AND FRIENDS
★★ **Genesis / GNP 2054**
★★★★ **On Tour / Atco 326**
Delaney and Bonnie Bramlett were Okla-homa-bred musicians who made mid-Sixties reputations in the Hollywood ses-sion scene (Delaney was a member of the Shindogs, who appeared on ABC's *Shin-dig).* They made their first album—not the GNP outtakes above—for Stax in 1968, in a kind of white gospel-funk mode to which Eric Clapton, among others, owes a great deal. In 1969, they formed a band to tour with Blind Faith that included Carl Radle, Leon Russell, Jim Price and Bobby Keys, all of whom went on to tour with Joe Cocker's Mad Dogs and Englishmen, an act of desertion that took the backbone

from the duo's career. Before that, how-ever, they made a couple of influential, laid-back tours of Europe (from which the live Atco LP, which features Clapton, is drawn) and the States.

The deleted LPs Delaney and Bonnie made for Elektra and Atlantic are all worthwhile listening for anyone interested in moderately impassioned white soul. The couple split up—artistically and mari-tally—in 1972 and both have since pursued solo careers. — D.M.

THE DELEGATES
★ **The Delegates / Mile. 100**
Heavy early-Seventies R&B verging on funk; "Funky Butt" was the single. (Now deleted.) — J.S.

THE DELLS
★★★ **Face to Face / ABC AA-1113**
★★★ **Love Connection / Mer. SRM-1-3711**
★★ **They Said It Couldn't Be Done, But We Did It / Mer. SRM-1-1145**
The Dells, with the Isley Brothers, are probably the oldest remaining group in rock. Their first hit, "Oh What a Night," made in a Chicago version of doo-wop harmony, appeared in 1956, and at least on the R&B charts, their success has contin-ued virtually unbroken, with occasional appearances on the pop charts as well. Surprisingly, the best overview of their ca-reer can be found on a now-deleted Trip album, *The Dells' Greatest Hits* (Trip X-9503).

In the Sixties, the Dells became a Temp-tations/Impressions-styled vocal group, and most of the (now deleted) Cadet/Chess albums represent that phase of their career. Aside from the driving "There Is," perhaps the best record they ever made, and the re-makes of the first two hits ("Oh What A Night" and "Stay in My Corner"), they rarely dented the pop charts, although they always remained important in the soul field. Since switching to Mercury in 1975, they have become more modern still, but since today's soul formulas place more of a premium on rhythm and less on singing, the records aren't as interesting. — D.M.

ROBERT DE NIRO
★★★ **Soundtrack from *Taxi Driver* / Ari. 4079**
Taxi Driver contains one monologue from the movie, the one with De Niro talking to himself in the mirror ("You talking to me? Ain't nobody else here!") and fingering

some stranger offcamera. A must for paranoids. — G.C.

SANDY DENNY
★★★★ Sandy / A&M 4371
★★★ The North Star Grassman and the Ravens / A&M 4317

Sandy Denny was a founding member of Fairport Convention, the landmark late-Sixties British group that combined elements of traditional English music with rock instrumentations. Denny's strong singing has its roots in plainsong, and Fairport's stolid, dirgelike march beat is derived from the music of the Church of England. Denny's solo albums, two of which are still in print, feature members of Fairport Convention in backup roles (notably the superb guitarist Richard Thompson) and give a good account of what Denny's music is about. Each album contains a magnificent interpretation of a Bob Dylan song ("Down in the Flood" on *Grassman,* "Tomorrow Is a Long Time" on *Sandy*). *Grassman* is sparser, while *Sandy* includes intriguing horn arrangments by Allen Toussaint, one of which works a wondrous, Band-like effect in a dialogue with Thompson's guitar toward the end of "For Nobody to Hear." Denny died after a tragic fall down a flight of stairs, in 1978. — J.S.

JOHN DENVER
★ Aerie / RCA LSP-4607
■ An Evening with John Denver / RCA CPL2-0764
■ Back Home Again / RCA AFL1-0548
★ Beginnings / Mer. SRM-1-704
■ Farewell Andromeda / RCA APL1-0101
★★ Greatest Hits, Vol. 1 / RCA AFL1-0374
■ Greatest Hits, Vol. 2 / RCA CPL1-2195
■ I Want to Live / RCA AFL1-2521
■ John Denver / RCA AQL1-3075
★★ Poems, Prayers and Promises / RCA AFL1-4499
★ Rhymes and Reasons / RCA AFL1-4207
■ Rocky Mountain Christmas / RCA AFL1-1201
★ Rocky Mountain High / RCA AFL1-4731
■ Spirit / RCA AFL1-1694
★ Take Me to Tomorrow / RCA AFL1-4278
■ Windsong / RCA AFL1-1183
★ Whose Garden Was This / RCA AFL1-4414

John Denver was one of the many pastoral singer/songwriters who proliferated in the early Seventies in the wake of James Taylor's initial impact. His thin, whiny voice, sophomoric writing and extremely limited instrumental facility made him far from the most interesting practitioner of the style, but his tenacity paid off. He reached a sort of creative highpoint with *Poems, Prayers and Promises,* then shortly after scored massive success with the single "Rocky Mountain High," a good song that far outshines Denver himself as well as anything else he's recorded. After the single, Denver was packaged as the latest TV star commodity, doing a double bill with Frank Sinatra and generally hamming it up on and off record. If his writing and performance left much to be desired before he made it, it positively festered once he became popular enough to stop trying. And he has. — J.S.

EUMIR DEODATO
★ Artistry / MCA 457
★ In Concert / CTI Q-6041
★ Love Island / War. BSK-3132
★★★ The First Cuckoo / MCA 491
★★ 2001: Also Sprach Zarathustra / CTI 7081
★ Very Together / MCA 410

Although wholly obedient to the laws of homogeneity, arranger/keyboardist/composer Eumir Deodato has written a new chapter in the history of elevator music. His albums consist of disco-charged orchestral pop/rock/jazz/TV theme/classical swirling. Deodato has drawn melodic structures from Ravel, Page, Marley and Mancini on which to hang striding and rather chichi production formulas.

Because they are so environmental in strategy, Deodato's records are particularly hard to distinguish one from another. His version of Richard Strauss' "Zarathustra" was a hit, but the best-defined LP is *The First Cuckoo,* which contains a pair of lesser pop successes, "Black Dog" and "Caravan/Watusi Strut." — B.T.

DEREK AND THE DOMINOS
★★★★★ Layla / RSO 2-3801

Derek and the Dominos—particularly because of the extensive participation of Duane Allman—gave Eric Clapton the context in which to demonstrate his prowess without unnecessarily calling attention to it. Clapton and Allman battled neck to neck (sometimes it's tough to figure out who is playing which guitar), and the sessions brought out the best in each player, with Clapton's rumbling leads segueing perfectly into Allman's lightning runs. The guitar call and response on "Why Does Love Got to Be So Sad?" and the molten-metal exorcism of "Layla" alone make this one of the premier guitar albums of all of rock & roll. The group (sans Allman) also made a live recording (deleted), which, while featuring some attractive, stretched-out soloing by Clapton, pales next to Siren *Layla.* — J.B.M.

DERRINGER
★★★ **Derringer / Blue S. PZ-34181**
★★★ **Derringer Live / Blue S. PZ-34848**
★★ **If I Weren't So Romantic, I'd Shoot You / Blue S. JZ-35075**
★★ **Sweet Evil / Blue S. PZ-34470**
The first band Rick Derringer has led since the demise of the McCoys at the end of the Sixties, Derringer showed fine potential on its first LP, with a twin guitar attack (new-comer Danny Johnson played second guitar), a fine rhythm section (Kenny Aronson, formerly of Dust and Stories, on bass and Vinny Appice on drums) and some tough, sturdy songs ("Beyond the Universe," "Sailor"). *Sweet Evil* and *If I Weren't So Romantic,* though, suffered from rather weak material. *Derringer Live,* a set of tracks from the first two LPs done in concert, is a fairly successful picture of a band apparently more at home in front of an audience than in a studio. — B.A.

RICK DERRINGER
★★★★ **All-American Boy / Blue S. PZ-32481**
★ **Spring Fever / Blue S. PZ-33423**
Rick Derringer's first solo album, *All-American Boy,* released in 1973, is a fine showcase of his often-inspired guitar playing and features, besides a fine rendition of "Rock and Roll Hootchie Koo" (originally done while he was with Johnny Winter And), such straight-ahead movers as "Teenage Love Affair" and "Slide on Over Slinky" and two fine ballads, "The Airport Giveth" and "Jump, Jump, Jump." The less said about *Spring Fever,* from its androgynous cover photo on down, the better. — B.A.

JACKIE DeSHANNON
★★★★ **New Arrangement / Col. PC-33500**
★★ **You're the Only Dancer / Amh. 1010**
DeShannon was something of a star during the Sixties, a gentle blond folk rocker whose authorship of songs like "When You Walk in the Room," for the Searchers, and "Don't Doubt Yourself, Babe," for the Byrds, supplanted that image with real resilience. Her own hits, all deleted (on Imperial or United Artists), included Burt Bacharach's "What the World Needs Now Is Love" and "Needles and Pins." The Columbia album, released in 1975, is first-rate singer/songwriter stuff; DeShannon has a better voice than Joni Mitchell, at least to these ears, and she gets more distance on her material. The Amherst album (1977), on the other hand, is a dismal disappointment, in which DeShannon's writing and performing are both reduced to contemporary singer/songwriter clichés. — D.M.

DETECTIVE
★★ **Detective / Swan 8417**
★★ **It Takes One to Know One / Swan 8504**
Credible but uneventful late-Seventies hard rock from a band led by ex-Yes keyboardist Tony Kaye. — J.S.

DETROIT EMERALDS
★★★★ **Feel the Need / Westb. 302**
★★ **Let's Get Together / Westb. 6101**
The best of what Detroit soul had left after Motown moved to L.A. in 1970 is reissued on the 1971 LP (original title: *You Want It, You Got It, Feel the Need*). The style is basically neoclassic soul (the Temptations and the Four Tops are reference points), and it produced a pair of Top Forty records in "You Want It, You Got It" and "Do Me Right." But the real gem here is "Feel the Need," one of the first records "made" by discos, which propelled the album track into semiclassic status. *Let's Get Together* is not up to that standard. — D.M.

MINK DEVILLE
★★★ **Mink DeVille / Cap. ST-11631**
★★★ **Return to Magenta / Cap. SW-11780**
Willie DeVille emerged from the same Bowery bar that produced Blondie, the Ramones, Talking Heads and Television, but has even less connection with any of them than they do with each other. What he really is, is a sort of (too?) late-Seventies Mitch Ryder, with tripled *angst.* Good voice, bad attitude—the same old story, but a good one. — D.M.

DEVO
★★ **Q: Are We Not Men? A: We Are Devo / War. 723**
A group of Captain Beefheart-influenced dadaists who have one joke (they act like

automatons) that they beat into the ground. They're not too funny, they're not much as players, and their sophomoric philosophizing (the group's name stands for de-evolution, which they argue is the present human condition) doesn't cover their lack of imagination. High point: a weird cover of "Satisfaction." — J.S.

NEIL DIAMOND

★ And the Singer Sings His Song / MCA 2227
★★ Beautiful Noise / Col. PC-33965
★★★★ Double Gold / Bang 2-227
★★★ Greatest Hits / Bang 219
★★★★ His 12 Greatest Hits / MCA 2106
★★★ Hot August Night / MCA 8000
★ I'm Glad You're Here with Me Tonight / Col. JC-34490
■ Jonathan Livingston Seagull / Col. KC-32550
★ Love at the Greek / Col. KC2-34404
■ Moods / MCA 2005
★ Neil Diamond Gold / MCA 2007
■ Rainbow / MCA 2103
★ Serenade / Col. PC-32919
★★ Stones / MCA 2008
★★★ Sweet Caroline / MCA 2011
★★ Tap Root Manuscript / MCA 2013
★★ Touching You, Touching Me / MCA 2006
★★ Velvet Gloves and Spit / MCA 2010
★★ You Don't Bring Me Flowers / Col. FC-35625

A moody singer/songwriter, blander than Dylan, darker than Bacharach. Diamond's pop hits are numerous—more than twenty singles in the Top Forty—but he has never established himself as a "serious" artist in the manner of Dylan, although that's obviously his deepest wish.

At Bang from 1966 to 1968, Diamond was produced by Jeff Barry and Ellie Greenwich, who co-wrote many of the Phil Spector hits. These records have a bright freshness: "Cherry Cherry," "Thank the Lord for the Nighttime" and "Kentucky Woman" are a definition of late-Sixties pop, as is "I'm a Believer," a hit for the Monkees.

At MCA (originally with the now-defunct subsidiary Uni), Diamond worked with a variety of producers before settling in with Tom Catalano, with whom he made his biggest hits, and worst music. His basic style hardly changed. A pleasant exuberance might give way to a brooding growl, depending on the lyric, but he was always accompanied by spare, driving rhythm sections, and additional elements—

choruses, horns, rarely strings—were kept to a minimum. Few of these records had the excitement of those early ones, though "Brother Love's Traveling Salvation Show" is a nice twist on the *Elmer Gantry* theme. But Diamond was writing potboilers, and his thirst was for Pulitzer-level poesy. Unfortunately, his imagination and the very blandness of his voice condemned him to setting a model for the radical-MOR singer/songwriter style of the Seventies. In this sense, he has superficially influenced everyone from James Taylor to Jim Croce.

Double Gold is an excellent representation of the Bang days, and of Sixties pop in general. (A caution, however: in the Sixties, pop was not always coincidental with rock.) *His 12 Greatest Hits* is a fair retrospective of the era, and the one that followed. Avoid *Neil Diamond Gold,* an execrable live album, and *Rainbow,* a pathetic attempt to interpret songs written by others. *Hot August Night* is, on the other hand, a classic live set—somewhere, Diamond summoned up passion and charisma, though for pretty hokey material.

The later MCA period was marked by an identity crisis. Like many commercially successful, artistically disdained pop singers in the rock era, Diamond longed for another kind of success. *Tap Root Manuscript,* his first attempt to break through to the realm of Dylan and Paul Simon, is almost comic—side two consists of a quasi-African "folk ballet," which sounds like ordinary AM pop extended to twenty minutes. Strangely, however, the record contains one of Diamond's biggest (and best) hits, the marvelous "Cracklin' Rosie."

At Columbia, where he was given a multi-million-dollar contract, this passion to become "serious" and respected reached absurd heights. His first album, the soundtrack to the flop movie *Jonathan Livingston Seagull,* was nearly as insipid as the book and movie that inspired it. But Diamond has a way with pop philosophy, and the record was a commercial smash. So was *Serenade,* though its dedication to Longfellow made it a bit much to take.

Since none of this had earned him the devotion of the Dylan camp, Diamond's next move was to shanghai Dylan's guitarist, Robbie Robertson of the Band, as producer of *Beautiful Noise.* But the result convinced more people that Robertson was a mercenary than that Diamond was an artist. *Beautiful Noise* is curious, however, as a rather affectionate attempt to assess the impact of the demise of Tin Pan Alley, Diamond's alma mater and the place from which the artistic particle of his talent derives. Strangely enough, however, it is Diamond's anti-Tin Pan Alley attitude that has invariably spiked his ambition; like so many of his pop predecessors, his talent is greatest when he reaches for less, not more. He has since returned to garden variety pop schlock (e.g., "You Don't Bring Me Flowers," with Barbra Streisand). — D.M.

DIAMOND REO
★ **Dirty Diamond / Kam. S. 2619**
Pittsburgh glamour rockers blow out a crude and unnecessary heavy-metal buzz. Others preferred. (Now deleted.) — J.S.

MANU DIBANGO
★★★ **Afrovision / Is. 9526**
DiBango is a soprano saxophonist who scored a hit in 1973 with the catchy instrumental "Soul Makossa" but failed to reproduce the hit formula on subsequent releases. This side is one of his more recent attempts, a pleasant synthesis of African rhythms and jazz-rock instrumental stylings. — J.S.

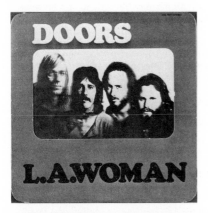

HAZEL DICKENS AND ALICE GERRARD
★★★★ **Hazel and Alice / Roun. 0027**
★★ **Won't You Come and Sing for Me / Folk. FTS 31034**
Hazel and Alice are two women who, in the early Sixties, formally entered the male-dominated bluegrass scene as singers, instrumentalists and, later, composers. The 1973 Rounder album is their best, encompassing a slightly broader country music range, their themes running from traditional mining songs to latter-day statements on women's consciousness. The 1967 Folk-

ways set is more straightforwardly bluegrass/old-timey-oriented. — I.M.

THE DICTATORS
■ **Manifest Destiny / Asy. 7E1109**
■ **The Dictators Go Girl Crazy / Epic KE 33348**
A new low—rock songs about wrestling and contempt, not just for the music and the audience, but even for themselves. Witlessly performed. — D.M.

BO DIDDLEY
★ **Bo Diddley / Chess 704**
★★★★ **Bo Diddley—16 All Time Greatest Hits / Check. 2989**
★★★★★ **Got My Own Bag of Tricks / Chess 2CH-60005**
Bo Diddley was one of the great fathers of rock & roll, ranking with such transitional blues artists as Fats Domino and Chuck Berry in both importance and influence. His most important songs included "I'm a Man/Bo Diddley," "Who Do You Love," "Mona" and "Road Runner"; these were among the building blocks of the English rock of the next decade, both in their eccentric rhythmic sense and in their often bizarre sense of humor. (One English blues group, the Pretty Things, went so far as to name themselves after one of his songs.)

Diddley (born Ellis McDaniel) was raised in the Mississippi Delta tradition, steeped in both blues and church music, but found his real place in Chicago, where he moved as a child. By 1955 he was ready to record for Chess, and his first record, "I'm a Man/Bo Diddley," became one of that year's major R&B hits, although it did not dent the pop charts. The biggest pop hit he ever had was "Say Man," which made the Top Twenty in 1959. No other Diddley single (there were dozens, many of them masterful) cracked the Top Fifty.

A great deal of this was due to his sensibility, based on outrage at a time when the vogue was relative conformity. If Chuck Berry had a vision of America as a comic-book paradise, Diddley—his nearest competitor at Chess—countered it with a view of all of life, but particularly sex, as a profound cosmic joke, played out at the expense of everyone, but particularly the solemn and pompous. So he wisecracked and cackled his way through songs with themes that bordered on the absurd: a botched stickup in "Cops & Robbers" and a series of crazed, sometimes demonic, love affairs, culminating in "Who Do You Love," the outlandish Willie Dixon song.

The music set it all up perfectly. The rhythmic attack was less sharp and direct than most other rock & roll and R&B of the era, but Diddley's strange beat—the Bo Beat, it was termed, though you know it as "Shave and a haircut/Two bits" electronified—made physical drive irrelevant, not that it couldn't be called upon when needed. A constant feature, in addition to Diddley's whipping guitar, was a pair of jiggling maracas, played by bassist Jerome Green, who was also a frequent verbal sparring partner ("Bring It to Jerome," "Say Man," "Hey Bo Diddley"). But as much as anything else, Bo's singing told the story. Cracking up, biting, sarcastic, jive and angry by turns, that voice often seemed to be putting on everything in the world, including itself.

Without Bo's beat, it is impossible to imagine the Rolling Stones, the Yardbirds or the Animals (whose "Story of Bo Diddley" is a perfect nutshell tribute to the man and a great history of the music). The best of it is contained on *Got My Own Bag of Tricks,* which includes all the familiar tunes from *16 Greatest Hits,* plus such rarities as "Cops and Robbers" and the hilarious "Bo Diddley Is Loose." The other two records still in print are, unfortunately, of more recent vintage. The early LPs (at least a dozen) can still sometimes be found as cutouts: especially recommended are *Go Bo Diddley, Bo Diddley Is a Gunslinger,* either of the records titled *Bo Diddley* on Checker (*not* the Chess above) and *Have Guitar Will Travel.* The titles say it all. — D.M.

DIGA RHYTHM BAND
★★★ Diga Rhythm Band / Roun.
　RX-LA600-G

An international drumming cooperative recorded under the auspices of the Grateful Dead, Diga plays long drumming pieces using tabla, folk drums, vibes, congas and bongos without dependence on lead instruments or even the usual rock snare-drum kit. Their music is happily eclectic, exotic and mildly hypnotizing. — B.T.

THE DILLARDS
★★★ Back Porch Bluegrass / Elek. 7232
★★★ Copperfields / Elek. 74054
★★★ Glitter Grass from the Nashwood Hollyville Strings / Fly. Fish 036
★★★ Live . . . Almost! / Elek. 7265
★★★ Pickin' and Fiddlin' / Elek. 7285
★★ Roots and Branches / Anth. ANS 590l

★★★ The Dillards vs. the Incredible Flying L.A. Time Machine / Fly. Fish 040
★★★ Tribute to the American Duck / Poppy LA175G

The Dillards hold a unique position in the genealogy of West Coast folk rock. Unlike the young folksingers who turned to rock because it was more familiar turf, the Dillards were dyed-in-the-wool country musicians from Missouri who met rock on their own terms and took only what they wanted from it. Originally made up of Douglas Dillard on banjo, Rodney Dillard on guitar, banjo and dobro, Dean Webb on mandolin and Mitch Jayne on bass, the Dillards were a souped-up bluegrass band featuring Doug as the fast-fingers virtuoso, and they charged their vibrant live performances with a healthy dose of cornpone yokel humor.

In 1963, while shopping around for a foothold in the booming folk scene, they were outcasts from both mainstream factions. Their country irreverence irritated the puritanical folk tradionalists and the serious social protest singers, yet their act was too "cracker" for the folk entertainers.

So the band was forced to find its own level, which it did brilliantly. The Elektra albums are lively and enjoyable sets that have held up. After *Back Porch Bluegrass,* their straightforward introductory album (which included a version of "Duelin' Banjos" a decade too early for *Deliverance*), the Dillards let it all hang out with a live recording, *Live . . . Almost!,* which showed them at their zaniest, cracking slick jokes and poking fun at Joan Baez (practically heresy at the time) between greased-lightning cutting matches and pristine country harmony vocals. They even included a version of Dylan's "Walkin' down the Line."

When the folk-rock style surfaced in 1965, the Dillards were midwife to its vocal arrangements. Rodney Dillard had been thinking of recording Beatles songs and was already arranging Dylan material for the band. The Byrds were well aware of the Dillards, and even toured with them in 1965. Rodney and Mitch helped out on the vocal arrangements for the Byrds' demo and Dean sang with Roger McGuinn on the "Mr. Tambourine Man" demo. The close relationship enjoyed by the early folk-rock bands with the comparatively veteran Dillards didn't end there. Drummer Dewey Martin went from working with the Dillards to completing the original Buffalo Springfield lineup.

After the third album, *Pickin' and Fiddlin',* recorded with fiddler Byron Berline, Doug left the band to hook up with the Byrds' Gene Clark. Ironically, the Dillards went on to make their most durable recording; *Wheatstraw Suite,* a now-deleted 1968 classic (Elektra), introduced Doug's replacement on banjo, Herb Pederson, and added a couple of drummers, an electric bass and a pedal steel guitar to their traditional instrumentation. The record is a brilliant rush of fierce playing and beautifully precise vocal harmonies with several excellent originals ("Nobody Knows," "Listen to the Sound") and covers of the Beatles' "I've Just Seen a Face" and Tim Hardin's "Reason to Believe." The next album, *Copperfields,* moved further away from the traditional roots and included covers of "Yesterday" and Eric Andersen's "Close the Door Lightly."

On the 1972 *Roots and Branches,* Billy Ray Latham replaced Pederson and the band moved more completely into country-rock style, recording Shel Silverstein's "Last Morning" and the energetic "Get Out on the Road." The following year's *Tribute to the American Duck* continued to mix rock and country material and featured the rousing spiritual "You've Gotta Be Strong." — J.S.

DILLINGER
★★ Babylon Fever / U. Artists LA-795-R
★★ Bionic Dread / Mango 9455
★★ C.B. 200 / Mango 9385
Middling reggae group, which is not terribly clever vocally or instrumentally. Regarded as one of the giants of dub. — D.M.

DINGOES
★ Five Times the Sun / A&M 4636
Efficient but boring Australian hard-rock band indicates on its 1977 debut album just how stale the genre can sound. — J.S.

MICHAEL DINNER
★ The Great Pretender /
  Fan. 9454
★★ Tom Thumb the Dreamer /
  Fan. 9512
Dinner's albums are polished products full of sweet harmony and tasteful guitar, but no amount of studio pizazz can pump life into his relentlessly predictable tunes. At best, the four-part harmony and intermittent reggae beat of *Tom Thumb the Dreamer* provide some diversion. With his twang, his fingerpicking and his smug, earnest lyrics, Dinner is reminiscent of Don McLean.

His mood is less sunny: he sees himself as a victim of women and includes a variety of social outcasts in his songs. But Dinner's visions, like his melodies, are secondhand. — A.S.

DION
★★★★ Dion's Greatest Hits / Col. C-31942
★★★★★ Everything You Always Wanted to Hear by Dion and the Belmonts / Laur. 4002
★★★ Return of the Wanderer / Lifes. JZ-35356
★★★ 60 Greatest of Dion and the Belmonts / Laur. SLP-6000
★★ Streetheart / War. B-1954
Dion DiMucci emerged from the Bronx in 1958. At first, he appeared with a vocal trio called the Belmonts; together, they made some of the greatest records of their era, beginning with "I Wonder Why" and including "A Teenager in Love." On his own, Dion hit with "A Lover's Prayer," "The Wanderer," "Runaround Sue" and "Lonely Teenager," and he also made some rare but mysteriously magnificent misfires, such as "Born to Cry" and "Sandy." He even attempted to create a dance craze with "The Majestic." Often dismissed as just another pretty face, Dion was much more accomplished than that. He was heavily influenced by Bobby Darin and black vocal groups, and only the nasality of his early records places him in the Fabian/Frankie Avalon league. In fact, he belongs with Darin as one of the first white R&B singers—smooth, cool, but committed.

Good selections of his greatest hits can be found on the Columbia LP and the Laurie *Everything* package. *60 Greatest* is more than anyone but the most rabid fan wants to hear.

After a nasty bout with heroin, Dion re-emerged in 1968 as a kind of folk-rock singer/songwriter. He scored an immediate hit with the haunting "Abraham, Martin and John," perhaps the best, and certainly the best received, protest song of all. The *Abraham* LP revealed enormous artistic growth, particularly a fascination with Robert Johnson-styled country blues; it is deleted but definitely worth seeking out. He signed with Warner Bros. in 1969 and cut a terrific first album, featuring the anti-drug classic "Clean Up Your Own Back Yard," but he was soon trapped in the company's pop-rock production mill. *Streetheart,* released in 1976, was meant to reestablish him as a writer and performer of importance. But hack production and arrangements buried several good songs, particularly the title track (inspired by the Richard Price novel, *The Wanderers,* which had in turn been inspired by his earlier hit) and "Queen of '59." Yet Dion remains one of the great underdeveloped talents in rock history. A third comeback would not be at all surprising, though, especially given the pleasures of the 1978 Lifesong LP, which includes the haunting "I Used to Be a Brooklyn Dodger." — D.M.

DIRE STRAITS
★★★★ Dire Straits / War. 3266
This monochromatic British blues group became one of the most celebrated bands of the late Seventies merely for championing Sixties musical values at a time when rock was in the violent throes of self-analysis. Group leader Mark Knopfler is a poor singer, an adequate guitarist out of the Peter Green/Eric Clapton school of British blues players, and a powerful songwriter. The stark, romantic visions expressed in songs like "Water of Love" and "Down Along the Waterline" (why does the guy wonder when interviewers ask him about his fascination with water imagery?) contrast eerily with songs of bitterness and persecution like "In the Gallery" and the hit "Sultans of Swing." Knopfler is probably too bitter for his own good, but he's calculating enough to understand the key to Fleetwood Mac's lifelong success—their supple and driving rhythm section. "Sultans" made it on that same rhythmic solidity. Expect more of the same from this crew. — J.S.

DIRTY ANGELS
★★ Kiss Tomorrow Goodbye / Priv. PS 2020
Despite production by the New Wave–associated Richard Gottehrer *(Blondie),* this is just more of the thump of standard American dumbbell hard rock. — D.M.

DIRTY TRICKS
★★ Hit and Run / Poly. PO-1-6104
★★ Night Man / Poly. 1-6082
Typically rudimentary British hard rock band relied on fuzzy-toned guitars, hoarse blues-based vocals and production by Tony Visconti. If that makes you curious, though, you probably already own a half-dozen records of this quality or better. — D.M.

DISCO TEX
★ Disco Tex and the Sex-O-Lettes Review / Chel. CHL 505
★ Manhattan Millionaire / Chel. CHL 516
Singer/hairdresser/hanger-on further debases self, but all in fun. A Johnny Carson favorite—as Monte Rock III in the Sixties—this sounds like his revenge on Trude Heller. — K.T.

DIXIE DREGS
★★★ Free Fall / Capri. 0189
★★★ What If / Capri. 0203
Experimental Southern rock group noted for its virtuosic instrumental technique and its debt to the Mahavishnu Orchestra. — J.S.

BONNIE DOBSON
★★★ Dear Companion / Prest. 7801
Dobson was one of those ethereal-voiced young women who popularized Child ballads in the early Sixties. More traditional than Judy Collins, more down to earth than the gloriously tragic Baez, Dobson never captured public imagination as firmly. Still, *Dear Companion* endures as pleasant, earnestly performed folk music. — A.S.

DR. BUZZARD'S ORIGINAL "SAVANNAH" BAND
★★★★ Dr. Buzzard's Original "Savannah" Band / RCA APL1-1504
★★ Dr. Buzzard's Original "Savannah" Band Meets King Pennett / RCA AFL1-2404
The most popular disco album of 1976, *"Savannah"* introduced a fresh approach to the idiom by reprising Big Band and earlier R&B in a sassy, arch Kurt Weill–influenced style. It contains the disco classics "I'll Play the Fool" and "Cherchez la Femme." But the *King Pennett* followup showed much less flair. — S.H.

DR. FEELGOOD
★★ Malpractice / Col. PC-34098
★★ Sneakin' Suspicion / Col. PC-34806
Simple to an extreme, these Britons emulate but fail to match the early R&B-influenced exploits of groups like the Rolling Stones. Their LPs sound like sparse backing for a lead musician who never appears. — C.W.

DR. HOOK
★ A Little Bit More / Cap. ST-11522

★★★ Bankrupt / Cap. ST-11397
★ Belly Up! / Col. C-32270
★ Dr. Hook and the Medicine Show / Col. C-30898
★ Dr. Hook and the Medicine Show Revisited / Col. C-34147
★ Sloppy Seconds / Col. C-31622

Hook's *oeuvre* is dominated by the songwriting of nonmember Shel Silverstein: cutsey, mannered crypto-country rock. The band itself is competent in a spunky barband way, and *Bankrupt* is its best because it contains the most non-Silverstein material. The group seems to pride itself on being vulgar, but it works against the music. *Revisited* is an all-Silverstein best-of package, and Dr. Hook's worst. — K.T.

DR. JOHN
■ Dr. John / Trip X-3507
★ Dr. John / Sp. 4018
★★★★★ Gris-Gris / Atco 234
★★★★★ Gumbo / Atco 7006
★★★ In the Right Place / Atco 7018
★★ 16 Greatest Hits / Trip TOP-16-1

After a healthy and respected career as a songwriter/arranger/pianist in New Orleans in the early Sixties, Mac Rebennack burst on the scene as a solo artist under the alias of Dr. John Creaux, the Night Tripper. *Gris-Gris,* his first album, features most of his fellow Bayou associates, albeit under voodoo-ized masks: Jesse Hill is Dr. Poo Pah Doo of destine tambourine and Harold Battiste is Dr. Battiste of Scorpio of bass clef. The entire crew is "dregged up from . . . under the eight visions of Professor Longhair reincanted in the charts of now." The record is a wild celebration of New Orleans' Magnolia Street mayhem, with such charmers as "I Walk on Gilded Splinters," "Gris Gris Gumbo Ya Ya" and "Croker Courtbouillion," and was easily one of the most bizarre LPs of the late Sixties, which is saying a lot.

The good Doctor's next few releases, however, did not match the spontaneity or excitement of *Gris-Gris. Remedies* (now deleted) includes a full-sided "Angola Anthem" which is unfocused and seemingly endless; *The Sun, Moon & Herbs* (now deleted), recorded in England with a host of guest stars (Eric Clapton, Mick Jagger), is also disappointing. With *Gumbo,* though, all is forgiven. Rebennack's piano playing, far too understated on previous albums, becomes the focal point as he pays tribute to Huey Smith, "Sugarboy" Crawford, Longhair and the entire New Orleans R&B

sound through versions of its classic songs. This impeccable strutting tour of New Orleans music features, besides Rebennack's impeccable piano playing and his best recorded vocals, marvelous horn arrangements from Battiste. *In the Right Place* is a record that on paper looked great—Dr. John hooked up with Allen Toussaint as producer and the Meters as backing musicians. But aside from the title track, Dr. John's only big hit single, it's a failure: much too slick and exacting. *16 Greatest Hits* is certainly not that; it's a jumble of demos from Rebennack's earlier years, some sung by him and others by unidentified artists. This is for diehards only. — B.A.

DOG SOLDIER
★ Dog Soldier / U. Artists LA-405-G

Featuring drummer Keef Hartley, guitarist Miller Anderson, plus three unknown Brits whose names emblazon the cover sticker, Dog Soldier played some of the most forgettable music of 1975. Fortunately, they were only a short-lived mistake. (Now deleted.) — A.N.

NED DOHENY
★★★ Hard Candy / Col. PC-34259
★★ Prone / Col. PC-34889

Doheny's R&B is a lot like Carole King's, white but not overly pale. His sweet but nearly colorless voice is the lesser element in an engaging confection of L.A. singer/songwriter melodies cum Philly soul and Steve Cropper's meticulously crisp and simple production. — P.H.

DOLENZ-JONES-BOYCE-HART
★ Dolenz-Jones-Boyce-Hart / Cap. ST-11513

In which two of the Monkees attempt a comeback by uniting with one of the Monkees' songwriting teams. Unfortunately, Mickey Dolenz and Davey Jones were far from the strongest members of the Monkees (Mike Nesmith was), and Tommy Boyce and Bobby Hart weren't the best of the Monkees' songwriters (Nesmith was). Eminently forgettable. (Now deleted.) — D.M.

FATS DOMINO
★★★★★ Fats Domino / U. Artists UAS 9958
★★ My Blue Heaven / Pick. SPC-3295

From 1950, when "The Fat Man" hit the charts, to his current semiretirement with sales of 65 million records behind him, Fats Domino has been an unmistakable and endearing presence in American music.

He came out of the New Orleans blues tradition, playing boogie-woogie piano against a gently pumping rhythm section. His flexible tenor was more than a match for the trumpet and sax sections that filled out his sound. Once he'd found the formula (with collaborator Dave Bartholomew), Fats never looked back. His first hit to cross over to white audiences was "Ain't That a Shame" (five years after its initial release in 1950), and many others followed. "I'm in Love Again," "Blueberry Hill," "Blue Monday" (all 1956) and "Walking to New Orleans" (1960) are as much a part of our collective rock memory as anything put out by Fats' only two peers in record sales—Elvis and the Beatles.

Fats Domino, from United Artists' well-annotated Legendary Masters series, is a nicely documented selection of twenty-eight of the best songs (although it does skip Fats' 1960 hit, "My Girl Josephine").

My Blue Heaven, a Pickwick reissue of Mercury's *Fats '65,* is a characteristically warm live set. Domino's 1968 *Fats Is Back* LP was spurred by his success with a "Lady Madonna" single, but is now out of print. This leaves the larger UA collection as a basic part of anybody's rock library. — F.S.

DON AND DEWEY
★★★ **Don and Dewey / Spec. 2131**
Fifties R&B. Don is "Sugarcane" Harris, who in the Sixties joined up with John Mayall for a brief spell, and Dewey is Dewey Terry, who handled most of the lead vocals. Their style was more light-hearted than raucous, more novelty than

straightforward. The duo is a footnote in R&B history—and a thoroughly enjoyable one. This contains their essential hits. — K.R.

DONOVAN
★★★ **A Gift from a Flower to a Garden / Epic 171**
★★★ **Barabajagal / Epic 26481**
★ **Donovan / Ari. 4143**
★★★★ **Donovan in Concert / Epic BN-26386**
★★★★ **Donovan's Greatest Hits / Epic 26836**
★ **Essence to Essence / Epic KE-32800**
★★★ **Hurdy Gurdy Man / Epic 26420**
★★ **Seven Tease / Epic PE-33245**
★★ **Slow Down World / Epic PE-33945**
Listening to Donovan's albums is like being consigned to relive the most insipid parts of the Sixties. But although the medieval-minstrel-flower-power-spiritual conceits have worn thin, Donovan's music from that era sounds remarkably pleasant, at least as background. So pleasant in fact that viewed from a jaded Seventies' perspective, it makes all the pretentious falderal charming.

The albums with a three-star rating are from Donovan's late-Sixties period of fancy bathrobes and peacock feathers. They each contain one or two memorable songs, but are worth the purchase only for aging nostalgics or students of cultural history (the latter will find them especially interesting as a type of laid-back music that didn't come from Los Angeles).

Greatest Hits and *Concert* are rated more highly because they have a higher concentration of hits. Even so, unless "Sunshine Superman" or "Mellow Yellow" are particularly important to you, you can easily get along without them. Unfortunately, Donovan's pre-electric, Dylan-influenced material ("Universal Soldier") is not available on LP in the U.S. Pye has a selection of that material, however, in its Golden Hour series, which is easily spotted in import bins.

The rest of the LPs are from Donovan's various comebacks in the Seventies. Oddly, most of them sound cynical; it's interesting that the Great Innocent may have turned sour, but so far it hasn't made for very interesting music. *Mellow Yellow,* Donovan's best Sixties album, is worth seeking out as a cutout—it was recorded just at the moment when folkies were all smoking pot and just going electric and when the economy of England was still in good shape.

That is, before Donovan was either innocent or cynical, and after he was political. — T.S.

THE DOOBIE BROTHERS

★★★★ Best of the Doobies / War. K-3112
★★★ Livin' on the Fault Line / War. K-3045
★★★★ Minute by Minute / War. K-3193
★★★ Stampede / War. BS4-2835
★★★ Takin' It to the Streets / War. B-2899
★★★ The Captain and Me / War. BS4-2694
★★ The Doobie Brothers / War. 1919
★★★★ Toulouse Street / War. BS4-2634
★★ What Were Once Vices Are Now Habits / War. WS4-2750

A tough San José street band that had a half-dozen hits in the mid-Seventies. Their sweeping, driving rhythms rivaled the Allmans, and the use of three singers created a distinctive harmonic style, epitomized by "Listen to the Music," from *Toulouse Street.* In addition, Patrick Simmons contributed some pleasant acoustic guitar work. *The Captain and Me* is dance music, and *What Were Once* is now mishmash, an eclecticism that had one success, the sneakily elegant "Black Water." With *Stampede,* Jeff Baxter (formerly of Steely Dan) replaced Tom Johnston on lead guitar, although the latter continued singing until *Takin' It,* when another ex-Steely Dan member, Michael McDonald, replaced him altogether. The harmonies remain, but the songs are often jazzy, and the keyboards challenge the guitars as lead instrument. *Best of the Doobies* collects the six hits, plus some all right filler. The 1979 *Minute by Minute* saw McDonald come into his own with some of the best California pop in years. — P.H.

THE DOORS

★★★★ Absolutely Live / Elek. 9002
★★ American Prayer / Elek. 5E-502
★★★★ Best of the Doors / Elek. EO-5035
★★★★★ L.A. Woman / Elek. 75021
★★★★ Morrison Hotel / Elek. 75007
★★★★★ Strange Days / Elek. 74014
★★★★★ The Doors / Elek. 74007
★★★ The Soft Parade / Elek. 75005
★★★★★ 13 / Elek. 74079
★★★★ Waiting for the Sun / Elek. 74024
★★★★ Weird Scenes Inside the Gold Mine / Elek. 8E-6001

Brash, courageous, intelligent, adventurous and exciting. The Doors were all this—and more. Of all the groups to emerge from the

West Coast in the late Sixties, only the Doors succeeded in consistently getting their often disturbing messages across to the core of America through both hit albums and singles. And the fact that they were able to do so without compromising their stance or their art only makes the accomplishments that much more incredible.

Various themes and images rang throughout all of the Doors' albums—deserted houses, strangers, endless highways, unsolvable mysteries, accents on sensuality and sexuality—and the group's intent was there even on the very first track of *The Doors*, their inital LP: "Break On Through (To the Other Side)." With Jim Morrison's vision leading the way, a vision that encompassed notions of both good and evil as viable alternatives in terms of human action and that was continually obsessed with exploration and search, the Doors played unique music: Ray Manzarek's keyboards, Robby Krieger's guitar and John Densmore's drums weaving around in support of the specific needs of each song. Investigations were never really completed in the Doors' music—the probe was the thing—and though many of the Doors' lengthy works ("The End," "When the Music's Over," "The Soft Parade") weren't wholly successful, they were admirable and fascinating, exemplary of the group's desire to further its horizons.

After *The Doors* and *Strange Days,* the Doors went into a moderately subdued period with *Waiting for the Sun* (in which Morrison began his Lizard King persona) and *The Soft Parade,* which, although their least cohesive record, still managed to include four hit songs. It also marked the band's experimentation with some unexpected genres: bluegrass ("Runnin' Blue") and jazz ("Touch Me"). *Morrison Hotel,* steeped in blues, saw a resurgence of the band's power, and *Absolutely Live,* a double LP, featured the prophetic theatrics of "Celebration of the Lizard." *L.A. Woman* was the final record with Morrison. Arguably the group's finest album, with two excellent long tracks (the title cut and "Riders on the Storm"), it forms a rather detailed composite sketch of everything that helped make the Doors such an intriguing band: blues and rock forged together, poetry mingled with standard rock lyrics, and a solid dose of inquiries into the unexplainable puzzles of life. *American Prayer* recycled some of Morrison's poetry (and phone calls) with tepid backing music added posthumously. — B.A.

DOUBLE EXPOSURE
★★★ Four Play / Sals. 8501
★★★ Ten Percent / Sals. 5503
Slick Spinners-like disco-soul group, great emphasis on harmonies but featuring terrific Philadelphia session playing. Excellent material includes contributions by Bunny Sigler and Holland-Dozier-Holland. — D.M.

CAROL DOUGLAS
★ Burnin' / Mid. Int. BKL1-3048
★★ Full Bloom / Mid. Int. BXL1-2222
★★ Haunted / Mid. Int. BKL1-2131
★★ Midnight Love Affair / Mid. Int. BKL1-1798
★★ Steppin' Out / Mid. Int. BKL1-2423
★★ The Carol Douglas Album / Mid. Int. BKL1-0931
Mildly popular disco singer whose biggest success came in 1974 with "Doctor's Orders," included on *The Carol Douglas Album.* — D.M.

LAMONT DOZIER
★★★ Peddlin' Music on the Side / War. B-3039
★★★ Right There / War. B-2929
Part of the famed Motown songwriting and production trio, Holland-Dozier-Holland, Lamont Dozier's Seventies solo albums have been uniformly tasteful and engaging, if not up to the level of greatness of his better-known Motown work. — J.S.

CHARLES DRAIN
★★★ Dependable / RCA APL1-1414
Chicago singer blended elements of Barry White and Wilson Pickett on this above-average 1976 debut LP. (Now deleted.) — D.M.

NICK DRAKE
★★★★ Bryter Layter / Ant. AN-7028
★★★★ Five Leaves Left / Ant. AN-7010
The late Drake offered gentle, delicately rich music that avoided fluffiness and resignation. His breathy, jazz-inspired, attractively cool singing reminded one of Donovan, but Drake's was more smoky and naturally delivered. *Five Leaves Left* was somewhat more somber and muted than *Bryter Layter,* which had smoother sound and instrumentation. Both relied strongly on Drake's acoustic guitar strumming for an arranging basis. Appealingly melancholy orchestration served both records well. (Now deleted.) — C.W.

THE DRAMATICS
★★★ Do What You Wanna Do / ABC AA1072
★★★ Joy Ride / ABC D-955
★★★★ Shake It Well / ABC 1010
★★★★ Whatcha See Is Whatcha Get / Stax 4111
Post-Motown Detroit soul quintet, led by singer Ron Banks, heralded something of a soul renaissance for that city, first in 1971-1972 with a pair of hits for Stax, "In the Rain" and "Whatcha See Is Whatcha Get" (reissued in 1978 on *Whatcha See*), later with *Shake It Well* in 1977. These are uniformly good records, though *Shake* seemed to lift them to a new plateau. The Stax LPs, which like the ABC discs were done with producer Don Davis, are well worth investigating for lovers of neoclassicism in soul. The group's first LPs for Cadet (many of which are now deleted) aren't quite as good, though *Dells vs. the Dramatics* is worth hearing. — D.M.

THE DRIFTERS
★★★★ Drifters' Golden Hits / Atl. 8153
★★★★ The Early Years / Atco SD33-375
There were actually two different groups who recorded for Atlantic under the name Drifters. Each has its own anthology; taken together they account for the early history of soul music. *Early Years,* showcasing Clyde McPhatter, provides one of the few observable transitions from post-World War II gospel singing through mid-Fifties R&B and, after widespread commercial success, pop styles. McPhatter was a giant among R&B singers, a strong influence on Smokey Robinson.

Golden Hits is closer to pop music. When producers Jerry Leiber and Mike Stoller added strings, a breakthrough sound—

"soul"—resulted. The album features a number of lead singers, most notably Ben E. King, and some of the finest tunes ever to emerge from the Brill Building—"On Broadway," "Save the Last Dance for Me," "Under the Boardwalk" and "Up on the Roof." — R.G.

JULIE DRISCOLL
★ **Julie Driscoll / Sp. SPB-4043**
A typically cheesy collection that features tin-can sound, no inner sleeve, absolutely no information on musicians, and twenty-two minutes of slushy R&B and pop. Of special interest is an early Randy Newman love song, "If You Should Ever Leave Me." (Now deleted.) — J.B.M.

JOE DROUKAS
★ **Shadowboxing / Southw. 6400**
New York session guitarist attempted to step forward on this 1975 solo debut with the usual direly tedious results. — D.M.

DUCKS DELUXE
★★★★ **Don't Mind Rockin' Tonite / RCA AFL1-3025**
One of the toughest outfits from the late lamented British pub-rock scene, the Ducks released one U.S. album with enough minor triumphs on it ("Coast to Coast," "Daddy Put the Bomp," "Fireball," "Hearts on My Sleeve," "West Texas Trucking Board") to ensure them a small niche in rock history. Amen. — J.S.

LES DUDEK
★★★ **Ghost Town Parade / Col. JC-35088**
★★★ **Les Dudek / Col. PC-33702**
★★★ **Say No More / Col. PC-34397**
Dudek is an extremely talented session guitarist noted for his work with Steve Miller and the Allman Brothers (he "ghosted" a Duane Allmanish lead on "Ramblin' Man"). But his solo albums, while featuring some fine playing, suffer from the characteristic sideman's dilemma. In this case, it sounds like fusion jazz and the standard Southern boogie, well turned but unadventurous. — J.S.

THE DUDES
★★ **We're No Angels / Col. PC-33577**
A spinoff from the Elektra groups the Wackers and Roxy, the Dudes could not match their devotion to English rock harmony singing with skillful execution of it. This 1975 LP was their only try. (Now deleted.) — D.M.

GEORGE DUKE
★★★ **From Me to You / Epic PE-34469**
★ **Live on Tour in Europe / Atco 18194**
★★★ **Reach for It / Epic JE-34883**
After a number of years jamming in West Coast clubs, Duke began his recording career as a jazz keyboardist with Jean-Luc Ponty in the early Seventies. Later, Duke joined Frank Zappa's band, where he started playing synthesizer, the instrument he's become known for. During his Zappa stint, Duke recorded his first solo records for MPS, all of which are now out of print. He switched to a straight-ahead R&B style on joining up briefly with Billy Cobham in 1976, playing some heavy funk influenced by James Brown and Sly Stone. The combination of players should have been fruitful, but it wasn't, as the *Live in Europe* album painfully demonstrates. His two Epic albums extend the funk strategy to much better effect. Duke finally achieved his goal—a hit single—with "Reach for It," a chanting, danceable blues funk pattern strongly reminiscent of Sly Stone's "Stand." — J.S.

DUKE AND THE DRIVERS
★★ **Cruisin' / ABC D-911**
★★ **Rollin' On / ABC D-942**
The Drivers have enthusiasm and taste, particularly in choosing cover material. The faults of the first album might be blamed on production, but the second's problems are entirely their own. A good bar band, but nothing more. (Now deleted.) — P.H.

LESLEY DUNCAN
★★★ **Maybe It's Lost / MCA 2274**
★★★ **Moon Bathing / MCA 2207**
Duncan had an English pop voice something like Olivia Newton-John's little-girl-lost sound, but redeemed by the excellent production and arrangements of her husband, Jimmy Horowitz. These two late-Seventies LPs went nowhere commercially, which shows where good taste gets you. (Now deleted.) — D.M.

CORNELL DUPREE
★★★★ **Teasin' / Atl. 7311**
Cornell Dupree melts the blues into dripping caramel; sweet and thick, it should cover the earth. The guitarist from King Curtis' rhythm section, who laid down the lines on Aretha's early Atlantic tracks with cohorts Richard Tee and Bernard Purdie, later earned a little more fame with Stuff,

but I prefer this album to both of that group's efforts. — A.G.

THE DUSTY CHAPS
★★★ Domino Joe / Cap. ST-11755
★★★ Honky Tonk Music / Cap. ST-11614
Perhaps because they woodshedded in Arizona for so long before recording these late-Seventies LPs, the Dusty Chaps were one of the better country-rock groups, though their attitude was no less reactionary than the rest. — D.M.

AMON DUUL II
★ Hijack / Atco 36-108
★★★ Made in Germany / Atco 36-119
Hijack is pretentiously weird. The strings, reeds, brass and guitars are deliberately dark and cold, but finally leaden as well. Though it is German, the group sings in English, resulting in frequently awkward lyrics, and the low-pitched vocals are an unwise idea. The record does contain a few spirited passages, and these become the base for the far superior *Made in Germany*. Lively beat, colorful instrumentation and, most importantly, no impulse to be overly arty or bizarre. — C.W.

RICHARD DYER-BENNETT
★★ Richard Dyer-Bennett, Vol. 4 / Dyer-Bennett 4
★★ Richard Dyer-Bennett Vol. 5 / Dyer-Bennett 5
A classically trained tenor, Dyer-Bennett uses simple Spanish guitar accompaniment to render old ballads ("Greensleeves," "Barbara Allen," and others). Considered a minstrel in the traditional sense of the term, he has recorded dozens of songs for his own label in addition to earlier efforts for others. Although few folksingers attempt this kind of formal presentation today, Judy Collins and Joan Baez can be cited as examples of contemporary artists who grew out of this stylized milieu. — I.M.

DYKE AND THE BLAZERS
★★★★★ Dyke's Greatest Hits / Orig. Sound 8877
Dyke (Arlester Christian) and the Blazers predated the Seventies funk explosion with a series of raw, gutbucket dance hits. Their first smash, "Funky Broadway" (covered by Wilson Pickett), brought the word "funky" into the popular vocabulary and subsequent singles were among the raunchiest soul records of the late Sixties. Dyke was shot to death in 1970. — J.MC.

BOB DYLAN
★★★★ Another Side of Bob Dylan / Col. PC-8993
★★★★★ Bob Dylan / Col. PC-8579
★★★★★ The Freewheelin' Bob Dylan / Col. PC-8786
★★★ The Times They Are a-Changin' / Col. PC-8905
When Bob Dylan (originally, Robert Zimmerman) arrived in New York from Minnesota in 1960, he was little more than the latest in the line of Woody Guthrie imitators. By the time he made his first album, *Bob Dylan,* in 1961, however, he was far beyond that, an amazingly original singer of traditional blues tunes (Blind Lemon Jefferson's "See That My Grave Is Kept Clean," for instance), country classics ("Highway 61") and his own original songs in the Guthrie talking-blues tradition: "Song to Woody" is stark and beautiful, "Talking New York" hilarious.

Freewheelin' (1962) contained some material in these veins, but was more notable for Dylan's emergence as the most inspired talent of the entire folk revival. His original love songs, particularly "Don't Think Twice, It's All Right" and "Girl from the North Country," were lyrically far beyond anything any other popular or folk writer had attempted, and while some of his "protest" songs were jejune ("Masters of War"), others were lovely affirmations of humanity, like the immediate classic "Blowin' in the Wind," or frankly sardonic but nonetheless perfect ridicules of the cold war mentality ("Talking World War Three Blues" and "I Shall Be Free"). Peter, Paul and Mary's pop hit with "Blowin' in the Wind" established Dylan as a cult figure.

The Times They Are a-Changin' is Dylan's most topical, or protest-oriented, record, and its temporal concerns make it in many ways his most dated. The title song particularly suffers from age—it now sounds self-righteous—though there is a maturity of political analysis in "Only a Pawn in Their Game" and "The Lonesome Death of Hattie Carroll" that helps them hold up. Still, the best songs here are more personal, less tied to issues, such as "One Too Many Mornings" and "Restless Farewell," in which Dylan indicates that he may not be around the protest scene anymore; the haunting love song "Boots of Spanish Leather"; and his reminiscence about his childhood in the Minnesota copper country, "North Country Blues."

Perhaps the most prophetic song on the record, however, is "When the Ship Comes

In," in theory a protest song, as chastising as an Old Testament sermon, but in fact an example of the surreal outpouring of imagery that would characterize Dylan's next period and the birth of folk rock. Although the next album, *Another Side of Bob Dylan* (1964), retained the simple instrumentation—Dylan accompanying himself on guitar, piano and/or harmonica—it opted for far less topical material, and instead painted a series of fecund portraits of urban street life. "Chimes of Freedom," "Spanish Harlem Incident," "I Shall Be Free No. 10," "My Back Pages" and "I Don't Believe You" were all fragments from an entirely new breed of songwriting, not romantic or topical but rather philosophic or purely emotive. There were definite themes to some of them—as well as to "All I Really Want to Do," a hit for Cher, and "It Ain't Me Babe," a smash for the Turtles—but the levels of meaning accelerated; if they can be given any definition at all, these songs are visionary. And Dylan's entire early work must be seen as a process of development that led inevitably to this uniquely personal vision, whose accessibility and applicability in the lives of his generational peers was none the less potent for all its abstraction.

★★★★★ **Blonde on Blonde** / Col. C2S-841

★★★★★ **Bringing It All Back Home** / Col. PC-9128

★★★★★ **Highway 61 Revisited** / Col. PC-9189

★★★★★ **John Wesley Harding** / Col. PC-9604

★★★★★ **The Basement Tapes** / Col. C2-33682

At the Newport Folk Festival in the summer of 1965, Dylan unveiled a new, electric approach, appearing onstage with members of the highly amplified Paul Butterfield Blues Band. Folk purists were enraged that Dylan had "sold out" to commercial rock & roll, but when *Bringing It All Back Home* was released that fall, most seemed to stay with him, and he added a horde of new fans. Dylan's imagery got really wild here, though it still maintained links—sometimes melodic, sometimes lyric—to the folk tradition and still festered with elliptical protest. "Maggie's Farm," the minor hit "Subterranean Homesick Blues" and the abstract ballads "Mr. Tambourine Man," "Love Minus Zero/No Limit" and "She Belongs to Me" were peppered with lines that became slogans for the emerging youth culture: "You don't need a weatherman to know which way the wind blows," "Don't look back," and a dozen more. More importantly, by fusing the Chuck Berry beat of the Rolling Stones and the Beatles with the leftist, folk tradition of the folk revival, Dylan really had brought it back home, creating a new kind of rock & roll (dubbed folk rock but soon pervasive everywhere, inspiring in part the Beatles' *Rubber Soul* and *Revolver* and the Stones' *Between the Buttons*) that made every type of artistic tradition available to rock. The message was libertarian and it was seized and spread by cover versions (the Byrds had a No. 1 hit with "Mr. Tambourine Man") and imitators like the Turtles and P. F. Sloan, who wrote slangy West Coast approximations of Dylan's "message" lyrics, such as "Eve of Destruction," and plain rock bands. Dylan opened up new country for everyone in popular music, because his songs were unrestricted in meter, because his lyrics were so untamed and because his singing voice, once described as sounding like "a cow with its leg caught in a fence," made it clear that there was a difference between the great voice and the great rock & roll voice.

Highway 61 Revisited and *Blonde on Blonde,* released within six months of each other in 1966, are Dylan's two best albums, and two of the greatest in the history of rock & roll. *Highway 61* is a series of parables and tall tales, founded on tough rock guitar lines and crashing, dense keyboards. Its highlight was "Like a Rolling Stone," a six-minute hit single that said everything that needed to be said about the social revolution of the Sixties in simple terms. For that alone, the album would be essential; with the addition of "Ballad of a Thin Man," "Just Like Tom Thumb's Blues" and the title song, among others, it was an immediate hit and major Sixties classic. *Blonde on Blonde,* recorded in Nashville, is a two-record set that stakes out much the same turf and takes it, if anything, even further. Dylan's songs, some of them ostensibly about love affairs but all possessed of a barbed wit and some imponderably profound aphorisms, hit their peak with "I Want You" (a Top Twenty hit), "Just Like a Woman" and "Visions of Johanna." This was rock & roll at the farthest edge imaginable, instrumentalists and singer all peering into a deeper abyss than anyone had previously imagined existed.

Not surprisingly, what followed was withdrawal. In June 1966, Dylan had a motorcycle accident that forced him to withdraw from public appearances for the next year and a half. While recuperating, he and his backup band (the Hawks, later to become the Band) worked on new material, released a decade later as *The Basement Tapes,* which included some formidable songs, including "This Wheel's On Fire," "Too Much of Nothing" and "Tears of Rage"; some flat-out rock & roll, such as "Please Mrs. Henry" and "Odds and Ends"; and dozens of others, some sketchy, many brilliant. The two-record set that finally appeared isn't even all-inclusive, and includes many songs that feature the Band without Dylan, but it is a brilliant document nonetheless, made more legendary because of the long delay between creation and release. (Bootleg copies surfaced throughout this period, of course.)

The record that did appear was Dylan's quietest, most modest in years. "John Wesley Harding" is an outlaw tale, similar in theme to Guthrie's "Pretty Boy Floyd." The rest of the record has a kind of acceptance of bizarre phenomena—"I Dreamed I Saw St. Augustine" and "All Along the Watchtower, " for instance—that indicated that Dylan had made some kind of reconciliation with the terms of his vision. *John Wesley Harding* is an intensely religious record, one that owes almost as much to country music as to rock. It is a lovely album, with a spirit of resilience beneath its placid surface.

■ **Dylan** / Col. PC-32747
★★★ **Nashville Skyline** / Col. PC-9825
★★★ **New Morning** / Col. PC-30290
★★★★ **Pat Garrett and Billy the Kid** / Col. PC-32460
★ **Self-Portrait** / Col. C2X-30050
Dylan's diminished energy cost him almost nothing in the way of adulation, but *Nash-*

ville Skyline, which painted a picture of a blissfully romantic, decidedly uninteresting fool, nearly did. (The legions of admirers would hold on, though not forever.) *Nashville Skyline* contained a couple of striking songs, notably the great ballad "Lay Lady Lay" and a charming duet on the early "Girl from the North Country" with Johnny Cash. But in general, the album succumbed quickly to the vices of country music, its central idiom, without much awareness of C&W's strengths. It is typified by such babble as "Country Pie."

If *Nashville Skyline* was failed country, *Self-Portrait* was a disaster that crossed all generic boundaries. For the first time, Dylan attempted to interpret the songs of some of the writers who had followed him in the folk-rock movement, making himself ridiculous with versions of Paul Simon's "The Boxer" and Gordon Lightfoot's "Early Mornin' Rain," surrounding these with a batch of wholly uninspired originals. As Greil Marcus put it at the time, "I once said I'd buy an album of Bob Dylan breathing hard. But I never said I'd buy an album of Dylan breathing softly." *Blonde on Blonde* is probably the best two-record set in the history of rock & roll; *Self-Portrait* is almost certainly the worst double set ever done by a major artist.

Dylan, released a couple of years later, is an act of vengeance, with outtakes from *Self-Portrait,* put out by Columbia while Dylan was recording for Asylum in 1974. It features Joni Mitchell's "Big Yellow Taxi" and a version of "A Fool Such as I," the Presley hit, both guaranteed to net only horselaughs. Dylan has lost his sense of humor in the Seventies; this is as close to a joke as has been available from him in the last decade.

Dylan's immediate response to the negative critical and commercial reception of *Self-Portrait* was *New Morning,* released only three months later. While the songs are occasionally exceptional—particularly "Went to See the Gypsy," an obvious Elvis parable—the music is too diffuse to be really effective. Far better is his soundtrack to *Pat Garrett and Billy the Kid,* the Sam Peckinpah film in which Dylan had a minor role. The title song isn't much, but "Final Theme" and "Knockin' on Heaven's Door" have an epic grandeur reminiscent of Dylan's best electric work, though they are much more modestly presented.
★★★★ **Before the Flood** / Asy. 201
★★★★ **Blood on the Tracks** / Col. PS-33235

★★★★ Desire / Col. PC-33893
★★★ Hard Rain / Col. PC-34349
★★ Planet Waves / Asy. 7E-1003
★★★ Street Legal / Col. JC-35453

In 1974, Dylan signed with David Geffen's Asylum Records; the company was then in the forefront of recording the singer/songwriter movement that was the most obvious inheritor of the songwriting tradition he'd founded in the Sixties. But his initial release there, *Planet Waves,* sounded hasty, unfinished. He was once more recording with the Band, something he had not done for a full album (except for the still mysterious—at that point—*Basement Tapes*), but there simply was not enough good material to produce the sort of major work expected from a performer of Dylan's stature. The best songs—"You Angel You," "Wedding Song," "Forever Young"—were simply adequate, and the rest were far less than that. *Before the Flood* is a two-record live set from the tour that followed the release of *Planet Waves.* Dylan reinterprets all of his old material drastically, singing the lyrics as though they either mean nothing at all or something very different from what we've always understood them to signify. This can be discomforting, but it is at least interesting, and with the able support of the Band, always at its best onstage, the record can reach the point of fascination.

Blood on the Tracks and *Desire* are the two best records Dylan has made since *John Wesley Harding.* The former is a bitter chronicle of love affairs gone wrong, whose best songs—"Tangled Up in Blue" and "Simple Twist of Fate"—might have been as great as anything he'd ever done if his band had offered him adequate support. Unfortunately, the playing was ragged and perfunctory; Dylan has never liked the strictures of modern recording technique,

and spontaneity has worked well for him in the past, but working with relative amateurs has kept his work from greatness here. Similarly, *Desire,* much more ambitious in scope, lacks only a great band. With love songs like "Sara," such topical numbers as "Hurricane" and "Joey" (about the imprisoned boxer Rubin "Hurricane" Carter and gangster Joey Gallo, respectively) and simple rockers like the ironic "Mozambique," it could have been a masterpiece. Still, these remain his best recent works. *Hard Rain,* the live album from Dylan's 1976 tour, the Rolling Thunder Revue, is simply inconsequential, without the differences of interpretation that make *Before the Flood* fascinating. *Street Legal* (1978) is weird beyond immediate comment.

★★★★ Bob Dylan's Greatest Hits / Col. PC-9463
★★★★★ Bob Dylan's Greatest Hits, Vol. 2 / Col. PG-31120

Dylan's first *Greatest Hits* package was assembled by Columbia while he was recuperating from the motorcycle accident: it contains all the obvious pre-*John Wesley Harding* material and is distinguished only because it marks the only LP appearance of "Postively 4th Street," the followup to "Like a Rolling Stone," and because the package contains a really horrible Milton Glaser poster of Dylan with rainbow-colored hair—a true psychedelic relic.

The second *Greatest Hits,* a two-record set, was compiled in 1973, this time with Dylan's cooperation. It's a model of the best of form, with unreleased tracks, a live cut, several previously uncollected singles and a smart selection of the most representative songs not included on the other set. In a way, *Greatest Hits, Volume 2* is the album that gives the best representation of what Bob Dylan has wrought in popular music, as a composer, lyricist and performer. Whatever his recent failures, he remains one of the greatest rockers of all time. — D.M.

THE DYNAMIC SUPERIORS
★★★ Dynamic Superiors / Mo. M7-822
★★ Give and Take / Mo. M7-879
★★ Pure Pleasure / Mo. M7-841
★ You Name It / Mo. M7-875

The Dynamic Superiors arrived at the right place, Motown, at the wrong time. About a decade too late, to be exact. By 1975 no one at the studio knew what to do with a traditional R&B vocal group, let alone one with a falsetto lead singer who is explicitly gay. So they were farmed out to writer/producers Nick Ashford and Valerie Simpson, then having career problems of their own. The resultant album, *Dynamic Superiors,* is better than anyone expected. Ashford and Simpson threw commercial considerations aside and crafted eleven lush, old-fashioned romantic ballads. Lead vocalist Tony Washington gave all of them masterful readings in the style of early Aretha Franklin.

Half of the next album, *Pure Pleasure,* was wasted on fair-to-middling disco-material, but it's not without its rewards. The followup, *You Name It,* was handled by an assortment of staff writers and producers and is unduly crass and impersonal. — R.G.

RONNIE DYSON

★ **(If You Let Me Make Love to You Then) Why Can't I Touch You / Col. C-30223**
★ **Love in All Flavors / Col. PC-34866**
★ **One Man Band / Col. KC-32211**
★ **The More You Do It / Col. PC-34350**

From teenaged *Hair*-graduate and one-hit wonder ("Why Can't I Touch You") to nightclub stylist produced by Natalie Cole's producers, Dyson has remained a bantamweight purveyor of Broadway soul. — S.H.

THE EAGLES

★★★ **Desperado** / Asy. 5068
★★★ **Eagles** / Asy. 5054

With "Take It Easy," the Eagles took to flight fueled by a pint of Jackson Browne, a case of tequila and commercial tastes honed by the highlights of L.A. country rock. There was a bed of rhythm guitars and deftly executed harmonies to soften the edges for pop tastes, and enough rock rhythms to attract the kid on the street. Their image was L.A. hippie/cowboy stud, and their lyrics matched—women were left behind with a recommendation to take it easy. With producer Glyn Johns, they conceived the rock band as outlaws in *Desperado,* a pleasurable concept piece that introduced "Tequila Sunrise" and the by-now-standard title tune.

★★★ **Hotel California** / Asy. 6E-103-A
★★★ **On the Border** / Asy. 7E-1004
★★★ **One of These Nights** / Asy. 7E-1039
★★★★ **Their Greatest Hits** / Asy.
  6E-105-A

With producer Bill Szymcyzk along to lend a hand, the Eagles sharpened their hit potential. More and more, the emphasis shifted to rock, with Glenn Frey's riffing guitar supplying the edge to songs like "Already Gone" (*Border*) and "One of These Nights." Like the rockers, Don Henley's ballads—most notably "The Best of My Love"—had appeal by virtue of their slick craftsmanship. The singles demanded immediate attention, and were increasingly the highlights of the albums. Lesser tunes were burdened by slick execution. With little lyrical depth to sustain them, they fell into the shadows of the singles, making *Greatest Hits* the essential Eagles LP. The Eagles had taken the folk rock of the Byrds and the early Burritos, mixed in a dose of jive Castaneda-like wisdom, and dressed it in boutique commerciality.

Hotel California was the Eagles' first album since Joe Walsh replaced Bernie Leadon, a move that gave them three lead guitarists steeped in rock. The album is built around the guitars, giving the usual battery of ballads and rockers a moodier, more electric sound. With nary a hint of responsibility in their voices, they sing of Los Angeles' decadent culture, and in the end personify the smugly detached professionalism of much of that city's music. — J.B.M.

EARTH QUAKE

★★★ **Earth Quake** / A&M 4308
★★★ **8.5** / Beserk. 0047
★★★ **Leveled** / Beserk. 0054
★★★ **Rockin' the World** / Beserk. 0045

The little San Francisco band that tried. The A&M debut LP is probably this mainstream group's least-affected album, since it was recorded in the early Seventies, while the band was still influenced by mid-Sixties pre-psychedelia and more interested in stylish harmonies than bludgeoning guitar. *Rocking,* a live LP, is a bit of a letdown, especially since it was released on the heels of a fine series of Beserkley singles (included on that label's compilation, *Chartbusters*). The band's heart is perennially in the right place (covers of everything from the Easybeats' "Friday on My Mind" to Lou Reed's "Head Held High") but the performances are plagued by a garage-band spirit of sameness. This band has it in them, if it just wouldn't try so hard. — M.G.

EARTH, WIND AND FIRE

★★★ **All 'n' All** / Col. JC-34905
★★★ **Another Time** / War. 2WS-2798
★★★ **Earth, Wind and Fire** / War. 1905
★★★★★ **Gratitude** / Col. PG-33694
★★★ **Head to the Sky** / Col. PC-32194
★★★★ **Last Days and Time** / Col.
  KC-31702

★★★ **Open Our Eyes** / Col. PC-32712
★★★★ **Spirit** / Col. PC-34241
★★★★ **That's the Way of the World** / Col. PC-33280
★★★★ **The Best of Earth, Wind and Fire, Vol. 1** / Col. FC-35647
★★★★ **The Need of Love** / War. 1958

Maurice White, the vocalist/percussionist who is the energy behind EW&F, put this band together from a bunch of Chicago slum kids. When it started back in 1971, its music was closer to the street than it has become over the years. At first impression the group was like a straighter R&B version of the Art Ensemble of Chicago. Mystic and celebratory, the songs bridged into loose, jazzlike horn colors and elongated rhythms the likes of which recent EW&F fans probably wouldn't recognize.

When EW&F switched labels, it changed personality. White has reworked the personnel, expanded the fold and turned EW&F into one streamlined hit-cutting factory. All the while that same religious spirit not only maintained but came through even more strongly, if only because the size of its audience grew. To see EW&F on stage was to behold a gospel experience that was an existential hosanna guaranteed to heal your ills. *Gratitude,* a two-disc set (one disc recorded live), presents the band in its truest environment. The latter Seventies have grown up with EW&F hits like "Shining Star," "Celebrate" and "Sing a Song," some of the most joyous moments in modern music. — B.M.

EBONYS
★★★ **Ebonys** / Phil. 32419

Along with the Intruders, the Ebonys represented the greasier side of Gamble and Huff's soul stable, an intriguing quartet that combined male falsetto and baritone leads with a breathy female voice. The *Ebonys* is a collection of Philadelphia International singles from the late Sixties and early Seventies. Though it's uneven, it has a number of charming and sweaty moments. — J.MC.

BILLY ECKSTINE
★★★★ **Mr. B and the Band** / Savoy 2214
★★ **The Modern Sound of Mr. B** / Trip 5567

Billy Eckstine was at one time America's permier baritone crooner. His rococo phrasing on songs like "Cottage for Sale" and "Jelly Jelly" influenced a score of later singers. Eckstine also carried a formidable bop showcase band that featured at various times Charlie Parker, Dizzy Gillespie, Dexter Gordon and Gene Ammons (to name but a few). The notables on the Savoy LP include Art Blakey, Sonny Stitt, Gordon and Ammons, and this double album covers Eckstine's career from 1945 through 1947—his peak years. The Trip album is a so-so ballad collection, a reissue of a 1964 Mercury set. Eckstine's voice had already frayed and the record is only of marginal interest. — J.MC.

ECSTASY, PASSION AND PAIN
★★★★ **Ecstasy, Passion and Pain** / Rou. 3103

Long-lasting Seventies soul vocal group hit its stride with this 1974 album, including three Top Twenty R&B hits: "I Wouldn't Give You Up," "Good Things Don't Last Forever" and "Ask Me." — D.M.

EDDIE AND THE HOT RODS
★★★ **Life on the Line** / Is. 9509
★★★★ **Teenage Depression** / Is. 9457

A pair of excellent, uncharacteristically lighthearted New Wave—not punk—albums from England, circa 1977-78. *Teenage Depression,* the debut, is a transitional effort, including some cover versions that are obvious relics of a pub-rock approach abetted by intelligent record collecting: not just "96 Tears" and "The Kids Are All Right," but also "Get Out of Denver," Bob Seger's Chuck Berry-style anthem. On *Life,* producer and cowriter Ed Hollis (oddly, the only Eddie in the band isn't a performer) takes a firmer hand, with results a bit more intense and not quite as satisfying. But the Rods do have one magnificent song on that record, the British hit single, "Do Anything You Wanna Do," which is pure and powerful mainstream rock, uncorrupted by its hedonistic message. — D.M.

THE EDDIE BOY BAND
★★ **The Eddie Boy Band / MCA 2153**
When your better-than-average bar band sets out to play in the styles of the current Top Ten FM playlist, they are usually pleasing. When they have Josh Leo's good spirits and a fresh, modest instrumental lineup, as does Eddie Boy, they can even make good derivative records. — B.T.

DUANE EDDY
★★ **Duane Eddy's 16 Greatest Hits / Jamie 3026**
★★ **Pure Gold / RCA ANL1-2671**
★★★ **The Vintage Years / Sire SASH-3707/2**
Unless you're a student of Fifties and Sixties rock guitar, these don't hold up well. Eddy's low, "twangy" guitar style imbued the instrumental single with Top Ten power, but most of his subsequent hits sound like reworkings of his first big one, "Rebel Rouser." The Sire LP has an interesting liner note by Greg Shaw, but its four sides of twang are numbing. — K.T.

RANDY EDELMAN
★ **If Love Is Real / Ari. AL 4139**
Despite guest appearances from an all-star session cast, Edelman never gets past the bad habits picked up from Elton John and Harry Chapin. — J.S.

THE GRAEME EDGE BAND
★★ **Kick Off Your Muddy Boots / Thresh. THS 15**
★★ **Paradise Ballroom / Lon. PS 686**
The Moody Blues drummer's seasoned outfit, including Adrian and Paul Gurvitz, plays lukewarm pop. The frequent orchestration damages matters further. There are some good chord changes and melodies, but the bulk is surprisingly unmemorable chaff. — C.W.

DAVE EDMUNDS
★★★★★ **Dave Edmunds and Love Sculpture—The Classic Tracks—1968/1972 / One Up/EMI OU 2047 (Import)**
★★★ **Get It / Swan 8418**
★★★ **Subtle as a Flying Mallet / RCA LPL1-5003**
★★★ **Tracks On Wax 4 / Swan 8505**
Edmunds is a sort of Welsh rock *Wunderkind,* noted as a guitarist, producer and minor pop-rock guru, whose work with Nick Lowe, Graham Parker, the Flamin' Groovies and others has helped keep the heart of the matter alive through a dolorous decade.

The EMI import includes not only much of the best from Love Sculpture, Edmunds'

Sixties band, a power trio which specialized in frantically paced urban blues and electrified versions of Bizet and Khachaturian, but also tracks from his excellent 1972 solo debut, *Rockpile.* Unfortunately, the three American LPs show Edmunds to slightly less advantage, as his obsession with recapturing the magic of the Sun records and Phil Spector productions of previous years becomes a mania for imitating them. Quite simply, these lack the bite of the earlier solo tracks. — M.G.

JOHN EDWARDS
★★★ **Life, Love and Living / Coti. 9909**
An unashamedly hardcore Southern soul album, *Life, Love and Living* is a creditable attempt by producer David Porter to update the mid-Sixties Memphis sound. Edwards is a malleable vocalist who seems most comfortable when imitating Al Green (and in early 1977, he joined the Spinners). Thoroughly derivative but fun. — J.MC.

JONATHAN EDWARDS
■ **Have a Good Time for Me / Atco 7036**
■ **Lucky Day / Atco 36-104**
■ **Rockin' Chair / Rep. 2238**
■ **Sailboat / War. BS 3020**
The most unctously dumb of all the hippie singer/songwriters. His hit, "Sunshine" (on a now-deleted Atco LP), sells what he usually does—peace and bliss in the country, contempt for anyone who's not following along. It is the best of a truly miserable body of work. — D.M.

STONEY EDWARDS
★★ **Blackbird / Cap. ST-11490**
★★★★ **Mississippi You're on My Mind / Cap. ST-11401**
Edwards' intense, grainy, Haggard-like voice is heard to best effect on *Mississippi,* which is marred only by his overly sentimental reading of the title song. Most of these tunes are quite sentimental, in fact, but Edwards has an unerring melodic flair that compensates handsomely—and "Jeweldene Turner (The World Needs to Hear You Sing)" is a brilliant slice of country life. While *Mississippi* is mainstream country, *Blackbird* is "progressive"; it's an interesting group of songs, but Chip Taylor's production is distractingly cute. — J.MO.

WALTER EGAN
★★★ **Fundamental Roll / Col. PC-34679**
★★★ **Not Shy / Col. JC-35077**
Fleetwood Mac's Lindsey Buckingham and Stevie Nicks produced *Fundamental* and

Buckingham did *Not Shy* alone, and there's enough of his guitar and her voice on both to make Egan's rather puerile songs seem an East Coast equivalent of the everyday California teen dream, from the backseat romance to the call of the freeway . . . almost. Finally, both crash under the weight of Egan's postured immaturity. Still, for *Rumours* fans, useful accessories. — D.M.

EL CHICANO
★★★ **Cinco / MCA 401**
★★ **El Chicano / MCA 69**
★★★ **Pyramid of Love and Friends / MCA 2150**
★ **The Best of Everything / MCA 437**
★ **Viva Tirado / MCA 548**
El Chicano mixes heavy traces of Latin heritage with equally strong North American Top Forty influences. Technically excellent, but too often overcome by filler that's mostly movie music with a Latin beat. *Cinco* is probably their best; *Pyramid* their most successful. — A.N.

ELECTRIC FLAG
★★★★ **A Long Time Comin' / Col. CS-9597**
★★ **The Best of the Electric Flag / Col. C-30422**
★ **The Electric Flag / Col. CS-9714**
Electric Flag pioneered the rock-horn-band style, but never seemed to know whether they were playing blues, pop or rock. The first album, *A Long Time,* is an inspired failure, with the four key members, guitarist Michael Bloomfield, singer Nick Gravenites, drummer/vocalist Buddy Miles and bassist Harvey Brooks, at the top of their form. *Electric Flag* loses Bloomfield, as well as inspiration. *Best of* is unnecessary, since the three tunes from the second album are turkeys. Get *A Long Time Comin'* instead. — P.H.

ELECTRIC LIGHT ORCHESTRA
★★★★ **A New World Record / Jet JZ-35529**
★★★★ **Eldorado / Jet JZ-35526**
★★★ **Electric Light Orchestra II / Jet JZ-35533**
★★ **Face the Music / Jet JZ-35527**
★★ **No Answer / Jet JZ-35524**
★ **Olé ELO / Jet JZ-35528**
★★★ **On the Third Day / Jet JZ-35525**
★★★ **Out of the Blue / Jet JZ-35530**
■ **The Night the Lights Went Out in Long Beach / War. 56-058-Z (Import)**
Roy Wood originally conceived ELO as an expansion of the Move's horizons—an em-

bracement of the semiclassical vision the Beatles discarded after "I Am the Walrus." *No Answer* was pedantic, boasting Wood's monotonous arrangements and few memorable melodies, and by the time *II* was recorded, Wood had departed and Movemate Jeff Lynne emerged as the group's resident leader/writer, all changes for the better. Lynne has a better ear for tying electric and chamber ensemble instrumentation; with recurring motifs and classy interludes (as with *Third Day*), the incessant rotation of string-heavy ballads and jarring rockers could become ponderous.

On *Eldorado,* Lynne concentrated more on his innate rocker's instincts and an uncontrollable urge for pilfering Beatle themes, including allusions to an epic story outline. *Face the Music,* on the other hand, eschewed the conceptual format and paid the price: it is ELO's most unctuous outing to date (not counting the live import and *Olé,* a premature greatest-hits package). But with *New World* (a Dvořák pun) and *Out of the Blue,* Lynne managed to blend his wit and nonpareil rock sensibilities in mini-orchestral fashion for the first time. — M.G.

ELEPHANT'S MEMORY
★ **Angels Forever / RCA APL1-0569**
★ **Sometime in New York City / Cap. SVBB-3392**
Elephant's Memory epitomizes the late-Sixties concept of leftist music from the streets. Gritty, hard-edged rhythm & blues, spiced by the raunchy sax playing of Stan Bronstein, is the band's meal ticket, rock & roll is its slogan, and the Hell's Angels and John Lennon are its patrons and compatriots. Unfortunately the band's recordings never captured its best qualities. *Angels Forever* is a production mess and the one moment of glory, backing Lennon on *Sometime in New York City,* was a sloppy, unfocused disaster that did neither justice. (Now deleted.) — J.S.

THE ELEVENTH HOUR
★★ **Hollywood Hot / 20th Cent. T-511**
★★★ **The Eleventh Hour's Greatest Hits / 20th Cent. T-435**
Ten years after "Music to Watch Girls By," Bob Crewe is found relaxing as a funk auteur too concerned with the comedic possibilities of controlling everything from writing to production to worry about the disco market. *Greatest Hits'* "Nasty," one of the funniest self-critical moves in production history, shows what common

ground John Entwistle, Frank Zappa and Flo and Eddie share with the Ohio Players. It also proves that disco and Fifties nostalgia are related trends. (Now deleted.) — J.S.

ELF
■ **Elf / Epic KE-31789**
Cheap platers too incompetent for as bad a judge of heavy-metal horseflesh as Ritchie Blackmore. Destined for the glue factory. — J.S.

YVONNE ELLIMAN
★★ **Love Me / RSO RS-1-3018**
★★ **Night Flight / RSO RS-1-3031**
Elliman played Mary Magdalene in *Jesus Christ Superstar,* and her version of "I Don't Know How to Love Him" was probably the best that befuddled gospel produced. Later, she toured as guitarist and singer with Eric Clapton, cutting several soul- and rock-influenced solo records that were better than these, which are straight out of the Bee Gees' breathless pop-disco mold. Although they squander her resources—at her best, Elliman's a belter—they did earn her a couple of hits, with a remake of Barbara Lewis' "Hello Stranger," and "If I Can't Have You," one of the soundtrack highlights from *Saturday Night Fever.* — D.M.

RAMBLIN' JACK ELLIOTT
★★★★ **Essential Jack Elliott / Van. VSD-89/90**
★★★★ **Hard Travelin' / Fan. 24720**
★★★ **Jack Elliott / Ev. 210**
★★★ **Jack Elliott / Prest. 7453**
★★★ **Ramblin' Jack Elliott / Prest. 7721**
★★★★ **Songs to Grow On / Folk. 7501**
Elliott was one of the most colorful figures in folk music in the Fifties and Sixties, a traveling companion of Woody Guthrie shortly before the latter was hospitalized, and a great influence upon the early Bob Dylan. The self-styled "last of the Brooklyn cowboys" (he was raised there) traded on an outlaw persona that was pure invention, but his singing is among the best the genre's recent adherents have to offer. *Hard Travelin'* is all Guthrie songs, the *Essential* a fine survey of his work on traditional material, while *Songs to Grow On* is a set of Guthrie's children's songs. All are affecting, but only a bit more so than his work on the other albums listed here, which contain more traditional material. Many other Elliott records are out of print, and worth seeking out, except perhaps for

the final flawed few he made for Warners in the late Sixties. — D.M.

JOE ELY
★★★★ **Honky Tonk Masquerade / MCA 2333**
★★★★ **Joe Ely / MCA 2242**
Terrifically talented Texas singer/songwriter/bandleader gives a pretty good approximation of the excitement his band can generate in a live performance on these late Seventies records. Ely's powerful voice handles honky-tonk stompers, ballads and Tex-Mex ranchero tunes with equal facility, and producer Chip Young gets it all down cold. This is about as good as country-rock playing gets, combining the bite and release of rock emotion with the rich musical foundation of country (Ely's band includes accordion and steel guitar).

The albums also present two fine songwriters in Ely ("I Had My Hopes Up High," "Gambler's Bride") and Butch Hancock ("She Never Spoke Spanish to Me," "Suckin' a Big Bottle of Gin," "Tennessee's Not the State I'm In"). — J.S.

EMERSON, LAKE AND PALMER
★★★★ **Brain Salad Surgery / Atl. 19124**
★★★ **Emerson, Lake and Palmer / Atl. 19120**
★★ **Love Beach / Atco 19211**
■ **Pictures at an Exhibition / Atl. 19122**
★ **Tarkus / Atl. 19121**
★★ **Trilogy / Atl. 19123**
★★ **Welcome Back, My Friends, to the Show That Never Ends / Mant. MC3-200**
★ **Works, Vol. 1 / Atl. 2-7000**
★ **Works, Vol. 2 / Atl. 19147**
Between Keith Emerson's organ-stabbing, flag-burning debut in the Nice and Greg Lake's involvement in the first screaming edition of King Crimson, folks had high hopes for this band. Drummer Carl Palmer's automaton frenzy was just icing on the cake. The first album (*Emerson, Lake and Palmer*) was a good debut, with some pretty romanticism from Lake's lyrics, and was generally more subdued than people expected. But there was something changing in Emerson—he seemed bent on earning a maestro award and often overreached himself. *Trilogy* was out-to-lunch *Sturm und Drang,* portentous, pretentious and about as distended as it comes. There was no viable excuse for *Pictures at an Exhibition.* It's hard to take in the spirit in which it was made (i.e., seriously), and if you look at it as comedy, it's at least . . . not funny. Then

came the three-year layoff, giving our beleaguered heroes some time to do whatever it is rock stars do when they get fat.

The comeback started inauspiciously enough with a crummy live album featuring Emerson and his grand piano doing somersaults in a stage show about a titan rock band (predating Kiss as definitive Marvel comics material). But *Brain Salad Surgery* was one breathless tour de force—"Karn" in particular was remarkably pyrotechnical entertainment. *Works* is appropriately titled, like a tuna-fish hero sandwich with so much glop on it you forget what you're eating. Talk about distended; this is like shouting at a void that couldn't care less. — B.M.

BUDDY EMMONS

★★★ Buddies (with Buddy Spicher) / Fly. Fish 041
★★★ Buddy Emmons Sings Bob Wills / Fly. Fish 017
★★★ Steel Guitar / Fly. Fish 007

Excellent steel guitarist on records that feature some of the best Nashville players in a less commercialized context than usual, and material including (besides great Bob Wills hits on 017) songs as diverse as Dylan's "Nothing Was Delivered," Ben E. King's "Spanish Harlem" and seventeenth-century German classical music. — D.M.

EMOTIONS

★★★ Chronicle / Stax 4121
★★★★ Flowers / Col. PC-34163
★★★ Rejoice / Col. PC-34762
★★★ Sunshine / Stax 4100

Flowers is a first-rate album, conceived by Earth, Wind and Fire's Maurice White who provides sparse and imaginative instrumental direction for the former Stax-Volt female trio. Lead singer Wanda Hutchison wrote the bulk of the songs, and her lead vocals add a moody, dark undercurrent to the album's flowery romanticism. *Rejoice* continues in that mold, though with less spectacular results; *Sunshine* is a collection from the group's work at Stax, released after "Best of My Love" (from *Flowers*) became a pop hit. — J.MC.

ENGLAND DAN AND JOHN FORD COLEY

★★ Dowdy Ferry Road / Big 76000
★ Fables / A&M 4350
■ I Hear the Music / A&M 4613
★ Nights Are Forever / Big 89517
★★ Some Things Don't Come Easy / Big 76006

Their thin, tightly harmonized voices slide neatly over their acoustic guitar-piano mix, the neat hooks highlighted by cautious studio players. Few have had the laid-back FM radio formula down quite so well as England Dan and John Ford Coley. If they sound like watered-down Eagles suffering from chronic car-radio ennui, this may be only appropriate to their obsessive theme: return. A whole army of traveling salesmen would be unlikely to spend so much time preparing for homecomings.

In sound, their albums have evolved steadily from a nearly folk lightness to full pop production (on *Nights Are Forever*) with elements derived from Southern rock bands (reflecting their touring experience). But there is no noticeable change in the quality of their very limited writing and performing. — B.T.

BRIAN ENO

★★★★★ Another Green World / Is. 9351
★★★★ Before and After Science / Is. 9478
★★★ Here Come the Warm Jets / Is. 9268
★★★★ Taking Tiger Mountain by Strategy / Is. 1-3001

After breaking with Roxy Music in 1972, Eno's solo albums earned him critical acclaim, a small cult following and an avant-garde reputation that has kept him away from the larger audience. His rock albums, comprising the third of his records still in print, reveal a fascination with lead-background relations and the more curious uses to which melody can be put. *Here Come the Warm Jets* redefined the Roxy style as a fantastic vehicle for Eno's surreal unsentimental irony. The electronically altered guitars of Robert Fripp and Ray Manzanera are devastating and Eno's vocals are a magical tour de force. *Taking Tiger Mountain by Strategy* is the perfection of Eno's rock mannerism, with guitars imitating machinery over a rhythm section of mesmerizing force and insistence.

Another Green World, a far more personal record, is the fruit of a series of experimental albums Eno made with Robert Fripp, including the deleted *Discreet Music*. On *Green World*, Eno's almost motionless settings become a kind of dreamlike pastorale meditation. Much of the music uses a well-ordered, though exotic, rhythm track under beautiful melodic fragments or wide washes of organ and synthesizer. But the wholly static piano-synthesizer duets (continued on *Low* and *Heroes*, Eno's collaborations with David Bowie) are what make *Green World* Eno's masterpiece. — B.T.

JOHN ENTWISTLE
★★★ **Mad Dog / MCA 2129**
★★★ **Smash Your Head against the Wall /**
MCA 2024

Who bassist John Entwistle had the misfortune to be a good songwriter in a group (the Who) with a great one. *Smash Your Head against the Wall* showcased his instrumental talents (bass, keyboards, trumpet, trombone, fluegelhorn) and proved that his ballads were as good as his hard-rock songs. Unfortunately his second and best solo album, *Whistle Rymes,* is now out of print. But *Mad Dog* is a witty and eclectic collection ranging from the early-Sixties girl-group parody of the title track to "Cell Number Seven," Entwistle's homage to the Montreal jail where the Who spent a night during their 1974 tour. — J.S.

EQUALS
★ **Unequaled Equals / Laur. 2045**
Pop-soul group struck in 1968 with "Baby Come Back," which is not included here (probably because it was recorded for RCA). — D.M.

ESCORTS
★★ **3 Down 4 to Go / Ali. 9106**
The Escorts capitalized on the fact that the members were prison inmates. (The title refers to their then-current status.) This is their second album, and it's ragged and none too original. But falsetto ballads find the Escorts shining. (Now deleted.) — J.MC.

ESPERANTO
■ **Danse Macabre / A&M 3624**
■ **Esperanto Rock Orchestra / A&M 4399**
■ **Last Tango / A&M 4524**
Don't you think that anyone who is capable of envisioning a world that speaks one language (the utopian Esperanto) ought to be bright enough to know that "rock orchestra" is an idiot's contradiction in terms? Me too. (Now deleted, in any language.) — D.M.

DAVID ESSEX
★★ **All the Fun of the Fair / Col.**
PC-33813
★★ **David Essex / Col. PC-33289**
★★ **Rock On / Col. PC-32560**

Essex was marketed as a Seventies teen idol, which garnered him one hit—"Rock On"—and the lead in a pair of rock & roll movies, *That'll Be the Day* and *Star-Dust,* playing sort of a cross between Paul McCartney, David Bowie and Donovan. Unfortunately, he never sang all that well, and his songwriting was even more miserable, though it dominated each of these records. — D.M.

BETTY EVERETT
★ **Happy Endings / Fan. 9480**
★★ **Betty Everett Starring . . . / Trad. 2073**
Neither of Betty Everett's two best-known hits, "You're No Good" and "It's in His Kiss," are included on the Tradition album, a collection of early-Sixties Vee Jay material. The record is a mixed bag: blues, novelties, ballads and three duets with Jerry Butler. Though they had a few hits, Butler and Everett don't really mesh as a vocal team and schmaltzy big-band arrangements mar all but a handful of songs. *Happy Endings* was done in conjunction with arranger Gene Page. Unfortunately some faceless charts and a rather nondescript choice of songs fail to give Everett much to work with. — J.MC.

THE EVERLY BROTHERS
★★★ **Golden Hits of the Everly Bros. /**
War. 1471
★★★★★ **The Everly Brothers' Greatest**
Hits / Barn. 6006
★★ **Very Best of the Everly Bros. / War.**
1554

The Everly Brothers took Fifties rock 'n' roll nearest to country, but also nearest to the deadly soft rock of the Sixties and Seventies. An important influence on such folk rockers as Simon and Garfunkel, a few of the hits they cut from 1957 to 1962 are among the best of rock's first era: "Bye Bye Love," "Wake Up Little Susie," "Bird Dog," "All I Have to Do Is Dream," "Problems," "('Til) I Kissed You," all cut for Cadence and included on the Barnaby collections. The Warner material, cut from 1962 to 1967, is thinner, but still includes a few good songs, notably "Cathy's Clown," "Walk Right Back" and "Crying in the Rain." The Barnaby LP is a must; the Warner LPs are a luxury. — D.M.

FABIAN
★ **16 Greatest Hits / Trip**
  TOP-16-20
Fabian's three 1959 hits ("Turn Me
Loose," "Tiger" and "Hound Dog Man")
are on one side of this collection. Along
with such matter as the egregiously tacky
"Kissin' and Twistin'," they provide a
time-capsule memoir of this instant asphalt
Elvis from Philadelphia. — F.S.

FABULOUS POODLES
★★★★ **Mirror Stars / Epic JE-35666**
Witty, energetic and a little absurd, the
Poodles combine elements from Ventures
and Yardbirds guitar lines to Kinks/Who
chord structures in the service of cleverly
written cameo songs. The title track became a minor hit in early 1979. — J.S.

FACES
★★ **Ooh-La-La / War. B-2665**
★★★★ **Snakes and Ladders: The Best of**
  Faces / War. B-2897
This is the Faces with Rod Stewart and
Ron Wood. Beginning in 1971, the group
originally known as the Small Faces (Ian
MacLaglan, Ronnie Lane and Kenny
Jones) began touring and recording with
the taller Stewart and Wood, making some
of the hardest-driving (albeit sloppiest)
rock of the decade. The group had an
enormous cult following, but its rather
loose spirit could hardly be contained on
record. Distressingly, only the group's least
successful original recording, *Ohh-La-La,*
remains in print, while the more creative
Long Player and *A Nod's as Good as a
Wink* are no more. *Snakes and Ladders* is,
for now, the definitive document: it includes the Top Forty hit "Stay with Me"
and most of what was best and brashest
from their other discs. — D.M.

JOHN FAHEY
★★★★★ **Best of John Fahey (1959-
  1977) / Tak. 1058**
★★★★★ **Blind Joe Death / Tak. 1002**
★★★ **Christmas with John Fahey, Vol. 2 /
  Tak. 1045**
★★★★ **Dance of Death and Other Planta-
  tion Favorites / Tak. 1004**
★★★★ **Death Chants, Breakdowns and
  Military Waltzes / Tak. 1003**
★★★ **Essential John Fahey / Van. VSD-
  55/56**
★★★★ **Fare Forward Voyagers / Tak.
  1035**
★★ **John Fahey Guitar / Van. 79259**
★★★★ **John Fahey/Leo Kottke/Peter
  Lang / Tak. 1040**
★★★ **Old Fashioned Love / Tak. 1043**
★★★★ **The New Possibility (Xmas Al-
  bum) / Tak. 1020**
★★★ **The Yellow Princess / Van. 79293**
A native of Takoma Park, Maryland,
Fahey is a self-taught guitarist who picked
up his encyclopedic knowledge of rural
blues and folk forms from field excursions
and intensive study in the Library of Congress. His early work was culled from a variety of influences, including Elizabeth
Cotten, Blind Willie Johnson, Charley Patton and Mississippi John Hurt. In 1958,
Fahey borrowed money to form his own
record company, named it after his hometown and proceeded to record the most famous obscure album of recent times, *Blind
Joe Death.* Even though there were only
ninety-five copies of the record available
for distribution, the album was extraordinary enough to plant the seeds of a
world-wide reputation for the guitarist.
Fahey later re-recorded the songs from that
LP and *Death Chants.*
  As he continued recording, Fahey began
to extend his performance and composition

under the influence of classical composers (especially the Russian romantics) and film soundtracks (he cites *The Thief of Baghdad* as a major influence). His catalogue, aside from the two rather uninspired attempts for Vanguard (which are repackaged as *Essential*), remains a magnificent selection of revitalized and experimental blues forms.

As if his exacting musical contribution weren't enough, Fahey has played an important entrepreneurial role as well. On successive field trips in the South, he rediscovered Bukka White (who he recorded for his own label) and Skip James. He also discovered guitar prodigy Leo Kottke and sponsored Kottke's recording career on Takoma. In the process of writing his master's thesis on bluesman Charley Patton, Fahey collaborated with the late musicologist/guitarist Al Wilson, whom he subsequently introduced to blues collector Bob Hite, inadvertently spawning the late-Sixties blues and boogie band, Canned Heat. — J.S.

BILLY FAIER
★★★ **Banjo / Tak. 1037**
Virtuoso banjo players are not exactly a common commodity, but Faier has long been a respected instrumentalist and composer. Unlike Bill Keith, Faier experiments with the sound of the instrument rather than with musical form. The result, as with John Fahey, is part classical, part folk. — I.M.

FAIRPORT CONVENTION
★★★★★ **Fairport Convention / A&M 4185**
★★★★★ **Unhalfbricking / A&M 4206**
The most distinctive and satisfying folk-rock LPs since the Byrds' first. Emerging in the late Sixties, the English Fairports were built around singer Sandy Denny and guitarist/vocalist Richard Thompson; they combined a timeless lyricism, an archivist's purism, rock & roll punch, Cajun good times, superb original songs and a sense of humor that led to marvelously idiosyncratic readings of obscure Dylan tunes. Their emotional commitment to their material was extraordinary. Had the Band been British, this is what it might have sounded like.
★★★ **Liege and Lief / A&M 4257**
Well-thought-out traditional fare, but save for Denny's astonishingly passionate "Matty Groves," lacking in excitement.
★★ **Full House / A&M 4265**

★ **Nine / A&M 3603**
Denny had left the group (Thompson would leave after *Full House*); she later made decent LPs with Fotheringay and the Bunch, plus two inconsistent solo discs, rejoining an in-name-only Fairport in 1975 for two desultory sets on Island (her best performance after *Liege and Lief* came with "The Battle of Evermore," on Led Zeppelin's *Zo-So* LP). Only Thompson's haunted "Sloth" rescues *Full House* from tedium; *Nine*, which followed other forgettable Fairport albums, is tedium itself.
★★★★ **Fairport Chronicles / A&M 3530**
Two discs that collect much of the best of the first three albums, plus highlights of later LPs ("Sloth") and solo projects. Eminently listenable and enduring. — G.M.

ANDY FAIRWEATHER-LOW
★★ **Be Bop 'n' Holla / A&M 4602**
★★ **La Booga Rooga / A&M 4542**
★★★ **Spider Jiving / A&M 3646**
English cult figure writes and sings hard rock and an occasional ballad. Primitive singing, sophisticated writing. Boozy, desperate, buffoonish. — S.H.

YVONNE FAIR
★★★ **The Bitch Is Black / Mo. 5-832**
Fair is a fiery singer who is fit into a world of Norman Whitfield arrangements. No style really dominates here, but some nice ballads, a red-hot funk song ("You Can Walk Out the Door if You Wanna") and a novel reworking of the Gladys Knight/Kim Weston chestnut, "It Should've Been Me," make the album more than a curiosity. — J.MC.

MARIANNE FAITHFUL
★ **Marianne Faithful / Lon. PS-423**
This ghoulish singer's greatest contribution to musical history is that she provided a suitable focus for Mick Jagger's contemplation of quiet evil. "As Tears Go By" (1965) is the product of that inspiration, and it's the Rolling Stones' version, not hers, that realizes its implications. Jagger later wrote "Sister Morphine" in memory of their feelings together. — J.S.

FAITH, HOPE AND CHARITY
★★★ **Faith, Hope and Charity / RCA APL1-1100**
★★ **Life Goes On / RCA APL1-1827**
This mixed trio (two women, one man) might be only vaguely soulful MOR singers if not for producer Van McCoy's typi-

cal disco embellishments, which make them sound slick and smooth. They scored big in 1975 on the R&B charts with "To Each His Own," which went to No. 1. — D.M.

RODERICK FALCONER
★ New Nation / U. Artists LA651–G
★ Victory in Rock City / U. Artists LA777–G

Falconer used to be poet Rod Taylor, but the fact that he's an aesthete with a decent sense of rhythm and melody doesn't excuse the way that his album graphics and song lyrics toy with totalitarian imagery. — D.M.

GEORGIE FAME
★ All Me Own Work / Rep. K-44183 (Import)
★★★★ Fame and Price Together / Col. 64392 (Import)
★★★ Georgie Fame / Is. 9293 (Import)

Georgie Fame was an anomaly in mid-Sixties British rock. His earlier hits, "Yeh-Yeh" and "Point of No Return" (both on the out-of-print Yeh-Yeh Imperial LP 12282), revealed the jazz vocal values of Jon Hendricks, Ray Charles and Mose Allison, while the 1968 "Ballad of Bonnie and Clyde" was a honky-tonk novelty.

By the Seventies, Fame's commerical light had dulled but his blues were sharpened, acquiring a howling urgency in the powerful *Shorty* (Epic BN 26563, also out of print). His pairing with fellow R&B devotee Alan Price on *Fame and Price Together* is a vibrant affair, each spurring the other to some of the most vaulting and mellifluent vocals either has ever recorded.

Fame's subsequent *All Me Own Work* is its own pronouncement: he is an interpreter, not a songwriter. The 1975 *Georgie Fame* spans the breadth of his influences, from scat to New Orleans dance blues, but most indelibly suggests that Fame could make it today by striking the same elegant R&B pose as Boz Scaggs. — M.G.

FANCY
★ Fancy Turns You On / RCA APL1-1482

This hard-rock outfit is best noted for its cover of the Troggs' "Wild Thing" and a 1974 hit, "Touch Me," both on the band's now-deleted Big Tree debut. The RCA set is a waste of time. (Now deleted.) — J.S.

THE FANTASTIC FOUR
★★★ Got to Have Your Love / Westb. 306
Detroit meets Philly soul, and the merger

succeeds on this 1977 LP by a Motor City vocal quartet. The obvious singing debt is to the Temptations, but while the Four owe far more to Motown-style singing than any of the Philadelphia International groups (even Harold Melvin and the Bluenotes), producer Dennis Coffey's arrangements are right out of Gamble and Huff's staple bag of Philly tricks. Perhaps as a consequence, a couple of ballads on side one are the record's highlights. — D.M.

FANTASTIC JOHNNY C.
★★ Boogaloo Down Broadway / Phil.-L.A. 4000

Johnny is another one-hit wonder. "Boogaloo Down Broadway," a chunky soul shuffle, broke into the Top Ten in late '67, so Johnny went into the studio and filled out an album's worth of cuts, most of which sound like attempts at remakes. He charted three other singles before disappearing altogether, but none of them made it past the Top Thirty, which means they didn't get much airplay and were quickly forgotten, as was Johnny. — J.S.

FARAGHER BROTHERS
■ Family Ties / ABC 1009
■ Faragher Brothers / ABC D-941
Tepid blue-eyed soul, poorly produced. — S.H.

DON FARDON
★★ The Lament of the Cherokee Indian Reservation / GNP 2044
The Raiders picked up on the title track and made it a big hit—having done it first (and better) is Fardon's chief claim to fame. The rest of the album is similarly oriented to pop-blues, about halfway between Eric Burdon and Tom Jones—sometimes an interesting place but more often precisely nowhere. — D.M.

MIMI AND RICHARD FARIÑA
★★ Best of Mimi and Richard Fariña / Van. 21/22
★★★ Celebrations for a Grey Day / Van. VSD 79174
★★ Memories / Van. 79263
★★★ Reflections in a Crystal Wind / Van. VSD 79204

Richard Fariña's novel, *Been Down So Long It Looks Like Up to Me,* is a slightly surreal classic of the transitional period between beatniks and hippies. His marriage to Joan Baez' sister, Mimi, was a folk-revival fairy tale; so was his death, on his birthday, in a motorcycle crash.

The albums are the relics of the first flowering of rock's self-conscious poesy, and they suffer from it. But Fariña's best songs ("Pack Up Your Sorrows" on *Celebrations,* for instance) could be as chilling as any of the other Dylan-inspired folk-rock singers, and he used rock rhythm sections more effectively on *Reflections* than any folk rocker except Dylan and the Byrds. *Memories* is a collection of leftovers, however, and the *Best of* doesn't hold up very well. The original albums, cut in 1964 and 1965, are interesting if dated period pieces. — D.M.

MIMI FARIÑA AND TOM JANS
★★ Take Heart / A&M 4310

Mimi Fariña joined with Jans, who was then a disc jockey, after the death of her husband, Richard Fariña. Jans has had a fairly successful solo career since then as a kind of country-rock writer and singer. Fariña and Jans' collaboration was brief and forgettable. — D.M.

MARK FARNER
★ Mark Farner / Atco 18232

Ex-Grand Funk Railroad guitarist/singer/songwriter extends his penchant for naive politics ("Ban the Man") and cheap hedonism ("Dear Lucy") into solo album territory with predictably rotten results. Outside the inspired amateur context of Grand Funk, Farner is just another misguided and overly sentimental hippie songwriter. — J.S.

FATBACK BAND
★ Man with the Band / Sp. 1-6717
★★ Night Fever / Sp. 6711
★★★ Raising Hell / Event 6905
★★★ Yum Yum / Event 6904

Better-than-average Seventies disco funk outfit. — J.S.

FAT LARRY'S BAND
★★ Feel It / WMOT WM 625

Pedestrian disco funk takeoff on Bill Cosby's TV hero, Fat Albert, who is both more naturally cool and more bearable (on Saturday-morning TV, at that, which is saying a lot). (Now deleted.) — D.M.

FELA AND AFRIKA 70
★★★★ Zombie / Mer. SRM-1-3709

Multi-instrumentalist (tenor and alto sax, piano) Fela leads a hot fourteen-piece band in a blend of African rhythms with Western melodic and harmonic elements. The side-long title track shows the band at its best. — J.S.

JOSÉ FELICIANO
★ And the Feeling's Good / RCA AFL1-0407
★ Compartments / RCA APD1-0141
★ Encore! José Feliciano's Finest Performances / RCA AFL1-2824
★★ Feliciano! / RCA AFL1-3957
★ Feliciano/10 to 23 / RCA AFL1-4185
★ Fireworks / RCA AFL1-4370
★ For My Love . . . Mother Music / RCA APL1-0266
★ José Feliciano / RCA AFL1-4421
★ Just Wanna Rock 'n' Roll / RCA APL1-1005
★★ Sweet Soul Music / Priv. 2022

This blind Latino's records are very uneven collections of indiscriminately selected material, some of it in Spanish. A virtuoso twelve-string guitarist and fiery singer, Feliciano puts his heart on his sleeve for a ballad, but his rockers are embarrassingly stiff. *Feliciano!* contains his first and biggest hit, "Light My Fire," and is a classic make-out album. *Sweet Soul Music,* coproduced by Jerry Wexler, almost succeeds in establishing an R&B base. — S.H.

DICK FELLER
★★★ No Word on Me / Asy. CM-1
★★★ Some Days Are Diamonds / Asy. 7E-1044

A populist in the extreme, Dick Feller worries about the common man—about his foibles and follies, his triumphs and tragedies—and is quick to spot a phony. Feller's most famous song is "Abraham Martin and John," a 1970 Dion hit, and like that one, his tales have real power ("Daisy Hill" on the deleted *Dick Feller Wrote* and "Cry for Lori" on *No Word on Me* are devastating chronicles of wasted lives). Feller, who surely checks his wallet when he encounters such praise, is careful to maintain a neat balance between the poignant and the humorous in his repertoire. Charlie McCoy, Johnny Gimble, Pete Drake and other redoubtable players lend to each record a superior quality of musicianship; but it's Feller's rich baritone voice, his haunting melodies and his compelling lyrics that endure and place him several cuts above the Harry Chapins of this world. — D.MC.

NARVEL FELTS
★★★★ Greatest Hits / Dot 2036
★★★ Inside Love / ABC 1080
★★★ Narvel / Dot 2095
★★★ Narvel the Marvel / Dot 2033
★★★ This Time / Hi 32098
★★★ Touch of Felts / Dot 2070
Felts is a melodramatic country singer strongly influenced by Roy Orbison and Charlie Rich. His quavering, strangely intoned singing makes for some flashy histrionics, especially on his ballads, and he covers a wide range of pop, soul and country material, but with formula country-pop productions. His version of "Drift Away" introduced him in 1973 to the country audience; his subsequent country hits have been "Reconsider Me," "Somebody Hold Me (Until She Passes By)" (1975) and "Lonely Teardrops" (1976). — J.S.

FREDDY FENDER
★ Are You Ready for Freddy / Dot-2044
★ Before the Next Teardrop Falls / Dot-2020
★★ Best of Freddy Fender / Dot 2079
★ If You Don't Love Me / Dot 2090
★ If You're Ever in Texas / Dot 2061
★ Merry Christmas from Freddy Fender / ABC 2101
★ Rock 'n' Country / ABC 2050
★ Swamp Gold / ABC AA-1062
Freddy Fender (formerly Baldemar Huerta) is a classic example of a man ahead of his time. Long a legend in South Texas, he was the typical Mexican-American rock & roller in the heyday of the Gulf Coast Sound, when Huey Meaux' productions of such people as Cookie and the Cupcakes and B. J. Thomas and the Triumphs set a standard for sentimental triplet-laden rock & roll. That Fender was in and out of prison only added to his stature. He was widely regarded—especially with Doug Sahm perpetuating his myth by constantly

performing Fender's superlative "Wasted Days and Wasted Nights"—as the big contender from Texas, if ever his energy could be harnessed by a major record company. His Texas records—in both Spanish and English, on small local labels—were brilliant, if erratic, examples of Tex-Mex rock & roll. His vibrato vocals (especially in person, since his records always sounded as if they were cut in a garage) were unmatched.

Then Meaux got Fender a deal with a major record company and turned him into not only a country singer but an overworked goose that strained to lay golden eggs. Even "Wasted Days and Wasted Nights" sounded weak and exhausted. His biggest hits—"Before the Next Teardrop Falls" and "Roses Are Red," from the *Teardrop* album—are good country songs but thin Freddy Fender. The entire series of albums above shows Fender to have turned into a competent if unexciting country singer; but that is not saying a great deal given the usual level of country albums. — C.F.

JAY FERGUSON
★★★ All Alone in the End Zone / Asy. 7E-1063
★★★ Thunder Island / Elek. 7E-1115
Ex-Spirit and Jo Jo Gunne leader Ferguson spices these more pop-oriented albums with all the things that made Jo Jo Gunne a fine band, albeit unsuccessful: short, high-energy pieces with great rock melodies, highlighted by appealing vocals. Guest appearances by Joe Walsh, Vitale and Lala. — A.N.

BRYAN FERRY
★★★ Another Time, Another Place / Atl. 18113
★★ In Your Mind / Atl. 18216
★★★ Let's Stick Together / Atl. 18187
★★★★ "These Foolish Things" / Atl. 7304
Bryan Ferry, the once and future Roxy Music vocalist, likes to shock, and what could be more shocking than to discover Bob Dylan's "A Hard Rain's a-Gonna Fall" side by side with Lesley Gore's "It's My Party" on an album called *"These Foolish Things"*? The point—and he made it best the first time—is the idea of pop as a unified spectrum encompassing everything from . . . well, from Bob Dylan to Lesley Gore. There was only one problem: instead of elevating Gore, Ferry chose to diminish Dylan.

Another Time, Another Place is a pointless but entertaining reprise of the same theme. *Let's Stick Together* is a compilation of flip sides from Ferry's British singles (many of them remakes of his Roxy Music material), noteworthy for its view of love as a masochist's playground.

On *In Your Mind,* the emphasis shifts from Ferry the bandleader to Ferry the solo star: this is his first solo album composed exclusively of original material. It's also a disappointment—partly because it searches for new routes to artiness, partly because it's sloppy. — F.R.

FEVER TREE
★★ **Fever Tree / MCA 551**
Houston band had one great hit ("Where Do You Go?" popularly known as "San Francisco Girls"), which stands as a nostalgic testament to the Summer of Love, and is included here. The rest is 1968's version of eclectic padding (Beatles, Buffalo Springfield, Wilson Pickett). — A.N.

W. C. FIELDS
★★ **Best of W. C. Fields / Col. CG-34144**
★★ **Further Adventures of Larson E. Whipshade / Col. KC-33240**
If you don't know his films, these bits seem funny in their incongruity, but not as funny in their intended way: a consummate blast of misanthropic sarcasm. Fields could do something no other comedian has ever done, which is to despise amusingly. The records never even suggest this ability. — K.T.

THE FIFTH DIMENSION
★★★ **Greatest Hits on Earth / Ari. 4002**
■ **Star Dancing / Mo. M7-896**
Choreographed bionic sepia. *Greatest Hits* contains the "essential" Sixties hits, "Aquarius," "Up Up and Away," etc. *Star Dancing* features the group without its lead vocal team, Marilyn McCoo and Billy Davis, Jr., and it is completely lackluster. — S.H.

MIKE FINNIGAN
★★★ **Black and White / Col. JC-35258**
★★★ **Mike Finnigan / War. B-2944**
Finnigan's list of keyboard session credits leading up to his 1976 solo debut is impressive. He played with the Jerry Hahn Brotherhood, Dave Mason, Maria Muldaur, Paul Simon, Jimi Hendrix and Doctor Hook. On his self-titled debut, Finnigan ranges through a variety of styles under the production direction of Jerry Wexler. *Black and White* is more of the same. The impact is of a pop R&B album. — J.S.

FIRE AND RAIN
■ **Living Together / 20th Cent. T-481**
Muzak for the Patchouli Suite at the Niagara Hilton. Could they possibly have listened to a noted singer/songwriter on that big night? — J.S.

FIREBALLET
★★ **Night on Bald Mountain / Pass. DQ 98010**
★★ **Two Too / Pass. PPSD-98016**
Synthesized versions of classical symphonic themes set to rock rhythms never were a particularly good idea, and Fireballet does nothing to aid that fashion's cause. You get the characteristic late-Seventies panoply of flashy keyboard licks, but without any good reason for their existence. — J.S.

FIREFALL
★★ **Firefall / Atl. 19125**
★★ **Luna Sea / Atl. SD 19101**
Firefall, the debut of this package of country-rock middleweight, presented a blandly smooth electric/acoustic pop: pleasant but dull, predictable melodies, chords and harmonies with the barest hint of a country background. Some of Larry Burnett's songs managed a rockish edge, but former Flying Burrito Brother Rick Roberts' were sugary and MORish. The electric guitar parts were surprisingly refreshing but the saxophone awkward. *Luna Sea* offered a few catchier instances but otherwise repeated those shortcomings. — C.W.

FIRESIGN THEATRE
★★★★★ **Don't Crush That Dwarf, Hand Me the Pliers / Col. C-30102**
★★★★★ **How Can You Be in Two Places at Once When You're Not Anywhere at All? / Col. CS-9884**
★★ **Waiting for the Electrician or Someone Like Him / Col. 9518**
Peter Bergman, Philip Proctor, David Ossman and Philip Austin first appeared in 1967 as a mutant hybrid of James Joyce, Monty Hall, Douglas MacArthur and Flash Gordon. They were the first, and remain the only, comedy group whose primary medium was the stereo phonograph record itself; thus, their best albums stand up to literally hundreds of listenings. Multitracked, multileveled, multidimensional— one never gets to the bottom of them. Consistent themes recur from LP to LP: that changing TV channels is the fundamental aesthetic and political experience of modern times; that aliens long ago took over California; that the U.S.A. lost World War II (we were *fighting* fascism, remember).

Electrician, their first outing, is only fair, but contains the incredible "Beat the Reaper," the first of several game-show parodies ("Hawaiian Sellout," "Give It Back"). *Two Places* features an excellent if limited Sam Spade satire, backed with the first full flowering of Firesign genius, a time trip involving a used-car salesman, W.C. Fields and the aforementioned author of *Ulysses,* who is liberally quoted. *Dwarf,* a complete work, scrambles a fascist future, high-school madness, old movies, the Korean War, ethnic humor and uncontrolled paranoia to emerge as the ultimate answer record to *Catcher in the Rye;* it is also the greatest comedy album ever made.

★★★ **I Think We're All Bozos on This Bus / Col. C 30737**
An ambitious, overly rational work about a future run by machines and populated by clones. Spooky, but a little too obvious. And, as the Firesigns would later claim, not insane, and that hurts.

★★ **Dear Friends / Col. PG 31099**
Transcriptions from the Firesign radio show. Sometimes funny, but very conventional.

★ **Not Insane or Anything You Want To / Col. KC 31585**
Further decline: witless, noisy, unfocused.

★★ **The Tale of the Giant Rat of Sumatra / Col. KC 32730**
A halfassed comeback containing only one good joke in the course of a meandering, pointless Sherlock Holmes parody.

★★★★★ **Everything You Know Is Wrong / Col. KC 33141**
The real comeback, in which daredevil Rebus Cannebus attempts to put out the sun in the center of the earth; slaves seize power; Erich von Daniken gets his; aliens get us; Nazis emerge from the South American jungles to eat moss; and the lights go out all over the world.

★★★★ **In the Next World, You're on Your Own / Col. PC-33475**
Based loosely on the popularity of Billy Jack Dog Food ("The kind Billy Jack eats") and Marlon Brando's refusal to accept an Academy Award; terrestrial destruction continues as media pigs eat flaming death; cop shows take over TV; aliens retreat into the central cortex; and the hero knocks over a floor display of P. J. Probé wine. A triumph.

★★★★★ **Forward into the Past / Col. PG-34391**
Two LPs of Firesign's best over the years, brilliantly selected and programmed. Horrifying, death-dealing, life-enhancing.

★★ **Just Folks . . . A Firesign Chat / Butter. FLY 001**
In the ups and downs of Firesigniana, another down: mostly pallid, single-tracked parodies of Jimmy Carterland, though there is that commercial for "Confidenz in the System," a new wonder drug, and a few random lines are inexplicably hilarious. A stall, perhaps—the future calls. — G.M.

FIRST CHOICE
★★★ **So Let Us Entertain You / War. BS 2934**
First Choice (a female trio) scored heavily on the R&B charts with three of the greatest early disco hits, "The Player, Pt. 1" (1974), "Smarty Pants" and "Armed and Extremely Dangerous" (both 1973). But somehow, when Philly Groove was absorbed by Warners, the albums that contained the hits (*Armed and Extremely Dangerous* and *Smarty Pants,* both with gloriously glitzy covers) were deleted. *So Let Us* isn't bad, but it isn't nearly so hot and danceable. — D.M.

WILD MAN FISCHER
■ **An Evening with Wild Man Fischer / Biz. 2XS-6332**
Larry "Wild Man" Fischer was a character in the late-Sixties L.A. rock scene. A former patient in a mental institution, he continually pounded his pathetic songs (imitations of the hits of the day played on a broken guitar and sung with a voice that made Bob Dylan sound like Pavarotti) outside the doors of record companies, on street corners and wherever else he could get a note in edgewise. Frank Zappa recorded him in the late Sixties, a particularly vicious example of Zappa's penchant for sadistic social commentary. The results are brutal, not funny except to the emotionally immature and the socially callous, and would constitute a deleted embarrassment in recorded history if the record industry had any shame. — D.M.

ROBERTA FLACK
★★★ **Chapter Two / Atl. 1569**
★★ **Feel Like Makin' Love / Atl. 18131**
★★★ **First Take / Atl. 8230**
★★ **Killing Me Softly / Atl. 19154**
★ **Quiet Fire / Atl. 1594**
★★★ **Roberta Flack and Donny Hathaway / Atl. 7716**
In the early Seventies, Roberta Flack brought a certain refinement and gentility

to popular black music that helped pave the way for the achievements of Stevie Wonder, Marvin Gaye and Maurice White, among others. These artists owe her a genuine debt for her success in freeing contemporary black music from the stranglehold of soul conventions. Additionally, of course, there are moments of genuine beauty in "First Time Ever I Saw Your Face," "Hey That's No Way to Say Goodbye" (from *First Take*), "Reverend Lee" (on *Chapter Two*) and "Be Real Black for Me" on her collaboration with Donny Hathaway. Unfortunately, more often than not Flack substitutes artifice for feeling, and as a whole her recorded career is terribly dull and dreary.

A classic example is her cover of Aretha Franklin's "Baby I Love You," on the Hathaway duet album, where she and Hathaway decide to add a little pizazz by vamping on the final "goodbye." The only problem is that "goodbye" is the one word that an intelligent interpretation would not emphasize—it destroys the meaning and thrust of the story line. The point seems trivial, but it helps explain why their version is so tedious. Flack's work is often tedious more from carelessness than anything else.

First Take and *Chapter Two* had a certain folk-and-funk verve that make them her best, but the success of "First Time Ever" destroyed Flack as an LP artist. From then on, her focus became smart, stylish singles and the albums became bloated, lifeless afterthoughts. — R.G.

FLAMIN' GROOVIES
★ Now / Sire K-6059
★★★ Shake Some Action / Sire 7521
★ Still Shakin / Bud. 5683
This is a curious group indeed: a second-wave San Francisco outfit that attempted a one-band British invasion. Unfortunately, they timed it wrong; in the early Seventies no one cared about their kind of rock revivalism. In 1976, however, they reappeared with *Shake Some Action,* as unabashedly derivative as ever but brighter, cleaner and infinitely more exuberant. Later in the year, Buddah raided its vaults for material from the 1970-71 sessions that had produced their long-since-deleted second and third albums. Released as *Still Shakin,* these tracks suggested reasons other than timing for their initial failure, and 1978's *Now* suggested that *Action* was a fluke. — F.R.

FLASH
★★ Flash in the Can / Cap./Sov. SM-11115
Tony Kaye is sort of a Seventies answer to Peter Best. It was Kaye who quit Yes in 1971, when it was just another band with a funny name, in order to form Flash. You know what became of Yes—Flash unfortunately fizzled after three albums, Kaye leaving after the first. But anyone hearing Flash in 1972 would have given them equal chances for success. Besides Kaye, Flash had a fluid, innovative guitarist in Peter Banks, and a very British vocalist in Colin Carter. Sounds like Yes in its formative years. A must for Anglo-rock historians, although only the second of the group's three LPs remains in print. — A.N.

FLASH CADILLAC
★★★ Flash Cadillac and the Continental Kids / Epic KE 31787
★★ Rock & Roll Forever / Epic PEG 33465
★ Sons of the Beaches / Priv. 2012
Flash Cadillac, like Sha Na Na, works under the burden of either covering oldies it can't really match in spirit or execution, or writing its own songs to compete with classic oldies. In each case, the attempt often fails, but Flash and the boys' introductory album (1972) is the best of the genre. Their cover of "Muleskinner Blues" is so rabid it works. The album's upbeat songs are randy and wry, the ballads full of reverb but free of coyness.

Their first producer was Kim Fowley. Later, producers Toxey French and Jerry Leiber, trying to sweeten the product, lost the essence. *Rock & Roll Forever* packages the first album with two additional sides of stolid remakes, and *Sons of the Beaches* offers one side of ersatz Beach Boying and another of petrified bubblegum. The group also appeared in *American Graffiti,* as the band at the hop. — F.S.

FLEETWOOD MAC
★★★ Fleetwood Mac in Chicago / Sire 2XS-6009
★★★ Then Play On / War. 6368
In its original incarnation, Fleetwood Mac was the best traditional band to arise from the late-Sixties British blues revival. The band was spearheaded by Peter Green, whose lean lead guitar cut with the precision of an Anglo B. B. King. Its first two albums on Epic (now deleted), and the sessions produced in Chicago with such great

traditional bluesmen as Willie Dixon and Otis Spann, revealed more than a trendy affection for the blues. The second album, *English Rose,* put blues chops to invigorating use, with such highlights as "Black Magic Woman" (made famous by Santana, who duplicated Green's solo) and the haunting British instrumental hit "Albatross."

Then Play On was Green's last album with Fleetwood Mac, and its deviation from pure blues ("Oh Well" segued from a blistering blues boogie to a near-classical ending) and strong rock contributions from guitarist Danny Kirwan pointed toward new directions for Mac. Even more bizarre changes were in the offing, though—Peter Green renounced the rock life for menial-laboring ascetic Christianity, and guitarist Jeremy Spencer, whose work with Mac was characterized by his lecherous voice and slide guitar, played on *Kiln House* and then became a Child of God. Thus ended the first chapter of one of the strangest career patterns in rock & roll.

★★★★ **Bare Trees / War. K-2278**
★★★★ **Future Games / War. 6465**
★★★ **Heros Are Hard to Find / War. 2196**
★★★ **Kiln House / War. 6408**
★★ **Mystery to Me / War. K-2279**
★★ **Penguin / War. 2138**

This long stretch of Fleetwood history, from 1970 to 1975, is a jumble of personnel changes, with the quality of the releases fluctuating accordingly. The crucial addition was Christine Perfect from a blues band called Chicken Shack. Perfect found both a singing and marital role in Fleetwood Mac as she married bassist John McVie. Her solid piano and smoky voice proved to be an exciting contrast to Kirwan's rocking sense. The latter had been the saving grace of *Kiln House,* which, despite its smooth playing, displayed an overwrought Buddy Holly fixation. *Future Games* and *Bare Trees* saw Mac gaining its sea legs in the pop-rock field, with McVie supplying the feminine warmth to contrast with Kirwan's more austere moodiness. The combination made the two records Fleetwood Mac's best work until Phase Three.

Penguin, recorded after Kirwan's departure to a solo career, found guitarist/vocalist Robert Welch taking up the compositional slack. But Welch wasn't as consistent as either Kirwan or Green, leaving Fleetwood Mac with a trio of rather lackluster albums with Christine McVie providing the best moments. While *Heros*

Are Hard to Find, Welch's final album with the group before founding the heavy-metal band Paris, showed definite improvement, his replacements prompted a change that almost nobody could have predicted.

★★★★ **Fleetwood Mac / War. K-2281**
★★★★ **Rumours / War B-3016**

Stevie Nicks, the bewitching vocalist, and Lindsey Buckingham, a muscular lead guitarist with a writing style influenced by California rock and Buddy Holly, were added in 1976, and it proved a magical catalyst. Suddenly possessing three strong writers and singers, the new Fleetwood Mac produced an album that spawned three singles and sold more than 4 million copies, becoming Warner Bros.' all-time best-seller. Drummer Mick Fleetwood and bassist John McVie, the respective Fleetwood and Mac of the group's name and the only founding members still in the band, suddenly found themselves recognized as one of the finest rhythm sections in rock. And Stevie Nicks found herself as rock's newest heartthrob and the voice of one of 1976's finest singles, "Rhiannon (Will You Ever)."

Rumours, which was recorded under typically bizarre circumstances (two romantic liaisons within the group broke up), proved that *Fleetwood Mac* wasn't a fluke. Rather, it showed what a formidable hit-making machine Mac had become, as their sound took on more of the characteristics of the best California rock without becoming stale or predictable. (The record was the runaway best-seller of 1977, selling more than 10 million copies.) McVie and Buckingham shine in particular, with her wonderfully seductive "You Make Loving Fun" and his tough-rocking "Go Your Own Way" highlighting the latest volume of a most peculiar rock & roll journey. — J.B.M.

FLO AND EDDIE

★★★★ **Illegal Immoral and Fattening / Col. PC-33554**
★★ **Moving Targets / Col. PC-34262**

Mark Volman and Howard Kaylan, the duo responsible for the Turtles, found a new niche in the early Seventies fronting Frank Zappa's Mothers of Invention under the monikers of the Phlorescent Leech and Eddie. Their subsequent solo efforts (two fine cutouts on Warner Bros. and this pair) combine elements of Zappa's soft-core porn and self-conscious parody with the slick professionalism of the Turtles. *Illegal,* the blueprint for their hilarious stage shows, is closer to their Zappa persona and is their most effective record. *Targets* is a collection of songs trying to be hits, including a remake of the Turtles' "Elenore" and some self-pitying looks at show biz. It adds up to their worst solo album. — J.S.

FLOATERS
★★★ Float On / ABC 1030
★★ Magic / ABC 1047

Imagine Barry White as a thin, four-piece group? Never mind—just remember that "Float On," this 1977 LP's hit single, is a leading contender in the Dumbest Popular Record in the Universe Sweepstakes, but it hums great. *Magic* has far fewer charms. — D.M.

THE FLOCK
★ The Flock / Col. CS-9911

Eclectic but disjointed jazz-rock. Wooden blues-based riffing, too much pointless soloing. The horns play some interesting charts but sound cold next to the dexterous violin of Jerry Goodman (later of the Mahavishnu Orchestra). — C.W.

EDDIE FLOYD
★ Experience / Mal. 6352

Eddie Floyd was one of the second rank of Stax Records stars, but he still managed a sizable body of Sixties R&B hits, most notably "Knock on Wood" and "Raise Your Hand," both often-covered bar-band staples. Floyd sang in a raw soul style only a bit less agitated than Otis Redding's, and his deleted Stax greatest-hits collection, *Rare Stamps,* is highly recommended. Until Fantasy gets around to re-releasing the old Stax masters, the 1977 Malaco album, a dismal attempt to go disco at the hands of the TK organization, is all that's left—not much. — D.M.

KING FLOYD
★★ Body English / Chim. 202
★★★ Well Done / Chim. 201

Well Done is notable for one magnificent song, "I Feel Like Dynamite," a tough slab of Southern funk honed from Floyd's biggest hit, "Groove Me" (1970). Mild reggae and less commanding funk songs make up the rest of that album and also *Body English.* — J.MC.

THE FLYING BURRITO BROTHERS
★★ Airborne / Col. PC-34222
★★★★ Burrito Deluxe / A&M 4258
★★★ Close Up the Honky Tonks / A&M 3631
★★ Flying Again / Col. PC-33817
★★★ Last of the Red Hot Burritos / A&M 4343
★★★ Sleepless Nights / A&M 4578
★★★★ The Flying Burrito Bros. / A&M 4295
★★★★ The Gilded Palace of Sin / A&M 4175

1969's *The Gilded Palace of Sin* is one of the earliest and best matchings of rock & roll and country & western, thanks to former Byrd Gram Parsons' achingly pretty and fragile tenor, tinged with a youthfully innocent Southern accent, and "Sneeky" Pete Kleinow's facile pedal steel, often enlivened with distortion effects.

Burrito Deluxe adds Bernie Leadon on guitar and a third ex-Byrd (joining Parsons and bassist Chris Hillman, Michael Clarke, on drums). The result is tougher, leaner, faster, more rocking music with Leadon and Kleinow in the forefront—less variety perhaps, but an improved group. *Sleepless Nights* (containing three non-Burrito tracks from Parsons and Emmylou Harris, recorded after the singer had left) has nine competent outtakes from sessions done at this time, and shows the more country-derived side of the hybrid.

Rick Roberts then joined, and his melodic singing and more pop-oriented writing gives *The Flying Burrito Bros.* a workable new direction. Chris Hillman assumed more control, both as a singer and writer; but the country influence was not decreasing.

The live *Last of the Red Hot Burritos,* released after the group disbanded, is an odd mixture: fiddle virtuoso Byron Berline leads a new lineup through "The Orange Blossom Special," while Hillman and Roberts play spirited but thin rock & roll. Kleinow had been replaced by Al Perkins.

Close Up the Honky Tonks, a two-record

set, is half material from the first two albums, and half passable outtakes spanning each phase of the group; adequate but unthrilling.

Flying Again marked a reassembling that had two originals (Kleinow and bassist Chris Ethridge) and another ex-Byrd, Gene Parsons. This record—along with the ensuing *Airborne,* with yet another ex-Byrd, Skip Battyn—gives only the barest hint of the earlier incarnations, instead offering faceless approximations of pop, rock and country: a weak shadow, possibly even an insult, to the pioneers of before. — C.W.

FLYING ISLAND
★ **Another Kind of Space / Van. 79368**
★ **Flying Island / Van. 79359**
Ersatz John McLaughlin, but without the fire—just the sonorous tedium of an overamped fiddle. It's stuff like this that makes nine out of ten music critics say, "When I hear the phrase 'jazz-rock,' I reach for my gun." I say it's spinach and I say the hell with it. (Now deleted.) — D.M.

FOCUS
★★★ **Focus Con Proby / Harv. ST-11721**
★★ **Focus Live at the Rainbow / Sire 7408**
★★★ **Focus 3 / Sire S-3901**
★ **Hamburger Concerto / Atco S-36-100**
★★ **Ship of Memories / Sire 7531**
The musical concepts of Focus, the first successful Dutch rock band, are roughly sketched out on the deleted *In and Out of Focus.* Although its debut album's title proved to be unnervingly prophetic in light of the band's erratic career, Jan Akkerman (guitars) and Thijs Van Leer (keyboards, vocal gymnastics) were immediately distinguishable for their obsessively eclectic instrumental skills, unabashed enthusiasm and demented sense of humor (read *I Jan Cremer* for Dutch cultural corollary) that reached its apogee on "Hocus Pocus," their first and only hit single.

"Hocus Pocus" actually appears on *Moving Waves,* also deleted, the most cohesive album of the group's early period. Besides this unlikely single—punctuated with manic yodels and frenetic guitar riffing—the LP's showcase track, "Eruption," laid the groundwork for much of the Focus music to come. A long instrumental piece in several movements, it blended jazz, rock and classical motifs with total impunity while providing a melodic context for one of Akkerman's most dramatic solos. Like many guitarists, Akkerman has always run hot and cold, his dazzling speed, versatility

and passion offset by a crushing right-hand attack and an unfortunate propensity for angular, pseudo-Coltrane lines that invariably clashed with Van Leer's softer, classical approach.

Focus 3, a double LP set, takes the extended instrumental concept (Focus was never known for vocals or lyrics that could be taken seriously) to its tenuous limits. Except for brief swells of excitement provided by selected solos on cumbersome tracks like "Answers? Question! Questions? Answers!" and "Anonymous II," this one is for hard-core fans.

Focus Live at the Rainbow, recorded at the height of the band's popularity in England, is primarily an energetic recapitulation of the first three albums with most of the crowd response coming from Akkerman's onstage pyrotechnics.

Hamburger Concerto oozes desperation from its grooves as our fun-loving Dutchmen strained for a contemporary hit feeling with some tepid disco-funk marked by Akkerman's conspicuous semi-involvement. *Ship of Memories* is essentially outtakes and filler, confirming the demise of the "original" Focus.

The "new" Focus, with Philip Catherine on guitar (he's much more graceful and fluid than Akkerman) and the venerable P.J. Proby on salubrious vocals, emerged on the ascendant with *Focus Con Proby.* With some real songs and a much more integrated instrumental approach, Focus appeared to be on the right track at last. — J.C.C.

DAN FOGELBERG
★ **Captured Angel / Epic PE-33499**
★★ **Home Free / Col. PC-31751**
★★ **Nether Lands / Epic PE-34185**
★★ **Souvenirs / Epic PE-33137**
Talented singer/songwriter and multi-instrumentalist records himself to sound like a one-man Crosby, Stills and Nash. Best when he's mooning softly, which is often. — S.H.

TOM FOGERTY
★★ **Excalibur / Fan. 9413**
Tom Fogerty, brother of John, was the first member to leave Creedence Clearwater, but his early exit hasn't helped. His songwriting is penny-dreadful, his singing not much better, and without Creedence's whiplash rhythm section, this music is just plain faceless. A nice guy winds up in the usual position. This is the only one of his four LPs still available. — D.M.

FOGHAT
★★ Energize / Bears. 6950
★★ Foghat / Bears. 2077
★★ Foghat / Bears. 2136
★★★ Foghat Live / Bears. K-6971
★★ Fool for the City / Bears. K-6980
★★★ Night Shift / Bears. BR-6962
★★★ Rock and Roll Outlaws / Bears. 6956
★★ Stone Blue / Bears. K-6977

One sun-baked stadium day, I saw Foghat flash the weapon that has made it a top Middle American rock attraction—Chuck Berry simplified and amplified into a bludgeoning torrent of chunky rhythms. The band's style hasn't really changed over the course of eight albums; rather, its attacks have become more sharply defined and the songwriting has improved. The band's appeal, nonetheless, rests on its particularly strong tunes; the rest of the album invariably reveals a wide gap in quality, and the live show is a predictable batch of them, from *Night Shift*'s 'Driving Wheel" to the title tunes from *Fool for the City* and *Rock and Roll Outlaws.*

Foghat scored an instant FM hit with its whining wah-wah treatment of Willie Dixon's "I Just Want to Make Love to You," a tune that essentially defines the style. Like Savoy Brown, from which two of the players came, Foghat's method is comparable to a meat-and-potatoes fighter who aims for the gut. The emotions of the tune are inevitably subservient to the big, metallic beat that brings in the kids. Consequently, while Foghat lacks the sense of humor to be one of Chuck Berry's best interpreters, it'll never be the worst.

Rock and Roll Outlaws is the most successful LP here; yet the qualitative difference between the live show and the records is lost in translation to the stage album. The other albums have highlights, but there's just too much retread here and not enough inspiration. — J.B.M.

FOOL'S GOLD
★★ Mr. Lucky / Col. PC-34828

Fool's Gold (once a backing band for Dan Fogelberg) fashions humdrum country rock by stealing a little from the Beatles and the Eagles, and a lot from Poco. Good background music with a breakfast of Raisin Bran, buttered toast and orange juice. Concentrate, however, on the breakfast. — D.MC.

FORCE OF NATURE
★ Unemployment Blues / Phil. PZ-34123

A forgettable record by a self-contained Philadelphia group. A memorable exception: "Do It (Till Your Back Ain't Got No Bone)," a stomping, Bohannon-styled slice of funk. — J.MC.

TENNESSEE ERNIE FORD
★★ America the Beautiful / Cap. SM-412
★★★★ Best Of / Cap. STBB-2949
★★ Book of Favorite Hymns / Cap. ST-1794
★★★ Country Hits . . . Feelin' Blue / Cap. SM-2097
★★ Faith of Our Fathers / Cap. SM-2761
★★ Great Gospel Songs / Cap. SM-2026
★★ He Touched Me / Word 8764
★★ Let Me Walk with Thee / Cap. STBB-506
★★ Make a Joyful Noise / Cap. ST-11290
★ Nearer the Cross / Cap. ST. 1005
★★ Precious Memories / Cap. SVBB-11382
★ Sing His Great Love / Cap. ST.-11495
★ Star Carol (Xmas) / Cap. SM-1071
■ Story of Xmas / Cap. SM-1964
★★ Sweet Hour of Prayer / Cap. STBB-506
★★ Tennessee Ernie Hymns / Cap. SM-756
★★ Tennessee Spirituals / Cap. SM-818
★★★ 25th Anniversary / Cap. STBB-11325

Ford's growling bass voice is employed for the most part on devotional hymns and specialty projects, but two white R&B classics, "Mule Train" and "Sixteen Tons," insure him a niche in rock & roll history. The rest is pretty much competent but forgettable. — C.F.

FOREIGNER
★ Double Vision / Atl. 19999
★★★ Foreigner / Atl. 18215

This group of British and American journeyman hard rockers, led by Spooky Tooth refugee Mick Jones, outdid most of its antecedents on its 1977 debut. It lacked all subtlety, but on that album, "Cold as Ice" and "Feels Like the First Time" transcended their limitations enough to become sizable pop hits. *Double Vision,* however, was a myopic rehash of the earlier LP, a formula approach that suggested the group belonged in the ranks of the simply banal. — D.M.

DAVID FORMAN
★★★ David Forman / Ari. 4084

A white New Yorker with an extraordinary R&B voice, Forman writes starkly arranged ballads with a tendency toward opulent imagery. Very often the street smarts triumphs over the romantic maunderings, and at such moments, Forman seems an intelligent merger of Smokey Robinson and Jackson Browne. Perhaps the best example on this 1976 LP is the oft-recorded "Dreams of a Child." — K.T.

FOTHERINGAY
★★ Fotheringay / A&M 4269
Uneven, unfocused and loosely performed, this is the sole effort by the defunct offshoot of Fairport Convention. Mainly Sandy Denny's British folk, with bits from co-member Trevor Lucas and covers of Dylan and Lightfoot. — C.W.

THE FOUR SEASONS
★★★★ Four Seasons Story / Priv. 7000
★ Helicon / War. B-3016
★ Who Loves You / War. B-2900
In the early Sixties, the Four Seasons battled it out with Motown, the Beach Boys and the Beatles for supremacy on the pop charts. Led by the piercing falsetto of vocalist Frankie Valli, they scored repeatedly with hits like "Sherry," "Walk Like a Man," "Big Girls Don't Cry," "Dawn," "Rag Doll" and "Stay." The songs epitomized the Fifties hangover era before a Sixties style developed, the era invoked by *American Graffiti*. The Private Stock collection includes all relevant Four Seasons material. The two Warner Bros. albums are lame attempts at reviving the group in the Seventies. — J.S.

THE FOUR TOPS
★★★★★ Anthology / Mo. M9-809
★★ Catfish / ABC D-968
★★★★ Four Tops: Greatest Hits / Mo. M7-662
★★★ Keeper of the Castle / Dun. DSX-50129
★★ Live and in Concert / Dun. DSX-50188
★★ Main Street People / Dun. DSX-50144
★★ Night Lights Harmony / ABC 862
★★ The Show Must Go On / ABC 1014
From their first hit, 1964's "Baby I Need Your Loving," the Four Tops were one of the grandest things about Motown. Lead singer Levi Stubbs had a huge, smoldering voice that set the group apart from the often airy music most other Motown acts made. But if the Tops' sound was not definitive, it was one of the best in Sixties soul music, as their long string of hits confirmed: "I Can't Help Myself," "It's the

Same Old Song," "Standing in the Shadows of Love." "Bernadette" and half a dozen others. The best of all was the terrifying melodrama, "Reach Out, I'll Be There," which Phil Spector called "black Dylan." Stubbs has been criticized for overemoting, but here his histrionics matched the material and the incredible production of Holland-Dozier-Holland perfectly. There are few more transcendent moments in American music.

As the Sixties waned, however, the Tops were unable to keep up with the accelerating changes fostered by the emergence of black stars like Sly and the Family Stone and Jimi Hendrix, or with the new production values brought to Motown by Norman Whitfield and Barrett Strong. Although they scored an occasional chart success, such as "Still Water (Love)" in 1970 and "MacArthur Park," of all things, in 1971, time had clearly passed them by. Moving to ABC/Dunhill in 1972 helped a bit— "Keeper of the Castle" was a Top Ten hit, and much less forced than their last few Motown discs—but soon, attempts to remain contemporary or to go pop, and confusion between the two, took a toll. While the group remains intact, with Stubbs still a distinctive singer, their recent albums have grown more and more irrelevant. — D.M.

PETER FRAMPTON
★★ Frampton / A&M 4512
★★ Frampton Comes Alive / A&M 3703
★★★ Frampton's Camel / A&M 4389
★ I'm in You / A&M 4204
★★ Somethin's Happening / A&M 3619
★★★★ Wind of Change / A&M 4348
Armed with several years of rock apprenticeship in the Herd and Humble Pie, a pretty face and an unusually seductive

electric guitar style, Peter Frampton leaped into a solo recording career with the kind of confidence that comes from knowing you have *all* the attributes to make it big. *Wind of Change,* his first—and still his best—solo effort, amply demonstrates that confidence, mingled with a sense of exhilaration at being freed from the heavy-metal exigencies of Humble Pie. The first, airy chords of "Fig Tree Bay" announce the arrival of an above average melodist but lightweight lyricist, and although the album is replete with fiery guitar work and some of Frampton's better songs ("It's a Plain Shame," "All I Want to Be," "The Lodger"), this unfortunate dichotomy was to persist in varying degrees on subsequent recordings.

Frampton's Camel featured the first Frampton group per se, and the music uncharacteristically dense and hard-edged. Troubled and autobiographical, *Camel* contains one of Frampton's most touching and durable ballads, "Lines on My Face" (to him, it *mattered*); "White Sugar"; and "Do You Feel like We Do," a typically friendly song that would become a staple in live performance.

Somethin's Happening was directionless, with little more than the gleaming title tune and some pleasant moments to recommend it. A growing Frampton trend toward one to three strong, commercial rock songs mingled in with elegant filler was becoming more apparent.

Kicking off a long and arduous American campaign of road trips, *Frampton,* his fourth LP, was infused with a languid, spacious feeling that harkened back to the first album and revitalized FM programmers' flagging interest.

Frampton Comes Alive, a double LP set complete with Frampton's best material, a *lot* of lead guitar and an adoring audience responding enthusiastically to his "nice" stage personality, did in fact capture the imagination of the listening populace and sold well over 8 million copies.

And, except for two passable Motown covers—"Signed, Sealed, Delivered (I'm Yours)" and "Roadrunner"—*I'm in You* merely confirmed the fact that Peter Frampton has little to say, but a very "pretty" way of saying it.   — J.C.C.

CONNIE FRANCIS
■ **Very Best of Connie Francis / MGM 4167**
People who missed the late Fifties may not know the answer to the question: "What's less funky than a Connie Francis movie?" The answer, in all its glitzy, depressing splendor, is right here.   — D.M.

BOB FRANK
★★★ **Bob Frank / Van. 6582**
Frank's a weedy songwriter/guitarist whose album is rife with bluesy folk tunes of boozers and dopers. Aside from his guitar playing, the only accompaniment to his singing is an occasional harmonica part.   — J.S.

ARETHA FRANKLIN
★★★ **All-Time Greatest Hits / Col. CG-31355**
★★ **Almighty Fire / Atl. 19161**
★★★★★ **Amazing Grace / Atl. 2-906**
★★★ **Aretha Franklin's Greatest Hits, Vol. 2 / Col. CS-9601**
★★★ **Aretha Live at Fillmore West / Atl. 7205**
★★★★★ **Aretha's Gold / Atl. 8227**
★★★★★ **Aretha's Greatest Hits / Atl. 8295**
★★★★ **Best of Aretha Franklin / Atl. 8305**
★★★★★ **I Never Loved a Man (The Way I Love You) / Atl. 8139**
★★★ **Laughing on the Outside / Col. CS-8879**
★★★★ **Songs of Faith / Check. 10009**
★★ **Sparkle / Atl. 18176**
★★★★ **Spirit in the Dark / Atl. 8265**
★★ **Sweet Passion / Atl. 19102**
★★★★ **Ten Years of Gold / Atl. 18204**
★★★ **The Great Aretha Franklin / Col. KC-31953**
★★★★ **Unforgettable / Col. CS-8963**
★ **You / Atl. 18151**
★★★★★ **Young, Gifted and Black / Atl. 7213**
Aretha Franklin is the greatest female singer of her generation, perhaps the great-

est all-around musical talent in black music since Ray Charles. Not only as a singer, but also as a pianist, Franklin's work is as impressive and influential as any artist's of the past two decades.

Franklin was already famous on the black gospel circuit in the late Fifties, mostly as a result of her singing at the Detroit church where her father, the Reverend C. L. Franklin (himself the author of more than two dozen preaching LPs), was pastor, but also partly as a result of the Checker LP above. In 1959, John Hammond, the legendary CBS talent scout, signed her to a pop recording contract with Columbia. Franklin's first sides there, produced by Hammond and included on *The Great Aretha Franklin,* present her as a jazz singer and sometime pianist, a limited approach given the range of her talents, but one that had excellent results. Unfortunately, almost all of her other Columbia sides were produced by a series of white pop producers, who tried to make her a black version of Barbra Streisand. This approach was generally disastrous, with an occasional thrilling exception, like "Lee Cross."

In 1967, Franklin moved to Atlantic, where she entered a long and profitable association with producer Jerry Wexler (later assisted by Arif Mardin and Tom Dowd). Her first record there, *I Never Loved a Man (The Way I Love You),* was an immediate success, not only on the R&B charts, where she had had occasional success before, but also on the pop charts, where it made the Top Ten. It was followed by a string of winners, including "Respect," a Number One hit, and the immediate followups (all of them Top Ten): "Baby I Love You," "Chain of Fools," "A Natural Woman," "Think," "(Sweet Sweet Baby) Since You've Been Gone," "The House That Jack Built" and "I Say a Little Prayer." Wexler produced Franklin in Muscle Shoals with the tremendously propulsive rhythm section he had developed while working with Wilson Pickett, capitalizing not only on her feeling for blues, but also her gospel roots, and giving her remarkable piano-playing skills more prominence. The pattern, in fact, was similar to what Ahmet Ertegun and Wexler had done with Ray Charles (another gospel-based R&B singer/pianist) in the late Fifties.

With the album *Soul '69,* Franklin began to expand her horizons ever further, into a variety of pop-jazz that was tremendously emotional and as singular as anything recent popular music has produced. Beginning in 1971, she created another series of Top Ten hits, including a brilliant gospel version of "Bridge over Troubled Water," a remake of Ben E. King's "Spanish Harlem," the driving "Rock Steady" and "Day Dreaming." But after 1974, the Wexler-Mardin-Dowd production team was discarded, first for a confusing album with Quincy Jones, *Hey Now Hey (The Other Side of the Sky),* which shared many of the flaws of her Columbia work despite the inclusion of her sister Carolyn's wonderful "Angel," and later for a series of contemporary, disco-oriented producers, including Lamont Dozier and Curtis Mayfield. The hits became much more minor and much less frequent, and Franklin, always an eccentric, seems at present to be floundering in search of a focus for her own genius.

Virtually everything Franklin has recorded is worth hearing, if only for the qualities of her voice, which is too remarkable for capsule description. The great bulk of her Columbia work remains in print, but as is usual for that company, Atlantic has allowed her catalogue to fall into disrepair. Of the first few albums she did for that label, only *I Never Loved a Man* remains in print. Now lost are such gems as *Aretha Now, Aretha Arrives* and the record that remains her supreme achievement, *Lady Soul,* which includes "Respect," "Chain of Fools," "Good to Me as I Am to You" (featuring a guitar obbligato by Eric Clapton), "Since You've Been Gone," "Ain't No Way" and Ray Charles' "Come Back Baby." All of these records are musts for soul fans, if only they can find them. Lacking that, settle for the various greatest-hits collections: *Gold* includes all the early hits, up to "The House That Jack Built"; *Greatest Hits* contains much of the best of the "Spanish Harlem" period, as well as some of the earlier records, while *Ten Years of Gold* includes the most prominent early hits and such recent near-misses as "Angel," "Until You Come Back to Me" and "Something He Can Feel."

Of the more sophisticated recent records, only the classic *Spirit in the Dark* and the more moderately successful *Young, Gifted and Black* remain. Gone are the mixed-bag *This Girl's in Love with You,* the adventurous and underrated *Soul '69,* and her two final albums with Wexler-Mardin-Dowd, *With Everything I Feel in Me* and *Let Me in Your Life* (the latter is particularly fine). *You* is a complete disaster—unredeemed even by her voice—while *Sparkle,* a Mayfield-produced soundtrack for a black-exploitation film, and the Lamont Dozier-produced *Sweet Passion* court catastrophe by not providing suitable channels for Franklin's occasionally wandering attention.

Live at Fillmore West features the only recorded collaboration between Franklin and Ray Charles, which makes it worthwhile, even though the band lacks focus; King Curtis' session with them, recorded at the same time and released as *King Curtis and the Kingpins Live at Fillmore West,* is better if less spectacular. Finally, *Amazing Grace,* a two-record set of gospel songs recorded live in Los Angeles in 1972, is a marvel in which the great star returns to her deepest roots and shines in total triumph over songs she has sung all her life. It is a perfect climax to any Franklin collection. — D.M.

CAROLYN FRANKLIN
★★★ **If You Want Me / RCA APL1-0420**
Although Carolyn Franklin has never enjoyed the commercial success of either of her sisters, she is a much richer and subtler stylist than Erma and has proved to be one of Aretha's best recent writers (most notably with "Angel"). This 1976 LP contains excellent, if unspectacular, performances of completely original tunes. (Now deleted.) — D.M.

ERMA FRANKLIN
★★ **Soul Sister / Bruns. 754147**
Erma Franklin's real claim to fame, besides being the sister of Aretha and Carolyn, is the pioneering version of "Piece of My Heart," not available on LP, which Janis Joplin turned into a Sixties anthem. On *Soul Sister,* Franklin essays late-Sixties standards, from soul numbers like "Hold On I'm Comin'" and "Son of a Preacher Man" to such instantly dated efforts as "By the Time I Get to Phoenix" and "Light My Fire." — D.M.

MICHAEL FRANKS
★★★ **Burchfield Nines / War. K-3167**
★★★ **Sleeping Gypsy / War. 3004**
★★★ **The Art of Tea / Rep. MS-2230**
Affectingly light, jazzy pop—smooth but not slick. Franks possesses a casual, slow, almost talking style of singing; his melodies and tempos are leisurely without dragging. The albums center on Joe Sample's relaxed electric piano, with generally only guitar, bass and drums accompanying. Occasional

sax and string arrangements are handled judiciously. *Sleeping Gypsy* is slightly more spacious and less restricted, though many of the same musicians appear on all of the records. — C.W.

STAN FREBERG
★ **Freberg Underground Show No. 1 / Cap. SM-2551**
★★★ **Stan Freberg Presents the United States of America / Cap. SM-1573**
★ **Stan Freberg with the Original Cast / Cap. SM-1242**
★★ **The Best of Stan Freberg / Cap. SM-2020**
These unfunny records almost conceal Freberg's small, arch sense of humor. Raised on radio, he never really overcame his contempt for television (as expressed overtly in "Tele-Vee-Shun" on *Best of* and embodied by *Underground,* half-seriously intended to bring back radio via record, or in Freberg's phrase, "pay radio"). Nowadays, this makes him sound petty and shortsighted. *Freberg Presents* is easily the best thing here, with Freberg populating the touchstones of American history (Columbus' voyage, the Boston Tea Party, etc.) with sarcastic puns in thick Jewish accents. He must be seen as an important precursor to the sublime self-consciousness of the Firesign Theatre.

These recordings do not preserve Freberg's more important and much funnier stuff: his TV commercials and ad compaigns. It was he who set Ann Miller to tap-dancing atop a Campbell's Soup can, and he who wrote the Sunkist Prune ads featuring Freberg as an off-camera interviewer pressing the new pitted prune on a disdainful fat man who, after munching one, acknowledges their deliciousness but then picks another one up and sniffs, "Still haven't gotten rid of those nasty wrinkles, though, have you?" — K.T.

JOHN FRED
★★★ **Judy in Disguise with Glasses/Agnes English / Paula 2197**
A genuine eccentric, Fred gathered a bunch of Louisiana sessionmen to fashion a sublimely commercial pop group called the Playboy Band in the late Sixties and early Seventies. "Judy in Disguise (with Glasses)" was their fluke hit single; for the rest, they purveyed a catchy white R&B sound that really rocked. Fred's immaculate taste led them to cover terrific songs by everyone from Mann and Weil to Willie Dixon, but it was on the all-original and

unfortunately final album, *Permanently Stated* (now deleted), that Fred hit his peak: delicate wit, immature romance and the purest American rock & roll.   — K.T.

FREE
★★★★ Best of Free / A&M 3663
★★★★ Fire and Water / A&M 4268
★★ Free / A&M 4204
★★ Free Live / A&M 4306
★★ Heartbreaker / Is. ILPS-9217
★★★★ Highway / A&M 4287
★★ Tons of Sobs / A&M 4198

At its best, Free walked on a tightrope of rolling drums—a voice skirting round and about the beat—and a dramatically sustained lead guitar. The music was taut and jaggedly rhythmic, with a much simpler production than most hard rock of the late Sixties—"All Right Now" squawked out of the box with raw bravado. Singer Paul Rodgers and drummer Simon Kirke brought some of these sensibilities to Bad Company, but they rarely matched the tastefully tense edge of the best Free music.

The debut album was standard British heavy blues, and the second showed potential, particularly on the slithery "I'll Be Creeping." But it wasn't until *Fire and Water,* which began with the stormy title cut and ended with "All Right Now," that Free hit its stride. Paul Kossoff established a guitar style that was simple in conception but inherently dramatic in execution, making Free an instant standout from much of the overplaying hard-rock competition. *Fire and Water* shows off Kossoff and Rodgers' burgeoning talents in their best hard-rock light; Rodgers' light, flexible blues voice took similar improvisational jumps that played off the other rhythms. *Highway* cooled down the burners, concentrating on

rhythmic cohesion with a bit more of a pop feel. With bassist Andy Fraser and Rodgers' best tunes yet ("The Highway Song," "Bodie") and the tough-riffing "The Stealer," it was probably their most consistent album.

Free subsequently lost its bearings, with a routine live album and a fairly heartless *Heartbreaker,* whose best song, the awfully hippie but nicely rocking "Little Bit of Love," is included on the *Best of Free.* Bad Company's success dwarfed Free, and Paul Kossoff died while playing with Back Street Crawler.   — J.B.M.

FREE BEER
■ Highway Robbery / RCA APL1-1733
■ Nouveau Chapeau / RCA APL1-2072

One of the singers sounds like Dylan, circa *Nashville Skyline,* with a frog in his throat; the playing is technically adequate, but lacks heart; only the dreaded Aztec Two-Step rivals this trio for lyrical vacuity.   — D.MC.

ACE FREHLEY
★★★ Ace Frehley / Casa. 7121

Kiss guitarist put together the best solo outing from that group, including the hit single, "New York Groove."   — J.S.

KINKY FRIEDMAN
★★★★ Lasso from El Paso / Epic PE-34304
★★★★ Sold American / Van. 79333

Friedman made a big splash with his '73 debut, *Sold American,* as much for his outrageous C&W stage persona, the "Texas Jewboy," as for his tremendous songwriting talents. His songs played off the self-deprecation of his ethnic joke for all it was worth, sometimes to riotous effect and sometimes into tasteless endgroove. "We Reserve the Right to Refuse Service to You" is a raucous tune that has him caught in the middle of the rednecks and Jews, a joking yokel outcast in both worlds, but "The Ballad of Charles Whitman" shows how tasteless he can be when he has a mind. The title cut is a no-nonsense classic, though, a poignant look at a washed-out cowboy star looking for a cheap rush and wondering where the glory went.

After a failed and now out-of-print second album for ABC, Friedman resurfaced on Epic in '76 with the happily indulgent smorgasbord *Lasso from El Paso.* It includes a live version of "Sold American," recorded in Colorado with Bob Dylan's

Rolling Thunder Revue, and an excellent version of Dylan's "Catfish." Texas producer Huey P. Meaux collaborated on several of the album's best tracks, such as the astoundingly funny, bad-taste parable "Men's Room, L.A.," which presents Ringo Starr in a cameo appearance as Jesus. — J.S.

FRIENDS OF DISTINCTION
★★ Greatest Hits / RCA LSP-4184
Black MOR pop of the early Seventies; funkier than the Fifth Dimension, but not much. *Greatest Hits* includes their two Top Ten singles, "Love or Let Me Be Lonely" and "Grazing in the Grass." — D.M.

FRIJID PINK
★★ All Pink Inside / Fan. F-9464
The band that grew from the late-Sixties Detroit scene, which also spawned MC5 and Stooges, had a 1970 hit with "House of the Rising Sun." This album is a few years post-hit and very ordinary. (Now deleted.) — A.N.

FRIPP AND ENO
★★★ Evening Star / Ant. AN 7018
★★ No Pussyfooting / Ant. AN 7001
Robert Fripp's intensely beautiful, heavily distorted guitar, on top of Brian Eno's hypnotically attractive electronic drones. Experimental yet realized—intriguing but eventually monotonous. The latter has shorter pieces and more variation. (Now deleted.) — C.W.

DONNIE FRITTS
★ Prone to Lean / Atl. SD 18117
They call Donnie Fritts the Legendary Alabama Leaning Man, and he got that reputation as one of Kris Kristofferson's pickers. Unfortunately, that's where he should have stayed. The most remarkable thing about this solo album is that it was one of Atlantic's unsuccessful forays into country music. Despite crisp production by Jerry Wexler and Kristofferson; despite the presence of such superior musicians and singers as Roger Hawkins, Tony Joe White, Billy Swan, Rita Coolidge and John Prine; despite such good Fritts compositions as "Three Hundred Pounds of Hongry" and "We Had It All," the album just doesn't work. Why? Fritts is not a lead singer, or any kind of vocalist at all. — C.F.

LEFTY FRIZZELL
★★★ ABC Collection / ABC 30035
★★★★ Lefty Frizzell's Greatest Hits / Col. CS-9288
★★★★ Remembering . . . / Col. KC-33882
★★★ The Classic Style of Lefty Frizzell / ABC D-861
Frizzell was a great honky-tonk country singer, influenced as a youngster by Jimmie Rodgers and later by Hank Williams. He emerged from the Texas oil country in the late Forties and had an immediate hit with his first record, "If You've Got the Money I've Got the Time." A string of country successes for Columbia followed, highlighted by "Long Black Veil" in 1959 and "Saginaw Michigan," a No. 1 hit in 1964. But honky-tonk singing fell out of commercial favor in the mid-Sixties (although Frizzell remained a favorite of such formidable C&W figures as Willie Nelson and Merle Haggard). Particularly after his move to ABC, Frizzell never again had much recording luck. He died in 1975. — C.F.

STEVEN FROMHOLZ
★★ Frolicking in the Myth / Cap. ST 11611
★★ Rumor in My Own Time / Cap. ST 11521
Fromholz is a figure in the Austin country-rock set, overrated by the genre's aficionados. He did do an excellent LP early in the Seventies with the group Frummox, but it is long deleted. These two recent albums reveal him as a good writer but lackluster performer. — C.F.

THE FUGS
★★★★ Fugs 4, Rounders Score / ESP 2018
★★★★ Golden Filth / Rep. 6396
★★★★ The Fugs / ESP 1028
★★★★ The Fugs' First Album / ESP 1018
★★★★ Virgin Fugs / ESP 1038
Only the Sixties could have produced high-quality pornographic rock. The Fugs were led by a pair of leftovers from the beat generation, poets Ed Sanders and Tuli Kupferberg, which accounts for the high-art eroticism of their first two albums (*The Fugs* and *The Fugs' First Album*), which include selections from the poetry of William Blake and A. C. Swinburne. But it was the full flowering of mass bohemia—hippiedom, if you like—that produced such carnal comedies as "Slum Goddess," "Coca-Cola Douche" and "Kill for Peace."

What's involved here is nothing less than a perfect mixture of sacrilege, scatology, politics and rock. (Among the players:

Richard Tee, Danny Kortchmar, Charles Larkey, Peter Stampfel.) The early records on ESP—all except *Fugs 4*—are a bit cruder but contain the best songs. *Golden Filth* features live re-recordings of many of them, with an all-star New York band. *Fugs 4* is the result of a liaison with the similarly mad Holy Modal Rounders.

The sound wanders from brutal, straight-ahead rock to countryish rags (particularly on the Rounders LP) to effective and af-fecting folk rock. But this isn't the pander-ing to tradition of Oscar Brand, with his "bawdy songs." The Fugs meant to be of-fensive in every way imaginable, from the political to the poetic, and they succeeded gloriously. If they haven't all been melted, it's worth looking for the several deleted LPs on Reprise, including *Tenderness Junc-tion, It Crawled into My Hand, Honest* and Ed Sanders' deleted solo LPs for that la-bel. — D.M.

FUNKADELIC
★★★ **Best of the Funkadelic Early Years /**
   Westb. WB 303
★★ **Hardcore Jollies / War. B-2973**

Best of the Funkadelic Early Years combines tracks from the first eight Funkadelic al-bums. The band, George Clinton's original spinoff from Parliament, was one of the first black bands to fuse Sly Stone and Jimi Hendrix, incorporating horn players, back-ing voices, strings, social science, science fiction song titles and Pedro Bell's sleazy mutant psychedelic covers. The combina-tion is daft, but fascinating—the deleted LPs are well worth seeking out, particular-ly *Let's Take It to the Stage* (the title track of which blasts more earnest funk competi-tors) and *Standing on the Verge. Hardcore Jollies* is a momentary lapse, coinciding with a change in record label affiliation. The music of Funkadelic is an urban soundscape—not always pretty or appeal-ing but perhaps the truest representation of urban life offered in black music. — J.MC.

FUNK FACTORY
★★ **Funk Factory / Atco 36-116**
This 1975 disco production by fusion band-leader Michal Urbaniak allows for some hot soloing but doesn't really go anywhere.

A failed experiment. (Now de-leted.) — J.S.

FUNKY KINGS
★★★ **Funky Kings / Ari. 4078**
Debut album by six-man L.A. group high-lights strong Jack Tempchin material. Sty-listically similar to the Eagles' first and just as impressive. (Now deleted.) — S.H.

RICHIE FURAY BAND
★ **Dance a Little Light / Asy. E-115**
★ **I've Got a Reason / Asy. 7E-1067**
Furay possesses a most engaging voice, perfectly suited to the melancholy country-rock love songs he wrote and sang while a member of Buffalo Springfield, Poco and the Souther-Hillman-Furay Band. But his lyrics have deteriorated with each succes-sive group, and on his solo LPs he hits rock bottom. His songs here are so flighty and devoid of any substance that the voice ceases to be sorrowful and becomes pitiful. The title song is the only redeeming item. — G.K.

LEWIS FUREY
★★ **Lewis Furey / A&M SP-4522**
★ **Lewis Furey: The Humours Of / A&M**
   SP-4594
Lewis Furey sings Seventies pop for per-verts. His cabaret of the surreal gives a fresh twist to the sophisticated trendiness of such pop nostalgia acts as Bette Midler and the Manhattan Transfer. Despite some intriguing compositions, however, his mu-sic is simply too erratic—and too obvi-ous—to succeed. It's *très avant,* yes—but *avant* what? — F.R.

FUSE
★ **Fuse / Epic 26502**
Forgettable Seventies hard rock featuring Cheap Trick's Rick Nielsen. (Now de-leted.) — D.M.

THE FUTURES
★★ **Past, Present and the Futures / Phil.**
   JZ-35458
This nondescript modern soul quintet would like to give Harold Melvin and the Bluenotes a run for their money, but it just doesn't have the chops. — D.M.

GABRIEL
- **Sweet Release / ABC D-972**
- **This Star on Every Heel / ABC D-885**

The only mystery about this horrible Seattle-area rock band is how it ever got to make *two* albums. — J.S.

PETER GABRIEL
★★★★ **Peter Gabriel / Atco 36-147**
★★★★ **Peter Gabriel / Atl. 19181**

The former Genesis vocalist's pair of identically titled solo LPs are far better than anything he did with the progressive rock band. The first (Atco) includes "Solsbury Hill," a wonderfully spirited allegory about his breakup with Genesis, and "Modern Love," a wild, Who-like rocker. "Here Comes the Flood," a piano-based melody reminiscent of Randy Newman, suggests an apocalyptic vision familiar to Jackson Browne fans. Gabriel is a witty singer and writer, and producer Bob Ezrin extracts unusual hard-rock drive from his rather diffuse songs. The second album, produced by Robert Fripp, is less accessible but more adventurous; the best songs ("D.I.Y.," "On the Air" and "Home Sweet Home") have a lucid vision and, with the addition of Fripp's guitar and electronic experimentation, mark a more complete synthesis of Genesis art-rock and the hard rock of the earlier disc. — D.M.

GALLAGHER AND LYLE
★★★ **Breakaway / A&M 4566**
★★ **Gallagher and Lyle / Cap. SM-11016**
★★ **Love on the Airwaves / A&M 4620**
★★ **Seeds / A&M 3605**
★★ **Showdown / A&M 4679**
★★ **The Last Cowboy / A&M 3665**
★★ **Willie and the Lapdog / A&M 4384**

Gallagher and Lyle was a light, melodic, somewhat bare and bland adaptation of American folk roots: tenor harmonies, acoustic guitars, harmonica, accordion, mandolin (mostly from the two Britons), bass, drums and occasional orchestration. Produced by Glyn Johns, as were *Willie and the Lapdog* (a concept album with slightly more spark) and *Seeds,* which retained most of the earlier approach yet edged toward more overt rock stylings and embellishments (saxophone, electric guitar, livelier tempos), but with infrequent success.

The Last Cowboy delved increasingly into fuller but overly scored, trivial, middle-of-the-road pop, effectively putting aside their origins. *Breakaway* all but shelved the duo's folk base. With David Kershenbaum's precise production, Gallagher and Lyle pursued the previous record's angle, only this time with little fluff, despite the blatantly pop approach, in either the melodies or the colorful, alive, more electric arrangements. The album included two of their best moments: the title cut and "Heart on My Sleeve."

Love on the Airwaves more or less duplicated its predecessor, but had weaker material and less biting playing. — C.W.

RORY GALLAGHER
★★★★ **Against the Grain / Chrys. 1098**
★★★★ **Calling Card / Chrys. 1124**
★★★ **Live in Europe / Poly. 5513**
★★★ **Photo-Finish / Chrys. 1170**
★★★ **Sinner . . . and Saint / Poly. 6510**
★★★★ **Tattoo / Poly. 5539**
★★★ **The Story So Far / Poly. 6519**

Gallagher is an Irish guitarist who has gained international (though not American) stardom as a blues/boogie shouter since the breakup of his original group, Taste, in 1971. Aside from *Live,* most of this is springy blues; the addition of piano on *Tattoo* adds depth. *Story* and *Sinner* are repackages of import LPs never or no longer available here. *Against* is standard stuff, but *Calling Card* attempts to diversify with notable success, partially because it is better crafted than Gallagher's usual, energetic spontaneity. — A.N.

THE GAP BAND
★ The Gap Band / Tattoo BJL1-2168
The gap this seven-piece, multiracial, post-R&B band would like to fill is the one left by the demise of Sly and the Family Stone. Unfortunately, this 1977 debut LP goes a long way toward confirming that Sly's eccentric ambiance isn't quite that susceptible to quick cash-ins. Thank goodness. — D.M.

JERRY GARCIA
★★ Cats under the Stars / Ari. 4160
★★ Garcia / Round 192
★★ Garcia / War. B-2582
★ Merl Saunders, Jerry Garcia, John Kahn, Bill Vitt: Live at the Keystone / Fan. 79002
★★★ Reflections / Round LA565-G/RX-107
Like other members of the Grateful Dead, when Jerry Garcia makes a solo album, it usually sounds like a mediocre Dead record. But since so much of the Dead's sound is keyed to his guitar, Garcia's LPs are generally the most interesting of the group's individual efforts.

His vocal range cracks at either end and shows all the expressiveness of a loaf of bread, so Garcia's charm clearly isn't his voice. The cover of *Reflections* depicts a body with the head of a guitar, and this neatly encapsulates his appeal. But most of these are only fodder for Dead fanatics. — J.B.M.

GARFIELD
■ Out There Tonight / Capri. 0193
A Toronto singer/songwriter, Garfield French teamed up with a crew of "progressive" musicians who operate as his synthesizer orchestra. As they stroll through trendy versions of French movie music, Garfield coughs, coos, caterwauls and generally renders his solipsistic ditties into tatters in an excruciating attempt to sound earnest. — B.T.

ART GARFUNKEL
★ Angel Clare / Col. PC-31474
★★ Breakaway / Col. PC-33700
★★ Watermark / Col. JC-34975

Expensively produced but chilly artifacts from the choirboy half of the immortal duo. "Breakaway" was a 1976 hit single (it's Gallagher and Lyle's song, not the Beach Boys'), and that LP also includes the Simon and Garfunkel reunion song, "My Little Town." *Watermark* includes Garfunkel's "Wonderful World," a rehash of the Sam Cooke tune that was a 1978 hit, but it's interesting mostly for the backing harmonies of Paul Simon and James Taylor. — D.M.

LEE GARRETT
★★ Heat for the Feets / Chrys. CHR 1109
Medium-cool soul singer with a decent grunty voice proves that wearing shades and banging a tambourine with your mouth open does not grant one Stevie Wonder's genius. Not even if you hire every great session player in Hollywood to help you out. (Now deleted.) — D.M.

LEIF GARRETT
■ Feel the Need / Scotti Bros. 7100
■ Leif Garrett / Atl. SD 19152
Okay, so Shaun Cassidy's versions of the Beach Boys aren't as bad as they seem. But that doesn't excuse *cloning* him. — D.M.

TERRY GARTHWAITE
★★ Terry / Ari. 4055
Technical overkill and emotional reticence combine to make this solo fling by the former Joy of Cooking warbler a dazzlingly cold affair. (Now deleted.) — S.H.

GASOLIN'
★★ Gasolin' / Epic PE 34149
A heartwarming debut from a Danish group that reveres Anglo-American rock customs with the same fervor its older brothers (parents?!) must have reserved for be-bop musicians: Gasolin' plays with just that much ingenuousness. This sampling of tracks recorded from 1974 to 1976 is the band's only American release, but while the spirit is fine enough, such rabid devotion seems a bit out of place this side of the water. (Now deleted.) — D.M.

DAVID GATES
★★ First / Elek. 75066
★★★ Goodbye Girl / Elek. 6E-148
★★★ Never Let Her Go / Elek. 7E-1028
If David Gates' music is predictable, it is also impressive in its own way. Above all, Gates displays a concern for lyrics and melody (indeed, for song structure) that is

nothing if not admirable and praiseworthy. But he can also be totally insipid: side two of *First* is an emotional wasteland. But if his tendency for romantic overkill is checked, Gates, as *Never Let Her Go* indicates, can be convincing both as a rocker and a balladeer. What all of this means is that it's hard to knock a guy who once had the audacity to write Bread's brilliantly sugary hits.   — D.MC.

LARRY GATLIN
★★ **High Time** / Monu. MC-6644
★★ **Larry Gatlin's Greatest Hits** / Monu. MG-7628
★★ **Larry Gatlin with Family and Friends** / Monu. MC-6634
★ **Love Is Just a Game** / Monu. MG-7616
★ **Oh, Brother** / Monu. MG-7626
★ **Rain-Rainbow** / Monu. 6633
★ **The Pilgrim** / Monu. MC-6632

Gatlin began as a folkish country writer/singer, much like a younger version of his initial sponsors, Johnny Cash and Kris Kristofferson. His 1974 debut album, *The Pilgrim,* contained a pair of fine songs, "Sweet Becky Walker" and "Penny Annie," plus notes by Cash, written in his Dylanesque, half-poetic style. Since the debut, however, he has treaded ever nearer the most saccharine banalities of Nashville country pop, something for which his rough-edged voice is hardly suited.   — D.M.

MAC GAYDEN
★★ **Hymn to the Seeker** / ABC D-960
★★★ **Skyboat** / ABC D-927

Competent session guitarist tries his hand at a solo career without much luck. His playing and songwriting are good, especially on his 1975 debut, *Skyboat,* but there's insufficient focus to give his delivery substance. (Now deleted.)   — J.S.

MARVIN GAYE
★★★★★ **Anthology** / Mo. M9-790
★★★★ **Greatest Hits** / Tam. T6-348
★★★★ **Here My Dear** / Tam. T-364
★★★ **I Want You** / Tam. T6-342
★★★★★ **Let's Get It On** / Tam. T5-329
★★★ **Live** / Tam. T6-333
★★★ **Marvin Gaye Live at the London Palladium** / Tam. T7-352
★★★★ **Marvin Gaye's Greatest Hits** / Tam. T7-252
★★★★ **Super Hits** / Tam. T5-300
★★★★★ **What's Going On** / Tam. T5-310

Marvin Gaye is perhaps the most underrated soul singer of the Sixties. He was by far the toughest and grittiest of all the male Motown singers, and he has influenced everyone from Mick Jagger to Rod Stewart and Stevie Wonder. His early hits—"Hitch Hike," "Ain't That Peculiar," "Can I Get a Witness" and "I'll Be Doggone"—rank with Otis Redding's for sheer power.

Those songs are collected on the various greatest-hits collections, of which the best is *Anthology,* which includes the duet recordings he made with Tammi Terrell, Kim Weston and Mary Wells. Of the others, *Super Hits* is the most interesting. But all of Gaye's deleted early Tamla albums had something to recommend them, and are worth seeking out in bargain centers.

His last hit in the standard Motown fashion was the 1968 blockbuster "I Heard It through the Grapevine." Beginning in 1970, he began to record on his own initiative, away from the company's production mill. *What's Going On* opened the company's music up, both in terms of lyrics and music (long, elliptical tracks with fluid grooves replaced the precision-molded songs of the past). "Mercy Mercy Me" and "Inner City Blues" were hardheaded but hopeful songs about black urban life that discarded the romanticism of Gaye's (and Motown's) past. In this respect, *What's Going On* was a couple of years ahead of its time, and obviously influential on such records as Stevie Wonder's *Innervisions* and Curtis Mayfield's *Superfly.*

After *What's Going On,* however, Gaye slipped back into the role of black sex idol. *Let's Get It On* is perhaps the best overtly sensual music anyone in rock has ever made; the title song was an enormous hit and its groove tells the whole story. Unfortunately, Gaye has yet to match its consistency, although "Got to Give It Up," from the *London Palladium* album, was a hit in 1977 and demonstrated that Gaye still had the knack. *Here My Dear,* released in late 1978, is an epic two-disc chronicle of his divorce, whose theme is alimony. While it doesn't have the focus of Gaye's best music, it is fascinating because black popular music is rarely so frankly personal.   — D.M.

CRYSTAL GAYLE
★ **Crystal** / U. Artists LA614-G
★ **Crystal Gayle** / U. Artists LA365-G
★ **I've Cried the Blue Right Out of My Eyes** / MCA 2334

★ **Somebody Loves You / U. Artists
LA543-G**
★★ **We Must Believe in Magic / U. Artists
LA771-G**
★ **When I Dream / U. Artists LA858-H**
Loretta Lynn's younger sister records in
Nashville, but that's about all they have in
common: where Loretta resists country
formulas, or explodes them from the inside,
Crystal just succumbs. As a result, "Don't
It Make Your Brown Eyes Blue," a 1977
pop hit from . . . *Magic,* sounds mostly like
Cher. — D.M.

GLORIA GAYNOR
★★ **Experience Gloria Gaynor / MGM
M3G-4997**
★★ **Glorious / Poly. 1-6095**
★★ **I've Got You / Poly. 1-6063**
★★★★ **Love Tracks / Poly. 1-6184**
★★★★ **Never Can Say Goodbye / MGM
M3G-4982**
★★ **Steppin' Out / Poly. 2-9007**
Gaynor is really only an average disco
singer, but 1975's *Never Can Say Goodbye*
scored a remarkable breakthrough in disco
production by treating the three songs on
side one ("Honey Bee," "Never Can Say
Goodbye," "Reach Out I'll Be There") as
one long suite, delivered without interrup-
tions of the dance beat that drove them.
This has since become a standard disco
format, but Gaynor's record not only did it
first, it was one of the greats: all three of
those songs are performed with shattering
intensity, and the Tony Bongiovi/Meco
Monardo/Jay Ellis production screams to
be repeated again and again. Gaynor finally regained the touch with the 1979 hit
"I Will Survive," and the excellent album
containing it, *Love Tracks.* — D.M.

DAVID GEDDES
■ **Run Joey Run / Big S-89511**
Dreck assembled around the title hit, the
tale of a teenager murdered by his lover's
father. (Now deleted.) — S.H.

THE J. GEILS BAND
★★★ **Bloodshot / Atl. 7260**
★★ **Blow Your Face Out / Atl. 507**
★★★ **Full House / Atl. 7241**
★★★★ **Monkey Island / Atl. 19130**
★★★★ **Nightmares (and Other Tales from
the Vinyl Jungle) / Atl. 10107**
★★★★ **Sanctuary / EMI SO-17006**
★★★★ **The J. Geils Band / Atl. 8275**
★★★ **The Morning After / Atl. 8297**
In the perennial quest for an American
equivalent to the Rolling Stones, the best
work of the J. Geils Band ranks at the top
of the heap; along with Lynyrd Skynyrd,
the Geils group perhaps came closest to
the Stones' synthesis of rhythm & blues,
bravado and a strong sense of outrage. The
dominant instrumental voices are the brilliant harp playing of Magic Dick, perhaps
the best white player on that instrument,
and the volatile guitar work of J. Geils
himself. But the group's real leader (and
with keyboardist Seth Justman, principal
writer) is former Cambridge disc jockey
and master of jive double-talk Peter Wolf.

Geils burst full grown from the Boston
rock scene with a 1970 debut LP (*The J.
Geils Band*) that was its most Stones-like,
incorporating several blues covers (notably
John Lee Hooker's "Serve You Right to
Suffer" and Otis Rush's "Homework"),
some hard-edged soul (Smokey Robinson's
"First I Look at the Purse," a wonderful
early example of Wolf 's ability to mock
black dialect) and a handful of similarly
oriented originals. Both there and on
Morning After, the approach is tough and
direct, and Geils had a rhythmic base so
eager to find a groove and keep it that almost everything worked almost all of the
time.

With *Full House,* however, the focus began to shift: on this live set, the group's
stage show has not just begun to jell, it has
begun to ossify. Wolf had developed a
stage persona that mixed the witty with the
obnoxious, and the group was slamming
out riffs as close to boogie as blues. There
was still more intelligence at work here
than in a band like Foghat, but the balance
between flair and respect for one's sources
had begun to tilt, dangerously. Still, *Full
House* is an enjoyable set, the band's first
commercial success and a first-rate document of rock & roll in the early Seventies.

Bloodshot contained the group's first single hit—a modified reggae, "Give It to
Me"—but aside from that song, the Show
Stoppers' venerable funk classic "Ain't
Nothin' but a House Party" and "Southside Shuffle," a good blues jam, the material was weaker than on any of the preceding records. Yet the album that followed,
Ladies Invited (now deleted) began to turn
the corner for the group: it successfully
mixed R&B with more pop-oriented rock
tunes. Unfortunately, the boogie following
the group had developed rejected the album, and this commercial failure put Geils
on the defensive. *Nightmares* contained another hit, the eerie "Must of Got Lost," but
with far too much hammerheaded fooling

around. *Hotline* (also deleted) deteriorated completely into an obviously condescending throwaway designed to placate the most elementary instincts of the band's followers. *Blow Your Face Out,* a two-disc live set, continued the process; only Eddie Floyd's "Raise Your Hand" and the Supremes' "Where Did Our Love Go" showed any of the old spark.

Monkey Island, then, came as a complete surprise, an album of very mature hard rock that revealed Justman and Wolf to be a trenchant songwriting team, with a dark vision behind all the good times. It contains sufficient R&B to keep it rooted firmly in the Geils style, but allows the group considerable artistic latitude. The final song, "Wreckage," seems both a metaphor for a career gone awry (but not lost altogether) and a statement of purpose. It ends in a welter of heavy-metal guitar that ought to be the envy of Led Zeppelin; an inspired and melodic conception, *Monkey Island* hinted that Geils might yet find a workable alternative to pandering to its audience, without sacrificing any of its manic energy. *Sanctuary* gave additional promise of resolution, continuing the band's adventurous music and reaching the gold record sales level. — D.M.

GENERATION X
★★★ **Generation X / Chrys. 1169**
This British punk band came up with one bright idea: "Your Generation," a 1977 answer record to the Who's earlier "My Generation," in which we are informed that the old wave is now irrelevant. Be that as it may, vocalist Billy Idol was a bit too slick to be effective on most of the rest of the record, and the band's second-best song, "Ready Steady Go," was a tribute to the British pop show of the Sixties, a complete contradiction of the earlier disc. Confusing but interesting for bedrock tastes. — D.M.

GENESIS
★★ **And Then There Were Three . . . / Atl. 19173**
★★ **A Trick of the Tail / Atco 38-101**
★★ **London Collector—In the Beginning / Lon. LC-50006**
★★★ **Seconds Out / Atl. 2-0002**
★★★★ **The Best of Genesis / Bud. 5659-2**
★★★ **The Lamb Lies Down on Broadway / Atco 2-401**
★★★ **Trespass / ABC X-816**
★★ **Wind and Wuthering / Atco 36-144**
One of the most adventurous and eventually most accomplished of the British art-

rock groups to come into prominence in the early Seventies, Genesis featured the songwriting and singing direction of Peter Gabriel; the studied, classically inspired arrangements of keyboardist Tony Banks; and the alternately angular and dulcet guitar playing of Michael Rutherford and Steve Hackett. The London album is made up of the earliest (1969) material, short tunes that are really failed pop songs and of interest only to the group's most ardent followers.

A characteristic sound that stretched out over complex arrangements began to emerge with the second LP, *Trespass,* highlighted by a bizarre and frightening epic of conquest and betrayal called "The Knife," which would later become the climax to the band's live performances.

Hackett joined up after *Trespass* and the group went on to record its best albums for Charisma Records. These are now out of print, but the *Best of* collection on Buddah is an excellent representation of that period.

The Lamb Lies Down on Broadway is the conceptual "masterpiece" Genesis had always been pointing toward, but it was predictably dense and overblown. Still, it did mark the group's commercial high point. Gabriel's fractured narrative style works to good effect on the extended poetics of such cameo songs as "Supper's Ready," "Watchers of the Sky" or "The Musical Box," but over a two-record set his obscurantism swamps the project.

Gabriel was not with the band for ensuing albums, and his place was not adequately filled by drummer Phil Collins. The live *Seconds Out* is much more effective due to the addition of drummers Bill Bruford and Chester Thompson, leaving Collins free to sing. *And Then There Were Three,* however, features the group without Hackett, which is nearly no group at all—maybe the next one should be called *Exodus,* or *The Incredible Shrinking Band.* — J.S.

GENTLE GIANT
★★★ **Acquiring the Taste / Vert. 1005**
★★★★ **Free Hand / Cap. ST-11428**
★★ **Giant for a Day / Cap. SW-11813**
★★★ **Interview / Cap. ST-11532**
★★ **Missing Piece / Cap. ST-11696**
★★ **Octopus / Col. PC-32022**
★★★ **Playing the Fool / Cap. SKBB-11592**
★ **The Power and the Glory / Cap. ST-11337**
★★★ **Three Friends / Col. PC-31649**

Despite releasing ten albums since 1970 (eight in the U.S.), Gentle Giant has never acquired more than a cult following. What support it does have is hardcore, attracted largely by the band's insistence on highly innovative song structures, superb musicianship and diverse styles. Weird but creative, this music demands active involvement from the listener.

Acquiring is historically their second album (the first is available only on import). Like the rest, it's a combination of contrasting classical, jazz and progressive rock (notably King Crimson) influences. It's probably their most accessible. *Three Friends* is ostensibly a concept album, though it's more instrumental than vocal. This one stars Kerry Minnear's keyboards, which compare stylistically with Keith Emerson's. It's uncharacteristically melodic. *Octopus* is based on the work of psychiatrist R. D. Laing and novelist Albert Camus, albeit with a medieval bent. Totally bizarre time signatures make it eclectic, intricate and showy, but not necessarily pleasant. *The Power and the Glory* is the band's most irritating, least listenable record, but *Free Hand* is Gentle Giant's answer to Yes' *Tales from Topographic Oceans.* It displays Jon Anderson's vocal shrieks, similarly complex time structures and the same unmelodious pitterpat music—yet it's probably their best record. *Interview* is similar, but not as accessible. *Playing the Fool* is live, a good sample. In sum: an acquired taste. — A.N.

THE GENTRYS
★ **The Gentrys / Sun 117**
Name that tune time. The present-day Gentrys (only vocalist Larry Hart remains from the "Keep on Dancing" group of 1965) are adept at flabby and unimagina-

tive rewrites of Rolling Stones, Yardbirds and Grass Roots songs, but they usually throw in a country ballad to keep you off balance. For lovers of elevator music only. — D.MC.

GERARD
★ **Gerard / Cari. PZ-34038**
Producer James William Guercio, the Buckinghams' Svengali in the Sixties and Chicago's in the Seventies, attempted to follow up with this rabidly eclectic ten-piece band, which made its only LP in 1976. Gerard's album features the same blowsy horn riffs one associates with Chicago, with perhaps a more transparent touch of Beach Boys (or was that Beatles?) influence on the lyrics. (Now deleted.) — D.M.

PAUL GEREMIA
★★★ **Just Enough / Folk. 31023**
Geremia's wry approach to blues and original folk-oriented material makes him much more attractive than the run-of-the-coffeehouse white folkie. It helps that this approach is directed more toward East Coast ragtime blues than the standard Mississippi Delta variety. — K.R.

ANDY GIBB
★★ **Flowing Rivers / RSO 1-3019**
★★ **Shadow Dancing / RSO 1-3034**
The young brother of the Bee Gees, Andy Gibb clicked commercially with both of these, mostly when his siblings were around for support, as writers or harmonizers. Anyway, couldn't he at least have had the sense of humor to record Dylan's "Watching the River Flow"? (Would that have made his debut LP a schlock-rock concept LP?) — D.M.

STEVE GIBBONS
★★★ **Any Road Up / MCA 2187**
★★★ **Caught in the Act / MCA 2305**
★★★★ **Down in the Bunker / Poly. 1-6154**
★★★ **Rollin' On / MCA 2243**
Veteran Birmingham rocker Steve Gibbons has a knife-edged voice and a cunning wit sharpened by years of slumming in the British Motor City's dank pubs before his discovery by the Who's Pete Townshend. His all-Birmingham group includes ex-Move bassist Trevor Burton, and his two studio albums include several minor successes ("Take Me Home," "Spark of Love," "Standing on the Bridge," "Please Don't Say Goodbye" and a cover of Chuck Berry's "Tulane"). *Caught in the Act* is a

live set that proves Gibbons' journeyman credentials without extending them. But *Down in the Bunker* (1978) is a small triumph of old-fashioned rock, driving and concise; it marks Gibbons as a sort of British Bob Seger, with a future potentially just as bright. — J.S.

NICK GILDER
★★★ City Nights / Chrys. 1202
★★ You Know Who You Are / Chrys. 1147
Frail British pop singer scored with oddly erotic "Hot Child in the City," from *City Nights,* in 1978. But the rest of his material is hardly up to that standard. — D.M.

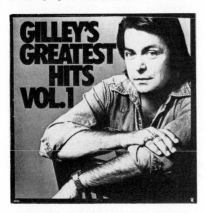

MICKEY GILLEY
★★★ City Lights / Play. KZ-34737
★★★ First Class / Play. KZ-34776
★★★★ Gilley's Smokin' / Play. KZ-34749
★★ Mickey Gilley at His Best / Play. 2224
★★★★★ Mickey Gilley's Greatest Hits, Vol. 1 / Play. KZ-34743
★★★★ Mickey Gilley's Greatest Hits, Vol. 2 / Play. KZ-34881
Gilley is Jerry Lee Lewis' cousin, and the two played together extensively when they were kids, but when Jerry Lee made the move to big-time entertainment in 1956, Mickey went to work as a laborer. It wasn't until twenty years later, after Gilley opened a Houston club featuring himself as the main performer and clicked with a beautifully relaxed version of "Roomful of Roses," that he caught up with his cousin's musical notoriety.

Since then, Gilley has become the voice of honky-tonk in the Seventies. His smooth vocal delivery and plunking piano playing engendered an impressive string of hit singles—"I Overlooked an Orchid," "City Lights," "Window up Above," "Bouquet of Roses," "Overnight Sensation," "Don't the

Girls All Get Prettier at Closing Time," "She's Pulling Me Back Again," "How's My Ex Treating You." Gilley is equally at home singing a maudlin tearjerker or pounding up a rockabilly storm. He'll never make people forget about Jerry Lee Lewis, but he more than holds his own. — J.S.

IAN GILLIAN BAND
★ Ian Gillian Band / Oys. OY-1-1602
★ Scarabus / Is. 9511
As the melodramatic Deep Purple lead singer and star of the original *Jesus Christ Superstar,* Gillian screeched with the best of them, but these solo outings leave it all behind. — J.S.

DAVE GILMOUR
★★★ Dave Gilmour / Col. JC-35388
Pink Floyd's guitarist goes the solo album route with results that are fairly impressive as these things go. Gilmour works better in the more balanced atmosphere of the band, but his compositions retain enough rock influence to make their jazz and avant-garde pretensions palatable. — D.M.

JOHNNY GIMBLE
★★★★ Johnny Gimble, Texas Dance Party / Lone KC-39284
This Texas fiddler/bandleader's 1976 live album presents his good-timey country & western swing in fine style. — J.S.

GIORGIO
★★ Battlestar Galactica / Casa. 7126
★★★ From Here to Eternity / Casa. 7065
★★ Knights in White Satin / Casa. 5006
Disco theoretician Giorgio Moroder is the man responsible for producing the electronic dance band called the Munich Machine, four Donna Summer albums and her computerized hit singles, "Love to Love You Baby" and "I Feel Love." Moroder's solo albums are comprised of nonstop synthesizer programs bleating narcotic trance patterns into infinity while disembodied voices chant themes in front of the endless sound system. Very odd, very catchy and very empty, Giorgio's songs get appropriate titles, such as "Utopia—Me Giorgio" and "Lost Angeles." An Italian working in Germany, Moroder creates austere but otherworldly productions that sound like futurist soundtracks for Fritz Lang's *Metropolis.* — J.S.

TOMPALL GLASER
★★★ The Wonder of It All / ABC 1036

★★★ **Tompall Glaser and His Outlaw Band / ABC 978**
Tompall Glaser's now-deleted MGM LPs are among the seminal works of so-called progressive C&W. *Charlie* is a landmark, one of the first of the outlaw LPs. Intensely personal, it's a dissenting look at the Nashville musical and social milieu, an explanation of why the outlaw movement was necessary. Though not as adventurous musically as subsequent Tompall works, it strikes a good balance between the new and the familiar, and grows with repeated listening. *Tompall* is stylistically similar, but all eleven songs are by Shel Silverstein, which is about eight too many for any album.

Then a Tompall style congeals. The Outlaw Band includes refugees from Bobby Bland's group; the sound is blacker, bluesier, with a solid dance beat and stinging dobros and guitar as well as elements of a rockabilly, New Orleans R&B and Western Swing. Tompall, with some degree of accuracy, calls it discobilly. He's perhaps Nashville's most flamboyant interpreter, tearing down such chestnuts as "Time Changes Everything" and rebuilding them from scratch, keeping only the feel of the original. His grainy voice is made to sound like total dissipation; he moans, groans and slurs as though he were about one step from his grave. — J.MO.

PHILIP GLASS
★★★ **North Star / Virgin PZ-34669**
Because this classical modernist is reaching out to a pop audience rather than withdrawing from mass appeal, his synthesizer approach seems warmer and more accessible than that of his nearest competitor, Brian Eno. But it would be silly to pretend that Glass understands the rock base of what he's doing as well as Eno does. Worthwhile for the adventurous. — D.M.

GLASSHARP
★ **Glassharp / MCA 293**
A Cleveland-based group, originally led by a sometimes spectacular guitarist, Phil Keaggy. Keaggy's appearances on the band's first two LPs (*Synergy* and *Glass Harp*, both Decca cutouts) had their moments, but after the second album he turned to religion, and the rest of this early-Seventies trio could not carry on even with the pedestrian post-Beatles guitar rock he made. Keaggy has since recorded a couple of forgettable LPs of white gospel music. — D.M.

ROGER GLOVER
★★ **Elements / Poly. PD 1-6137**
★★ **Roger Glover / Oy. OY1-1605**
Two undistinguished solo LPs from the Deep Purple vocalist. Stick with the original band. — D.M.

TONY GLOVER
★★★★ **Blues-Harp / Folk. 83358**
This is essentially an instruction record, but Glover's basso voice and deadpan delivery, plus his mastery of blues harmonica playing, makes it something special. Not up to his work with the occasionally inspired Koerner, Ray and Glover trio, but worth hearing anyway. — D.M.

KEITH AND DONNA GODCHAUX
★ **Keith and Donna / Round 101**
For hippies and/or Dead heads only. Donna has a fairly attractive voice, but she lacks a sense of dynamics and the meandering melodies don't help. Keith's keyboards and the rest of the instrumentalists (Jerry Garcia is along on guitar) are adequate but fairly ho-hum. Includes a ridiculous cocktail-lounge version of "River Deep Mountain High." Proof positive that the Grateful Dead (of which the Godchauxs have been a part for several years) lacked soul; only white people would sing like this. — J.B.M.

ANDREW GOLD
★★ **All This and Heaven Too / Asy. 6E-116**
★★★ **Andrew Gold / Asy. 7E-1047**
★★ **What's Wrong with This Picture? / Asy. 7E-1086**
The L.A. studio musician's debut, *Andrew Gold,* is a gorgeous collection reminiscent of mid-Sixties Anglo-rock: beautifully rich, ringing guitars and melodies. Gold plays nearly all instruments. The followups switch to glossy orchestration—less bounce and little edge, a step toward MOR. The second album, *What's Wrong,* has "Lonely Boy," a 1977 hit that tells a perfect pop-psychology fable about a psychotic teenager. — C.W.

BARRY GOLDBERG
★★ **Barry Goldberg and Friends Recorded Live / Bud. 5684**
Goldberg has played some hot keyboard tracks on a variety of sessions, and with collaborator Gerry Goffin he's written some nice pop songs. But this project is simply aimless, a waste of his (and his cronies') chops. — D.M.

GOLDEN EARRING
★★ **Mad Love / MCA 2254**
★★★ **Moontan / MCA 2354**
★★ **Switch / MCA 2139**
★★ **To the Hilt / MCA 2183**
Highly derivative Dutch band that finally
got a break when "Radar Love" (from
Moontan) became a big hit in 1974. "Ra-
dar" is a great radio song, a fusion of
Canned Heat and Kraftwerk, but unfortu-
nately atypical of Earring's other work, a
well-produced bag of riffs borrowed from
other European rock groups, notably Pink
Floyd and Jethro Tull. The other three
LPs are energetic and competent but face-
less progressive rock. — A.N.

THE GOLLIWOGS
★★ **Golliwogs Pre-Creedence / Fan. 9474**
A collection of singles recorded by Creedence Clearwater Revival just before the
band adopted that name and found success.
The key difference is that Tom Fogerty,
not brother John, sings almost everything
here. When John sings a couple of numbers you can spot the increase in inspiration instantly. For hard-core devotees of
CCR only. — D.M.

GONZALEZ
★★★ **Our Only Weapon Is Our Music /
EMI ST-11644**
★★★ **Shipwrecked / Cap. SW-11855**
Gonzalez is an all-star band of British session players led by Chris Mercer, with
Mick Eve and Bud Beadle on reeds, guitarist Steve Waller and drummer Preston
Heyman. The sound is what you might expect—terse, snappy R&B-influenced jazz
arrangements with occasional spaces for
the soloists to stretch out. This formula is
broken up by the singles, which are heavily
arranged, pop-oriented progressive R&B in
the manner of Stevie Wonder. — J.S.

PHILLIP GOODHAND-TAIT
★★ **Oceans Away / Chrys. 1113**
★★ **Teaching an Old Dog New Tricks /
Chrys. 1146**
A mediocre singer but a pretty and occasionally haunting pop melodist who could
use more spirited and varied backup and
production. But Robert Kirby's orchestrations on *Oceans* are nicely done. — C.W.

DICKIE GOODMAN
★ **Mr. Jaws / Cash 6000**
Since the Fifties, Goodman has been a
master of a tiny genre: loony question-and-
answer narratives, questions from Good-

man (often on vogue topics), answers from
snatches of pop songs. Thus, Goodman:
"What should you do if you're bitten by a
shark?" Van McCoy: "Do the Hustle."
Worth two chuckles as singles, unlistenable
but staggeringly impressive as an entire album. Includes the original pastiche,
"Flying Saucer," and the more recent "Energy Crisis" and "Mr. Jaws." — K.T.

STEVE GOODMAN
★★ **Jessie's Jig and Other Favorites / Asy.
7E-1037**
★ **Say It in Private / Asy. 7E-1118**
★★ **Somebody Else's Troubles / Bud. 5121**
★★ **Steve Goodman / Bud. 5096**
★★★ **The Essential Steve Goodman / Bud.
5665-2**
★ **Words We Can Dance To / Asy.
7E-1061**
Steve Goodman is the perfect master of the
latter-day urban folk scene—and its perfect
fool. From the effortless grace of his guitar
work to the ingenious elegance of his lyrics, he radiates technique and taste—and
they nearly choke him. As a songwriter
(best known for "City of New Orleans"),
Goodman has a gift for wry commentary,
such as "Chicken Cordon Blues" (*Essential*)—a palate-rending tale of macrobiotic
deprivation—or the caustic "Banana Re-
publics" (*Words*).
  As a singer he's most at home with the
country-flavored songs that predominate
his earlier albums for Buddah. Since *Jessie's Jig* (his Asylum debut) he's favored
slicker, more contemporary songs and arrangements. But though Goodman doesn't
sound like a folkie anymore, he's kept the
insular aesthetics of the coffeehouse—topical references, in jokes ("Daley's Gone" to
the tune of "Delia's Gone"). Technology is
suspect in his lyrics and his choice of material suggests that the old is automatically
good. Unlike Arlo Guthrie (who successfully maintains both a folk and a pop
audience), Goodman confuses taste with
style and substitutes the accepted values of
a small community for a personal voice.
He's deservedly a cult figure selling small
subtleties and limited perfections, though
his cult may not be willing to follow him
through the strings and studio singers he's
using now. — A.S.

THE GOOD OLD BOYS
★★★ **Pistol Packin' Mama / Round
RX-LA597-G**
Traditional country music performed by
one of the strangest-looking quintets in his-

tory: one looks forty years old and must weigh 300 pounds; another is the same age, but slimmer; the remaining three are moderately hip in attire and physiognomy. Produced by the Grateful Dead's Jerry Garcia, the album was released on the Dead's now defunct label, but is far superior to any of the Dead's C&W efforts. — D.M.

GOOSE CREEK SYMPHONY
★★ **Goose Creek Symphony** / Cap. SM-444
★★ **Welcome to Goose Creek** / Cap. ST-690
★★ **Words of Ernest** / Cap. ST-11044

Like many country-rock bands, Goose Creek Symphony can't be faulted on technical grounds, but can't be praised on emotional ones, either. These albums are continually promising but never quite deliver, leaving Goose Creek in the ranks of the perennial also-rans. — D.M.

ROBERT GORDON
★ **Fresh Fish Special** / Priv. 7008
★ **Robert Gordon with Link Wray** / Priv. 2030
★ **Rock Billy Boogie** / RCA AFL1-3294

Gordon would like to be a rockabilly revivalist, but since he understands none of the nuances of the genre, he is finally hopeless. Reducing some of the greatest American music ever created to a matter of mannerism insults it, and when Gordon attempts to interpret a modern song in the idiom (e.g., Bruce Springsteen's "Fire," on *Fresh Fish Special*), he simply sounds confused. Well-intentioned but inept. — D.M.

LESLEY GORE
★★ **The Golden Hits of Lesley Gore** / Mer. SR 61024

"It's My Party (and I'll Cry If I Want To)" is as succinct a declaration of emotional independence as you can find. The followup, "Judy's Turn to Cry," shows how quickly petulance can turn to revenge. Lesley Gore didn't need assertiveness training ("You Don't Own Me" is a prefeminist anthem), but then she was a Sarah Lawrence girl. — A.S.

GRAHAM CENTRAL STATION
★★★ **Ain't No Bout-A-Doubt It** / War. BS4-2876
★★★ **Graham Central Station** / War. BS-2763
★★★ **Mirror** / War. B-2937
★★★ **My Radio Sure Sounds Good to Me** / War. K-3175

★★★ **Now Do U Wanta Dance** / War. BS-3041
★★★ **Release Yourself** / War. BS-2814

When it began recording in 1972, GCS was almost alone in carrying on and developing Sly Stone's visionary R&B invention of the late Sixties. But others have since caught up and left these guys in the dust. Three acts that quickly come to mind are George Clinton's Funkadelic/Parliament/Rubber Band school of mind-twisting funk; Earth, Wind and Fire, with its emotional and instrumental intensity; and ex-James Brown hornman/arranger Fred Wesley's brass adventurists, the JB's (now the Horny Horns). Which leaves ex-Sly bassist Larry Graham's congregation as merely an expert dance band. In the not too creative but professional footsteps of their fellow East Bay Oaklanders, Tower of Power, they do what they do well, but it just doesn't grow. — B.M.

GRAND FUNK RAILROAD
★ **Caught in the Act** / Cap. SABB-11445
★★ **Closer to Home** / Cap. SKAO-471
★ **E Pluribus Funk** / Cap. SW-853
★ **Good Singin', Good Playin'** / MCA 2216
★★ **Grand Funk** / Cap. SKAO-406
★★ **Grand Funk Hits** / Cap. ST-11579
★★ **Live Album** / Cap. SWBB-633
★★ **Mark, Don and Mel 1969-1971** / Cap. SABB-11042
★★ **On Time** / Cap. ST-307
★★ **Phoenix** / Cap. SMAS-11099
★ **Shinin' On** / Cap. SWAE-11278
★★★ **Survival** / Cap. SW-764
★★★ **We're an American Band** / Cap. MAS-11207

Grand Funk Railroad created an immediate and enormous following with its appearance at the 1969 Atlanta Pop Festival, then parlayed that popularity into national notoriety by exploiting the extraordinarily abrasive critical attacks on the band. It was really the first attack on the dichotomies that had lain dormant within the Sixties rock community, for all its vision of peace and hope, and as such, the antipress campaign became a marvelous portent of things to come.

The group was a power trio, in some senses a surrogate for those who'd missed being bludgeoned by Cream's dissemblings upon blues themes. Drummer Don Brewer, bassist Mel Schacher and guitarist Mark Farner were archetypal Midwestern rock & rollers, long-haired, impolite and sweaty, with a kind of radical cheek orientation that was more naive and divisive than sophisticated or analytical. For Grand Funk, and many similar "heavy-metal" bands of the era, "Power to the People" was a slogan that justified rampant consumerism, as long as the consumer smoked pot, a perfect misunderstanding of populism.

Wretched was the word to describe Grand Funk's music. Although the group ocasionally achieved an interesting song— "I'm Your Captain" was about the best of the early ones—the playing was never much more than energetic, always dull in its meter, and the singing was completely hopeless. The production of Terry Knight, formerly a recording artist in his own right, mostly took a back seat to some clever promotions.

By 1972, the group and Knight were embroiled in a nasty lawsuit, and Grand Funk rarely came up with anything quite so ingenious, despite a succession of producers that included Jimmy Ienner and Frank Zappa. Only Todd Rundgren could do much with them, producing a masterful hard-rock hit single in 1973 with *We're an American Band*'s title track. When the group left Capitol in 1976, it was obvious GFR was near the end of the line; the group recorded one album for MCA and folded. (Farner, the band's frontman, has since recorded an awful Atlantic solo LP.)

Among the discs available, it is hard to choose; most are simply unlistenable without the cult fervor that once surrounded the band. *Survival,* however, contains a sledgehammer version of the Rolling Stones' "Gimme Shelter." *Grand Funk Hits,* which has "We're an American Band," is about the best bet, although why anyone except professional nostalgists would still be interested is mystifying. This is one legend whose rehabilitation is highly unlikely. — D.M.

GRASS ROOTS
★★★ **Golden Grass / Dun. 50047**
★ **Lovin' Things / Dun. 50052**
★★ **More Golden Grass / Dun. 50087**
★ **Move Along / Dun. 50112**
★★★ **Their 16 Greatest Hits / Dun. DSX-50107**
★ **Where Were You When I Needed You / Dun. DSX-50011**

Had the Grass Roots faded away after their first two pop-punk hits, "Let's Live for Today" (1967) and "Midnight Confessions" (1968), they might be fondly remembered. Unfortunately, the group stuck around through most of the Seventies, with records progressively more mediocre in the same half-rock, half-schlock manner. They finally gave up in 1975, after a career not nearly so interesting as the best pop groups of their day (Three Dog Night, for instance). — D.M.

GRATEFUL DEAD
★★★ **Anthem of the Sun / War. 1749**
★★★ **Aoxomoxoa / War. 1790**
★★ **Grateful Dead / War. 1689**
★★★ **Live Dead / War. 1830**

More than any other psychedelic-era band, the Grateful Dead epitomized the hippie in rock & roll. In terms of pure music, this could be a detriment: the Dead is nothing if not self-indulgent, and while its instrumentalists are capable of sparkling jams, they are just as likely to wander aimlessly. In addition, only a bunch of hippies could survive this long without a first-class singer. But it's the Dead's image that has sustained it. Dead heads congregate as much to rekindle that Sixties spirit as to see the band create something new.

The Dead's most cogent musical asset is Jerry Garcia, whose long, circular lead lines, characterized by the round, sustained tone preferred by West Coast guitarists, spearhead its best performances and save its worst. The debut album, *Grateful Dead,* found the Dead working over rock and R&B-based tunes, highlighted by a handful of rockers displaying more energy than was to become customary. *Anthem of the Sun* featured extended pieces patched together from studio and live recordings and captured the Dead in its acid-gobbling element. The swirling guitars and melodies have the feel of a cultural document, as if they constituted an additional chapter to Tom Wolfe's *Electric Kool-Aid Acid Test* (the Dead, of course, was Kesey's acid-test band).

Aoxomoxoa brought this trippiness into

the studio, and offered a pair of Dead classics in the riffing "St. Stephen" and the more delicate "China Cat Sunflower." But just as often, the ambiance of psychedelic hip marred the flow of the music, and while this problem cropped up on parts of *Live Dead,* it was overshadowed by that record's moments of brilliance. "Dark Star" is the Dead at its best, with Phil Lesh's bass providing a resonant contrast to Garcia's rolling lead. Though the group rarely achieved such heights, the rush of Garcia's guitar flying out of a percussive crescendo in the song's belly is a peak moment of rock jamming and Sixties music in general.
★★★ **American Beauty / War. 1893**
★★★ **Workingman's Dead / War. 1869**
With a reputation solidified by environmental live performances, the Dead produced its most commercial records by moving to acoustic-based country rock. *Workingman's Dead* is the gruffer of the two, and includes the Dead's throat-stretching impersonation of Crosby, Stills and Nash ("Uncle John's Band"); a naive (or shamelessly self-serving, depending on who's asked) answer to the Altamont disaster ("New Speedway Boogie"); and another druggy anthem ("Casey Jones"). *American Beauty,* which further smoothed the edges of the Dead's new style, was centered on gently rocking tunes ("Sugar Magnolia," "Friend of the Devil"); a pipeful of gentle hippie sentiments ("Box of Rain," "Ripple"); and an autobiographical sketch of a rock band on the run ("Truckin' "). Of all Dead records, these have dated the least, and are unarguably the band's most consistent recordings.
★★★ **Best of—Skeletons in the Closet / War. 2764**
★★ **Blues for Allah / Grate. LA494-G**
★★ **Europe '72 / War. 3WX-2668**
★★ **Grateful Dead / War. 1935**
★★★ **Greatest Hits / War. 2W-3091**
★ **History of . . . Vol. 1 / War. B-2721**
★★ **Steal Your Face / Grate. LA620-J2**
★★ **Wake of the Flood / Grate. 01**
★★★ **What a Long, Strange Trip It's Been / War. 2W-3091**
I don't mean to lay any bum trips, but it's mostly downhill from here. Of these nine records (including *Skeletons,* a well-chosen best-of collection), four are live albums, bringing the total to eight live discs of the good old Grateful Dead. These records offer conclusive proof that the Dead's the absolute worst interpreter of Chuck Berry to ever take the rock & roll stage. They're

also not a very good rhythm and/or blues band, as *History of . . . Volume 1* documents. Nor are they notable interpreters of country standards. The Dead is, well, the Dead. It evolved into a sporadically successful big-time jam band, and the stage show garnered a reputation for great length and relatively little musical precision. There were flashes of the old flame—snatches of the Europe collection and "Bertha" and "The Nine" from *Skeletons*—but the rest was hopelessly mediocre.
Wake of the Flood and *Blues for Allah* were two studio albums recorded on the Dead's own label (since liquidated), and they revealed a band grasping for a style. The sound was disarmingly thin, and musical and lyrical ideas were infrequent. The highlights ("Eyes of the World" from *Flood*) were drowned in the general lack of direction. The Dead continues to exist because it is linked to our cultural past, and even the most cynical among us can agree with a good number of the band's communal ideals. But the farther we get from those innocently innocuous times, the more the Dead seems to be sleepwalking through the Seventies.
★★ **Grateful Dead from the Mars Hotel / Grate. 102**
★★ **Shakedown Street / Ari. 4198**
★★★ **Terrapin Station / Ari. 7001**
Back in the corporate fold with Arista, the Dead rebounded strongly with a fine albeit one-sided album, *Terrapin.* The side-long title tune was the trick. The album returned to the extended-suite format of *Anthem of the Sun,* and the differences between the two are telling. Where anarchy once reigned, now the progressions are crystal clear, with Paul Buckmaster's solid orchestration leading the way. The success of *Terrapin Station* is measured by the fact that it's over before you even start to get restless. But *Mars Hotel* and *Shakedown Street* weren't even up to that slight standard. — J.B.M.

CARL GRAVES
■ **Carl Graves / A&M 3410**
Hopelessly lame arrangements of some fairly decent songs (notably "My Whole World Ended," and Neil Sedaka's "Breaking Up Is Hard to Do") aren't all that mar this first and only record by a singer who sounds like he's still auditioning. — D.M.

DOBIE GRAY
★★★ **Midnight Diamond / Inf. 9001**
★★ **New Ray of Sunshine / Capri. 0163**

Dobie Gray is best known for his spectacular renditions of "Loving Arms" and "Drift Away," the title songs to two MCA albums that are unfortunately no longer in circulation. *New Ray* and *Midnight Diamond* can't sustain that earlier brilliance, mostly because of poor material. Gray's expressive baritone is wasted on standard country-rock songs, and when he does get something passable to sing, thin production robs him of much of his power. — C.F.

AL GREEN
★★★★ **Al Green Gets Next to You / Hi 32062**
★★★ **Green Is Blues / Hi 32055**
Green Is Blues, Al Green's Hi debut and a so-so collection of soul and pop standards, caused little reaction on its release. Few predicted that his very next album would see the emergence of the heir to the Sam Cooke-Otis Redding throne. To the delight of those who favor Redding over Cooke, *Gets Next to You* is rough. The smoothing of style and delivery was yet to come, a fact evident from Green's hokey get-up on the cover of his second LP.
★★★★★ **Call Me / Hi 32077**
★★★★ **I'm Still in Love with You / Hi 32074**
★★★★★ **Let's Stay Together / Hi 8007**
Call Me and *Let's Stay Together* are surely the best Al Green records. He didn't turn out to be the next incarnation of Otis Redding, but rather a vocalist who flaunted a cuddly persona in the face of those who liked their soul rugged and harsh. *Let's Stay Together* is still closer to old-fashioned Stax-Volt soul than the followups would ever be. Both "Old Time Lovin'" and "It Ain't No Fun for Me" suggest Stax; the choked rhythm guitar on "Ain't No Fun" and the unwashed gospel of "Old Time Lovin'" are as pure as the rawest Redding or Sam and Dave record. *I'm Still in Love with You* finds few holes in producer Willie Mitchell's seam and one real moment of boredom: a six-and-a-half-minute version of "For the Good Times." But if *Let's Stay Together* recalls Stax, *Call Me* manages to distill Green's affection for Sam Cooke and Claude Jeter. The subtlety of both technique and mood change is as astounding as it is difficult to perceive.
★★★★ **Al Green Explores Your Mind / Hi 32087**
★★★★★ **Greatest Hits / Hi 32089**
★★★★ **Livin' for You / Hi 32082**
Not only does *Livin' for You* mark the first evidence of creative decline, but it also

contains the first of many Al Green songs that mix oblique sexual and religious metaphors ("Sweet Sixteen"). *Explores Your Mind* finds its true moment of greatness in such a song—the blues shuffle "Take Me to the River." While a gospel song had been included on previous records, Green's obsession with religion dominates *Explores Your Mind*, as it would in albums to follow. *Greatest Hits* was released almost simultaneously with *Explores Your Mind*. It includes a small but delightful bonus: two extra minutes of "Let's Stay Together."
★★★★ **Al Green Is Love / Hi 32092**
★★★★ **Full of Fire / Hi 32097**
★★★ **Have a Good Time / Hi 32103**
Al Green Is Love is enigmatic and adventurous. Green and Mitchell attempt to loosen the formula: the crack Hi rhythm section is spotlighted on the thundering "Love Ritual," while at other times Green is seemingly caught in some private hell ("Love Sermon"). Both *Full of Fire* and *Have a Good Time* are a return to more conventional territory, and Green's paranoia becomes full-blown on "Keep Me Crying," a song from *Good Time.*
★★★★ **The Belle Album / Hi 6004**
★★★★ **Truth 'n' Time / Hi 6009**
These albums, released in late 1977 and late 1978 respectively, are Green's most adventurous. Producer Mitchell was gone; Green now produced himself. And the music swung drastically from the straight soul of Mitchell's conception to smoldering funk, hot disco changes and intimations of pure blues. Green himself was sometimes featured on guitar. The songs are intimate and percussive and suggest an incomplete resolution of his previous religious and paranoid musings. "Belle," the first album's attempt for a hit, wasn't the chartbuster it deserved to be but the approach of both these records suggest that Green's eccentricities might have found a new focus. — J.MC./D.M.

THE GREENBRIAR BOYS
★★ **Best of the Greenbriar Boys and John Herald / Van. 79317**
★★★ **Better Late Than Never / Van. 79233**
★★★ **Ragged but Right! / Van. 79159**
The Greenbriar Boys paved the way for the city bluegrass scene of the Sixties. John Herald and Bob Yellin headed up the band, with a succession of members that included Eric Weissberg, Ralph Rinzler, Frank Wakefield, Jim Buchanan and Dian Edmondson. The various artists shared a

sophisticated respect for the music, were accomplished musicians (bluegrass being a virtuouso form) and displayed an originality in material and its execution that was rarely paralleled.

Highlighted by Herald's unique high tenor, the music is as convincing today as then. And their scholarly quest for new sources made the Boys' own records sources for others. "Take a Whiff on Me," "Ragged but Right" and "Stewball" rapidly became staples of bluegrass and folk-rock groups. *Ragged* and *Better* are more representative of the *group's* talents than the Herald-dominated *Best of.* — I.M.

MIKE GREENE
★★ **Midnight Mirage / Mer. SRM-1-1100**
Recorded in Atlanta, the album has a sound closer to noodling jazz rock than to the Allmans or Skynyrd. Greene's singing and lyrics are about the worst of it, but even they are so innocuous that the record is more harmless than annoying. But who needs harmless music? (Now deleted.) — D.M.

GRIN
★★ **Gone Crazy / A&M 4415**
Grin (Nils Lofgren, guitar, keyboards and vocals; Bob Berberich, drums and vocals; Bob Gordon, bass and vocals; and, later, Tom Lofgren, guitar) was a first-class early-Seventies band that never achieved wide success; *Gone Crazy,* an eviscerated farewell made after the group left Spindizzy/CBS following three LPs, shows little of its talent. Their best work is on *1 + 1,* a lovely blend of tough hard rock ("Moon Tears," "End Unkind") and ironic teen-heartbreak ballads ("Lost a Number"). It can still be found in bargain bins, as can *Best of Grin,* an erratic collection of tracks from the slight *Grin, 1 + 1* and the overproduced, strained *All Out.* — G.M.

GRINDERSWITCH
★★ **Honest to Goodness / Capri. 0135**
★★ **Macon Tracks / Capri. 0150**
★★ **Pullin' Together / Capri. 0173**
★★ **Redwing / Atco 152**
Fervid Southern boogie, performed thunderously and unfeelingly, just the sort of thing that gave the genre a bad name. Stick with the Allmans, Lynyrd Skynyrd or, at the outside, Wet Willie; this stuff is for Charlie Daniels addicts only. — D.M.

LARRY GROCE
■ **Junkfood Junkie / War. B-2933**

The fact that the title song (a 1976 hit about a closet burger freak in a vegetarian world) took the wind out of the sanctimonious health-food cult doesn't excuse an album that's the aural equivalent of a Big Mac diet. — D.M.

HENRY GROSS
★ **Henry Gross / A&M 4416**
★ **Love Is the Stuff / Lifes. JZ-35280**
■ **Plug Me into Something / A&M 4502**
■ **Release / Lifes. PZ-34995**
★ **Show Me to the Stage / Lifes. PZ-35002**
Working in realms far beyond the derivative, Gross takes Rolling Stones-type rockers, Beatlesque ballads, Lou Reed-styled documentaries, songwriterish laments, Southern rock and phony C&W and turns them all into flavorless FM fodder. Gross does do a passable Beach Boys imitation ("Shannon," from *Release,* was a smash in 1976), but his idea of rock is facile doodling, and his love songs are gruesome propositions at best.

Cashman and West, who own Lifesong, are the ideal producers for Gross. Their obsessively tasteful and genuinely indifferent approach pulls the gutless whole together under a fine gelatin of functionalist studio technique. (They even disguise Gross' wholly dumb guitar playing—a good trick.)

Gross' music stays on the radio by means of his tunes' subliminal appeal to their half-remembered predecessors, making him a good bet for distracted listening. — B.T.

THE GROUP WITH NO NAME
■ **Moon over Brooklyn / Casa. 7033**
A decent marketing strategy since mystery is supposed to be sexy. But this 1976 album was performed with all the passion of a set by understudies from *Hair,* so who cares who's responsible? — D.M.

GRYPHON
★★★ **Red Queen to Gryphon Three / Ari. 4018**
Elegantly reserved yet sprightly mix of British Isles folk, classics and rock. Drums and electric instruments, but also bassoon, recorder and krumhorn. Long but attention-keeping compositions; no singing. (Now deleted.) — C.W.

THE GUESS WHO
★★ **American Woman / RCA LSP-4266**
★★★★★ **Best of the Guess Who / RCA AFL1-2594**

★★★ Best of the Guess Who, Vol. 2 /
RCA APL1-0269
★★★★ Canned Wheat / RCA ANL1-0986
★★★ Greatest of the Guess Who / RCA
APL1-2253
★ No. 10 / RCA APL1-0130
★ Road Food / RCA APL1-0405
★ Rockin' / RCA ANL1-2683
★★ Shakin' All Over / Spri. 4022
★★★ Share the Land / RCA LSP-4359
★ The Way They Were / RCA
APL1-1778
★★★ Wheatfield Soul / RCA ANL1-1171

The title of the first Guess Who album,
Wheatfield Soul, was a pun on the band's
western Canadian roots, but even though
the musicians were somewhat provincial,
they were far from amateurish. Led by guitarist Randy Bachman and fronted by lead
singer Burton Cummings, the Guess Who
coined a fairly substantial, jazz-inflected
R&B sound similar to contemporary
Southern bands, such as the Classics IV.

Bachman's chord structures and Cummings' lyrics created the group's first hit,
"These Eyes." And while the rest of the
debut record was more experimental and
included Cummings' blatant Jim Morrison
imitation on the melodramatic "Friends of
Mine," the followup album, *Canned Wheat,*
paid more attention to the singles formula
and produced a string of pop-rock hits—
"Laughing," "No Time" and "Undun."

American Woman turned out to be the
band's psychedelic LP, and was accordingly loud, fuzz-guitar drenched and repetitive. It sounds dated today, despite the
title track's tremendous success as a hit
single. Until that album, the Guess Who
was a quartet with Bachman firmly in control of its musical direction. After Bachman left in 1970 to form Brave Belt and
later Bachman-Turner Overdrive, Cummings took full control, added two guitarists to replace Bachman, and the Guess
Who began to grind it out.

The title track of *Share the Land* was the
band's last well-written hit, and it's all
downhill from there. Of the eleven subsequent albums, *Road Food, No. 10, Greatest
of* and the previously unreleased demos
from *Way They Were* are all that's left in
print. *Greatest* makes the most sense by
culling the good moments from this
group's erratic but occasionally brilliant
career. *Shakin' All Over* is the pre-Cum-
mings band; the title track, a 1965 hit, is
first-rate, but everything else is filler. — J.S.

GIB GUILBEAU
★★ Gib Guilbeau Sings / Als. 5287
Louisiana songwriter and (briefly) member
of the Flying Burrito Brothers, best known
for writing "Big Bayou," covered by both
Rod Stewart and Ron Wood. — D.M.

THE GUN
★ The Gun / Epic 26468
Unpolished, overly eager Sixties power trio
led by Adrian and Ben Curtis (read Gur-
vitz). Awkward strings and brass in spots.
(Now deleted.) — C.W.

JO JO GUNNE
★★★★ Jo Jo Gunne / Asy. SD 5053
This band grew from the breakup of Spirit.
Built around Jay Ferguson and Mark
Andes, they released four superb albums
between 1972 and 1974, all uniformly ex-
cellent except for the second, which is now
deleted. High energy tromp. — A.N.

ARLO GUTHRIE
★★★ Alice's Restaurant / Rep. 6267
★★★★★ Amigo / Rep. 2239
★★ Arlo / Rep. 6299
★★★ Arlo Guthrie / Rep. 2183
★★★★ Hobo's Lullaby / Rep. MS-2060
★★★★ Last of the Brooklyn Cowboys /
Rep. MS4-2142
★★★ Running down the Road / Rep. 6346
★★ The Best of Arlo Guthrie / War.
K-3117
★ Together in Concert (with Pete See-
ger) / Rep. 2R-2214
★★ Washington County / Rep. 6411
Arlo Guthrie's "Alice's Restaurant," an
eighteen-minute underground hit in 1967,
immediately established him as the inheri-
tor, and perhaps the fulfillment, of the folk-
music tradition pioneered by his father,
Woody. "Alice" was funny, leftishly politi-

cal as well as folk-based, but it was also up-to-date in a way that implied his absorption of those on whom Woody had had his greatest influence: Bob Dylan, Jack Elliott and other early Sixties folkies. And if Arlo's first attempts at serious material were weaker than his humorous songs, the lovely "Chilling of the Evening" indicated that that wouldn't always be so.

Yet *Arlo,* a live album that followed the success of "Alice," emphasized the hit novelty status, partly because it was framed by similar, shaggy, hippie story-songs, partly because the musical arrangements were too skeletal, partly because the original material was weak. The album's best track, in fact, is the Ernest Tubb country standard, "Try Me One More Time."

Perhaps this was obvious to the artist himself, for with *Running down the Road* almost everything shifted. Arlo began working with producer Lenny Waronker, whose roots were more pop than folk, and rather than writing all of his own material, he became an interpretive singer, recording songs by his father, Mississippi John Hurt, Pete Seeger and Gus Cannon, as well as originals. The latter are mostly dated, but the dope-smuggling anthem "Coming into Los Angeles" remains among his best-known work. In 1970, *Running* seemed a breakthrough; today, it seems dated and slightly out of focus.

Hobo's Lullaby, released in 1972, was almost entirely interpretive, and contains Guthrie's best-known post-"Alice" number, Steve Goodman's "City of New Orleans," which immediately became a sort of singer/songwriter standard. "City" was brilliant, a song that extended rather than merely invoked the tradition Woody had founded, and it became Guthrie's first "serious" Top Twenty hit. This is a near-perfect interpretive folk-rock LP—listen to the rocking sax on Hoyt Axton's "Lightning Bar Blues"—and the folk-rock genre has produced the best interpretive singing in rock.

But with *Washington County,* Arlo once more attempted to write all his own material, and the project fell flat. Its best moments are instrumental, not exactly what we came for. To really fulfill the tradition, Guthrie needed a more direct approach. *Last of the Brooklyn Cowboys,* a designation swiped from Jack Elliott, provided just the remedy, opening with an Irish reel and including songs by Woody, plus country, ragtime, white gospel, Stephen Foster jazz-like waltz-time pop-blues, and even some

Latin and cowboy-Mexican accents. This is Guthrie's most eclectic LP, and a great deal of its success is due to outside forces: co-producers Waronker and John Pilla and the cast of L.A. studio pros who played on it. The biggest flaw is Dylan's "Gates of Eden," perfect for Arlo's reedy voice but a truly bad song.

Arlo Guthrie was more uneven: "Presidential Rag" is perhaps the greatest and certainly the most vicious anti-Nixon song. Unlike most other topical songs of our era, it hasn't dated a bit, much like Woody's protest masterpiece, "Deportees," which is also included. More striking was "Children of Abraham," a song about the Arab-Israeli dispute that made sense of that political mess by relying on just the sense of tradition Guthrie had brought to *Brooklyn*'s music. Most of the rest, however, was not nearly as strong.

The *Together in Concert* LP was a barely mitigated disaster. Guthrie's sense of folk tradition was too natural and free-flowing to jell with Pete Seeger's pedantic and sanctimonious approach, and the two-record set does little but expose the worst of both men's weaknesses.

But in 1976, Guthrie released an album that finally connected all the links of the chain: *Amigo* spanned the folk tradition with the same assurance that *Brooklyn* had, and by adding a piece of pure rock & roll in the Rolling Stones' "Connection," Guthrie brought it all back home as no one since early electric Dylan had been able to do. In this context, a song about the martyred Chilean poet, Victor Jara, meshed seamlessly with more personal concerns expressed in songs like "Manzanillo Bay" and "Massachusetts." *Amigo* is Guthrie's triumph, and although the public never picked up on it, one looks forward to its successors (with the exception of the formulaic and ill-chosen *Best of*) with great anticipation. — D.M.

WOODY GUTHRIE

★★★★★ **A Legendary Performer** / RCA CPL1-2099

★★★★ **Cowboy Songs** / Stin. 32

★★★★★ **Dust Bowl Ballads** / Folk. 5212

★★★★ **Early Years** / Trad. 2088

★★★★ **Folk Songs by Woody Guthrie and Cisco Houston** / Stin. 44

★★★★ **Immortal Woody Guthrie** / Olym. 7101

★★★★ **Legendary Woody Guthrie** / Trad. 2058

★★★★ **Poor Boy** / Folk. 31010

★★★★ Songs to Grow On / Folk. 7005
★★★★ Songs to Grow On, Vol. 2 / Folk. 31502
★★★★ Songs to Grow On, Vol. 3 / Folk. 37027
★★★★ This Land Is Your Land / Folk. 31001
★★★★ Woody Guthrie / Ev. 204
★★★★ Woody Guthrie / War. 2999
★★★★★ Woody Guthrie: Library of Congress Recordings / Elek. 271/272
★★★★ Woodie Guthrie Sings Folk Songs / Folk. 2483
★★★★ Woody Guthrie Sings Folk Songs, Vol. 2 / Folk. 2484

Woody Guthrie ranks with the half-dozen most important names in the history of American music. After his childhood in Oklahoma, he went west to California, the very incarnation of Steinbeck's Tom Joad (in *The Grapes of Wrath*), about whom he wrote a ballad. Throughout the Thirties and Forties, and into the Fifties until felled by Huntington's chorea, Guthrie was the most influential songwriter on the American political left, a remarkable, energetic figure whose creations include literally hundreds of songs, dozens of poems, exhaustive journals, novels and other autobiographical material as well as one of the classic hobo legends. All of this would serve to inspire not only his peers—particularly such singers as Lee Hays, Pete Seeger, Cisco Houston and Ramblin' Jack Elliott—but also the Beats and, of course, the folk and leftist movements that became the Sixties counterculture.

Guthrie's musical approach was raw and primitive, generally amounting to just a voice and acoustic guitar, sometimes adding a harmonica but never more. The naiveté he enjoyed projecting is totally belied by the quality of his songs and the intensity of his performances. It was no dumb Okie who wrote "Deportee," as subtle a picture of discrimination against migrant workers as has been done to date, or "This Land Is Your Land," as beautiful a portrayal of American natural glory as has been created in any medium. Throughout these songs, from the outlaw ballads like "Pretty Boy Floyd," to the depictions of

the dust bowl in Guthrie's many songs about that catastrophe, to the children's tunes and the political calls-to-arms, there is a singular artistic vision at work, one of the greatest of its generation. No wonder the greatest American composer of our era, Bob Dylan, began his career in total, awestruck emulation of Guthrie.

The basic Guthrie document is the *Library of Congress Recordings,* which contains much conversation between Guthrie and Alan Lomax, as well as a good share of both original and traditional tunes. *Dust Bowl Ballads* and *This Land Is Your Land,* as well as the RCA *A Legendary Performer* (which was also previously known as *Dust Bowl Ballads*), are the best selections of his material, although there is no one record that presents all of Guthrie's best work; there's simply too much of it for that. The Stinson material is largely devoted to traditional songs, often featuring Guthrie accompanied by one of his many sidekicks—Cisco Houston, Leadbelly, Sonny Terry and Brownie McGhee, or Pete Seeger. The recordings on Tradition, Everest, Olympic, and Warners basically recapitulate the approaches above. (*Legendary Woody Guthrie* on Tradition repeats much of what's available on the Everest LP.) *Songs to Grow On,* finally, is a series of some of the greatest children's recordings ever made—both Guthrie's wonderfully amusing original children's songs and some of the folk tunes he grew up with.   — D.M.

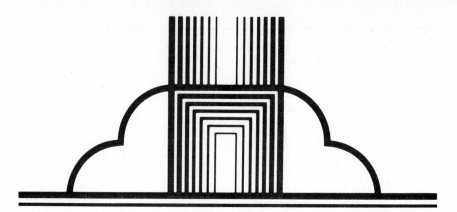

STEVE HACKETT
★★ Please Don't Touch / Chrys. 1176
★★ Voyage of the Acolyte / Chrys. CHR 1112

Genesis guitarist tries his hand at solo outings with middling success. Hackett is technically proficient, but his classically inspired instrumental meanderings are bereft of any dynamic focus. — J.S.

SAMMY HAGAR
★★★ Musical Chairs / Cap. ST-11706
★★ Nine on a Ten Scale / Cap. ST-11489
★★★ Sammy Hagar / Cap. ST-11599
★★★ Sammy Hagar Live / Cap. SMAS-11812

Hagar was lead singer in Montrose before leaving to form his own band in late 1975. His first album, Nine on a Ten Scale, was notable mostly for a version of Van Morrison's "Flamingos Fly." But Hagar is a capable hard rocker of the generation weaned on Cream albums, and his brusque singing fits well with the polished crunch of his band. Backed by a group built around former Montrose members, Hagar charges through a variety of spotty material, including a number of songs he claims are destined for some future space opera, and covers items as diverse as Donovan's "Catch the Wind" and the Paul Revere and the Raiders' hit, "Hungry." The results are often pedestrian, but just as often enjoyable. — J.S.

MERLE HAGGARD
★★ A Tribute to the Best Damn Fiddle Player in the World / Cap. ST-638
★★ A Working Man Can't Get Nowhere Today / Cap. ST-11693
★★★ Eleven Winners / Cap. ST-11745
★★★ High on a Hilltop / Cap. STBB-707
★★★ His 30th Album / Cap. ST-11331
★★★ If We Make It Through December / Cap. ST-11276
★★ I Love Dixie Blues / Cap. ST-11200
★★★ I'm a Lonesome Fugitive / Cap. SM-2702
★★ It's All in the Movies / Cap. ST-11483
★★ Keep On Movin' / Cap. ST-11365
★★ Merle Haggard's Christmas Present / Cap. SM-11230
★ My Farewell to Elvis / MCA 2314
★★ My Love Affair with Trains / Cap. SM-11823
★★★★ Okie from Muskogee / Cap. ST-384
★★ Pride in What I Am / Cap. SM-168
★★ Ramblin' Fever / MCA 2267
★★ Same Train, a Different Time / Cap. SWBB-223
★★ Sing a Sad Song / Cap. STBB-707
★★★★★ Songs I'll Always Sing / Cap. SABB-11531
★★★★ The Best of Merle Haggard / Cap. ST-2951
★★★★★ The Best of the Best of Merle Haggard / Cap. ST-11082
★★★★ The Fightin' Side of Me / Cap. ST-451
★★ The Roots of My Raising / Cap. ST-11586

Merle Haggard has been compared to Woody Guthrie (for the populist streak in his songwriting) and such country heroes as Bob Wills, Jimmie Rodgers and Lefty Frizzell. Both comparisons are correct, but beyond his inheritance and the notoriety that "Okie from Muskogee" brought him, Haggard has made consistently listenable (and sometimes classic) country music since he began recording in 1963.

Haggard's parents drifted from dust-bowl Oklahoma to Bakersfield, California, in the early Thirties. Born in 1937, he was only fourteen when his father died of a brain tumor; he soon ran away from home, and a year later landed in reform school. In 1957, after several years of odd jobs and jail visits, the nineteen-year-old Haggard was sentenced to one to fifteen years in San Quentin on a safecracking rap.

When he was released, Haggard played guitar for Wynn Stewart, who gave him "Sing a Sad Song" to record as a single. Released on the obscure Tally label, it went to No. 19 on the country charts in 1963. Two years later, "(All My Friends Are Gonna Be) Strangers" became a hit and won him a Capitol contract.

The early *Sing a Sad Song* and *High on a Hilltop* (sometimes found as a twofer) contain those first two hits and such classics as "Swinging Doors" and "The Bottle Let Me Down." But those two, and *I'm a Lonesome Fugitive,* are effectively boiled down to the fine selection found on *The Best of Merle Haggard.*

Haggard recorded "Okie from Muskogee" in late 1969; the song, framed by a Muskogee crowd's applause, appears on the record of that title, a concert disc that also has good treatments of several Hollywood cowboy anthems: "White Line Fever," "Silver Wings," "Mama Tried" and "Working Man Blues," among others. *The Fightin' Side of Me,* a second live LP, documents a sometimes-uproarious Philadelphia show from 1970. Haggard's ex-wife, Bonnie Owens, fluffs Woody Guthrie's "Philadelphia Lawyer," and Merle runs through parodies, tributes and hits; "I Take a Lot of Pride in What I Am," along with "Okie from Muskogee" and "If We Make It Through December," the 1975 recession anthem, are the songs that made him something of a standard bearer of the so-called silent majority.

Haggard's tribute records—to Bob Wills (*Fiddle Player*), Elvis and Jimmie Rodgers (*Same Train*)—are adept but often mawkishly narrated, and superfluous except as shills for the originals. *I Love Dixie Blues,* which features him live in New Orleans with a Dixieland brass section, joins these derivative efforts as a curio.

Such marginal albums as *My Love Affair with Trains* enabled Haggard to release *30th Album* in 1974, only eleven years after his recording career began. The latter contains the salty "Old Man from the Mountain" and "Honky Tonk Night Time Man," which join "Living with the Shades Pulled Down" (from *Movies*) as studies of fatheaded but funny redneck libertinism.

The pick of Haggard's formidable output is contained in the two-disc *Songs I'll Al-*ways *Sing* and *The Best of the Best of*; *Eleven Winners* has similar intentions but is only a passable sampling whose release coincided with his 1977 departure from Capitol. His initial MCA release, and most recent album, *Ramblin' Fever,* contains only two of his own songs, which indicates that Haggard's career may be at a transitional stage. But his best songs reveal a composer/performer who is not only one of country music's glories but enduringly important on anyone's terms. — F.S.

BILL HALEY AND HIS COMETS
★★★ **Golden Hits / MCA 2-4010**
In 1954, Bill Haley assembled the bones of a synthesis of country swing, R&B, Big Band and Dixieland elements. He brought it all down on the second and fourth beats, and white rock 'n' roll was born as a popular phenomenon.

It took Elvis to put flesh on those bones, but the freshness and danceability of the medium Haley had outlined was not lost on the white audiences that began boogieing to "Rock around the Clock." (And not only whites—Haley made two of the five records by white singers that made the R&B charts in 1950-1955.)

The reasons for his success are still audible. If his breakthroughs (technical and commercial) seem tame and quaint today, they are still very listenable period pieces. And occasionally, a song like "Shake, Rattle and Roll" will ineluctably loosen up your legs. Excepting a few odds and ends, *Golden Hits* gets it all down in twenty-four quick doses. — F.S.

DARYL HALL AND JOHN OATES
★★★ **Abandoned Luncheonette / Atl. 19139**
★★★★ **Along the Red Ledge / RCA AFL1-2804**
★★★ **Beauty on a Back Street / RCA AFL1-2300**
★★★ **Bigger Than Both of Us / RCA AFL1-1467**
★★ **Daryl Hall and John Oates / RCA AFL1-1144**
★★★ **Livetime / RCA AFL1-2802**
★★★ **No Goodbyes / Atl. 18213**
■ **Past Times Behind / Chel. 547**
★ **War Babies / Atl. 18109**
★ **Whole Oats / Atl. 7242**
It may very well be true, as critic Paul Nelson has suggested, that Daryl Hall is so chic that, were he writing *Moby Dick,* he'd make the whale off-white. But this Philadelphia-based duo owes more to hard rock and street-corner soul than any of its disco-

based hits indicate; because their albums present such a decorative surface, songs sometimes blend together in an unnecessarily mellow mélange.

Their early records for Atlantic are erratic (the Chelsea sides include a goodly number of Daryl Hall demos and very little of his work with John Oates). The high point is, of course, the oft-recorded "She's Gone," an upbeat soul ballad worthy of the Spinners; it's included on both *Abandoned Luncheonette* and *No Goodbyes,* a collection released by Atlantic to cash in on the greater success the team has enjoyed with RCA.

With RCA, they've had better luck. Their biggest hit, "Sara Smile," is on *Bigger Than Both of Us,* but beginning with *Beauty on a Back Street,* hard rock re-entered the mix in a more forceful way. *Livetime,* a concert LP, presented their pop-soul in a most driving context, and *Red Ledge,* the most recent album, has one side of tough soul songs somewhat in the Gamble and Huff mold and another side of flat-out rockers, which include guest appearances from Rundgren, Robert Fripp, George Harrison and Cheap Trick's Rick Nielsen, all on guitar. — D.M.

TOM T. HALL

★ About Love / Mer. SRM-1-1139
★ Country Is / Mer. SRM-1-1009
★★ Faster Horses / Mer. SRM-1-1076
★★ For the People in the Last Hard Town / Mer. SRM-1-687
★★★ Greatest Hits, Vol. 2 / Mer. SRM-1-1044
★★ I Wrote a Song about It / Mer. SRM-1-1033
★★★★ In Search of a Song / Mer. SRM-1-61350
★ Magnificent Music Machine / Mer. SRM-1-1111
★ New Train—Same Rider / RCA AHLI-2622
★★★★ Rhymer and Other Five and Dimers / Mer. SRM-1-668
★★ Songs of Fox Hollow / Mer. SRM-1-500
★★★ The Storyteller / Mer. SRM-1-61368
★★★★★ Tom T. Hall's Greatest Hits / Mer. SRM-1-61369
★★★ We All Got Together and . . . / Mer. SRM-1-61362

Hall got his start as house songwriter for a Nashville country music publishing firm in the mid-Sixties and built a reputation for writing controversial material after Jeannie C. Riley turned his "Harper Valley P.T.A." into a pop hit single in 1968. By the time he started recording, Hall had already turned out more than 500 songs, and he wasted no time getting as much of it onto record as he could (sixteen albums' worth at last count). A number of Hall's songs, especially on his first four (now-deleted) albums, are well-drawn dramas about down-and-out and alienated characters. "Ballad of Forty Dollars," "Homecoming," "A Week in a Country Jail" and "Salute to a Switchblade" justify Hall's reputation for incisive storytelling. But much of the rest of his material is the hackneyed observation and freeze-dried sentiment of processed MOR country music.

Jerry Kennedy's excellent production of Hall's albums brought together many of Nashville's top session players (including Bob Moore, Buddy Harman, Charlie McCoy and Pig Robbins), and the earlier albums are also hot instrumental sessions, unencumbered by the ruthless country pop mixes of the later LPs, where saccharine but militant string sections drown out the backing band's ambiance.

Hall and Kennedy continued their successful formula until *Last Hard Town,* but since that record, Hall's writing has become more and more gimmicky while the production has turned to the maudlin strings and glossy postures of standard country-pop. Even at his worst, Hall still has enough wit to turn out an occasional gem like "Lying Jim" (from *I Wrote a Song about It*). But lately it seems he's more interested in selling pickup trucks than writing good songs. — J.S.

DIRK HAMILTON

★★★ Alias I / ABC 976
★★★ Meet Me at the Crux / Elek. 6E-125
★★★ You Can Sing on the Left or Bark on the Right / ABC D-920

A post-folk singer with a tenor that seems to emanate from the core of his Adam's apple, Hamilton has a gift for terse, evocative imagery that can be simultaneously bitter and magnanimous. Also loony (progressively more so with each album). Needless to say, he isn't well known, but *Alias I,* with its novel delineations of an ambitious, frustrated loner, and *Crux,* which has an even crazier cast, are hilarious and chilling albums. *You Can Sing on the Left* is uneven, but "She Don't Squash Bugs" juggles adoration and fear of women with admirable frankness and wit. — K.T.

HAMILTON, JOE FRANK AND DENNISON
■ **Love and Conversation / Play. PZ-34749**
More insipid than the originals, if you can believe that. (Now deleted.) — D.M.

HAMILTON, JOE FRANK AND REYNOLDS
★ **Fallin' in Love / Play. PZ-34741**
The title song, a No. 1 pop hit in 1975, was the sequel to their 1973 opus, "Don't Pull Your Love Out On Me Baby." Nonetheless, this is about as aggravating as white pop can get—phony soul grunts without a shred of feeling. — D.M.

HAMMERSMITH
★ **Hammersmith / Mer. SRM-1-1040**
★ **It's for You / Mer. SRM-1-1102**
As the name suggests, this is an overbearing Seventies hard-rock band. It is also a waste of time. (Now deleted.) — J.S.

ALBERT HAMMOND
■ **My Spanish Album / Cay. 1493**
Hammond had a sort of junky singer/songwriter hit in "It Never Rains in Southern California." This album, then, must have been recorded with the Spanish plains in mind—which does not help. — D.M.

JOHN HAMMOND
★★ **Big City Blues / Van. 79153**
★★ **Country Blues / Van. 79198**
★★ **Footwork / Van. 79400**
★★ **John Hammond / Van. 2148**
★★ **John Hammond Solo / Van. 79380**
★★★ **So Many Roads / Van. 79178**
★★★ **Southern Fried / Atl. 8251**
★★★ **The Best of John Hammond / Van. VSD11/12**
Son of famed talent scout John Hammond, Sr., this John Hammond comes by his de-

votion to country blues honestly enough, and performs with a pedant's rectitude. But Hammond has never developed the individual performing personality that is the mark of the true bluesman, black or white, and the result is that his albums sound more like exercises than the real thing. The exceptions are *So Many Roads* and *Southern Fried,* where he is backed by excellent bands, including members of the Band and the Rolling Stones on the latter. — D.M.

BO HANSSON
■ **Attic Thoughts / Sire SRK 7525**
■ **Watership Down / Sire K-6044**
More synthesizer doodlings from the man who made a "rock" version of J. R. R. Tolkien's *The Hobbit.* These aren't even that interesting. — D.M.

HAPPY THE MAN
★★ **Happy the Man / Ari. 4120**
Belated 1977 American release from a mediocre British art-rock band. (Now deleted.) — J.S.

LINDA HARGROVE
★★ **Impressions / Cap. ST-11685**
Middleweight Seventies country-pop singer. — J.S.

STEVE HARLEY AND COCKNEY REBEL
★ **Best Years of Our Lives / EMI ST-11394**
★ **Closer Look / EMI ST-11456**
★ **Face to Face / EMI SKBB-11661**
★★ **Love's a Prima Donna / EMI ST-11596**
★★ **Psychomodo / EMI ST-11330**
★ **Timeless Flight / EMI ST-11500**
When he first hit the scene in 1974, Harley was supposed to be a hard-rocking David Bowie, but concept albums and all, he's never amounted to much more than a mannequin, combining the worst qualities of Steve Marriott's strained vocals with the most nitwit Bowie-styled verbal concepts. Balderdash for sure. — D.M.

ROY HARPER
★★★ **One of Those Days in England / Chrys. 1138**
★★★ **When an Old Cricketer Leaves the Crease / Chrys. 1105**
Harper's roots are folk, but his product is more rock. The Briton has several import albums and has attracted such stars as Jimmy Page and Keith Moon as sidemen. His two most recent LPs mostly rock hard with

meaty electric guitar chords, but his self-indulgence mars the proceedings: he writes too many lyrics. The backup includes Bill Bruford, Chris Spedding, Dave Gilmour and John Paul Jones. — C.W.

DON "SUGARCANE" HARRIS
★★★ Sugarcane / Epic 30027

As half of the venerable R&B duo Don and Dewey, Harris has some claim to rock (well, doo-wop) fame. But here he engages himself as a violinist in a context closer to mood-jazz . . . nothing to scare Jean-Luc Ponty or Jerry Goodman, or even a Cajun crazy like Doug Kershaw, all of whom are more imaginative performers on the same instrument. — D.M.

EMMYLOU HARRIS
★★ Elite Hotel / War. MS-2286
★★★ Luxury Liner / War. K-3115
★★★★ Pieces of the Sky / War. K-2284
★★★ Profile / War. K-3258
★★ Quarter Moon in a Ten-Cent Town / War. K-3141

Emmylou Harris earned her reputation accompanying the late Gram Parsons, but her solo albums have brought her a country-pop following of her own. *Pieces of the Sky* is Harris' best; it flows at a consistently easy pace, the melodies soar and all that well-wrought sorrow makes her vulnerability seem almost voluptuous. Heartache and her gentle twang were made for each other, but in Harris' mouth, bravado comes perilously close to bathos. The hyper, hard-drinking, good-time loving songs she introduces on subsequent albums make her sound like a little girl in someone else's clothes. *Quarter Moon* and *Elite Hotel* are the most disjointed, but *Luxury Liner* similarly fails to establish Harris as the versatile country queen she'd like to be. She's all willow and no oak. The gumption, unusual in a backup singer, that Harris displayed with Bob Dylan (on *Desire*) and Parsons dissolves under the front and center spotlight. — A.S.

MAJOR HARRIS
★★ How Do You Take Your Love / RCA AFL1-2803
★★★ My Way / Atl. 18119

Like many Philadelphia singers, Major Harris has a limited range and a tendency to sing flat. *My Way* includes "Love Won't Let Me Wait," a hit whose selling point was the orgiastic moaning of an anonymous female. The album is a fair sampling of mid-Seventies Philly soul, but the fol-lowups are without distinguishable material or production gimmicks. — J.MC.

RICHARD HARRIS
★★ A Tramp Shining / Dun. DSX 50032
★★ His Greatest Performances / ABC Dun. DSX 50139
■ The Prophet, by Kahlil Gibran / Atl. SD 18120
★ The Richard Harris Love Album / Dun. DSX 50074

It's one thing for a breathless singer to rasp his way through Jim Webb's pop baroque pillow fights. There are compensations when Webb's overripe melodies get the orchestral exploitation of *A Tramp Shining.* "MacArthur Park," the hilarious masterpiece of the Webb-Harris collaboration, became a 1968 hit and revolutionized MOR by adapting John Lennon's "A Day in the Life" to the sentiments of an Erich Segal novel. Very effective.

However, it's another thing to try stretching such diva turns into a sustained musical enterprise. Which makes the rest of these simply embarrassing; he even makes *The Prophet* seem more pop-platitudinous than it was in print. — B.T.

DON HARRISON
★ Not Far from Free / Mer. SRM-1-1185

Harrison seems to be one of those journeyman rockers who had one great moment in him. It came in a song called "Living Another Day," a description of those journeyman travails. It's on the first Don Harrison Band album, not on this set of Hollywood pop-rock formulas. — D.M.

THE DON HARRISON BAND
★★ Red Hot / Atl. 18206
★★★ The Don Harrison Band / Atl. SD 18171

Clean, sharply focused, post-Creedence rock, courtesy of ex-Creedence drummer Doug Clifford and bassist Stu Cook, plus guitarist Russell Dashiell and Harrison himself—the latter an unreconstructed Southern rocker now based in California. The first album, *The Don Harrison Band,* is graced by "Living Another Day," Harrison's lovely, unassuming tale of the days he spent as a janitor in a recording studio, listening to everybody's music but his own. *Red Hot,* unfortunately, is cooled off. — G.M.

GEORGE HARRISON
★★★★★ All Things Must Pass / Apple STCH-639

A grand gesture—philosophically (check the title), musically (with Ringo Starr, Billy Preston, Dave Mason, Eric Clapton and Phil Spector), spiritually and morally. Coming at the end of 1970, the year the Beatles broke up, this three-record set established George as a heavy mystic and an ex-Beatle with a future. Cynics will note the presence of the same sanctimoniousness that has marred his later work; what saves this set is humility, respect for the audience and Phil Spector's typically Wagnerian production. A monumental album that makes a nice signpost for the Seventies.

★★★★ **The Concert for Bangladesh / Apple STCX 3385**
Harrison and friends (Clapton, Preston, Leon Russell, Ringo, Ravi Shankar and Bob Dylan, again with Spector producing) stage an overblown concert spectacular for the starving masses of Bangladesh, some of whom were to have benefited from the proceeds. Bob Dylan's is the best of the six sides.

★★ **Best of George Harrison / Cap. ST-11578**
★ **Dark Horse / Apple SMAS-3418**
★ **Extra Texture (Read All about It) / Apple SW-3420**
★★★ **Living in the Material World / Apple SMAS-3410**
★★ **Thirty-Three and 1/3 / Dark 3005**
With few exceptions, Harrison's post-Bangladesh work has been preachy, sophomoric and dull. Is that because of his tendency to work with mediocrities like Tom Scott, Billy Preston and Gary Wright? Partly—but the real conclusion seems to be that his bout with Indian mysticism has simply been too much for what were always limited entertainment abilities at best. — F.R.

GEORGE HARRISON
ALL THINGS MUST PASS

WILBERT HARRISON
★★ **Soul Food Man / Chel. 523**
Harrison is best known as the most successful popularizer of "Kansas City," which he took to No. 1 in 1959 over competing versions by James Brown and Hank Ballard. His only other Top Forty hit in 1969 was the bouncy blues "Let's Work Together," and the album released under that name (on the now-defunct Sue label) is well worth finding. *Soul Food Man* is an ineffective mid-Seventies attempt to recapture his sound, an unfortunate sole remnant for such an interesting if minor artist's career. — D.M.

JOHN HARTFORD
★★★★ **Aero-Plain / War. 1916**
★★★ **All in the Name of Love / Fly. Fish 044**
★★★ **Glitter Grass from the Nashwood Hollyville Strings / Fly. Fish 036**
★★★ **Mark Twang / Fly. Fish 020**
★★★ **Nobody Knows What You Do / Fly. Fish 028**
★★★ **Tennessee Jubilee / Fly. Fish 012**
Glen Campbell's former banjo player claimed a half-acre of Opryland for the freaks with the easygoing *Aero-Plain,* which features first-rate musicianship from Tut Taylor, Norman Blake and Vassar Clements. Since then, he's developed that obscure but witty turf over the five Flying Fish albums, which are samey but, taken one at a time, amusing. — A.E.G.

KEEF HARTLEY BAND
★★★ **Halfbreed / Deram DES 18024**
★★ **The Battle of North West Six / Deram DES 18035**
★★ **The Time Is Near / Deram DES 18047**
★★ **Through the Years / Lon. 2PS-600-1**
An interesting castoff from John Mayall's Bluesbreakers, Hartley's band gave the world such sub-luminaries as Savoy Brown's Miller Anderson, Uriah Heep's Gary Thain and other names known only to liner-note readers. *Halfbreed* is highly recommended to British blues fans; it features lots of unspectacular but solid keyboard work and some aptly pugnacious guitar. The other albums listed (the remnants of a half-dozen early Seventies releases) are cluttered by extraneous horns and flutes. Despite Hartley's American Indian obsession (which parallels Mayall's own), this was a decent workingman's blues band, in the mold of early Fleetwood Mac and Savoy Brown. (Now deleted.) — A.N.

DAN HARTMAN

★★★ **Instant Replay / Blue S. JZ-35641**
Former Edgar Winter bassist (he wrote
"Free Ride") turns to disco self-production
with catchy if inconsequential results. — D.M.

LISA HARTMAN

★ **Lisa Hartman / Kir. PZ-34109**
A regrettable stab at star-making by pop
entrepreneur Don Kirshner. Lisa is that
rarity, an almost completely talentless
singer. — J.S.

ALEXANDER HARVEY

★★ **Preshus Child / Kam. S. 2618**
★★ **Purple Crush / Bud. 5696**
Perhaps the most mild mannered of all the
country music outlaws, Harvey produced a
series of albums for a variety of labels in
the mid-Seventies. *Preshus Child,* a 1976 effort, is the most recent.

At his best, Harvey sings exactly like
Johnny Cash, a neat trick but hardly worth
investment of time or money. His most
well-known song, "Delta Dawn," was one
of the outstanding numbers on Bette Midler's debut LP. — D.M.

THE SENSATIONAL ALEX HARVEY BAND

★★★ **Live / Atl. 18184**
★★★ **Next / Vert. 1017**
★★ **The Impossible Dream / Vert. 2000**
★★ **Tomorrow Belongs to Me / Vert. 2004**
The penultimate (pre-Sex Pistols) British
working-class-hero band, SAHB is almost
unknown in the U.S. except to cultists.
Prime resources: raunch, energy, sweat.
SAHB (led by forty-three-year-old Alex
Harvey) exemplified the punk attitude long
before it was fashionable. Unfortunately,
most of what it did was better seen live
than endured on vinyl. *Tomorrow* includes
a bizarre one-act play, "Tale of the Giant
Stoneater." The Atlantic LP is definitive,
including extended versions of their crowd-
pleasers, "Vambo," "Tomahawk Kid" and
"Delilah." (Now deleted.) — A.N.

ANNIE HASLAM

★ **Annie in Wonderland / Sire 6046**
This high-pitched singer's solo debut tries
to play off the fairy-tale image central to
the success of her parent group, Renaissance. Even production from Annie's ge-
nius/eccentric husband, Roy Wood, fails to
make this banal set interesting. — J.S.

DONNY HATHAWAY

★★★ **Donny Hathaway / Atco 360**
★★★ **Donny Hathaway Live / Atco 386**
★★★ **Everything Is Everything / Atco 332**
★★★★ **Extension of a Man / Atl. 7029**
Hathaway is a fairly accomplished singer/
songwriter/keyboardist best known for his
duets with Roberta Flack. On his own, he
leans to the MOR side of the R&B axis.
His first two early-Seventies albums present him as a glib interpreter of pop material from "I Believe in Music" to "He Ain't
Heavy He's My Brother" and a fairly good
arranger. The 1973 album, *Extensions of a
Man,* is his major work, a stylistic hodgepodge with autobiographical overtones.
His version of Al Kooper's "I Love You
More Than You'll Ever Know" is very
good, and excellent instrumental support
from guitarists David Spinozza and Cornell
Dupree, bassist Weeks Willie and percussionist Ralph MacDonald rounds things
out. The live album is an unaffected and
spirited set of recordings from the Troubadour in Hollywood and the Bitter End in
New York. — J.S.

RICHIE HAVENS

★ **End of the Beginning / A&M 4598**
★ **Mirage / A&M 4641**
★★★ **Mixed Bag / MGM 4698**
Havens is one of the few singers who can
handle depressing material without resorting to melodramatics or self-pity. "Morning, Morning" and "I Can't Make It
Anymore," the best tracks on *Mixed Bag,*
demonstrate this beautifully. In a sense,
they captured, better than anything else,
the sadness behind the seeming ebullience
of the Woodstock era, and it's no accident
that it took a *black* folk-rock singer to do
it.

In subsequent years, however, Havens
has repeated this approach ad nauseum,
and little of value has emerged; the A&M
releases are recent and typical. — R.G.

DALE HAWKINS

★★★ **Dale Hawkins / Chess 703**
A solid set of Fifties rock 'n' roll—the
straight stuff—highlighted by the original
big hit, "Suzie Q." Most notable for the
driving guitar playing and Hawkins' overpowering vocals, which are an early
prophecy of John Fogerty's. — D.M.

RONNIE HAWKINS

★★★ **The Best of Ronnie Hawkins / Rou. 42045**

Hawkins was an early-Sixties rockabilly flash; his backing group, the Hawks, surfaced in 1965 behind Bob Dylan and came forth as the Band in 1968. This set collects material from Hawkins' several pre-1965 albums, most notably his titanic assault on "Who Do You Love" (fired by Robbie Robertson's historic guitar solo). After the success of the Band, Hawkins cut two smooth LPs for Atlantic and two drooling rockers for Monument, one of which, *Rock and Roll Resurrection* (out of print), offers the seminal fluids of rockabilly uncorrupted by overdubbed strings, tender love songs or good taste. (Now deleted.) — G.M.

HAWKWIND
★ **Doremi Fasol Latido / U. Artists LA001**
★★ **Hawkwind / U. Artists 5519**
★ **In Search of Space / U. Artists 5567**
★ **Quark, Strangeness and Charm / Sire K-6047**
★ **Space Ritual Live / U. Artists LA120-H2**
England's answer to acid rock, Hawkwind is primarily the medium for Bob Calvert's visions of science-fiction apocalypse. Concept overshadows music pretty drastically throughout the Hawkwind opus, and whatever social importance the band might have been credited with has dissipated over the years. Anachronistically, they still plug on. — J.S.

ISAAC HAYES
★★★ **Chocolate Chip / ABC D-874**
★★ **Disco Connection / ABC D-923**
★ **Groove-a-Thon / ABC D-925**
★ **Juicy Fruit / ABC D-953**
★ **Man and a Woman / ABC D-996**
★ **New Horizon / Poly. 1-6120**
Isaac Hayes first appeared, chains draped across his bare chest and calling himself Black Moses, as the last big-time proponent of the declining Memphis Sound. Though no heir to the tradition of Sam and Dave (for whom he wrote some great songs with partner David Porter), Hayes did gradually pick up steam by groaning long intros into truly gruesome ballads, which were expanded into huge workouts by his band, the Movement. Then in 1970, "Theme from *Shaft*," aided by Curtis Mayfield's "Superfly," put the disco seal of fate on soul music. But most of the *Shaft* album was bad movie music, and Hayes' first full disco album (his oldest still in print), *Chocolate Chip*, is alternately a lush and pushy party record, though Hayes unfortu-

nately dropped his ballad intros just as Barry White picked upon the gimmick. The followup, *Disco Connection*, is so evenly programmed for dancing that Hayes is almost absent, except for the rare growl. He returns, however, to torpedo *Juicy Fruit* with already horrific self-parody, whether conscious or not no one has ever determined. Subsequent Hayes is nothing but factory simulacrum, easily ignored and rather dadaistic in his overblown obsequiousness to the disco style and scene he at least partly fathered. — B.T.

JUSTIN HAYWARD
★★ **Songwriter / Deram DES 18073**
The Moody Blues guitarist hits an acceptable if unspectacular balance between the sugary and the hard. Catchy tunes and instrumentation, good guitars—similar but finally inferior to the best of the group. — C.W.

JUSTIN HAYWARD, JOHN LODGE
★★ **Bluejays / Thresh. 14**
Two ex-Moody Blues members make what sounds like a Moodies album, but a mediocre one. Lazy tempos, dull strings, syrupy lyrics, sameness. — C.W.

LEON HAYWOOD
★★ **Double My Pleasure / MCA 2322**
R&B producer-turned-singer had some moderate R&B chart success with his self-produced disco effort following up a couple of more successful earlier singles ("Strokin' Pt. II," "Just Your Fool") for 20th Century-Fox. — D.M.

EDDIE HAZEL
★★★★ **Game, Dames and Guitar Thangs / War. B-3058**
Hazel is a guitarist for Parliament/Funkadelic, and this 1977 solo effort, produced by Parliament/Funkadelic king George Clinton, is an exemplary addition to that group's black-rock vision. Hazel stretches out not only on the usual crazed originals, but also on a couple of Sixties favorites, John Lennon's "I Want You," from *Abbey Road,* and the Mamas and the Papas' "California Dreamin'." — D.M.

HEAD EAST
★★★ **Flat as a Pancake / A&M 4537**
★★★ **Gettin' Lucky / A&M 4624**
★★★ **Get Yourself Up / A&M 4579**
★★★ **Head East / A&M 4680**
★★★ **Live / A&M 6007**

St. Louis hard rockers forced themselves into the national spotlight after phenomenal regional popularity in the mid-Seventies. Though the band tends to be flatulent, there are good moments on all of these records. — J.S.

MURRAY HEAD
★ Say It Ain't So / A&M 4558
Head played Bob in *Sunday Bloody Sunday* (a brilliant piece of acting) and Judas in the original cast recording of *Jesus Christ Superstar* (enough to make you want to quit show biz altogether). He's got a penchant for sensitive and intense operatic muddles like this album, derived from the script of an unpublished musical called *Atlantis,* which Head couldn't sell. At least his out-of-print *Nigel Lived,* in which Head's protagonist lived a very emotional odyssey through late-Sixties London, was saved by its expert session musicianship. — B.M.

ROY HEAD
★★★★ A Head of His Time / Dot 2066
★★★ Head First / Dot 2051
★★★ Tonight's the Night / ABC 1054
Once a fine vocalist in the blue-eyed soul vein ("Treat Her Right" was a '65 hit), Roy Head has re-emerged a country singer—but of a different sort. The title of his second album (*Time*) is an ironic and intentional pun: a singer equally at home with country, rock, soul and Broadway show tunes—all of which are represented here—still waits his just due, critically and commercially. For its display of sheer vocal prowess, *A Head of His Time* stands as the definitive Roy Head album. — D.MC.

THE HEADHUNTERS
★★ Straight from the Gate / Ari. AL 4146
★★ Survival of the Fittest / Ari. AL 4038
Herbie Hancock's electric backup band tried its hand at disco funk with poor results. — J.S.

HEADSTONE
★★★ Headstone / 20th Cent. T-483
Intelligent British pop-rock, sophisticated yet accessible. The acoustic and electric guitars and violins weave imaginative textures around the catchy melodies, mostly from guitarist/lead singer Mark Ashton. Tight production from John Anthony. (Now deleted.) — C.W.

HEART
★★★ Dog and Butterfly / Por. FR-35555
★★★ Dreamboat Annie / Mush. 5005
★★ Little Queen / Por. PR-34799
★ Magazine / Mush. 5008
Take Ian Anderson and Robert Plant, endow them with mammaries, and you have the essence of Heart. *Dreamboat Annie* is a sharp, tolerably echoic first effort, unfortunately diluted by crosscurrent heavy-metal and anemic folk bents; *Little Queen* completely loses whatever focus the first set had, and *Magazine* sounds like what the group claimed it was: unfinished demos. *Dog and Butterfly* is a bit of a rebound. — M.G.

HEARTSFIELD
★★★ Heartsfield / Mer. SRM-1-688
★★ The Wonder of It All / Mer. SRM-1-1003
Passably interesting Seventies country-rock band. — J.S.

HEATWAVE
■ Central Heating / Epic JE-35260
★ Too Hot to Handle / Epic PC-34761
Despite the presence on *Too Hot* of a major 1977 hit single, "Boogie Nights," the most fitting subtitle here would seem to be: "Too Boring to Be Believed." Much less listened to for any length of time. — D.M.

RICHARD HELL AND THE VOIDOIDS
★★ Blank Generation / Sire 6037
Hell achieved New Wave notoriety as Tom Verlaine's foil in Television, before either man recorded. When he left that group, Hell took his apathy anthem, "Blank Generation," with him, parlaying it into a reputation as the voice of alienated American youth. Bull-oney. In the first place, Jack Kerouac said everything here first, and far better. In the second place, Hell is about as whining as Verlaine is pretentious. Stick with the Ramones, or someone else with a sense of humor. (God, I miss Keith Moon.) — D.M.

HELLO PEOPLE
■ Bricks / ABC D-882
■ The Handsome Devils / ABC/Dun. 50184
The ultimate evidence that mime acts should not be allowed to make records. Especially if they don't know enough to keep their mouths shut. (Now deleted.) — D.M.

LEVON HELM
★★★ Levon Helm / ABC 1089
★★★★ Levon Helm and the RCO All Stars / ABC 1017

Former Band drummer Helm's first solo outing (*Levon Helm and the RCO All Stars*) is aptly named, providing a vital context for blues harpist Paul Butterfield, keyboardist/guitarist Mac "Dr. John" Rebennack, guitarists Steve Cropper and Fred Carter Jr., bassist Donald "Duck" Dunn and a crack horn section led by Howard Johnson on baritone sax and tuba. Helm's Band cohorts Robbie Robertson and Garth Hudson also guest on the record. The session is a relaxed, semi-jam with basic arrangements that give everybody a chance to blow to their hearts' content. Helm's craggy vocals and Butterfield's harp pretty much steal the show, and the surprise inclusion of two of Rebennack's best tunes, "Washer Woman" and "Sing Sing Sing," flesh out a sturdy set of standards. The followup is not as hot. — J.S.

BOBBY HELMS
★★★ **My Special Angel / Voc. 73874**
Helms had a Top Ten hit in 1957 with the title cut, a nicely crooned R&B ballad, and followed it up with the Christmas novelty "Jingle Bell Rock." He hasn't been heard of since, except between Thanksgiving and New Year's. — D.M.

JIMI HENDRIX
★★★★★ **Are You Experienced? / Rep. 6261**
★★★★★ **Axis: Bold as Love / Rep. 6281**
★★★ **Band of Gypsys / Cap. STAO-472**
★★★ **Crash Landing / Rep. 2204**
★★★★ **Electric Ladyland / Rep. 6307**
★ **Isle of Wight / Poly. 2302-016 (Import)**
★ **Jimi Hendrix, Vol. 1 / Trip 3505**
★ **Jimi Hendrix, Vol. 2 / Trip 3509**
★ **Jimi Hendrix in Concert / Sp. 4031**
★ **Loose Ends / Bar. 80491 (Import)**
★★ **Midnight Lightning / Rep. 2229**
★★★★ **Smash Hits / Rep. K-2276**
★★★ **Soundtrack from *Experience*, Vol. 1 / Ember NR-5057 (Import)**
★★ **Soundtrack from *Experience*, Vol. 2 / Ember NR-5061 (Import)**
★ **Soundtrack from the Film *Jimi Hendrix* / Rep. 2RS-6481**
★★★★ **The Cry of Love / Rep. MS-2034**
★★★ **The Essential Jimi Hendrix / Rep. 2RS-2245**

Jimi Hendrix was the most innovative and momentous instrumentalist of the last decade. Perhaps more than any other jazz or rock musician, he personified the tension between a musician's facultative roles—intuition, intellect and technique—and his public image. If frustration over the latter

may have contributed to his tortuous life and too-early death, his triumph over the former transformed his brief career into a durable legend.

Nothing in Hendrix' early recorded output (which includes recordings with the Isley Brothers, Little Richard and the lamentable Curtis Knight releases) prepares one for the extraordinary metamorphosis that produced *Are You Experienced?, Axis: Bold as Love* and *Electric Ladyland,* or the Experience's assaultive live shows (best documented on the Monterey Festival LP shared with Otis Redding and on the imported *Experience* soundtrack). No electric guitarist since then—not Peter Townshend or Jimmy Page, nor John McLaughlin or Larry Coryell—has played without reflecting Hendrix' influence.

He redefined the guitar's parameters and, in the process, the scope of rock ensembles. By assigning Noel Redding's bass to a role more rhythmic than harmonic, Hendrix afforded drummer Mitch Mitchell the mobility to explore and color his surroundings in much the same way jazz drummers like Elvin Jones and Tony Williams did with John Coltrane and Miles Davis. The latitude suited Hendrix's boundless melodic and tonal imagination and, on those first three LPs, the Experience trio formulated a musical vision that melded the verve of rock to the nerve of jazz.

Those initial LPs also reveal Hendrix as much more than a technically innovative musician. He was a deeply moving and highly spiritual (although some of his more recklessly psychedelic metaphors now seem silly) songwriter, who took on big subjects (death, for instance, in "I Don't Live Today") with as much aplomb as he explored the backroads of sexual braggadocio (in "Fire," for example, and the great twelve-bar blues "Red House"). Yet he was capable of enormous tenderness: "The Wind Cries Mary," "Little Wing" and "Castles Made of Sand" are replete with well-executed, Dylan-styled, romantic-religious imagery. If Hendrix was a Super Spade who came along at just the right moment for a young white generation prepared to idolize black culture, he was always and decidedly his own man.

Although Hendrix continued to write and record prolifically, only one other record, *Band of Gypsys,* was released in his lifetime. Recorded live at the Fillmore East on New Year's Eve 1970, this is an intriguing but failed attempt to reduce Hendrix's music to its common denominator in soul.

Of the posthumous issues, *The Cry of Love,* the first, is a solid fusion of singing and songwriting, made more poignant for its air of parting. The bulk of the remaining releases—comprised of vapid studio outtakes and concert performances of varying quality—were slovenly assembled, falling deaf upon the ears of even the most ardent Hendrix idolater.

In an attempt to "set the record straight," veteran jazz producer Alan Douglas (who supervised some still-unreleased jams between Hendrix, Larry Young and John McLaughlin) negotiated with Reprise, which deleted the posthumous albums under the condition that Douglas cull ten sides of first-rate material from a cache of recently discovered tapes. But by overdubbing rhythm and vocal sections (and in some cases, a second lead guitarist), Douglas fanned rather than cooled the flames. *Crash Landing* works, *Midnight Lightning* doesn't, and neither can be trusted as "true" Hendrix. Worse, *The Essential Jimi Hendrix,* Douglas' repackaging of the earlier releases, does a disservice to Hendrix's best work, concentrating on such a limited perspective of the man's work— his abilities as a technologist of strings and studio—that it is almost worthless. The best Hendrix anthology remains *Smash Hits,* which includes the redoubtable blues, "Red House," and much of what's best from the first three LPs. — M.G.

NONA HENDRYX
★★★★ **Nona Hendryx** / Epic 34863
The former member of Labelle comes up with a solo disc that is somewhere between her old group's avant-garde R&B and heavy rock, à la the Who. This is admirable, winning stuff, maybe the hardest rock ever made by a woman (black or white), but it slipped through the cracks of record marketing clichés—how to promote a black woman on FM radio? how to promote hard rock on black radio?—so naturally there hasn't been a followup — D.M.

CLARENCE "FROGMAN" HENRY
★★★★ **Clarence "Frogman" Henry** / Rou. 42039
"Frogman" was a title that Henry earned with his hits "Ain't Got No Home" and "But I Do," classics of Fifties New Orleans R&B. The voice is incredibly croaking, the backing as funky as the best of that city's music. Unfortunately, this album doesn't include "Ain't Got No Home," though "But I Do" and a number of other fine

tracks are included. (Now deleted.) — D.M.

HENRY COW
★ **Henry Cow** / Virgin V2005
Secondhand *Bitches Brew,* from an avant-garde ensemble formed at England's Cambridge University. (Now deleted.) — A.N.

KEN HENSLEY
★ **Eager to Please** / War. B-2863
Uriah Heep vocalist/keyboardist/guitarist Hensley improves on his mediocre *Proud Words on a Dusty Shelf* (issued by Mercury, now deleted) but not by much. (Now deleted.) — A.N.

THE HEPTONES
★★★ **In Love with You** / U. Artists UA-LA805-R
★★★★ **Night Food** / Is. 9381
The Heptones come closer than any other reggae performers—even Toots and the Maytals—to completely merging the Jamaican idiom with American soul. Although the rhythm has the characteristic hesitation beat, the trio's vocals are patterned closely on the model of Stax and Motown groups; as if in tribute, they include the Four Tops' "Baby I Need Your Lovin'" on *Night Food.* Their leader, LeRoy Sibbles, is an excellent composer in his own right, and a more convincing polemicist than most of his Rasta brethren.

Night Food also contains versions of some of their earlier hits, including "Book of Rules" and "Mama Say." — D.M.

HERMAN'S HERMITS
★ **Herman's Hermits XX (Their Greatest Hits)** / Abkco 4227
If you need conclusive evidence that not everything that followed the Beatles out of

Britain in 1964–65 was brilliant, by all means hear this. The Hermits had plenty of hits—"No Milk Today" was about the best, the worst is a tossup between "Henry the Eighth" and "Silhouettes"—all in a sort of sub-English music-hall style. It would be cheaper, and no more unpleasant, to record yourself in the shower while holding your nose. Yecch. — D.M.

HERO
■ **Boys Will Be Boys / 20th Cent. 573**
Hard rock from the folks who brought you Shaun Cassidy and Debby Boone. Don't be deceived: this album's "The Kids Are All Right" is not a version of the Who's masterwork but some dumbbell's "original." — D.M.

JOHN HIATT
■ **Overcoat / Epic KE 33190**
Hiatt is about as ill at ease and forced as an R&B-based white singer/songwriter can get, which is awfully ill at ease and horribly forced. One suspects that *Overcoat*, released in 1975, will soon go the way of Hiatt's out-of-print debut LP. (Now deleted.) — D.M.

JOE HICKERSON
★★★ **Drive Dull Care Away, I / Folk-Leg. 58**
★★★ **Drive Dull Care Away, II / Folk-Leg. 59**
★★★ **Folk Songs and Ballads / Folk-Leg. 39**
As head of the Archive of Folk Song at the Library of Congress, Hickerson has access to an awesome reservoir of recorded and printed folk materials. More than access, however, Hickerson has a love of folk music that keeps him forever researching, writing bibliographies and, most importantly, singing and sharing songs that would otherwise be lost in the card files. His major contribution is not so much as a recording artist, but as an available source to others interested in folk music. A pleasant-voiced tenor, Hickerson is at his best with a group of friends singing on the choruses of both familiar and obscure numbers. Extensive notes on the songs' backgrounds accompany all three LPs. — J.M.

HICKORY WIND
★★★★ **Crossing Devil's Bridge / Fly. Fish 074**
★★★★ **Fresh Produce / Fly. Fish 018**
Excellent progressive bluegrass band. — J.S.

DAN HICKS AND HIS HOT LICKS
★★★ **It Happened One Bite / War. K-3158**
■ **Original Recordings / Epic 26464**
★★ **Striking It Rich / Blue Th. 36**
★★★ **Last Train to Hicksville / Blue Th. 51**
Is Dan Hicks Haight-Ashbury's answer to Jim Kweskin? No. Hicks and the Hot Licks have more up the sleeves of their seedy furs than hip camp and cabaret. The violin virtuosity of Sid Page, the spiffy harmonies of Maryann Price and Naomi Eisenberg and all those quotable sources, from Western Swing to Fifties cool, serve Hicks' curmudgeon's-eye view of life in the breakdown lane. Hicks gives nostalgia a mordant, modern voice. His ear for a piquant idiom extends beyond the last fifty years of popular song to the stuff of conversation. Hicks has cultivated a twang, a yodel and an air of gum-chewing innocence that fools no one—if he can help it. Probe his sentimentality and you find a sneer.
Warning: the forgettable *Original Recordings* are pre-Price and Eisenberg. The live *Where's the Money* (now deleted), on the other hand, is their moment of glory—durable, original, as feverish as a speed rap, as wryly romantic as a sloe gin fizz. — A.S.

HIGH COTTON
★★ **High Cotton / Is. 9395**
Discovered and produced (perhaps a bit prematurely in the group's development) in 1975 by the venerable Allen Toussaint and Marshall Sehorn, High Cotton is a seven-piece working-class band that plays Southern rock with a brassy edge. Despite a couple of hot white R&B originals (most notably "Ain't It a Shame") and a fine Allman-like ballad ("Meet Me at the Junction"), this debut LP fails to distinguish the band from the rest of the genre and was duly forgotten almost as soon as it was released. — G.K.

HIGH INERGY
★★ **Steppin' Out / Gor. G7-982**
★★ **Turnin' On / Gor. G6-978**
Late-Seventies R&B group came up with a big pop hit, "You Can't Turn Me Off," in late 1977. — D.M.

DAN HILL
★ **Dan Hill / 20th Cent. 500**
★ **Frozen in the Night / 20th Cent. 558**
★★ **Hold On / 20th Cent. 526**
★★ **Longer Fuse / 20th Cent. 547**

This Canadian singer is a cloying but (among young females) compelling performer of adolescent love songs. The atavistic lyrics and Hill's gasped vocals are complemented by strings, which set the tone of lonely-boy-in-the-woods romance. Hill's forte is using Poetic Statements to puff up seductions in pleasant surroundings. *Longer Fuse* (the title is apparently meant to evoke Jackson Browne's "The Fuse") is more of the same, but without pop-song relief, making it Hill's most self-important and confused LP, but also his most commercially successful, thanks to an Elton John–styled ballad, "Sometimes When We Touch." — B.T.

Z. Z. HILL
★★★ Dues Paid in Full / Kent 560
★★★ Let's Make a Deal / Col. JC-35030
★★★ Pure Soul / Kent 517
★★★ Soul Stirring Z. Z. Hill / Kent 518
★★★★ The Brand New Z. Z. Hill / Mank. 201
★★★ Whole Lot of Soul / Kent 526

Z. Z. Hill is an underrated vocalist with a lazy, relaxed singing style and a voice that resembles Bobby Bland's. The Kent LPs above are collections of Kent singles recorded in mock-Bland style; the arrangements are often less than imaginative, and overbearing horns tend to clutter many of the songs.

After leaving Kent, Hill recorded with a wide range of producers, each in a slightly different and offbeat vein, usually successfully. *Brand New* sports a Jerry "Swamp Dogg" Williams production; *Deal* is Philly-oriented disco material. Williams offered Hill a standard Muscle Shoals background with a catch: side one is linked by a thematic concept called Blues at the Opera, predating Millie Jackson's similar concept recordings.

What may be Hill's very best record, *Keep On Lovin' You*, has been deleted by United Artists. Production work is divided by Allen Toussaint, Lamont Dozier and Matt Hill, the singer's brother. Z.Z. proves to be a pliable stylist who fits well into the imaginative settings offered by all three mentors. — J.MC.

STEVE HILLAGE
★★ L / Atl. 18205
★★ Motivation Radio / Atl. 19144

Psychedelic God-consciousness meets electric guitar, and the mating nearly sinks mysticism. The former Gong lead guitarist, Hillage evangelizes a stoned, sophistic, hippie philosophy for the Seventies amid a permissive aural environment. In *L*, God meets Todd Rundgren (producer) and Utopia (musicians). To nobody's surprise, Todd wins, imbuing Hillage's music with a clarity and fever often missing in his own. If you like *High Times*, you'll like Steve Hillage. — M.G.

CHRIS HILLMAN
★★ Clear Sailin' / Asy. 7E-1104
★ Slippin' Away / Asy. 7E-1062

Within the context of the Byrds and the Flying Burrito Brothers, Hillman sang harmonies, wrote an occasional song and took the odd lead vocal, but he simply does not possess the vocal or lyrical talent to sustain interest over an entire album. Even with the assistance of virtually every "name" session musician in Los Angeles, neither of Hillman's solo albums really get off the ground. Typically, the two best cuts on 1976's *Slippin' Away* have fatal flaws: "Step On Out" is a rocking love story ruined by war metaphors, while an otherwise affecting lament, "Falling Again," is hampered by a gushy synthesizer. *Clear Sailin'* (1977) is bouncier, which at least makes it more listenable and "Quits" is a solid ballad. But on both albums Hillman is forced to cover his weakness as an emotive singer with harmonies on every chorus, thereby removing any tension or drama from the songs. As a luxury item in a group of greater talents, Hillman could be gratifying, but his solo career is strictly a mistake. — G.K.

JUSTIN HINES AND THE DOMINOES
★★★ Jezebel / Is. 9416

Relatively slick Jamaican reggae group, which places more emphasis on horns than is customary. The lyrical concern is as sociological as is usual for reggae, though not as sharp as the best of the genre. — D.M.

JOE HINTON
★★★ Duke-Peacock Remembers Joe Hinton / Duke X-91
★★★ Funny / Back. 60

Joe Hinton was an early-Sixties soul crooner whose most memorable song was an interpretation of "Funny," a country standard that featured an ear-splitting, falsetto finale. Hinton's songs had the same blustery, Big Band charts that were prominent in the music of fellow Duke artists Bobby Bland and Junior Parker. He died in 1965. — J.MC.

SAM HINTON

★★★ **I'll Sing a Story / Folk. 7548**
★★★ **Sam Hinton Sings Songs of Men / Folk. 2400**
★★★★ **Wandering Folk Songs / Folk. 2401**
★★★ **Whoever Shall Have Some Good Peanuts / Folk. 7530**

Hinton is a thoroughgoing folk historian, a walking oral history whose repertoire extends to more than a thousand American folk songs. His interests are often academic and not limited to folk music (he has also written several scientific texts), but his experience as a folklorist/entertainer goes as far back as the mid-Thirties, when he performed in vaudeville and on radio. He recorded several albums that are now out of print, but his Folkways catalogue is useful. Much of his material comes under the heading of children's songs, but the title is misleading—the wit and cultural interest of this material is enduring. *Wandering Folk Songs* is of particular interest because Hinton traces several songs through their historical development. — J.S.

HI RHYTHM

★★★ **On the Loose / Hi 32099**

As a backup unit for Al Green, Syl Johnson and Ann Peebles, Hi Rhythm has developed a reputation as a crew of tasteful and first-rate soul session players. This solo album, however, is hardly tame. Here the band opts for a refreshingly wacky and adventurous sensibility (including a song called "Superstar" that sports a banjo solo and a lyric that pokes fun at Green). — J.MC.

CATFISH HODGE

■ **For Free / 20th Cent./Westb. 202**

Can blue men sing the whites? Hodge is as tedious as they come. (Now deleted.) — J.S.

ROSCOE HOLCOMB

★★★★ **The High Lonesome Sound / Folk. 32368**

Holcomb was one of the greatest discoveries of the folk music revival of the early Sixties. This 1965 LP is the only recording still in print (he made two others), but it's a winner: Holcomb's voice is the essence of the title, and he's an adept banjo player as well. In addition, there's interview material—taped for the 1962 film of the same name—which gives a look at the sociology of the eastern Kentucky mountains. His answer about rock & roll is a classic—per-

haps one reason why Bob Dylan was one of this album's enthusiasts back when it was first released. — D.M.

THE HOLLIES

★★ **Distant Light / Epic KE-30958**
★★★★★ **Greatest Hits / Epic PE-32061**
★★ **Hollies / Epic PE-32574**
★★★ **Romany / Epic KE-31992**
★ **Words and Music by Bob Dylan / Epic BN-26447**

The Hollies never overcame the reputation they earned during the British Invasion as masters of finely crafted pop hits that made magic as singles but could make LPs tedious. In fact, some of the group's early Imperial albums (all deleted) were fairly solid, but more recently, they have seemed pop stylists rather than pop artists. The difference is crucial, perhaps best expressed by Graham Nash's need to leave the group in the late Sixties to escape its frothy limitations. (Crosby, Stills and Nash owes a good deal of its more substantial froth to what Nash learned with the Hollies, however.)

The Hollies' bright instrumentation and cheery harmonies thrive in catchy pop frameworks; when the formula was applied to more serious-minded interpretations, as on the Dylan album, the effect could be disastrous. The problem has never been performance—their harmonies are inevitably attractive and the instrumental accompaniment universally competent—but their material has often been at odds with their distinctly pop sound.

Greatest Hits, however, is a gem, even featuring versions of the Imperial hits ("Look through Any Window," "Bus Stop," "Carrie-Anne") along with the more recent "Long Cool Woman" and "The Air That I Breathe." This is undeniable proof that the two-minute-and-thirty-second single is the most potent rock & roll medium. Impeccably crafted, and as pleasurable as an ice cream cone on a blistering day, these songs hold a lot of teenage memories that are jogged and enlivened with each listening. — J.B.M.

BUDDY HOLLY

★ **A Rock and Roll Collection / MCA 2-4009**
★★★★★ **Buddy Holly / MCA CDLM 8034 (Import)**
★★★★★ **Buddy Holly—Legend / MCA CDMSP 802 (Import)**
★ **Buddy Holly—Portrait in Music / MCA COPS 4408-D/1-2 (Import)**

★★ **Buddy Holly—Portrait in Music, Vol. 2 / MCA COPS 5616-D/1-2 (Import)**
★ **Buddy Holly's Greatest Hits / MCA CDLM 8007 (Import)**
★★★ **Buddy Holly—The Nashville Sessions / MCA CDLM 8038 (Import)**
★ **Rave On / MCA MFP-50176 (Import)**
★★★★★ **The "Chirping" Crickets / MCA CDLM 8035 (Import)**
★ **The Great Buddy Holly / Cor. 20101**
★★★★ **Twenty Golden Greats / MCA 3040**

If any major rock figure was ever worse served by his record company than Buddy Holly, I'd sure like to hear about it. When he died (on February 3, 1959) in a plane crash near Clear Lake, Iowa (which also claimed Ritchie Valens and the Big Bopper), Holly had released only three American LPs. The first two (*The "Chirping" Crickets* and *Buddy Holly*) were long ago discontinued in America, but are still available as British imports under their original titles. The third (originally titled *That'll Be the Day*) was subsequently released as *The Great Buddy Holly* (on both Vocalion and Coral) minus one song, "Ting-a-Ling." It's still available, but what's more amazing is that the same album is available as an import (*The Nashville Sessions*) with "Ting-a-Ling" reinstated and, as a bonus, with a second, alternative rendition of "Rock around with Ollie Vee." Both versions of "Ollie Vee" are on *Nashville Sessions;* the first with Sonny Curtis (who wrote it) on lead guitar. The second was cut with the great country guitarist Grady Martin and with sax player Boots Randolph giving it a more raucous sound. The album is a real pastiche (the version of "That'll Be the Day" here is from 1956 and bears little resemblance to the one recorded with the Crickets, which was a radio hit in 1957), but shows Holly's great versatility while he was forming and settling into his rockabilly style.

Holly was actually on three record labels: He was first signed by Decca, which dropped him after the singles resulting from the Nashville sessions had no commercial impact. In 1957 he went to Norman Petty, who had a little studio in Clovis, New Mexico. Holly and his newly formed Crickets were sure that if they recut "That'll Be the Day," they would have a hit. Holly's Decca contract prohibited him from rerecording anything he had cut for that label. So they recorded the song under the Crickets' name and sold it to

Brunswick—a Decca subsidiary. At the same time, Holly began recording as a solo artist for Coral—yet another Decca subsidiary. The Crickets themselves did not sing; vocal backings were either by Holly overdubbing himself or by the Picks or the Roses, two New Mexico groups.

There was only one Crickets album, and it is a classic, with "That'll Be the Day," "Oh Boy," "Not Fade Away," "Maybe Baby" and "Tell Me How." Although Crickets came and went (Waylon Jennings among them), the essential band was Holly singing and playing astounding lead guitar, Joe Mauldin on standup bass and Jerry Allison on drums.

The same basic lineup yielded the second album, *Buddy Holly.* Even while "That'll Be the Day" was on the charts as the first hit, Holly was readying his masterpiece. "Peggy Sue" is the cornerstone of *Buddy Holly,* with Holly's yearning vocals soaring over Allison's drums, which sound like distant rolling thunder, and Holly's savage guitar breaks. That was not just a one-hit album, though, as so many rock LPs were in the Fifties. "Listen to Me" is one of the most haunting rock ballads ever recorded. "Everyday" sounds as fresh and clear today as it did then. "Rave On"—well, there've been few better rock songs recorded since. "Words of Love" remains one of the most underrated songs in rock history.

The third album, all material from 1956, was apparently rushed out to capitalize on Holly's success. Then he died. That's when the confusion started. What little material Holly had finished was rushed into release. What was not finished was shortened, lengthened, overdubbed or plastered over with strings and background vocals. Entire bands recut the instrumentals (the Fireballs were one group), and the material was otherwise altered, in many cases mutilated and distorted. Scraps of songs that Holly had taped were turned into "new material."

Eventually Coral (then Decca and MCA) issued ten more albums. All, fortunately, are now out of print except *The Great Buddy Holly* and *A Rock and Roll Collection.* The latter, a double album intended to be MCA's definitive Holly reissue, is a disgrace. No liner notes, no key as to who played on what cut or even when and where they were recorded. Worse, many of his best songs are left off. In addition, overdubbed versions of the songs released after his death are used instead of the originals. It's simulated stereo, instead of the mono originals. Finally, the version of "Love's Made a Fool of You" does not even have Holly singing on it; it was recorded by the Crickets without Holly. Avoid this album at all costs.

Collection is basically a reshuffled version of *Portrait in Music,* a two-record German import. *Portrait* itself should be avoided. *Portrait in Music, Volume 2* (also a two-record set) is interesting for its inclusion of two early recordings never available in America: "Queen of the Ballroom" and "Baby It's Love." It also includes some of the last songs Holly recorded in his New York apartment shortly before his death: "That's What They Say," "That Makes It Tough" and "Crying, Waiting, Hoping." (Recently, MCA released the excellent *Twenty Golden Greats* to cash in on the success of *The Buddy Holly Story* film.)

There have been massive box sets of Holly recordings released (at equally massive prices) in both Germany and England—where Holly's memory is clearly more revered than in America—but a basic Buddy Holly library is not that complicated. Three imports will suffice: *Buddy Holly, The "Chirping" Crickets* and *Legend* cover his career quite well.

Legend is a recent two-record set from England and, thankfully, it includes mono versions except where Holly originally recorded in stereo. It's also the most representative of Holly collections, with thirty-three cuts covering all the phases of his career, from Lubbock, Texas, to Nashville to Clovis to New York City. Holly was a complex musician and composer, not easily pigeonholed or catalogued, and *Legend* shows that well: if he borrowed here and there from Elvis or Fats Domino or Mickey and Sylvia, he gave much more of himself—and you can hear traces of what the Rolling Stones, the Beatles and even the Who would later borrow from him.

Despite a recording career that lasted only about eighteen months, despite being treated by his record company in a manner that makes "insensitive" an understatement, despite never having a No. 1 chart record in America ("Peggy Sue" hit No. 3), Holly remains an authentic rock & roll genius. Even Mick Jagger once said of him, "Buddy Holly, as far as I'm concerned, was the only original *white* rock & roller. All the rest borrowed from the blacks. Even Elvis. But Holly was original." — C.F.

HOLLYRIDGE STRINGS
■ **Beach Boys' Song Book / Cap. SM-2156**
■ **Beatles' Song Book / Cap. SM-2116**
Instrumental cover versions, pure schmaltz for those who can still remember the good old days (pre-Elvis). — S.H.

RUPERT HOLMES
★ **Pursuit of Happiness / Priv. 7006K**
★★ **Rupert Holmes / Epic KE 33443**
★ **Singles / Epic PE 34288**
★★ **Widescreen / Epic KE 32864**
Holmes—a bubblegum rocker turned pop revivalist—would probably like to be Barry Manilow with class. He started with something called "film rock," which was like ordinary rock except that it tried to be cinematic. Unfortunately, he forgot that easy listening means the music must be easy to listen to. He got the message in time for *Singles,* but he still didn't know what to do with it. — F.R.

HOLY MODAL ROUNDERS
★★★★ **Holy Modal Rounders, Vol. 1 / Prest. 7720**
★★★★ **Indian War Whoop / ESP 1068**
★★★★ **Stampfel and Weber / Fan. 24711**
Steve Weber (guitar and vocals) and Peter Stampfel (fiddle, banjo and vocals) were cocreators and lone practitioners of the genre known as acid folk. Stampfel, who has a working knowledge of almost every song ever written, and Weber, who only sometimes has a working knowledge of his own compositions, teamed up in the early Sixties and have produced such classics as "Boobs a Lot," "Half a Mind," "The I.W.W. Song" and "Bird Song" (one of the standouts on the *Easy Rider* soundtrack). *Indian War Whoop* has playwright Sam Shepard on drums, and its first side is a conceptual affair entitled "Jimmy and Crash Survey the Universe." Any of their albums are musts for lovers of out-of-control mind warp, although their best LP, *The Moray Eels Eat the Holy Modal Rounders* (Elektra), is sadly out of print. It features Michael Hurley's legendary "Werewolf" and a fractured rendition of the old jug-band favorite, "Mobile Line," not to mention "The STP Song" or "My Mind Capsized." — B.A.

HONK
★★ **Honk / Epic KE-33094**
★★ **Honk / 20th Cent. T-406**
Honk's debut album (Epic) was melodic, light pop with an occasional taste of coun-

try & western, advisedly not slick or syrupy. Modest (if undistinguished) arranging included guitars, keyboards, reeds and lots of vocals. Lively and unimitative, but usually unmemorable. The identically titled followup stuck to the same format but shed the C&W, recalling at times the smoothness of Boz Scaggs. — c.w.

HOODOO RHYTHM DEVILS
★★ All Kidding Aside / Fan. F-9543
★★★ Safe in Their Homes / World 9201
Although this San Francisco-based rock band has recorded on and off throughout the Seventies, these are their records that remain in print. Fortunately, *Safe* is their most deserving, featuring an interesting cover of Bob Dylan's "Tangled Up in Blue" and guest appearances by Ronnie Montrose, Steve Miller, the Pointer Sisters and the venerable Link Wray. *All Kidding Aside* suffers from the band's inability to recognize its complete lack of understanding of the mechanics of funk. — d.m.

HOOKFOOT
★★★ Good Times a Comin' / A&M SP 4338
Passingly interesting Seventies British rock band with strong R&B instrumental influence. Led by Elton John guitarist Caleb Quaye. (Now deleted.) — j.s.

LINDA HOPKINS
★★ Me and Bessie / Col. PC-34032
From a stylistic point of view, this album—and the Broadway show from which it originated—should have been labeled "Me and Aretha." Hopkins' singing owes nothing in style or spirit to Bessie Smith and everything to the melodramatic, melismatic gospel approach of Franklin and her predecessor, Clara Ward. Consequently,

the album's only success is a chilling, down-home rendering of "Fare Thee Well," a tune not associated with Smith. But "Fare Thee Well" is so good it almost compensates for the shallowness of the rest of the project. — r.g.

NICKY HOPKINS
★ No More Changes / Mer. SRM-1-1028
Hopkins, pianist to the stars (Beatles, Stones, Who, Rod Stewart, Jeff Beck and Jefferson Airplane, among others), drops into complete mediocrity with his solo album, which is probably the worst context in which to hear him. For collectors only. (Now deleted.) — b.t.

HORSLIPS
★★ Aliens / DJM 16
★★ The Book of Invasions / DJM 10
★★ The Man Who Built America / DJM 20
Heavy-handed rock adaptations of traditional Irish folk music: inappropriately dirty guitars, muddy production and a general lack of polish cover up the occasional inspired passages. — c.w.

JOHNNY HORTON
★★★ Honky-Tonk Man / Col. CS-8779
★ Johnny Horton Makes History / Col. CS-8269
★★ Johnny Horton's Greatest Hits / Col. CS-8396
★★ The Spectacular Johnny Horton / Col. CS-8167
★★★ The World of Johnny Horton / Col. CG-30893
Johnny Horton catapulted to national fame in May 1959 on the strength of the No. 1 hit "The Battle of New Orleans." He went on to quickly establish himself as the singer of history-oriented novelty songs, vignettes of life in Alaska and other oddities. But ironically, he had little serious album success until several months after his death in an automobile accident in Texas on November 5, 1960.

Blessed with a rough-edged voice that slipped easily into falsetto, and an infectious enthusiasm that helped him pull off his historical narratives on record, Horton was an early example of an artist who attracted both the country and pop audiences. Interestingly, he seemed to be turning away from pop/novelty items and settling into an unpretentious honky-tonk country vein when he died.

The Spectacular Johnny Horton, his debut Columbia album (after several singles for independent labels), found him with a strong voice but no direction. The country roots are there, but all the attention was garnered by "Battle of New Orleans" and "When It's Springtime in Alaska." Horton carried the musical chronicles genre to its furthest extreme on *Johnny Horton Makes History,* which, although it must be regarded as camp to be appreciated today, is indispensable for those patriots who thought the Bicentennial was the experience of their lifetimes. Subtitled "Action Tales of Battles, Heroes and Epic Events," the album did yield three hit singles, "Sink the Bismarck," "Johnny Reb" and "Johnny Freedom." His successful string of singles continued with the irrepressible "North to Alaska," the theme song of the movie of the same title. All these 45s were thrown together to create Horton's first hit album, *Greatest Hits.* It was the next two singles, however, "Sleepy-Eyed John" and "Honky-Tonk Man," that represented a move into a more indigenous country territory for Horton, and the posthumously released *Honky-Tonk Man* is generally considered his best.

If you're looking for one package that summarizes Horton's short but trenchant career, the best bet is the 1971 *World of Johnny Horton.* This double album includes not only the earlier novelty hits, but also much of the later honky-tonk, quasi-rockabilly material. — G.K.

BILL HORWITZ
★★ **Lies, Lies, Lies / ESP 3020**
Marxist—well, at least anticapitalist—folk-rock singer/songwriter, whose music was already an anachronism when released in 1975, but fine for those who like such things. — D.M.

LARRY HOSFORD
■ **AKA Lorenzo / Shel. 2132**
■ **Crosswords / Shel. 52003**
If this modish country singer/songwriter had satiric intentions, he'd be great. As it is, he's just another romantic macho on the make. George Harrison's presence on *Crosswords* can't begin to redeem its effusive embrace of every cliché in the book. (Now deleted.) — D.M.

HOT
★★ **Hot / Big 89522**
★★ **If That's The Way You Want It . . . You Got It / Big BT 76005**
One of the more interesting soul successes of 1977, Hot's hit single, "Angel in Your Arms," was a trashy mixture of girl-group nostalgia and contemporary rhythm that was only barely resistible. The rest of *Hot* and all of the followup was just the trash. — D.M.

HOT CHOCOLATE
★★ **Cicero Park / Big 89503**
★★ **Every 1's a Winner / Inf. 50002**
★★★ **Greatest Hits / Big 76002**
★★ **Hot Chocolate / Big 89519**
★★ **Man to Man / Big 89512**
English pop group of the mid to late Seventies, with an interesting mix of black and white members and influences. Its most important achievement has probably been writing the pop-reggae gem, "Brother Louie," which Stories made a U.S. hit. Others included "You Sexy Thing" and "Don't Stop It Now." Because the group had nothing to say when it stretched out, *Greatest Hits* is by far the best bet. — D.M.

HOT TUNA
★★ **America's Choice / Grunt BXL1-0820**
★★ **Burgers / Grunt FTR 1004**
★★ **Double Dose / Grunt CYL2-2545**
★ **First Pull Up, Then Pull Down / RCA LSP-4550**
★★★ **Hoppkorv / Grunt BXL1-1920**
★★ **Hot Tuna / RCA AFL1-4353**
★★ **The Phosphorescent Rat / Grunt BXL1-0348**
★★ **Yellow Fever / Grunt BXL1-1238**
When Jefferson Airplane guitarist Jorma Kaukonen and bassist Jack Casady conceived this band, they wanted to call it Hot Shit, but RCA wouldn't hear of it. Too bad. That endearing appellation was tailor-made for this band.

Kaukonen and Casady's blues excursions always seemed incongruous and circumscribed in the context of Airplane, and Hot

Tuna was originated as an outlet for such fantasies. Although the first album came from a live session, it prescribed the two sources from which the band would obtain its material: country and gospel blues standards and Kaukonen's occasional romantic songwriting. With *First Pull Up,* also a live recording, drummer Sammy Piazza and Airplane violinist Papa John Creach signed on, and Kaukonen plugged in his guitar, but none of this helped dispel the band's innate dispassion. In particular, Kaukonen's nasal, taciturn vocals and the excessive, meandering jams belied the assertions of blues spirit.

In spite of the departure of Creach and the replacement of Piazza with Bob Steeler, little progress was made from *Burgers* to *Yellow Fever.* Hot Tuna's dirge-like blues-rock became increasingly insular, and the musicianship, never to be faulted for technique, was now simply perfunctory. Kaukonen, once a biting, economical guitarist, now favored four-minute traipsing solos, and Casady's rumbling bass impeded the dynamics even more. *Hoppkorv* is unarguably the band's most aggressive LP, because its staggered layers of combative guitars, female harmonies and keyboard embellishments lend Hot Tuna a badly needed textural variety, something never approached (and rarely attempted) elsewhere in the band's work. — M.G.

CISCO HOUSTON
★★ Cisco Houston / Ev. 205
★★ Cisco Houston Sings American Folk Songs / Folk. 31012
★★★ Cisco Houston Sings Songs of Woody Guthrie / Van. 2131
★★★ Cowboy Ballads / Folk. 2022
★★★★ Cowboy Songs (with Woody Guthrie) / Stin. 32
★★★ Hard Travelin' / Folk. 2042
★★★ I Ain't Got No Home / Van. 73006
★★★ Railroad Ballads / Folk. 2013
Cisco Houston's main claim to fame is as Woody Guthrie's sidekick; he recorded many other albums with Guthrie, although his equal billing on *Cowboy Songs* was rare. Houston's best recordings are of Guthrie songs, but his vocal prowess wasn't particularly suited to the populist folk genre. He was halfway between a slick cowboy vocalist like Gene Autry and a pop singer of the late Forties–early Fifties era (when most of these sides were made). This made him a perfect vehicle for the pop-folk production on the Vanguard recordings, made during the Kingston Trio craze in the late Fifties. — D.M.

THELMA HOUSTON
★★★★ Anyway You Like It / Tam. 345
★★ Ready to Roll / Tam. T7-361
★★★ The Devil in Me / Tam. T7-358
★★ Thelma and Jerry / Mo. M7-887
★★ Two to One / Mo. M7-903
Thelma Houston is one of a handful of genuinely talented vocalists to emerge from the Seventies disco phenomenon. Before her big hit, "Don't Leave Me This Way," Houston had spent nearly a decade in obscurity, completing pop albums in Hollywood with Jimmy Webb and Joe Porter (now deleted) and turning in a perfunctory appearance on the soundtrack to Motown's *Bingo Long and the Travelling All-Stars.* All the while, she was perfecting her own gospel-based pop style, which has a chilling precision and nuance of phrasing rare in soul music.

By the time "Don't Leave Me This Way" clicked in 1976, Houston was more than ready; the rest of *Anyway You Like It,* and much of *The Devil in Me,* is a bit too mechanical to be considered successful, but her handling of ballads and standards is masterful. *Thelma and Jerry* was conceived as a reprise of Marvin Gaye's duets with Tammi Terrell, but Jerry Butler's failing voice and talents don't couple well with Houston's skill and zest. The other albums are exercises in competence. — R.G.

JAMES NEWTON HOWARD
★★ James Newton Howard / Kam. S. KSBS-2602
This multi-keyboardist's 1974 solo experiment is overstuffed but earnest, and occasionally interesting. His acoustic piano playing is pretty sharp here, but his monochromatic synthesizer washes don't work. Howard was later to gain notoriety as a keyboardist in Elton John's band. (Now deleted.) — J.S.

CATHERINE HOWE
★★ "Harry" / RCA LP1-5091
This 1975 one shot by an English actress turned singer/songwriter has its best moments with Tom Jans' "Loving Arms" and Bob Dylan's "To Be Alone with You." As far as her own writing goes, however, Howe remains an actress. — D.M.

STEVE HOWE
★★ Beginnings / Atl. 18154

The rough draft of a Yes album, from the group's guitarist. Howe is typically expert (except on bass). The backing is creditable, and an occasional passage shines, but most of the songs are too loose, his singing weak and the lyrics naive. — c.w.

REUBEN HOWELL
★★★ **Rings** / Mo. M6-799S1
Motown is a strange place to find an album by a white soul singer who covers songs by writers as diverse as Jeff Barry, Barry Mann, Cynthia Weil, Paul Williams, Allen Toussaint and Stevie Wonder. The material isn't much, but Howell's potent voice and the always excellent backing of the Muscle Shoals Sound Rhythm Section (strange place to find them, too) make this 1974 one shot more than passable. (Now deleted.) — d.m.

RAY WYLIE HUBBARD
★ **Ray Wylie Hubbard and the Cowboy Twinkies** / War. 2231
Hubbard was yet another of the Texas artists signed in the wake of the pop success of Willie Nelson's *Red-Headed Stranger.* Whatever charisma Hubbard has in person was not transferred to this record: turn instead to Jerry Jeff Walker. (Now deleted.) — c.f.

AL HUDSON AND THE SOUL PARTNERS
★★★★ **Cherish** / ABC 1035
★★★ **Do Ya Feel Like Dancin'** / ABC 12317
★★ **Especially for You** / ABC 1001
Especially and *Do Ya* aren't much, but 1977's *Cherish* is a highlight of recent Chicago soul—not disco, but not dated either. So far Hudson's appeal has been restricted to the soul market, but he's worth checking out by more than just cultists. — d.m.

THE HUDSON BROTHERS
★★★ **Ba-Fa** / R. PI 6-2169
★ **Totally Out of Control** / MCA 460
These three brothers bobbed momentarily on the waves of TV stardom with a variety show and they churned out typical Video Teen Idol singles to cash in on it. Atypically, the singles didn't sell well. The series was eventually canceled, and the boys made *Ba-Fa,* produced by Elton John lyricist Bernie Taupin. *Ba-Fa* is very good. The single from it, "Rendezvous," was marvelously tough, kinetic pop, but it bombed. The album has a blend of emo-

tional innocence and technical sophistication that recalls middle-period Beach Boys, but with a nice urban crassness. (Now deleted.) — k.t.

HUDSON-FORD
★★★★ **Free Spirit** / A&M 3652
★★★ **Nickelodeon** / A&M 3616
★★★ **Worlds Collide** / A&M 4535
Fronted by ex-Strawbs John Ford and Richard Hudson, Hudson-Ford is an appealing blend of tuneful stolen riffs, spry vocal harmonies and more enthusiasm than ten blocks' worth of Children of God. *Free Spirit* is one of the most instantly likable, accessible and good-timey pop-rock albums of the mid-Seventies. The other two LPs rate lower, because the songs are less appealing. The craftsmanship is equally adept, however, and fans of pop-folk music could do worse than to pick up on at least one of these. (Now deleted.) — a.n.

THE HUES CORPORATION
★★★ **Best of the Hues Corporation** / RCA APL1-2408
★★ **I Caught Your Act** / War. B-3043
★★★ **Rock the Boat** / RCA ANL1-2147
★★ **Your Place or Mine** / War. K-3196
"Rock the Boat" (1974), this vocal group's big hit, was a nicely bouncing pop-R&B number that they could never repeat. The band has since become more pop, without becoming more listenable. — d.m.

HUMBLE PIE
★★★★ **As Safe as Yesterday Is** / A&M 3513
★★★ **Eat It** / A&M 3701
★★★ **Humble Pie** / A&M 4270
★★★★ **Performance: Rockin' the Fillmore** / A&M 3506
★★★ **Rock On** / A&M 4301
★★ **Smokin'** / A&M 4342
★★ **Street Rats** / A&M 4514
★★ **Thunderbox** / A&M 3611
★★★ **Town and Country** / A&M 3513
Formed in 1968 by ex-Small Face Steve Marriott and future superstar Peter Frampton, Humble Pie enjoyed massive popularity until its timely demise in 1975. *As Safe* is fantastically progressive, similar to the best work of the Small Faces. *Town and Country* is uneven—here, they're clearly seeking direction. *Humble Pie* and *Rock On* mark the end of Frampton's studio contributions; both have a transitional feel, somewhere between intelligently crafted progressive rock and boogie excess. With

Rockin' the Fillmore, the group exploded commercially; mainly because of its success, the Pie concentrated thereafter on boogie. "I Don't Need No Doctor" and "Rolling Stone" became FM-radio and beer-party favorites—unfortunately, they also trace the decline of Marriott's voice, and simply bludgeoned the more melodically oriented Frampton.

Minus Frampton, *Eat It* had only Marriott's R&B perversions to rely on. Side four of this is live; the studio sides feature a black female chorus and a half-dozen R&B standards. The final pair of albums, *Thunderbox* and *Street Rats,* simply play out the string, with numbers by Chuck Berry and the Beatles pasted in to finish up a project that was as over as they come. — A.N.

HUMMINGBIRD
★★★ Hummingbird / A&M 4536
★★★★ We Can't Go On Meeting like This / A&M 4595

Vocalist Bobby Tench, bassist Clive Chapman and keyboardist Max Middleton first got together as early-Seventies sidemen for Jeff Beck. After their work with Beck, they formed Hummingbird with guitarist Bernie Holland and drummer Conrad Isidore, who was soon replaced by session genius Bernard Purdie. *We Can't Go On,* featuring Purdie, is as sizzling a studio fusion of jazz and rock as anyone has made. — A.N.

IAN HUNTER
★★ All American Alien Boy / Col. PC-34142
★★★★ Ian Hunter / Col. PC-33480

As lead singer and songwriter for Mott the Hoople, Hunter mined rock history for influences, looking for some mythic connection between Bob Dylan, the Kinks, Doug Sahm and Lou Reed. It turns out that Mott the Hoople *was* that connection, and though Hunter's penchant for self-indulgence eventually doomed his association with that group, he took the band's identity with him when he left. *Ian Hunter,* his 1975 solo debut, stands as a personal high point, a rocking extravaganza that features some of Hunter's toughest songwriting (from such gut crunchers as "Once Bitten Twice Shy," "Who Do You Love" and "I Get So Excited" to the pensive "It Ain't Easy When You Fall"). Mick Ronson's production and guitar-playing support is the perfect complement to Hunter's approach. The alarming slide guitar solo on "The Truth, the Whole Truth, Nuthin' but the

Truth" is one of Ronson's best moments on record.

All American Alien Boy seems to lack the desperation that charged *Ian Hunter,* and aside from several obligatory hot tracks (like the title cut), it's a forgettable album. — J.S.

IVORY JOE HUNTER
★★★ Ivory Joe Hunter / Ev. 289

Hunter, born in Texas and first recorded there by Alan Lomax in 1933 (for the Library of Congress), became an important R&B writer and singer after he moved to California in the Forties. As a writer, he had Fifties successes with songs for Nat Cole, the Five Keys, Pat Boone and Elvis Presley. As an artist, his biggest hits came in the mid-Fifties with Atlantic; unfortunately, most of these are out of print, although "Since I Met You Baby"—his only Top Twenty record—is available on several anthologies. (His earlier "I Almost Lost My Mind," a 1950 hit, was a No. 1 for Boone in 1956 as well.) Hunter's style is heavily derivative of Cole's, and on the early tracks included on Everest's LP, this is more apparent than ever. His silken crooning, in fact, anticipates much of what would later be incorporated into soul when it succeeded R&B as the basic black idiom with pop. — D.M.

ROBERT HUNTER
★★★ Tales of the Great Rum Runners / Round 101
★★★ Tiger Rose / Round 105

Hunter is a Grateful Dead lyricist, and his solo album is similar to records by other spinoffs of that group: at its height, it comes in a tad below the best Dead; at its worst, it exaggerates the aspects that make the Dead notoriously inconsistent. Hunter sings his admirably varied set of tunes like Jerry Garcia trying to imitate Randy Newman. Not exactly easy listening. — J.B.M.

MICHAEL HURLEY
★★★★ Long Journey / Roun. 3011

Hurley comes from Bucks County, Pennsylvania, where he used to hang out with Jesse Colin Young. When Young put together Raccoon Records in the early Seventies, he released two Hurley solo albums, now out of print and highly prized collector's items. Hurley's songwriting provided the focal point for the great 1976 *Have Moicy* album, which debuted the Unholy Modal Rounders and Jeffrey Fredericks and the Clamtones. The surprising success of that record led Rounder to commission Hurley's third solo album, *Long Journey,* featuring his characteristic catalogue of bizarre songs about twisted characters. "Reconciled to the Blues," "Hog of the Forsaken" and "The 8-Ball Cafe" are brilliant descriptions of human acceptance of degradation as a neutral, even interesting, condition. The musicians include Peter Stampfel on banjo and stalwarts from Hurley's sometimes backup band, the Redbirds: Morgan Huber, Robert "Frog" Nickson and Al Zangler. — J.S.

HUSTLER
★★★ **High Street** / A&M 4504
★★★ **Play Loud** / A&M 4556
They just don't make hard rock like this anymore—outrageous, shoe-stomping Anglo-raunch. At best, Hustler's got all the organ-heavy madness of the Nice's *Emerlist Davjack,* plus the metallic propulsion of peak Deep Purple and the passion of Free. There are too few bands currently mining this late-Sixties vein. The albums are produced by old-timer Pete Gage (formerly of Vinegar Joe), a man who understands what it means to get sodden, which is a complementary arrangement. Both records sound like they just finished a decade of charcoal-mellowing in a keg of Pinch. — B.M.

WILLIE HUTCH
★★ **Color Her Sunshine** / Mo. M7-871
★★★ **Havin' a House Party** / Mo. M7-874
★★ **In Tune** / Whit. K-3226
All of Hutch's albums have a stylistic similarity that can be traced to his first and best Motown record, the soundtrack to *The Mack.* Unfortunately, the best records by this limited vocalist/songwriter are out of print. These albums, like much of his other work, are too dependent on clichés to be of more than minor interest. — J.MC.

LEROY HUTSON
★★★ **Closer to the Source** / Cur. K-5018
★★★ **Feel the Spirit** / Cur. 5010
★★★ **Hutson II** / Cur. 5011
★★ **Leroy Hutson** / Cur. 5002
★★★ **Love Oh Love** / Cur. 5020
Hutson composes, arranges, produces, plays keyboards, sings (without real distinction) and poses for the album jackets. In the rhythmic scheme of things, he lies somewhere between the Brothers Johnson and Barry White, which probably would look more ridiculous (like twin blimps) than it sounds. He develops some nice grooves, but the songs tend to be overlong. Donnelle Hagan on drums and Benny Scott on bass are the stars; most of these have a good beat and you can definitely dance to them. That's the point. — A.G.

HYDRA
★★★ **Hydra** / Capri. CP 0130
★★★ **Land of Money** / Capri. CP 0157
★★ **Rock the World** / Poly. PD-1-6096
Hydra was routine but capable and varied blues-based rock: short songs, plenty of hard guitars (but no boogie excesses), occasional horns. The Allmans' influence (such as dual lead guitars) was evident but, to this Southern quartet's credit, hardly exploited. Wayne Bruce's vocals often resembled Johnny Winter's. *Land of Money* (produced by Johnny Sandlin) generally followed suit, although with some subtle nods to heaviness. *Rock the World,* the group down to a trio, extended this path, erring with bottom-heavy engineering and overly loud bass. (Now deleted.) — C.W.

IAN AND SYLVIA

★★★ **Four Strong Winds / Van. 2149**
★★★★ **Greatest Hits, Vol. 1 / Van. VSD-5/6**
★★★★ **Greatest Hits, Vol. 2 / Van. 23/24**
★★★ **Ian and Sylvia / Van. 79215**
★★★ **Ian and Sylvia: Early Morning Rain / Van. 79175**
★ **Nashville / Van. 79284**
★★★ **Northern Journey / Van. 79154**
★ **The Best of Ian and Sylvia / Col. CG-32516**
★★★ **The Best of Ian and Sylvia / Van. 79269**

Although they weren't nearly as well known as some of their peers in the early-Sixties urban folk movement, Ian and Sylvia were both a major force within it and deeply influential on the generation of rock and folk singers who followed them out of Canada. Much of Ian Tyson's phrasing can be heard in the work of Gordon Lightfoot, and in a less direct way, in Neil Young's. His wife, Sylvia, would seem to have had her share of influence on Joni Mitchell and the McGarrigle sisters.

The duo originally sang mostly traditional ballads, with voice and guitar occasionally augmented by autoharp or acoustic bass. But as early as their second album (*Four*) they recorded Dylan's "Tomorrow Is a Long Time," and Tyson wrote the title song. Sylvia's "You Were on My Mind"—from *Northern Journey*—became a pop hit for We Five during the folk-rock craze, and by *Early Morning Rain,* the duo was deeply into the day's leading folk-based songwriters, introducing the world to Lightfoot's classic title song and "For Lovin' Me," both hits for Peter Paul and Mary, and making a bow to country & western with Johnny Cash's "Come in Stranger."

Throughout, the pair's style was distinc-tive, the deep, rolling resonance of Ian's voice a perfect foil for Sylvia's soprano, often evoking Canada as a kind of successor to the Wild West. But when they tried to go fully country & western on *Nashville,* the results were dismal. The original songs weren't good, and even the pair of Dylan tunes ("The Mighty Quinn" and "Wheels on Fire") were better done elsewhere. (The deleted *Play One More* is a better exposition of this aspect.) They recorded briefly for Columbia (whence that label's *Best of*), with dire results.

The Vanguard *Best of* is a one-record collection that has some of their best work. But the *Greatest Hits* collections contain two discs each for the price of one. The first is an especially fine representation of their music. — D.M.

JANIS IAN

★ **Aftertones / Col. PC-33919**
★★★ **Between the Lines / Col. PC-33394**
★ **Janis Ian / Poly. 6058**
★ **Miracle Row / Col. PC-34440**
■ **Present Company / Cap. SM-683**
★★ **Stars / Col. PC-32857**

Postadolescent sob sister is three parts Susan Hayward to one part T. S. Eliot. *Janis Ian* contains "Society's Child," the protest song that made her a teen sensation in 1967. Her four Columbia albums are painstaking Rorschachs of bitter, humorless self-pity. *Between the Lines* contains Ian's best songs, "At Seventeen" and "Watercolors." — S.H.

ICE

★★ **Ice / Pass. 10075**
★★ **Import/Export / Pass. 10096**

The usual blips, squeaks and mechanical moans of European art rock, as manifested in the synthesizer effects of the late Seventies. — D.M.

IF
★★★ Not Just Another Bunch of Pretty Faces / Cap. ST-11299
This talented English jazz-rock band released about six albums between 1970 and 1975. *Not Just* is one of their last, recorded after personnel changes had altered the band almost completely. Still, worth a listen, mainly on the strength of Dick Morrissey's reed work. (Now deleted.) — A.N.

THE IMAGINATIONS
★★★ Good Stuff / 20th Cent. 497
★★★ The Imaginations / 20th Cent. 453
Solid disco music with undistinguished vocals but strong dance rhythms. — D.M.

IMPACT
★★★ Impact / Atco 36-135
★★★ The 'Pac Is Back / Fan. 9539
Impact is headed by a former second-generation member of the Temptations, Damon Harris, who sounds too much like Eddie Kendricks to be anything more than an interesting derivative. Still, these records have moments when they outdo Kendricks' own Philadelphia-produced albums. — J.MC.

THE IMPRESSIONS
★★★★ Best of the Impressions / ABC 654
★★ First Impressions / Cur. 5003
★★★★★ Impressions 16 Greatest Hits / ABC 727
★★ It's about Time / Coti. 9912
★★ Loving Power / Cur. 5009
★★★★ The ABC Collection—Curtis Mayfield and the Impressions / ABC AC-30009
★★★ The Fabulous Impressions / ABC 606
★★★★★ Vintage Years—The Impressions featuring Jerry Butler and Curtis Mayfield / Sire H-3717
★★★ We're a Winner / ABC 635
The Impressions were one of the greatest harmony vocal groups of the soul era. Formed in Chicago during the late Fifties, their earliest recordings were made with a group that included songwriter/guitarist/vocalist Curtis Mayfield and the brilliant singer Jerry Butler, resulting in beautifully constructed songs like "For Your Precious Love."

After Butler left, Mayfield gave the group a socially conscious gospel style that would remain unequaled until the Staples Singers turned to secular material in the early Seventies. Mayfield's high falsetto came to dominate the sound, and his songwriting certainly provided its most inspirational moments, raising the Impressions to a level matched only by the Temptations among Sixties black vocal groups. "Amen," "We're a Winner," "Gypsy Woman," "I'm So Proud," "Keep On Pushin' " and "People Get Ready" are all classic hits from this era.

Mayfield went solo in 1970, and the remaining members have carried on with disappointing results, first at Curtom (Mayfield's own label) and later with Cotillion, where attempts to modernize their style have faltered.

Of the records available, the well-annotated Sire collection is the top choice—it has the greatest historical scope. *The ABC Collection*, the *Best of* and *16 Greatest Hits* are all adequate documents, however, and none of the ABC material is less than respectable. The Curtom and Cotillion LPs ought to be avoided. — D.M.

DON IMUS
★ This Honky's Nuts / Bang 407
★ 1,200 Hamburgers to Go / RCA LSP-4699
Imus is indeed an outrageous disc jockey, entertainingly rude, opinionated and intentionally sloppy. He apparently needs the strict boundaries of AM radio to thrash within, however; freed to make uncensored records, he just dribbles on with a variety of unfunny sketches that rely on poorly rendered dialects and cheap topical jokes. — K.T.

THE INCREDIBLE STRING BAND
★★★ The 5000 Spirits or the Layers of the Onion / Elek. 74010
★★★★ The Hangman's Beautiful Daughter / Elek. 74021
★ The Incredible String Band / Elek. 7322
Like other mid-Sixties folkies, Robin Williamson and Mike Heron started out fitting personal chronicles and self-righteous protests to blues and fiddle tunes, though by their second ISB album they'd begun to forge an original style from a variety of traditions. Williamson favored the rhythmic liberties of acappella ballads and the weird shading of Middle Eastern quarter tones and used them brilliantly in "The First Girl I Loved." Heron preferred calypso accents and exuberant innocence. *The Hangman's Beautiful Daughter* is their most eclectic and most experimental album, a pattern (never equaled) for all the rest. Abstruse fantasies, reminiscences and parables are set to melodies that draw on everything

from spirituals to Gilbert and Sullivan. Unlike the later albums, *Hangman*'s sweetness and light is balanced by humor and vestiges of protest.

★★ **Changing Horses / Elek. 74057**
★ **I Looked Up / Elek. 74061**
★★ **Relics / Elek. 7E-2004**
★★ **The Big Huge / Elek. 74037**
■ **U / Elek. 7E-2002**
★★ **Wee Tam / Elek. 74036**

Middle-period String Band records are a tribal love feast—the whole family playing and singing about reincarnation and nature's way. Female participants Rose and Licorice (as befits their subordinate positions, presumably) are never listed with last names, but their piccolo-thin, high harmonies add an awkward grace to Heron and Williamson's frantic display on every kind of stringed instrument. It's spirit, not technique or playing in tune, that counts, and the String Band doesn't sacrifice communalism to aesthetics—voices may shrill and fiddles screech, but they're never discreetly buried on a track. At their best— "You Get Brighter" (*Wee Tam*), "Greatest Friend" (*Big Huge*), "Sleepers, Awake!" (*Changing Horses*)—the group transcends spiritual propaganda in songs that have the spacious simplicity of folk hymns. And Heron and Williamson's lively, resonant melodies rescue more songs than deserve it from self-indulgence and vapid mysticism. It's a tribute to their obsessive antiformalism that even their most accessible songs— from *Hangman* on—lose something when strung together on *Relics* (a two-volume collection spanning all seven earlier albums). The String Band goes nowhere if not with the flow. — A.S.

INNER CIRCLE
★★ **Ready for the World / Cap. ST-11664**
★★ **Reggae Thing / Cap. ST-11574**

When reggae albums this mediocre began being released in the U.S., it was a sign that the Jamaican genre had come of age as a multinational commodity. Although they're said to be a big thing back home, Inner Circle's American releases, at least, have all the rhythm but none of the exhilaration of the best reggae. — D.M.

NEIL INNES AND ERIC IDLE
★ **Rutland Weekend Television Song Book / ABC 98018**

Weird English humor that isn't terribly funny to Yank ears, plus parodies of pop music by a pair of former associates of the Bonzo Dog Band and Monty Python, respectively. For public-television addicts only. (Now deleted.) — D.M.

INTRUDERS
★★★★ **Save the Children / TSOP ZX-31991**

One of the first vocal groups to get the Gamble-Huff Philly-soul-production treatment. This is the only Intruders LP remaining in print, and it's a good one, with hot rhythm tracks, wonderful harmonies and an utter absence of the sodden religious philosophizing that mars recent Gamble-Huff lyrics. There's even a hit on the 1973 disc: "I'll Always Love My Mama," sentiments which seem much more appropriate to pop music than today's mystical mumbo jumbo. — D.M.

IRON BUTTERFLY
★★ **In-A-Gadda-Da-Vida / Atco 250**
■ **Iron Butterfly—Live / Atco 318**

Some might call the Iron Butterfly rock & roll semiologists for arriving at a mythic description of 1968's psychedelic heavy-metal *Zeitgeist* with the side-long title track from the first album, *In-A-Gadda-Da-Vida.* Others might argue that the track is a mock-epic Eden analogue. But the album that at one point outsold everything else in the Atlantic/Atco catalogue quickly became as forgettable an artifact as the group itself, so speculation as to its worth is pointless. It's now garbage. — J.S.

ISIS
★★ **Ain't No Backin' Up Now / Bud. 5626**
★ **Isis / Bud. 5605**

One of the early hopes for a female-based, and implicitly feminist, woman's band, Isis started stridently with its first album. Isis left room for development, even if it is wholly pedestrian. But instead of developing, Isis was sent to New Orleans to be remade by Allen Toussaint. *Ain't No Backin' Up Now* is predictably polished, and quite competent, Toussaint funk, but leader Carol MacDonald might as well be anyone from the sound of it, and that betrays the group's original concept. — B.T.

ISLEY BROTHERS
★★★★ **Forever Gold / T-Neck PZ-34452**
★★★ **Go for Your Guns / T-Neck PZ-34432**
★★★ **Harvest for the World / T-Neck PZ-33809**
★★★ **Live It Up / T-Neck PZ-33070**
★★ **Rock Around the Clock / Camd. ACL1-0861**

★★★ Showdown / T-Neck JZ–34930
★★★★ The Best of the Isley Brothers /
  Bud. 2-5652
★★★★ The Heat Is On / T-Neck
  PZ–33536
★★ The Very Best of the Isley Brothers /
  U. Artists LA–500–G
★★★ This Old Heart of Mine / Pick. 3398
★★★★ 3 Plus 3 / T-Neck PZ–32453
One of the longest-lasting groups in rock
history, the Isley Brothers have been making hits since the Fifties, and in a variety
of styles. Their first records were raucous,
sometimes delirious call-and-response affairs. "Shout," available on *Rock Around
the Clock,* provided the group with both its
first hit and also a signature song for the
frenzied gospel style. But despite an impressive number of single releases (including several that featured Jimi Hendrix as a
session guitarist), the Isleys' early-Sixties
output seemed a bit too raw for the marketplace; the exception was the remake of
"Shout," now considered a rock classic,
"Twist and Shout" (contained in the U.A.
set), which is as often covered as any song
of its era. (Perhaps the most notable version is the Beatles'.)

After shifting to Motown midway
through that decade, the group had one
other major hit, "This Old Heart of Mine"
featuring Ronnie Isley's wild, barely controlled tenor lead vocal, which gave the
group's sound an intensity rare for a Berry
Gordy act. (The Pickwick LP is a collection from the Motown period.)

The group was one of the first to form
its own label, T-Neck, in the early Seventies, giving it greater artistic control just at
the moment when soul was developing an
expanded consciousness. The early records
for Buddah—T-Neck's first distributor—
are typified by "It's Your Thing," a slice of
simple, hard-edged funk that was a hit in
1973. Gradually, with the addition of
younger Isleys (Ernie on guitar, Marvin on
bass and keyboard player Chris Jasper) the
conception broadened, and the influences
of Sly Stone, Jimi Hendrix and white hard
rock were incorporated. When T-Neck
switched to CBS as its distributor, its first
reward was a smash pop hit, "That Lady"
(from *3 Plus 3*), which set the pace for
most of the uptempo songs that followed:
infectious, snaky funk, highlighted by Ernie
Isley's sinewy guitar solo. Subsequent albums have shown the redundancy of the

young Isley's guitar playing and the group
hasn't developed the sound much past the
ideas presented on *3 Plus 3*. But such artistic conservatism has paid off: they may be
the products of a formula, rather than a
creative context, but all of the T-Neck/
CBS LPs are also in the platinum and gold
commercial range. — J.MC.

PETER IVERS
★★ Peter Ivers / War. B–2930
★★ Terminal Love / War. B–2804
An embittered Jonathan Richmond meets
Sigmund Freud. Peter Ivers might have
been a forebear of Television or Talking
Heads—if they'd ever heard of him. Ivers
is more concerned with rock & roll as
metaphor than music. His instrument is
the amplified blues harp, which he plays
without a single reference to the blues. It's
a second mechanical, atonal voice beside
his own. As a form-buster, proto-punk and
black ironist ("Felladaddio" and "You
Used to Be Stevie Wonder" are a couple of
his more inspired titles), Ivers is interesting. Listenable? Another story. Thrill seekers will enjoy his long-dead album of jazz
harmonica, *Knight of the Blue Communion*
(Epic). (Now deleted.) — A.S.

BURL IVES
★★ Burl Ives' Greatest Hits / MCA 114
★★★ The Best of Burl Ives / MCA 2-4034
■ The Times They Are A-Changin' / Col.
  CS-9675
Although his biggest hits—"A Little Bitty
Tear," "Call Me Mr. In-Between" and
"Funny Way of Laughin' "—came in the
early Sixties, Ives' real contribution came
in the post-World War II period. Having
performed solo as he traveled around the
country during the Thirties, and having
sung with the Almanac Singers on occasion, his postwar solo outings helped develop a public consciousness of folk and
folk-based material that would open the
way for the Kingston Trio and the hootenanny craze.

The *Best of* is an excellent children's album, with renditions of "Blue Tail Fly,"
"Hush Little Baby" and others, while
Greatest Hits is a career sampler spanning
twenty years, which includes his 1945 recording of "Foggy Foggy Dew" and the
three hits cited above. *The Times* is Ives'
condescending (at best) mid-Sixties attempt
to be contemporary. — I.M.

PAUL JABARA
★★ **Perils of Paul / Casa. 7055**
Disco concept LP in which an attempt is
made to turn a white soul singer into a
male answer to Donna Summer. The beat's
right, but the story doesn't match Summer's *Once upon a Time,* and the singing's
just this side of wretched. — D.M.

CHUCK JACKSON
★★★ **Needing You, Wanting You / All Pl.**
3014
★★★ **Patty / Stang 1027**
Chuck Jackson's early-Sixties hits, which
included "Any Day Now" and "I Don't
Want to Cry," combined an "uptown" production style (strings, heavy choral
backups and nondescript band tracks) with
his muscular baritone. Jackson is not the
most flexible of vocalists; consequently the
feel of those songs (available on a deleted
Wand *Greatest Hits* album) is too homogeneous. But the quality of the lyrics and the
intensity of performance lend them vitality.
"Needing You," a 1975 soul hit, was a welcome re-creation of the old style. The subsequent album is anachronistic and often
crude, but not without charm. — J.MC.

THE JACKSON 5
★★★★★ **Anthology / Mo. M7-868**
★★★★★ **Greatest Hits / Mo. M7-741**
When twelve-year-old Michael Jackson
first hit the airwaves in November 1969 as
lead singer of a quintet composed of five
brothers from Gary, Indiana, he was the
least likely rock hero to end the decade.
But Jackson was, and remains, an instinctively great soul singer, steeped in gospel
and capable, eventually, of drawing on all
that had come before, from Ray Charles
and Smokey Robinson to Sly Stone and
Jerry Butler. "I Want You Back," the first
J5 hit, has one of the greatest guitar lines

in soul history, and it was followed by a
remarkably energetic string of hits, including "ABC," "The Love You Save," "Never
Can Say Goodbye" and "Little Bitty Pretty
One," interspersed with Michael's solo
hits, "Ben," "Got to Be There" and
"Rockin' Robin."
   The J5 was one of the few soul groups
that made the transition to Seventies dance
structures easily. Their reputation as the
first black teen idols unfortunately tends to
obscure the sophistication of their music.
When the band left Motown for Epic in
1975—leaving behind brother Jermaine,
who'd married Motown owner Berry
Gordy's daughter—Motown chose to delete
all J5 records, except *Greatest Hits,* in favor
of *Anthology,* which includes Michael's
now-deleted hits. — D.M.

JERMAINE JACKSON
★★ **Feel the Fire / Mo. M7-888**
★ **Frontiers / Mo. M7-898**
★ **My Name Is Jermaine / Mo. M7-842**
Is there any significance to the fact that
brother Michael's best-sellers have been
deleted since he left the label, while the
Jackson family's sole Motown loyalist, Jermaine, finds his far less worthy albums still
in distribution? Oh, well, *Fire* has a few
nice riffs. — D.M.

MILLIE JACKSON
★★★★ **Caught Up / Spring 1-6703**
★★★ **Feelin' Bitchy / Spring 1-6715**
★★★ **Free and in Love / Spring 1-6709**
★★★ **Get It Out 'Cha System / Spring**
1-6719
★★★ **It Hurts So Good / Spring 1-5706**
★★★ **Lovingly Yours / Spring 1-6712**
★★★★ **Still Caught Up / Spring 1-6708**
Jackson first scored with a pair of fairly
conventional soul singles in 1972: "My
Man, a Sweet Man" and "Ask Me What

You Want." Those records are no longer available on LPs. *It Hurts So Good,* which followed in 1973, was notable principally for containing a couple of songs from the blaxploitation flick *Cleopatra Jones,* but it was less than exceptional.

With *Caught Up*, released the next year, Jackson and producer Brad Shapiro hit their stride. *Caught Up,* and most of what followed it, was based on a simple concept: Jackson rapping her way through one side as a seductress, daring the wife to keep her man; and on the flip, as the wife, challenging the temptress to take him. *Caught Up* interspersed a revamped version of Luther Ingram's R&B adultery hit, "If Loving You Is Wrong . . ." with original material to achieve her best effect. *Still Caught Up* continues the story, with material only slightly less fine. *Free and in Love* features a first-rate version of "Feel Like Making Love," doubly impressive because Jackson is interpreting Bad Company's song, not Roberta Flack's.

Lovingly Yours and *Feelin' Bitchy* seemed to have taken the concept to its limit—the latter's contents were so explicit that the album required an airplay warning on the DJ copy. But Jackson is obviously bold enough, and a sharp enough singer, to find a way out of even that dead end. Her saga, distinct from the triangular love affairs she sings about, is one of the most fascinating stories of the decade. — D.M.

PYTHON LEE JACKSON
★★ **In a Broken Dream / Cres. 2066**
This obscure Australian group's sole album probably would never have been released in America had it not been that when it was recorded, the band lacked a vocalist for the title track. A then (1970) unknown singer named Rod Stewart stepped in, and the result, while not terribly impressive as part of Stewart's body of work, became a hit following the U.S. success of "Maggie May." — D.M.

THE JACKSONS
★★ **Destiny / Epic JE-3552**
★★★ **Goin' Places / Epic JE-34835**
★★ **The Jacksons / Epic PE-34299**
In moving from Motown's production to Gamble and Huff's, something got lost. It wasn't the absence of Jermaine, who stayed behind, but the failure to come up with interesting vehicles for Michael's maturing voice. The groove is right for dancing, but that was also true of the old stuff, which had a lot more to offer. — D.M.

SHAWNE JACKSON
★★★ **Shawne Jackson / RCA APL1-1320**
Shawne Jackson was the singer in a short-lived mid-Seventies band led by ex-Mandala Soul Crusade, Bush and Guess Who lead guitarist Domenic Troiano. Troiano dominates the record, producing, arranging and writing most of the material, with his guitar the principal solo voice. The result is a kind of high-water mark for the Toronto R&B scene. (Now deleted.) — J.S.

WALTER JACKSON
★★ **Feeling Good / Chi-S. CH-LA656-G**
★★ **Good to See You / Chi-S. CH-LA844-G**
★★ **I Want to Come Back as a Song / Chi-S. CH-LA733-G**
★★★ **Walter Jackson's Greatest Hits / Epic E-34657**
A moody baritone crooner, Jackson made his reputation in the early Sixties as part of Okeh's Chicago soul stable; those R&B hits are included on the Epic collection. Only "It's All Over," from 1964, made any substantial dent in the pop charts, however.

Feeling Good, Jackson's Chi-Sound debut, includes a re-recording of "Welcome Home," his 1965 hit. But the rest of that album, and the others on Chi-Sound, are marred by rather wooden arrangements. — J.MC.

JADE WARRIOR
★★ **Jade Warrior / Vert. 1007**
★★ **Kites / Is. ILPS 9393**
★★★ **Last Autumn's Dream / Vert. 1012**
★★★ **Released / Vert. 1009**
★★★ **Waves / Is. ILPS 9318**
An intriguing, almost unknown English progressive rock band, heavily influenced by King Crimson, Jethro Tull and British jazz-rock. The LP covers are characterized by Chinese motifs that rarely carry over into the music. The Island albums, from the middle Seventies, are more experimental than the Vertigo ones of a few years earlier; *Kites* even manages "Teh Ch'eng," which finally realizes the group's Oriental flourishes. — A.N.

JAGGERZ
★ **We Went to Different Schools Together / Kam. S. 2017**
This is about as low as a one-hit wonder can get. The hit was "The Rapper," which made it to the second spot on the record charts in 1970. The album is the pits. — J.S.

THE JAM
★★★★ All Mod Cons / Poly. 1-6188
★★★★ In the City / Poly. 1-6110
★★★★ This Is the Modern World / Poly.
  1-6129
The most Who-influenced of all the late-
Seventies English punk bands, the Jam was
a trio led by Paul Weller, who had an
amazing ability to mimic and update Pete
Townshend's early song ideas. *In the City* is
perhaps too derivative, even including
"Batman Theme" as a sort of obscure
homage to one of Keith Moon's obsessions,
but the late 1977 *This Is the Modern World*
laid firm claim to its own turf, particularly
since the Jam was able to turn in the acceptable cover of Stax/Motown R&B ("In
the Midnight Hour") that the Who were
never able to manage. Potentially one of
the best bands of the Eighties, the Jam already ranks with the finest items the New
Wave has to offer. — D.M.

ETTA JAMES
★★★ At Last / Cadet 4003
★★ Come a Little Closer / Chess 60029
★★★★ Deep in the Night / War. K-3156
★★ Etta Is Betta Than Evah / Chess 19003
★★★★★ Peaches / Chess 2CH 60004
★★★★ Tell Mama / Cadet 802
★★★ Top Ten / Cadet 4025
The *New York Times* called Etta James "a
soul star who has been intense and intelligent about soul music for longer than anyone since Ray Charles." Others have called
her one of the great ballad singers of the
century on the basis of such classics as "At
Last," "I'd Rather Go Blind" and recent
treatments of Randy Newman's "God's
Song" and her own "Moanin'."
   Yet unlike Charles', James' record career
is an utter shambles, containing frequent
confrontations with hack producers and
some of the most unlikely, inappropriate
material imaginable. Even *Peaches,* an anthology of her early work and the one indispensable James album, is a mess. Tracks
were put together with complete disregard
for both historical continuity and listenability. Revved-up neo-Motown material
alternates with Southern soul ballads in
completely chaotic fashion. Yet if you pick
up and put down the needle at the right
spots, you can hear one of the two or three
deepest, most profound voices in rhythm &
blues.
   Of the other albums, *Tell Mama*—produced by Rick Hall in Muscle Shoals a
couple of years after that studio's success
with Aretha Franklin—is by far the best,

but also the hardest to find. It has a touch
of the flavor of Aretha's *I Never Loved a
Man* and features her most popular hit,
"Tell Mama," as well as "I'd Rather Go
Blind" and Otis Redding's "Security." *At
Last* and *Top Ten,* two early albums consisting of almost identical material, are
both better than one would expect. Both
were recorded in the early Sixties and feature decent, down-home renderings of
standards alongside some reasonably intelligent blues numbers. Both albums have
more than their share of junk, though, particularly the Motown-inspired numbers.
   Come a Little Closer is a comeback attempt engineered by former Three Dog
Night producer Gabriel Mekler. It's an
ambitious failure, with a stunning version
of "St. Louis Blues" ruined by a Mitch
Miller-style chorale background. But she
does well by Randy Newman, and the self-
penned, wordless "Moanin' " is a neglected
soul classic. *Etta Is Betta Than Evah,* on
the other hand, tries to be raunchy. It succeeds in that regard, but without much
quality. There's something forced about a
1975 album trying to capture 1962 loose-
ness, and too much is underdeveloped.
   While the great Etta James album is yet
to be made, *Deep in the Night,* produced by
Jerry Wexler and released in 1978, is more
intelligently assembled than anything else
here. Her readings of such pop hits as
"Only Women Bleed" and "Take It to the
Limit" are superb, and the arrangements
provided by Barry Beckett and Wexler are
excellent. James sings from the bottom of
her soul and this time, at least, it pays
off. — R.G.

JAMES GANG
★ Live in Concert / ABC X-733
★★★★ Sixteen Greatest Hits / ABC
  X-801
★★★ The Best of the James Gang/Joe
  Walsh / ABC X-774
★★★★ The James Gang Rides Again /
  ABC X-711
This version of the James Gang featured
guitarist/singer/songwriter Joe Walsh, a
gifted interpolater of West Coast and Brit-
ish rock styles who mightily impressed the
Who's Pete Townshend during a set in
Cleveland, the band's hometown. The first
album (*James Gang,* ABC 688, deleted)
shows their roots: a combination of Buffalo
Springfield's and the Yardbirds' guitar
styles. *Again,* the second LP, demonstrates
what Townshend responded to in Walsh's
playing. Walsh had figured out a rhythm/

lead-guitar technique that became the most significant post-Cream power-trio strategy. As side one of *Rides Again* indicates, he picked up a lot of cues from Townshend and Jeff Beck.

But Walsh was bored with the trio format. Side two of *Rides Again* presents him as a songwriter, leading the band on keyboards for a more layered effect reminiscent of late-period Beatles recordings. His facility with country-rock modes anticipates the trademark sound of the Eagles, which Walsh joined in 1976. *Rides Again* is one of the most important rock records of the Seventies.

By the time of the live album, though, Walsh's heart was no longer in the material. And since the band didn't have hits, the anthologies aren't particularly useful.
★ **Bang / Atco 7037**
★ **Jesse Come Home / Atco SD-36-141**
★ **Newborn / Atco SE-36-112**
★ **Straight Shooter / ABC X-741**
Drummer Jim Fox continued the James Gang but was never really able to find a suitable replacement for Walsh. The result was turgid Midwestern heavy metal. — J.S.

JIMMY JAMES AND THE VAGABONDS
★★ **Life / Casa. 7054**
This is a soul harmony group name, and in 1968, when "Come to Me Softly" was a big R&B hit, that is what this gang was. By 1977, when *Life* was released, disco was the name of the game, and they played it, probably wisely but not terribly well. — D.M.

SONNY JAMES
★★★ **Biggest Hits of Sonny James / Cap. SM-11013**
★★ **Country Male Artist of the Decade / Col. KC-33846**
★★ **If She Just Helps Me Get Over You / Col. KC-32291**
★★ **In Prison, in Person / Col. KC-34708**
★★ **Is It Wrong / Col. KC-32805**
★★ **Little Bit South of Saskatoon / Col. KC-33428**
★★ **Sonny James Sings the Greatest Country Hits of 1972 / Col. KC-32028**
★★★★ **The Best of Sonny James / Cap. SM-2615**
★ **The Guitars of Sonny James / Col. KC-33477**
★★★ **Traces / Cap. SM-11108**
★★★ **200 Years of Country Music / Col. KC-34035**

★★★ **When Something Is Wrong with My Baby / Col. KC-34309**
★★ **You're Free to Go / Col. KC-34472**
James' first hit was the soft-rock tear-jerker "Young Love," a 1956 rockabilly ballad smash, for Capitol. He has never repeated that pop success, but his country hits have been frequent, including a run of C&W No. 1s that lasted from 1967 to 1971. In 1972 he moved to Columbia, and that label's production mill has produced more hits but less satisfactory ones. James' voice is now much deeper than when he cut "Young Love," so he sounds somewhat like Johnny Cash. At his best—or simply when he is given a challenging project, like *Something Is Wrong*, which includes some soul-based songs and some rockabilly, or on the collection of classic and traditional songs, *200 Years*—he is still a surprisingly affecting performer. — D.M.

TOMMY JAMES
★★★ **Cellophane Symphony / Rou. 42030**
★★ **Crimson and Clover / Rou. 42023**
★ **In Touch / Fan. 9509**
★ **Midnight Rider / Fan. 9532**
★★ **Mony Mony / Rou. 42012**
★★ **My Head, My Bed and My Red Guitar / Rou. 3007**
★★★★ **The Best of Tommy James / Rou. 42040**
★★ **Tommy James / Rou. 42051**
★★ **Travelin' / Rou. 42044**
Tommy James' late-Sixties pop hits, with his group the Shondells and on his own, were actually first-rate AM rock. "I Think We're Alone Now," "Crimson and Clover" and "Crystal Blue Persuasion," a transparent allegory about his involvement with amphetamines, were interesting, if totally lightweight, radio fare. Had James come along at a time when the rock audience

was less self-conscious about the distinction between hit singles and concept albums, he might have turned himself into a precursor of Elton John and Neil Diamond. Unfortunately, Roulette's rather hidebound approach to marketing and his drug problem conspired against such respectability. His *Best of* album and *Cellophane Symphony,* where he does stretch out a fraction, remain worth hearing. But the rest, particularly the mid-Seventies Fantasy sets, in which he tries to become to Linda Ronstadt what Ford is to General Motors, are dull and dismal. — D.M.

JAN AND DEAN
★★★ Gotta Take That One Last Ride / U. Artists UA-LA341-H2
★★★★ Legendary Masters / U. Artists 9961

Jan and Dean, of course, were the principal competitors of the Beach Boys (whose Brian Wilson helped write many of their hits) in the surf-and-hot-rod scene of the pre-Beatles Sixties. Their hits included "Dead Man's Curve," "Surf City," "Drag City" and scads more, most of them pretty wacky. Neither Jan Berry nor Dean Torrance was an accomplished singer—they *looked* right, though—but they got by on nerve and sheer madness, which is better than well represented on side four of *Legendary Masters.* That record also includes the group's first hit, the pre-surf "Baby Talk." — D.M.

JANICE
■ Janice / Fan. 9492
Nice girls finish last, too. — D.M.

BERT JANSCH
★★★★ Jack Orion / Van. 6544
Jansch is a central figure of the British folk-rock scene, both on his own and as a member of Pentangle. He is one of that genre's most accomplished guitarists, and *Jack Orion* is his best and most influential recording. It features almost exclusively folk music of the British Isles, most of it completely solo but with occasional assistance from John Renbourn. A wide selection of other Jansch albums is available on import. — C.W.

BERT JANSCH AND JOHN RENBOURN
★★★★ Stepping Stones / Van. VSD-6506
Two spirited, agile and subtle acoustic guitarists; no backing. Mostly original instrumentals incorporating blues, jazz, British

Isles folk and Indian ragas. Occasional vocals from Jansch. — C.W.

TOM JANS
★★ Dark Blonde / Col. PC-34292
★★ Eyes of an Only Child / Col. PC-33699
★★ Tom Jans / A&M 3644
Best known for his collaboration with Mimi Fariña, Jans later had a Seventies career as a sort of macho California-based hip country singer. He developed a small cult, which apparently found sustenance in his plaints about the tough life of an All-American stud. *Eyes* has his best song, "Struggle in Darkness." — D.M.

AL JARREAU
★★★ All Fly Home / War. K-3229
★★★ Glow / Rep. 2248
★★★ Look to the Rainbow / War. 2BZ-3052
★★★ We Got By / Rep. 2224
Often hailed as a jazz singer, Al Jarreau is a protean vocalist still in search of a personal style. He can simulate virtually any horn or reed instrument with disarming accuracy, and his breathing maneuvers are nearly enough to send even Al Green back to yoga school. But thus far his techniques surpass his skills. His scatting swings with all the dexterity of a lumberjack, and his songwriting is rarely more than a flashy weave of passable soul fundamentals. *We Got By* is all original Jarreau and flows better than *Glow*, with its misplaced emphasis on pop warhorses ("Fire and Rain," "Your Song"). *Rainbow* is live. — M.G.

THE JEFFERSON AIRPLANE
★★★ After Bathing at Baxter's / RCA AFL1-4545
★★★★ Bless Its Pointed Little Head / RCA AFL1-4133
★★★ Crown of Creation / RCA AFL1-4058
★★ Early Flight / Grunt BXL1-0437
★★★★ Flight Log 1966-1976 / Grunt CYL2-1255
★★★ Jefferson Airplane Takes Off / RCA AFL1-3584
★★★★ Surrealistic Pillow / RCA AFL1-3766
★★★ Thirty Seconds over Winterland / Grunt BXL1-0147
★★★★★ Volunteers / RCA AFL1-4238
★★★ Worst of the Jefferson Airplane / RCA AFL1-4459
In the mid-Sixties an ambitious San Francisco artist/musician named Marty Balin

decided to put together a band to play at his club, the Matrix. The band eventually became the Jefferson Airplane, the first of the San Francisco bands that would become famous in the 1967 acid-rock era. Initially the Airplane was a folk group, with Balin singing lead and a woman vocalist, Signe Anderson, backing him. *Jefferson Airplane Takes Off* is dominated by Balin's pensive ballads and a decidedly folk-rock feel.

Surrealistic Pillow established the band's subsequent sound and put the group over the top commercially. Anderson was replaced by Grace Slick, who brought two of her own songs from her former group, the Great Society, both of which became hit singles. "White Rabbit" and "Somebody to Love" became the Airplane's trademarks, and Slick took much of the attention away from Balin, despite his inclusion of songs like "3/5 of a Mile in Ten Seconds" and "Plastic Fantastic Lover."

After Bathing at Baxter's attempted to capture the psychedelic aura of the Airplane's live performances on record. The record was divided into sections, but everything ran together into a seamless whole. There were some great moments, such as "The Ballad of You, Me and Pooneil" and "Won't You Try"/"Saturday Afternoon." The density of the album's production was truly staggering, but it was an attempt doomed to ultimate, even if heroic, failure. You can't record an LSD trip, so the album ends up sounding like a bizarre indulgence.

The Airplane went back to single tracks for *Crown of Creation*. The band had already begun to fragment, and Balin's lyrics to "The House at Pooneil Corners" provided a chilling science-fiction metaphor for its disintegration. Slick contributed two strange and poetic songs, "Greasy Heart" and "Lather." But Kantner's title song was the most significant track because it indicated the band's future direction into science fiction.

The live album, *Bless Its Pointed Little Head,* did everything it was supposed to do, and a lot of what *Baxter's* couldn't. The band took a lot of chances live and consequently was not always very good, but when it was right, it was awesome; this record gets those moments down for posterity. Guitarist Jorma Kaukonen, bassist Jack Casady and drummer Spencer Dryden are the stars on this set, and they set up their post-Yardbirds, metal electro-attack with sublime logical frenzy.

Volunteers is the band's best studio album. It was also its last gasp as a group. The Balin/Kantner political anthem, "Volunteers," and its companion piece, Kantner's "We Can Be Together," were written and performed at the height of the Vietnam War resistance movement and provided a stirring tribute to the utopian idealism of the late Sixties. A lot of similar sentiments have dated badly since then, but these songs stand, if only for their naive realism and refusal to despair. The album also includes the definitive version of the apocalyptic "Wooden Ships," written by Kantner with help from David Crosby and Stephen Stills. Instrumentally, the band was never sharper, with Kaukonen and Casady playing up a firestorm, and Kaukonen's adaptation of the traditional "Good Shepherd" was terrific, a precursor of his best moments in his own band, Hot Tuna.

After Balin left, the group literally fell apart. A cursory listen to the wretched *Bark* (deleted) will prove the point. The band had added violinist Papa John Creach and replaced Spencer Dryden with Joey Covington, but there were major problems with material and overall focus. *Thirty Seconds over Winterland* was better because it was live and unburdened by the need for new material, but it wasn't as good as *Bless Its Pointed Little Head.* The greatest-hits collections are what you might expect, but this band is not best represented by such anthologies, although *Flight Log* is almost comprehensive enough to do the trick. — J.S.

THE JEFFERSON STARSHIP
★★★★ Blows Against the Empire / RCA AFL1-4448
★★★ Dragon Fly / Grunt BXL1-0717
★★ Earth / Grunt BXL1-215
★★★★ Gold / Grunt BZL1-3247
★★★★★ Red Octopus / Grunt BXL1-0999
★★ Spitfire / Grunt BXL1-1557

The Jefferson Starship is the most obvious byproduct of the chemical breakdown of the Jefferson Airplane. When Airplane founder Marty Balin quit the group, the band splintered into two factions, the Paul Kantner/Grace Slick songwriting axis and the Jorma Kaukonen/Jack Casady instrumental duo (Hot Tuna). *Blows Against the Empire* was really a Kantner solo album recorded while the Airplane was in its death throes. Jefferson Starship was the name Kantner used for the assemblage of San Francisco players on the album (including Slick; Jerry Garcia, Bill Kreutzmann and Mickey Hart from the Grateful Dead; and Kaukonen's brother, Peter) and the name stuck when the Airplane foundered and Kantner kept going.

Dragon Fly was really the first Starship album. Kantner and Slick fronted the group, bringing only violinist Papa John Creach with them from the Airplane. Ex--Quicksilver Messenger Service member David Freiberg alternated on bass and keyboards with Pete Sears; John Barbata was the drummer; and Craig Chaquico played lead guitar. The instrumental personality of the Airplane was reduced to typical Seventies functional competence, making the band much less interesting but more disciplined than the Airplane. "Ride the Tiger" was as good a song as anything Kantner or Slick wrote for the Airplane, and "That's for Sure" was also good. But the rest was filler, with one major exception: Kantner's collaboration with Marty Balin, "Caroline," the album's best song, on which Balin performed a tremendous vocal.

When Balin agreed to lend a more complete hand to the making of *Red Octopus,* the Starship came into its own. Balin contributed to five songs and wrote a blockbuster ballad, "Miracles," which became the biggest hit single the Starship or Airplane ever produced. His presence inspired the rest of the band to excellence. Slick came up with two of her best songs in years, "Play on Love" and "Fast Buck Freddie." *Red Octopus* was a triumph for Balin, Kantner and Slick, one of the best albums of 1975 and proof positive that rock musicians can age gracefully.

Spitfire and *Earth* were disappointments after *Red Octopus.* They suffered not only by comparison, but from apparent fatigue. Slick sounds strained, Kantner overstuffed (on *Earth,* he's almost absent) and Balin either muzzled or uninterested. Creach was gone altogether. — J.S.

GARLAND JEFFREYS
★★★★ Ghost Writer / A&M 4629
★★★★ One-Eyed Jack / A&M 4681
A mulatto rock singer from New York, Jeffreys blends the cityscape into almost everything he's written. On *Ghost Writer* (1977), "Cool Down Boy" finds him moving from rock to reggae without losing a beat, and the mix of influences characterizes the album, which includes the great "Wild in the Streets," a single for Atlantic some years previously. *One-Eyed Jack* is cooler, the influences more nearly absorbed into a standard American rock format, but

it has some fine moments; the dedication to Jackie Robinson is appropriate, for Jeffreys triumphs through a similar mix of nerve and verve. — J.B.M.

JELLY
★★★ A True Story / Asy. 7E-1096
They look terribly unlikely—a pop vocal trio shouldn't contain a very plain woman, a tweedy John Le Carré type and a hirsute, bespectacled third party who could pass for an unfrocked minister—but they sound fairly swell. Now, if only some wag at Asylum hadn't persisted in booking them with the company's other big pop act, Bread. Thank God the Peanut Butter Conspiracy folded during the psychedelic era. — D.M.

SNUFFY JENKINS AND PAPPY SHERRILL
★★★ Crazy Water Barn Dance / Roun. 0059
★ 33 Years / Roun. 0005
Basically a novelty act of exceptional technical competence, Jenkins (banjo) and Sherrill's (fiddle) second Rounder LP, *Crazy Water,* is a much livelier and more virtuoso set than their first. Jenkins, though not as commercially successful as Earl Scruggs, is probably equally responsible for the development of the three-finger banjo style that became one of the backbones of bluegrass. — I.M.

WAYLON JENNINGS
★★★ Are You Ready for the Country / RCA AFL1-1816
★★ Country Boy & Country Girl / RCA APL1-1244
★★★ Dark Side of Fame / Camd. ACL-7019
★★★★ Dreamin' My Dreams / RCA AFL1-1062
★★★ Good Hearted Woman / RCA LSP-4647
★★ Heartaches by the Number / Camd. CAS-2556
★★★ Honky Tonk Heroes / RCA APL1-0240
★★ I've Always Been Crazy / RCA AFL1-2979
★★★ Ladies Love Outlaws / RCA LSP-4751
★★★ Lonesome, On'ry & Mean / RCA LSP-4854
★★ Mackintosh & T.J. / RCA APL1-1520
★★★★ Ol' Waylon / RCA APL1-2317
★★ Ruby, Don't Take Your Love to Town / Camd. 2608

★★★ **Singer of Sad Songs / RCA
LSP-4418**
★★ **The Best of Waylon Jennings / RCA
ASP-4341**
★★ **The Only Daddy That'll Walk the
Line / RCA ACL1-0306**
★★ **The Ramblin' Man / RCA AFL1-0734**
★★★ **The Taker/Tulsa / RCA LSP-4487**
★★ **This Time / RCA AFL1-5039**
★★★★ **Waylon and Willie / RCA
AFL1-2686**
★★ **Waylon Jennings / Voc. 73873**
★★★ **Waylon Live / RCA AFL1-1108**

The central fact of Waylon Jennings' career is not his status, along with Willie Nelson's, as one of country music's outlaws, but the power and durability of his big, rolling voice. He can use that voice to belt and purr; sometimes, as on his two versions of "MacArthur Park," his gruff fervor seems almost ludicrous, but he can also convey enough passion and vulnerability to elevate much mediocre pop and country vehicles as "Sweet Caroline" or "Ruby, Don't Take Your Love to Town."

Born in West Texas in 1937, Waylon found work as a teenage disc jockey in Lubbock and became Buddy Holly's protégé. He became bass player for the Crickets in 1958, but Holly died the next year in the legendary Iowa plane crash (Jennings had given his seat on the fatal flight to the Big Bopper) and Waylon began working bars in Phoenix, where he first met Willie Nelson.

In 1965, Waylon signed with RCA and moved in with Johnny Cash just outside of Nashville. The folk-tinged country albums he cut over the next four years are mostly out of print; *Heartaches by the Number* culls "country favorites" from that phase, but "Nashville Bum," from *The Only Daddy That'll Walk the Line,* makes early mock of the system he came to loathe.

The Best of Waylon Jennings (1970) marked the end of that period, and within a year Waylon said goodbye to the Opry shitkickers with *Singer of Sad Songs* ("Honky Tonk Woman") and *The Taker/Tulsa* ("Sunday Mornin' Comin' Down" was one of its four Kristofferson songs).

Waylon broadened his mystique with help from Willie Nelson on *Good Hearted Woman* (1972) and, still working with name sessionmen in Nashville, enlisted such quirky songwriters as Mickey Newbury and Billy Joe Shaver on his next three albums (all cut in one year of expanding crossover popularity). *This Time* and *The Ramblin' Man* (both 1974) showed

Waylon retrenching, using sparer arrangements for sets of introspective songs. *Dreamin' My Dreams* (1975), produced by Waylon with Jack Clement, completed his shift out of the RCA studio formula. The resolute beat of "Are You Sure Hank Done It This Way" and "Waymore's Blues" (in part a tribute to Jimmie Rodgers) joined with "Bob Wills Is Still the King" (live and fierce in Austin) to showcase a determinedly history-minded Waylon.

The first weeks of 1977 saw the release of *Outlaws,* an anthology on which Waylon joined with Willie Nelson, Tompall Glaser and his own wife, Jessi Colter, to affirm their collective image as outsiders—and to prove their marketability. The Waylon-Willie duet, "Good Hearted Woman," became a hit single.

As a result of the attention paid *Outlaws,* Waylon was ready, six months later, to address a new audience with a Neil Young title song: *Are You Ready for the Country* is laced with rock guitar, but as with 1977's *Ol' Waylon,* the real message is that the singer need not concern himself with labels.

Waylon is still tugging up roots; *Are You Ready*'s "Old Friend" celebrates Buddy Holly's enduring presence, and *Ol' Waylon* contains an Elvis medley and two tributes to the Willie/Waylon/Texas axis.

With *Waylon and Willie,* released early in 1978, the two veterans earned their credentials as reclusive pop stars. But the good news, as Waylon's cover of Stevie Nicks' "Gold Dust Woman" shows, was his easy power on both rockers and ballads. A planned collaboration with Pete Townshend, Eric Clapton and Bernie Leadon could be the seal to Waylon's crossover to stardom after twenty years of struggle. — F.S.

JETHRO TULL
★★★ **Aqualung / Chrys. CH4-1044**
★★★ **Benefit / Chrys. 1043**
★★★ **Bursting Out / Chrys. 2-1201**
★★ **Heavy Horses / Chrys. 1175**
★★★★★ **Living in the Past / Chrys. 1035**
★★★ **Minstrel in the Gallery / Chrys.
1082**
★★★ **MU—The Best of Jethro Tull /
Chrys. 1078**
★★ **Passion Play / Chrys. 1040**
★★★ **Repeat / Chrys. K-1135**
★★★ **Songs from the Wood / Chrys. 1132**
★★★★ **Stand Up / Chrys. 1042**
★★ **Thick as a Brick / Chrys. 1003**

★★★★ This Was / Chrys. 1041
★★ Too Old to Rock 'n' Roll; Too Young
to Die / Chrys. 1111
★★ War Child / Chrys. CH4-1067
Jethro Tull was originally, at best, a gut-busting fusion of jazz, R&B and progressive rock. Nothing the group has done since can equal the energy of the first album, *This Was,* a 1969 release that featured guitarist Mick Abrahams. *Stand Up* replaces Abrahams with Martin Barre, but like all subsequent Tull releases, it is dominated by flutist/vocalist Ian Anderson. *Stand Up* contains some of Tull's best music, but here is also the beginning of their characteristic diddling around.

Benefit finds Anderson still conceiving three- and four-minute songs, but *Aqualung* begins the slide into semi-autobiographical morality plays. Typically, *Aqualung* can be hummed, though it is not danceable. *Thick as a Brick* is a single song divided over two sides, with relatively undifferentiated movements. *Living in the Past* recapitulates the first five, adds some previously unavailable British singles and a live side from Carnegie Hall in 1970, which is based on "Dharma for One," off *This Was.* It is the essential package.

The rest are mostly interesting because of the pomposity of their themes. *War Child* is partially orchestrated and thoroughly eclectic; *Minstrel* has Anderson's most successful fusion of Elizabethan and rock structures; *Too Old* is a canard. *MU* spans their work from 1972 to 1975, but the selections are poorly chosen, especially compared to the well-executed *Living.* *Songs from the Wood* abounds with unadulterated Elizabethan boogie; this album owes more than most Tull to the Fairport Convention/Steeleye Span school of British folk rock. But all of those groups were better at it all along, probably because they didn't have to suffer under a dictatorial Pharisee like Anderson. — A.N.

JIGSAW
★★★ Jigsaw / 20th Cent. 545
"Sky High" was a major pop hit in 1975, and it's included here. The rest is of a similar pop-soul ilk, though not quite up to the standards of the hit, perhaps because the material is a bit weaker. — D.M.

JIM AND JESSE
★★★ Diesel on My Tail / Epic 26314
Country singing duo that's more interesting than most, because it has folk roots and a sense of history. — D.M.

JIVA
★ Jiva / Dark SP 22003
Premature outing from a faceless bass/drums/two-guitar quartet sponsored by George Harrison. Clean-cut approach: understated guitars, plodding rhythm section. (Now deleted.) — C.W.

J. JOCKO
■ That's the Song / Kam. S. KSBS 2604
Don't you think that if a member of an oldies act like Sha Na Na does a solo album, he ought to be able to turn in a decent performance of an oldie like Hank Ballard's "Work with Me Annie," at the very least? I do, too. — D.M.

BILLY JOEL
★★★ 52nd Street / Col. FC-35609
★ Piano Man / Col. C-32544
★ Streetlife Serenade / Col. PC-33146
★★★ The Stranger / Col. JC-34987
★★ Turnstiles / Col. PC-33848
This Long Island singer/songwriter and virtuoso keyboardist has earned an avid cult following by wasting his talent with self-dramatizing kitsch. At least that's the story with the first three albums (*Piano Man, Streetlife Serenade, Turnstiles*), which together have one good song, "New York State of Mind," on *Turnstiles. The Stranger* (1978) was a considerable improvement. Joel's singing, which has often and aptly been compared to the monotone of Harry Chapin, was given more effective support, which gave him a pair of hits, "Just the Way You Are" and "Only the Good Die Young," which also seemed to reflect an increasingly mature lyrical perspective. *52nd Street* went further toward rock, though even its best numbers—"Big Shot," "52nd Street," "My Life"—were closer to Paul McCartney pop. — D.M.

ELTON JOHN

★★ Blue Moves / MCA 2-11004
★★ Captain Fantastic and the Brown Dirt Cowboy / MCA 3009
★★★★ Caribou / MCA 3006
★★★ Don't Shoot Me, I'm Only the Piano Player / MCA 3005
★★ 11/17/70 / MCA 3002
★★★ Elton John / MCA 3000
★★ Empty Sky / MCA 3008
★★★★ Goodbye Yellow Brick Road / MCA 2-10003
★★★★★ Greatest Hits / MCA 3007
★★★ Greatest Hits, Vol. 2 / MCA 3027
★★★★ Honky Château / MCA 3004
★★★ Madman across the Water / MCA 3003
★★★★ Rock of the Westies / MCA 3010
★★★ Single Man / MCA 3065
★★★★ Tumbleweed Connection / MCA 3001

One of the most massively popular stars of the mid-Seventies, Elton John offends purists for reveling in his fame, for being sloppy in matters of technique and for indulging in extreme sentimentality. He attained his stardom by encouraging just these "faults," however, and by combining them with a fan's enthusiasm for the opulence of rock, he has produced some of the catchiest and most durable pop rock ever made.

His debut American album, *Elton John,* displays none of the above flaws, save a bracing wallow in sentimentality. *Elton John* presents John as a quiveringly sensitive singer and pianist, thoughtful and romantic, if lyrically soft-headed. For this last, Elton could not entirely be blamed; his words are provided by Bernie Taupin, a fellow Englishman with an obsession with the American West and sledgehammer metaphors. "Your Song," melding one of John's most succinct, pretty melodies and Taupin's most terse lyrics, was their first American hit.

Tumbleweed Connection revealed a few more sides of John's personality. His piano playing on "Burn Down the Mission" and "Amoreena" is extravagant, and the entire record allows Taupin to portray scenes of rural Americana that range from ludicrous realism ("Ballad of a Well-Known Gun") to touching fantasy ("Country Comfort").

A live album, *11/17/70,* follows. It laid the foundation for anti-Johnists: a cheerfully idiotic and self-indulgent mess, culminating in an eighteen-minute version of "Burn Down the Mission" that also worked in hysterical salutes to two of Elton's heroes, Elvis and the Beatles—pass it by.

The next three albums established Elton John as a dependable purveyor of hit singles. *Madman across the Water*'s title song and "Levon," *Honky Château*'s "Rocket Man" and *Don't Shoot Me, I'm Only the Piano Player*'s "Daniel" anchored his dreamy style, heavy on the lugubrious piano and John's ballad voice, which sounds as if he's trying to sing into his stomach and draws out syllables beyond recognition. The fast songs on these albums rank with the best radio music of the period: "Crocodile Rock," "Honky Cat" and "Teacher I Need You" are, when coherent, vapidly adolescent, ranting with unfulfilled lusts and flushed with the thrill of petty rebellion—in short, pop rock in the classic mold.

For a pair of self-conscious moralists like John and Taupin, *Goodbye Yellow Brick Road* is a surprisingly provocative double album, even more miraculous for the fact that its four sides all deal in some way or another with that dull subject, the vicissitudes of public life. *Goodbye* is wildly uneven: a ditheringly bitter song, "Funeral for a Friend," which begins ponderously and concludes with a smash of rock fury, leads off the album. There are commercial triumphs ("Bennie and the Jets," "Saturday Night's Alright for Fighting") alongside inexplicably overlooked sure-shots like "Jamaica Jerk-Off " (they could have changed the title for the radio) and "Your Sister Can't Twist (But She Can Rock 'n' Roll)." The title song is Taupin at his most maudlin, and "Candle in the Wind," a "tribute" to Marilyn Monroe, is so unrelievedly embarrassing that it actually exerts a certain queer fascination that impels listening, which a lilting chorus encourages.

Caribou is the aural equivalent of the outlandish eyeglasses and stage dress Elton sported at the time. The album's prime weirdie is "Solar Prestige a Gammon," banal nonsense lyrics redeemed by a melody both spirited and malevolent. *Caribou* also contains John's most endearing misogynist tune, "The Bitch Is Back," which may not despise women at all: Elton's voice so parodies the blithe macho of Taupin's lyric that it undermines the song entirely. Instead, Elton makes "Bitch" a slap at, if anyone, himself—the superstar more than capable of bitchiness. "Bitch" is the archetypal Elton John hard-rock number—one vast hook, with inseparable melody and chorus. John pumps away at the piano like the bizarre nephew of Jerry Lee Lewis that he is; Davey Johnstone lays down a cushy bed of vibrating lead guitar; and Nigel Olsson slides in precise and wry drumming. This is the way it is on every great fast Elton single.

Empty Sky is the American release of the first LP of wimpy introspection that John recorded in the late Sixties. His real first album, and in the face of what followed, easily dismissed.

Captain Fantastic and the Brown Dirt Cowboy is a lumpy concept album, one of Taupin's typically muzzy parables about stardom versus the normal life, and Taupin never means it ironically. *Captain* follows a quite rigid rule: when the melodies are attractive, the lyrics repel, and vice versa. Big exception: "Meal Ticket," one of John's very hardest rockers; Taupin's sketch of a desperate young prole is witty and bitter and has the ring of authenticity—a real marvel.

Rock of the Westies appeared just as John's public appeal reached its zenith. As with all gigantically popular stars, Elton peaked, and *Westies'* sales suffered for it. *Westies* is, however, one of the best records Elton John has made, crammed with passion both nasty and hilarious. He has never been this unguarded, this totally committed a rock & roller, this frantically magnanimous with his passion for fast music. *Westies'* hooks are artfully entwined with John's smoothest, quickest melodies, and for once Taupin's lyrics are succinct and functional. *Rock of the Westies* is one of the most darkly funny and moving hardrock records of the Seventies.

The publicity that peaked just before *Westies* created a backlash, a fact that would be irrelevant except that its effect suffuses John's next collection, *Blue Moves,* a double album that wobbles with selfdoubt, self-pity and self-hatred. Within John's dirge-paced melodies, Taupin spins a line of pretentious obfuscation and non sequitur lamentation. *Blue Moves* is not just not fun, it's boring, something that heretofore seemed impossible from the irrepressible Elton John.   — K.T.

JOHNNY'S DANCE BAND
■ Johnny's Dance Band / Wind. BHL1-2216
Conclusive evidence that, despite Bruce Springsteen, Patti Smith and Southside Johnny, not everything that came from South Jersey in the Seventies was very good. This is so downright awful that even John Denver's record label doesn't deserve it.   — D.M.

GENERAL JOHNSON
★★★ General Johnson / Ari. 4082
The former Chairman of the Board lead singer, General Johnson is also a creditable songwriter ("Patches," "It Will Stand"). This solo album is a bit limited in scope and includes some annoyingly stock arrangements, but it also has its share of nice moments—"All in the Family," for instance.   — J.MC.

SYL JOHNSON
★★★★ Back for a Taste of Your Love / Hi 32081
★★★★ Total Explosion / Hi 32095
Syl Johnson's music is one of the last soul styles to incorporate Southern soul with a bluesman's sensibility. His first Hi album, *Back for a Taste of Your Love,* is in an Al Green mold. "We Did It" and "Back for a Taste" are seamless and uptempo, like the Green hits of the period (1973), though "The Love You Left Behind" is brash and rugged—a Hi anomaly. *Total Explosion,* recorded three years later, is even rougher and more assertive; it shows scarcely a hint of Green's influence. The album's two hit singles, "Take Me to the River" and "I Only Have Your Love," are blues shuffles with harmonica intros. (Now deleted.)   — J.MC.

BRUCE JOHNSTON
★ Going Public / Col. PC 34459
Sappy '77 solo album from the former auxiliary Beach Boy who wrote Barry Manilow's execrable "I Write the Songs." Plodding pop, without a trace of rock; features a disco version of the Sixties surf hit "Pipeline," one of the silliest moments in recorded history.   — D.M.

JO JO GUNNE
★★★★ Jo Jo Gunne / Asy. 5065

High-energy rock from a band that grew from the breakup of Spirit. Built around Jay Ferguson and Mark Andes, also the central members of Spirit, Jo Jo Gunne released four superb albums between 1972 and 1974, all (except this second one) now deleted. — A.N.

GEORGE JONES

★★★ **All Time Greatest Hits, Vol. 1** / Epic KE 34692
★★★ **Alone Again** / Epic KE-34290
★★★ **Best of George Jones** / Epic KE-33352
★★★★★ **Double Gold George Jones** / Musi. X-4602
★★★ **George Jones** / Epic BG-33749
★★★ **Grand Tour** / Epic E-33083
★★★ **I Wanta Sing** / Epic KE-34717
★★★★ **Memories of Us** / Epic KE-33547
★★★ **Nothing Ever Hurt Me** / Epic KE-32412
★★★ **Picture of Me** / Epic BG-33749
★★★★ **Sixteen Greatest Hits** / Trip TOP-16-15
★★★★★ **The Battle** / Epic KE-34034

George Jones is known to the popular audience for his 1965 crossover country hit, "The Race Is On," and as Tammy Wynette's ex-husband. (He has recorded several duet LPs with Wynette, and another series with Melba Montgomery.) But Jones is really the last pure country singer. He still sings as he did when growing up in the Forties in East Texas honky-tonk territory; he is the most uncompromising of country artists, blithely ignoring every trend. His songs, which lean heavier to the romantic rather than boozing side of the honky-tonk tradition, are perhaps best known to concert audiences; he has never been a particularly huge record seller.

Jones' early-Sixties sides for Musicor are certainly his most consistent work. Such hits as "All I Have to Offer You Is Me," "White Lightning," "The Race Is On," "Window Up Above" and "Good Year for the Roses" established him as an influence among other country artists beyond his commercial stature. His Epic sides are much less raw, smoothed out by Billy Sherrill's formula productions. Still, he made his best album with Sherrill, *The Battle,* an album-long eulogy for his marital breakup with Wynette. The title song is a classic, as is the album's cover, which features framed portraits of Jones and Wynette on either side of a white bed, at the foot of which is a pair of empty boots. It seems to say everything, at least until he sings. — D.M.

GEORGE JONES AND GENE PITNEY

★★★ **It's Country Time Again** / Musi. MS 3065

This is just the kind of stuff Jones did with Melba Montgomery (and later, Tammy Wynette), but here Pitney's falsetto takes the female role—no small task for an Italian kid from the Bronx. It works, though. The material runs to country standards (a terrific "Mockin' Bird Hill") with one solo number apiece. A weird but often excellent record; worth digging up if you dig country, Pitney or both. — D.M.

GRACE JONES

★ **Fame** / Is. 9525
★ **Portfolio** / Is. 9470

No-talent singer whose camp posturing made her a Bette Midler-style favorite with the gay community. You had to be there, I guess. — J.S.

SPIKE JONES

★★★ **Spike Jones in Stereo** / War. WS 1332
★★★★★ **Spike Jones Is Murdering the Classics** / RCA LSC-3235
★★★★ **The Best of Spike Jones** / RCA ANL1-1035e

"Spike Jones made hundreds of records, nearly every one of them a total outrage," writes Dr. Demento in the notes to *Dr. Demento's Delights,* a collection of madcap recordings that includes Jones' hysterical gem from 1949, "Ya Wanna Buy a Bunny." Unlike Stan Freberg, whose parodies of rock & roll were born of hatred and misunderstanding, Jones loved the music he sent up—his aim was to take an honest poke at its pomposities.

Of the hundreds of records Jones and his City Slickers recorded, only three are now in print, but all of them are terrific. Most outrageous and most indispensable: *Spike*

Jones Is Murdering the Classics, which features the City Slickers' unforgettable interpretations of the "William Tell Overture" and "Dance of the Hours," complete with gargles, coughs, wheezes, sneezes and hiccups punctuated by shots from Jones' Smith & Wesson .22. The *Best of* album includes such bits of inspired lunacy as "Cocktails for Two" and "Laura." *Spike Jones in Stereo* teams Jones with Dracula and Vampira, Frankenstein, the Mad Doctor, Alfred Hitchcock ("Poisen to Poisen") and, in a "Spooktacular Finale," the Entire Ghastly Cast. To explain further would be, like the music, sheer insanity. — D.MC.

TOM JONES
★ **Fever Zone / Par. X-71019**
■ **Help Yourself / Par. X-71025**
★ **Memories Don't Leave Like People Do / Par. PAS 71068**
★ **Say You'll Stay Until Tomorrow / Epic PE-34468**
★ **This is Tom Jones / Par. X-1028**
★★★ **Tom Jones' Greatest Hits / Lon. PS 430**
★ **Tom Jones Live / Par. X-71014**
★ **Tom Jones Live in Las Vegas / Par. X-71031**
★ **What a Night / Epic JE-35023**
Tom Jones is the missing link between Elvis Presley and middle-class sex-symbol clones like Engelbert Humperdinck and Mac Davis. But this hunky Welshman is a bit better than the rest of the pack: he pushes as hard as his awkward voice allows, never hitting a blue note in the process. But his triumphs in singles like "It's Not Unusual" and "Delilah" have earned him a permanent niche in the annals of nursing-home rock. — J.S.

JANIS JOPLIN
★ **I Got Dem Ol' Kozmic Blues Again, Mama / Col. PC-9913**
★★ **Janis / Col. PC-33345**
★★★ **Janis Joplin's Greatest Hits / Col. PC-32168**
★★ **Joplin in Concert / Col. C2X-31160**
★★★★ **Pearl / Col. PC-30322**
The same air of desperation that kindled Janis Joplin's best performances left her screeching ineffectually through others. These glories and excesses can often be found side by side in one song. Her work in 1967-68 with Big Brother and the Holding Company established Joplin as the type of culture hero whose death by overdose in 1970 would seem sadly logical.

Her first solo album (*I Got Dem Ol' Kozmic Blues Again, Mama*) is uneven. The studio band is sometimes listless and the album's three best songs—"Try," "Maybe" and "Kozmic Blues"—appear later in livelier versions. Her only other studio album, *Pearl,* benefits from the sympathy and chops of the Full Tilt Boogie Band. Even though four of its songs are included on *Greatest Hits,* the nicely paced *Pearl* is still a necessity for her urgent "A Woman Left Lonely" and "My Baby."

Joplin in Concert salvages the early, brutal "Down on Me," plus versions of "Piece of My Heart," "Summertime" and "Ball and Chain." All these are available as studio takes on *Greatest Hits,* and much of the rest on the live album is dreck.

The movie soundtrack *Janis* likewise draws heavily on earlier recordings; but it is worthwhile for snatches of her simultaneously funny and heartbreaking raps, and for two surprisingly warm and listenable sides of Janis singing country blues in a noisy bar in Austin, Texas, around 1963-64.

Greatest Hits is a bumpy ride through her best-known songs ("Me and Bobby McGee"). It boasts ten classic Joplin cuts, but the rich, mature *Pearl* is still the one indispensable item from this great-hearted singer who came and left so abruptly. — F.S.

LOUIS JORDAN
★★★★★ **Louis Jordan's Greatest Hits / MCA 274**
★★★★★ **The Best of Louis Jordan / MCA 2-4079**
Louis Jordan was an enormously popular Forties bandleader whose style ranged from bemused blues to goofy novelty songs and hot jump tunes. Though often ignored or uncredited by rock historians, Jordan's infectious brand of jump and blues was an important foundation in the development of rock & roll; Chuck Berry has cited his singing as his inspiration. — J.MC.

MARGIE JOSEPH
★★★ **Feeling My Way / Atco 19182**
★★★ **Hear the Words, Feel the Feeling / Coti. SD-99006**
Margie Joseph's early Atlantic recordings were produced by Arif Mardin, who treated her like a poor man's Aretha Franklin, with disastrous results. Those records are now deleted; her sole remaining LP is also her best.

Hear the Words was produced by La- mont Dozier, who seemed to know exactly what to do with her. Dozier supplied mate- rial, arrangements, vocal backups and structure in a tight, Motown-derived set- ting. All Joseph had to do was follow his directions and sing.

The title track was her best single ever; for the first time in her career, Joseph sounds self-assured. One wishes the overall level of the material on the rest of the al- bum were higher, but a few numbers— "Don't Turn the Lights Off," for in- stance—succeed on their own limited level and she sings with some of the tenderness and conviction that was hidden for so long.   — R.G.

JOURNEY
★★★ **Infinity** / Col. JC-34912
★★★ **Journey** / Col. PC-33388
★★★ **Look into the Future** / Col.
   PC-33904
★★★ **Next** / Col. PC-34311
Journey owed much to Santana, via former members Gregg Rolie (keyboards, vocals) and Neal Schon (guitars). But the sound was more open and echoed, less complex and more rock than jazz; good playing but bland singing. *Look into the Future* was more song- than instrument-oriented, al- though Schon in places took off admirably. The keyboards were understated, the beat livelier—a denser, brighter, more pop-di- rected angle, although heavy-metal ex- cesses marred spots. *Next* and *Infinity* effec- tively combined the approaches of the previous two: colorful and tuneful meet- ings of catchy and well-played (if some- times lengthy) rock, with synthesizer in a growing role.   — C.W.

THE JOY
★★★ **The Joy** / Fan. 9538
In 1977, Toni Brown and Terry Garthwaite attempted to reform Joy of Cooking, with a slightly altered name but the same folkish funk sound. This album was the result; they didn't quite pull it off, but not for want of trying. The Joy remains the only reasonably interesting rock group led by women, but that hardly justifies its aimless- ness.   — D.M.

JOY OF COOKING
★★★ **Castles** / Cap. ST-11050
★★★ **Closer to the Ground** / Cap.
   SMAS-828
★★★ **Joy of Cooking** / Cap. ST-661
In the early Seventies, the Berkeley-based Joy of Cooking was a provocative blend of folk and rock, women and men. Toni Brown and Terry Garthwaite were not only the vocalists and songwriters of the group but also the instrumental leaders of a five-piece band.

What's surprising is how well these rec- ords hold up. Though the idea of a women-led band is no longer novel, Brown and Garthwaite's energy and air of de- lighted discovery survives and unites their sometimes fragmented intentions. As, well, foremothers, they touched most of the bases Fleetwood Mac, the McGarrigles and Heart now divvy up among them- selves: personal commentary with a pop beat, sweet harmonies and hardheaded ro- manticism, a fusion of pastoral and urban visions. The sound on these albums is often thin (only *Castles* is enriched by horns and strings), the arrangements are more homey than honed, but the songs—proud without being preachy, woman-oriented but not ex- clusionary—transcend the times that pro- duced them.   — A.S.

JUDAS PRIEST
★ **Sad Wings of Destiny** / Janus-7019
★ **Sin after Sin** / Col. PC-34787
★ **Stained Glass** / Col. JC-35296
Grunting, flailing Seventies hard rock, as vulgar as its name, but less euphonious. For lovers of recycled Led Zeppelin riffs only.   — D.M.

BILL JUSTIS
★★★★ **Raunchy** / Sun 109
One of Sam Phillips' ablest sessionmen during Sun Records' early days, Bill Justis is a prime example of a rock & roll saxo- phonist whose searing melodiousness is tempered beautifully by a craftsman's pre- cision. Nowhere is this demonstrated better than on his landmark 1964 instrumental, "Raunchy," which is the cornerstone of his lively, first and sole in-print Sun al- bum.   — D.MC.

KALEIDESCOPE
★ **When Scopes Collide / PFA 102**
Semi-legendary late-Sixties San Francisco
band is not well represented by this Seventies revival attempt. The earlier version of
the group did several fine LPs on Epic,
which merged blues, country and Middle
Eastern music, and gave instrumentalist
David Lindley his start. — J.S.

KANSAS
★★ **Kansas / Kir. PZ-32817**
★★★ **Leftoverture / Kir. JZ-34224**
★★★ **Masque / Kir. PZ-33806**
★★ **Point of Know Return / Kir. JZ-34929**
★★★ **Song for America / Kir. PZ-33385**
★★ **Two for the Show / Kir. PZ2-35660**
Kansas is an American counterpart to such
European groups as Yes and King Crimson, constructing understated pastiches of
rock and the classics. Admittedly less colorful and imaginative than many similar
groups, nonetheless the band is viable. The
compositions are ordinary and lack complexity, but the arrangements are beautiful.
Robbie Steinhardt's fluid violin belies the
rarity of the instrument in a rock context,
and the other players are both stately and
precise. The only consistent error lies in
the save-the-world lyrics, epitomized by
the sophomoric philosophizing of "Dust in
the Wind," the 1977 hit from *Point.*
  Kansas at once contains the poppish and
the arty, in a recognizable and mature
manner for a debut; only a long heavy-metal song hurts. *Song for America* realizes the
group's more ambitious ideals, with haunt-
ingly pretty instrumental passages and a
sharp sense of organization and dynamics.
The lengthy, finely tailored title cut exemplifies the entire genre well.
  Masque explores the possibilities of hard
rock embellished with art-rock sensibilities—fewer long instrumental sections and
ornate touches.

Leftoverture takes the same course to
slightly better ends. The guitars are in the
forefront but do not dominate. Much of the
accessible yet lofty spirit of the second album shows through. A simpler pursuit perhaps, but a worthy one. — C.W.

GABRIEL KAPLAN
★★ **Holes and Mellow Rolls / ABC D-815**
The pre-*Welcome Back Kotter* TV hero was
an offensive nightclub comic, with a remarkable anal fixation and an incompre-
hension of women that was not merely unfunny but pathetic. (Now deleted.) — K.J.

JORMA KAUKONEN
★★★ **Quah / Grunt BXL1-0209**
Jefferson Airplane/Hot Tuna guitarist
Kaukonen's first solo album is an all-
acoustic guitar set. Kaukonen does some
vocals, and some instrumental tunes and
duets with guitarist Tom Hobson. Kaukonen was a folk guitarist before plugging
in with the Airplane; his acoustic solo,
"Embryonic Journey," on *Surrealistic Pillow* and the first acoustic Hot Tuna album
are preparation for *Quah,* on which Kaukonen fares better than on the most recent
Hot Tuna stuff. — J.S.

RYO KAWASAKI
★★★ **Juice / RCA APL1-1855**
Kawasaki is a virtuoso Japanese electric
guitarist who justifies his reputation with
his playing, writing and arrangements on
this debut album. The instrumental support from keyboardist Tom Coster is exemplary, but the rest of the accompaniment
and production makes this sound like an
ordinary fusion record. — J.S.

KAYAK
★ **Phantom of the Night / Janus 7039**
★ **Royal Bed Bouncer / Janus 7023**
★ **Starlight Dancer / Janus 7034**

Are these "concept" LPs by mid-Seventies European art-rockers so lame because the Dutch quintet that made them doesn't understand its own English lyrics? Or is it just that pompous clowns like these had complete contempt for anyone who'd listen to this type of pop, which they were making only because the "serious music" they preferred wouldn't make them rich? — D.M.

THE KAY GEE'S
★★ Find a Friend / Gang 102
★★★ Keep On Bumpin' and Master
   Plan / Gang 101
The Kay Gee's are protégés of Kool and the Gang. Not surprisingly, their records sound markedly like their mentors'. *Keep On Bumpin'* has the Gang's burping vocals, loony atmosphere and staccato horn riffs. Its successor, *Find a Friend,* is milder and reflects Kool and the Gang's preoccupation with the ethereal. — J.MC.

JOHN KAY
★ All in Good Time / Mer. SRM-1-3715
Impossible listening abounds on this solo album by the former Steppenwolf lead vocalist, who without his leathers would be indistinguishable from any semipro beginner. Nasty, but in all the wrong ways. — D.M.

KC AND THE SUNSHINE BAND
★★★ Do It Good / TK 600
★★★ KC and the Sunshine Band / TK 603
★★ Part / TK 605
★★ Who Do Ya / TK 607
The Sunshine Band's early recordings, found on *Do It Good,* were ambitious and fresh. At the time, the group consisted of just two members, Rick Finch and H.W. Casey, who were given free rein in the TK studios to explore their eccentric funk vision. *Do It Good* is ragged, but the energy expounded borders on the maniacal. The best of it is "Queen of Clubs," runaway Miami funk that blends Finch's machine-gun bass line, surging Junkanoo horns and George McCrae's falsetto banshee wail.

Pop success began with "Get Down Tonight," and since then Finch and Casey have whittled the music down to its lowest common denominator: a pile-driving, percussive groove and hook lines as simple as any in pop. The result: bubblegum funk. — J.MC.

THE KEANE BROTHERS
★ Taking Off / ABC AA-1122
★ The Keane Brothers / 20th Cent. T-536

Preteen pop singers who didn't learn the only important lesson the Osmonds had to teach: if you gotta fake it, lift your ideas from somebody as talented as the Jackson 5. The Keanes' fake Elton John moves aren't any better just because they aren't old enough to know that the originals are synthetics, too. — D.M.

SPEEDY KEEN
★★★ Y'Know Wot I Mean? / Is. 9338
Good rock & roll, though inferior to the Thunderclap Newman album on which Keen debuted. One side hard, the other introspective and reserved. He plays an assortment of instruments; his Who-like singing is better than ever. Backup includes half of Back Street Crawler. (Now deleted.) — C.W.

BILL KEITH
★★★ Something Auld, Something New,
   Something Borrowed, Something Blue-
   grass / Roun. RB-1
As banjoist for Bill Monroe, the Jim Kweskin Jug Band and others, Keith almost single-handedly expanded the scope of bluegrass banjo. Taking Earl Scruggs' work for starters, he added chromatic breaks, a new peg system and post-ragtime jazz to the idiom. — I.M.

PAUL KELLY
★★★ Stand on the Positive Side / War.
   B-3026
Kelly's first hit, "Stealing in the Name of the Lord," created a sensation in soul music in 1970, partly because Kelly is such a fine Sam Cooke–derived singer, partly because the lyrics accused preachers of ripping off the black community. This 1977 LP isn't bad—there are a few gritty, funny Joe Tex songs mixed in with the ballads—but it isn't as fine as "Stealing." — D.M.

ROBERTA KELLY
★★ Gettin' the Spirit / Casa. 7089
★★ Trouble Maker / Oasis 5005
★★ Zodiac Lady / Casa. NBLP-7069
Roberta Kelly fronts for the disco beat of the Musicland Studios of Munich, West Germany, much as Donna Summer does in America. Unfortunately, Kelly does not have Summer's voice or her brilliant production. This has a heavy beat, but that's about it. — D.M.

EDDIE KENDRICKS
★★★ All by Myself / Tam. T7-309S1
★★★★ Eddie Kendricks at His Best /
   Tam. 77-35451

★★★ Goin' Up in Smoke / Tam.
   I7-346-S1
★★★ He's a Friend / Tam. T7-343S1
★★★ People . . . Hold On / Tam.
   T7-315S1
★★★ Slick / Tam. T7-356S1
★★★ Vintage '78 / Ari. AB-4170

Kendricks was the higher pitched of the Temptations' two lead vocalists—David Ruffin was the other—and his leads on songs like "Beauty Is Only Skin Deep" helped establish a certain type of soul singing. But after leaving the Temptations, Kendricks has operated in a very updated Philadelphia rhythm style that uses the front man more as a chant leader than as a crooner. Kendricks' first hit in this disco-oriented mode came in 1973, with "Keep On Truckin'." Since then, he's rarely been out of sight. In late 1977, he signed with Arista, where he's made one adequate LP. Only time will tell whether his departure from the Tamla/Motown rhythm mill will be productive.   — D.M.

THE KENTUCKY COLONELS
★★★ Livin' in the Past / Tak.
   BT-7202
★★★ The Kentucky Colonels /
   Roun. 0070
★★★★ The White Brothers (The New
   Kentucky Colonels) / Roun. 0073

This seminal Southern California bluegrass band yielded such low-profile L.A. stalwarts as Clarence White (Byrds), Billy Ray Latham (Dillards) and Roger Bush (Country Gazette), as well as Roland White, who made similar inroads in Nashville playing for Bill Monroe and Lester Flatt. The first two LPs are surprisingly good quality tapes of the Colonels' snappy, almost scat-influenced style while still plucky youths. Playing with incredible speed and agility, the Colonels display a fresh ebullience and professional abandon rare in usually staid bluegrass bands. The last LP is a live album from a 1973 Swedish reunion tour, where the instrumental facility and upbeat style of the Colonels has matured like a vintage wine. Throughout the three sets, the late Clarence White plays superb guitar. If he had lived, the Colonels would no doubt have gained their rightful public acclaim in bluegrass circles. A footnote in rock history worth savoring.   — R.P.

DOUG KERSHAW
★★ Alive and Pickin' / War. B-2851
★★ Devil's Elbow / War. B-2649
★★ Doug Kershaw / War. 1906
★★ Douglas James Kershaw / War.
   B-2725
★★ Louisiana Man / War. K-3166
★★ Mama Kershaw's Boy / War. B-2793
★★ Spanish Moss / War. 1861
★★ Swamp Grass / War. B-2581
★★ The Cajun Way / War. 1820
★★★ The Ragin' Cajun / War. B-2910

Kershaw is a white Cajun fiddle player who in 1961 had two regional country hits that also made the country charts, "Louisiana Man" and "Diggy Diggy Lo." But he's never attained a sizable following because he's just too weird—with his wild shoulder-length black hair atop a warlock's face that houses a paranoid's eyes. Onstage, Kershaw writhes, whoops and rips the strings of his fiddle to shreds before settling down to any *serious* sawing. Thus he is off-putting to, say, Johnny Cash's audience, and too exotically rural to open for, say, Jefferson Starship's. In this limbo between country and rock, Kershaw remains an erratic novelty in search of a style. His albums jump from genre to genre: *Douglas James Kershaw* features insipid string arrangements, *Swamp Grass* is quasi-rock, *Devil's Elbow* is crypto-psychedelia. They all contain one or two extraordinary, banshee-inspired numbers, and the rest are uniformly tedious mixes of progressive MOR and off-key yowling. It is only on *Ragin' Cajun,* easily the best of these, that he has abandoned this stylistic self-consciousness and just lets the music blare and moan as it will. As if to confirm the rightness of this decision, *Ragin'* yielded his first hit single since the Sixties, "It Takes All Day (To Get Over Night)," again heard only on country stations.   — K.T.

KGB
★★ KGB / MCA 2166
★ Motion / MCA 2221

This was supposed to be a supergroup with Barry Goldberg and Michael Bloomfield playing the points. But Bloomfield is smothered on the first album, gone altogether by the second, and the whole thing turned out to be a waste of time.   — J.S.

GREG KIHN
★★★ Greg Kihn / Beserk. 0046
★★★ Greg Kihn, Again / Beserk. 0052
★★★ Next of Kihn / Beserk. 0056

Greg Kihn aspires to be a cross between Buddy Holly and Bruce Springsteen, and though these albums reveal some rough edges, they contain a handful of tunes that show strong potential. The first album is highlighted by "Worse or Better," a wonderfully infectious pop-rocker, while "Satisfied" takes on the same thumpiness in a rock-reggae context. The second album is more consistent, boasting a fine cover of Springsteen's "For You" (Kihn gives Springsteen's most Dylanesque song an appropriate Byrds-like treatment), and a beautifully wistful original called "Island." Though still in the process of development—he and his band sound better on the lighter material than on the rockers, and Kihn's lyrics are sometimes heavy-handed—Kihn represents a healthy strain of West Coast rock & roll. But 1978's *Next of Kihn,* a set of original material, is better; both Kihn and his band find deeper, more confident grooves here.   — J.B.M.

ANDY KIM
★★★ **Andy Kim / Cap. ST-11318**
Sultry-voiced singer/songwriter got the full California session treatment on this 1974 set (guitarist Larry Carlton, drummer Ed Greene, keyboardist Michael Omartian). The result was a No. 1 hit, "Rock Me Gently," which serves as an apt self-description. Kim has had earlier pop hits—including a remake of "Be My Baby"—which are entirely forgettable.   — J.S.

BEN E. KING
★★★★ **Ben E. King's Greatest Hits / Atco 165**
★★★ **Benny and Us (with the Average White Band) / Atco 19105**
★ **I Had a Love / Atco 18169**
★★★ **Let Me Live In Your Life / Atco 19200**
★★★ **Supernatural / Atco 18132**
In the annals of soul music, Ben E. King ranks only slightly behind Smokey Robinson, Curtis Mayfield and Aretha Franklin. From his first single ("There Goes My Baby," with the Drifters), he left an indelible mark on the genre, and on rock in general. "There Goes My Baby"—co-written by King—was the first soul hit to use strings, and his other Drifters' records were equally influential, partly because of the brilliant production by Jerry Leiber and Mike Stoller (and occasionally the young Phil Spector). On his own, King had a series of major hits, including "I (Who Have Nothing)" and "Don't Play That Song for Me." The most notable of them all was the brilliant "Stand by Me," one of the starkest love songs ever written—it too was self-penned; its opening bass solo alone is among rock's great moments. *Greatest Hits*

collects his solo sides, and is invaluable to anyone who would understand early-Sixties soul.

The hits ran out in the latter part of that decade, but King returned, talent intact, with *Supernatural,* in 1975. The title track was a major hit in the early days of disco, and one of its best. But the rest of the album, as well as *I Had a Love* and *Benny and Us,* the 1976 and 1977 followups, buried King in an excess of production and rhythm. One is left wondering when his producers will stand aside and simply let the man sing again.   — D.M.

KING BISCUIT BOY
★★★ **King Biscuit Boy / Epic KE-32891**
Ex-Ronnie Hawkins sideman Richard Newell (a.k.a. King Biscuit Boy), a local favorite blues shouter and harmonica player in Canada, meets Allen Toussaint and the Meters, and comes up on the short end. A good album, but more Toussaint's than Biscuit's—more funky New Orleans than bluesy Chicago. (Now deleted.)   — A.N.

CAROLE KING
★★★ **Fantasy / Ode PE-34962**
★★★★ **Her Greatest Hits / Ode JE-34967**
★★★ **Music / Ode PE-34949**
★★★★ **Really Rosie / Ode PE-34950**
★★★ **Rhymes and Reasons / Ode PE-34950**
★★ **Simple Things / Cap. SMAS-11667**
★★★★★ **Tapestry / Ode 77009**
★★★★ **Thoroughbred / Ode PE-34963**
★★ **Welcome Home / Cap. SW-11785**
★★★ **Wrap Around Joy / Ode PE-34953**
★★★ **Writer: Carole King / Ode PE-34944**
Carole King was one of the most important pop and rock songwriters of the Six-

ties, numbering among her hits (written with lyricist and first husband Gerry Goffin) the Drifters' "Up on the Roof" and "Some Kind of Wonderful," the Byrds' "Goin' Back," the Shirelles' "Will You Still Love Me Tomorrow," Aretha Franklin's "You Make Me Feel like a Natural Woman," and virtually numberless others. These were great songs, but after she and Goffin split, their teenage romantic fantasies ended, though they continued to write together. King moved to California, where she married bassist Charles Larkey and raised a family. In 1970, she returned to music, as a performer.

Writer, her first solo album, attracted some critical notice but not much public acknowledgment, although in retrospect it contains some of her finest work, particularly the remodeled "Goin' Back." With *Tapestry,* however, King broke wide open—the record remains one of the half-dozen biggest sellers in history, and its major hits—"It's Too Late," "I Feel the Earth Move" and "You've Got a Friend," which scored biggest for friend James Taylor—are classics of their type.

The Taylor connection is not coincidental—he appeared on both records, and together, Taylor and King defined what was quickly labeled the singer/songwriter school. The emphasis was on craftsmanship as much as artistry, but the focus was also much more intensely personal than earlier pop: a song like "Goin' Back" has much heavier emotional connotations if there is no distance between singer and writer. The music, too, was distinctly stylized; King emphasized piano, Taylor guitar, but otherwise the songs relied on light drums and acoustic guitars (with a bit of light electric) to create a homey "living room" feeling. The watchword was intimacy, and on that scale, *Tapestry* is one of the best LPs ever made.

But as the records that followed showed, there were limits with what even King could so with the singer/songwriter approach. *Music* contained some fine songs—particularly "Sweet Seasons" and "Some Kind of Wonderful"— but as King exhausted her reserve of material, the new songs began to seem repetitious in their celebrations of the domestic virtues. King's voice was consistently pleasant, and each of the records has some striking moments, but what is most apparent is a kind of musical and lyrical redundancy. Toni Stern's lyrics predominated over Goffin's, and their addition of a female perspective, so

rare in rock, could be revelatory, but only in a relative sense.

A kind of nadir was reached with *Wrap Around Joy,* in 1974. Saddled with an inferior lyricist in David Palmer, and much more adventurous settings, featuring horns and heavy vocal choruses, King turned in only one really outstanding song, "Jazzman." The rest is pretentious muck, unleavened with humor and overburdened with quasi-poetic metaphor.

King rebounded somewhat with *Really Rosie.* Written as the soundtrack to a TV special based on the Maurice Sendak story, it is the best children's rock album, and the music is so worthwhile that it is exceptionally appealing to adults as well. *Thoroughbred,* the record which followed her breakup with Larkey, was her best since *Tapestry.* The arrangements were a bit tougher—closer to rock—and Goffin once more became her principal collaborator, although King had turned to writing much more of her material herself. At least one song, the splendid "Only Love Is Real," seemed to capture the essence of King's entire body of work, both in its lyric and melody, which left one with the feeling—or at least the hope—that King's future work might regain the mass resonance of her pop hits and *Tapestry.* But her Capitol albums, released in 1977 and 1978 respectively, are guru-mad: King trying to sell her audience universal utopia. I liked her better when she only offered perfect romantic bliss. — D.M.

KING CRIMSON
★★★★ In the Court of the Crimson King / Atl. 19155
★★★ In the Wake of Poseidon / Atl. 8266
★★ Islands / Atl. 7212
★★ Lizard / Atl. 8278
★★★ Starless and Bible Black / Atl. 7296
★★★ USA / Atl. 18136

In the Court of the Crimson King helped shape a set of baroque standards for art-rock, merging angry frenetic guitars and saxophones, delicate woodwinds and other acoustic instruments, and the symphonic majesty of the Mellotron. It works, through the cohesive arranging and superb musicianship of guitarist/leader Robert Fripp and his ensemble. Ian McDonald was at the center, playing every instrument except guitar, bass (Greg Lake, who also sang) and drums (the nimbly, even melodically inventive Michael Giles). This is wonderfully colorful music, reaching a variety of moods, tones, volumes and tempi; Peter

Sinfield's magical lyrics enhance the musical aura. The songs are long, but to worthwhile purpose.

McDonald then left, and much of *In the Wake of Poseidon* seems to be Fripp's attempt to rework the debut his way. Competent but finally inferior, the LP's color and breadth don't quite measure up. Elsewhere, there's Fripp's effectively dark Mellotron and Keith Tippet's fresh, jazz-tinged piano. *Lizard* is similar, despite more personnel changes (of the original lineup, only Fripp remained), but the more pronounced jazz influence is somewhat cold and aimless; the brass and reed solos tend to meander. *Islands* continues this icy abstractness, stressing playing over composing at a time when more changes had left the group at its weakest: Fripp and saxist/flautist Mel Collins play well, but Boz Burrell (bass, vocals) and Ian Wallace (drums) lack the necessary precision. The arrangements are more spare and dull.

Larks' Tongues in Aspic (now deleted) emerged with a tight new quintet: Fripp, future Yes-man Bill Bruford on drums, John Wetton (later of Roxy Music) on bass and vocals, David Cross on violin and Jamie Muir on percussion; Sinfield was gone, replaced by Richard Palmer-James. The sound is less ornate; sharper and weightier, it deserved more than the mediocre compositions accorded it here. The same lineup, minus Muir, was intact for the far superior *Starless and Bible Black,* where the emphasis is less on ornamentation than on sheer power, abrasive but firmly controlled. The writing matches the playing, showing a subtle influence from such fusionists of rock and jazz as the Mahavishnu Orchestra. *USA,* from the same quartet, is a capable live set that improves on three of *Larks'* pieces, and includes one new cut. *Red* (now deleted) saw the group out in a blaze of glory: a tautly energetic finale and realization of their last directions, driven by Fripp's distorted guitar and Wetton's similarly aggressive bass. Bruford punctuates magnificently. Supplemented by the Mellotron, *Red* gives new meaning to the concept of a trio. — C.W.

KINGFISH
★★ Kingfish / Round RX-LA564-G
★★ Live 'n' Kickin' / Jet JG-LA-732-G
★★ Trident / Jet 7Z-35479

Hippie C&W blues band led by New Riders of the Purple Sage bassist Dave Torbert and Grateful Dead vocalist/guitarist Bob Weir. It's a live album with the usual endless undulating San Francisco jams. An excellent soporific. (Now deleted.) — J.S.

KING HARVEST
★★ King Harvest / A&M SP-4540

King Harvest's only hit, the 1972 "Dancing in the Moonlight," is not included in this 1975 album, but the pop-rock formula of vocal harmony and jingling piano is about the same. Light, airy pop produced skillfully by veteran Jeff Barry. Guest appearances by Chicago's Peter Cetera and Mike Love and Carl Wilson of the Beach Boys still can't make the record more than fluffy, though. (Now deleted.) — D.M.

KINGSTON TRIO
★★★ The Best of the Kingston Trio, Vol. 1 / Cap. 1705

With the demise of the Weavers in the early Fifties and the blacklisting of Pete Seeger in the McCarthy years, it was not until the Kingston Trio's 1959 hit, "Tom Dooley," that professional folk performance recaptured a hold on American pop music.

"Tom Dooley" was a traditional ballad from Frank Proffitt's repertoire, and represented one aspect of the Trio's work—carefully arranged, edited versions of traditional folk songs. The Kingston Trio, however, also found material from contemporary songwriters such as Seeger ("Where Have All the Flowers Gone"), Bob Dylan ("Blowin' in the Wind") and Will Holt ("Lemon Tree") as well as drawing on such commercially familiar sources as Lerner and Loewe ("They Call the Wind Maria") and the Julius Monk satirical revues ("Ballad of the Shape of Things").

This breadth gave Dave Guard, Nick Reynolds and Bob Shane's group broad appeal and opened the way for Peter, Paul and Mary, the Chad Mitchell Trio and a host of imitators, and for the songwriters whose work they performed. John Stewart replaced Guard in 1961, and although a group with Reynolds continues to tour under the name, the Kingston Trio can really be said to have disbanded in 1968. — I.M.

THE KINKS
★★★★ Arthur / Rep. 6366
★★★ Everybody's in Showbiz, Everybody's a Star / RCA VPS-6065
★★★★★ Greatest Hits! / Rep. 6217
★★★ Greatest Hits—Celluloid Heroes / RCA APL1-1743
★★★★ Kink Kronikles / Rep. 2SX-6454
★★★ Kinks-Size / Rep. 6158

★★★★★ Lola Versus Powerman and the Moneygoround / Rep. 6423
★★★ Misfits / Ari. 4167
★★★ Schoolboys in Disgrace / RCA AFL1-5102
★★ Soap Opera / RCA ALP1-5081
★★★★★ Something Else / Rep. 6279
★★★ Sleepwalker / Ari. 4106
★★★★ The Live Kinks / Rep. 6260
★★★★★ The Kinks Are the Village Green Preservation Society / Rep. 6327
★★★ You Really Got Me / Rep. 6143

There never had been a rock & roll sound like the one introduced by the Kinks with their first hit, "You Really Got Me." With one simple riff, Ray Davies and brother Dave Davies virtually invented power-chord rock. The furious sound of that record should be contrasted with the velvet-suit, ruffled-shirt outfits members of the band wore at the beginning of their career, which gave immediate notice that the Kinks were a complex unit. Their early albums contained, besides a few monumental hits like "All Day and All of the Night," "Tired of Waiting for You" and "I Need You," the usual blues reworkings common to the era. But by their fifth album, *Kink Konstroversey* (out of print), it was clear that songwriter Ray Davies was growing by leaps and bounds. Here, in addition to the chaos of "Till the End of the Day" and "Milk Cow Blues," were some poignant ("The World Keeps Going Round"), self-mocking ("I'm on an Island") starkly beautiful ("Ring the Bells") compositions.

Davies' use of narrative came to full maturity on the classic *Face to Face* (out of print), arguably rock's first concept album. Looking around at the often drab, sometimes melodramatic day-to-day occurrences of average people, Davies concocted his own peculiarly English microcosm of the world, and proof of his brilliance and eloquence as a writer resides in such tracks as "Rosie Won't You Please Come Home," "Too Much on My Mind" and "Rainy Day in June." "Sunny Afternoon," a vaudevillian tune, was a hit for the band, their last for a long time.

Something Else continued Davies' masterful combination of rock and pop, with the ethereal "Waterloo Sunset" leading an album of uniformly excellent songs, among them "Afternoon Tea," "David Watts," "Situation Vacant" and brother Dave's "Death of a Clown." Another conceptual album, *Village Green,* followed, and again the group produced a very quiet and modest masterpiece. Davies zeroed in on the

inhabitants of a sleepy English town and revealed their broken dreams and fading hopes through a collection of expertly assembled vignettes.

Although the group had been making uncannily fine albums, their audience had all but disappeared, heading for the psychedelic sounds of the late Sixties. With the band at its lowest point commercially in 1970, Davies was asked to write a score for a British television special about the decline of the British Empire. The album's soundtrack, *Arthur,* put the Kinks back on the map, and as the Kinks began to rock again, with songs like "Victoria," "Australia" and "Brainwashed," things began looking up. *Lola* gave them their first hit in five years, and with a song about a transvestite, at that. The band forged on, combining tough, tongue-in-cheek numbers like "Top of the Pops" and "Apeman" with haunting ballads such as "A Long Way from Home" and "Get Back in Line."

After *Lola,* the Kinks moved to RCA records; their initial LP for the label, *Muswell Hillbillies* (deleted), found them once again in softer territory. But Davies' songwriting talents helped produce an album that stands as his signature statement. There were splashes of the music hall ("Skin and Bones") and the legitimate theater ("Alcohol," "Holiday"); elements of rock ("Twentieth Century Man"), blues ("Acute Schizophrenia Paranoia Blues"), ballads ("Oklahoma U.S.A.") and country ("Holloway Jail"). Davies' infatuation with theatricality, however, soon began to dominate the group's records. *Everybody's in Showbiz,* while containing the lovely "Celluloid Heroes," was the first Kinks album in a long time with any truly weak tracks, and the live disc included in the set relies more on Davies' camp stage act than good music for its success. (The earlier *Live Kinks,* recorded in 1966, has that *plus* some ferocious music.) From there, it was inevitable that Davies compose a full-bodied, plotted extravaganza. *Preservation,* a two-part, three-record affair (only half of which remains available) was hampered by its rather involved and self-absorbed plot. Another concept LP, *Soap Opera,* followed, but it too was a bit thin and ineffective. The main problem with both works is that they contained no distinguished compositions. *Schoolboys in Disgrace* brought Davies back to straight unconnected song settings, with fairly good results. Dave Davies' reemergence on guitar helped quite a bit on *Schoolboys* and on the band's first record for Arista, *Sleepwalker,* which has, in "Juke Box Music," the best song Davies had composed in years. *Misfits* follows the same pattern, with similar success. — B.A.

DANNY KIRWAN
★★ **Danny Kirwan / DJM 9**
★★ **Second Chapter / DJM 1**
Kirwan was the first addition to the basic lineup of Fleetwood Mac and one of the first members to leave; he helped make some of their early albums (particularly *Kiln House*) as good as they were. But without that group's fine rhythm section, his solo albums wander aimlessly, just another good guitarist in search of something to play and something to say. — D.M.

KISS
★★★ **Alive / Casa. 7020**
★★ **Alive 2 / Casa. 7076**
★★★★ **Destroyer / Casa. 7025**
★★★ **Double Platinum / Casa. 7100**
★ **Dressed to Kill / Casa. 7016**
★ **Hotter than Hell / Casa. 7006**
★ **Kiss / Casa. 7001**
★ **Kiss—The Originals / Casa. 7032**
★★ **Love Gun / Casa. 7057**
★★ **Rock and Roll Over / Casa. 7037**
The power riffing, the exuberance, the innate humor—even the subtlety—marking such early Kiss classics as "Deuce," "Strutter" and "Nothin' to Lose" are lost in production so muddy it renders the group's first three albums, *Kiss, Hotter than Hell* and *Dressed to Kill* (and *The Originals* collection), unlistenable. When Kiss needed to establish itself on record, *Alive* was released. By capturing the real thunder of the group in concert, *Alive* justifies much of Kiss's popularity, and contains one of rock's indisputably great anthems in "Rock and Roll All Nite."

Destroyer was a logical step forward. Paired for the first time with a forceful producer in Bob Ezrin—who is both a master of studio technology and a classically trained musician—Kiss came forth with a concept album that explored the psychological ramifications of the members' stage personas via music that is by turns driving and dynamic, chilling and introspective. Moreover, *Destroyer* is sophisticated in a manner apart from standard heavy-metal fare: the intricate time signatures of "Detroit Rock City," for example, present a challenge to any rock musician.

Kiss's return to minimalism, *Rock and Roll Over,* produced by the passive Eddie Kramer, lacks *Destroyer*'s distinctive production and memorable material, save a quintessential Kiss song in "I Want You." The rest merely reworks the fire-breathing formula. — D.MC.

KLAATU
★ **Hope / Cap. ST-11633**
★ **Klaatu / Cap. ST-11542**
★ **Sir Army Suit / Cap. SW-11836**
Named for a robot in a science-fiction movie, Klaatu's only claim to fame came through rumor: its self-titled first LP was reported to be the re-formed Beatles, a 1976 scam perpetuated by the group members' refusal to identify themselves. When word leaked out that it was only a batch of anonymous Canadian session players, reality asserted itself: mediocrity runs rampant through each of these discs, even the attempt to make *Sir Army Suit* a Northland *Sgt. Pepper's.* Good for a laugh—barely. — D.M.

ROBERT KLEIN
★★★★ **New Teeth / Epic PE-33535**
Klein is a young college-educated comedian who emulates tough old Jewish saloon comics like Rodney Dangerfield and Henny Youngman. Klein structures his bits more—they're not strings of one-liners—but not much; it all comes out in an urgent, articulate, conversational rush. His targets are ordinary—TV commercials, dentists—but his style is not: brutally accurate mimicry, bitter sarcasm and boyish charm, all from a genuine moralist. A comedy album that bears repeated listenings. — K.T.

GLADYS KNIGHT AND THE PIPS
★★★★ **Anthology / Mo. M7-792**
★★ **Bless This House / Bud. 5651**
★★★ **Claudine / Bud. 5602**

★★ Early Hits / Sp. 4035
★★ Gladys Knight and the Pips / Trip 3500
★★ Gladys Knight and the Pips / Up Fr. 185
★★★★ Gladys Knight and the Pips' Greatest Hits / Bud. 5653
★★★ Gladys Knight and the Pips' Greatest Hits / Soul S7-723
★★ How Do You Say Goodbye / Sp. 4050
★★★ I Feel a Song / Bud. 5612
★★★★ Imagination / Bud. 5141
★★★ Love Is Always on Your Mind / Bud. 5689
★★ Miss Gladys Knight / Bud. 5714
★★★★ Neither One of Us / Soul S7-737
★★ Pipe Dreams / Bud. 5676
★★★ Second Anniversary / Bud. 5639
★★★ Standing Ovation / Soul S7-736
★★★ Still Together / Bud. 5689

Gladys Knight and the Pips began singing together as teenagers. By 1961, they clicked twice on the pop charts with "Letter Full of Tears" and "Every Beat of My Heart," in a Fifty-ish vocal group mode. Those records, done for Fury, are classics, but what surrounds them—on repackages on Trip, Up Front and Springboard—is mostly mush. The versions included on Motown's *Anthology,* however, are re-recorded and to be avoided.

At Motown's subsidiary, Soul, the group, beginning in 1967, recorded a batch of tough, gritty sides, closer to Martha and the Vandellas than to the frothy Supremes. The first of them was "Everybody Needs Love," and the series included what is perhaps the best version of "I Heard It Through the Grapevine," "The End of Our Road," "Nitty Gritty" and "Friendship Train" through 1969. In 1970, the group teamed up with producer Johnny Bristol for an adult soul ballad, "If I Were Your Woman," which set the mold for the rest of their career. Rather than the shouting histrionics that had characterized Knight's singing on her early records, these featured elaborate productions, more sentimental and sensual than in the past; "Woman" was the highlight, but "I Don't Want to Do Wrong" and "Neither One of Us (Wants to Be the First to Say Goodbye)" were in the same mold.

Knight was now the dominant force in the group, stepping ever more out front, and when they went to Buddah, she adopted an even more adult persona, much more like Dionne Warwick than the hoarse belter of the past. The group recorded songs by Barry Goldberg and Gerry Goffin, who contributed "I've Got to Use

My Imagination," and Jim Weatherly, who penned several Knight hits (including her greatest, "Midnight Train to Georgia"); 1973 was probably their peak year. The hits continued through 1975, but a spiral of banality begun on *Second Anniversary* with a medley of "The Way We Were/Try to Remember" reigned unchecked. A brief association with Curtis Mayfield (*Claudine,* a soundtrack) helped a bit but didn't really orient them. Since then, the records have been more formulaic, though the beauty of Knight's performances can occasionally cut through.

Anthology is the ideal collection of the years at Soul; *Greatest Hits,* on Buddah, is a more than adequate retrospective of the Buddah syndrome, though *Imagination,* which contains both of her 1973 hits, is just about as definitive. *Pipe Dreams,* the soundtrack to the film in which Knight made her acting debut, is probably the weakest of the post-Vee Jay discs. Of late, the Pips have begun to record on their own, which may presage a similar move by Knight herself. — D.M.

REGGIE KNIGHTON
★ Reggie Knighton / Col. PC-34685
Poor man's Randy Newman. Sample song title: "VD Got to Idi." We never did like protest music. — D.M.

JOHN KOERNER
★★★★ Running Jumping Standing Still (with Willie Murphy) / Elek. 74041
★★★ Spider Blues / Elek. 7290
As a member of Koerner, Ray and Glover, John Koerner earned a reputation as a fine blues guitarist, whose approach involved the eccentricity of playing a seven- (rather than the usual six- or twelve-) string guitar. *Spider Blues* is a solo album of guitar work

from the early-Sixties folk revival period. *Running* is the result of a collaboration with fellow Minnesotan Willie Murphy from the late Sixties, and it rocks a lot harder—a fine example of white blues at its best. — D.M.

KOERNER, RAY AND GLOVER
★★★★ **Blues, Rags and Hollers / Elek. 240**
★★★★ **Lots More Blues, Rags and Hollers / Elek. 7267**
John Koerner (seven-string guitar), Dave Ray (twelve-string guitar) and Tony Glover (harmonica) were from the same University of Minnesota folk scene that produced Bob Dylan in the early Sixties. They were the finest white blues group in the entire folk revival of that era, and these albums (along with the now-deleted *Return of Koerner, Ray and Glover*) were highly influential on aficionados of black American folk music. Ray was a formidable twelve-string stylist, the best of his era, and Koerner's approach to blues was fairly unbeatable, while Glover's emulation of Sonny Boy Williamson kept the rhythm going at a hot pace. — D.M.

KOKOMO
★★★ **Kokomo / Col. PC-33442**
★★★ **Rise and Shine! / Col. PC-34031**
Average White Band by vegetative propagation, Kokomo is basically Joe Cocker's old Grease Band (bassist Allan Spenner's seal imitations still steal the show), along with the extra-muscular saxophones of ex-- King Crimson reedman Mel Collins and a trio of very black-sounding British singers. Any band with the wit to coin the chant "It ain't kool to be kool no mo' " has a lot more going for it than just good dance music. (Now deleted.) — B.M.

BONNIE KOLOC
★★★ **After All This Time / Ova. QD-14-21**
★★★★ **Bonnie at Her Best / Ova. 1701**
★★★ **Bonnie Koloc / Ova. QD-14-29**
★★★★ **Close-Up / Epic PE-34184**
★★★ **Hold on to Me / Ova. QD-14-26**
★★★ **Wild and Reclusive / Epic JE-35254**
★★★ **You're Gonna Love Yourself in the Morning / Ova. QD-14-38**
Female interpretative singer who is commendable on all accounts: excellent production, sensitive playing and knowing, deeply felt vocals. Koloc's values are traditionalist, in much the same way as Bonnie Raitt's, but she's also capable of moving toward pop without becoming as flimsy as Linda Ronstadt and her ilk. — D.M.

KOOL AND THE GANG
★★★★★ **Kool and the Gang Spin Their Top Hits / De-Lite DSR-9507**
★★ **Open Sesame / De-Lite DSR-2025**
★★ **The Force / De-Lite DSR-9501**
★★★ **Wild and Peaceful / De-Lite 2013**
As the first important funk and horn band of the Seventies, predating even James Brown's JB's, Kool and the Gang derived from the soul revues of the Sixties. Most of the major soul acts of the time carried large bands that verged on being orchestras, in which the most prominent solo instrument was the saxophone. While the crowd piled in, the band would often warm up by playing whatever pop-jazz pieces were then fashionable.

Kool and the Gang, with their obvious affection for jazz, added a party atmosphere to such instrumentals that gave their songs a deranged flavor; the horns sputter a staccato riff, while in the background, band members whoop and holler in seemingly uncontainable delight. After the first few successful instrumentals, Kool (bassist Robert Bell) and the Gang added loose vocal lines. On "Who's Gonna Take the Weight," there is a short spoken intro about worldly responsibility that leads into a driving track punctuated periodically by shouts of the title. "Funky Man" was an even more crazed vision—a good-humored song whose principal character is a man whose clothes stink.

The group has made more than a dozen LPs, and what's left is hardly representative of nearly a decade's work. The zenith of the approach is *Wild and Peaceful*, in which burping vocals and good-time horn charts are anchored by a metronomic beat. Songs like "Hollywood Swingin' " and "Funky Stuff" found an unexpected home with the white disco audience. Subsequent records have seen little variation from that formula; although spiritual concerns have seeped into the lyrics, the albums all revolve around similar sounding instrumentals—with an incessant rhythmic approach and horn charts that haven't altered in years. — J.MC.

AL KOOPER
★ **I Stand Alone / Col. 9718**
★ **Kooper Session / Col. CS-9951**
★ **Live Adventures of Al Kooper and Mike Bloomfield / Col. PG-6**
★★★ **Super Session / Col. CS-9701**
★ **Unclaimed Freight / Col. PG-33169**

At first glance, Al Kooper's solo career would seem to divide into two impulses: the "session" albums and the elaborate "pop" productions. On closer inspection, however, all of Kooper's albums collapse into a failure of the Grand Pop that Kooper first envisioned as leader of the original Blood Sweat and Tears.

Despite their commercial success, the "session" albums manage to insult everyone involved. The most famous, *Super Session,* features Stephen Stills (guitar only) on one side and Mike Bloomfield on the other. Kooper took the finished "session" tapes and then added horns and production to highlight his amateurish vocals and organ playing. His psychedelicized production of the Stills side shoves Stills' feeble needles-and-pins guitar solos onto the rhythm track. Bloomfield's work (also in settings imposed by Kooper afterward) is sterling, perhaps the last great performance of Bloomfield's career. On this side, Kooper's contributions consist of inept Jimmy Smith imitations on the organ, horn charts to cover the dead spots, and his patented thin-pipe soul vocals.

Kooper's subsequent attempts to re-create the original session, *Live Adventures* and *Kooper Session* with Shuggie Otis), merely repeat the mistakes and stretch out the dead spots.

The Kooper pop canon is a hugely arrogant, incredibly inflated and totally misconceived version of Blood, Sweat and Tears' *Child Is Father to the Man* concept, using studio musicians in place of a stable band. The latest of these, *Act Like Nothing's Wrong* (United Artists; deleted), after a hiatus of several years, at least shows that Al Kooper is on to himself as a joke, but it is still lousy. — B.T.

ALEXIS KORNER
★ **Get Off of My Cloud / Col. PC-33427**
In the early Sixties, Korner and Cyril Davies were the godfathers of London's blues cult; Brian Jones met Mick Jagger and Keith Richards while all three were apprenticing in Korner's band, from which John Mayall also emerged. Unfortunately, this album—the only U.S. representation of Korner's music—was recorded in 1975, by which time Korner had become a sort of elder statesman and relic of the early Stones era. Keith Richards appears on the Stones standard that serves as the title cut, but even he can't redeem Korner's gravelly, almost toneless growl. (Now deleted.) — D.M.

LEO KOTTKE
★★★ **Burnt Lips / Chrys. 1191**
★★★ **Chewing Pine / Cap. ST-11446**
★★ **Dreams and All That Stuff / Cap. ST-11335**
★★★★★ **Greenhouse / Cap. ST-11000**
★★★★ **Ice Water / Cap. ST-11262**
★★★★ **Leo Kottke / Chrys. 1106**
★★★ **Leo Kottke 1971-1976/"Did You Hear Me?" / Cap. ST-11576**
★★★ **Mudlark / Cap. ST-682**
★★★★★ **My Feet Are Smiling / Cap. ST-11164**
★★★★ **Six and Twelve-String Guitar / Tak. C-1024**
★★★ **The Best of Leo Kottke / Cap. SWBC-11867**
Although Kottke is often mentioned in the same breath with John Fahey, a more appropriate comparison is with the late country blues guitarist Sam McGee. Unlike Fahey, a highly idiosyncratic artist whose career has lately taken a turn away from American folk music, Kottke remains a staunch traditionalist. Like McGee's, his career bespeaks a profound commitment to the simple virtues of harmony, melody, and if you will, plain talk found in country, folk and blues songs. The bristling energy of Kottke's early albums is due in large part to a redoubtable and curious penchant for finding new possibilities within the oldest genres. This often culminates in beautiful surprises, foremost among them being his exquisite, moving rendition of Bach's "Jesu, Joy of Man's Desiring" (first heard on the Takoma album; repeated on *My Feet Are Smiling*). *My Feet Are Smiling,* a live album, signals the end of Kottke's musical free-spiritedness; subsequent recordings have found him striving, most unsuccessfully, for a more commercial middle ground. As he does this he sings less,

which is unfortunate, despite Kottke's protests to the contrary. While not an adept singer technically, he is blessed with a deep, resonant voice capable of great emotive power. It is no accident that his best albums—*Greenhouse, My Feet Are Smiling, Ice Water*—contain his finest vocal performances. And of five post-live albums, only *Ice Water,* graced by a superb interpretation of Tom T. Hall's "Pamela Brown," approaches vintage Kottke. However, a label change in 1977 proved fruitful. *Leo Kottke,* complete with orchestra and Jack Nitzsche arrangements, is, aesthetically speaking, Kottke's most fully realized work since *Greenhouse.* — D.MC.

ERNIE KOVACS
★★ **The Ernie Kovacs Album / Col.**
  PC-34250
Kovacs was the first video surrealist, right? So what can you see of his stunts on a record? — K.T.

KRAAN
★★★ **Let It Out / Pass. PPSD-98015**
★★★ **Widerhoren / Elect. 32110**
German instrumental band mixes Seventies jazz, British progressive rock and German machine rock (à la Kraftwerk) into a surprisingly listenable stew. A British cult favorite. — A.N.

KRAFTWERK
★★★★ **Autobahn / Mer. SRM-1-3704**
★★★ **Man Machine / Cap. SW-11728**
★★★ **Radio-Activity / Cap. ST-11457**
★★★ **Trans Europe Express / Cap.**
  SW-11603
This German band didn't invent the synthesizer but *Autobahn,* a sonic portrait of a drive along the world's second most famous roadway (after Route 66), went a long way toward popularizing the instrument. Complete with whooshes resembling passing autos, repeated refrains and droning choruses, "Autobahn" is a 22-minute composition that encapsulates the hypnotic redundancy of a twelve-hour drive. Valuable as both a musical oddity and background music for watching tropical fish sleep.

The other albums repeat the latter's musical themes with varying motifs, and are hence unnecessary. — A.N.

KRIS KRISTOFFERSON
★ **Border Lord / Col. PZ-31302**
★★ **Easter Island / Col. JZ-35310**
★ **Jesus Was a Capricorn / Col. PZ-31909**

★★ **Me and Bobby McGee / Col.**
  PZ-30817
★ **Spooky Lady's Sideshow / Col.**
  PZ-32914
★ **Surreal Thing / Col. PZ-35254**
★★ **The Silver-Tongued Devil and I / Col.**
  PZ-30679
★ **Who's to Bless and Who's to Blame /**
  Col. PZ-33379
Country-rock's only Rhodes scholar and its best film actor (*A Star Is Born, Pat Garrett and Billy the Kid*) is also a key figure in the rejuvenation of Nashville. As a songwriter in the late Sixties, Kristofferson contributed tunes like "Help Me Make It through the Night," "Me and Bobby McGee" and "Sunday Morning Coming Down" to singers such as Roger Miller, Janis Joplin and Johnny Cash, opening new possibilities of sexual frankness and emotional honesty to the C&W field.

But as a performer, he is a questionable talent. Even when the material is as strong as it is on his first two albums, *Me and Bobby McGee* and *Silver-Tongued Devil,* Kristofferson's aphoristic tales soon wear thin, as does his rough singing style—which is minimal, to put it charitably. — S.H.

KRIS KRISTOFFERSON AND RITA COOLIDGE
★ **Breakaway / Col. PZ-33278**
★ **Kris and Rita Full Moon / A&M 4403**
The Nelson Eddy–Jeanette MacDonald of rock, except that he can hardly sing and she sounds like she's only half trying. — S.H.

JIM KWESKIN
★★★ **Best of Jim Kweskin / Van. VSD**
  79270
★★★ **Greatest Hits / Van. VSD 13/14**

★★ Jim Kweskin / Van. 79234
★★★ Jim Kweskin and the Jug Band /
Van. 2158
★★ Jug Band Music / Van. VSD 79163
★★ Jump for Joy / Van. VSD 79243
★★★★ Relax Your Mind / Van. VSD
79188
★★ Whatever Happened to the Good Old
Days at Club 47 / Van. 79278
This selection includes what remains from the heyday of the Jim Kweskin Jug Band, the early-Sixties folk revival and Kweskin's solo material from the same period. The solo stuff isn't worth much, but the Kweskin Jug Band, besides being Boston's major contribution to the folkie scene, was a formidable array of talent and by far the best of the short-lived jug-band revival. It included Maria Muldaur (whose "Woman" on *Relax* presages her Seventies approach); her husband, Geoff; bassist Fritz Richmond; and a then unknown, Mel Lyman, who later created a psychedelic dictatorship in Boston. — D.M.

L.A. EXPRESS
★ **L.A. Express / Cari. PZ-33940**
★ **Shadow Play / Cari. PZ-34355**
Hybrid pop-jazz-rock. As competent as it is dull. The group is led by sometime Joni Mitchell arranger/saxophonist Tom Scott. — S.H.

L.A. JETS
★ **L.A. Jets / RCA APL1-1547**
For terminal West Coast rock fans only. The Jets magically gathered all of the genre's clichés under one wing for this debut. As if you couldn't guess, they are pale ghosts of the Jefferson Airplane, sporting male/female harmonies, hippie sensibilities and a general lack of direction. — J.B.M.

SLEEPY LABEEF
★★★ **1977 Rockabilly / Sun 1004**
LaBeef is the last of the real rockabillies, and this album—recorded a decade after the genre was in full bloom—should make such contemporary poseurs as Robert Gordon hang their heads in shame. Full-throated, energetic, hampered only by the fact that LaBeef's bass voice is sometimes a bit too solemn. — D.M.

LABELLE
★★ **Chameleon / Epic PE-34189**
★★★★ **Nightbirds / Epic KE-33075**
★★ **Phoenix / Epic PE-33579**
A brilliant but erratic Seventies group, this trio of magnificent women vocalists included the high-pitched histrionics of Patti LaBelle, the hard-edged belting of Nona Hendryx and the sultry soul singing of Sarah Dash, who had earlier performed as Patti LaBelle and the Bluebells. In a way, their problem was they were too good: they were capable of accomplishing so much that Labelle never developed a consistent, focused style. The deleted *Pressure*

Cookin' was one peak, fronting a relaxed but airtight R&B band and covering an amazing range of material, including a marvelous medley of "Something in the Air" and "The Revolution Will Not Be Televised." The commercial high point was the Allen Toussaint-produced "Lady Marmalade" from *Nightbirds*, but Toussaint couldn't find the handle outside of that brilliant single, and subsequent attempts found Labelle floundering through a number of unsatisfactory strategies. Eventually this lack of direction led to the trio's dissolution. — J.S.

PATTI LABELLE
★★★ **Tasty / Epic JE-35335**
★★★★ **Patti LaBelle / Epic 34847**
Patti LaBelle's triumphant solo debut marks this singer's third career (in her first two she led Patti LaBelle and the Bluebells and Labelle). There are two instant classics here—"Joy to Have Your Love" and "Dan Swit Me"—a spunky version of Bob Dylan's "Most Likely You'll Go Your Way and I'll Go Mine" and an all-stops-out rendition of "Since I Don't Have You." Producer David Rubinson gives Patti the consistent pop R&B setting that always just eluded her with Labelle. *Tasty*, though, is merely competent. — J.S.

BILL LA BOUNTY
■ **This Night Won't Last Forever / War. B-3206**
It's only when you hear a pop singer this bad that you can completely appreciate how skillful—I didn't say good—hacks like Barry Manilow and Tony Orlando are. — D.M.

LA COSTA
■ **Get on My Love Train / Cap. ST-11345**
■ **Lovin' Somebody / Cap. ST-11569**

■ **With All My Love / Cap. ST-11391**
I know this should be a group, but it's a
featherweight country singer (female) instead. Also, it butchers songs by talents as
diverse as Billy Joel, Neil Diamond and
Jagger-Richards ("Honky Tonk Woman").
You try to forgive her, I can't. (Now deleted.) — D.M.

CHERYL LADD
■ **Cheryl Ladd / Cap. SW-11808**
Would that this Charlie's Angel had sufficient imagination to have created jiggle-
rock. Instead, she sounds like she recorded
after completing a stint in the lounge at the
Holiday Inn in Passaic, New Jer-
sey. — D.M.

PETER LA FARGE
★★★ **As Long as the Grass Shall Grow /
Folk. 31013**
★★★ **Peter La Farge, on the Warpath /
Folk. 2535**
An American Pima Indian who died in
1965 at the age of thirty-four, La Farge
wrote the poignant "Ballad of Ira Hayes"
(among other songs), which was recorded
by such artists as Bob Dylan, Patrick Sky
and Johnny Cash. Although La Farge had
written, performed and become familiar
with folk music prior to his service in Ko-
rea, it was evidently that experience, combined with his own sense of heritage, that
forged him into a writer who voiced the
plight of American Indians as no other has
done. These two (of five) Folkways sets express the anguish and strength of his music
in its most basic form. — I.M.

DAVID LA FLAMME
■ **Inside Out / Amh. 1012**
■ **White Bird / Amh. 1007**
La Flamme's original group, It's a Beautiful Day, was easily the lamest band ever to
emerge from Fillmore West and environs:
all pretty hippie pretensions and a complete absence of energy. "White Bird," the
title track of La Flamme's initial solo outing, was a hit for It's a Beautiful Day and
serves as both warning and (one dreads to
suppose) recommendation for the somnolent virtues of both these albums — D.M.

DENNY LAINE
★ **Holly Days / Cap. ST-11588**
Ex-Moody Blues and current Wings sing-
er/guitarist. This tribute to Buddy Holly is
an ill-conceived set that doesn't present
Laine at his best and insults Holly's memory. Produced by Paul McCartney. — J.S.

CORKY LAING
★★ **Makin' It on the Streets / Elek.
7E-1097**
Apparently Laing knows nothing about the
title subject, which figures: he used to be
the drummer in Mountain and in West,
Bruce and Laing, which only saw the street
from the back seats of limousines. — D.M.

LAKE
★ **Lake / Col. PC-34763**
★ **Lake 2 / Col. PC 5289**
Competent meld of German synthesizer
and L.A. harmony Muzak, circa 1977-78:
the Eagles meet Tangerine Dream. Bad
idea nets the predictable result. — D.M.

ROBERT LAMM
★★ **Skinny Boy / Col. KC-33095**
Good songs straddling rock and MOR, but
the Chicago keyboardist's rudimentary piano chording can't carry the lean arrangements. Anonymous vocals. To date, the
only Chicago solo excursion, and this without the trademarked horns. (Now deleted.) — C.W.

MAJOR LANCE
★ **Now Arriving / Soul S7-751**
Does not contain "The Monkey Time" or
other great hits. — D.M.

RONNIE LANE
★★★★ **Any More for Any More /
GML-1017**
★★★ **Mahoney's Last Stand / Atco 36-126**
★★★★ **One for the Road / Is. 9366**
★★★★ **Ronnie Lane's Slim Chance /
A&M 3638**
When Ronnie Lane left the Faces in 1973,
it was carnival music he wanted to make—
sprightly, spontaneous and exquisitely sim-
ple. He succeeded; but it cost him his audi-
ence, which is why only his first album,
Slim Chance, was released in the States.
Mahoney's Last Stand is blues and rock
from the Faces (principally Ron Wood)
and friends (Rick Grech, Pete Townshend)
minus Rod Stewart. Much filler, sometimes
sloppy, but can at least boil water. Lane
sounds on Townshend's Rough
Mix. — F.R.

PETER LANG
★★ **Lycurgus / Fly. Fish 014**
★★★★ **The Thing at the Nursery Room
Window / Tak. 1034**
Lang is an interesting folk- and classical-
based acoustic guitarist of the John Fahey
school; the Takoma album lacks all of Fa-

hey's warmth and invention but is still admirably soothing music. On the Flying Fish set, he makes the mistake of singing and stepping out on some relatively boogie-woogie tunes. — D.M.

NICOLETTE LARSON
★ **Nicolette / War. SK-3243**
A protégé of Linda Ronstadt's and a featured backing singer with Neil Young, Larson epitomizes the worst of L.A. Seventies pop-rock. So laid-back it's a wonder she can stand up. Her debut album is a certified snore, and of course, a commercial smash circa 1978-1979. No, rock isn't dead, but anyone who remembers Little Eva may wish it were after hearing this. — D.M.

DENISE LASALLE
★★★ **Here I Am Again / Westb. 209**
★★ **Second Breath / ABC D-966**
★★ **The Bitch Is Bad / ABC 1027**
Denise LaSalle is a sensitive Southern soul singer/songwriter whose style, like that of Candi Staton, occasionally suggests a heavy C&W influence. Though her best work, *Trapped by a Thing Called Love* (Westbound), is out of print, *Here I Am Again* is fair representation: a sturdy collection of ballads and rugged midtempo Memphis soul. The ABC albums are less assured. LaSalle seems at a loss for direction, and the music is an uneasy collage of Motown, country and diluted Southern soul. — J.MC.

THE LAST POETS
★★ **Delights of the Garden / Casa. 7051**
This quartet of black poets first appeared in the early Seventies with *The Revolution Will Not Be Televised*, a remarkable out-of-print album that featured political versions of black street raps set to jazz rhythms. The interplay of voices in such a context had striking force, especially given the vulgar vernacular of so many of the "lyrics." Ideological rifts typical of the Seventies Left ensued, and who knows which version of the group this is. There's nothing here as inspired as the title track of the first record, which is worth digging up if if you can find it. — D.M.

LATIMORE
★★★ **Dig a Little Deeper / Glades 7515**
★★★ **It Ain't Where You Been . . . / Glades 7509**
★★★ **Latimore / Glades 6502**
★★★★ **Latimore III / Glades 7505**
★★★ **More, More, More / Glades 6503**

Miami's Benny Latimore is an accomplished keyboard player and distinctive vocalist who evinces an intriguing persona, combining elements of storyteller Oscar Brown Jr. and cabaret blues singer Lou Rawls with the earthy sexiness of traditional soul singers. The sparsely produced *More, More, More* includes blues and soul ballads, highlighted by Latimore's biggest hit, the smoldering "Let's Straighten It Out." Its followup, *Latimore III,* shows a real evolution of style. Latimore had a hand in writing five of the eight songs, and the best, "Keep the Home Fire Burnin' " and "There's a Redneck in the Soul Band," show a real ear for both wit and originality. *It Ain't Where You Been* has the same type of fluid, seamless groove as *Latimore III,* but the songs, while attractive, are longer and tend to sound alike. — J.MC.

LAW
★★★★ **Breakin' It / MCA 2240**
★★★ **Hold On to It / MCA 2306**
Because Law records for Roger Daltrey's Goldhawke Productions, it's not surprising that its speciality is an updated version of white soul. (Two of the five members are black, which helps.) Ex-James Gang singer Roy Kenner is occasionally a ringer for the Small Faces' Steve Marriott, and the modern soul attempts are at least as adept as Average White Band's, and much better sung. — D.M.

LEADBELLY
★ **Easy Rider / Folk. 2034**
★★★★ **Good Mornin' Blues / Bio. 12013**
★ **Leadbelly / Cap. SM-1821**
★★★ **Leadbelly / Fan. 24714**
★★ **Leadbelly Sings Folk Songs / Folk. 31006**
★★★★★ **Leadbelly's Last Sessions, Vol. 1 / Folk. 2941**
★★★★★ **Leadbelly's Last Sessions, Vol. 2 / Folk. 2942**
★ **Leadbelly's Legacy, Vol. 3 / Folk. 2024**
★★★★ **Leadbelly's Library of Congress Recordings / Elek. 301-2**
★ **Take This Hammer / Folk. 31019**
Biographies of Leadbelly (Huddie Ledbetter) can be found with almost all of these albums, and in any number of books about blues and/or American folk music. For present purposes, it is most important to note his authorship of such songs as "Goodnight Irene" (a three-month No. 1 hit for the Weavers in 1950, a year after Leadbelly's death), "Rock Island Line," "Give Me Li'l Water Sylvie" and "Take

This Hammer," plus literally hundreds of other ballads, shouts, hollers and blues that he either wrote or preserved through constant performance and recording.

A master of the twelve-string guitar, Leadbelly is additionally credited with developing the "walking bass" style of playing. His influence on such contemporaries as Woody Guthrie, Cisco Houston, Sonny Terry (all three sing with him on *Sings Folk Songs*), Pete Seeger, Oscar Brand and countless others is inestimable. And his songs, although sometimes appearing under the copyright of Alan Lomax (the man who first "discovered" and recorded Leadbelly, but who later wrote what many considered an offensive and inaccurate biography), are a part of the fabric of American folk tradition.

In 1933, Leadbelly made 78 rpm recordings of some 135 selections for the Library of Congress. The Elektra three-record set is drawn from these and later sessions, also cut by Alan and John Lomax. The difference the tape-recording process made is evident when comparing the Elektra set with Folkways' *Last Sessions*, recorded in 1948. On the latter collections (two discs each), Leadbelly's friend and folk-music enthusiast/scholar Frederic Ramsey, Jr., in whose apartment the recordings were made, speaks with the singer and encourages little monologues and asides. Although the Lomaxes tried to do the same for the Library of Congress, they had to contend with the time limitations of 78 rpm disc-cutting equipment (about five minutes per side).

Ramsey had originally hoped that the three nights of recording that became *Last Sessions* would be the first of a series, but Leadbelly died before further sessions could be arranged. Variations on given songs, sometimes in snatches used to illustrate a point, are left in, and both for quality of recording and range of material, *Last Sessions* constitutes the most highly recommended of Leadbelly's records.

The Biograph album is also of interest. It has been remastered with great care, and side one (circa 1940) features Woody Guthrie as a quasi-narrator for what is believed to have been an audition for a radio program featuring Leadbelly. Side two consists of half a dozen tunes recorded in 1935 that represent his first commercial efforts. None of this material has been previously available. The Fantasy set is made up of tracks variously recorded for Musicraft, Disc and Asch between 1939 and 1944.

Sings Folk Songs is spirited, what with its three-man backup team, and includes some lesser-known songs. As usual (and as with *Take This Hammer),* original mono versions are preferable to the stereo.

Easy Rider and *Legacy,* both ten-inch discs, date from the mid-1930s. The Capitol set, recorded in Hollywood in 1944, lacks the warmth exuded on the later *Last Sessions,* but does not have a few rare tracks that find Leadbelly playing piano instead of guitar. — T.M.

BERNIE LEADON
★★ **Natural Progressions** / Asy. 7E-1107
The former Eagle and Flying Burrito Brother turns in a solo LP that is the very model of washed-out California rock. Oh so country-funky, and oh so dull. Excesses exceeded only by fellow Eagle exile Randy Meisner's dismal affair. — D.M.

LEBLANC AND CARR
★★ **Midnight Light** / Big 89521
Pete Carr is the best guitarist the Muscle Shoals Sound Rhythm Section has had since Duane Allman left town; check his solo on Rod Stewart's "Tonight's the Night" for proof. Lenny LeBlanc is a singer based in the same Deep South region whose most notable compositional credit is the Elvis tribute, "Hound Dog Man." Unfortunately, on this 1977 duo debut, their talents never quite jell—primarily because LeBlanc is not strong enough vocally to pull off versions of "Johnny Too Bad," "Something about You" and "Desperado" better than the Jimmy Cliff, Four Tops and Eagles originals. Carr's playing and production (he also engineered) is more than adequate in this context, but he can't rescue the project. The easy-listening "Falling" was a Top Ten hit in 1978. — D.M.

LENNY LEBLANC
★★★ **Hound Dog Man / Big 76003**
The title track, a tribute/plea to Elvis begging him to return to rock, enjoyed a brief vogue after Presley's death in 1977. LeBlanc is, in fact, a Muscle Shoals guitarist and writer, although a better writer than player or singer. — D.M.

LED ZEPPELIN
★★★★ **Houses of the Holy / Atl. 7255**
★★★★ **Led Zeppelin / Atl. 19126**
★★★ **Led Zeppelin II / Atl. 19127**
★★★★ **Led Zeppelin III / Atl. 19128**
★★★ **Physical Graffiti / Swan 2-220**
★★★★ **Presence / Swan 8416**
★★★ **The Song Remains the Same / Swan 2-20**
★★★★ **Untitled / Atl. 7208**
When Led Zeppelin's debut album appeared in 1969, the anticipation built up among knowledgeable music fans, excited over the prospects of Jimmy Page (the Yardbirds' last guitarist) leading his own group, was replaced by an equally king-sized disgust. Here was a band that, when not busy totally demolishing classic blues songs, was making a kind of music apparently designed to be enjoyable only when the listener was drugged to the point of senselessness. Page, a young veteran of the mid-Sixties guitar wars, had somehow made two very important discoveries: spaced-out heavy rock drove barely pubescent kids crazy; the Sixties were over. And so, with virtually no critical support, Led Zeppelin was soon the biggest new band on earth.

Led Zeppelin II was somewhat weaker than its predecessor, leaving skeptics optimistic that soon all the superhype (also the name of Page and singer Robert Plant's song-publishing company) would be over, and the minor commercial flop of *Led Zeppelin III* seemed to support that feeling. Yet there were some strange things going on there. While side one covered usual Zep territory, from the absurd ("Out on the Tiles") to the ridiculous ("Immigrant Song"), side two, done mostly acoustically, represented the band's turning point.

Plant's voice had come down from the hysteria range, and backed by Page on everything from Banjo ("Hangman") to mandolin ("That's the Way") to steel guitar ("Tangerine"), new directions were being formed. "Tangerine" formed the musical basis of "Stairway to Heaven," which would become to the Seventies what "Satisfaction" had been to the Sixties. The song was the centerpiece of *Untitled,* arguably

Zeppelin's finest album (although one is tempted to give the band's initial LP an extra notch for sheer chutzpah value). That fourth album showed all sides of the group, with the indescribably chaotic "Black Dog," the stark and powerful "When the Levee Breaks" (the first Zep blues rework that didn't sound like a bizarre parody) and respites from the frenzy like "Going to California," on which Plant's hippie stance was finally bared.

Houses of the Holy was a fine successor, ranging from murky and foreboding ("No Quarter") to rollicking ("Dancing Days," "D'yer Mak'er") to idiotic ("The Crunge"). *Physical Graffiti,* a double set, has plenty of filler, but Page's "Kashmir" is a masterpiece of controlled tension, full of the Eastern influence that's been in his playing since the Yardbirds days. *Presence,* done quickly after a car accident prevented the band from touring in 1975-76, is probably its most down-to-earth LP, with the band drawing on all the band's resources—a little soul ("Royal Orleans"), a little blatant macho ("Candy Store Rock"), a little heavy mania ("Achilles Last Stand") and a little guitar rave-up ("Hots on for Nowhere"). *The Song Remains the Same* is a nice souvenir of the concert film, though nothing extraordinary. — B.A.

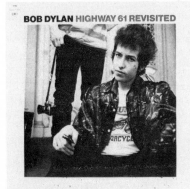
BOB DYLAN HIGHWAY 61 REVISITED

ALVIN LEE
★★★★ **In Flight / Col. PG 33187**
★★★ **Pump Iron / Col. PC 33796**
★★ **Rocket Fuel / RSO 1-3033**
In Flight—two live records with most of the soul group Kokomo as backup—was largely vintage rock & roll led admirably by former Ten Years After guitarist Alvin Lee. His often Presley-like vocals and economic but spirited guitar—no Ten Years After-style showing off—resulted in short songs and neat playing, which wasn't a

throwback or an imitation. *Pump Iron* used different musicians (some of Britain's better players) and retained the earlier records' approach in a studio setting—good but lacking the same verve. *Rocket Fuel* was much more disorganized—more akin to Ten Years After's boogie excesses. — c.w.

ALVIN LEE AND MYLON LEFEVRE
★★★ On the Road to Freedom / Col. C-32729
Good potpourri of American rock and rhythm & blues from mostly British rockers. (LeFevre, however, is American.) Traces of bluegrass and C&W. LeFevre's expressive voice resembled Dickey Betts'; Lee's guitar was agile and varied, avoiding the showoff tendencies of Ten Years After. Pleasingly pastoral and rustic. Steve Winwood, Ron Wood, Mick Fleetwood, George Harrison offer support. — c.w.

BRENDA LEE
★★★★ Brenda Lee Story / MCA 4012
★ L.A. Sessions / MCA 2233
★ Sincerely, Brenda Lee / MCA 477
★★★ Ten Golden Years / MCA 107
Brenda Lee was the best white female rock singer of the Fifties. Such hits as "Sweet Nothin's," "Dum Dum," "Rockin' Around the Christmas Tree" and "I'm Sorry" were as tough, if as sentimental, as the best of any male rock & roller, and far beyond the capacity of any of her peers. The evidence is on *Brenda Lee Story,* a two-record set, and *Ten Golden Years,* a single disc, both of which collect her best work of that period.
L.A.Sessions and *Sincerely, Brenda Lee* unfortunately reflect the kind of artistic disintegration so many country-based white rockers of the Fifties went through in recent years. They are totally tame, formulaic country albums, with virtually nothing to recommend them except the odd pleasure of Lee's still sobbing voice. — d.m.

BYRON LEE AND THE DRAGONAIRES
★ Disco Reggae / Mer. SRM-1-1063
It would be easy to dismiss Byron Lee as the Neil Hefti or Mantovani of reggae for his featherweight, effortless Jamaican records, among which only this LP was released in the U.S. (1975). But as a producer and creative force behind Kingston's Dynamic Sounds Recording Studio, Lee is a seminal figure in reggae's development. Which doesn't excuse him for the false advertising here: it's all watered-down reggae

except for one track, a reggae-ized version of "The Hustle." — g.k.

LAURA LEE
★★★ I Can't Make It Alone / Inv. KZ-33133
Laura Lee is a tough, gravel-voiced singer capable of transmitting intense, raging hurt. Though her best-known records— "Dirty Man" (Chess), "Women's Love Rights" and "Rip Off" (both Hot Wax)— are out of print, this Eddie and Brian Holland-produced album has some memorable moments (i.e., the torrid "I Need It Just as Bad as You"). (Now deleted.) — j.mc.

JOHN LENNON
★★★★★ John Lennon/Plastic Ono Band / Apple SW-3372
An instinctively popular artist, Lennon has always been an angry man, caught between a desire to please his audience and to assault it. This contradiction, muted in his Beatles days, surfaced immediately in his solo work and has since marked his career with desperation, smugness and confusion. No resolution is in sight.
Lennon began his break from the Beatles well before the formal dissolution of the group in 1970. In 1969, he and Yoko Ono, his then-love-soon-to-be-wife, put out two so-called "unfinished music" tape-buzz LPs: *Two Virgins,* with the scandalous prefall Adam and Eve cover, and *Life with the Lions,* which commemorated Yoko's miscarriage of that year.
The Wedding Album (also 1969), a narcissistic boxed set, celebrated John and Yoko's marriage, after which the duo embarked on a worldwide crusade for "peace," which produced *Live Peace in Toronto 1969* (released 1970), featuring one side of first-class raving rock (Lennon's pickup band included Eric Clapton) and one side of Yoko's avant-garde ravings. Singles—notably "Give Peace a Chance," the stunning "Cold Turkey" and "Instant Karma"—also came out of this period.
But it was *John Lennon/Plastic Ono Band* (released in conjunction with the shattering "Lennon Remembers" interviews in *Rolling Stone)* that revealed Lennon as a new man, liberated by the fall of the Beatles. Primal scream therapy, which John had then recently undergone, now dates the LP, but it also inspired its vital extremism: the record was a full, blistering statement of fury, resentment and self-pity, and Lennon's proof that the true power of rock as music is to be found in stripping it as bare as primal

therapy was supposed to strip the soul. Thus there was virtually no instrumentation beyond a primal rock band composed of Lennon on rough lead guitar, Ringo on drums, Klaus Voorman on bass and Billy Preston's occasional keyboards: the music didn't cut, it bit. Nearly a decade later, "Well Well Well" particularly holds its power, though "Working Class Hero" too remains a favorite; John's singing on the last verse of "God's Song" may be the finest in all of rock. A lot of people hated *JL/POB*, but few have really forgotten it; it stands as John's strongest, most sustained piece of work in the Seventies.

★★★ **Imagine / Apple SW-3379**
If *JL/POB* was sparked by the cry "The dream is over," the message of *Imagine*, a much more accessible pop album, was "Long live the dream": as a popular artist, the angry man simply could not endure without a dose of utopianism in his music, his sense of romance and his politics. *Imagine*, despite its notorious attack on Paul McCartney ("How Do You Sleep?"), felt like a breath of fresh air in 1971; "Gimme Some Truth," a nasty rocker, "Oh Yoko," an almost girl-groupish ditty and the lovely "Jealous Guy" still do. At this point, John seemed to know where he was going, and to be going in a good direction.

★★ **Mind Games / Apple SW-3414**
★ **Some Time in New York City / Apple SVBB-3392**
★★ **Walls and Bridges / Apple SW-3416**
It didn't seem that way after *Some Time* (1972), a disastrous collaboration between John, Yoko and the leftish rock band Elephant's Memory. This was a two-LP set divided between horrendous Phil Spector-produced protest epics and live recordings (some with Frank Zappa): the politics were witless and the live jams mindless. After John's ideological flip-flops of the previous years (from the Maharishi to "peace" to primal therapy, each embraced as an absolute Answer), it was hard to take his new political commitments seriously; here, the question of taking his music seriously never came up.

Both *Mind Games* (1973) and *Walls and Bridges* (1974) were drastic retreats from the anti-pop stance of *Some Time*, and both produced hits: "Mind Games," the trendy "Whatever Gets You Thru the Night" and "#9 Dream." The sound was lush and conventional, the singing assured, but there was no real point of view at work—no point at all, in fact, save for continuing a career for its own sake; only "Going Down

on Love" (*Walls*) recalled the gutty realism of *JL/POB*, which seemed very far away. Like so many veterans of the Sixties trapped in the Seventies, Lennon (by then the subject of a brutal but accurate parody on the National Lampoon's *Radio Dinner* LP) had no idea of how to relate to his audience: with what appeared to be panic, he substituted production techniques for soul, building a bridge to his listeners with his sound but erecting a wall around himself with empty music.

★★ **Rock 'n' Roll / Apple SK-3419**
Lennon knew it; he just didn't know what to do about it, and so, again like many others, he tried to escape a dead end by going back to his roots with an oldies album. *Rock 'n' Roll* (1975, a year that also saw John popping up on a couple of Elton John 45s) began as a collaboration with Phil Spector, who needed a shot of rhythm & blues as much as John did, but the partnership soon came to grief—as did most of the album. Remakes of "Stand by Me" and "Just Because" were deeply touching, but with the rest of the tunes—mostly classic hard rockers—John never found a groove. And so, no doubt tired of his helpless drift back and forth between adventure (*JL/POB, Some Time*) and retreat (*Imagine, Mind Games, Walls, R'n'R*), Lennon shut up, his battle with Paul McCartney apparently conceded. On record, John has not been heard from since.

★★★ **Shaved Fish / Apple SW-3412**
A short-term epitaph: collected singles since 1969, omitting the *R'n'R*. Highlights are still "Cold Turkey," "Instant Karma" and "Power to the People" (a nervy 45 from 1971). John's first solo LP remains his testament: divided, bitter and utterly uncompromising, qualities that one expects to emerge again as Lennon makes his way into the Eighties. — G.M.

MIKE LESLEY
★★ **Mike Lesley / Big 89516**
Where Big Tree finds its stable of clean-cut late-Seventies throwbacks to mid-Sixties pop rock is a mystery. Perhaps they've cloned Brian Hyland? This one is interchangeable with Lobo and Lenny LeBlanc, David Geddes and the rest. (Now deleted.) — D.M.

JULIUS LESTER
★★ **Departures / Van. 79261**
★★ **Julius Lester / Van. 79199**
One of the few black performers to come out of the early-Sixties folk-songwriting

boom spearheaded by Bob Dylan, Lester is
better known as a page poet. As can easily
be heard here, the reputation is justified,
although one senses a more authentic radi-
calism here than in many of the opportun-
ists who sniffed around Dylan during the
period. (Now deleted.) — D.M.

LES VARIATIONS
★ **Cafe de Paris / Bud. 5625**
★★ **Moroccan Roll / Bud 5601**
"Paint It Black," french-fried and stretched
over two albums. — J.S.

GARY LEWIS AND THE PLAYBOYS
★★ **The Greatest Hits of Gary Lewis and
the Playboys / Power 311**
Would you buy a used diamond ring from
this man? Gary Lewis sang like his father
acts—goofy—and without Dean Martin for
a straight man. But that doesn't mean we
can't treasure his handful of pathetic contributions to Sixties rock, generally written
and arranged (in collaboration) by a duck-
tailed Leon Russell. "This Diamond Ring"
is what you remember, but there's also
"Everybody Loves a Clown," "She's Just
My Style" and the rest of Lewis' Beatles-
era pop hits, a high point in mainstream
masochism. — M.G.

JERRY LEE LEWIS
★★★★ **A Taste of Country / Sun 114**
★★★★★ **Best of Jerry Lee Lewis / Smash
67131**
★★★★ **Best of Jerry Lee Lewis, Vol. 2 /
Mer. SRM-1-5006**
★★★ **Country Class / Mer. SRM-1-1109**
★★★ **Country Memories / Mer.
SRM-1-5004**
★★★★ **Golden Hits of Jerry Lee Lewis /
Smash 67040**
★★★ **Jerry Lee Lewis / Elek. 6E-184**

★★★ **Jerry Lee Lewis / Ev. 298**
★★★★ **Jerry Lee Lewis' Golden Cream of
the Country / Sun 108**
★★★★★ **Jerry Lee Lewis' Original
Golden Hits, Vol. 1 / Sun 102**
★★★★★ **Jerry Lee Lewis' Original
Golden Hits, Vol. 2 / Sun 103**
★★★★★ **Jerry Lee Lewis' Original
Golden Hits, Vol. 3 / Sun 128**
★★★★ **Jerry Lee Lewis' Rockin' Rhythm
and Blues / Sun 107**
★★★★ **Memphis Country / Sun 120**
★★★★★ **Monsters / Sun 124**
★★★★ **Ole Tyme Country Music / Sun
121**
★★★★ **Sunday Down South / Sun 119**
Of all the rock & roll singers who followed
Elvis Presley into Memphis and Sam Phil-
lips' Sun Records in the late Fifties, the
greatest was undeniably Jerry Lee Lewis.
He would tell you so himself, for Lewis is
a master of the Bunyanesque brag, a swag-
gering piano stomper whose arrogance is
as legendary as his vanity, though neither
is quite a match for the enormity of his talent.

Lewis' two biggest hits were his first,
"Whole Lotta Shakin' Going On" and
"Great Balls of Fire," both released on Sun
in 1957. Those songs presented fundamentalist gospel imagery as sexual innuendo,
and Lewis portrayed, through his romping,
stomping, incessant piano backbeat and his
heated singing, a kind of Elmer Gantry out
for action and trouble be damned. Lewis
was the very incarnation of what Northerners feared about the South—the most
arrogant and unregenerate of the all the
Fifties rockers. Compared to Lewis, Elvis
Presley's humility seems absolutely overweening. And it was this triumph of the id,
which has made so much of Lewis' music
so forceful, that proved his undoing.

Lewis had only two other Top Forty hits
in the rock & roll era: "Breathless" and
"High School Confidential," both in 1958.
After that, he virtually dropped out of
sight, for he had married his fourteen-year-
old third cousin, an irreparable violation of
social taboo. He still made records, including some more than faintly great ones, covered everybody from Elvis to Chuck Berry
and often cut them on their own songs—
but few heard him, because the radio simply wouldn't play his music.

If Lewis' music of this period could be
compared to anyone else's (besides Presley,
to whom everything in rock is comparable), the most apt alter ego would be Little
Richard. Like Lewis, Richard's focus was

a pounding piano, with a kind of primitive boogie-woogie approach and more than a hint of the church in his vocals. But Lewis parted company as a vocalist; Little Richard shouted, but Jerry Lee sang like a demented choirboy, so that even the licentious lyrics of "Great Balls of Fire" got a properly rounded enunciation. This was part of Lewis' greatest implicit boast: that he could cut anybody at anything, and if necessary, when it comes to music, he could cut everybody all at once.

Banished from pop radio, Lewis turned to cutting country songs, where his natural instincts and his really quite exquisite voice already made him at home. By 1967, his excellent country records (made with producer Jerry Kennedy in Nashville for Mercury's country line, Smash), were beginning to become heavy factors on the country charts. Since then, he has cut a number of the best country songs of the era, including "What Made Milwaukee Famous Has Made a Loser Out of Me," "She Even Woke Me Up to Say Goodbye," "You Belong to Me" and "Who's Gonna Play This Old Piano." He hardly ever sings rock & roll anymore, but whenever he wants to, he's still great at it. And even his country records are pretty untamed; Jerry Lee Lewis has never surrendered. — D.M.

LINDA LEWIS
★ **Not a Little Girl Anymore / Ari. 4047**
Histrionic, squealing R&B vocalist. — J.S.

LIBERTY
★★ **Liberty / Wind. BHL1-1006**
In some respects, this vocal-dominated country and jazz-influenced group is the very best that John Denver's record label has to offer. The material is mostly first-rate, incorporating such standards as "Sitting on Top of the World" and "Ain't Misbehavin' " as easily as eccentric pop oldies ("I Remember You"). On the other hand, even given the slick production overseen by Denver and his producer, Milton Okun, this is terribly soulless stuff, including the final tune, dedicated to Guru Maharaj Ji—more like mystical Peter, Paul and Mary than anything really substantial. — D.M.

LIBRA
■ **Libra / Mo. M-6847**
■ **Winter Day's Nightmare / Mo. M-6864**
Libra is a very sloppy Seventies space-rock band that manages to combine the worst impulses of a Michael Quatro with the

technological baggage of an age obsessed with wires. Its music, which resembles an annoying drizzle as heard inside a tin house, has neither a center nor a periphery. (Now deleted.) — B.T.

LORI LIEBERMAN
★ **Becoming / Cap. ST-11203**
★ **Letting Go / Millen. 8005**
★ **Lori Lieberman / Cap. ST-11081**
Ineffectual Laura Nyro imitation. — J.S.

LIFESTYLE
★★★ **Lifestyle / MCA 2246**
Philadelphia soul group modeled on the O'Jays, but without their distinctive production or excellent material. Still, this relatively unnoticed 1977 LP is at least listenable. (Now deleted.) — D.M.

GORDON LIGHTFOOT
★★ **Back Here on Earth / U. Artists 6672**
★★★ **Best of Gordon Lightfoot / U. Artists 6754**
★★ **Best of Gordon Lightfoot, Vol. 2 / U. Artists 5810**
★★ **Cold on the Shoulder / Rep. MS4-2206**
★★★ **Don Quixote / Rep. 2056**
★★ **Endless Wire / War. K-3149**
★★★ **Gord's Gold / Rep. 2RS-2237**
★★★★ **If You Could Read My Mind / Rep. 6392**
★★★ **Lightfoot / U. Artists 38-6487**
★★ **Old Dan's Records / Rep. 2116**
★★ **Summer Side of Life / Rep. MS-2037**
★★★ **Summertime Dream / Rep. 2246**
★★★ **Sunday Concert / U. Artists 6714**
★★ **Sundown / Rep. MS4-2177**
★★★ **The Way I Feel / U. Artists 6587**
Born into a well-to-do family from the London, Ontario, area—English Canada's Tory stronghold—and brought up as a

classically trained choirboy, singer/song-writer Gordon Lightfoot has had a long, successful career, first as a "folksinger," then in the Seventies as *the* Canadian musical institution. These two phases in Lightfoot's career are marked less by a change in style than by a switch of record companies, from United Artists to Reprise/Warner Bros., and by the increasing slickness of his producer, Lenny Waronker.

Lightfoot, his first album, introduced Lightfoot's style in a mature form: firm, fast strumming on guitar and a smooth baritone voice. It was a style that made Lightfoot one of the most engaging singers to come from the Sixties folk boom. This first album also contains several songs that have since become frequently recorded standards: notably "Early Morning Rain"; "For Lovin' Me," penned by Lightfoot; and "The First Time," by Ewan McColl. The subsequent U.A. albums may now seem more formulaic than they did when first released. Lightfoot's lyrical sophistication, forceful melodies and stolid posture remain admirable, but the major topical songs, "Black Day in July" and "Canadian Railroad Trilogy," sound glossy and over-written. Too many of the ballads ("If I Could" and "Mountains and Marion") are so reflectively vague that they verge on being folkie Tin Pan Alley. This is, in fact, the tendency that overtakes Lightfoot on several of his Reprise/Warner albums.

Although beautifully produced and featuring Lightfoot's most consistent collection of songs, *If You Could Read My Mind* was a sleeper until the title song became a smash hit single in 1970 and Lightfoot was rediscovered by a public who remembered him only by way of cover versions of his early songs, such as Peter, Paul and Mary's "Early Morning Rain." Stylistically, *If You Could* recast Lightfoot's mixture of ballads and topical songs into a blend of elements from both genres. Typically, "Sit Down Young Stranger" takes on a highly personal tone to welcome American draft dodgers and deserters to Canada. The song also points to Lightfoot's growing semi-official status in Canada. The "Railroad Trilogy," having led to a whole catalogue of Canadian songs, also led to Lightfoot's Seventies position as his country's songwriter laureate, with "Alberta Bound" and "Christian Island (Georgia Bay)" finally leading to the masterful epic "Wreck of the Edmund Fitzgerald" (on *Summertime Dream).*

Even when Lightfoot's ballads are tired and indulgent, which is often on *Summer Side of Life* and *Cold on the Shoulder,* Lenny Waronker's production has been able to screen the albums so pleasingly that even the most minor later Lightfoot is listenable. (But the converse is *Gord's Gold,* on which he rerecords his Sixties songs in a way that makes them sound minor as well.) On the most recent album—*Endless Wire,* Lightfoot seems, at last, aware of his gradual drift into well-crafted post-folk Muzak: the studio players are as strongly highlighted as his indifferent vocals, leaning heavily on medium-tempo tunes and strings. Now approaching middle age, Lightfoot is apparently satisfied with his role as a Canadian institution, writing one or two superior songs a year and gliding easily over the rest of his annual album and tour. In the off months, Lightfoot occasionally plays Las Vegas or Lake Tahoe; in mid-winter he does a sold-out week at Toronto's Massey Hall. — B.T.

LIGHTHOUSE
★ **Best of Lighthouse** / Janus JXS-7025
Canada's answer to Blood, Sweat and Tears and Chicago—closer to the former, unfortunately, which means the electrified Big Band charts are totally uninspired and that the singing is, in a word, lame. "One Fine Morning," however, was an across-the-border hit. (Now deleted.) — D.M.

DENNIS LINDE
★ **Under the Eye** / Monu. MG-7608
Linde's entire reputation rests on having penned Elvis Presley's last rock hit, "Burning Love," in 1972. Since then, he's recorded several times, but no one has done his work a similar favor. This is what's left, and it's not much. — D.M.

LINDISFARNE
★★★ **Back and Fourth** / Atco 33-108
Competent Seventies folk rock from a band based in the North of England that has made better records (for Elektra and Buddah) which are now unfortunately deleted. — D.M.

BUZZY LINHART
★ **Best of Buzzy Linhart** / Kam. S. BS-2-2615
Linhart, a hippie of the most droolingly uncouth variety, wrote "Friends," which is Bette Midler's theme song. But the abrasiveness Midler makes charming, Linhart takes straight. These are some of the most

annoying songs in existence. (Now deleted.) — D.M.

LIQUID PLEASURE
★★ **Steppin' Out / Midl. BKLI-2423**
Late-Seventies disco pop outfit fairly slides off your turntable. Pass. — J.S.

LITTLE BEAVER
★★ **Black Rhapsody / Cat 1602**
★★★★ **Little Beaver / Cat 1601**
★★★★ **Party Down / Cat 2604**
★★ **When Was the Last Time / Cat 2609**
This Miami session guitarist's debut album has so far proved to be his most satisfying. Beaver's moody vocals and delicate guitar soloing are highlighted on *Little Beaver*—a set of sinewy blues songs. As a guitarist, he favors single-note playing with a clear tone reminiscent of Wes Montgomery. *Black Rhapsody* is Beaver's tribute to Montgomery; it even includes a song called "Tribute to Wes." Unfortunately, the rhythm section is a little stiff and the instrumentals are only mildly satisfying—excepting for a tough, funk number called "Hit Me with Funky Music." Little Beaver found commerical success in "Party Down," a sultry dance song. The *Party Down* album is filled with variations on the theme. The relaxed mood proves to be the perfect setting for his oozing solos. After a two-year hiatus, *When Was the Last Time* found the guitar mixed low and the emphasis on romantic crooning. — J.MC.

LITTLE FEAT
★★★★ **Dixie Chicken / War. 2686**
★★★ **Feats Don't Fail Me Now / War. B-2784**
★★★★ **Little Feat / War. 1890**
★★★★ **Sailin' Shoes / War. B-2600**
★★★ **The Last Record Album / War. B-2884**
★★★ **Time Loves a Hero / War. 3015**
★★★ **Waiting for Columbus / War. 2B-3140**
Little Feat was formed in 1970 by Lowell George and Roy Estrada of the Mothers of Invention, Ritchie Hayward of the Fraternity of Man and Bill Payne, a Texas piano player. George was the group's chief writer, and on *Little Feat,* they turned in a fine set of post-psychedelic country-influenced rock, with one standard, "Willin'," which has been covered by nearly everyone in the L.A. barfly scene.

Estrada left after *Sailin' Shoes,* the second album, and with Ken Gradney, Sam Clayton and Paul Barrere as new members, the group made its best album, *Dixie Chicken,* in 1973. But in the absence of commercial success, George seemed to lose interest in Little Feat, playing a great many sessions while the band's product withered. The group's cult has made it imperative to continue, however, and commercial success seems eventually assured. But Payne and Hayward now dominate the band, which is traversing some of the territory between jazz and rock staked out by Steely Dan. The result of this, and whether George will retain his association, remains to be seen. — D.M.

LITTLE MILTON
★ **Friend of Mine / Glades 7508**
★★★★ **Greatest Hits / Chess 50113**
One of the most gravel-voiced of Chicago rhythm & blues singers, Little Milton Campbell in fact owes more to Howlin' Wolf than Curtis Mayfield. Because he recorded for Chess and plays guitar as well as sings, Milton has often been described as a blues artist, but he managed to retain his popularity on the soul scene in the Sixties while most harder blues performers lost theirs. A good deal of this is due to his whimsically sensual material, notably the hits "Grits Ain't Groceries" and "We're Gonna Make It." The Chess album is masterful, presenting Milton as a sort of Northern equivalent to Bobby Bland.

But in 1971 Milton left Chess, and began recording for Stax. He had some commercial success there, but after the label folded, he was left adrift, conceptually and contractually. His 1977 LP for TK's Glades subsidiary is perfunctory funk, far from the blues and gritty R&B Milton sings at his best. — D.M.

LITTLE RICHARD
★★★ **His Biggest Hits / Spec. 2111**
★★★★ **Little Richard / Spec. 2103**
★★★ **Little Richard's Greatest Hits / Trip 8013**
★★★★★ **Little Richard's Grooviest 17 Original Hits / Spec. 2113**
★★★★★ **The Fabulous Little Richard / Spec. 2104**
★★★★★ **Well Alright! / Spec. 2136**
Little Richard's music remains among the most vital rock & roll two decades after it was first recorded. His wild pumping piano style (matched only by Jerry Lee Lewis in the annals of world history), his braggadocio singing, with its gospel-derived screams and hollers, and his manic songs—"Long Tall Sally," "Lucille," "Jenny Jenny,"

"Tutti Frutti" and the rest—are all models for later performers. But on record, Richard remains indubitably Richard.

His Specialty sides are the originals, recorded in the middle and late Fifties before he changed his name back to Richard Penniman and became a minister. *Grooviest 17 Original Hits* is the definitive collection, although *His Biggest Hits* is available in pristine monaural sound, which is preferable. *Well Alright!* and *The Fabulous Little Richard* are excellent compilations with some rare tracks; the latter includes the version of "Kansas City" on which the Beatles based theirs.

Little Richard's career as a gospel singer is unfortunately no longer represented on records. Nor is his 1970s comeback for Warners, although *The Rill Thing,* which contains the marvelous "Freedom Blues," an unrestrained rocker in the grand tradition, frequently shows up in bargain bins. The Trip collection is the rerecordings of the Fifties hits that Richard cut for Vee-Jay during the Sixties; they are vastly inferior. Better to look for Epic's *Cast a Long Shadow,* a reissue of a live-in-the-studio set for Okeh in the Sixties. A-wop-lop-a-loo-bop-a-wop-bam-boom. — D.M.

LITTLE RIVER BAND
★★ **Diamantina Cocktail / Harv. SW-11645**
★★ **Little River Band / Harv. ST-11512**
★★ **Sleeper Catcher / Harv. SW-11783**
Guitar-dominated Australian sextet performing passable melodic hard rock, with a tendency for two-chord clichés. — C.W.

IAN LLOYD
★★ **Ian Lloyd / Poly. 1-6066**
Correct but uninspired hard rock, though Lloyd's sandpapery voice is in good form.

Greg Diamond co-wrote most of the material with Lloyd, and he drums solidly. Good sax from Ian McDonald. (Now deleted.) — C.W.

LOBO
★★ **The Best of Lobo / Big 89513**
Lobo had a string of pop hits, most notably 1971's "Me and You and a Dog Named Boo" and 1972's "I'd Love You to Want Me." It is surprising that Lobo of Spanish origin sings in a gentle, José Feliciano style of folk pop. All the hits are here, for anyone who still cares. — D.M.

JOHN LODGE
★ **Natural Avenue / Lon. PS-683**
From the Moody Blues bassist, sweet but forgettably airy melodies, plain orchestration, flat engineering; weak and precious. — C.W.

NILS LOFGREN
★★★ **Cry Tough / A&M 4573**
★ **I Came to Dance / A&M 4628**
★★ **Night After Night / A&M 3707**
★★ **Nils Lofgren / A&M 4509**
This fondly regarded but marginally popular rock & roll gypsy was first noticed as leader of Grin and as an occasional sessionman for Neil Young. His debut solo effort, *Nils Lofgren,* with its jut-jawed "Back It Up," showed off Nils' speed and taste on electric guitar. "Keith Don't Go" and a cover of the Byrds' version of Carole King's "Goin' Back" were a fan's notes on rock. They joined the pick of his Grin work on 1975's "authorized bootleg," a document of a hot live set for a San Francisco FM station.

Cry Tough, which came out in '76, sported more of Nils' shifty, rhythmic guitar. His thin, smoky voice, mixed up front, was just right for the punk snideness of "Incidentally . . . It's Over" and "Mud in Your Eye."

But the Yardbirds' "For Your Love" strained him vocally, and early 1977's *I Came to Dance* featured a foot-dragging misreading of idol Keith Richards' "Happy." The rest of that album forsook polish for attempted funk, and *Night After Night,* an indifferent double-record live set, left Nils at a career impasse. — F.S.

LOGGINS AND MESSINA
★★ **Finale / Col. JG-34167**
★ **Full Sail / Col. PC-32540**
★★★ **Loggins and Messina / Col. PC-31748**

★★★ **Loggins and Messina Sittin' In / Col. PC-31044**
★ **Mother Lode / Col. PC-33175**
★ **Native Sons / Col. PC-33578**
★★★ **On Stage / Col. PG-32848**
★ **"So Fine" / Col. PC-33810**
★★★ **The Best of Loggins and Messina/ Friends / Col. PC-34388**
Originally this was Jim Messina's laid-back escape hatch from Poco. But Poco virtually invented laid-backness, so there wasn't too much further to go by the time Messina decided to join forces with West Coast folkie Kenny Loggins. Messina's career high points were his marginal contributions to the Buffalo Springfield and the first two Poco albums, which were about as high energy as this peculiarly tired genre comes. Thus Loggins and Messina became spokesmen for the "easy" aesthetic.

There's no question that the first two duo LPs were warm and rocking. So it's little wonder that nearly 80 percent of the final *Best of* album was comprised of songs that originally appeared on those two LPs. "Vahavella" (even better in its broiling reincarnation on the live album), "Angry Eyes" and their most essential hit, "Your Mama Don't Dance," were infectious if unassuming pop. But the unassumingness snowballed over the years into total snore. Loggins and Messina didn't stop—they just faded away. — B.M.

DAVE LOGGINS
★ **Apprentice (in a Musical Workshop) / Epic KE 32833**
★ **Country Suite / Epic PE 33946**
★ **One Way Ticket to Paradise / Epic PE-34713**
★ **Personal Belongings / Van. 6580**
Acoustical singer/songwriter whose only hit, "Please Come to Boston," is on *Apprentice*. Earnest schlock. — S.H.

KENNY LOGGINS
★★ **Celebrate Me Home / Col. PC-34655**
★★ **Nightwatch / Col. JC-35387**
On his own, without Jim Messina to provide some effervescence, Loggins is as flat as a day-old open can of beer. This is to Loggins and Messina's lightweight MOR what the Art Garfunkel solo albums are to Simon and Garfunkel's heavyweight MOR: a sad reflection of a once enjoyable past. — D.M.

JACKIE LOMAX
★★★ **Did You Ever Have That Feeling / Cap. ST-11668**

One of the smoothest purveyors of blue-eyed soul, Jackie Lomax is still waiting for his luck to turn. Several lively albums on Apple and Warner Bros. are no longer in print, but Lomax' late-Seventies records show his tart voice in good form over a range of serviceable, if unspectacular, material. This is unfortunately, all that's left. — J.S.

LON AND DERREK
★ **Who Do You Out Do? / A&M 4507**
A: We are not Devo. — D.M.

LOST GENERATION
★★★ **Sly, Slick and Wicked / Bruns. 754164**
★★ **Young, Tough and Terrible / Bruns. 54178**
Modern soul group recorded these two albums in the early Seventies, after scoring a Top Forty pop hit with "Sly, Slick and Wicked." Moderate R&B, no pop success followed, and like most such items, this group disappeared. — D.M.

LOST GONZO BAND
★★ **Lost Gonzo Band / MCA 487**
★★ **Signs of Life / Cap. SW-11788**
★★ **Thrills / MCA 2232**
Jerry Jeff Walker's backup band plays a credible version of the raucous country-rock bar-band music that Walker and his Austin cronies helped popularize in the Seventies. Unfortunately, the group lacks the personality or songwriting ability to make it on its own. — J.S.

LOTHAR AND THE HAND PEOPLE
★★★ **Lothar and the Hand People / Cap. SM-2997**
As if you couldn't guess from the title, this is a relic of the psychedelic era. Lothar and company were an early synthesizer combo that used to appear in Greenwich Village during the late Sixties— it is impossible to remember them except in a druggy haze, which actually isn't a bad description of what their first and only album sounds like. — D.M.

LOVE
★★★★★ **Forever Changes / Elek. 74013**
A light classic from the late psychedelic era. Released in 1967, *Forever Changes* is all that survives of almost a dozen Love LPs, most of them harder-rocking and less worthwhile. This is rather like a soundtrack from an LSD movie—lead singer Arthur Lee is a bizarre composer whose song

titles tell a good deal of the story: "A House Is Not a Motel," "The Good Humor Man He Sees Everything Like This," "Bummer in the Summer," "You Set the Scene." Although it's similarly dated, the music has an exotic frothiness and the string settings are among the most gorgeous in rock history. Even the lyrics, while occasionally demented, were usually too inchoate to be anything but curiously passionate love songs. Indescribably essential. — D.M.

LOVE SCULPTURE
★★ Forms and Feelings / Prod. 71035
Believe it or not, prototype pub and punk rocker Dave Edmunds began his career as guitarist with this group, playing some of the most godawful boogie blues in history. Actually, if you like amphetamine-style guitar playing, it's not half bad, and tremendously amusing at this late date. — D.M.

LOVE UNLIMITED
★★ He's All I've Got / Unli. U-101
★★ In Heat / 20th Cent. 443
★★ Under the Influence of Love Unlimited / 20th Cent. 414
Barry White's subsidiary vocal group scored on the charts with a couple of tidbits, but mostly served as a kind of pretty fluff for White's macho-horny growl. He married one of 'em. And he can keep 'em. — D.M.

LOVE UNLIMITED ORCHESTRA
★ Music Maestro Please / 20th Cent. 480
★ My Musical Bouquet / 20th Cent. 554
★ My Sweet Summer Suite / 20th Cent. 517
★★ Rhapsody in White / 20th Cent. 433
★ White Gold / 20th Cent. 458
The Orchestra's hit, "Love's Theme," sounded like some dreamy movie music for a Diana Ross flick in 1974, but by now their sound has become as unbearably odious as that of the chubbo they back up. And Barry White is (you know, baby) pretty (uh-huh) goddamn lame. — D.M.

THE LOVIN' SPOONFUL
★★★★★ Best of the Lovin' Spoonful / Kam. S. 2608-2
It's a real shame that a group that contributed so heavily to folk rock and the general resurgence of the rock & roll spirit in the mid-Sixties should have all of its original albums out of print. The band produced such hits as "Do You Believe in Magic,"

"Summer in the City" and "Daydream," and had a fine songwriter in John Sebastian, plus a real rocker in Zal Yanovsky. The remaining anthology is recommended, but only as an introduction; any of the group's first five albums, especially *Daydream* and *Hums of the Lovin' Spoonful,* are worth hunting down. — B.A.

NICK LOWE
★★★★ Pure Pop for Now People / Col. JC-35329
The English title of this album is *Jesus of Cool,* which overstates the case even if Lowe is Carlene Carter's boyfriend. Actually, Brinsley Schwarz' former bassist/songwriter has become a pop dilettante of the first water, thanks mostly to his association with Dave Edmunds and Rockpile. These songs are witty and the playing is forceful, more so than Lowe's productions of Graham Parker but about as brutal as his work with Elvis Costello. Highlights include "Heart of the City," which Edmunds and Lowe will probably record until doomsday if it doesn't become a hit; "Marie Provost," a beastly tale; and "Rollers Show," which is only halfway a joke, I'll bet. Intriguing, to say the least, but not for the faint of heart, which includes fans of Foreigner and Boston. — D.M.

L.T.D.
★ Gittin' Down / A&M 3660
★ Love to the World / A&M 4589
★★★ Love, Togetherness and Devotion / A&M 3602
★★ Something to Love / A&M 4646
★ Togetherness / A&M 4705
Slick Seventies ensemble R&B group enjoyed disco crossover popularity. — J.S.

L.T.G. EXCHANGE
★ Susie Heartbreaker / RCA APL1-1046
This record, written by L.T.G. keyboardist Walter Chiles, was called, in all seriousness, a "black rock operetta" on its release. In reality, it is a mindless set of funk vamps hardly worth the vinyl it's stamped on. (Now deleted.) — J.S.

JON LUCIEN
★★★ I Am Now / RCA ANL1-2193
★★★ Mind's Eye / RCA APL1-0493
★★★ Premonitions / Col. KC-34255
★★ Rashida / RCA APL1-0161
★★★★ Song for My Lady / Col. PC-33544
Jon Lucien is a baritone singer who croons his spiritual and love songs in fashionably

glossy pop-jazz settings. He is also some-times an instrumentalist and songwriter ca-pable of writing unashamedly mushy love songs. Arrangements differ little from al-bum to album, and their lushness often gives his music an unnecessary MOR bent. On romantic ballads, Lucien's phrasing is reminiscent of Johnny Hartman, but he tends to be at his most imaginative on up-tempo songs. — J.MC.

LUCIFER'S FRIEND
★ **Banquet / Pass. SO-98012**
■ **I'm Just a Rock 'n' Roll Singer / Bill. BG-1008**
■ **Mind Exploding / Janus JXS 7030**
Classic European Seventies hackwork, with influences acquired, but not absorbed, from Genesis, Led Zeppelin, Grand Funk and the nether world of jazz rock. The group is composed of a typical "progres-sive" rock mixture of Germans and Eng-lishmen, whose artistic pretensions consis-tently outrace their ability to sing a song. Real bad stuff. — D.M.

BASCOM LAMAR LUNSFORD
★★ **Music from South Turkey Creek / Roun. 0065**
Lunsford, who wrote "Old Mountain Dew" about his brief tenure as a full-time lawyer, sings and plays banjo (two-finger style) on the first side of this LP. He is credited with several hundred items in the Archive of American Folksong, although relatively little has been recorded. George Pegram and Red Parham are on side two. — I.M.

ELLIOT LURIE
★★★ **Elliot Lurie / Epic KE 33337**
Former lead singer for Looking Glass ("Brandy") invests his epicurean sensibility

in the disco idiom, with splendid results. Lurie never sacrifices his insinuating vocal temper or lyrical acuity to the genre's cus-tomary emotional overkill and insipid rhet-oric, even when celebrating discos as churches for the common man. (Now de-leted.) — M.G.

LUTHER
★★ **Luther / CTI 9907**
★★ **This Close to You / Coti. 9916**
R&B backup singer attempts a career as a leader by making his own disco albums. He's not bad, but he might as well stay in the studio—the money's better. — J.S.

CHERYL LYNN
★ **Cheryl Lynn / Col. JC-35486**
Because it is every white, middle-aged rec-ord executive's dream to discover a hot looker with a hook, the 1979 success of this wretched pop vocalist perhaps portends a trend. But that doesn't mean anyone ought to follow it. — D.M.

LORETTA LYNN
★★★ **Back to the Country / MCA 471**
★★★★ **Coal Miner's Daughter / MCA 2342**
★★★★ **Don't Come Home A-Drinkin' / MCA 113**
★★★ **Home / MCA 2146**
★★★ **Hymns / MCA 5**
★★★★ **I Remembered Patsy / MCA 2265**
★★★★★ **Loretta Lynn's Greatest Hits / MCA 2341**
★★★★ **Loretta Lynn's Greatest Hits, Vol. 2 / MCA 2353**
★★★ **Somebody Somewhere / MCA 2228**
★★★ **They Don't Make 'Em Like My Daddy / MCA 444**
★★★★ **When the Tingle Becomes a Chill / MCA 2079**
★★★ **Who Says God Is Dead? / MCA 7**
★★★ **You Ain't Woman Enough / MCA 6**
Loretta Lynn is one of the most perplexing of all country women performers. A major star for the past decade, she seems torn be-tween the raw roots of her Kentucky up-bringing—"Coal Miner's Daughter" is her story—and the middle class demands of modern Nashville. But within this series of contradictions (and with the exception of her often pallid duet work with Conway Twitty), Lynn has recorded some of the most consistently appealing music to come from Nashville in this decade.

Mostly this has meant her hits, which in-clude tough woman songs that are nearly female honky-tonk, like "You Ain't

Woman Enough," such social commentary items as "The Pill" and "One's on the Way," both examples of instinctive working-class feminism; and country weepers like "When the Tingle Becomes a Chill" and "They Don't Make 'Em Like Daddy." If Lynn were ever granted artistic rather than purely commerical production values, she might become the most important female singer of her generation.   — D.M.

LYNYRD SKYNYRD
★★ **Gimme Back My Bullets** / MCA 3022
★★ **Nuthin' Fancy** / MCA 3021
★★★★ **One More from the Road** / MCA 2-8001
★★★ **Pronounced Leh-Nerd Skin-Nerd** / MCA 3019
★★★★ **Second Helping** / MCA 3020
★★★ **Skynyrd's First . . . And Last** / MCA 3047
★★★★ **Street Survivors** / MCA 3029

Plugging in hard-rock influences, where most other Southern bands place country roots, a mix of British rock sensibilities and hard-drinking Southern boogie established Lynyrd Skynyrd as top contenders for the mid-Seventies Southern rock throne.

Second Helping is the band at its chunky best, with rhythm and lead licks fairly bursting from the seams of songs like "The Needle and the Spoon" and the tongue-in-cheek "Workin' for MCA." Lead singer Ronnie Van Zant's reputation as a rabble-rousing hero was solidified with "Sweet Home Alabama," Skynyrd's breakthrough single (and an ostensible reply to Neil Young's "Southern Man").

When producer Al Kooper was dumped for Tom Dowd's cleaner sound, after

Nuthin' Fancy, Skynyrd also lost some if its distinction. While there were still some strong tunes—"Saturday Night Special" cracked like the gun it was named after—there wasn't the sort of combustion that drove the first two albums. *Gimme Back My Bullets* continued this trend with a few notable tunes and a clutter of well-executed but otherwise lackluster performances. The fact that the bulk of the tough-rocking live double album, *One More from the Road,* was drawn from the first two LPs indicates that while Skynyrd reached its commercial peak through incessant touring, it was at a critical point in its recording career—when creative growth was straining to match popular appeal. The soaring beauty of "Free Bird" was matched by its ascent as an FM standard, but Ronnie Van Zant's writing was suffering.

Skynyrd met the challenge with *Street Survivors,* the band's hardest-rocking studio album since *Second Helping.* But the victory was wrested from its   asp by a plane crash within weeks   e album's October 1977 release. (Va. zant, uita. Steve Gaines and singer Cassy Gaines died in the wreck.)

"That Smell," a maniacally propulsive tune from *Street Survivors* dealing with the perils of the rock & roll trail, served as the band's epitaph. At least until the release of *First and . . . Last* a year later. That album, compiled from tapes made before Al Kooper discovered the band, contains some of Van Zant's best writing; it was far from a ploy to market the remains of a rock ghost. And Van Zant's true epitaph is contained in its best song, "Was I Right or Wrong," in which a singer, spurned by his family, finds success and returns home to find his parents dead.   — J.B.M.

JIMMIE MACK
★★★ **Jimmie Mack / Big 76007**
Hard rock that's high energy without being heavy metal, by the former Montrose lead singer. Jimmie Mack is no relation to the fella Martha and the Vandellas sang about, but he's an above-average white screamer. — D.M.

LONNIE MACK
★★★ **Lonnie Mack with Pismo / Cap. ST-11703**
Semi-legendary rock guitarist Lonnie Mack is best known for his 1963 instrumental hit with Chuck Berry's "Memphis." *With Pismo* is in a laid-back country vein that's pleasant but does nothing to further his reputation for hot licks, although it does include a guest appearance by the able sessionman David Lindley. Elektra's reissue of the original Mack album—*For Collectors Only* (now deleted)—is more worth tracking down. — J.S.

UNCLE DAVE MACON
★★★ **Early Recordings / Coun. 521**
★★★ **Wait 'Til the Clouds Roll By / Hist. 8006**
A pioneer in the field of commercial country music, Macon was a superb banjo player and vocalist who surrounded himself with excellent backup musicians (Sam and Kirk McGee, the Delmore Brothers) or performed solo, whether on record, in concert or during his twenty-seven years as a star on *The Grand Ole Opry.* These are remasters of Twenties and Thirties 78s, drawn from the two hundred titles he cut for various labels. Both are technically well handled and offer sufficient background information for a first-time listener. — I.M.

CLEDUS MAGGARD
★★ **Two More Sides / Mer. SRM-1-1112**

★★★ **White Knight / Mer. SRM-1-30176**
Commercial jingles writer/adman Jay Huguely recorded a 1976 single, "The White Knight," under the name of Cledus Maggard as part of an investigation into the pop-song possibilities of CB radio. Produced by Nashville session mastermind Jerry Kennedy, the song became a No. 1 hit on country stations, and Huguely became a recording artist. (Now deleted.) — J.S.

MAGMA
■ **Kohntarkosz / A&M 3650**
★ **Mekanik Destruktiw Kowmmandoh / A&M 4397**
★ **Udu Wudu / Toma. 6001**
Christian Vander, a German gypsy who was taught to play drums by Elvin Jones and Chet Baker and has played with Chick Corea and John Coltrane, had this typically Teutonic concept: a musical ensemble that would embody the *Gessamkunstwerk,* or music for all mankind, accessible on manifold levels. Magma was the medium.

Vander also invented his own language, a sort of universalist Esperanto called Kobayan, which comes from Kobaia, an imaginary planet where there's room for revolutionary thought and where "Univeria Zekt," the new man, finds greater energy and meaningfulness.

Vander claims this music comes from the deep Polish and Baltic forests, and it undeniably sounds as if it just climbed out from under a rock. He's also into voodoo, exorcism, trance music, German and Russian neoromanticism and classical Greek tragedy. But for all its pretensions, Magma sounds like the worst possible sloweddown clone of Deep Purple or Tangerine Dream undergoing a bout of colitis. Do the locomotion. (Now deleted.) — B.M.

TAJ MAHAL
★★★★ Anthology, Vol. 1 / Col. PC-34466
★ Brothers / War. B-3024
★★ Evolution (The Most Recent) / War.
   K-3094
★★★★ Giant Step/De Old Folks at
   Home / Col. CG-18
★★ Happy Just to Be Like I Am / Col.
   C-30767
★★ Mo' Roots / Col. KC-33051
★ Music Fuh Ya' (Musica Para Tu) / War.
   B-2994
★ Music Keeps Me Together / Col.
   PC-33801
★★ Oooh So Good 'n' Blues / Col.
   KC-32600
★ Recycling the Blues (and Other Related
   Stuff) / Col. C-31605
★ Satisfied 'n' Tickled Too / Col.
   PC-34103
★★★ Taj Mahal / Col. CS-9579
★★★ The Natch'l Blues / Col. CS-9698
★★★ The Real Thing / Col. CG-30619

Few artists can boast a catalogue that so specifically chronicles changes in personal musical conception and social attitudes. Taj Mahal began as a blues interpreter, but his music has since encompassed rock, traditional Appalachian sounds, jazz, calypso, reggae and a general tendency toward experimentation and assimilation.

For example, take the four-man string section on the live *The Real Thing,* or Jesse Ed Davis' superbly complementary guitar work on any number of these albums. Mahal performs with bands, orchestras and as a soloist. Through his understanding of contemporary tastes, he has brought the music of his heritage to a mass audience. A self-taught musician who took it upon himself to explore the roots of his music academically, Mahal brings a rare historical perspective to his work, and while he is dedicated to educating his fans, he's never preachy about it.

His debut, *Taj Mahal,* is his least-defined LP. Although Davis and Ry Cooder are among the backup troupe, Taj sounds a bit lost in the recording studio. Musically, the set lacks the focus he was subsequently able to develop. But it does include his landmark, "The Celebrated Walking Blues." *Giant Step/De Old Folks at Home* is a two-record set that incorporates smooth country blues and understated rock rhythms. The second LP is a solo disc, on which Taj plays harmonica, guitar and banjo in addition to singing. The record suffers from poor production: fuzzy vocals and a severe stereo mix that places banjo

completely on the left speaker, voice completely on the right.

The Natch'l Blues is just that, although rather than interpreting traditional bluesmen, Mahal himself is the principal songwriter, in addition to rearranging such tunes as "The Cuckoo" and "Corinna." *The Real Thing* is a two-disc live album that features little material from the earlier sets; the regular band is augmented by a tuba section that doubles on other brass. Rather than Mahal's usual three- to four-minute renditions of blues themes, this album includes a number of extended jams. The studio set, *Happy Just to Be,* also includes the tuba/brass section and draws a clear picture of the relationship between blues and rock. Listen to what happens to "Oh Susanna" and the title track.

Oooh So Good 'n' Blues, Satisfied 'n' Tickled Too, Mo' Roots and *Recycling the Blues* represent various stages of Mahal's discovery of other blues forms and an increasing fascination with Caribbean music. *Mo' Roots* is the most ambitious in its variations on calypso and reggae themes.

Anthology is the first of a projected three-part series Columbia will assemble, tracing Mahal's career while he recorded for that label. The LP is concerned with his early blues and country-blues recordings, and it's excellent.

In addition to his own albums, Taj has done several film scores, the best known being *Sounder,* in which he also played a minor acting role. *Brothers,* based on the lives of George Jackson and Angela Davis, also features a score by Taj consisting of both background music and original songs. The two Warner Bros. albums continue his fascination with Caribbean sounds, with mixed results. But as always, his next step is unpredictable. — I.M.

MAHOGANY RUSH
★★★ Child of the Novelty / 20th Cent. 451
★★★ Live / Col. JC-35257
★★★ Mahogany Rush IV / Col. PC-34190
★★ Maxoom / 20th Cent. 463
★★★ Strange Universe / 20th Cent. 482
★★★ World Anthem / Col. PC-34677

Frank Marino, so the story goes, was involved in a serious car accident somewhere around 1970 or 1971 and lapsed into a deep coma for several days. A nonmusician before the crash, he was supposedly visited while in a coma by the spirit of the late Jimi Hendrix, who endowed the poor Canadian with a soupçon of his deceased talent. Marino awoke, picked up a guitar and started playing riffs in a very familiar style. He acquired a bassist and drummer and cut *Maxoom* for Montreal's tiny Kot'ai label (later reissued on 20th Century-Fox).

This is an interesting story, but unfortunately, listening doesn't support it. Marino is obviously a pretty fair guitarist and a devout, almost maniacal Hendrix fan, but unless Jimi regressed to his Curtis Knight days while crossing the Styx, his amalgamation with Marino's physical being is doubtful. Lots of *Axis: Bold as Love* feedback and sound effects and a poignant Hendrix homage ("Buddy") make *Maxoom* a nifty curiosity, but not much more.

With *Child of the Novelty,* however, Marino lowers his voice an octave, and his songwriting and guitar are more accessible, in the fashion of *Electric Ladyland.* Since then, beginning with *Strange Universe,* Marino's playing has grown more fluid and varied, even taking a run at a jazz riff on occasion. But nobody tells the Hendrix tale much any more. After six or seven years, it's apparent that Marino will never be an innovator, and at best, he's just a competent mime. — A.N.

MAIN INGREDIENT
★★ Afrodisiac / RCA LSP 4834
★★ Euphrates River / RCA APLI-0335
★★★ Greatest Hits / RCA APL1-0314
★★ Music Maximus / RCA APL1-1558
★★ Rolling Down a Mountainside / RCA ANL1-2667
★★ Shame on the World / RCA LSP 4412
★★ Spinning Around / RCA LSP 4412
Black MOR, a little tougher and funkier than the Fifth Dimension, but not by much. The hits—particularly "Everybody Plays the Fool"—were about the best of it, but in general, this is a good example of how characterless black pop has become in the past decade. — D.M.

MALLARD
★★★ In a Different Climate / Virgin PZ-34489
Mallard is a former Captain Beefheart backing band from the northern California town of Eureka. But they haven't quite found it, after all; this is derivative of Beefheart's innovations, all right, but of his less inspired later ones rather than the bizarrely brilliant early stuff. Some quirky pleasures here, but not quite enough. — D.M.

MAMA CASS
★★ Dream a Little Dream / Dun. DSX-50040
★★ Make Your Own Kind of Music / Dun. DSX-50071
★★ Mama's Big Ones / Dun. DSX-50093
As a member of the Mamas and the Papas, Cass Elliott was a highly visible star during the more complex and ethereal moments of folk rock. But these albums, made in the waning days of the group, are all too characteristic of her and their style: light, sentimental pop with a veneer of rock rhythm. Only for those who also miss Sopwith Camel. — D.M.

THE MAMAS AND THE PAPAS
★★ A Gathering of Flowers / Dun. DSY-50073
★★★ Farewell to the First Golden Era / Dun. 50025
★★ The Mamas and the Papas / Dun. X-50006
★★★ The Mamas and the Papas: Sixteen of Their Greatest Hits / Dun. 50064
★★★ The Mamas and the Papas' Twenty Golden Hits / Dun. X-50145
★★ The Papas and the Mamas / Dun. X-50031
The Mamas and the Papas mastered a very slick form of Sixties folk rock, a kind of West Coast version of Simon and Garfunkel, although this quartet's chief songwriter, John Phillips, lacked the sardonic edge of Paul Simon. The group was formed by four veterans of the Greenwich Village folk scene—Phillips; his wife, Michelle; Mama Cass Elliott; and Denny Doherty—while they were down and out in the Virgin Islands in 1965. After relocating to the Los Angeles area and hooking up with producer Lou Adler, the band scored a formidable series of hit singles from 1966 to 1968: "California Dreamin'," "Monday Monday," "Dedicated to the One I Love" (a sweet cover of a Shirelles hit), "Creeque

Alley" (a sometimes hilarious parable of the band's career before stardom) and "Twelve Thirty."

The Mamas and the Papas represented folk rock's rapprochement with conventional pop music. Adler surrounded them with the best Hollywood sessionmen of the day, and while sometimes cloyingly sentimental, the records are always highly professional. By typifying hippies in the most harmless sort of way, the group reached a commercial peak of acceptability that more authentic practitioners were denied. And because their singing was so good, and because Phillips and Adler were astute commercially, the band acquired a considerable reputation in hippie-era music circles, helping organize the momentous Monterey International Pop Festival in 1967.

Since then, Phillips has gone on to a rather dissolute career as a pop aristocrat (his most notable achievement has been acting as producer for Robert Altman's *Brewster McCloud*). Michelle, who was divorced from John in 1968 around the time the group broke up, has engaged in a similar career, with spurts of acting (best in *Dillinger,* but not all that great at any time). Cass Elliott, the band's most visible symbol, died in London in 1971; she had a couple of hits on her own. Doherty is no longer present on the recording scene.

Of the albums still available, almost all are anthologies, and the original LPs are not the best the group made. (That honor goes to *If You Can Believe Your Eyes and Ears,* their first.) Any LP rated three stars is a decent sampler. — D.M.

MAMA'S PRIDE
★ **Mama's Pride / Atco 36-122**
★ **Uptown and Lowdown / Atco 36-146**
The virtual nadir of Southern rock. The ecstasy of Skynyrd's "Free Bird" and the Allman's "Mountain Jam" reduced to the sort of boring sludge that guarantees a headache. — D.M.

MAN
★★ **Back into the Future / U. Artists LA-179-H**
★★ **Be Good to Yourself / U. Artists LA-077-G**
★★★ **Rhinos, Winos and Lunatics / U. Artists LA-247-G**
This is the most famous rock band ever to come from Wales, although the music it played had more to do with psychedelic San Francisco. The chief pleasure Man had to offer was guitarist Deke Leonard,

who is absent from the first two albums above but dominates *Rhinos.* The group also recorded several deleted LPs, but nothing it did had much impact inside the U.S., although the band had sizable followings in the Bay Area and in England and Germany. It broke up in 1976. Leonard's *Iceberg* solo album can also sometimes be found as a cutout. — D.M.

MELISSA MANCHESTER
★★ **Better Days and Happy Endings / Ari. AQ-4067**
★★ **Bright Eyes / Ari. 4011**
★★ **Don't Cry Out Loud / Ari. 4186**
★ **Help Is on the Way / Ari. 4095**
★★ **Home to Myself / Ari. 4006**
★★★ **Melissa / Ari. AQ-4031**
★ **Singin' / Ari. 4136**
At her best, this one-time backup singer for Bette Midler sounds like a cross between the Divine Miss M and Dionne Warwick. Her first two albums are intimate, if somewhat unsure. *Melissa,* her most outgoing set, contains the hit "Midnite Blue." From here on, Vini Poncia's inept, overblown productions undermine Manchester's charm. — S.H.

MANCHILD
★ **Feel the Phuff / Chi.-T. LA872-H**
★ **Power and Love / Chi.-T. LA765-G**
Dull, tepid jazz riffs mingle with Chicago soul harmonies to no apparent purpose. — D.M.

MANDALABAND
★ **Mandalaband / Chrys. 1095**
Focus gets religion. (Now deleted.) — A.N.

HARVEY MANDEL
★★★ **Baby Batter / Janus 3017**

★★★ **The Best of Harvey Mandel** / Janus
7014
★★★★ **The Snake** / Janus 3037
Mandel is a phenomenal blues-rock guitarist with jazz technique and chops. He
recorded a number of solo albums in addition to these still in print and has also
done many sessions. John Mayall tapped
him for *U.S.A. Union,* Canned Heat used
him as lead guitarist on one of that band's
best records, *Future Blues* (the last LP featuring the great guitarist Al Wilson) and
Mandel led Pure Food and Drug Act with
violinist Don "Sugarcane" Harris.
   The Janus albums were produced by
Canned Heat's Skip Taylor and use musicians from Canned Heat and Pure Food
and Drug Act as sidemen. *Best of* duplicates material from *Snake* and *Baby Batter*
as well as the out-of-print *Shangrenade. The
Snake* is Mandel's best solo effort. "Ode to
the Owl," a solo tribute to Wilson, is the
outstanding track, yet it is not reproduced
on the *Best of* album.   — J.S.

MANDRILL
★★ **New Worlds** / Ari. 4195
★★★★ **The Best of Mandrill** / Poly. 6047
★★ **The Greatest** / Ari. 7000
★★ **We Are One** / Ari. 4144
This septet originated in Brooklyn's Bed-
ford-Stuyvesant section and played a
streetwise amalgam of funk, salsa and rock
elements organized around a loosely Latin-
jazz format. On later albums, the range was
extended to include disco and heavily arranged ballads, and the band's instrumental
capability matured, especially on the now
out-of-print *Mandrilland.* All the band's
best work is on the cutout records done for
Polydor and United Artists, so the *Best of*
collection is the only remaining set worth
hearing. Mandrill's three Arista albums are
fairly pointless compared to much of the
band's earlier material.   — J.S.

THE MANHATTANS
★★★★ **It Feels So Good** / Col. 34450
★★ **That's How Much I Love You** / Col.
KC-33064
★★★ **The Manhattans** / Col. 33820
★★★ **There's No Good in Goodbye** / Col.
JC-35252
★★★★ **There's No Me without You** / Col.
C-32444
The Manhattans are a low-key group that
rarely extends itself beyond what it does
best: rumbling, old-fashioned soul ballads
like "Kiss and Say Goodbye." Gerald Al-
ston, the lead singer, has a tenor that is

modest at best, yet the Manhattans' consistency and taste in the genre has few rivals.
The records are packed with a real sincerity and soulfulness. The five Columbia albums are produced by Philadelphia perennial Bobby Martin, with the exception of
one side on *That's How Much,* which is
filled with five mediocre songs from the
group's De Luxe days. *It Feels So Good* is
their strongest album yet, marred only by
Blue Lovett's spoken, Barry White–styled
intros on just about every song.   — J.MC.

THE MANHATTAN TRANSFER
★★★ **Coming Out** / Atl. 18183
★★ **Jukin'** / Cap. ST-11405
★★★ **Pastiche** / Atl. 19163
★★★ **The Manhattan Transfer** / Atl. 18133
Picking up where Bette Midler fell apart,
the Manhattan Transfer lifts nostalgia out
of the Continental Baths and into the Wal-
dorf. Pert and debonair, these well-
groomed exponents of recherché schmaltz
may lack Midler's penchant for the outrageous, but that's okay; they sing effortlessly, and they distance themselves from
their illusion without puncturing
it.   — F.R.

BARRY MANILOW
★ **Barry Manilow** / Ari. 4007
★ **Barry Manilow Live** / Ari. 8500
★ **Barry Manilow 2** / Ari. 4016
★ **Even Now** / Ari. 4164
★ **Foul Play** / Ari. 9501
★★ **This One's for You** / Ari. 4090
★ **Tryin' to Get the Feeling** / Ari. 4060
Impeccably crafted records in which the
king of MOR treats the pop song as adver-
tisement. Every day is Christmas at
Macy's. Manilow has become the epitome
of soulessness as a pop singer whose great-
est artistic achievement is not his former

role as Bette Midler's onstage musical director or his flock of flavorless housewife hits, but his singing—not even composing—the McDonald's "You Deserve a Break Today" commercial. — S.H.

BARRY MANN
★★ Joyride / U. Artists LA-784-H
★★ Survivor / RCA APL1-0860
Solid if unexceptional albums by the male half of the legendary Mann/Cynthia Weil songwriting team. (Now deleted.) — S.H.

MANFRED MANN
★★★ Get Your Rocks Off / Poly. 5050
★★ Glorified, Magnified / Poly. 5031
★★★★ Manfred Mann's Earth Band / Poly. 5015
★★ Nightingales and Bombers / War. B-2877
★★ Solar Fire / Poly. 6019
★★★★ The Best of Manfred Mann / Cap. M-11688
★★★★ The Best of Manfred Mann / Janus 3064
★★ The Good Earth / War. B-2826
★★ The Roaring Silence / War. BK-3055
★ Watch / War. K-3157
Manfred Mann's original band (represented on the essentially identical Janus and Capitol/EMI collections) was a late-blooming part of the post-Beatles British Invasion and less notable for keyboardist/arranger Manfred Mann himself than for the singing of Paul Jones, one of the best vocalists of that era.

The group's best-known American songs—"Do Wah Diddy," "Sha La La" (both 1964) and "Pretty Flamingo" (1966)—feature Jones' smooth but resonant vocals. On LP, Mann was known for his flirtation with jazz (on one early album, the group did a perfectly dreadful version of Herbie Hancock's "Watermelon Man") and as a frequent interpreter of Bob Dylan material. The later tendency reached its height in 1978, when Mann turned Dylan's "Mighty Quinn" into a splendid Top Ten hit. By then, however, Jones had been replaced by the more flexible but less enduring Mike D'Abo, who went on to write Rod Stewart's early signature song, "Handbags and Gladrags." And numerous other personnel shifts resulted in a drastic change of direction for the group, which was known (beginning with the eponymous 1972 LP on Polydor) as the Earth Band. The Earth Band specialized in extravagant reworkings of pop songs, including terrific versions of Randy Newman's "Living

without You" and Dylan's "Please Mrs. Henry" on the Manfred Mann's Earth Band album, and John Prine's "Pretty Good" and Dylan's "Get Your Rocks Off" on Get Your Rocks Off (1973). The result could be termed jazz rock, though all of it is much more oriented toward pop vocals than any of the other jazz-rock fusion attempts.

A switch to Warner Bros. in 1974 coincided with Mann's discovery of Bruce Springsteen as an artist equally susceptible to remodeling in this manner, and in 1976 Mann scored his most recent pop hit with "Blinded by the Light," a Springsteen song from The Roaring Silence. By then, however, a great deal of the novelty had worn off and, as Chris Hamlet-Thompson's vocals were none too endearing (they were rather emotion-starved, in fact), the Earth Band seemed simply a curiosity, and a shopworn one at that, by the time of 1978's live set, Watch. — D.M.

MAN'S THEORY
★ Just Before the Dawn / MCA 2250
Why is it that this sort of five-piece funk band never seems to make any popular headway? Maybe because it's all rhythm and no blues. (Now deleted.) — D.M.

PHIL MANZANERA
★★★★ Diamond Head / Atco 36-113
★★★ K-Scope / Poly. 1-6178
★★★ Listen Now / Poly. 1-6147
The Roxy Music guitarist enlists Britain's best—John Wetton, Brian Eno and many others—for expert, proudly electric rock permutations. Manzanera's chords are sharp and silvery, his single notes thick with distortion and sustain. The material spans rock, R&B, electronics and an acoustic guitar/oboe arrangement. (Now deleted.) — C.W.

DIANA MARCOVITZ
★★ Horse of a Different Feather / Col. KC-33063
★ Joie de Vivre / Kam. S. 2614
This goofy singer/songwriter would be more comfortable in an off-Broadway Streisand musical parody than warming up an audience for, say, Phoebe Snow. Horse has some funny moments, such as "The William Morris Agency," but Marcovitz can't sing too well and she's not funny enough to carry a listener through more than a song or two. — J.S.

MARCUS
★ Marcus / U. Artists LA-668-G

Cheap, derivative, Detroit-based hard-rock band recorded in 1976 with help from ex-Vanilla Fudge and BBA bassist Tim Bogert. (Now deleted.) — J.S.

MARIAH
★ **Mariah / U. Artists LA-493-G**
Typically mediocre, Eagles-influenced mid-Seventies MOR rock, complete with seven love songs and a version of the group's rise to "prominence," "Rock and Roll Band," which sounds like every other "I believe in music" song ever recorded. This is the kind of thing that turned rock & roll into a product instead of a social force, a movement or something that might be interesting to sentient humans. — D.M.

JON MARK
★★ **Songs for a Friend / Col. PC-33339**
A slightly more energetic version of the MOR pablum in which Mark's recordings with Johnny Almond specialized. So smooth and relaxing, you'll wonder if you've been drugged. (Now deleted.) — D.M.

MARK-ALMOND
★★ **Mark-Almond 2 / Blue Th. 32**
★★ **Other People's Rooms / A&M 730**
★★ **Rising / Col. C-31917**
★★ **The Best of Mark-Almond / Blue Th. 50**
★★ **To the Heart / ABC D-945**
Guitarist Jon Mark and reed man Johnny Almond (alumni of John Mayall's group) play the most lightweight vocal jazz rock imaginable—mood music for the Valium set. This sort of sound has neither peaks nor valleys, just the same dull threnody, a passionless evocation of life's most minute pleasures. Despite a brief vogue in the early Seventies, this batch of easy-listening rock is probably as boring as any comparable catalogue in recorded history. — D.M.

MARK AND CLARK BAND
★ **Double Take / Col. PC-34498**
Late-Seventies hard-rock version of early Simon and Garfunkel: the sanctimoniousness without the melody or the insight, that is. (Now deleted.) — D.M.

STEVE MARRIOTT
★★ **Marriott / A&M 4572**
The first and only solo album by the former leader of Humble Pie and the Small Faces exhibits transatlantic schizophrenia. The British side is hard, heavy guitar rock—no wrong notes but little inspiration

or variety. The American side offers R&B-based studio slickness: horns, strings, vocal choruses—quite professional but just as routine. — C.W.

PENNY MARSHALL AND CINDY WILLIAMS
★ **Laverne and Shirley Sing / Atl. 18203**
So do I, and just as badly, but do I put out a record? Stars of a sitcom set in the Fifties do appropriate oldies inappropriately. Unfunny. — K.T.

MARSHALL TUCKER BAND
★★★ **A New Life / Capri. 0124**
★★★ **Carolina Dreams / Capri. K-0180**
★★★ **Greatest Hits / Capri. N-0214**
★★★ **Long, Hard Ride / Capri. 0170**
★★★★ **Searchin' for a Rainbow / Capri. 0161**
★★★ **The Marshall Tucker Band / Capri. 0112**
★★★ **Where We All Belong / Capri. 2C-1045**
The Marshall Tucker Band was one of the first of the so-called Southern boogie bands of the Seventies. Their music is indeed Southern, it definitely boogies (albeit quite sensitively at times), and it's a band in the strictest sense of the word: five years up the road and most rock fans couldn't name a single member. Limited in scope, Marshall Tucker is invariably spirited and has never made a poor LP.

Like other bands of this ilk, the music is heavy and riff-oriented, yet it depends more on melody and affected vocals than on jamming. The occasional use of Jerry Eubanks on alto sax and flute gives the band distinctive depth uncharacteristic of the genre. The constant instrumental highlight, though, is guitarist Toy Caldwell.

Of these albums, *Where We All Belong* and *Greatest Hits* are the best introduction for the uninitiated. The latter includes the group's best-known songs, such as "Heard It in a Love Song," while *Where We All Belong* includes a live disc paired with a studio session, both of which feature Caldwell prominently, especially on the twelve-minute "Every Day I Have the Blues." But the band hit a creative apex with *Searchin'*, a comparatively laid-back affair featuring several solid country numbers; the albums since then have principally been repetitions of the formula established there. — A.N.

MARTHA AND THE VANDELLAS
★★★★★ **Anthology / Mo. M7-778**

Martha Reeves was the most blues-oriented of all of Motown's Sixties female singers, and her triumphs—"Dancing in the Streets" and "Heat Wave" particularly—are among that label's longest-lasting. The approach is brassy and rocking, and there isn't a clinker among the many hits collected here, which include (in addition to the anthems listed above) "Livewire," "Quicksand" and "Come and Get These Memories." Reeves has gone on to an undistinguished solo career in the Seventies, but these songs will outlive her as dance and party records and great examples of Motown's high-spirited Sixties vision. — D.M.

MARTIN BOGAN AND ARMSTRONG
★★★ Barnyard Dance / Roun. 2003
★★★ Martin Bogan and Armstrong / Fly. Fish 003

Founded in the Thirties, this black string band re-formed in 1970 to play precisely the same rags, pop songs, country blues and jazz. Mandolin, fiddle, guitar and bass constitute the instrumentation, and the style is untouched by age. The quartet has played the festival route in recent years, and has recorded with Steve Goodman. The infectious vitality of Carl Martin, Ted Bogan, and Howard and Joe Armstrong (father and son) is best witnessed in person, but these discs are rare chronicles of a nearly extinct form. — I.M.

MOON MARTIN
★★★ Shots from a Cold Nightmare / Cap. SW-11787

Martin's chief claim to fame is writing "Rolene" and "Cadillac Walk" for Mink DeVille, but there is more authentic toughness to this debut solo disc than almost anything that has come from Los Angeles in years. Not exactly soulful, but definitely rocking. — D.M.

STEVE MARTIN
★★★★ A Wild and Crazy Guy / War. HS-3238
★★★★ Let's Get Small / War. K-3090

Let's Get Small, full of the coy asides ("I'm so mad at my mother") and frantic burlesques ("Excuse me") that mark Martin's stage and TV work, can't be quite as funny as seeing him. But it is full of neurotic laughs, and the mad-dog speed of Martin's Johnny Duke routine (on "Vegas") is a physical feat that demanded documentation. Includes professional banjo playing. His second album, Wild, is the one to buy, though; it features his great hit single, "King Tut." — F.S.

HIRTH MARTINEZ
★★ Big Bright Street / War. B-3031
★★ Hirth from Earth / War. B-2867

A Robbie Robertson discovery, Martinez is a sort of minor-league Captain Beefheart. He has the bizarre world view, that is, but lacks an equivalently devastating musical vision. The Robertson-produced Hirth from Earth flirted with several idioms, and usually emerged as clever and quirky but finally inconsequential, jazzy pop: cute tunes but too many strings and horns. Vocally, Martinez often recalls Dr. John, and Big Bright Street, produced by John Simon, stripped away much of the arranging chaff for a more direct, harder sound. — C.W.

JOHN MARTYN
★★★★ One World / Is. 9492
★★★★ So Far So Good / Is. 9484

After a few ordinary albums, Scottish folksinger John Martyn evolved an elliptical style of writing and playing in the mid-Seventies and started singing in a sensuous, low-key rock-blues voice. Pentangle bassist Danny Thompson lends the folk-jazz feel that underlays these delightful records. So Far So Good is a compilation that draws heavily on his best (but deleted) record, Bless the Weather. Jazz studio players and a subtle rhythm section on most cuts show Martyn cautiously and effectively extending Nick Drake's fluid manner. However, Martyn's "other" style, an overblown jazz rock, has yet to develop beyond the experimental instrumental "Glistening Glyndebourne." Several near misses are included on So Far. — B.T.

MARVELETTES
★★★★★ Anthology / Mo. M7-827
The Marvelettes were a mysterious Motown "girl" group that lasted almost a decade and sported a number of lead singers and a raft of Motown production styles. *Anthology* is a splendid document of the evolution of Motown in the Sixties as well as a must for anyone who has ever felt the emotional pull of "Forever" or "When the Hunter Gets Captured by the Game" or earlier hits like "Please Mr. Postman," "Beechwood 4-5789" and "Don't Mess with Bill." — J.MC.

MARVIN, WELCH AND FARRAR
★★ Second Opinion / Sire 7403
Hank Marvin and Bruce Welch were part of the British instrumental group the Shadows. The band was noted for Marvin's guitar style, exemplified by the 1960 hit "Apache," which influenced the generation of British guitarists led by Pete Townshend, Keith Richards and Eric Clapton. Unfortunately, this album with Australian John Farrar has nothing to do with that music, presenting instead an ersatz country-rock vocal harmony group. (Now deleted.) — J.S.

GROUCHO MARX
★★ An Evening with Groucho / A&M 3515
He painted a mustache on his face and walked funny for a reason—see the movies. A genius maligned, this. — K.T.

MASHMAKHAN
★★★ The Family / Epic 30813
Montreal underground celebrities, Mashmakhan surfaced in the U.S. only with this occasionally pretty but mostly just competent LP of basic early-Seventies progressive pop. (Now deleted.) — D.M.

BARBARA MASON
★★★ Give Me Your Love / Bud. 5117
★★ Lady Love / Bud. 5140
★★ Locked in This Position / Cur. 5014
★★ Love's the Thing / Bud. 5628
★★ Sheba, Baby / Bud. 5634
★★★ Transition / Bud. 5610
Barbara Mason is Philadelphia's true first lady of soul. It also happens that she's been almost without competition for nearly a decade, but that's beside the point. Mason is no great shakes as a singer, but her off-key cooing and breathy phrasing give her an attractive vulnerability. Her early hits for Arctic ("Yes I'm Ready," "Oh How It Hurts") are long out of print, but her Buddah albums are often quite appealing in small doses.

Give Me Your Love, Mason's best in-print album, is mostly ballads (the title song is seductive, but uptempo), some with neat hook lines and titles ("Bed and Board," "You Can Be with the One You Don't Love"). *Transition,* the other exceptional disc here, finds Mason waxing philosophic about our times (she wrote all but one of the songs). — D.M.

DAVE MASON
★★★ Alone Together / Blue Th. 29
★★ Certified Live / Col. PG-34174
★★★ Dave Mason / Col. PC-33096
★★★ Dave Mason at His Very Best / ABC TD-880
★★ Dave Mason Is Alive / Blue Th. 54
★★ Headkeeper / Blue Th. 34
★★★ It's Like You Never Left / Col. PC-31721
★★ Let It Flow / Col. PC-34680
★★ Mariposa de Oro / Col. JC-35285
★★ Split Coconut / Col. PC-33698
★★★ The Best of Dave Mason / Blue Th. 6013
Mason was a key member of Traffic in its first and a couple of subsequent incarnations. *Alone Together* staked out the solo territory from which Mason has rarely strayed: a rather relaxed and reserved take-off from hard rock, featuring somber, bittersweet melodies, basic guitar/keyboard arrangements, as well as Mason's restrained vocals and blues-derived though not bluesy electric guitar. His acoustic rhythm guitar accounted for the driving lightness of the songs, which moved but without breakneck tempos or flashy playing; some, however, were a trifle lengthy.

Side one of *Headkeeper* contained more alive but also unpolished continuations of his debut. The other side had fairly spirited live versions of earlier songs, plus a Traffic number, "Pearly Queen." *Dave Mason Is Alive* was almost entirely selections from his debut; adequate if unspectacular and somewhat rough, it benefited from Mark Jordan's tasteful piano and organ.

Best of and *At His Best* are almost identical compilations of the early studio material. *It's Like You Never Left* smoothed out some of the singer's few edges, while simultaneously picking up pace: it has more polished and full scoring but little bite. Still, the record had some of Mason's best writing. The backup band included Graham Nash singing and Stevie Wonder on harmonica. *Dave Mason* experimented with additional instrumentation: pedal steel, horns, strings, etc., which usually disguised and spoiled the continuing quality of Mason's material. But he erred with covers of Dylan and Sam Cooke, and his new band played without verve or flair, Mason no longer on lead guitar. *Split Coconut* shelved the orchestration and rocked out more with guitars. The band's plainness remained, although Mark Jordan made guest appearances, as did Crosby and Nash and, oddly, the Manhattan Transfer on a reggae-influenced Buddy Holly cover. Again, good material squandered, this time by overanxious arranging.

Certified Live unfortunately relied on the thin anonymity of the guitars/keys/bass/drums lineup. The surfeit of mediocre guitars from Mason and Jim Krueger detracted further, as did Mason's further attempts at husky soulful singing. Several weak covers were included; Mason's own songs spanned his whole career (including Traffic) but emphasized the earlier styles.

Let It Flow and *Mariposa de Oro* are Mason's softest efforts, padded with plenty of extra orchestration in an apparent pitch to MOR tastes. Nonetheless, the capable composer in Mason was evident though submerged. — C.W.

JAE MASON
★ Crossroads / Bud. 5604
★ Tender Man / Bud. 5640
Inconsequential singer/songwriter who later became famous as the bouncer at New York's Bottom Line. — J.S.

MASQUERADERS
★★ Everybody Wanna Live On / ABC D-921
★★ Love Anonymous / ABC 962
The Masqueraders are best known for two Sixties soul classics: "I'm Just an Average

Guy" and "I Ain't Got to Love Nobody Else." Isaac Hayes' production on their comeback albums is labored and wooden, but "Traveling Man," a whimsical ballad from *Everybody*, stands out. — J.MC.

MASS PRODUCTION
★ Believe / Coti. 9918
★ Three Miles High / Coti. 5205
★ Welcome to Our World / Coti. 9910
Seventies disco funk with, as the name implies, more of a grind than a groove. — D.M.

MASTERS OF THE AIRWAVES
★★★ Masters of the Airwaves / Epic KE-33060
Appealing if not ground-breaking hard rock—some hints of heaviness—highlighted by Jimmy Berick's interestingly noncountrified steel guitar. But somewhat overblown vocals and slightly thin production drag it down. (Now deleted.) — C.W.

IAN MATTHEWS
★★ Go for Broke / Col. PC-34102
★★★ Some Days You Eat the Bear . . . / Elek. 75078
★★★ Stealin' Home / Mush. 5012
★★★ Valley Hi / Elek. 75061
An original member of Fairport Convention (and one of the first to leave), Ian Matthews owns a winsome tenor voice that has rarely been sufficiently aggressive for the kind of folk-rock material ("Brown-Eyed Girl," for instance) that he likes to sing. His best effort, in fact, came on *Tigers Will Survive*, a now-deleted Vertigo LP that included his closest shot at a hit single, a splendid version of the Crystals' "Da Doo Ron Ron." *Tigers* is worth digging up; the Elektra sets are worth it for folk-rock fans and the Columbia and Mushroom records are mostly notable because Matthews consistently chooses all the right songs, then sings and arranges them wrong. — D.M.

JOHN MAYALL
★★★★ A Hard Road / Lon. PS-502
★★★ Bare Wires / Lon. PS-537
★★★★★ Bluesbreakers / Lon. LC-50009
★★★★★ Bluesbreakers / Lon. PS-492
★★★★ Blues from Laurel Canyon / Lon. PS-545
★★★★ Crusade / Lon. PS-529
★★ Diary of a Band / Lon. PS-570
★★★ The Blues Alone / Lon. PS-534
These records were all made between 1966 and 1968, when Mayall did some of his most memorable work with a collection of

young musicians who would go on to their own successful careers. Although this period is early in his recording history, Mayall had already been playing the blues for twenty years when he recorded *Bluesbreakers* with Eric Clapton on guitar and John McVie on bass. Many still consider this one of Clapton's finest moments. (LC-50009 is identical to PS-492, with the addition of historical notes by Billy Altman and a revised cover.)

A Hard Road is another remarkable blues album, with Peter Green taking over from Clapton on guitar and Aynsley Dunbar playing drums. McVie and Green formed Fleetwood Mac after recording this LP. On *Crusade,* Mayall introduced yet another brilliant young guitarist, Mick Taylor, added drummer Keef Hartley and used horn arrangements for the first time. On *The Blues Alone,* Mayall plays all instruments except drums, once again handled by Hartley. The results are for Mayall fanatics only. *Diary of Band* is the cream of sixty hours of live tapes from small club dates throughout Europe and the British Isles. More interesting as a historical document than for musical value, unless you collect Mick Taylor solos.

Bare Wires is a transitional album on which Mayall begins to move away from the blues and toward more progressive rock and jazz modes. It is supposed to be a concept album, and while the playing, especially Taylor's, is interesting, the concept is not. After most of the *Bare Wires* band, led by drummer John Hiseman and saxophonist Dick Heckstall-Smith, left to form Colosseum, Mayall went to the West Coast, where he recorded *Blues from Laurel Canyon* with some local musicians led by Canned Heat's Larry Taylor. Its easy modes, occasional haunting guitar and soft boogie passages make it a great late-night album, and it has lost little of its appeal over the years.

★★★ Down the Line / Lon. PB-618/619
★★ Live in Europe / Lon. PS-589
★★★★ Looking Back / Lon. PS-562
★★ Primal Solos / Lon. LC-50003
★★ Raw Blues / Lon. PS-543
★★★ Thru the Years / Lon. 2PS-600/601
These records are all reissues compiled after Mayall became established and left London for other labels. *Looking Back* catalogues all the singles issued by London from 1964 to 1969, which makes it valuable to collectors in that none of it is otherwise easily available. Much of the material is strong, particularly "Sitting in the Rain"

with Green and "Stormy Monday," which includes Jack Bruce. *Thru the Years* is an anthology with some previously unissued material. *Down the Line* is a two-record set, one disc of selected tracks from the London records listed above, the other a rerelease of *John Mayall Plays John Mayall,* his first (1964) album, which compares well with early Rolling Stones for R&B excitement. *Primal Solos* is previously unreleased live tapes of the (1966) Clapton-Bruce (1968) *Crusade* and *Laurel Canyon* lineups. *Raw Blues* and *Live in Europe* scrape the bottom of London's barrel.

★★★★ Banquet in Blues / ABC D-958
★★ Hard Core Package / ABC 1039
★★★ Jazz Blues Fusion / Poly. 5027
★★ Last of the British Blues / ABC 1086
★★ Lots of People / ABC D-992
★★ New Year, New Band, New Company / ABC BTSD-6019
★★★ Notice to Appear / ABC D-926
★★★★ The Best of John Mayall / Poly. 2-3006
★★★★ The Turning Point / Poly. 4004
These records cover Mayall from 1969 to the present, and generally trace his decline. *The Turning Point* (recorded live at Fillmore East) is blues without drums and electric guitar leads; it depends on bass and Jon Mark's acoustic guitar for its rhythms, with Mayall's vocals and/or harmonica or Johnny Almond's flutes and saxes laying jazzy riffs on top. *Jazz Blues Fusion* is a live set featuring jazz trumpeter Blue Mitchell.

The Best of John Mayall contains selections from almost all of the deleted Polydor releases (there are seven mostly insignificant cutouts) and serves as an adequate sampler of his work from this period. *New Year, New Band, New Company* sounds really tired. The big surprise here is the addition of a female vocalist, Dee McKinnie, who was added because Mayall, at forty-two, had begun to lose his falsetto voice. Mayall's vocals on *Notice to Appear* are incredibly shot, but the album has a few good points—production and strong new material from Allen Toussaint, more vocal help from McKinnie, a few hooks and even a Beatle song.

Banquet in Blues features more sidemen (twenty-four—most of them old friends) than there is space to list, and it offers a spunky rebirth for Mayall. His vocals are surprisingly strong, the various groupings cook, and his decision to stick with other people's material pays off well. This largely overlooked effort should be part of every Mayall fan's library. *Lots of People* is a live recording of a fifteen-piece band. The scenario is loose and funky, as are the jams. But there is little here (or on *Hard Core Package* and *Last of the British Blues*) that has not been heard before, and the LP is another indication that Mayall must think everything he puts on tape has historical significance and therefore should be released. — A.N.

CURTIS MAYFIELD
★★ **America Today** / Cur. 5001
★★★ **Do It All Night** / Cur. K-5022
★★★ **Give, Get, Take and Have** / Cur. 5007
★★★★ **Let's Do It Again** / Cur. 5005
★★★ **Never Say You Can't Survive** / Cur. 5013
★★ **Short Eyes** / Cur. 5017

With the Impressions, Mayfield was one of the most inspired writers and singers of Sixties soul. His falsetto style was suitably modernized on his first few solo albums for Curtom when it was distributed by Buddah. *Superfly*, the soundtrack to the blaxploitation film, was a simply great record, with marvelous singing and lyrics that undercut the film's lionization of dope dealing. "Freddie's Dead" and "Superfly" were major hits from that anti-decadent disco record, but it has somehow been deleted; find it if you're at all interested in Seventies black rock—it was one of the germinal albums, as important in its way as Marvin Gaye's, Stevie Wonder's and Sly Stone's stuff. The rest of these albums aren't nearly so good; *Let's Do It Again,* a soundtrack dominated vocally by the Staple Singers, is about the best. The rest is meandering funk that can usually be lived without, although occasionally Mayfield's chirping voice or his stinging guitar reappear for a few worthwhile moments. — D.M.

MAZE
★★ **Golden Time of Day** / Cap. ST-11710
★★ **Inspiration** / Cap. SW-11912
★★ **Maze** / Cap. ST-11607
★★ **The Hitter** / Cap. SW-11920

This lazy jazz-funk ensemble, featuring vocalist/producer Frankie Beverly, managed several pop-R&B hits in 1977 and 1978—"Workin' Together," "While I'm Alone" and "Lady of Magic"—none of them terribly distinguished. The best parts of both albums are merely mediocre soul music. The worst would be laughed out of a cocktail lounge. — D.M.

DAN McCAFFERTY
★ **Dan McCafferty** / A&M 4553
Nazareth's vocalist makes a solo album. A Rod Stewart growler without the charm, McCafferty is for Nazareth fans only. — A.N.

CASH McCALL
★★ **Omega Man** / Paula 2220
Hard R&B singer, heavily influenced—almost to the point of parody—by B. B. King. Sample title: "Hard Head (Makes a Sore Behind)." — D.M.

C. W. McCALL
★ **Black Bear Road** / MGM M3G-5008
★★ **C.W. McCall's Greatest Hits** / Poly. 1-6156
★ **Roses for Mama** / Poly. 1-6125
★ **Rubber Duck** / Poly. 1-6094
★ **Wolf Creek Pass** / MGM M3G-4989

McCall cashed in on the mid-Seventies CB craze with "Convoy," written in 10-4-type lingo, then repeated it to death on this series of albums. "Convoy" was better as a movie; here, it's just one long drawl, probably destined to be remembered only in the trivia contests of the Eighties. — D.M.

TOUSSAINT McCALL
★★ **Nothing Takes the Place of You** / Ronn 7527

Like "Boogaloo down Broadway" and "Why Can't We Live Together," McCall's "Nothing Takes the Place of You" is a homemade one-shot that transcends its own technical limitations. McCall is an organist, and this ballad-centered album is better than you might expect. — J.MC.

PAUL McCARTNEY AND WINGS
★★★★★ **Band on the Run** / Apple SO-3415

★★★ **London Town** / Cap. SW-11777
★★ **McCartney** / Cap. SMAS-3363
★★★★ **Ram** / Cap. SMAS-3375
★ **Red Rose Speedway** / Apple
SMAL-3409
★★★★ **Venus and Mars** / Cap.
SMAS-11419
★★★ **Wild Life** / Cap. SW-3386
★★★ **Wings at the Speed of Sound** / Cap.
SW-11525
★★★★ **Wings over America** / Cap.
SWCO-11593

A home-produced solo excursion, *McCartney* was designed to publicize the official (1970) breakup of the Beatles, and Paul used it more as a forum for his own self-obsession (he is the album's sole musician) than as a vehicle for good material. His playing is rough and disingenuous, and there's only one good song on the record, "Maybe I'm Amazed."

Ram, on the other hand, is an all-out production effort that comes closer to reproducing the Beatles sound than any other solo album, and it includes a scattering of excellent material ("Smile Away," "Monkberry Moon Delight," "Uncle Albert/Admiral Halsey"). *Wild Life* has a crude but effective sound, since McCartney went right into the studio with wife Linda, Denny Laine and Denny Seiwell and laid down the tracks as quickly as possible. This boils down to a Wings audition.

Red Rose Speedway emphasizes the worst aspects of McCartney as solo artist and bandleader. The album is rife with weak and sentimental drivel and lacks any musical focus. But he turned around from that disaster and made a great album, *Band on the Run,* recorded in Nigeria. With only sparse help from Linda and a faithful Denny Laine, this turned out to be the real one-man show, and McCartney came up with aces, playing most of the instruments and writing his strongest collection of post-Beatles material—"Jet" and "Helen Wheels" especially.

Venus and Mars introduced a new Wings lineup, adding drummer Joe English and guitarist Jimmy McCullogh. Recorded in New Orleans, the album is a solid collection of good songs (particularly "Rock Show" and "Listen to What the Man Said") played well by the band and featuring some fine horn arrangements by Tony Dorsey. *Venus and Mars* pretty much served as a blueprint for the band's concert strategy, a successful plan judging by results of the Wings tour, documented by the three-record live set, *Wings over America.*

McCartney's road show had a little something for everyone, but most of all the band proved it could rock and McCartney proved he hadn't forgotten his Little Richard imitation. The live set is also notable for the inclusion of Denny Laine's classic "Go Now" and the otherwise unreleased encore, a fiery rocker called "Soily."

Wings at the Speed of Sound, recorded in a hurry while the band was preparing for the tour, proves that they were sure enough of themselves to go on instinct and make a good album under extreme pressure. The McCartney wit is sharp on "Silly Love Songs," powered by one of his most melodic bass patterns. And chestnuts like "Beware My Love," Laine's pungent "Time to Hide" and the frolicking "Let 'Em In" give the record substance.

But *London Town,* released in 1978 after the group had been off the road for a while, finds McCartney and company succumbing to their vices: fake rock, pallid pop and unbelievable homilies make an unreal hodgepodge that's barely listenable next to Wings' best work.   — J.S.

DELBERT McCLINTON
★★★★ **Genuine Cowhide** / ABC D-959
★★★ **Love Rustler** / ABC 991
★★★ **Second Wind** / ABC 0201
★★★★ **Victim of Life's Circumstances** /
ABC D-907

McClinton makes consistently strong albums, though he isn't for everyone. A product of Texas and Louisiana roadhouses, he comes off a bit greasy, a bit compulsive, a bit dangerous but basically a vulnerable and big-hearted guy just trying to stay one step ahead of whatever's chasing him, be that his shadow, a woman or some guy he just antagonized in a bar. *Victim,* containing brilliant originals, is in a "progressive country" mold, but a decidedly nonhackneyed one that thinks nothing of mixing Bobby Bland–type horns with pedal-steel guitar. *Genuine Cowhide* has but two originals; the others are rock & roll or rhythm & blues favorites. *Love Rustler* and *Second Wind* are mostly oldies or contemporary songs by other writers, with only one original. Like their predecessors, they are blue-eyed Southern soul that has little to do with country music, progressive or otherwise.   — J.M.

MARILYN McCOO AND BILLY DAVIS, JR.
★★★ **I Hope We Get to Love in Time** /
ABC D-952

★★ **Marilyn and Billy / Col. JC-35603**
★★ **Two of Us / ABC 1026**
McCoo and Davis were the most identifiable voices of the Fifth Dimension, and these albums continue that MOR approach to black pop. Their big hit, "You Don't Have to Be a Star," came with their first album, in the summer of 1976. The rest is thoroughly dispensable. — D.M.

CHARLIE McCOY
★★ **Charlie McCoy / Monu. MC-6624**
★★ **Charlie McCoy Christmas / Monu. MC-6645**
★★ **Charlie McCoy's Greatest Hits / Monu. MG-7622**
★★ **Charlie My Boy / Monu. MC-6628**
★★ **Country Cookin' / Monu. MG-7612**
★★ **Fastest Harp in the South / Monu. MC-6626**
★★ **Good Time Charlie / Monu. MC-6625**
★★ **Harpin' the Blues / Monu. 6629**
★★ **Nashville Hit Man / Monu. MC-6627**
★★ **Play It Again, Charlie / Monu. MC-6630**
★★ **The Real McCoy / Monu. MC-6623**
The fabled Nashville harmonica player, who made a rock reputation with his sometimes astonishing work on Bob Dylan's *Blonde on Blonde,* has never gone beyond tepid pop-country instrumentals with his own LPs, all of which are competent and dull. — D.M.

VAN McCOY
★ **Dancin' / SSS 33**
★★ **From Disco to Love / Bud. 5648**
★★ **Lonely Dancer / MCA 3071**
★★ **My Favorite Fantasy / MCA 3036**
★★★ **The Hustle / H&L 69016**
Veteran soul producer cashed in early on Seventies dance crazes with "Disco Kid"

and "The Hustle," both pop as well as R&B hits. McCoy is probably better known as a producer, and these records show why—they're all boogie-able party tracks, but they're also completely interchangeable. — D.M.

THE McCOYS
★★ **Hang On Sloopy / Bang 212**
★★ **You Make Me Feel So Good / Bang 213**
Led by Rick Derringer (then known as Rick Zehringer), the McCoys were a slightly above average mid-American garage band when "Hang on Sloopy" turned them into overnight stars in 1965. Their two Bang albums are populated mostly by energetic covers with a few tasty surprises (the Pretty Things' "SF Sorrow Is Born," "Stormy Monday") that gave clues to the band's possible growth. Their finest work came a bit later, though, on their two Mercury releases, *Infinite McCoys* and *Human Ball* (both out of print). — B.A.

GEORGE McCRAE
★★★ **Diamond Touch / TK 606**
★★★ **George McCrae / TK 602**
★★★★ **Rock Your Baby / TK 501**
★★★ **We Did It / TK 610**
The record was "Rock Your Baby," the year was 1974, and it established Miami's TK Records as a force in black popular music—in fact it did a much better job establishing TK, and producers H. W. Casey (of KC and the Sunshine Band) and Rick Finch, than it did establishing McCrae, who has never quite lived up to it. "Rock Your Baby" remains, though, one of the great hit singles of the decade, a rolling soul groove with a marvelous falsetto trill. — D.M.

GEORGE AND GWEN McCRAE
★★★ **Together / Cat 2606**
In which the leading husband-and-wife team (the only one) of Miami R&B do a Marvin Gaye and Tammi Terrell turn, not without some effect, but not with particularly terrific results, either. — D.M.

GWEN McCRAE
★★ **Let's Straighten It Out / Cat 2613**
★★★★ **Rockin' Chair / Cat 2605**
★★ **Something So Right / Cat 2608**
Gwen McCrae is a tough, brassy singer who has been a mainstay of Miami's TK soul stable. *Rockin' Chair* is a collection of early TK singles, including her lone Top Forty hit, the title song. The records are

hot, a little raunchy and mostly very good. Little Beaver is featured on guitar. But the other albums are de-energized. Beaver is absent, the tracks are limp, and they're weighed down by dull horn and string charts. — J.MC.

MARY McCREARY
★ **Butterflies in Heaven** / Shel. 52026
★ **Jezebel** / Shel. 52027
Leon Russell's ex-wife provides yet another argument against nepotism. (Now deleted.) — J.S.

ED McCURDY
★ **The Best of Ed McCurdy** / Trad. 2051
McCurdy's best-known song, "Last Night I Had the Strangest Dream," is not included on this record. Nonetheless, there is a certain sense of the man: sentimental, humorous, boisterous and gentle—a Western version of Dave Van Ronk. He is assisted by Erik Darling and Billy Faier. — I.M.

COUNTRY JOE McDONALD
★★★ **Country Joe** / Van. 79348
★ **Goodbye Blues** / Fan. 9525
★★ **Hold On It's Coming** / Van. 79314
★ **Incredible—Live** / Van. VSD-79316
★ **Love Is a Fire** / Fan. 9511
★ **Paradise with an Ocean View** / Fan. 9495
★ **Paris Session** / Van. 79328
■ **Rock and Roll Music from the Planet Earth** / Fan. 9544
★★★ **The Essential Country Joe McDonald** / Van. VSD-85/86
★★★ **Tonight I'm Singing Just for You** / Van. 6557
★★★ **Tribute to Woody** / War. 2W-3007
★★ **War War War** / Van. 79315
Country Joe McDonald has retained the strengths he displayed when he debuted with the Fish in 1967—wit, a steady tone of populist outrage about war and things unecological, and a solid journeyman's musicianship. None of these virtues, unfortunately, has proved mightier than his flaws—a shortage of originality and raw talent.

His story is one of persistence: eight albums with the Fish from 1969 to 1971 and fourteen solo LPs from 1971 till the present. Tellingly, the first two solo efforts, which are Joe's renditions of classics from Woody Guthrie (*Thinking of Woody*) and various country greats (*Tonight I'm Singing Just for You*), are the best. After that, beyond the wryly mesmerizing title track from 1971's *Hold On It's Coming*, there are

very few standout tracks among these albums, which are full of complaints both personal ("Entertainment Is My Business") and political ("Tear Down the Walls"). An attempt to be a late-blooming rock & roller (*Rock and Roll from the Planet Earth*, 1978) was the most unnerving try from a man whose career was already out of joint with the times. — F.S.

KATHI McDONALD
★★ **Insane Asylum** / Cap. ST-11224
The horror-movie album cover warns you off this veteran backup singer's failed 1974 attempt at a blues-tinged solo statement. The title cut was written by Willie Dixon (for Koko Taylor), and Neil Young wrote "Down to the Wire" for this album, which is all that distinguishes it. — F.S.

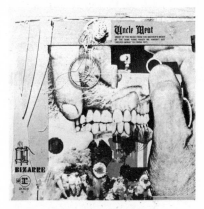

McDONALD AND GILES
★★★★ **McDonald and Giles** / Coti. 9042
A very respectable album by two renegades from the original King Crimson. Ian McDonald, whose explosive reeds helped put Crimson on the map, absconded with that group's inventive drummer, Mike Giles, to produce this colorful album. The raucous, double-tracked tenor-sax maneuvers on the swinging finale to McDonald's "Suite in C" are guaranteed ear candy, and sort of McDonald's trademark. Giles' bassist brother, Peter, anchors down an effervescent rhythm section underpinning Stevie Winwood's heavenly piano. Where Winwood isn't playing keyboards, McDonald is—and he adds flute, guitar and a brilliant zither.

Seven years later, McDonald is finally getting the attention he deserves, as a co-leader of Foreigner. But perhaps what is most important about this obscure get-together are the goofy, cryptic lyrics, which should be preserved in formaldehyde as the perfect example of at least one era's stony innocence. — B.M.

KATE AND ANNA McGARRIGLE
★★★★ Dancer with Bruised Knees / War. B-3014
★★★★ Kate and Anna McGarrigle / War. B-2862
★★★ Pronto Monto / War. K-3248

Two sisters from Montreal make music that's crisp, nonelectric and utterly magical. Singing now in English, now in French, they suffuse their records with brightness and wit, proving that the inspired amateurism of the mid-Seventies can be dazzling. — F.R.

PARKER McGEE
★★ Parker McGee / Big 89520

Another one of the pretty young faces from Big Tree's seemingly endless stable of pop singers. No better and no worse than most of the rest. — D.M.

MAUREEN McGOVERN
★ Nice to Be Around / 20th Cent. 439

Uninteresting woman singer noted for the late-Seventies hit "Morning After," which is not included here. — J.S.

BAT McGRATH
★★ From the Blue Eagle / Amh. 1005
★★ The Spy / Amh. 1011

The present-day folksinger refuses to die. The difference between McGrath and his equally average predecessors (Eric Andersen, David Blue et al.) is the influence of the Southern California rock of Jackson Browne in addition to Bob Dylan and Woody Guthrie. No big deal, just a spruced-up time warp. — D.M.

ROGER McGUINN
★★★★ Cardiff Rose / Col. PC-34154
★★★ Peace on You / Col. KC-32956
★★★ Roger McGuinn / Col. C-31946
★★★ Roger McGuinn and Band / Col. PC-33541
★★★ Thunderbyrd / Col. PC-34656

Roger McGuinn's solo career is a stylistic extension of the final versions of the Byrds, which he put together. McGuinn's distinctive, twangy voice and trademark rhythm-guitar harmonics give an overall evenness to his work that makes all but his least-inspired material sound pretty good. At his best, as on most of *Cardiff Rose* and bits and pieces from all the rest of his solo outings, McGuinn is a true original, one of the finest examples of a mature folk-rock stylist who isn't a sap. — J.S.

BARRY McGUIRE
★★★ Eve of Destruction / Dun. 50003
★ Jubilation / Myrrh A-6555
★ Jubilation, Too / Myrrh 6568
★ Lighten Up / Myrrh A-6531
★ Seeds / Myrrh A-6519
★ To the Bride / Myrrh X-6548

In the mid-Sixties, McGuire scored with the strident protest-song epic "Eve of Destruction." He went on to become a Jesus freak and write his sermons more directly. — J.S.

ELLEN McILWAINE
★★★ Honky Tonk Angel / Poly. 5021
★★★ The Real Ellen McIlwaine / Kot'ai 3306
★★★ We the People / Poly. 5044

McIlwaine is a pretty-voiced young woman who also plays fine slide guitar; with both, she does a crazy little chordal thing worth hearing (listen to "Toe Hold" on *Honky Tonk Angel*, "Higher Ground" on *The Real* and "Sliding" on *We*). McIlwaine cares slightly more for music than lyrics and loves to rearrange blues and R&B songs for just her voice and guitar. But is that a flaw? — M.R.

McKENDREE SPRING
★ McKendree Spring / MCA 277
★ 3 / MCA 44

A truly rotten Seventies art/gimmick rock band led by the flatulent violin histrionics of Michael Dreyfuss, McKendree Spring is notable for recording the most obnoxious cover of Neil Young's oft-mangled wimp anthem, "Down by the River." This band's version was even worse than Buddy Miles'. — J.S.

SCOTT McKENZIE
★ Stained Glass Morning / Ode 77007

Folksy singer/songwriter scored with the late-Sixties hippie paean "San Francisco" (in which he advised visitors to the city to wear flowers in their hair), then quickly disappeared. This record does not include the hit. (Now deleted.) — J.S.

MURRAY McLAUCHLAN
★★★ Boulevard / True 9423
★★★ Hard Rock Town / True 9466

McLauchlan started out as a plucky Canadian folkie capable of great penny-novel-prose songwriting. These two albums represent his very late graduation into rock & roll, which lends his crudely drawn songs much needed power. *Hard Rock Town* actually finds McLauchlan leading a band, and with that album, the harsh realism of *Boulevard* achieves a poetic elegance and McLauchlan finally liberates himself from a certain regional primitivism. — B.T.

DON McLEAN
★★★ **American Pie** / U. Artists 5535
★★★ **Don McLean** / U. Artists 5651
■ **Homeless Brother** / U. Artists LA-315-G
★ **Playin' Favorites** / U. Artists LA-161-G
★ **Prime Time** / Ari. 4149
★★ **Solo** / U. Artists LA-652-H2
★ **Tapestry** / U. Artists 5522
"American Pie" is a tightly coded, symbolically charged "critical history" of rock & roll that serves as McLean's justification for saying goodbye to rock in favor of folk music. But McLean delivers it with such conviction that it becomes an anthem in spite of itself; in 1971, it seemed to sum up what a strange journey rock had taken us upon and how far adrift it had left us. "Vincent," McLean's followup ode to Vincent Van Gogh, shows his tendency to inflate insight into dogma, which is a lot more typical of his post-*Pie* work. McLean's chief concerns, the City as Babylon and Nature as Eden, are stifled by his New York liberal moralism. Although he found his most important lyrical sources in Phil Ochs and Bob Dylan, his tone is pure Pete Seeger, and emotionally he conveys a collegiate anger that might better be described as sophomoric petulance. His love songs sound like notes from the garret, and his odes to nature are mere catechism. Sanctimonious as he may be, however, McLean's not a purist: he's used folk in combination with rock, Dixieland and even ragtime, always to suit didactic ends. — B.T./D.M.

PENNY McLEAN
★★ **Lady Bump** / Atco 36-130
German disco containing a mid-Seventies hit (the title track) and its followup. — J.S.

ANNIE McLOONE
★★ **Fast Annie** / RCA APL1-1362
Boston-based white soul singer tried hard without quite connecting; funkier than Linda Ronstadt, but the tracks aren't nearly as hot. (Now deleted.) — D.M.

RONNIE McNEIR
★★★ **Love's Comin' Down** / Mo. M-870
Ronnie McNeir produced himself as well as wrote his own material (with a variety of collaborators). He emerges as a weak-voiced but interesting amalgam of Motown sources, most heavily influenced by Marvin Gaye. — D.M.

CHRISTINE McVIE
★★★ **The Legendary Christine Perfect Album** / Sire 6022
Rereleased after Fleetwood Mac's pop ascendance, this is the blues album that Christine Perfect (soon to be McVie) made after leaving Chicken Shack for a brief solo career before joining Mac. It's a solid and enjoyable set that features standard British blues playing and McVie's sublimely controlled blues voice. — J.B.M.

MEAT LOAF
★★★ **Bat out of Hell** / Epic PE-34974
Frenetic hard rock played at breakneck speed by ex-Ted Nugent lead singer Meat Loaf (rock's first 300-pound star since Leslie West) and written by his partner, Jim Steinman. Production and backup support for this 1977 extravaganza was provided by Todd Rundgren. New York Yankees announcer Phil Rizzuto does a cameo commentary that coincides with the album's climax, "Paradise by the Dashboard Light." That song and "Two Out of Three Ain't Bad" were two of 1978's less likely hits—ersatz Bruce Springsteen featuring performances by some members of the E Street Band. — J.S.

MECO
★★ **Encounters of Every Kind** / Millen. 8004
★★★★ **Star Wars and Other Galactic Funk** / Millen. 8001
★★ **The Wizard of Oz** / Millen. 8009
Disco producer/*auteur* Tony Bongiovi's stable of session players clicked with this semi-solo strategy of covering the immensely popular themes from *Star Wars*, *The Wizard of Oz* and *Close Encounters of the Third Kind*. Rather than do the usual mindless ripoffs, however, the Meco versions are so cleverly arranged that the themes, when they do appear, work as surprise elements that are quite effective. The band's best moment is the side-long "Other Galactic Funk" from the first album, an interesting disco vamp based on a New Orleans second-line marching drum pattern. — J.S.

BILL MEDLEY
★ Lay a Little Lovin' On Me / U. Artists LA-929-H
★ Wings / A&M 3503

Talking about half of the Righteous Brothers is like talking about one Siamese twin, and listening to one is little improvement. — D.M.

RANDY MEISNER
★ Randy Meisner / Asy. 6E-140

Laid-back drivel from the former Eagle. Makes John David Souther sound like Led Zeppelin. — D.M.

MELANIE
★★★ Best of Melanie / Bud. 5705
★★★ Phonogenic—Not Just Another Pretty Face / Mid. Int. 3033
★★ Photograph / Atl. 18190

Melanie epitomized the flower child folksinger of the late Sixties. Her vocal range is in fact quite exceptional, and her phrasing often more sophisticated than she is given credit for, but the determined innocence and ingenuousness of her songs, their firm faith in good vibes conquering all, was obnoxious when she began recording and is now rather hilariously dated in its naiveté.

Her first commercial success came when she recorded "Candles in the Rain," a 1970 hit that called forth the spirit of Woodstock itself. (As those who saw the movie will recall, the emcee asked everyone in the crowd to light matches as a sign of solidarity—or something.) Her only other substantial hit came with "Brand New Key," a 1972 hit. "Candles" is on the Buddah *Best of* package, "Key" on the deleted ABC *From the Beginning* set. *Phonogenic* and her most recent album, *Photograph,* are much more mature, and include several good interpretations of contemporary songs. The earlier material, however, is recommended only for freshman mentalities, and only those which are terribly romantic, at that. — D.M.

HAROLD MELVIN AND THE BLUE NOTES
★★★★ Black and Blue / Phil. KZ-32407
★★★★ Collector's Item / Phil. PZ-34232
★★★ Harold Melvin and the Blue Notes / Phil. KZ-31648
★★ Now Is the Time / ABC AA-1041
★★ Reaching for the World / ABC 969
★★★★★ To Be True / Phil. KZ-33148
★★★★ Wake Up Everybody / Phil. ZX-33809

The lead singer's name was Theodore Pendergrass, and he turned out some of the strongest records produced by Kenny Gamble and Leon Huff since their work with Jerry Butler. The brilliant "Bad Luck," "If You Don't Know Me by Now" and "Wake Up Everybody" were among the greatest disco-soul records of the middle Seventies, with hot tracks and really ferocious vocal attack. After the group broke up in 1976, Melvin's regrouped forces churned out inferior imitations for ABC, while Pendergrass kept on with the real thing for Gamble and Huff. — D.M.

MEMPHIS HORNS
★★★ Get Up and Dance / RCA APL1-2198
★★★ High on Music / RCA APL1-1355
★★★ The Memphis Horns Band II / RCA APL1-2643

Moderately inventive mid-Seventies funk from the session musicians left over on the soul side of town after the Stax empire collapsed. — D.M.

NEIL MERRYWEATHER
■ Neil Merryweather . . . John Richardson and Bores / Kent 546

One of the most useless relics of Sixties West Coast psychedelic blues. Merryweather actually made a fairly listenable record once: *Word of Mouth "A Two Record Super-Jam,"* circa 1970, was bearable, but only because of the contributions of Steve Miller, Dave Mason, Barry Goldberg and a couple of others. Melt this one down. — D.M.

THE METERS
★★★★ Cabbage Alley / Rep. 2076
★★★★ Cissy Strut / Is. 9250
★★★ Fire on the Bayou / Rep. 2228
★★★ New Directions / War. B-3042
★★★★★ Rejuvenation / Rep. 2200
★★ Trick Bag / Rep. 2252

The Meters' early style (represented on *Cissy Strut*) was revolutionary. As a quartet, the New Orleans-based group developed a bare-boned, quirky brand of funk that leaned heavily on clipped rhythms and syncopated accents. The languid, off-center groove of songs like "Sophisticated Cissy" proved to be the forerunner of Seventies funk.

The group's Reprise albums sport an expanded approach, with congas, acoustic piano and horns often incorporated. *Cabbage Alley* features mild reggae, second-line funk, ballads, rolling Professor Longhair piano chords (played by Art Neville) and some tasty horn charts by Allen Toussaint. *Rejuvenation* maintains their heavy commitment to New Orleans music, while at the same time taking dead aim at early-Seventies Sly Stone funk innovations. The album is a masterpiece. But not one of the albums since then has been able to expand on the possibilities suggested on *Rejuvenation*. *Trick Bag* is particularly disappointing because it shows a band stalled for lack of direction. — J.MC.

AUGIE MEYERS AND THE WESTERN HEAD BAND
★★★ Live at the Longneck / Tex. 1002
Good-timey rock, Texas style, with keyboardist Meyers retaining the substance, and some of the sound, of the original Sir Douglas Quintet, to which he belonged. Augie's group can play a polka, a rock arrangement of Merle Haggard or Hank Williams, a Ricky Nelson oldie, or an original like the title song with equal gusto. Some weak vocals, but an irresistible barroom ambiance. — J.M.

MFSB
★★ Love Is the Message / Phil.
  KZ-32707
★★ MFSB / Phil. KZ-32046
★★★ Philadelphia Freedom! / Phil.
  PZ-33845
★★ Summertime / Phil. PZ-34238
★★ The End of Phase 1 / Phil. PZ-34658
★★ Universal Love / Phil. KZ-33158
MFSB is the driving instrumental force—horns and rhythm section—behind the remarkable Philadelphia soul sound of producer Kenny Gamble and Leon Huff. But aside from "TSOP (The Sound of Philadelphia)," a major 1973 pop and R&B hit, and a decent version of "Philadelphia Free-

dom," this is a long way from the heyday of Booker T. and the MGs. For the most part, it's just competent dance funk. — D.M.

LEE MICHAELS
★★★★ Lee Michaels / A&M 4199
★ Tailface / Col. 32846
An organist/vocalist with an eccentric approach—his band consisted of himself and a huge drummer, Frosty—Michaels' repertoire consisted of about thirty numbers, most of which sounded precisely the same. Because he attacked the organ with such verve and the vocals with such total disregard for his larynx, Michaels earned an unlikely amount of prosperity in the late Sixties and early Seventies. His best stuff was done for A&M, and the only remaining item in that label's catalogue contains two of his best-known numbers, "Stormy Monday" and "Heighty Hi" (but not his best single, the touching "Do You Know What I Mean"). The Columbia album represents a pathetic attempt at a mid-decade comeback. — A.N.

BETTE MIDLER
★★ Bette Midler / Atl. 7270
★★ Broken Blossom / Atl. 19151
★★★ Live at Last / Atl. 2-9000
★ Songs for the New Depression / Atl.
  18155
★★★★ The Divine Miss M / Atl. 7238
When Bette Midler first began appearing in New York nightclubs, she was revelatory: a cabaret performer who was truly funny and had a firm grasp of rock and its offshoots. As a Seventies answer to Barbra Streisand, she was perfect. The flawed but historic first album captures her in all her gum-snapping, wisecracking naiveté—everything from the pathos of John Prine's "Hello in There" to the Andrews Sisters' "Boogie Woogie Bugle Boy" is here. This is the album that created nostalgia as we currently know it.
  But Bette wilted in the spotlight, and little that she has come up with since is sufficient to explain her rabid cult. The readings grow more camp and turgid with each new album, and Midler seems less committed as well. There are bright spots: the spontaneous, screamingly funny dialogue on the *Live* album, which is also enhanced by her studio recording of "You're Moving Out Today." A few more songs like that and her hysterical, mismanaged career might finally amount to something. — D.M.

MIGHTY DIAMONDS
★★★ Ice on Fire / Virgin PZ-34454
★★★ Right Time / Virgin PZ-34235
Right Time is smooth but not slick reggae—
sweetly flowing vocal harmonies and appealingly conservative rhythm arrangements and occasional horns. All original
material; many lyrics concern Marcus Garvey, the Rastafarian cult hero.

Ice on Fire, produced neatly by Allen
Toussaint and Marshall Sehorn, features
subtle, slightly more complex (if perhaps
less pure) music—half the songs are
American rhythm & blues, adapted smartly
to reggae beats. — C.W.

BUDDY MILES
★★★ Carlos Santana and Buddy Miles
Live / Col. C-31308
★★★ Them Changes / Mer. 61280
The solo career of this clownish, heavy-
handed ex-Electric Flag drummer is a series of incredible gaffes, the likes of which
have seldom been witnessed in the annals
of popular music. His taste is awful, his
playing almost always overbearing and he
manages to make more judgmental errors
than seem possible. "Them Changes" is his
anthem, and a decent funk song, which in
this context is miraculous. — J.S.

JOHN MILES
★ Rebel / Lon. 660
★ Stranger in the City / Lon. PS 682
★ Zaragon / Ari. 4176
Eclectic English pop star borrows from
everyone from Elton John to Yes. Slick,
flashy, often pretentious. — S.H.

FRANKIE MILLER
★★★ Double Trouble / Chrys. 1174
★★★ Full House / Chrys. 1128

★★★ High Life / Chrys. 1052
★★★ Once in a Blue Moon / Chrys. 1036
★★★ The Rock / Chrys. 1088
A raspy rhythm & blues belter, Miller resembles other singers (Otis Redding, Bob
Seger, Joe Cocker, Paul Rodgers) but sings
mainly his own R&B-based material. *Once
in a Blue Moon* enlists the pub-rock of
Brinsley Schwarz—tight and subtle, and
very derivative of the Band. For *High Life,*
Miller went to Georgia to team up with
producer/arranger/writer Allen Toussaint
and a good studio team, including the Atlanta Rhythm Section's fine guitarist, Barry
Bailey. Miller's own more rock-directed
quartet made the meatier though less distinguished *The Rock. Full House* contains
much the same band, but also used studio
aces like Chris Spedding and John "Rabbit" Bundrick. Here, with mixed results,
Miller resorts more than usual to nonoriginal material that goes beyond the limits of
straight R&B. But *Double Trouble* returns
him to his own material. — C.W.

JACOB MILLER
★★★ Dread, Dread / U. Artists
LA-806-H
Your basic late-Seventies reggae: a rhythm
machine for Rastafarians and other der-
vishes. — D.M.

ROGER MILLER
★★★★ Golden Hits of Roger Miller /
Smash 67073
★★ Off the Wall / Wind. BXL1-2337
★★★★ The Best of Roger Miller / Mer.
61361
These days, Roger Miller is perhaps best
known for being the proprietor of Nashville's largest and most garish hotel, the
King of the Road Inn—a little slice of Vegas right in the heart of Music City, whose
cocktail lounge symbolizes country-as-
banal-pop music. But from 1964, when he
scored with "Dang Me," to 1966, when his
success more or less faded out with "You
Can't Roller Skate in a Buffalo Herd,"
Miller was a genuine pop-country eccentric whose recordings both epitomized the
warm folksiness of country's good side and
quickly capitulated to the homogeneous
homeyness of its dark, pre-outlaw days.

"King of the Road" and "Kansas City
Star"—both released in 1964—were the
height of Miller's writing and performing.
The former, sung in a choking twang, was
the story of a hobo; the irony was deliberate and endearing, much more humane

than the kind of thing Randy Newman would get away with ten years later. "Kansas City Star," which was a pun on that city's most famous newspaper, was a sign that his creativity was fading fast and that he at least suspected it. The song is a marvelous description of a television personality who's content to be a hero in a small environment and doesn't really want the pressure of the big time. As Miller sang it, there was no doubt that the metaphor was personal.

But thereafter, Miller's knack for the vernacular evaporated into the usual pop-country unctuousness and sanctimony. Sojourns at Columbia and John Denver's Windsong Records didn't help much. But for a couple of years, Roger Miller was a working-class hero. — D.M.

THE STEVE MILLER BAND
★★★★ **Brave New World** / Cap. SKAO-184
★★★ **Children of the Future** / Cap. SKAO-2920
★★★★ **Living in the U.S.A.** / Cap. STBB-717
★★★★ **Sailor** / Cap. STBB-2984
Diehards contend that this was the Steve Miller Band's prime, and it's awfully hard to dispute the point. Produced by Glyn Johns, with Boz Scaggs contributing songs and vocals, these albums are unusually "British," particularly for a late-Sixties, San Francisco-based band. From the beginning, Miller knew his formula—well-produced bunches of songs that ran together like rock & roll suites—and it's the same method that has made him a multi-platinum artist in the late Seventies.

The blues orientation of the first album, *Children of the Future*, softened by Scaggs'

wistful "Baby's Calling Me Home," contrasts effectively with the rocking *Sailor*, which was highlighted by Miller's satiric raver, "Living in the U.S.A.," and Scaggs' all-stops-out "Dime-a-Dance Romance." *Living in the U.S.A.* is a twofer compilation of *Sailor* and the initial *Children* set.

Brave New World, without Scaggs but with an often puzzling Boz-like presence, continues in the seamless blues-rock style of the first two albums, with "Space Cowboy" and the title tune aptly capturing Miller's cogent, if occasionally banal, world view.
★★★★ **Anthology** / Cap. SVBB-11114
★★ **Number Five** / Cap. SKAO-436
★★★ **Recall the Beginning** / Cap. SMAS-11022
★★ **Rock Love** / Cap. SW-748
This is a long and sleepy middle period in which the formula became tired and passé. Enlivened by an occasional standout tune, like "Your Saving Grace," this is generally a boring string of records in which Miller dabs bits of the blues and country into his rock formula, but fails to bring it to a full pop shine.
★★★★ **Book of Dreams** / Cap. SD-11630
★★★★ **Fly Like an Eagle** / Cap. ST-11497
★★★ **Steve Miller Band's Greatest Hits** / Cap. SOO-11872
★★★ **The Joker** / Cap. SMAS-11235
The simple blues figure that defined "The Joker" was to become the pattern for the albums that would secure Miller's mass success. The album, though, lacks the immediacy of the single—something that can't be said of the two LPs that followed.

Eagle and *Dreams,* recorded at the same time, are perfectly constructed albums, regurgitating old riffs with an undeniably professional polish that makes their derivation almost meaningless. Such singles as "Rock 'n' Me" (recycled Free, from *Eagle*) and "Jet Airliner" (based on Cream's "Crossroads" riff, from *Dreams*) were obviously retreads, but that didn't diminish the assured grace with which they monopolized AM radio in 1977 and 1978. Like Fleetwood Mac, Jefferson Starship and Bob Seger, Miller was a prototype late-Seventies rock phenomenon: a rocker who honed his craft in the Sixties and bided his time until the market was right for his well-produced encyclopedia of riffs. Seamless and smooth in style and presentation, Miller has ascended with the confidence that comes from thinking that you've always belonged there. — J.B.M.

MILLINGTON
★ **Ladies on the Stage / U. Artists
LA-821-G**
The Millington sisters' first group, Fanny, seemed to be a prospective great feminist hope in the early Seventies. This album, recorded half a dozen years and half a dozen albums down the line, makes apparent their real desire: to be pop stars at any cost. The tragedy is that their original ideas were so far superior to this formula Hollywood trash. — D.M.

STEPHANIE MILLS
★★ **For the First Time / Mo. M6-859**
The teenage Mills was a sensation as Dorothy in *The Wiz*, the 1975 Broadway play that revived *The Wizard of Oz*. Unfortunately, her big voice was a bit too stagy and immature to carry off a pop record, even one nicely written and arranged by Burt Bacharach and Hal David. (Now deleted.) — D.M.

MINK DEVILLE
★★★★ **Mink DeVille / Cap. ST-11631**
★★★★ **Return to Magenta / Cap.
SW-11780**
Singer Willy DeVille is cleverly derivative—he sounds like everyone from Lou Reed to the Isley Brothers. The caliber of his material has made the Mink DeVille albums an immediate punk/New Wave standout, though DeVille's roots are more clearly in New York's seamy R&B past. The highlights are the first album's "Mixed Up Shook Up Girl," a streetwise romance, and *Magenta*'s wild dance item, "Soul Twist." — J.B.M.

THE MIRACLES
★★ **City of Angels / Tam. T6-339**
★★ **Do It Baby / Tam. T6-334**
★★★ **Don't Cha Love It / Tam. T6-336**
★★★ **Love Crazy / Col. PC-34450**
★★ **Miracles / Col. JC-34910**
★★★ **Miracles Greatest Hits / Tam.
T6-357**
★★ **Power of Music / Tam. T6-344**
★★★ **Renaissance / Tam. 325**
Without Smokey Robinson, the Miracles have had difficulty achieving a comfortable identity. *Renaissance* finds Robinson's replacement, William Griffin, attempting to imitate his predecessor's vocal style. Yet, working with a variety of producers (Marvin Gaye, Willie Hutch, Freddie Perren) and some good songs, *Renaissance* is a commendable soft-soul effort. *Do It Baby* again features a host of producers and

some not-too-distinctive material, with one exception: the title song, produced by Perren, became the group's first post-Robinson hit single.

Perren produced all of *Don't Cha Love It*, mostly in the vein of *Do It Baby*—fluffy ballads and midtempo songs with snappy hooks. Perren also produced *City of Angels* a concept album with songs written exclusively by the group. The lyrics are often embarrassingly trite, but Perren's arrangements are among his best, including the Griffin-led "Love Machine," the Miracles' biggest hit. The last Motown album, *Power of Music,* is also their first in-group production since the Robinson days. It sports neither distinctive songs nor arrangements. The Columbia albums reflect this independence, but without scoring heavily either artistically or commercially. — J.MC.

MISSISSIPPI
★ **Mississippi / Fan. 9438**
Great title for a hot delta blues band. Too bad this isn't it—or much of anything else, for that matter. (Now deleted.) — D.M.

MISSISSIPPI SHEIKS
★★ **Stop and Listen Blues / Maml. 3804**
Made up of Lonnie Chatmon (fiddle) and Walter Vinson (guitar), the Sheiks were a black Thirties string band that catered to white audiences. "Sitting on Top of the World" was the Sheiks' "hit," and Vinson, who claimed to have written it, is also said to have taught Charlie McCoy mandolin. — I.M.

MR. BIG
★ **Photographic Smile / Ari. 4083**
Hard rock at its most wrongheaded and overweening, and without either rhythm or emotion. — D.M.

JONI MITCHELL
★★★★ Clouds / Rep. 6341
★★★ Joni Mitchell / Rep. 6293
★★★ Ladies of the Canyon / Rep. 6376

At first encounter, Joni Mitchell came on like an enlightened but somewhat precious folkie, writing striking vignettes of romance but presenting them in an uncomfortably sterile manner. The first album, *Joni Mitchell,* did show effectively the varied hues that her later work would reflect: an alluring boisterousness ("Night in the City"), a sure hand at storytelling ("Marcie") and an almost mythic concept of romantic love ("Michael from Mountain"). Her second album, *Clouds,* found her singing with more confidence, and the songs reveal a developing maturity. Such tunes as "I Don't Know Where I Stand" and "That Song about the Midway" capture the emotional confusions of weakening romanticism.

Ladies of the Canyon, while it can't boast the extraordinary consistency of the songwriting on *Clouds,* nonetheless find Mitchell expanding musically, with added instrumentation pushing her toward her most fruitful period.

★★★★★ Blue / Rep. 2038
★★★★★ Court and Spark / Asy. 7E-1001
★★★★ For the Roses / Asy. 5057

With *Blue,* Mitchell's lyrical outlook became much more entwined with her own emotions, quickly establishing her as the most significant of the confessional singer/songwriters. Her delicate but ever-adventurous vocals, bolstered by the album's quiet but assured instrumentation, left the songs to speak for themselves. The giddy hopefulness of "All I Want," the bittersweet regret of "Last Time I Saw Richard" and the sheer romantic wisdom of the title tune spoke eloquently.

For the Roses, a musically artier set than *Blue,* dealt with the romantic dilemma from an overtly feminine standpoint, even for Mitchell. Though occasionally ponderous—"Judgment of the Moon and Stars," in particular, suffers from this—the sweeping lyricism of "Cold Blue Steel and Sweet Fire" and the quiet intimacy of "Lesson in Survival," as well as the independence of will in *Roses'* every groove, make it one of her best.

Court and Spark remains Mitchell's most musical album: here the lyrics were pared to the essential bone, and the music accentuated the words as never before. We not only felt the romance in her voice on "Help Me," but the well-paced music of

Tom Scott and crew sent a shiver of recognition up our spines. The emotional rushes that such a union created, such as the breathless bridge of "The Same Situation," gave Mitchell's songs a power far beyond mere words.

★★★ Don Juan's Reckless Daughter / Asy. BB-701
★★★★ Hejira / Asy. 7E-1087
★★★ Miles of Aisles / Asy. 202
★★ The Hissing of Summer Lawns / Asy. 7E-1051

Recorded with Tom Scott and the L.A. Express, *Miles of Aisles* placed Mitchell in a cushy concert situation, where she could prove her newfound vocal chops. And on the early tunes, like "Cactus Tree" and "Rainy Night House," the updating is welcome. "Jericho," a song that later appears on *Don Juan,* is also a highlight, with the sturdy pop feel of the best of *Court and Spark.* A secondary, if entertaining, package.

Summer Lawns finds Mitchell spreading her introspective wings with sadly mixed results. Some of the songs are embarrassingly overdrawn, as if Mitchell reasoned that her stories could be better explained by too many details rather than a few well-chosen gems. The jazz feel she was developing was much better applied on *Hejira,* an album obsessed with lonesome revelry on a mythic and romantic highway. Here, Mitchell's increasingly airy voice blended with Jaco Pastorius' bass to create some sweeping moments of revelation. Despite an occasional lyrical gaffe, such songs as "Refuge of the Road" and "The Hissing of Summer Lawns" effectively embodied the mean contradictions with which an aging romantic must deal.

Don Juan's Reckless Daughter, a double album that should have been a single disc, seems to be another transitional LP, choking as it is with overblown ideas and an obsessively loose musical framework. But though Mitchell might be regretfully inconsistent of late, the spirit of romantic and artistic wanderlust that percolates through her work makes her an important standard-bearer in the confessional singer/songwriter genre. — J.B.M.

WILLIE MITCHELL
★★★ Best of Willie Mitchell / Hi 2-32068/9
★★★ Hold It / Hi 32021

Mitchell has never had any hits of his own, and these albums contain only pedestrian funk. He is of interest chiefly as the producer of Al Green, Ann Peebles and many of the other Hi soul artists, as a first-rate mainstream-soul songwriter/producer and as the leader of the Hi Rhythm Section. — D.M.

MOBY GRAPE
★★★ Great Grape / Col. CS-31098
★★★★★ Moby Grape / Col. CS-9498
★ Wow / Col. CXS-3

Moby Grape made only one good album, but what an album it is. That its debut LP is as fresh and exhilarating today as it was when it exploded out of San Francisco during 1967's summer of love is testament to the band's visionary concept of eclectic American music. Swirling within *Moby Grape* are elements of jazz, country, blues and plain old rave-up rock & roll. Yet all of it is so well integrated into the group's execution (five members who all sing, write and play brilliantly) that it's impossible to pigeonhole any of the album's thirteen songs. Lead guitarist Jerry Miller and bassist Bob Mosley propelled the band instrumentally, but the two rhythm guitarists, Skip Spence and Peter Lewis, and drummer Don Stevenson also contributed heavily.

The Grape's rapid downhill slide remains one of the mysterious tragedies of the late Sixties. *Wow* was a complete failure, a double album that included a "bonus" jam LP that made absolutely no sense in terms of the group's strongest point: tight song construction. A half-dozen other albums are no longer available; they vary from solid country- and blues-influenced rock to sheer musical confusion. *Great Grape* is a moderately well-chosen anthology, but that first LP is really the one that matters. — B.A.

MODERN LOVERS
★★★★ Modern Lovers / Beserk. 0050

Lead singer Jonathan Richman, a precursor of the late-Seventies New Wave, is a perfectly innocent rock visionary whose best work is represented here on sides originally recorded in 1971 for Warner Bros. John Cale's production lends an ominous undercurrent to such songs as "Road Runner," a charmingly gauche tribute to AM radio, and "Pablo Picasso," a wryly corny lament about the rock artist and his attempt to attain respect. Richman went on to a solo career so ingenuous it became simply silly, while keyboard player Jerry Harrison joined up with Talking Heads. — D.M.

THE MODULATIONS
★★★ It's Rough Out Here / Bud. 5638

It's Rough Out Here is mid-Seventies Philly soul with a touch of grease. The Modulations sound a bit like the Persuaders ("Thin Line between Love and Hate") and mix a rough-hewn lead singer, whiny falsetto and raspy baritone. Appealing to fans of the genre. — J.MC.

KATY MOFFATT
★ Katy / Col. KC-34172
★ Kissing in the California Sun / Col. JC-34774

Moffatt can't seem to make up her mind whether to be an interpreter of singer/songwriters and soft rock like Linda Ronstadt or a honky-tonk country singer like Marshall Chapman. Maybe because Moffatt isn't really very good at either. — D.M.

ESSRA MOHAWK
★★ Essra / Priv. 2024
★★★ Essra Mohawk / Elek. 7E-1023

Better-than-average female singer/songwriter whose most distinctive characteristic is a bizarre streak she picked up from a brief Sixties stint with the Mothers of Invention. Her 1974 set for Elektra, *Essra Mohawk,* is her best work. — J.S.

THE MOMENTS
★★★ Look at Me / Stang 1029
★★ Moments with You / Stang 1030
★★★ Patty / Stang 1027
★★★ Sharp / Stang 1034
★★★★ The Moments' Greatest Hits / Stang 1033

The Moments deserve better. For almost ten years, they've kept a steady string of hits on the charts in a genre (sweet soul) where groups come and go in the flicker of one hit 45. While the memory of faded groups like the Delfonics and Stylistics lingers, the Moments remain almost unknown outside of their primary audience: urban teens. Their clout is narrow, but intense. Not only is their list of soul hits enviable, but the group also writes and produces much of its own material, often with quite interesting results.

Though their 45s are impressive and lots of fun, the albums tend to be spotty, with a couple of exceptions: the most outstanding is *Greatest Hits,* which only recently was restored to the Stang catalogue. The other superior LP, *My Thing,* is unavailable. Of what's left, *Look at Me* features the frothy but delightful "Girls," as well as the

creamy smooth title song. The other LPs
are expendable. Anyway, if you've read
this far, you probably have already heard them
all, including *The Moments Live at the New
York State Women's Prison.* — J.MC.

EDDIE MONEY
★★★★ Eddie Money / Col. PC-34909
★★ Life for the Taking / Col. PC-35598
Money sings in the hard-rock mold of Bob
Seger and Bruce Springsteen, although
with a lighter, more pop feel. His self-titled
debut album earned him two of 1978's best
rock hits, "Baby Hold On" and "Two
Tickets to Paradise." But *Life for the Taking* strained too hard to follow it
up. — D.M.

THE MONKEES
★★★★ The Monkees' Greatest Hits / Ari.
4089
Okay, the Monkees were TV's synthetic response to the Beatles, a mass-produced
imitation of something relatively natural
and important. That doesn't mean they
weren't good—in fact, the group sometimes
got excellent material and production from
a variety of sources, notably Neil Diamond, Tommy Boyce and Bobby Hart, and
group member Michael Nesmith. As
drippy as Davy Jones' ballads could be,
"Another Pleasant Valley Sunday," "I'm a
Believer," "(I'm Not Your) Steppin'
Stone" and several of the other upbeat singles rank with the best pop-rock of the
mid-Sixties era, which is saying something. — D.M.

BILL MONROE
★★★★★ Bean Blossom / MCA 2-8002
★★★★ Bill and Charlie Monroe / MCA
124
★★★ Bill Monroe and His Bluegrass
Boys / Cor. 1065
★★★ Bill Monroe's Country Music Hall
of Fame / MCA 140
★★★★ Bill Monroe's Greatest Hits /
MCA 17
★★★ Bill Monroe Sings Bluegrass Body
and Soul / MCA 2251
★★★ Bill Monroe Sings Country Songs /
Cor. 20099
★★★ Bluegrass Instrumentals /
MCA 104
★★★ Bluegrass Ramble / MCA 88
★★★★ Bluegrass Special / MCA 97
★★★ Bluegrass Style / Cor. 20077
★★★ Bluegrass Time / MCA 116
★★★★ I'll Meet You in Church Sunday
Morning / MCA 226

★★★ Kentucky Bluegrass / MCA 136
★★★★ Mr. Bluegrass / MCA 82
★★★ Road of Life / MCA 426
★★★★ The High, Lonesome Sound of Bill
Monroe / MCA 110
★★★★ Uncle Pen / MCA 500
★★★ Voice from on High / MCA 131
★★★ Weary Traveller / MCA 2173
They call Monroe the "father of bluegrass"
not because he invented that variant of
country & western, but because he was its
most adventurous pioneer. The Kentucky
native began performing in the mid-Twen-
ties with his brother Charlie as the Monroe
Brothers. The album *Bill and Charlie Monroe* represents their early work, and some
of Monroe's best. Bill played what he
called "potato bug mandolin"; Charlie
played "houn' dog guitar." Their first hit,
written by Bill, was "Kentucky Waltz"
(1934), which gained them and their backing group, the Bluegrass Boys, a wide
country audience. Monroe's instrumental
style was characterized by peculiar tuning
and intricate timing; among his best-known
instrumentals are "Get Up John," "Blue
Grass Ramble" and "Memories of You."
Bill went solo in 1938 (Charlie retired after World War II) and joined the Grand
Ole Opry a year later. He and the Bluegrass Boys were among the troupe's featured artists through the Sixties. The Bluegrass Boys were one of country's seminal
groups, serving as a training ground for
Lester Flatt, Earl Scruggs, Clyde Moody,
Don Reno and many others. Monroe's
best-known tune, "Blue Moon of Kentucky," was one of Elvis Presley's first
great Sun records. Other memorable Monroe compositions include "Uncle Pen,"
"Gotta Travel On" and "Cheyenne."
Of the albums still available, the most
exceptional are *Bean Blossom,* which is
live, the best format for bluegrass; *I'll Meet
You in Church,* a fine gospel recording; and
several compilation albums of classic material (all rated four stars). Monroe's other
material is spotty and sentimental, but at
his best, he is the invigorating spirit of
bluegrass itself. — D.M.

THE MONTCLAIRS
★★★ Dreaming Out of Season / Paula
2216
A soft-soul group from East St. Louis, the
Montclairs made only album, which is
given over almost exclusively to creamy,
falsetto ballads—all written by group member Phil Perry. Pre-disco, teenage love music. — J.MC.

THE JAMES MONTGOMERY BAND
★★ The James Montgomery Band / Is.
9419

Long, repetitious, riff-dominated rhythm &
blues by this Boston-based bar band squander Allen Toussaint's carefully tailored
production. Montgomery's smoothly nonchalant vocals work, but his capable harmonica playing is strangely
scarce. — C.W.

MONTROSE
★★★ Jump on It / War. B-2963
★★★ Open Fire / War. K-3134
★★ Paper Money / War. B-2823
★ Montrose / War. K-3106
★★ Warner Brothers Presents . . . Mon-
trose / War. B-2892

Considering Ronnie Montrose's rather impressive credentials as a guitarist (he's
worked with Herbie Hancock, Van Morrison and Edgar Winter), the music he's
made with his namesake band is disappointing. The group has had two incarnations, the first (represented on *Montrose*
and *Paper Money*) featuring Sammy Hagar
on lead vocals. *Montrose* is rehashed
Mountain without even an update, although Ronnie is no Leslie West, and neither is Hagar. *Paper Money* tries to sound
more progressively English and winds up
equally redundant in a different field.

Stage two followed Hagar's departure,
the 1975 breakup of the original unit and
the re-formation later that year. The new
singer, Bob James, was obviously chosen
for his resemblance to Hagar. Like its
predecessors, *Presents* is faceless, unimaginative and plodding—ordinary in the extreme. *Jump on It* and 1978's *Open Fire* are
improvements. The former is uptempo
hard rock, the latter benefits from Edgar
Winter's production, which adds funk and

an ethereal touch. Nothing blindingly
original, but competence has been achieved
at last. — A.N.

MONTY PYTHON
★★ Live at City Center / Ari. 4073
★★★ Matching Tie and Handkerchief /
Ari. 4039
★★ The Album of the Soundtrack of the
Trailer of the Film of Monty Python and
the Holy Grail / Ari. 4050
★★★ The Worst of Monty Python / Bud.
5656-2

Puns, transvestites, double talk, studio effects and a smattering of obscenity from a
clutch of English university grads. The live
album's sound is very muddled and *Holy
Grail* is dumb (though that's not true of the
film), but *Matching Tie* contains a couple of
bits of timeless genius: a cheese shop that
contains no cheese and a marital squabble
over rat-flavored pie. The early work on
the Buddah set is Monty Python's best, although it may be too English (in approach
and content) to be intelligible to non-
Anglophilic Americans. — K.T.

THE MOODY BLUES
★★ Go Now: The Moody Blues #1 / Lon.
LP 428

This 1965 album is now interesting mainly
for the wonderful hit single "Go Now" and
its near-hit followup, "From the Bottom of
My Heart." The other ten songs are as thin
and inept as anything by the Dave Clark
Five. But as a souvenir of young adoles-
cence, this timeworn LP is irreplaceable
magic.
★★★ A Question of Balance / Thresh. 3
★★★★ Days of Future Passed / Deram
18012
★★★ Every Good Boy Deserves Favour /
Thresh. 5
★★★ In Search of the Lost Chord /
Deram 18017
★★ Moody Blues Caught Live Plus Five /
Lon. 2PS-690/1
★★★ Octave / Lon. PS-708
★★★ On the Threshold of a Dream /
Deram 18025
★★★★ Seventh Sojourn / Thresh. 7
★★★ This Is the Moody Blues / Thresh.
2-12/13
★★★ To Our Children's Children's Chil-
dren / Thresh. 1

Slightly reorganized, the Moodys reappeared in 1967 with the landmark *Days of
Future Passed,* the first of many attempts to
unite the pop group with the symphony orchestra. Pretentious as it was (especially

the spoken "poetic" introductions), it also has moments of real splendor in "Nights in White Satin" and "Tuesday Afternoon," both hits. Like all the group's material, the songs sound better with age.

The other albums follow a similar pattern. By mixing puerile philosophies (best/worst example: "Om" from *Lost Chord*) with easy, memorable melodies, and pleasant English vocal harmonies with the lessons learned from the London Festival Orchestra (expressed on Mellotron), the Moody Blues became gurus for a whole generation of illicit undergraduate pot smokers. Most of these sold millions, but contain little real imagination. "Ride My See-Saw," from *Chord,* is one exception, but the ideas came to a virtual dead end with *Seventh Sojourn,* and what's followed since the group's recent regrouping is dispensable, even on these pretentious terms. *This Is* is a good compilation for the uninitiated. — A.N.

KEITH MOON
★★ **Two Sides of the Moon / MCA 2136**
The Who's late drummer ill-advisedly enlisted dull West Coast sidemen to back his weak singing of well-chosen but poorly performed Sixties rock covers. (Now deleted.) — C.W.

MOONDOG
★★★★ **Moondog 1 / Col. MS-7335**
Louis Hardin, a.k.a. Moondog, is a blind musician/composer who built up a reputation for standing on street corners in midtown Manhattan dressed in archaic European garb. The marvelously eclectic symphonic work on this album is an obscure but worthwhile find. His melodic structures are classically inspired, while his use of percussion suggests a relationship with the more outside elements of rock and jazz rhythms. Moondog successfully sued Alan Freed in the late Fifties, forcing Freed to change the name of his radio show, originally called *Moondog's Rock and Roll Party.* — J.S.

MOONGLOWS
★★★★ **Moonglows / Chess 701**
One of the greatest R&B vocal groups of the Fifties, led by Bobby Lester and Harvey Fuqua. (Fuqua went on to become an important Motown producer/arranger/writer.) This doesn't contain "Sincerely," their huge 1955 hit, but it does have "Ten Commandments of Love," the 1959 smash, and a gaggle of other smooth, soulful

croonings, including a previously unreleased gem, "Sweeter than Words." Fun and fundamental. — D.M.

MOONQUAKE
★★ **Moonquake / Fan. 9450**
★ **Starstruck / Fan. 9486**
Your usual mid-Seventies rock: dull and conservative. (Both now deleted.) — D.M.

MOONRIDER
★★★ **Moonrider / Anchor 2010**
Guitarist John Weider, formerly with Eric Burdon and the Animals, leads an honest band that delivers modestly. Their two-guitar framework is tasteful, some of their material is sturdy and Weider's soloing saves the rest. (Now deleted.) — J.S.

DOROTHY MOORE
★★ **Dorothy Moore / Mal. 6353**
★★★ **Misty Blue / Mal. 6351**
★★ **Once Moore with Feeling / Mal. 6356**
"Misty Blue" is one of those records—like Barbara Mason's "Yes I'm Ready"—that overpowers with its starkness, directness and simplicity. The album that followed up the single showed that Moore has the potential to do more with ballads, though mediocre material is a definite problem. The other two LPs are a bit more pop-oriented, and also rather aimless. — R.G.

JACKIE MOORE
★★★★ **Make Me Feel Like a Woman / Kayv. 801**
Though Moore's best work was done for Atlantic ("Precious Precious") and is currently out of print, this comeback album serves her well. She is a blustery vocalist, and producer Brad Shapiro combines hardy lyrics with some tasteful, if not

completely imaginative, arrangements. — J.MC.

MELBA MOORE
★ A Portrait of Melba / Bud. 5695
★ I Got Love / Mer. SRM-1-61287
★ Melba / Bud. 5677
★ Melba / Epic JE-35507
★★ Peach Melba / Bud. 5629
★ This Is It / Bud. 5657

Melba Moore screeches, even more than Minnie Riperton did. One's tolerance for her albums depends on one's tolerance for the shrill. Nightclub cognoscenti seem to love it. *Peach Melba* does have a couple of reasonably modulated ballads and the title tune of the Van McCoy disco album, *This Is It,* is reasonably pleasant. But her version of "Lean On Me" (the McCoy version) and "The Long and Winding Road" are nightmares. — R.G.

TIM MOORE
★★ Behind the Eyes / Asy. 7E-1042
★★ Tim Moore / Asy. 7E-1019
★ White Shadows / Asy. 7E-1088

This pop singer/songwriter won at the 1974 American Song Festival with "Charmer," from his first album, *Tim Moore,* a fine blend of MOR and rock with a Philly soul slant. The third LP, *White Shadows,* shows a marked decrease in song quality. — S.H.

PATRICK MORAZ
★★ i / Atl. 18175

Moraz is a former member of Refugee and later replaced Rick Wakeman in Yes. His solo album features all manner of keyboards, often matched with Latin percussion. Intriguing arranging and technique, but generally mediocre composing. (Now deleted.) — C.W.

VAN MORRISON
★★★ A Period of Transition / War. B-2987
★★★★★ Astral Weeks / War. 1768
★★★★ Best of Van Morrison / Bang 222
★★★★ Blowin' Your Mind / Bang 218
★ Hard Nose the Highway / War. B-2712
★★★ It's Too Late to Stop Now / War. 2B-2760
★★★★★ Moondance / War. K-3103
★★★★ St. Dominic's Preview / War. B-2633
★★★ T.B. Sheets / Bang 400
★★★★ Tupelo Honey / War. 1950
★★★★ Van Morrison, His Band and Streetchoir / War. B-1884
★★★★ Veedon Fleece / War. B-2805
★★★ Wavelength / War. K-3212

Van Morrison has never been a terribly successful public artist, although he has occasionally sold a great many records, and some of his songs are well known. But his influence on musicians and critics has been enormous ever since he emerged from Belfast in 1966 with his band, Them, and its rock & roll masterpiece, "Gloria." (Even then, Van was upstaged; the Shadows of Knight's near-identical version made the American Top Ten.)

With Them, Morrison was a rough and tumble R&B singer—he sports a black eye on the cover of their second LP—who was capable of bringing Irish soul to Bob Dylan's "It's All Over Now Baby Blue" and demonic frenzy to the great harmonica-driven instrumental "Mystic Eyes." On his own, the soul sources have deepened and expanded, so that Morrison now seems less a great white R&B singer than like one of the very few rock artists who has invented a personal emotional equivalent of the blues.

The Bang sides were his post-Them solo debut, which produced one terrifically catchy single, "Brown-Eyed Girl" (1967), and several dreamy, Latin-rhythm personal songs, most notably "T.B. Sheets," "Ro Ro Rosey" and "He Ain't Give You None," all remarkably erotic in the best blues tradition. (The other Bang LPs are merely reworkings of the debut.)

Following the death of Morrison's producer, Bert Berns, the owner of Bang but best known as a soul writer/producer, Van moved to Warner Bros. Already living in America (*Blowin'* was made while Van lived in Cambridge, Massachusetts; he's since spent time in Woodstock, New York; Marin County, California; and L.A.), Morrison began to see himself as an immigrant everyman with a heavily mystical streak: he calls the result "Caledonia soul." *Astral Weeks,* a gorgeous song-cycle that appeared in 1968, was the first manifestation of this style. The record is nearly perfect, deeply emotive, elusively lyrical, musically both powerful and gentle.

Moondance was closer to straight soul, but the compact construction of songs like "Stoned Me," "Moondance," "Crazy Love" and the rest couldn't hide their searching spiritual concerns. *His Band and Streetchoir,* which contains his only Warners Top Ten hit, "Domino," and a pair of minor successes, "Blue Money" and "Call Me Up in Dreamland," is musically based in the sweet romantic soul of Curtis Mayfield and Smokey Robinson, though there is a devilish undercurrent of Fats Domino's New Orleans music as well.

Tupelo Honey was his last album of brief songs and contains some of his finest moments, particularly the hard-rocking "Wild Night." By now, however, Morrison was on the track of a truly personal voice, extremely singular, with roots in jazz as well as R&B. Always a part of his sound, these elements came to an exhilarating head in *St. Dominic's Preview.* That album's best songs—particularly the growling "Listen to the Lion" and the heart-wrenching "St. Dominic's Preview" and "Almost Independence Day"—are as soul-searching and soulful as any modern music.

Hard Nose the Highway was a failed sidestep, a compromise between the visionary demands of Morrison's work and his desire for a broad-based audience, a compromise more nearly perfected by *It's Too Late to Stop Now,* which weaves together his entire career, beginning with "Gloria," into a seamless act of will and devotion. *Veedon Fleece,* released in 1974, was more idiosyncratic—half a send-up of the superstardom that had eluded him, half a metaphysical voyage into his ancestry as a man and an artist. Its lack of public acceptance apparently pushed Morrison into a three-year retreat, broken by 1977's *A Period of Transition,* which more than lived up to its name. There are hints (notably "It Fills You Up" and "Heavy Connection") of a final, successful rapprochement between accessibility and vision, but the record finally falls short of its goal.

But all of this is of little consequence for those who know Morrison's songs and his singing. The bass playing of Richard Davis on *Astral Weeks,* which predates jazz-rock fusion by four years; Jack Schroer's beautiful sax work on several of the early Warners records; the constant drive of Morrison's songs, which often belies their tender sentiments—all mark him as an artist to be reckoned with. His influence has held considerable sway over such contemporaries as the Band, and he has, in fact, spawned a whole school of rock singers, which includes such notables as Bruce Springsteen, Bob Seger, Graham Parker, Frankie Miller and Thin Lizzy's Phil Lynott. Yet none of these has yet taken the spiritual basis of rock and R&B and the blues so far into an almost religious concept. Van Morrison remains unique, a great artist crying to be heard. — D.M.

MOSE JONES
★★★ **Blackbird** / RCA AFL1-2793
In 1973 this group worked as Al Kooper's backup band and signed to Sounds of the South records, which released their first two (now deleted) records. This time around they sound more polished and studio smart than on their first outings, and the connection with the Atlanta Rhythm Section's Studio One accounts for the commercial sound in a similar mold to the ARS. — J.S.

MOTHER'S FINEST
★★ **Another Mother Further** / Epic PE-34699
★★ **Mother Factor** / Epic JE-35546
★ **Mother's Finest** / Epic PE-34179
Like many musical crossbreeds in their early stages, Mother's Finest is a sound in search of an audience. Neither rock, soul nor disco, Mother's Finest bridges the gaps between Earth, Wind and Fire, Labelle and any number of white boogie bands. Of the group's three albums, the 1976 debut, *Mother's Finest,* is a lesser effort, with a sound far less integrated than the group itself (which has four black members, two white ones). Familiar rock riffs are coated with glossy, superfunk harmonies. *Another Mother Further,* the 1977 followup, is smoother and less frantic, with producer Tom Werman (who also works with Ted Nugent) rounding out the sound with strings and extensive use of synthesizer. Not coincidentally, the best two tracks are the shortest ones: "Piece of the Rock" and "Hard Rock Lover," both pure stud rockers. — G.K.

THE MOTHERS OF INVENTION / FRANK ZAPPA
★★★★ **Absolutely Free** / Verve V/V6-5013X
★★★★ **Freak Out** / Verve V6-5005-2
★★★ **Mothermania** / Biz./Verve V6-5068
★ **The Worst of the Mothers** / Verve SE-4754
★★★★★ **We're Only in It for the Money** / Verve V6-5045X
The Mothers of Invention, led by Frank Zappa, shocked the Sixties "underground" into early self-recognition with the intellectual arrogance and wit of *Freak Out.* Here, at last, was an album that interjected the ironic modes of pop art (as practiced by Rosenquist, Warhol and Dine) into rock & roll and made it work. Dylan's lyrics had already put down love-song clichés, and others had attempted arty experiments

with rock, but Zappa took the whole form through a grand mutation.

One disc of the double record consists of robust parodies of mid-Sixties suburbia. Zappa knew his pop ready-mades well enough to render them into effective songs like "You Didn't Try to Call Me" and "How Could I Be Such a Fool," but it was Ray Collins' extraordinary pop-operatic vocals that best conveyed the not-so-mock rage.

The other disc is rock's first experimental music masterpiece, influenced mainly by such modern composers as Edgar Varèse, but with an anarchist aggression that is far more defiantly celebratory than arty. "Help, I'm a Rock" and "The Return of the Son of Monster Magnet" created an enduring aural landscape over which Zappa's mythic heroes—from Suzy Creamcheese to his current Sadean libertine of "The Torture Never Stops"—have quested in various stages of numbed distress ever since.

Stuck in among these avant-garde excursions is "Trouble Comin' Everyday." Zappa's own brilliantly ugly vocal growls over the Mothers' lunging ancestor, heavy-metal rock. Along with "Help, I'm a Rock," "Trouble" darkly anticipates the political themes of imprisonment and suffocation that obsess Zappa on *Absolutely Free* and *We're Only in It for the Money.*

Both of those albums should have dated badly. While often hailed for Zappa's "montage" editing, which turned regular rock-song forms inside out, the popularity of the LPs rests on satire. Surprisingly, they have dated very little. Aside from a few topical references, the prison/insane asylum/shopping mall algebra still stings and the essentially structural intelligence of Zappa's montage remains awesome.

Absolutely Free takes on "straight" America with "Brown Shoes Don't Make It," "Plastic People" and "America Drinks and Goes Home" to create a pop horror show worthy of Hans Bellmer's dolls, whose violent overtones Zappa was deliberately evoking in his live shows.

We're Only in It for the Money was intended to serve as a Brechtian (as in "alienation effect") answer to *Sgt. Pepper's Lonely Hearts Club Band,* and it is a relentless savaging of "hip" America, for which the Beatles' album was providing an appropriately naive soundtrack. Zappa's tone is never less than ominous. His montage techniques are now perfected, and he weaves chillingly munchkin pop-song sec-

tions into white noise, spoken sections and Varèsian segments mounting up to his horrific "The Chrome Plated Megaphone of Destiny." The suitable text, he tells us in his liner notes, is Kafka's "In the Penal Colony," while the music itself is a frightening indication that if Zappa expected anything of the Sixties, it was the antichrist, not the Aquarian Age. Still, "Mother People" posits a cautiously rationalist humanism as something to which his fans might aspire. As he would reveal with his next albums, Zappa wasn't really the Dada nihilist of his public reputation.

The compilation albums should be avoided. Zappa was working in a strict album format, although he himself put *Mothermania* together, which makes it preferable.

★★★★ **Burnt Weeny Sandwich / Biz. 6370**

★★★★★ **Uncle Meat / Biz. 2MS-2024**
★★★★ **Weasels Ripped My Flesh / Biz. 2028**

Uncle Meat, the last album recorded by the original Mothers, was part of Zappa's sustained effort to use *musical* means to create extended works. (*Lumpy Gravy,* Zappa's deleted first solo album, is also part of this process.) Although the montage techniques are still used to great advantage, they are now joining together longer and more discrete elements. The effect achieved is a blend rather than a collision. As the Mothers grew into a superb instrumental ensemble, Zappa also worked in extended, jazzlike solos, and his appropriations from modern composers also continued.

Here, Zappa the moralist-satirist temporarily disappears, replaced by an incarnation as metaphysician. The vocal fragments, spoken parts and even the songs consist largely of autobiographical allusions, poetic texts, linguistic games and gnomic manifestoes on aesthetics. The result is Zappa's most personal work. *Meat* and the later-released *Weeny* and *Weasels* (consisting of selections from the vast career retrospective Zappa once planned) are the best records by Zappa and the Mothers of Invention.

The missing artifact from this period is *Ruben and the Jets,* the set of doo-wop parodies that are autobiographical in another way. The set is deleted, which is unfortunate, although Zappa's sincere affection for doo-wop's aching sweetness was overwhelmed by sheer weariness and a dry sense of something neither Zappa nor the Mothers could emotionally entertain.

★ **Just Another Band from L.A. / Biz. 2075**
★★ **Mothers Live at the Fillmore East—**
June 1971 / Biz. 2042
★★★ **The Grand Wazoo / Rep. 2093**
This is Zappa's most disorganized period,
because so much of his work immediately
following the dissolution of the Mothers is
deleted. The best album, *Hot Rats* (Bizarre), was a long-awaited guitar showcase
for Zappa, who had previously repressed
his own playing on records. *Chunga's Revenge* featured Flo and Eddie, and was recorded just before the formation of a second Mothers lineup. Zappa's sarcastic
intelligence is indefatigable here, but it's
quite clear that both his icy anger and serious imagination were spent before *Chunga*
was recorded.

The band that recorded *Live at the Fillmore* and *Just Another Band* had taken on
the character of a cynical joke. These
Mothers could play excitingly and entertainingly, but in the end, the albums witness a woeful attenuation of Zappa's best
ideas and instincts. *The Grand Wazoo* is a
return to the full horn-section arranging
he'd almost forsaken after *Uncle Meat*. In
its modest way—Zappa has seldom been so
understated—*Wazoo* is a fusion-music gem
that almost manages to sound like art rock.
★★ **Bongo Fury / Discr. 2234**
★★★ **One Size Fits All / Discr. 2216**
★★★ **Over-Nite Sensation / Discr. K-2288**
★★ **The Roxy and Elsewhere / Discr.**
2DS-2202
On these albums, Zappa achieves a nicely
formulaic plateau. Having discarded, or
stored away, most of his compositional experiments, Zappa now writes regular rock
songs that in turn resemble Chicago, Santana and John McLaughlin in structure,
though usually a quirk beat change or keyboard flourish acts as a signature. The lyrics are cozily scatological, casually pornographic or smugly satirical. As *Roxy*
demonstrates, Zappa has found a congenial
audience that considers him a showbiz eccentric in between the heated mathematical
guitar solos that have become his main order of business. The studio albums are better, simply because they're more amply
produced and cleverly arranged than *Roxy*.

Bongo Fury is a collaboration with Captain Beefheart and a depressing edition of
more-of-the-same, a very minor *Trout
Mask Replica* lyrically, with the band restlessly twanging.

All these records are enjoyable, if only
for the pleasure of Zappa being very much
his competent self. However, they do sug-

gest that the cautiously rational humanist
in him has overcome his imagination. — B.T.

THE MOTORS
★★★★ **Approved by the Motors / Virgin**
JZ-35348
★★★★ **Motors / Virgin PZ-34924**
Blazing hard-rock band led by ex-Ducks
Deluxe pub rockers. The Motors' 1977 de-
but was one of the best straight rock rec-
ords out of England during a year when
New Wave bands, Elvis Costello and Gra-
ham Parker dominated the head-
lines. — J.S.

MOTT THE HOOPLE
★★★★ **All the Young Dudes / Col.**
PC-31750
★★★★ **Brain Capers / Atl. 8304**
★ **Drive On / Col. PC-33705**
★★★ **Greatest Hits / Col. PC-34368**
★★★★★ **Mott / Col. PC-32425**
★★★★ **Mott the Hoople / Atl. 8258**
★ **Mott the Hoople Live / Col. PC-33282**
★ **Shouting and Pointing / Col. PC-34236**
★★★ **The Hoople / Col. PC-32871**
Mott the Hoople, the group's 1969 debut, is
an amazing record, one of the most perfect
emulations of Dylan's *Blonde on Blonde* pe-
riod; dense roller-rink organ blues and vo-
calist Ian Hunter's droning voice create a
perfect atmosphere. The band did not have
much to say ("Rock and Roll Queen" is
the sole good original song), but the outside material included Sonny Bono's
"Laugh at Me," which finally made sense
without self-pity in this context; Doug
Sahm's dramatic ballad, "At the Crossroads"; and the Kinks' "You Really Got
Me," done as an overpowering instrumental. *Wildlife,* the group's disastrous second
album for Atlantic, is now thankfully de-

leted. But on *Brain Capers,* the third, the band made one of the best heavy-metal records of the early Seventies: pounding and intelligent (if you can handle a song called "Death May Be Your Santa Claus"). All this time, Hunter's domination of the group was subtle but obvious; drummer Dale "Buffin" Griffin, bassist Overend Watts and particularly guitarist Mick Ralphs also played key roles.

When the band moved to Columbia in 1972 (after almost breaking up in the wake of its remarkable lack of success in both England and America), it was accompanied by producer David Bowie, who cleaned up the sound, moved it to a point midway between heavy metal and *Blonde on Blonde* (an interesting and innovative niche) and gave the group two great songs: "All the Young Dudes," an explicitly gay anthem written by Bowie that almost became a U.S. hit, and Lou Reed's wonderful "Sweet Jane," a hymn of praise to the rock & roll muse.

Mott was even better, full of meditations on the group's artistic and commercial failures ("The Ballad of Mott the Hoople"), rock legends ("All the Way from Memphis," which Martin Scorsese used over the opening credits of *Alice Doesn't Live Here Anymore*) and English folk-rock psychological whimsy ("I Wish I Was Your Mother"). This is one of the great lost masterpieces of modern rock, ranking with Love's *Forever Changes* as a perfect mood piece.

Unfortunately, the group was never able to follow it up: *The Hoople,* Mott's immediate successor, was spotty, largely because of Ralphs' departure. And the rest was worse, leading up to *Drive On* and *Shouting and Pointing,* made after Hunter left for a solo career; both are shrill and pointless. The Columbia *Greatest Hits* anthology can't really bring all this together in a way that makes emotional sense; Atlantic's deleted collection of early Hoople material, *Rock and Roll Queen,* does a little better for the pre-*Dudes* stuff. But contemporary fans of mainstream rock could do worse than to pick up the four- and five-star records above while they remain in print; they're a profound influence on much of what has gone on with the New Wave of the late Seventies. — D.M.

MOUNTAIN
★★ **Avalanche / Col. C-33088**
★★★ **The Best of Mountain / Col. PC-32079**

★★ **Twin Peaks / Col. PC-32818**
The cream of American heavy metal in the early Seventies, Mountain had the formula down cold, building a plodding bass/ drums/keyboards rhythmic foundation for ex-Vagrant guitarist Leslie West's equally plodding leads. Felix Pappalardi (who helped launch heavy metal as Cream's producer) did his best Jack Bruce imitation on bass and wrote one of the band's best songs, "Theme from an Imaginary Western." That and the band's best-known song, "Mississippi Queen," are on the *Best of* collection. — J.S.

THE MOVE
★★★★ **California Man / Elect. 054-05696 (Import)**
★★★★ **Fire Brigade / MFP 5276 (Import)**
★★★★★ **The Best of the Move / A&M 3625**
★★★ **The Move / MFP 50158 (Import)**
The Move was formed in 1965 in Birmingham, England, and opened at the Marquee Club in London the next year. They created immediate excitement with a pop-art stage show heavily influenced by the Who, as was their sound. The group had a number of hit singles in Britain, beginning with "Night of Fear" in 1967, but never achieved more than a small cult following in the United States. As a result, most of the band's recorded history is to be found on imports.

The Best of the Move repackages the group's 1967 debut; it's an intriguing blend of pop melodies with loud but controlled drumming and Roy Wood's understated yet accomplished guitar, along with a dozen brilliant B sides, outtakes and failed singles. The import albums are also collections: *California Man* is the group's final material, including the excellent title single and "Do Ya," the band's best song and closest approximation of an American hit. *Fire Brigade* and *The Move* are more scattershot collections that include songs from several phases of the band's career.

Although they never achieved respectability at home—despite such autodestruct antics as smashing a TV set to smithereens as part of the act—the Move was highly influential on American art-rock bands. By 1970, the group was falling apart. Vocalist Jeff Lynne took the place of Jeff Wayne, with Wood and drummer Bev Bevan then forming Electric Light Orchestra, from which Wood soon departed for his own group, Wizzard. The band's later songs include most of the concepts ELO would make famous, the combination of classical motifs and Beatles melodies. — C.W.

THE MOVIES
★ **The Movies / Ari. 4085**
For everyone who fondly remembers the new suit of clothes that good little boys once got to wear for the holidays. *Clean* pop music, but without the drama or the humor of soap opera. Compared to this, Barbie dolls are radical chic. (Now deleted.) — D.M.

MOXY
★ **Moxy / Mer. SRM-1-1087**
★ **Moxy II / Mer. SRM-1-1115**
★ **Ridin' High / Mer. SRM-1-1161**
★ **Under the Lights / Mer. SRM-1-3723**
The (very) poor man's Aerosmith. Makes Rush look like an intellectual's concept. — J.S.

GEOFF MULDAUR
★ **Motion / Rep. 2255**
Muldaur, the former Jim Kweskin Jug Band vocalist/instrumentalist, has never enjoyed much popular success, either on this solo album (or his other deleted LP) or with his wife, Maria, who's done better by herself. Eclectic and witty though he is, Muldaur has never achieved sufficient direction to give his music focus. — I.M.

GEOFF AND MARIA MULDAUR
★★★ **Pottery Pie / Rep. 6350**
★★★ **Sweet Potatoes / Rep. 2073**
The former Jim Kweskin Jug Band vocalists made this pair of duet albums in the early Seventies, before Maria struck gold with "Midnight at the Oasis." The records hold up surprisingly well, both in terms of performance and material, which ranges from Hoagy Carmichael's "Lazybones" to

Son House's "Death Letter Blues" to some originals. The arrangements are contemporary pop-folk, without losing sight of the traditional material's roots. — I.M.

MARIA MULDAUR
★★★★ **Maria Muldaur / Rep. 2148**
★ **Southern Winds / War. K-3162**
★★★★ **Sweet Harmony / Rep. 2235**
★★ **Waitress in a Donut Shop / Rep. 2194**
Formerly teamed with husband Geoff, this veteran of the Boston folk scene (Kweskin Jug Band) emerged in 1974 as a mature, sensual stylist of great depth and versatility. Her solo debut, *Maria Muldaur,* boasted definitive versions of excellent songs by Dolly Parton, Kate McGarrigle and Wendy Waldman among others, though it was David Nichtern's "Midnight at the Oasis" that earned her an enormous pop hit.

Waitress followed a similar format, but the material and production were weaker. *Sweet Harmony* ranged farther afield than the debut for its material—the title song is a Smokey Robinson ballad—and it was more sophisticated, highlighted by a brilliant remake of Mildred Bailey's theme song, "Rockin' Chair." But *Southern Winds,* a 1977 attempt at contemporary funk produced by Chris Bond (Hall and Oates), was a catastrophically wrongheaded disc, with weak material and inept arrangements that strained where Muldaur had formerly projected with ease. — S.H.

MARTIN MULL
★ **Days of Wine and Neuroses / Capri. 0155**
★ **I'm Everyone I've Ever Loved / ABC 997**
★ **In the Soop / Van. 79338**
★ **Martin Mull / Capri. 0106**

★ **Martin Mull and His Fabulous Furniture** / Capri. 0117
★ **No Hits, Four Errors** / Capri. 0195
★ **Normal** / Capri. 0125
★ **Sex and Violins** / ABC 1064

The best way to torpedo this artist-turned-TV-star (he's had conceptual art exhibits at major galleries and starred in the syndicated *Fernwood 2Night*) is to give some samples of his wit as it appears in his song titles: "Noses Run in My Family," "Jesus Christ Football Star," "Ego Boogie." Another tune is said to be recorded by the Below Average White Band. Mull does *not* have to be seen to be dismissed unless you're just leaving your sophomore year. Smug and obvious. — K.T.

MICHAEL MURPHEY

★ **Blue Sky Night Thunder** / Epic PE-33290
★★★ **Cosmic Cowboy Souvenir** / A&M 4388
★ **Flowing Free Forever** / Epic PE-34220
★★★ **Geronimo's Cadillac** / A&M 4358
★ **Lonewolf** / Epic JE-35013
★★ **Michael Murphey** / Epic KE-32835
★ **Swans Against the Sun** / Epic PE-33851

A "Cosmic Cowboy" country rocker with a strong satirical thrust in his early songs, Murphey moved relentlessly into banal John Denver territory. "Geronimo's Cadillac" is his best and best-known song, but it's been done better by others (notably Hoyt Axton). — S.H.

ELLIOTT MURPHY

★★★ **Just a Story from America** / Col. PG-34653

Murphy made his first and best album for Polydor in 1973 (*Aqua Show*, deleted). Since then, he's developed a remarkable lyrical style—F. Scott Fitzgerald out of Lou Reed—but hasn't added a discernible musical approach. This is his most recent (1977) album, an excellent investigation of the mythical basis of twentieth-century American culture without sufficient musical interest to make the songs as interesting as they'd need to be to enter that mythology themselves. (Now deleted.) — D.M.

WALTER MURPHY BAND

■ **A Fifth of Beethoven** / Priv. 2015
■ **Phantom of the Opera** / Priv. 7010
■ **Rhapsody in Blue** / Priv. 2028

Hooking classical and semi-classical melodic clichés around disco arrangements isn't a new idea by any means—classical quotes have been clipped for popular song themes throughout the century. But celebrating the banal use of these clichés is pretty pointless. Pass these along to your aunt, who'll feel hip rather than rooked. — J.S.

ANNE MURRAY

★★ **Country** / Cap. ST-11324
★ **Danny's Song** / Cap. ST-11172
★★★ **Highly Prized Possession** / Cap. ST-11354
★ **Keeping in Touch** / Cap. ST-11559
★★ **Let's Keep It That Way** / Cap. ST-11743
★★★ **Love Song** / Cap. ST-11266
★★ **New Kind of Feeling** / Cap. SW-11849
★★ **Snowbird** / Cap. ST-579
★★ **Talk It Over in the Morning** / Cap. ST-821
★ **Together** / Cap. ST-11433

Murray is a Canadian with a deep, throaty voice that delivers an intense emotionalism belied by her calm, polite performing demeanor. A former high school phys. ed. teacher, her record company has always tagged her with a girl-next-door image, and this has been reinforced by the bulk of her material, which is average MOR. But Murray also has an exciting, even dark, side to her: she has a strong cult among gay women, who have astutely perceived her firm independence of men even as she sings gloppy hetero-hymns to them—again, it is her voice that always rings out honestly.

Murray has also done a number of terrific Beatles covers, culminating in her gloriously tough and cheerful version of "You Won't See Me," on *Love Song,* her best album, though *Highly Prized Possession* is a close second (she makes "Day Tripper" her own on that one). The rest of these drown in the oily slickness of their production. This is nearly tragic, because Murray could be a great pop singer in a feminist era. Currently she is a moderately unpopular MOR tool. — K.T.

JUNIOR MURVIN

★★★ **Police and Thieves** / Mango 9499

Murvin isn't that great, but "Police and Thieves," the politicized reggae song that became his 1976 British hit and was later covered by the Clash, is a masterpiece. The album rates this highly on the strength of that song alone. — D.M.

MUSCLE SHOALS HORNS
★★★ Born to Get Down / Bang 403
★★★ Doin' It to the Bone / Ario.-Amer.
 ST-50021
Muscle Shoals is better known for its
rhythm sections than its horns, but this is
surprisingly hot-blooded funk without
much embellishment, something like a Seventies version of the Mar-Keys. Highlights
are the first (Bang) album's torrid title
track and a cover of the J. Geils Band's
reggae hit, "Give It to Me." — J.MC.

MUSIC EXPLOSION
★★★ Little Bit O' Soul / Laur. 2040
The title track, a mid-Sixties hit, was a
great R&B-pop one-shot propelled by a
snappy bass riff and excellent AM production. It hardly matters that the rest of the
band's output is worthless. — J.S.

MYLES AND LENNY
★ Myles and Lenny / Col. KC-33366
Bad California pop, without the precision
necessary to pull off either the harmonies
or the backing tracks that are the genre's
saving grace. Save your dough for an old
Fleetwood Mac album—at least one of
those will have a couple of good Christine
McVie songs. (Now deleted.) — D.M.

MYSTIQUE
★★★ Mystique / Cur. 5012
Competent 1977 vocal group led by singer
Ralph Johnson, who was in the Impres-
sions from 1973 to 1976. — J.S.

GRAHAM NASH
★★ **Songs for Beginners / Atl. 7204**
★ **Wild Tales / Atl. 7288**
This former Hollie and Crosby, Stills and Nash staple confuses simplicity with triteness. *Beginners* contains the prototypical "Simple Man." — S.H.

JOHNNY NASH
★★★ **I Can See Clearly Now / Epic KE-31607**
★★ **My Merry-Go-Round / Epic KE-32158**
Possessed of a strikingly affecting high tenor and a rich gift for soulful phrasing, Johnny Nash has nonetheless been the victim of his own arrangements, which push him toward the corny and commercial. Nash, who would eventually settle in London, moved from the United States to Jamaica to make his 1972 hit, "I Can See Clearly Now." The album of the same name—that contains three Bob Marley songs, two by John "Rabbit" Bundrick and one co-written by Marley with Nash—uses reggae rhythms to effectively capture Nash's oddly innocent eroticism.

Despite Bundrick's percolating keyboard work, an intrusive and almost bubblegum-style production job by Nash mars 1973's *My Merry-Go-Round,* which reels between Philly soul, reggae and Stax-Volt attacks that never cohere. — F.S.

THE NATIONAL LAMPOON
★★ **Animal House / MCA 3046**
★★ **Gold Turkey / Epic PE-33410**
★★ **Goodbye Pop / Epic PE-33956**
★★★★ **Lemmings / Blue Th. 6006**
★★★ **Radio Dinner / Blue Th. 38**
Like the magazine that spawned them, this series of comedy albums begins brilliantly and then peters out into material so pathetic it gives new meaning to the term "sophomoric." *Lemmings,* based on the touring revue that launched the careers of many of *Saturday Night Live*'s Not Ready for Prime Time Players, is an inspired takeoff on rock pomposity; the John Lennon, Bob Dylan and Joan Baez parodies are sheer genius. *Radio Dinner* keeps it up almost as relentlessly. But the Epic albums disintegrate into cheap shots at the counterculture, pop culture and just culture in general; they're more exploitative of collegiate sensibility than reflective of it. *Animal House,* the soundtrack to the sometimes brilliant first *Lampoon* movie, falters for several reasons, not least of which is because the version of "Louie Louie" included here has been censored; John Belushi's marvelously filthy lyrics in the film deserve permanent enshrinement on disc. — D.M.

NATURAL ESSENCE
★ **In Search of Happiness / Fan. 9440**
Dreary Seventies funk. — D.M.

THE NATURAL FOUR
★★ **Nightchaser / Cur. 5008**
A mildly interesting minor-league soul group with a spotty track record, the Natural Four manages to come up with a soul hit every few years. *Nightchaser* was produced by the Chuck Jackson/Marvin Yancy team (which also works with Natalie Cole) with an ear toward funk and disco. Somehow things just never get off the ground. *Heaven Right Here on Earth,* the group's other Curtom album, is also deleted, but it's better: nothing too ambitious, just a falsetto lead with harmonizing. (Now deleted.) — J.MC.

NATURAL GAS
★★ **Natural Gas / Priv. 2011**
What could a group of second-line British musicians do in 1976 except pull out a

bunch of outmoded heavy-metal riffs? Not much, apparently. (Now deleted.) — D.M.

NAVARRO
★ Listen / Cap. ST-11670
★ Straight to the Heart / Cap. SW-11784
The backup band for Carole King's recent albums (her worst) makes God-consciousness albums that are about as transcendently intense as three-day-old milk. — D.M.

NAZARETH
★ Close Enough for Rock and Roll / A&M 4562
★ Expect No Mercy / A&M 4666
★★ Hair of the Dog / A&M 4511
★ Hot Tracks / A&M 4643
★ Loud 'n' Proud / A&M 3609
★ No Mean City / A&M 4741
★ Play'n' the Game / A&M 4610
★ Rampant / A&M 3641
★ Razamanaz / A&M 4396
Dog food. Among the most mediocre of successful mid-Seventies British hard-rock groups, Nazareth's biggest claim to fame is a 1975 hit,"Love Hurts," which bears not a smattering of resemblance to the great Everly Brothers song of the same name. Dreadful stuff. — D.M.

FRED NEIL
★★★★ Everybody's Talkin' / Cap. SM-294
★★★ Little Bit of Rain / Elek. 74073
★★★★ The Other Side of This Life / Cap. SM-657
Reclusive Sixties folk-jazz singer/composer who played an avuncular role in relationship to folk rock—both Eric Burdon and Jefferson Airplane recorded Neil's "The Other Side of This Life"—but is perhaps better known for "Everybody's Talkin'," which Harry Nilsson made a hit on the soundtrack to *Midnight Cowboy. Everybody's Talkin'*, on which Stephen Stills plays a pre-Buffalo Springfield guest role, also contains two marvelous little-known songs, "The Dolphins" and Neil's version of "Cocaine." Neil never had much commercial success and retreated by the mid-Sixties to Coconut Grove, Florida, where he has been peripherally engaged in dolphin research but has played little music ever since. — D.M.

NEKTAR
★★ A Tab in the Ocean / Pass. 98017
★★ Down to Earth / Pass. 98005
★★ Magic Is a Child / Poly. 1-6115

★★★ Recycled / Pass. 0811
★★ Remember the Future / Pass. 98002
These five Britons made their initial recordings for the German Bellaphon label, but they didn't begin enjoying any real success until the import-bin gnomes who enjoyed the group's psychedelic-style freakouts (a kind of bastard son of Hawkwind and the Grateful Dead, only more melodic) turned Nektar into a fairly successful cult band.

The debut, *A Tab*, released in 1972, features Roy Albrighton's hot guitar and screechy vocals over a tape-loop rhythm section; it's nearly fifty minutes of pure noise, a must for anyone who's ever passed out with headphones on and volume up full. *Remember* is a concept album about an extraterrestrial bluebird who lets a blind boy see the future: pure *National Lampoon* rock opera. *Down* and *Magic* are variations on similar themes, but *Recycled* gives some hope of the band's eventual maturity: less blitzkrieg stomp, more Genesis/Camel/Caravan-style melodic improvisation. — A.N.

BILL NELSON AND RED NOISE
★★★ Sound-on-Sound / Harv. ST-11931
This initial outing from guitarist Nelson's post-Be Bop Deluxe band features the same blend of avant-garde art-rock ideas and hot licks done by the earlier group, but it doesn't surpass them. A cautious first step. — D.M.

RICKY NELSON
★★ Intakes / Epic PE-34420
★★★★★ Legendary Master Series / U. Artists UAS-9960
Because he first appeared on television's *Ozzie and Harriet* (which starred his parents) and began his rock & roll career in the same place, Nelson has been unjustly underrated. In fact, he was a first-rate rock singer—if not a great one, he was at least leagues superior to the Bobby Vee/Fabian/Paul Anka finger-pop axis. Hits like "Travelin' Man," "Hello Mary Lou," "Teenage Idol" and "Poor Little Fool" were among the best in post-Elvis rock of the late Fifties. Nelson was supported by a terrific band, led by guitarist James Burton, who a decade later joined up with the King himself. If Nelson was a little closer to a crooner than a shouter, his work still holds up well. Had Pat Boone been this good, he wouldn't have had to go Christian.

The *Legendary Master Series* is a model

of a reissue: excellent graphics and liner notes by Ed Ward say it all. It's not easy to find, though, and unfortunately, all of Nelson's Decca albums, including a pair of pretty good ones—the 1972 *Garden Party,* which contains the title cut, his last hit; and the 1970 *In Concert,* which features some terrific Dylan material—are out of print altogether. The 1977 LP, *Intakes,* is not up to that level, but Nelson is definitely an artist worth hearing, one of rock's lost resources. — D.M.

SANDY NELSON
★★★ **Big Bad Boss Beat** / Orig. Sound 8871
★★★ **Let There Be Drums** / Imper. 10280
In the post-Elvis, pre-Beatles rock world, Sandy Nelson held top rank with the Ventures as an instrumental influence. His axe was drums, and "Teen Beat," his 1959 hit for Original Sound, and "Let There Be Drums," a Top Ten smash for Imperial in 1961, were typically silly instrumentals of the period, which helped prepare an entire generation for such later episodes of ridiculous infatuation with instrumentals as Ginger Baker's Cream solo, "Toad," and the Surfaris' immortal "Wipe Out." Not an entirely benign historical force, but good for a laugh. — D.M.

TRACY NELSON
★★ **Deep Are the Roots** / Prest. 7726
★★ **Homemade Songs** / Fly. Fish 052
★★★ **Poor Man's Paradise** / Col. KC-31759
★★★ **Sweet Soul Music** / MCA 494
★★ **Time Is on My Side** / MCA 2203
As lead vocalist of Mother Earth, Tracy Nelson established herself as an acoustic blues and C&W singer with a large cult following. Members of Mother Earth were mostly from Texas, and steeped in rural tradition; Nelson grew up in Madison, Wisconsin, a college town where she became a folksinger. Together, she and the group made two superb (and long deleted) Mercury albums, *Living with the Animals* (1968) and *Make a Joyful Noise* (1969). But Nelson's solo albums often only suggest, rather than deliver, the full-throated power that has made her so popular.

Deep Are the Roots is a 1965 tribute to Ma Rainey and Bessie Smith. Nelson's strong, stately singing and Charley Musselwhite's fine harp work make it more than a period curio. *Poor Man's Paradise* (1975) encapsulates the country-rocking melancholy Nelson's roving sensibility also embraced in 1975's *Sweet Soul Music,* and 1976's *Time Is on My Side* shows her convincing way with bluesier tunes.

From 1967 to 1971, Nelson enjoyed a tenuous commercial viability, culminating in the fine religious-pastoral suite, *Bring Me Home,* and the deleted albums from that period include some real show-stoppers: "Down So Low," "Soul of the Man," "I Need Your Love So Bad" and "You Win Again" are specimens of her strength and versatility. The available albums are products of a rich but quirky output. But it remains to be seen if Tracy Nelson's sometimes petulant intelligence will overshadow her strengths indefinitely. — F.S.

WILLIE NELSON
★★★ **Columbus Stockade Blues** / Cam. 7018
★★★ **Country Willie** / U. Artists LA410-G
★★★★ **Phases and Stages** / Atl. 7291
★★★ **Shotgun Willie** / Atl. SD-7262
★★★ **Spotlight on Willie Nelson** / Cam. ACL1-0705
★★★★ **Stardust** / Col. JC-35305
★★★ **The Best of Willie Nelson** / U. Artists LA086-G
★★★★★ **Red Headed Stranger** / Col. KC-33482
★★★ **The Sound in Your Mind** / Col. KC-34092
★★★★ **The Troublemaker** / Col. KC-34112
★★★★ **To Lefty from Willie** / Col. KC-34695
★★ **What Can You Do to Me Now** / RCA APL1-1234
★★ **Willie/Before His Time** / RCA APL1-2210
★★★ **Willie Nelson and His Friends** / Plant. 24
★★★ **Willie Nelson Live** / RCA APL1-1487
★★ **Wishing You a Merry Christmas** / RCA ANL1-1952
★★ **Yesterday's Wine** / RCA ANL1-1102
Like many of his peers, Willie Nelson began his career singing in Texas honky-tonks in the late Fifties, before moving on to Nashville in the early part of the next decade, where he quickly acquired a reputation as a versatile country songwriter ("Night Life") and wrote at least one soul standard, "Funny (How Time Slips Away)," as well. Nelson also wrote "Crazy" for Patsy Cline and Faron Young's "Hello Walls." His early recordings—rep-

resented on the United Artists packages, they were originally done for Liberty— were also country hits, although they were a bit too raw for pop tastes. By 1964, Nelson was a fixture in the country establishment, a regular on the Grand Ole Opry and an RCA recording artist. But his talents didn't adapt well to the formula productions then the vogue, and by the early Seventies his dissatisfaction led him back to Texas, where he and Waylon Jennings, among others, spawned the so-called outlaw movement that returned country closer to its roots.

In 1972 Nelson became the first country artist signed to Atlantic Records. *Phases and Stages,* his first release for the label, gave him more latitude artistically than he'd been used to, and he used it well. But the soul- and rock-oriented company didn't really know what to do with him. After a disheartening second LP, *Shotgun Willie,* he moved to Columbia, with enough artistic autonomy to ensure his escape from the clutches of the CBS production pulverizer, Bill Sherrill.

His first Columbia release, *Red Headed Stranger,* was a genuine triumph that immediately brought country up to date with the trends in other forms of popular music. A concept album that owed as much to rock opera as to C&W, *Red Headed Stranger* was moving on several levels: as an allegorical autobiography, a religious parable and a fine country album that featured the hit single, "Blue Eyes Crying in the Rain." Yet while that album had won him a rock following as rabid as his country cult, Nelson hasn't quite been able to match *Red Headed Stranger.* The Columbia albums all have some worthwhile music, and they're far more adventurous than almost any other country records of recent years. But in the end, they seem to prove that even outlaw notions can be regulated and turned into formula. — D.M.

MICHAEL NESMITH
★★★ **And the Hits Just Keep On Comin'** / **Pacif. 116**
★★★ **Compilation** / **Pacif. 106**
★★★ **From a Radio Engine to the Photon Wing** / **Pacif. 107**
★★★ **Pretty Much Your Standard Ranch Stash** / **Pacif. 117**
★★★ **The Prison** / **Pacif. 101**

Nesmith earned his name as a member of the Monkees, but his list of credits is more than enough to dispel the idea that he's as faceless as that band. Besides many of the Monkees' best songs, he also wrote "Different Drum" for the Stone Poneys (Linda Ronstadt's first hit); released a series of critically acclaimed country-rock albums for RCA (all out of print) after leaving the Monkees; and produced albums by Bert Jansch, Linda Hargrove and Ian Matthews. These albums give a good account of Nesmith's performance talents, although his most pompous tendencies coalesce on the concept album, *The Prison,* which is accompanied by a book and was later turned into a stage production. — J.S.

NETWORK
★★ **Network** / **Epic PE-34979**
★★★ **Nightwork** / **Epic JE-35476**

A seven-piece hard-rock band with middleweight credentials (Mike Ricciardella, the drummer and chief writer, came from Barnaby Bye; guitarist Mike Coxton played with the Illusion), Network's first album is screeching keyboard-oriented hard rock. But the second, *Nightwork,* settles down, thanks to better writing, George Bitzner's impressive keyboard work and a nice cover of "Halfway to Paradise." — D.M.

THE NEVILLE BROTHERS
★★★ **The Neville Brothers** / **Cap. ST-11865**

The Nevilles have been among New Orleans' hottest rhythm sections for years, forming the backbone of the Wild Tchoupitoulas, among others. But this album, produced by Allen Toussaint, doesn't quite live up to their potential for drive and fire. Still, Toussaint makes the Nevilles seem a passing fair rock group, which isn't bad at all. — D.M.

THE NEWBEATS
■ **Big Beat Sounds** / **Hick. 122**

★ **Bread and Butter** / Hick. 120
★ **Run Baby Run** / Hick. 128
This Nashville pop-rock trio produced two hits, the title songs of the second and final LPs above, in 1964 to 1965. This kind of average-to-poor stuff makes one wonder about those years being called the "golden age" of rock. (And why, pray the Lord, are all the Newbeats albums and only half of Ray Charles in print?) — D.M.

NEW BIRTH

★★ **Behold (The Mightly Army)** / War. B-3071
★★ **Best of the New Birth** / RCA AHL1-1021
★★ **Birth Day** / RCA ANL1-2145
★★★ **Blind Baby** / Bud. 5636
★ **Love Potion** / War. B-2953
★★ **Reincarnation** / RCA APL1-1801
A self-contained vocal and instrumental group, New Birth has never enjoyed much pop success, and it has scored only sporadically on the R&B charts: "Dream Merchant," on the Buddah album, made it to No. 1 in 1975, and the group enjoyed a few other Top Twenty singles during that period, but never established a real identity. With good reason: the sound wavers from pure MOR (like the Main Ingredient or Fifth Dimension) to a version of soul harmony and straight funk groove. Lacking a really distinctive vocalist, this stuff just never jells. — D.M.

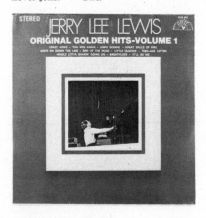

MICKEY NEWBURY

★★★ **Frisco Mabel Joy** / Elek. 74107
★★★ **Heaven Help the Child** / Elek. 75005
★ **His Eye Is on the Sparrow** / ABC 44021
★★★ **I Came to Hear the Music** / Elek. 7E-1007
★★★★ **Live at Montezuma Hall/Looks Like Rain** / Elek. 7E-2007

★★ **Lovers** / Elek. 7E-1030
★★ **Rusty Tracks** / ABC 44002
Newbury is one of the best of the new breed of Nashville singer/songwriters who came into prominence in the Seventies. Like his peers, Newbury specialized at first in writing material for other people—the Kenny Rogers and the First Edition hit, "Just Dropped In (To See What Condition My Conditon Was In)," was his first big break, and since then his material has been covered by people as diverse as Jerry Lee Lewis, Roger Miller, Tom Jones, Pat Boone and Andy Williams. Perhaps Newbury's best-known song since then is "Heaven Help the Child," but his best album is the double LP of a live set recorded at Montezuma Hall coupled with a reissue of his first album, the Jerry Kennedy-produced *Looks Like Rain*. — J.S.

NEW LOST CITY RAMBLERS

★★★ **American Moonshine and Prohibition** / Folk. 5263
★★★ **Depression Songs** / Folk. 5264
★★★ **Modern Times** / Folk. 31067
★★★ **New Lost City Ramblers, Vol. 1** / Folk. 2396
★★★ **New Lost City Ramblers, Vol. 2** / Folk. 2397
★★★ **New Lost City Ramblers, Vol. 3** / Folk. 2398
★★★ **New Lost City Ramblers, Vol. 4** / Folk. 2399
★★★ **New Lost City Ramblers, Vol. 5** / Folk. 2395
★★★ **New Lost City Ramblers** / Folk. 2492
★★★ **"New" New Lost City Ramblers** / Folk. 2491
★★★ **On the Great Divide** / Folk. 31041
★★★ **Remembrance of Things to Come** / Folk. 31035
One of the most important groups of the early Sixties folk revival, the New Lost City Ramblers specialized in old-timey music, the sound of the Appalachian hills, the root stock from which commercial country & western music was developed in the late Twenties. Rather than the standard material developed by the Carter Family and Jimmie Rodgers, however, the Ramblers concentrated on older, less well-known songs that are the Carters' and Rodgers' source points or which were spun off from their reworkings of the tradition. The group was formed in the late Fifties by folklorist Mike Seeger (Pete's brother), who had done field recordings of some of the material; photographer John Cohen;

and mathematician Tom Paley, who left the group in the early Sixties to pursue a teaching career and was replaced by Tracy Schwartz. All of the Ramblers' records are competent, and some of them are very high-spirited; the series, called simply *New Lost City Ramblers*, is the earliest and probably the best of their catalogue. — D.M.

RANDY NEWMAN
★★★★ **Good Old Boys** / Rep. MS4-2193
★★★★ **Little Criminals** / War. K-3079
★★★★ **Randy Newman** / Rep. 6286
★★★★ **Randy Newman Live** / Rep. 6459
★★★★★ **Sail Away** / Rep. 2064
★★★★★ **Twelve Songs** / Rep. 6373

Randy Newman is one of the most eccentric and talented of the late Sixties pop performer/composers, possessed of an unusual melodic sense (derived not only from rock and blues but movie scores of the Thirties and Forties) and a pungently sardonic sense of humor. His first album, *Randy Newman,* was such an oddity when released in 1969 that Reprise attempted to give it away though a series of tongue-in-cheek advertisements. That didn't help much commercially. *Twelve Songs,* which followed in 1970, was even more striking; Newman's sense of humor (in songs like "Suzanne," about an obscene telephone call; "Lucinda," about a girl swept up by a bleach cleaner; and "Mama Told Me Not to Come," later a hit for Three Dog Night, which concerned an improbable orgy attended by a naif) was more fully developed. The pathos he would bring to his best later work also began to emerge ("Let's Burn Down the Cornfield," "If You Need Oil") as his fascination with the South made its first appearance in "My Old Kentucky Home," a sort of backhanded tribute to Stephen Foster, among

other things. But the most engaging aspect of the album is the playing of guitarist Ry Cooder and Newman's ragged-edged singing, which make everything from blues to pop songs fit together perfectly.

Newman has never been prolific, and *Live* was released in 1971 to fill the gap between *Twelve Songs* and *Sail Away*. It's a pleasant exposition of the songs on the first two albums, with a couple of minor additions. *Sail Away* was much more than that, a tour de force of social satire and some of Newman's best music. The title cut was an imaginary voyage on a slave ship, with the ship's captain promising Africans streets paved with gold; "Burn On," a tribute to the polluted Cuyahoga River, Cleveland's famous burning stream; "Dayton, Ohio—1903" an elliptical romance taking place in that town at the time of the Wright brothers' discovery of flight; and a couple of more puerile numbers, "Political Science" ("Let's drop the big one") and "God's Song," in which the Lord appears as a monster who delights in holocaust. Despite slight flaws—those last two songs are a bit obvious, closer to Tom Lehrer than Bob Dylan in their targets and commentary— *Sail Away* is Newman's triumph.

Good Old Boys was Newman's first attempt at a cycle of thematically linked songs, and although it was much more popular than his earlier albums, its success was problematic. It is a series of sketches of the South, including "Rednecks," an imaginary defense of Lester Maddox against "smartass New York Jews," the offensiveness of which is not redeemed by Newman's Jewishness. The humor is exploitative of a region and people Newman comprehends less than well, although a couple of songs are both striking in their imagery and emotionally moving: "Louisiana 1927," about a famous flood; "A Wedding in Cherokee County," about a backwoods marriage to a freak; and the plaintive love song "Marie."

1977's *Little Criminals* contained the hit single, "Short People," which offended plenty of people for the wrong reasons; it typified, however, a strain of smugness and cruelty that had developed in Newman's work. Accompanied by the Eagles and some really gorgeous string arrangements, he whipped his way through a batch of songs that lacked his usual bite, with only a couple of examples of the kind of nonformula pop his fans had come to expect. "Sigmund Freud's Impersonation of Albert Einstein in America" was about the best; it was originally written for the film of E. L. Doctorow's novel *Ragtime*. Nonetheless, *Little Criminals* won Newman a much larger audience than he had previously enjoyed. What he does with it will certainly prove fascinating. — D.M.

THUNDERCLAP NEWMAN
★★★★★ Hollywood Dream / MCA 354
This remarkable one-shot assembled some of the strangest rock & roll minds of the past decade. Produced and recorded by Peter Townshend (who also played bass), the record combines Townshend protégés Andy Newman on piano and horns, Jimmy McCulloch (later of Stone the Crows and Wings) on guitars, and Speedy Keen on drums and vocals. Keen also wrote the songs, some of which are enduring ("The Reason," "Look Around," "Accidents," "Something in the Air"). The band also does a neat cover of an obscure Dylan tune, "Open the Door, Homer." — J.S.

THE NEW RIDERS OF THE PURPLE SAGE
★★★ Adventures of Panama Red / Col. PC-32450
★★★ Best of / Col. PC-34367
★★ Brujo / Col. PC-33145
★★ Gypsy Cowboy / Col. KC-31930
★ Home, Home on the Road / Col. PC-32870
★ Marin County Line / MCA 2307
★ New Riders / MCA 2196
★★★ New Riders of the Purple Sage / Col. PC-30888
★★ Oh What a Mighty Time / Col. PC-33688
★★★ Powerglide / Col. C-31284
★ Who Are Those Guys? / MCA 2248
This band got its start as the Grateful Dead's official warmup group during the Dead's performing heyday in the early Seventies. The Dead fans loved the Riders if only because Jerry Garcia would often sit in on steel guitar. So even though the Riders were a disorganized, second-rate country-rock outfit without a decent lead singer, the band gained instant recognition and a widespread following. The Riders traded off their hippie outlaw image deftly, drawing out their version of the cowboy caricature fairly successfully before running completely out of gas. If you want appropriate background music for rustic keg parties in the wilderness, *NRPS*, *Powerglide* or *Panama Red* will do the trick. Otherwise, the New Riders are guaranteed to put you to sleep. — J.S.

NEW ROTARY CONNECTION
■ Hey Love / Cadet 50006
After Minnie Riperton left, so did the amusement. — D.M.

THE NEW SEEKERS
★ Best of the New Seekers / Elek. EQ-5051
The kind of pop group that would turn a Coca-Cola commercial ("I'd Like to Teach the World to Sing") into an international hit. Yecch. — D.M.

JUICE NEWTON AND THE SILVER SPUR
★ Come to Me / Cap. ST-11682
★ Well Kept Secret / Cap. SW-11811
Boring rock band fronted by an emotionally empty female singer who leads them where even fools would fear to tread, most nobably into a rotten version of Bob Segar's "Fire Down Below," on *Come to Me*. — D.M.

OLIVIA NEWTON-JOHN
■ Clearly Love / MCA 3015
■ Come On Over / MCA 3016
■ Don't Stop Believin' / MCA 3017
■ Have You Never Been Mellow / MCA 3014
■ If You Love Me, Let Me Know / MCA 3013
■ Let Me Be There / MCA 3012
■ Making a Good Thing Better / MCA 3018
■ Olivia Newton-John's Greatest Hits / MCA 3028
★ Totally Hot / MCA 3067
Not only does this Australian country-pop singer possess the blank, open face of a Barbie doll, she also has what the French call *une voix chuchotante mannequinée*,

which means (roughly) "a whispering fashion model voice" and denotes the kind of model turned pop singer—of which Twiggy is another example—who is a proliferous species in Europe. Each of Newton-John's hit singles—"If You Love Me, Let Me Know," "Have You Never Been Mellow," "Let Me Be There," and a blasé reading of Dylan's "If Not for You" are the most notorious—has made her place on the throne of the dude ranch/ski lodge subgenre of Seventies mass-market pap more secure. These albums are almost indistinguishable from one another: you have only to buy one to know if you need music to go with your marshmallow sundaes. — B.T.

NEW YORK CITY
★★★ **Soulful Road / Chel. 500**
Producer Thom Bell gave this group a hit in 1973 with "I'm Doin' Fine Now." *Soulful Road* is the follow-up album and Bell's last production of this minor group. At the time of the LP's release, many described the songs as leftovers from a Spinners session. (Now deleted.) — J.MC.

THE NEW YORK DOLLS
★★★ **New York Dolls / Mer. SRM-1-675**
★★★ **Too Much Too Soon / Mer. SRM-1-1001**
If there was ever a band before its time, it was the New York Dolls, the early Seventies precursors of the punk scene. Caught between the glitter and punk eras, the Dolls squawked out hard rock that most often recalled the Stones and MC5, though they also had clear, if sonically obscure, R&B roots. Their debut, while featuring such standouts as "Looking for a Kiss" and "Personality Crisis," was marred by Todd Rundgren's heavy production hand. Shadow Morton had a tighter grasp on *Too Much Too Soon,* and the result was a frenetic attack. The unlikely highlight was a cover of Archie Bell and the Drells' "There's Gonna Be a Showdown." With singer David Johansen pouting out the song like an adolescent Mick Jagger, the title of the album told it all. (Now deleted.) — J.B.M.

NEW YORK MARY
★ **A Piece of the Apple / Ari./Free 1035**
★★★ **New York Mary / Ari./Free 1019**
A tight jazz-funk horn band in the style of the Brecker Brothers, but not as strong conceptually or improvisationally (which is not necessarily something to be ashamed

of). The debut album, *New York Mary,* avoids clichés, but *Piece* wallows in 'em. — M.R.

THE NEW YORK ROCK ENSEMBLE
★★★★ **Roll Over / Col. 30033**
This is the group that made its name by wearing tuxedos, playing society gigs and trying to adapt Bach to rock. They failed miserably at all that overblown stuff, then went out and made this tremendous rock & roll album. "Running Down the Highway," "Anaconda" and "Field of Joy" are all top-notch songs, and the band plays with good taste and fire. — J.S.

THE NICE
★★ **Elegy / Mer. SRM-1-61324**
The Nice began life as a backup quartet for British singer P. P. Arnold, whom they often upstaged with their showmanship. Two of the members, keyboardist Keith Emerson and drummer Brian Davison, had been part of Gary Farr and the T-Bones, an early British R&B act. Guitarist David O'List was in the original Roxy Music, although he left before they made their first LP, while bassist Lee Jackson and Davison later appeared in Jackson Heights and Refugee, respectively. Emerson, of course, went on to Emerson, Lake and Palmer.

Nice's approach was more similar to ELP than any of the rest: they revamped jazz and classical themes with a heavy rock bias. The group's most famous numbers were evergreens like "Rondo" and "America" (from *West Side Story*), which gave Emerson all the room he needed for his flamboyant antics. Unfortunately, the group's most representative recordings were made for Andrew Loog Oldham's now-defunct Immediate label, and the Mercury set that's left in print hardly does Nice justice. *Elegy* features awkward covers of Bob Dylan and Tim Hardin songs and a peculiarly weak rendition of the once spirited "America." The key to the future—Emerson's anyway—is a horribly simplistic and colorless Tchaikovsky adaptation. (Now deleted.) — D.M.

MAXINE NIGHTINGALE
★★ **Night Life / U. Artists LA731-G**
★★★ **Right Back Where We Started From / U. Artists LA626-G**
"Right Back Where We Started From" was one of the most infectious hits of 1976, the best sort of pop R&B. Recorded in England, it is Nightingale's sole first-rate song. The rest of the album named for it,

as well as *Night Life,* the 1977 followup, is conventional and unexplosive. — D.M.

JOHN JACOB NILES
★★★★ John Jacob Niles Sings Folk
  Songs / Folk. 2373
★★ The Best of John Jacob Niles / Trad.
  2055

Crossing Kentucky mountain tradition with a vocal style that is reminiscent of Elizabethan balladeers, Niles was a concert artist performing folk songs some fifty years before the genre came into vogue. As a composer he is responsible for "I Wonder as I Wander," "Go 'Way from My Window" and the popular melody for "Black Is the Color of My True Love's Hair." His high tenor is magnificently captured on "I'm So Glad Trouble Don't Last Always," from the Folkways set (mostly reissues of 78 material). Joan Baez is probably the most prominent recorded practitioner of this style of folk interpretation. — I.M.

HARRY NILSSON
★★ Aerial Ballet / RCA AFL1-3956
★★ A Little Touch of Schmilsson in the
  Night / RCA AFL1-0097
★ Early Tymes / Sp. 4099
★★ Harry / RCA AFL1-4197
★★ Knnillssonn / RCA AFL1-2276
★★★★ Nilsson/Greatest Hits / RCA
  AFL1-2798
★★★★ Nilsson Schmilsson / RCA
  AFL1-4515
★★★★ Pussy Cats / RCA CPL1-0570
★★ Son of Schmilsson / RCA AFL1-4717
★★ . . . That's the Way It Is / RCA
  APL1-1119
★★★ The Point / RCA LSP-4417
★★ The World's Greatest Lover / RCA
  ABL1-2709

Aerial Ballet and *Harry,* art-pop songwriter Harry Nilsson's first two albums, display him as a whimsical moralist who made music so wry it forced either smiles or grimaces; the principal instrument was his soft, high, perfectly pitched voice, while the imagery in his lyrics was cleverly domestic. Lots of aging urban folkies enjoyed these early-Seventies recordings, because they seemed sensibly progressive: traditional songwriting tastefully orchestrated. On his second album, Nilsson covered Randy Newman's "Simon Smith and the Amazing Dancing Bear," to this day the most chirpily soup-headed song Newman's written. When *Nilsson Sings Newman* (now incomprehensibly out of print) followed, it

seemed clear what Nilsson was aiming for: mass success achieved by deleting the bitterness from Newman's odd melodies and impeccable wordplay.

The Point, the soundtrack of a television cartoon, further embedded Nilsson's cuteness. *Nilsson Schmilsson,* however, was his artistic breakthrough: where once his songs had been shy and chiding when they wanted to criticize ("Don't Leave Me," "Together," "I Guess the Lord Must Be in New York City"), here he decided to rock out, with all the energy and passion without prettiness that phrase implies. He hadn't totally abandoned the lovely lilting, but in a dreamy confection like "The Moonbeam Song," he inserted one word— "crap"—that made the whole thing work, both as a good song and a good MOR parody.

Son of Schmilsson is a clutch of unbearably clever and/or willfully cheesy outtake *manqués,* while *A Little Touch* is the opposite: a numbingly careful rendering of smooth crooning in styles and songs of the Twenties, Thirties and Forties. To make it authentic, Nilsson used orchestrator/arranger Gordon Jenkins, who has performed the same tasks for Sinatra, Garland, Nat Cole and others. Given what had just preceded it, *A Little Touch* was bizarre: Was Nilsson serious? Was it camp? Was it a monumental sneer? Or a repentance? But the album was too cool and slick to make such questions interesting.

There ensued a two-year silence, during which Nilsson lived out the slob Schmilsson persona; according to the headlines, he was always ready to carouse with new pals John Lennon and Ringo Starr. (He had first received attention because the debut album had some Paul McCartney soundalikes that were shocking in their verisimilitude.) He thrashed back with the Lennon-produced *Pussy Cats,* which, in its limning of rock agony and absurdity, finds equals only in Lennon's own *Plastic Ono Band* and Neil Young's *Tonight's the Night.* An assemblage of offbeat covers ("Loop de Loop," "Subterranean Homesick Blues," "Rock around the Clock"), *Pussy Cats* is inspiring in its rage and heartbreaking in its cheerfulness. For someone who's never fully achieved stardom, Harry Nilsson knows and articulates more about it than almost anyone in rock.

That's the Way It is is another burp from the dyspepsia that resulted in *Pussy Cats,* but it lacks the discipline that made *Cats* so scarily anarchic, the firmness that's essential to portraying a person out of control. Nilsson has become a whimsical amoralist, an artist who cannot find salvation or even much comfort in his art unless he is savaging it. All that prevents him from becoming an L.A. Artaud is his small protests: he likes to sleep late, he doesn't like to shave and he's almost proudly lazy. — K.T.

NITTY GRITTY DIRT BAND
★ ★ **All the Good Times** / U. Artists
UAS-5553
★ ★ ★ **Dirt, Silver and Gold** / U. Artists
LA670-13
★ ★ **Dream** / U. Artists LA469-G
★ ★ **Stars and Stripes Forever** / U. Artists
LA184-J2
★ ★ **The Dirt Band** / U. Artists LA854-H
★ ★ **Uncle Charlie and His Dog Teddy** /
Lib. LST-7642
★ ★ ★ ★ **Will the Circle Be** Unbroken /
U. Artists UAS-9801

Unlike other country-rock groups (Poco or even the Eagles) who merely added country trappings to their light rock & roll, the Nitty Gritty Dirt Band began with a firmer commitment to bluegrass and rural C&W, blending in the electrified accouterments of rock. Formed in Long Beach, California, in 1965, the group has an underlying musical focus that's helped keep the Dirt Band (as it is now called) together through myriad personnel changes (Jackson Browne is one of many one-time group members) and ever-changing musical climates.

The Dirt Band's first album, *The Nitty Gritty Dirt Band,* yielded a hit single, "Buy for Me the Rain," by far their most middle-of-the-road 45. But that album, as well as their next three, are no longer available, leaving 1970's *Uncle Charlie and His Dog Teddy* to begin the story. *Uncle Charlie* demonstrated the band's savvy for picking material by up-and-coming songwriters. No less than three hit singles were culled from it: Michael Nesmith's "Some of Shelley's Blues," Kenny Loggins' "House at Pooh Corner" and the million-selling version of Jerry Jeff Walker's "Mr. Bojangles."

But it was not until the band moved from Los Angeles to Aspen, Colorado, that its identity became fixed and its albums began to gain a consistency of forethought and execution. *All the Good Times* (parts of which were recorded live) reflected not only the Dirt Band's new rural roots but also its affinity for modernized corn-pone

humor. That album also produced the last thing even approaching a hit single for the band, a swinging version of Hank Williams' "Jambalaya." The Dirt Band's acknowledged masterstroke, however, came in 1972. *Will the Circle Be Unbroken,* a three-record set, brought together three generations of musical Americana in a well-conceived, ornately packaged supersession. Traditional classics such as "Keep on the Sunny Side," "Orange Blossom Special" and "I Saw the Light" are performed with relish by country institutions like Mother Maybelle Carter, Earl Scruggs, Doc Watson, Roy Acuff, Merle Travis and Vassar Clements.

By their next album, *Stars and Stripes Forever* (1974), the group was whittled down to a quartet (Jeff Hanna, John McEuen, Jim Ibbotson and Jimmie Fadden), and managed to represent its live show on two records. But this was a less successful attempt to sum up the band's career than the subsequent hits LP, *Dirt, Silver and Gold* (1976), another three-record set, this one including early hits, unreleased masters and some new material. Between those two compilations was a single album, *Dream* (1975), which stands as the band's last attempt to remain faithful to its bluegrass and country roots, including the obligatory Hank Williams song ("Hey Good Lookin'," with Linda Ronstadt on vocals) and an almost-hit version of the Everly Brothers' "(All I Have to Do Is) Dream."

On the surface, it would seem that the Dirt Band finally gave in to commercial pressures on its latest album, simply entitled *The Dirt Band.* It was a six-man band by now, with Jim Ibbotson exiting and Merle Bregante, Al Garth (both of Loggins and Messina's band) and Richard Hathaway entering the fold. The LP is more song-oriented than its predecessors, and bluegrass influences give way to supplemental horns and strings, and to speculation that the Dirt Band is on the verge of a new era. — G.K.

NO DICE
★ ★ ★ **No Dice** / Cap. ST-11733
Although the cover shows the band members posing as punks, this 1978 album by a young British band owes more to the relentless riffing of recent Rolling Stones–style music. Which is just fine. No Dice's blues-based hard rock was one of the year's most convincing mainstream debuts. — D.M.

NOTATIONS
★★★★ Notations / Gemigo 5501
A varied, intelligent and fun album from a
veteran second-line Chicago soul quartet.
Despite several moderately big soul hits,
this album was unjustly ignored when released. Producers include the Chuck Jack-
son/Marvin Yancy team. (Now deleted.) — J.MC.

THE NOT READY FOR PRIME TIME PLAYERS
★★★ Saturday Night Live / Ari. 4107
This is the gang from NBC's TV show—
including John Belushi in a nonsinging
performance, Gilda Radner doing her most
celebrated characters and the rest filling in
with more imagination than almost anyone
else recording comedy LPs in 1977. You'll
probably recognize most of the bits from
the show—Chevy Chase doing Gerald
Ford, a great Lily Tomlin monologue,
some "Weekend Update" material and, of
course, the marvelous "News for the Hard
of Hearing." Not as good as the show—
you need a video disc for that. But not
bad. — D.M.

NOVA
★★★ Sun City / Ari. 4203
★★★ Vimania / Ari. 4110
★★★ Wings of Love / Ari. 4150
An Italian band influenced by the Maha-
vishnu Orchestra's acoustic stylings,
Wayne Shorter's soprano sax attack, and
British art-rock vocalizing. The resultant
fusion is airy and pleasant, and on *Vima-
nia,* guest drummer Narada Michael Wal-
den pushes things incisively and contrib-
utes a catchy chart. — M.R.

NRBQ
★★★ NRBQ at Yankee Stadium / Mer.
SRM-1-3712
The initials originally stood for New
Rhythm and Blues Quartet, but in fact
these funky New York street guys play a
mix of jazz and rock that swings and bops
pretty hard, with a quirky sense of humor
of the Michael Hurley variety. NRBQ
made a series of Columbia albums, all now
out of print, that are worth investigating,
but this 1978 set is fine as well, in a modest
way. — D.M.

TED NUGENT
★★★★ Cat Scratch Fever / Epic
JE-34700
★★★★ Double Live Gonzo! / Epic 35069
★★★ Free-for-All / Epic PE-34121

★★ Marriage on the Rocks/Rock Bottom / Poly. 6073
★★★ Ted Nugent / Epic PE-33692
★★★ Ted Nugent and the Amboy Dukes /
Main. 421
★★★ Weekend Warriors / Epic FE-35551
Ted Nugent has been recording since the
mid-Sixties, when his Detroit-based band,
the Amboy Dukes, had hits with a version
of "Baby Please Don't Go" and their own
quasi-psychedelic "Journey to the Center
of the Mind." The original Dukes were a
well-balanced rock band, typical of the
time, with a decent singer, sloppy drummer
and a half-inspired guitarist in Nugent.
Subsequent editions of the group (the first
recorded for Mainstream; later, they made
discs for Polydor and Warner Bros.) leaned
more and more heavily on Nugent, a real
wild man who viewed everything as a
background for his undisciplined excursions into Jimi Hendrix fantasyland.
It wasn't until Nugent reached Epic
Records and producers Tom Werman and
Lou Futterman that he achieved some focus for his sheets of notes and piles of
chords. Nugent is a formidable stylist in
the heavy metal/psychedelic styles of the
late Sixties and early Seventies. But if it
weren't for his carnivorous and hysterical
showmanship—and his unrestrained boast-
fulness about his alleged talents—he'd
probably seem more old-fashioned than
celebrated. As it is, he has become a star
by making albums that capture all the
frenzy of a convention of armed lunatics.
Nugent's demeanor is not inspired by
drugs, but by sex and, he says, hunting—
his blood lust and skills with rifle and bow
and arrow are legendary. Oddly enough,
this out-of-control image matches his playing so perfectly that his best records are his
most recent, particularly the 1978 *Double
Live Gonzo!,* which also serves as an
excellent historical retrospective of his
career. — D.M.

NUTZ
★★ Hard Nutz / A&M SP-4623
★★ Nutz / A&M SP-3648
Yet another English hard-rock quartet:
heavy rhythm section, standardized riffs,
gritty vocals. Instrumentally competent but
unnecessary unless you plan to collect the
whole set of 1,001 British boogie
bands. — A.N.

LAURA NYRO
★★★ Christmas and the Beads of Sweat /
Col. PC-30259

★★★★ **Eli and the Thirteenth Confession / Col. PC-9626**
★★★★ **Gonna Take a Miracle / Col. PC-30987**
★★ **Nested / Col. JC-35449**
★★★ **New York Tendaberry / Col. PC-9737**
★★ **Season of Lights / Col. PC-34786**
★★ **Smile / Col. PC-33912**
★★★ **The First Songs / Col. C-31410**
Laura Nyro was the hottest American songwriter in the pop and pop-R&B fields for a period in the late Sixties and early Seventies. She wrote "Stoney End" for Barbra Streisand; "Stoned Soul Picnic," "Sweet Blindness" and "Wedding Bell Blues" for the Fifth Dimension; and Blood, Sweat and Tears' "And When I Die." But her own performances were not as well received: booed off the stage at the Monterey Pop Festival in 1967, she has never recovered, and remains one of the current music scene's most sheltered and enigmatic figures.

Nyro has certain problems—a tendency to be both obtuse and precious, platitudinous and opaque—but of all the American singer/songwriters of her era, she is certainly the most soulful. Her best records—*Eli*, *The First Songs* and the collaboration with Labelle, *Gonna Take a Miracle*—fuse rock and poetry with far more conviction and emotional honesty than, say, Patti Smith.

After *Miracle* was released in late 1971, Nyro did not record or make public appearances again until late 1975, when *Smile* appeared. Nyro still sounded about the same, but in many ways that simply meant that she was outdated, and she has not regained her large cult or expanded it into anything like mass success with the relatively mediocre LPs that have followed. — D.M.

PHIL OCHS

★★ **All the News That's Fit to Sing / Elek. 7269**

★★★ **I Ain't a'Marchin' Anymore / Elek. 7287**

★★★★ **Phil Ochs in Concert / Elek. 79184**

As a former journalism student, Phil Ochs' decision to become a "topical" songwriter was appropriate. He started off in the Sixties as an imitator of Bob Gibson, more out of convenience than any sense of tradition. By the time he recorded his first album, he was already staking out his special territory, a kind of Romantic New Left patriotism.

Despite the fast-fingered playing of Danny Kalb (later lead guitarist for the Blues Project), *All the News That's Fit to Sing* is rather drab, aside from Ochs' emulation of Woody Guthrie, "The Power and the Glory" and an inspired adaptation of Edgar Allan Poe's "The Bells." On *I Ain't a'Marchin'*, Ochs' second album and solo this time, he hits his stride; the John Kennedy assassination and the escalation of the Vietnam War created an ethos of patriotic concern and protest in which Ochs worked best. "Draft Dodger Rag" and "I Ain't a'Marchin' Anymore" became antiwar theme songs, while "Here's to the State of Mississippi" and "In the Heat of the Summer" show just how much passion Ochs could bring to the topical song.

On *Phil Ochs in Concert,* Ochs delivers his strongest collection of protest songs, but his voice—freed of the restraints of folk-music vocals—soars away from the melodies into dramatic phrasing. The influence of Bob Dylan, moreover, prompted Ochs to pen several slightly "abstract" political songs like "There But for Fortune" (a hit single for Joan Baez), "Canons of Christianity" and his first major narrative works, "The Ringing of Revolution" and

"Santo Domingo," both of which are still amazingly moving. Although *In Concert* offers his most advanced collection of protest songs, and the most droll between-song remarks ever recorded by anyone, it was the lone love song, "Changes," which caught the most attention.

★★★ **Chords of Fame / A&M 4599**

★★★ **Pleasures of the Harbor / A&M 4133**

★★★★ **Rehearsals for Retirement / A&M 4181**

★★★ **Tape from California / A&M 4148**

Ochs' *Pleasures of the Harbor* was an all-too-grand attempt to create his own *Blonde on Blonde* and become a major songwriter/poet. If Dylan could create a successful song cycle by drawing on the poetics of Verlaine and Rimbaud, then Ochs could pursue Keats and Byron and the music of the nineteenth-century art song. While they may work well enough as baroque meditations on idealism (in concert they did), "Cross My Heart," "I've Had Her," "Pleasures of the Harbor" and "Flower Lady" sink into a slow melodrama with their Mozart-like piano awash in dense strings. The most intriguing song on the album is "Crucifixion," which is a mythic narrative about the politics of assassination from Christ to Kennedy.

However much Ochs wanted to be the songwriter/poet, *Pleasures* attains its special charm through three comedy songs, "The Party," "Miranda" and the celebrated "Small Circle of Friends," with which his public reputation is forever linked. The arrangements here, unlike the "exalted" serious songs, played Dixieland and cocktail-piano stylings off Ochs' splendidly deadpan vocals.

The opening title track of *Tape from California* is Ochs' first, and quite successful, foray into rock & roll, helped by producer Van Dyke Parks. Then there is the straight folkie "Joe Hill," an autobiographical ballad and two beautifully martial antiwar songs, the last of which, "The War Is Over," was Ochs' most eccentric contribution to the mounting antiwar movement. The second side opens and closes with two very bad songs, "The Harder They Fall," based on elaborate puns, and a shy return to the themes of *Pleasures,* "The Floods of Florence." The centerpiece, however, is Ochs' explosive answer to Dylan's "Desolation Row"—"When in Rome." The song does nothing less than symbolically rewrite the entire history of the United States as a chaotic and apocalyptic epic, with Ochs playing all the lead parts in the first person. Performed solo, it marks the early stages of Ochs' personal disintegration, and it's brilliant.

The madness really breaks out on *Rehearsals for Retirement,* Ochs' bitter and extraordinary self-examination as a Sixties American hero. The Chicago Democratic Convention was a trauma from which Ochs, ever the sentimental patriot, never quite recovered. "My Life" closes the album like a door slamming on a cell, and not even the wit of "Where Were You in Chicago" defuses the scorched depression of the rest.

Rehearsals has all the marks of an epitaph, but it is here that Ochs' wit, politics and poetic intentions ultimately meet and their vehicle is rock & roll, scruffily produced by Larry Parks. On this album, Ochs actually succeeds in becoming an American Romantic, a scarred veteran of the Sixties with his soul still intact.

However, his psyche was shot, and his next project, an exploration of Americana, floundered on *Greatest Hits* (deleted). Van Dyke Parks' arrangements are too heavy, and the rapid decay of Ochs' writing, now that his political demons had departed to leave only anomie, brought the album down to numb sentimentality.

Released only in Canada, *Shoot Out at Carnegie Hall* (A&M SP-9010) was Ochs' last gesture. Dressed in gold lamé and backed by a band (made up of the *Rehearsals* crew), he sang his best songs, "Okie from Muskogee" and medleys of Elvis Presley and Buddy Holly hits. Much of this material, but not the medleys, can be found on *Chords of Fame,* an anthology released after Ochs' suicide and distinguished by the alternate versions of sensual songs, including a march-band single of "Power and Glory," the live solo version of "Cru-

cifixion" and the madcap singles (with Paul Rothchild producing) of songs from his first two albums. — B.T.

ODETTA
★ **Odetta at the Gate of Horn** / Trad. 1025
★★★ **The Essential Odetta** / Van. VSD-43/44

Odetta is one of the most powerful folksong stylists this country has produced. That her numerous recordings—some solo, some with rhythm section and some attempting folk rock, most out of print—have never aired the emotional intensity she reaches in live performance is sad. Perhaps a video disc would show her to better effect.

Odetta at the Gate of Horn is not the live album for which one would have hoped, and her voice matured considerably after the LP was made. *The Essential* was compiled from Carnegie Hall and Town Hall concerts, and because it's two discs long, it is more representative of her repertoire. — I.M.

ODYSSEY
★ **Hollywood Party Tonight** / RCA AFL1-3031
★★★ **Odyssey** / RCA AFL1-2204

"Native New Yorker" and "Weekend Lover," Top Forty hits for this two-man, three-woman black singing group in 1978, were both very much in the spirit of early Motown—cheery, soulful pop. Unfortunately, *Hollywood Party Tonight* tries to follow disco trends; it is simply inept. — D.M.

MICHAEL O'GARA
★ **Michael O'Gara** / Lon. PS-660
London Records called him *"the* poet of 1975." Even Rod McKuen did not tremble, much less real poets. As for music . . . pffft. — D.M.

OHIO PLAYERS
★ **Angel** / Mer. SRM-1-3701
★★ **Best of the Ohio Players Early Years, Vol. 1** / Westb. 304
★★★ **Contradiction** / Mer. SRM-1-1088
★★★★ **Fire** / Mer. SRM-1-1013
★★ **Honey** / Mer. SRM-1-1038
★★ **Jass-Ay-Lay-Dee** / Mer. SRM-1-3730
★★ **Mr. Mean** / Mer. SRM-1-3707
★★ **Ohio Players** / Cap. SM-11291
★★ **Ohio Players** / Trip X-3506
★★ **Ohio Players** / Up Fr. 167
★★★★ **Ohio Players Gold** / Mer. SRM-1-1122
★★★ **16 Greatest Hits** / Trip TOP-16-23

Dayton, Ohio's answer to the bizarre, post-Sly Stone funk of Parliament/Funkadelic. Formed in the early Seventies by reedman Clarence "Satch" Satchell, the band recorded a couple of inconsequential albums for Westbound Records, *Pain* and *Pleasure* (now out of print), known as much for the bondage cover art as for the music inside. The band's first hit single, a monotonous vamp called "Funky Worm," remains in print on the *Best of the Early Years* collection. When the Players switched to Mercury Records and adopted a more overtly Sly Stone-influenced style, immediate mass success followed. "Skin Tight" and "Fire" kicked off a series of monster R&B hits. Eventually, the band ran out of hooks and degenerated into just another grinding wheel. *Fire* and the Mercury *Gold* collection present the group at its best. — J.S.

THE O'JAYS
★★★★★ Back Stabbers / Phil. ZX-31712
★★★★ Family Reunion / Phil. PZ-33807
★★ Live in London / Phil. KZ-32953
★★★ Message in the Music / Phil.
    PZ-34245
★★★ O'Jays Collector's Items / Phil.
    PZG-35024
★★★★ Ship Ahoy / Phil. KZ-32408
★★★ So Full of Love / Phil. JZ-35355
★★★ Survival / Phil. KZ-33150
★★★ The O'Jays / Up Fr. 168
★★★ The O'Jays in Philadelphia / Phil.
    KZ-32120
★★★ Travelin' at the Speed of Thought /
    Phil. PZ-34684
The O'Jays were probably the most faceless of all the groups who were the tools of Philadelphia soul producers Kenny Gamble and Leon Huff, but they have also been the most consistently successful, beginning

with a string of R&B hits including "Lipstick Traces" (1965) and "I'll Be Sweeter Tomorrow" (1967), which are repackaged on the Up Front collection along with similar R&B hits of the period.

Their early-Seventies recordings for Gamble and Huff's Neptune label (collected on *In Philadelphia*) reached much the same audience, but it was their 1972 hits "Back Stabbers" and "992 Arguments" (from *Back Stabbers*) that set the tone for the Philly International success story. Growling vocals rode on top of huge, complex productions that antedate disco but pick up on many of the seminal components of that sound, particularly the drums, which are mixed ever louder on succeeding releases. The group's string of singles successes has continued virtually unabated— "Love Train" and "Put Your Hands Together" in 1973, "For the Love of Money" in 1974, "I Love Music" in 1975 and so on.

The group's albums have been consistently danceable and the singing is always powerful, although recent LPs (you can tell which ones from the titles) have succumbed somewhat to the specious quasi-mystical preaching of Gamble and Huff, who seem to have decided that disco is also the ideal medium for a kind of elusive spiritualism that smacks of the hippie rhetoric prevalent among Sixties white rock bands. None of this mars, however, the really awesome power of the best O'Jays music; *Back Stabbers* ranks with the best albums released in any genre in the past decade. — D.M.

DANNY O'KEEFE
★ American Roulette / War. B-3050
★★ Breezy Stories / Atco 7264
★★★ Danny O'Keefe / Coti. 9036
★ So Long Harry Truman / Atco 18125
Erratic singer/songwriter whose moment of glory, "Good Time Charlie's Got the Blues" (from *Danny O'Keefe*), was more than enough to base a career on. — J.S.

OKLAHOMA
★★ Oklahoma / Cap. ST-11646
Small-time boys remain small-time. — D.M.

OLD AND IN THE WAY
★★★★ Old And In The Way / Round 103
This live string band recording (from the Boarding House in San Francisco in 1973) is a treat. Old And In The Way was best known for presenting Grateful Dead guitarist Jerry Garcia in a nonelectric context.

Though this was a convenient promotional hook, Garcia didn't really lead the band. Instead he played banjo and sang harmony vocals along with David Grisman, who added his excellent mandolin playing to the ensemble as well. Guitarist/vocalist Peter Rowan fronted the band and contributed its two liveliest songs, "Midnight Moonlight" and "Panama Red." John Kahn played string bass, and bluegrass violin virtuoso Vassar Clements put on the finishing touches as featured soloist (his break on "Midnight Moonlight" is terrific). — J.S.

MIKE OLDFIELD
★★ **Ommadawn** / Virgin PZ-33913
★★ **Tubular Bells** / Virgin PR-13116
Oldfield, who had played bass and lead guitar in Kevin Ayers' band, was Virgin's first artist in 1973, and *Tubular Bells,* an ambitious fifty-minute composition, was an immediate success in Britain. The album consists of short, uncompelling melodies—based on rock, classical and British folk themes—repeated over and over at sluggish tempos, with various instruments (mostly fretted or keyboard) playing the same part. It's simplistic, monotonous and far too long, but fragmented into a 45 and released as the theme song from the film *The Exorcist,* it also became a pop smash in America.

The followup, *Hergest Ridge* (now deleted), was similar, although it emphasized the folk derivation and offered more colorful and pastoral textures and phrases. But *Ommadawn* capitalized on its predecessor's improvements, and added livelier, more forceful playing, as well as more catchy phrases. Still, it lacks sufficient imagination to sustain the composition over an entire LP. — D.M.

NIGEL OLSSON
★★ **Nigel Olsson** / Col. JC-35048
★★ **Nigel Olsson** / R. PIG-2158
Highly orchestrated, lushly produced, tuneful AM pop. A surprisingly expressive singer, Elton John's former drummer chooses good material, but the backup is too predictable, sugary and safe. — C.W.

OLYMPIC RUNNERS
★★ **Don't Let Up** / Lon. PS-668
★★ **Hot to Trot** / Lon. PS-678
Mitch Mitchell and Ric Grech once planned a supergroup that would have featured themselves and a guitarist they'd discovered, Joe Jammer. That plan fizzled,

but Jammer went on to form the Olympic Runners, with Pete Wingfield (former Keef Hartley, Van Morrison, Colin Blunstone and Maggie Bell keyboardist). The format was transcendent disco. but it was sustained only for the group's first two albums, *Put the Music Where Your Mouth Is* and *Out-in-Front,* both of which London has deleted. What's left doesn't have the hot playing, although it does contain samples of Jammer's artfully Spartan guitar jabbing. Wingfield left to go solo, and made the 1976 hit, "Eighteen with a Bullet," in a vein similar to the Runners' early work. — B.M.

OMEGA
★★ **Omega** / Pass. 98007
For everyone who'd like to grow up to be a synthesizer. — D.M.

OPEN WINDOW
★ **Open Window** / Van. 6515
Folk rock with tired blood. (Now deleted.) — D.M.

ROY ORBISON
★★★★★ **All-Time Greatest Hits** / Monu. MP-8600
★★★ **Golden Hits** / Buckboard BBS-1015
★★★ **Greatest Hits** / Monu. MC-6619
★★★★ **In Dreams** / Monu. MC-6620
★★★ **More of Roy Orbison's Greatest Hits** / Monu. MC-6621
★★★ **Regeneration** / Monu. MG-7600
★★★ **The Original Sound of Roy Orbison** / Sun 113
★★★★ **Very Best of Roy Orbison** / Monu. MC-6622
Roy Orbison was one of the most singular rock stylists of the Fifties and Sixties; his string of hits is full of maundering, literally paranoiac self-pity, redeemed time and

again by the extraordinary power of his quavering voice and the eccentric dynamism of the musical arrangements, which range from hard-edged rock & roll to the plushest ballads.

At Sun in the Fifties, Orbison was a journeyman rockabilly, heavily influenced by Elvis Presley both as a writer and as a singer. His hits were minor—"Rock House" and "Ooby Dooby" have lasted—but he occasionally came up with a track of gripping proportions: "Domino" features surf-style guitar five years too soon, while "Devil Doll" sets the stage for his truly major accomplishments of the next decade.

When he moved to Monument, where he was produced by Frank Foster, Orbison's style quickly divided into two parts: On the one hand, there was the nearly snarling blues/country shouter, whose quintessential movement comes with the seductive snarl on "Oh Pretty Woman." That song, and others like it, including "Mean Woman Blues" and "Candy Man," had a fair share of influence on the Beatles (who toured with him) and the rest of British rock & roll.

But Orbison's most fascinating records are chronicles of deep lust and even deeper fear: "Running Scared," "Love Hurts," "Only the Lonely"—these titles tell the story. In "Running Scared," the music builds from a whisper to a scream as Orbison recites an ultimate paranoid fantasy, imagining what might happen if his girl *possibly* saw someone who *might* attract her more than him, an anxiety rendered completely ironic because at the end he imagines that she doesn't. In general, these records were accompanied by the same surging Nashville rhythm section used for the other songs, but often abetted by female choruses and usually using strings to accentuate the rhythm. Only Phil Spector came close to this orchestral style of music, and only Spector matched Orbison's paranoia.

The Buckboard and Sun compilations are of the material Orbison did for Sun in the Fifties, including the hits "Ooby Dooby" and "Rock House." The Monument *All-Time* is one of rock's more indispensable anthologies—its two records contain all the hits and a fair share of other oddities ("Leah" and "Shadaroba" reveal an unlikely bent for Orientalism). *Very Best* is a good one-disc sampling of the hits, while the other Monuments have been rendered redundant. The exception is *Regen-*

eration, the 1977 album that reunited Orbison and producer Frank Foster; it's less inspired than competent, but it is also always listenable. — D.M.

ORCHESTRA LUNA
★★ **Orchestra Luna / Epic KE-33166**
Excellent, varied composing with the flair and catchiness of a Broadway score. Randy Roos' inspired guitar is fleet and frequently jazz tinged. But the singing is too theatrical for rock; the narrations and orchestrations detract. Interesting and unusual, but fey and uneven, even for American art rock of the mid-Seventies. (Now deleted.) — C.W.

THE ORIGINALS
★★ **Another Time, Another Place / Fan. 9546**
★★ **Come Away with Me / Fan. 9577**
★★ **Down to Love Town / Soul S7-749**
The Originals have recorded two classic records, "The Bells," and "Baby I'm for Real," both produced by Marvin Gaye. Sad to say, neither are in print (except perhaps on collection albums) and these albums don't do the group justice. Without Gaye's guidance, the Originals lack distinctive personality and direction. — J.MC.

TONY ORLANDO AND DAWN
■ **Before Dawn / Epic BG-33785**
★★ **Greatest Hits / Ari. 4045**
★ **He Don't Love You / Asy. 7E-1034**
★ **The World of Tony Orlando and Dawn / Ari. 9006**
■ **To Be with You / Elek. 7E-1049**
Until he met up with producers Hank Medress and Dave Appel, Tony Orlando worked for CBS Records as a publishing executive. With the enormous success of "Tie a Yellow Ribbon 'Round the Old Oak Tree" in 1973, he became a national celebrity, but one utterly without substance. The singles weren't the worst of it—imagine what the filler sounded like—but they were bad enough: one hoarse-throated throwback to the days of Frankie Laine after another. Garbage redeemed only slightly by success. — D.M.

ORLEANS
★ **Before the Dance / ABC 1058**
★★ **Let There Be Music / Asy. 7E-1029**
★ **Waking and Dreaming / Asy. 7E-1070**
Supposedly the intelligent person's alternative to Eagles-Ronstadt-L.A.-session-rock, Orleans is masterminded by narcissists, John and Joanna Hall, and is, if anything,

more hollow and slick than that to which it is supposed to be an alternative. — K.T.

ORPHAN
★★ **Everyone Lives to Sing / Lon. XPS-614**

Competent Boston-area country-rock band aligned with singer/songwriter Jonathan Edwards, who guested on the out-of-print *More Orphan Than Not* album. *Everyone Lives* does not represent the band at its best, which wasn't much to begin with. (Now deleted.) — J.S.

OSIBISA
★ **Ojah Awake / Ant. 7058**
★★★★ **Osibisa / MCA 32**
★★ **Welcome Home / Ant. 7051**
★★★★ **Woyaya / MCA 43**

A quartet of Ghanaians transplanted to London, Osibisa makes music about happiness. At the core of the group's synthesis of intense, complex and primitive African rhythm and modern electric instrumentation (plus a wizard horn section) lies infectious joy. You can't tell it from the lyrics—most of which are in Swahili—but it's in the nature of their high-stepping Afro-Anglo blues jazz.

The group put out three Warner albums, all of which are deleted, but MCA has kept their first and best two albums in print. These albums represent a fine introduction to the rites of hypnotic rhythm that define Osibisa. The recent stuff for Antilles is an embarrassment; to hear such brilliant players head for the disc formula is more than disappointing. Though they've never made a discernible commercial impact in America—despite having done the soundtrack for the second *Superfly* flick—Osibisa did make an important contribution by inventing a Western form of Patanga (Swahili for improvisation) atop a bed of Nigerian-style "high-life" music that isn't easily forgotten. — B.M.

LEE OSKAR
★★ **Before the Rain / Elek. 6E-150**
★★ **Lee Oskar / U. Artists LA-594-G**

War's only white member, this Dutch harp player recorded these LPs in 1976 and 1978, well after the band had peaked. Passing interest for diehard fans of War only. — D.M.

DONNY OSMOND
■ **Alone Together / MGM 4886**
■ **Disco Train / Poly. 1-6067**
■ **Donald Clark Osmond / Poly. 1-6109**
■ **Donny Osmond Album / MGM 4782**
■ **My Best to You / MGM 4872**
■ **Portrait of Donny / MGM 4820**

This is not the reincarnation of Shaun Cassidy. Well-crafted garbage—trash is too elevated a description. — D.M.

DONNY AND MARIE OSMOND
■ **Donny and Marie / Poly. 6068**
■ **I'm Leaving It All Up to You / MGM M3G-4968**
■ **Make the World Go Away / MGM M3G-4996**
■ **New Season / Poly. 1-6083**
■ **Winning Combination / Poly. 1-6127**

The only people I've ever heard who deserved Andy Williams. Sometimes I wish they'd learn to ski, and meet his ex-wife. — D.M.

MARIE OSMOND
■ **Paper Roses / MGM 4910**
■ **This Is the Way That I Feel / Poly. PD-1-6099**
■ **Who's Sorry Now / MGM M3G-4979**

Wretched excess, accent on wretched. — D.M.

THE OSMONDS
■ **Around the World Live in Concert / MGM M3JB-5012**
■ **Brainstorm / Poly. 1-6077**
■ **Osmonds' Christmas Album / Poly. 2-8001**
■ **Osmonds' Greatest Hits / Poly. 2-9005**
■ **Phase Three / MGM ISE-4796**
■ **The Proud One / MGM M3G-4993**

For Mormon Tabernacle Choir fans only. Some of these were hits; all of them deserve to be melted, except maybe the occasional Jackson 5 imitations. The heavy rock on *Phase Three* epitomizes stupidity. — D.M.

JOHNNY OTIS

★★★★ Cold Shot / Kent 534
★★★ Guitar Slim Green's Stone Down
    Blues / Kent 549
★★★ Live at Monterey / Epic BG-30473
★★★★ The Original Johnny Otis Show /
    Savoy 2221

One of the most important figures in R&B
history, Otis' list of accomplishments is impressive. The drummer/pianist/vibraphon-
ist played with the Count Basie Orchestra
before becoming a bandleader himself and
scoring with the 1946 hit "Harlem Nocturne." This early work is represented on
the Savoy collection. He later opened the
first R&B club in Los Angeles and his ribald jam sessions discovered and included
such talents as Little Esther Phillips, Big
Mama Thornton, Etta James, Hank Ballard and the Midnighters, and Jackie Wilson. The available material dates from
Otis' comeback in the late Sixties. *Cold
Shot* is the best Otis available, featuring
Don "Sugar Cane" Harris and Otis' guitar
prodigy son Shuggie. The Monterey album
(from the jazz, not pop, festival) features
many of same associates, including Little
Esther from the old days.   — J.S.

SHUGGIE OTIS

★★★ Freedom Flight / Epic E-30752
★★★ Here Comes Shuggie Otis / Epic
    26511
★★★ Inspiration Information / Epic
    KE-33059
★★★★ Kooper Session / Col. CS-9951
★★★ Preston Love's Omaha Bar-B-Q /
    Kent 540

This blues-based guitarist was well tutored
by his father, legendary R&B bandleader
Johnny Otis. *Here Comes,* Shuggie's debut,
with white gospel singer Al Kooper, is of
particular interest. On his own albums,
Shuggie's performance suffers somewhat
from his rather poor vocal ability.   — J.S.

THE OUTLAWS

★★★ Bring It Back Alive / Ari. 8300
★★★ Hurry Sundown / Ari. 4135
★★★ Lady in Waiting / Ari. 4070
★★★ Outlaws / Ari. 4042
★★★ Playin' to Win / Ari. 4205

A totally synthetic band who sound like
every country boogie outfit from the Byrds
to Poco and the Eagles, the Allmans to
Marshall Tucker. Their chief songwriter,
Henry Thomasson, is a master of the cut-
and-paste method (a snippet of Richie
Furay here, a soupçon of Bernie Leadon
there). With excellent production by Paul

Rothchild, and adequate musicianship, all
Outlaws albums are full of Good Things
from the Recording Industry. Or the Sara
Lee banana cake of rock & roll.   — A.N.

BUCK OWENS

★★ Best of Buck Owens, Vol. 3 / Cap.
    SM-11677
★★ Buck 'Em / War. B-2952
★★★ Sixteen Greatest Hits / Trip
    TOP-16-10
★★ The Best of Buck Owens / Cap.
    SM-11827

Owens came out of the Bakersfield, California, country music scene that also produced Wynn Stewart and Merle Haggard;
he had an enormously popular series of
country hits in the mid-Sixties, most of
which were as much pop as country but
only one of which—"I've Got a Tiger by
the Tail"— made the pop Top Forty. Later, he went on to star with Roy Clark on
TV's *Hee Haw.* Capitol deleted most of his
albums when he left the label for Warner
Bros. in 1977—why not?—and leased the
best early hits (including "Tiger") to Trip,
which is the "essential" Owens album. The
rest are pretty dull.   — D.M.

THE OZARK MOUNTAIN
DAREDEVILS

★★★ Don't Look Down / A&M 4662
★★★★ It'll Shine When It Shines / A&M
    3654
★★★ Men from Earth / A&M 4601
★★★★ The Car over the Lake Album /
    A&M 4549
★★★ The Ozark Mountain Daredevils /
    A&M 4411

A tribe of good old boys who came out of
the Missouri hills and Arkansas playing a
mixture of traditional mountain music and
bona fide American pop, the Ozark Mountain Daredevils sound like what might
have happened if Jed Clampett had bought
himself the Eagles to make records with.
They've had several sizable pop hits, notably "If You Wanna Get to Heaven" from
the eponymous first album (1973). The
Daredevils really hit their stride, though,
on *Shine* and *Car over the Lake,* released in
1974 and 1975, respectively. Since then
they've been repeating a formula that has
grown progressively more slick and less interesting.   — A.N.

OZO

■ Listen to the Buddah / DJM 4

Post-psychedelic garbage. (Now deleted.)   — J.S.

PABLO CRUISE
★★★ Lifeline / A&M 4575
★★ Nadia's Theme / A&M 3412
★★ Pablo Cruise / A&M 4528
★★ Place in the Sun / A&M 4625
★★★ Worlds Away / A&M 4597
Mellow West Coast white R&B from a
quartet of vets from failed groups. Bassist
Bud Cockrell was in It's a Beautiful Day at
that band's low point, and the other three
(keyboardist Cory Lerios, guitarist David
Jenkins and drummer Steve Price) were in
Stoneground. Jenkins is the best player of
the lot and the second album, *Lifeline,* in-
cludes a couple of songs written by Ron
Nagle, a little-known but interesting songwriter. But *Worlds Away* scored big with a
1978 single, "Love Will Find a Way," sort
of a blander version of Boz Scaggs' later
work. — J.S.

TOM PACHECO
★★ The Outsider / RCA APL1-1887
Pacheco believes in the mythological
America of Woody Guthrie, hobos in rail
yards and cowboy/outlaws as ingenuously
and completely as anyone since Bob Dylan
and Ramblin' Jack Elliott. Unfortunately
he doesn't have the talent to bring this vision to life. At best, Pacheco sounds like a
manic-depressive Arlo Guthrie; at worst,
he's bone-dull and tuneless to boot. (Now
deleted.) — D.M.

PACIFIC GAS AND ELECTRIC
★★ Get It On / Kent 547
A soul-based band from the heyday of San
Francisco rock. Strident funk without pur-
pose. A couple of earlier albums for Co-
lumbia are deleted. — D.M.

GENE PAGE
★★ Close Encounters / Ari. 4174
★★ Lovelock / Atl. 18161
Veteran Philadelphia soul arranger makes
his Barry White move, without the moans
but with the same Muzak dance feel. Lush
and empty. — D.M.

PAICE, ASHTON, LORD
★★★ Malice in Wonderland / War.
B-3038
A Deep Purple splinter group that suc-
ceeds on the strong Baldrey/Cocker-like
vocals of Tony Ashton and the white Eng-
lish blues-rock keyboard playing of veteran
Jon Lord and his underrated crew includ-
ing Ian Paice on drums and ex-Babe Ruth
Bernie Marsden on guitar. — A.N.

PALEY BROTHERS
★★★ Paley Brothers / Sire K-6052
Teen thrill music from aging Boston rich
kids. At the advent of the Seventies, when
these guys were called the Sidewinders and
Lenny Kaye produced their first LP (for
RCA, now deleted), they were as catchy as
their best song, "Rendezvous." Now, having remained unwrinkled for nearly ten
years, the Paleys seem a little embarrassing, like Dorian Gray without the
venom. — D.M.

ROBERT PALMER
★★ Double Fun / Is. 9476
★★ Pressure Drop / Is. 9372
★★★ Sneakin' Sally through the Alley / Is.
9294
★★ Some People Can Do What They
Like / Is. 9420
White soul for snobs. Palmer's first album,
Sneakin' Sally, was more than promising,
influenced equally by reggae, Allen Tous-
saint's New Orleans rhythms and Little
Feat's bizarre attitudes. But each succeed-
ing album has been more narcissistic, as
Palmer—generally decked out in duds so
ornately expensive they'd make Al Green

blush—began a treatise on high culture and soul slumming that made Bryan Ferry's odyssey seem tame. Revered by the sort of rock critics who think that the sophomoric jokes of Sparks are the epitome of art rock, Palmer is in fact virtually soulless, the Fraud of Funk. — D.M.

FELIX PAPPALARDI

★ Felix Pappalardi with Creation / A&M 4586

Noted producer Pappalardi (Cream, Mountain) teams up with four of the world's skinniest Japanese rock & rollers (named Sugar, Flash, Thunder and Daybreak) for the least successful Japanese/Italian coalition since World War II. (Now deleted.) — A.N.

PARIS

★★ Big Towne, 2061 / Cap. ST-11560
★ Paris / Cap. ST-11464

Paris was raucous, monotonous heavy metal, due mostly to excesses by former Fleetwood Mac guitarist/singer/songwriter Bob Welch, whose smooth vocal timbre was sadly miscast as well. Bassist Glenn Cornick (an early member of Jethro Tull) and drummer Thom Mooney couldn't overcome the self-righteous songs and noisy playing.

The followup was a slight improvement as Welch toned down his guitar noise. But the songs remained repetitious and laden with simplistic riffing. The band broke up after *Big Towne,* and Welch has gone on to solo success. — C.W.

GRAHAM PARKER

★★★★★ Heat Treatment / Mer. SRM-1-1117
★★★★★ Howlin' Wind / Mer. SRM-1-1095
★★★★ Stick to Me / Mer. SRM-1-3706
★★★ The Parkerilla / Mer. SRM-2-100

Howlin' Wind and *Heat Treatment,* both released in 1976, are extraordinary works of neoclassic rock & roll that draw their anger and emotional intensity from Bob Dylan, Van Morrison and the Rolling Stones, and at the same time anticipate the unsullied, scabrous explosion of punk. These are tough, passionate and hungry albums in which Parker refuses to accept anybody's vision of himself except his own. What his first two albums share with punk is the frightening implication that the culture around him is collapsing, that there is nothing to hold on to. If Parker's abnegation isn't as extreme as the punks', his best

songs ("Pourin' It All Out," "Fool's Gold," "Don't Ask Me Questions") bray with danger and defeat, and even his most romantic songs ("Heat Treatment" and "Hold Back the Night") have a fierce edge.

Where Parker differs from the punks and what he shares with Bruce Springsteen, Southside Johnny and Mink DeVille—the new guardians of rock & roll past—is his relation to rock history. This is more than a matter of choosing heroes (Van Morrison versus Iggy, say) or forms (R&B versus minimalism or primitivism, or whatever you want to call it). Parker sees rock & roll as a way out—in his case, as a way out of being a gas-station attendant—and rock tradition as a way of establishing order in a culture that has lost much of its meaning. The Rumour, Parker's five-piece band, turn almost every song into an epic stand of R&B belligerence and operatic intensity. By placing so much emphasis on traditional rock values, Parker avoids the pessimism of punk and the passivity of pop. The sound is steel-eyed and gritted-teeth.

On *Stick to Me* Parker's compromise comes close to collapsing. Bitterness reverts to impudence ("Problem Child"); sentiment turns maudlin ("Watch the Moon Come Down"); and for the first time, he has written throwaways ("The Raid," "New York Shuffle"). The situation is exacerbated by Nick Lowe's pollution of a mix, which buries the album's best cuts ("Soul on Ice," "Clear Head"). There are moments when Parker's vocals are barely audible. But for all its problems—most of which came about because the album was cut in a week—the record does live up to its title. It takes a while, but like the best method actors, Parker works by the accumulation of gesture and detail, and in the end *Stick to Me* has a power that can't be dismissed.

Parker followed *Stick to Me,* however, with a set that was undeniably disappointing. *The Parkerilla,* a two-disc live LP, merely rehashed the first two albums (only two songs are from *Stick*), added a sort of disco-single version of "Don't Ask Me Questions," which opened the set and had already appeared on the second album, and failed completely to convey the power of his public appearances. No oldies, nothing special—it was a remarkably shoddy set from a man of so much principle, and it undercut his credibility, even if the ostensible reasoning behind it was to escape the Mercury contract. That's no excuse for stealing money from fans with an inferior

LP. Parker has a switch-blade voice, but *Parkerilla*'s a mugging. — K.R./D.M.

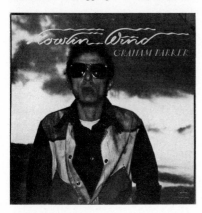

WAYNE PARKER
★★★ **Oklahoma Twilight / Ari. ST-5005**
In 1975 this country-based singer (who actually wrote a song called "I Can't Stand Country Music") seemed a promising potential outlaw (despite production by Mike Curb). Without a followup, he's merely a pleasant eccentric, although one whose return to recording would not be unwelcome. (Now deleted.) — D.M.

VAN DYKE PARKS
★★ **Clang of the Yankee Reaper / War. B-2878**
★ **Song Cycle / War. 1727**
Parks is supposed to be one of the cryptic geniuses of mid-Sixties rock-into-art. Unfortunately, it is not genius but his tendency to be gaseously enigmatic and pretentiously hip that propels these albums. As a lyricist, Parks is as overrated as his best-known song (the Beach Boys' "Surf's Up"), and the coyness that would like to pass for innocence on *Song Cycle* (1968) renders it hopelessly out of date. *Clang* (his third album, *Van Dyke Parks Discovers America*, is deleted) dabbles in Caribbean rhythm, with essential purposelessness. Parks' reputation is really built more on a few minor achievements (producing Randy Newman's and Ry Cooder's debut albums, playing keyboards on "Eight Miles High" by the Byrds and Judy Collins' "Who Knows Where the Time Goes"), plus the famous Brian Wilson critical smokescreen, than on anything his solo projects have revealed. Overrated, to say the least. — D.M.

PARLIAMENT
★★★ **Chocolate City / Casa. NBLP-7014**
★★★★ **Funkentelechy vs. the Placebo Syndrome / Casa. NBLP-7084**
★★★ **Get Down and Boogie / Casa. NBLP-7042**
★★★ **Mothership Connection / Casa. NBLP-7072**
★★★★ **Motor Booty Affair / Casa. NBLP-7125**
★★★ **Parliament Live / Casa. NBLP-7053**
★★★★ **The Clones of Dr. Funkenstein / Casa. NBLP-7034**
★★★ **Up for the Down Stroke / Casa. NBLP-7002**
Parliament was the seedling from which the Parliafunkadelicment empire of maestro George Clinton grew. Originally a late-Sixties Detroit soul group ("[I Just Wanna] Testify" was their hit), Clinton has since taken the band (and its various offshoots, including Funkadelic, Bootsy's Rubber Band and the Horny Horns) into a nether world of black rock & roll. Funkadelic and Bootsy are more outrageously entertaining—a good deal of their music is simply power rock with a dance beat—but Parliament has been used for Clinton's major statements: *The Clones of Dr. Funkenstein* suggests a rather unpleasant vision of the future, while *Funkentelechy vs. the Placebo Syndrome* is actually a prescriptive manifesto concerning the sad state of the Seventies music world. Fascinatingly vulgar, like all of Clinton's projects, but also engaging in a rather diffuse way. — D.M.

ALAN PARSONS PROJECT
★★★ **I, Robot / Ari. 7002**
★★★ **Pyramid / Ari. 4180**
★★ **Tales of Mystery and Imagination / 20th Cent. 539**
A dubious pretext for music, *Tales* (based on Poe's short stories) nonetheless has inspired moments from Pilot's infectious Beatles-derived rock, Andrew Powell's ornate arranging and Parsons' marvelously precise engineering. But melodramatic lyrics hurt. *I, Robot* and *Pyramid* are more rocking, less orchestrated versions of the same approach, with superb performances from Pilot, Allan Clarke and many others. — C.W.

GENE PARSONS
★★★ **Kindling / War. B-2687**
The former Byrd and Flying Burrito Brother offers mostly self-penned and self-played bluegrass with lots of overdubbing. Parsons' soothing baritone also brings in catchy pop melodies. Among others, guitarist Clarence White backs. Few electric

instruments; appealingly unambitious and simple. — c.w.

GRAM PARSONS
★★★ G.P. / Rep. 2123
★★★ Grievous Angel / Rep. 2171
★★★ Sleepless Nights / A&M 4578
There are many who would agree that Gram Parsons' name should be appended, not just to these three records but to the entire body of country rock. *Safe at Home,* Parsons' 1967 record with the International Submarine Band, is an out-of-print treasure that shows the start of his Dynaflow mix of Merle Haggard and Arthur Crudup.

In 1968, Parsons joined with a Byrds incarnation that included Roger McGuinn, Chris Hillman and Clarence White to make the landmark *Sweetheart of the Rodeo*; "Hickory Wind," a song about his South Carolina boyhood that is perhaps his finest creation, is on that album. His 1970 collaboration with the Flying Burrito Brothers lent nine tracks to *Sleepless Nights*; the remaining three songs, bolstered by Emmylou Harris' loving attentions, are from the 1973 sessions for *Grievous Angel,* which was released in 1974.

G.P., released in 1973, is a sometimes lovely, sometimes wavering collection, with backups by Elvis Presley's band and Emmylou Harris; the same team made *Grievous Angel,* and the latter record shares the same mix of glories and thin spots. Parsons did a solo tour in support of that album in the winter and spring of 1973. His self-destructive ways stopped his heart and fixed him as a legend in October of that year. "His exit was perfect," says Elvis Costello with a certain sad truth. Parsons' influence is wide, deep and likely to last. — F.S.

DOLLY PARTON
★★★ All I Can Do / RCA APL1-1665
★★★★ Bargain Store / RCA APL1-0950
★★★★ Coat of Many Colors / RCA LSP-4603
★★★ Dolly / RCA APL1-1221
★★★ Dolly Parton in Concert / RCA CPL2-1014
★★ Heartbreaker / RCA AFL1-2797
★★ Here You Come Again / RCA AFL1-2544
★★★ In the Beginning / Monu. MG 7623
★★ I Wish I Felt This Way at Home / Camd. ACL-7002
★★★★ Jolene / RCA APL1-0473
★★ Just the Way I Am / Camd. 2583
★★★★ Love Is Like a Butterfly / RCA APL1-0712
★★ Mine / Camd. ACL1-0307
★★★★ My Tennessee Mountain Home / RCA APL1-0033
★★★★ New Harvest . . . First Gathering / RCA APL1-2188
★★ Release Me / Power. 299
★★★★★ The Best of Dolly Parton / RCA APL1-1117
★★★★★ The Best of Dolly Parton / RCA LSP-4449

In many ways, Dolly Parton is the perfect country singer, because she has all the right qualifications: she came from a poor family in the Tennessee mountains, and her stunted childhood has resulted in prolific songwriting about same. She's also the possessor of a stunning soprano voice and of a remarkable resemblance to the Big Rock Candy Mountain that all Southern kids were convinced actually existed. Dolly Parton *is* the South to many people; her lyrics are the embodiment of the proper Southern virtues of fundamental religion, respect for the family, worship of one's parents, praise for the right husband/lover and weepy, heartfelt laments over the wrongs suffered at the hands of a callous/drinking/running-around husband. Many country songwriters take all that and make it corny; Dolly makes it real and believable.

For many years she led a twin recording and performing career, solo and as half of a successful duo with Porter Wagoner. In 1973 she left the Porter Wagoner show, although he continued to produce her albums. Then in 1976 she left Wagoner completely and began to gear her career toward pop audiences. By 1978 she had succeeded, and *Here You Come Again* was her first gold album. It was also her least pleasing in years, with its slick California arrangements and production. That was a point she cheerfully conceded but argued convincingly that it gave her the pop audience she wanted and, simultaneously, that success afforded her the freedom to do whatever she wanted in the future.

The best representation of her work is contained in the two *Best of Dolly Parton* albums. So prolific is she that the albums are equally good, even though no one song appears on both. — C.F.

STELLA PARTON
★ Country Sweet / Elek. 7E-1111
★ Stella Parton / Elek. 6E-126
Yeah, she's Dolly's sister. No, they don't have anything in common, musically or (ahem) physically. — D.M.

PASSPORT
★★ Cross-Collateral / Atco 36-107
★★ Iguacu / Atco 36-149
★★ Infinity Machine / Atco 36-132
★★ Looking Thru / Atco 7042
★★ Sky Blue / Atl. 19177
On each of its albums, this German group plays similar-sounding fusion music. Built around leader Klaus Doldinger's tenor and soprano sax playing, and favoring somber yet steadily pulsing tunes, Passport is a poor man's Weather Report, but with much less percussive and compositional nuance. Competent but dull. — M.R.

SANDY AND CAROLINE PATON
★★ Sandy and Caroline Paton / Folk-Leg. EGO-30
As founders (along with Lee Haggerty) of the Folk-Legacy label, the Patons' influence on contemporary folk revivalists has been a combination of hospitality and song swapping. The label was the first to record Rosalie Sorrels and Mary McCaslin. The

Patons' own disc is simple, with the emphasis on traditional ballads. — I.M.

BOBBY PATTERSON
★★★ It's Just a Matter of Time / Paula 2215
For a couple of years in the early Seventies, Patterson was Jewel/Paula's man for all seasons. His lone album is stylistically varied, though centered in old-fashioned Southern soul. — J.MC.

BILLY PAUL
★★ Ebony Woman / Phil. KZ-32118
★★★ Feelin' Good at the Cadillac Club / Phil. KZ-32119
★★★★ Going East / Phil. KZ-30580
★★★ Got My Head on Straight / Phil. ZX-33157
★★ Let 'Em In / Phil. PZ-34389
★★ Live in Europe / Phil. KZ-32952
★★ Only the Strong Survive / Phil. PZ-34923
★★★ 360 Degrees of Billy Paul / Phil. KZ-31793
★★★ War of the Gods / Phil. KZ-32409
★★★ When Love Is New / Phil. PZ-33843
When Billy Paul recorded *Feelin' Good* (originally for Gamble Records), he was a nimble-voiced cabaret-jazz singer. Despite the title, it is not a live album; instead, Paul scats his way through standards ("Bluesette," "Billy Boy") backed by an adept acoustic rhythm section. Since then, Paul's baritone has frayed around the edges and his singing often finds him parodying his own affectations.

Ebony Woman and *Going East* continue loosely in the cabaret vein. The former is filled with lightweight pop and jazz standards while *Going East* is a successfully ambitious attempt to flesh out Paul's persona. With the possible exception of "Magic Carpet Ride," the choice of songs on *Going East* is judicious while the arrangements combine sophisticated horn and string charts with a crisp but not cumbersome rhythm section.

Since then, Paul's music has been recorded with MFSB's backup. "Me and Mrs. Jones," a pop smash, found him treading the line between MOR, cabaret and soul. It's a formula that Gamble and Huff have turned to time and again for his albums. As a result, there's little to choose among them. The songs are either lushly romantic or filled with pop social statements; both varieties have equally erratic lyrics. Vocally, Paul tends to fall back on familiar mannerisms. The only album to avoid completely, however, is *Live in Europe,* which is bogged down by a lumbering orchestra. — J.MC.

LES PAUL
★ **Guitar Tapestry / Proj. 6019-20**
★ **Les Paul Now / Lon. SP-44101**
★★ **New Sound, Vol. 2 (with Mary Ford) / Cap. SM-286**
★★ **The World Is Still Waiting for the Sunrise / Cap. SM-11308**
Les Paul is one of the most influential figures in rock—he perfected guitar amplification and built one of the great blues guitars, the Gibson Les Paul—but his records aren't much. The Capitol sets, with former wife Mary Ford, are interesting period pieces from the pre-Presley Fifties, but the rest are sheer mood music, for Mantovani fans more than rockers. — D.M.

PAVLOV'S DOG
★★ **At the Sound of the Bell / Col. PC-33694**
★★ **Pampered Menial / Col. PC-33552**
Blue Oyster Cult on laughing gas. David Surkamp's extraordinary, if hard-to-take, voice (Marty Balin crossbred with a vacuum cleaner) never quite jelled with the band's technologically informed heavy-metal attack. A few songs survive—"Late November" from the first album, *Pampered Menial* (1975), and the wonderful Mersey-like ballad, "Mersey," from the second, *At the Sound of the Bell* (1976)—but this will be remembered mainly for its eccentric qualities. (Now deleted.) — J.B.M.

TOM PAXTON
★ **Heroes / Van. 79411**
★ **Morning Again / Elek. 74019**
★ **New Songs from the Briarpatch / Van. 79395**
★ **Outward Bound / Elek. 7317**
★ **Ramblin' Boy / Elek. 7277**
★★ **The Compleat Tom Paxton / Elek. 7E-2003**
★ **The Things I Notice Now / Elek. 74043**
A smugly sanctimonious product of the early Sixties folk movement, Paxton's performance abilities are extremely meager. His best-known song, "The Last Thing on My Mind," was written in 1963; after that, he quickly declined into sentiment and a kind of ham-handed political sermonizing about obvious subjects. Somehow, this has earned him a cult following in England, although America still can't be bothered. The Elektra anthology (*Compleat*) is an overview for historians of the milieu in

which Dylan was nurtured. The rest are up for grabs to anyone who cares. — D.M.

FREDA PAYNE
★★ **Out of Payne Comes Love / ABC 901**
★★ **Payne and Pleasure / Dun. X-50176**
★★ **Stares and Whispers / Cap. ST-11700**
Payne made a couple of great soul singles for Holland-Dozier-Holland's Invictus label in the early Seventies, notably the cryptic "Band of Gold" and the antiwar song, "Bring the Boys Home." But the rest of her work is closer to Nancy Wilson than Martha Reeves—it would be unfair to classify her as a bad soul singer, but as a pop stylist, she's none too distinctive either. — D.M.

JOHN PAYNE BAND
★★ **Bedtime Stories / Ari. 1025**
★★ **Razor's Edge / Ari. 1036**
Payne's chief claim to fame is that he has frequently been a Van Morrison horn player. On his own, he plays a blend of folk and funk that's peculiar though rarely exciting. — D.M.

PAZANT BROTHERS AND BEAUFORT EXPRESS
★★ **Loose and Juicy / Van. 79364**
A self-contained horn group, the Pazant Brothers have made some interesting singles in their time. Sad to say, *Loose and Juicy* is tame soul and quasi-jazz instrumentals. (Now deleted.) — J.MC.

PEACHES AND HERB
★★ **2 Hot! / Poly. 1-6172**
Not one of the great disco hits, but a nice comeback for Herb Fame and Francine Barker, the R&B vocal team that scored in the mid-Sixties with "Let's Fall in Love," "Close Your Eyes," "United" and "For Your Love." "Shake Your Groove Thing" was the 1979 hit that sparked this album's ascent to the pop Top Ten, and it was worth it. — D.M.

PEARLS BEFORE SWINE
■ **Balaklava / ESP Disk 1075**
★★ **One Nation Underground / ESP Disk 1054**
Between arty New York folk rock and the San Francisco eruption of 1967 there lay in wait a half-dozen bands like this. *One Nation Underground,* graced with a detail cover from Hieronymus Bosch's *Garden of Delights* that made the poster a big hit, is a classic example of wimp aggression. Between Tom Rapp's lisp, his rubber-band

box guitars, windy eight-minute poetry lessons and kiss-off songs in Morse code, Pearls Before Swine's debut was, and remains, a disaster. On *Balaklava,* Rapp drops even the pretense of constituting a rock band and starts his long groan of pretentious Muzak. All his other attempts save *Balaklava* were mercifully deleted some time ago. This one is distinctive, anyway, in its insane compulsion to garnish liberally with sound effects. — B.T.

ANN PEEBLES
★★★ **If This Is Heaven** / **Hi 6002**
★★★ **Part Time Love** / / **Hi 8005**
★★★ **Straight from the Heart** / **Hi 8009**
★★★ **Tellin' It** / **Hi 32091**
★★★ **The Handwriting Is on the Wall** / **Hi 6007**

Born in East St. Louis in 1947, Ann Peebles grew up singing in her father's Baptist choir, a group estimable enough to back Mahalia Jackson (Peebles' idol) when she toured the Midwest. Peebles was discovered by Willie Mitchell, Al Green's producer, when she sat in with a club act while visiting Memphis. In 1970 she made *Part Time Love* with Mitchell, whose economical string and horn accompaniments were the ideal complement to a bottom-heavy rhythm section and Peebles' gritty, direct vocal style. Her debut, more straightforwardly bluesy than later sessions, bore little resemblance to Green's work with the same band—rather than recalling his keening melismata, she spoke out like the young Aretha Franklin.

1972's *Straight from the Heart,* instrumentally a bit slicker than the 1970 record, cut even deeper vocally: "I Feel Like Breaking Up Somebody's Home Tonight" states a theme—loneliness—that is nicely underpinned by the concupiscent spunk of "99 Pounds" (a number written by her husband, Don Bryant).

Although Peebles' 1972 "I'm Gonna Tear Your Playhouse Down" had sold half a million copies in R&B markets, and several other singles had done well, 1974's brooding "I Can't Stand the Rain" (the excellent album of the same name is out of print) sold a surprising million copies as a crossover hit. In 1978, Cream Records began buying the rights to the above albums as well as *If This Is Heaven* (1977). Peebles has never cut any weak numbers, so anything available is recommended. 1975's *Tellin' It,* while it helps Peebles stake a claim as a songwriter, shows her as a somewhat domesticated stylist. Her first

Cream release, *The Handwriting Is on the Wall,* is said by Willie Mitchell to be her best piece of work (it uses Mitchell's new production team). If so, Peebles' peak is still to come. — F.S.

DAVID PEEL AND THE LOWER EAST SIDE
★ **Have a Marijuana** / **Elek. 74032**

The Sixties relic to end all Sixties relics: New York street freak arouses anthropological instincts of hip record company, who sends specialists to capture him in native environment. As the record that demolished the ban on drug references, this one gets high marks in the blow-for-artistic-freedom department. — F.R.

PELE
★ **Pele** / **Atl. 18231**

Pele is said to be one of the nicest guys in the world, and if he wants to put his name on an album so lame that even he barely appears on it (singing execrably behind Sergio Mendes and Brasil '77), who are we to kick? — F.S.

TEDDY PENDERGRASS
★★★★ **Life Is a Song Worth Singing** / **Phil. JZ-35095**
★★★★ **Teddy Pendergrass** / **Phil. PZ-34390**

Pendergrass was the original lead singer of Harold Melvin and the Blue Notes; his solo albums, the first (*Teddy Pendergrass*) released in 1977, the second (*Life Is a Song*) in 1978, have kept up the consistently high quality he showed there. Pendergrass is perhaps more confident as an uptempo stylist than as a ballad singer, but he acquits himself well on all sorts of material. One of the best products of the Gamble and Huff soul stable. — D.M.

PENGUINS
★★★ **Cool Cool Penguins** / **Dooto 242**

Their hit was "Earth Angel," a model of R&B harmony group slickness; the rest is similar but less inspired. — D.M.

LYDIA PENSE
★ **Lydia Pense** / **ABC 917**

Take my cold blood. Please. (Now deleted.) — J.B.M.

THE PENTANGLE
★★★ **Sweet Child** / **Rep. 6334**
★★★★ **The Pentangle** / **Rep. 6315**

The original Pentangle idea was to bring together John Renbourne and Bert Jansch, two stellar British folk guitarists, Jacqui McShee, a crystal-voiced traditional ballad singer, and the jazz-oriented rhythm team of bassist Danny Thompson and drummer Terry Cox in order to breathe some life back into English folk music, a genre that was quite played out by the late Sixties.

The Pentangle, the band's first album, went further than could be hoped. The active jazz bottom, Renaissance-music harmonies and the spirited exchanges between Renbourne and Jansch made Pentangle a virtuoso unit creating a terse, instrumentally based new folk style. Sparing use of McShee's voice brings out the mysteriously laconic circularity of the ballads, while the acoustic guitar duets converge with Cox and Thompson into occasionally powerful kinesics.

Sweet Child successfully experiments with minor variations on the group's basic formula. A double, half-live/half-studio album, *Child* features Renbourne on solo guitar doing short pieces which anticipate his extraordinary *Lady and the Unicorn* album, and Jansch, too, presents some of his nongroup songs (see *Bert Jansch Sampler,* on import). Cox and Thompson, after their own solo curios, lead the band through several excellent instrumentals which clearly show that their presence in Pentangle is the crucial ingredient. However, *Child*'s high points are still the full ensemble readings of traditional ballads.

★★★ **Basket of Light** / Rep. 6372
★★ **Cruel Sister** / Rep. 6430
★ **Reflection** / Rep. 6463
★★ **Solomon's Seal** / Rep. 2100

While *Basket of Light* marks the perfection of what had over the first two albums become Pentangle's characteristic ensemble sound, totally accommodating the traditional ballad to its flying instrumentals (and even incorporating "Sally Go Round the Roses" into the style), the album also marks the first step in the gradual withdrawal of Thompson and Cox into mere backup. Period-style percussion begins to predominate on *Basket* and Pentangle begins progressively to lose its jazz feeling, and with it, its early conciseness and daring.

Nevertheless, *Cruel Sister* is the true dividing line. Side one serves as a retrospective of past achievements in style, completed with Renbourne's tender and very moving reading of "Lord Franklin" (the source of "Bob Dylan's Dream"). But the other side drags a side-long treatment of "Jack Orion" into the mistake of a grand

"folk suite," an idea which has brought down several other English folk groups, including Fairport Convention. At some point, Pentangle had started taking itself too seriously as an institution.

Reflection and *Solomon's Seal* have their bright spots, but these belong to individual members. With these records, Pentangle ceases to operate as a unit. The unusual amount of original material on *Reflection* suggests that they grew tired of the ballads. But the new material is ill-suited to the chemistry of the group. Cox and Thompson seem to have lost all interest, Renbourne and Jansch seem only less distracted and the album is overproduced. But the most telling mark is that Jacqui McShee, who was the haunted voice of the group, has reverted to mere folksinging. *Seal* suggests some sort of rebirth, particularly in the vocals, but that hope has proved short-lived. — B.T.

PEOPLE'S CHOICE
★★★ **Boogie Down U.S.A.** / Phil. KZ-33154
★★★ **Turn Me Loose** / Phil. JZ-35363
★★★ **We Got the Rhythm** / Phil. PZ-34124

People's Choice is a black rock band with limited scope, which just shows that limited doesn't always mean wretched. *Boogie Down*'s "Do It Anyway You Wanna," an unlikely pop hit in 1975, is typical of the group's songs: tough, clean, Philadelphia mix and some simple chanting. Lead singer Frankie Brunson often sounds like Screamin' Jay Hawkins and combined with the band's updated, Philadelphia version of Booker T. and the MGs, usually does well. There's little to choose between these albums, all of which are mindless but fun. — J.MC.

PERIGEO
★ **Fata Morgana** / RCA TPL1-1228
★ **Genealogia** / RCA TPL1-1080
★ **Valley of the Temples** / RCA TPL1-1175

Italian progressive/jazz-rock Muzak. For cosmopolitan mood-music fans only. (Now deleted.) — D.M.

CARL PERKINS
★★★★★ **Blue Suede Shoes** / Sun 112
★★★ **Ol' Blue Suede's Back** / Jet KZ-35604
★★★★ **Original Golden Hits** / Sun 111

Perkins was one of the original great stars of Sam Phillips' Sun Records. Along with Jerry Lee Lewis, Elvis Presley and Johnny

Cash, he put the stamp on rockabilly, a wild man's music. His best-known song is "Blue Suede Shoes" (although even that is often claimed as Presley's), but the standout track that reveals Perkins' rather astonishing guitar-playing ability is the more obscure "Dixie Fried." *Ol' Blue Suede's Back* is a 1978 comeback attempt (Perkins has more recently appeared in Cash's combo) that isn't bad, though the old stuff far surpasses it. — D.M.

CARL PERKINS AND NRBQ
★★★★ **Boppin' the Blues / Col. 9981**
Excellent mix of rockabilly and English-influenced Sixties rock featuring lots of guitar. New and old cuts by Perkins, NRBQ and the singer and the group together. A smart matching. — C.W.

FREDDIE PERREN
★★ **Record City / Poly. 1-8002**
Perren is a Hollywood soul and disco producer who's done great things with the Sylvers and Tavares. On his own, he relies more on thump than coloration, which makes this danceable but dull. — J.MC.

THE PERSUADERS
★★ **It's All about Love / Calla PZ-34802**
The Persuaders had a fantastic hit with "Thin Line between Love and Hate" in 1971 (on Atlantic, where it's available on some anthologies), but have never followed it up. This is far later material than that, and not nearly so worthwhile. — D.M.

THE PERSUASIONS
★★★★★ **Chirpin' / Elek. 7E-1099**
★★★★ **Street Corner Symphony / Cap. ST-872**
★★★★ **We Came to Play / Cap. SM-791**
The last (only?) great a cappella R&B group. Frank Zappa rescued the Persuasions from a life of total obscurity in Brooklyn about 1970, and recorded a pair of albums for his Bizarre label, which are now deleted. But the group was interesting enough to latch on to a Capitol contract almost immediately. Both of those albums (while they sold only barely enough to remain in the catalogue) contain some fine singing—perhaps the best track is "Buffalo Soldier" from *Street Corner Symphony.* But the deleted A&M and MCA albums that followed the Capitol don't really do the Persuasions justice.

Chirpin', released in 1977 and one of the best albums in any genre put out in that year, is a complete triumph, as moving and evocative of street life as the best soul music, as energetic as early rock & roll. In "Looking for an Echo," the group found a song that told its story perfectly; in "To Be Loved," Joseph Russell came up with a great solo vehicle, nearly cutting Jackie Wilson's masterful original; "Sixty Minute Man" and "It's Gonna Rain Again" were simply great reflections of what such street-corner harmonies were always all about. There isn't a bad track on *Chirpin',* and everyone vaguely interest in the amateur roots of rock ought to own it. — D.M.

PETER AND GORDON
★★★ **The Best of Peter and Gordon / Cap. SM-2549**
Peter Asher was the brother of actress/model Jane Asher, Paul McCartney's first famous girlfriend, which encouraged McCartney to write "A World without Love" and give it to Asher's group, Peter and Gordon. It was a smash hit in 1964. But most of what Peter and Gordon did could be described as pre-folk-rock—their first album included "Freight Train" and "500 Miles" for instance. Their hits—"A World without Love," "I Don't Want to See You Again," "I Go to Pieces"—all had a folkish feel. But the group's best-known hit is probably "Lady Godiva," which is about the famous nude horsewoman, a puerile novelty.

Peter and Gordon are of current interest mostly because Asher went on to become the producer/manager of James Taylor and Linda Ronstadt. — D.M.

JIM PETERIK
★★★ **Don't Fight the Feeling / Epic PE-34196**
Peterik, a Chicago rocker who enjoyed brief success with the Ides of March ("Ve-

hicle"), epitomizes a Midwesterner's approach to pop-rock—a little Raspberries, a little Chicago and a properly rocking edge on the guitar and arrangements. The album is a bit bloated, particularly on the ballads, but the craft and performance is Second City solid. (Now deleted.) — J.B.M.

PETER, PAUL AND MARY
★★★ A Song Will Rise / War. 1589
★★★ Album 1700 / War. 1700
★★ Best (Ten Years Together) / War. 2552
★ Late Again / War. 1751
★★ Peter, Paul and Mary / War. 1449
★★ Peter, Paul and Mary in Concert / War. 2-1555
★★★ Peter, Paul and Mary in the Wind / War. 1507
★ Peter, Paul and Mary Moving / War. 1473
★ Peter, Paul and Mommy / War. 1785
■ Reunion / War. K-3231
★ See What Tomorrow Brings / War. 1615
★ The Peter, Paul and Mary Album / War. 1648

Listening to Peter, Paul and Mary today, one finds it difficult to fathom the profound effect that their highly staged, impeccably arranged music had on the early Sixties. Having emerged from the Greenwich Village folk scene at about the time Bob Dylan, Tom Paxton, Eric Andersen and a host of others were developing their songwriting and performing abilities, they had an enormous fountain of new as well as traditional material at their disposal. And in combination with manager Albert Grossman and musical director Milt Okun, they hit upon the right songs at the right time.

Given the late-Fifties success of people such as the Kingston Trio and Harry Bela-

fonte, and the definition of folk music that derived from that success, it was a natural progression to the slickly stylized work of Peter Yarrow, Paul Stookey and Mary Travers, even if they were introducing the songs of people who were shortly to become known as "protest singers." Bob Dylan's version of "Blowing in the Wind" wouldn't have sold the way it did without being dressed up in PP&M's three-part harmonies, with crisp dual-guitar accompaniment.

The civil-rights movement made social consciousness acceptable at the mass level, and gave focus to the general dissatisfactions of the new breed of white, middle-class socio-musical commentators. PP&M were among the first to put their popularity at the service of the cause. (And vice versa.)

In the Wind, for example, pictures them at the 1963 March on Washington, performing before the hundreds of thousands of people who lined the mall between the Lincoln Memorial and the Washington Monument. *In Concert,* the group's next set (and first live album), exposed their political concerns a little more directly, though not as pronouncedly or as exploitatively as say, the Chad Mitchell Trio.

A Song Will Rise was not one of their better-selling albums, though it did much for revitalizing a number of traditional and blues tunes, adding "Motherless Child," "San Francisco Bay Blues" (sparking interest in Jesse Fuller) and "Cuckoo" to the standard pop-folk repertoire.

It was *1700,* however, that finally brought the political overtones into the foreground. The civil rights movement had been overshadowed by the Vietnam War, and once again PP&M were among the leading singing protesters. In addition, although they sneered in fear at the growing importance of rock with "I Dig Rock and Roll Music" (as they had done earlier with "Blue" on *In Concert*), their sound matured considerably.

It was at this point too, though, that the group began to move in individual directions, Peter Yarrow in particular wanting to assume a more political stance. The two albums that followed *1700* were, for all intents and purposes, throwaways. *Ten Years Together* marked the formal end, the trio regrouping on rare occasions for benefit performances, more as a symbol of political unity than of group allegiance. — I.M.

TOM PETTY AND THE HEARTBREAKERS

★★★★ **Tom Petty and the Heartbreakers / Shel. 52006**

★★★★ **You're Gonna Get It / Shel. 52029**

Petty operates on the fringe of the New Wave, but hews much closer to the mainstream than the archetypal punk could stand. If anything, he is a Roger McGuinn protégé—"American Girl" is the best song he's written, and it is a ringer for the Byrds circa 1966—but there are also a host of Sixties pop and rock influences in his writing, arranging and singing. Both of these albums are too explicitly derivative to earn full five-star honors, but each of them is full of solid songs and enough hot licks to make them worthwhile additions to most mainstream rock collections. — D.M.

PEZBAND

★★ **Laughing in the Dark / Pass. 9826**

★★ **Pezband / Pass. 9821**

Powerful, if not terribly distinctive pop from a Chicago-based rock band; its roots are more in British pop-rock like Sweet and Amen Corner than in America, however, despite an appearance by Bruce Springsteen's saxman Clarence Clemons on the debut set, *Laughing in the Dark*. — D.M.

P.F.M.

★★★ **Chocolate Kings / Asy. 7E-1071**

★★★ **Jet Lag / Asy. 7E-1101**

These are supposed to be Italy's top progressive musicians, and in fact the P.F.M. sound is comparable to the best of a topflight English progressive group like Genesis. The vocals are studied Peter Gabriel copies, too. The group has a great deal of other material available on earlier, deleted U.S. albums for Manticore (Emerson, Lake and Palmer's label) or on import. — A.N.

ANTHONY PHILLIPS

★★★ **Private Parts and Places / Pass. 7905**

The original lead guitarist of Genesis returned in the mid-Seventies with a pleasant fusion of that group's art-rock pastoralism, and his own avant-garde notions. Not rock & roll, but not everything needs to be . . . I suppose. — D.M.

ESTHER PHILLIPS (LITTLE ESTHER)

★★★ **All About Esther Phillips / Mer. SRM-1-3733**

★★★ **Alone Again (Naturally) / Kudu 09**

★★★ **And I Love Him / Atl. 8102**

★★★ **Black-Eyed Blues / Kudu 14**

★★★★ **Burnin' / Atl. 1565**

★★ **Capricorn Princess / Kudu 31**

★★★ **Confessin' the Blues / Atl. 1680**

★★★ **From a Whisper to a Scream / Kudu 05**

★★★ **Little Esther Phillips / Power. 268**

★★★ **You've Come a Long Way Baby / Mer. SRM-1-1187**

Esther Phillips, a Texas-born blues and jazz singer, first emerged into the national spotlight as Little Esther in 1950, with "Cupid's Boogie" on Savoy. (That material is included on the Powerpak LP.) Extremely talented, with a sensual streak derived from Dinah Washington, she has rarely repeated even R&B chart success: "Ring a Ding Doo" for Federal in 1952 and "Release Me," an R&B reworking of a country standard that made R&B Top Ten in 1962 for Lenox, are her only other R&B Top Ten hits. Phillips worked steadily with Johnny Otis' soul revue, however, and in 1964 came close to a hit with the Beatles' "And I Love Him" for Atlantic. She did a series of smoldering sides for that label (most notably the live LP, *Burnin'*) before moving into a more modern pop-jazz groove with her Seventies LPs on Kudu, all of which are pleasant examples of contemporary pop and jazz vocalizing. — D.M.

MICHELLE PHILLIPS

★ **Victim of Romance / A&M 4651**

The former member of the Mamas and Papas turns in a dismal Hollywood pop album as a sort of 1978 comeback. Personally, I liked her better when she was married to Dennis Hopper—but then that only lasted a week. — D.M.

SHAWN PHILLIPS
★★ Bright White / A&M 4402
★ Collaboration / A&M 4324
★★★ Contribution / A&M 4241
★★★ Do You Wonder / A&M 4539
★★ Faces / A&M 4363
★★★ Furthermore / A&M 3662
★★★ Rumplestiltskin's Resolve / A&M 4582
★★★ Second Contribution / A&M 4282
★★ Spaced / A&M 4650
★★ Transcendence / RCA AFL1-3028

Phillips was signed to A&M in 1969, when he delivered a trio of homemade albums to the company; the label boiled them down to form *Contribution.* Mostly, he has mined a similar vein since then: folk and folk rock of the sort pioneered by Buffalo Springfield and Crosby, Stills and Nash. At his worst, Phillips is a quavering wimp; his philosophy is the usual muck of romanticism and ecology. But at his best, he deals comfortably with producer Paul Buckmaster's relatively lush arrangements, and on *Furthermore,* he collaborates capably with the British rock band Quartermass for some folk-classical mood music. — A.N.

BRUCE (U. UTAH) PHILLIPS
★★ El Capitan / Philo 1016
★★ Good Though / Philo 1004

Phillips is a better entertainer and performer than either of these LPs indicates. Though his vocal and guitar abilities are severely limited, he is both an aficionado and a raconteur as regards railroads, hobos and the West. Rosalie Sorrels, Joan Baez and a number of progressive bluegrass and country bands have recorded his material. "The Telling Takes Me Home" and "Daddy, What's a Train?" are favorites along the summer folk festival route. — I.M.

BOBBY PICKETT
★★★ Monster Mash / Par. X-71063

"Monster Mash," the hit takeoff on the Sixties dance song craze, is one of the greatest novelty songs ever. (It's been revived on radio a couple of times.) Bobby "Boris" Pickett and the Crypt Kickers do it in mock Boris Karloff style (Zacherle later did a cover version), with memorable lines like "It was a graveyard smash." The rest of the record is similar and, as you might expect, not as good. Great for Halloween parties, though. — J.S.

WILSON PICKETT
★★★ A Funky Situation / Big 76011
★★ Join Me and Let's Be Free / RCA ANL1-2149
★★★★★ The Best of Wilson Pickett / Atl. 8151
★★★ Wickedness / Trip 8010
★★★★★ Wilson Pickett's Greatest Hits / Atl. 2-501

Wilson Pickett's work on Atlantic in the Sixties defined a style of soul music. Bold and cocky, Pickett—like James Brown—seemed to symbolize soul music at its most kinetic. His hits are among the period's most memorable and include "In the Midnight Hour," "Mustang Sally" and "I'm in Love." The songs on *Greatest Hits* span almost a decade and range from the unleashed fury of "I Found a True Love" (sung with the Falcons) to slicker but still powerful, Gamble-and-Huff-produced performances like "Don't Let the Green Grass Fool You."

Wickedness is a collection of songs from Pickett's pre-Atlantic tenure on the Double L label. Undisciplined and raw, the ballads remain forceful and moving. Included are his first two solo hits, "If You Need Me" and "It's Too Late." The RCA album—like its deleted brethren and the album Pickett made for his own Wicked label—lacks direction and distinctive material. It's representative of the musical identity crisis experienced not only by Pickett but by other soul stars of the Sixties struggling to find a niche in the mid-Seventies. Pickett came as close to a complete rapprochement with current styles as anyone with *A Funky Situation,* produced by Rick Hall in Pickett's Sixties stomping ground, Muscle Shoals. The record manages to update the tracks—including the inspired "Lay Me like You Hate Me," a summation of Pickett's philosophy of romance—without losing the singer's distinctive style, as most recent veteran soul recordings have done. — J.MC.

RANDY PIE
★★★ Kitsch / Poly. 6518

Various Europeans (Frenchmen, Germans, Belgians) sing in English—the first Common Market jazz-rock band. *Kitsch* is less striking than the group's deleted, eponymous debut, but both display a witty, polished fusion synthesis. — A.N.

PIERCE ARROW
★ Pierce Arrow / Col. PC-34805

Ersatz Crosby, Stills and Nash mingles with Eagles hard rock, circa 1977. A totally formulaic approach to California rock, although the group also has New York roots—Doug Lubahn and Jeff Kent were in Dreams, the group that also featured Billy Cobham and the Brecker Brothers; David Buskin had a failed solo singer/songwriter career; Robin Batteau had appeared in Batteaux with his brother; Werner Fritzsching had been in Cactus and Dave Mason's backup band; Bobby Chouinard came from Orphan. However, a supergroup this ain't.   — D.M.

JOHN PILLA
★★ Southbound / Van. 79213
Only a middling folksinger, Pilla is justifiably much better known for his production work with Arlo Guthrie.   — D.M.

PILOT
★★★★ Morin Heights / EMI 779
Like Badfinger, Pilot specialized in brilliant re-creations of the high harmonies, memorable melodies and ringing guitars of the early Beatles. Its first two albums (now deleted) displayed the singing and writing of Billy Lyall and David Paton; the debut also contained an AM hit, "Magic." Lyall was gone by the time of *Morin Heights,* but Paton more than fills the gap, with the aid of Ian Bairnson's hard-edged guitar. Roy Thomas Baker's clear production works well.   — c.w.

MICHAEL PINDER
★★ The Promise / Thresh. 18
The former member of the Moody Blues comes across like a relaxed, introspective singer/songwriter: agreeable but unimpressive arranging and playing, light though not fluffy tempos and volume.   — c.w.

MIKE PINERA
★ Isla / Capri. 0202

From a guy who was in both Iron Butterfly and Blues Image you expected what— genius?   — D.M.

PINK FLOYD
★★★ A Nice Pair / Harv. SABB-11257
★★★ A Saucer Full of Secrets / Cap. ST-6279
★★ Atom Heart Mother / Harv. SKAO 382
★★★★ Meddle / Harv. SMAS 832
★ More / Cap. STW-1198
★★ Obscured by Clouds / Harv. STW-11078
★ Relics / Harv. SW-759
★★ The Piper at the Gates of Dawn / Tower ST-5093
★★★ Ummagumma / Harv. STBB-6318
Because they're a cult band with a mass audience, Pink Floyd has enjoyed a career of soaring ups and plummeting downs. The sound originated in late-Sixties British psychedelia, and Floyd's first two albums (*Piper* and *Saucer*) tortured song forms in the post-*Sgt. Pepper* manner. But those records also offered several instrumental space-rock seedlings that sprouted on *Ummagumma.*

At first, under Syd Barrett's leadership on *Piper,* the emphasis was on crazed songwriting. But with the harder rock sound of *Saucer,* the band developed a fruitful relationship between mannered experimentalism and aching lyricism, which it has never abandoned. However, these twin strains are not successfully synthesized until *Meddle.*

Ummagumma, a two-disc set, is a failed but fascinating experiment in the construction of avant-garde rock. On the studio sides, noise (electronic and documentary sounds), drone effects, mixed tempos and weirdly twisted song forms are mixed into sequences of fragmented pieces. It's something of a Pink Floyd notebook. The concert sides portray a very much advanced editing of the band that made *Saucer* the peak of its powers. It's here, incidentally, that Floyd creates the sounds of space-rock later developed into a major European genre by Hawkwind, Can, Tangerine Dream and others.

The lyrical soundtracks, *More* and *Obscured by Clouds,* are collections of light, often quasi-folkie ballads suggestive of impressionist sketches. Both were made to accompany European art films. The band retreats into polite but awkward poeticism and turns out music far more sentimental than the films.

Side one of *Atom Heart Mother* is an orchestral rethinking of the studio sides of *Ummagumma*. Not unlike something by the middle-period Deep Purple, Floyd breaks up into its component soloists and sets them in the context of a large orchestra playing a score of light classical fanfares. Even the several avant-garde sections late on the side fail to redeem the music's middle-brow pretensions. Side two is a rehash of ballad ideas left over from the movie scores.

The organization of *Meddle* is similar, but here the band has at last achieved a stylistic union of its aimless experimentalism and bland ballads. *Meddle*'s title track, which covers a whole side flows out of a primal beep to create a play of stasis/hypnosis and pulse/pathos. Strangely, after several failed soundtracks, this music achieves its own cinematic mood, in a decidedly sci-fi genre. Unfortunately, side two is filler, mostly ballads, although this time they don't suffer from *Atom Heart Mother*'s indifferent performances.

A Nice Pair repackages *Piper* and *Saucer*. *Relics* collects singles from *Piper* through *More* and is of little interest.
★★★★ Animals / Col. JC-34474
★★★★★ Dark Side of the Moon / Harv. SMAS-11163
★★★ Wish You Were Here / Col. PC-33453
Dark Side of the Moon is Pink Floyd's masterpiece. The band improved its sound immeasurably (helped by engineer Alan Parsons) and took the leisure to develop its songs into perfect vehicles for its instrumental procedures. While the main interest on *DSOTM* is to maintain a rich lyricism (aided by Dick Parry's saxophone and Clare Torry's vocals), the album also reintroduces *Ummagumma*'s experiments with noise and speech. These, together with bassist Roger Waters' lyrics, break *DSOTM*'s smooth surface with the flaky-epic urgency typical of the band's late albums.

Wish and *Animals* continue to work inside the style of *DSOTM*, but on those albums older Floyd ideas, like faster songs and harsh aural violence, are introduced into the majestic sweep. In these last albums, Waters' lyrics become progressively bitter in their rather smug pessimism: *Animals* is little more than one long execution by Orwellian allegory. With a great deal of spotlighted solo space, all three albums document guitarist David Gilmore's emergence as Floyd's major instrumentalist,

while keyboardist Rick Wright moves into the increasingly deep recesses of the band's music as the prime mover of Floyd's aural stagecraft.

Pink Floyd is a band that's never thrown away a single idea. While this may have resulted in a dearth of imagination and a kind of standardization, as cited by its many critics, this narrowness has also kept Floyd from the dilettantism of its art-rock colleagues (Moody Blues; Emerson, Lake and Palmer) who lapse inexorably into glossy sentiment. — B.T.

PIPER
★★ Can't Wait / A&M 4654
★★ Piper / A&M 4615
Potentially good rock & roll from a Boston-based quintet succumbs to heavy arranging: too many loud guitars doing too little. Yet a fresh pop sensibility and an occasional catchy tune surface. *Can't Wait* generally reduces *Piper*'s guitar blare (one song convincingly evokes the early Who), but elsewhere the embellishments are clumsy and out of place. — C.W.

PIRATES
★★ Out of Their Skulls / War. K-3155
★★ Skull Wars / War. K-3224
With the late Johnny Kidd as vocalist, the Pirates cut a seminal British rock single, "Shakin' All Over," and helped spawn the guitar styles of Townshend, Page, Beck et al. This 1978 recording, much of it live, includes a decent version of "Shakin' " (though not nearly as good as those by the Who and Guess Who) and a lot of rockabilly filler. Historians only. — D.M.

GENE PISTILLI
★ Jukin' / Cap. 11405
Pistilli's a pop singer whose main claim to fame is being part of Cashman, Pistilli and West, the trio that produced Terry Cashman and Tommy West, Jim Croce's producers. This is dull, dull, dull. — D.M.

GENE PITNEY
★★★ A Golden Hour of Gene Pitney / Musi. 60-3233
★★★ Big Sixteen / Musi. 2008
★★★ Big Sixteen, Vol. 2 / Musi. 3043
★★★★ Double Gold: The Best of Gene Pitney / Musi. X-4600
★★★ Gene Pitney / Sp. 4057
★★★ It Hurts to Be in Love / Musi. 3019
★ Just for You / Musi. 2004
★ Looking Through the Eyes of Love / Musi. 3069

★★★ Only Love Can Break a Heart / Musi. 3003

★★ Pitney '75 / Bronze 9314 (Import)

★ She's a Heartbreaker / Musi. 3164

★★ Sings Bacharach / Musi. 3161

★★★ 16 Greatest Hits / Trip TOP-16-16

★★ The Country Side of Gene Pitney / Musi. 3104

★★ The Gene Pitney Story / Musi. M2S-3148

★★★ The Golden Hits of Gene Pitney / Musi. 3250

★★★ This Is Gene Pitney (Singing the Platters' Golden Platters) / Musi. 3183

★ Young and Warm and Wonderful / Musi. 3108

★★★ World Wide Winners / Musi. 3005

Gene Pitney is a very strange case. At times he seemed to be one of the classic minor rock singers—listen to "(I Wanna) Love My Life Away," on which he played every instrument, overdubbed his own voice a dozen times, and added a devastating cymbal clash to the final bar of every chorus, a remarkable feat for 1961. Others of his hits present him as a fine ballad singer, almost a male counterpart of Dionne Warwick—"Only Love Can Break a Heart," "Town without Pity," "Half Heaven, Half Heartache" and even "Mecca" all fit here. But he also recorded country songs, operated as a falsetto in duets with George Jones, and sang Italian love songs and the schlockiest Tin Pan Alley ballads. It's confusing, but "Love My Life Away," "Last Chance to Turn Around," "The Man Who Shot Liberty Valance," "Mecca" and a few others make Pitney's importance unmistakable, if rather ineffable.

Pitney also had some importance as a writer—notably, "Hello Mary Lou," for Ricky Nelson—and as a discoverer of songwriters. He recorded as many Burt Bacharach and Hal David tunes as Warwick, although she was better known for it; had Carole King and Gerry Goffin songs in his repertoire; and was first to record Al Kooper's finest composition, "Just One Smile," later done by Blood, Sweat and Tears. Even Mick Jagger and Keith Richards wrote a song for him, the odd "That Girl Belongs to Yesterday"—and Pitney recorded with the Rolling Stones on their second album, along with crony Phil Spector. He is a significant figure for those reasons, as well.

Of these albums, the two-disc *Best of* is clearly the most worthy, although all of the *Greatest Hits* and other anthologies have

much to recommend them. *Best of*, however, leans a little more heavily toward his hard-edged material, including "Love My Life Away," the rockingest number he ever did, and stays away from the country-Italian junk. *Golden Hour* is almost as good, but is dragged down by a few Italian songs.

The *Country Side of* is interesting but inferior to the George Jones duets. *It Hurts* contains the Jagger-Richards "That Girl Belongs to Yesterday," and is of value to collectors. (The song was an English hit for Pitney.) Avoid *Looking Through, Just for You,* and particularly *Young and Warm and Wonderful,* all of which emphasize his Anka-esque roots. Most of the rest are relics of the early-Sixties era and consist of hits sandwiched with junk. *World Wide Winners* almost constitutes a greatest-hits LP, and has one of the classic schlock covers of the period. *This Is* is a curious experiment—Pitney as R&B vocalist—that almost works. *Pitney '75* was recorded after a long layoff, and gets an extra star just because his voice is in shape, which is more than can be said for either the material or arrangements. He is rumored to be recording again, but nothing has resulted since 1975. — D.M.

MARY KAY PLACE

★ Aimin' to Please / Col. PC-34908

★ Tonite! At the Capri Lounge—Loretta Hagers / Col. PC-34353

Place portrayed Loretta Haggers, a housewife who aspires to be a country-music star, in the TV series *Mary Hartman, Mary Hartman.* She gave both dignity and broad humor to what must have been a nasty caricature on paper. Here, she plays it straight as a country singer—it is typical of Place's honesty that she has tried to make these more than novelty cash-ins—but the music is mediocre. — K.T.

THE PLATTERS

★★★ Double Gold Platters / Musi. X-4601

★★★★ Encore of Golden Hits / Mer. 60243

★★★★ Sixteen Greatest Hits / Trip TOP-16-11

★★★ The Platters / Sp. 4059

One of the slickest R&B groups of the Fifties, the Platters were probably the most palatable to straight pop (or antirock) tastes, the logical successors to the Mills Brothers and the Ink Spots. But at their best, with "Smoke Gets in Your Eyes," "Harbor Lights," "Only You" and "The Great Pretender," the group perfected the kind of funky smooch music that Curtis Mayfield's Impressions and Smokey Robinson's Miracles would later make an art form. — D.M.

PLAYER

★ Danger Zone / RSO 1-3036
★★★ Player / RSO 1-3026

One of the several great singles from the hit disco movie *Saturday Night Fever,* "Baby Come Back" was probably a one-shot from this perfectly faceless Hall and Oates clone. For sure, as palatable as the self-titled debut album may be, it's also instantly forgettable; pop music as Chinese food. *Danger Zone* is less of the same. — D.M.

PLEASE

■ Manila Thriller / Lon. PS-672

Someone reading this book in the twenty-first century may need to know that the Thriller in Manila was the third Muhammad Ali-Joe Frazier prize fight, held in the Philippines' capital in 1975. No one else will care about such mediocre funk. (Now deleted.) — D.M.

PLEASURE

★★ Accept No Substitutes / Fan. 9506
★★ Dust Yourself Off / Fan. 9473
★★ Get to the Feeling / Fan. 9550
★★ Joyous / Fan. 9526

Another dance-yourself-to-death concoction. In the late Seventies, of course, it is often hard to tell whether compulsive joggers or obsessive dancers are more obnoxious. Pleasure's mindless funk, however, seems to swing the issue strongly toward the latter. — D.M.

POCKETS

★ Come Go with Us / Col. PC-34879
★ Take It On Up / Col. JC-35384

Utterly obnoxious black pop from 1977-78. The bottom of the Philadelphia funk barrel. Only for diehard dancers who've worn out everything else—including their shoes. — D.M.

POCO

★★★★ A Good Feelin' to Know / Epic PE-31601
★★★★ Cantamos / Epic PE-33192
★★★ Crazy Eyes / Epic PE-32354
★★★ Deliverin' / Epic PE-30209
★★★★ From the Inside / Epic KE-30753
★★★★ Head over Heels / ABC D-890
★★★ Indian Summer / ABC 989
★★★ Legend / ABC AA-1099
★★★ Live / Epic PE-33336
★★★★★ Pickin' Up the Pieces / Epic BXN-26460
★★★ Poco / Epic E-26522
★★★ Rose of Cimarron / ABC 946
★★★ Seven / Epic KE-32895
★★★★ The Very Best of Poco / Epic PEG-33537

Poco was founded in 1968 by two former members of Buffalo Springfield, Richie Furay and Jim Messina, along with three Coloradans, Rusty Young, Randy Meisner and George Grantham. Their first album, *Pickin' Up,* was an excellent combination of Beatles-inspired harmony, melody and beat with country & western's then-untapped rock possibilities. Furay's gorgeous tenor, Young's rockified pedal steel and an imaginatively tasteful mix of acoustic and electric guitars trademark the debut. Meisner then left to join first Ricky Nelson's Stone Canyon Band and later the Eagles, and Tim Schmit replaced him as bassist on *Poco,* which streamlined but somewhat reduced the sound with more electricity. But that album also wasted almost a whole side with an unthrilling instrumental. *Deliverin'* was a faithful but routine live album, and after it, Messina left to form Loggins and Messina. He was replaced by Paul Cotton, who had been in Illinois Speed Press. The Steve Cropper-produced *From the Inside* lacks some of the early exuberance, but the care and sheer professionalism with which it was made echoes the debut.

Cotton pushed the group in a somewhat harder, simpler direction and *A Good Feelin' to Know* took this several steps further. Recorded with a ragged toughness usually reserved for hard rock, the country influence seemed nearly abandoned—disorienting but good, if a bit drawn out. *Crazy Eyes,* though, had no apparent course: tepid covers of Gram Parsons and J. J. Cale songs and a lengthy, orchestrated, cryptic title cut bogged it down in correctness that left little room for excitement.

Seven suffers severely from the departure of Furay. Schmit was now the most important member—Furay wasn't replaced—and while the songs were good enough, the playing was too long and wimpy. But *Cantamos* brought back much of the old excitement; it marked Young's emergence as a writer and the more generous solo passages rocked hard and fresh. *Very Best* is an excellent sampler of this period; the subsequently released *Live* has adequately performed material from several of the earlier discs.

Head over Heels had densely arranged and recorded short songs—a modest excellence rarely reached—but *Rose of Cimarron* lacks raunch and drive. *Indian Summer* perks up a bit but lacks the subtleties and imagination of the group's best work. When Schmit became an Eagle (once more replacing Meisner), the Poco saga was completed, although *Legend* eked out a hit in "Crazy Love." — C.W.

POINT BLANK
★ **Point Blank / Ari. 4087**
★ **Second Season / Ari. 4137**
Pointless late-Seventies formula hard rock. — J.S.

BONNIE POINTER
★★ **Bonnie Pointer / Mo. M7-911**
Those who try to tell you that this cast-off Pointer Sister is a late-Seventies model of the great Motown singers of the Sixties either do not own *Mary Wells' Greatest Hits* or have not listened to it lately. Not bad, sort of tuneful, spritely melodies, but a long way from the genius of yesteryear. Says the purist. — D.M.

THE POINTER SISTERS
★★★ **Best of the Pointer Sisters / Blue Th. BTSY-6026**
★★ **Energy / Planet P-1**
★★ **Having a Party / Blue Th. 6023**
★★ **Live at the Opera House / Blue Th. 8002**
★★★ **Pointer Sisters / Blue Th. 48**
★ **Steppin' / Blue Th. 6021**
★★ **That's a Plenty / Blue Th. 6009**
Black woman vocal group whose gimmick was singing updated Andrews Sisters-type material from the Forties. The idea worked well enough in the early Seventies to net them a hit single, "Yes We Can Can." It

was all downhill from there, except for their Top Ten 1978-79 hit, the Richard Perry production of Bruce Springsteen's "Fire," from *Energy.* — J.S.

THE POLICE
★★★ **Outlandos d'Amour / A&M 4753**
Three-piece New Wave/punk/power pop/whatchamacallit band from England scored biggest hit in (you figure out the name of the genre) with their Top Forty hit, "Roxanne," in 1979. Leader Sting—another one-named rocker—copped the starring role in the Who's film of *Quadrophenia,* which is all the clue you need to know where this band's loyalties and roots lie. Not bad, but far more ingenious than inspired. — D.M.

MICHEL POLNAREFF
★ **Lipstick / Atl. 18178**
★★ **Michel Polnareff / Atl. 18153**
This singer/songwriter and multi-instrumentalist is apparently *le derrière du chat* in his native France, but his premier American release is most notable for the who's who of musician's musicians that back him up. The songs have commercial potential (which remains unrealized), and Polnareff sounds like a continental David Gates. *Lipstick* is a full-blown motion picture score (it starred Margaux Hemingway and it sucked) and has very little to do with rock & roll. (Now deleted.) — A.N.

DAVID POMERANZ
■ **It's in Everyone of Us / Ari. 4053**
Jazz-pop singer/songwriter (who made earlier albums for MCA) comes a cropper with this shriekingly pretentious pop album. (Now deleted.) — S.H.

CHARLIE POOLE
★★ **Legend of Charlie Poole / Coun. 516**
★★★ **Old Time Songs, I / Coun. 505**
★★ **Old Time Songs, II / Coun. 509**
Banjoist Poole and his North Carolina Ramblers were exponents of pre-bluegrass, country string-band music. Poole played his instrument using thumb and three fingers—as compared to the thumb and two-finger style later developed by Earl Scruggs. Known today as old-timey music, an idiom revitalized by the New Lost City Ramblers, these recordings (1925–1930) have been carefully remastered. The variations on traditional or "composed" pieces from the era ("Take a Whiff on Me" is heard as "Take a Drink on Me" on *Old Time Songs, I*) are of interest to both the scholar and the musician. — I.M.

IGGY POP
★★★ Lust for Life / RCA AFL1-2488
★ The Idiot / RCA APL1-2275
★ TV Eye—1977 Live / RCA AFL1-2796
Iggy Pop was once the leader of the
Stooges, the seminal punk-rock prototype.
Here he's produced by David Bowie, who
dominates on *The Idiot*, retreats on *Lust for
Life* and nearly disappears on *TV Eye*. By
the time Iggy got this far, his maniacal in-
spiration was gone. Better to search for the
now-deleted and sometimes brilliant
Stooges albums—*Fun House* and *The
Stooges* on Elektra, *Raw Power* on Colum-
bia, all available as imports—and then only
if you thought the Sex Pistols were mellow.
Some did.   — D.M.

PORTSMOUTH SINFONIA
★ Portsmouth Sinfonia Play the Popular
  Classics / Col. KC-33049
An orchestra of fifty-odd musicians, mostly
untrained, attacks the William Tell Overture, Beethoven's Fifth and seven others,
with predictably devastating results. This is
a by-product of Brian Eno's experiments
into the nature of the accident in music.
Perhaps the worst record ever made; best
dismissed as an intellectual joke. Liner
notes, however, a must-read.
■ Hallelujah / Ant. 7002
An orchestra of fifty-odd musicians, mostly
untrained, attacks an audience at the Royal
Albert Hall. A by-product of Brian Eno's
experiments into the nature of the accident
in music. Perhaps the worst record ever
made; best dismissed as an intellectual joke
not worth repeating.   — F.R.

JIM POST
★ Colorado Exile / Fan. 9401
★ Looks Good to Me / Fan. 9451
★ Rattlesnake / Fan. 9425
★ Slow to 20 / Fan. 9408
The definition of the mediocre singer/song-
writer.   — D.M.

POUSETTE-DART BAND
★★ Amnesia / Cap. SW-11608
★★★ Pousette-Dart Band / Cap.
  ST-11507
★★ Pousette-Dart Band 3 / Cap.
  SW-11781
Not quite folk, not quite rock. Jon Pousette-Dart's haunting melodies and raw yet
tasteful electric slide guitar distinguish
much of the debut, *Pousette-Dart Band,* as
does Norbert Putnam's clear, spacious production. Yet at the same time a blandness
lurks in other songs and Pousette-Dart's

voice. But John Curtis' acoustic guitar is a
neat complement.
   Amnesia and *Pousette-Dart Band 3* follow
the earlier record's worst tendencies and
the slide is mostly missing. These are more
rock orientated, with a slightly (and uncon-
vincingly) heavier beat in parts. The sax
and flute parts suggest interesting possibilities, which remain unexploited.   — C.W.

PRATT AND McCLAIN
★ Pratt and McClain, featuring "Happy
  Days" / War. MS-2250
The 1975 hit, spun off from the theme song
of the TV show. When that goes off the
air, this goes off the market. None too soon
either.   — D.M.

ANDY PRATT
★★★ Andy Pratt / Col. PC-31722
★★★★ Resolution / Nemp. 438
★★★ Shiver in the Night / Nemp. 443
Andy Pratt is a promising prodigy in the
pop school headmastered by the Beatles
and the Beach Boys; he plays pop rock
that is defined by its simple but catchy
melodies, thick harmonies and finely
glossed production. The Columbia album
boasted some of Pratt's melodic talents—
"Avenging Annie," unquestionably the album's highlight, ebbs and flows with the
assurance of only the best pop—but his
frail voice and occasionally cloying lyrics
were emphasized by the tentative production. Done with producer Arif Mardin,
though, *Resolution* is everything a pop album should be—simultaneously pretty and
melodically compelling, sincere and yet
self-aware, and clearly an effort of both
pleasurable and professional expertise.
Shiver is too baroque. Neither Mardin nor
Pratt can really rock out, and they
shouldn't have tried.   — J.B.M.

ELVIS PRESLEY/Early Years
★★★★★ A Date with Elvis / RCA
AFL1-2011
★★★★★ Elvis / RCA AFL1-1382
★★★★★ Elvis Presley / RCA AFL1-1254
★★★★★ For LP Fans Only / RCA
AFL1-1990
★★★★ King Creole / RCA AFL1-1884
★★★★ Lovin' You / RCA AFL1-1515
★★★★★ Sun Sessions / RCA APM1-1675
Elvis Presley is by far the most important
single figure in the history of rock & roll,
and possibly the most important in American popular music, a giant of the modern
era. We lean perilously close to toppling
into blathering fandom, and thus dispense
with historical detail, at least for this stage
of his career. Presumably, every reader
knows the outline of his initial success
from "That's All Right" through "Heartbreak Hotel" and the great early RCA and
Sun singles that accompanied them. If not,
the poor soul is referred to the bibliography appended to this volume; he or she
has some basic catching up to do.

Suffice it to say that these records, more
than any others, contain the seeds of everything rock & roll was, has been and most
likely what it may foreseeably become. The
most important of them by far are *The Sun
Sessions,* the ten songs released by Sam
Phillips' Memphis label before the Presley
contract was sold to RCA, and *Elvis* and
Elvis Presley, the first two RCA LPs. *A
Date* and *For LP Fans* contain a mixture of
Sun and early RCA material; they were released during his incarceration in the
Armed Forces. *King Creole* and *Loving You*
are the soundtracks to his early movies.
Each has some brilliant moments, thanks
to the excellence of Jerry Leiber and Mike
Stoller's songs, but they are nonetheless
soundtrack LPs, with hints of the limitations discussed more thoroughly below.

ELVIS PRESLEY/The Soundtracks
★★★ Blue Hawaii / RCA AFL1-2426
★★ Clambake / RCA APL1-2565
★★★ Double Dynamite / Camd.
DL2-5001
★★ Double Trouble / RCA AFL1-2564
★★★ Elvis Sings "Flaming Star" and Oth-
er Hits from His Movies / Camd. 2304
★★★ Elvis Sings Hits from His Movies /
Camd. 2567
★★ Frankie and Johnny / RCA
APL1-2559
★★ Fun in Acapulco / RCA AFL1-2756
★★★ G.I. Blues / RCA AFL1-2256
★★ Girl Happy / RCA AFL1-3338

★★★ Girls! Girls! Girls! / RCA
AFL1-2621
★★ Harum Scarum / RCA APL1-2558
★★ It Happened at the World's Fair /
RCA APL1-2568
★★ Kissin' Cousins / RCA LSP 2894
★★ Paradise, Hawaiian Style / RCA
AFL1-3643
★★ Roustabout / RCA AFL1-2999
★★★ Speedway / RCA AFL1-3989
★★★★ Spinout / RCA APL1-2560
Elvis made nearly forty movies, not count-
ing concert films and TV shows; almost all
of them were completely dismal, and the
LPs named after them, despite the occa-
sional inclusions of studio "bonus" tracks,
aren't much better. However, and this is
crucial, there are exceptions: *G.I. Blues* has
Presley fresh from the Army, before he got
worn down by mediocre scripts and banal
songs; *Girls! Girls! Girls!* has "Return to
Sender," a great single; *Spinout* has some
tough blues and a fine interpretation of a
Dylan song, "Tomorrow Is a Long Time."
Most of the rest of these are incompetent
on all levels; Presley isn't trying, probably
the wisest course in the face of material
like "No Room to Rumba in a Sports Car"
and "Rock-a-Hula Baby." When he does
try, though, which is mostly when he's
given something to try *with,* he's still one of
the greats.

**ELVIS PRESLEY/Post-Army Studio
Albums: The Sixties**
★★★ Almost in Love / Camd. 2440
★★★ Elvis for Everyone / RCA
AFL1-3450
★★★★ Elvis Is Back / RCA LSP-2231
★★★★ Elvis Sings the Wonderful World
of Christmas / RCA ANL1-1936
★★★ I Got Lucky / Camd. 2533
★★★ Pot Luck / RCA AFL1-2523

★★★ **Somethin' for Everybody** / RCA
AFL1-2370

It's hard to admit it, but Presley did manage to sandwich a few indications of his vast natural talent on almost all of the studio albums released during the doldrums of the Sixties. This is most apparent on *Elvis Is Back,* recorded immediately following his release from the Army, when something (his future) was at stake. Although the power of his first recordings is diluted, it's still a fine record. Unlikely as it may seem, so is the Christmas LP, which contains a couple of strong blues and some convincing renditions of traditional songs. The rest is average, with an occasional surprise; worth looking into for the obsessed.

ELVIS PRESLEY/Gospel and Inspirational LPs
★★★★★ **He Touched Me** / RCA
AFL1-4690
★★★ **He Walks Beside Me** / RCA
AFL1-2772
★★★★★ **His Hand in Mine** / RCA
ANL1-1319
★★★★★ **How Great Thou Art** / RCA
AFL1-3758
★★★★ **You'll Never Walk Alone** / Camd.
2472

Those who doubt that Presley was an intensely religious man have not heard these albums, almost all of which are among the most heartfelt he recorded. Except for the Camden, which lends toward secular inspirational songs, all are white gospel music and Presley's singing is nothing less than sublime; *How Great* even garnered a hit single, "Crying in the Chapel." *He Walks Beside Me* is a reissue of assorted gospel material with a couple of poor live songs added. It's noteworthy as one of RCA's first posthumous Presley releases but is otherwise dismissible.

ELVIS PRESLEY/The Great Comeback
★★★★★ **Elvis** / RCA AFM1-4088
★★★★ **Elvis Back in Memphis** / RCA
AFL1-4429
★★★★★ **From Elvis in Memphis** / RCA
AFL1-4155
★★★★ **From Memphis to Vegas** / RCA
LSP-6020

In 1968, Elvis withdrew from Hollywood, although he'd still make a couple more films there, to recenter his activities around live performances. This was first marked by a return to Memphis for recording sessions, and the initial album of the return, *From Elvis in Memphis,* is a masterpiece in which Presley immediately catches up with pop music trends that had seemed to pass him by during the movie years. He sings country songs, soul songs and rockers with real conviction, a stunning achievement. His Christmas 1968 TV special was even more remarkable, the first time in ten years Presley fans had been able to see him outside of a movie theater. He rose to the occasion magnificently, and rather than the banal show-business extravaganza that would have been so typical of his recent work, he came through with a set of hard-rocking blues and rock, represented on the show's soundtrack (*Elvis*). The other two albums attempt to continue such successes, with spottier results. The two-record *From Memphis to Vegas,* one disc of which was recorded live from his initial main-room casino shows, gave a hint of the uneven quality of what was to follow. Still, Presley had reestablished himself as the king of rock & roll, and he quickly became a major draw on both the concert circuit and in Vegas.

ELVIS PRESLEY/Live Albums
★★★ **As Recorded at Madison Square Garden** / RCA AFL1-4776
★★★ **Elvis Aloha from Hawaii (Via Satellite)** / RCA CPD2-2642
▪ **Elvis Having Fun on Stage** / RCA
AFM1-0818
★★★ **Elvis in Concert** / RCA APL2-2587
★★★ **Elvis in Person** / RCA AFL1-4428
★★★ **Elvis Recorded Live on Stage at Memphis** / RCA AFL1-0606
★★★★ **On Stage—February 1970** / RCA
AFL1-4362
★★★★★ **That's the Way It Is** / RCA
AFL1-4445

Live concerts gave Presley an ideal method to make equally speedy and shoddy recordings, a perfect substitute for soundtrack albums. Although only eight are represented here, there are far more than any other rock performer has ever released, and RCA probably has a few more shows in the can. Most of them are spotty, based on pseudo-events: a satellite broadcast to fifty countries (*Aloha*), his first-ever concert in New York (*Madison Square*), another return to *Memphis.* The best is *That's the Way It Is,* which is both a concert recording and a soundtrack, being the music from his final feature, a documentary of one of his shows, with a tremendous closing number, "Bridge over Troubled Water," the best version ever done of that warhorse. Being earlier than the others, *On Stage—*

February 1970 also isn't bad. The worst by far is *Having Fun on Stage,* two sides of tape-recorded byplay—bad jokes and about 10,000 requests for a glass of water.

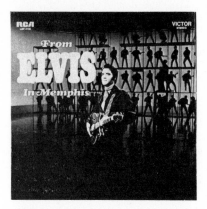

ELVIS PRESLEY/Studio LPs of the Seventies
★★★ **Elvis Good Times / RCA AFL1-0475**
★★★ **Elvis Now / RCA LSP-4671**
★★ **Elvis Raised on Rock/For Ol' Times Sake / RCA AFL1-0388**
★★★★ **Elvis Today / RCA AFL1-1039**
★★★ **From Elvis Presley Boulevard, Memphis, Tennessee / RCA AFL1-1506**
★★★★ **I'm 10,000 Years Old / RCA AFL1-4460**
★★★ **Love Letters from Elvis / RCA AFL1-4530**
★★★ **Moody Blue / RCA AFL1-2428**
★★★★ **Promised Land / RCA AFL1-0873**
★★★ **Welcome to My World / RCA AFL1-2274**

Although the live albums replaced the soundtracks as Presley's Seventies method of shrugging off his ability, his studio albums were of better quality than the ones he made in the previous era. Partly this was a matter of the variety of superior material available to him—a song like Billy Swan's "I Can Help" is tailor-made for the rollicking interpretation Elvis gives it on *Today,* which is sort of an updated rockabilly album. But Presley also did better with country sources (*10,000*) and the usual thrown-together assortments. Even something as ostensibly wrongheaded as *From Elvis Presley Boulevard* contains a magnificent performance of Timi Yuro's early-Sixties hit, "Hurt." Although rarely discussed, each of the albums in this group has more than a little to recommend it, and very few things to be said against it. Presley doesn't sound inspired very often, but he does

sound committed, which is generally enough.

ELVIS PRESLEY/Compilations
★★ **Burning Love / Camd. 2595**
★★★★★ **C'mon Everybody / Camd. 2518**
★★★★ **Elvis: A Legendary Performer, Vol. 1 / RCA CPL1-0341**
★★★★ **Elvis: A Legendary Performer, Vol. 2 / RCA CPL1-1349**
★★★★★ **Elvis' Golden Records, Vol. 1 / RCA AFL1-1707**
★★★★★ **Elvis' Golden Records, Vol. 2 / RCA AFL1-2075**
★★★★★ **Elvis' Golden Records, Vol. 3 / RCA AFL1-2765**
★★★★★ **Elvis' Golden Records, Vol. 4 / RCA AFL1-3921**
★★ **Elvis Separate Ways / Camd. 2611**
★★ **Let's Be Friends / Camd. 2408**
★★★ **Pure Gold / RCA ANL1-0971**
★★★★★ **World Wide Fifty Gold Award Hits, Vol. 1 / RCA LPM-6401**
★★★★ **World Wide Fifty Gold Award Hits, Vol. 2 / RCA LPM-6402**

Presley's songs have been frequently reassembled into a variety of packages, most of them tossed together without much consideration or respect. The leading offenders are the Camden packages, a hit or two (at most) surrounding pure trash; *Burning Love,* for instance, cashes in on Presley's last big pop hit (1972) by putting it on an album with lame songs from the movies. But at least the Camden packages have budget prices. *Pure Gold* tosses together some good hits, some bad, without annotation or reason; there's some decent music here, but the range is neither focused enough to be insightful nor broad enough to give a complete outline of Presley's skills.

The four-volume *Golden Records* series is far better. It isn't annotated either, but the covers are great—Volume 2, subtitled *Fifty Million Elvis Fans Can't Be Wrong,* features the King in his gold lamé suit, allegedly worth $10,000—and together the four discs provide all the hits, major and minor, through the mid-Sixties. The *World Wide Fifty Gold Award Hits* packages, which are four discs each, take the Presley story (or its highlights) through 1969, the final side of the great Volume 1 containing "In the Ghetto," "Kentucky Rain," "Suspicious Minds" and the other brilliant sides Presley made in his early return to Memphis recording studios. Volume 2 is weaker, since it is mostly B sides, but does contain the songs from his three early EPs, all of them worth having. But neither of these are annotated either; perhaps RCA feels commentary would be superfluous, gilding an obvious lily.

The real gems of this genre, however, are the two *Legendary Performer* albums, which are not only annotated (not particularly well) but also include things like photographs of the early days, pictures of Presley memorabilia, RCA contractual documents and the like. They also contain enough variety to give a true picture of Presley's career—famous mediocrities like "Blue Hawaii," alongside outtakes from the fabled Sun sessions. RCA could do worse than to continue to construct such packages from the man's massive *oeuvre*—God knows how much unreleased Presley there may be. But a year after his death, there's absolutely no indication that the company (or Colonel Tom Parker, who presumably still controls the Presley recorded legacy) are ready to pay him the artistic homage he deserves. Yet as the *Legendary Performer* sets, as well as so much else here, indicate, Elvis Presley was the king of rock & roll not only because he was first and most influential, but also because he was the best singer and the most creative personality that the music has produced. — D.M.

BILLY PRESTON
★★ A Whole New Thing / A&M 4656
★★ Billy / A&M 4587
★★ Everybody Likes Some Kind of Music / A&M 3526
★★ Gospel in My Soul / Pick. 179
★★ It's My Pleasure / A&M 4532
★★ I Wrote a Simple Song / A&M 3507
★★ Kids and Me / A&M 3645
★★ Music Is My Life / A&M 3516
★★★ Original Billy Preston—Soul'd Out / GNP 2-2071
★★★ The Genius of Billy Preston / Sp. 4034
★★★ The Wildest Organ in Town / Cap. SM-2532

Billy Preston was a gospel-music prodigy—he played the young W. C. Handy in the film *St. Louis Blues*—and in his teens, he toured with Little Richard and Sam Cooke; he recorded his first album for the latter's Sar Records in 1964, then won a regular spot on ABC-TV's *Shindig*. Ray Charles then became his patron, and he made an album with Charles' aid, which resulted in the British hit single, "Billy's Bag." Later in the Sixties, George Harrison took Preston under his wing (an odd exam-

ple of Krishna/Christian ecumenicalism), and Preston participated in the Beatles' *Get Back* and *Let It Be* sessions. For Apple, he made his first record to receive much white American attention, "That's the Way God Planned It," a pleasant gospel-rock attempt.

But it was after leaving Apple for A&M that Preston became a star. His initial A&M LP, *Simple Song*, earned him a No. 1 hit with "Outa Space" and his next two records (*Music Is My Life, Everybody Likes Some*) also produced hits, "Will It Go Round in Circles" and "Space Race." The records weren't much—tepid funk riffs with bellowed vocals and vaguely spiritual lyrics—but they kept him chic enough to earn a bid to appear as the Rolling Stones' keyboardist on the band's 1975 American tour. But his music since then has merely reworked the pallid formula established on the earlier records. Perhaps his most interesting work is the pre-Apple material available on the Springboard and GNP sets. — D.M.

THE PRETTY THINGS
★★★ Real Pretty / Rare R7-549
★★★ Silk Torpedo / Swan 8411

The Pretty Things were originally a spinoff from the Rolling Stones when bassist Dick Taylor (who'd been an original Stone) and guitarist Phil May formed the band in 1963. Their early sides, unavailable here but represented on the import collection *Attention! The Pretty Things!* (Fontana Special 6438 059, German), are raw-edged white R&B, drawing heavily on Bo Diddley, Chuck Berry and similar black urban R&B shouters. Today that style is dated but enormously attractive for its visceral energy and the streak of wildness that made the Prettys seem ribald even as the Stones edged ever nearer to the socially acceptable.

The group later expanded its base into psychedelia for a rock opera, *S.F. Sorrow,* released a year before *Tommy* but without much apparent influence on it. Taylor left shortly thereafter, and while some of the group's material since is well regarded in Anglophile rock circles, it's really only competent and conventional hard rock. One suspects the recent LPs for Led Zeppelin's Swan Song label were made more out of Jimmy Page's sense of historical obligation than because the band rates such attention these days. — D.M.

DORY PREVIN
★★★ Dory Previn / U. Artists 5336

★★ Dory Previn Live at Carnegie Hall /
U. Artists LA-108-Z
★★★ Mary C. Brown and the Hollywood
Sign / U. Artists 5657
★★ Mythical Kings and Iguanas / Media.
41-10
★★ On My Way to Where / Media. E1-1
★★ We're Children of Coincidence and
Harpo Marx / War. B-2908
A talented if somewhat overbearing and
verbose songwriter with a horrible voice,
Dory Previn's cult status never evolved
into anything larger-scale. She has more to
offer devotees of Tin Pan Alley and soap
operas than rock & roll fans. — J.S.

ALAN PRICE
★★★ Alan Price / Jet LA-809-G
★★★★ O Lucky Man / War. B-2710
★★★ This Price Is Right / Par.
PAS-71018
Former organist for Animals was one of
the first to record Randy Newman (*This
Price*). His song cycle for *O Lucky Man*
soundtrack uses rock as nastily witty
Greek chorus commentary on the film's
scenario. But its worthy Warner followup,
Between Today and Yesterday, is a cutout.
Price's later albums were never released in
the U.S. and are available only via import,
except for the mediocre 1978 set on
Jet. — S.H.

LLOYD PRICE
★★★★ Sixteen Greatest Hits / ABC
X-763
★★★ Sixteen Greatest Hits / Trip
TOP-16-5
★★★★ The ABC Collection / ABC
AC-30006
His two big rock-era hits, "Personality"
and "Stagger Lee," were characteristic of
the sophisticated R&B Price was doing
with rhythm and blues throughout the Fif-
ties. (The best hit was probably "Lawdy
Miss Clawdy" for Specialty in 1952.) Ei-
ther of the ABC albums will fill you in;
Price was more than occasionally terrific at
Jackie Wilson-era soul music. The Trip is
unnecessary unless the ABC's are unavail-
able. — D.M.

RAY PRICE
★★ Christmas Album / Col. CS-9861
★★ Danny Boy / Col. CS-9477
★★★ Hank 'n' Me / Dot 2062
★★★ Help Me / Col. KC-34710
★★★ If You Ever Change Your Mind /
Col. KO-33560
★★ Like Old Times Again / ABC D-871

★★★ More Ray Price's Greatest Hits /
Col. CS-9470
★★ Rainbows and Tears / Dot 2053
★★★★ Ray Price's All Time Greatest
Hits / Col. CG-31364
★★★★ Ray Price's Greatest Hits / Col.
CS-8866
★★★ Reunited / Dot 2073
★★ Say I Do / Dot 2037
★★★ She's Got to Be a Saint / Col.
KC-32033
★★★★ The Best of Ray Price / Col.
KC-34160
★★★★ The World of Ray Price / Col.
CG-28
★★ Welcome to My World / Col.
CG-30878
★★ You're the Best Thing That Ever Hap-
pened to Me / Col. KC-32777
Ray Price was known as the Cherokee
Cowboy, not because he was part Ameri-
can Indian, but because he came from
Cherokee County in East Texas, the same
territory that produced Jim Reeves, whose
songs his early honky-tonk weepers some-
times resemble. Price began recording in
the late Forties, but it wasn't until he
signed on with Columbia and with the
Grand Ole Opry, in 1952, that he won a
wide audience. In 1956, "Crazy Arms" became his first No. 1 national hit; it remains
a country standard, as do "Same Old Me"
and "Heartaches by the Number," among
his grab bag of other hits in the Fifties.
"Make the World Go Away" was his best
Sixties recording, but while Price was continually commercially successful in that
decade, he was one of the first honky-tonk-
ers to resort to using strings and other pop
arrangements on his records, with results
that were at first energizing and later bathetic. The later sessions for ABC are exercises in mild competence. — D.M.

JOHN PRINE
★★★★ Bruised Orange / Asy. 6E-139
★★★ Common Sense / Atl. 18127
★★★ Diamonds in the Rough / Atl. 7240
★★★ John Prine / Atl. 8296
★★ Prime Prine / Atl. 18202
★★★★ Sweet Revenge / Atl. 7274
After over five albums of original songs,
John Prine has evolved from a sentimental
but witty folkie to a nihilistic but thought-
ful soft rocker. Prine comes from working-
class Chicago, and he's not only worked
for the post office but served in the Army;
all of that experience is reflected in his
songs. His first album was his most popular, containing both "Sam Stone" and

"Hello in There," which remain his best-known songs. The abuse of Vietnam vets and the neglect of old people, respectively, were just the sort of subjects a socially conscious folk-based singer/songwriter should have strummed about in 1971, but because of Prine's corrosive cynicism and withering imagery, the songs soon seemed too pat. The far better things about the album were its shiveringly accurate feeling for white working-class life, as depicted in "Far from Me" and "Six O'Clock News," and an inclination toward lean, gutbucket country music that no young performer until Gary Stewart could equal.

The soupy melodrama of "Hello in There" increased on *Diamonds in the Rough,* which nonetheless included "Yes I Guess They Oughta Name a Drink after You," a glorious Hank Williams throwback.

Prine's disappointment at not becoming a star was palpable. On the cover of *Sweet Revenge,* he sprawled unshaven in the front seat of a convertible, pointy-toed cowboy boots thrust out and a hungover fuck-you expression beneath his shades. The music here is harder with country melodies, more smoothly complex lyrically, and more bitter and unforgiving in content. The soft-hearted songs, "Grandpa Was a Carpenter" and "Christmas in Prison," were redeemed by a modicum of sentimentality and a maximum of terse description.

Common Sense is Prine's greatest commercial failure but it is also his most daring and intermittently triumphant album. To those who loved "Sam Stone," *Common Sense* made no sense—Prine's sidewalk yowl and rock rhythms were unpalatable to old fans, and no new rock fans paid attention. In fact, Prine was thrashing around for a new stance, a deceptively cheerful equivalent to Neil Young's *Tonight's the Night. Common Sense* concludes with a driving, hoarse version of Chuck Berry's "You Never Can Tell," which served both as a warning admonition (would Prine continue in this electric vein in a further—probably doomed—stab at becoming a late Seventies folk rocker?), or has he been consumed by his bitterness? *Prime Prine,* the best of album released during the two-year silence which followed, clarified nothing, being predictably chosen and folkie-minded.

Bruised Orange, released in mid-1978, was quiet, almost somber, a grouping of eccentric vignettes of urban working life, love songs and one hilarious blast at record-business promotional ploys, "Sabu Visits the Twin Cities Alone." The best of the love songs, "If You Don't Want My Love," was written with Phil Spector, but Prine's best work was done on his own, abetted by Steve Goodman's perfect production touch. "Fish and Whistle," "That's the Way that the World Goes 'Round" and "Crooked Piece of Time" mask the toughness of their locales and stories with whimsical, gentle singing. *Bruised Orange* is an oddity, almost completely ignored by the public and radio alike, but it is nearly John Prine's masterpiece, a complete statement of one of the most interesting visions the Seventies has produced. — K.T./D.M.

PETER PRINGLE
★★★ **Peter Pringle** / Rep. 2243
Passable Hollywood singer/songwriter (probably not the heir to the potato chip fortune). Songs forgettable, accompaniment distinguished (Bill Payne from Little Feat; producer Brian Ahern on bass; Linda Ronstadt on a backup vocal turn) but essentially ditto. Lush and empty. (Now deleted.) — D.M.

FREDDIE PRINZE
★★★ **Looking Good** / Col. PC-33562
Prinze was the first Latin stand-up comic to become a star, but except for a couple of autobiographical bits that bite, Prinze borrowed heavily from black stylists—Pryor, Foxx and Cosby—rather than evoking anything especially Puerto Rican. He also copped his philosophy from Lenny Bruce, a big mistake that only further confused his ethnic/comedic point of view. Genuine laughs when he speaks lovingly of his mother, though. (Now deleted.) — K.T.

MADDY PRIOR AND JUNE TABOR
★★★★ **Silly Sisters** / Chrys. 1101
Terrific one-shot in which Steeleye Span's Prior teams up with the similarly inclined Tabor for a set of medieval to modern English folk music, but with far more bounce and joy than any of the Steeleye records. Much ironic commentary on male-female relationships, marital and otherwise. Splendid Sunday morning music for apostates. — D.M.

PRISM
★ **Prism** / Ario. ST-50020
★ **See Forever Eyes** / Ario. SW-50034
Portentous progressive rock: a dab of Genesis, a smidgen of Yes. For synthesizer clones only. — D.M.

PROCOL HARUM

★★★★★ **A Salty Dog / A&M 4179**
★★★★★ **A Whiter Shade of Pale / A&M 4373**
★★ **Broken Barricades / A&M 4294**
★★★★ **Exotic Birds and Fruit / Chrys. 1058**
★★★ **Grand Hotel / Chrys. 1037**
★★★★ **Home / A&M 4261**
★★ **Live with the Edmonton Symphony Orchestra / A&M 4335**
★★★ **Procol's Ninth / Chrys. 1080**
★★★★ **Shine On Brightly / A&M 4151**
★★★ **Something Magic / Chrys. 1130**
★★★★ **The Best of Procol Harum / A&M 4401**

A Whiter Shade of Pale (originally released on Deram as *Procol Harum*) presented an imaginative, realized, and (for 1967) wholly unlikely combination of styles: Gary Brooker's excellent vocals echoed blues wailers like Ray Charles; Robin Trower's thickly distorted guitar recalled Eric Clapton's blues-based work with Cream; Matthew Fisher's cathedral organ borrowed from the seriousness, precision and majesty of classical composers; B. J. Wilson was a nimble and individual drummer; Keith Reid's lyrics owed much to Dylan's surrealistic *Blonde on Blonde* phase. The constant combination of piano (Brooker) and organ was largely unknown in rock at the time. *Shine On Brightly* continued this approach and included a long, shifting, multi-segmented magnum opus, one of rock's first.

Less a one-man show for Brooker (who had been writing almost all the music), *A Salty Dog* took many chances and succeeded brilliantly: grand orchestrations, subtle sound effects, quaint and somewhat rustic instruments, Fisher's gentle vocals, and ruder and more pared-down blues variations.

Fisher then quit and was replaced by Chris Copping (who doubled on bass), an adequate player but one without his predecessor's imagination. *Home* thus lacked the maturity, sweep and variety of earlier Procol, but did press further into harder rocking territory.

Broken Barricades erratically extended the heavier direction, failing twice with ragged, simplistic and poorly sung cuts from Trower. Elsewhere, the group was stale or long-winded, despite the prettiness of the title track, at the finish of which Wilson turns in some of his finest signatures.

Trower then left, and his successors have offered competent but not excellent similarity. The live LP had no new songs, and only smoothed out and drained the old arrangements with tasteful but sterilizing orchestration—too polite an approach for what was finally a rock group, whatever its obvious classical inspirations.

The Best assembled superior tracks from the previous six albums, as well as some fine B sides and never-released tracks.

Grand Hotel had Brooker back in control, but except for Wilson, it's a faceless cast, and the record was only a pale reflection of the band's past. But *Exotic Birds and Fruit* nearly matched the best of the Fisher/Trower days with its energetic paces, gentle melodies, gritty engineering and unabashed confidence. Given inspiring material, Procol showed it could still rise to the occasion.

Procol's Ninth (actually their tenth, including *The Best*) tried new tacks with some success: production from Jerry Leiber and Mike Stoller all but ignored the classical influence yet kept the group's basic sound intact. A horn-enlivened rock & roll song worked, as did an organ simulating bagpipes, but the Beatles' "Eight Days a Week" didn't.

Something Magic offered unconvincing and disjointed dollops of previous stylings; side two was a lengthy, boringly narrated indulgence. — C.W.

PROCTOR AND BERGMAN

★★★ **Give Us a Break / Mer. SRM-3719**
★★★★ **TV or Not TV / Col. KC-32199**
★★ **What This Country Needs / Col. PC-33687**

The performing half of the Firesign Theatre melds its characteristic Joycean wit with some hilarious slapstick routines. Their first album (*TV*) is the most successful of all the Firesign Theatre's side projects. — J.S.

PROFESSOR LONGHAIR
★★★★ Live on the Queen Mary / Harv.
  SW-11790
★★★★ New Orleans Piano / Atco 7225
Roy Byrd, a.k.a. Professor Longhair, is
widely acknowledged as the greatest New
Orleans dance-hall pianist in the post--
World War II era. His raucous, bawdy,
half-chanted vocals over the wildest barrelhouse keyboard pounding you're ever
likely to hear has strongly influenced New
Orleans pianists, from Fats Domino to
Mac Rebennack (a.k.a. Dr. John) and Allen Toussaint. Byrd's influence can be
gauged, in fact, by comparing the 1953 version of "Tipitina" on the Atco set (*New Orleans Piano*) to Dr. John's early Seventies
tribute on *Gumbo.*

New Orleans Piano collects Longhair's
Atlantic sides from 1949 and 1953, including some previously unissued goodies like
"Ball the Wall" and "Longhair's Blues
Rumba." Many characteristic sides for various obscure Southern labels are unfortunately unavailable (import pressings turn
up from time to time), but this is a more
than adequate representation of Byrd at
the height of his powers. *Queen Mary,* recorded in 1975 at a party for Paul McCartney, shows how little those talents have diminished in twenty years. The material
here is more traditional than on the Atco
set, but it's still exciting, as is Byrd's relentless performance. — J.S.

FRANK PROFFITT
★★ Frank Proffitt Sings Folk Songs /
  Folk. 2360
★★★ Reese, North Carolina / Folk-Leg. 1
It was Proffitt's version of the traditional
ballad "Tom Dooley," made world-famous
by the Kingston Trio, that is credited with
formally launching the late Fifties folk revival. Proffitt himself, however, was a wellspring of ballads, first tapped by Frank
Warner and later recorded by Sandy Paton, who went to Proffitt's home to make
the tapes that resulted in both these albums. A tobacco farmer, carpenter and instrument maker, Proffitt was also known in
folk circles for the fretless banjos he built
and played. His own rendition of "Tom
Dooley" is on the Folk-Legacy
LP. — I.M.

BRIAN PROTHEROE
★★★ I/You / Chrys. 1108

An eclectic stylist, Protheroe suggests,
though doesn't copy, other artists (Beatles,
Donovan, Jethro Tull, et al.) but has yet to
forge his own musical identity. This LP,
like his earlier deleted pair, skips from
hints of jazz to rock to music hall to various permutations thereof. His keen and
fresh melodies and bright tenor voice determine the music, and the spare arrangements (usually with his keyboards, and
acoustic guitar in front), as well as Del
Newman's sleek production, are nicely
complementary. — C.W.

RICHARD PRYOR
★★★ Are You Serious / Laff 196
★★★★ Bicentennial Nigger / War. K-3114
★★★ Black Ben / Laff 200
★★★★ Craps / Laff 146
★★★ Down-in-Dirty / Laff 184
★★★ Is It Something I Said? / Rep.
  K-2285
★★★ Richard Pryor / Rep. 6325
★★★ Richard Pryor Meets Richard and
  Willie and the S.L.A. / Laff 188
★★★ Richard Pryor's Greatest Hits / War.
  BK-3057
★★★ That Nigger's Crazy / Rep. K-2287
Richard Pryor is by far the most inspired
and hilarious of all the Seventies black co-
medians, just this side of genius in a good
many of his movie roles. On record, he's
more erratic, with a tendency to fall back
on the puerile sexual and racial stereotypes
of under-the-counter party albums, of
which Laff's series is typical. For Warner
Bros., he's changed little, although on his
best record, *Bicentennial Nigger,* he pulls off
some bits (particularly the title piece) that
are frightening in their bitterness and rage
and funny only to the truly paranoid. At
such moments, Pryor is easily the funniest
man in America. — D.M.

ARTHUR PRYSOCK
★★★ All My Life / Old Town 74-12004
★★ Arthur Prysock '74 / Old Town
  73-12001
★★★ Best of Arthur Prysock / Verve
  6-5011
★★ Love Makes It Right / Old Town
  74-12002
★★★ Silk and Satin / Poly. 2-8901
★★★ This Is My Beloved / Verve 6-5070
Prysock was only sort of a blues singer in
the Delta to uptown sense; he was really a
part of the jazz scene. His biggest hit, "I
Didn't Sleep a Wink Last Night," came in
1952, although he was on the fringes of the
R&B scene, as a sort of minor-league

Jimmy Rushing, for many years thereafter. — D.M.

PURE FOOD AND DRUG ACT
★★★ Choice Cuts / Epic E-31401
Better-than-average early-Seventies blues-rock group with some inclination to jazz complexity, led by guitarist Harvey Mandel and violinist Don "Sugar Cane" Harris. Now deleted. — J.S.

PURE PRAIRIE LEAGUE
★★★ Bustin' Out / RCA AFL1-4769
★★ Dance / RCA APL1-1924
★★★ If the Shoe Fits / RCA AFL1-1247
★★★ Just Fly / RCA AFL1-2590
★★★ Pure Prairie League / RCA
  AFL1-4650
★★★ Takin' the Stage / RCA CPL2-2404
★★★★ Two Lane Highway / RCA
  APL1-0933
Pure Prairie League's leaders, Craig Fuller and George Powell, come from Kentucky. Their debut (the self-titled LP) and *Bustin' Out* were agreeably quiet and modest blends of pop-rock songs with C&W arrangements; Fuller's writing and singing

added a special gentleness. Fuller left before *Two Lane Highway,* where the group honed its earlier approaches, beefed up the guitars and investigated related stylings for greater variety. The other albums are slight variations on this approach. *Takin' the Stage* is a live LP. — C.W.

THE PURIFY BROTHERS
★★ James and Bobby / Mer.
  SRM-1-1134
The Purify Brothers are best known for their 1966 Top Ten hit, "I'm Your Puppet." But this album, released much later, should be better. Despite good songs and inspired vocals, *James and Bobby* is sabotaged by dull production. (Now deleted.) — J.MC.

PUZZLE
★ Puzzle / ABC 671
Third-rate pop-rock from the progressive Seventies, which proves that neither Elvis Presley nor Alan Freed made a damn bit of difference: there's still one born every minute, and most of them become record-company executives. — D.M.

Q

★★ **Dancin' Man / Epic PE-34691**
1977's answer to Mother's Finest: a black-oriented rock band about half as funky as it likes to proclaim it is. — D.M.

SIDNEY JOE QUALLS
★★ **I Enjoy Loving You / Dakar 76914**
How about an entire album by somebody who's made a career of sounding exactly like Al Green? The title song was a minor soul hit. — J.MC.

BILL QUATEMAN
★★ **Night after Night / RCA AFL1-2027**
★★ **Shot in the Dark / RCA APL1-2434**
An expressive rock singer and versatile multi-instrumentalist from Chicago. His performing skills far outweigh his writing abilities. — S.H.

MICHAEL QUATRO
■ **Getting Ready / Prod. P7-10016**
A former concert promoter (in Detroit, where else?) decides he can do it better himself. The result is a hash of overworked classical clichés, amplified beyond endurance. Quatro's chief claim to fame is that he is the brother of Anglo-American pop tart Suzi Quatro, and although this is his third album, the relationship is destined to remain the same. If ever records deserved to be melted . . . — D.M.

QUEEN
★★★ **A Day at the Races / Elek. 6E-101**
★★★ **A Night at the Opera / Elek. 7E-1053**
★★ **Jazz / Elek. 6E-166**
★★ **News of the World / Elek. 7E-112**
★★ **Queen / Elek. 75064**
★★ **Queen II / Elek. 75082**
★★★ **Sheer Heart Attack / Elek. 7E-1026**

This quartet of British college boys was assembled in 1972, and between the androgynous rich-kid posturings of vocalist Freddie Mercury and the metallic extravagances of Brian May's guitar, it bridged the gap between Led Zeppelin and David Bowie quite effectively, becoming one of the highest-grossing bands of the current era.

The debut albums are mostly fast, loud, guitar-dominated heavy rock, but taken considerably further than the genre's traditional blues base. *Queen II* has richer arrangements and a slightly less frenzied approach, which isn't always a blessing. The group's flamboyance couldn't always compensate for the weakness of its songwriting.

Sheer Heart Attack is streamlined: shorter songs, which are more hard than heavy, with an often simplified framework, although the ornate flourishes still obtrude. Mercury's piano playing also comes to the fore here. *A Night at the Opera,* which contains the classical hodgepodge "Bohemian Rhapsody," and *A Day at the Races* sharpened the now-varied attack. Queen effectively mimicked all the big-time British bands, moving through Zeppelin-like heaviness, Mercury's breathy vocals and piano, and May's more mainstream rock singing and guitar work. But *News of the World* took the band back closer to its heavy-metal base; the arrangements lack variety and the songs aren't just simple, they are redundant. Jazz was another bombastic farce. — D.M.

THE QUICK
■ **Mondo Deco / Mer. SRM-1-1114**
Huysmans would roll over in his oversensitive grave to listen to this premature version of decadence. The lead guitar player sings about "my purgatory years" and it

sounds like they're not over yet. (Now deleted.) — B.M.

QUICKSILVER MESSENGER SERVICE
★★★ Anthology / Cap. SVBB-11165
★★ Comin' Thru / Cap. SMAS-11002
★★★★ Happy Trails / Cap. ST-120
★★ Just for Love / Cap. SMAS-498
★★ Quicksilver / Cap. SW-819
★★★ Quicksilver Messenger Service / Cap. ST-2904
★★★ Shady Grove / Cap. SM-391
★★ Solid Silver / Cap. SM 11820
★★ What about Me / Cap. SMAS-630

Quicksilver was probably the most overrated of the original batch of San Francisco groups. Its personnel was somewhat stellar—Dino Valenti wrote "Hey Joe" (under a pseudonym) and Jefferson Airplane's "Let's Get Together"; David Freiberg is now a member of Jefferson Starship; and English session veteran Nicky Hopkins appeared with the band during the *Shady Grove* period. But the group made only one noteworthy record, *Happy Trails,* which catches them live, at their peak, on versions of "Who Do You Love" and "Mona." Both tracks feature guitar extravaganzas by John Cipollina that are among the best instrumental work any San Francisco band did. They are the only hint available about where Quicksilver earned its reputation. — D.M.

QUIET SUN
★★★ Mainstream / Ant. 7008

Hard-hitting jazz rock—emphasizing the latter—paced by Phil Manzanera's stingingly exotic guitar and Dave Jarrett's shimmering keyboards. Open arrangements leave plenty of soloing room, with solid ensemble playing underneath. Accessibly eccentric. (Now deleted.) — C.W.

JIMMY RABBIT AND RENEGADE
★★ **Jimmy Rabbit and Renegade / Cap. ST-11491**
Disc jockey turned country singer leads a country-rock group through predictable paces. (Now deleted.) — D.M.

RABBITT
★★ **Boys Will Be Boys / Capri. 0175**
★★ **Croak and a Grunt in the Night / Capri. 0190**
Blues-rock keyboardist and guitarist notable as a session player in Britain (and in 1979, semi-official shadow member of the Who) takes on Southern funk with unexciting results. Do not open until Easter. — J.S.

TREVOR RABIN
★★ **Trevor Rabin / Chrys. 1196**
The 1978 vogue term for Rabin's brand of pop-rock was power pop, which meant that he had a cheery voice and a heavily chorded electric guitar to back up his numbing songs about romance and dance. — D.M.

THE RACING CARS
★★★ **Bring on the Night / Chrys. 1178**
★★ **Downtown Tonight / Chrys. 1099**
★★ **Weekend Rendezvous / Chrys. 1149**
English pop-rock band has never risen above the level of nice humdrum melodies, tasteful playing; it's the group's blandness—its aggravating and unrelenting good taste—that does it in. — D.M.

MARK RADICE
★★ **Ain't Nothin' but a Party / U. Artists LA629-G**
★★ **Intense / Road. LA788-G**
Prodigy began recording at age seven for RCA. Later produced three cuts for Donovan, appeared with B.T. Express and Brass

Construction. Now focuses on Moog synthesizer, piano, clavinet. Fundamentally tedious. — D.M.

RADIO BIRDMAN
★★ **Radios Appear / Sire K-6050**
Punk with spunk, but without imagination. And *all* punk has spunk. — D.M.

GERRY RAFFERTY
★★★ **Can I Have My Money Back? / Blue Th. 6031**
★★★★ **City to City / U. Artists LA840-G**
As a member of Stealers Wheel, Rafferty turned in an engaging British variation of Dylan's folk rock. On his own, he's done a more placid version of the same, highlighted by *City to City*'s "Baker Street," one of the most pleasant hit singles of 1978. The sax solo there is worth the price of admission, and the rest of the record follows suit. — D.M.

THE RAIDERS
★★ **Greatest Hits, Vol. 2 / Col. C-30386**
★★ **Indian Reservation / Col. C-30768**
After their hard-rocking beginnings as Paul Revere and the Raiders, this Seattle-bred, L.A.-based group settled into a more conventional mold, turning most of the proceedings over to vocalist Mark Lindsay, whose greatest aspiration, apparently, was to beat B. J. Thomas at his own game. "Indian Reservation" was the best they did, and it wasn't bad—but far inferior to the early stuff. — D.M.

BONNIE RAITT
★★★★ **Bonnie Raitt / War. 1953**
★★★★ **Give It Up / War. 2643**
★★★ **Home Plate / War. B-2864**
★★ **Streetlights / War. B-2818**
★★ **Sweet Forgiveness / War. B-2990**
★★★★ **Takin' My Time / War. B-2729**

Bonnie Raitt, the daughter of Broadway singer John Raitt, was playing on the Cambridge, Massachusetts, folk scene as early as 1967. Because she was managed by Dick Waterman, who also represented a number of country-blues figures (among them, Fred McDowell, John Hurt, Sippie Wallace and Son House), she frequently appeared with them in concert, which only fueled her ambition to become an authentic white blues performer.

Raitt began recording in 1971; her debut album, *Bonnie Raitt,* which was recorded at Dave Ray's studio in Minnesota and features Chicago bluesmen A. C. Reed and Junior Wells, is a straight blues affair, both engaging and sensitive. But it was with *Give It Up* that she came closest to perfecting her approach: she mingled her blues resources with a variety of contemporary and folk-oriented songs, coming up with classics in "Been Too Long at the Fair" and Eric Kaz's "Love Has No Pride." Her version of the latter remains definitive, despite the many subsequent covers. *Takin' My Time* is along the same lines, with a touch more electricity, highlighted by Jackson Browne's "I Thought I Was a Child" and Randy Newman's "Guilty."

But since then, Raitt's recordings have generally been frustratingly inadequate. All of these records represent strategies designed to make her a star, and while Raitt's emotional sincerity is never called into question, the process has had less than salutary effects on the tone of her work.

Streetlights is the product of a collaboration with vetran soul producer Jerry Ragavoy and his philistine imagination. He came up with promising R&B-oriented material, but the arrangements are far too slick to accommodate Raitt's native funkiness. The record's most interesting moment is Joni Mitchell's "That Song about the Midway," a song whose involuted ambiguity couldn't be further from Raitt's bright-eyed irony.

Both *Home Plate* and *Sweet Forgiveness* were produced by Paul Rothchild, a man who should be consigned to making airline commercials; they are inexcusably banal attempts to turn Raitt into a Linda Ronstadt *manquée.* The fact that Raitt nearly overcomes on *Home Plate* doesn't excuse the concept. Rather than allowing herself to be melodramatic, Raitt is steamrollered, flattened out to accommodate a song selection that would enervate anyone. *Sweet Forgiveness* contained a remake of Del Shannon's "Runaway," which, while quite awful, was nearly a hit single; presumably the streamlining homogenization will continue after that "success." — B.T.

RAM JAM
★ **Portrait of the Artist / Epic JE-35287**
★ **Ram Jam / Epic PE-34885**
Ram Jam is a godawful version of studio heavy metal, courtesy of former bubblegum producers Kastenatz-Katz. How this synthetic group got to make a second album is anybody's guess, but it probably has something to do with the fact that Ram Jam scored a minor hit single in 1977 with a reworking of Leadbelly's "Black Betty." — D.M.

THE RAMONES
★★★★ **Leave Home / Sire 6031**
★★★★ **Road to Ruin / Sire K-6063**
★★★★ **Rocket to Russia / Sire 6042**
★★★★ **The Ramones / Sire 6020**
Is this America's greatest rock band? Certainly it's the most amusing. Of all the Seventies punk rock bands, the Ramones were also the first latter-day punks to record. The Ramones know only one tempo—accelerated; their lyrical subject matter is puerile and inane, and the singer ain't real tuneful. As a result, they are great, the embodiment of the amateur passion of rock & roll at a moment when it has nearly died out. — D.M.

WILLIS ALAN RAMSEY
★★★ **Willis Alan Ramsey / Shel. 52013**
The name ought to belong to a sissy singer/songwriter, but Ramsey's made of slightly sterner stuff: he's a modern cowboy singer, modifying the usual laid-back folkie stance with some hobo and range-riding themes. He could still use a least a hint of belligerence, rather than the resignation that seems to be the guiding emotion of this LP. — D.M.

ELLIOTT RANDALL
★★★ **Elliott Randall's New York / Kir. PZ-34351**
A New York studio guitarist makes a solo album that rocks hard enough to justify his chops. — D.M.

TOM RANIER
★ **Ranier / War. BSK 2946**
Mood music à la Tom Scott. (Now deleted.) — D.M.

KENNY RANKIN
★★ **Inside / Li. Dav. 1009**

★★ **Like a Seed** / Li. Dav. 10003
★★ **Silver Morning** / Li. Dav. 3000
★★ **The Kenny Rankin Album** / Li. Dav.
1013
MOR jazz-pop crooner is as bland as he is
skillful at interpreting his and others' songs
in a mellow, light scat style. Good mood
music. Early Mercury albums, including
minor classic, *Mindclusters,* out of
print. — s.h.

RARE BIRD
★★ **As Your Mind Flies By** / ABC 716
Originally experimenters with classical/
rock fusion, these guys have since retrenched into the standard British rock formula: a bit of melody, a shred of predictable improvisation, not much feeling to
any of it. It rocks a mite, but so does
everything these days. (Now deleted.) — d.m.

RARE EARTH
★ **Band Together** / Prod. P7-10025
★ **Ecology** / Rare R7-514
★★ **Get Ready** / Rare R7-507
★ **Rare Earth** / Prod. P7-10019
■ **Rare Earth in Concert** / Rare R7-534
Although they had some hits in the early
Seventies (the most notable was a cover of
the Temptations' "Get Ready," on the album of the same name), Rare Earth remain remarkable because they were perhaps the worst white-soul bar band ever
formed, and prospered on a Motown subsidiary. Where was Berry Gordy—out to
lunch? — d.m.

THE RASCALS
★★★★★ **The Rascals' Greatest Hits/
Time-Peace** / Atl. 8190
The (Young) Rascals grew up in New Jersey, but were discovered on Long Island,
playing white R&B to socialites in the
summer of 1965. Their gimmick was supposed to be that they dressed in Edwardian
costume, but what gave them a string of
great white soul hits was the vocal prowess
of Eddie Brigati and Felix Cavaliere.
Brigati, Cavaliere (who played keyboards
as well as sang) and guitarist Gene Cornish
had originally played with Joey Dee and
the Starlighters ("Peppermint Twist") at
the Peppermint Lounge, the home of the
twist; drummer Dino Danelli was added
when the trio split from Dee. Signed to Atlantic Records in 1965 and coupled with
the production team of Arif Mardin and
Tom Dowd—which would later assist Jerry Wexler so ably in making Aretha

Franklin's masterful records—the group's
first single, "Ain't Gonna Eat Out My
Heart Anymore," came close to breaking
out. But it was the second, the rousing
"Good Lovin'," which went to No. 1 in
early 1966, that really brought them to
fame. This spawned a string of hits, the
best known of which are the reflective and
sinuous "Groovin' " (1967) and "People
Got to Be Free" (1968), by which time the
name had been changed, from Young Rascals to the Rascals.
"People Got to Be Free" was included
in an album that sowed the seeds of the
group's demise, *Freedom Suite,* which reflected an attempt to join the psychedelic
craze and particularly Cavaliere's growing
infatuation with Eastern mysticism. In a
pattern typical of so many of the group's
contemporaries, the Rascals' musical worth
declined as its ambition soared, and by the
early Seventies, the band faded out, after
switching to Columbia for one ill-fated LP.
All that now remains in print is this glorious chronicle of a group that ranks with
Mitch Ryder and the Detroit Wheels, and
the Righteous Brothers among white
American soul singers. — d.m.

THE RASPBERRIES
★★★★ **The Raspberries' Best (Featuring
Eric Carmen)** / Cap. ST-11524
An exquisite anthology of Seventies pop-
rock that's a throwback to the heyday of
the Beatles and Beach Boys. The Raspberries came out of Cleveland in 1972 with a
sound that was already brilliantly homogeneous—"Go All the Way" and "Tonight"
(their first two singles hits) were ringers for
Paul McCartney, thanks to Eric Carmen's
vocals, and the songs that followed lived
up to a similar standard. Such romanticism
and nostalgia had no great depth, but it
was great entertainment. But in 1974, when
Carmen despaired of ever breaking
through to more substantial recognition, he
came up with a last-ditch effort called
"Overnight Sensation (Hit Record)" that
painted his aspirations with perfect blunt-
ness. "Overnight Sensation" *is* the radio
that leads to Carmen's street of dreams,
and in it, his vision of himself as the true
inheritor of the innocence of early-Sixties
rock is justified completely.
Unfortunately, "Overnight Sensation"
and the inspired album from which it came
(*Starting Over,* now deleted) were both relative commercial failures, and Carmen soon
left the band (which has since contributed
members to Fotomaker and Tattoo) for a

solo career in which he has, despite occasional hit singles, seemed more and more like Barry Manilow for the prematurely senile. — D.M.

GENYA RAVAN
★★★ **Urban Desire / 20th Cent. 562**
As Goldie of Goldie and the Gingerbreads, Genya Ravan toured with the early Rolling Stones; later she led an abominable horn band, Ten Wheel Drive. But in the late Seventies, she became enamored of New Wave rock and after producing the Dead Boys debut LP, made this heavy-breathing affair on her own. It's more notable for street smarts than anything approaching melody, but it's tough enough to get by—with a little help from such pals as Lou Reed. — D.M.

LOU RAWLS
★★★★ **All Things in Time / Phil. PZ-33957**
★ **Merry Xmas, Ho Ho Ho / Cap. SM-2790**
★★★ **Naturally / Poly. 1-6081**
★★★ **Lou Rawls Live / Cap. SM-2459**
★★★ **Soulin' / Cap. SM-2566**
★★★ **Stormy Monday / Cap. SM-1714**
★★★★ **The Best from Lou Rawls / Cap. SKBB-11585**
★★★★ **The Best of Lou Rawls / Cap. SM-2948**
★★★★ **Unmistakably Lou / Phil. PZ-34434**
★★★★ **When You Hear Lou, You've Heard It All / Phil. JZ-35036**
Rawls is one of the many R&B singers trained in gospel groups. He got his start with the Pilgrim Travelers, then was signed as a pop singer by Capitol. In the Sixties, Rawls had several hits: "Dead End Street" and "Tobacco Road" pointed him out as one of the best new vocalists of his time. Capitol tried to mold Rawls in the same style as Nat King Cole, but ended up overproducing him and negating his talent, although the hits have a certain vitality.

It took Rawls a few label switches and some years to regain his composure after being slotted as a Las Vegas lounge act, but in the mid-Seventies he hooked up with Philadelphia International producers Gamble and Huff. They wrote and produced his next record, and suddenly Rawls had found himself once more. The high point of the collaboration so far is the 1977 smash hit, "You'll Never Find Another Love Like Mine," a magnificent performance that shows Rawls in top form and in-dicates that he still may not have tapped his full potential as a vocalist. He has also been seen and heard as the voice of Budweiser beer on commercials, from which *When You Hear* stems. — J.S.

RAYDIO
★★★ **Raydio / Ari. AB 4163**
★★★ **Rock On / Ari. 4212**
Tight, funky horn band from Detroit scored pleasurable 1978 pop hit with re-working of "Jack and Jill" nursery rhyme. — D.M.

CHRIS REA
★★★ **Whatever Happened to Benny Santini / U. Artists LA879-H**
Smooth sax and organ-based version of what Springsteen and Seger did better. Gus Dudgeon-produced debut was promising, but much more pop than the real thing. "Fool" was a Top Forty hit. — D.M.

JOHN DAWSON READ
★★ **Read On / Chrys. 1102**
Sticky-sweet English pop. (Now deleted.) — D.M.

EUGENE RECORD
★★★ **Eugene Record / War. B3018**
★★ **Trying to Get to You / War. K-3097**
Record was the guiding light (songwriter and lead vocalist) of the Chi-Lites, last of the sweetly classic soul vocal groups. On his own, he's still a fine songwriter, and on his first solo album, he nearly matches the Chi-Lites' romantic enthusiasm. The second, however, shows a tendency to dawdle off into instrumental irrelevancies. — D.M.

REDBONE
★★★ **Come and Get Your Redbone (The Best of Redbone) / Epic PEG-33456**

★★ Cycles / RCA AFLI-2352
★★ Redbone / Epic EGP-501
★★ Wovoka / Epic E-32462
The only rock band led by full-blooded
North American Indians, Redbone was,
however, less influenced by Native American culture than soul music. Pat and Lolly
Vegas were good songwriters (P. J. Proby
had a hit with "Niki Hoeky" in the Sixties)
but more limited performers. Despite such
fine material as "The Witch Queen of New
Orleans" and "Niki Hoeky," the strained
vocals make a good deal of this unbearable. In "Come and Get Your Love,"
though, the singing was perfect, in a Marvin Gaye mold, and the song became a
Top Ten hit in 1974. The RCA record is a
misguided comeback from 1978; the one to
have, if you're interested in the boundaries
of rock and soul, is *Come and Get Your
Redbone.* — D.M.

LEON REDBONE
★★ Champagne Charlie / War. K-3165
★★★ Double Time / War. B-2971
★★★★ On the Track / War. B-2888
Redbone, a mysterious late Sixties–early
Seventies folk scene fixture who numbers
Bob Dylan among his admirers, coupled
with producer Joel Dorn and came up
with *On the Track,* a lovely album of
pre–World War II American music, with
the ambiance of an old 78. But *Double
Time,* the followup, made the approach
seem more like a pose than a commitment,
and smugly self-conscious pose at that.
And *Champagne Charlie* made the debacle
complete. — D.M.

THE RED CLAY RAMBLERS
★★★ Stolen Love / Fly. Fish 009
★★ The Red Clay Ramblers / Folk. 31039
★★★ Twisted Laurel / Fly. Fish 030
This North Carolina group of college-educated traditional music buffs earned its recognition by providing the music for a
Broadway play, *Diamond Studs.* On vinyl,
the Ramblers have moved from an almost
musicological sense of tradition to a
greater awareness of taping technology and
modern nuance. Their facility with the
two-step string-band idiom is perhaps the
most accessible form of old-timey music
being performed in modern America. Comfortably accomplished instrumentalists and
singers, the Ramblers both pay tribute to,
and infuse with new life, neglected segments of our musical heritage. — R.P.

NOEL REDDING BAND
★ Blowin' / RCA APLI-1863
Ex-Jimi Hendrix Experience bassist's solo
album is a washy blues rock set. (Now deleted.) — J.S.

OTIS REDDING
★★★★★ History of Otis Redding / Atco
261
★★★★ Otis Redding Live in Europe /
Atco 286
★★★★★ The Best of Otis Redding / Atco
2-801
★★★★★ The Immortal Otis Redding /
Atco 252
Otis Redding was probably the most influential soul singer of the late Sixties, and on
talent alone, he ranks with Marvin Gaye,
Smokey Robinson, James Brown and Curtis Mayfield as one of the greatest. Redding's style was grittier and more maturely
emotional than any of these, without
Brown's hysteria or Mayfield's reserve; his
hoarse shouting left a deep imprint on the
music, which it has not yet fully discarded.
   Despite this, Redding never achieved a
major pop hit until after his untimely death
in a plane crash in December 1967. Until
the release of "Dock of the Bay," in early
1968, he was best known for having written
Aretha Franklin's first No. 1 hit, "Respect," and for having wowed the hipsters
at the Monterey Pop Festival the summer
before. Yet Redding had recorded since
1962, and his songs include several now regarded as classics: "I've Been Loving You
Too Long," "Mr. Pitiful" and "Try a Little
Tenderness," the latter actually a reworked
Forties ballad. But despite frequent cover
versions of his songs, by Franklin, the
Rolling Stones and many others, Redding
never reaped the benefits of his genius. His
version of "Satisfaction," in which he re-
paid the Stones' several cops from him,
came close. But "Dock of the Bay," a
moody, introspective piece that set him
solo against Steve Cropper's guitar and a
very spare arrangement, was the song that
put him over. It was almost as though radio and the public were atoning for ignoring Redding when he was alive.
   Yet, as demonstrated by these albums,
and the many deleted Atlantic and Volt recordings from which they are derived,
Redding was a marvel: one of the great
live showmen (*Live in Europe* is better than
any other live rock or soul album I can
think of), a masterful ballad singer and a
true rocker in the spirit of his boyhood
hero, Little Richard. Everything the man
recorded—not only these albums but the
cutouts as well—demands to be
heard. — D.M.

HELEN REDDY
★★ **Ear Candy / Cap. SO-11640**
■ **Free and Easy / Cap. ST-11348**
★ **Helen Reddy / Cap. ST-857**
★★ **Helen Reddy's Greatest Hits / Cap. SW-11467**
★★ **I Am Woman / Cap. ST-11068**
★ **I Don't Know How to Love Him / Cap. ST-762**
★ **Long Hard Climb / Cap. SMAS-11213**
★ **Love Song for Jeffrey / Cap. SO-11284**
★ **Music, Music / Cap. ST-11547**
★ **No Way to Treat a Lady / Cap. ST-11418**
★ **We'll Sing in the Sunshine / Cap. SW-11759**

Helen Reddy could have been a feminist hero. Her 1972 No. 1 hit, "I Am Woman," was an anthem that signified the increasing political awareness of women, and Reddy might have commanded the loyalty of such people if she'd wanted to. Instead, she drifted off into the worst kind of romantic pop, even allowing her image to be reduced to a simple double entendre with *Free and Easy*. Since she was never any great shakes as a song stylist or interpreter anyway, the loss is her own. — D.M.

JEAN REDPATH
★★ **Frae My Ain Countrie / Folk-Leg. 49**
★★ **Songs of Robert Burns / Phil. 1037**
Shortly after Redpath moved to the U.S. from Scotland in 1961, she found herself amidst the folksingers and songwriters in Greenwich Village, and performing at Gerde's Folk City: Jack Elliott, Bob Dylan, the Greenbriar Boys and others. Her own Scottish roots and songs were an entrée into the "folk revival," and she recorded for Prestige and Elektra at that time.

Frae My Ain Countrie has the sort of ballads and other material she did on those now-deleted LPs, while the Burns set features her singing the poet/songwriter's words to the semi-classical folk-based music of Serge Hovey. — I.M.

REDWING
★★★ **Beyond the Sun and Stars / Fan. 9488**
★★ **Dead or Alive / Fan. 9459**
★★★ **Redwing / Fan. 8409**
★★ **Take Me Home / Fan. 9439**
★★★ **What This Country Needs / Fan. 9405**
Redwing is a classic little band—talented enough to develop a small record buying cult (an old friend and I are the only members I know), while recorded on a small la-

bel not known for its rock acts. The debut album sounded admirably like Fantasy's only other rock heavyweight, Creedence Clearwater Revival, with an insistent rock edge that was never duplicated. They quickly began mixing in a bit of country with the second album—as tasty an example of the country-rock genre as anyone's made. What other band could cook up something as melodic and tasteful as "Reaching Out" and then turn around for a funky version of "Walking the Dog." The succeeding pair of albums saw the balance tipping toward country, though, which essentially denied the band's stronger rocking side. The proper mix was back on *Beyond the Sun*. The title tune is a fine example of soul-influenced rock & roll.

Unfortunately, Redwing also suffered from another "classic little band" limitation—though the group possessed a couple of good songwriters (guitarists Tom Phillips and Ron Floegel), it had only one superior singer (lead guitarist Andrew Samuels), who sang only about a quarter of the time. — J.B.M.

BLIND ALFRED REED
★★★★ **How Can a Poor Man Stand Such Times and Live? / Roun. 1001**
An outstanding reissue of the Depression era singer/composer/fiddler's work. The sides were originally recorded for RCA between 1927 and 1929, and they reflect a strong sense of humor, topicality and musicality. The line to Woody Guthrie and Phil Ochs is readily evident. — I.M.

JERRY REED
★★ **Alabama Wild Man / Camd. ACL1-7024**
★★ **Both Barrels / RCA APL1-1861**
★★ **East Bound and Down / RCA AHL1-2516**
★ **Jerry Reed in Concert / RCA CPL2-1014**
★★ **Jerry Reed Rides Again / RCA AHL1-2346**
★★ **Me and Chet / RCA ANL1-2167**
★★ **Me and Jerry / RCA AHL1-4396**
★ **Paper Roses / Camd. ACL1-0533**
★★ **Red Hot Picker / RCA APL1-1226**
★★★ **The Best of Jerry Reed / RCA AHL1-4729**
★★ **Tupelo Mississippi Flash / Camd. ACL1-0331**
★★★ **When You're Hot, You're Hot / RCA ANL1-1345**
Reed is a Nashville session guitarist who had two big hits—"When You're Hot, You're Hot" in 1971, "Amos Moses" in

1970—that he has never followed up, despite nearly a decade of trying. Mostly because his picking and singing are strictly by formula—except on those singles, where he really sounds like an Alabama wild man. — D.M.

LOU REED
★★★★ **Coney Island Baby** / RCA
ANLI-2480
★★★ **Lou Reed** / RCA AFLI-4701
★★★ **Lou Reed Live** / RCA APLI-0959
★ **Rock and Roll Heart** / Ari. 4100
★★★★★ **Rock 'n' Roll Animal** / RCA
APLI-0472
★★★★★ **Street Hassle** / Ari. 4169
★★★ **Take No Prisoners—Lou Reed**
Live / Ari. 8502
★★★ **Transformer** / RCA AFLI-4807
★★ **Walk on the Wild Side** / RCA
AFLI-2001

The temptation to put in a disclaimer in regard to the ratings above is strong. One's opinion of Reed's solo work changes constantly, because his constant shifts of stance and style continually confound any sense of perspective. And there's always the mental match-up between any new work by Reed and his undeniably brilliant efforts as the leader of the Velvet Underground.

Take *Metal Machine Music,* which RCA has unfortunately deleted. *Metal Machine Music* was a two-disc set consisting of nothing more than ear-wrecking electronic sludge, guaranteed to clear any room of humans in record time. In retrospect, one might easily have given the album four stars for sheer nerve and guts, for its deafening blip-and-bleep is a statement, a bitter rail against record companies, fans' notions of image and the entire workings of the music industry. (On the other hand, *Metal*

Machine Music might be nothing more than a rather perverse and elaborate joke, replete with a cover that implies a concert recording and liner notes written in deadpan electronic mumbo jumbo.) Everything considered, it's probably a combination of the two—hence the dilemma.

Nonetheless, certain Reed albums do stand out, for better or worse. *Lou Reed,* the first (1972) solo LP, has a nonchalant charm and grace that remains untarnished. The ridiculously uneven *Transformer* includes Reed's only hit single, "Walk on the Wild Side," as well as the lovely "Satellite of Love" and the ethereal "Perfect Day." (*Berlin,* which followed *Transformer,* is deleted, but its grandiose, decadent Bob Ezrin production helps make it one of the most depressing records ever made, and oddly beautiful in its own awful way.)

Rock 'n' Roll Animal is a live album and it's a riveting tour de force; Reed wrenches forth chilling vocals while the one-two guitar punch of Steve Hunter and Dick Wagner overpowers everything in its way. (*Lou Reed Live,* a second volume taken from recordings of the same concert tour, suffers from a weaker song selection.) Oddly, Reed's biggest commercial success, *Sally Can't Dance,* has been deleted by RCA; there, Reed let his soul urges come to the forefront musically, though there is an incredible amount of hostility lurking in the lyrics to songs like "Animal Language," "Ennui" and "Kill Your Sons."

Coney Island Baby is, on the whole, a very soft affair that (since it was the followup to *Metal Machine Music*) might be construed as Reed's attempt to affect a reconciliation with his audience. The accent is on simplicity, and songs like "Charley's Girl" and the beautiful title cut brought a return to the warm, positive songwriting that had been one of Reed's strongest points as a member of the Velvet Underground.

Rock and Roll Heart, however, is Reed's most careless and ineffective record. But *Street Hassle* is unquestionably his finest effort—intense, demanding and unflinching in its on-the-corner scenarios. Songs like "Dirt" and "I Wanna Be Black" reveal a sense of humor that had been notable only in its absence through most of Reed's tortured solo career. Of course, you can never be certain which way Reed will turn next—sometimes one suspects that the uncertainty of his supporters is built into Reed's master plan. In a word: complex. — B.A.

MARTHA REEVES
★ We Meet Again / Mile. 9549
Martha Reeves' career since departing from the Vandellas has been a sad series of now-deleted conceptual mishaps shaped up by smartass auteurist producers: Richard Perry did a notable boondoggle for MCA in the mid-Seventies and no less than four producers turned executioner for her 1977 Arista set, *The Rest of My Life.* Reeves called that LP's gimmicky clutter "disco-designed," which is probably what she would say about this Milestone set, too. No excuse. — B.T.

THE REFLECTIONS
★★★ Love on Delivery / Cap. ST-11460
The Reflections carry a rugged baritone lead singer whose raspy voice adds some needed rough edges to adequate production. The title song and "Three Steps from True Love," based on the melody of the Detroit Emeralds' "Do Me Right," are the highlights. (Now deleted.) — J.MC.

CLARENCE REID
★★★ On the Job / Als. 4404
Reid is a mainstay of the TK Records soul complex as Betty Wright's producer, and under his pseudonym, Blow Fly, he has also recorded a hilariously obscene series of R&B party albums in which he converts soul and disco chart-toppers into risqúe expressions that verge on comedic pornography. His work on this album isn't that imaginative, but the songs are written with wit and Reid's performances have a kind of gravelly intensity that makes them memorable. — D.M.

JOHN REID
★★ Facade / Col. PC-34298
A member of the Classics IV who didn't make it to the Atlanta Rhythm Section now pays the price: pure pop drivel on his only solo album, a deservedly forgotten item. (Now deleted.) — D.M.

TERRY REID
★★★★ Bang, Bang, You're Terry Reid / Epic 26427
★★ Rogue Waves / Cap. SW-11857
★★★ Terry Reid / Epic 26477
When he debuted in America, opening for Cream in 1968, Reid was only nineteen. *Bang, Bang,* produced by British pop veteran Mickie Most, introduced his high pitched, often improvisatory and sometimes excessive singing. The songs—a mix of drawn-out rock standards and good

originals, some of which echo Donovan—usually had only adequate instrumentation from Reid's guitar-organ-drums trio. *Terry Reid* sharpened these approaches with better material and strong playing, though Most's pop-oriented production leaves it oddly dated.

After disastrous efforts for Atlantic and ABC (Graham Nash produced *Seed of Memory* for the latter label), Reid turned up in 1978 with *Rogue Waves,* a clear attempt to return to the relative focus of his first two LPs. Despite a version of the Ronettes' "Do I Love You," it didn't work. Like his other albums after the first two, it was too loose and sluggish to achieve the necessary force. — C.W.

CARL REINER AND MEL BROOKS
★★★ 2000 and Thirteen / War. B-2741
★★★ 2000 Years with Carl Reiner and Mel Brooks / War. 3XX 2744
The premise in anyone else's hands would be trivial, lending itself to but a few quick yoks. But Mel Brooks portraying a 2,000-plus-year-old man inspires a blitz of dialect and absurdist humor that is surpassed only by Richard Pryor. Unlike Pryor, though, Brooks is apolitical, and the ancient Jew he impersonates bounces off things banal (food, historical celebrities) and abstract (the evolution of language, the family and religion). They say it was unrehearsed, but genial Reiner's questions sound carefully phrased and ordered; this does not spoil anything, however. — K.T.

RENAISSANCE
★★ A Song for All Seasons / Sire K-6049
★ Ashes Are Burning / Cap. ST-11216
★ In the Beginning / Cap. SWBC-11871
★★ Live at Carnegie Hall / Sire 2XS-6029
★ Novella / Sire 6024

★★★★ Prologue / Cap. SMAS-11116
★★★ Scheherazade and Other Stories / Sire 6017
★★★ Turn of the Cards / Sire 6015

This classical rock group was originally spawned by former Yardbird vocalist Keith Relf and drummer Jim McCarty in 1969. But (although the group did make one album for Elektra then) both the former Yardbirds had departed by 1972, when *Prologue* was released. This set is atypical—John Tout's piano actually stars over Annie Haslam's soprano vocal flights, which are used more for flavoring than for carrying lyrics. *Ashes* goes a bit too far the other way, the band assuming a completely subordinate position to Haslam.

Turn and *Scheherazade* represent Renaissance at is zenith. Haslam's singing has gained self-assurance, the band is more solid and precise and the orchestral touches are judicious. "Song of Scheherazade," which covers all of side two of the album named for it, is a fable set to music; curiously, the group has never pursued this direction. The live album, instead, offers heavily orchestrated reworkings of the material from the first four LPs, and it is notable for the relentless seriousness with which the band now takes itself. Since then it's been mostly downhill. — A.N.

JOHN RENBOURN
★★★★ Faro Annie / Rep. 2082
★★★ John Renbourn / Rep. 2-6482
★★★ Sir John—Alot of Merrie Englandes / Rep. 6344
★★★ The Lady and the Unicorn / Rep. 6407

Renbourn and fellow folk guitarist Bert Jansch were moving forces in the British folk-rock group Pentangle, which was sort of a mellow man's Fairport Convention in the late Sixties and early Seventies. These LPs feature a lot of flashy guitar work, but it's ultimately somnolent: all of it good, and *Faro Annie* especially so, but nothing really breathtaking as this kind of folk music can be at its best. — D.M.

R.E.O. SPEEDWAGON
★★ Lost in a Dream / Epic PE-32948
★★ R.E.O. / Epic PE-34143
★★★ R.E.O. Speedwagon / Epic E-31089
★★ R.E.O. Speedwagon—Live: You Get What You Play For / Epic PEG-34494
★★★★ R.E.O./T.W.O. / Epic PE-31745
★★★ Ridin' the Storm Out / Epic PE-32378
★★ This Time We Mean It / Epic PE-3338
★★ You Can Tune a Piano But You Can't Tuna Fish / Epic JE-35082

It took R.E.O. Speedwagon seven albums to earn a gold record, which makes it one of America's least successful but longest-lived bands commercially as well as aesthetically. Without a distinctive vocalist or material that's more than humdrum, R.E.O. Speedwagon has steadfastly maintained its status as a poor man's Jo Jo Gunne, a perennial opening act that's never quite qualified as a headliner.

The 1971 debut, *R.E.O. Speedwagon,* is interesting primarily for its "bar band makes good" atmosphere, complete with Jerry Lee Lewis piano riffs. *T.W.O.* showed added maturity and power; the version of "Little Queenie" is marred only by weak singing. But the three albums that followed (*Ridin' the Storm Out, Lost in a Dream,* and *This Time We Mean It*) are slicker and less energetic, a rejection of heavy-metal beginnings for a stab at Doobie Brothers-style pop-rock. In 1976, with *R.E.O.,* the group returned to the *T.W.O.* approach, modified by some of the California influences of the three previous LPs. And while the 1977 *Live* seemed risky at the time—a two-record set for a band that had never been able to come across effectively on one?—it brought them gold, perhaps because of its predictability, which includes every breadbasket heavy-metal cliché down to the Chuck Berry encore. It was followed by *You Can Tune,* which is about as fresh as its title. — A.N.

REVELATION
★★★ Revelation / RSO 4810

A New York group with a gospel flavor. Lead singer Benny Diggs has a robust baritone that is used to good effect on several hot Philadelphia tracks. Slower songs are not as inspired. (Now deleted.) — J.MC.

PAUL REVERE AND THE RAIDERS
★★★★ All-Time Greatest Hits / Col. CG-31464

Although they're best remembered as a sort of American answer to the British Invasion, the Raiders were actually around for several years before the Beatles struck; they even had a local hit, "Like Longhair," in the Pacific Northwest in 1961. In 1965, Dick Clark tapped them for his L.A. rock show, *Where the Action Is,* and there the group's Revolutionary War costumes and lead singer Mark Lindsay's ponytail made them seem a sort of British Invasion band satire: not unlike a pre-packaged Monkees. But the Raiders began grinding out a series of hits in 1965, with "Steppin' Out" and "Just like Me," that continued through 1967. The group's best-known song is "Kicks," an anti-drug song written by Barry Mann and Cynthia Weil, which manages to convey its message without losing its cool.

The Raiders continued as a band of sorts until the nether end of the Sixties, when Mark Lindsay assumed command and the name was shortened. Thereafter, they pursued a pop-rock direction that was much less satisfying. — D.M.

MALVINA REYNOLDS
★★ Malvina / Cass. 2807
"The singing grandmother," Reynolds wrote the anti-housing tract "Little Boxes," among scores of other sociopolitical commentaries, ballads and children's songs. The rhythm section and extra guitars on this disc are superfluous, for it is the emotional involvement rather than the music per se that's important to her approach. — I.M.

THE RHEAD BROTHERS
★ Dedicate / Harv. ST-11669
Sappy Seventies easy-listening rock. Others preferred. — J.S.

RHINESTONES
★★★ Rhinestones / 20th Cent. 489
Crack group of top session players in a loose blues-rock context led by veteran bassist Harvey Brooks. (Now deleted.) — J.S.

RHYTHM HERITAGE
★★ Disco-fied / ABC 934

★★ Last Night on Earth / ABC 987
★★ Sky's the Limit / ABC 1037
Faceless funk from the folks who brought you a Top Ten TV tune, "Theme from S.W.A.T." in the early disco daze. — D.M.

ALLAN RICH
★ Allan Rich / Epic KE-33078
★ Glass Heart / Col. PC-34153
Charlie Rich's son seems confused: should he head for MOR country, as his father has done in the Seventies, or settle in as a country rocker, as his father did earlier? Answer: neither. Reason: can't sing as well as Pop. (Now deleted.) — D.M.

CHARLIE RICH
★★★★ A Time for Tears / Sun 123
★★★ Arkansas Traveller / Power. 245
★★★★ Behind Closed Doors / Epic PF-32247
★★★★ Big Boss Man/My Mountain Dew / RCA APLI-2260
★★★★ Boss Man / Epic E-30214
★★ Classic Rich / Epic JE-35394
★★ Classic Rich, Vol. 2 / Epic JE-35624
★★ Every Time You Touch Me / Epic PE-33455
★★★ Greatest Hits / Epic PD-34240
★★★ Greatest Hits, Vol. 1 / Power. 248
★★★ Greatest Hits, Vol. 2 / Power. 249
★★ I Still Believe in Love / U. Artists LA876-H
★★★★ Lonely Weekends / Sun 110
★★ Rollin' with the Flow / Epic KE-34891
★★★★ Set Me Free / Epic 26376
★★★ She Loved Everybody but Me / Camd. 2417
★ Silver Lining / Epic KE-33545
★★★★ So Lonesome I Could Cry / Hi 8006
★ Take Me / Epic KE-3444
★★★★ The Best of Charlie Rich / Epic PE-31933
★★★★ The Early Years / Sun 132
★★★★★ The Fabulous Charlie Rich / Epic JE-26516
★★ The Silver Fox / Epic PE-33250
★★★ Tomorrow Night / RCA ANL1-1542
★★★ Too Many Teardrops / Camd. 7001
★ Very Special Love Songs / Epic PE-32531
Charlie Rich was perhaps the most inspired of all the singers who followed Elvis Presley and Jerry Lee Lewis out of Sam Phillips' Sun Studios, the birthplace of rockabilly. He is not only a first-rate rock singer—"Lonely Weekends" is his masterpiece in the genre—but also an adept country vocalist, a superb jazz-influenced

pianist and a moving blues crooner. His early career was checkered, and many of that period's recordings are now released on a variety of repackages (Sun, Powerpak, Camden, RCA, Hi). Its peaks were "Lonely Weekends" (Sun, 1958) and "Mohair Sam" (Smash, 1963). The best sides he cut were done for Sun, but his best country singing was done at Smash, with producer Jerry Kennedy. Later, he recorded for RCA's Groove subsidiary, and did a single album for Hi that is one of the fundamental country-meets-the-blues LPs.

In the late Sixties, Rich moved to Epic Records in Nashville and hooked up with producer Billy Sherrill. Their early collaborations were superb: culminating in *The Fabulous Charlie Rich* (1970), which contains perhaps the greatest song ever written about a working-class loser—"Life Has Its Little Ups and Downs," written by Charlie's wife, Margaret Ann. But it was not until 1973's "Behind Closed Doors" that Rich became a big star. That song and a couple of the followups were excellent pop music, though not nearly as country as their high ranking on that genre's charts would indicate. But after hitting the big time, Rich succumbed—to his drinking problem, and to the blandishments of Vegas big bucks, which meant equally bathetic arrangements, to which Sherrill was already prone in any case. The last few years have been sad ones; a change of label to United Artists in early 1978 didn't seem to help much. — D.M.

CLIFF RICHARD
★★★ **Every Face Tells a Story / R. BXL1-3045**
★★ **Green Light / R. BXL1-3045**
★★★ **I'm Nearly Famous / R. 3004**
★★ **It's All in the Game / Epic BN-26089**
Before the Beatles, Cliff Richard was England's answer to American rock. He began as a sort of mini-Elvis, with a backup group called the Shadows, who included a guitarist, Hank Marvin, an important influence on many British guitarists of the Sixties. But Richard converted to England's variety of fundamentalist Christianity, and whatever spark of spunk had been in his music was snuffed, though he continued to make the British charts throughout the Sixties. In the mid-Seventies, Rocket, Elton John's label, signed him up, and "I'm Nearly Famous" became his most successful American single. Unfortunately, neither album he did for that label amounts to much, just a more or less uninspired ver-

sion of Elton's own style of pop-rock vision. — D.M.

TURLEY RICHARDS
★★ **West Virginia Superstar / Epic PE-34306**
Run-of-the-mill country singer, with some pretensions to rock because of his gospel roots. (Now deleted.) — D.M.

JONATHAN RICHMAN
★★ **Jonathan Richman and the Modern Lovers / Beserk. 0048**
★★ **Modern Lovers "Live" / Beserk. 0055**
★★ **Rock and Roll with the Modern Lovers / Beserk. 0052**
In his original incarnation as the hyperthyroid lead singer of the Modern Lovers, Richman gave new hope to the socially inept. He looked like the kid who stumbled over his own feet in the high school lunchroom and got the shit kicked out of him by the football team on general principles: short hair, sloppy clothes, no cool. But a real genius for apt metaphor, expressed in songs like "Road Runner," "Pablo Picasso" and "Government Center."

On these two albums, Richman loses his vision and becomes once more a teenage twerp, warbling about Veg-a-Matics and other garbage, replacing the Lovers' flat punk rock with even flatter folkie music. Now you know *why* everybody picked on that kid in high school. — D.M.

THE RIGHTEOUS BROTHERS
★★★★★ **The Righteous Brothers' Greatest Hits, Vol. 1 / Verve 6-5020**
Blue-eyed soul was all the rage from 1963 to 1966, thanks to the Rascals, Mitch Ryder and this duo. The Righteous Brothers were only Bill Medley and Bobby Hatfield, but they often sounded like a choir, adapt-

ing the approach of the Isley Brothers and Ike and Tina Turner to a male team sound. Their first hit, "Little Latin Lupe Lu," which also scored for Ryder, came on Moonglow Records in 1963. But in 1964, they joined Phil Spector's Philles label and immediately recorded one of the giants of the blue-eyed soul genre, "You've Lost That Lovin' Feelin'," which remains one of the best-produced rock records ever made, and one of the most wildly emotive. "Lovin' Feelin' " set a pattern for the group's other hits—Spector's Wall of Sound and tremulously paranoid lyrics in a call-and-response pattern were also the format of such hits as "Ebb Tide," "Just Once in My Life," "Soul and Inspiration" and "Go Ahead and Cry." All of these are here and none of them miss a trick. Anyone who likes Hall and Oates, for instance, should faint when they hear *this* stuff. — D.M.

BILLY LEE RILEY
★ **Billy Lee Riley in Action / Cres. 2028**
Riley was once a hot session guitarist for Sam Phillips at Sun, accompanying Jerry Lee Lewis, Roy Orbison and others in the heyday of rockabilly, and recording a few masterful sides himself. (The most well-known of them is the delightful "Flying Saucers Rock 'n' Roll," in which little green men come to this planet to boogie.) Such gems of nonsense and power are available on many of the Sun rockabilly compilation albums. The album above, recorded ten or more years later, is not so much mistitled as misspelled: *Billy Lee Riley Inaction* is more like it. — D.M.

JEANNIE C. RILEY
★★ **Country Girl / Plant. 8**
★★ **Country Gold / Plant. 250**
★★ **Country Queens / Plant. 508**
★ **Generation Gap / Plant. 11**
★ **Girls Girls Girls / Plant. 519**
★★★ **Harper Valley P.T.A. / Plant. 1**
★★ **Jeannie / Plant. 16**
★★ **Jeannie C. Riley's Greatest Hits / Plant. 13**
★ **Things Go Better with Love / Plant. 4**
★ **Yearbooks and Yesterdays / Plant. 2**
Jeannie C. Riley is famous for her cover of Tom T. Hall's anti-hypocrisy classic, "Harper Valley P.T.A." The song was hot enough to launch her career and prompt her manager, Shelby Singleton, to start a new record label (Plantation) behind it. But Riley never came up with another vehicle as good, and she slowly faded into country music history. — J.S.

RIMSHOTS
★★★ **Down to Earth / Stang 1028**
★★★ **Party / Stang 1027**
Competent funk, for all those who think that the primary musical sound at the core of the universe is probably "shooogity-boogity-shoop." And who knows, it might be true. — D.M.

JERRY RIOPELLE
★★★ **Jerry Riopelle / Cap. SM-732**
★★ **Second Album / Cap. SM-863**
★ **Take a Chance / ABC D-886**
Average and occasionally pleasant Seventies singer/songwriter with a penchant for understated funk arrangements. — J.S.

RIOT
★ **Welcome to the World of Riot / Mo. M6-806**
Talk about not living up to your name. This mindless funk assemblage doesn't live up to Asleep at the Wheel's name. (Now deleted.) — D.M.

MINNIE RIPERTON
★★ **Adventures in Paradise / Epic PE-33454**
★ **Come to My Garden / Janus 7011**
★★★ **Perfect Angel / Epic KE-32561**
★★ **Stay in Love / Epic PE-34191**
Riperton had a multi-octave voice, which made her the Yma Sumac of progressive soul. "Lovin' You" from *Perfect Angel* was a hit in 1975, but everything from then until her death from cancer in 1979 was downhill. — D.M.

THE RITCHIE FAMILY
★★ **African Queens / Marlin 2206**
★★ **American Generation / Marlin 2215**
★★ **Arabian Nights / Marlin 2201**
★★ **Life Is Music / Marlin 2203**
Miami soul's all-female answer to the Jackson 5 lacks either the distinctive vocal personality of Michael Jackson or the group's excellent material. The tracks are hard, funky and tight, in the characteristic TK-combine fashion, but there's not enough coloration to make them worthwhile. — D.M.

JEAN RITCHIE
★★★ **A Folk Concert / Folk. 2428**
★★ **None But One / Sire 7530**
Ritchie hails from the Cumberland Mountains of Kentucky and was largely responsible for the popularization of the moun-

tain dulcimer during the Sixties. *None But One* attempts, with intermittent success, to bridge the traditional/contemporary gap— a rock rhythm section just doesn't always adapt to her original or traditional songs. The 1959 *Folk Concert* is shared with Oscar Brand and David Sear, and is more representative of her vocal and instrumental style (listen to "Shady Grove") than the 1977 Sire LP, although the recording quality of the Folkways set is exceptionally poor. — I.M.

TEX RITTER
★★★ **An American Legend** / Cap. SKC-11241
★★★ **Blood on the Saddle** / Cap. SM-1292
★★★ **Hillbilly Heaven** / Cap. SM-1623
★★★ **The Best of Tex Ritter** / Cap. DT-2595

The John Wayne of country music—although Ritter wasn't as formidable a singer as Wayne was an actor. But like Wayne, Ritter has a reputation as both a cowboy and a reactionary of the old school. Ritter's best-known song, aside from a large repertoire of cowboy classics, was "Hillbilly Heaven," a maudlin epic that describes a dream in which Tex sees all the deceased heroes of country music. It has spawned innumerable parodies since, though it would be going too far to describe the song as influential—weird and gushingly sentimental are closer to the truth. — D.M.

SCARLET RIVERA
★ **Scarlet Rivera** / War. 3060
★ **Scarlet Fever** / War. K-3174

Bob Dylan's Rolling Thunder Revue violinist makes a discofied gypsy music album, more notable for its pretentiousness than its charm. — D.M.

JOHNNY RIVERS
★★★ **A Touch of Gold** / Imper. 12427
★★★ **Blue Suede Shoes** / U. Artists LA075-G
★★ **Changes** / Imper. 12334
★★★★ **Johnny Rivers** / U. Artists UXS-93
★★★★ **Johnny Rivers' Golden Hits** / Imper. 12324
★★ **L.A. Reggae** / U. Artists 5650
★★ **New Lovers and Old Friends** / Epic PE-33681
★★ **Outside Help** / Soul C. 76004
★★ **Wild Night** / U. Artists LA486-G

In the early Sixties, Rivers played the Los Angeles club circuit and eventually caught on at the Whiskey A Go Go, where the celebrity-studded crowds ate up his Baton Rouge-cum-New York white funk vocals and heavily rhythmic John Lee Hooker-derived boogie guitar playing. A live recording of Chuck Berry's "Memphis," from one of his Whiskey shows, became a hit, and Rivers was able to follow it with a couple more dance records (now all out of print) and singles ("Mountain of Love," "Maybellene," "Secret Agent Man," "I Washed My Hands in Muddy Water"), available on *Golden Hits.*

Rivers went on to become an MOR crooner, having some success with "Poor Side of Town" and "Tracks of My Tears"; a record executive (responsible for discovering the Fifth Dimension); and later a socially conscious Seventies singer/songwriter, covering James Taylor and recording "Come Home America," George McGovern's campaign song. — J.S.

HARGUS "PIG" ROBBINS
★★ **Country Instrumentalist of the Year** / Elek. 7E-1110
★★ **Pig in a Poke** / Elek. 6E-129

Robbins is a blind pianist who is one of Nashville's foremost sessionmen; he made his mark on rock by playing many of the piano parts on *Blonde on Blonde,* although his blindness apparently so intimidated Dylan that he was afraid to call Robbins by his studio nickname, "Pig." But these two LPs of C&W MOR don't do his talents justice; they're faceless Muzak for hayseeds. — D.M.

MARTY ROBBINS
★★ **Adios Amigo** / Col. KC-34448
★★★★ **All-Time Greatest Hits** / Col. CG-31361
★ **Christmas Album** / Col. CG-30763
★★ **Don't Let Me Touch You** / Col. KC-35040
★★★ **El Paso City** / Col. KC-34303
★★★ **Gunfighter Ballads** / Col. CS-8158
★★ **I Walk Alone** / Col. CS-9725
★★ **Marty's Country** / Col. CG-15
★★★ **Marty's Greatest Hits** / Col. CS-8639
★★ **Marty's Greatest Hits, Vol. 3** / Col. C-30571
★★ **More Greatest Hits** / Col. CS-8435
★★★ **More Gunfighter Ballads** / Col. CS-8272
★★ **My Woman, My Woman, My Wife** / Col. CS-9978
★★ **No Signs of Loneliness** / Col. C-33476
★★ **Return of the Gunfighter** / Col. CS-8872

★★ **The Alamo / Col. CS-8358**
★★★ **The Drifter / Col. CS-9327**
★★★ **The World of Marty Robbins / Col. CG-30881**
★★★ **What God Has Done / Col. CS-9248**

Best known today as a conventional country singer, Marty Robbins was a successful ballad singer in the mid-Fifties who helped bridge the gaps between country and rockabilly country and straight pop. His 1954 version of Arthur Crudup's "That's All Right" outsold Elvis Presley's superior Sun recording. But Robbins reached his pop peak in 1957, with "White Sport Coat," a Top Three hit, and enjoyed a string of weepers that had considerable chart success and earned him the sobriquet "Mr. Teardrop."

Always more western-oriented than most country or rock singers, Robbins earned a No. 1 in 1959 with "El Paso," a gunfighter ballad of his own composition that led to the interesting series of *Gunfighter Ballads* and other cowboy-anthem albums. More recently, he has recorded formula country songs, earning some occasional big country hits but not much pop success. — D.M.

BRUCE ROBERTS
★★ **Bruce Roberts / Elek. 7E-1119**
This New York dandy is best known as one of lyricists Carole Bayer Sager's collaborators, but his sole solo LP is distinguished more by Tom Dowd's perfect MOR production than by anything Roberts contributes. — D.M.

RICK ROBERTS
★★ **She Is a Song / A&M 4404**
★★ **The Best of Rick Roberts / A&M 4744**
★★ **Windmills / A&M 4372**
Roberts replaced Gram Parsons in the Flying Burrito Brothers, though not in the hearts of the group's fans. He cut these solo LPs between his stint with that group and the formation of Firefall, his current band. Both feature plain pop melodies with country and bluegrass overtones, delivered with neither flair nor conviction and at usually lazy tempos. The few rocking moments lack strength. Roberts sports a sweet but unmoving tenor, and as an instrumentalist, favors dull acoustic guitar strumming. Only the sometimes stellar backup musicians—David Crosby, Jackson Browne, Byron Berline and various Eagles—helps raise this above the level of the really awful. — C.W.

PAUL ROBESON
★★ **Ballad for Americans, Carnegie Hall Concert, Vol. 2 / Van. VSD-79193**
★★★★ **The Essential Paul Robeson / Van. VSD-57/58**
A former All-American football player at Rutgers, a lawyer, concert artist, actor, humanitarian and leftist political activist, Paul Robeson was probably the most influential black performer of the late Forties and early Fifties for white audiences. His style, however, owes more to conventional operatic and popular singing than to any of the blues or gospel traditions of black culture. His rich baritone is best remembered for the searing interpretation of Jerome Kern's "Old Man River" and for the Earl Robinson cantata "Ballad for Americans." *The Essential* is a repackage of Volume 1 of his farewell Carnegie Hall concert (1958), coupled with another previously available LP of folk and classical concert pieces, in addition to "Ballad for Americans." The other set includes more from the concert and some other material recorded about the same time. — I.M.

THE ROBINS
★★★★ **Best of the Robins / Cres. 9034**
Excellent mid-Fifties R&B harmony group, whose reputation is enhanced by the fact that the same quartet later became the Coasters. "Smokey Joe's Cafe" is the big hit from this one. — D.M.

EARL ROBINSON
★★ **A Walk in the Sun / Folk. 2324**
Although rock will best remember Robinson as the composer of Three Dog Night's "Black and White," he was, more importantly, responsible for such cantatas as "Ballad for Americans" and "The Lonesome Train," and numerous TV and film scores. "Joe Hill," the labor anthem, and "The House I Live In" are also his compositions. The LP is monotonous, but the songs are models of the craft. — I.M.

SMOKEY ROBINSON
★★★★ **A Quiet Storm / Tam. T7-337**
★★★ **Big Time / Tam. T7-355**
★★★ **Deep in My Soul / Tam. T7-350**
★★★ **Love Breeze / Tam. T7-359**
★★★★ **Pure Smokey / Tam. T6-331**
★★★★ **Smokey's Family Robinson / Tam. T7-341**
★★★ **Smokin' / Tam. T9-363**
As the leader of the Miracles, Smokey Robinson had as much as anyone, even Berry Gordy, to do with formulating the

Motown sound. When Smokey stepped away from the Miracles in the early Seventies (to become a Motown corporate vice-president), he swore he didn't want to make solo records, but his first, the now-deleted *Smokey* (Tamla 328), wasn't long in arriving. Interesting but erratic, it set the pattern for what followed. All of these albums have something to recommend them—most often Robinson's smooth tenor voice. But the best of all are those on which he wrote the material, generally much more reflective and personal than anything he tried with the Miracles. *Pure Smokey,* for instance, contains "Virgin Man," a fascinating attempt to explore male sexual inexperience and insecurity; *A Quiet Storm* is as romantic as songs he wrote for the Miracles, but more personally involved, and features one terrific groove, "Baby, That's Backatcha," for his voice; *Family Robinson* manages to make Robinson's sweetness come to terms with the contemporary black rock idiom, an explosive combination. All three of these are recommended to those with tastes in Sixties soul crooning; the other LPs are for more limited palates only. — D.M.

SMOKEY ROBINSON AND THE MIRACLES
★★★★★ **Anthology / Mo. 793**
★★★★ **Greatest Hits from the Beginning / Tam. 254**
★★★★★ **Greatest Hits, Vol. 2 / Tam. 280**
★★★ **Tears of a Clown / Pick. 3389**
Motown has deleted almost its entire catalogue of Sixties albums, except greatest-hits packages. The Miracles' *Hits from the Beginning* is the oldest Motown album still in print. It contains twenty-two songs, all from the Miracles' earliest days. The material is ballad-oriented, and Smokey Robinson's falsetto sounds wildly erotic on songs like "You Can Depend On Me" and "I've Been Good to You." *Volume 2* is centered on the group's "classic" period, at the height of Robinson's powers as a songwriter, and includes mid-Sixties favorites like "The Tracks of My Tears," "I Second That Emotion" and "Going to A Go-Go." The *Anthology,* a three-record set, covers the Miracles from selected early hits through Robinson's departure. Naturally, there is a great deal of duplication among the first two greatest-hits sets and the *Anthology.* While the Sixties albums are no longer in the Motown catalogue, several have been reissued on Pickwick—but with modifications, including sleazier covers and fewer cuts per LP—nine songs from the

original eleven to twelve. It seems a shoddy way to present some of soul's greatest music. — J.MC.

TOM ROBINSON BAND
★★★★ **Power in the Darkness / Harv. STB 11778**
★★★ **Tom Robinson Band TRB II / Cap. ST-11930**
Overtly gay New Wave rocker from England 1978. Robinson is a bitter leftist polemicist, and songs like "Right on Sisters" are too full of rhetoric to be satisfying to any but the most doctrinaire ears. But the title song has a real majesty, and the group's English hit singles, "Grey Cortina" and "2-4-6-8 Motorway," have a raw hard-rock vitality that makes them work—and enhances the band's politics. Robinson could become one of the most important artists of the Eighties. — D.M.

VICKI SUE ROBINSON
★★ **Half and Half / RCA AFL1-2294**
★★★ **Never Gonna Let You Go / RCA APL1-1256**
★★ **Vicki Sue Robinson / RCA APL1-1829**
She started as an aspiring Broadway singer/actress, which may account for the uptown energy of "Turn the Beat Around," a truer "Boogie Down Broadway." The rest of *Never Gonna Let You Go* alternates ballads and Gloria Gaynor-type romps. Her second and third albums have Vicki moving downtown to the cabaret. It's "strictly for lovers," but she earns a shot on the *Johnny Carson Show* before retiring to Atlantic City. — B.T.

ROCCO
★★ **Rocco / 20th Cent. 505**
Undistinguished disco-funk from 1976. (Now deleted.) — D.M.

MAGGIE AND TERRE ROCHE
★★★★ **Seductive Reasoning / Col.
KC-33232**
This pair of New Jersey sisters operates in
the Seventies post-folk idiom in much the
same manner as Loudon Wainwright, joking their way through life's turmoil. Although they're a steady draw on the folk
circuit (lately accompanied by a third sister, Suzze), this 1975 LP is their only disc.
But it's a winner. The Roches have a special interest in sexual neurosis that adds to
their wit, and Maggie has a knack for getting away with outrageous rhymes: "clear
to ya" and "cafeteria," for instance. The
backup, by the Muscle Shoals Rhythm
Section mostly, is superb and the production—including a few tracks done by Paul
Samwell-Smith and one by Paul Simon—is
first-rate. Interesting for aficionados of the
strange. — D.M.

ROCKIN' HORSE
★★★ **Rockin' Horse / RCA APL1-0937**
Competent mid-Seventies hard rock. (Now
deleted.) — D.M.

JESS RODEN
★★★★ **Blowin' / Is. 9496**
★★ **Keep Your Hat On / Is. 9349**
★★★ **Player Not the Game / Is. 9506**
Roden's a better-than-average blue-eyed
soul singer from England whose recorded
work is spotty. *Player Not the Game* is a
decent studio effort, but the live set,
Blowin', shows him and band in excellent
form, a funk complement to Robert
Palmer. — J.S.

JIMMIE RODGERS
★★★★ **A Legendary Performer / RCA
CPL1-2504**
★★★★★ **Best of the Legendary Jimmie
Rodgers / RCA AHL1-3315**
★★★★★ **Country Music Hall of Fame:
Jimmie Rodgers / RCA AHM1-2531**
★★★ **Jimmie the Kid / RCA AHM1-2213**
★★★★ **My Rough and Rowdy Ways /
RCA ANL1-1209**
★★★★ **My Time Ain't Long / RCA
AHM1-2865**
★★★★ **Never No Mo' Blues / RCA
AHM1-1232**
★★★★ **Short but Brilliant Life of Jimmie
Rodgers / RCA AHM1-3094**
★★★★ **This Is Jimmie Rodgers / RCA
VPS-6091**
★★★★ **Train Whistle Blues / RCA
AML1-1640**
With the exception of Hank Williams, Jim-
mie Rodgers is undoubtedly the most im-

portant figure in country & western music;
he was discovered in 1927, in the same
Cumberland Mountains area where the
Carter Family was also beginning its career. As the Singing Brakeman, it was
Rodgers—far more than Woody Guthrie—
who was the true voice of the Depression.
Among his greatest records were "Blue
Yodel," "Mule Skinner Blues," "Yodeling
Cowboy Blues" and "Somewhere Down
Below the Dixon Line," although dozens
of his songs have entered the standard
country and folk music repertoire.
　Rodgers had been suffering from TB for
several years before his first recordings,
and he died in 1933 of that disease. This
helped enhance his legend, and set the pattern for a great many other white recording
stars (Hank Williams, Elvis, etc.) who
burned out young. But his records remained best sellers through the Fifties and
into the Sixties, which is why his career is
so exceptionally well documented even
now. (It helps that all of his records were
made for one company, RCA.) Each of
them is of more than moderate value, although the *Legendary Performer* set is perhaps the best annotated. — D.M.

JIMMIE RODGERS
★★ **Yours Truly / Roul. 42006**
Not the country singer but a pop-folk stylist with the same name who had a few hits
in the late Fifties; "Honeycomb" and
"Kisses Sweeter than Wine" are the best
known. His career ended after an alleged
police beating. — D.M.

JOHNNY RODRIGUEZ
★★★★ **Great Hits of Johnny Rodriguez /
Mer. SRM-1-1078**
★★ **Just for You / Mer. SRM-1-5003**
★★★ **Introducing Johnny Rodriguez /
Mer. 61378**

★★ **Practice Makes Perfect** / Mer.
SRM-1-1144
★★ **Reflecting** / Mer. SRM-1-1110
Chicano country singer got his start as gui-
tarist in Tom T. Hall's band and eventually
became Hall's protégé. Producer Jerry
Kennedy went to work on him and Rodri-
guez soon had a string of Seventies country
pop hits: "Pass Me By," "Ridin' My
Thumb to Mexico," "That's the Way
Loves Goes," "Just Get Up and Close the
Door," "Hillbilly Heart" and "If Practice
Makes Perfect." Like Freddy Fender,
Rodriguez's signature is to alternate sing-
ing Spanish and English verses. — J.S.

TOMMY ROE
★★ **Energy** / Monu. MG-7604
★★ **Full Bloom** / Monu. MG-7614
Dull attempts at a Seventies comeback by
the kid who did "Dizzy" and "Sweet Pea,"
which were obnoxiously catchy pop-rock
hits of the middle Sixties. — D.M.

D. J. ROGERS
★★★ **D. J. Rogers** / Shel. 52025
★★★ **Love Brought Me Back** / Col.
JC-35393
★★★ **Love, Music and Life** / RCA
APL1-2218
D. J. Rogers is a former member of gospel
singer James Cleveland's choir, and Cleveland's influence still holds sway over Rogers' vocal delivery and phrasing. Also like
Cleveland, Rogers possesses an unremit-
tingly harsh singing voice. His albums are
rhythmically stiff and tend to fall back on
funk clichés, but midtempo songs and ballads reveal a rude power that transcends
much of the studio junk. Rogers is also a
capable songwriter. — J.MC.

KENNY ROGERS
★ **Daytime Friends** / U. Artists
LA754-G
★ **Kenny Rogers** / U. Artists LA689-G
★ **Kenny Rogers and the First Edition's
Greatest Hits** / Rep. 6437
★ **Love Lifted Me** / U. Artists LA607-G
★★ **Ten Years of Gold** / U. Artists
LA835-H
Who would have thought, when Kenny
Rogers and the First Edition scored a 1968
hit with "Just Dropped In to See What
Condition My Condition Was In," that this
prime-time psychedelia would later evolve
into pop-country superstardom via the pro-
war "Ruby Don't Go to Town"? Who
would have cared? For *Hee Haw* devotees
only. — D.M.

ROLLING STONES / The Early Years
★★★★★ **Around and Around** / Decca
SLK 16315-P (Import)
★★★★★ **Big Hits (High Tide and Green
Grass)** / Lon. NPS-1
★★★ **December's Children (And Every-
body's)** / Lon. PS-451
★ **Got Live If You Want It** / Lon. PS-493
★★★★ **Out of Our Heads** / Lon. PS-429
★★★★ **The Rolling Stones** / Lon. PS-375
★★★★★ **The Rolling Stones, Now!** / Lon.
PS-420
★★★★ **12 × 5** / Lon. PS-402
As everyone past infancy should know, the
Rolling Stones in their initial incarnation
were the greatest white blues and R&B
band that ever was. This is not legend; it is
fact. Unfortunately, the magnitude of their
talent did not prevent them from making
frequently spotty albums. Even in 1964,
when the group first recorded, Keith Richards was the world's greatest Chuck
Berry–style guitarist, Charlie Watts and
Bill Wyman the most existentially funky
rhythm section in music, and Brian Jones
served as blues freak extraordinaire and
musical director. But the early Mick Jagger's charisma could not make up for a
lack of confidence and stylistic range. Although modeled after Muddy Waters, Slim
Harpo, Solomon Burke and Otis Redding,
too many of his vocals simply miss the
mark. Worse, some of the early songs written by Jagger/Richards miss by more.
Around and Around, the import, is a
fabulous look at the early days; it includes
"Poison Ivy," the Stones' astounding version of Chuck Berry's "Bye Bye Johnny,"
and Jagger/Richards' best early song,
"Empty Heart." It contains much of what's
on *12 × 5* but is more coherently organized, and the liner photo of Jagger and
the cop is a scream. On the other hand, the

first LP (subtitled *England's Newest Hit-makers*) is the hardest R&B the Stones (or anyone) ever recorded. Besides "Not Fade Away," their first U.S. hit, it has another Berry marvel, "Carol"; "Tell Me," another strong original; and some first-rate Chicago blues. But it is also padded (with an instrumental version of "Can I Get a Witness," for one). *Now* is not—it is spare but powerful, and includes some benchmark Stones material: the obligatory Berry tune is "You Can't Catch Me," but the finest songs here are "Mona" and "Everybody Needs Somebody to Love," expropriated from Bo Diddley and Solomon Burke, respectively. *12 × 5* ranges from the wonderful "Time Is on My Side"—a true portent—to the simply silly "Under the Boardwalk."

Out of Our Heads and *December's Children* let the focus slide slightly from blues/R&B to rock & roll. *Heads* includes some archetypal Jagger poses—"Satisfaction," "Play with Fire," "The Last Time," "The Under Assistant West Coast Promotion Man," as well as Burke's "That's How Strong My Love Is," Jagger's best pure soul vocal. It's padded, though, with a couple of jams. *Children,* despite "Get Off My Cloud" and "I'm Free," takes a distinct dip; "Route 66" and "As Tears Go By" haven't aged well, and the original writing is weak while the cover material scrapes the barrel bottom.

High Tide and Green Grass is both brutal and beautiful, one of the finest rock & roll collections ever assembled, not to mention its photography, which captures the essence of the early Rolling Stones completely. Besides being the cream of the six early American LPs, it also featured the first LP appearance of "19th Nervous Breakdown," which set the stage for the psychotic rock that would dominate the group's passions through *Aftermath* and much of the rest of its career. (Regrettably, it does not include the group's two other similar 1966 hits, "Mother's Little Helper" and "Have You Seen Your Mother Baby Standing in the Shadow.")

ROLLING STONES / The Middle Years
★★★★★ **Aftermath / Lon. PS-476**
★★★★★ **Beggar's Banquet / Lon. PS-539**
★★★★ **Between the Buttons / Lon. PS-499**
★★★ **Flowers / Lon. PS-509**
★★★★ **Hot Rocks 1964—1971 / Lon. 2PS-606/7**
★★★★ **Let It Bleed / Lon. NPS 4**
■ **Metamorphosis / Abkco ANA 1**

★★★★★ **More Hot Rocks (Big Hits and Fazed Cookies) / Lon. 2PS 626/7**
★★★ **Their Satanic Majesties Request / Lon. NPS-2**
★★★ **Through the Past, Darkly (Big Hits, Vol. 2) / Lon. NPS-3**

With *Aftermath,* the change begun with *Out of Our Heads* was complete. No longer were the Stones simply recycling the blues and R&B of the masters; now they had evolved a rock & roll form of their own. It was still rooted in black music (in some ways, Richards' giant, fuzzy guitar tones were a compensation for the band's lack of horns), but now the style was distinctly their own.

Aftermath has everything: "Paint It Black," a tormented and demented hit: the misogyny of "Stupid Girl"; and "Under My Thumb," which made Jagger infamous; dark brooding stuff like "Flight 505" and "Goin' Home." The instrumentation is remarkably diverse—Brian Jones chips in with dulcimer and sitar, and there are a variety of keyboards—while Jagger's singing begins to reach maturity. The album's one flaw is its tendency to pander to the Stones' audience's flagellant tendencies, but I'm not sure that's the Stones' fault.

Between the Buttons is almost lighthearted in contrast, a kind of demonic folk-rock record. There are a number of obscure treasures here—"My Obsession," "Connection," "All Sold Out," "Complicated"—as well as the hits "Ruby Tuesday" and "Let's Spend the Night Together." *Flowers* includes those songs, plus "Have You Seen Your Mother," "Mother's Little Helper" and *Aftermath's* "Lady Jane," not to mention one of the most embarrassing white-soul fiascoes on disc, "My Girl." It does have "Ride on Baby," "Sittin' on a Fence" and "Backstreet Girl." So does the English version of *Buttons* (Decca SKL 4852), which is a recommended alternative.

Satanic Majesties is a bad idea gone wrong. The idea of making a truly druggy answer to the cherubic joyousness of the Beatles' *Sgt. Pepper* was silly enough. Doing so by fuzzing up some pretty good songs with tape loops and early synthesizer experiments is thoroughly unforgivable. Only "2000 Man," "In Another Land" and "She's a Rainbow" redeem this one.

Beggar's Banquet is closer to what *Satanic* aimed for anyway. Its theme is dissolution, and from the opening song—the infamous "Sympathy for the Devil"—to the final number—the bathetically charming "Salt of the Earth"—it is terrifying. "Street

Fighting Man" is the keynote, with its teasing admonition to do something and its refusal to admit that doing it will make any difference; as usual, the Stones were more correct, if also more faithless, philosophers than any of their peers.

Through the Past, Darkly has been rendered redundant by the *Hot Rocks* sets. The first of those collections is a hodgepodge of the obvious, but *More* contains some gems and rarities: the B side, "Child of the Moon" is available nowhere else; side four—which features blues numbers, some Chuck Berry and R&B remakes like "Fortune Teller" and "Poison Ivy"—has been available only on foreign LPs. *Metamorphosis* was assembled by the group's former manager, and consists of useless demos, outtakes from the 1968 to 1970 era, and a lot of sheer garbage. An early version of "Memo from Turner" is interesting, and "Don't Lie to Me" is decently done, but a wise person would pass this up, if only out of respect for the group.

Let It Bleed is a transitional LP. It could as easily fall into the Seventies grouping, although one or two of its key tracks— "Midnight Rambler" and the title track, particularly—are leftovers of *Aftermath*-style demonism. Some of the most frightening and beautiful music the Stones have made is here—"Gimme Shelter" encapsulates the former, "You Can't Always Get What You Want" the latter, until you listen closely, at which point the categories revise themselves still more. But, perhaps because Brian Jones had died and Mick Taylor was not fully integrated as his replacement, the record is erratic. Richards' vocal on "You Got the Silver" is evocative, but "Monkey Man" is silly, "Country Honk" an abomination in the face of the original "Honky Tonk Women" single. Some of the rest is just okay. A good one, though—you wouldn't want to be without "You Can't Always Get What You Want" and "Gimme Shelter," which are about as terminal as the Sixties got.

ROLLING STONES / The Seventies
★★★ **Black and Blue / Rol. NPS-3**
★★★★ **Exile on Main Street / Rol. 2900**
★★★★ **'Get Yer Ya-Ya's Out!' The Rolling Stones in Concert / Lon. NPS-5**
★ **Goat's Head Soup / Rol. COC-39106**
★★★ **It's Only Rock 'n' Roll / Rol. 79101**
★★★ **Love You Live / Rol. 2-9001**
★★ **Made in the Shade / Rol. COC-39107**

★★★ **Some Girls / Rol. 39108**
★★★★ **Sticky Fingers / Rol. 39105**
This is a muddled era, framed by concert albums that contain some of the greatest music the Stones have made, and some of the most dreadfully disconcerting. If such a long-lived and volatile rock & roll band can be said to be in transition, then that's the explanation; others say it was over the moment Mick Taylor joined the group, replacing Brian Jones. (Jones died several weeks later.)

Taylor appeared on one track of *Let It Bleed,* but he made his presence felt with the Stones' 1969 tour of America, and with *Ya-Ya's* (one result of it). Partly as a result of Jones' absence, partly because of Taylor's stinging slide guitar and blues background, the group became much less pop-oriented, concocting instead a salacious and brutal rock sound. "Stray Cat Blues" was nasty on *Beggar's Banquet,* but on *Ya-Ya's* it is malicious. So is a good deal of Jagger's posing, which is an embarrassment eight years later. Still, there were moments in that show (including "Carol," "Love in Vain," "Little Queenie" and the twin classics that frame this album, "Jumpin' Jack Flash" and "Street Fighting Man") when one could believe, love and fear every aspect of the Stones' myth.

Sticky Fingers, then, came as something of a shock. Aside from "Brown Sugar" and "Bitch," which open the respective sides, it is the most subdued Rolling Stones record ever made. But its gentler side hides real fury: "Moonlight Mile" is beautiful, but listen closely and you'll hear a ravaged tale. "Wild Horses" is not so much wistful as bitter, and the rest is a restless rush in search of a self-assurance that never comes. Richards and Taylor work together well, while Paul Buckmaster's strings and Watts' drumming on "Moonlight Mile" are rock & roll landmarks.

Exile on Main Street made the mood of rebelliousness grown stale that dominated *Sticky Fingers* more explicit. It was an attempt to break past the limits maturity imposed, and about half the time it succeeded: "Rocks Off," "Rip This Joint" and Keith's sardonic "Happy" are truly fearsome—just plain mean. But even the Stones couldn't sustain that much spite for four sides; too much of *Exile* is simply forgettable, though the best of what's there is as essential as any Stones' music—which is to say, as any music at all. "Tumbling Dice," incidentally, may be the best thing they've ever recorded.

Goat's Head Soup is a mistake, a jumble or the beginning of the end, depending on whom you ask. Jagger's poses are encapsulated—or should I say, embalmed—forever here, with claptrap like "Dancing with Mr. D.," which wouldn't scare a four-year-old. Only "Heartbreaker" and "Angie" are up to the usual level.

Only Rock 'n' Roll managed to avoid the questions of decline by tossing together the usual recycled Chuck Berry with a terrific reggae song, "Luxury," and a knife-in-the-back ballad, "If You Really Want to Be My Friend." It's full of filler, but it is also the Rolling Stones as we know them, no small thing.

Black and Blue is the Rolling Stones as we may have to learn to like them. The hard rock they drew from Chuck Berry is dissipated here—only "Crazy Mama" and "Hand of Fate" show a hint of it. There are some interesting, if eventually tedious, rhythm numbers, like "Hot Stuff," a reggae not half so good as "Luxury," and not much else. Except that Jagger sings better than ever—in fact, it could even be said that he sings, in the traditional sense, for the first time, on songs like "Memory Motel" (a half-mocking sequel to "Moonlight Mile"), "Melody" and "Fool to Cry." He's also stepping away from his devilish image, as befits someone nearing forty. The combination may prove fascinating. *Love You Live* is a live album, has no new material (unless some old Fifties blues numbers count) and reveals nothing, though the playing is far superior to the group's dreadful 1975 U.S. tour. What will be interesting, though, will be whether rock's most famous (did someone say best?) group can survive to middle age.

Some Girls, released in 1978, was the group's biggest seller ever, thanks to market expansion and a hit single in "Miss You," which took the discofied accents of *Black and Blue*'s "Hot Stuff" and tightened them up. But the old energy of the Stones is gone for good—tracks like "Shattered" and "When the Whip Comes Down" are hollow echoes of the Stones' best moments. Only Keith Richards' scabrous "Before They Make Me Run" has any sort of emotional power, and then only because of Richards' then-current heroin bust. (He seems to have gotten off almost scot-free, hardly an outlaw's comeuppance.) What the Stones may do in the future may be an open question, but *Some Girls* demonstrates that it probably won't matter much except to the diehards. — D.M.

MAX ROMEO
★★ **Open the Iron Gate / U. Artists LA803-H**
★★★ **War Ina Babylon / Is. 9392**
Romeo was known early on for making the most risqué kind of reggae; it's got a tough rhythmic bite but isn't useful except as a dance mechanism, as the U.A. LP demonstrates. By the time of the Island set, he'd switched his concerns to include Rastafarian politics (Babylon is everywhere except Jamaica and mythic Ethiopia) with a considerable improvement in interest value. — D.M.

MICK RONSON
★★ **Play Don't Worry / RCA APL1-0681**
Good Beck-influenced guitar from former David Bowie sideman Ronson, but otherwise ordinary playing and singing, little economy and mediocre material. Backup included other former Bowie sidemen. (Now deleted.) — C.W.

LINDA RONSTADT
★★★★ **A Retrospective / Cap. SKBB-11629**
★★★ **Different Drum / Cap. ST-11269**
★★★ **Don't Cry Now / Asy. 5064**
★★★★ **Greatest Hits / Asy. 6E-106**
★ **Hand Sown / Cap. ST-208**
★★★ **Hasten Down the Wind / Asy. 7E-1072**
★★★★★ **Heart Like a Wheel / Cap. SW-11358**
★★ **Linda Ronstadt / Cap. SMAS-635**
★★ **Living in the U.S.A. / Asy. 6E-155**
★★★★ **Prisoner in Disguise / Asy. 7E-1045**
★★ **Silk Purse / Cap. 407**
★★★ **Simple Dreams / Asy. 6E-155**
Linda Ronstadt's the prototypical Seventies pop-country-rock voice and also rock's

major sex symbol as it enters the Eighties. Both voice and image are ripe, throbbing, with a heartbroken emotional edge. Ronstadt had her first hit in 1967, when she sang with the Stone Poneys. Her subsequent Capitol albums, until *Heart Like A Wheel,* were thinly produced, uneven collections that show much untapped potential. The two-record *Retrospective* collects everything valuable from this period; *Different Drum* is a one-record selection.

Heart Like a Wheel, produced by Ronstadt's manager, Peter Asher, and featuring arrangements by supersideman Andrew Gold, finally matched the voice with ideal material and sensational production values. "You're No Good," "When Will I Be Loved" and Anna McGarrigle's touching title song are among *Heart*'s gems. Though just as opulently recorded, *Prisoner* and *Hasten* lack *Heart*'s perfect consistency, and because it does not include the title songs of *Heart* and *Prisoner,* *Greatest Hits* is not the greatest Ronstadt.

In fact, *Hits* was premature. Ronstadt and Asher quickly developed a formula that made her the leading female vocalist of the age, cutting across barriers into country as well as pop. Their willingness to record excellent songs by then-unknown writers such as Karla Bonoff and Warren Zevon and Asher's perfect selections of Buddy Holly and Motown oldies gave her a continuing stream of both hit singles and smash LPs. But with *Simple Dreams,* the formula began to turn stale, and with 1978's *Living in the U.S.A.,* the pair seemed to have reached a conceptual dead end. Chuck Berry's "Back in the U.S.A." was so embalmed that it flopped as a single, although the album was again a commercial winner. Only Elvis Costello's "Alison" redeemed it artistically. Whether Ronstadt and Asher can find a way out of this remains to be seen. — S.H.

ROOMFUL OF BLUES
★★ Roomful of Blues / Is. 9474
Boston-based big band defines blues as a medium with horns, a rare thing in rock. They swing it a bit, but the material is too conventional and the singing too uninspired to make this the imaginative success it deserves to be. Future is worth watching, though. — D.M.

ROOT BOY SLIM AND THE SEX CHANGE BAND
★ Root Boy Slim and the Sex Change Band / War. 3160

Truly wretched 1978 version of the kind of college prank that would have been mildly funny in 1961. Slim growls, but not so handsomely as Howlin' Wolf, and the band plays with absolute lack of feel. Another gem for the second-year men. — D.M.

ROSE ROYCE
★★★ In Full Bloom / Whit. 3074
★★★ Rose Royce Strikes Again / Whit. 3227
This nine-man progressive soul band was formed by Norman Whitfield to back up his latter-day Temptations productions. Whitfield named the group, added female vocalist Gwen "Rose" Dickey, then used them as the soundtrack artists for *Car Wash,* which gave them their first hit singles, "Car Wash" and "I Wanna Get Next to You." The subsequent releases haven't been as successful as the *Car Wash* theme, which went to No. 1. But the group's popularity has endured for more than a year, and that's something in the late Seventies. — D.M.

ROSETTA STONE
★ Rosetta Stone / Priv. 7011
The key to nothing except a nice big English rock snooze. Formed by a former Bay City Roller, yet. Some supergroup. — D.M.

ROSIE
★ Last Dance / RCA APL1-2415
Manhattan Transfer for the tone deaf, or those hopelessly addicted to the usual cabaret melange of pop, jazz and R&B. Which is probably the same group of people anyway. — D.M.

DIANA ROSS
★★ An Evening with Diana Ross / Mo. M7-877
★★★ Baby It's Me / Mo. M7-890
★★★★ Diana Ross / Mo. M7-861
★★★★ Diana Ross' Greatest Hits / Mo. M7-869
★★★★ Lady Sings the Blues / Mo. M7-758
★★★ Mahogany / Mo. M7-858
★★★ Ross / Mo. M7-907
Ross' career since she left the Supremes in 1970 has been checkered, but not as spotty as what's left undeleted among her solo LPs. *Baby It's Me* is a 1977 super-production job by the always bombastic Richard Perry, which works half the time, more or less. The live set is predictably dull. The soundtracks are also middling: *Mahogany*

has that film's hit single plus lots of filler, *Lady Sings the Blues* some remarkable (although probably unpalatable to fans of the originals) versions of Billie Holiday songs crowded together with Michel Legrand's pop-jazz bathos, which fills out the score. *Diana Ross,* from 1976, is one of her best solo LPs, including "Mahogany" and "Love Hangover"; "Good Morning Heartache," the best song from *Lady*; and her great early hits, "Ain't No Mountain High Enough" and "Reach Out and Touch Somebody's Hand," as well as her two worst hits, "Touch Me in the Morning" and "Last Time I Saw Him." — D.M.

DIANA ROSS AND MARVIN GAYE
★★★★ Diana and Marvin / Mo. M7-803
Essentially a reworking of the old Marvin Gaye and girl singer cliché, which he'd made work before with such lesser lights as Mary Wells, Kim Weston and the scintillating Tammi Terrell. This one has some moments, especially the singles, "Don't Knock My Love" and "My Mistake"— more moments, in fact, than most of the LPs either Ross or Gaye has recorded separately since 1973, when this one was released. — D.M.

ROTARY CONNECTION
★ Dinner Music / Cadet 328
★ Peace / Cadet 318
★★ Rotary Connection / Cadet 312
★ Rotary Connection / Cadet 317
★ Songs / Cadet 322
Late-Sixties pop-psychedelia from a mostly black group featuring the whining multi-octave voice of Minnie Riperton, who here sounds (at her best) like a Mixmaster gone berserk. "Amen," from the first album (Cadet 312), was a standby in the early days of FM radio rock, but all of these are barely period pieces by now. — D.M.

ROTO ROOTER
★ The Roto Rooter Goodtime Christmas Band / Van. 79347
Any group that does lame parodies of both Jimi Hendrix and Brahms (not to mention "The Beer Bottle Polka") *deserves* to be named after a septic-tank cleaning service. (Now deleted.) — D.M.

ROUGH DIAMOND
★ Rough Diamond / Is. 9490
A 1977 minor-league all-star band featuring vocalist David Byron, a man so talented that he was thrown out of Uriah Heep, unquestionably the worst rock band

ever to earn a gold album. Rough Diamond isn't any improvement. — D.M.

DEMIS ROUSSOS
★ Demis Roussos / Mer. SRM-1-3724
★ Happy to Be / Mer. SRM-1-1086
★ Magic / Mer. SRM-1-1162
Big-Time European pop singer fails to cash in on U.S. market. In some countries, this Greek-born pop singer is outsold only by Abba. Here, he looks like a hairier Kojak, and though his singing is passable, it's nothing that Johnny Carson and Ed McMahon (even) could get shook up about. — D.M.

THE ROWANS
★ Jubilation / Asy. 7E-1114
★ Sibling Rivalry / Asy. 1073
★ The Rowans / Asy. 7E-1038
Jerry Garcia called this group of Marin County wimps the California Beatles when the boys' first album was released in the early Seventies. One presumes he was tripping at the time. The most godawful hippie mindlessness since It's a Beautiful Day. — D.M.

ROXY MUSIC
★★★★ Country Life / Atco 36-106
★★★ For Your Pleasure . . . / Atco 36-134
★★★★ Greatest Hits / Atco 38-103
★★ Roxy Music / Atco 36-133
★★★★★ Siren / Atco 36-127
★★★★ Stranded / Atco 7045
★★★★ Viva! Roxy Music / Atco 36-129
Roxy Music was one of the most intelligent and musically compelling rock groups to come out of Britain in the Seventies, and given the fact that the original band housed singer Bryan Ferry and experimental wizard Brian Eno, it was also one of the most influential. Yet Roxy was, superficially, primarily Ferry's vehicle—with his mannered singing and lyrics drenched in self-aware ennui, his songs and visual style made him Chairman of the Board.

Roxy's first two albums are groping for a style. While Ferry's songs were generally strong, there was a disparity between Eno's attraction to eccentric instrumentation and Ferry's relatively straightforward tunes. *For Your Pleasure* found Ferry's songs and the band's treatment of them coming closer to fruition, but following its release, Eno left to pursue a solo career while Eddie Jobson was added on keyboards and electric violin. Roxy proceeded to make its best music.

At its high point Roxy came on like the

Concorde, sleek and metallic. *Stranded* fairly exploded with rockers like "Street Life" and "Serenade," while more unusual uptempo tunes like "Amazona" crackled with sustain-drenched electricity. What set Roxy apart from other progressive and art-rock bands, though, was its incredible drive, sustained by saxophonist Andrew MacKay and guitarist Phil Manzanera, but founded in the drumming of Paul Thomas, and the band's various bassists, most often John Wetton, a King Crimson veteran. The slower, more tortured tunes further developed Ferry's lonely Everyman persona, an image that burst with fury from *Country Life*'s opening track, "The Thrill of It All." The slickest and most accomplished Roxy music yet, *Country Life* found the group at the peak of its maturity.

Siren's title is appropriate; it has that sort of effect on the listener. It is Roxy's masterpiece, calling the listener back by virtue of its finely honed instrumental attack and compelling lyrical attitude. "Love Is the Drug," Roxy's nearest approximation to an American hit single, set the scene of transitory love in a plastic world, while "She Sells" and "Sentimental Fool" pictured the participants in the charade as simultaneously pathetic and heroic. It is the album's music, though—steely sleek and fiery to the core—that makes it a touchstone album of Seventies art-rock. While *Viva!* captured the group at its onstage best, and the *Greatest Hits* set is a fine sampler, *Siren* remains the album by which their best work will be remembered, at least for now. Although the group broke up in 1977, in late 1978, they were rumored to be re-forming. — J.B.M.

THE ROYAL GUARDSMEN
★ **Return of the Red Baron** / Laur. 2039
■ **Snoopy and His Friends** / Laur. 2042
■ **Snoopy for President** / Laur. 2046
■ **Snoopy vs. the Red Baron** / Laur. 2038
One tepidly interesting comic-strip spinoff hit ("Snoopy vs. the Red Baron," 1966) does not excuse four albums of the same variety of insipid drivel. — D.M.

ROY C.
★★ **More Sex and More Soul** / Mer. SRM-1-1192
★★ **Sex and Soul** / Mer. SRM1-678
Anyone daft enough to make reggae on Long Island, in a Hempstead garage, deserves points for bravado. If Roy C. weren't so patently exploitative of women,

he might get a lot more for his music, which is propulsive but formulaic. — D.M.

RUBEN AND THE JETS
★★★ **Ruben and the Jets** / Verve 6-5055
This album of brilliantly rendered Fifties R&B vocal tunes indicates Frank Zappa's love for the form and his consummate stylistic chops despite the fact that many people took the whole thing as a joke. Of course Zappa's sardonic wit does play a role here, but that's in the fictional casting of the Mothers of Invention as a pre-*American Graffiti* Fifties cultural parody, not in the music itself. (Now deleted.) — J.S.

RUBINOOS
■ **Rubinoos** / Beserk. PZ-34778
Rotten Berkeley-based pop group that does not vindicate itself by covering Tommy James' bubblegum classic "I Think We're Alone Now." Shlock has its place, but not as cheap nostalgia. — J.S.

RUBY AND THE ROMANTICS
★★ **Greatest Hits Album** / MCA 541
"Our Day Will Come" was their only claim to fame, and one is probably well advised to pick up that girl-group staple on the multitudinous oldies collections. — R.G.

DAVID RUFFIN
★★★ **David Ruffin at His Best** / Mo. M7-895
★★ **Everything's Coming Up Love** / Mo. M7-866
★ **In My Stride** / Mo. M7-885
★ **Who I Am** / Mo. M7-849
When David Ruffin left the Temptations in 1969 and scored an immediate success with "My Whole World Ended (The Moment You Left Me)," his future seemed as bright

as any singer in soul. His raspy leads on
many Temptations songs had earned him a
wide following—Rod Stewart draws heavily on Ruffin's singing in his interpretations of soul songs—that needed only nur-
ture (adequate production, good material)
to flower. Unfortunately, he began to suffer
from a program of benign neglect from the
Motown production corps, which tossed
him around like a hot potato, and he's never lived up to a fraction of that promise.
There are a few good moments on the *Best
of,* but nothing any ordinary singer
couldn't do on the rest. — D.M.

RUFUS
★★★★ Ask Rufus / ABC 975
★ Numbers / ABC 1098
★★★ Rags to Rufus / ABC 809
★★ Rufus / ABC 783
★★★ Rufus . . . Featuring Chaka Khan /
  ABC AB-909
★★★★★ Rufusized / ABC D-837
★★★ Street Player / ABC 1049
In reality Rufus *is* Chaka Khan. No one
else in the group has anywhere near her
distinctive talent. But the fact that she has
always had a group behind her, to write
with, tour with and work out arrangements
with seems to have saved her from some of
the hysterical, narcissistic excesses of a
Natalie Cole or Melba Moore. From album to album, she's grown as a singer. At
the time of "Tell Me Something Good"
and "You Got the Love," she was a powerful, somewhat freakish AM singer, with
an incredible range. By the time of "Sweet
Thing" (on *Rufus . . . Featuring Chaka
Khan*) and *Ask Rufus,* she's become a
rhythmical sophisticated stylist. Her theme
is always unrequited love, or at least uncertain love, and in all her best songs—
"You Got the Love," "Stop On By,"
"Sweet Thing," "Better Days," "Ain't
Nothing but a Maybe"—she's addressed
herself to uninterested or indifferent men.
  Her lucky break came during the afternoon when Stevie Wonder sat in on their
recording session, and cooked up "Tell Me
Something Good," a ditty that outsold his
own current singles. *Rags to Rufus* was
something more than a showcase for its
two hit singles—including "Smoking
Room"—but not that much more. The
next album, *Rufusized,* was a fully realized
piece of work in what was to become a
new genre—the middle ground between
rock and soul. Khan had obviously been
doing some thinking about Janis Joplin,
but her sensibility was as different from

Joplin's as from Aretha Franklin's or
Gladys Knight's. There's a spacey, moody
air about the woman that doesn't easily fit
into any established genre. On *Numbers,*
without Chaka, the band is lost. — R.G.

THE RUMOUR
★★★ Max / Mer. SRM-1-1174
Competent solo set from Graham Parker's
backing band, which includes former members of Brinsley Schwarz and Ducks Deluxe. Never as inspired as the Brinsleys,
never as driving as Ducks, never as visionary as Parker, the Rumour must be seen
live to understand this eccentric offering.
Further releases are unlikely but might resolve the issue: is this the Band of the
Eighties? (Answer so far: probably not, but
then Parker isn't Dylan, either.) — D.M.

THE RUNAWAYS
★★ Queens of Noise / Mer. SRM-1-1126
★★ The Runaways / Mer. SRM-1-1090
★★ Waitin' for the Night / Mer.
  SRM-1-3705
Put together by Kim Fowley, the Runaways were meant to be a female punk rock
band. They have yet to achieve either a
musical style or the visual arrogance to
make one unnecessary, so they remain a
subcultural cartoon show. Their first album
has all the marks of an Alice Cooper ripoff, including sequences from an imaginary
girls' prison movie. On *Queens of Noise* the
band manages a lumpen Mott the Hoople
instrumental manner, while Joan Jett sings
most of the lead vocals. — B.T.

TODD RUNDGREN
★★★ A Wizard, a True Star / Bears. 2133
★★★ Another Live / Bears. 6961
★★★ Back to the Bars / Bears.
  2BRX-6986

★★★ Faithful / Bears. 6963
★★ Hermit of Mink Hollow / Bears. 6981
★★ Initiation / Bears. 6957
★★ Oops, Wrong Planet / Bears. 6970
★★★ RA / Bears. 6965
★★★★★ Something/Anything / Bears.
  2BX-2066
★★★ Todd / Bears. 2B-6952
★★ Todd Rundgren's Utopia / Bears.
  BSV-6954

Todd Rundgren is an artist caught between two worlds: he is a student of modern technology, capable of turning out densely experimental music that relies more on form and process than content, but he is also an incurable romantic with a penchant for writing light, soulful ballads. As a result, his recorded work has been remarkably inconsistent. A whiz in the studio (Rundgren learned his engineering and production crafts while fronting Philadelphia's Nazz in the late Sixties), the early part of his studio career found him more often than not making albums almost totally on his own, playing all (or almost all) the instrumental parts and singing both lead and background vocals. *Something/Anything*, his third album (*Runt* and the beautiful *The Ballad of Todd Rundgren* are both Ampex cutouts), featured only him on three of its four sides. It remains the definitive Rundgren opus, an ambitious, challenging and completely successful venture into everything from Motown parodies ("Wolfman Jack") to pop ("Saw the Light," a hit single) to hard rock ("Black Maria"). *A Wizard* crammed almost an hour's worth of music onto its two sides, with mixed results. The ethereal "Sometimes I Don't Know What to Feel" demonstrated Rundgren's keen understanding of Philly soul, and "International Feel" and "Just One Victory" rose to anthemic proportions as progressive rock classics. Yet such mindless electronic noodlings as "Dogfight Giggle" and "Rock and Roll Pussy" demolished the album's flow. *Todd*, another two-disc set, sought to place both sides of the Rundgren persona into a more cohesive and less manic format. But the songwriting was weak, for the first time in Rundgren's prolific career, and since that record, he has shunted back and forth from group leader (Utopia) to solo performer. For the last few years, Rundgren has seemed adrift, without focus. *RA* is Utopia's clearest work, reminiscent in spots of the Nazz; *Faithful*, which sported one side of cover versions of such Sixties standards as "Good Vibrations" and the Beatles'

"Rain," is the best recent solo effort. — B.A.

RUSH

■ A Farewell to Kings / Mer. SRM-1-1184
■ All the World's a Stage / Mer.
  SRM-2-7508
★ Caress of Steel / Mer. SRM-1-1046
★ Fly by Night / Mer. SRM-1-1023
★★ Hemispheres / Mer. SRM-1-3743
★ Rush / Mer. SRM-1-1011
■ Rush Archives / Mer. SRM-23-9200
★★ 2112 / Mer. SRM-1-1079

This Canadian power trio, which boasts a vocalist who sounds like a cross between Donald Duck and Robert Plant, reached its pinnacle of success the day it was discovered by *Circus* magazine and turned into fanzine wall-decoration material. Rush is to the late Seventies what Grand Funk was to the early Seventies—the power boogie band for the *16* magazine graduating class. *Rush Archives*, a reissue of the first LPs, is docked one star for pointlessness. — A.N.

MERILLEE RUSH

■ Merillee Rush / U. Artists LA735-G

Rush had a late-Sixties hit with Chip Taylor's "Angel of the Morning," a marvelously winsome one-shot. This 1978 comeback effort is not only ten years too late. It would have been wretched even in the hippie daze. — D.M.

TOM RUSH

★★★ Blues, Songs, Ballads / Prest. 7374
★★★★ Classic Rush / Elek. 74062
★★ Ladies Love Outlaws / Col. KC-33054
★★★ Merrimack County / Col. C-31306
★★ Mind Rambling / Prest. 7536
★★★ The Best of Tom Rush / Col.
  PC-33907

★★★★★ **The Circle Game** / Elek. 74018
★★★ **Tom Rush** / Col. CS-9972
★★★ **Tom Rush** / Elek. 7288
★★ **Tom Rush** / Fan. 24709
★★★★ **Tom Rush—Take a Little Walk
with Me** / Elek. 7308

Primarily known as an interpreter of other songwriters' material, Tom Rush is one of a handful of singers who helped alter the definition of folksinger in the Sixties. His early work on Prestige/Fantasy placed him squarely in the folk-blues vein of contemporaries John Hammond and Koerner Ray and Glover. But when he moved to Elektra in the mid-Sixties, Rush began experimenting both with different types of songs and stylistic approaches. *Take a Little Walk with Me* featured one side of rockers arranged by Al Kooper, with fine versions of Bo Diddley's "Who Do You Love" and Buddy Holly's "Love's Made a Fool of You." *The Circle Game* is Rush's high-water mark, with songs by then-unknown Joni Mitchell, Jackson Browne and James Taylor, as well as a standout original composition, "No Regrets." The atmosphere is exemplified by Rush's version of Mitchell's "Urge for Going." Its low-key, sparse arrangement characterizes the educated, wistful and warm style Rush had evolved. Moving to Columbia at the end of the decade, Rush found immediate success with *Tom Rush,* which included one of his best known pieces, "Lost My Drivin' Wheel." Unfortunately, he was becoming progressively more mellow and laid-back each time out, and his last few releases were pleasant but innocuous. — B.A.

RICHARD RUSKIN
★★★ **Microphone Fever** / Tak. 1044
★★★ **Richard Ruskin** / Tak. 1039
★★★ **Six String Conspiracy** / Tak. 1057

West Coast acoustic guitarist records for John Fahey's Takoma label but doesn't play like Fahey, using shorter melodic fragments and covering standards with droll but effective humor. *Richard Ruskin*

includes a version of "Teddy Bear's Picnic." — J.S.

LEON RUSSELL
★★ **Asylum Choir 2** / Shel. 52010
★★★★ **Best of Leon Russell** / Shel.
52004
★★★ **Carney** / Shel. 52011
★★★ **Leon Russell** / Shel. 52007
★★★★ **Leon Russell and the Shelter
People** / Shel. 52008
★★ **Will o' the Wisp** / Shel. 52020
★★★ **Hank Wilson's Back** / Shel. 8923

Russell was a session piano player in Los Angeles in the mid-Sixties. In his spare time, he recorded his own material at his home studio, including the two Asylum Choir albums that were released years later. After touring and recording with Delaney and Bonnie, he met Joe Cocker's producer, Denny Cordell. Russell was signed to work on Cocker's second album. Russell went on to lead Cocker's touring band, Mad Dogs and Englishmen, and to record a couple of fine solo albums, *Leon Russell* and *Leon Russell and the Shelter People.* The latter is his best record, combining three different bands on a variety of material including two of his best originals ("Stranger in a Strange Land," "Home Sweet Oklahoma") and interesting covers of Bob Dylan's "It's a Hard Rain Gonna Fall" and "It Takes a Lot to Laugh, It Takes a Train to Cry."

Russell's material thinned out and his abrasive singing could not save average songs, so his later albums suffer. His only worthwhile record in recent years was the tribute to Hank Williams, *Hank Wilson's Back.* — J.S.

THE RUTLES
★★★ **The Rutles** / War. H-3151

A marvelously precise Beatles parody, done by ex-Bonzo Dog Band member Neil Innes, former Monty Python collaborator Eric Idle and, among others, lonesome George Harrison. — D.M.

CAROLE BAYER SAGER

★★★ **Carole Bayer Sager / Elek. 7E-1100**
Working with a variety of collaborators—
most notably Marvin Hamlisch—Sager has
written hit songs for a number of pop performers, including Barbra Streisand, which
makes the young composer a sort of Seventies Carole King. But her solo debut, despite Brooks Arthur's tasteful production,
lacks King's vision and beautiful voice. Interesting but minor. — D.M.

DOUG SAHM

★★★★ **Best of the Sir Douglas Quintet /**
Tribe TRS-47001
★★ **Doug Sahm and Band / Atl. 7254**
★★★ **Honkey Blues / Smash**
SRS-67108
★★★ **Mendocino / Smash SRS-67115**
★★★★ **1 + 1 + 1 = 4 / Phi. 600-344**
★★★ **Rough Edges / Mer. SRM-1-655**
★★ **Texas Rock for Country Rollers / Dot**
D-2057
★★★ **Texas Tornado / Atl. 7287**
★★★ **The Return of Doug Saldana / Phi.**
600-353
★★★★★ **Together After Five / Smash**
SRS-67130
Doug Sahm is a walking encyclopedia of
Texas music—blues, country, Western
Swing, vintage rock & roll, Cajun, R&B,
even Mexican border music—all of which
is melted into a bright, pulsating sound no-
body else has ever matched. Unfortunately,
the only album combining these elements
that remains in print is the Dot set, a halfhearted attempt to cash in on the progressive country fad.

The other LPs are listed because they
rank with some of the most interesting and
influential recordings of the late Sixties and
early Seventies, and are fairly easy to scare
up in bargain bins. The Tribe album contains mid-Sixties British-influenced rock

(the hit was "She's About a Mover") anchored by Augie Meyer's simple, rhythmic
Farfisa organ. With its classic bar-band
sound, this can legitimately be considered
the only example of Texas punk rock. *Together,* with its relaxed and easygoing
groove, its unlikely combination of cover
versions and spacey originals and its irrepressible spirit, is perhaps Sahm's most coherent and consistent album. In this case,
the sloppiness only adds to the atmosphere;
1 + 1 + 1 = 4 is more bluesy, more country
and more precise, as well as better produced, but the Texas soul still carries it. In
this period (1969 to 1970), Sahm's voice
was at its richest and most commanding.
His lyrics are also a perfectly natural min-
gling of the cosmic and the earthy; they often make a moral point but are seldom
moralistic.

Honkey Blues, on which horns augment
the Quintet, is what happens when the
white blues move from San Antonio to Big
Sur. It revels in all that was good with the
psychedelic experience, but because this
expression is rooted in blues, it never gets
too far gone. *Mendocino* is a denser version
of the original Tribe sound, with its Cajun
two-step and Tex-Mex rhythms. The album is largely composed of demos not intended for release, and is thus another
slapdash affair, but it hardly suffers for
that.

The same is true of *Rough Edges,* a compilation of outtakes that doesn't sound ap-
preciably worse than Sahm's finished products. The *Saldana* LP is a much-celebrated
return to his roots, on the west side of San
Antonio, via "Wasted Days and Wasted
Nights" and the like. The greasy barroom
songs are among his best records, but the
album's strength is diminished by a couple
of ill-conceived and aimless acoustic ditties.

The first Atlantic album (*Doug Sahm and Band*) is a super session, produced by Jerry Wexler with help from Bob Dylan, but as sterile and bloodless as Sahm's early work was sloppy and full of life. Though some rock and blues are included, it's also his first overtly country album. Side two of *Texas Tornado* is prime Sir Doug in style and substance, heavy on Chicano influence, but the first side is pretty dull. — J.MO.

SAILOR
★★ **Sailor / Epic KE-33248**
★★ **Trouble / Epic PE-34039**
Ersatz Roxy Music. Sailor's chief innovation was a calliope, the first and only band to use that instrument as a regular part of its sound. Didn't help much. (Now deleted.) — D.M.

BUFFY SAINTE-MARIE
★★ **Fire and Fleet and Candlelight / Van. 79250**
★★ **Illuminations / Van. 79300**
★★ **I'm Gonna Be a Country Girl Again / Van. 79280**
★★★ **It's My Way / Van. 79142**
★★★ **Little Wheel Spin and Spin / Van. 79211**
★★★ **Many a Mile / Van. 79171**
★ **Moonshot / Van. 79312**
★★★ **Native North American Child (An Odyssey) / Van. 79340**
★ **Quiet Places / Van. 79330**
★★ **She Used to Wanna Be a Ballerina / Van. 79311**
★ **Sweet America / ABC D-929**
★★★ **The Best of Buffy Sainte-Marie / Van. VSD-3/4**
★★ **The Best of Buffy Sainte-Marie, Vol. 2 / Van. VSD-33/34**
Buffy Sainte-Marie is best known as a Native American (Indian) folksinger and lately as a frequent member of the cast of *Sesame Street.* But the best of her songs—"Universal Soldier," "Many a Mile" and especially "Until It's Time for You to Go"—have a convincing universality. As a participant in the folk-music revival of the early Sixties, Sainte-Marie was respected as much for the "authenticity" of her Cree background as for her rather underestimated talents as a writer. Her voice, a soprano with heavy vibrato, is perhaps too eccentric to gain her mass popular acceptance. And in recent years, as she has attempted to bridge the gap between the narrow world of folk and the broader horizons outside it, she has been subject to some

egregious gaffes: *Moonshot,* in which she plays a sex-kittenish role, is downright embarrassing. The best of her work remains her early Vanguard albums, particularly *Many a Mile* and *It's My Way.* — D.M.

THE SAINTS
★★ **I'm Stranded / Sire 6039**
Punk rock from Down Under, 1978 style. For decibel junkies only. — D.M.

SALSOUL ORCHESTRA
■ **Charo and the Salsoul Orchestra / Sals. 5519**
★★★ **Magic Journey / Sals. 5515**
★★★ **Nice 'n' Naasty / Sals. 5502**
★★★ **Salsoul Orchestra / Sals. 5501**
★★ **Up the Yellow Brick Road / Sals. 8500**
A hot disco band, not really an orchestra. Most of the time, this group's very facelessness is an advantage; nothing gets in the way of the steaming tempos. But when they make attempts to expand their horizons—on the godawful *Charo* set and *The Wizard of Oz* fiasco—the results have been pretty dire. Covers are often fascinating for their blatant sexism; chief case in point is *Nice 'n' Naasty.* — D.M.

SAM AND DAVE
★★★★★ **The Best of Sam and Dave / Atl. 8218**
Once Sam and Dave stood side by side with Otis Redding as the most formidable purveyors of Memphis soul. But Redding's death marked the beginning of a sharp decline for the two-fisted, double-punch brand of soul that Sam Moore and Dave Prater proffered, and in the Seventies the pair has all but disappeared. Though their peak was brief (1965-1969), the hits ("Soul Man" and "Hold On I'm Comin' " were the biggest) gathered on the *Best of* are landmark Sixties pop music. — J.MC.

DAVID SANCIOUS AND TONE
★★ **Dance of the Age of Enlightenment / Ari. 4130**
★ **David Sancious / Chel. 548**
★★★ **Forest of Feelings / Epic KE-33441**
★★ **Transformation / Epic PE-33939**
Sancious has served as an extremely able sideman for an unlikely combination of Seventies stars: Bruce Springsteen and Stanley Clarke (he recorded only with the former). The *David Sancious* LP was made during his tenure with Springsteen and is less directly jazz rock than the others. *Forest* is the most appealing of the rest, incorporating the variety of jazz, classical, rock

& roll and African modes that made Sancious a special favorite with Springsteen
cultists. — D.M.

CARL SANDBURG
★ **Carl Sandburg Sings Americana / Ev.
309**
★★ **The Great Carl Sandburg / Lyr. 766**
The poet/historian/folklorist periodically
recorded some of the songs he compiled in
his book *American Songbag,* and an out-of-
print album of that name (Caedmon
TC-2025) is really preferable to the two
currently available LPs. There is a gentleness in his voice that communicates enormous warmth, and *Songbag* (book and record) served as a source of traditional songs
for many a latter-day folkie. The Lyrichord
set features more tracks than the Everest,
with six cuts duplicated on each. — I.M.

SANFORD-TOWNSEND BAND
★★ **Duo Glide / War. K-3081**
★★★ **Smoke from a Distant Fire / War.
B-2966**
This white-soul songwriting team's funk-
rocking 1976 debut *Smoke from a Distant
Fire* was produced by Jerry Wexler and
Barry Beckett at Muscle Shoals Sound Studios in Alabama and lives up to that studio's reputation for fine R&B sessions. The
band is tight and inspired; several of the
songs (particularly "Smoke from a Distant
Fire," a 1977 hit single) are good, and the
Wexler-Beckett production glosses it all
beautifully without stifling the players. The
second record, *Duo Glide,* is less inspired,
as the two seem unsure of themselves without the direction of Wexler and Beckett. — J.S.

SAMANTHA SANG
★★ **Emotion / Priv. 7009**
Sang was a virtual unknown until Bee Gee
Barry Gibb took her to Criteria Studios in
Miami and produced her LP's title song,
which became a Top Ten hit in early 1978,
during that year's Bee Gees explosion. The
sound is pure Bee Gees, and one wonders
just what the singer contributed beyond
her disembodied vocal. The rest of the album, produced by Miami vets Albhy Galu-
ten and Karl Richardson, lacks even this
much interest. — D.M.

SANTA ESMERALDA
★★★★ **Don't Let Me Be Misunderstood /
Casa. 7080**
★★★ **House of the Rising Sun / Casa.
7088**

This Spanish disco group reworked white
rhythm & blues hits of the British Invasion
for the late-Seventies disco market—and
with good effect. "Don't Let Me Be Misunderstood," an eight-minute suite of the
Animals' 1965 hit, is the best of the group's
work, thanks to a ferocious lead singer, Leroy Gomez. The *Don't Let Me* album also
contains a remarkable version of Van Morrison's "Gloria." *House of the Rising Sun,*
released in 1978, is less skillful, mostly because of Gomez' departure. Nonetheless, it
probably is more attractive to most rock
fans' ears than other disco products. — D.M.

SANTANA
★★★★ **Amigos / Col. PC-33576**
★★★ **Borboletta / Col. PC-33135**
★★★★ **Caravanserai / Col. PC-31610**
★★★ **Festival / Col. PC-34423**
★★★ **Moonflower / Col. C2-34914**
★★★★ **Santana / Col. PC-9781**
★★★★ **Santana: Abraxas / Col. PC-30130**
★★★★ **Santana's Greatest Hits / Col.
PC-33050**
★★★★ **Santana 3 / PC-30595**
★★★ **Welcome / Col. PC-32445**
Carlos Santana, a Mexican guitarist from
the Tijuana region, went to San Francisco
during the hippie daze and first earned rec-
ognition playing on the second Al Koop-
er-Mike Bloomfield super session. With a
variety of other Latin musicians from the
area, most notably the poll-winning Central American percussionist José "Cepito"
Areas and drummer Mike Shrieve, he
formed his own band and recorded an
eponymous debut LP (Col. PC-9781) in
1969.
  An appearance at Woodstock set the
stage for great commercial prosperity.
Abraxas, the second album, featured a re-

working of Latin master Tito Puente's "Oye Como Va," which garnered them a hit single. *Santana 3* added Coke Escovedo and guitar protégé Neal Schon to the lineup; it was the culmination of the band's early style. Since then, Santana albums have alternated between Carlos Santana's solo LPs and his occasional collaborations, including one with Mahavishnu John McLaughlin, with whom he shares a guru, Sri Chinmoy.

With *Caravanserai* (1972), Santana became a jazz-rock fusion band, with emphasis on Latin percussion devices. The lineup included Schon, Areas, Shrieve and several additions, most prominently conga players James Mingo Lewis and Armando Peraza. *Borboletta* was a disappointing followup. But *Amigos* is more interesting, as Santana attempted to recapture his Latin roots. *Festival,* unfortunately, was thoroughly ordinary. Still, Santana remains one of the pioneers of both Latin-jazz electric fusion and jazz rock. — D.M.

CARLOS SANTANA
★ Carlos Santana and Buddy Miles Live / Col. C-31308
★★ Illuminations / Col. C-32900
★★★ Love, Devotion, Surrender / Col. C-32034
These are the Mexican-American guitarist's solo LPs, which are more conceptually adventurous but generally less listenable than his work with the Santana group. The album with Miles is essentially a casual jam; *Illuminations* (with Alice Coltrane) and *Love, Devotion, Surrender* (with John McLaughlin) attempt to do for guitar what John Coltrane did for saxophone, with only middling success at best. — D.M.

SASSAFRAS
★★★ Wheelin' and Dealin' / Chrys. 1076
A Welsh band whose brutal embrace of the work ethic (virtually a gig a night since 1973 on the British school circuit) guarantees a solid workout. Compares well with the Brinsleys, Ace and others of the eight-days-a-week pub-rock ilk. (Now deleted.) — A.N.

MERL SAUNDERS AND JERRY GARCIA
★★★ Live at the Keystone / Fan. S-79002
The association between Jerry Garcia, guitarist, vocalist and composer for the Grateful Dead, and Merl Saunders, a Northern California keyboardist of some renown,

does not really deliver much on this extra-mellow album recorded live at San Francisco's Keystone. Combining old and new standards like "Positively 4th Street," "That's All Right, Mama" and "My Funny Valentine" with indolent funk-rock instrumental treatments, this band often threatens to succumb to blissful torpor. Saunders plays a lot of swirling chords, but Garcia never really rises to the level of inspiration he's often shown with the Dead. — J.C.C.

SAVOY BROWN
★★★ A Step Further / Par. 71029
★★★ Blue Matter / Par. 71027
★★ Boogie Brothers / Lon. APS-638
★★ Getting to the Point / Par. 71024
★★★ Hellbound Train / Par. X-71052
★ Jack the Toad / Par. X-71059
★★ Lion's Share / Par. 71057
★★ Looking In / Par. 71042
★★★ Raw Sienna / Par. 71036
★ Skin 'n' Bone / Lon. PS-670
★★★ Street Corner Talking / Par. 71047
★ Wire Fire / Lon. PS-659
Despite countless personnel changes, Savoy Brown's one constant, guitarist Kim Simmonds, endures with his fluid boogie-blues style. The first four albums (*Point, Matter, Further* and *Sienna*) feature a strange, croaking blues vocalist, Chris Youlden; both *A Step Further* and *Blue Matter* also contain some live recordings, and "Savoy Brown Boogie" from the former is the band's definitive statement, although the basic premise is better presented through Youlden's vocal on "Train to Nowhere" on *Blue Matter.*

Dave Peverett, later of Foghat, replaced Youlden on *Looking In,* and he was fully integrated over the next three albums. But with *Jack the Toad* a decline set in, partially because another capable vocalist, Dave Walker, had left. The rest is simply a matter of playing out the string of tired, recycled blues riffs. — A.N.

RAY SAWYER
★★ Ray Sawyer / Cap. ST-11591
Dr. Hook's singer in a solo outing with that characteristic mixture of sleazy humor and country-music sentiment his band is noted for. (Now deleted.) — J.S.

SKY SAXON BLUES BAND
★ A Full Spoon of Seedy Blues / GNP 2040
The Sonny Bono of the psychedelic age. — B.A.

LEO SAYER
★ **Another Year** / War. B-2885
★★★ **Endless Flight** / War. K-3101
★★★ **Just a Boy** / War. B-2836
★★ **Leo Sayer** / War. K-3200
★★★ **Silverbird** / War. B-2738
★★ **Thunder in My Heart** / War. K-3089

An excellent English pop-rock singer, Sayer is only a fair writer. His first two albums, *Silverbird* and *Just a Boy,* were done during a period when Sayer appeared onstage in mime makeup, exploiting a lonely Pierrot persona. With *Endless Flight* Sayer went Hollywood, thanks to Richard Perry's lush production, and scored two No. 1 hits, "You Make Me Feel Like Dancing" and "When I Need You." Since then, he's learned to grin on talk shows and generally act so cute it's revolting, and not even Perry's studio expertise has been able to save him from banality. — s.h.

BOZ SCAGGS
★★★★ **Boz Scaggs** / Atl. 19166
★★★ **Boz Scaggs and Band** / Col. C-30796
★★★ **Down Two, Then Left** / Col. JC-34729
★★★ **Moments** / Col. 30454
★★★★ **My Time** / Col. PC-31384
★★★★ **Silk Degrees** / Col. PC-33920
★★★ **Slow Dancer** / Col. PC-32760

After leaving the Steve Miller Band in the late Sixties, Boz Scaggs recorded a solo album in Muscle Shoals, Alabama, that earned him instant notoriety. *Boz Scaggs* (produced by *Rolling Stone*'s Jann Wenner) featured that town's crack rhythm section, led by guitarist Duane Allman, whose extended solo on "Loan Me a Dime" is one of the high points of both men's careers. Scaggs has an easy, lilting voice and a knack for writing terrific rock & roll hooks into his songs. His subsequent recordings switched back and forth between hard rock and ballad R&B (*My Time* has two burning rockers, "Dinah Flo" and "Full-Lock Power Slide") before settling into softer material. His reputation as a crooner grew slowly until he scored big in 1976 with the hit single "Lowdown," from *Silk Degrees. Down Two, Then Left* attempted to continue that cool R&B success a little too cautiously, leaving Scaggs a bit too cold for comfort. — j.s.

JANNE SCHAFFER
★★ **Earmeal** / Col. JC-35508

Schaffer is a sideman for Abba; he's responsible for the bell-like guitar on many of that Swedish group's early hits. But given the opportunity to stretch out with an LP of his own, he heads for the usual sideman-turned-soloist territory: pointless riffs that haven't the heart to qualify as true jazz and haven't the guts to rock. — d.m.

SCORPIONS
★★ **Fly to the Rainbow** / RCA AFLI-4025
★★ **In Trance** / RCA AFLI-4128
★ **Taken by Force** / RCA AFLI-2628
★ **Tokyo Tapes** / RCA CPL2-3039
■ **Virgin Killer** / RCA AFL1-4225

German hard-rock band influenced by Deep Purple and Uriah Heep. Guitarist Michael Schenker later joined UFO. — j.s.

TOM SCOTT
★★ **Blow It Out** / Epic PE-34966
★★★ **Great Scott!** / A&M 4330
★★ **New York Connection** / Ode 77033
★★★ **Tom Cat** / Ode 77029
★★★ **Tom Scott and the L.A. Express** / Ode 77021
★★ **Tom Scott in L.A.** / Fly. BXL1-0833

Reedman Scott, perhaps the best known L.A. studio horn player, brought functionally tasty licks and arrangements to a host of albums. But only one of his own—*Great Scott!*—features him as a soloist and conceptualizer of any note. *Great Scott!* isn't just one thing; at times it features a little late-Sixties space sensibility, but it also includes modal jazz and a bit of rock. Still, it's elegantly musical, and Scott does better than his usual antiseptic copping of original styles.

The two L.A. Express albums (*Tom Cat*'s the second) are heavily arranged (not strings, but with a certain density), small-group fusion, featuring nice, if brief, solos by the Express members (who include guitarists Larry Carlton and Robben Ford, bassist Joe Sample and drummer John Guerin). There's plenty of guitar-horn dueling and ample funky backbeat. On the similar *Connection,* made with East Coast studio pros, the tunes aren't as striking.

Tom Scott in L.A. resembles *Great Scott!* in places, but the material ("Age of Aquarius") dates it. — M.R.

GIL SCOTT-HERON
★★★★ Bridges / Ari. 4147
★★★★ First Minute of a New Day / Ari. 4030
★★★ From South Africa to South Carolina / Ari. 4044
★★★ It's Your World / Ari. 5001
★★★ Pieces of Man / Fly. BXL1-2834
★★★ Secrets / Ari. 4189
★★★ The Revolution Will Not Be Televised / Fly. BXL1-0613

Scott-Heron began recording in the early Seventies as one of those black jazz poets who bop along every few years; he was more politically astute than most, though hardly more musical. But in 1974 Scott-Heron and his partner, Brian Jackson, composed "The Bottle," a savage attack on drugs and alcohol in minority communities. It was a pop hit, and deservedly so: the *First Minute* album shows why, particularly given Scott-Heron's newfound ability (willingness?) to actually sing. *Bridges* contains his best song since "The Bottle," the utterly chilling anti-nuclear ode, "We Almost Lost Detroit." — D.M.

EARL SCRUGGS
★★★ Anniversary Special, Vol. 1 / Col. PC-33416
★★★★ Banjoman / Sire 7527
★★★ Dueling Banjos / Col. C-32268

★★ Earl Scruggs—His Family and Friends / Col. CS-30584
★★★ Earl Scruggs Revue / Col. KC-32426
★★★ Earl Scruggs Revue, Vol. 2 / Col. PC-34090
★★★ Earl Scruggs Revue Live from Austin City Limits / Col. PC-34464
★★★ Family Portrait / Col. PC-34336
★★★ I Saw the Light / Col. KC-31354
★★ Live at Kansas State / Col. KC-31758
★★ Nashville's Rock / Col. CS-1007
★★★ Rockin' 'Cross the Country / Col. KC-32943
★★ Strike Anywhere / Col. KC-34878
★★ Where the Lilies Bloom / Col. C-32806

As half of Flatt and Scruggs, Earl Scruggs was one of the most important popularizers of bluegrass and a significant banjo stylist. On his own, the influence continues, but the output hasn't been as good. — D.M.

GARY AND RANDY SCRUGGS
★★ The Scruggs Brothers / Van. 6579

The sons of Earl Scruggs attempt to adapt their father's bluegrass style to a rock format, with dismal results. Not lively enough to be one or the other, the album is too condescending to effect a workable merger. — D.M.

SEA LEVEL
★★★ Cats on the Coast / Capri. 0198
★★★ On the Edge / Capri. 0212
★★★★ Sea Level / Capri. 0178

When Chuck Leavell, the former Allman Brothers keyboard player, put together his own band following the group's demise, he came up with a terrific pun for its title (C. Leavell, get it?) and an interesting approach: adapting the Allman's modal blues-rock to the jazz from which it was derived. The debut album (0178) seemed like a new, bluesier direction for fusion, but having seen the light, Sea Level was apparently unable to follow it. *Cats on the Coast* and *On the Edge* simply meander in search of focus. — D.M.

SEALS AND CROFTS
★★ Diamond Girl / War. BS4-2699
★★ Get Closer / War. BS-2907
★ I'll Play for You / War. BS4-2848
★★★ Seals and Crofts Greatest Hits / War. K-3109
★★ Seals and Crofts 1 and 2 / War. 2WS-2809
★ Sudan Village / War. B-2976

★★ Summer Breeze / War. BS4-2629
★ Takin' It Easy / War. K-3163
★ Unborn Child / War. WS4-2761
★★ Year of Sunday / War. B-2568

Folk-rock duo spins contemporary MOR
of above-average intensity, relying on
pretty tunes with exotic flourishes ("Summer Breeze" and "Diamond Girl" were
their biggest mid-Seventies hits) and a
spiritual angle: both are members of the
Bahai faith, which got them into considerable trouble with their viciously antifemi-
nist "Unborn Child," which derided abor-
tion. *Get Closer* (1976) tried to bring them
nearer to MOR soul, an attempt that
clicked for the title song, and not much
else. Since then, they've returned to their
previous style. — D.M.

TROY SEALS
★★ Troy Seals / Col. KC-34271

Seals is best known as a writer of country
cowboy songs, and on the basis of this solo
LP, it's likely to remain that way. — D.M.

SEATRAIN
★★★ Marblehead Messenger / Cap.
 SMAS-829
★★ Seatrain / A&M 4171
★★ Seatrain / Cap. SMAS-659

Seatrain was formed in California by bass-
ist/flautist Andy Kulberg and drummer
Roy Blumenfeld after the Blues Project
broke up. But their Capitol debut album,
which earned considerable critical acclaim
in 1969, placed heaviest emphasis on violinist Richard Greene, who had experience
with Bill Monroe's bluegrass group and the
Jim Kweskin Jug Band. Greene was missing on *Marblehead Messenger,* recorded in
London with George Martin producing,
and on the A&M LP, so these albums are
considerably less attractive. — D.M.

JOHN SEBASTIAN
★★★ John Sebastian / Rep. 6379
★ Welcome Back / Rep. 2249

After Lovin' Spoonful broke up, Sebastian
recorded a self-titled solo album for Reprise that, while pleasant listening, was the
epitome of strained, tie-dyed soulfulness.
This approach continued for a series of
now-deleted efforts, each of which reduced
the memories of "Do You Believe in Magic?" and "Summer in the City" a bit further. The last straw, however, was "Welcome Back," the theme song for Gabe
Kaplan and John Travolta's TV show. The
song was a hit, but both it and the album
are nearly worthless artistically. — D.M.

SECTION
★★ Fork It Over / Cap. ST-11656

Some of the hottest sidemen in Hollywood
in an almost unbelievably dull jazz-rock
exercise. Lots of chops, no vision. — D.M.

NEIL SEDAKA
★★★ Breaking Up Is Hard to Do / Camd.
 ACL-7006
★★★ Neil Sedaka's Greatest Hits / R.
 BXL1-3050
★★★ Neil Sedaka Sings His Greatest
 Hits / RCA AFL1-0928
★★★ Oh Carol / RCA ANL1-0879
★★★ Pure Gold / RCA ANL1-1314
★★★★ Sedaka's Back / R. BXL1-3046
★★★ Sedaka: The Fifties and Sixties /
 RCA AFL1-2254
★★ Song / Elek. 6E-102
★★ Steppin' Out / R. BXL1-3049
★★★ The Hungry Years / R. BXL1-3047
★★ The Many Sides of Neil Sedaka /
 RCA AFL1-2524

After a promising beginning as a classical
pianist (Artur Rubenstein selected him as
the best New York classical player in
1956), the Brooklyn-born Sedaka conceived
an interest in writing pop songs. He
teamed up with a high-school crony, Howard Greenfield (Sedaka was the melodist;
Greenfield added lyrics), and began selling
songs to LaVern Baker, the Tokens and
Dinah Washington. He scored biggest,
however, with "Stupid Cupid" by Connie
Francis in 1958.

Like Carole King and Jerry Goffin, Ellie
Greenwich and Jeff Barry and others, Se-
daka/Greenfield soon became a familiar
New York composing team of the pop hits
of the era. But in 1959 Sedaka turned to recording his own material; "The Diary" was
his first hit, but it was minor compared to
the international best-seller that followed—
"Oh Carol," written for King. Sedaka followed this with a succession of nasal teen-
dream items, including "Happy Birthday
Sweet Sixteen," "Calendar Girl" and the
best of them, "Breaking Up Is Hard to
Do." These and the other, lesser songs Sedaka made during the post-Presley, pre-
Beatles years are collected on the various
RCA and Camden anthologies.

In 1973, after a ten-year layoff, Sedaka
began performing again. He recorded three
albums in the U.K.—*Solitaire, The Tra La
Days Are Over* and *Laughter in the Rain*—
before getting a compilation of them released on MCA (now Rocket 3046)
through the auspices of Elton John.
"Laughter in the Rain" became a major hit

for him, and Captain and Tennille scored even bigger with his "Love Will Keep Us Together." The first album Sedaka made for John's Rocket Records, the mistitled *The Hungry Years,* seemed to reestablish him as a major pop writer/performer. Sedaka had also been a more attractive singer than his teen-idol competitors, and his early Rocket work seemed to indicate that he had matured into an Elton-like pianist/vocalist. But subsequent releases have shown him to be much more like a second-rate Barry Manilow, without much of John's hard-rocking sensibility. — D.M.

THE SEEDS

★★★ **A Web of Sound / GNP 2033**
★★ **Fallin' Off the Edge / GNP 2107**
★ **Future / GNP 2038**
★★ **Merlin's Music Box / GNP 2043**
★★★ **The Seeds / GNP 2023**

"Two great chords—five great albums!" reads the epitaph at the beloved Seeds' mythical grave site, a spot in Southern California where marijuana plants and magic mushrooms grow wild, and toward which most God-fearing punk bands of the Seventies bow at sunset each day.

That the Seeds were able to parlay their distinctly limited talents as writers, singers and musicians into a rather long and successful career is one of the more miraculous stories in rock fabledom. Lead singer Sky Saxon's world view was limited to two subjects—sex and drugs—and his snarling vocals were accompanied by some of the most amateurishly oddball music ever recorded by modern recording equipment—in particular, the organ and piano of Daryl Hooper, whose idea of a creative solo was to play the same riff over and over at varying octaves. It is highly doubtful that their music could have been any worse than it was. Their singular charm lay in the fact that, due to their lack of skills, their music could not have been any better, either.

The Seeds sports their biggest hit, "Pushin' Too Hard," and Saxon's best composition, "Can't Seem to Make You Mine," but true believers usually rally around their second LP, *A Web of Sound.* This LP includes plenty of psychedelic numbers, like "Rollin' Machine," "Tripmaker" and "Mr. Farmer," and the band's magnum opus, "Up in Her Room," a fourteen-and-a-half-minute account of love-making that features two breaks for cigarettes (Saxon obviously worked fast).

Future is the group's flower-power concept album, and its best track, "Two Fin-

gers Pointing On You," was performed by the band in *Psych Out,* their lone film appearance (the movie starred Jack Nicholson as the ponytailed leader of an acid-rock band in Haight-Ashbury during the summer of love; of such stuff, friends, are legends made). *Merlin's Music Box* is supposed to be a "live" album, but sounds curiously like outtakes from previous LPs with prerecorded audience screams. Still, the record does include the classic "900 Million People Daily All Making Love," and Saxon's Arab getup on the back cover does pre-date Dylan by a good eight years.

Fallin' Off the Edge is a recent release consisting of more outtakes and previously unreleased songs, taking the place of *A Full Spoon of Seedy Blues,* a blues LP with liner notes by Muddy Waters ("I sincerely believe that at last America has produced a group to be another Rolling Stones"). That all records but *Full Spoon* are still available is proof positive that there is, at times, justice in the universe. Pass the hookah. — B.A.

MIKE SEEGER

★★★ **American Folk Songs / Folk. 2005**
★★★ **Old Time Country Music / Folk. 2325**
★★★ **Tipple, Loom and Rail / Folk. 5273**

Since the mid-Fifties, Mike Seeger—son of ethnomusicologist Charles Seeger, brother of Peggy and half-brother of Pete—has carried on his family's folk-music tradition, with a special interest in the Appalachian Mountain music that forms the basis of C&W.

In the early Fifties, he traveled through the rural South, collecting folk songs and discovering a number of important performers, including Dock Boggs. Beginning around 1955, he began performing such material at a variety of coffeehouses and festivals; by 1958 he had helped form the most important old-timey group of the folk revival, the New Lost City Ramblers. His solo albums include the same kind of material, which is performed with musicological expertise, but also with a great deal of authentic emotion, lacking the sanctimonious politicking of Pete's similar recordings of international folk music. — D.M.

PEGGY SEEGER AND EWAN MacCOLL

★★★★ **At the Present Moment / Roun. 4003**
★★★★ **Folkways Record of Contemporary Songs / Folk. FW 8736**

It was ironic for MacColl to win a Grammy in 1972 as a writer of "The First Time Ever I Saw Your Face." For more than a decade the song had been a standard of the contemporary folk repertoire. It was symbolic, however, of the scant attention the songwriter/singer/interpreter has received here. Similarly, Seeger's work is better known and respected in Britain, where the two reside. (She is, of course, the sister of Mike and half-sister of Pete Seeger.) They have recorded dozens of albums of radical protest songs composed in the folk idiom, traditional ballads and other works. Both MacColl and Seeger inspired many of the protest singers of the Sixties folk revival, and they themselves remain vital commentators to this day. — I.M.

PETE SEEGER
★★ **American Favorite Ballads III / Folk. 2322**
★★ **American Favorite Ballads IV / Folk. 2323**
★★ **American Favorite Ballads V / Folk. 2445**
★★★ **Broadside / Folk. 5302**
★★ **Dangerous Songs / Col. CS-9303**
★★ **Original Talking Union / Folk. 5285**
★ **Pete Seeger at the Village Gate, Vol. 2 / Folk. 2451**
★ **Pete Seeger's Greatest Hits / Col. CS-9416**
★★ **Pete Seeger Sings American Ballads / Folk. 2319**
★★ **Pete Seeger Sings Leadbelly / Folk. 31022**
★★ **Pete Seeger Sings Woody Guthrie / Folk. 31002**
★ **Pete Seeger with Memphis Slim and Willie Dixon at the Village Gate / Folk. 2450**
★ **Pete Seeger with Sonny Terry at Carnegie Hall / Folk. 2412**
★ **Sing with Seeger / Disc 1101**
★ **Songs of Struggle and Protest: 1930-1950 / Folk. 5233**
★★ **The World of Pete Seeger / Col. KG-31949**
★★★ **3 Saints, 4 Sinners and Six Other People / Odys. 32-16-0266**
★★★ **Waist-Deep in the Big Muddy and Other Love Songs / Col. CS-9505**
★★★★ **We Shall Overcome / Col. CS-8901**
★★ **Young vs. Old / Col. CS-9873**

Carl Sandburg called Seeger "America's tuning fork." Although he would no doubt deny it, Seeger more than anyone was responsible for the sparks that ignited the folk revival of the Fifties and Sixties. During the earlier decade, Seeger's radical belief in humanitarian socialism found him at odds with both Senator Joseph McCarthy and the House Un-American Activities Committee. Seeger's refusal—on Fifth Amendment grounds—to testify before the committee resulted in his being blacklisted by television and radio, although Columbia continued to record him.

Despite his lack of media exposure, Seeger was at the forefront of the civil-rights and anti-Vietnam War movements. Throughout the Sixties, he reached audiences by touring constantly in this country and abroad; through his travels and concerts, he taught more people the choruses of such songs as "We Shall Overcome," "Little Boxes," "A Hard Rain's A-Gonna Fall," "Where Have All the Flowers Gone" and "Guantanamera"—among dozens of others—than could reasonably have been expected of a single human being.

Seeger has neither an exceptional voice nor an outstanding banjo or guitar style. What he does possess is the unique ability to make friends of total strangers, using his music and gestures as common denominators. In fact, Americans may have more trouble than anyone else with Seeger, for his entertainment, while educational, can also be preachy and sanctimonious on political issues.

Seeger has recorded extensively. The list here represents perhaps half of what he has put on disc as a soloist. There are also recordings by him and the Almanac Singers (which included Lee Hays, Woody Guthrie and Millard Lampell) and the Weavers. This list is only a sampling, but it is impressive on several levels. Each LP, whether recorded live or in a studio, is a concert unto itself. Seeger is a master of programing and of the sing-along, and his concerts always strike a balance between traditional ballads, international folk songs, freedom songs, political commentaries and satires, instrumentals, new songs in the folk idiom and others. With the exception of the *American Favorite Ballads* series, on which Seeger becomes a human songbook, that kind of balance is struck throughout his catalogue. The emphasis may shift slightly, but the effect is always of a broad overview of life. Even when the same songs overlap from LP to LP, the performances change sufficiently to keep them fresh.

The Folkways titles are generally self-explanatory, although when other performers share the billing, their roles are generally minor. Memphis Slim and Willie Dixon are barely audible, for instance. The sound quality of the Folkways LPs, most of which have been recorded with a single microphone, is also poor. And on the reprocessed stereo of the Leadbelly and Guthrie collections, the electronic effect robs the albums of naturalness. However, all of these records are historically most valuable. *Broadside* is particularly recommended as an example of Seeger's excellent ear for material from the "topical" songwriters of the early Sixties.

The Columbia recordings, dating through the mid-Sixties, are generally well recorded. *We Shall Overcome,* loaded heavily with the freedom songs of the civil-rights movement, is perhaps Seeger's best concert recording. It was obviously a highly emotional night and Seeger was at his peak vocally.

"Waist-Deep in the Big Muddy" was the song that brought Seeger back to national television after seventeen years, with two appearances on *The Smothers Brothers Comedy Hour.* The first time, censors nixed the anti-Vietnam War song; the ensuing uproar gained him a return invitation and he sang the song.

3 Saints is a set of story songs, excellent for children or adults. *World* and *Greatest Hits* are collections of material associated with Seeger, although many were popularized by other artists. They're both satisfactory introductory sets. — I.M.

THE SEEKERS
★★ **Best of the Seekers / Cap. SM-2746**
Australian pop-folk group hit in the middle Sixties with the theme from *Georgy Girl* and "I'll Never Find Another You." They produced fluffy Peter, Paul and Mary-style vocals, then faded out to reappear a couple of years later as the New Seekers, equally banal. — D.M.

BOB SEGER
★★★ **Beautiful Loser / Cap. ST-11378**
★★★★ **Live Bullet / Cap. SKBB-11523**
★★★ **Mongrel / Cap. ST-499**
★★★★★ **Night Moves / Cap. SW-11557**
★★★ **Ramblin' Gamblin' Man / Cap. ST-172**
★★★★ **Seven / Cap. ST-11748**
★★★★ **Smokin' O.P.'s / Cap. ST-11746**
★★★★ **Stranger in Town / Cap. SW-11698**

From 1965, when he made his first single for Cameo-Parkway, through 1977, Bob Seger was rock's foremost case of talent in the wilderness. In those years, Seger made a series of great rock singles in a style influenced by Dylan, the Stones, John Fogerty and Wilson Pickett. An adept writer and a brilliant vocalist, Seger still could not get a hit—outside of his native Detroit, where most went Top Ten. And along the way, a fine series of LPs for Warner Bros., particularly *Back in '72*, has been allowed to disappear. But *Night Moves* turned the corner for Seger in 1977, and he is now highly regarded almost everywhere.

Of the albums remaining in print, *Ramblin' Gamblin' Man* (1968) and *Mongrel* (1970) sound relatively dated, although Seger's "Ramblin' Gamblin' Man," a white R&B song, is a gem, and *Mongrel*'s Creedence-like "Lucifer" is nearly as good. *Smokin' O.P.'s* contains only one Seger original, "Heavy Music," which had been a Detroit hit in 1967. The rest of this eccentric 1972 LP is diverse—Chuck Berry's "Let It Rock," Stephen Stills' "Love the One You're With," plus staples like "Bo Diddley" and "Turn on Your Lovelight"— but it's notable mostly for Seger's voice and some guitar work by Bobby Bland veteran Mike Bruce.

Seven and *Beautiful Loser* are the albums that paved the way for Seger's breakthrough; on the former, he assembled the Silver Bullet Band, and on the latter, he attempted some ballad material that, although too crude to work perfectly, at least allowed him some additional range. Each, of course, contains a hard-rock hit (in Detroit only): *Beautiful* has "Katmandu," *Seven* has "Get Out of Denver."

Live Bullet is one of the best live albums ever made, and a fitting documentary history of Seger's career. In spots, particularly during the medley of "Travelin' Man"/

"Beautiful Loser" on side one, Seger sounds like a man with one last shot at the top. The desperation, oddly enough, was what pushed the record far past a concert LP's ordinary boundaries, paving the way for *Night Moves,* that wonderful chronicle of the moments when age becomes irrelevant and innocence gains experience. *Stranger in Town,* released in mid-1978, picked up where *Night Moves* left off, perfectly balancing Springsteen-affected ballads with brutally hard rock. Seger now seems guaranteed a permanent place in the rock pantheon, a place he earned long before he received it. — D.M.

SELDOM SCENE
★★★ Act 1 / Rebel SLP 1511
★★★ Act 2 / Rebel SLP 1520
★★★ Act 3 / Rebel SLP 1528
★★★ Old Train / Rebel 1536
★★★ Recorded Live / Rebel SLP 1547/ 1548
★★★ The New Seldom Scene Album / Rebel SLP 1561

This is bluegrass' most promising light, as evidenced by the group's topping the polls of *Muleskinner News* as best group for the last few years. Dobro player Mike Auldridge is an accomplished sessionman and solo artist; Ben Eldridge is a facile and intelligent banjo stylist; and singers John Duffey and John Starling are notable for their warm, rich vocals. Given to mixing traditional tunes with contemporary material by such writers as Tom Paxton, Rodney Crowell, Herb Pederson and Steve Goodman, the Seldom Scene cross the bluegrass generation gap: the group is adored by both young and old fans.

Of special interest are the resonant *Live* set, recorded at Washington's Cellar Door club, and *The New Seldom Scene* LP, which includes vocal harmonies by Linda Ronstadt, who also featured Starling on her own albums. The epitome of low-key, friendly, down-home hip, Seldom Scene is fast becoming a bluegrass institution. — R.P.

THE SEX PISTOLS
★★★★ Never Mind the Bollocks, Here's the Sex Pistols / War. K-3147

The Sex Pistols were unquestionably the most radical new rock band of the Seventies. Their initial single, "Anarchy in the U.K.," was widely banned in England, got them thrown off their first record label (EMI) and still made the Top Ten. The group's nihilistic politics, coupled with their basic punk-rock musical approach, was startling, the best example of deliberate vulgarity rock has ever produced. Stretched over an album, the relentless power of Johnny Rotten's scabrous vocals, Steve Jones' stinging guitar and the blitzkrieg of sound can become a bit wearing, but the best tracks, including "Anarchy," "God Save the Queen" and "Pretty Vacant," are as challenging as anything recorded since the advent of Elvis Presley himself. Not for the faint of heart, but if that's your problem, you may have wandered into this volume by mistake. The group broke up, appropriately enough, after making only this record, and bassist Sid Vicious died an ugly death in early 1979, but Rotten continues as a soloist. — D.M.

SHADOWFAX
★★ Watercourse Way / Pass. 98013

Like Synergy, Shadowfax was an attempt to make an American version of Europe's mechanized, synthesizer-oriented art rock. Like Synergy, it mostly struck out, though on slightly less pretentious grounds. (Now deleted.) — D.M.

SHAKERS
★ Yankee Reggae / Asy. 7E-1057

Berkeley's only contribution to reggae was a batch of white boys who couldn't quite get the beat right, sang miserably and, in short, lived up to the generally impoverished Bay Area rock tradition. — D.M.

SHAM 69
★★★ Tell Us the Truth / Sire K-6060

Punk group with an admirably brittle sound, but given to lyrics of the most ideologically pure political stripe. For safetypin leftists, or anyone who thinks the Clash are too pop. — D.M.

SHA NA NA
★ Sha Na Na Is Here to Stay / Bud. 5692

In 1969, when Sha Na Na was formed by a group of students at Columbia University, the notion of nostalgia for Fifties rock was still reasonably novel. Onstage, the group's slick choreography and its impersonations of the look of such greaser archetypes as Gene Vincent and Eddie Cochran was at least amusing. But in the studio, the group had nothing new to add: the harmonies were purified and lost all soul. Despite a successful appearance at Woodstock (oh, irony!), the group never developed sufficient original material or personality to become more than cartoons of real rock. This junk-food aroma was only enhanced when the group somehow managed to acquire a network TV show in 1976. Only one member of the group, original guitarist Henry Gross, has gone on to anything like authentic success. — D.M.

DEL SHANNON
★★★ **Del Shannon Live in England /** **U. Artists LA151-F**
★★★★ **The Vintage Years / Sire Y3708-2**
Shannon is an underrated composer ("I Go to Pieces" was a Peter and Gordon hit) and singer whose music may have been the missing link between Fifties American and early-Sixties British rock & roll. The live album is a 1972 recording that features all of his hits ("Runaway," "Hats Off to Larry," "Little Town Flirt," "Stranger in Town" and "Keep Searchin' "), but in versions that are too hurried and nostalgic for comfort. The Sire package is marvelous: all the original recordings, and excellent notes by Greg Shaw. (Now deleted.) — B.A.

DEE DEE SHARP
★★★ **Happy 'Bout the Whole Thing / Phil.** **PZ-33839**
★★★ **What Color Is Love / Phil.** **PZ-34437**
Famed for her tinny (and mostly forgettable) Cameo-Parkway novelty songs of the early Sixties ("Ride," "Mashed Potatoes"), Sharp teamed up with husband Kenneth Gamble's Philadelphia soul production team for these pleasant, if unexceptional, offerings. — J.MC.

BILLY JOE SHAVER
★★★ **Gypsy Boy / Capri. 0192**
★★★★ **Old Five and Dimers like Me /** **Monu. MG-7621**
★★★ **When I Get My Wings / Capri. 0171**
Shaver is one of the most celebrated of the new breed of Nashville singer/songwriters led by Kris Kristofferson and Waylon Jennings. He wrote most of the material for Jennings' *Honky Tonk Heroes* album and has had his songs covered by Kristofferson, Tom T. Hall, Willie Nelson, Bobby Bare and Tex Ritter. *Old Five and Dimers* is his classic set, which his Capricorn albums cannot match, despite the presence of better than average material and production assistance from Bob Johnston. — J.S.

MARLENA SHAW
★★★ **Acting Up / Col. JC-35073**
★★ **From the Depths of My Soul / Blue N.** **LA143-G**
★ **Just a Matter of Time / Blue N. LA606**
★ **Marlena / Blue N. 84422**
★★★ **Sweet Beginnings / Col. PC-34458**
★★★ **Who Is This Bitch Anyway / Blue N.** **LA397**
Marlena Shaw sounds like the soft side of Esther Phillips; she's capable of the same sardonic phrasing, the same sexuality, but she also has a yearning and coyness reminiscent of the young Nancy Wilson. It's been hard for Shaw to find a proper studio setting for her talent, and as a result, her career has more misses than successes.

Marlena is an abomination; her salty vocals are constantly warring with Wade Marcus' sugary strings, and her attempts to sing behind the beat clash with the rigid orchestrations. *Depths* is a slight improvement, because the material is more contemporary, a tentative compromise between Shaw and her arranger.

It wasn't until *Bitch*, an album she largely cowrote with Bernard Ighner, that Shaw wallowed to show off her stuff, especially her improvisational raps. Here, one gets the sense of an intelligent woman doing the singing, with a nasty but nice sense of humor. But lackluster sales sent her back to a factory-like disco approach with producer Bert deCoteaux. DeCoteaux supplied her with a variety of current and slightly out-of-date soul songs and a conventional female backup trio. It just didn't work: singing the Spinners, Shaw sounds silly. But the Columbia albums modulated that approach. *Beginnings* featured an improvised monologue on "Go Away Little Girl," which became her first hit single. Shaw and deCoteaux now seem to have established some type of sensible working relationship. — R.G.

SHEER ELEGANCE
★ **Sheer Elegance / ABC D-963**
More pointless disco. (Now deleted.) — D.M.

SHERBERT
★★★ **Howzat / MCA 2226**
★★★ **Magazine / MCA 2304**
Australia's top pop group racked up nine consecutive gold albums and eighteen hit singles Down Under, but it has yet to make much of an impression in the U.S. Led by a singer (Daryl Braithwaite) with a voice somewhere between Blood, Sweat and Tears' David Clayton-Thomas and Chicago's Peter Cetera, Sherbert has a knack for hooks, and plays in a variety of styles, but it's nothing Three Dog Night

hasn't done better. (Both now deleted.) — J.S.

JOHN SHINE
★★★ **Songs for a Rainy Day / Col. PC-33518**
Pleasant 1975 country-pop album recorded in Nashville with an excellent cast of musicians, including Kenny Buttrey (drums), David Briggs (piano), Pete Wade and Mac Gayden (guitars) and Terry Garthwaite and the Pointer Sisters (backing vocals). Shine's songs are nice, if not great, and the meticulous production makes the package work fairly well. (Now deleted.) — J.S.

THE SHIRELLES
★★★★★ **The Shirelles Sing Their Very Best / Sp. 4006**
In the late Fifties and early Sixties, the Shirelles spearheaded the "girl group" movement, which also included the Crystals, Ronettes, Chiffons, Orlons and scads of others. The Shirelles were the first of these and one of the best, numbering among their hits such legitimate classics of the era as "Soldier Boy," "I Met Him on a Sunday," "Will You Love Me Tomorrow," "Baby It's You" and a half-dozen other statements of romantic adolescent innocence. This set contains almost all of them, though some of the group's original, but now deleted, collections on Scepter are more attractively presented. — D.M.

THE SHIRTS
★★ **The Shirts / Cap. SW-11791**
Like Mink DeVille, the Shirts wound up at CBGB's not because the group was terribly New Wave in its approach but because the joint happened to be in the neighborhood. But unlike DeVille, the Shirts aren't motivated by a soul crusade, just a desire to

make pop music. Pleasant but formulaic pop-rock. — D.M.

SHO NUFF
★★ **From the Gut to the Butt / Stax 4107**
The title says it all. This is from Stax's rejuvenation at the hand of the Fantasy Records combine, and it kinda makes you glad most of the classic acts have gone, one way or another, without being reduced to this shoogity-boogity mindlessness. — D.M.

SHOTGUN
■ **Good, Bad and Funky / ABC 1060**
■ **Shotgun / ABC 979**
■ **Shotgun III / ABC 1118**
These guys play like somebody took a .12 gauge to their instruments. Seventies rock at its dumbest. — J.S.

SIDE EFFECT
★★ **Goin' Bananas / Fan. 9537**
★★ **Side Effect / Fan. 9491**
★★ **What You Need / Fan. 9513**
The poor man's Dr. Buzzard's Original "Savannah" Band. Since the concept of Broadway soul only carried Buzzard through one album successfully, this is for addicts only. — D.M.

BEN SIDRAN
★★★ **A Little Kiss in the Night / Ari. 4178**
★★★ **Free in America / Ari. 4081**
★★★ **Puttin' in Time on Planet Earth / Blue Th. 55**
★★★★ **The Doctor Is In / Ari. 4131**
Benjamin Sidran, a Ph.D. in philosophy/ musicology, grew up in Racine, Wisconsin, joined up with Steve Miller and Boz Scaggs at the University of Wisconsin (they taught him that rock & roll wasn't dirty), then traveled to England to write his doctoral thesis on the growth of black music in the U.S. (it was published in 1971 as *Black Talk*). But along with his studies, Sidran has found time to play session piano (and vibes) with Miller, Scaggs, Eric Clapton, Peter Frampton, the Rolling Stones and Tony Williams. He has also produced albums by Miller, Williams and Jon Hendricks, and while producing Miller's *Brave New World* he helped corral Paul McCartney to play drums on "Kow Kow" and sing on "My Dark Hour."

When Sidran decided to take the solo plunge, it was sort of casual and nonprofit funk-filled jazz and goofiness that he came up with. These albums are exemplary "easy swinging," laid-back professionalism. His piano turns a nasty trick and his vocals and lyrics owe a great deal to the wit and slow-burn contortions of his mentor, Mose Allison. — B.M.

PAUL SIEBEL
★★★ Jack-Knife Gypsy / Elek. 74081
★★★ Woodsmoke and Oranges / Elek. 74064
Good Woodstock-area folksinger and songwriter. — J.S.

SIEGEL-SCHWALL BAND
★★ Say Siegel-Schwall / Van. 79249
★★ Shake / Van. 79289
★ Siegel-Schwall '70 / Van. 6562
★★ The Best of Siegel-Schwall / Van. 79336
★★ The Siegel-Schwall Band / Van. 79235
★ Three Pieces for a Blues Band / Deutsche Grammophon 2530309
This was Chicago's "other" white blues group of the Sixties, but unlike their neighbors the Butterfield Blues Band, Siegel-Schwall was not steeped in blues tradition, but emphasized a kind of neo-psychedelic improvisation on blues themes that has weathered the years with little grace. Still, the early Vanguard sets are far superior to the later one ('70) and the windy, pretentious symphonic fraud for Deutsche Grammophon recorded in this decade. — D.M.

SIERRA
★★★ Sierra / Mer. SRM-1-1179
Strong but failed country-rock album combines the talents of Sneeky Pete Kleinow (ex-Flying Burrito Brother) on steel guitar, Floyd "Gib" Guilbeau (ex-Burrito, Linda Ronstadt) on rhythm guitar and Micky McGee (ex-Ronstadt, Goose Creek Symphony) on drums. The band's frontman, ex-Steppenwolf guitarist Bobby Cochran, simply doesn't fit. — J.S.

BUNNY SIGLER
★★★ I've Always Wanted to Sing . . . / Gold 9503
★★★★ Keep Smilin' / Phil. PZ-33249
★★★ My Music / Phil. PZ-34267
★★★ That's How Long I'll Be Loving You / Phil. PZ-32859
Bunny Sigler's first two Philadelphia International albums were released only months apart. Despite the fact that *Keep Smilin'* has only three songs not found on *That's How Long,* the additions do wonders, making the "rerelease" a smart, iconoclastic gumbo of modern Philly soul. *Keep Smilin'* not only reflects such sources of inspiration as Marvin Gaye, the early Impressions and street-corner doo-wop, but it also is imbued with infectious good humor—quite apart from the increasingly ponderous paeans of mentors Gamble and Huff. Though *My Music* has several outstanding songs, including one bit of zaniness about a trip to Ghana, the LP is disappointing. Many of Sigler's more eccentric impulses have been curtailed in favor of stock Philly disco charts. Still, *Keep Smilin'* and a handful of earlier singles remain as a testament to Bunny Sigler's talents. — J.MC.

SILVER
■ Silver / Ari. 4076
Slick Hollywood dreck. (Now deleted.) — S.H.

SILVERADO
★ Silverado / RCA APL1-1792
★ Taking It All in Stride / RCA APL1-2421
Execrable Seventies rock band. — J.S.

SILVER CONVENTION
■ Golden Girls / Mid. Int. BXL1-2296
★★ Love in a Sleeper / Mid. Int. 3038
★★ Madhouse / Mid. Int. BXL1-1824
★★★ Save Me / Mid. Int. BXL1-1129
★★★ Silver Convention / Mid. Int. BXL1-1369
★ Steppin' Out / Mid. Int. BXL1-2423
Silver Convention is a premier example of tightly formularized disco that works. Their sound is precision tooled, by the German team of Michael Kunze, Stephan Preager and Sylvester Levay, from a design first sketched by Gloria Gaynor's *Never Can Say Goodbye.* Silver Convention's sound-alike big hits—"Save Me," "Get Up and Boogie" and "Fly, Robin, Fly"—are typical of almost all their records. Cunning chants are repeated endlessly over a metronomic funk mechanism greased carefully

by strings and hooted along by an occasional sax solo. The whole operation is modest, clean and pleasantly functional.

The vacancy of Silver Convention's three vocalists, Penny McLean, Ramona Wolf and Linda Thompson (later replaced by Rhonda Heath), who invariably sing in unison with all the style of distracted typists, suggests the singing-along of disco dancers themselves, and it may well be the key to the group's success in creating aural presence.

Although no one would want to own more than one of their LPs, Silver Convention's earlier singles collections, *Silver Convention* and *Save Me,* contain their best work. The songs, of course, are virtually identical, creating a kind of meta-single. *Madhouse* is a misdirected concept album about dehumanization, more proof that Germans have no sense of irony, since the very sound of Silver Convention is inconceivable except in a dehumanized context. The three singers try out some Motown-type harmonies on *Golden Girls,* while the production edges ever so slightly in the direction of lushness. Both moves gum up the works and the album is a disaster. — B.T.

SHEL SILVERSTEIN

★ **Freakin' at the Freakers Ball / Col. C-31119**

Silverstein is a *Playboy* cartoonist who has contributed many novelty songs (most notably Loretta Lynn's "One's on the Way" and Dr. Hook's "Cover of Rolling Stone") to the country and pop charts. As a singer, however, he's mostly a pretty good draftsman. — D.M.

SIMON AND GARFUNKEL

★★★★ **Bookends / Col. PC-9529**
★★★★ **Bridge over Troubled Water / Col. PC-9914**
★★★★ **Parsley, Sage, Rosemary and Thyme / Col. PC-9363**
★★★★★ **Simon and Garfunkel's Greatest Hits / Col. PC-31350**
★★ **Sounds of Silence / Col. PC-9269**
★★ **The Graduate / Col. CS-3180**
★★ **Wednesday Morning, 3 A.M. / Col. KCS-9049**

With their socially relevant but gentle folk rock, Simon and Garfunkel quietly bridged the Sixties generation gap. *Wednesday Morning,* their 1965 debut, made no waves until producer Tom Wilson grafted an electric guitar to a song called "Sounds of Silence," which proceeded to become one of the biggest and best folk-rock hits. Paul Simon's elliptical, imagistic writing soon became very big on the rock-lyrics-are-poetry circuit, but he was really an expert popular-song craftsman, influenced by both folk and rock but owing allegiance to neither. A string of hits followed, many featuring Art Garfunkel's beautiful tenor voice. *Parsley,* an early if vague concept album, contained more than its share of successes: the beautiful "Homeward Bound," the Eleanor Rigby-like "For Emily Whenever I May Find Her," and "59th Street Bridge Song (Feelin' Groovy)," a big hit for Harper's Bizarre.

Ironically, "Scarborough Fair/Canticle," an adaptation of a pair of traditional songs, made Simon and Garfunkel superstars when it and an additional number written by Simon, "Mrs. Robinson," were used as themes for Mike Nichols' 1968 film, *The Graduate.*

It was on the next two albums, *Bookends* and *Bridge,* that the pair really hit their stride, however. *Bookends* was more directly conceptual than even *Parsley,* a kind of snapshot album of American life in the late Sixties: "Mrs. Robinson," "America," "Fakin' It" and "At the Zoo" were hits (all were written by Simon, of course). "Bridge over Troubled Water" was perhaps the most influential and certainly the most recorded number of the latter half of the Sixties; it is an almost breathtakingly perfect song, and its roots in black gospel enable it to escape the sometimes cloying sweetness of the rest of the album. *Bridge* became an unheard-of success, selling four million copies in the U.S. and many millions more abroad.

Unfortunately, that saccharine tendency makes many of these records seem extremely dated today. *Greatest Hits* remains the best example of Simon and Garfunkel's work together. Simon's solo recordings, however, are far superior to all except two or three of the duo's best songs. — D.M.

CARLY SIMON

★ **Anticipation / Elek. 75016**
★ **Carly Simon / Elek. 74082**

After several false starts (including an album with sister Lucy as the Simon Sisters on Columbia), Carly Simon's recording career began with these inflated, clumsily revisionist folkie albums in 1970 and 1971. Successive left-field summertime hits, "That's the Way I Always Heard It Should Be" and "Anticipation," later a ketchup commercial, probably saved both albums from the remainder bins, and the frequently flat-voiced Simon from immediate obscurity. Despite lifeless performances, both singles proved to be pop masterpieces expressive of the *Viva*-type postfeminist woman—sexually independent but still expecting to find the easy permanence of romantic marriage someday soon.

Although prophetic of Simon's career, these singles were not typical of the first two albums. The rest of the songs have no such thematic redemptions, except for the pop-star snapshot "Legend in Your Own Time." The Paul Simon-styled "Reunions" and "Dan, My Fling," not to mention the apocalyptic "Share the End," are way outside Carly's reach both as performer and songwriter (even with poet/collaborator Jacob Brackman).

★★ **Hot Cakes** / Elek. EQ-1002
★★★ **No Secrets** / Elek. 75049
★ **Playing Possum** / Elek. EQ-1033
Richard Perry was the perfect producer to give shape to Carly Simon's vast confusions. His slick cut-and-paste production gives both her writing and her studio performances a semblance of form; his massed but subtly deployed studio firepower covered Simon's anemic vocals with pleasant salvos of sound. However, that marvel of female sarcasm and Simon's real claim to pop genius, "You're So Vain" (from *No Secrets*), is untypical. Most of Simon's songs continue the themes of her early singles, but in a postmarital mode: proud family chronicles—from both childhood and her marriage to James Taylor—some vague pop feminism and some ambivalent love songs.

Perry's work with Simon starts strongly with *No Secrets,* almost an autobiographical concept album, slips into hit-and-miss with *Hot Cakes,* practically a James Taylor-Carly Simon duet LP, and falls apart with *Playing Possum,* in which Perry presses a variety of unsuitable stylized settings, from disco to lounge jazz, on Simon, who winds up panting for breath.

★★★ **Another Passenger** / Elek. 7E-1064
★★★ **Boys in the Trees** / Elek. 6E-128
★★★ **The Best of Carly Simon** / Elek. 6E-109
On *Another Passenger,* produced by Ted Templeman, Simon achieves a narrow but solid new start. Co-writer Jacob Brackman returns after a long absence, and she has picked up some needed lessons in phrasing, mostly from James Taylor. On the best songs, including the title cut, Simon uncovers herself and reflects her age and her

class. (She is the daughter of one of the founders of Simon and Schuster.) She has abandoned the inane persona of a college-educated housewife about to enter transactional analysis that had progressively taken over her songs. The lessons learned from Perry aren't forgotten, but Simon at least seems really comfortable. At times, she is even conversant with the arrangements. *Boys in the Trees* is something of a compromise between Perry's lushness and Templeman's relatively sparse approach, thanks to the guiding hand of Arif Mardin. If Simon is never quite as soulful as she'd like to be, she's given consistently appropriate support.

The *Best of* collection is Simon's best album, since she is primarily a singles artist. Here, her early singles can be heard without suffering through the albums. Some fans, however, have probably found alternative favorites. — B.T.

PAUL
SIMON

JOE SIMON
★★★ **A Bad Case of Love** / Spring 1-6716
★★★ **Easy to Love** / Spring 1-6713
★★★ **Get Down** / Spring 6706
★★★ **Joe Simon Today** / Spring 6710
★★★★ **The World of Joe Simon** / Sound. S. SP-5000
Joe Simon is a smooth-voiced soul singer whose immense popularity has diminished only slightly since he began recording for Sound Stage Seven in 1966. With producer John Richbourg (best known as disc jockey John R.), Simon scored a series of brilliantly mellow soul hits, including "Teenager's Prayer," "Nine Pound Steel" and "The Chokin' Kind," the latter a 1969 million-seller. Since he's moved to his own label, Spring, Simon's career has been more erratic in terms of quality. "Drowning in the Sea of Love," produced by Gam-

ble and Huff, was a smash in 1972 on both pop and soul stations, but since then he's been more confined to black audiences. Unfortunately, a great deal of his early and superior work for Spring has been deleted, and the Sound Stage Seven LP remains the only collection of his early work. — D.M.

PAUL SIMON
★★★★ Greatest Hits, Etc. / Col.
  JC-35032
★★★ Live Rhymin' / Col. PC-32855
★★★★★ Paul Simon / Col. PC-30750
★★★★★ Still Crazy After All These
  Years / Col. PC-33540
★★★★★ There Goes Rhymin' Simon /
  Col. PC-32280

Paul Simon was one-half of Simon and Garfunkel, which understates the matter considerably: he was the duo's writer, and it is for their songs, more than anything, that Simon and Garfunkel are remembered. Since he struck out on his own, in 1971, he has recorded a series of albums (the most recent in 1976) that are among the greatest popular music anyone in the current era has attempted.

Paul Simon, the first LP, set the stage for his growth: it is rougher and more expansive than any of the Simon and Garfunkel recordings, with several quirky reggae numbers made in Jamaica and a sense of lost innocence that says much about the necessity for the group's demise. *There Goes Rhymin' Simon* is based on blues and gospel music; the record's biggest hit, "Loves Me Like a Rock," was recorded with the Dixie Hummingbirds, which makes it as close to real gospel as a Jewish kid from Queens is ever likely to come. *Still Crazy* is a chronicle of experience, frequently using broken marriage as a metaphor; it is Simon's most mature work, and his most musically sophisticated, relying, for instance, on interrelationships of notes from song to song for part of its cohesion and emphasizing piano rhythms over guitar figures. In "50 Ways to Leave Your Lover," "My Little Town" (the Simon and Garfunkel reunion), the title cut and several other songs, Simon's writing reached a new level of sophistication.

Unfortunately, he has produced nothing since then. *Live Rhymin'* was released to fill the temporal gap between the second and third solo albums, and *Greatest Hits, Etc.,* which contained a pair of good new songs, "Stranded in a Limousine" and "Slip Slidin' Away," perhaps serves the same function at present. For the past two years,

Simon has been working on a film, writing both script and music; presumably this accounts for the delay. — D.M.

NINA SIMONE
★★★ Baltimore / CTI 7084
★★★★ Here Comes the Sun / RCA
  AFL1-4536
★★★ It Is Finished / RCA APL1-0241
★★★★ The Best of Nina Simone / Phi.
  PHS 600298
★★★★ The Best of Nina Simone / RCA
  AFL1-4374
★★★★ The Finest of Nina Simone / Beth.
  BCP-6003

Dusky-voiced singer/keyboardist earned her nickname, "The High Priestess of Soul," through deeply personal interpretations of everything from Gershwin to Dylan to African folk songs. One of the most intellectual soul singers of her generation, Simone metamorphosed from a moody jazz-pop stylist into a political voice whose expressions of black rage and pride remain unmatched in their emotional intensity.

Simone debuted in the late Fifties on Bethlehem, for whom she had her first and biggest hit, "I Loves You Porgy." The Philips *Best of* collects highlights from six albums recorded between 1964 and 1967 and includes "I Put a Spell on You" and Simone's searing black-consciousness manifesto, "Four Women." RCA's *Best of* seems a somewhat arbitrary selection from her next half-dozen albums (from 1967 to 1971). — S.H.

FRANK SINATRA
★ A Man Alone / Rep. 1030
★ All Alone / Rep. 1007
★★ All the Way / Cap. SM-1538
★★★★ Come Dance with Me / Cap.
  SM-1069

★★★★ Come Fly with Me / Cap. SM-920
★ Concert Sinatra / Rep. 1009
★ Cycles / Rep. 1027
★ Days of Wine and Roses / Rep. 1011
★★ Francis A. Sinatra and Edward K. Ellington / Rep. 1024
★★ Frank Sinatra and Strings / Rep. 1004
★★ Frank Sinatra and Swingin' Brass / Rep. 1005
★★ Frank Sinatra/Antonio Carlos Jobim / Rep. 1021
★★★ Frank Sinatra's Greatest Hits / Rep. K-2274
★★ Frank Sinatra's Greatest Hits, Vol. 2 / Rep. K-2275
★★ Frank Sinatra Swings / Rep. 1002
★★★ Greatest Hits, Vol. 1 / Col. CS-9274
★★★ Greatest Hits, Vol. 2 / Col. CS-9372
★ I Remember Tommy / Rep. 1003
★★★★ In the Beginning (1943-1951) / Col. KC-31358
★★ It Might as Well Be Swing / Rep. 1012
★ Moonlight Sinatra / Rep. 1018
★ My Kind of Broadway / Rep. 1015
★★★★ My One and Only Love—Sentimental Journey / Cap. STBB-724
★★★★ Nice 'n' Easy / Cap. SM-1417
★★★ Ol' Blues Eyes Is Back / Rep. ES4-2155
★★★★ One More for the Road / Cap. ST-11309
★★★ Ring-a-Ding Ding / Rep. 1001
★★★ Round No. 1 / Cap. SABB-11357
★★★★★ September of My Years / Rep. 1014
★★★ Sinatra—A Man and His Music / Rep. 2-1016
★★ Sinatra and Basie / Rep. 1008
★ Sinatra and Company / Rep. 1033
★ Sinatra at the Sands / Rep. 2-1019
■ Sinatra '65 / Rep. 6167
★★ Sinatra's Sinatra / Rep. 1010
★ Softly, as I Leave You / Rep. 1013
★ Some Nice Things I've Missed / Rep. 2195
★★★★ Songs for Swingin' Lovers / Cap. SM-653
★★ Strangers in the Night / Rep. 1017
★★★★ Swingin' Affair / Cap. SM-11502
★★★ Swingin' Session / Cap. SM-1491
★ That's Life / Rep. 1020
★ The Main Event / Rep. 2207
■ The World We Knew / Rep. 1022
★ Watertown / Rep. 1031
★★★★★ What Is This Thing Called Love? / Cap. STBB-529

In the Forties, "The Voice" was the purest bel canto baritone—a distillation of the home-front American dream in wartime. Even the song titles reinforced fantasy: "If You Are but a Dream," "Dream," "Put Your Dreams Away." Sinatra personified the gallant prince who yearned to waken Sleeping Beauty with a kiss. No male pop star before or since has offered eroticism so tenderly.

Sinatra's earliest recordings with Tommy Dorsey are available on RCA Victor and RCA Camden. After leaving Dorsey, he began recording with Columbia, but most of his nearly 250 Columbia sides are out of print. *In the Beginning,* which contains twenty cuts, duplicates Columbia's greatest-hits collections and sticks to Sinatra's more successful singles; they were seldom his best records. But though the material is crassly chosen and the sound poorly rechanneled, the beauty of Sinatra's voice over and over again illuminates banal material with an almost mystical hope and sadness.

Sinatra moved to Capitol in 1953 and abruptly changed his persona from questing romantic to worldly sophisticate. At Columbia he worked almost exclusively with one arranger/conductor (Axel Stordahl), but at Capitol he used three. With Gordon Jenkins (*The Night We Called It a Day,* formerly *Where Are You*), Sinatra's ballad singing exuded a towering *angst* that bordered on the sepulchral. With Billy May (*Come Fly with Me, Come Dance with Me*), he revived Big Band swing. With Nelson Riddle (*Songs for Swingin' Lovers, Nice 'n' Easy*), he took a middle path between reflection and aggression.

Many of the albums Sinatra made for his own record company, Reprise, beginning in 1961, were simultaneous exercises in nostalgia and attempts to improve on past performances. But though Sinatra continued to refine his style, the voice itself had frayed, and his choices of new songs and of new writers to boost (Rod McKuen? Bob Gaudio and Jake Holmes?) became very uneven. On turning fifty, Sinatra reteamed with Gordon Jenkins to make *September of My Years,* a pop masterpiece that summed up the punchy sentimentality felt by a whole generation of American men. The highlight, "It Was a Very Good Year," is an exceptionally eloquent expression of middle-aged sexist nostalgia.

Like Presley and Dylan—the only other white American singers since 1940 whose popularity, influence and mythic force have been comparable to his—Sinatra will last indefinitely. He virtually invented modern pop song phrasing.   — S.H.

STEPHEN SINCLAIR
★★ A Plus / U. Artists LA767-G
★★ Sad and Lonely Saturday Night /
MCA 2171
Yet another mediocre Seventies singer/songwriter. — J.S.

SISTER SLEDGE
★★ Circle of Love / Atco 36-105
★★ Together / Coti. 9919
★★★ We Are Family / Coti. 5209
This talented teenage family group has been unable to come up with a hit record, partly because of material that usually lacks distinction. The disco-based *We Are Family* is their 1979 commercial breakthrough. — J.MC.

THE SKATALITES
★★★ African Roots / U. Artists LA799-H
The Skatalites were the foremost band playing ska, the predecessor of reggae. This is a little rugged on Yankee ears, but the fundamentals for what the Wailers and Maytals would later make popular are firmly embedded here. — D.M.

PATRICK SKY
★★★ Patrick Sky / Van. 79179
■ Songs That Made America Famous /
Adel. R-4101
★★ Two Steps Forward—One Step Back /
Lev. 2000
As a singer/songwriter during the Sixties (as represented on the Vanguard LP), Sky combined an offbeat sense of humor with a serious love of traditional music. But after two albums for Vanguard (the second is deleted) and two for MGM (also out of print), Sky did *Songs That Made America Famous* on his own. He claimed that the language and subject matter were too offensive and vulgar for any major label to

release it, but with the exception of Mike Hunt's "The Pope," the record just isn't really funny. Sky is currently concentrating on traditional music and building Irish uilleann pipes, and that's the side of his career chronicled on the Leviathan LP. — I.M.

SKYBAND
★★ Skyband / RCA APLI-0839
Faceless mid-Seventies power trio writes standard riff plodders and lacks an interesting soloist. (Now deleted.) — J.S.

SKYHOOKS
★★★ Ego Is Not a Dirty Word / Mer.
SRM-1-1066
★★★ Living in the Seventies / Mer.
SRM-1-1124
Demented Australian band that depends on theatrics and visual effects and hence is pretty ineffective on these two mid-Seventies LPs. Skyhooks does play some interesting, light jazz-tinged rock, and they coax some good rhythms from the standard guitar/drums/vocals lineup. (Now deleted.) — A.N.

SKY KING
★ Secret Sauce / Col. KC-33367
Dave Brubeck's sons run through their earnest but predictable version of jazz rock. (Now deleted.) — J.S.

SKYLARK
★★ Skylark / Cap. ST-11048
Like the Band and Crowbar, Skylark is also made up of Ronnie Hawkins alumni. Based in Vancouver, Skylark had an international hit in 1973 with the wimp ballad "Wildflower" and then disappeared, leaving as a legacy this very ordinary MOR pop album. — A.N.

SKYLINERS
★★★★ Since I Don't Have You / Orig.
Sound 8873
The title track was one of the best moody pop ballads of 1959; it sounded so funky, in a manner derived from the Platters, that it was hard to believe the quintet was white. Subsequent singles, collected here from the originals released on Calico, still featured the resonant lead singing of Jimmy Beaumont but lacked the great spark of the first hit. — D.M.

SLADE
★ Nobody's Fools / War. B-2936
★ Sladest / Rep. 2173

A number of people were briefly convinced in the early Seventies that Slade, a group of working-class louts from the English Midlands, were about to be the Next Big Thing. They were, at least in England, thanks to such trebly, metallic shouters as "Mama Weer All Crazee Now" and "Gudbuy T'Jane" (the spelling is theirs, not ours). Those moments came a few years before the over-the-hill-and-soon-to-be-faraway *Sladest* and *Nobody's Fools*. The highwater marks for this quartet of ferocious hardcore rockers were a pair of deleted LPs, *Slade Alive* and *Slayed?*, whose straight-for-the-gut approach has influenced a number of later bands, most notably Kiss. Produced and managed by former Animals bassist and Jimi Hendrix manager Chas Chandler. — B.A.

NELSON SLATER
★★ **Wild Angel / RCA APL1-1306**
An S&M odyssey produced by Lou Reed, the venerable godfather of sexual and other kinkiness in rock. There's nothing here, unfortunately, that Reed hasn't done better, wittier and more succinctly. (Now deleted.) — D.M.

SLAVE
★★★ **Slave / Coti. 5200**
★★★ **The Concept / Coti. 5206**
★★ **The Hardness of the World / Coti. 5201**
This ten-piece disco band's first album, *Slave*, got some exposure in dance palaces, where its all-out thump made up for the utter inanity of the rest of it. *The Hardness of the World* lacked panache, but *The Concept* snapped with Parliafunkadelic-styled wit and imagination. — D.M.

PERCY SLEDGE
★★★ **I'll Be Your Everything / Capri. 0147**
★★★★ **The Best of Percy Sledge / Atl. 8210**
Through the middle Sixties, Percy Sledge, along with producers Quin Ivy and Marlin Greene, made a series of melodramatically heart-rending soul ballads—"Warm and Tender Love," "When a Man Loves a Woman," "Out of Left Field," "Take Time to Know Her"—that remain emotional classics for romantics of all ages. Sledge's tenor voice was fitted to gospel-like backgrounds, which gave the often maudlin lyrics a properly portentous cast. This is a bit dated, in terms of approach and message, but truly wonderful stuff; the Atlantic collection has the great majority of Sledge's

worthwhile sides. The Capricorn album, released in 1974, reunites Sledge with Quin Ivy, and although there aren't any masterpieces, it's a smoothly listenable update of the approach. — D.M.

GRACE SLICK
★★★ **Collectors Item / Col. CG-30459**
★★★ **Conspicuous Only in Its Absence / Col. CS-9624**
★★ **Manhole / Grunt BHL1-0347**
The two Columbia albums are essentially the same: material from Slick's pre-Jefferson Airplane band the Great Society, including elongated versions of "White Rabbit" and "Somebody to Love." *Manhole* is Slick's only solo album, recorded during the days of the Jefferson Airplane's disintegration and bearing the appropriate scars of the time. — J.S.

THE SLICK BAND
★★★ **Razor Sharp / Cap. 11570**
★★ **The Earl Slick Band / Cap. 11493**
Before forming this band, Earl Slick was best known as David Bowie's guitarist, circa the *Young Americans* LP. Although singer Jimmie Mack wrote most of the material, the group's apparent purpose is to create a setting for Slick's firestorm guitar playing. In that capacity, it serves well, grinding out solid, simple bottom. Mack works inside the Anglo-screamer rock tradition and writes passable lyrics about barroom sex and violence.

On *Earl Slick,* the band is apparently still figuring out its basic strategy, and Mack's songs overuse the Bad Company midtempo strategy; Slick botches the multi-tracked guitar technique developed in his Bowie stint. *Razor Sharp* is much improved, reducing Mack's role to something more functional, and the band pushes steadily to showcase Slick's searing solos and flash fills. (Both now deleted.) — B.T.

SLY AND THE FAMILY STONE
★★★ **A Whole New Thing / Epic 30335**
★★★ **Dance to the Music / Epic E-30334**
★★★ **High Energy / Epic 33462**
★★★★ **Life / Epic E-30333**
A Whole New Thing was an apt title; with one album, Sly Stone and his sexually and racially integrated band assaulted black music conventions and irreparably changed its direction and focus. Sly built songs like "Dance to the Music" and "Life" on James Brown's rhythmic innovation while adding fresh elements: disembodied group vocals,

scattershot horn charts and lyrics with a point of view. The early Sly Stone records are undisciplined, but they contain a ferocious spirit and energy that borders on the anarchic.

★★★★★ **Greatest Hits / Epic PE-30325**
★★★★★ **Stand! / Epic 26456**
Both *Stand!* and *Greatest Hits* exuded an optimism that was fitting for the time. "Stand," "Everybody Is a Star" and "Hot Fun in the Summertime" were as representative of the Woodstock sensibility (and mood) as any twenty-minute Grateful Dead guitar jam. The optimism wasn't confined to the lyrics or stance, either. The brashness of early singles like "Dance to the Music" was replaced by a gentler tone that one might guess meant peace of mind.

★★★★★ **There's a Riot Goin' On / Epic 30986**
There are few pop albums this powerful. Though the record yielded two hit singles, white listeners were alienated by it, perhaps purposely. Sly made fun of his old songs; the remake of "Thank You Falettinme Be Mice Elf Again" as "Thank You for Talkin' to Me Africa" is chilling. The title cut was timed at 0:00, and through most of the record, Sly sounded stoned. Not a pleasant buzz either, but something a whole lot more vicious. Greil Marcus said it best: "The record was no fun." Woodstock was over.

★★★★ **Fresh / Epic KE-32134**
★★★ **Heard Ya Missed Me, Well I'm Back / Epic PE-34348**
★★★ **High on You / Epic 33835**
★★★ **Small Talk / Epic 32930**
Sly hasn't been quite the same since *Riot. Fresh* featured a glossy Richard Avedon cover and "If You Want Me to Stay," a hit single that beat a hasty retreat from the wormy truths of "Family Affair." Black funk, rock and disco groups borrowed heavily from *Riot*'s rhythms but ignored the message for the trappings. By *Small Talk,* Sly was competing with a host of imitators who could do Sly Stone better than Sly. And with the Ohio Players, an audience didn't have to worry about hearing what it didn't want to hear, confronting what was most painful to confront. A 1976 issue of *Jet* magazine provided the final irony: Sly Stone, on whose back the Seventies black music explosion was built, was broke. (But in late 1978, Warner Bros. announced that he would be recording for that label. *Heard Ya Missed Me* may still be his most prophetic title.) — J.MC.

THE SMALL FACES
★★★ **First Step / War. 1851**
★★★★ **Ogden's Nut Gone Flake / Abkco 4225**
★ **Playmates / Atl. 19113**
★★ **78 in the Shade / Atl. 19171**
This hardly looks like the catalogue of an important British rock band, but the Small Faces (later, simply the Faces) never had much luck in the States. All of their early mod R&B records are out of print in the U.S. (a deleted Sire anthology is well worth picking up), as is the group's first Immediate album, *There Are but Four Small Faces,* which contained their pop-psychedelic hit, "Itchykoo Park."

The equally psychedelic concept album, *Ogden's Nut Gone Flake,* a strange combination of program music, fairy tale and soul-based rock, remains, and it's fairly wonderful, one of the least pretentious and most artistically successful spinoffs of the *Sgt. Pepper* era. Lead singer Steve Marriott never sounded more leprechaunish. *First Step* is the group's first album with Rod Stewart and Ron Wood replacing Marriott (who left to form Humble Pie). It's back to rock and soul, quite admirably done but nowhere near as much fun as the band's stage show.

Playmates, released in 1977, presents the original group (Marriott, Ian McLagan, Kenny Jones) minus bassist Ronnie Lane, who's virtually dropped out of sight. *Playmates* is a disaster, mostly because of the shoddy material, though the fact that Marriott blew out his voice in the latter stages of Humble Pie's boogieing days doesn't help. *78* is a minor rebound, but with the departure of drummer Kenny Jones to join the Who, probably a last gasp. — D.M.

SMALL WONDER
★★ **Growin' / Col. PC-34425**
★★★ **Small Wonder / Col. PC-34100**
Led by violinist/vocalist Henry Small, Small Wonder grew from the ashes of the little-known Canadian band Scruballo Caine. As a beery Saturday-night bar band extolling the virtues of modern dance, the group was nearly unbeatable. But the transition to record was less spectacular, hampered by halting production and inconsistent material. The self-titled first LP (1976) is superior for its innocent freshness and for the inclusion of "Why Walk When You Can Dance," a potential anthem for all leftover longhairs who still enjoy a drunken boogie. (Both now deleted.) — A.N.

BUFFALO BOB SMITH
■ **Live at Fillmore East / Proj. 5055**
This nightmarish bit of nostalgia offers Howdy-smokes-pot jokes. Perhaps if promoter Bill Graham had played W.C. Fields to Smith's Edgar Bergen, it would have worked. (Now deleted.) — J.S.

PATTI SMITH
★★★★ **Easter / Ari. 4171**
★★★★ **Horses / Ari. 4066**
★ **Radio Ethiopia / Ari. 4097**
Patti Smith began her career as a poet and critic, published in a variety of periodicals, but mostly *Creem* and *Rolling Stone.* At her best, those vocations have an expansive effect on her approach to music; at her worst, she's an arrogant amateur, with more pretenses than anyone in the history of rock & roll. Which is to say that even at her worst, she's one of the most interesting figures in contemporary rock & roll and potentially the first really compelling female rocker since Janis Joplin.

Horses, her 1975 debut LP, is Smith at her most overtly poetic, perhaps because several key songs were developed in the context of poetry readings, in which Smith would be backed only by Lenny Kaye's electric guitar. Her version of "Gloria" is one of the most remarkable ever done, and "Land," a takeoff on Wilson Pickett's "Land of 1,000 Dances," is a psychic horror story unmatched by anyone since Jim Morrison. Smith's voice is never more than winsomely evocative, but on this album she uses it to good effect. Not so on *Radio Ethiopia:* the Kaye-led group, inferior to her in imagination if not technique, simply overwhelms her and drowns her out.

The 1978 LP, *Easter,* returns Smith to the forefront with amazing success. "Because the Night," a composing "collaboration" with Bruce Springsteen, became a Top Twenty hit single, hardly what the ordinarily scatological Smith could have been expected to turn out; the rest of the album is hard-driving rock, as eerie as anything she'd done before, and more sensual. Her flaws aren't completely tamed, naturally, but *Easter* at least points the way to a sound that is both palatable and uncompromising. — D.M.

SMOKIE (SMOKEY)
★★★ **Bright Lights, Back Alleys / RSO 1-3029**
★★★ **Smokey / MCA 2152**
★★★ **Smokie—Midnight Cafe / RSO 1-3005**
Last in the long line of outlets for the British songwriting/production team of Chinn and Chapman (Sweet and Suzi Quatro were the other notable incarnations), Smokie is an adequate purveyor of some of Chinnichap's most palatable yet least commercially rewarded efforts. Although primarily aimed at the teen and even preteen market, the songs are so full of hooks, and Chapman's production is so flawless, that their appeal easily spans the pop music spectrum. Worth a listen. — A.N.

MICHAEL SMOTHERMAN
★ **Michael Smotherman / Wind. BXL1-2416**
Another slushy pop singer from John Denver's label. Hard to believe there are so many inferior specimens of Denver's rancid formula around, isn't it? — D.M.

PHOEBE SNOW
★★ **Against the Grain / Col. JC-35456**
★★ **It Looks Like Snow / Col. PC-34387**
★★ **Never Letting Go / Col. JC-34875**
★★★★ **Phoebe Snow / Shel. 52017**
★★★ **Second Childhood / Col. PC-33952**
An eccentric but talented writer with a great jazz-pop voice, Snow scored with the confessional "Poetry Man," from her first album (for Shelter). Though the stylistic collisions in her singing sometimes result in confused mannerism, Snow is a true original. Unfortunately, since the debut LP, the confusions have dominated. — S.H.

SOFT MACHINE
★★★ **Fourth / Col. C-30754**
★★★ **Seven / Col. C-32716**
★★★ **Six / Col. PG-32260**
★★★★★ **Third / Col. CG-30339**
Soft Machine was the most prestigious and musically accomplished of the experimental groups to come out of England in the Sixties, melding rock, jazz and classical styles into a kind of noncommercial, prefusion music. Led by the brilliant percussionist Robert Wyatt, this band's first three albums are landmarks in experimental rock. Unfortunately the first two are now out of print, but the breakthrough record, *Third,* remains. On that one, the band expanded from a trio to eight pieces and fomented an instrumental interlace seldom heard in a rock context. At one time, four different horn lines race each other while the twisted rhythm section chugs it all along like crazy clockworks. Wyatt's "Moon in June" is a masterpiece.

Wyatt departed after *Third,* leaving the conceptual reins to organist Mike Ratledge. Under his direction, the band was less inspired, playing the sort of aimless noodling that eventually gave this kind of music a bad name. — J.S.

SOLUTION
★ **Cordon Bleu / R. 2189**
Worthless pop group from Elton John's handlers. — J.S.

BERT SOMMER
★ **Bert Sommer / Cap. 11684**
Hippie writer/singer. The most obscure, least worthy performer to appear at the Woodstock festival, a distinction he earns. (Now deleted.) — D.M.

SONNY AND CHER
★★ **Sonny and Cher "Live" / MCA 2009**
★★★ **The Beat Goes On / Atco 11000**
★★★★ **The Best of Sonny and Cher / Atco 219**
★★ **The Two of Us / Atco 2-804**
Having learned the ropes of the music business as a percussionist with Phil Spector's studio orchestra, Sonny Bono was able to successfully re-create Spector's Wall of Sound on many of his early hits, written by him and performed with his wife, Cher. Their pre-Seventies material holds up rather well. The *Best of* collection features the duo's string of Top Ten smashes in the mid and late Sixties ("Bang Bang," "Baby Don't Go"); *The Beat Goes On*'s title track is a classic period piece of pop culture, and "Laugh at Me," Sonny's lone solo hit, is a disarming let-me-do-my-thing anthem; the *Live* double LP is from their Vegas act and is a souvenir of prime-time Sonny and Cher, replete with Cher's constant rank-outs of Sonny. In light of subsequent events, it's hard to say just what was acting and what was real. Recommended mostly for those with a taste for the perverse. — B.A.

SONS OF CHAMPLIN
★★★ **Circle Filled with Love / Ario. 50007**
★★★★ **Follow Your Heart / Cap. 675**
★★★ **Loosen Up Naturally / Cap. SWBB-200**
★★★ **Loving Is Why / Ario. 50017**
★ **Sons / Cap. 332**
★★★ **Sons of Champlin / Ario. 50002**
The Sons of Champlin bill themselves as the longest-living Marin County rock band. They've consistently eschewed the spotlight since their inception in 1965 and became one of the first rock groups to use horns for soloing in a jazz-influenced context. The double set, *Loosen Up Naturally,* includes some pretty hot playing and sounded very good when released in the late Sixties, though it's awfully dated a decade later. The band indulges in some inane cosmic lyrics and falls prey to the noodling tendencies that often plague such efforts. *Follow Your Heart* is the most focused record and it's aged well. The Ariola albums date from the band's mid-Seventies comeback, but by that time the group wasn't offering anything novel and had to rest on its status as a hippie legend. — J.S.

SOPWITH CAMEL
■ **The Miraculous Hump Returns from the Moon / Rep. 2108**
This San Francisco-area band was one of the first of that region's groups to score with a hit, the vaudevillian "Hello Hello." Such minuscule success was hardly an excuse for this Seventies reunion album, which is predictably atrocious. — D.M.

ROSALIE SORRELS
★★ **Always a Lady / Philo 1029**
★★★ **If I Could Be the Rain / Folk-Leg. 31**
★★ **Moments of Happiness / Philo 1033**
Sorrels drifts in and out of view, her infrequent albums appearing on various labels. A singer, songwriter, raconteuse and poet, she adds great sensitivity to her music, whether she is singing any of the title tracks here or one of Bruce "Utah" Phillips' union or train songs. Phillips' songs are well represented on the 1967 Folk-Legacy set, on which Sorrels is accompanied by Mitch Greenhill. Some of the stories ("Mehitabel's Theme" on *Always a Lady*) work better in concert than on record, but when Sorrels is singing, she can swing on a jazz beat or rock with a country flavor along with the best. — I.M.

THE SOUL CHILDREN
★★★ **Where Is Your Woman Tonight? / Epic PE-34455**
The Soul Children are a durable Southern trio with a twist: each member (two male, one female) is a qualified lead vocalist. The group specializes in an intense, rugged brand of gospel soul, a style long out of fashion in black music. Still, they've managed to keep an audience, like many others in the genre, through a series of other-man, other-woman love songs. But *Where Is Your Woman Tonight?* suffers from the oc-

casionally intrusive and sloppy production of David Porter. The Don Davis–produced *Finders Keepers* is concise and truer to the verities of the genre, but it's an Epic cutout. Meanwhile, the group has been making a variety of uptempo dance singles for Fantasy's revived Stax label. — J.MC.

SOUL TRAIN GANG
★ **Soul Train / Soul T. BVL1-1287**
★ **Soul Train Gang / Soul T. BVL1-1844**
The problem is, on LP you can't watch 'em dance. Wait for the video disc. — D.M.

JOE SOUTH
★★★★ **Joe South's Greatest Hits / Cap. SM-450**
In the early Sixties, South made his reputation in Atlanta and Nashville as a top-notch session guitarist and songwriter. Among his hits are "Games People Play," "Walk a Mile in My Shoes," "Hush," "Down in the Boondocks" and "I Never Promised You a Rose Garden." Unfortunately, most of his catalogue is out of print, but well worth looking for in the cutout bins, especially his groundbreaking 1968 classic, *Introspect.* — J.S.

JOHN DAVID SOUTHER
★ **Black Rose / Asy. 7E-1059**
★★ **John David Souther / Asy. 5055**
Talented Texas singer/songwriter (he co-wrote "The Best of My Love" for the Eagles and "Faithless Love" for Linda Ronstadt) followed a promising solo debut with the whiny *Rose* LP. — S.H.

THE SOUTHER-HILLMAN-FURAY BAND
★★ **The Souther-Hillman-Furay-Band / Asy. 7E-1006**
★ **Trouble in Paradise / Asy. 7E-1036**
This was supposed to be a supergroup: Chris Hillman made his reputation as a Byrd, Richie Furay as a member of the Buffalo Springfield and Poco, John David Souther as a kind of Jackson Browne *manqué* who also wrote songs for sometime girlfriend Linda Ronstadt. But it never jelled, and what seemed promising in 1975 was all through by 1976. The three subsequently pursued solo careers. — S.H.

SOUTHSIDE JOHNNY AND THE ASBURY JUKES
★★★★ **Hearts of Stone / Epic JE-35488**
★★★★ **I Don't Want to Go Home / Epic PE-34180**
★★★★ **This Time It's for Real / Epic PE-34668**
Because they're from Asbury Park, New Jersey, are produced by Miami's Steve Van Zandt of the E Street Band, and have recorded several of Bruce Springsteen's songs, Southside Johnny and the Asbury Jukes have been identified with Springsteen's musical style. This is far from an apt comparison: Springsteen's antecedents are much broader than this combination of doo-wop and Stax/New Orleans rhythm & blues.

But all of these records are charming, and with *Hearts of Stone,* Southside and Van Zandt have begun to exert a vision of their own. The first album, *Go Home,* which features Springsteen's monumental "The Fever" and guest appearances by Lee Dorsey and Ronnie Spector, is perhaps slightly superior to the second for its energy and enthusiasm, although *This Time* has better Van Zandt material. But the group's best LP is *Hearts* : the horns have the punch of rock & roll guitars; Southside sings with great assurance; the material is superlative (the Springsteen title track and Van Zandt's "This Time Baby" are pop songs Leiber and Stoller could envy); and the rhythm and guitar sections have all the drive great rock requires. — D.M.

SPARKS
★★ **Big Beat / Col. PC-34359**
★ **Introducing Sparks / Col. PC-34901**
★★ **Kimono My House / Is. 9272**
★ **Sparks / Bears. 2048**
★ **Woofer in Tweeter's Clothing / Bears. 2110**
All-American weirdos Ron and Russ Mael (*Sparks*) go to England to get rich and famous (*Woofer in Tweeter's Clothing*). The objective is to hit it big in a foreign land and then return home to conquer the masses who ignored them before they went to England to get rich and famous. The plan goes awry when they bomb in the U.S. after scoring hits in the U.K. (*Kimono My House*). They decide to move back home to California, assuming that the failure was caused by losing touch with their roots. They abandon the speeded-up music-hall approach and opt for somewhat less *outré* rock (*Big Beat*). No one seems to care. They then decide to start from scratch again (*Introducing Sparks*), but old fans have disappeared and new ones are few and far between.

Docked one star per album for being somewhat responsible for Queen. — B.A.

PHIL SPECTOR
★★★★★ **Phil Spector's Christmas LP /**
  Spector 9103
★★★★★ **Phil Spector's Greatest Hits /**
  Spector 2SP 9104

Both of these albums contain performances by a variety of artists, but they are really the result of only one man's work and vision. Phil Spector, rock's first boy genius, made the producer a cult hero with his Sixties Wall of Sound singles on his own Philles Records. (Earlier, he had been the protégé of Leiber and Stoller and had worked with the Drifters and Ben E. King.) The *Christmas* album is a masterpiece of sentimentality that achieves a trio of unbelievable peaks: Darlene Love's keening "Christmas (Baby Please Come Home)"; the Crystals' atomic reworking of "Santa Claus Is Comin' to Town"; Spector's maudlin voiceover "thank you" and benediction on the final track, "Silent Night," which presages Simon and Garfunkel's *Parsley, Sage, Rosemary and Thyme* move by several years.

The cream, though, is really on *Greatest Hits.* Spector's good-bad-but-not-evil genius was perfectly suited to singles, so the compilation album is his grandest idiom. This package includes the best songs he did with the Ronettes ("Be My Baby," "Walking in the Rain" and "Baby, I Love You"), the Crystals ("Da Doo Ron Ron," "Then He Kissed Me," "He's a Rebel," "Uptown"), and Darlene Love ("[Today I Met] The Boy I'm Gonna Marry," "Wait 'Til My Bobby Gets Home"), who were his major performers at Philles. Also on the LP are majestically paranoid Righteous Brothers hits ("You've Lost That Lovin' Feelin'," "Unchained Melody," "Just Once in My Life," "Ebb Tide") and a host of one-shots: a bizarre version of "Zip-a-Dee-Doo-Dah" by Bobb B. Soxx and the Blue Jeans; Curtis Lee's swinging "Pretty Little Angel Eyes"; the Teddy Bears' "To Know Him Is to Love Him," Spector's initial hit and the one for which he took the title from his father's tombstone; Ike and Tina Turner's classic flop, "River Deep—Mountain High," the most overrated rock single ever made; and a final blast of bombast, Sonny Charles and the Checkmates' "Black Pearl." Genius in every groove, and only one sin: Spector must be the only man in the world who thinks he produced Ben E. King's "Spanish Harlem," as well as co-writing it with Jerry Leiber. — D.M.

CHRIS SPEDDING
★★★ **Chris Spedding / EMI SRAK-519**
Superlative English session guitarist hoisted by his own petard: should he go for the Anglo-flash technique he helped pioneer or the raw rock & roll he obviously admires? The answer is to the left of Dave Edmunds and the right of Brian Eno, which ain't nowhere, but also isn't terribly satisfying. — D.M.

JIMMIE SPHEERIS
★ **Isle of View / Col. C-30988**
★ **Jimmie Spheeris / Col. KC-32157**
★ **Ports of the Heart / Epic PE-34276**
★ **The Dragon Is Dancing / Epic**
  PE-33565
The hippie ethic refuses to die, as demonstrated by the catalogue of this character, so laid-back that he gives new meaning to the word limpid. — D.M.

SPIDER-MAN
★ **Rock Reflections of a Superhero / Lifes.**
  6001
This was the second attempt by Marvel Comics' Stan Lee to marry his most popular comic-book character to the rock audience. (The first was *The Amazing Spider-Man*, which Buddah billed as the first rock-comic, before cutting it out of its catalogue. But Buddah President Neil Bogart went on to put out more comics, with Kiss.) A bunch of competent New York studio musicians help make this a sprightly, passable rock album, despite Stan Lee's lifeless narration. John Romita, one of the top artists in Marvel's stable, does the cover art, and the best thing about the album (perhaps because it's visual) are his depictions of our favorite superheroes in the studio: The Incredible Hulk on Drums! Mighty Thor on Trumpet! Background Vocals by the Fantastic Four! And Strings by Conan and the Barbarians! (Now deleted.) — G.K.

SPINNERS
★ **Happiness Is Being with the Spinners /**
   Atl. 18181
★★★★ **Mighty Love / Atl. 7296**
★★★ **New and Improved Spinners / Atl.**
   18118
★★★★★ **Pick of the Litter / Atl. 18141**
★★★★★ **Spinners / Atl. 7256**
★★ **Spinners/8 / Atl. 19146**
★★★★ **Spinners Live / Atl. 2-910**
★★★★ **The Best of the Spinners / Atl.**
   19179
★★ **Yesterday, Today and Tomorrow / Atl.**
   19100

A decade ago, trying to analyze his feelings
about the two most fashionable New Wave
film directors, critic Andrew Sarris concluded that while Jean-Luc Godard was
decidedly more brilliant, more innovative
and more profound, as time went by, the
gentle, leisurely insights of François Truf-
faut became more valued. I don't think the
metaphor has to be stretched very far to
apply to the Spinners. They've never received the praise addressed to the O'Jays,
the Blue Notes or Al Green; the very
smoothness and gentleness in their music
has often been used against them. Yet few
soul albums of the Seventies are as genuinely pleasurable as *Pick of the Litter,
Mighty Love* and *Spinners.* The critic inside
us tends to condemn them for being so instantly likable, so easy to listen to. But the
Spinners have a definite, strong resonance
and an intelligence that goes deeper than
their supposedly bubblegum surface.

The key to their success has always been
writer/producer/arranger Thom Bell. He
saw in the Spinners a chance to expand beyond the overly ornate falsetto groups he
had previously worked with (the Delfonics,
for example). *Spinners,* their first album,
contains four classic singles—"I'll Be
Around," "Could It Be I'm Falling in
Love," "One of a Kind (Love Affair)" and
the meditative "How Could I Let You Get
Away." It still sounds more like a collection of singles than a genuinely conceptual
album, but the singles are so great that it
hardly matters.

On *Mighty Love,* Bell created his first listenable and coherent LP, allowing Philippe
Wynne to stretch out and explore his gospel roots. *New and Improved* sounds a bit
old and tired and is salvaged mainly by
Dionne Warwick's guest shot on "Then
Came You." On that number, the Bell/
Spinners style—with its call-and-response
structure imposed upon cascading strings
and vocal backups—reaches its pinnacle.
Pick of the Litter was the collaboration's

last great success; there are no monumental
songs on it, but the group sang with utter
professionalism. And many of the songs
are very good: "Just as Long as We Have
Love" with Warwick, and "Honest I Do,"
for example. There's something so tight
about the record, including its deep understanding of counterpoint, the grace with
which the singers switch leads and, most of
all, its ability to express joy simply and
directly.

Despite awkward orchestrations and a
lame rhythm section, the *Live* album allowed Wynne to show off on the ballads.
Happiness was the beginning of the end, although *Yesterday, Today and Tomorrow* is
in many respects worse, save for Wynne's
swan song, "Throwing a Good Love
Away," a number that owes as much to
Gene Kelly as Otis Redding, but nevertheless works.

Spinners/8 features Jonathan Edwards
replacing Wynne. Edwards is monstrously
talented—he plays Willie Mays to Wynne's
cool Joe DiMaggio—and onstage he can
really spark the group, but Bell seems at a
loss for what to do with him here. The
sound never jells; if it did, the Spinners
could still deliver a plenitude of pleasure.
The 1978 anthology of hits certainly does,
though not so much as *Spinners, Mighty
Love* and *Litter,* which have a force all
their own. — R.G.

DAVID SPINOZZA
★★★ **Spinozza / A&M 4677**
Hot young New York session guitarist
turns in a surprisingly effective set of jazz
rock. Powerful and concise like Spinozza's
best backup work. — D.M.

SPIRIT
★★★★ **Best of Spirit / Epic KE-32271**
★ **Feedback / Epic E-31175**

★★★★ **Spirit** / Epic EG-31457
★★★ **The Family That Plays Together** /
Epic E-31461
★★★★ **Twelve Dreams of Dr. Sardoni-**
cus / Epic PE-30267

Spirit was one of the strangest and best bands to come out of the anything-goes attitude that surrounded California rock in the late Sixties. Drummer Ed Cassidy was a jazz journeyman who'd played with Gerry Mulligan, Thelonious Monk and Cannonball Adderley and was old enough to be the father of all the other players in the band. In fact, he later became the stepfather of Spirit's guitarist, Randy California, who studied with Jimi Hendrix just as that guitarist was codifying his amazing style. Keyboardist John Locke, bassist Mark Andes and vocalist Jay Ferguson rounded out a strange lineup that played jazz-rock hybrid long before anyone thought of matching those styles.

Best of, which duplicates the first album but adds the otherwise unavailable *Clear Spirit,* is recommended. *The Family That Plays Together* includes the group's most accessible single, "I Got a Line on You." *Twelve Dreams* is the band's most adventurous and probably best record, notable for advanced production technique and a few excellent songs: "Nothin' to Hide," "Nature's Way," "Animal Zoo" and "Mr. Skin." The band splintered, Ferguson and Andes forming Jo Jo Gunne, California going solo, while Cassidy recruited new players and kept on. *Feedback* is all that remains from that period.

Cassidy and California later re-formed Spirit to record for Mercury, but the records were parodies of the band's former greatness, laying out every psychedelic cliché imaginable. All of them are now deleted. — J.S.

SPLIT ENZ
★★★ **Dizrhythmia** / Chrys. 1145
★★★ **Mental Notes** / Chrys. 1131

Impressive, wacky avant-garde rock from New Zealand. Sort of the Bonzo Dog Band of Down Under, although the more obvious debt is to the Australian group Skyhooks. — D.M.

SPLINTER
★★ **Two Man Band** / Dark 3073

George Harrison discovery. Placid, pleasant, purposeless. — D.M.

MARK SPOELSTRA
★ **Mark Spoelstra** / Folk. 3572

In the Sixties folk movement, Spoelstra was known for having done alternative service time as a conscientious objector, long before Vietnam became a hot issue. This gave his first records for Elektra special interest, but by the time he made this early-Seventies Folkways album, Spoelstra seemed just another dated folkie, locked permanently out of time with too much integrity and not enough music to get him to the next stop. — D.M.

SPOOKY TOOTH
★ **Ceremony** / A&M 4225
★★★★ **Spooky Two** / A&M 4194
★★★★ **The Last Puff** / A&M 4266
★★ **The Mirror** / Is. 9292
★★★ **Tobacco Road** / A&M 4300
★★★ **You Broke My Heart So I Busted Your Jaw** / A&M 4385

If there was ever a *heavy* band, Spooky Tooth had to be it. Featuring two vocalists prone to blues-wrenching extremes (Gary Wright and Mike Harrison) and an instrumental attack composed of awesomely loud keyboards and guitars, Spooky Tooth came on like an overwhelming vat of premedicated goo. *Tobacco Road,* which put the title tune and Janis Ian's "Society's Child" into this bluesy heavy-metal context, contained the germ of the style. But with *Spooky Two,* the band applied the bombastic combination with more dramatic panache; the result is an album that's still heavy after all these years.

Spooky Two's blockbuster was "Evil Woman," with growling stretches of lead guitar roaring out of the song's belly, which itself was framed by a cathedral-loud blues organ. Totally overdone, and perhaps because of that, a total knockout. Whether it was a ballad ("Hangman Hang My Shell on a Tree") or riff-rocker ("Better by You, Better by Me"), *Spooky Two* played it at full throttle. Similarly, *Ceremony,* a concept LP done with the French electronic musician Pierre Henry, went full tilt; the cumbersome musical and lyrical concept made this last album sound like it was done by a bunch of gentle-hearted folkies. *Ceremony* was a dreadful musical and commercial tailspin; Gary Wright left to go solo.

Harrison re-formed Spooky Tooth to include guitarist Henry McCulloch and keyboardist Chris Stainton from the Grease Band; the album that resulted, *The Last Puff,* was a smashing comeback, though it failed to revive the commercial fires. A spritely cover of Elton John's "Son of

0

Your Father" and a doomsday interpretation of the Beatles' "I Am the Walrus" brandished all the chutzpah of the best Spooky Tooth. Though subsequent moments would sometimes hit these peaks (Harrison rejoined for *You Broke My Heart* and left the memorable "Wildfire"; Mick Jones was a part of this band), Spooky Tooth would remain the right band at the wrong time. — J.B.M.

DUSTY SPRINGFIELD

★★★★ **Dusty Springfield's Golden Hits /**
Phi. 600220
★★★ **It Begins Again / U. Artists**
LA791-H
★★ **Never Trust a Man in a Rented Tux-**
edo / U. Artists LA932-H

Dusty Springfield was one of the most ingratiating of the Sixties "girl" singers—the breathy romanticism of her hits ("I Only Want to Be with You," "Stay Awhile," "You Don't Have to Say You Love Me" "Wishin' and Hopin' ") demands she be thought of as a girl, rather than a woman, too. Those hits are on the Philips LP.

Since then, Springfield has been recorded several times in a more mature style, as a sort of rock & roll Peggy Lee. Only the United Artists attempts remain in the catalogue, and they're rather bland. But her (deleted) 1969 Atlantic LP, *Dusty in Memphis,* was a genuine pop classic, including a version of "Son of a Preacher Man" that comes close to cutting Aretha Franklin's. — D.M.

BRUCE SPRINGSTEEN

★★★★★ **Born to Run / Col. PC-33795**
★★★★★ **Darkness on the Edge of Town /**
Col. JC-35318
★★★ **Greetings from Asbury Park, New**
Jersey / Col. KC-31093
★★★★ **The Wild, the Innocent, and the E**
Street Shuffle / Col. PC-32432

Record companies often like to tout verbally imaginative young songwriters as "the new Bob Dylan," which is a phrase now widely regarded as the kiss of death. Among many other things, Bruce Springsteen is the exception that proves the rule. He is the most brilliant American rock & roll performer of this decade, with a truly remarkable verbal facility. But Springsteen's lyrical talent is only the equal of his strengths as a composer, as a live performer and as a guitarist. Although Columbia pushed his *Greetings* debut as a "Dylan"-styled album because of its astonishing verbosity, Springsteen was a rocker

from the beginning, in a league with English writer/performers like Keith Richards, Pete Townshend and Van Morrison. He was much more than any postfolkie word wizard.

Greetings is a collection of excellent songs whose public rejection has more to do with overhype and underproduction than with the music that's on it. Springsteen immediately established his feel for both street scenes and human relationships in such songs as "Growin' Up," "For You" and "Blinded by the Light." The latter became a hit (in a bowdlerized version) for Manfred Mann's Earth Band in 1976. Springsteen's producer wanted a singer/songwriter-oriented album, and the conflict between this approach and the performer's R&B and English rock roots finally drags the record down, but not without some remarkable moments.

The Wild, the Innocent, and the E Street Shuffle, released in late 1973, resolved the musical conflict, leaving Springsteen with a fine soul-based band to complement a set of songs intimately linked conceptually. Side two of this album is practically a suite, beginning and ending with scenes of urban poverty and romance ("Incident on 57th Street," "New York City Serenade"); the rock anthem "Rosalita," a hilarious statement of purpose, is sandwiched between them. Springsteen continued his interest in both character and narrative in the lyrics, and his song structures, which used multiple bridges, varying choruses and meter stretched until it almost snapped, were easily the most influential and inventive since Van Morrison's.

Still, *Wild* had little or no commercial impact, despite the fact that Springsteen's stage show had attracted a particularly rabid cult in the Northeast and among critics. *Born to Run,* released in September 1975, was so widely anticipated that it landed Springsteen on the covers of both *Time* and *Newsweek* during the same week in October. The album popped him loose commercially and with good reason: it is a production masterpiece, a celebration of the joys of the street, rock & roll and the ecstasy of life lived on its sweet edge.

Born to Run was a concept album in every important sense—its Phil Spector-influenced production gave it a continuity of sound, and the progression from the opening "Thunder Road" to the final "Jungleland" was not only diurnal but (despite the many characters involved) really one long story. But in achieving this homogeneity of purpose, Springsteen sacrificed nothing, made no concessions to nonrock: "Born to Run," the record's hit single, is the crust of classic rock & roll, and numbers like "Backstreets," "She's the One" and "Tenth Avenue Freezeout" dig even deeper. *Born to Run* was Springsteen's assertion that he could do it all, that he was not just another rocker but a truly great one; clarity of purpose and mammoth ambition drip from the grooves.

Springsteen did not release another LP until the late spring of 1978. *Darkness on the Edge of Town* rejected the production embellishments of *Born to Run* for a hardnosed sound driven by Springsteen's furious guitar and aching vocals. On it, the E Street Band, Springsteen's backing group, could finally be heard as one of rock's great supporting combos, but more importantly, both music and lyrics told stories that meant that Springsteen had begun to reach maturity. The bite of *Darkness* makes the Spectoresque *Born to Run* sound practically mushy; Springsteen finally begins to assert himself as a guitarist in the spirit of Jimi Hendrix and Jimmy Page. In the lyrics, he evidences a perspective that is newly mature and more deeply compassionate than his earlier fantasies of a sweet life. *Darkness* is in some sense an album about revenge—"Adam Raised a Cain" is its keynote—but it is also filled with innocence and hope and compassion: Springsteen asserts both the pain of lost innocence and the ache of a hope against hope.

There is a messianic streak to all Springsteen criticism; this occurs mostly because he seems, to his fans, so much the fulfillment of the hopes and dreams of the rock tradition as handed down from Presley. Time will judge that matter more clearly, but for now, Springsteen is unquestionably a major force in the development of that tradition. — D.M.

CHRIS SQUIRE
★★★★ **Fish Out of Water / Atl. 18159**
The Yes bassist presents a fine approximation of the whole group, even down to his Jon Anderson–inspired singing. Squire prefers long cuts that excellently and subtly vary the same passage. His loud, thick bass is both an anchor and a lead instrument; few guitars, lots of majestic orchestrations. Ex-Yes member Bill Bruford is on drums. — C.W.

STACKRIDGE
★★★ **Extravaganza / Sire D-7509**

Short songs with smart melodic twists and chord changes; tight, varied and colorful ensemble playing with few solo excursions. A piano centers most arrangements; guitars and brass also appear. Hints of music-hall-inspired gaiety, as well as art-rock grandeur and exoticism. (Now deleted.) — C.W.

JIM STAFFORD
★ **Jim Stafford / Poly. 6072**
Stafford enjoyed a brief mid-Seventies vogue, which earned him a summer replacement TV show and a hit record, "Spiders and Snakes," a wretched pop interpretation of the Garden of Eden story. If you must, the hit's here—along with gallons of other garbage. — D.M.

STALLION
■ **Hey Everybody / Casa. 7083**
■ **Stallion / Casa. 7040**
Imitation Chicago. The worst. — S.H.

MICHAEL STANLEY BAND
★★ **Cabin Fever / Ari. 4182**
★ **Friends and Legends / MCA 372**
★★★ **Ladies' Choice / Epic 33917**
★★★ **Stagepass / Epic 34661**
★★ **You Break It . . . You Bought It / Epic PE-33492**
Although it has yet to make a dent outside its native Ohio, MSB is a competent band, though it's hampered by the lack of a unique sound. *Friends and Legends* was actually a Stanley solo album, released in 1973, before he put the group together. *You Break It,* released in 1975, is pleasant but restrained; *Ladies' Choice* (1976) is more adventurous, with solid riffs, some added and well-done synthesizer work and even a dash of reeds. Like most live albums, *Stagepass* is a good souvenir for staunch

fans but offers little for the uninitiated. — A.N.

MAVIS STAPLES
★★★ **A Piece of the Action / Cur. 5019**
As the lead singer with the Staple Singers,
Mavis Staples is one of the most remarkable voices in soul and gospel. On this
soundtrack album produced by Curtis
Mayfield, unfortunately, she is rather un-
derutilized. There are high points here, but
they pop up infrequently and unexpectedly
from the tepid vocal and instrumental riffing that fills out the disc. — D.M.

STARBUCK
★★★ **Rock 'n' Roll Rocket / Priv. 2027**
★★★ **Searching for a Thrill / U. Artists
LA918-H**
Atlanta-based seven-piece pop group
scored a 1976 hit with "Moonlight Feels
Right." Generally the band is thin-sound-
ing but with some good ideas; slick pro-
duction is provided by Steve Clark and
Rodney Mills at the Atlanta Rhythm
Section's Studio One in Doraville,
Georgia. — J.S.

STARCASTLE
★★ **Citadel / Epic PE-34935**
★★ **Fountains of Light / Epic PE-34375**
★ **Real to Reel / Epic JE-35441**
★ **Starcastle / Epic PE-33914**
Starcastle is one of those pre-Boston
American bands that couldn't quite come
up with a distinctive synthesis of English
progressive rock. In desperation (or inspiration, depending on your taste), the group
became an almost completely literal, note-
for-note copy of Yes. This has brought
them a bit of success, though someday,
public memory being what it is, it may result in a windfall. — D.M.

STARDRIVE
★ **Stardrive / Col. KC-33047**
A nightmare at the planetarium. (Now
deleted.) — J.S.

STARLAND VOCAL BAND
■ **Late Night Radio / Wind. BXL1-2598**
■ **Rear View Mirror / Wind. BXL1-2239**
■ **Starland Vocal Band / Wind.
BXL1-1351**
John Denver's first payoff from having his
own record label was this group, which
scored with a bouncy piece of meringue,
"Afternoon Delight," in the summer of
1976. Denver did this stuff better, a judg-
ment one can't often make. Starland is as

nearly worthless as anything that ever hit
the charts. — D.M.

EDWIN STARR
★★ **Clean / 20th Cent. 559**
★★ **Edwin Starr / 20th Cent. 538**
As a minor-league Motown singer, Starr
had a couple of fine moments in the late
Sixties: "25 Miles" was a good Wilson
Pickett derivative, and "War" helped introduce social commentary into soul. But
these middle-Seventies albums reduce
Starr's once-powerful voice to a mannerism, and the arrangements don't give him
the space to belt. Look for the old
stuff. — D.M.

RINGO STARR
★★ **Bad Boy / Por. JR-35378**
★★★ **Beaucoups of Blues / Cap.
SMAS-3368**
★★★ **Blast from Your Past / Cap.
SW-3422**
★★★ **Goodnight Vienna / Cap. SW-3417**
★★★★★ **Ringo / Cap. SWAL-3413**
★★ **Ringo's Rotogravure / Atco 18193**
★★ **Ringo the 4th / Atco 19108**
★★★ **Sentimental Journey / Cap.
SW-3365**
Of all the Beatles, Ringo Starr seemed the
least likely to pursue a successful solo ca-
reer after the group broke up. His first solo
records were accordingly strange—*Senti-
mental Journey,* a catalogue of pop stan-
dards done with lush string arrangements,
and *Beaucoups of Blues,* a straight country
album produced by Pete Drake.
  Then producer Richard Perry assembled
a spectacle of an album around the goofy
Beatles drummer, and when the dust settled, *Ringo* yielded two blockbuster singles,
"Photograph" and "You're Sixteen." Ringo's solo career was made. *Goodnight Vienna,* the followup, included a cameo by
John Lennon on the title track, which he
wrote, and another hit with "Nono Song."
Despite ambitious production and able studio backing, Ringo's albums for Atco and
Portrait are lifeless, much inferior to the
Capitol solos. *Blast* is a nice greatest-hits
set that includes the previously unavailable
single written about the Beatles breakup,
"Early 1970." — J.S.

RUBY STARR AND GREY GHOST
★ **Ruby Starr and Grey Ghost / Cap.
ST-11427**
★ **Smokey Places / Cap. ST-11643**
Starr and company hung out a lot with
Black Oak Arkansas, which must make her

some sort of heavy-metal queen. If she had a voice that sounded less like a power-driven socket wrench, these wretched discs might have had a chance. But she didn't. — D.M.

STARRY EYED AND LAUGHING
★★ Thought Talk / Col. PC-33837
A mediocre Byrds imitation. (Now deleted.) — J.S.

STARWOOD
■ Homebrew / Wind. BHL1-1125
■ Starwood / Col. PC-34785
More useless than Starland Vocal Band, if only because it never even hit the charts, Starwood is John Denver's idea of a rock act, I think. — D.M.

STARZ
■ Attention Shoppers / Cap. ST-11730
■ Coliseum Rock / Cap. ST-11861
■ Starz / Cap. ST-11539
■ Violation / Cap. SW-11617
Miniaturized Kiss, in comparatively worse taste. — J.S.

CANDI STATON
★★ House of Love / War. K-3207
★★ Music Speaks Louder than Words / War. B-3040
★★ Young Hearts Run Free / War. B-2948
Candi Staton's early, Rick Hall–produced recordings (for Fame) remain her best work, though all are out of print. These albums feature different producers, none wholly sympathetic to Staton's special gifts, although "Young Hearts Run Free" was a 1976 pop hit. Bob Monaco, producer of *Music,* sabotages the singer with watery charts, while Dave Crawford, who did the other two LPs, found himself so bankrupt for rhythm ideas that he used the same me-

lodic hook on three *Young Hearts* songs. The most impressive item here is a beautiful gospel song, "Take My Hand, Precious Lord" on *House of Love.* — J.MC.

STATUS QUO
★★★ Hello / A&M 3615
★★★ Live / Cap. SKBB-11623
★★★ On the Level / Cap. ST-11381
★★★ Piledriver / A&M 4381
★★★ Quo / A&M 3649
★★★ Rockin' All Over the World / Cap. ST-11749
★★★ Status Quo / Cap. ST-11509
In 1968, Status Quo had a worldwide hit with "Pictures of Matchstick Men," a phased-guitar rocker. They did not resurface until 1972, having changed in the meantime from arty pop to full-tilt boogie band. *Piledriver,* with riff-riddled boogie grunge like "Don't Waste My Time" and "Oh Baby," inspired massive boot-thumping in England and a somewhat smaller following in the U.S. The rest of the records repeat the formula: strongly accented beat with noxiously simple guitar chords and a few shouted catch phrases. — A.N.

STEELEYE SPAN
★★★★ All Around My Hat / Chrys. 1091
★★★ Below the Salt / Chrys. 1008
★★★★ Commoner's Crown / Chrys. 1071
★★★★ Hark! The Village Wait / Chrys. 1120
★★★★ Now We Are Six / Chrys. 1053
★★★ Parcel of Rogues / Chrys. 1046
★★★★ Please to See the King / Chrys. 1119
★★ Rocket Cottage / Chrys. 1123
★★★ Storm Force Ten / Chrys. 1151
★★★★ Ten Man Mop or Mr. Reservoir Butler Rides Again / Chrys. 1121
★★★★ The Steeleye Span Story—Original Masters / Chrys. 2-1136
Steeleye Span was one of the earliest and most prolific groups to combine rock with traditional British Isles folk music. *Hark! The Village Wait* featured acoustic fretted instruments with lots of vocal harmonies; occasional electricity, as well as a session drummer, gave the rock setting. Two duos—Gay and Terry Woods, Tim Hart and Maddy Prior—provided depth and variety; ex-Fairport Conventioneer Ashley Hutchings played bass.

The Woodses then left. Martin Carthy, a mainstay in acoustic folk until then, and fiddler Peter Knight joined. *Please to See the King* and *Ten Man Mop* gave the quintet a sharper, more electric timbre, with

Prior's vocals in the forefront. No drummer appeared, but the group often utilized miscellaneous percussion instruments for strong rhythm.

Hutchings then left, as did Carthy, and the group took a decidedly more muscular, rockish turn. But newcomer Bob Johnson's electric guitar was too loud and raw. The previous subtlety and distinction were gone, and thus *Below the Salt* and *Parcel of Rogues* suffered: these have the same spirit, but a somewhat different and inferior presentation.

Now We Are Six added Nigel Pegrum on drums, as well as wind instruments and even synthesizer, and Steeleye Span had never sounded better or cleverer. But three throwaways—two cuts from a primary-school choir and an inexplicable remake of "To Know Him Is to Love Him," with David Bowie on saxophone—marred the album. Technically, however, the record benefited from its production consultant: Ian Anderson of Jethro Tull.

Commoner's Crown topped them all: thoughtful, imaginative and varied arranging—a masterful synthesis of folk and rock, neither overshadowing the other. Peter Sellers, of all people, added a slice of whimsy to one cut.

All Around My Hat plunged more deeply into rock, largely through Mike Batt's production and louder guitars. For the first time, Steeleye Span sounded like rock turning to folk, rather than the reverse—a less adventurous approach perhaps, yet handled well. But *Rocket Cottage* continued the trend to a poor end. The six were heavy-handed, almost clumsy—a pale reduction of their past triumphs.

Story is an excellent two-record set spanning all previous albums. — C.W.

STEELY DAN
★★★ **Aja / ABC 1006**
★★★★ **Can't Buy a Thrill / ABC 788**
★★★★ **Countdown to Ecstasy / ABC 779**
★★★ **Katy Lied / ABC D-846**
★★★★ **Pretzel Logic / ABC D-808**
★★★ **The Royal Scam / ABC D-931**
Steely Dan's first two albums (*Can't* and *Countdown*) presented the group as a polished studio rock band, which scored a couple of hit singles, including "Do It Again" and "Reeling in the Years," despite a penchant for obscure lyrics and dissonant guitar patterns. With *Pretzel Logic*, the dissonance and beatnik poesy began to take over, and while the band was still capable of something as fine as "Rikki Don't Lose That Number," it was also growing much more pompous.

After *Pretzel*, Steely Dan became the exclusive province of songwriters Walter Becker and Donald Fagen; the results, *Katy Lied* and *Royal Scam*, have been defended as innovation and as ideology, but not necessarily as listenable. Steely Dan's art rock was by now edging ever closer to jazz, the vocals had deteriorated, the lyrics were often obscure for their own sake and the group's stature seemed to infect the records with an unparalleled pretentiousness. *Aja*, the most recent album, reflects some musical lightening up: it is more frankly into musical merger, with less pretense about being a rock band and with liner notes just sophomoric enough to undercut the grad-school inflations of the lyrics. Not the greatest American rock band (by a long shot), Steely Dan remains unquestionably the weirdest. — D.M.

DIANNE STEINBERG
★★★ **Universal Child / ABC 1011**
How does the daughter of a soul-queen disc jockey (Detroit's legendary Martha Jean the Queen) make a soulless pop record? Easy: she gets hooked up with a true mediocrity like David Pomeranz. Fortunately, Steinberg's first album, for Atlantic, was somewhat better; unfortunately, but quite naturally, it's deleted. Her appearance in the *Sgt. Pepper* film ought to discredit her forever, though. — D.M.

STEPPENWOLF
★★★ **ABC Collection / ABC AC 30008**
★ **At Your Birthday Party / Dun. X-50053**
★ **Early Steppenwolf / Dun. X-50060**
★★ **For Ladies Only / Dun. X-50110**
★ **Hour of the Wolf / Epic PE-33583**

★ **Reborn to Be Wild / Epic PE-34382**
★★★ **16 Greatest Hits / Dun. X-50135**
★★★ **16 Great Performances / ABC
D-4011**
★★★★ **Steppenwolf / Dun. X-50029**
★★★ **Steppenwolf Gold / Dun. X-50099**
★★ **Steppenwolf Live / Dun. X-50075**
★ **Steppenwolf Seven / Dun. X-50090**
★★★ **Steppenwolf the Second / Dun.
X-50037**

Steppenwolf evolved from a Canadian group of legendary freneticism, Sparrow. Their first two albums made them mid-Sixties biker favorites, thanks to such items as "Born to Be Wild" and "Magic Carpet Ride." Leader John Kay then tried his hand at a political-commentary concept album (the awful and deleted *Monster*) and trailed off into anachronism, moving from Dunhill to Epic along the way. The self-titled first LP (50029) remains the best, and should be picked up in lieu of one of the virtually identical greatest-hits repackages. — J.S.

CAT STEVENS
★★ **Buddah and the Chocolate Box /
A&M 3623**
★★★ **Catch Bull at Four / A&M 4365**
★★★ **Cat's Cradle / Lon. LC-50010**
★★★★ **Cat Stevens' Greatest Hits / A&M
4519**
★★ **Foreigner / A&M 4391**
★ **Izitso / A&M 4702**
★★★ **Mona Bone Jakon / A&M 4260**
★ **Numbers / A&M 4555**
★★★★ **Tea for the Tillerman / A&M 4280**
★★★ **Teaser and the Firecat / A&M 4313**

Stevens began recording for Deram (now released on London) in 1966; his second single, "Matthew and Son," was a Top Ten hit in his native England in 1967. But in 1968, Stevens contracted tuberculosis and spent a year recuperating in a clinic. He recovered in time to release *Mona Bone Jakon* in 1970, perfectly timed for the beginning of the singer/songwriter era.

Stevens was recording with a basic rock band (guitar, bass and drums), and together with producer Paul Samwell-Smith they made his next album, *Tea for the Tillerman,* a classic of British pop. Stevens had a knack for writing sensitive but straightforward songs like "Father and Son" and his first American hit, "Wild World." The album established him in America. *Tea* was followed by another strong set, *Teaser and the Firecat.* But since then, he's become infatuated with Eastern mysticism, numerology and a pretentious, light classical mu-

sical approach. He has not handled much of this complexity well, and the simple warmth of his early songs is now buried in a mass of needless ostentation. — D.M.

RAY STEVENS
★★ **Feel the Music / War. B-2997**
★★ **Just for the Record / War. B-2914**
★★ **Nashville / Barn. 5005**
★★★ **Ray Stevens' Greatest Hits / Barn.
5004**
★★★ **Very Best of Ray Stevens / Barn.
6018**

Stevens began his career as a rock novelty singer whose biggest hit was a semibrilliant comic turn, "Ahab the Arab," recorded back about 1962; phase two (the Barnaby LPs) found him a pop-country singer with several hits on the C&W chart; phase three finds him floundering at Warner Bros., not turning out anything distinctive. The "Ahab" era novelties are on Barnaby's hits anthologies, but in rerecorded versions; search for Mercury's cutouts, which have the originals and a spark of imagination. — D.M.

B. W. STEVENSON
★★ **B. W. Stevenson / RCA AFL1-4685**
★ **Lost Feeling / War. B-3012**
★★ **The Best of B. W. Stevenson / RCA
APL1-2394**

Stevenson clicked in 1973 with "My Maria" and "Shambala," both on the RCA albums. These were the very best sort of folkish Seventies rock: tough vocals, driving backings. They deserved their chart status. Unfortunately, since moving to Warner Bros. he has not come up with anything half so interesting. — D.M.

AL STEWART
★★ **Modern Times / Janus 7012**

★★ Past, Present and Future / Janus 3063
★★ The Early Years / Janus 2-7026
★★★★ The Year of the Cat / Janus 7072
★★★ Time Passages / Ari. 4190

Scottish singer/songwriter who has been recording for a decade but enjoyed his biggest success with the title song from *The Year of the Cat,* in 1976. *Past, Present and Future* is a concept album about European history, though Stewart seems without the insight to make such an outrageous proposition more than amusing. The Arista album is his most recent. — D.M.

BARON STEWART
★★ Bartering / U. Artists LA419-G

California singer/songwriter with a soft spot in his heart for ducks. (Now deleted.) — J.S.

BILLY STEWART
★★★★ Billy Stewart Remembered / Chess 1547
★★★ Billy Stewart Teaches Old Standards New Tricks / Chess 1513
★★★ Cross My Heart / Cadet 50059
★★★ I Do Love You / Chess 1496
★★★ Summertime / Chess 1499

Stewart had perhaps the most eccentric vocal style in the history of soul. He weighed 300 pounds, but his range was extremely high and he was capable of amazing trills at the upper end of it. Such glossolalia brought an extremely weird dimension to "Summertime," the *Porgy and Bess* standard he made a hit in 1966. That, and "I Do Love You," a hit in both 1965 and 1969, were the highlights of his career. Stewart died in 1960. (Now deleted.) — D.M.

GARY STEWART
★★★ Little Junior / RCA AHL1-2779
★★★★ Out of Hand / RCA APL1-0900
★★★ Steppin' Out / RCA AHL1-1225
★★★ You're Not the Woman You Used to Be / MCA 488
★★★★ Your Place or Mine / RCA AHL1-2199

For anyone who likes both honky-tonkin' country music and basic rock & roll, Gary Stewart is a dream come true. He combines both genres seamlessly into something more elusive than ordinary country rock. His ferocious mountain tenor, heavy on the vibrato, attacks songs like a rocker's voice, but his records are clearly a product of Nashville (although they've progressed away from the Music City mainstream). Stewart sings drinking, fighting and cheating songs, but he keeps his distance: he's paying tribute to the country forms he loves, not singing about himself.

The MCA album is old demos released after he became a star; the singing is vibrant but not fully developed. But the songs represent his most fanciful storytelling on record. Of the RCA albums, *Out of Hand* is an unbeatable collection of honky-tonk songs on which his singing overcomes a slightly muddled production. *Steppin' Out* is a more self-conscious country primer: a bluegrass song, a standard, some stinging Southern rock, some "progressive" songs. *Your Place* is Stewart's most subtly distinctive yet—big-beat country that's harmonically reminiscent of *Blonde on Blonde* (of all things); on the up-tempo numbers, Stewart's singing even evokes the mid-Sixties Dylan. *Little Junior* isn't quite that fine, but it does reflect Stewart's growing comfort with his unique formal merger. — J.MO.

JOHN STEWART
★★★ California Bloodlines / Cap. SM-203
★★ Cannons in the Rain / RCA AFL1-4827
★★ Fire in the Wind / RSO 1-3027
★★★ Phoenix Concerts / RCA CPL2-0265
★ Willard / Cap. ST-540
★ Wingless Angels / RCA APL1-0816

One man's Americana, deeper than John Denver's, but still laced with corn, appropriately enough for a former member of the Kingston Trio. — S.H.

ROD STEWART
★★★★ A Night on the Town / War. K-3116
★★★★ Atlantic Crossing / War. K-2875
★★★ Best of Rod Stewart / Mer. SRM-2-7507
★★★ Best of Rod Stewart, Vol. 2 / Mer. SRM-2-7509
★★ Blondes Have More Fun / War. K-3261
★★★★★ Every Picture Tells a Story / Mer. SRM-1-609
★★★ Foot Loose and Fancy Free / War. K-3092
★★★★ Gasoline Alley / Mer. 61264
★★★★ Never a Dull Moment / Mer. SRM-1-646
★★★ Sing It Again, Rod / Mer. SRM-1-680
★★ Rod Stewart and Steampacket / Sp. 4063
★★ Rod Stewart and the Faces / Sp. 4030

★★★★ **The Rod Stewart Album** / Mer. 61237

Rod Stewart is one of the great rock singers of the Seventies. He began his career in England, performing with a variety of small-time bands (some of his early material is represented on the Springboard packages) before joining the Jeff Beck Group in 1969, where he established himself. By 1970 he had joined the Faces and begun recording a memorable series of solo albums; the Faces broke up in 1975 and Stewart has continued on his own since then.

The Rod Stewart Album, his debut, and *Gasoline Alley,* which followed, reveal more of Stewart's folk roots than he would ever show again. But it was with *Every Picture Tells a Story* that he finally realized his full promise, turning in a diverse collection of vocals, including folk-rock numbers like Tim Hardin's "Reason to Believe"; flat-out rock like the title cut, which is as imaginatively lyrical as the best of Jerry Lee Lewis and (thanks to Mickey Waller's drumming) just as powerful; and the poignant ballad "Maggie May," his first hit single. Stewart also toyed with soul music, recording the Temptations' "Losing You" in a style that reflected the influence of both the Tempts' David Ruffin and soul master Sam Cooke. *Never a Dull Moment* repeated this mix with slightly less successful results. The Mercury repackages (the two *Best of*s and *Sing It Again, Rod*) also include material from his fourth and weakest solo LP, *Smiler,* now deleted.

In 1975, Stewart moved to Warner Bros., where he began working with veteran producer Tom Dowd, who teamed him with a variety of American sessionmen. *Atlantic Crossing,* the first of their collaborations, was spotty, but *A Night on the Town* was terrific, revealing Stewart's skills as both writer and interpreter, and at the same time gaining him a second and even bigger hit single, "Tonight's the Night." But he then decided to become a sex symbol rather than a rock & roller, and *Foot Loose and Fancy Free,* while not truly awful, came as a real disappointment to those who knew the vitality of his early work. At his best, Stewart remains one of the most moving singers of the current era, capable of both hard rock and deep emotion. But at his worst, he's just another Mick Jagger *manqué.* — D.M.

STEPHEN STILLS

★ **Down the Road** / Atl. 7250

★ **Illegal Stills** / Col. PC-34148
★★★ **Manassas** / Atl. 2-903
★★★ **Stephen Stills** / Atl. 7202
★ **Stephen Stills** / Col. PC-33575
■ **Steven Stills Live** / Atl. 18156
★★★ **Stephen Stills 2** / Atl. 7206
★★★ **Still Stills** / Atl. 18201
★★ **Thoroughfare Gap** / Col. JC-35380

As a member of the Buffalo Springfield and Crosby, Stills, Nash (and Young), Stephen Stills was always a more notable guitarist than writer, and his singing ranged from moving to limpid. It remained in the latter category, and his writing was only occasionally worthwhile, on his solo discs. The best of them are the first Atlantic LP (7202), which includes "Love the One You're With," the second, which has "Change Partners," and *Still Stills,* an anthology that has both plus his "Go Back Home" collaboration with Eric Clapton. *Manassas* isn't really a solo LP at all—it's a rock band, featuring ex-Byrd and Flying Burrito Brother Chris Hillman, and it has its moments. The Columbia stuff is garbage, the relic of a burnt-out career. — D.M.

STILLS-YOUNG BAND

★★ **Long May You Run** / Rep. 2253

Stephen Stills and Neil Young in a collaboration that's a long way from their days in the Buffalo Springfield. The album is redeemed only by Young's biting title track, a mock tribute to a car and a girl—in that order. — D.M.

STILLWATER

★ **I Reserve the Right** / Capri. 0210
★ **Stillwater** / Capri. 0186

Anonymous Southern folk rock. — J.S.

STONEGROUND

★ **Hearts of Stone** / War. K-3187

Dull San Francisco band under the illusion that it's funky. — D.M.

THE STONE PONEYS

★★★ **The Stone Poneys Featuring Linda Ronstadt** / Cap. ST-11383

Linda Ronstadt as a green but strong-voiced lead singer in a folk-rock band noted primarily for the hit "Different Drum," written by Monkee Mike Nesmith. — J.S.

STRANGELOVES

★★ **I Want Candy** / Bang 21

Billing itself as Australian to cash in on the 1965 British invasion, this New York City trio crossed "Hand Jive" with a typical high-school football cheer to produce the pulsatingly delightful "I Want Candy." Today, the song is wonderfully dated, invoking blissful, nostalgic tingles—the highlight of an otherwise laughably weak collection of the same song rewritten a dozen times. — A.N.

STRANGLERS
★★ Black and White / A&M 4706
★★ IV Rattus Norvegicus / A&M 4648
★★ No More Heroes / A&M 4659
New Wave band strongly reminiscent of one of the original Sixties punk-rock groups, the Music Machine, but with additional Jim Morrison pretensions. — J.S.

THE STRAWS
★★★ Burning for You / Oy. 1-1604
★★★ Bursting at the Seams / A&M 4383
★★★ Deadlines / Ari. 4172
★★★★ Deep Cuts / Oy. 1-1603
★★★ From the Witchwood / A&M 4304
★★★ Ghost / A&M 4506
★★★★ Grave New World / A&M 4344
★★★ Hero and Heroine / A&M 3607
★★★★ Just a Collection of Antiques and Curios / A&M 4288
★★★ Nomadness / A&M 4544
★★★ The Best of the Strawbs / A&M 6005
The Strawbs came out of the same English folk-rock scene that produced Steeleye Span and Fairport Convention, with whom they shared singer Sandy Denny. The group also gave Rick Wakeman his start. But the real leader of the band was vocalist/guitarist Dave Cousins, and it is Cousins' range of interests, from classical to folk to art rock, that makes the Strawbs one of the more interesting—if least commercially viable—folk-rock groups of the Seventies. — D.M.

STREET CORNER SYMPHONY
★★ Harmony Grits / Bang 406
★★★ Little Funk Machine / ABC 974
Harmony, the first album by this five-piece soul-singing group, isn't much, but the second is a pleasant surprise, mostly because of production by Willie Hutch and a rhythm section that includes drummer James Gadson and bassist James Jamerson, studio stalwarts of Motown's heyday. — D.M.

STREETWALKERS
★★★ Red Card / Mer. SRM-1-1083
★★★ Streetwalkers / Mer. SRM-1-1060

★★ Vicious but Fair / Mer. SRM-1-1135
Roger Chapman's gruff, almost frighteningly intense voice is among rock's best; guitarist Charlie Whitney's writing subtly combines rock, R&B and folk. (Not surprisingly, Streetwalkers remind strongly of the pair's earlier and vastly superior group, Family.) Most of the arrangements here are hard, loud and lacking variation—better than the average heavy-metal outfit, but below Chapman and Whitney's capabilities. Rarely is vocalist/guitarist Bob Tench well utilized.
Streetwalkers is most Family-like; except for a long, solo-ridden piece and a rather unnecessary blues, it's a strong album. *Red Card* is more unified and mature, but less haunting and colorful. *Vicious but Fair* suffers from weak material and arranging, and possibly the growing pains from the addition of three new members. (All three now deleted.) — C.W.

BARBRA STREISAND
★ A Happening in Central Park / Col. PC-9710
★ A Star Is Born (Soundtrack) / Col. JS-34403
★★★ Barbra Joan Streisand / Col. PCQ-30792
★ Barbra Streisand/A Christmas Album / Col. CS-9557
★ Barbra Streisand and Other Musical Instruments / Col. PC-32655
★ Barbra Streisand Live Concert at the Forum / Col. PC-31760
★★★★★ Barbra Streisand's Greatest Hits / Col. PC-9968
★★★★ Barbra Streisand/The Third Album / Col. PC-8954
■ Butterfly / Col. PC-33005
★ Color Me Barbra / Col. PC-9278
★★ Funny Girl (Original Cast) / Cap. STAO-2059
★★ Funny Girl (Soundtrack) / Col. BOS-3220
★ Funny Lady (Soundtrack) / Ari. AQ-9004
★ Je m'appelle Barbra / Col. PC-9347
★★★ Lazy Afternoon / Col. PC-33815
★★ My Name Is Barbra / Col. PC-9136
★★ My Name Is Barbra, Two / Col. PC-9209
★★ People / Col. PC-9015
★★ Simply Streisand / Col. PC-9482
★★★★ Stoney End / Col. PC-30378
★★★ Streisand Superman / Col. JC-34830
★★★ The Barbra Streisand Album / Col. PC-8807

★★ **The Second Barbra Streisand Album /
Col. PC-8854**
★★★ **The Way We Were / Col. PC-32801**
■ **The Way We Were (Soundtrack) / Col.
JS-32830**
★ **What About Today? / Col. PC-9816**
In 1963, at age twenty, Streisand catapulted
a minor Broadway success into a major recording career. *The Barbra Streisand Album*
typecast her as a theatrical diva of capri-
cious temperament and inexhaustible will.
For freshness and sheer chutzpah, Streisand hasn't topped her ironic version of
"Happy Days Are Here Again" on the debut. Through the Sixties, Streisand remained fixed in the firmament: a musically
conservative force with a vast nonrock following that included a camp cult. *Greatest
Hits* reprises most of the high points of this
period, with "People" and "Free Again"
the pinnacles. During this time, Streisand
worked most frequently with Peter Matz, a
first-rate arranger/conductor.

Stoney End was the first of two albums
made with producer Richard Perry. Both
incorporated contemporary pop and "rock"
material (the single version of Laura
Nyro's "Stoney End" was a major hit in
1970). *The Way We Were* brought back the
"old" Streisand, sounding more confident
than ever. *Streisand Superman* showed her
at last able to handle rock without sounding too uncomfortable. Released after the
commercial success (and artistic disaster)
of her home movie, *A Star Is Born,* it
showed Streisand at the peak of her powers and with a "contemporary" audience at
last in tow.   — S.H.

STRETCH
★★ **Elastique / Anchor 2014**
★★ **You Can't Beat Your Brain for Enter-
tainment / Anchor 2016**

Competent British R&B. (Both now deleted.)   — J.S.

STRONGBOW
★★ **Strongbow / Southw. 6401**
Country rock at its worst.   — J.S.

ALICE STUART
★★ **Believing / Fan. 9412**
★★ **Full Time Woman / Fan. 8403**
Like most West Coast funk, Stuart's is
more than sort of forced—calling it histrionic isn't taking things too far. One gets
the idea she'd be happier singing folk
songs, though that wasn't the vogue in the
mid-Seventies, when these LPs were
made.   — D.M.

STUFF
★★★ **More Stuff / War. B-3061**
★★★ **Stuff / War. B-2968**
★★★ **Stuff It / War. K-3262**
A group of top pop and soul studio musi-
cians (bassist Gordon Edwards, keyboard-
ist Richard Tee, guitarists Cornell Dupree
and Eric Gale, drummer Christopher
Parker). The playing is predictably slick
and fiery.   — J.S.

THE STYLISTICS
★★★★ **Best of the Stylistics / H&L 69005**
★★★★ **Fabulous Stylistics / H&L 69013**
★★★ **Heavy / H&L 69004**
★★★ **In Fashion / Mer. SRM-1-3727**
★★★★ **Let's Put It All Together / H&L
69001**
★★★ **Once upon a Juke Box / H&L 69015**
★★★★ **Rockin' Roll Baby / H&L 11010**
★★★ **Round 2 / H&L 11006**
★★★ **Stylistics / H&L 33023**
★★★ **Thank You Baby / H&L 69008**
★★★ **Wonder Woman / H&L 69032**
★★★ **You Are Beautiful / H&L 69010**
In the early to middle Seventies, the Stylis-
tics, along with the Chi-Lites and very few
others, perfected a neoclassic soul-group
harmony sound, which owed a debt to the
Temptations and the Impressions without
ignoring the changes wrought by Sly and
the Family Stone. Van McCoy, later to
make a name for himself as a disco performer, arranged and conducted a series of
hits produced by Hugo and Luigi (responsible for many of Sam Cooke's pop hits),
but the real highlight of such chart-busters
as "Rockin' Roll Baby," "Let's Put It All
Together" and the group's other smashes
was lead tenor Russell Thompkins Jr.,
whose style is an updated model of what
Eddie Kendricks had done with the Temp-

tations. This is romantic, lush music for anyone who values soul as a pop-music source-point. — D.M.

STYX
★★ Best of Styx / Wood. BXL1-2250
★★★ Crystal Ball / A&M 4604
★★★ Equinox / A&M 4559
★★★ Grand Illusion / A&M 4637
★★ Man of Miracles / Wood. BXL1-0638
★★ Pieces of Eight / A&M 4724
★ Styx / Wood. BXL1-1008
★★ Styx II / Wood. BXL1-1012
★★ The Serpent Is Rising / Wood. BXL1-0287

Styx is a superbly teenage American response to the flashy British art rock (Yes, etc.) that blended unusual melodies, spirited vocals and just enough technical gymnastics to score heavily in the teen market. The Wooden Nickel records came before the rise, and aren't worth much. *Equinox* and *Crystal Ball* gave the group its first successes, although the latter repeats most of the former. *Grand Illusion,* the third in the series, also exposed the band's limitations as writers—further progress seems unlikely. — A.N.

SUGARLOAF
★★★ Don't Call Us, We'll Call You / Clar. 1000

This Colorado band had an early-Seventies pop hit, "Green-Eyed Lady," then faded from sight. Trying to regain a recording deal, it was spurned rather imperiously by CBS. This resulted in Jerry Corbetta's amusing song, "Don't Call Us, We'll Call You," in which the CBS phone number is spelled out—touch-tone style—for the world. That was another hit, but the band quickly dropped from sight anyway. CBS has since changed its number. — D.M.

YMA SUMAC
★★ Inca Taqui / Cap. SM-684
★★ Legend of the Sun Virgin / Cap. SM-299
★★★ Voice of the Xtabay / Cap. SM-684

Sumac arrived in the mid-Fifties from the Peruvian mountains, and immediately became an unpronounceable household name because of her eight-octave range. (*Xtabay*—now re-released as side A of a disc that also includes *Inca Taqui*—was her hit, or milestone, or whatever.) Patti Smith for xenophiles. — D.M.

DONNA SUMMER
★ A Love Trilogy / Oasis 5004
★★ I Remember Yesterday / Casa. 7056
★ Live and More / Casa. 7119
★ Love to Love You Baby / Oasis 5003
★★ Once upon a Time / Casa. 7078
★ The Four Seasons of Love / Oasis 7038-V

Produced by Pete Bellotte in Munich, Donna Summer's first album (5003) consists of the full sixteen-minute discoid moans and sighs of her hit title song and a few limp soul numbers. Interestingly, only "Love to Love You Baby" is actually disco, serving as a novelty dance number. But it's too slow for dancing and too long for the recorded multiple orgasms not to become self-parodying.

A Love Trilogy formularizes Summer's silky pliancy into a "mood" album, but its feeble pumping is rather boring beside *Four Seasons of Love,* which is more spirited because Bellotte and his Munich Machine have finally worked out their oily European variant of the disco genre. *I Remember Yesterday* proves a complete surprise. Here, Summer presents herself as a pleasantly competent soul singer; the randy Siamese posing of her earlier records disappears before her affectionate replays of Ronettes, Supremes and ballad styles, concluding with a Kraftwerk-derived dance tune, "I Feel Love." *Once upon a Time* presents her as Cinderella, a ridiculously gauzy move that almost works. The live album, despite containing a major hit in "MacArthur Park" (no less), is dismal. — B.T.

SUN
★★★ Live On, Dream On / Cap. ST-11461
★★ Sunburn / Cap. ST-11723
★★ Sun-Power / Cap. ST-11609

This post-Sly Stone hard-disco group from Dayton, Ohio, came from a parent group called the Overnight Low Show Band, which contributed three members to the Ohio Players. The band's sound is hard-edged funk and features tightly arranged ensemble riffing in the manner of the Commodores. "Wanna Make Love (Come Flick My Bic)" from *Live On* became a substantial hit in 1976. — J.S.

SUPERTRAMP
★★★ Crime of the Century / A&M 3647
★★★ Crisis? What Crisis? / A&M 4560
★★★★ Even in the Quietest Moments ... / A&M 4634
★★ Indelibly Stamped / A&M 4311
★★ Supertramp / A&M 4665

After its classic period (*The Yes Album* through *Close to the Edge*), Yes left a mid-Seventies void in art rock that has been filled by Genesis and Supertramp. Both bands have the capacity to turn out well-honed avant-garde technotronics with a minimum of murky subterfuge. They also stretch out (but not too far), and on occasion get fairly outside (but they know how and when to reel it back in). The most substantial difference between the two is that Supertramp can write a hook, the missing element in the genre since the early days of Yes. Another important distinction is that while Genesis has grown less creative over the years, Supertramp has grown exponentially, improving as players while perfecting the hit formula epitomized by "Ain't Nobody but Me." — B.M.

THE SUPREMES
★★★★★ **Anthology: Diana Ross and the Supremes / Mo. M9-794**
★ **Supremes / Mo. M7-873**
★★ **The Supremes at Their Best / Mo. M7-904**

When Holland-Dozier-Holland stopped writing and producing the Supremes in the late Sixties, many looked at it as the end of an era. Together, that trio plus Diana Ross had created a remarkable string of hit singles in the mid to late Sixties that were the epitome of the Motown sound; they are included on the *Anthology* package and are virtually all great. The other albums, however, feature little by Holland-Dozier-Holland, and nothing at all by Ross. As a result, there's little here of more than cursory interest. — R.G.

SURPRISE SISTERS
★★ **Surprise Sisters / RCA APL1-1404**
Four women attempt to be funky, aided by Tony Visconti's orchestrations. A couple of times, they almost make it. (Now deleted.) — D.M.

SUTHERLAND BROTHERS AND QUIVER
★★★ **Down to Earth / Col. JC-35293**
★★★ **Reach for the Sky / Col. PC-33982**
★★★ **Slipstream / Col. PC-34376**
Prior to their amalgamation, the Sutherland Brothers (Gavin and Iain) had made two folk-rock albums, while Quiver had made a pair of undistinguished hard-rock LPs. In 1973, the collaboration sparked a Top Twenty hit (on Island) called "You Got Me Anyway," which felt like the best kind of Dylanesque rock. Although the Sutherlands received some British acclaim as authors of Rod Stewart's "Sailing," the group itself never again made much U.S. impact. *Reach* has a fantastic song, "Arms of Mary," surrounded by lots of passable ones; *Slipstream* is just the passable stuff, while *Down to Earth* finds the remnants of Quiver altogether absent, leaving the field entirely to the Sutherlands, who lack punch. — D.M.

SWAMP DOGG
★★★ **Finally Caught Up with Myself / MCA 2504**
★★★★ **Swamp Dogg / Wiz. 1306**
Jerry Williams, a.k.a. Swamp Dogg, has for several years been soul music's chief eccentric, applying his gravelly voice and trenchant wit to all manner of unlikely subjects, many of them bizarre tales of philandering. In a weird way, he's like a less obscene version of Clarence Reid's Blowfly persona, or a more humorous but equally macho parody of Wilson Pickett. Either way, these records are worth hearing for those with sufficiently diverse taste. — D.M.

BILLY SWAN
★★★★★ **Billy Swan / Col. PZ-34183**
★★★ **Billy Swan at His Best / Monu. MG-7629**
★★★ **Four / Col. PC-34473**
★★★★ **I Can Help / Col. PZ-33279**
★★★ **Rock and Roll Moon / Col. PZ-33805**
★★★ **You're OK, I'm OK / A&M 4686**
Swan is labeled "progressive rockabilly"—definitely for lack of a better term. He owes a lot to the Beatles for ideas about harmony singing and to Motown or Forties jump-blues bands for ideas about using horns. It's a modern Southern roadhouse sound, greatly influenced by the music of the original rockabilly artists (Presley, Jerry Lee Lewis et al.), but in Swan's hands it sounds something like the Beatles singing Buddy Holly. Though he has a fondness for novelty tunes, Swan's specialty is the adult love song; his urgent, nervous singing style somehow makes him sound guarded and outreaching at the same time, a truly Seventies attitude.

"I Can Help" is his best-known song, and the album marks an impressive debut. Though perhaps his most country-sounding, it owed obvious debts to Memphis rockabilly, and the material is outstanding. The second, *Moon,* is clearly a descendant of the first, but rocks a little harder. The

third, *Billy Swan,* on which his sound finally jells, is one of the great lost Seventies
albums—passionate songs and singing with
white-hot musicianship. *Four* was cut in
Muscle Shoals, Alabama, and has more of
a soul feel, with increased use of strings
and horns. *You're OK, I'm OK* finds Swan
shifting his recording base to L.A. and
nearly becoming swamped in psychobab-
ble. The result was that he found himself
back where he started, playing keyboards
for Kris Kristofferson. — J.B.M.

SWEET
★★★ **Desolation Boulevard / Cap.
S-11395**
★★ **Give Us a Wink / Cap. ST-11496**
★★ **Level Headed / Cap. SKAO-11744**
★★ **Off the Record / Cap. STAO-11636**
Sweet made Who-like pop-rock singles
that were massive hits in England from
1973 through 1975, the prepunk heyday of
bands like Slade. Sweet was slicker and
flashier than those, but also less inspired;
the real story was the songs of Nicky
Chinn and Mike Chapman, who also wrote
for Suzi Quatro. In America, Sweet scored
mildly with "Action" (from *Wink*), "Blockbuster" (their best song), "Little Willy"
and *Desolation*'s "Fox on the
Run." — D.M.

THE SYLVERS
★★★ **Best of the Sylvers / Cap.
ST-11868**
★★ **Forever Yours / Casa. 7103**
★★★ **New Horizons / Cap. ST-11705**
★★ **Showcase / Cap. ST-11465**
★★★ **Something Special / Cap. 11580**
After a career largely kept alive by one
Foster Sylvers hit ("Misdemeanor") and
innumerable appearances on the cover of
the black teen magazine *Right On!*, the Syl-
vers found consistent commercial success
in the mid-Seventies with former Jackson
Five producer Freddie Perren. Perren's
production style harks back to the classic
Motown sound, and his hot, concise tracks,
coupled with some appropriately frothy
Keni St. Lewis lyrics, have given this fam-
ily group a string of sometimes annoying
("Boogie Fever") and sometimes fun ("Hot
Line") pop hits. — J.MC.

SYLVESTER
★★★ **Stars / Fan. 9579**
★★ **Step Two / Fan. 9556**

★★ **Sylvester / Fan. 9531**
When he first began recording in 1973, for
Blue Thumb, Sylvester was disco's only
screaming black drag queen. But in recent
years, he's modified his sexual thrust and
come up with a trio of hot dance albums,
lightly likable except for his more mannered exhortations. — D.M.

TERRY SYLVESTER
★ **Terry Sylvester / Epic KE-33076**
The Hollie who is neither Graham Nash
nor Allan Clarke, and who sounds mundane without the benefit of the others'
harmonies. Definitely for Hollies fanatics
and album pack rats only (Now
deleted.) — A.N.

SYLVIA
★ **Brand New Funk / Vibr. 143**
★ **Lay It on Me / Vibr. 131**
★ **Sylvia / Vibr. 129**
The original heavy-breathing disco, from
the former distaff member of Mickey and
Sylvia ("Love Is Strange"). She also owns
All-Platinum Records, of which Vibration
is a subsidiary. The hit was "Pillow Talk"
from *Sylvia.* — J.S.

SYNERGY
★ **Cords / Pass. 6000**
★ **Electronic Realizations for Rock
Orchestra / Pass. PPSD-98009**
★ **Sequencer / Pass. PPSD-98014**
Not really a group at all, just New Jersey
synthesizer whiz Larry Fast and his mul-
tiple machines. Truly pompous antirock
b.s. — D.M.

SYREETA
★★★ **One to One / Tam. T7-349**
★★★ **Rich Love, Poor Love / Mo.
M7-891**
★★★ **Syreeta / Mo. M7-808**
Stevie Wonder's former wife was produced
by him on *Syreeta,* and she turned in her
best work. The Tamla LP is not as successful, mostly because she's only an average
vocalist who lacks inspiration. A latter
duet with G.C. Cameron was slightly more
successful. — D.M.

HERMAN SZOBEL
★★ **Szobel / Ari. AL-4058**
Classically trained, Zappa-influenced
pianist; nephew of the Fillmore's Bill
Graham. (Now deleted.) — J.S.

TALKING HEADS
★★★ **More Songs about Buildings and Food / Sire K-6058**
★★★★ **Talking Heads '77 / Sire 6036**
Led by guitarist/songwriter/singer David Byrne, Talking Heads have made two of the best albums to come out of the New York New Wave. Musically, the band seems most influenced by the slightly soul-dipped bubblegum music of the late Sixties (Crazy Elephant and the 1910 Fruitgum Company are clear reference points). Combined with Byrne's almost-off-the-edge vocals, and his often tongue-in-cheek lyrics ("Don't Worry about the Government," for instance), both these records are unique and entertaining. Brian Eno produced the second, *More Songs*. — B.A.

JAMES TALLEY
★★★ **Ain't It Somethin' / Cap. ST-11695**
★★★ **Tryin' like the Devil / Cap. ST-11494**
Talley's 1975 debut (*Got No Bread*), a self-produced and financed disc, was a warm-spirited evocation of the populist part of country music tradition. It was more senti-mental, less tough-minded than the Way-lon Jennings/Willie Nelson outlaw ap-proach, but derived from the same country roots, and as such, stands as one of the key links between the new country sounds of recent years and the leftist folk tradition. Subsequent albums, however, have been more didactic, and Talley sometimes seems to be striking a working-class pose, rather than standing as a true example of that sensibility. The basic feel of the music is still loose and gentle, with a fundamental warmth not found in more sophisticated productions, but the political commentary begins to seem more forced—just as it did in some of the more self-conscious urban

folk music of the early Sixties. Whether Talley can find an audience for his point of view—and whether he can overcome his more dogmatic instincts—remains open to question. — D.M.

TALTON/STEWART/SANDLIN
★★★ **Happy to Be Alive / Capri. 0617**
Capricorn fundamentalists, a little better than the usual Macon funk excursion. Liner notes by critic/producer Jon Lan-dau. (Now deleted.) — J.S.

TAMS
★★★ **Tams / ABC 481**
Group that scored in 1963 with "What Kind of Fool?" is ineffectively revived for a mid-Seventies dance record. Boo-wop. — D.M.

TANGERINE DREAM
★★★ **Encore—Tangerine Dream Live / Virgin PZG-35014**
★★★ **Stratosfear / Virgin PZ-34427**
Kings of the synthesizer, German-style, or the machine takes over. These are neither much better, nor much worse, than the group's import albums, but they *are* cheap-er. For technocrats and energy brats. — D.M.

TARGET
★★ **Captured / A&M 4652**
★★ **Target / A&M 4607**
More ho-hum hard rock. — D.M.

A TASTE OF HONEY
★★ **A Taste of Honey / Cap. ST-11754**
★★ **The Hitter / Cap. SW-11920**
Disco group notable principally for having a pair of women instrumentalists and scor-ing a major 1978 hit with "Boogie Oogie Oogie," almost but not quite the "Surfin' Bird" of the new beat. — D.M.

TATTOO
★ Tattoo / Prod. PS-10014
Non-Eric Carmen Raspberry remnants in a band that sounds rawer, rather than better. (Now deleted.) — D.M.

TAVARES
★★★★ Check It Out / Cap. ST-11258
★★★ Future Band / Cap. SW-11719
★★★ Hard Core Poetry / Cap. ST-11316
★★★ In the City / Cap. ST-11396
★★★★ Love Storm / Cap. STAO-11628
★★★ Madame Butterfly / Cap.
   SW-11874
★★★ Sky High! / Cap. ST-11533
★★★★ The Best of Tavares / Cap.
   ST-11701
Tavares is a family soul quintet without a particularly distinctive vocal personality. Nevertheless, as a vehicle for two sets of producers, the group has made several first-rate contributions to the pop-soul arena in the middle and late Seventies.

Tavares' first three albums (*Check It Out, Hard Core Poetry*, and *In the City*) were produced by Brian Potter and Dennis Lambert, who downplayed traditional two- and three-part soul harmonies in favor of a more homogenized unison approach. With intelligent song selection and tasteful (if sometimes bland) production, Lambert and Potter gave Tavares a string of mildly soulful ballad hits ("Check It Out," "She's Gone").

Ex-Motown producer Freddie Perren took over after *In the City,* and while he too works a pop-soul bag, the difference is noticeable. Perren's tracks are hotter (in the classic Motown mold), and his arrangements tend to feature more old-fashioned soul group devices. The lyrics are often lightweight ("Whodunit"), but the songs have a spirit and energy missing from Lambert and Potter's work. — J.MC.

CHIP TAYLOR
★★ Chip Taylor's Saint Sebastian / Cap.
   ST-11909
★★ Some of Us / War. K-2824
★★ Somebody Shoot Out the Jukebox /
   Col. CP-34345
Taylor is best known as a songwriter: in the Sixties, two of his songs, "Wild Thing" and "Angel of the Morning," became big one-shot pop hits for the Troggs and Merilee Rush, respectively. On his own, the sound's closer to C&W, laconic but not terribly effective because he isn't a particularly impressive singer. (Now deleted.) — D.M.

JAMES TAYLOR
★★★★ Gorilla / War. BS4-2866
★★ In the Pocket / War. B-2912
★★★★ James Taylor's Greatest Hits /
   War. 2979
★★★★ JT / Col. 3481
★★★ Mud Slide Slim and the Blue Horizon / War. 2561
★★ One Man Dog / War. BS4-2660
★★★★★ Sweet Baby James / War. 1843
★★ Walking Man / War. 2794
The prototypical Seventies singer/songwriter, Taylor blends folk, traditional, R&B and jazz influences into an acoustically based pop song style, as expressive as it is understated. Taylor's auspicious 1969 Apple debut is out of print. *Sweet Baby James* (1970), which made him a star, introduced the famous "Fire and Rain"; it holds up as a spare, compelling musical statement. *Mud Slide Slim* (1971) reflects, often eloquently, the confusion that followed success.

On *Gorilla* (1975), Taylor broke out of a downward drift with some pure R&B ("How Sweet It Is") and a steamy masterpiece, "You Make It Easy." *JT* (1977) contains a great interpretation of the Jimmy Jones R&B hit, "Handy Man," and a sly gem, "Secret O' Life." Taylor's singing has gained in strength over the years, as evidenced by the stunning remakes of "Carolina on My Mind" and "Something in the Way She Moves," on the *Greatest Hits* collection. A fine writer who has produced at least a handful of modern standards, Taylor is perhaps an even finer singer; his assimilation of American-roots styles evokes classic male American types. — S.H.

JOHNNIE TAYLOR
★★ Disco 9000 / Col. PS-38004
★★★ Eargasm / Col. PO-33951
★★ Ever Ready / Col. JC-35340
★★ Rated Extraordinaire / Col. PC-34401
★★ Reflections / RCA APLI-2527
★★★★ The Johnnie Taylor Chronicle /
   Stax 88001
Taylor's early Stax hits (collected on *Chronicle*) are riveting Southern funk, highlighted by "Who's Making Love." But he is also a warm balladeer with a relaxed, easygoing delivery derived from his biggest vocal influence, Sam Cooke. *Eargasm* is largely in one mold—heavily produced blues ballads—though "Disco Lady," a catchy novelty hit (1976) crammed full of sexual innuendo, pointed the unfortunate direction for the rest of what's here, summed up by *Rated Extraordinaire*'s air-

brushed sleaze ("Your Love Is Rated X"). — J.MC.

LITTLE JOHNNIE TAYLOR
★★★ **Open House at My House** / Ronn 7832

Though often confused with his better-known namesake, the Johnnie Taylor who did "Disco Lady," Little Johnnie Taylor has carved his own distinct identity. The title song was a novelty blues hit (perhaps the last of its kind), and the album features a cross section of ballads, Southern R&B and blues. Taylor has a grainy, dry voice that's most effective on his half-spoken, half-sung blues songs. — J.MC.

KATE TAYLOR
★ **Kate Taylor** / Col. JC-35089

Kate Taylor once seemed the most promising member of her musical family, which includes brothers James, Livingston and Alex. But that was with her early Seventies album on Atlantic. On this 1978 album, she attempts to go the Linda Ronstadt oldies route and it just doesn't work; she hasn't the feeling for old rock that Ronstadt and producer Peter Asher contrive, and seems more at home with the kind of singer/songwriter material brother James writes. — D.M.

LIVINGSTON TAYLOR
★★★ **Three Way Mirror** / Epic JE-35540

Livingston made a pair of earlier albums produced by critic Jon Landau in the early Seventies, when recording James' siblings was all the rage. The 1979 LP is just as laid-back, featuring the same minimal attempts at going funky, as his brothers' and sister's records. But Liv's singing is a bit less apathetic. — D.M.

TED TAYLOR
★★ **Keepin' My Head Above Water** / MCA 3059
★★ **Shades of Blue** / Ronn 7528
★★ **Taylor Made** / Ronn 7531
★★ **You Can Dig It** / Ronn 7529

Taylor is a Southern R&B singer with an affecting nasal falsetto. These albums collect vintage Taylor recordings from the late Sixties; the production is sometimes cheesy, but a strolling blues on *Shades of Blue* ("Days Are Dark") and some pop-R&B ballads are of interest. — J.MC.

TUT TAYLOR
★★ **Dobrolic Plectoral Society** / Tak. D-1050

★★ **Friar Tut** / Roun. 0011
★★★ **The Old Post Office** / Fly. Fish 008

Taylor is Nashville's premier dobro player who, together with guitarist Norman Blake, is responsible for much of the back-up work on any number of country and country-rock albums recorded in that city. Among others, John Hartford has featured them on his solo outings. Although the dobro is essentially an accompanying instrument, it holds up surprisingly well in its featured role here. The Takoma set has the most varied instrumentation (the bass is unduly prominent), but the Flying Fish album is the one most closely linked to the latter-day "progressive/hot licks" school of bluegrass—flashy but always tastefully executed. — I.M.

WILLIE TEE
★★★ **Anticipation** / U. Artists LA-655

Though Willie Tee has recorded a handful of notable soul singles, including "Teasin' You" (his biggest hit, in the Sixties for Atlantic), and has made an LP produced by Cannonball Adderley, only *Anticipation* remains in print. The record is an easy-to-swallow (though sometimes clichéd) blending of New Orleans second-line music and more contemporary black styles. (Now deleted.) — J.MC.

TELEVISION
★★★ **Adventure** / Elek. 6E-133
★★★ **Marquee Moon** / Elek. 7E-1098

Somewhat mysteriously, Television was the most widely touted band to emerge from the New York New Wave. But *Marquee Moon* showed the group as the exclusive project of guitarist Tom Verlaine, an interesting Jerry Garcia-influenced guitarist who lacked melodic ideas or any emotional sensibility. After releasing a similar LP

(*Adventure*) in 1978, the group broke up, though Verlaine is expected to continue recording. — D.M.

JACK TEMPCHIN
★ **Jack Tempchin / Ari. 4193**
Tempchin is best known as one of the key songwriters in the L.A. cowboy school: he wrote "Peaceful Easy Feeling" for the Eagles, "Slow Dancing" for Johnny Rivers. This album is so laid-back you'll wonder if it was recorded posthumously. Every cliché in the Hollywood book—which is a *lot* of clichés. — D.M.

TEMPTATIONS
★ **A Song for You / Gor. G7-969**
★★★★★ **Anthology with Diana Ross and the Supremes / Mo. M9-794**
★ **Bare Back / Atl. 19188**
★★★ **Cloud Nine / Gor. G7-939**
★★ **Do the Temptations / Gor. G7-975**
★ **Hear to Tempt You / Atl. 19143**
★★★★ **Temptations' Greatest Hits, Vol. 1 / Gor. G5-919**
★★★★ **Temptations' Greatest Hits, Vol. 2 / Gor. G7-954**
The best-known and commercially most successful of all the male Motown groups of the Sixties, the Temptations have had an erratic career that runs the full range from post-doo-wop harmony to Sly Stone-influenced modern funk and includes more than its share of hits.

The Temptations released their first records in 1961 and had their first hit, "Dream Come True," the next year, but it wasn't until 1964, with Smokey Robinson's "The Way You Do the Things You Do" (contained on the remarkable but, sadly, deleted Gordy LP, *The Temptations Sing Smokey*), that the group began to achieve consistent success, largely through the brilliance of lead vocalists Eddie Kendricks (tenor) and David Ruffin (baritone). Through 1968, the group had a streak of major hits, most notably 1965's "My Girl" and "Since I Lost My Baby," 1966's "Ain't Too Proud to Beg," "Beauty Is Only Skin Deep" and "I Know I'm Losing You," the next year's "You're My Everything" and 1968's "I Wish It Would Rain." But with "Cloud Nine," which began to venture farther from basic group harmony, Ruffin left the group and was replaced by Dennis Edwards from the Contours. The Temptations were now teamed with Norman Whitfield, a producer heavily influenced by Sly and the Family Stone's innovations, who earned them another series of hits in a

looser, funkier style including "Get Ready," "I Can't Get Next to You," "Psychedelic Shack" and "Ball of Confusion." But after "Just My Imagination," a 1971 return to the ballad style, Kendricks also left to go solo. Kendricks was never satisfactorily replaced, and although the Temptations' 1972 hit "Papa Was a Rollin' Stone" is a landmark Seventies recording that helped usher in an age of increased sophistication both lyrically and musically for black pop music, the group has really never been the same. Currently, the group is recording disco-oriented material for Atlantic while Kendricks and Ruffin record solo with sporadic success. — D.M.

10 C.C.
★★ **Bloody Tourists / Poly. 1-6161**
★★ **Deceptive Bends / Mer. SRM-1-3702**
★★ **How Dare You / Mer. SRM-1-1061**
★★ **Live and Let Live / Mer. SRM-2-8600**
★★ **Original Soundtrack / Mer. SRM-1-1029**
★★ **The Things We Do for Love / Poly. 1-6186**
A melange of art-rock smarminess and pop-song parodies that have occasionally clicked as hits ("I'm Not in Love" was the most notable). Critically overrated, mostly because the group's fascination with pop formulas and studio technology is sufficiently pretentious to seem imposing to a bunch of college boys. — D.M.

TEN YEARS AFTER
★★★ **A Space in Time / Col. PC-30801**
★ **Alvin Lee and Company / Deram X-18064**
★★ **Goin' Home: Their Greatest Hits / Deram 18072**
★★★ **London Collector: Ten Years After / Lon. LC-50013**
★ **Positive Vibrations / Col. C-32851**
★★ **Recorded Live / Col. C2X-32288**
★★★ **Rock and Roll Music to the World / Col. C-31779**
★★★ **Ten Years After / Deram 18009**
★ **The Classic Performances of Ten Years After / Col. PC-34366**
★★★ **Undead / Deram 18016**
Ten Years After began performing in 1967 (a decade after Elvis became a star), with a blues/jazz fusion led by Chick Churchill's Brian Auger-inspired organ and Alvin Lee's Jim Hall-like guitar. Early on, Lee established himself as the focus of the group, with a hyperkinetic, staccato guitar solo style. (See "Spoonful," from *Ten Years After*.) *Undead* contained the first of the

group's classic numbers, however: "I'm Going Home." Thereafter, the group began to move away from blues and jazz stompers (on *Undead*, they'd actually recorded Woody Herman's "Woodchopper's Ball") toward writing their own rock-blues-based material.

With *Sssh, Cricklewood* and *Watt*, TYA hit its popular peak. (Those albums are now replaced with a selection on *London Collector*.) Lee had made a big impression on the guitar-struck masses with his performance at Woodstock (and later, in the movie). His reputation as a blazingly fast guitarist came to dominate the group's image, much to Lee's own displeasure. The music grows repetitious, though the group has become more technically adept. *Alvin Lee and Company* and *Goin' Home* are both scrapings from the bottom of the barrel, released when the group left to join Columbia in 1972.

The Columbia records feature some change of direction: on the first two, Lee tones down, attempting to accommodate his fiery style to the band, even toying with strings and electronic effects. *Recorded Live* regressed: this 1973 set included virtually nothing that wasn't being done in 1969. By the time of *Positive Vibrations*, Lee was already out touring under his own name and Columbia simply used *Classic Performances* as a mop-up reissue from the band's waning days. — A.N.

TEXAS PLAYBOYS
★★★ Live and Kickin' / Cap. ST-11725
★★★ Texas Playboys Today / Cap. ST-11612
Bob Wills' old band has carried on the Western Swing tradition since his death. That's what these discs are about, and for what they are, they're good, although one is not as likely to be surprised by the band without Wills. — D.M.

JOE TEX
★★★ Another Woman's Man / Power. 305
★★★ Bumps and Bruises / Epic PE-34666
★★★ London Collector—Super Soul / Lon. LC-50017
★★★ Rub Down / Epic JE-35079
Joe Tex is a journeyman Southern soul singer with a flair for down-home storytelling. While his voice has lost the falsetto edge that marked his classic hits ("Hold What You've Got," "The Love You Save," available on his deleted Atlantic albums), the Epic albums are charmingly anachronistic LPs spurred by a hot Nashville ses-

sion band. The Powerpak album features sides recorded for Mercury, between the Atlantic and Epic periods. The London album features obscure Sixties singles. — J.MC.

THEE IMAGE
■ Inside the Triangle / Mant. MA6-506
■ Thee Image / Mant. MA6-504
From the folks who brought you Iron Butterfly via Emerson, Lake and Palmer's record label. As Marty Robbins once said, "El Paso." (Now deleted.) — D.M.

THEM
★★★ Backtrackin' / Lon. PS-639
★★★ The Story of Them / Lon. LC-50001
★★★★ Them / Par. 71005
★★★ Them Again / Par. 71008
★★★★ Them Featuring Van Morrison / Par. BP-71053-54
This hard-nosed Irish R&B band made minor inroads in the British Invasion with several hits—"Gloria," "Here Comes the Night" and "Mystic Eyes." Their recording career spanned only three years, and the group might well be forgotten if it weren't for lead singer Van Morrison. Thanks to Morrison, Them's sound was as tough and sinewy as the Animals and Stones, and Morrison himself was particularly fierce at this stage.

Van was an original even then, and his raspy, vaguely threatening vocals fit Them's punch-it-out approach perfectly. *Them* is the album that spawned all three hits and the band is never better than on "Mystic Eyes"—pounding, relentless drums and bass anchoring a rhythm section stretched by organ washes and incessant staccato guitar. Morrison carries the load: shaking maracas, bleating through his talking harmonica, singing in an unrestrained growl that twists to a climactic, inarticulate scream. The true source of raw power, this is some of the most visionary music ever made. *Them Again* includes more of the same, with horns added for James Brown's "Out of Sight" and Morrison at his interpretive best on Bob Dylan's "It's All Over Now Baby Blue."

Them Featuring Van Morrison reissues the first two records (minus two tracks each) in a single package. *Backtrackin'* and *The Story of Them* collect previously unavailable material from British singles and albums. The title track from *Story of Them* is a minor classic in the autobiographical talking-blues vein also used by the Animals

("The Story of Bo Diddley") and Rolling Stones ("Stoned"). A must for fans of Van Morrison's brooding defiance, as are all of these. — J.S.

THIN LIZZY
★★★ Bad Reputation / Mer. SRM-1-1186
★★ Fighting / Mer. SRM-1-1108
★★★★ Jailbreak / Mer. SRM-1-1081
★★★ Johnny the Fox / Mer. SRM-1-1119
★★★ Live and Dangerous / War. 2B-3213
★★ London Collector: Rocker / Lon. LC-50004
★★ Night Life / Mer. SRM-1-1107
This Irish quartet has been kicking around the British Isles since the early Seventies, led by Phil Lynott's throaty, Van Morrison-like vocals and songwriting. Most of the time, it's been nothing much more than a good bash, but the group reached a commercial-artistic peak in 1976 with *Jailbreak,* which included a hit single, "The Boys Are Back in Town," which remains the best absorption of Bruce Springsteen's Morrison influence to date. Since then, it's been back to the hammer and tongs approach, (*Johnny the Fox,* a concept LP, notwithstanding). The *London Collector* set represents the group's first recording, which has a tendency to stray in the direction of art rock; the Warner Bros.' live set is a 1978 compendium of the band's best material over the years, including "The Boys . . ." and a nice version of Bob Seger's "Rosalie." — D.M.

THIRD WORLD
★ Journey to Addis / Is. 9554
★ 96 Degrees in the Shade / Is. 9443
★★ Third World / Is. 9369
Perfectly mediocre reggae, emblematic of the music's decline in recent years. When this half-white, half-rasta band plays "Slav-

ery Days," the Burning Spear classic, all the ominous elements are discarded, leaving nothing but sinewy dance music, slick but not devoid of deep emotion. — D.M.

. 38 SPECIAL
★★★ Special Delivery / A&M 4684
★★ . 38 Special / A&M 4638
Soft-focus Lynyrd Skynyrd led by Ronnie Van Zant's younger brother, Donnie. — D.M.

B. J. THOMAS
★★ B. J. Thomas / MCA 2286
★★★ B. J. Thomas Sings His Very Best / Sp. 4005
★★ Help Me Make It / ABC DP-912
★★ Reunion / ABC DP-858
★★★ Sixteen Greatest Hits / Trip TOP-16-18
★★★★ The ABC Collection / ABC 30028
This Oklahoma-based country-rock singer had a series of pop ballad hits from 1966 through 1972, many of them of surprisingly high quality. The first was a version of Hank Williams' "I'm So Lonesome I Could Cry" in 1966. This was followed by "Hooked On a Feeling" in 1968, the No. 1 "Raindrops Keep Falling on My Head" in 1969 and "I Just Can't Help Believing" in 1970. But the best of all was the final one, "Rock and Roll Lullabye," which appropriated some Beach Boys falsetto for its final chorus.
  The ABC Collection is far more interesting than the Trip or Springboard sets, and the other albums are mere country pop, not worth bothering with. — D.M.

CARLA THOMAS
★★★★ The Best of Carla Thomas / Atl. 8232
The queen of Memphis soul during its mid-Sixties heyday has hardly been visible in the Seventies. Never a major talent on a level with Sam and Dave or Otis Redding (with whom she cut "Tramp"), Thomas did develop a soft, vulnerable persona (best expressed in "B-A-B-Y") that was a refreshing contrast to the raw, gritty music of her Stax-Volt stablemates. Her father is pioneer Memphis singer/DJ Rufus Thomas. (Now deleted.) — J.MC.

RAY THOMAS
★ From Mighty Oaks / Thresh. 16
★★ Hopes, Wishes and Dreams / Thresh. 17
From Mighty Oaks was generally schmaltzy MOR: glossy orchestration and an unap-

pealing naiveté to the singing of this member of the Moody Blues. The melodies were airily and emptily pretty, the dull tempos neither fast nor slow enough. Sentimental and thinly theatrical, the songs were written by Thomas and Nicky James. The followup (*Hopes, Wishes and Dreams*) had the same composers and much of the same backup. Yet it was more stately and mature as well as less saccharine; the music rocked more, with added punch and sharpness. — C.W.

RUFUS THOMAS
★★ **I Ain't Gettin' Older, I'm Gettin' Better** / Avid 6046
★★ **If There Were No Music** / Avid 6015
Former Memphis disc jockey who made a name for himself as a recording artist with a string of salaciously comedic soul numbers for Stax: "Do the Funky Penguin" and "Walking the Dog" are probably the best known. The Avid discs contain none of these, and the Stax items are out of print. Thomas is the father of soul singer Carla Thomas. — D.M.

TIMMY THOMAS
★★★ **The Magician** / Glades 7510
★★★ **Touch to Touch** / Glades 7513
★★★ **You're the Song I've Always Wanted to Sing** / Glades 6504
Minor Florida soul singer, from the same stable that produced Betty Wright and K.C. and the Sunshine Band, but inferior to most of the rest. Interesting groove, but not enough distinction. — D.M.

RICHARD AND LINDA THOMPSON
★★★ **First Light** / Chrys. 1177
★★★★ **Live (More or Less)** / Is. 9421
Former Fairport Convention lead guitarist and his wife released several albums on Island, but *Live*, a two-record set, is all that's left in print. One of the discs is a very good live album; the other is Thompson's first solo record, previously unavailable in the U.S. *First Light* is a 1978 LP that's a pleasure for committed folk-rock fanciers but whose pleasures may be a bit too subtle for everyone else. — J.S.

ROBBIN THOMPSON
★ **Robbin Thompson** / Nemp. 440
Virginia seaboard singer/songwriter, with country inflection, vague Bruce Springsteen connection (he appeared briefly in Springsteen's pre-CBS band, Steel Mill). Thompson was done in by the hack producer, Jim Mason, as much as anything;

Poco-style clichés abound, ruining some fairly decent songs. — D.M.

THOR
■ **Keep the Dogs Away** / Mid. Int. 2337
The cover features the muscle-bound singer fighting off attack dogs. Listeners may be excused from hoping he loses. Unlistenable. — D.M.

THREE DOG NIGHT
★★ **American Pastime** / ABC D-928
★ **Captured Live** / Dun. X-50068
★★★★ **Joy to the World—Greatest Hits** / Dun. D-50178
★★★ **Three Dog Night** / Dun. X-50048
From about 1969 through the mid-Seventies, Three Dog Night was the slickest Top Forty singles band in America. Fronted by three lead singers (the best known of whom was Cory Wells), the group presented a modified soul revue as polished as a Vegas lounge band's, for white audiences who had often never seen anything like it.

At their best (on singles, rarely on LPs), Three Dog Night were skillful reductionists, giving mass appeal to songwriters as eccentric as Randy Newman ("Mama Told Me Not to Come"), Laura Nyro ("Eli's Coming") and Harry Nilsson ("One") long before most of the hard-rock in-crowd picked up on them. The group was also capable of a certain kind of R&B stylization; in their hands, Otis Redding's "Try a Little Tenderness" might have lost most of its specific gravity, but it was Three Dog Night's version which introduced the song to most Americans.

But on LP, the group was never able to produce anything substantial. Production extravaganzas, farcical concepts and other attempts at artistic outreach all went wanting; the result is that of the LPs left in the catalogue, only *American Pastime* (their last) and *Three Dog Night* (their first) are not collections of their hits (which is what the live LP amounts to). — D.M.

PERCY "THRILLS" THRILLINGTON
★ **Thrillington** / Cap. ST-11642
This is Paul McCartney's idea of a joke: a Muzak instrumental version of Wings' *Ram* album. Sounds great in elevators, but that's the only place. — D.M.

TIGER
★★★ **Goin' Down Laughing** / EMI 3153
Going down, anyway. This British band might have made it, if they'd boogied with more grace and a lot less sweat. — D.M.

JOHNNY TILLOTSON
★★★ **Johnny Tillotson** / U. Artists
LA758-G
Pop-country singer covers a fairly good
range of material, including a credible version of Jesse Winchester's "Mississippi
You're on My Mind." The production and
backup arrangements by Jerry Crutchfield
are slick without being stifling. Tillotson
earned his reputation with the Sixties hits
"Send Me the Pillow You Dream On" and
"It Keeps Right on a-Hurtin'," neither of
which is included here. — J.S.

SONNY TIL
★★★ **Straighten Up and Fly Right** / New
W. 261
Sonny Til's cool tenor vocals with the Orioles helped found doo-wop R&B in the
late Forties and early Fifties, particularly
with the great "Crying in the Chapel," a
1953 hit. This Seventies album is not
nearly so good or important as those, but
Til retains some of his vocal prowess,
which might make it worthwhile for doo-
wop buffs. (Now deleted.) — D.M.

TIMBERLINE
★★ **Timberline—The Great Timber Rush** /
Epic PE-34681
1977 country-rock album by a group of
fairly accomplished instrumentalists led by
Jim and Chuck Salestrom. The performance is spirited but the material is pretty
weak. — J.S.

LIBBY TITUS
★★★ **Libby Titus** / Col. PC-34152
Titus is Levon Helm's ex-wife and a crony
of many stars. None of this diminishes her
vocal skills or sense of humor, which are
considerable, but it contributed to making
this album (she cut one earlier one, long
since deleted) a bit more of a jumble than
it needed to be. Tracks are produced not
only by the estimable Phil Ramone, but by
Paul Simon (his "Kansas City" is the record's highlight), the Band's Robbie Robertson and Carly Simon. In the late Seventies,
when female singers were all the rage, Titus was one of the more sophisticated, and
for my money, a sight more mature than
any of the West Coast contenders. — D.M.

TOBY BEAU
★★ **Toby Beau** / RCA AFL1-2771
Awful Midwestern rock band that found a
following (God knows how) in the late
Seventies with this ridiculously hammer-
headed debut LP. — D.M.

LILY TOMLIN
★★★ **And That's the Truth** / Poly. 5023
★★★★ **Lily Tomlin on Stage** / Ari. 4142
★★★★ **Modern Scream** / Poly. 6051
★★★ **This Is a Recording** / Poly. 4055
Tomlin is the greatest comic monologuist
since Ruth Draper. Her first two albums,
Recording and *Truth,* feature the most
popular characters she created on TV's
Laugh-In, Ernestine and Edith Ann. *Modern Scream* (1975) is a more ambitious aural collage (Tomlin interviews herself playing a variety of characters), which includes
some of the material that went into her
1977 Broadway triumph, captured with *On
Stage.* Tomlin's stand-up comedy dissolves
in and out of social criticism and tour-de-
force acting—hilarious, astute, occasionally
chilling. — S.H.

TOMPALL AND THE GLASER BROTHERS
★★★ **Greatest Hits** / MGM SE-4946
A sort of pop-rockabilly harmony trio out
of Nashville and popular in the Sixties,
this group was modestly progressive in
both lyrics and arrangements. So the LP
contains several small gems. But it also
contains some pure schmaltz, and its
creamy smoothness undermines even its
best material. (Now deleted.) — J.MC.

GARY TOMS EMPIRE
★ **Blow Your Whistle** / Pip 6814
★ **Let's Do It Again** / Mer. SRM-1-3731
★ **Turn It Out** / MCA 2289
One of hundreds of one-shot disco acts, the
Empire had its moment with "Blow Your
Whistle," a raucous Kool and the Gang
derivative. — J.MC.

TONIO K.
★★★ **Tonio K.** / Epic JE-35545
If Warren Zevon is Jackson Browne as
werewolf, what's this guy? How about
Warren Zevon as simple smartass? Rocks
pretty hard considering the L.A. origins,
but a bit too glib for its own
good. — D.M.

TOOTS AND THE MAYTALS
★★★★★ **Funky Kingston** / Is. 9330
★★★★ **Reggae Got Soul** / Is. 9374
Toots Hibbert is unquestionably one of the
greatest vocalists to appear in popular music in the past decade. Together with the
Maytals, he helped found reggae (and gave
it its name) in the Sixties, and the group's
series of singles is one of the most pleasurable things to be found in the Jamaican

idiom. As a singer, Toots is sort of a sweet Antilles version of Otis Redding—he occasionally sings Redding's material in concert and the effect is startling.

Funky Kingston is virtually a greatest-hits album, released years after most of the material became popular in Jamaica. It includes three of the finest reggae vocals ever made ("Time Tough," "Pressure Drop," "Pomp and Pride") plus a couple of amazing American pop covers, "Louie Louie" and "Country Road." *Reggae Got Soul* is an awkward but moving compromise between reggae and North American soul music—a rapprochement more effective, at least, than Bob Marley's recent attempts to make himself an International Boogie King. — D.M.

TOPAZ
★★ Topaz / Col. PC-34934
When Rob Stoner and friends backed up Bob Dylan in the Rolling Thunder Revue, they were called Guam. On this album, produced by Dylan's sometime producer Don DeVito, they not only change their name but their style: Stoner, who made some rockabilly singles for Epic a few years earlier, has given up on driving rock for a pale country-funk approach, and it doesn't really work. The level of skill is high, but nobody seems to know quite what to do with it. (Now deleted.) — D.M.

TORNADER
★★★ Hit It Again / Poly. 1-6098
Ex-Edgar Winter and Larry Young guitarist Sandy Torano and songwriter/vocalist Larry Alexander combine for a surprisingly fine debut album of white R&B. The stellar session band assembled by producer Jack Richardson includes guitarists Johnny Winter and Joe Beck, Average White Band

drummer Steve Ferrone and the Brecker Brothers on horns. — J.S.

RICHARD TORRANCE AND EUREKA
★ Anything's Possible / Cap. SW-11660
★ Bareback / Cap. SW-11610
★ Double Take / Cap. SW-11699
Mediocre Seventies folk rock. Bor-ing. — J.S.

PETER TOSH
★★★★ Bush Doctor / Rol. 39109
★★★★ Equal Rights / Col. PC-34670
★★★★ Legalize It / Col. PC-34153
One of the original Wailers (along with Bob Marley and Bunny [Livingston] Wailer), Tosh's solo albums, although they've never had much non-Jamaican airing, are excellent, pure reggae, truer to the spirit and form of the music than Marley's more celebrated recent work. *Equal Rights* is the best of these, if only because it has a version of the Wailers' "Get Up, Stand Up." *Bush Doctor* features a duet with Mick Jagger on the Temptations' "Don't Look Back" but also a softening of Tosh's raw musical and abrasive political posture. Not a sellout but enough to sow seeds of doubt. — D.M.

TOTO
★ Toto / Col. JC-35317
This latest conglomeration of L.A. session musicians made a hit out of a debut album that is all chops and no brains. Formula pop songs, singing that wouldn't go over in a Holiday Inn cocktail lounge. — D.M.

TOUCH OF CLASS
★★★ I'm in Heaven / Mid. Int. BKL1-1821
★★★ Steppin' Out / Mid. Int. BKL1-2423
Although they never had much commercial appeal, this black vocal group had a spritely pop-soul sound that makes these LPs worth looking into. — D.M.

ALLEN TOUSSAINT
★★★ Life, Love and Faith / Rep. 2062
★★★ Motion / War. K-3142
★★★★ Southern Nights / Rep. 2186
Legendary New Orleans R&B producer's recent solo albums (he recorded now unavailable material for a number of small labels) are exemplary versions of mellow Southern soul. The only problem is that Toussaint sometimes gets too mellow, but his songwriting and arrangement genius overcomes any conceptual problems. The title track from *Southern Nights,* his best

record, was covered by Glen Campbell
with remarkable success. — J.S.

TOWER OF POWER
★★★ **Ain't Nothin' Stoppin' Us Now / Col.
PC-34302**
★★★★ **Back to Oakland / War. B-2749**
★★★ **Bump City / War. B-2616**
★★★ **In the Slot / War. B-2880**
★★★★ **Tower of Power / War. B-2681**
★★★★ **Tower of Power Live and in Living
Color / War. B-2924**
★★★★ **Urban Renewal / War. B-2834**
★★★ **We Came to Play / Col. JC-34906**
This Oakland-based big band is noted for
its super-funky live performances and has
managed to translate a good deal of that
energy onto vinyl. Though the band was
always tight and the trademark five-piece
horn section could blow up a storm from
the start, it wasn't until the third album,
Tower of Power, that the sound jelled. Vocalist Lenny Williams provided the focal
point for the band's energy, and the three
albums that feature him fronting the band,
T of P, Back to Oakland and *Urban Renewal,* are as fine a set of R&B records as
have been released in the Seventies. Williams gave the band tremendous breadth
on ballad material, but his uptempo vocals
(as on the hit "What Is Hip") really took
off. A couple of different vocalists have
tried to fill Williams' shoes since then
without much success, so the band has relied on its instrumental firepower and arrangement sense to make up the difference.
The live set shows just how hot they can
get in concert. — J.S.

PETER TOWNSHEND
★★★★★ **Rough Mix / MCA 2295**
★★★★ **Who Came First / MCA 2026**
The Who's guitarist and principal song-
writer is one of the most important figures
in the past fifteen years of rock & roll. His
two solo albums (*Rough Mix,* the second, is
actually a collaboration with a former
Face, Ronnie Lane) are more overtly involved with his spiritual master, Meher
Baba, than his group efforts can afford to
be. On the first, this is not necessarily an
advantage: Townshend's version of Jim
Reeves' "There's a Heartache Following
Me" is fine and moving, but his version of
Baba's prayer, "Parvadigar," is a bit wearing to heathen ears. But the album is saved
by the rock numbers. "Pure and Easy,"
contained on the Who's *Odds and Sods* in a
group version, is one of the best songs
Townshend's ever written, and "Nothing Is

Everything" is far superior to the Who's
version of the same song, "Let's See Action."
Rough Mix is a triumph: "Street in the
City" ranks with Townshend's most adventurous productions, and "My Baby Gives
It Away" is a classically styled rocker,
while Lane's eccentric fusion of British
folk and hard rock is consistently moving,
particularly on such songs as "Annie." — D.M.

TRAFFIC
★★★ **Heavy Traffic / U. Artists LA421-G**
★★★★ **John Barleycorn Must Die / U.
Artists 5504**
★★★ **Last Exit / U. Artists 6702**
★★ **More Heavy Traffic / U. Artists
LA526-G**
★★★★ **Mr. Fantasy / U. Artists 6651**
★★★★ **The Best of Traffic / U. Artists
5500**
★★ **The Low Spark of High Heeled Boys /
Is. 9180**
★★★★★ **Traffic / U. Artists 6676**
★★ **Traffic on the Road / Is. 2**
★★★ **Welcome to the Canteen / U. Artists
5550**
★★★ **When the Eagle Flies / Asy. 7E-1020**
Traffic was a band with talent to burn. Its
nominal figurehead, Stevie Winwood, pow-
ered the group with his searing blues singing and intelligent keyboard and guitar
playing. Dave Mason, whose singing, songwriting and guitar playing would have
made him the focal point of most other
bands, was overshadowed here by Winwood, and the lineup was completed by the
angular funk drumming of Jim Capaldi
and hipster fills from saxophone-flautist
Chris Wood.
At its best, Traffic was a band to be
reckoned with. The first two Traffic albums

are late-Sixties classics, an eclectic combination of blues, folk, jazz and rock that was polyglot without ever becoming overextended. *Mr. Fantasy,* released shortly after *Sgt. Pepper* and masterfully produced in similar fashion by Jimmy Miller, is one of the most durable products of that very dated era. *Traffic* was more fully mature. "Feelin' Alright," "Who Knows What Tomorrow May Bring" and "You Can All Join In" are timeless songs, some of the best moments of their era.

After Mason's departure for a solo career, Traffic was never really the same. *John Barleycorn* was Winwood's swan song as a major talent; the album concentrated more on the folk and jamming elements of the band, and it was particularly effective as a trio record. It includes three stand-out songs: the title track, "Empty Pages" and "Freedom Rider." *Canteen* added a new rhythm section, Latin percussion and reunited Dave Mason with the band for a one-shot tour. The record's fairly good, especially in comparison to the lethargic *On the Road.* Traffic's later work is desultory, with Winwood apparently just going through the motions after his disastrous flirt with superstardom in Blind Faith. He even wrote a song called "Sometimes I Feel So Uninspired," an accurate account of his creative powers. Some of the old spark seemed to return for *When the Eagle Flies* (1977), but nothing has appeared since then.

Since all of Traffic's important work is on the first two albums, the compilation packages are redundant. — J.S.

TRAMMPS
★★ **Disco Inferno / Atl. 18211**
★★★ **The Best of the Trammps / Atl. 19194**
★★★ **The Legendary Zing Album / Bud. 5641**
★★ **Trammps III / Atl. 19148**
★★★ **Where the Happy People Go / Atl. 18172**

The Trammps have been one of disco's most idiosyncratic groups. The band's early singles on Buddah updated ancient R&B classics and featured Jimmy Ellis' straining, gritty tenor against the basso profundo of Earl Young, a style continued on the group's best (though unfortunately deleted) LP, *Trammps* (Golden Fleece 33163). But when the dictates of disco began to demand longer songs, the group foundered on bloated workouts. The Buddah singles are stretched to six-minute-plus lengths on the

Zing album and the Atlantic LPs feature similarly inflated material. Despite some hot tracks ("Where the Happy People Go," "Disco Inferno") and the appeal of Ellis' voice, the excess baggage becomes wearing. — J.MC.

TRANQUILITY
■ **Silver / Epic KE-31989**
■ **Tranquility / Epic 7801**

Pastoral Renaissance-type muck is the aim and feeble latter-day Byrds impressions is the game. This band showed up at the tail end of the country-rock explosion. And missed the boat. It's like the Bonzo Dog Band spoofing Poco. — B.M.

TRAPEZE
★ **Final Swing / Thresh. THS 11**
★ **Hot Wire / War. B-2828**
★★ **Medusa / Thresh. 4**
★ **Trapeze / Thresh. 2**
★★ **You Are the Music . . . We're Just the Band / Thresh. 8**

Trapeze was the only band signed to the Moody Blues' Threshold label. The first album, recorded in 1970 and produced by Moody John Lodge, shows heavy influences from the parent group in its musical and lyrical pretensions. After the initial disaster, Trapeze pared down to a trio that featured heavy, Grand Funk–style power trio rushes and bassist Glenn Hughes' rather studied Steve Marriott screeches and yelps. All of it, stunningly witless and minor-league, is congealed in *Final Swing,* a collection from the first three LPs.

In 1974, Hughes split to shore up Deep Purple, and guitarist Mel Galley and drummer David Holland added a pair of guitarists, Pete Wright and Bob Hendrik, to create, instead of an inferior power trio, an inferior heavy-metal version of the dime-a-dozen guitar-vocal outfits. — A.N.

HAPPY AND ARTIE TRAUM
★★★ **Hard Times in the Country / Roun. 3007**
★★★ **Mud Acres, Music Among Friends / Roun. 3001**
★★★ **Woodstock Mountain / Roun. 3018**

Together or as soloists, backup musicians and songwriters, the Traums were all-around participants in the folk revival. Although two fine Capitol albums are out of print, these LPs represent the traditional foundations and contemporary folk influences that contribute to their sound. Though *Mud Acres* also features Maria Muldaur, Eric Kaz and John Herald, it is the Traums who shape the tone and whose folk-blues-country mesh is one of the building blocks of a Northeastern sound further developed by Dylan, the Band, the Muldaurs and others. — I.M.

PAT TRAVERS
★★★ **Heat in the Streets / Poly. 1-6170**
★★★ **Makin' Magic / Poly. 1-6103**
★★★ **Pat Travers / Poly. 1-6079**
★★★ **Putting It Straight / Poly. 1-6121**
Technically adept Canadian blues-rock guitarist has the standard Eric Clapton fixation but seems to be able to take it somewhere. — J.S.

MERLE TRAVIS
★★★ **Merle Travis and Joe Maphis / Cap. SM-2102**
★★★★ **Merle Travis' Guitar / Cap. SM-650**
★★★★★ **The Best of Merle Travis / Cap. SM-2662**
Merle Travis is influential both as a writer—responsible for "Sixteen Tons" and "Dark as a Dungeon" among others—and as a guitarist. He adapted five-string banjo picking to guitar playing, a style now called "Travis picking." The Capitol *Best of* contains his finest work, including the originals of "Sixteen Tons" and "Dark as a Dungeon." — D.M.

JOHN TRAVOLTA
★★ **Can't Let You Go / Mid. Int. BXL1-2211**
★★ **John Travolta / Mid. Int. BXL1-1563**
The pop face of 1978 actually began recording a couple of years previously, though no one noticed much until *Saturday Night Fever* and *Grease.* Frankly, though, Travolta's a lot more interesting dancing to the Trammps and the Bee Gees than he is slogging his way through modernized Frankie Avalon concoctions. — D.M.

TREMELOES
★ **Shiner / DJM 2**
Like a lot of English pop groups, the Tremeloes have some sort of cult reputation because they existed at the same time as the Beatles and had British hits without any American ones. This is no excuse for such banality. After all, Jay and the Americans aren't forgiven because they existed simultaneously with the Beach Boys and Four Seasons. (Now deleted.) — D.M.

T. REX
★★★ **Electric Warrior / Rep. 6466**

★★★ **The Slider / Rep. 2095**
Marc Bolan formed Tyrannosaurus Rex during the English hippie craze, and made a couple of delightful pop-mystical LPs in a psychedelic folkie vein. But in the early Seventies, Bolan aimed for bigger game—the teen idol market—which required more punch. He built "Bang a Gong," the highlight of *Electric Warrior,* around a Pete Townshend-style fuzz chord riff, and the abbreviated T. Rex had an international hit in 1971. But despite a succession of followups in the same innocently slinky mold, Bolan was never able to follow up his one chart success, and *The Slider* is the only other LP still in print. Bolan died in 1977. — D.M.

TONY TRISCHKA
★★★ **Bluegrass Light / Roun. 0048**
★★ **Heartlands / Roun. 0062**
Banjo player Trischka takes his cues from Bill Keith, combining technique, imagination and a willingness to experiment with traditional styles, and carries bluegrass into new territory. Though Kenny Kosek (fiddle) and Andy Statman (mandolin and saxophone) deserve considerable credit for stylistic and playing innovations here, Trischka makes these LPs his own through the writing and production. *Heartlands* is better recorded and occasionally reaches beyond the themes stated on *Bluegrass Light,* but it lacks the spirit of adventure that marks the earlier LP. — I.M.

TRIUMVIRAT
★ **A La Carte / Cap. ST 11862**
★ **Illusions on a Double Dimple / Harv. ST-11311**
★ **Mediterranean Tales / Elect. 29441**
★ **Old Love Dies Hard / Cap. ST-11551**
★ **Pompeii / Cap. ST-11697**

★ **Spartacus / Cap. ST-11392**
Finland's contribution to Seventies progressive rock. For Focus fans or complete xenophiles only. — J.S.

DOMENIC TROIANO
★★★ **Burnin' at the Stake / Cap. ST-11665**
★★★ **The Joke's on Me / Cap. ST-11772**
Excellent Canadian guitarist who's played with a variety of bands (notably the James Gang and Guess Who) turns in an estimably interesting pair of solo LPs, with lots of hot licks but too few solid songs for real distinction. — D.M.

TROOPER
★ **Knock 'Em Dead / MCA 2275**
★ **Thick as Thieves / MCA 2377**
■ **Trooper / MCA 2149**
★ **Two for the Show / MCA 2214**
Randy Bachman's mid-Seventies heavy-metal discovery. Senescent Bachman-Turner Overdrive. — J.S.

ROBIN TROWER
★★★ **Bridge of Sighs / Chrys. 1057**
★★ **Caravan to Midnight / Chrys. 1189**
★★★ **For Earth Below / Chrys. 1073**
★★★ **In City Dreams / Chrys. 1148**
★★★ **Long Misty Days / Chrys. 1107**
★★★ **Robin Trower—Live! / Chrys. 1089**
★★ **Twice Removed from Yesterday / Chrys. 1039**
Procol Harum's original guitarist, Robin Trower earned a respectable following on both sides of the Atlantic for his powerful and incisive style. He had a knack for shaping a thick, rich sustain from his vintage Les Paul guitar with total control, building towering lead-guitar passages that perfectly complemented the big, keyboard-dominated sound of Procol Harum.

By the time of Procol's *Broken Barricades* LP, Trower had switched to a Fender Stratocaster and a totally different style. This would take him away from the group and on to a solo career. It was definitely fashioned from the Jimi Hendrix school, although Trower cleaned things up and refined certain nuances in terms of bent notes and finger vibrato. *Twice Removed from Yesterday*'s material and execution was still at a nascent stage, and the aura of Hendrix hung too thick for most to penetrate.

But the audience obviously appreciated Trower's aesthetic of continuity and he continued to refine his sound on subsequent albums. *Bridge of Sighs* and *For Earth Below* had better songs, and the addition of drummer Bill Lordan on the latter album helped tighten things up. *Live!*, recorded in Sweden, gave Trower more space to stretch out his improvisations. Concentrating on subtle vibrato and long, shaped notes, he does his best work on slower tunes like "Daydream," where his lyricism prevails. Faster and more popular numbers like "Rock Me Baby" and "Little Bit of Sympathy" have a certain energy, but they suffer from comparison with the originals.

The last few albums exhibit a softer, more understated approach that lacks the fire of Trower's earlier work. For hardcore rock guitar fans. — J.C.C.

ROGER TROY
★★★ **Roger Troy / RCA APL1-1910**
Troy, who played in the 1975 re-formation of Mike Bloomfield and Nick Gravenites' Electric Flag, is a fine white funk singer. This modest solo LP is from the next year. The material limits him, as does the somewhat dated production approach. (Now deleted.) — D.M.

ANDREA TRUE CONNECTION
★ **Steppin' Out / Mid. Int. BKL1-2423**
★ **White Witch / Bud. 5702**
Former porno starlet actually came up with a hit disco single, "More More More," for Buddah, but the rest of these are pretty mediocre no matter how you like to do the do. — D.M.

ERNEST TUBB
★★★ **Ernest Tubb's Golden Favorites / MCA 84**
★★★ **Ernest Tubb's Greatest Hits / MCA 16**
★★★★ **The Ernest Tubb Story / MCA 2-4040**
Tubb is the link between Jimmie Rodgers and Hank Williams in the honky-tonk country tradition. Tubb and Rodgers never met, but Tubb's family became friendly with Rodgers' widow in San Antonio, and she gave him Rodgers' old guitar and arranged for Tubb to record for RCA's Bluebird subsidiary in 1936. In 1940, Tubb signed with Decca Records, for whom he has recorded for nearly forty years, although these are his only remaining catalogue LPs. Tubb became a regular member of the Grand Ole Opry in 1943, after a couple of appearances in Westerns. Later in the Forties, he became one of the first country stars to sing at Carnegie Hall.

Tubb has never been a giant record seller; rather, he is a key influence on many rockabilly and country performers of the present (Asleep at the Wheel in particular). His best-known songs include "Walking the Floor over You," "Our Baby's Book," "My Tennessee Baby," "Have You Ever Been Lonely," "Take Me Back and Try Me One More Time," "Tomorrow Never Comes" and a couple of duets: "Goodnight Irene," the Leadbelly song, sung with Red Foley in 1950, and "Mr. and Mrs. Used to Be" with Loretta Lynn in 1964. *Story* is from 1959; *Golden Favorites* from 1961; *Greatest Hits* from later in the Sixties. — D.M.

THE TUBES
★ Now / A&M 4632
■ The Tubes / A&M 4534
★ What Do You Want from Live / A&M 6003
■ Young and Rich / A&M 4580

The Tubes are a San Francisco troupe that *earns* the title shock-rock. They specialize in a kind of satirical cabaret that emphasizes ambisexuality, *outré* social and political humor, and hard rock twisted into comedic shape. Their best-known song, "White Punks on Dope," is an unlikely freaks' anthem, but most of the time, this material doesn't deserve preservation on wax. What's funny when spontaneous and visual becomes turgid and shrill on repeated listenings, and vocalist Fee Waybill has the most unique range in rock: two notes, both flat. — D.M.

TANYA TUCKER
★★★ Delta Dawn / Col. KC-31742
★★ Here's Some Love / MCA 2213
★★ Lovin' and Learnin' / MCA 2167
★★ Ridin' Rainbows / MCA 2253
★★ Tanya Tucker / MCA 2141
★★★★ Tanya Tucker's Greatest Hits / Col. KC-33355
★★★ Tanya Tucker's Greatest Hits / MCA 3032
★★★ TNT / MCA 3066
★★★ What's Your Mama's Name / Col. KC-32722
★★★ Would You Lay with Me / Col. KC-32744
★★★ You Are So Beautiful / Col. KC-34733

Tanya Tucker began recording in 1972 when she was only thirteen, in a pop-country style developed with producer Bill Sherrill. She immediately scored two minor pop crossover hits, "Would You Lay with

Me in a Field of Stone" and "Blood Red and Going Down." But when she left Columbia and Sherrill, and as she aged, she lost much of her popular attraction. Whether she will ever regain a substantial audience is still open to question. — D.M.

TUFANE AND GIAMMARESE
★★ Other Side / Ode PE-34969

This twosome is a lightweight but—thanks to Jack Richardson's excellent production—more than acceptable entrant in the pop flotsam sweepstakes, edging out the Alessi Brothers by a lot more than a nose. For everyone who wishes Fabian and Frankie Avalon had recorded duets. (Now deleted.) — D.M.

TUFF DARTS
★ Tuff Darts / Sire K-6048

Group that spawned Seventies rockabilly idolater Robert Gordon, recorded long after he'd left the band. Result is perhaps the most mediocre of all American New Wave LPs. — D.M.

IKE AND TINA TURNER
★★★★ Ike and Tina Turner's Festival of Live Performances / Kent 538
★★★★ Ike and Tina Turner's Greatest Hits / U. Artists LA592-G
★★★★ Please, Please, Please / Kent 550
★★★★★ River Deep—Mountain High / A&M 4178
★★ Sixteen Great Performances / ABC BTD 4014
★★★★ The Soul of Ike and Tina Turner / Kent 519
★★★★ The World of Ike and Tina Turner / U. Artists LA064-G2
★★★★ Too Hot to Hold / Sp. 4011
★★★ What You Hear Is What You Get / U. Artists 9953

Ike Turner began his career as an A&R man for a variety of labels, turning over talent to Modern and Sun among others. (Howlin' Wolf was among his discoveries.) He joined forces with his wife, Tina, in the mid-Fifties, and they had several hits through the early Seventies in a variety of R&B styles. The early records for Sun are perhaps their best, but the remakes of such classics of that period as "A Fool in Love" (on *River Deep*) and the United Artists' *World of* aren't bad.

A 1969 tour with the Rolling Stones won the duo a white rock following, which was both deserved (they had one of soul's most dynamic shows) and finally ruinous (it encouraged Tina's tendency to screech rather than sing and incited the Turners' dual capacity for silly salacious byplay). Nonetheless, the recordings for United Artists in this period are solid, although the Blue Thumb material recorded a bit later is far weaker.

The Kent records are solid Sixties R&B, featuring Tina's voice above Ike's always tight rhythm arrangements, with a band led by his fine guitar playing. *River Deep* is a Phil Spector production and one of the true anomalies of rock & roll; the title song's failure to become a hit single drove Spector into retirement for several years. Yet when the album was finally rereleased in the early Seventies, it was a hodgepodge in which Turner's bluesy productions clash with Spector's silken Wall of Sound. It never lives up to what Spector claimed for it, although it occasionally comes close enough to be a must for fans of either performer or producer. — D.M.

SPYDER TURNER
★ **Music Web / Whit. K-3124**
Turner earned his legend with a late-Sixties one-shot, a version of Ben E. King's "Stand by Me" into which he interpolated the styles of King, Sam Cooke, Otis Redding, Smokey Robinson, James Brown and other soul heroes of the day. (And inspired a monumentally silly but famous rock essay by Sandy Pearlman—later Blue Oyster Cult's producer—called "The Raunch Epistomology of Spyder Turner.") This is a 1977 "comeback" LP, but Turner didn't really have anywhere to go back *to.* — D.M.

TINA TURNER
★★★ **Acid Queen / U. Artists LA495-G**
★★★ **The Queen / Sp. 4033**
Without Ike Turner's grand sense of groove and melody, Tina is left on her own to shout and screech without much purpose. Stick with the Ike and Tina sides. (Now deleted.) — D.M.

THE TURTLES
★★★★ **Greatest Hits / Sire H-3703-2**
The only one in the catalogue is the only one you could ever want. Complete with liner notes from former Turtles Flo and Eddie, the collection runs the gamut from the seminal folk-rock "It Ain't Me Babe" to the memorable pop-schlock "Elenore" and "Happy Together" to a look at where they are now (a 1966 Warren Zevon song called "Outside Chance," performed like a cross between the Rolling Stones and ? and the Mysterians). Period music to be

sure, but what a fine period! (Now deleted.) — J.B.M.

TWIGGY
★★ **Please Get My Name Right / Mer. SRM-1-1138**
★★ **Twiggy / Mer. SRM-1-1093**
Sings better than she used to look when she was faking it as the mistress of Carnaby Street. But still not good enough. (Now deleted.) — D.M.

DWIGHT TWILLEY
★★★ **Sincerely / Shel. 52001**
★★★ **Twilley / Ari. 4214**
★★★ **Twilley Don't Mind / Ari. 4140**
Beatles and Byrds influences abound in this Tulsa band's albums. The best moment is on the first (Shelter) album: their 1975 hit single, "I'm on Fire," rockabilly for moderns. — J.S.

CONWAY TWITTY
★★ **Conway Twitty's Honky Tonk Angel / MCA 406**
★★ **Georgia Keeps Pulling On My Ring / MCA 2328**
★★★★ **Greatest Hits, Vol. 1 / MCA 2345**
★★★★ **Greatest Hits, Vol. 2 / MCA 2235**
★★★ **Hello Darlin' / MCA 19**
★★★ **High Priest of Country Music / MCA 2144**
★★ **I'm Not Through Loving You Yet / MCA 441**
★★ **I'm Not Used to Loving You / Cor. 20000**
★★ **I've Already Loved You in My Mind / MCA 2293**
★★ **Linda on My Mind / MCA 469**
★★ **Now and Then / MCA 2206**
★★★ **Play Guitar Play / MCA 2262**
★★★ **To See My Angel Cry / MCA 18**
★★ **Twitty / MCA 2176**
★★ **You've Never Been This Far Before / MCA 359**
Twitty originally scored with "It's Only Make Believe," a 1958 No. 1 hit. He followed it the next year with "Mona Lisa," before tripping over from rockabilly into straight country where he has become a major force, albeit a conservative one. His records continually top the country charts, and occasionally when he combines his big baritone voice, still acute guitar playing and his top-notch group, The Twitty Birds, he makes a record that breaks through the stifling conventions of current country pop. — D.M.

TYLA GANG
★★ **Moonproof / Beserk 0059**

★★★ **Yachtless / Beserk 0057**
New Wave-associated studio group, led by
Sean Tyla, shares Nick Lowe's affection
for the inside joke as pop song, but lacks
his imagination and inspiration. Not bad,
but they ran out of ideas after the first record. — D.M.

BONNIE TYLER
★ **Diamond Cut / RCA AFLI-3072**
★★ **It's a Heartache / RCA AFLI-2821**
★ **The World Starts Tonight / Chrys. 1140**
Tyler's Chrysalis debut LP makes her
sound like an ersatz Janis Joplin, screeching loudly but without discipline. She
toned down for her first RCA album,
Heartache, and earned a Rod Stewart
sound-alike hit in early 1978 with "It's a
Heartache," but the rest of the record is
too bland for comfort, a style that continued on *Diamond Cut.* — D.M.

THE TYMES
★★★ **Best of the Tymes / Abkco 4228**
★★ **Diggin' Their Roots / RCA
APL1-2406**
★★ **Turning Point / RCA APL1-1835**
A very late, somewhat minor doo-wop
group from Philadelphia, the Tymes first
scored in 1963 with "So Much in Love"
and followed it up with "Wonderful Wonderful." But by the end of 1964, they were
on their way back to obscurity. The Abkco
collection is the one to get—the RCA discs
are recent attempts to revive the group
with a more modern style. — D.M.

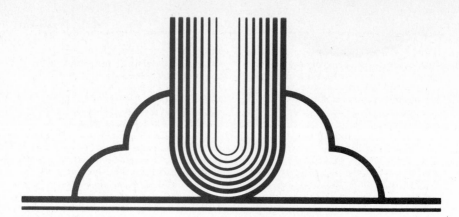

PERE UBU
★ **Dub Housing / Chrys. 1207**
Art rock with a New Wave face is no less
pompous, pretentious or irrelevant because
of its claim to association with Johnny
Rotten. Anti-rock for anti-rockers.
Boo. — D.M.

UFO
★★ **Force It / Chrys. 1074**
★★ **Lights Out / Chrys. 1127**
★★ **No Heavy Petting / Chrys. 1103**
★★ **Obsession / Chrys. 1182**
★★ **Phenomenon / Chrys. 1059**
★★ **Strangers in the Night / Chrys. 1209**
UFO began as a power trio with lead vo-
calist; its chief distinction was the thick
chording and agile (if unrevolutionary)
lead guitar playing of Michael Schenker.
Phenomenon, Force It and *No Heavy Petting*
were produced by Leo Lyon, of Ten Years
After. TYA keyboard player Chick
Churchill also turns up on *Force It.* With
Petting, a permanent keyboardist was
added to flesh out the sound; subsequent
releases used more artillery—horns and
strings even—in attempt at greater substance. Not much of it worked. — C.W.

U.K.
★★★ **Danger Money / Poly. 1-6194**
★★★ **U.K. / Poly. 1-6146**
Progressive rock supergroup led by former
Yes/King Crimson percussionist Bill Bu-
ford and ex-Roxy Music synthesizer whiz
Eddie Jobson turned in competent job with
first two LPs, all the rage among techno-
philes in 1978. — D.M.

U.K. SQUEEZE
★ **Cool for Cats / A&M 4759**
★ **U.K. Squeeze / A&M 4687**
Not be be confused with U.K., this group
produces anonymous, pedestrian hard rock

of the same vintage as the other's. By the
end of 1978, this band was so defeated it
changed its name to the simpler
Squeeze. — D.M

ULTRAVOX
★★★ **Systems of Romance / Ant. 7069**
★★★ **Ultravox / Is. 9449**
Passable late-Seventies hard rock by Brit-
ish quintet. — D.M.

UNDISPUTED TRUTH
★★ **Method to the Madness / Whit. 2967**
Led by Chaka Khan's sister, Taka Boom,
this group scored a great early-Seventies
hit for Motown in "Smiling Faces Sometimes," but has never reached that level
since. The album to look for is the now-deleted Motown debut, which also features
the weirdest version of "Like a Rolling
Stone" ever made. — D.M

UNICORN
★ **One More Tomorrow / Cap. ST-11692**
This British folk-rock quartet, produced by
Pink Floyd's David Gilmour, released a
versatile and engaging record in 1976 (*Unicorn II*), which is now out of print. But
leader Ken Baker seemed to run out of
songwriting inspiration by the time they
recorded this third album, and the hasty
inclusion of John Fogerty's "Have You
Ever Seen the Rain" does little to salvage
it. The only two songs of interest, "So
Hard to Get Through" and "The Night,"
show a decided Dylan influence on Baker's
writing that he would probably do well to
cultivate. (Now deleted.) — J.S.

UNION GAP
★ **Lady Willpower / Col. EN-13093**
★★★ **Union Gap's Greatest Hits / Col.
CS-1042**

Powered by Gary Puckett's searing lead vocals, the Union Gap racked up a series of hits from 1967 to 1968—"Woman, Woman," "Young Girl," "Lady Willpower" and "Over You." The group was strictly a singles band, so the *Greatest Hits* set is the only one that makes sense. — J.S.

UNIQUES
★★★ Golden Hits / All Pl. 2208
★★★ Uniquely Yours / All. Pl. 2190
★★★ Uniques / All Pl. 2204
More post-doo-wop Jersey rhythm & blues, à la the Montclairs and Sylvia. — D.M.

UNIVERSE CITY
★ Universe City / Mid. Int. BKL1-1368
Not the *Star Wars* of rock & roll exactly, but if there's a disco in heaven, maybe the angels boogie to this. God help 'em. (Now deleted.) — D.M.

PHIL UPCHURCH
★★★ Feeling Blue / Mile. 9010
★★ Phil Upchurch / Cadet 826
★★ Phil Upchurch / Mar. 2209
★★ The Way I Feel / Cadet 840
Upchurch is from Chicago, and his guitar playing is basically derived from blues and funk, with an undercurrent of Charlie Christian in his phrasing. His early albums show off a tough guitar sound with spurts of inventiveness bouncing off occasionally inappropriate choral and orchestral backgrounds.

Unfortunately, most of Upchurch's career has been marked by formula playing and funk anonymity. Upchurch's style is fluid and clean but colorless. A tendency to become a guitar chameleon (too many sessions) is best expressed on the Marlin *Phil Upchurch*, his latest and most commercial effort. The first side is produced by John Tropea, and Upchurch unconsciously assumes a Tropean style. On side two, George Benson produces, and guess who Phil turns into as of the first few notes? *Feeling Blue* is the only recommendation here. — J.C.C.

UPP
★★ This Way Upp / Epic PE-34177
★★ Upp / Epic KE-33439
Jeff Beck-inspired band (he produced the first album, *Upp*, and plays on the second) gets swamped in obeisance to Beck's own *Blow by Blow* for average late-Seventies fusion music. — J.S.

UPSETTERS
★★ Super Ape / Is. 9417
If reggae were plagued with boring disco records, this is probably what they'd sound like. Fortunately, most reggae is exciting dance music, which is all the less reason to listen to this assemblage of unfocused riffs. — D.M.

URIAH HEEP
★ Best of Uriah Heep / Mer. SRM-1-1070
★ Demons and Wizards / Mer. SRM-1-630
■ Fallen Angel / Chrys. 1204
■ Firefly / War. B-3013
■ High and Mighty / War. B-2949
■ Innocent Victim / War. K-3145
★ Look at Yourself / Mer. SRM-1-614
■ Magician's Birthday / Mer. SRM-1-652
■ Return to Fantasy / War. B-2869
■ Salisbury / Mer. 61319
■ Sweet Freedom / War. B-2724
■ Uriah Heep / Mer. SRM-61294
■ Uriah Heep Live / Mer. SRM-2-7503
■ Wonderworld / War. 2800
A mutant version of Deep Purple, Uriah Heep has to be considered one of the worst commerically successful bands of the Seventies. Good points: sincerity and an organist (Ken Hensley) far more intelligent and capable than the group. Bad points: one of the most strident and annoying singers (David Byron) in rock history. The problem is that Byron gets the material he deserves. — J.S.

U-ROY
★★★★ Dread in-a Babylon / Virgin PZ-34234
One of the original masters of the reggae-derived "dee jay" style, U-Roy's a scabrous conversationalist with a more than funky beat, but definitely not the thing for the

faint of heart or those with any antipathy to marijuana, which he treats as a true sacrament. — D.M.

URUBAMBA
★ ★ ★ ★ **Urubamba / Col. KC-32896**
This album of Peruvian folk music was recorded by Paul Simon, who has used this group on some of his recordings, both solo and with Simon and Garfunkel. It is sur-prisingly charming, the South American flute and drums carrying a series of high-pitched but soothing melodies that are calm without becoming Muzak. (Now deleted.) — D.M.

UTOPIA
■ **Utopia / Kent 566**
Todd Rundgren's idea of a joke—synthe-sizer psychodrama. Ugh. — J.S.

VALDY
★★ **See How the Years Have Gone By /**
A&M 4538
★★ **Valdy and the Hometown Band /**
A&M 4592

Valdy is a minor Canadian pop music institution who has successfully played out
the semi-amateur folksinger role for almost
a decade. Despite the slickness of his records, Valdy's songs are moral rather than
mellow, full of message rather than mellif-
luence. His performances are notorious for
their arrogant displays of "country man"
sermonizing.

After recording two studio LPs and one
live one in Canada, Valdy went to L.A. to
record a U.S. greatest-hits package, *See
How the Years.* Producer Paul Rothchild
offers a tastefully dressed-up L.A. session
band and Valdy sounds quite at ease, if a
bit comatose.

Valdy and the Hometown Band, produced
by Claire Lawrence, marks a slight change
in Valdy's writing. Instead of posing as
Legendary Canadian Mountain Man,
Valdy becomes a trans-Canada tourist and
produces full-color, National Film Board
songs. The Hometown Band, a very flexible Vancouver-based group that also records on its own, provides an intelligently
eclectic backup without the pretensions of
ponderous rootsiness that are Valdy's usual
stock in trade. — B.T.

FRANKIE VALLI
■ **Frankie Valli Is the Word / War.**
K-3233

In plain English, that word means garbage.
Despite his association with the Four Seasons, Valli's career is really notable because he has managed to extend the nasal
whining of the Fabian/Frankie Avalon
style well into the Seventies. Pure pop for
poor fools. — D.M.

VANCE OR TOWERS
★ **Vance or Towers / A&M 4551**
California singer/songwriter team whose
songs bear titles like "Scream Bloody Robbery" and "Education Blues." The limpest
of the wimps. (Now deleted.) — J.S.

VAN DER GRAAF GENERATOR
★★★ **H to He Who Am the Only One /**
Dun. X-50097
Van Der Graaf Generator was formed in
England's Manchester University in 1967,
and has been together, off and on, in one
form or another, ever since. *H to He,* a
1970 release, is the group's only American
catalogue item, although Mercury has released and deleted three others. This one
sports a rich, elegant reserve, not unlike a
less majestic Procol Harum or a more
preened King Crimson. The songs are
long, serious and delicate, though not
weak. The somber, almost menacing arrangements are paced by Hugh Banton's
careful and exact piano, organ and pedal
bass, and Guy Evans' neatly energetic
drumming. But guitarist/leader Peter Ham-
mill's affected and bathos-laden lyrics and
singing too often obscure the music. David
Jackson's simple, subtly jazz-tinged saxophone is, however, good punctuation. Robert Fripp's guitar graces one cut. — C.W.

LON AND DERREK VAN EATON
★★ **Who Do You Out Do / A&M 4507**
Passable melodic pop, unambitious and
unindividual. Economic arranging, medium
tempos, lots of vocal harmonies. Suitably
modest production from Richard Perry and
Bill Schnee. (Now deleted.) — C.W.

VANGELIS
★ **Albedo 0. 39 / RCA AFL1-5136**
★ **Beaubourg / RCA AFL1-3020**
★ **China / Poly. 1-6199**

★ **Heaven and Hell / RCA AFL1-5110**
★ **Spiral / RCA AFL1-2627**
Greek piano prodigy makes his records in
England. Allegedly this is rock, but if that's
true, then the guy who wrote the soundtrack for *2001* is Buddy Holly. Classical
mediocrity. — D.M.

VAN HALEN
★★★ **Van Halen / War. K-3075**
★★ **Van Halen 2 / War. HS-3312**
1978's heavy-metal surprise was a Southern
California band that grinds out a variety of
variations on the basic "Louie Louie"
thump theme, most notably a version of
the Kinks' earlier variation, "All Day and
All of the Night." The second album is as
imaginative as its title. — D.M.

VANILLA FUDGE
★★★ **Vanilla Fudge / Atco 224**
One of the most absurd albums ever
made—soul music, "In-A-Gadda-Da-Vida"
style. In 1968, when this album was released, the notion of a psychedelic version
of the Supremes' "You Keep Me Hangin'
On" was so perfect that the Fudge actually
found itself with a hit single. Grand organ
playing, lugubrious drumming, vocals that
define wretched excess, pure period fun.
Ages better than some "serious" art rock of
the era. — D.M.

GINO VANNELLI
■ **A Pauper in Paradise / A&M 4664**
★ **Brother to Brother / A&M 4722**
■ **Crazy Life / A&M 4395**
★ **Powerful People / A&M 3630**
★ **Storm at Sunup / A&M 4533**
■ **The Gist of the Gemini / A&M 4596**
Teamed with his keyboardist brother,
John, and under the tutelage of Herb Al-
pert, Gino Vannelli has progressed from
mere schlock to monumental vulgarity,
creating a mammoth new "My Way" out
of MOR melodies and his brother's
post-Pink Floyd Muzak.

Vannelli is primarily a crooner, but capable of twisting loudly in the sonic wind
whooshing from the synthesizers. He is a
parody of romantic agony, a pop Prome-
theus unbound by taste or prodded by
imagination. Studio technology, the budget
to use it, and Gino's temperamental self-
image are the sole sources of development
from the suburban wedding music of *Crazy
Life* to the errant disco of *Powerful People*
to the unavoidable crystallization of style
begun with *Storm at Sunup*. Perhaps a few
of Vannelli's epic arrogations might work,

were it not for his lyrics that extend bot-
tomless narcissism and chilling stupidity
beyond sodden sentimentality straight into
complete hilarity. — B.T.

DAVE VAN RONK
★ **Black Mountain Blues / Folk. 31020**
★★★ **Dave Van Ronk / Fan. 24710**
★ **Dave Van Ronk Sings Earthy Ballads
and Blues / Folk. FA-2383**
★★ **In the Tradition / Prest. 7800**
★★★ **Sunday Street / Philo 1036**
This is just a bare sampling of Van Ronk's
recorded work. One of the majors behind
the folk revival, both as a performer and as
host to many would-be folkies newly arrived in New York, Van Ronk's initial
loves were blues and jazz. Eventually he
integrated the songs of contemporary writers—Bob Dylan, Joni Mitchell, even
Jacques Brel—into his gruffly tender style.

The Folkways sets are more interesting
for material than sound quality, which is
poor, and Van Ronk's often instructive
blues guitar work is largely inaudible. The
Fantasy two-disc set is a repackaging of his
first two Prestige LPs, *Folksinger* and *Inside,* both recorded in 1962. They feature
some of his best-known interpretations—
most notably "Cocaine Blues," "He Was a
Friend of Mine" (perhaps the first cover of
a Dylan song), "Motherless Child" and
"Fair and Tender Ladies." *In the Tradition*
finds Van Ronk singing as part of the Red
Onion Jazz Band (Dixieland, of course) on
six songs and performing solo blues on the
remainder.

Sunday Street, released in 1976, is representative of Van Ronk's periodic forays
into a sound that links his traditional efforts to the pop idiom—which is not to say
that it's a pop record. But together with a
now out-of-print Polydor LP, it covers his
performing repertoire (he has often re-recorded songs over the years as his approach to them changes) in a faithful yet
accessible fashion. — I.M.

TOWNES VAN ZANDT
★★★ **Delta Momma Blues / Toma. 7013**
★★★ **Flyin' Shoes / Toma. 7017**
★★★ **High, Low and In-Between / Toma.
7012**
★★★ **Our Mother, the Mountain / Toma.
7015**
★★★ **The Late, Great Townes Van
Zandt / Toma. 7011**
★★★ **Townes Van Zandt / Toma. 7014**
★★★ **Townes Van Zandt Live / Toma.
2-7001**

The Jackson Browne of Texas. Which means that Van Zandt's country inflection is a bit more authentic, his mysticism is firmly grounded in pop psychology, his melodies have a hummable sameness, and he isn't much of a vocalist. On the other hand, Townes is a hell of a lot better alternative than, say, John David Souther. — D.M.

TÁTA VEGA
★★ **Full Speed Ahead / Tam. T7-347**
★★★ **Totally Táta / Tam. T7-353**
★★ **Try My Love / Tam. T7-360**

Táta Vega is an exception to the glut of current, anonymous Motown acts. Though her debut LP, *Full Speed Ahead,* is perfunctory disco, *Totally Táta* shows intelligence and some varied ideas. The influences on *Totally Táta* include Stevie Wonder, Marvin Gaye and Jackson Five, but the album's unfortunate commercial failure may preclude any further musical ambitiousness. — J.MC.

MARTHA VELEZ
★★ **American Heartbeat / Sire 6040**
★★★ **Escape from Babylon / Sire D-7515**
★★ **Matinee Weepers / Sire 7409**

Velez is a veteran New York Latin-soul singer with a more than passing interest in rock trends. In 1975, she made *Escape* with Bob Marley as producer; it survives as one of the more eccentric moments in either career, a hybrid of soul and reggae that could have been great if Velez had a mite more voice. *Matinee Weepers,* however, is simply forced and none too soulful—whatever Velez learned in Jamaica, she left it there before returning to Manhattan. — D.M.

THE VELVET UNDERGROUND
★★★★★ **Loaded / Coti. 9034**
★★★★★ **1969 Velvet Underground Live / Mer. SRM 2-7504**
★★★★★ **The Velvet Underground and Nico / Verve 6-5008**
★★★★ **The Velvet Underground Live at Max's Kansas City / Coti. 9500**

Few groups in the history of popular music have broken down as many barricades as the Velvet Underground did in its all-too-brief existence. The Velvets' foresight into the directions that electric music was taking (dissonance, feedback, extended improvisation) and their forays into taboo lyrical subject matter (the decadence of the idle rich, the horrors and joys of drugs, the realities of life on the street) were so out of step with what was going on in the music world around them in the late Sixties and early Seventies that they never gathered more than a very small cult following. Yet the Velvets' influence hovers over all present music seeking to do more than merely entertain. Leader Lou Reed's almost *cinéma véurité* songwriting style rang with an honesty and compassion that few songwriters ever reach, and the band's uncompromising, committed playing is arguably *the* source of most punk/New Wave music.

The group's first album, *The Velvet Underground and Nico,* with its famous Andy Warhol banana cover, features such classics as "Waiting for the Man," "Heroin," "Venus in Furs" and "I'll Be Your Mirror," with the ever-mysterious Nico on lead vocals on several tracks, and John Cale's viola and piano helping to shape the various moods and images evoked by the band's music. The second and third LPs, *White Light White Heat* and *The Velvet Underground* (both out of print), are also masterpieces, though on completely different levels. *White Light* is a turbulent, almost chaotic assault of electric music. *The Velvet Underground* is the most low-key of the group's records, with several beautiful ballads ("Candy Says," "I'm Set Free," "Pale Blue Eyes") and some extraordinary rhythm guitar by Reed on "What Goes On."

Loaded is the final testament, recorded at a time (1970) when things were looking up for the band. It's the most accessible of the Velvets' records, featuring such charged rockers as "Rock and Roll" and "Head Held High" and some passionate ballads ("New Age," "Oh! Sweet Nuthin' ").

Of the two live albums released after the band's demise, the Mercury double-LP set is recommended slightly above the Max's record because it features a few previously unrecorded songs and captures neatly the often-overlooked ability of the group to rock out gracefully without compromising its music or attitudes. Reed's heartfelt singing, Sterling Morrison's sympathetic lead work, Doug Yule's innocent, supportive vocals and fine bass work (he replaced Cale after the second album), and Maureen Tucker's primitive, solid drumming are displayed here to the fullest and make the set a glorious document of the music. — B.A.

THE VENTURES
★★★ **Golden Greats by the Ventures / Lib. 8053**
★★★ **Tenth Anniversary Album / Lib. 35000**
★★★ **The Ventures Play Telstar and Lonely Bull / Lib. 8019**
★★★ **TV Themes / U. Artists LA717-G**
★★★★ **Walk Don't Run / Lib. 8003**
Textbook instrumental rock & roll, West Coast school, brought to us through the Sixties courtesy of Bob Bogle (guitar/bass), Nokie Edwards (guitar), Don Wilson (guitar) and Mel Taylor (drums). These four journeyman musicians helped blaze a path for many aspiring rockers through their tough, no-nonsense treatment of rock & roll classics and popular movie and TV themes of the day.

The Ventures' big hit, "Walk Don't Run," is a marvel of rock & roll balance, with the dark and echoey lead guitar part that put the Mostite Company on the map; it survives as the era's signature sound. The current discography is confused to say the least, and you're more likely to find out-of-print Ventures albums in the cutout bins than anything on this list. But rejoice in the fact that they all sound the same, so it really doesn't matter anyway. Stiff snare and cymbal sound, pulsing bass and metallic guitars spitting out popular melodies through a wash of echo and vibrato. What more could the young musician ask for? — J.C.C.

VIGRASS AND OSBORNE
■ **Steppin' Out / Epic KE-33077**
This duo's 1974 album is about as low as you can get. Vigrass is yet another British art school product, whose claim to fame is having worked with Tim Rice and Andrew Lloyd Weber. Osborne is a burnt-out psychedelic holdover from the Chocolate Watchband. Together they managed to write a newspaper song called "Daily Depress" that actually includes the line

"That's all water under the gate." (Now deleted.) — J.S.

THE VILLAGE PEOPLE
★★★ **Cruisin' / Casa. 7118**
★★★ **Go West / Casa. 7144**
★★★ **Macho Man / Casa. 7096**
★★ **Village People / Casa. 7064**
Late-Seventies disco group (all male) raised the gay visual stereotype to an art form: an Indian, a leather freak, et cetera. Everything but a sissy, which would not have worked, because their big hit was "Macho Man," a dumb but inspired dance chant. It was followed by "YMCA," which was more frank and just as stupid, if equally danceable. Kiss for grown-ups. — D.M.

GENE VINCENT
★★★ **Gene Vincent's Greatest / Cap. SM-380**
★★★★ **The Bop That Just Won't Stop / Cap. SM-11826**
Minor but influential Fifties rockabilly artist who is best known for (a) his hit single, "Be-Bop-a-Lula," one of the raunchiest white records of the first rock decade, and (b) being injured in the car crash that killed Eddie Cochran. Between the two, Vincent managed a career that spanned the early Seventies—he died in 1971. These are his best, and while they aren't as expansive in scope as Buddy Holly's or Elvis Presley's, they still are important groundwork rock & roll. A real wild man. — D.M.

VOLUNTEERS
★ **Volunteers / Ari. 4103**
A four-man singer/songwriter team whose most notable partner, Wayne Berry, had a couple of (now-deleted) solo LPs for RCA in the mid-Seventies. But Berry's talents are stifled here, partly by the mediocrity of

the other contributions, mostly by the execrably hackneyed production of Jim Mason. (Now deleted.)   — D.M.

ERIC VON SCHMIDT
★★ **Eric Von Schmidt with Rolf Cahn /**
Folk. 2417
★★ **The Folk Blues of Eric Von Schmidt /**
Prest. 7717
A composer, blues interpreter and artist/illustrator, Von Schmidt sang intermittently throughout the Fifties and early Sixties, although music took second place to his artistic pursuits. He was immortalized by an aside about him that Bob Dylan offered on his debut album. Both of these sets date from the early Sixties, the Folkways LP offering a more interesting song selection, the Prestige recording featuring blues and jug-band style support from Geoff Muldaur, Robert Jones and Fritz Richmond.   — I.M.

PORTER WAGONER
★★★ **Porter / RCA AHL1-2432**
★★★★★ **The Best of Porter Wagoner /
RCA ANL1-1213**
★★★★ **The Best of Porter Wagoner, Vol.
2 / RCA LSP-4321**
Wagoner has been a major country star
since 1955, when he hit with "Satisfied
Mind." He joined the Grand Ole Opry in
1957 and started his own TV show in 1960.
His hits in the Sixties included "Cold Dark
Waters," "Misery Loves Company,"
"Green Green Grass of Home," "Skid
Row Joe" and "The Cold Hard Facts of
Life." In 1968, he began performing duets
with Dolly Parton. He remains an influen-
tial, if eccentric, mainstream country per-
former. — D.M.

BUNNY WAILER
★★★★ **Black Heart Man / Is. 9415**
Bunny Wailer (né Livingston) was one of
the Wailers' original members, and as
such, a crucial figure in the development of
reggae. After Bob Marley converted that
group to mere backup in the mid-Seventies, dispensing with Bunny and Peter Tosh
except for special occasions, Bunny recorded this remarkable record, darker and
yet more listenable than much of Marley's
recent guitar-noodling. It contains more
than its share of Rastafarian religious rhetoric (even a song called "Armageddon"),
but Bunny is still a better singer on his
own than Marley. — D.M.

BOB MARLEY AND THE WAILERS
★★★ **Babylon by Bus / Is. 11**
★★★ **Birth of a Legend / Calla
ZX-34759**
★★★★ **Burnin' / Is. 9256**
★★★★ **Catch a Fire / Is. 9241**
★★★ **Early Music / Calla ZX-34760**
★★★ **Exodus / Is. 9498**

★★★ **Kaya / Is. 9517**
★★★★★ **Live / Is. 9376**
★★★★ **Natty Dread / Is. 9281**
★★★ **Rastaman Vibrations / Is. 9383**
The Wailers have been the most important
group in reggae since the late Sixties; their
only real challengers are Toots and the
Maytals, Bob Marley, Peter Tosh and Bunny Livingston (who now records as Bunny
Wailer) joined together in the mid-Sixties
and recorded several primordial singles
(collected on the Calla packages), including the brilliant "Trench Town Rock."
Catch a Fire was the group's first American
release, but while it got excellent critical
notices, it received little airplay or public
attention. With *Burnin',* Tosh and Livingston left the group and Bob Marley, who
had been the group's principal guitarist,
took the band over. Under his direction, it
continued to make some of the most exciting music of the Seventies, climaxing
with the 1976 London concert captured
on *Live.*

But thereafter, as Marley became more
prominent among rock listeners, he took
the band in the direction of superstar guitar. Marley is an estimable guitarist, but
his compositions are meandering (*Exodus*
is a perfectly self-descriptive LP title), his
lyrics exploit the usual Rastafarian politi-
cal/religious imagery less effectively than
they did when he was aided by Tosh and
Livingston, and his singing simply can't
carry the group. By the time of 1978's
Kaya, he seemed more like a popularizer of
the form, much as Cream was for blues
rock, than one of its elder statesmen. The
group's best songs, particularly "No
Woman No Cry," "Get Up Stand Up" and
"I Shot the Sheriff," remain exciting, but
the more recent work is tame in comparison to the Marley-Tosh-Livingston collaborations. — D.M.

LOUDON WAINWRIGHT III
★★★ Album II / Atl. 8291
★★★★ Album III / Col. C-31462
★★★ Attempted Mustache / Col.
C-32710
★★ Final Exam / Ari. 4173
★★★ Loudon Wainwright III / Atl. 8260
★★ T-Shirt / Ari. 4063
★★ Unrequited / Col. PC-33369

Acoustic singer/songwriter and brilliant middle-class satirist. Onstage, Wainwright is Chaplin through the eyes of Artaud, filtered through Dylan. *Album III* has his only hit, the bizarre one-shot, "Dead Skunk." The Atlantic albums contain his least comic, most mordant material; the Arista LPs have his most bitter and freakish. — S.H.

GENEVIEVE WAITE
■ Romance Is on the Rise / Proj.
QD-5088

Cutie-pie singer who played little girl Gracie Allen dumbbell to former Papa John Phillips' posthippie George Burns. Nice decadent move, but in the postfeminist age, it's offensive. (Now deleted.) — D.M.

TOM WAITS
★★★★ Blue Valentine / Asy. 6E-162
★★★★ Closing Time / Asy. 5061
★★★★ Foreign Affairs / Asy. 7E-1117
★★★ Heart of Saturday Night / Asy.
7E-1015
★★★ Nighthawks at the Diner / Asy.
7E-2008
★★★ Small Change / Asy. 7E-1078

Tom Waits is probably the most beatnik-influenced figure in rock & roll—his best work is a cross between one of Jack Kerouac's amphetamine verbal rambles and a psychotic short-order chef's midnight diatribe. This obscures, unfortunately, his talents as a composer (*Small Change* and *Closing Time* each contain several winning songs), and his gravel-voiced poetic renditions can become tedious for all but cultists. Waits is a punk of the old school, hard-bitten and determinedly scrounging, worth watching, if not always able to transcend his own excessive wordiness. *Blue Valentine*, a 1978 album that contains a remarkable version of *West Side Story*'s "Somewhere" and a lot of actual music instead of polysyllabic monotone mumble, is his best effort since the debut. — D.M.

RICK WAKEMAN
★★★ Journey to the Center of the Earth /
A&M 3621

★★ Myths and Legends of King Arthur /
A&M 4515
★★ No Earthly Connection / A&M 4583
★★ Rick Wakeman's Criminal Record /
A&M 4660
★★★ Six Wives of Henry VIII / A&M
4361
★★ White Rock / A&M 4614

Classically trained ex-Strawbs and Yes keyboardist lets his imagination run wild on these bloated solo efforts full of wholesale clips from his favorite composers. Wakeman's attempt at making program music for the various themes the albums are supposed to represent is ludicrous, but enough decent playing surfaces through the smoke screen to save this stuff from the recycling vat. His first solo outing, *Six Wives*, remains Wakeman's best. — J.S.

WENDY WALDMAN
★★ Gypsy Symphony / War. B-2792
★★★★ Love Has Got Me / War. B-2735
★★ Main Refrain / War. K-2974
★★ Strange Company / War. K-3178
★★ Wendy Waldman / War. B-2859

LA singer/songwriter heavily influenced by Laura Nyro has yet to fulfill the potential shown by her first album, *Love Has Got Me* (1973). — S.H.

JERRY JEFF WALKER
★★★ A Man Must Carry On / MCA
2-8013
★★★ Contrary to Ordinary / MCA 3041
★★★★ It's a Good Night for Singin' /
MCA 2202
★★★ Jerry Jeff / Elek. 6E-163
★★★ Jerry Jeff Walker / MCA 2358
★★★ Ridin' High / MCA 2156
★★★ Viva Terlingua / MCA 2350
★★★★ Walker's Collectibles / MCA
2355

Walker's best-known song is "Mr. Bojangles," a 1970 hit for the Nitty Gritty Dirt Band. Associated with the Austin, Texas, outlaw country scene, his band—The Lost Gonzos—is perhaps the best in the genre. His records tend to sound too similar, and they have a tendency toward hippie sentimentalism and sanctimoniousness. But at his best he is a wryly humorous and moving performer, worth hearing by country-rock buffs. — D.M.

JIMMIE (J.J) WALKER
★ Dyn-O-Mite / Bud. S-5635

A young black comic whose stage persona is quite different from the sunny, sassy character portrayed on TV's *Good Times*, the role that made his club career commercially viable. He spins out already dated one-liners about black style. (Now deleted.) — K.T.

JUNIOR WALKER AND THE ALL STARS
★★★★★ Anthology / Mo. M2-786
★★★★ Greatest Hits / Soul S7-718
★★★★ Shotgun / Pick. 3391
★ Smooth / Soul 750
★ Whopper Bopper Show Stopper / Soul S7-748

Even in his salad days, Junior Walker was a soul-music anomaly. As a member of the mid-Sixties Motown stable, Walker managed a steady stream of hot party hits ("Shotgun," "I'm a Roadrunner") using a honking saxophone style that had its roots in late-Forties and early-Fifties R&B. Walker's voice and saxophone shared a similar tone: both gruff and ragged with an appealing affability. Though his early Motown hits resembled the records of his label counterparts only in the velocity of the band tracks, by the late Sixties, Walker was funneled into more muted and produced settings. With increased emphasis on vocals and more lyrical saxophone solos, Walker maintained his popularity with ballad and midtempo hits like "What Does It Take (To Win Your Love for Me)."

After a commercial decline and a recording absence of several years, Walker was resurrected by Motown in the mid-Seventies, when party hits (as a part of disco) became a black pop staple again. *Whopper Bopper* and *Smooth* are both results of that era, but the best of the comeback LPs, *Hot Shot* (produced by Brian Holland and emphasizing Walker's gruffer side) is out of print. — J.MC.

PETER WALKER
★★★ Second Poem to Karmela / Van. 79282

Mood music for hippies, played on a variety of stringed instruments. The title of Walker's best-known album, *Rainy Day Raga,* gives the idea of this Haight-Ashbury smooch music, though that record is no longer in print. (Now deleted.) — D.M.

SAMMY WALKER
★ Blue Ridge Mountain Skyline / War. B-3080
★ Song for Patty / Folk. 4310

Walker was originally presented to the world under the aegis of the late Phil Ochs as yet another "new Bob Dylan." But in

Walker's hand, Dylan's influence became a matter of studied mannerism, too crude for belief. Rather than extending the styles Dylan originated, Walker simply mimics Dylan's style, with all its many limitations. The result is something worse than mediocre—it's as insulting as unintentional parody gets. — D.M.

JOE WALSH
★★★ But Seriously Folks . . . / Asy. 6E-141
★★★ So What? / Dun. DSD-50171
★★★ The Best of Joe Walsh / ABC AA-1083
★★★ The Smoker You Drink, the Player You Get / Dun. X-50140
★ You Can't Argue with a Sick Mind / ABC D-932

The former James Gang lead guitarist takes his band, Barnstorm, through a collection of fiery rockers and cool, sweaty neofunk instrumentals on the ABC albums. The classic is "Rocky Mountain Way" from *The Smoker. Sick Mind* is a live album made while Barnstorm was on the wane. *But Seriously Folks* is a riotous disc, made after Walsh joined the Eagles; it contains his 1978 hit single, "Life's Been Good," which may be the most important statement on rock stardom anyone has made in the late Seventies. — J.S.

DEXTER WANSEL
★★★ Life on Mars / Phil. PZ-34079
★★★ Voyager / Phil. JZ-34985
★★★ What the World Is Coming To / Phil. PZ-34487

Gamble-Huff arranger/keyboardist Wansel's three solo albums with the house band for that team's Philadelphia International label are better-than-average instrumental sets, highlighted by Wansel's accomplished

synthesizer work and the usual funk wallpaper that characterizes such projects. — J.S.

WAR
★★★ **All Day Music** / U. Artists 5546
★★★ **Deliver the Word** / U. Artists
LA128-F
★★ **Galaxy** / MCA 3030
★★ **Love Is All Around** / ABC B-988
★★★ **Platinum Jazz** / Blue N. LA690-12
★★★★ **The World Is a Ghetto** / U. Artists
5652
★★ **War Live** / U. Artists LA193-12
★★★★ **War's Greatest Hits** / U. Artists
LA648-G
★★★★ **Why Can't We Be Friends** /
U. Artists LA441-G
★★★ **Youngblood** / U. Artists LA904-H
War is perhaps the most underrated black
band of the Seventies; its best songs out-
strip even the Commodores and the Isley
Brothers for sheer funk power.

The septet began recording with Eric
Burdon (of the Animals) in 1970 and immediately scored with "Spill the Wine." By
1971, Burdon was exhausted but the band
carried on. "All Day Music," the title song
of their second album, was a 1971 hit and
established their lean style: creaking electric backup underneath powerful vocal
shouts. But it was the second hit, "Slippin'
into Darkness," that signified War's ability
to capture the mood of its time. That song,
like "The World Is a Ghetto," its brilliant
followup, is nothing less than haunting.

The ABC album is recycled Burdon
tracks and mediocre, as is the MCA album
released in 1978. But the United Artists albums are of uniformly high quality, stinging and angry at their peaks, with a throbbing beat that qualifies them as a variety of
disco but without any of the mechanistic
menace normally associated with that
genre. — D.M.

JENNIFER WARNES
★★ **Jennifer Warnes** / Ari. 4062
L.A. singer with strong Ronstadt resemblance, lavishly produced. "Right Time of
the Night" was a 1977 hit. — S.H.

DIONNE WARWICK
★★★ **Dionne** / War. B-2585
★★★★★ **Dionne Warwick: More Greatest
Hits** / Sp. 4032
★★★★ **Dionne Warwick Sings Her Very
Best** / Sp. 4002
★★★★ **Dionne Warwick Sings One Hit
After Another** / Sp. 4003
★★★ **Just Being Myself** / War. B-2658
★★★ **Love at First Sight** / War. B-3119
★★★ **Only Love Can Break a Heart** /
Musi. 2501
★★★★ **The Golden Voice of Dionne War-
wick** / Sp. 4001
★★★ **Then Came You** / War. BS4-2846
★★★ **Track of the Cat** / War. B-2893
Dionne Warwick was something of an
anomaly in Sixties pop music. She was
black, yet not an R&B singer, though she
wasn't a straight pop interpreter like
Nancy Wilson, either. Instead, Warwick
walked a thin line between the genres, and
the result, thanks to her long collaboration
with producer/writers Burt Bacharach and
Hal David, was an impressive stream of hit
records. The string began in 1962 with
"Don't Make Me Over," continuing with
"Anyone Who Had a Heart," "Walk On
By," "You'll Never Get to Heaven," "Who
Can I Turn To," "Message to Michael,"
"Trains and Boats and Planes," "I Just
Don't Know What to Do with Myself"
and "Alfie," among many others, before it
petered out in 1971 with "Make It Easy on
Yourself." This is among the best romantic
music ever made. and Warwick's best singles as collected on the various Springboard repackages (the originals were on
Scepter) still make fine listening. But when
she began recording for Warner Bros. in
1972, she lost her touch, and except for
"Then Came You," a single recorded with
the Spinners in 1976, she's never quite regained it, despite a succession of approaches and producers. — D.M.

WATER AND POWER
★★★ **Water and Power** / Fan. 9494
Better-than-average vocal trio's offering is
slickly produced and well written and performed R&B. Nothing really stands out,

which is the only thing keeping this from being a spectacular debut.   — J.S.

DOC WATSON
★ **Doc and the Boys** / U. Artists LA601-G
★★ **Doc Watson** / Van. 79152
★★★★ **Doc Watson and Son** / Van. 79170
★★ **Doc Watson on Stage** / Van. VSD-9/10
★ **Good Deal! (In Nashville)** / Van. 79276
★★ **Home Again!** / Van. 79239
★★★ **Memories** / U. Artists LA423-H2
★★★★ **Southbound** / Van. 79213
★★ **The Essential Doc Watson** / Van. VSD-45/46

Doc Watson is frequently heralded as the best flat-picking guitarist in the country. It is not simply the breakneck speed at which he is capable of playing, but rather that every tune comes from deep within him, growing out of the Carter Family/Clarence Ashley/Jimmie Rodgers traditions on which he was raised.

Watson came to national prominence during the early Sixties, playing the Newport Folk Festival as well as clubs and concerts in Los Angeles, New York and all points between. Although his repertoire— in number of songs—seems endless, Doc has generally limited himself to items within the country traditions mentioned above. His occasional forays into more contemporary songs (other than original compositions) have rarely been successful. Rhythm sections and other extraneous instruments take too much away from Doc's own playing.

Similarly, his best recorded work has featured himself solo or with his son Merle or guitarist John Pilla and perhaps a string bass. Thus *Doc Watson and Son* and *Southbound,* though among his earliest sets for Vanguard (1966 and 1967, respectively), remain the most representative of his playing. Doc's vocals have become surer over the years, and the flash of his flat-picking has somehow mellowed without losing its cutting edge. But the repertoire on each is a good cross section of the types of songs Doc performs best—from "Deep River Blues" to "Tennessee Stud" to "Little Darling Pal of Mine."

On Stage and *The Essential* are both live sets—no date on the former, the latter emanating from Doc's Newport appearances in 1963 and 1964. Other than the applause, however, they have nothing on *Southbound* or *Doc Watson and Son.*

Memories is an interesting concept album put together by Merle, reflecting the tradi-

tional roots of Doc's music and, in the case of "You Don't Know My Mind Blues," accounting for a certain boomerang effect: "Our arrangement of this old Bar-B-Q Bob tune," writes Merle on the inner sleeve, "shows the Allman Brothers' influence in our blues." Merle was most assuredly smiling when he wrote those words. Once again, though, the rhythm section (as on *Good Deal!*) is intrusive rather than supportive.

As for the remaining albums in the catalogue, Doc couldn't make a *bad* album if he tried. It's more a matter of the similarity in the kinds of tunes and the occasional re-recordings of favorites making them somewhat redundant. His impact on people ranging from John Herald (who played on *Doc Watson*) to the Allmans, however, is undisputed. And his ability to make tradition breathe is unequaled.   — I.M.

JOHNNY GUITAR WATSON
★★★ **A Real Mother for Ya** / DJM 7
★★★ **Ain't That a Bitch** / DJM 3
★★★ **Funk beyond the Call of Duty** / DJM 714
★★★ **Gangster of Love** / Power. 306
★★★ **Giant** / DJM 19
★★ **I Cried for You** / Cadet 4056
★★★ **I Don't Want to Be a Lone Ranger** / Fan. 9484
★★★ **Listen** / Fan. 9437

After a recording career that included frantic B. B. King–styled guitar blues, soul duets with Larry Williams and cocktail blues piano (*I Cried*), Johnny Guitar Watson emerged on Fantasy in the mid-Seventies with a unique concoction of blues, funk and middle-class soul. Like Junior Walker, Watson has a matching vocal and instrumental tone: lean and sandpaper grainy. To his credit, Watson uses a deft, small band on his records, avoiding studio overkill. His best songs ("I Don't Want to Be a Lone Ranger," "Real Mother") are either tongue-in-cheek or just plain silly, and all the recent albums are infused with a humor that, while neither profound nor transcendent, makes them just plain fun.   — J.MC.

WAH WAH WATSON
★★★ **Elementary** / Col. PC-34328

Watson played for years as a session guitarist with Motown (he was on the Jackson Five's *ABC* album) before branching out to record with Barry White, the Pointer Sisters, Herbie Hancock and others. *Elementary* puts him out front in a disco-funk set that shows him to be a pretty decent singer and features an impressive list of sidemen, including guitarist Ray Parker Jr., Hancock on keyboards, Bennie Maupin on soprano sax, Ollie Brown on drums and Joe Sample on piano. — J.S.

WEAPONS OF PEACE
★ Weapons of Peace / Play. PZ-34747
Late-Seventies urban soul trying to emulate Stevie Wonder vocal postures and disco-rhythmic programing unsuccessfully. It all ends up sounding like a bad Moody Blues album. (Now deleted.) — J.S.

JIM WEATHERLY
★ Pictures and Rhymes / ABC 982
Writer of mid-Seventies Gladys Knight hits is too mild-mannered to put over his own songs. — S.H.

THE WEAVERS
★★ Reunion at Carnegie Hall, 1963 / Van. 2150
★★★★★ The Weavers at Carnegie Hall / Van. 6533
★★★ The Weavers' Greatest Hits / Van. VSD-15/16
★★ The Weavers' Reunion, Part Two / Van. 79161
★ The Weavers' Songbook / Van. 73001
For anyone interested in the roots of the folk revival of the Fifties and Sixties, the Weavers are the group to hear. The original incarnation—Pete Seeger, Ronnie Gilbert, Lee Hays and Fred Hellerman—was an outgrowth of the Almanac Singers of the Forties. The songs were carefully arranged for multipart harmony and the performances were sparked by spiritual energy. Though Erik Darling, the first replacement for Seeger when the latter set

out on his own, was an able banjoist and singer, it is clear today that Seeger provided the intangible element that made the Weavers hitmakers ("Goodnight Irene," "On Top of Old Smokey," both for Decca in 1950).

The original Carnegie Hall concert LP stands as testimony to the sharp image cut by the quartet. It is one of the few recordings from that era that still holds tremendous emotional power. Recorded Christmas Eve, 1955, the renditions of "Kisses Sweeter Than Wine," "Rock Island Line" and "Goodnight Irene" (there are twenty songs altogether) are definitive in the context of a commercial folk idiom that didn't betray its origins.

The reunion LPs feature the original quartet plus Darling, Bernie Krause and Frank Hamilton (also members at various times). They were recorded in 1963. Seeger leads a sing-along on Tom Paxton's "Ramblin' Boy," and "San Francisco Bay Blues" and "Guantanamera" are also added to the repertoire. But the enlarged ensemble doesn't always adapt to the highly structured arrangements.

Greatest Hits consists of live takes with the original members. Poor in sound quality, the two studio LPs lack the enthusiasm of the live ones. — I.M.

JIMMY WEBB
★★★ El Mirage / Atl. 18218
★★★ Land's End / Asy. 5070
Major Sixties songwriter ("By the Time I Get to Phoenix," "Wichita Lineman," "MacArthur Park," "Up, Up and Away," "Didn't We," etc.) is a quirky but expressive interpreter of his own ultraromantic material. His three out-of-print Reprise albums, especially *Letters,* are also worth scouting out. — S.H.

WE FIVE
★ Take Each Day as It Comes / A.V.I. 6016
★★ You Were on My Mind / A&M 4111
Australian folk-rock singers who had a hit with the title cut for the A&M LP in the mid-Sixties, an Ian and Sylvia song that was arranged in a way that gave early indication of how Tin Pan Alley would co-opt the supposedly pristine American folk-rock movement. This is We Five's sole interest a decade later, and it is more socio-political than musical. — D.M.

BOB WEIR
★★★ Ace / War. B-2627

★★★ **Heaven Help the Fool / Ari. 4155**
Grateful Dead lead singer and rhythm guitarist Weir was the first member of that band to release a solo album. *Ace* was more of a Grateful Dead album than any of the band's other solo offshoots, featuring the Dead as players and including a number of songs (particularly "Playing in the Band" and "One More Saturday Night") that became concert standards for the group.

   Heaven Help the Fool was Weir's attempt to break away from the Grateful Dead image. The album was recorded with a harder-edged band and presents Weir as a Boz Scaggs-style crooner. The title track, "Bombs Away" and "Salt Lake City" are the album's stand-outs. — J.S.

TIM WEISBERG

★★ **Dreamspeaker / A&M 3045**
★ **Hurtwood Edge / A&M 4352**
★★ **Listen to the City / A&M 4545**
★★ **Live at Last / A&M 4600**
★★ **Rotations / U. Artists LA857-H**
★★★ **Tim Weisberg / A&M 3039**
★★ **Tim Weisberg Band / U. Artists LA773G**
★★ **Tim Weisberg 4 / A&M 3658**
This talented but mellow flautist insists on turning jazz chops and a rock background into undifferentiated Muzak mush. He should play his concerts in supermarkets. — J.S.

TIM WEISBERG AND KENNY LOGGINS

★★ **Twin Sons of Different Mothers / Epic JE-35339**
Smooth, post-rock cocktail-lounge Muzak made a big hit in 1978. Whatever blandness Loggins lacks, Weisberg makes up for in spades. The combination ought to be marketed as an insomnia cure. — D.M.

BOB WELCH

★★★ **French Kiss / Cap. ST-11663**
★★ **Three Hearts / Cap. SO-11907**
Welch was a key member of Fleetwood Mac in the years immediately preceding that band's sudden rise to fame. His presence in the group yielded mixed results— Welch is a good guitarist and has written some very good songs, but he never seemed to be able to put it all together. When he left Fleetwood Mac and formed Paris, a boring power trio, it seemed he'd succumbed to his own worst instincts.

   French Kiss, however, has its moments. Half the songs are pretty good, Welch handled most of the difficult production and arrangement tasks himself with good results, and some of the Fleetwood Mac crew joined up to remake Welch's best song with that band, "Sentimental Lady" (originally on Mac's *Bare Trees*). Fittingly enough, Welch's version became a substantial hit single this time around. *Three Hearts* was an ineffective followup. — J.S.

LENNY WELCH

★★★ **Since I Fell for You / Col. CS-9230**
Welch had a 1963 hit with the title song of this collection, a Forties Tin Pan Alley ballad that never sounded soulful before or since. Unfortunately, neither here nor anywhere else was Welch able to achieve such a mellow rapprochement between R&B and pop. (Now deleted.) — D.M.

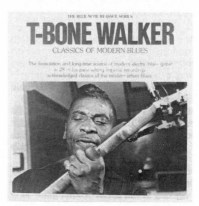

CORY WELLS

★★ **Touch Me / A&M 4673**
Former Three Dog Night lead singer sounds forlorn without the rest of the pack. Strained and soulless. — D.M.

KITTY WELLS

★★★ **Dust on the Bible / MCA 149**
★★★ **Kitty Wells' Greatest Hits / MCA 121**
★★★★ **Kitty Wells Story / MCA 2-4031**
From 1952 straight through the Sixties, Kitty Wells was the almost undisputed queen of country music. She earned her stature with "It Wasn't God Who Made Honky Tonk Angels," continued it with a series of hits including "Making Believe," "One by One" and "I Can't Stop Loving You" in the Fifties, and sustained it in the Sixties with "Day into Night," "Unloved Unwanted" and "Will Your Lawyer Talk

to God." The best of her music is collected on *Story*. — D.M.

MARY WELLS
★★★★ Mary Wells' Greatest Hits / Mo. M7-616

One of Motown's early teen queens, Wells had a first-rate series of early-Sixties hit singles: "My Guy," "The One Who Really Loves You," "Two Lovers" and "You Beat Me to the Punch." All of them would have been sultry if her breathlessness hadn't rendered them adolescently harmless. They're still fun to listen to, though, and this is one of Motown's better collections. — D.M.

WEREWOLVES
★★ Ship of Fools (Summer Weekends and No More Blues) / RCA AFL1-3079
★★ The Werewolves / RCA AFL1-2746

Fairly undistinguished Seventies American hard rock. Band's chief distinction is production by former Rolling Stones' mentor, Andrew Loog Oldham. Perfect song title: "Waking Up Is Hard to Do." — D.M.

DAVID WERNER
★ Imagination Quota / RCA APL1-0922
Midwestern glitter rock. (Now deleted.) — S.H.

HOWARD WERTH AND THE MOONBEAMS
★★★ King Brilliant / R. 2180

When Elton John formed his own record label in the mid-Seventies, he decided he needed a hard-rock band for its roster. This amalgam of Rolling Stones clichés was his solution. Which says more about Elton than Werth. (Now deleted.) — D.M.

FRED WESLEY
★★★ A Blow for Me, A Toot to You / Atco 18214

Ex-James Brown trombonist and horn-section captain turns in a neat but directionless solo outing with a lot of funk riffing and some (but not enough) hot playing. — J.S.

WEST, BRUCE AND LAING
★★★ Live 'n' Kickin' / Col. KC 32899
★★ Whatever Turns You On / Col. C-32216
★★ Why Dontcha / Col. KC-31929

A grotesque attempt to revive Cream using the basest of retreads, Mountain, as a foundation. Leslie West's guitar playing is laughably inept in comparison with Eric Clapton's, but as power trios go, the presence of Jack Bruce on bass helps this one approach respectability (only on the live record). — J.S.

HEDY WEST
★★★ Old Times and Hard Times / Folk-Leg. 32

Best known as the author of "500 Miles," West's repertoire here is descended from her Georgia family, including lyrics composed by her father, the poet-activist Don West. West was looked to by folk-revival singers and topical songwriters as a first-hand source of lore and information concerning the Appalachian coal miners and their union struggles. — I.M.

WET WILLIE
★★★ Dixie Rock / Capri. 0148
★★★ Drippin' Wet / Capri. 0113
★★★ Keep On Smilin' / Capri. 0128
★★★ Left Coast Live / Capri. 0182
★★★★ Manorisms / Epic JE-34983
★★★★ The Wetter the Better / Capri. 0166
★★ Wet Willie / Capri. 0138
★★★ Wet Willie II / Capri. 0109
★★★ Wet Willie's Greatest Hits / Capri. 0200

Rock & roll is chronically derivative, but nowhere was this as obvious as during the South's rise to rock prominence after the Allman Brothers Band's breakthrough—nearly everybody seemed to be flogging the same whipping post with a blues-rock style applied to the jamming sensibilities of hard, heavy-metal rockers like Cream. Soon enough, the wheat was separated from the chaff, and though a long career with Capricorn resulted in only minimal commercial success, Wet Willie proved itself one of the region's most vibrant and consistent bands.

Most other Southern bands seasoned their blues rock with country influences, but Wet Willie fired its with hard-biting R&B. Though the band's debut album, *Wet Willie*, jelled into little more than a studied blueprint of the approach, with *II*, Willie could deliver credible covers of tunes like Otis Redding's "Shout Bamalama" alongside its own cookers like "Red Hot Chicken." The highly charged live album, *Drippin' Wet*, showed that the band's barroom approach effectively complemented the beer-swilling nature of its music. With his combination of a rocker's dynamics and a soul man's restraint, Jimmy Hall became the best vocalist of the Southern school.

Mass acceptance almost came with the

single success of "Keep On Smilin'," which added a thicker slice of gospel styling to Willie's synthesis. "Dixie Rock," the title tune of the LP that followed, pushed Wet Willie to another level—this was the most rocking tune they'd done, owing as much to British hard rock as to the Stax sound. Though this element never dominated, the stylistic addition pushed the band toward its best Capricorn work.

The Wetter the Better cooked everything up right—Ricky Hirsch's guitar was sharper than ever and new singer/keyboardist Michael Duke contributed two stand-out rockers, "No, No, No" and "Teaser." The highlight, though, was "Everything That 'Cha Do (Will Come Back to You)," which found Hall's voice and Hirsch's guitar effortlessly binding the circular rhythms of this song about karma. *Left Coast Live,* the last album on which Hirsch appears (he left to join Gregg Allman), again effectively captured the band's dynamism and particularly shows Hirsch's growth during his tenure with the band.

Regrouping with a new contract at Epic (Jimmy Hall and Michael Duke remain principals), Wet Willie returned with *Manorisms.* It's the band's most heavily produced album (thanks to Gary Lyons), but the high gloss did nothing to diminish the rhythmic soul of "Make You Feel Love Again," the Spector cum Springsteen Wall of Sound of "Rainman" and the homespun joy of "Streetcorner Serenade." After eight albums, Wet Willie remains so true to its roots that the band keeps finding new ones. — J.B.M.

WHA KOO
★★ **Berkshire / ABC 1043**
Pedestrian California rock group led by former Steely Dan vocalist David Palmer. — D.M.

WHISPERS
★★★ **Headlights / Soul T. BXL1-2774**
★★★ **One for the Money / Soul T. BXL1-1450**
★★★ **Open Up Your Love / Soul T. BXL1-2270**
Soul vocal groups come and go, but the Whispers, led by Wallace and Walter Scott, have had remarkable staying power for a group that's never had a major hit. (A deleted Janus *Greatest Hits* set collects a number of their minor soul hits.) The Whispers are essentially convincing if limited street-corner balladeers. The albums above are Philadelphia productions that

combine old-fashioned soul-group grease with some strong Norman Harris production work. — J.MC.

ALAN WHITE
★★ **Ramshackled / Atl. 18167**
Mostly undistinguished popish jazz rock—though without funk or electric fireworks—led by Yes's drummer. Most instrumentation is competent but cold. Jon Anderson sings a William Blake poem. Quite unlike Yes. (Now deleted.) — C.W.

BARRY WHITE
★★★ **Barry White Sings for Someone You Love / 20th Cent. 543**
★★★ **Barry White's Greatest Hits / 20th Cent. 493**
★★★ **Can't Get Enough / 20th Cent. 444**
★★★ **Is This Whatcha Want / 20th Cent. 516**
★★★ **I've Got So Much to Give / 20th Cent. 407**
★★★ **Rhapsody in White / 20th Cent. 433**
★★★ **Stone Gon' / 20th Cent. 423**
★★★ **The Man / 20th Cent. 571**
★★★ **The Message Is Love / Unli. J2-35763**
White enjoyed a brief vogue in the mid-Seventies with a series of steamy seduction records in which he promised his baby virtually everything, in a way still acceptable to the FCC. He might have reigned forever as a black matinee idol, and held the title as king of smooch disco, had he not revealed himself to be the possessor of one of music's most corpulent frames. Somehow, the modern Rudolph Valentino shouldn't weigh three hundred pounds and wear a cluster of huge rings.

You pick from these records. They literally all sound the same: pleasant pop-funk riffs over which White can growl, the aural equivalent of static on your baby's telephone wire. — D.M.

WHITE HORSE
★★★★ **White Horse / Cap. ST-11687**
This unlikely trio of folk-derived rockers was spearheaded by Billy Nichols, whose songs nicely dominate the record. In addition, "Give It Up" displays Nichols' latent ability to rock out. John Lind and Kenny Altman also contribute material. Guitarist Caleb Quaye and keyboardist Bill Payne figure prominently, too. (Now deleted.) — J.S.

JOSH WHITE
★ **In Memoriam: Josh White / Trad. 2084**

Part jazz vocalist, part folksinger, White's polished nightclub style has influenced such diverse figures as Don McLean and Arthur Prysock. His Elektra catalogue (a small part of his overall output) is officially in print but difficult to find; this, sadly, isn't a very good representation of his work. — I.M.

TONY JOE WHITE
■ Tony Joe White / 20th Cent. 523
White looked like a formidable songwriter in the early Seventies, after hitting with his own "Polk Salad Annie" and writing bayou-style rock songs for a variety of other performers. But he's never lived up to his initial promise, the early (and sometimes excellent) albums for Monument and Warners are out of print and what's left—this . . . *thing*—is an abomination. — D.M.

WHITE WITCH
★★ Spiritual Greeting / Capri. 0129
★ White Witch / Capri. 0107
Mid-Seventies Southern answer to Black Sabbath led by guitarist Buddy Richardson. The only thing this group had going for it was the fine production of Ron and Howard Albert at Miami's Criterion Recording Studios, on *Spiritual Greeting*. — J.S.

THE WHO
★★★★ Happy Jack / MCA 2-4067
★★ Magic Bus—The Who on Tour / MCA 2-4068
★★★★ Meaty, Beaty, Big and Bouncy / MCA 3025
★★★★ Odds and Sods / MCA 2126
★★★★ Quadrophenia / MCA 2-10004
★★★★ The Who by Numbers / MCA 3026
★★★★ The Who Live at Leeds / MCA 3023
★★★★ The Who Sell Out / MCA 2-4067
★★★★★ The Who Sing My Generation / MCA 2-4068
★★★★ Tommy / MCA 2-10005
★★★★ Who Are You / MCA 3050
★★★★★ Who's Next / MCA 2023
The early Who albums present one of the most interesting problems posed in rock & roll history. The band was considered at the time to be much better in live performance than on record, yet these records transcend their flaws. *The Who Sing My Generation* (now available only in tandem with *Magic Bus*) is one of the most influential rock albums ever released. The generation of punk rockers takes its cue from this

record. Roger Daltrey's singing is crude and the recording quality leaves a lot to be desired, but the energy of the record is unbelievable. Two songs, "My Generation" and "The Kids Are Alright," became anthems for the Mods in England yet went almost unnoticed in the U.S. Guitarist (and songwriter) Pete Townshend's feedback technique made "My Generation" and the instrumental "The Ox" sonic marvels of the time. Bassist John Entwistle, for whom the latter track was named, added subtly to the mayhem as drummer Keith Moon cascaded his rolls through it all at breakneck speed.

Happy Jack (now available only in tandem with *Sell Out*) presents better-conceptualized material, but it's less energetic than the first record. The title track became the Who's first American hit. Entwistle unveiled his exceptional songwriting ability and multi-instrumental prowess with "Boris the Spider" and "Whiskey Man." More importantly, the album includes a suite of songs, "A Quick One While He's Away," that Townshend referred to as a "mini-opera." In "A Quick One," Townshend worked out organizational ideas and musical themes he would later use in *Tommy*.

The Who Sell Out is a failed concept album, but it's a brilliant failure. The idea was to re-create the ambiance of AM radio programing, fusing new Who songs with fake commercials written by Townshend. Side one pulls this off, climaxing with what may be the Who's most powerful single, "I Can See for Miles." The concept breaks down, however, on the second side. "Real," the last song on the album, is another mini-opera that anticipated *Tommy* directly, with a long instrumental break that was reproduced in *Tommy* as "Underture."

Magic Bus—The Who on Tour was a quickie package thrown together by MCA because *Tommy* was overdue. There are several good songs on the record, particularly "Magic Bus," "Pictures of Lily" and "Call Me Lightning," but this is really for collectors only. *Meaty, Beaty, Big and Bouncy* shows what the Who could really do with the singles anthology idea.

Tommy is Townshend's acknowledged masterpiece, the record that put the Who on the map. Using a few standard Who chord progressions as motifs, Townshend constructed a virtual theory of essential rock forms, running each progression through its possibilities. But the record was only a blueprint for what *Tommy* would become when the Who performed it live. The story line is a bit fractured, and it's further confused by the inclusion of two John Entwistle songs, but the band's instrumental work is exemplary, especially Moon's relentless drumming. "Pinball Wizard" became a huge hit single.

Live at Leeds gives an indication of what the Who was capable of in concert. It's a remarkably powerful, if diffuse, record, a good example of the kind of energy that the Who generates live. Side one lines up the killer combination of "Young Man Blues," "Substitute," "Summertime Blues" and "Shakin' All Over." The album was packaged as a mock bootleg and includes a lot of interesting scrapbook material, including Townshend's notes for "My Generation," the contract for the band's engagement at the Woodstock festival, a receipt for a case of smoke bombs and a poster advertising the band's early gigs at the Marquee Club in London.

Townshend's big problem at this point was trying to come up with a sequel to *Tommy.* He finally settled on a science fiction film project called *Life House,* which would include a live Who performance and expand the band's stage concept to include prerecorded tapes for backing rhythm. The project broke down in production, and the Who went into the studio to salvage what it could of the wealth of material Townshend had written for it. When they finished, they had what may well be the finest rock record ever made.

Who's Next is so different from what the band had put out on record before it sounds like it was recorded by a different group. For the first time the Who was able to capture the live energy of a concert in the studio, and the result was devastating. Glyn Johns engineered and deserves a lot of credit, but *Who's Next* is an indiviudal triumph for each individual in the band as well as a solid group effort. Some of Townshend's most beautiful songs are here—"Bargain," "Song Is Over," "Goin' Mobile" and "Won't Get Fooled Again." Entwistle's "My Wife" is his best song and a lot of people's favorite track on the record. Moon faced the difficult task of maintaining his abandoned drumming style while matching the rigid rhythmic structure of the backing tapes on "Baba O'Riley" and "Won't Get Fooled Again." The tapes added the promised technological edge to the band's sound, and Townshend's use of a guitar distortion device called an envelope follower on "Goin' Mobile" is amazing. But the final and most convincing triumph is Daltrey's. His singing had improved on *Tommy,* the first album on which he really came to life, and of course all his screaming blood and thunder was dutifully caught on *Live at Leeds.* Daltrey's singing on *Who's Next,* however, is stunning, and definitely one of the strongest rock vocal performances on record. His scream at the climax of "Won't Get Fooled Again" is a moment of pure rock transcendence.

Meaty, Beaty, Big and Bouncy is the album that proves what a great singles band the Who is. The British and American hits—"I Can't Explain," "The Kids Are Alright," "Happy Jack," "I Can See for Miles," "Pinball Wizard," "The Magic Bus" and "Substitute"—are all here, as well as gems like "I'm a Boy," "Anyway, Anyhow, Anywhere," "Boris the Spider," "Pictures of Lily" and "The Seeker."

Quadrophenia was Townshend's recapitulation of the Mod years in the form of a concept album. Here he took the use of electronic tapes to extend the limits of the Who's sound as far as he could, programing dense, symphonic textures throughout the record. As he did in *Tommy,* Townshend used motifs throughout the record, but this time in a much more complex formula. He also had Entwistle overdub entire horn sections. The project was so ambitious that it swamped the Who in its scope and ended up more like a Townshend solo project, with the Who as session musicians, than a full-fledged Who album. Daltrey's vocals are strained and often buried in the mix. Despite this flaw, *Quadrophenia* remains a rich and rewarding listening experience, especially on headphones. "The Real Me," "The Punk Meets the Godfather" and all of side three are classic Who performances.

Odds and Sods assembles a number of semi-legendary Who songs that never made it to albums. It's not what you'd call the band's most timeless work, but all of it is interesting and some of it is great. Entwistle's sardonic account of life on the road, "Postcard," leads off. Townshend's antismoking commercial written for the American Cancer Society, "Little Billy," is also here, as well as "Glow Girl," a part of the original idea for *Tommy,* and a trio of songs from the *Life House* project which were left off *Who's Next:* "Pure and Easy,"

"Naked Eye" and "Long Live Rock." Also included is the first single recorded by the band when they were called the High Numbers, "I'm the Face."

The Who by Numbers is the strangest and one of the most moving Who albums. Townshend's songs were written at a point when he was feeling depressed and frustrated, and deal directly with the problems faced by an aging rocker who wonders if he can still keep it together. "However Much I Booze," "How Many Friends" and "In a Hand or a Face" reflect Townshend's angst. "Dreaming from the Waist," a powerful rock song with Daltrey's best vocal on the record, seems to lament the characteristic impulsiveness of rock & roll stardom, while "Blue Red and Grey" openly denounces the crazy lifestyle in favor of a measured life in which every moment is savored. "Slip Kid" and "Squeeze Box" are neat little songs written as potential singles ("Squeeze Box" was released as a single and did well, though not spectacularly). Entwistle's one contribution, "Success Story," is almost an answer piece to Townshend's soul-searching. The autobiographical track pounds away furiously as Entwistle makes wry observations about various aspects of his band's career, then gives a heartfelt defense of rock & roll at the end.

Who Are You picks up where the song leaves off. Released in 1978, after a three-year hiatus, it shows the Who drastically changed but seemingly revitalized. Moon's drumming lacks power, but Daltrey has never sung better than on "Guitar and Pen," "Trick of the Light," a brilliant Entwistle heavy-metal pastiche, and the winding title track, which became a midsummer hit. The album's topic was sustaining rock & roll past thirty, and while this angered many Who fans, who felt that eternal youth is the rock & roll promise, it fit with the band members' situation. And Townshend left the record open-ended: if "Music Must Change," on which Moon doesn't even play, seemed the end of the band's basic approach, "Love Is Coming Down" promised at least that there would be more of the relentless honesty the Who had always delivered. "Who Are You" itself lived up to that promise, a pounding statement of identity lost and found.

Unfortunately, Keith Moon died of a drug overdose only weeks after the record's release. While he had been replaced—by former Faces drummer Kenny Jones—by

year's end, the future of the band remains in question. — J.S.

WIDOWMAKER
★★ **Too Late to Cry** / U. Artists LA723-G
★★ **Widowmaker** / U. Artists LA642-G
Routine hard/heavy rock cum blues led by the adequate guitar of Ariel Bender (Luther Grosvenor), with Steve Ellis singing on the debut, John Butler on the second. Lots of guitar, common tunes and chords—a general anonymity. A bad Led Zeppelin, perhaps. (Now deleted.) — C.W.

WIGGY BITS
★★ **Wiggy Bits** / Poly. 1-6081
This group meant to be an American art-pop ensemble, like Zeppelin or Yes. Boston beat them to it for a reason: Tom Scholz rocks a lot harder, and writes much better songs, than anybody here. (Now deleted.) — D.M.

WILD CHERRY
★ **Electrified Funk** / Epic PE-34462
★ **I Love My Music** / Epic JE-35011
★ **Wild Cherry** / Epic PE-34195
White boys playing quintessentially unfunky music. The hit (1976) was "Play That Funky Music (White Boy)." — K.T.

THE WILD TCHOUPITOULAS
★★★★ **The Wild Tchoupitoulas** / Is. 9360
The Wild Tchoupitoulas is American roots music—an ebullient album of hard-core, second-line New Orleans funk. The Tchoupitoulas are a street gang who long ago put down their weapons for songs and Mardi Gras parade costumes. The Meters provide instrumental backup and production assistance. A remake of the Meters' "Hey Pocky-A-Way" is the high point. — J.MC.

DENIECE WILLIAMS
★★★ Songbird / Col. JC-34911
★★★★ That's What Friends Are For /
Col. JC-35435
★★★★ This Is Niecy / Col. PC-34242
Best known for her 1978 duet with Johnny
Mathis, Williams benefits from Maurice
White's sparse and restrained production
on all three of these albums. Williams has
a billowy soprano perfect for the pleasant
love songs she favors, although the aim is
sometimes prettiness rather than sub-
stance. — J.MC.

DON WILLIAMS
★★★ Country Boy / Dot. 2088
★★★ Don Williams, Vol. 1 / Dot
DOSD-2014
★★★ Don Williams, Vol. 2 / Dot
DOSD-2018
★★★ Don Williams, Vol. 3 / Dot
DOSD-2004
★★★ Expressions / ABC 1069
★★★★ Greatest Hits / Dot DOSD-2035
★★★ Harmony / Dot DOSD-2049
★★★ You're My Best Friend / Dot
DOSD-2021
Williams' deep bass voice and soulful song-
writing made him one of the most success-
ful country-pop performers of the mid to
late Seventies, during which time he re-
corded a string of hits that were as good as
they were popular—"Amanda," "I
Wouldn't Want to Live if You Didn't Love
Me," "Say It Again," "She Never Knew
Me," "Ties That Bind," "Till the Rivers
All Run Dry" and "We Should Be Together." Williams' songs have come to the
attention of rock musicians and have been
recorded by Eric Clapton and Peter Townshend. — J.S.

HANK WILLIAMS JR.
★★★ 14 Greatest Hits / MGM
MG-1-5020
★★★ New South / War. B-3127
★★★ One Night Stands / War. B-2988
Hank Williams Jr. faced an impossible
task: as the son of the greatest figure in
country music history he was expected to
live up to (and perhaps live out) the grandeur and tragedy of his father's career. Although his father died when he was only
four, Williams has been performing his father's music in concert, from his preadoles-
cent years.
More recently, after a stint recording
conventional country for MGM, Williams
has begun to break into the outlaw country
mold. The process began with his final

MGM album, the deleted *Hank Williams
Jr. and Friends*, one of the landmarks of recent country. It is both personal and potent, with more of a rock tinge than anything since. After a mountain-climbing
accident in 1976, in which he nearly lost
his life, Williams came back to record the
Warner Bros. albums listed above, both of
which have strong moments but lack the
consistent sense of breakthrough which
characterizes *Friends*. — D.M.

HANK WILLIAMS SR.
★★★ Hank Williams Live at the Grand
Ole Opry / MGM MG-1-5019
★★★★ Hank Williams Sr.'s Greatest
Hits / MGM 3918
★★★ Home in Heaven / MGM M3G-4991
★★★★ I Saw the Light / MGM 3331
★★★★★ 24 Greatest Hits, Vol. 2 / MGM
5401
★★★★★ 24 of Hank Williams' Greatest
Hits / MGM 4755
★★★★ Very Best of Hank Williams /
MGM 4168
Only Jimmie Rodgers can compare with
Hank Williams as a country music figure,
and even Rodgers is outstripped by Williams' influence on later developments in
rock & roll; Elvis Presley, Buddy Holly
and Bob Dylan, to name just three, owe a
great deal to his writing and singing style,
to his lyrical vision and to his itinerant-
minstrel way of life. Williams recorded for
only six years—from 1947 to 1953—yet
even today, twenty-five years after his
death, he is regarded with semi-religious
awe in Nashville.
Williams has been called a folksinger,
which is not altogether inaccurate. His
sound was very basic, his voice and guitar
backed by a band without drums. But the
yodeling and the perspective of his singing

could only have come from the tradition founded by Jimmie Rodgers and the Carter Family.

But unlike most country musicians, Williams did not sing songs of resignation and despair but of exhilaration, resilience, and occasionally, nearly mystical illumination. The greatest of them include: "I'm So Lonesome I Could Cry," "Cold Cold Heart," "Moaning the Blues," "Long Gone Lonesome Blues," "Kawliga," "I'll Never Get Out of This World Alive," "Jambalaya," "Honky Tonk Blues" and "Settin' the Woods on Fire." Williams never found a way out of the social dead end of country, but in his songs are the seeds of rock & roll, which in the hands of Elvis Presley, Holly and others became the exit for thousands. — D.M.

LARRY WILLLIAMS
★ *That* Larry Williams / Fan. 9553
Williams was a Fifties novelty R&B singer who had hits with "Bony Moronie" and "Dizzy Miss Lizzy," the latter covered by the Beatles. This is a 1978 comeback LP and contains nothing but mediocre funk. — D.M.

LENNY WILLIAMS
★★★ Choosing You / ABC 1023
Ex-Tower of Power vocalist goes solo in a much mellower context with good results. — J.S.

MASON WILLIAMS
★ Feudin' Banjos / Olym. 7105
★ Hand Made / War. 1838
★ Mason Williams Listening Matter / Ev. 3265
★★ Mason Williams Phonograph Record / War. 1729
Williams earned a reputation as a writer/performer on the Smothers Brothers' late-Sixties television show. He wrote some fairly interesting pop songs—"Classical Gas" from *Phonograph Record* was a hit—but never quite broke through. *Phonograph Record* was an early attempt to record a pop-folk song cycle, something like Van Dyke Parks' first album, but much less interesting. The rest is mere silliness. — D.M.

ROBIN WILLIAMSON
★★ American Stonehenge / Fly. Fish 062
★★ Journey's Edge / Fly. Fish 033
Pleasant, quiet post-folk-rock music from a former member of the Incredible String Band. — D.M.

PAUL WILLIAMS
★ Classics / A&M 4701
■ Here Comes Inspiration / A&M 3606
★ Just an Old Fashioned Love Song / A&M 4327
■ Life Goes On / A&M 4367
■ Little Bit of Love / A&M 3655
■ Ordinary Fool / A&M 4550
★ Phantom of the Paradise / A&M 3653
■ Wings / A&M 3503
Williams is the most facile and bubble-headed of Seventies pop writers; his melodies are straight from advertising, and his lyrics are unctuous statements of things he may know about but has never felt. If one must suffer his banalities, it is far better to do so in the versions recorded by artists like the Carpenters and Three Dog Night. At least they can vocalize a bit; the composer cannot. — D.M.

WILLIE JOHN
★★★★ Fifteen Original Hits / King 5004
One of soul music's greatest voices, although his best shot at a hit single, "Fever," was stolen by Peggy Lee. Willie John's gospel-like falsetto was a major influence on James Brown (who recorded a tribute LP in the late Sixties after John died in a West Coast prison), and because of Brown, on a whole generation of singers. "Talk to Me," "All Around the World" and the other songs here stake Willie's claim as one of rock's least-remembered fathers. — D.M.

BOB WILLS AND HIS TEXAS PLAYBOYS
★★★ Bob Wills and His Texas Playboys / MCA 526
★★★★★ Bob Wills Anthology / Col. PG-32416

★★★★ Bob Wills in Concert / Cap.
SKBB-11550
★★★ Bob Wills in Person / MCA 550
★★★★ Bob Wills Plays the Greatest
String Band Hits / MCA 152
★★★ Bob Wills Sings and Plays / Lib.
7303
★★★ Fathers and Sons / Epic BG-33782
★★★ For the Last Time / U. Artists
LA216-J2
★★★ King of the Western Swing / MCA
543
★★★ Living Legend / MCA 546
★★★★ Remembering . . . / Col.
KC-34108
★★★ The Best of Bob Wills and His
Texas Playboys / MCA 153
★★★ The Best of Bob Wills and His
Texas Playboys / MCA 2-4092
★★★ Time Changes Everything / MCA
545
★★★ 24 Great Hits / MGM 2-5303
★★★ Western Swing Along / RCA 73735
Born in 1905, by 1933 Bob Wills had be-
come a major bandleader in Texas and
Oklahoma, leading the twenty-five-piece
Texas Playboys on radio stations through-
out the region, and recording for Columbia
in a fashion of his own device. Essentially,
Wills merged country & western music
with swing jazz; the resultant combination
was far from hick and numbered Charlie
Parker, among others, among its afficiona-
dos.

Wills' band emphasized both stringed instruments (guitars and his own fiddle) and
a horn section, which makes it unique in
C&W styles. Among his great hits, the best
of them recorded for Columbia in the Thirties, were "Rose of San Antone," "Texas
Playboy Rag," "Mexicali Rose," "Take Me
Back to Tulsa" and "The Yellow Rose of
Texas." The familiarity of those titles
speaks as well as anything for the remarkable power of his music. Along with Hank
Williams Sr. and Jimmie Rodgers, Wills is
one of the grandfathers, on the country
side, of rock. — .D.M.

AL WILSON
★★ I've Got a Feeling / Play. 410
Al Wilson is a contemporary singer with a
voice and style that treads a watery line
between Las Vegas gloss and urban soul.
Without a distinctive vocal personality,
Wilson has nevertheless managed to score
several hits with unassuming, midtempo
material. Listening to an Al Wilson record
is like eating at Howard John-
son's. — J.MC.

BILL WILSON
★ Ever Changing Minstrel / Col. KC-32535
Aren't you glad the folk boom—not to
mention the singer/songwriter boom—is
over? What a pompous pud! (Now deleted.) — D.M.

DENNIS WILSON
★★★ Pacific Ocean Blue / Cari. PZ-34354
A Beach Boy turns in that group's first
solo LP: a solid, if not overwhelming, rock
effort. — D.M.

JACKIE WILSON
★★ Baby Workout / Bruns. 754110
★★ Beautiful Day / Bruns. 754189
★★★ Body and Soul / Bruns. 754105
★★ Do Your Thing / Bruns. 754154
★★ I Get the Sweetest Feeling / Bruns.
754138
★★ It's All a Part of Love / Bruns. 754158
★★★★ Jackie Wilson Sings the Blues /
Bruns. 754055
★★ Jackie Wilson Sings the World's
Greatest Melodies / Bruns. 754106
★★★★ Jackie Wilson's Greatest Hits /
Bruns. 754185
★★ Manufacturers of Soul (with Count
Basie) / Bruns. 754134
★★★★ My Golden Favorites / Bruns.
754058
★★★★ My Golden Favorites, Vol. 2 /
Bruns. 754155
★★ Nobody but You / Bruns. 754212
★ Nowstalgia / Bruns. 754199
★★★ Spotlight on Jackie Wilson / Bruns.
754119
★★★ Whispers / Bruns. 754122
★★ You Got Me Walking / Bruns. 754172
Despite his vocal and performing genius
(he may have been the best pure vocalist of
his generation), Jackie Wilson led an aim-
less and uneven recording career. With few

exceptions, Wilson's output suffered from hack, over-orchestrated arrangements, heavy-handed choral accompaniment and dubious song selection. Still, the sheer power and virtuosity of Wilson's voice overcame many of the obstacles. Consider his biggest hit: "Night," backed with "Doggin' Around." "Night" is a supper-club ballad that borders on schmaltz, but Wilson turns it into a real showstopper, flaunting his operatic range (a gimmick he used to even greater effect on his version of "Danny Boy"). The flip side, "Doggin' Around," is a quasi-blues song that he reworks into a wrenching emotional showpiece.

Wilson's early LP output mixes melodramatic ballads with brassy uptempo dance numbers ("Baby Workout" was his biggest hit in that mold) and the occasional blues (one of his best albums is the hard to find *Sings the Blues*). The titles—*World's Greatest Melodies, Body and Soul*—reflect the bent.

In the mid-Sixties, Wilson found a sympathetic producer, Chicago soul entrepreneur Carl Davis, to produce two of his more memorable hits: "Whispers" and the ageless "Higher and Higher." For a time, the association gave Wilson's career a needed shot in the arm, but by 1970, the Davis-produced records were mediocre at best. Wilson had some minor Seventies hits but scarcely anything of interest to anyone but devoted fans. It's somehow fitting that the album released just prior to his heart attack and subsequent complete incapacitation was a tribute to Al Jolson. A hodgepodge of previously unreleased, Davis-produced singles came out a year later.   — J.MC.

JESSE WINCHESTER
★★★ **A Touch on the Rainy Side** / Bears. K-6984
★★★ **Learn to Love It** / Bears. 6953
★★★ **Let the Rough Side Drag** / Bears. 6964
★★★ **Nothing but a Breeze** / Bears. 6968
★★★ **Third Down 110 to Go** / Bears. 2102
Winchester grew up in Memphis, a serviceman's son, but when he became eligible for the draft in 1967, he split to Canada. In 1970, he met the Band's Robbie Robertson and Robertson induced his then-manager, Albert Grossman, to record Winchester. The resulting album, produced by Robertson and on the long-defunct Ampex label, was widely acclaimed, mostly for its fine collection of songs including

"Yankee Lady," "Biloxi" and "The Brand New Tennessee Waltz."

Winchester didn't return to vinyl until 1972, when he recorded a Todd Rundgren-produced LP, which was not so enthralling. But 1974's *Learn to Love It* fared better, and since then he's recorded fairly prolifically in a mildly interesting country-rock vein. Although he became a Canadian citizen in 1973, Winchester did not return to this country until the Carter amnesty of 1977. Since he'd never been around before, it wasn't much of a comeback, but he continues to work steadily in both countries today.   — D.M.

WINDY CITY
★ **Let Me Ride** / Chi-S. LA691-G
Although they've appropriated the name, this is neither as funky nor as elegant as the Chicago soul of Jerry Butler, Curtis Mayfield and the Impressions. Instead, it's pedestrian Midwestern Seventies funk that probably owes more to Dayton's Ohio Players.   — D.M.

WING AND A PRAYER FIFE AND DRUM CORPS
★★ **Babyface** / Wing 3025
★★ **Babyface Strikes Back** / Wing 3026
Competent New York funk ensemble scored in 1975 with a disco reworking of the Forties standard "Babyface," and later with a version of "Ease On Down the Road" from the Broadway musical *The Wiz*.   — D.M.

EDGAR WINTER
★★★ **Edgar Winter Group with Rick Derringer** / Blue S. PZ-33798
★★★★ **Edgar Winter's White Trash** / Epic E-30512
★★ **Entrance** / Epic 26503

★★ Jasmine Nightdreams / Blue S.
  PZ-33483
★★★ Recycled / Blue S. PZ-34858
★★★★ Roadwork / Epic PEG-31249
★★★ Shock Treatment / Epic PE-32461
★★★★ They Only Come Out at Night /
  Epic PE-31584

In the beginning (about 1970), Edgar Winter was just the older brother of Johnny Winter, who was then heralded as the greatest white blues guitarist of them all. *Entrance,* an eccentric Texas jazz-rock combination, made that distinction seem the only one Edgar was likely to earn. But a bit later, he put together one of the most soulful white horn bands ever assembled, White Trash, and together they made a pair of fine records—*Edgar Winter's White Trash* (which includes "Keep Playin' That Rock and Roll") and the live *Roadwork.* This music had its roots in Southwestern roadhouses and kicked just that viciously. Edgar came up with a huge hit in 1973, with "Frankenstein," from *They Only Come Out at Night,* heavy rock recorded with the band that included Derringer. He's never repeated that success, however. — D.M.

JOHNNY WINTER
★★★★ About Blues / Janus 3008
★★★ Austin, Texas / U. Artists LA319-G
★★★ Before the Storm / Janus 2-3056
★★★ Captured Live / Blue S. PZ-33944
★★★ John Dawson Winter III / Blue S.
  PZ-33292
★★★★ Johnny Winter / Col. CS-9826
★★★★ Johnny Winter And / Col. C-30221
★★★ Live / Col. PC-30475
★★★★ Nothin' but the Blues / Blue. S.
  PZ-34813
★★★ Saints and Sinners / Col. PC-32715
★★★★ Second Winter / Col. KCS-9947
★★★★ Still Alive and Well / Col.
  KC-32188
★★★ White Hot and Blue / Blue S.
  JZ-35475

Johnny Winter came out of Texas in 1969 after woodshedding there for the better part of a decade, and was immediately heralded as America's best young white blues guitarist—the acclaim was all the more powerful because he, like his brother Edgar, is an albino. He was almost immediately signed by Columbia to a lucrative long-term contract. But—because he was more committed to blues than rock, and because of a nasty heroin problem—Winter never realized his commercial promise.

The Janus and United Artists packages are recordings made in Texas during the mid-Sixties; they are straight blues and not bad, although the two-record Janus package (*Before the Storm*) is pretty thin. Winter's best blues playing is on *Johnny Winter,* the first Columbia LP, and *Nothin' but the Blues,* cut with some of the same people who made Muddy Waters' *Hard Again* (produced by Johnny). His rock ventures peaked early, with *Second Winter,* which includes a wonderful version of Bob Dylan's "Highway 61 Revisited," and *Johnny Winter And,* recorded with the remnants of the McCoys, including Rick Derringer. *Still Alive and Well,* his first album after being cured of his addiction, is also an interesting pop collection, with more than the usual share of straight blues work. — D.M.

JOHNNY AND EDGAR WINTER
★★★★ Together / Blue S. PZ-34033
A fine collaboration between the two Texas albino blues singers, in which Johnny's guitar and Edgar's voice and keyboards give each other more room to stretch out than could have been expected. — D.M.

WINTERS BROTHERS BAND
★★ Coast to Coast / Atco 38-106
★★ Winters Brothers Band / Atco 36-145
This has nothing to do with Johnny and Edgar Winter; it also has only a tenuous connection with the Allman Brothers Band, on whose name it would also like to capitalize. Mediocre Southern boogie music, more like Charlie Daniels than any of the fairly illustrious names above. — D.M.

JONATHAN WINTERS
★★ Laugh Live / Col. PG-31985
Winters' way with a sound effect is incomparable and unerring, but much more effective, naturally, if you can see him doing the impossible. His records unfortunately tend to emphasize Winters' least appealing character—a despised, lisping homosexual. For the rest, inspired mimicry with uninspired premises to showcase it. — K.T.

STEVE WINWOOD
★★★ Steve Winwood / Is. 9494
Winwood's extensive keyboard overdubbing quietly embellishes the modest simplicity of his R&B-derived songs and vocals. Moving, but not driving or obvious; relaxed, but not burnt out. — c.w.

WIRE
★★★★ Pink Flag / Harv. ST 11757

There's a cleanness of line and lack of distortion to this music that belies its place in the punk-rock pantheon; its motives are too self-consciously arty for that. But the British quartet plays at the furious pace of a punk group, cramming more than twenty songs—almost all of them intelligent ones—on this debut LP. The followup, *Chairs Missing,* available only as an import, slows the breakneck pace a fraction, but confirms the initial impression that this is one of the major groups of the Seventies' New Wave. — D.M.

WISHBONE ASH
★★★ Argus / MCA 2344
★★ Front Page News / MCA 2311
★★ Live Dates / MCA 2-8006
★ Locked In / Atl. 18164
★ New England / Atl. 18200
★ No Smoke Without Fire / MCA 3060
★ Pilgrimage / MCA 36
★★ Wishbone Ash / MCA 2343
★★ Wishbone Four / MCA 2348
Wishbone Ash never quite fit into any rock genre. They were simply a British hard-rock act, with overtones of art rock (like Yes) and boogie music (like Ten Years After), without a central personality, but capable of slugging it out on one-night stands throughout the U.S. and U.K. They earned their share of fans that way, but without developing any distinct musical style. *Argus* came closest to giving them an identity. Of the rest, the Atlantics are mush; the live LP is probably the next best bet for the curious. — D.M.

BILL WITHERS
★★★ 'Bout Love / Col. JC-35596
★★★ Making Music / Col. PC-33704
★★★ Menagerie / Col. JC-34903
★★★ Naked and Warm / Col. PC-34327
Withers began recording in 1972 for Clarence Avant's Sussex label, after serving in the Navy and as a computer operator. His early songs (recorded for Sussex Records), while funky enough, had an almost folkish feel, and he scored with several warm, pop-styled soul numbers, including "Ain't No Sunshine," the gospelly "Lean on Me" and "Use Me," both of which made the Top Ten. Since joining Columbia in 1975, however, he has lost his touch, caught between the macho of disco and his own artistic diffidence—he's too shy to be Barry White, and his natural demeanor is currently out of vogue. Some pleasant moments here, but the Sussex records are the ones worth tracking down. — D.M.

WOLFMAN JACK
■ Fun 'n' Romance / Col. KC-33501
Disc jockeys should be heard not seen, as Wolfman's Midnight Special appearances demonstrate. His album proves another immutable law of rock: disc jockeys should play records, not make them. (B. B. King and Waylon Jennings notwithstanding.) (Now deleted.) — D.M.

BOBBY WOMACK
★★★ Communication / U. Artists 5539
★★★ Understanding / U. Artists 5577
Too often, Bobby Womack seems the musical equivalent of baseball star Dick Allen. Like Allen, whose statistics have never kept pace with his abilities, Womack has never been as consistent as his considerable talent might allow. After years of indifferent success as a solo singer, he recorded *Communication* and *Understanding* in sessions only a few days apart. Though erratic, those LPs show a matured singer/songwriter and sport some of Womack's best work, including "That's the Way I Feel About 'Cha" and "Woman's Gotta Have It."
★★ Bobby Womack Goes C&W / U. Artists LA638-G
★★★★ Facts of Life / U. Artists LA043-G
★★ Lookin' for a Love Again / U. Artists LA199-G
★★★★ Greatest Hits / U. Artists LA346-G
★★★ I Don't Know What the World Is Coming To / U. Artists LA353-G
Though he's had success in an uptempo vein ("I Can Understand It," "Lookin' for a Love"), Womack works best in a narrative ballad approach. On one side of *Facts of Life,* he collects a string of such cuts, believable love songs that have the type of subdued passion that marked many Sam Cooke hits. A cover of "The Look of Love" is also included on *Facts,* and on other albums he takes awkward stabs at C&W and rock. As his own producer, Womack doesn't always temper such musical ambition with good taste.
★★★ Home Is Where the Heart Is / Col. PC-34384
★★★ Pieces / Col. JC-35083
★★★★ Safety Zone / U. Artists LA544-G
In an attempt to curb his excesses, U.A. contracted David Rubinson to produce *Safety Zone.* Using an L.A. session band, Rubinson concocted some smart rhythm tracks and with the exception of one slip into plastic psychedelia, *Safety Zone* sticks close to the feel of Womack's earlier work.

Womack's Columbia albums are returns to self-production, and the problems of the past creep up again: strong original tunes are mixed with misguided cover material. — J.MC.

THE WOMBLES
★★ **Remember You're a Womble / Col. KC-33140**
The Wombles were furry British TV creatures obsessed with picking up garbage; this pop-rock children's album isn't quite that bad. (Now deleted.) — D.M.

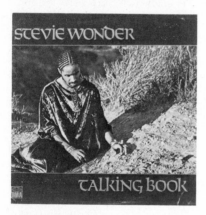

STEVIE WONDER
★★★★ **Fulfillingness' First Finale / Tam. T7-332**
★★★★★ **Innervisions / Tam. T7-326**
★★★★★ **Looking Back / Mo. M-804**
★★★★★ **Music of My Mind / Tam. T7-314**
★★★★★ **Songs in the Key of Life / Tam. T13-340**
★★★★ **Stevie Wonder's Greatest Hits / Tam. T7-283**
★★★★ **Stevie Wonder's Greatest Hits, Vol. 2 / Tam. T7-313**
★★★★★ **Talking Book / Tam. T7-3197**
Stevie Wonder has been a major star in black popular music since 1963, when "Fingertips Pt. 2," his third single, became a No. 1 hit. But in recent years, he has recorded music of such dazzling beauty, complexity and accessibility that he is now widely regarded as the most important popular composer of this era.

Wonder's early records generally fell well within the boundaries of the Motown formula sound: if "Fingertips," with its raucous harmonica and wild shouts, was at the raw edge of the company's recording spectrum, such ballads as "Castles in the Sand" and "I Was Made to Love Her"

went all the way in the other direction. In these, Wonder, though still a teenager, showed a remarkable resemblance to Ray Charles, which has something to do with the fact that both are black and blind, but more to do with a remarkably similar sense of time and pitch. His best Sixties singles included "I Was Made to Love Her," "Uptight" and "Contract on Love"; they are collected on the greatest-hits anthologies and on a later collection, *Looking Back,* which renders the former almost superfluous.

Beginning in 1971, Wonder took a more progressive direction, breaking out of the Motown formula with some of the most adventurous music of this decade. *Music of My Mind* in 1972 not only contained an enormously popular hit, "Superstition," but also reflected the influences of Sly Stone, Curtis Mayfield, Jimi Hendrix, Gamble and Huff and everyone else who had been involved in helping soul music break past the limits of its previous formulas. The production on all of the subsequent albums has been revelatory, and Wonder's singing is lighter and clearer than in his adolescence. Only *Fulfillingness' First Finale,* recorded after a 1974 car crash, is less than extraordinary. His most recent LP, *Songs in the Key of Life,* reestablishes Wonder as a major musical force: three years in the making, consisting of two LP discs and a seven-inch EP, it's a tour de force of the possibilities of modern recording, with an enormous amount to teach everyone who hears it. — D.M.

RON WOOD
★★★ **I've Got My Own Album to Do / War. B-2819**
★★★ **Mahoney's Last Stand / Atco 36-126**
★★★ **Now Look / War. B-2872**
Wood was the bassist in Jeff Beck's 1969 group. When the band split up, he and vocalist Rod Stewart joined the Faces, where Wood played guitar, and in 1975, after Stewart left the Faces, Wood became a Rolling Stone. The way to Stones-hood was paved by *I've Got My Own,* Wood's first (1974) solo album, which includes guest appearances by Keith Richards and Mick Jagger, among others. But his 1975 solo LP, *Now Look,* is better; his version of Gib Guilbeau's "Big Bayou" actually cuts Stewart's. Most of this is loose, energetic and more attractive for its feel than its precision—Wood is a cracked-voice singer, but his slide-guitar style is stinging and distinctive. *Mahoney's Last Stand* was a

soundtrack collaboration between Wood and Face Ron Lane; the movie was released only in Canada, but the music has the same jaunty appeal as the solo records. — D.M.

NANETTE WORKMAN
★★★ **Nanette Workman / Big 89514**
A guitar-based band makes a crazed album of what live, and very drunken, disco might sound like in a very much unhinged Montreal bar. Nanette Workman plays her thin-voiced part as the band's singer with round-heeled and passionate abandon. Actually recorded in Montreal, this album is a great example of the "other" style of Quebec rock. The first is the Harmonium, art-song type, and the "other" is the sleaze style epitomized by this and Michel Pagliaro. — B.T.

BETTY WRIGHT
★★★ **Betty Wright Live / Als. 4408**
★★★★ **Danger: High Voltage / Als. 4400**
★★★ **Explosion / Als. 4402**
★★ **This Time for Real / Als. 4406**
An energetic, spunky performer, Betty Wright hasn't been able to transfer her considerable talents into sustained commercial success. Her early hits ("Clean Up Woman," "The Babysitter") are gritty novelty records, but they're out of print and the albums are a mixed bag. *Danger: High Voltage* is the best; it's a cross section of exuberant, varied dance songs and poignant ballads, recorded during the peak of Miami soul. The subsequent albums show a distressing lack of direction and often bog down with hack productions. — J.MC.

GARY WRIGHT
★★ **Dream Weaver / War. 2868**
★ **Light of Smiles / War. B-2951**
★ **Touch and Gone / War. K-3137**
English keyboardist, a veteran of Spooky Tooth, hit big in 1975 with a syrupy ballad, "Dream Weaver," from the album of the same name. Since then, he's indulged himself with increasing flatulence in a spacey, mystical froth of synthesizers and remarkably poor vocalizing. — D.M.

O. V. WRIGHT
★★★★ **A Nickel and a Nail/Ace of Spades / Back. 70**
★★★ **Bottom Line / Hi 6008**
★★★ **Into Something I Can't Shake Loose / Hi 6001**
★★★★ **Memphis Unlimited / Back. X-72**

★★★ **Nucleus of Soul / Back. X-67**
★★★ **O. V. Wright / Back. 61**
O.V. Wright's best records are the Sixties soul sides he made for Backbeat, particularly the sometimes chilling "Ace of Spades." His voice is unique, a dark and moody instrument that's a holdover from the heyday of Southern soul. Both of the Hi albums contain strong performances marred by Willie Mitchell's dreary string charts. — J.MC.

BILL WYMAN
★★★ **Monkey Grip / Rol. COC-79100**
★★★ **Stone Alone / Rol. COC-79103**
The Rolling Stones' bassist is more production- than performance-minded on these two discs, and it shows: they sound a bit like demos of studio effects. There is a good sense of groove to both, however, and Stones' fans will undoubtedly enjoy listening to the personal quirks of the band's least-known member. (Now deleted.) — D.M.

TAMMY WYNETTE
★★★ **Another Lonely Song / Epic KE-32745**
★★★ **Bedtime Story / Epic BC-33773**
★★★ **Christmas with Tammy / Epic E-30343**
★★★★ **D-I-V-O-R-C-E / Epic 26392**
★★★ **First Songs of the First Lady / Epic BG-30358**
★★★ **I Still Believe in Fairy Tales / Epic KE-33582**
★★★ **Inspiration / Epic 26423**
★★★ **Kids Say the Darndest Things / Epic KE-31937**
★★★★ **Stand by Your Man / Epic BG-33773**
★★★★ **Tammy's Greatest Hits / Epic 26486**

★★★ **Tammy's Greatest Hits, Vol. 2 / Epic E-30733**
★★★ **Tammy's Greatest Hits, Vol. 3 / Epic KE-33396**
★★★ **Till I Can Make It on My Own / Epic KE-34075**
★★★ **Woman to Woman / Epic KE-33246**
★★★ **You and Me / Epic KE-34289**
★★★ **Your Good Girl's Gonna Go Bad / Epic 26305**

A former hairdresser from Tupelo, Mississippi, Tammy Wynette had become the most important female vocalist in country music by the end of the Sixties. She began recording in 1966 and quickly turned out a series of hits, including "Your Good Girl's Gonna Go Bad," "D-I-V-O-R-C-E," "Take Me to Your World" and "Stand by Your Man." Through the Seventies, and despite her marriage to champion honky-tonker George Jones, Wynette has settled into a formula country approach, abetted by producer Billy Sherrill's rather treacly taste in arrangements and material. But both *D-I-V-O-R-C-E* and *Stand by Your Man* are modern country LPs worth hearing, and the first *Greatest Hits* collection is a must. — C.F.

PHILLIPE WYNNE
★★★ **Starting All Over / Coti. SD-9920**
As lead vocalist for the Spinners, Wynne did some wonderful things. But on his own, he can't match them, at least not in his initial solo outing. Disappointing. — D.M.

STOMU YAMASHTA
★★★★ Go / Is. 9387
★★★ Go—Live from Paris / Is. 10
★★★ Go Too / Ari. 4138
★★★ Red Buddah / Van. 79343
Japanese composer/percussionist whose bizarre ideas and musical eclecticism have made him well respected in varied musical circles but keep him a mystery to the general public. Yamashta's musical productions (all his records are related to one of several multimedia presentations he has either put together or is still planning) combine elements of jazz, rock, classical and electronic music deftly, and sometimes arbitrarily—hence his difficulty in reaching a mass audience. *Man from the East,* a strange but fascinating stage show featuring elements of Japanese Kabuki theater, spawned the *Red Buddah* album, which is the best demonstration of Yamashta's astounding technique as a percussionist. The other records are part of a project that Yamashta intends as a recapitulation of all his influences. *Go,* which includes a fine performance on keyboards from Steve Winwood, is the most accessible record Yamashta has made. — J.S.

GLENN YARBROUGH
■ The Best of Glenn Yarbrough / RCA
  AFL1-4349
■ The Best of Glenn Yarbrough / Trad.
  1054
Less appropriate titles could not have been found for either of these LPs. Although Yarbrough had a hit with "Baby the Rain Must Fall" (around which the RCA collection is built), his best work was unquestionably as a member of the Limeliters. That group's RCA catalogue is out of print, but it was a typical example of early-Sixties pop folk. The Tradition LP is slightly more in tune with the Limeliters style than the obnoxiously orchestrated,

MOR RCA set. Better to check the cutout bins for RCA's Limeliters releases. — I.M.

THE YARDBIRDS
★★★★ Eric Clapton and the Yardbirds /
  Sp. 4036
★★★ Eric Clapton and the Yardbirds with
  Sonny Boy Williamson / Mer. 61271
★★★ Shapes of Things / Sp. 4039
★★★★★ The Yardbirds Great Hits / Epic
  PE-34491
★★★★★ Yardbirds Favorites / Epic
  E-34490
One of the great Sixties rock groups, the Yardbirds were influential on other musicians beyond the bounds of their own commercial impact, which in this country amounted mostly to a handful of hit singles: "Heart Full of Soul," "I'm a Man," "For Your Love" and "Shapes of Things." These were rock at a certain edge, beginning to prepare itself for the massive guitar frenzy and experimentation of the psychedelic age.

Keith Relf was probably the most limited singer in any of the significant British groups, but the Yardbirds' guitarists—Eric Clapton, Jeff Beck and Jimmy Page, in sequence—were all true originals: Clapton's fiery blues style dominates the Springboard LPs, while Beck and Page take over on the Epic repackages. The Yardbirds helped introduce almost every significant technical innovation in the rock of their period: feedback, modal playing, fuzztone, etc. Their influence can't be overestimated. Cream, Led Zeppelin and heavy metal in general would have been inconceivable without them. — D.M.

YELLOW SUNSHINE
■ Yellow Sunshine / Gam. KZ-32405
Another Seventies "Philadelphia Soul" disco project. So slick the needle won't stay on the record. (Now deleted.) — J.S.

YES
★★★★★ Close to the Edge / Atl. 7244
★★★★ Fragile / Atl. 7211
★★★★ Going for the One / Atl. 19106
★★★★ Relayer / Atl. 18122
★★★★ Tales from Topographic Oceans /
  Atl. SD2-908
★★★★★ The Yes Album / Atl. 8283
★★★ Time and a Word / Atl. 8273
★★★ Tormato / Atl. 19202
★★★ Yes / Atl. 8243
★★★ Yessongs / Atl. 3-100
★★★ Yesterdays / Atl. 18103

Yes introduces a varied virtuosity: beautiful high-keyed vocal harmonies led by John Anderson, and a contrasting rhythm section led by Chris Squire's loud, thick, trebly bass guitar, and Bill Bruford's firm, deft and imaginative drumming. Ethereal yet rocking, most of this colorful and complex material was original. *Time and a Word* follows similar paths, often employing tasteful orchestrations. *Yesterdays* assembles cuts from both albums, and adds songs unavailable elsewhere.

The Yes Album has a harder, cleaner, faster sound. Newcomer Steve Howe's bitingly imaginative guitar propels the band electrically and acoustically. The songs are generally longer but not meandering.

Fragile signals a slightly new approach. Whereas Tony Kaye's keyboards had been relatively simple, tonally bracing fills, newcomer Rick Wakeman's sport a rich, nimble flamboyance, similar in concept to Howe's guitar. Remarkably, no one interferes with anyone else, although solo sections take up a good deal of the record. *Close to the Edge* is more a group effort and the natural and ultimate outcome of the approach: technically brilliant, many-hued and free, but still within a definite framework. Perhaps most importantly, it rocks.

The three-record live *Yessongs* (Alan White replacing Bruford on must cuts) is certainly competent, but lacks the vital depth and sonority of the studio.

Tales from Topographic Oceans—a lengthy and ponderous double album—slows down and widens their earlier moves: one deliberately paced song per side. A certain spark is gone, but an agreeable calm emerges—subtle, though hardly dull, it rarely rocks. A dissatisfied and mystified Wakeman left, replaced by Patrick Moraz. The ensuing *Relayer* shows more vitality and hardness; Howe stepped forward, as Moraz was more a quietly effective texturist than a centerpiece.

Going for the One, recorded after a three-year hiatus and with Wakeman back, is a celebratory, crisply recorded return. The uptempo sections rock as hard as their finest moments, while the more quiet interludes again demonstrate the beautiful subtleties and complexities that Yes had so effortlessly poured out before. The material is both long and short. No new ground is broken, to be sure, and some of the hard moments do seem almost simple in comparison to, say, *Close to the Edge.* Nonetheless, it's a more than adequate display. — C.W.

CHRIS YOULDEN
★★ City Child / Lon. PS-642
Ex-Savoy Brown lead singer's second solo album presents him in fairly energetic blues voice, but his first, *Nowhere Road,* is better and well worth looking for in cutout bins. (Now deleted.) — J.S.

JESSE COLIN YOUNG
★★ American Dreams / Elek. 6E-157
★★ Light Shine / War. B-2790
★★ Love on the Wing / War. B-3033
★★ On the Road / War. B-2913
★★ Song for Juli / War. B-2734
★★ Songbird / War. B-2845
★★ The Soul of a City Boy / Cap.
  ST-11267
★★ Together / War. B-2588
Young was a quixotic force as leader of the Youngbloods, one of the more eccentric manifestations of late-Sixties folk rock. On his own, he was a lot more like a soap-opera caricature of northern California hippies—rusticated without relief or groove or much more than the usual pious combination of good times and happy vibes. This extensive catalogue is one long, numb muddle. — D.M.

JOHN PAUL YOUNG
★★★ John Paul Young / Mid. Int. BXL1-2535
★★ Love Is in the Air / Scotti 7101

Young, who is produced by the Vanda-Young team that made the Easybeats' hits, is one of Australia's current sensations. But up here in the big time, he looks like just another Paul Rodgers impersonator, with less than Bad Company-style backing. — D.M.

NEIL YOUNG
★★★★ After the Gold Rush / Rep. K-2283
★★★ American Stars 'n' Bars / Rep. 2261
★★★ Comes a Time / Rep. K-2266
★★★★★ Decade / Rep. RS-2257
★★★★★ Everybody Knows This Is No-where / Rep. K-2282
★★★★ Harvest / Rep. K-2277
★ Journey Through the Past / Rep. 2XS-6480
★★★ Neil Young / Rep. 6317
★★ On the Beach / Rep. 2180
★★★ Time Fades Away / Rep. 2151
★★★★★ Tonight's the Night / Rep. 2221
★★★★ Zuma / Rep. 2242

Young was already a hero when he split from the Buffalo Springfield in the late Sixties. His solo career played out the moves he'd already demonstrated with that band while borrowing a few new ones from Bob Dylan. *Neil Young* features the Dylan-esque epic dirge, "The Last Trip to Tulsa" and Young's alienation anthem, "The Loner." He then made some records with his backup band, Crazy Horse, the best of which is *Everybody Knows This Is Nowhere.* "Cinnamon Girl" from that album is the finest rock & roll song Young has ever recorded, and several other tracks from the record—"Cowgirl in the Sand," the title cut and "Down by the River"—have since become FM radio classics.

After the death of Crazy Horse guitarist Danny Whitten, Young returned to a softer, country-oriented style and made his most popular album, *Harvest,* in Nashville. "Heart of Gold" became Young's first hit single.

His album projects since *Harvest* have been erratic and very personal, with a wide range of material—from other Nashville-produced items to stark rock songs recorded in his California studio with long guitar solos. *Tonight's the Night,* an eerily brilliant set of drug-culture observations dedicated to Whitten, is his most difficult, yet the most gripping and durable work of this period. This period was really inaugu-

rated by *Time Fades Away,* one of the most audacious live albums ever made.

Young softened once more with the 1978 release, *There Comes a Time,* which included the most optimistic songs he's recorded in years. "Human Highway" was one song in particular that Young fans had been waiting to hear for a while, and "Goin' Back" and "Look Out for My Love" were two of his best lyric exercises. The album also includes a cover version of Ian Tyson's "Four Strong Winds."

Journey Through the Past was a regrettable collection assembled as a soundtrack to the movie of the same name. *Decade* is one of the best greatest-hits packages ever assembled, a three-record set that covers Young's best songs from the Springfield days to *Zuma,* including pertinent material unavailable on other albums and featuring Young's brief descriptions of the circumstances surrounding each song on the record. *Decade* includes virtually all the Neil Young songs that matter. — J.S.

STEVE YOUNG
★★★★ No Place to Fall / RCA AHL1-2510
★★★★ Renegade Picker / RCA AHL1-1759
★★★ Seven Bridges Road / Blue C. 505

Young is some kind of country songwriter. His "Lonesome, On'ry and Mean," with its loping pace and grim evocation of the plight of a drifter pursued by inner demons, is the best thing Waylon Jennings ever recorded. Young's own version of it (on *Renegade Picker*) approaches Jennings' intensity; he possesses the same kind of husky baritone and remarkable ability to sustain notes. A fine, overlooked, underrated country performer. — C.F.

YOUNG-HOLT UNLIMITED
★★ **Beat Goes On** / Bruns. 754128
★★ **Funky But** / Bruns. 754141
★★★ **Just a Melody** / Bruns. 754150
★★ **Soulful Strut** / Bruns. 754144
★★★ **The Great Soul Hits of Young-Holt Unlimited** / Bruns. 754129
★★★ **Young-Holt Unlimited on Stage** / Bruns. 754125
★★★ **Young-Holt Unlimited Plays "Super Fly"** / Paula 4002

Jazz-funk group scored with the Sixties hit "Wack Wack" (it was then known as the Young-Holt Trio), then went on to make this endless series of boring funk wallpaper records. Still, the patterns aren't bad for wallpaper. — J.S.

THE YOUNGBLOODS
★★★★ **Best of the Youngbloods** / RCA AFL1-4399
★★★★ **This Is the Youngbloods** / RCA AFL1-6051

★★★ **Youngbloods** / RCA AFL1-4150
One of the best of the late-Sixties bands to come under the psychedelic umbrella, the Youngbloods played music that was really much too conservative by the standards of the day to be called acid rock. Led by reconstructed folkie Jesse Colin Young, the band was more a white R&B outfit than anything else. After knocking around for a while, a version of "Get Together" became a hit and the band enjoyed moderate popularity. Young put together his own label, Raccoon Records, released a pair of great albums by Michael Hurley and some Youngbloods projects, then promptly went broke.

At various times the Youngbloods have had quite a few albums out, but now most of them, even the legendary *Elephant Mountain,* are deleted. The remaining records, especially the *This Is* compilation, do give a good, if fractured, account of the band. — J.S.

ZZ TOP
★★ Fandango / War. K-3171
★★ First Album / War. K-3268
★★ Rio Grande Mud / War. K-3269
★★ Tejas / War. K-3272 •
★★★ The Best of ZZ Top / War. K-3273
★★ Tres Hombres / War. K-3270

This Texas boogie band enjoyed a vogue during 1975 and 1976, when its concerts broke attendance records set by the Beatles, among others. But on record, ZZ Top was never more than a poor man's Lynyrd Skynyrd—some rural feeling but mostly just numbing guitar drive. Rock & roll can be mindless fun, but it never deserved to be this empty-headed. — D.M.

ZAGER AND EVANS
★ In the Year 2525 / RCA ANL1-1077

Space-pop. The hit was "2525," less notable for its synthesizer work than for the eerie but dumb vocal; a pleasantly forgettable chart fluke. — D.M.

WARREN ZEVON
★★★★ Excitable Boy / Asy. 6E-118
★★★★★ Warren Zevon / Asy. 7E-1060

Zevon is one of the best young writer/performers to emerge in the past few years, and one of the toughest rockers ever to come out of Southern California. *Warren Zevon,* his 1976 debut LP, received a great deal of attention because of Jackson Browne's production, but Zevon has a tougher, more ribald style than Browne, both lyrically and musically. "Carmelita," one of his best songs, is about a lonesome L.A. drug addict, and both "Desperados under the Eaves" and "Mohammed's Radio" paint less than flattering portraits of Hollywood life. *Excitable Boy,* which con-

tains Zevon's hit single, "Werewolves of London," was not quite as successful as the first LP, even though it was more popular. Producers Browne and Waddy Wachtel aided Zevon in firming up his sound, but the material on side two is terribly weak— among the most obvious filler any major rock artist has recorded. Still, "Roland the Head Thompson Gunner," "Excitable Boy" and "Lawyers, Guns and Money" make even the second album substantial. — D.M.

THE ZOMBIES
★★ Time of the Zombies / Epic PEG-32861

During the British Invasion, the Zombies hit with an ethereal love song, "Tell Her No," which spawned careers for Russ Ballard and Rod Argent. In the late Sixties, after a long hiatus, the group came up with "Time of the Season," the keynote of this mediocre comeback effort. "Tell Her No" was on Parrot, and it's the one to have. — D.M.

ZOOM
■ Zoom / A&M 3402

Inconsequential Seventies pop. — J.S.

ZUIDER ZEE
★ Zuider Zee / Col. PC-33816

Wooden and uninteresting 1975 album from a group with an *Abbey Road*-era Beatles fixation. (Now deleted.) — J.S.

ZULEMA
★★ R.S.V.P. / RCA APL1-1152
★★ Suddenly There Was You / RCA APL1-1423

Competent black female vocalist can't get beyond her idolatry of Aretha Franklin. — J.S.

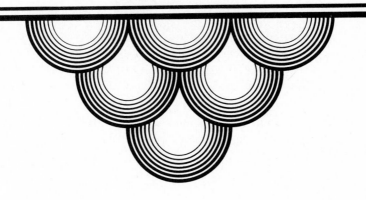

BLUES

LUTHER ALLISON
★★★ **Love Me Mama / Del. 625**
★★★ **Luther's Blues / Gor. 967**
★ **Night Life / Gor. 974**
Youngish Chicago blues guitarist who has
never been able to consolidate his raw talent into a truly workable recording style.
Motown's Gordy subsidiary is an odd
place to find Allison, and the label's pop
orientation proves disastrous on *Night Life,*
where he's asked to truck with soul music.
The others are better, but their preponderance of hot guitar licks lacks
focus.   — D.M.

BIG BILL BROONZY
★★ **Big Bill / Folk. 3586**
★★★ **Big Bill Broonzy / Ev. 213**
★ **Big Bill Broonzy Sings Country Blues /**
 Folk. 31005
★★★ **Big Bill Broonzy Sings Folk Songs /**
 Folk. 2328
★★★ **Blues / Folk. 3817**
★★★ **Do That Guitar Rag / Yazoo L-1035**
★★ **Feelin' Low Down / Cres. 10004**
★★★ **Lonesome Road Blues / Cres. 10009**
★★★★ **1932-42 / Bio. C-15**
★★★ **Young / Yazoo 1011**
A strong singer who doubled on guitar and
fiddle, Broonzy was widely recognized as
one of the greatest folk bluesmen before his
death in 1958. His style is languid yet
charged with emotion, with plenty of space
left between notes to develop tension. He
traveled the classic country-blues route
from Mississippi to Arkansas and finally to
Chicago, playing while holding down odd
jobs and occasionally recording. Broonzy is
the key transitional figure between the delta style of Robert Johnson and the modern,
electric Chicago blues of Muddy Waters.
The Everest, Biograph, Yazoo and Crescendo sides assemble some of the pertinent material he did during the Thirties

and Forties, but nowhere near encompass
the range of his repertoire, which is considered to include over 350 original compositions. The Folkways material, recorded
shortly before his death and released posthumously, shows that Broonzy was still a
powerful singer despite his failing health
and a throat operation. *Blues* is with Sonny
Terry and Brownie McGhee.   — J.S.

BIG MACEO
★★★★ **Chicago Breakdown / Blueb.**
 AXM2-5506
This double album spotlights the moving
vocals and strong left-handed playing of a
blues pianist perhaps second only to Otis
Spann.   — J.MO.

BIG MAYBELLE
★★ **Last of Big Maybelle / Para. 2-1011**
★★ **The Amazing Big Maybelle / Up. Fr.**
 162
★★★ **The Gospel Soul of Big Maybelle /**
 Bruns. 754142
★★★ **The Great Soul Hits of Big May-**
 belle / Bruns. 754129
A strong-voiced belter in the Bessie Smith
tradition, on record Big Maybelle never
really showed what she was capable of.
Her live performances were legendary, and
you do get a sense of her power on the
Brunswick records, but the Up Front and
Paramount sides simply don't capture her.
It's worth checking up on her pop sides re-
corded for Savoy in 1956, which are an-
thologized on *The Roots of Rock 'n' Roll.*
"Candy," a hit for that label, is the best she
sounded on record.   — J.S.

JUKE BOY BONNER
★★★ **Juke Boy Bonner / Arhoo. 1036**
Texas/California bluesman of the Forties;
relatively formless songs, effectively performed in the Lightnin' Hopkins mold, but

with a tinge of black social consciousness. — D.M.

LEROY CARR
★★★★ 1934 / Bio. C-9

Carr was one of the most influential Chicago bluesmen of the Thirties. His 1928 version of "How Long, How Long Blues" was quite popular and widely admired by other musicians, and Carr's reedy, cynical voice carried the themes of loneliness and desperation convincingly. The Biograph session captures him at the height of his powers, a year before his death in 1935. — J.S.

LEROY CARR AND SCRAPPER BLACKWELL
★★★★ Naptown / Yazoo 1036

Accompanied by the equally sophisticated guitar playing of Scrapper Blackwell, Leroy Carr put across an impressive array of music from 1928 to 1934, some of the best of which is included here. — J.S.

BO CARTER
★★★★★ Greatest Hits 1930-40 / Yazoo L-1014
★★★★★ Twist It Babe / Yazoo 1034

Carter popularized the Mississippi hokum blues in the Thirties on his own and with his band, the Mississippi Sheiks. Carter was a humorous and raunchy, if limited, vocalist, but a superb guitarist and violinist with an exemplary arrangement sense that enabled him to codify a lot of the white string-band and standard country-blues ideas others (notably Tommy Johnson and John Hurt) used, while still maintaining his own distinctive style.

Greatest Hits and *Twist It Babe* collect his best work from the Thirties and give a really good indication of what the locals were digging back in those days. On *Twist It Babe,* Carter accompanies his own singing on a National steel guitar. Other members of the Sheiks double on guitar and violin on various songs in the *Greatest Hits* set, which shows Carter in his best boasting, bawdy and drinking attitude. He even dabbles in humorous political protest here on "Sales Tax," with a hilarious intro that has Carter and a pal going in to buy a pack of cigarettes. When they find out about the sales tax, Carter's pal observes that there's a lot of things being sold that the government doesn't know anything about. — J.S.

JAMES COTTON
★★ Cut You Loose / Van. 79283
★★★ High Energy / Bud. 5650
★★★ 100 Per Cent Cotton / Bud. 5620
★★★ Super Harp—Live and on the Move / GRT 5661
★★ Taking Care of Business / Cap. SM-814

Cotton's story is the stuff of blues legend. He ran away from home when he was nine to find blues harmonica player Sonny Boy Williamson, met up with him in Arkansas and was taken in as a member of the family. When he was thirteen, Cotton became (along with Junior Parker) one of two blues harpists in Howlin' Wolf's Arkansas band. Cotton was the harpist on Wolf's first sessions for Chess Records, and went on to play for over a decade with Muddy Waters in Chicago, before forming his own group in 1965.

Cotton's earliest recordings with his own band on Verve/Forecast are now out of print. What remains is uneven, often more pop-oriented than blues-rooted, and mostly recorded with a series of session players. Oddly, the two more commercial Buddah albums stand out—Cotton's playing, singing and instrumental backup are in good form, though not always classic blues.

100 Per Cent Cotton (1974) was recorded with his band at the time; *High Energy* was produced by Allen Toussaint at his New Orleans studio and blends Cotton's sophisticated Chicago blues style to good effect with the steamy funk of New Orleans R&B. — J.S.

ARTHUR "BIG BOY" CRUDUP
★★★ Crudup's Mood / Del. 621
★★★ Look on Yonder's Wall / Del. 614
★★ Mean Ol' Frisco / Trip 7501

Country-blues singer best known for providing Elvis with his debut song, "That's

All Right." Crudup was never more than a journeyman bluesman—Elvis cut him to bits, however scandalous the royalty arrangements—but his late-Sixties Delmark recordings are interesting for a lightness of tone that neither the Trip nor a deleted RCA guilt anthology (*The Father of Rock and Roll*) possesses. — D.M.

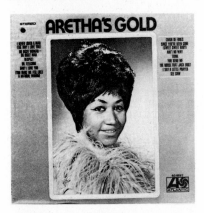

REVEREND GARY DAVIS
★★ **Lord I Wish I Could See / Bio. 12034E**
★★★ **Reverend Gary Davis / Bio. 12030E**
★★★ **Reverend Gary Davis, 1935–1949 / Yazoo 1023**
★★ **When I Die I'll Live Again / Fan. 24704**
Davis became an ordained minister in 1934 at the age of thirty-eight, whereupon he excised from his repertoire all "sinful" songs. But while the subject matter changed, the influence of the delta blues he'd heard and played in his youth (Leadbelly, Sonny Terry, Brownie McGhee) represented a substantial influence on the blind preacher's gospel singing and playing—six- and twelve-string guitars—for which Davis became best known. The Yazoo set chronicles the years Davis spent as a Harlem street singer. The other discs date from the Fifties and Sixties, by which time his gospel-blues style had become a major staple of the folk circuit. Davis taught (David Bromberg was among his students) and performed until shortly before his death in 1972 at the age of seventy-six. — I.M.

WILLIE DIXON
★★ **Catalyst / Ova. QD-14-33**
★★ **I Am the Blues / Col. CS-9987**
★★ **What Happened to My Blues / Ova. QD-1441**
Dixon is one of R&B's most important songwriters. He composed some of Bo

Diddley's best songs, including "I'm a Man" as well as a number of important Muddy Waters and Howlin' Wolf numbers, such as "Hoochie Coochie Man" and "Wang Dang Doodle." As a performer, he is definitely less interesting. — D.M.

GEORGIA TOM DORSEY
★★★★ **Come On Mama / Yazoo 1041E**
As the Reverend Thomas Dorsey, this man would become the greatest songwriter black gospel music has known. Here he is found in his sinful incarnation of the Twenties, performing first-rate country blues. — D.M.

CHAMPION JACK DUPREE
★★★★ **Blues at Montreux / Atco 1637**
★★★★ **Champion Jack Dupree / Ev. 217**
★★★★ **Happy to Be Free / Cres. 10006**
★★★★ **Tricks / Cres. 10001**
★★★★ **Women Blues of Champion Jack Dupree / Folk. 3825**
Dupree is more interesting as a stylist than a virtuoso, but he got the most out of his talent, and his records provide fine listening. A New Orleans native, Dupree learned to play barrelhouse piano as a kid from a guy named Drive 'Em Down, began playing on his own in the Thirties and supported himself by boxing, which is how he picked up his nickname. His postwar Forties recordings are notable for the drive and energy of his piano playing and powerful singing. The Everest and Crescendo recordings are not marked with dates, but the recording quality suggests they are sides from the late Fifties or Sixties. Fortunately, Dupree's powers did not wane with age, as the fine Sixties recording for Atco (saxophonist King Curtis is also on it) proves. — J.S.

SNOOKS EAGLIN
★★★ **Possum up a Simmon Tree / Arhoo. 2014**
Eclectic Louisiana blues performer, uses tom-toms and washboard in addition to guitar. Material ranges from spirituals to shoeshine-boy chants to bad-man ballads. Includes two Arthur Crudup songs, Elvis' first record, "That's All Right" and "Rock Me Mama," the hillbilly standard "This Train" and "John Henry." — D.M.

SLEEPY JOHN ESTES
★★ **Broke and Hungry / Del. 608**
★★ **Brownsville Blues / Del. 9613**
★★ **Electric Sleep / Del. 619**

★★ **Legend / Del. 9603**
★★★★ **1929-40 / Folk. RBF-8**
Estes was a fair guitarist and a good moaning-style singer from Brownsville, Tennessee, whose technique was similar to delta players. His best recorded work, done in the Thirties, is collected on the *1929-40* reissue. Despite stories he cut records with Sam Phillips in the Fifties that were never released, Estes was believed lost until Delmark got hold of him to make a generally uninspired series of comeback LPs in the Sixties. — J.S.

BLIND BOY FULLER
★★★ **1935-40 / Blues Cl. 11**
Fuller was a Carolina blues player whose singing was meant to be backed up by his guitar playing rather than a central element of the music, as it was for most Tennessee and Mississippi players. The ragtime-influenced picking style is heard to good effect on this reissue, which includes his essential recordings during the period. — J.S.

JESSE FULLER
★★★ **Brother Lowdown / Fan. 24707**
★★★ **The Lone Cat / Good T. S-10039**
Known primarily as the composer of "San Francisco Bay Blues," which was popularized by Peter, Paul and Mary, among others, Fuller was a vaudeville-like one-man band who was capable of playing guitar, cymbal, fotdella (a foot-controlled bass contraption he invented) and harmonica-kazoo at the same time. He sang in a blues style, but his music was also influenced by jazz and gospel forms. Both sets (the Fantasy is a repackage of two Prestige LPs) were recorded in the early Sixties and are appropriately annotated and moderately well recorded. — I.M.

LOWELL FULSOM
★★★ **Hung Down Head / Chess 408**
★★★ **Let's Go Get Stoned / Kent 558**
★★★★ **Lowell Fulsom / Chess 205**
★★★ **Lowell Fulsom . . . Now / Kent 531**
★★★ **Soul / Kent 516**
★★★ **The Tramp / Kent 520**
Lowell Fulsom (often spelled Fulson) is a hard R&B performer, verging closer to pure blues than almost any other well-known singer of the Sixties except Bobby Bland. His guttural voice and twanging guitar can be charming but lack the resonance or depth of Bland and his material. Fulsom's best-known songs include "Tramp," which Otis Redding and Carla

Thomas converted into a soul hit in 1966, and "Reconsider Baby." Chess 205, despite an ugly cover, contains the best of his work. — D.M.

BUDDY GUY
★★★ **Hold That Plane / Van. 79323**
★★★★ **Man and the Blues / Van. 79272**
★★★★ **This Is Buddy Guy / Van. 79290**
★★ **Through the Woods / Chess 409**
One of the younger Chicago bluesmen, Guy began recording in the Sixties after serving an apprenticeship in Muddy Waters' band. A flashy guitarist influenced by B. B. King and Elmore James and a good vocalist in the Bobby Bland style, Guy enjoyed a lot of crossover success with white audiences and covered a number of popular R&B songs ("Knock on Wood") in addition to blues staples. *This Is* is a fairly hot live set. Guy now tours jointly with harpist Junior Wells. — J.S.

SLIM HARPO
★★★ **Slim Harpo Knew the Blues, Vol. 2 / Ex. 28030**
Harpo was a little-known but influential Fifties and Sixties blues singer, whose R&B hits included "I'm a King Bee" and "Baby Scratch My Back." "King Bee" and his "Hip Shake" were recorded by the Rolling Stones, and his vocal-harmonica style had a heavy influence on Mick Jagger's. Unfortunately, Volume 1 of this set is out of print. Although Volume 2 is a two-record set, it lacks all of his important songs in favor of more obscure material, including covers of "Mohair Sam" and John Lee Hooker's "Boogie Chillun." (His own hits are available on several blues anthologies.) An intense, smokily erotic singer, Harpo deserves better representation. — D.M.

EARL HOOKER
★★★ **First and Last Recordings / Arhoo. 1066**
★★★ **Funk: The Last of the Great Earl Hooker / Ant. 7024**
★★★ **Hooker and Steve / Arhoo. 1051**
★★★ **Two Bugs and a Roach / Arhoo. 1044**
A fine slide guitarist but weak singer, Hooker was at his best on instrumentals. Born in Mississippi, where he learned slide guitar from Robert Nighthawk, Hooker was a prominent Chicago sideman and leader throughout the Fifties and Sixties. *Hooker and Steve* features him with Steve Miller. — D.M.

JOHN LEE HOOKER

★★★ **Best of John Lee Hooker** / Cres.
10007
★★★★ **Black Snake** / Fan. 24722
★★★★ **Boogie Chillun** / Fan. 24706
★★★ **Boogie with Hooker 'n' Heat** / Trip
3501
★★★★★ **Greatest Hits of John Lee
Hooker** / Kent 559
★★★★★ **It Serves You Right to Suffer** /
Imp. 9103
★★★ **John Lee Hooker** / Ev. 222
★★★★ **John Lee Hooker** / Kent 525
★★★★ **John Lee Hooker Alone** / Spec.
2125
★★★ **John Lee Hooker's Endless Boogie** /
ABC 720
★★★★ **Mad Man Blues** / Chess 2-60011
★★★ **Real Blues** / Trad. 2089
★★★★ **Whiskey and Wimmen** / Trip
X-9504

Hooker was probably the most eccentric of
the electric, urban bluesmen who emerged
in the late Forties and early Fifties. First of
all, he was based in Detroit, rather than
Chicago; more importantly, he never restricted himself to strict twelve-bar formats,
treating blues more as a feeling than a
form, more an emotional resource than a
binding tradition.

Hooker began recording for Modern
Records in 1948; he had an almost immediate, if moderate, success with "Crawling
King Snake Blues," but his big breakthrough did not come until 1951, with "I'm
in the Mood." Although he recorded prolifically for Modern and later Vee Jay
throughout the Sixties, he did not have another big hit until "Boom Boom," in 1962.
But his eccentric, thumping rhythms—a
fundamental source of what rockers call
"boogie"—and gravelly voice were enormously influential on early British R&B
bands, particularly Eric Burdon and the
Animals, who popularized both "Boom
Boom" and Hooker's more obscure "I'm
Mad Again" for white audiences. Later,
Canned Heat would record his "Whiskey
and Wimmen," first made for Vee Jay in
the early Sixties. During that decade,
Hooker recorded principally for ABC/
Bluesway, although only *Endless Boogie,* an
early Seventies affair, and *It Serves You
Right to Suffer,* a classic moaning blues recorded for ABC's jazz-oriented subsidiary,
Impulse, remain in print.

Hooker also recorded for a number of
other labels, sometimes under assumed
names. The Crescendo LP was originally
issued for that record company; the Trip

sides were recorded for a variety of labels,
mainly Vee Jay; the Fantasy recordings
were originally made for Prestige; the Everest and Tradition albums are collections
of his earliest work for Modern. As a result, there are dozens of out-of-print
Hooker LPs, almost all of which contain
something worthwhile. Hooker—who still
performs but has not recorded in several
years—is a crucial pivotal figure, both for
the transition from urban blues to R&B
and for the adoption of the blues form by
white bands. — D.M.

LIGHTNIN' HOPKINS

★★★★ **Autobiography** / Trad. 1040
★★★★ **Best** / Trad. 2056
★★★★ **Best of Texas Blues Band** / Prest.
7714
★★★ **Blues** / Main. 311
★★★ **Blues** / Prest. 7811
★★★ **Country Blues** / Trad. 1035
★★★ **Dirty Blues** / Main. 326
★★★★ **Double Blues** / Fan. 24702
★★★★ **Early Recordings** / Arhoo. 2007
★★★ **Early Recordings, Vol. 2** / Arhoo.
2010
★★★★ **Greatest Hits** / Prest. 7592
★★★★ **Gotta Move Your Baby** / Prest.
7831
★★★★ **Hootin' the Blues** / Prest. 7806
★★★★ **In Berkeley** / Arhoo. 1063
★★★★ **Lightnin' Hopkins** / Arc. Folk 241
★★ **Lightnin' Hopkins** / Trip 8015
★★★ **Lightnin' Sam Hopkins** / Arhoo.
1011
★★★★ **Lightnin' Strikes** / Trad. 2013
★★★ **Low Down Dirty Blues** / Main. 405
★★★ **Roots** / Folk. 31011
★★ **Talkin' Some Sense** / Jewel 5001
★★★★ **Texas Blues Man** / Arhoo. 1034
★★ **With Brothers and Barbara Dane** /
Arhoo. 1022

The last of the great country-blues singers,
Hopkins didn't even start recording until
he'd been playing for over twenty years at
country picnics and parties in Texas. Hopkins learned to play watching Blind Lemon
Jefferson, who taught him a few tricks, as
did Hopkins' cousin, "Texas" Alexander.
Hopkins went to Houston to record in
1946 and did a series of duets with piano
player "Thunder" Smith. After a few tries,
Hopkins finally clicked when he recorded
solo for Gold Star Studio, accompanying
himself on guitar. A single, "Short Haired
Woman" backed with "Big Mama Jump,"
became a huge regional hit.

Hopkins played around and built up a
reputation as a renegade who would accept

payment for recording only in cash and insisted on being paid after recording each song before he'd go on to the next one. He accumulated and spent plenty this way, because over the years the prolific Hopkins has become the most frequently recorded bluesman in history. The remarkable thing is that his records are of such consistently high quality—his ragged, urgent voice and deft guitar playing always come off well on the rambling, autobiographical stories he spins during sessions. Hopkins' glibness, his narrative force and smooth, relaxed delivery, provided an obvious model for much of Bob Dylan's early style. — J.S.

BIG WALTER HORTON
★★★ **Big Walter Horton with Carey Bell /** **Alli. 4702**

Horton is one of the masters of blues harmonica, ranking with the two Sonny Boy Williamsons (John Lee Williamson, Rice Miller), Little Walter and Junior Wells as the instrument's major innovators. He has recorded only twice as a leader, however, and this 1972 LP is the only one of those two that remains available. (The other LP, now extremely rare, was cut for Argo in 1964.) Horton has recorded as a sideman for Willie Dixon, Otis Rush, J. B. Hutto, Johnny Shines and Muddy Waters (he replaced the great Junior Wells), among others. (Other solo sides were recorded for the Chicago-based States and Cobra.) This record, which often features Horton in harp duets with Bell, is rugged, pure and free, although the constant focus on harmonica, coupled with Horton's nondescript vocal style, can make it a trifle wearing. — D.M.

SON HOUSE
★★ **Father of the Folk Blues / Col.** **CS-9217**

★★★ **Real Delta Blues / Blue G. 2016**
★★★★★ **Son House / Arhoo. 9002**

Although the Columbia and Blue Goose records were made in his dotage, Alan Lomax' field recordings for the Library of Congress (released on Arhoolie) mark House as one of the central figures in Mississippi blues. His stark, soulful singing and ringing, open-tuned, bottleneck guitar style made him a legend in the small Mississippi delta towns where he played house parties in the late Twenties and Thirties. He came to the attention of Charlie Patton, who set up House's first recording session with Paramount. House took up performing with Patton's friend Willie Brown, and built up a following that included the young Robert Johnson. It's a tribute to his powers that House still sounds vibrant on Blue Goose material, recorded privately by Nick Perls in the Sixties. — J.S.

MISSISSIPPI JOHN HURT
★★ **Last Sessions / Van. 79327**
★★★ **Mississippi John Hurt—1928—His** **First Recordings / Bio. BLP-C4**
★★ **Mississippi John Hurt—Today / Van.** **79220**
★★★ **The Best of Mississippi John Hurt /** **Van. 19/20**
★★ **The Immortal Mississippi John Hurt /** **Van. 79248**

His thrumming one-two guitar beat, his warm, hushed baritone, and his quiet joyfulness combined to make Mississippi John Hurt a welcome presence at a church picnic, college concert or recording session.

He lived a sharecropper's life in the delta town of Avalon, Mississippi, for most of his seventy-four years. Born in 1892, Hurt was brought to New York in 1928 to record some sides for Okeh Records (these sides, plus two cuts from Memphis sets, are on a fine Biograph disc). But the Depression hit the next year, and he returned to obscurity for over thirty years, until folk enthusiast Tom Haskins found him, aged seventy, in Avalon.

The country bluesman then resumed his career, playing concerts at Newport in 1963 and 1964 (he appears on Vanguard's recordings of these events). Before his death in November 1966, he made three studio albums.

Today has the unusually somber "Louis Collins" and the shiningly affirmative "Beulah Land." *The Immortal Mississippi John Hurt*'s "Tender Virgins" and "Hip Joint" are devilish next to a fervent "Nearer My God to Thee." On *Last Sessions*

Hurt pants and labors heartbreakingly, but his spirit is undimmed. *The Best of Mississippi John Hurt* is a two-record set, recorded at a 1965 college concert; Hurt is strong, salty and happy as he works through such traditional tunes as "Candy Man" and "C. C. Rider," plus his own quirky marvels like "Coffee Blues" and "Chicken." — F.S.

J. B. HUTTO
★★★★ **Hawk Squat / Del. 617**
★★★ **Master of Modern Blues / Test. 2213**
★★★ **Slidewinder / Del. 636**
Excellent contemporary Chicago blues guitarist heavily influenced by Elmore James. *Hawk Squat* is with pianist Sunnyland Slim. — J.S.

LITTLE WALTER JACOBS
★★★★★ **Boss Blues Harmonica / Chess 2CH-60014**
★★★★ **Confessin' the Blues / Chess 416**
★★★★ **Hate to See You Go / Chess 1535**
★★★★★ **Little Walter / Chess 2-202**
★★★★ **Super Blues / Check. 3008**
Little Walter's contribution to modern blues, rhythm & blues and rock is inestimable. For twenty years, from 1947, when he made his first recordings, until his death in a fight in 1968, he was known as the greatest harmonica player in history and was the most popular Chicago-based bluesman aside from Muddy Waters.

Jacobs got his training as blues harpist with Waters' band in the Forties and Fifties. When he put together his own group, it became apparent that Jacobs was not only a virtuoso instrumentalist but a first-class singer and bandleader as well. He released relatively few records, but everything he recorded is of the highest quality as far as arrangement, vocal-instrumental performance and band sound go. There are no bad Little Walter albums, and the two compilations, especially the magnificent *Boss Blues Harmonica,* get the nod for sheer bulk of material.

Every harmonica player after Little Walter has in some way been influenced by his style, especially rock players, from John Mayall to Magic Dick of the J. Geils Band. Jacobs was able to take hard bop melodic ideas from contemporary saxophonists and match them to a simpler but more forceful blues rhythm with heavily emphasized guitar parts, suggesting a further link between bop-era jazz players and rock & roll. The Little Walter harmonica style thus transposed saxophone ideas into terms compatible with and influential on guitars. — J.S.

ELMORE JAMES
★★★★ **Anthology of the Blues: Legend of Elmore James / Kent 9001**
★★★★ **Anthology of the Blues: The Resurrection of Elmore James / Kent 9010**
★★★ **Elmore James / Kent 522**
★★★★ **History of Elmore James, Vol. 1 / Trip 8007**
★★★★ **History of Elmore James, Vol. 2 / Trip 9511**
★★★ **Whose Muddy Shoes (with John Brim) / Chess 1537**
Elmore James recorded for only eleven years, from 1952 until his death in 1963, but his influence was far greater than such a brief span would suggest. His slide-guitar style was perhaps the most important in the translation of that technique into rock's version of blues. A good number of his stinging, whiplash songs, from his signature tunes "It Hurts Me Too" and "Dust My Broom" to the dance number "Shake Your Moneymaker" and the spiritually ravaged "The Sky Is Crying," have been covered again and again, by Eric Clapton, Fleetwood Mac and dozens of others. Either the Kent or Trip collections suffice as introductions—chances are, once you're familiar with James' brilliant slide playing and keening voice, you'll want to hear the rest as well. — D.M.

SKIP JAMES
★★★★ **Early Blues Recordings—1931 / Bio. 12029**
★★★ **Skip James: Greatest of the Delta Blues Singers / Melo. 7321**
James (1902-1969) was one of the greatest guitarists, pianists and singers to work within the frame of Mississippi delta blues, but because he was also one of the more idiosyncratic, his formal influence has been much less than that of Robert Johnson, Charlie Patton, Son House or even Tommy Johnson. His impact has been as an *inspiration*—on hearing him play, either on his original recordings or, after his rediscovery in 1964, in live performance, any number of musicians were moved to deepen the passion and commitment of their own music.

Early Blues collects a number of James' original recordings for Paramount, including his magnificent "Devil Got My Woman" and "If You Haven't Any Hay," which features James' wild, almost absurdist piano work. It is one of the central documents of delta blues. *Greatest* was cut in 1964, and while it demonstrated that James had lost none of his powers over the years, the best was yet to come.

★★★★★ Devil Got My Woman / Van. 79273

★★★★★ Skip James Today! / Van. 79219
These two modern recordings are among the most important blues albums ever made. The sound is full of presence, and the performance full of life—charged with bitterness, love, desire and a sense of fun (most evident on *Today!* with "I'm So Glad," first recorded by James in the Thirties and later made famous by Cream). James' high, ghostly voice pierces the night air—it always seems like night when these albums are playing—and his guitar shadows the moon.

If one must choose, the edge here goes to *Devil*, if only for the staggering version of the title song, which delves as deeply into the heart of American mystery as any tune ever has—and seals James' status as one of the finest, most aware folk artists of all time. Perhaps the reason so few of his songs have been recorded by others is that most musicians understand that the original performances simply can't be topped. — G.M.

BLIND LEMON JEFFERSON
★★ Black Snake Moan / Mile. 2013
★★★ Blind Lemon Jefferson / Mile. 47022
★ Master of the Blues, Vol. 1 / Bio. 12000
★ Master of the Blues, Vol. 2 / Bio. 12015
Jefferson is probably the single most influential country blues artist of the Twenties. Both his guitar and vocal styles were emulated by others immediately, and his impact continues to be felt today via such far-ranging blues-based musicians as John Hammond Jr., David Bromberg, Jerry Lee

Lewis, B. B. King and any number of others.

All of the above recordings were originally made as 78s for Paramount between 1926 and 1929. The elimination of surface noises without distorting the tonal quality is best accomplished on the Milestone sets—guitar lines are readily discernible, lyrics generally comprehensible with little extra effort. The Biograph material is flatter sounding and less dynamic in its treble range, making it chiefly of historical rather than musical value. — I.M.

LONNIE JOHNSON
★★ Losing Game / Prest. 7724
★★★★ Mr. Johnson's Blues / Maml. 3807
★★★★ Tomorrow Night / King 1083
Johnson was one of the most accomplished blues guitarists of the Twenties and Thirties, when he accompanied singers like Bessie Smith, recorded instrumentals on guitar, played fiddle on blues sessions and even sang quite well on his own blues records. Johnson is credited with adding jazz influences to blues technique, a suggestion borne out by his work on records with Louis Armstrong, Duke Ellington and Eddie Lang. His early work is unfortunately not well documented, but *Mr. Johnson's Blues* gives a good account of that facet of his playing.

The final testimony to Johnson's versatility came when he cut a hit R&B record for King in 1948, "Tomorrow Night." The album of the same name, though electronically reprocessed for stereo, shows Johnson in excellent pre-rock & roll form. — J.S.

ROBERT JOHNSON
★★★★★ King of the Delta Blues Singers / Col. 16-54
★★★★★ King of the Delta Blues Singers, Vol. 2 / Col. 30034
These records document the work of a man universally regarded as the greatest practitioner of the country blues genre identified with the Mississippi delta area, where so much of it was nurtured. Johnson synthesized the styles of Skip James, Henry Townsend, Son House and other blues greats before him. Johnson was undoubtedly at the height of his powers when these sides were recorded in 1935 to 1936, and he seems to make magic, his performance is so driven. His voice and slide-guitar playing complement each other perfectly as he provides a running commentary on the troubles that plague him and would eventually lead to his violent death in 1937.

Johnson's shadowy legend and brutal, dead-serious explication of it in song constitute one of the most emotional chapters in blues history, and it's all here in two neat packages. Even aside from the great songs, his bottleneck guitar playing alone is worth listening to, because it's influenced virtually everyone who's played in that style since. — J.S.

FLOYD JONES—EDDIE TAYLOR
★★★ **Masters of Modern Blues, Vol. 3 /**
   Test. 2214
Jones and Taylor each have a side as featured vocalist-guitarist on this 1966 Chicago blues LP. They're only middling performers in the genre, but they've backed up some much bigger names. And with accompanists such as Big Walter Horton, the redoubtable Otis Spann and drummer Fred Below, this is almost a Muddy Waters session without the boss. — D.M.

ALBERT KING
★★ **Albert / Utopia BUL1-1731**
★★★ **Albert Live / Utopia CYL2-2205**
★★★ **Door to Door / Chess 1538**
★★★ **King of the Blues Guitar / Atco 8213**
★★★ **The Pinch / Stax 4101**
★★★ **Truckload of Lovin' / Utopia**
   BUL1-1387
★★★ **Years Gone By / Stax 2010**
Of the three blues-singing and guitar-playing (though unrelated) Kings, Albert was clearly the inferior, in both approach and influence, in comparison with either B.B. or Freddie. Indeed, his style was almost entirely derived from B.B.'s—although that could also be said of half the other blues guitarists, black and white, of the Sixties and Seventies.

King began recording for King Records in 1961, when he had a Top Twenty R&B chart hit, "Don't Throw Your Love on Me So Strong." But his two most familiar songs, "Born under a Bad Sign" and "Cross Cut Saw," were both cut in 1967. "Born under a Bad Sign," the best and most widely covered (notably by Cream and Creedence Clearwater Revival) of the two, was written by Booker T. Jones and William Bell, and recorded for Stax; it is now available, along with most of the best of King's work, on the Atco album. "Born under a Bad Sign" might have been a simple soul song, but King's straight twelve-bar approach, rough-edged voice and raw guitar accented the tragedy, and minimized the self-pity, of the lyric's rather fantastic imagery.

King's series of albums for Stax, almost all of which are worthwhile, are now out of print. The current Stax sets are of new material released under Fantasy's Stax reissue program; hopefully, the company will re-release Stax sides as well. The Utopia LPs were recorded in the Seventies and produced by Bert de Coteaux and Tony Silvestre, who attempt to modernize King's approach without taking him into straight modern black music. The result is interesting but not as effective as his pure blues playing. — D.M.

B. B. KING
★★★★ **Anthology of the Blues—B. B.**
   King 1949-50 / Kent 9011
★★★★★ **B. B. King Live / Kent 565**
★★★★★ **B. B. King Live at the Regal /**
   ABC 724
★★★★★ **B. B. King Live in Cook County**
   Jail / ABC 723
★★★★★ **Back in the Alley / ABC D-878**
★★★★ **Better Than Ever / Kent 561**
★★★★ **Blues Is King / ABC D-704**
★★★★ **Blues on Top of Blues / ABC**
   D-868
★★★★ **Boss of the Blues / Kent 529**
★★★★ **Completely Well / ABC D-868**
★★★★ **Confessin' the Blues / ABC 528**
★★★ **Doing My Thing, Lord / Kent 563**
★★★ **Electric B. B. King / ABC D-813**
★★★ **Friends / ABC D-825**
★★★★★ **From the Beginning / Kent 533**
★★★★ **Greatest Hits of B. B. King / Kent**
   552
★★★★ **Guess Who / ABC XQ-759**
★★★★ **Incredible Soul of B. B. King /**
   Kent 539
★★★★ **Indianola Mississippi Seeds / ABC**
   713
★★★★ **King Size / ABC 977**
★★★★ **L.A. Midnight / ABC XQ-743**

★★★★ Let Me Love You / Kent 513
★★★★ Live and Well / ABC D-819
★★★★★ Live, B. B. King on Stage / Kent 515
★★★★ Lucille / ABC D-712
★★★★ Lucille Talks Back / ABC D-909
★★★★ Mr. Blues / ABC 456
★★★★ Original "Sweet Sixteen" / Kent 568
★★★★★ Pure Soul / Kent 517
★★★★ The Best of B. B. King / ABC XQ-767
★★★★★ The Jungle / Kent 521
★★★★ To Know You Is to Love You / ABC X-794
★★★★ Together Again . . . Live / Imp. 9317
★★★★ Together for the First Time / Dun. 7-51090
★★★ Turn On with B. B. King / Kent 548
★★★★★ Underground Blues / Kent 535

B. B. King is perhaps the greatest figure on the postwar urban blues scene, a powerful performer, a consolidator of blues styles, a great bandleader, an even greater singer and an innovative guitarist who's influenced virtually every blues guitarist to come after him. His clean, economical style can be heard quite clearly in the work of Eric Clapton and Michael Bloomfield, to use two standout examples among rock players.

King's intelligence and consummate professionalism have made him revered by a black audience that looks to his performance as the standard all else must be judged against. Although King never made direct attempts to pander to a white audience, his reputation grew in the Sixties after his impact on rock players became obvious, and King played a series of enthusiastically received dates at the Fillmores East and West.

The key to King's success is the wide range of ideas he brings in very squarely under the umbrella of blues playing. As a child, he heard a great deal of gospel music and listened to recordings by Blind Lemon Jefferson; the Texas guitar style of Jefferson and T-Bone Walker became B.B.'s foundation. But King's musical exposure was extensive, and he appended many disparate elements to that base: Jimmy Rushing's singing with the Count Basie orchestra; Al Hibbler's singing with Duke Ellington; the guitar playing of jazz stars Django Reinhardt and Charlie Christian; other blues players like Bukka White, Lowell Fulsom, Elmore James and Johnny Moore and the Three Blazers.

In 1948 King became a Memphis disc jockey, quickly gained a reputation for playing great records that couldn't be heard elsewhere, and began to piece together ideas for his own recording career. King's ear for great material led him to cover a number of songs that did far better for him than for the original writers. His first hit, in 1950, was with Lowell Fulsom's "Three O'clock Blues." Later in his career, he turned Memphis Slim's "Every Day I Have the Blues" and Robert Nighthawk's "Sweet Little Angel" into such personal statements that most people think King wrote them himself. King also successfully covered Arthur Crudup's "Rock Me Mama," Joe Turner's "Sweet Sixteen" and Roy Hawkins' "The Thrill Is Gone."

King's first Memphis band included vocalist Bobby Bland, who credits King as a major influence on his singing, pianist Johnny Ace and drummer Earl Forrest. Once King began touring behind the success of his first records, he developed a sophisticated band setup built around a solid rhythm backup and featuring tight horn sections to punctuate his highly emotional "crying" blues style and expressive guitar playing.

Over the years, King has recorded prolifically, yet he's kept his ideas varied and the emotional content well focused enough so that he never sounds stale. He has practically never cut a bad record.

His earliest available work is on the Fifties and Sixties Kent albums. Kent continued to release previously rejected material after King left for ABC, but in general the Kent records are very good. The ABC material is more far-ranging, as King expanded into using session musicians and augmented lineups. Some of these records, particularly several produced by Bill Szymczyk (*Completely Well, Indianola Mississippi Seeds*), show how many different things can be done within the seemingly tight restrictions of the blues.

King's best records, though, are the live sets, where the electricity of audience/performer interaction spurred King on to elaborate vocal and instrumental histrionics, and he demonstrated his total control over the concert experience. *Live at the Regal* is the generally acknowledged classic. — J.S.

FREDDIE KING
★ Burglar / RSO SO-4803
★★ Freddie King (1934-1976) / RSO RS-1-3025

★★★ **Larger than Life** / RSO SO-4811
★★ **The Best of Freddie King** / Shel. 2140
Freddie King's sudden death in December
1976 (he was forty-two) robbed blues and
rock of an active cross-pollinator. He left
his prophetically titled final release, *Larger
than Life*, as a barrelhousing live-in-Texas
epitaph. *Burglar* and *Freddie King
(1934-1976)*, a posthumous collection, were
both cut with British sessionmen and offer
less. Freddie's brassy singing and speedy
picking also survive on Shelter's *Best of*
("Palace of the King" is the peak of his
late-Sixties collaboration with Leon Russell). But his out-of-print sides for King
Records, which date from the Fifties, especially the Eric Clapton touchstone, *Hideaway* (containing Billy Myles' "Have You
Ever Loved a Woman"), remain the best
evidence of an electric guitar that roamed
from Texas to Chicago. Unfortunately, the
King albums are extremely difficult to
find. — F.S.

FURRY LEWIS
★★ **Back on My Feet Again** / Prest. 7810
★★ **Fabulous Furry Lewis** / So. 3
★ **Furry Lewis Blues** / Folk. 3823
★★★★ **In His Prime** / Yazoo 1050
★★ **Shake 'Em on Down** / Fan. 24703
Lewis made some interesting recordings in
the late Twenties, which are preserved on
the Yazoo set. His singing was good if not
spectacular, and he had a broad range of
material, but it was his sloppy yet engaging
slide-guitar work that set him apart from
other Memphis-based blues figures of his
time. Lewis was resurrected during the early-Sixties blues revival and subsequently
became a character actor, appearing on the
Johnny Carson TV show and in Burt
Reynolds' films. At that point he was more
of a comedian than a musician, and while

he got a lot of mileage out of dirty jokes,
the attempt to remake him into a recording
artist was a dismal failure. Only the Yazoo
set, appropriately titled, does Lewis justice
as a musician. — J.S.

MANCE LIPSCOMB
★★★ **Texas Sharecropper and Songster** /
Arhoo. 1001
★★★ **Texas Songster in a Live Performance** / Arhoo. 1026
★★★ **Texas Songster, Vol. 4** / Arhoo. 1033
★★★ **Texas Songster, Vol. 5** / Arhoo. 1049
★★★ **Texas Songster, Vol. 6** / Arhoo. 1069
In 1960, when Arhoolie's Chris Strachwitz
first recorded the Navasota, Texas, songster (the term Lipscomb himself used to
describe the range of material he performed), the guitarist/singer was already
sixty-five years old and had been a musician for more than fifty years. The first
Arhoolie album marked the beginning of a
semiprofessional career; Lipscomb was
soon in great demand, along with such
contemporaries as Furry Lewis and Mississippi John Hurt, at folk festivals, coffeehouses and folk-music clubs, in addition to
continuing to play for friends and relatives
at parties and dances.
    Almost all of the material Lipscomb re-
corded for Arhoolie was done solo, although an occasional cut features a second
guitar, or as on *Volume 5*, two cuts that
find him accompanied by drums and bass.
Lipscomb was a bottleneck guitarist of
great strength, and each of these LPs tends
to distribute his attention among ballads,
spirituals, blues, ragtime, jazz, children's
songs and dance tunes. *Volume 6* was recorded when Lipscomb was seventy-seven
years old, and stands as a remarkable
testament to a man kept young by his
music. — I.M.

ROBERT JR. LOCKWOOD
★★★ **Contrasts** / Trix 3307
★★★ **Robert Jr. Lockwood Does 12** / Trix
3317
★★★ **Steady Rollin' Man** / Del. 630
Excellent twelve-string guitarist who often
appeared as sideman to better-known performers (Little Walter and Sonny Boy Williamson in particular). Lockwood came
from the delta (where Robert Johnson allegedly was his stepfather—thus the Junior) but is best known as a Chicago performer. — D.M.

MISSISSIPPI FRED McDOWELL
★★ **A Long Way from Home** / Mile. 93003

★★ **I Do Not Play No Rock and Roll /
Cap. ST-409**
★★★★ **Keep Your Lamp Trimmed and
Burning / Arhoo. 1068**
★★ **Live in New York / Oblivion 1**
★★★ **Mississippi Fred McDowell / Arhoo.
1027**
★★ **Mississippi Fred McDowell and His
Blues Boys / Arhoo. 1046**
★★★ **Somebody Keeps Callin' Me / Ant.
7022**

Between the Rolling Stones' rewrite of Mc-
Dowell's "You've Got to Move" on *Sticky
Fingers* and Bonnie Raitt's general support
of his music (she asked him to tour with
her at one point and frequently performs
his songs), McDowell reached a far greater
number of people than one would ordinarily expect of such a harsh-sounding rural
bluesman. His own Capitol LP, *I Do Not
Play No Rock and Roll,* was probably his
best-selling album, but while it remains officially in print, it's difficult to track down
in stores.

Keep Your Lamp, Somebody, and *Live*
were all issued posthumously, the live set
recorded shortly before McDowell's death.
Keep Your Lamp, however, was culled from
various sessions (1965 to 1969) and features
McDowell in a variety of settings—solo;
with Johnny Woods on harmonica; with
the Hunter's Chapel Singers; with Mike
Russo and John Kahn on guitar and bass.
It is his most representative album.

The Antilles material dates from the
same sessions from which *I Do Not Play
No Rock and Roll* emerged, while *Long
Way from Home* was recorded by Pete
Welding in 1966. The remaining Arhoolie
sets (there are other Arhoolies as well as
still more albums on other labels, most deleted—this listing is only a sampling of the
best) are from the mid-Sixties; Arhoolie
1046 features Russo, Kahn and drummer
Bob Jones. The repertoire throughout
moves smoothly from blues to gospel and
back. — I.M.

BROWNIE McGHEE AND SONNY
TERRY

★★★★ **Back to New Orleans / Fan. 24708**
★★ **Brownie McGhee and Sonny Terry
Sing / Folk. 2327**
★★ **Brownie McGhee Sings the Blues /
Folk. 3557**
★★★ **Live at the 2nd Fret / Prest. 7803**
★★★★ **Midnight Special / Fan. 24721**
★★ **Preachin' the Blues / Folk. 31024E**
★★ **Sonny Terry: Harmonica and Vocal
Solos / Folk. 2035**

★★ **Sonny Terry's Washboard Band /
Folk. 2006**
★★ **The Best of Brownie McGhee and
Sonny Terry / Prest. 7715**

"Theirs is a unique form of song based
strongly on the traditional country blues,
modeled by the changing social climate
and polished for a more universal appeal.
Fortunately the tradition has not been subordinated to the shaping and polishing."

So wrote Gene Shay in his notes to *Live
at the 2nd Fret,* in 1962. Harmonica player
Terry and guitarist McGhee have been
playing and singing together since 1939,
with occasional timeouts for solo endeav-
ors; for Terry to portray Lost John, the
harp player in Broadway's *Finian's Rainbow;* and for them to spend two years acting together in *Cat on a Hot Tin Roof,* also
on Broadway.

As close friends of Leadbelly (with
whom they lived for a while), Woody
Guthrie (with whom they appeared as the
Woody Guthrie Singers) and Pete Seeger
(with whom Sonny toured—a live album of
their Carnegie Hall concert is on Folkways), they were never at a loss for material or engagements. And a great deal of
their work is documented on record. The
above sampling, however, dates approxi-
mately from 1952 through the mid-Sixties.
There have been subsequent albums, including one in the early Seventies for
A&M, but these represent Terry and
McGhee, solo and together, in their prime.

A drummer is used on some of the sessions (*Sing* and the second of the two discs
of *Back to New Orleans*), but is so distant in
the mix that he remains unobtrusive. Indeed, part of the problem with some of the
Sixties dates was that too many other musicians were thrown in to "compensate" for
McGhee's and Terry's age. Yet, onstage
even today, the pair remains as exuberant
and forceful as ever.

The original mono version of *Sing* is
preferable to its artificial stereo reissue, as
Preachin' the Blues and the various solo albums (*Washboard Band* and *Harmonica and
Vocal Solos* are ten-inch records) are suggested primarily as reference points to the
breadth of Terry's and McGhee's endeav-
ors and as an indication of where the duo
sound came from.

The two Fantasy sets are excellent
remasterings and repackagings of early
Prestige/Bluesville material and beautifully
illustrate the "modeling, shaping and polishing" process that has made Brownie's
and Sonny's appeal extend well beyond the

cult of blues fanatics. Theirs is a timeless music. — I.M.

BLIND WILLIE McTELL
★★★★ Atlanta Twelve String / Atl. 7224
★ Last Session / Prest. 7809
★★★ 1927-1935 / Yazoo 1037
★★★★ The Early Years: 1927-1933 / Yazoo 1005
★★★ Trying to Get Home / Bio. 12008

A blind street singer and twelve-string guitarist, McTell played blues, religious and country songs, ballads and pop tunes. He recorded under a variety of names for many labels, and although little is known of his life, much of the music remains readily available. And almost every young blues singer and interpreter has been influenced by McTell's guitar techniques and songwriting. His "Statesboro Blues," "Dying Crapshooter Blues" and "Trying to Get Home" are classics.

The Yazoo records are in amazingly good condition—the sound is crisp and clear throughout. *Trying to Get Home* and *Atlanta Twelve String* were recorded in 1949; the latter includes two cuts that had originally been released under the pseudonym Barrelhouse Sammy. Both LPs capture McTell pretty much at his peak. Recorded in a record shop in Atlanta, the 1956 *Last Session* is a rather sad footnote. McTell is caught at a point when the frustration of his lack of commercial success, liquor and age had overcome his physical and vocal dexterity. — I.M.

MA RAINEY
★★★ Blame It on the Blues / Mile. 2008
★★★ Blues the World Forgot / Bio. 12001
★★★ Down in the Basement / Mile. 2017
★★★★ Immortal / Mile. 47021
★★★★ Ma Rainey / Bio. 12011
★★★★ Oh My Babe Blues / Bio. 12032
★★★★ Queen of the Blues / Bio. 12032

The so-called Mother of the Blues, Rainey was one of the finest classic blues singers of the early part of the century, and influenced greats such as Bessie Smith. Her most famous song, "C. C. Rider," probably adapted from an obscure folk source, has become one of the most-covered blues songs, making the transition to a rock hit in Chuck Willis' and Mitch Ryder's versions much later. She recorded a number of sides in the Twenties with barrelhouse pianist Georgia Tom Dorsey and guitarist Tampa Red. — J.S.

JIMMY REED
★★★ Cold Chills / Ant. 7007
★★★★ History of Jimmy Reed / Trip 8012
★★★ Jimmy Reed / Ev. 234
★★★ The Best of Jimmy Reed / Cres. 10006
★★★ Wailin' the Blues / Trad. 2069

One of the most influential urban bluesmen of the Fifties, particularly on white rock musicians, Jimmy Reed developed his style as a youth in Mississippi, and perfected it after moving north and becoming a foundry worker in Gary, Indiana, just outside Chicago. His style is typified by a steady four-bar beat, a walking bass line and his own distinctive vocals, halfway between a moan and a shout. This approach was later adapted and presented under various guises; it pops up in the early records of the Who, the Animals and even the Rolling Stones.

Reed's best-known songs, "Ain't That Loving You Baby," "Baby What You Want Me to Do," "Bright Lights Big City" and "Big Boss Man," were all recorded for Vee Jay in the Fifties and early Sixties, and are included in the Trip package. But his style was so homogeneous that it rarely faltered, and almost any of the records here will give a decent glimpse of his accomplishments. — D.M.

FENTON ROBINSON
★★★★★ I Hear Some Blues Downstairs / Alli. 4710
★★★★★ Somebody Loan Me a Dime / Alli. 4705

Robinson is an exceptionally talented singer/guitarist working in the urban blues tradition out of Chicago. He has been intelligently recorded by Alligator, one of the best labels for contemporary blues, and his sure-fire, challenging solo style continues to push the boundaries of blues improvisation past previously recognized limits. Robinson is also a marvelous singer, who is equally adept at writing his own material as he is at covering standards. But it's his sometimes-incredible guitar playing that marks him as an original in a medium that prides itself on influence and imitation. — J.S.

OTIS RUSH
★★★★★ Right Place, Wrong Time / Bull. 301

If you think the horror stories so common to blues legend are a thing of the past, a quick account of the troubles that plagued Otis Rush will set you straight. Widely recognized as one of the finest contemporary blues guitarists/singers/bandleaders, Rush was bounced around from label to label and almost always treated with the utmost shabbiness until Albert Grossman landed him a long-term recording contract with Capitol in 1971. Under the direction of ex-Electric Flag vocalist Nick Gravenites, Rush went into the studio and recorded a blockbuster album with a tremendous band that spotlighted his bright, economical guitar playing. Capitol never released the master, and Rush finally had to bargain with the company to buy the tapes so he could release the record elsewhere. Bullfrog finally put the set out in 1976, and the record stands as a modern blues classic. — J.S.

SON SEALS
★★★★ Midnight Son / Alli. 4708
★★★★ Son Seals Blues Band / Alli. 4703

One of the best of the new generation of Chicago blues guitarists. He started off as a drummer, backing Robert Nighthawk, before switching to guitar and eventually joining Earl Hooker's band. Albert King later hired him as a drummer, and Seals' drumming in King's band is on the *Live Wire/Blues Power* album. In the Seventies, Seals took over Hound Dog Taylor's gig at Chicago's Expressway Lounge and began whipping his band into shape. Records show Seals to be a good blues singer in the Junior Parker tradition and an excellent, sure-toned guitarist. His lightning-fast runs will undoubtedly delight fans of better-known white blues guitarists who aren't as good. — J.S.

JOHNNY SHINES
★★ Johnny Shines / Advent 2803
★★★ Johnny Shines and Company / Bio. 12048

Howlin' Wolf and Robert Johnson (said to be his stepfather) were the major influences on this bluesman, who is equally at home with a traditional rural sound and with the electric Chicago blues. The Biograph set was produced by David Bromberg. The Advent collection, recorded about the same year (1974), features Shines among West Coast musicians. The Biograph LP is a touch more eclectic, and Shines' vocals are a little more powerful. — I.M.

BESSIE SMITH
★★★★★ Any Woman's Blues / Col. CG-30126
★★★★★ Empty Bed Blues / Col. CG-30450
★★★★ Nobody's Blues But Mine / Col. CG-31093
★★★★★ The Empress / Col. CG-30818
★★★★★ The World's Greatest Blues Singer / Col. CG-33

These records are the crown jewels of Columbia's ambitious jazz repackaging program, the John Hammond collection. Five double sets cover virtually the entire recorded history of one of the greatest, most influential musicians of the twentieth century. Bessie Smith's impact is so widespread it's almost impossible to gauge. She turned the blues into a modern jazz form, outdistancing most of her accompanists with her uncanny sense of phrasing and clear, powerful tone. The young Louis Armstrong played with Smith and was undoubtedly affected. Billie Holiday brought Smith's style into a jazz vocal context and passed it on to all those who, in turn, followed her, while Smith's impact on straight blues comes down through Mahalia Jackson and Big Mama Thornton.

World's Greatest covers Smith's first and last sessions, in 1923 and 1933. The first recordings were extremely crude, but the 1933 set, produced by Hammond, combines Smith with a fine band composed of trumpeter Frankie Newton, trombonist Jack Teagarden, Benny Goodman on clarinet, tenor saxophonist Chu Berry, Buck Washington on piano, Bobby Johnson on guitar and Billy Taylor on bass.

The other records present Smith in a variety of contexts, often accompanied by the solo piano of James P. Johnson. Some of the collection's best moments, however, are the exchanges between Smith and Louis Armstrong, the only musician at the time who could nearly match Smith's uncanny ability to bend notes and completely personalize even the most trite material. The version of W. C. Handy's "St. Louis Blues," done in 1925, is an amazing recording. — J.S.

OTIS SPANN
★★★★ Blues Never Die / Prest. 7719
★★★★ Chicago Blues / Test. 2211
★★★ Cryin' Time / Van. 6514
★★★ Otis Spann / Arc. Folk 216
★★★ Otis Spann vs. the Everlasting Blues / Spivey 1013
★★★★ Otis Spann with Luther Johnson, Muddy Waters Blues Band / Muse 5008

A tremendous piano player and fine singer, Spann nailed down the keyboard spot in

Muddy Waters' highly influential Fifties and Sixties outfit, and he played on many of the Waters classics. His high-powered, technically dazzling style created the standard for postwar hard blues piano, and thus for the rock keyboardists (especially the English ones), who picked up cues from the blues revival of the Sixties. Spann backed such notable white blues players as Paul Butterfield and Mike Bloomfield (on the landmark *Fathers and Sons* album, with Waters) and Fleetwood Mac.

Spann's own records are high-energy sets, recorded with a wide range of sidemen, including Robert Lockwood Jr. and, often, members of the Waters band. Waters gave him plenty of space but naturally Spann's separate efforts offer even greater opportunity to show off his fast-fingers roll. Vocally he was no slouch either, singing in a smooth but edgy voice influenced no small amount by Waters. Spann died in 1971 at age forty, but left a recorded legacy that testifies to his powers. — J.S.

VICTORIA SPIVEY
★ **Blues Is Life / Folk. 3541**
★★ **Queen and Her Nights / Spivey 1006**
★★ **Recorded Legacy of the Blues / Spivey 2001**
★★ **Victoria Spivey and Her Blues / Spivey 1002**
★ **Victoria Spivey with the Easy Riders Jazz Band / GHB 17**
Spivey was a blues sex symbol of the Twenties, but her records, even with the remarkable guitarist Lonnie Johnson, were inconsistent and mostly forgettable. The available material is little more than historical notation. — J.S.

ROOSEVELT SYKES
★★★ **Blues / Folk. 3827**
★★★★ **Country Blues Piano Ace 1929–1932 / Yazoo 1033**
★★★ **Feel like Blowing My Horn / Del. 632**
★★★ **Honeydripper / Prest. 7722**
Sykes is regarded as one of the key developers of the modern blues piano style—a combination of barrelhouse boogie, prominent right-handed rhythm patterns and twelve-bar blues structure. He is also a formidable blues singer and a prolific songwriter.

The albums listed above represent various phases of his career. The Yazoo set traces his early accomplishments, solo as well as with a number of vocal accompanists. The Prestige and Folkways LPs were

made in the early Sixties; the former draws on the jazz aspect of his talents (and features King Curtis on tenor sax), while the latter concentrates on Sykes' bluesier side (solo and with his protégé, Memphis Slim). The Delmark album, recorded in 1973, places him in a modified Chicago blues context.

Oddly, Sykes' lifelong theme song, the self-composed "Honeydripper," a hit for him in the Thirties, isn't on any of these albums, though another of his popular numbers, "The Night Time Is the Right Time," can be found on a set he shares with Little Brother Montgomery (*Urban Blues,* Fantasy 24717). — I.M.

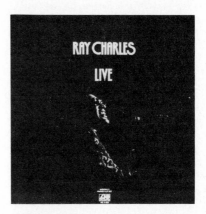

TAMPA RED
★★★ **Bottleneck Guitar 1928–1937 / Yazoo L-1039**
★★★★ **The Guitar Wizard / RCA AXM2-5501**
★★★ **The Guitar Wizard 1935–1953 / Blues Cl. 25**
One of the most popular and frequently recorded urban blues performers of the late Twenties, Thirties and Forties, Tampa Red has been credited by Big Bill Broonzy with inventing the slide-guitar blues technique, and his adaption of the Hawaiian guitar sound to blues playing was very effective. He earned his living playing for nickels and dimes on the streets of Chicago, where he picked up his nickname (he was raised in Tampa).

His second record, "It's Tight Like That" (1928) became one of the most popular "race" records of all time. He was accompanied on his early material by pianist Georgia Tom Dorsey, and this period is well documented on the Yazoo album. The two *Guitar Wizard* releases, which don't duplicate each other despite having the same title, feature Red's later work (mid-Thirties to Fifties). These spirited records include a wide range of styles, from simple blues to hokum jumpers. His records with the Chicago Five were very popular with white audiences and included a lot of kazoo playing. Red's importance as a scene-maker in Chicago blues circles over the years is shown in the selection of sidemen on these dates, ranging from pianists Black Bob and Big Maceo to blues harpists Willie "Sonny Boy" Williamson and Walter "Shakey" Horton. — J.S.

HOUND DOG TAYLOR
★★★★ Beware of Dog / Alli. 4707
★★★★ Hound Dog Taylor and the House-rockers / Alli. 4701
★★★★ Natural Boogie / Alli. 4704
Excellent Chicago slide guitarist plays no-holds-barred barroom boogie, and plays it as well as it comes. The posthumously released live album, *Beware of Dog,* captures Taylor at his hottest, in front of a club full of dancing, howling fans. — J.S.

KOKO TAYLOR
★★★ I Got What It Takes / Alli. 4706
★★★ The Earthshaker / Alli. 4711
Taylor is that rarity, a contemporary *female* Chicago blues performer. She's been around town for twenty years as a sort of gravel-voiced, distaff answer to Howlin' Wolf—her early Chess singles, collected on a single deleted Chess LP, include a definitive version of Willie Dixon's "Wang Dang Doodle," which is principally associated with Wolf. The Alligator albums date from the Seventies and both present her in fine form. *Earthshaker* features a remake of "Wang Dang Doodle," and somewhat stronger material overall than *I Got What It Takes.* — D.M.

BIG MAMA THORNTON
★★★★ Big Mama Thornton with the Chicago Blues Band / Arhoo. 1032
★★★ Jail / Van. 79351
★★ Sassy Mama / Van. 79354
★★ She's Back / Back. 68
It was Willie Mae "Big Mama" Thornton's recording of the Jerry Leiber and Mike Stoller song, "Hound Dog," that first rocked the charts, although it was Elvis Presley's later version that topped them. Fronting Johnny Otis' band at the time, and appearing on package shows with Little Esther (Phillips), Thornton also wrote "Ball and Chain," later popularized by Janis Joplin.

The Chicago Blues Band of the Arhoolie LP features Muddy Waters, James Cotton and Otis Spann, and the excitement of the moment is readily sensed, even though the staple songs of Thornton's career aren't included. Thornton has a big voice, in the traditions of Bessie Smith and Ma Rainey, and in 1966, when the Arhoolie sessions were done, she was still in relatively full command of it.

The subsequent albums lack the urgency of her earlier work—the Backbeat set was done in the early Seventies, the Vanguards in 1975—and the backup groups (unidentified on Backbeat, various top session musicians on the Vanguard LPs) lack the cohesiveness that comes from years of playing together or at least from playing in the same idiom. *Jail,* however, does have her singing "Hound Dog," "Ball and Chain" and "Little Red Rooster." — I.M.

BIG JOE TURNER
★★★★ Have No Fear, Big Joe Turner Is Here / Savoy 2223
Joe Turner qualifies as one of the unjustly ignored fathers of rock & roll. Part of the reason Turner's not as celebrated as he might be is that Atlantic, where he made his most fundamental rock records, has no Turner collection in print. *His Greatest Recordings,* now deleted from that label's catalogue, is worth seeking out, since it contains his two most influential hits, the original version of "Shake, Rattle and Roll," and his reworking of "Corrina Corrina" as well as a strong "Flip Flop and Fly," among others.

Turner was one of the key figures in the transition from country blues and boogie-woogie to modern R&B and soul. He teamed with pianist Pete Johnson in Kansas City during the city's jazz heyday in the Thirties and came to New York in 1938, where he was a central figure in the boogie-woogie revival of 1938-1941. The Savoy record is a collection of sides he made for National, a label owned by Atlantic co-founder Herb Abramson, from 1945-1947. It's excellent, with splendid biographical liner notes. — D.M.

EDDIE "CLEANHEAD" VINSON
★★★ Eddie Cleanhead Vinson / Trip 5590
One of the best Southwest blues singers, Vinson hails from Houston, Texas, and made a name for himself singing and playing alto saxophone in Cootie Williams' band. He scored a hit in 1945 with "Kidney Stew Blues" and a cover of Joe Tur-

ner's "Cherry Red." Vinson's strong voice and falsetto tricks carried him easily into the Sixties and Seventies blues contexts. — J.S.

T-BONE WALKER
★★★★★ **T-Bone Walker / Blue N. LA533-H2**
★★★★ **The Truth / Bruns. 754126**

T-Bone Walker was the most influential of the Texas blues guitarists, and his style can be heard in B. B. King, Eric Clapton, Albert King, Buddy Guy, Albert Collins, Freddie King and dozens of others. When he began recording in the Thirties, the blues was a rural and acoustic genre, but by the time he died in 1975, he'd helped turn it into something electric, faster, jazzier and much more modern.

Walker played with both large jazz orchestras and on his own, his voice and electric guitar (which he helped pioneer) accompanied by a brass section. In the end, he ranks with Muddy Waters and B. B. King, Robert Johnson and Blind Lemon Jefferson, and Charlie Patton as one of the kings of blues; today, his influence is evident everywhere. The Blue Note collection is truly his best music, with excellent liner notes and discographical information compiled by Pete Welding. — D.M.

MUDDY WATERS
★★★ **After the Rain / Chess 320**
★★★★ **Can't Get No Grindin' / Chess 50023**
■ **Electric Mud / Chess 314**
★★★ **Fathers and Son / Chess 50033**
★★★★ **Folk Singer / Chess 1483**
★★★★ **Hard Again / Blue S. PZ-34449**
★★★ **I'm Ready / Blue S. JZ-34928**
★★★★★ **McKinley Morganfield / Chess 60006**
★★ **Mud in Your Ear / Musi. 5008**
★★★★ **Muddy Waters / Chess 2-203**
★★★ **Muddy Waters at Newport, 1960 / Chess 1449**
★★★ **Muddy Waters at Woodstock / Chess 60035**
★★★ **Muddy Waters Live / Chess 50012**
★★★★★ **Sail On / Chess 1539**
★★★★ **The London Muddy Waters Sessions / Chess 60013**
★★★★ **They Call Me Muddy Waters / Chess 1553**
★★★ **Unk in Funk / Chess 60031**

The first and last of the great Chicago bluesmen. Waters grew up on a Mississippi plantation (as McKinley Morganfield),

where he made some field recordings during World War II. In the mid-Forties, he arrived in Chicago, and in 1948 he burst on the city's blues scene.

Through the years, he became widely hailed as one of America's great musical resources. Among Chicago bluesmen, only Howlin' Wolf could match Waters for vision, authority and dignity. Because he was also a formidable bandleader, Waters would appear to have a slight edge as the more influential of the two, but their rivalry was legendary.

From Waters' bands came a host of blues stars: Otis Spann, Little Walter, Junior Wells, Fred Below, Walter Horton, Jimmy Rogers, James Cotton, Leroy Foster and Buddy Guy, among many others. And from his guitar, voice and harp came a flow of classic blues songs: "Hoochie Coochie Man," "Mannish Boy," "Got My Mojo Workin'," "Rollin' Stone" and "You Shook Me" are only some of the more famous numbers Waters either wrote or popularized. Waters was beloved and venerated not just in Chicago's blues community, but also by the folk revivalists of the late Fifties and early Sixties, and by the white rock musicians, particularly English ones, of the Sixties: the Rolling Stones, of course, named themselves after his great song.

Waters has made his greatest music for Chess; the cream of it is collected on the two-disc *McKinley Morganfield*. More recently, Waters has recorded two LPs for the Blue Sky label, produced by Johnny Winter, that feature a number of his former sideman (notably Cotton and Rogers) and both old songs and new ones. Though in his sixties, Muddy Waters is still as vital as men twenty years younger. His mojo's working overtime. — D.M.

JUNIOR WELLS
★★★★ **Blues Hit Big Town / Del. DL-640**
★★★ **Comin' at You / Van. 79262**
★★★★★ **Hoodoo Man Blues / Del. DS-612**
★★★★ **It's My Life, Baby / Van. 79231**
★★★ **On Tap / Del. DS-635**
★★★ **Southside Blues Jam / Del. DS-628**

Junior Wells replaced Little Walter on harmonica in Muddy Waters' influential Chicago blues band during 1954, then did a stint in the Army. He really hit his stride as a recording artist with *Hoodoo Man Blues* in 1965, one of the best Chicago blues recordings. Wells is a master showman, and his performances with guitarist

Buddy Guy have been among the best received by the rock audience. But his style is sometimes a deterrent here: he is too flashy for some of the blues' more stately traditions. When held in check, as on the *Hoodoo Man* session and the four-star performances above, he is an excellent harmonica stylist and a better-than-average vocalist as well. — D.M.

BUKKA WHITE
★★★ Big Daddy / Bio. 12049
★★★ Sky Songs, Vol. 1 / Arhoo. 1019
★★★ Sky Songs, Vol. 2 / Arhoo. 1020
White was one of the earliest delta country-blues musicians, roughly contemporaneous with the great Charlie Patton and even greater Robert Johnson. White lived longer, but his output wasn't quite as magnificent. Still, these recordings are an important source of delta styles. — D.M.

SONNY BOY WILLIAMSON
★★★★ Bummer Road / Chess 1536
★★★★ One Way Out / Chess 417
★★★★ Sonny Boy Williamson / Chess 2-206
★★★★★ This Is My Story / Chess 2CH 50027
This is the second Sonny Boy (real name, Rice Miller); the first (real name John Lee Williamson) barely survives on records. The second Sonny Boy, like the first, was one of the best harmonica players the blues has produced. Williamson was a convincing lyricist as well, and a formidable vocalist. Several of his songs—"Don't Start Me to Talkin' " most prominently, but also "One Way Out," "Nine Below Zero" and "Fattening Frogs for Snakes"—have become rock-bar and blues-band staples.

Williamson was born in rural Mississippi, and like so many others, followed a seemingly inevitable route to Chicago in the late Forties. He was supported by many of the genre's best players (Muddy Waters, Willie Dixon, Robert Jr. Lockwood, Otis Spann, Fred Below, Buddy Guy and Jimmy Rogers, among others), all of whom seemed to have learned a great deal from his novel approach to blues. In Williamson, the medium is at its most lyrical without ever sacrificing any of its raw power. The best of the Chess LPs, *This Is My Story,* is a classic of the blues, and a fundamental source point of rock. — D.M.

JIMMY WITHERSPOON
★★★★ Best of Jimmy Witherspoon / Prest. 7713

★★★ Blue Spoon / Prest. 7327
★★★ Blues for Easy Livers / Prest. 7475
★★★ Goin' to Chicago Blues / Prest. 7314
★★★ Goin' to Kansas City Blues / RCA ANL1-1048
★★★ Groovin' and Spoonin' / Orig. Jazz 7107
★★★ Mean Old Frisco / Prest. 7855
★★★ Some of My Best Friends Are the Blues / Prest. 7356
★★★ Spoonful / Blue N. LA534-G
★★★ Spoon in London / Prest. 7418
★★ The Spoon Concerts / Fan. 24701
Jimmy Witherspoon is perhaps the best-known survivor of the Kansas City blues scene that produced so much fine music in the Thirties. He is a more jazz-oriented bluesman than the Chicago and delta performers, using more sophisticated arrangements—often featuring horn charts.

Witherspoon, whose best-known song is "Ain't Nobody's Business," was probably most influential on such R&B singers as Bobby Bland, although he also made a (now-deleted) LP with Eric Burdon for MGM. — D.M.

HOWLIN' WOLF
★★★★★ Evil / Chess 1540
★★★★ Howlin' Wolf: Chess Blues Masters / Chess 2ACMB
★★★★★ Original Folk Blues / Kent 526 / 5026
★★★★ The Legendary Sun Performers: Howlin' Wolf / Charly 30134 (Import)
Howlin' Wolf (1910-1976) was a truly heroic figure; a bitter angry man with roots in the early country blues of the Mississippi and a career in Chicago that lasted until his death. Born in Mississippi, he first recorded in the late Forties and early Fifties in and around Memphis, mostly for Sam Phillips, who leased sides to Chess and Modern. Wolf moved to Chicago in 1952 and remained with Chess thereafter. Crude, rough, impassioned, vulgar—Wolf made Muddy Waters seem like David Niven—he possessed enormous presence and authority, and could put across material as diverse as Robert Johnson's "Hellhound on My Trail," or Willie Dixon's lugubrious "300 Pounds of Joy" with equal conviction.

The early Memphis recordings are scattered over more than a dozen albums: *Original Folk Blues* and the Charly LP, which features mostly previously unissued performances, are exciting, loud and representative. Wolf's first hit, the blistering "How Many More Years," was also re-

corded in Memphis; it is included on both
Evil and *Chess Blues Masters,* a two-disc
survey of Wolf's best-known work from
1951 through 1965. Given the atrocious
fake stereo used on *Blues Masters, Evil* and
the deleted *Howlin' Wolf* (Chess 1469, identifiable by the rocking chair on the cover)
are more strongly recommended. The rocking chair LP, which can still be found, may
be the finest of all Chicago blues albums: it
includes "Red Rooster," "Spoonful,"
"Wang Dang Doodle," "Goin' Down
Slow," "Back Door Man," "Down in the
Bottom" and "You'll Be Mine," and features the kind of band the Rolling Stones
have always dreamed of sounding like.
★★★ **Change My Way / Chess CHV 418**
★ **Live and Cookin' at Alice's Revisited /
Chess CH 50015**
★ **Message to the Young / Chess CH
50002**
★★★★ **The London Howlin' Wolf Ses-
sions / Chess CH 60008**
Wolf's career in the late Sixties and early
Seventies was troubled. His label forced a
white, teenage rock band on him for one
LP (the anti-classic *This Is Howlin' Wolf's
New Album—He Doesn't Like It*) and bur-
dened him with third-rate soul music on
Message. Live, one of his last LPs, was a
hideously recorded and poorly performed
attempt to capture the man onstage.
Change, which collects singles from 1958
through 1966, is better, though it suffers

from weak material; highlights are "Do the
Do" and "I Ain't Superstitious." The great
exception to this waste is *London Sessions,*
cut in 1970 with Charlie Watts, Bill Wyman, Eric Clapton, Ian Stewart and other
Englishmen. Wolf soared and the musicians kept up with him. Unfortunately, little new material was used, but when Wolf
and Clapton took for the hills on "Do the
Do," one forgot about such failings. You'd
have to go back to Lend-Lease for a better
example of Hands across the Seamanship.
★★★★ **The Back Door Wolf / Chess
50045**
Wolf's last album, released in 1973, and
shockingly one of his greatest moments.
Again the band played real blues—spare,
dramatic, understated—and Wolf howled
for the moon on which he promised would
one day sit a coon. The songs ranged from
the Twenties to the Seventies—Wolf celebrated the black man who caught the Wa-
tergate burglars—and altogether rang with
pride, defiance and life. R.I.P.   — G.M.

MIGHTY JOE YOUNG
★★ **Chicken Heads / Ova. QD-14-37**
★★ **Love Gone / Ova. QD-1443**
★★ **Mighty Joe Young / Ova. 1706**
A rather pedestrian young Chicago blues
guitarist, Young earned his nickname more
for his obesity than for his guitar style, a
rather bland synthesis of Freddie King and
Luther Allison.   — D.M.

JAZZ

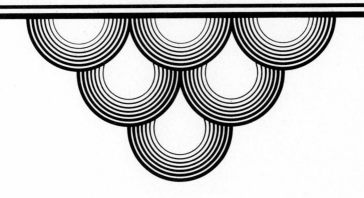

JOHN ABERCROMBIE
★★★ Friends / Oblivion OD 3
★★★ Gateway / ECM/Poly. 1061
★★★★ Sargasso Sea / ECM/Poly.
1080
★★★★ Timeless / ECM/Poly. 1047
Abercrombie's incredible range and technique make him one of the finest electric guitarists currently recording and one of the most sought-after session players for challenging new material. A founding member of Dreams, he worked as a sideman with Chico Hamilton, Barry Miles, Gil Evans and Jack DeJohnette, and in 1972 he collaborated on a remarkable quartet record, *Friends*, with saxophonist Mark Cohen, bassist Clint Houston and guitarist Jeff Williams. Abercrombie's playing on that session is a perfect illustration of the bridge between jazz and rock guitar technique.

Timeless, Abercrombie's first solo effort for ECM, was recorded in 1974 with DeJohnette on drums and Jan Hammer on organ, synthesizer and piano. Hammer, especially, plays with astounding fire and grace on this session, some of the finest organ playing he's recorded. *Gateway*, recorded in 1975 with DeJohnette and bassist David Holland, is more serene and uses subtler electronic effects from Abercrombie's guitar. *Sargasso Sea* is a 1976 duet with Oregon's virtuoso guitarist Ralph Towner. The alternately pensive and vibrant electric/acoustic interplay between these two master guitarists makes this a classic album of guitar duets.   — J.S.

MUHAL RICHARD ABRAMS
★★★ Levels and Degrees of Light / Del.
DS-413
★★★★ Sightsong / Black S. BSR 0003
★★★ Things to Come from Those Now
Gone / Del. DS-430

★★★★ Young at Heart/Wise in Time /
Del. DS-423
Throughout the Fifties, Richard Abrams (b. 1930) was one of Chicago's most sought-after local pianists when visiting jazz stars needed support. With the formation of his Experimental Band in 1961 and the Association for the Advancement of Creative Musicians (AACM) in 1965, Abrams (who began calling himself Muhal at the decade's end) led many young Chicago players into a new phase of avant-garde expression that stressed a thorough knowledge of black music tradition and an endless series of new formats.

Abrams' albums all have powerful and exciting moments, but leave the overriding impression that we have only heard a portion of the man's musical universe. *Levels and Degrees of Light* features an intriguing first side with wordless vocal and several AACM mainstays (Anthony Braxton, Maurice McIntyre), but falls apart in the poorly recorded wall of sound that covers side two. *Young at Heart/Wise in Time* is better, with a long example of Abrams' reflective piano and a tighter group performance by an excellent AACM quintet (Leo Smith, Henry Threadgill, Abrams, Lester Lashley, Thurman Barker).

Things to Come from Those Now Gone captures Abrams and the AACM in the middle of this decade running the gamut between chamber ballads, hard bop, electronics, mock opera and high energy. Fascinating, but too many bits and pieces. *Sightsong* is a more successful survey from 1975, with Art Ensemble bassist Malachi Favors along to help Abrams explore the AACM's roots.   — B.B.

CANNONBALL ADDERLEY
★★★★ Beginnings / Mer./Em.
EMS-2-404

★★ **Big Man** / Fan. 79006
★★★ **Cannonball Adderley and Friends** /
Cap. SVBB-11233
★ **Cannonball Adderley and Strings** / Trip
5508
★★★ **Cannonball in the Land of Hi-Fi** /
Trip TLP 5573
★★★★★ **Country Preacher** / Cap. SKAO-
404
★★ **Inside Straight** / Fan. 9435
★★★ **Live!** / Cap. SM-2399
★★ **Lovers** / Fan. 9505
★ **Love, Sex,and the Zodiac** / Fan. 9445
★★★★★ **Mercy, Mercy, Mercy!** / Cap.
SM-2663
★★★ **Music, You All** / Cap. ST-11484
★ **Phenix** / Fan. 79004
★★★ **Somethin' Else** / Blue N. LA169-G
★ **Soul Zodiac** / Cap. 11025
★★★ **Spontaneous Combustion** / Savoy
2206

Cannonball Adderley (1928–1978) first began to attract attention when he played in
the late Fifties with Miles Davis' first supergroup, which included John Coltrane,
Philly Joe Jones, Red Garland (later Bill
Evans) and Paul Chambers. But Adderley
began recording in 1955, just days after he
arrived in New York. He had learned from
Charlie Parker how to sail comfortably
against the rhythm, how to swing sixteenth
notes through scales arranged like mine
fields, and how to bend his lip around the
blues until he'd squeezed them dry. In fact,
Adderley is partly responsible for institu-
tionalizing Parker, by playing Parker-like
lines that were easier for listeners to follow.

The recordings on Savoy and EmArcy
(some of whose sessions were reissued by
Trip) chronicle the period before he joined
Davis. Later he found a more soulful
groove, with compositions that relied heavily on the blues and a driving beat. While
dedicated jazz listeners were turning to the
power saxophonists such as Ornette Coleman and John Coltrane, Adderley was
finding funky piano players such as Bobby
Timmons, Joe Zawinul and George Duke
more to his liking. Zawinul, who later
joined Miles' late-Sixties band, then formed
Weather Report, brought Adderley to his
most popular point in the late Sixties with
"Mercy, Mercy, Mercy!" (a pop hit) and
"Country Preacher," songs with their roots
in Memphis soil. And all along the way,
brother Nat Adderley was always to be relied upon for a few new themes and dart-
ing cornet choruses.

As tastes changed, so did Adderley, and

although he never left the blues behind, a
few projects in search of an audience were
less than artistic successes. But for session
players Dave Sanborn, Tom Scott and
many lesser-known musicians, there's nothing quite as righteous as the sound of Cannonball preachin'. They've emulated his
deep-fried attack and fancy-free howl. And
so traditions are born. — A.E.G.

AIRTO
★★★★ **Fingers** / CTI 6028
★★★★ **Free** / CTI 6020
★★★ **Promises of the Sun** / Ari.
AL-4116
★★★★ **The Essential Airto** / Bud. BDS 2-
5668

Airto arrived in the U.S. in time to lead a
small explosion of interest in Seventies-
style Brazilian rhythms. His first recordings in the States with Miles Davis and
Chick Corea's original Return to Forever
displayed a taste for extraordinary percussion work. *Essential* is decidedly cooler
than his later work, with more folk melodies than jazz rhythms, but the contributions of his fellow Brazilian musicians,
Ron Carter on bass and Flora Purim's
clear, unadorned vocals, make for some
compelling music.

Free joins the CTI all-stars with ringers
Keith Jarrett and Return to Forever members Stan Clarke, Chick, Flora and Joe
Farrell, who provide most of the excitement on this set. *Fingers* is less distinctive.
Several of the tunes are more bossa nova
pop than progressive jazz and the sound is
a little thin until David Amaro's guitar
sparkles through. *Promises of the Sun* lacks
intensity, but Airto still displays his talent
for creating musical hooks, and the inventiveness on many of his instruments that
has made him *Downbeat* magazine's num-

ber one percussionist six years in a
row. — A.E.G.

MOSE ALLISON
★★★★ Best of / Atco 1542
★★★ Creek Bank / Prest. 24055
★★★ Down Home Piano / Prest. 7423
★★★ I've Been Doin' Some Thinkin' /
Atco 1511
★★★ Jazz Years / Atco 2-316
★★★ Mose Alive / Atco 1450
★★★ Mose Allison / Prest. 24002
★★ Mose Allison Plays for Lovers / Prest.
7446
★★★ Mose in Your Ear / Atco 1627
★★★ Prestige Twofer Giants / Prest.
PRP-1
★★★ Retrospective / Col. C-30564
★★★ Seventh Son / Prest. 10052
★★★★ Your Mind Is on Vacation / Atco
1691

Mose Allison is the embodiment of the
cool jazzman. His blues-based, boogying
yet laid-back piano noodlings and laconic,
semidetached vocal style made him patron
saint of the beatnik lounge buffs (he'll cram
all the syllables from a line into the beginning of a measure, then sustain the last
note over a cascading piano response).
Gnossos Papadoupolis, hero of Richard
Farina's *Been Down So Long It Looks Like
Up to Me,* played an Allison record as the
selected soundtrack through his constant
Kerouac hustle. Later, Allison's "Young
Man Blues" became a standard remake for
the Who. His playing, attitude, song selection and instrumentation have been fairly
standard over his twenty-year career,
which has paralleled the life span of rock
& roll. Allison was not popular in the mid-
Seventies until the extraordinary 1976 Atlantic release, *Your Mind Is on Vacation,* on
which he steamed through a variety of new
and old tunes at comparatively breakneck
speed, augmented by a horn section featuring Joe Farrell (tenor sax), Dave Sanborn
(alto sax), Al Porcino (trumpet) and Al
Cohn (tenor sax). — J.S.

LOUIS ARMSTRONG
★★★★ Ambassador Satch / CSP
JCL-840
★★★ Best of / Audio Fi. 6132
★★★★ Best of / MCA 2-4035
★★★ Definitive Album / Audio Fi. 6241
★ Disney Songs the Satchmo Way / Buena
S-4044
★★★ Early Portrait / Mile. 22010
★★★ Ella—and Louis / Verve 6-8811
★★★ Essential / Van. VSD-91/92

★★★★★ Genius of Louis Armstrong,
Vol. 1 / Col. CG-30416
★★★★ Great Jazz Composers—Louis
Armstrong Plays W.C. Handy / CSP
JCL-591
★★★ Hello Dolly / MCA 538
★★★ Here's Louis Armstrong / Voc.
73851
★★★ High Society / Cap. SW-750
★★★ I Will Wait for You / Bruns. 754136
★★★★ Jazz Odyssey / Col. C3L-33
★★★ Louis Armstrong / Audio Fi. 6241
★★ Louis Armstrong / Trip 5814
★★★★ Louis Armstrong, Vol. 1 / CBS Fr.
(Import) 64218
★★★★ Louis Armstrong, Vol. 2 / CBS Fr.
(Import) 65379
★★★★★ Louis Armstrong, Vol. 3 / CBS
Fr. (Import) 65380
★★★★★ Louis Armstrong, Vol. 4 / CBS
Fr. (Import) 65421
★★★★★ Louis Armstrong and Earl Hines
1928 / Smithsonian (Album available by
mail only from Smithsonian, Box 10230,
Des Moines, Iowa 50336)
★★★★ Louis Armstrong and His All
Stars / CBS Fr. (Import) 62614
★★★ Louis Armstrong and His Friends /
Audio M. 12009
★★★★★ Louis Armstrong and King
Oliver / Mile. M-47017
★★★ Louis Armstrong at the Crescendo /
MCA 2-4013
★★★ Louis Armstrong Greatest Hits /
Col. CS-9438
★★★ Louis Armstrong Greatest Hits Re-
corded Live / Bruns. 754169
★★★ Louis Armstrong Historical Perfor-
mances / Ev. 3312
★★★★★ Louis Armstrong July 4,
1900-July 6, 1971 / RCA VPM-6044
★★★★★ Louis Armstrong-Sidney Bechet
with the Clarence Williams Blue Five /
CBS Fr. (Import) 63092
★★★★ Louis Armstrong Special / CBS
Fr. (Import) 65251
★★★★★ Louis Armstrong Story, Vols.
1-4 / Col. CL-851-4
★★★ Louis Armstrong V.S.O.P. / CSP
JEE-22019
★★ Mame / Pick. 3229
★★★★ Mostly Blues / Olym. 7124
★★★★ On the Sunny Side of the Street /
CBS Fr. (Import) 62902
★★★ One and Only Louis Armstrong /
Voc. 73871
★★★ Porgy and Bess / Verve 2-2507
★★★★ Satchmo / MCA 4-10006
★★★ Satchmo / Ev. 258
★★★ Satchmo, Vol. 2 / Ev. 312

★★★★ Satchmo at Symphony Hall /
   MCA 2-4057
★★★ Satchmo the Great / CSP JCL-1077
★★★★ Satch Plays Fats / CSP JCL-708
★★ Treasury / Cor. 20027
★★★ What a Wonderful World / ABC 650
★★★★★ Young Louis Armstrong / RCA
   AXM2-5519

Louis Armstrong (1900–1971) may well be
the single most important figure in twentieth-century music. With a brilliant blues
sense, he took the oral tradition available
in New Orleans and developed a radical
solo voice on the cornet and a rhythmic
blueprint for the small jazz ensemble that
laid the cornerstone for later developments
in jazz, blues, country and rock playing.

Armstrong's unique phrasing and his lucid combination of rhythmic and melodic
elements enabled him to become the first
important jazz soloist, and arguably the
first major soloist in any American music.
His influence has been felt by countless
musicians over the years. Armstrong's version of "St. Louis Blues," recorded in 1929,
is as steeped in rock & roll spirit as anything by the Rolling Stones—in fact, it
wouldn't be a bad idea for the Stones to
record an album of Armstrong classics.

Armstrong's brilliant powers as soloist,
vocalist—he is said to have invented scat
singing, or wordless vocals, and his raspy-
throated growl has been widely imitated—
and personality have almost always overshadowed his accompaniment. It seems less
that Armstrong was not a good bandleader
than that he was just too good for virtually
all his peers. Many of his performances in
the Twenties and Thirties have been frequently called avant-garde, and no less a
figure than Miles Davis has claimed that
Armstrong's playing covered everything
subsequently done in jazz, right up to the
present era. It's understandable, then, that
Armstrong's records, despite the often miraculous nature of his own playing, are often not very good by virtue of the inad-
equacy of the rest of the players on the
session.

Fortunately, Armstrong recorded prolifically at the height of his creative genius in
the Twenties and Thirties. As an accompanist, his work in his mentor King Oliver's
band and his recordings with the classic
blues singer Bessie Smith stand out. He recorded quite a few other tracks with female
blues singers of varying skill for Okeh records, and much of this material, which is
certainly of historical interest, is reproduced on the French CBS sets.

The best of the CBS imports is the album Armstrong recorded with Sidney
Bechet and the Clarence Williams Blue
Five. While Armstrong's bands were often
unable to keep up with him, there was usually one musician in each of his combos
who worked with and pushed Armstrong's
ideas. Bechet's superb soprano saxophone
playing is one example.

Armstrong's most memorable work was
recorded in the Twenties and Thirties with
the Hot Five, Hot Seven and the Louis
Armstrong Orchestra. Pianist Earl Hines
collaborated brilliantly with Armstrong
during this period.

After Armstrong became an international celebrity in the Thirties, the quality
of his records suffered; he became more interested in entertainment than in musical
values. Even at his worst, however, Armstrong is far better than detractors say. Far
from being an Uncle Tom, Armstrong was
a ground-breaking personality who proved
that jazz and popular music in general
could take a place of cultural preeminence
in society.

Armstrong went back to a small-group
context in the late Forties and Fifties with
remarkable success. Not only did his vocal
and instrumental powers continue undiminished, he scored even more impressive
popular triumphs as he went on, climaxing
with the astounding feat of knocking the
Beatles out of the top spot in the pop
charts with his riveting version of the show
tune "Hello Dolly."

The French CBS imports, the records
with King Oliver and Earl Hines, Louis
Armstrong Story, and Genius of Louis Armstrong are the best collections of Armstrong's famous Twenties and early-Thir-
ties recordings. Mostly Blues, with Fats
Waller on piano, is a fairly hot set recorded in 1938. The RCA and MCA sets
take Armstrong through the Forties and
into the Fifties. Satchmo (MCA) is a well-
annotated historical overview from Armstrong's own perspective, including remakes of some of his important recordings
with his comments on them. The Everest
material is from the Fifties, while Hello
Dolly, the Columbia Greatest Hits and the
live Essential are Sixties recordings.   — J.S.

HORACEE ARNOLD
★★★★ Tales of the Exonerated Flea /
   Col. KC-32869
★★★★ Tribe / Col. KC-32150

Drummer Arnold apprenticed with Bud
Powell, Charles Mingus, Stan Getz and

Chick Corea before recording his first LP, *Tribe,* as a leader in 1973. It is a beautiful record offering superb Afro-Latin accompaniment from percussionists David Friedman and Ralph McDonald, reedmen Joe Farrell and Billy Harper, bassist George Mraz and acoustic-guitar virtuoso Ralph Towner. The 1974 set, *Flea,* featuring excellent performances from Jan Hammer (synthesizer), John Abercrombie and Towner (guitars), Dom Um Romao (percussion) and Sonny Fortune (soprano sax and flute), remains an exemplar of fusion music at its finest. Hammer's synthesizer work here is some of his best ever. — J.S.

ART ENSEMBLE OF CHICAGO
★★★★★ Art Ensemble of Chicago with Fontella Bass / Prest. PR-10049
★★ Certain Blacks / Inner IC-1004
★★★ Chi-Conga / Paula LPS-4001
★★★★★ Les Stances à Sophie / Nessa N-4
★★★★★ People in Sorrow / Nessa N-3
★★★★ Phase One / Prest. 10064
★★★ The Paris Session / Ari./Free AL-1903

If asked to name the most innovative jazz group of the past decade, I would probaby choose the Art Ensemble of Chicago. Growing out of the Association for the Advancement of Creative Musicians, the AEC first appeared as Roscoe Mitchell's Art Ensemble in 1967, with Mitchell on alto sax, Lester Bowie on trumpet and Malachi Favors on bass—everyone also plays numerous "little instruments." Reedman Joseph Jarman joined in April 1969, making the band the Art Ensemble, and drummer Don Moye was also added.

The albums currently available in America are from the AEC's European years (1969-71). The best of these is their master-piece, *People in Sorrow,* a forty-minute example of how the group's menagerie of instruments and spontaneous approach to structure can create clearly delineated, precisely shaded and starkly emotional music. Nearly as impressive are *Art Ensemble of Chicago with Fontella Bass* and *Les Stances à Sophie,* both of which feature the singing of former soul star Bass. *Les Stances* has some of the group's most varied playing. *Phase One* is important for "Ohnedaruth," a rare piece using the familiar series-of-soloists format, but the other side is a shrill free form made shriller by bad recording. The double album *The Paris Session* has good duets and one successful extended work, but also contains tiresome theatrics. *Chi-Conga* is simply the band on one of its lesser sessions, while *Certain Blacks* adds Chicago bluesmen to no one's benefit. — B.B.

ROY AYERS
★★★★ Daddy Bug and Friends / Atco 1692
★ Everybody Loves the Sunshine / Poly. 1-6070
★★ Mystic Voyage / Poly. 6057
★★★ Red, Black and Green / Poly. 1-6078
★★★ Tear to a Smile / Poly. 6046

Vibraphonist Roy Ayers built a reputation out of his playing on Herbie Mann's albums from *Impressions of the Middle East* (1967) to *Memphis Two Step* (1971). Mann produced two solo albums for Ayers during that time, the best tracks of which are now condensed into *Daddy Bug and Friends,* Ayers' best record. *Red, Black and Green* comes close, matching Ayers' speed to a tensile front line of Sonny Fortune's soprano sax, Charles Tolliver's trumpet and Garnett Brown's trombone. Subsequently Ayers found commercial succes with disco by minimizing soloing and composition in favor of urgent, bass-dominated rhythm patterns, but the price he's paid for fame is our boredom. — J.S.

ALBERT AYLER
★★★★ Albert Ayler in Greenwich Village / Imp. AS-9155
★★★ First Recordings / GNP 9022
★★★★ Love Cry / Imp. AS-9165
★★ Music Is the Healing Force of the Universe / Imp. S-9191
★★★★ My Name Is Albert Ayler / Fan. 86016
★★ New Grass / Imp. AS-9175
★★★★★ New Wave in Jazz / Imp. AS-90

★★★★★ **Vibrations / Ari./Free 1000**
★★★★★ **Witches and Devils / Ari./Free 1018**

Albert Ayler (1936-1970) shot like a comet through jazz—from unknown to avant-garde extreme, then early jazz-R&B fusion and (possibly) suicide in a mere eight years. As *First Recordings* and *My Name Is Albert Ayler* (both made during his early-Sixties European period) show, post-bop formalities were not totally alien to his muse, but the oversized vibrato and expansive emotion of his tenor-sax work demanded the freer situation he found in a brief stay with Cecil Taylor (unfortunately not recorded).

Ayler's style came together on several brilliant 1964 recordings; with the essential ESPs out of print, the available pair on Arista-Freedom offer the best view of his stark and extreme conception. *Witches and Devils* has the tenor-trumpet-bass-drum format, the themes which are simple to the point of naiveté, the unfettered tonal and rhythmic energy of Ayler's tenor, and the perfectly supportive cataclysmic drumming of Sunny Murray. *Vibrations* unites Ayler and Murray with bassist Gary Peacock—these three are the quintessential Ayler trio—and trumpeter Don Cherry, who adds some contrasting reserve. The empathy among the players, and two takes of Ayler's anthem "Ghosts," make this the Ayler album to get first.

Ayler's affiliation with Impulse in the final years of his life saw a strange decline, from the collective exorcism of his 1965 "Holy Ghost" performance in the *New Wave in Jazz* anthology (also featuring John Coltrane, Archie Shepp and others) to the tedious blues-rock-energy-message muddle of 1969's *Music Is the Healing Force of the Universe,* where Ayler collaborates with lyricist Mary Maria. In between are two notable collections, a cut below the Freedom-ESP sessions, and one grand change of direction that might be simply ludicrous if it weren't so prophetic of jazz-rock trends. *Albert Ayler in Greenwich Village* adds violin and cello for a touch of the European, with stunning effect on the brooding "For John Coltrane" (where Ayler plays alto); "Change Has Come" is more characteristically incendiary. *Love Cry* is a studio date with the old format—an excellent free-rhythm section (Alan Silva, bass; Milford Graves, drums), Albert's brother and frequent collaborator Donald on trumpet, and the bizarrely baroque harpsichord of Call Cobbs—but the energy

sounds as if it has already begun to be depleted.

New Grass has to be the greatest turnaround in new music history, with Ayler verbally denouncing his past excesses in favor of a raunchy R&B approach which could easily pass for Maceo Parker among the JBs. The skeptics had to admit that Ayler could play the tenor, and numerous less esoteric jazz artists would take a similar course in the Seventies, but the musical results are disturbing. Ayler's true motivation regarding this and his last Impulse recordings are as clouded as the circumstances that led to his being found in the East River (tied, according to some accounts, to a jukebox). — B.B.

GATO BARBIERI
★★★ **Confluence / Ari. 1003**
★ **Gato Barbieri Quartet / ESP 1049**
★★★ **The Third World / Fly. BXL1-2826**

Gato Barbieri's throaty, lyrical tenor-saxophone style owes as much to the experimental jazz albums that reached his ears as to the cultural environment of his Argentinian homeland. His first notable work was on Don Cherry's decidedly avant-garde *Complete Communion.* Two years later he recorded his first album as a leader, *Gato Barbieri,* for ESP Disk, and though his performance is erratic, he is still an emotionally hard-hitting soloist in the tradition of others on that label, Albert Ayler and Frank Wright. *Confluence,* the 1968 duet recorded in Milan with South African pianist Dollar Brand, continues his exploration into the free-jazz vocabulary. Barbieri returned to America to record the last of his new music experiments, *The Third World.* The album's Afro-Latin theme indicated Barbieri's future direction.
★★★ **Bolivia / Fly. BXL1-2830**

★★★ **El Pampero / Fly. BXL1-2828**
★★★ **Fenix / Fly. BXL1-2827**
★★★ **Last Tango in Paris / U. Artists
US-LAO45-G**
★★★ **The Legend of Gato Barbieri / Fly.
FD-10165**
★★★★ **Under Fire / Fly. BXL1-2829**
★★★ **Yesterdays / Fly. BXL1-0550**
When Barbieri dropped his free jazz ex-
periments in 1971 for a completely Afro-
Latin style, he didn't so much change his
playing as its context. Only keyboardist
Lonnie Liston Smith remained, and the ac-
cent was now completely on native Latin
American rhythms. *Fenix* successfully em-
ploys two percussionists, drummer Lenny
White, bassist Ron Carter and guitarist Joe
Beck to evoke a lush atmosphere. *El Pam-
pero* is a live set recorded at the Montreux
Jazz Festival with Barbieri soloing fiercely
throughout. *The Legend of Gato Barbieri*
collects essential cuts from *The Third
World, Fenix* and *El Pampero.*

Under Fire is Barbieri's crowning
achievement in this phase, a verdant rain
forest of rhythmic ideas. Bassist Stanley
Clarke delivers a memorable performance
that links the support function of the
rhythmic foundation with the melodic responsibilities of the solo improvisers.

Under Fire and its followup with the
same band, *Bolivia,* were overshadowed by
Barbieri's soundtrack for Bernardo Berto-
lucci's *Last Tango in Paris,* which attempted to match a groaning Brando's
mute screaming to Barbieri's stifled cries.
Yesterdays, an almost traditional set of improvisations, is a tribute to John Coltrane's
hymnal ballad style.

★★★ **Caliente! / A&M 4597**
★★★★ **Chapter One: Latin America /
Imp. AS-9248**
★★★ **Chapter Two: Hasta Siempre / Imp.
9363**
★★★★ **Chapter Three: Viva Emiliano
Zapata / Imp. ASD-9279**
★★★ **Chapter Four: Alive in New York /
Imp. AQD-9303**
★★★ **El Gato / Fly. BDL1-1147**
Recorded in Buenos Aires with an excel-
lent band of South American musicians,
Chapter One: Latin America burns with ex-
otic rhythms and passionate playing. *Chap-
ter Two,* recorded in Los Angeles with
roughly the same musicians, is not quite as
successful, but Barbieri's collaboration
with the brilliant arranger Chico O'Farrill,
Chapter Three, is a remarkable set of or-
chestrated Latin American songs. The
Chapter Four Bottom Line recording is no-

table just for Barbieri's interplay with
Howard Johnson's tuba. *El Gato* is a
Flying Dutchman collection from *Under
Fire* and *Bolivia* with one previously unre-
leased track.

Herb Alpert helped popularize Latin
American music in the United States ten
years ago with his MOR hits, but he didn't
have to ask Barbieri to recut "Spanish
Flea" to make *Caliente!* commercial. Producer Alpert assembled a studio orchestra
of staggering proportions for Barbieri's
A&M debut, and though it's far from Barbieri's most challenging work, the album is
certainly accessible.   — J.S.

GARY BARTZ
★★ **Another Earth / Mile. 9018**
★★★ **Follow, the Medicine Man / Prest.
10068**
★★★ **Harlem Bush Music—Taifa / Mile.
9031**
★★★ **Harlem Bush Music—Uhuru / Mile.
9032**
★★★★ **Home / Mile. 9027**
★★★★ **I've Known Rivers / Prest. 66001**
★★ **Juju Street Song / Prest. 10057**
★★★ **Libra / Mile. 9006**
★★ **Love Affair / Cap. SW-11789**
★★★ **Music Is My Sanctuary / Cap.
ST-11647**
★ **Singerella—A Ghetto Fairy Tale / Prest.
10083**
★★ **The Shadow Do / Prest. 10092**
Bartz is one of the many young jazz musi-
cians nurtured in the late Sixties and Seventies who came up through the traditional
musicians' hierarchy, mastering their instruments in post-bop combos, yet saw
their rock and R&B contemporaries making money with commercial music and decided to have a go at it themselves. His
best work as an apprentice was with

McCoy Tyner on *Excursions.* Some of the
Bartz albums that feature him playing solo
(*I've Known Rivers, Home*) indicate that he
is one of the finer contemporary saxophonists. Yet Bartz tried to come up with a
hook, and chose the political-commentary
route on other Milestone and Prestige albums with little success. He also started
singing, a major mistake. Bartz reached a
low point with *The Shadow Do,* sinking
into self-parody.

His Capitol records are still attempts at
crossover, but at least they are done without image gimmicks; Bartz even sneaks a
few hot sax licks in between the funk ensemble singing and disco-R&B rhythm section.   — J.S.

COUNT BASIE

★★★★ Afrique / Fly. 10138
★★★ Basie-Eckstine Inc. / Rou. 42017
★★★★ Basie Jam / Pablo 2310718
★★★★ Basie Live! / Trip 5818
★★★★ Basie's Best / Olym. 7121
★★★★★ Best of / MCA 2-4050
★★ Broadway—Basie's Way / Camd.
  QD-40004
★★★ Count Basie and His Kansas City 7 /
  Imp. 15
★★★ Count Basie and Sarah Vaughan /
  Rou. 42018
★★★ Count Basie and Zoot / Pablo
  2310745
★★★★★ Count Basie at the Savoy
  Ballroom / Ev. 318
★★★★ Count Basie Big Band / Pablo
  2310756
★ Count Basie Meets Bond / Solid St.
  18032
★★★ Count Basie's in the Bag / Bruns.
  754127
★★ Count Basie Straight Ahead / Dot
  25902
★★★ Count Basie Swings and Joe Wil-
  liams Sings / Verve 6-8488
★★★ Echoes of an Era—Basie, Getz and
  Vaughan Live at Birdland / Rou. RE-126
★★★★ Echoes of an Era—Best of Count
  Basie / Rou. RE-118
★★★ Echoes of an Era—Count Basie
  Vocal Years / Rou. RE-107
★★★★ Echoes of an Era—Count Basie
  Years / Rou. RE-102
★★★ Fantail / Rou. 42009
★★★ First Time / Col. CS-8515
★★★★ For the First Time / Pablo 2310712
★★★ From Broadway to Paris / ABC
  X-773
★★★★★ Good Morning Blues / MCA
  2-4108

★★★★ I Told You So / Pablo 2310767
★★ It Might as Well Be Swing / Rep. 1012
★★★ Jazz at the Santa Monica Civic '72 /
  Pablo 2625701
★★★ Kid from Red Bank / Rou. 42015
★★★ Master's Touch / Savoy 12071
★★★★ Montreux Collection / Pablo
  2625707
★★★★ Montreux-Count Basie Jam /
  Pablo 2310750
★★★ One O'Clock Jump / CSP JCL-997
★★★★ Satch and Josh / Pablo 2310722
★★★ Sixteen Men Swinging / Verve
  VE2-2517
★★★★★ Super Chief / Col. CG-31224

William "Count" Basie (b. 1904) is one of
the most important jazz figures because of
his understanding of the use of the rhythm
section in Big Band arrangements, his perfection of the concept of riffing (repeating
an insistent melodic statement, usually
voiced by the horns in Basie's group,
against a strong basic rhythm), which has
filtered down to become an essential rock
& roll element, and for his adaptation of
the blues to large-band formats. Basie's
keyboard playing set up the architecture of
his band's sound by stripping all melodic
ideas down to their essential elements, an
antitechnical practice which did much to
loosen the idea of jazz arrangements and
has also filtered down through the years
into rock song structures.

After studying organ under Fats Waller
and learning to play stride piano at New
York nightspots, Basie took off to Kansas
City, where he hooked up with one of the
more raucous examples of the big beat
coming out of the Southwest, Bennie Moten's band. After gigging with that group
for a while, Basie formed his own organization out of elements of the Moten band
and other musicians in the Kansas City
area. In 1936 Basie brought this group to
New York at John Hammond's suggestion
after Hammond heard a radio broadcast of
the band from Kansas City. Within a year
Basie's organization won international acclaim. The personnel was one of the greatest collections of twentieth-century musicians: vocalists Billie Holiday and Jimmy
Rushing (Holiday was replaced by Helen
Humes and Mildred Bailey); saxophonists
Lester Young, Herschel Evans and Earl
Warren; trumpeters Buck Clayton and
Harry Edison, trombonists Benny Morton
and Dicky Wells; and the most astounding
rhythm section of Basie at keyboards,
drummer Jo Jones, guitarist Freddie Green
and bassist Walter Page.

With certain alterations, that's the band assembled on the live radio broadcast from 1937, *At the Savoy Ballroom.* Introduced as "ultra-modern rhythm," this set gives good indication of the impact this music had on the jazz world. Billie Holiday is also on the mixed bag of sessions from the late Thirties assembled on *Super Chief,* but is not on the full-scale sessions Basie's band recorded for Decca. These sides, collected on *Best of* and *Good Morning Blues,* show Basie and Co. in full swing, and include standards like "One O'Clock Jump," "Jumpin' at the Woodside," "Good Morning Blues" and "Hey Lawdy Mama."

Basie's Best and *Basie Live!* are also radio broadcasts. *Basie's Best* is from a date at the Meadowbrook in Cedar Grove, New Jersey, in November 1937, while the Trip *Live!* set combines tracks from the Meadowbrook and Savoy recordings with a 1940 set from Boston.

Basie's postwar bands introduced trombonist J. J. Johnson and a series of tremendous saxophonists, including Illinois Jacquet, Don Byas, Lucky Thompson, Paul Gonsalves and Frank Foster. While these groups still met high standards, they naturally suffered in comparison with the brilliant, free-swinging late-Thirties outfit. The Verve and Roulette sides from the Fifties and Sixties are not particularly relevant to a rock audience, and the Sinatra collaborations in the Sixties for Reprise might seem like the kind of thing rock & roll was invented to combat.

Basie's outstanding taste and musical chops can never be called into question, however, and he has released a series of excellent records for Flying Dutchman and Pablo in the Seventies. *Afrique* is an engaging conceptual album in an Afro-Cuban style compatible but not identified with Basie's own rhythmic experiments. Oliver Nelson's arrangements for that set are quite nice. The Pablo series features Basie in small- and large-group contexts and includes much excellent playing.   — J.S.

SIDNEY BECHET
★★★★★ **Jazz Classics, Vol. 1 / Blue N. 81201**
★★★★★ **Jazz Classics, Vol. 2 / Blue N. 81202**
★★★★★ **Master Musician / RCA AXM2-5516**
★★★★ **Sidney Bechet and Mezz Mezzrow / Class. 28**
New Orleans native Bechet (1897–1959) is one of jazz's true originators. A broad-

toned, florid improviser, he worked often on clarinet but spent most of his time on soprano sax, creating the definitive approach to the straight saxophone until the arrival of Steve Lacy and John Coltrane. After early fame and an eclipse, which most of his contemporaries also met during the Depression, Bechet had a resurgence during the traditional revival of the Forties and spent his last years in Europe as a revered celebrity.

The Bechet albums above also make room for numerous exceptional contributors. *Master Musician,* covering 1932–41, features the New Orleans Feetwarmers with trumpeter Tommy Ladnier; Earl Hines, Red Allen, Willie "The Lion" Smith, Rex Stewart, Kenny Clarke and others; plus early examples of studio overdubbing as Bechet becomes a six-piece one-man band. *Jazz Classics* spans 1939–51, has Bunk Johnson, Meade Lux Lewis, Sid Catlett and Frankie Newton among the greats, and includes classic Bechet solos on "Summertime" and "Blue Horizon." Mezzrow's featured presence brings down the level of the Classic Jazz double album, recorded between 1945 and 1947.   — B.B.

JOE BECK
★★★ **Beck / Kudu KU-2151**
★ **Watch the Time / Poly. PD-6092**
A longtime studio guitarist and arranger, Beck can probably play anything. But he's a surprisingly run-of-the-mill solo artist. True, *Beck,* with a dynamic, pressurized feel, features clean but raw jazz-rock guitar, engagingly melodic charts and powerful Dave Sanborn alto solos. But there is nothing distinctive about the pop R&B-rock of *Watch.* Beck's guitar is not prominent or unusual enough, and most of the tunes are fronted by Tom Flynn's irritating vocals.

There are also some Beck LPs out of print. Best is the 1969 *Nature Boy* (Verve-Forecast FTS-3081), a virtual one-man show that's a bit dated now. With his vocals multitracked, Beck sounds like the Mamas and the Papas. Still, *Boy* is strangely pleasant listening; parts of it, obviously conceptually progressive for their time, hold up nicely.   — M.R.

GEORGE BENSON
★★ **Bad Benson / CTI 6045**
★★ **Benson and Farrell / CTI 6069**
★★★★ **Benson Burner / Col. CH-33569**
★★★ **Beyond the Blue Horizon / CTI 6009**
★★★★ **Body Talk / CTI 6033**

★★★ Breezin' / War. K-3111
★★★★ Good King Bad / CTI 6062
★★★ In Flight / War. BK-2983
★★★★★ It's Uptown / Col. CS-9325
★★ Shape of Things to Come / A&M 3014
★★ Tell It Like It Is / A&M 3020
★★★ The George Benson Cookbook / Col. CS-9413
★★★ The Other Side of Abbey Road / A&M SP-3028
★★ White Rabbit / CTI 6015

Breezin' was the first jazz album ever to "go platinum"—sell more than a million copies—and that event released a flood of criticism. "Why Benson," some have asked, "and not a hundred others before him? After tons of lame numbers, cushioned in fluffy pillows of strings and horns, and a philosophy seemingly based on personal mercantilism rather than musical value, why should he get the honor?"

Well, why not? First of all, platinum is sales, not honor, and besides, Benson happens to be one of the best jazz guitarists alive. He is a consistent player: most of the more recent albums feature some of the best funk and jazz session players in the business. His predilection for pop-sounding material is as much a result of having served Brother Jack McDuff for years before going solo (Lonnie Smith carried the organ tradition onto Benson's early Columbia albums), as well as Benson's genuine comfort in a rhythmic rock & roller role, as it is commercial design.

What made Benson a big hit, finally, was his singing voice, not his guitar playing. For my part, I'd rather hear a guitarist who knows how to use solo space—who organizes his featured spots with a beginning, middle and end, building plunks of notes into octave strums in the manner of Wes Montgomery, with infallible rhythm, playing runs and scales—than sustained, feedbacked second-generation Clapton and Stills. Even if his blues has turned a trifle white-collar. If the pop thing stops clicking, he can always fall back on his talent. — A.E.G.

BUNNY BERIGAN
★★★ Take It Bunny / CSP JLN-3109
Big Band trumpeter made a name for himself in the Thirties with the Dorsey Brothers, Benny Goodman and Tommy Dorsey before forming his own group. A legendary drinker, Berigan (like Bix Beiderbecke) epitomized the myth of the self-destructive musical genius. The Pigpen of his era. — J.S.

LEON "CHU" BERRY
★★★★★ Chu / CSP JEE-22007
The only album available under the name of Leon "Chu" Berry (1910–1941), perhaps the greatest Coleman Hawkins disciple of the swing era, is *Chu.* The tenor saxophonist is heard with small groups and the Cab Calloway orchestra, where he was featured from 1937 until his death. But see also Fletcher Henderson and especially the Lionel Hampton boxed set on Bluebird. — B.B.

BLACKBYRDS
★★ City Life / Fan. 9490
★★★★ Flying Start / Fan. 9472
★★★★ The Blackbyrds / Fan. 9444
★ Unfinished Business / Fan. 9518
After working as Donald Byrd's backup band, the Blackbyrds recorded under their own name as a jazz-funk fusion group. *Blackbyrds* and *Flying Start* show them at their commercial peak. The rhythmic bottom was irresistibly solid and danceable, the vocals were appropriately sparse and the instrumentation—particularly the horn charts—was melodically adventurous and fulfilling. After the success of *Flying Start,* the Blackbyrds began to view themselves as a disco attraction rather than a progressive, jazz-trained R&B act. *City Life* exhibited a dispiriting reliance on recycled riff-hooks and an embarrassing bent for hollow social and psychocybernetic commentary. The one instrumental track was a dud, and the vocals were depressingly imitative. Any traces of the Blackbyrds' Howard University jazz training had been erased by the time of *Unfinished Business.* The horn arrangements were inaudible, the rhythm tracks commensurate with the slavish vocals, and synthesizer bromides reigned to the point of nausea. — M.G.

EUBIE BLAKE
★★★ **Eighty-Six Years of Eubie Blake /**
Col. C2S-847
This is a fairly comprehensive representation of Blake's output. A better than average ragtime pianist, Blake covered standards like "Maple Leaf Rag" before
making it big in the Twenties as a nightclub performer, then later as a vaudeville
act with Noble Sissle. He and Sissle co-
wrote a number of popular songs, the most
famous of which was "I'm Just Wild about
Harry." — J.S.

ART BLAKEY
★★★★★ **A Night at Birdland with the Art**
Blakey Quintet, Vol. 1 / Blue N. 81521
★★★★★ **A Night at Birdland with the Art**
Blakey Quintet, Vol. 2 / Blue N. 81522
Abdullah Ibn Buhaina, better known as
Art Blakey, has two claims on jazz immor-
tality: as one of the most incendiary drummers in history, the man who reawakened
interest in the most basic African sources
of jazz percussion; and as the leader of the
Jazz Messengers, a band that, at its incep-
tion in 1954, ushered in the hard-bop era,
and to this day continues to provide an un-
compromising forum for new talent.
   The *Night at Birdland* albums, from 1954,
have the seeds of the first Jazz Messenger
band (Horace Silver is on piano and the
chief composer), plus the lucid horns of
Lou Donaldson (alto) and Clifford Brown
(trumpet). Volume 1, with Brown's classic
"Once in a While," has the slight edge.
★★★★ **The Jazz Messengers at the Cafe**
Bohemia, Vol. 1 / Blue N. 81507
★★★★★ **The Jazz Messengers at the**
Cafe Bohemia, Vol. 2 / Blue N. 81508
The first classic Jazz Messenger band con-
tained Blakey, Silver, trumpeter Kenny
Dorham, tenor saxophonist Hank Mobley
and bassist Doug Watkins. Their trend-set-
ting studio work is now available under
Horace Silver's name (on Blue Note
81518); these live 1955 recordings are al-
most as good. Volume 2 contains "Like
Someone in Love," a hard-bop archetype
pop-song transformation.
★★★ **Art Blakey Big Band / Beth.**
BCP-6015
★★★★★ **Art Blakey's Jazz Messengers**
with Thelonious Monk / Atl. S-1278
★★★ **At the Jazz Corner of the World,**
Vol. 1 / Blue N. 84015
★★★★★ **At the Jazz Corner of the**
World, Vol. 2 / Blue N. 84016
★★★ **Messages / Rou. RE-131**
★★★★ **Moanin' / Blue N. 84003**

★★★ **Paris Concert / CSP JLN-3109**
★★★ **Percussion Discussion / Chess**
2ACMJ-405
Between 1956 and 1959, many fine soloists
(Jackie McLean, Hank Mobley, Johnny
Griffin, Lee Morgan) passed through the
Messengers, but the records often descended into a blowing session rut. The
meeting with Monk is notable for the sublime interaction between drums and piano,
and some good Griffin tenor. *Moanin'* has
the original of pianist Bobby Timmons' title hit (one of the first "soul-jazz" pieces
along with Silver's work) and the first
flowering of Lee Morgan's brilliant trumpet.
★★★★★ **A Night in Tunisia / Blue N.**
84049
★★★★ **Like Someone in Love / Blue N.**
84245
★★★★ **Meet You at the Jazz Corner of**
the World (2 vols.) / Blue N. 84054/5
★★★★ **Roots and Herbs / Blue N. 84347**
★★★★ **The Big Beat / Blue N. 84029**
★★★★ **The Freedom Rider / Blue N.**
84156
Blakey's 1959–61 quintet was one of his
best, with a maturing Morgan and Timmons and the then-raucous tenor sax of
Wayne Shorter. All of the soloists composed and all played their tails off. *Night in
Tunisia* gets highest marks for the most
bacchanalian version of the title piece ever
recorded, as well as "So Tired," one of
Timmons' best soul pieces; but this group
never made a bad record.
★★★ **Jazz Message / Imp. 45**
★★★★★ **Jazz Messengers! / Imp. 7**
★★★ **The African Beat / Blue N. 84097**
Impulse 7 is a transition album, with Cur-
tis Fuller's trombone making the band a
sextet. The group's reading of "Invitation"
is a ballad classic. *Jazz Message,* a quartet
with Sonny Stitt and McCoy Tyner, is surprisingly routine, while *African Beat* is a
drum ensemble workout for percussion fanatics only.
★★★★ **Buhaina's Delight / Blue N. 84104**
★★★★ **Caravan / Riv. 6074**
★★★★★ **Free for All / Blue N. 84170**
★★★★ **Mosaic / Blue N. 84090**
★★★★★ **Thermo / Mile. 47008**
The last great Blakey group is a sextet with
Freddie Hubbard, Shorter and Fuller in
the front line and pianist Cedar Walton
and bassist Jymie Merritt, or Reggie
Workman, joining Blakey in the rhythm
section. The band, which stayed together
from 1961 to 1964, may have been Blakey's
most consistent. While all of the above are

recommended, *Thermo* contains a particularly fired-up live Birdland set where Walton cuts the excellent horns.

★★★ Anthenagin / Prest. 10076
★★ Backgammon / Rou. 5003
★★★ Buhaina / Prest. 10067
★★★ Buttercorn Lady / Trip 5505
★★ Child's Dance / Prest. 10047
★★ Gypsy Folk Tales / Rou. 5008
★★★ Jazz Messengers '70 / Cata. 7902
★★ Live! / Trip 5034

The last decade has seen a decline in Blakey's personnel, and a formularization that has led him to place undue emphasis on repeating old hits. Still, for fans of blowing sessions there is always some strong soloing. *Buttercorn Lady,* from 1966, has special interest, for the Messengers of the time contained Chuck Mangione on trumpet and Keith Jarrett (heard here in his recording debut). Woody Shaw, Cedar Walton and Stanley Clarke participated in the early-Seventies Prestige sessions, and longtime Blakey associate Bill Hardman displays growing trumpet prowess on a couple of the others.

Blakey can be heard with countless other jazz leaders, including most of the people who have recorded for Blue Note, but special attention should be paid to his work with Silver, Monk and Miles Davis. — B.B.

CARLA BLEY
★★★ Dinner Music / Watt 6
★★★★★ Escalator over the Hill / JCOA EOTH-3
★★★★ 13 and 3/4 / Watt 3
★★★ Tropic Appetites / Watt 1

This co-founder, sustainer and confounder of the Jazz Composers Orchestra is known almost exclusively for her infrequent recordings. And so each album appears by surprise, like a flash flood or a train wreck. They can seem just as momentous; each is a complete work, another strong offering on her own independently financed and distributed label, with each part carefully integrated. But she composes from a musical background so diverse and with a musical community so close to lunacy that her music remains tousled and untamed.

Her most accomplished talent may be her mixology—she has combined opera singers with singing tuba players, Linda Ronstadt with a singing string bassist, members of Ornette Coleman's band with Jack Bruce and John McLaughlin, English rock stars with Gato Barbieri, and everybody with her kid. Most of the above happens on *Escalator*, a massive, durable three-record set. *Tropic Appetites* is a similar dish (words again by Paul Haines, whose images are as brittle and jagged as Carla's attack) in a scaled-down version, featuring Julie Tippetts (née Julie Driscoll) as vocalist.

Her half of *13 and 3/4* (husband Mike Mantler wrote "13") is an orchestral piece in which musicians are added and subtracted like swirls in a runaway spiral. *Dinner Music* is some shoutin' in the woods with the funk section known as Stuff.

Carla Bley is a composer and a pianist. She loves the sound of low brasses and buzzy reeds. NRBQ, Robert Wyatt and others have recorded her music, but the influence rock has had on her is more important. She is a musician who likes to have fun, and takes her humor seriously. — A.E.G.

ANTHONY BRAXTON
★★★★ For Alto / Del. DS-420/421
★★★★★ 3 Compositions of New Jazz / Del. DS-415

Braxton is one of the most interesting and certainly the most publicized musician to come out of Chicago's Association for the Advancement of Creative Musicians. His compositions create a diverse series of unique improvisational situations for a wide range of ensembles, and draw on contemporary European techniques as well as the Afro-American tradition. As a player, Braxton has led the way in making the unaccompanied saxophone recital an accepted form.

The above Delmark albums were made in Chicago before Braxton left for Europe in 1969. *3 Compositions* introduced four of the finest AACM players—Braxton, trumpeter Leo Smith, violinist Leroy Jenkins and pianist Richard Abrams. *For Alto,* two albums of unaccompanied sax, is historically important, although several of the solos sound like exercises in the more extreme avant-garde techniques.

★★★★ **Duo 1 (with Derek Bailey) / Eman. 3313**
★★★★ **Duo 2 (with Derek Bailey) / Eman. 3314**
★★★ **In the Tradition / Inner 2015**
★★★ **In the Tradition, Vol. 2 / Inner 2045**
★★★★ **Saxophone Improvisations/Series F / Inner 1008**
★★★ **Together Alone / Del. 428**
★★★★★ **Trio and Duet / Sack. 3007**

Braxton recorded prolifically during his European sojourn (1969–74), a period that found him hustling chess in order to make ends meet and pay for occasional concerts of his own work. His best recordings of the period were made with the collectives Creative Construction Company and Circle, though the solo album (Inner 1008) and duo concerts with innovative British guitarist Bailey are interesting. *In the Tradition* is Braxton with a post-bop rhythm section playing jazz standards, which works pretty well when Braxton is not playing his contrabass clarinet. The Sackville album, a Canadian import, features his best work with synthesizer (played by frequent collaborator Richard Teitelbaum; Leo Smith is also present), plus three duets with bassist David Holland on Tin Pan Alley material.

★★★★★ **Creative Orchestra Music 1976 / Ari. 4080**
★★★★ **Duets 1976 (with Muhal Richard Abrams) / Ari. 4101**
★★★★ **Five Pieces 1975 / Ari. 4064**
★★★★★ **New York, Fall 1974 / Ari. 4032**
★★★★ **The Montreux/Berlin Concerts / Ari. 5002**

Since signing with Arista, which has provided him with a commendable range of performing situations, Braxton has come to stand for the contemporary jazz vanguard. While all of his Arista recordings are worthwhile, *Creative Orchestra Music* is his masterpiece, a vibrant blending of open-ended structures, swinging extensions of Big Band tradition and even an abstract march; among the impressive personnel can be found Abrams, Holland, Leo Smith, Roscoe Mitchell and George Lewis. The *New York* album is also singled out because it is the most varied of Braxton's small-group works, with a clarinet/synthesizer duet and a composition for four saxophones. *Five Pieces* and the concert album

have Braxton's excellent quartets with Holland, drummer Barry Altschul and either trumpeter Kenny Wheeler or trombonist George Lewis.

Braxton has also recorded with Abrams, Holland, Marion Brown and Teitelbaum and on the *Wildflowers* anthology. — B.B.

BRECKER BROTHERS
★★ **Back to Back / Ari. AQ-4061**
★★★ **Brecker Brothers / Ari. 4037**
★★★★ **Heavy Metal Be-Bop / Ari. 4185**

This is the perfect illustration of how sidemen become leaders. The Breckers are the most ubiquitous New York session players: Randy is Miles Davis' only peer on electronic trumpet; Michael is recognized as being among the best of countless young tenor saxophonists. They formed their band with other New York sessioneers and proceeded to track a first album calculated to appeal to the disco market, giving themselves a commercial leg up when "Sneaking Up Behind You" became a minor hit. Their formula took over as the group went on, and by *Back to Back,* the playing is pure funk process. They remained vital in live performance, as *Heavy Metal Be-Bop* indicates. — J.S.

STAN BRONSTEIN
★★ **Living on the Avenue / Muse 5113**
★★ **Our Island Music / Muse 5072**

Elephant's Memory saxophonist tries his hand at leading conventional jazz sessions. — J.S.

CLIFFORD BROWN
★★★★ **Big Band in Paris/1953 / Prest. 7840**
★★★★ **Brownie Eyes / Blue N. LA267-G**
★★★★★ **Clifford Brown in Paris / Prest. 24020**

★★★★★ Quartet in Paris/1953 / Prest.
  7761
★★★★ Sextet in Paris/1953 / Prest. 7994
Trumpeter Clifford Brown (1930–1956)
could improvise with the flowing equilib-
rium of Fats Navarro, the crackling excitement of Dizzy Gillespie and more than
enough potent ideas of his own. Had he
not been killed in an auto accident, he undoubtedly would have grown even further;
as it is, he left a modest number of recordings and never sounded less than very
good.
  In 1953 Brown made his first impression
on the jazz world, first in some studio sessions collected on the Blue Note album,
then on some European albums made
while he toured with Lionel Hampton's
band. *Clifford Brown in Paris* is a twofer
that contains the master takes found on the
three other more exhaustive Prestige volumes (masters plus all alternate takes).
★★★★★ The Quintet, Vol. 1 / Em. 403
★★★★★ The Quintet, Vol. 2 / Em. 407
From 1954 until his death, Brown co-led a
band with drummer Max Roach, which
also contained George Morrow on bass,
Bud Powell's brother Richie on piano and
either Harold Land or Sonny Rollins on
tenor sax. The spectacular solo work of
Brown, Roach and (later) Rollins, Powell's
imaginative arrangements and the introduction of several classic compositions
(Brown's own "Joy Spring" and "Daa-
houd" among them) made this one of the
decade's premier groups. Both of the above
double albums are excellent, with better
tunes on Volume 1 and Rollins on Volume
2; the same material is currently available
on *At Basin Street* (Trip 5511), *Brown and
Roach Inc.* (Trip 5520), *Jordu* (Trip 5540),
Remember Clifford (Mercury 60827E) and
Study in Brown (Trip 5530).
★★★ Best Coast Jazz / Trip 5537
★★★ Clifford Brown All Stars / Trip 5550
★★★ Clifford Brown with Strings / Trip
  5502
★★★★★ The Beginning and the End /
  Col. C-32284
All Stars and *Best Coast* are from a 1954
jam session by Brown, Roach and five others; the tracks are long and typical of the
era's loose blowing encounters. Neal Hefti
wrote some economical string arrangements to showcase Brown's strong tone
and the results are pretty, though low on
improvisation. *Beginning and End,* on the
other hand, is essential Brown: two 1952
R&B tracks by Chris Powell's Blue Flames
which contain the trumpeter's first re-

corded solos, and three lengthy jams taped
in a Philadelphia music store the night before his death. Brown's passionate, life-
affirming spirit overcomes any potential
irony the performances might
carry. — B.B.

DAVE BRUBECK
★★★★ All the Things We Are / Atl.
  SD-1684
★★★ Brother, The Great Spirit Made Us
  All / Atl. SD-1660
★★★ Brubeck and Desmond—1975: The
  Duets / A&M/Hori. SP-703
★★★ The Art of Dave Brubeck / Atl.
  2-317
★★★★ The Dave Brubeck Quartet at
  Carnegie Hall / Col. C2S-826
★★ Time In / Col. CS-9312
★★★★ Time Out / Col. CS-8192
★★★ Two Generations of Brubeck / Atl.
  1645
In Brubeck's early-Fifties recordings, when
he was still playing jazz and Broadway
standards, he was generally overshadowed
by his masterly alto saxophonist, Paul Desmond. Brubeck, who was classically
trained under the tutelage of Darius Mil-
haud, has often been criticized for his approach to improvisation from a theoretical
rather than swinging basis. *The Art of* is a
collection of two 1953 concerts, remarkable
mostly for Desmond's contribution.
  Time Out is Brubeck's most popular and
durable album, and ample evidence of his
poignant maturity as a composer. Released
in 1960, it has acquired an undeserved
reputation as the first jazz work to explore
"compound time," something Max Roach
and others had long pursued. *Carnegie Hall*
is probably the best Brubeck quartet sampler from the mid-Sixties, with sterling performances of standards like "Take Five,"

"Blue Rondo à la Turk" and "For All We Know." Their rapport was telepathic by this time, particularly Brubeck's coy piano forays and Desmond's sly alto counterpoint. *Time In* is more memorable for its reflective ballads than its halfhearted uptempo efforts. *Time In* was the last significant statement from the original Brubeck quartet, and even a cursory listen will reveal that all was not well—the offhand performance, sloppy endings and Desmond's reticence all smack of hurried first takes.

Nowhere is Brubeck's vitality more apparent than on the recordings with his sons, Chris, Darius and Danny. Occasionally their attempts to update a standard like "Blue Rondo à la Turk," from *Two Generations,* with its Ponty-esque violin, extraneous blues guitar and harp, and electric bop piano, falter embarrassingly. On balance, their exuberance and integrative excellence make up for the blind spots.

The Duets merely affirmed something most critics had been saying all along: the best part of the old Brubeck quartet was Paul Desmond. A few moments connect, but it's mostly one-dimensional, calculatedly saccharine stuff. Dave, especially, needs the accompaniment of a rhythm section. *Brother* presents more of Brubeck's familial flirtations with jazz rock, enhanced by spacious, thoughtful improvisations and hardbop harmonic complexities, something Dad never accomplished with any group before. If *All the Things We Are* isn't the best Brubeck recording, it's certainly his bravest. One side features Dave trading ideas with Anthony Braxton, Lee Konitz and Roy Haynes, while the other is devoted largely to a stirring Jimmy Van Heusen medley, with perennial comrades Jack Six and Alan Dawson. Brubeck shines on both counts. — M.G.

GARY BURTON
★★★ Alone at Last / Atl. 1598
★★★★ Gary Burton and Keith Jarrett / Atl. 1577
★★★ Good Vibes / Atl. 1560
★★★★ Paris Encounter / Atl. 1597
★★ Throb / Atl. 1531
★★★★ Turn of the Century / Atl. 2-321

This conservatory-trained (Berklee College of Music) vibraphonist emerged in the Sixties as an accomplished soloist, bandleader and composer. As a soloist he perfected the technique of playing vibraphone with four mallets, and his classical training gave his ensemble work an understated, richly melodic chamber-music quality that was un-

usual amid the strident freneticism of most experimental music of the time.

Even though he was understated, Burton was an experimentalist himself. His landmark quartet albums for RCA featuring electric guitarist Larry Coryell explored the melodic possibilities of a musical fusion between jazz, rock and country in delightfully subtle ways. (Unfortunately all the work of this period is out of print.)

The next phase of Burton's career, represented by the five albums recorded for Atlantic between 1969 and 1972, remains in print. During this time Burton worked in a variety of contexts, keeping only bassist Steve Swallow from his previous lineup. *Throb,* which features guitarist Jerry Hahn and violinist Richard Greene, shows a country-music influence. *Good Vibes,* which adds guitarists Sam Brown and Eric Gale, drummer Bernard Purdie, keyboardist Richard Tee and bassist Chuck Rainey, is an out-and-out R&B record. Burton is at his best in collaboration with another gifted improvisationalist or as a soloist, where his pristine melodicism is shown off to best effect, so *Gary Burton and Keith Jarrett, Paris Encounter* (with the legendary French violinist Stephane Grappelli) and *Alone at Last* (a solo album featuring Burton's set from the 1971 Montreux Jazz Festival) are among his finest albums. *Turn of the Century,* a compilation of several tracks from each of the five Atlantic albums, is a serviceable recap of this period.

★★★★★ Crystal Silence / ECM/Poly. 1024
★★★ Dreams So Real / ECM/Poly. 1-1072
★★★ Hotel Hello / ECM/Poly. 1055
★★★ In the Public Interest / ECM/Poly. PD-6503
★★★★ Matchbook / ECM/Poly. 1056
★★★★ Passengers / ECM/Poly. 1-1092
★★★★ Ring / ECM/Poly. 1051
★★★★ The New Quartet / ECM/Poly. 1030

At ECM/Polydor, Burton found in Manfred Eicher a producer whose attitude toward music and recording fit perfectly with the vibraphonist's sensibility. Burton's sense of classical form and chamber-music delicacy has enabled him to benefit tremendously from Eicher's meticulous recording technique. Burton's ECM debut, *Crystal Silence,* a series of magnificent duets with pianist Chick Corea, picks up where his best work on Atlantic left off and is arguably a recording high point for both musicians, whose deft touch and lyricism complement each other perfectly. *The New Quartet* introduces guitarist Michael Goodrick, bassist Abraham Laboriel and drummer Harry Blazer on a number of compositions by Corea, Steve Swallow, Carla Bley and longtime Burton songwriter Michael Gibbs.

Burton's most prolific year was 1974. In May he reunited with Swallow from his old quartet for an ECM duet album, *Hotel Hello.* He collaborated with Gibbs on *In the Public Interest* for Polydor, a project of Gibbs compositions scored for a large (twenty-two musicians) ensemble. Then, in a four-day period that July, Burton recorded two albums for Eicher, the first—*Ring*—with a group made up of Goodrick, new guitarist Pat Metheny, percussionist Bob Moses and two bassists, Steve Swallow and Eicher's star instrumentalist, Eberhard Weber. After recording that set he went back into the studio with guitarist Ralph Towner to make a duet record, *Matchbook*, mostly of Towner's compositions (including the Winter Consort standard "Icarus"). The album closes with a stately reading of the Charles Mingus elegy for Lester Young, "Goodbye Pork Pie Hat."

Dreams So Real uses the Moses/Swallow rhythm section and both Goodrick and Metheny on guitars on a selection of Carla Bley material. *Passengers* combines drummer Dan Gottlieb with bassists Weber and Swallow and guitarist Metheny. Metheny contributes three songs and Swallow and Weber one each, but the high point of the record is Chick Corea's "Sea Journey." Burton has a special affinity for Corea's light-spirited melodicism and turns in a beautiful performance on this song.   — J.S.

CAB CALLOWAY
★★★★ The Hi De Ho Man / Col. CG-32593

In the Thirties and Forties Calloway became almost as well known among whites as a Big Band leader as Duke Ellington but for the opposite reasons. Against Duke's perfect impassiveness and grandeur, he posited pure jive and a hell of a lot of Betty Boop soundtrack music. This is charming, not quite as disingenuous as it seems. Special for potheads: "Reefer Man," from the 1933 film *International House.*   — D.M.

BENNY CARTER
★★★ Alto Artistry / Trip 5543
★★★★ Benny Carter—1933 / Prest. 7643

★★★★ Carter, Gillespie, Inc. / Pablo 2310781
★★★★ Early Benny Carter / Ev. 225
★★★ Further Definitions / Imp. 12
★★★ Jazz Giant / Contem. 7555
★★★★ King / Pablo 2310768
★★★★ Swing 1946 / Prest. 7604

Current pop music fans might know Benny Carter for the arrangements and support work he did for Maria Muldaur on her *Waitress in a Donut Shop* album and its accompanying tour, but Carter has a long and illustrious history as a soloist, bandleader and arranger. In the Thirties his alto-saxophone playing with a number of bands, including Duke Ellington's and Fletcher Henderson's organizations, gave him the reputation needed to form his own Big Band, which can be heard on the Prestige (7643) reissue. Since then he has worked off and on in a variety of different contexts, playing in many different groups and developing his arrangement technique while working on movie soundtracks. His alto playing remained fresh and lyrical right through the excellent series of recordings with the likes of Dizzy Gillespie and Art Tatum for Pablo in the Seventies.   — J.S.

BETTY CARTER
★★★★★ Betty Carter / Bet-Car MK-1001
★★★★★ Betty Carter Album / Bet-Car MK-1002
★★★★ What a Little Moonlight Can Do / Imp. 9321

Betty Carter is, in the words of Carmen McRae, "the only real jazz singer," an incredible interpreter of ballads and a fierce swinger who takes daring tonal and rhythmic liberties but never loses the musical thread. Rock fans began to notice her with the 1976 reissue of *What a Little Moonlight*

Can Do, a double album from the late Fifties that reveals her already formed style over a medium-sized combo and overblown Big Band.

Carter has owned her own Bet-Car label since 1971 and has produced two albums of her own songs and uncommon standards. *Betty Carter,* with Betty and trio at the Village Vanguard, contains her Charlie Parker medley, a spellbinding "Body and Soul" and two extended bouts of scatting. *Betty Carter Album* gathers many of her best originals ("I Can't Help It," "Happy," "Tight") plus more slow singing that approaches free-form. — B.B.

RON CARTER
★★★★ **All Blues** / CTI 6037
★★★ **Alone Together** / Mile. 904
★★★ **Anything Goes** / Kudu 25
★★★★ **Blues Farm** / CTI 6027
★★★★ **Magic** / Prest. 24053
★★★ **Out Front** / Prest. 7397
★★★ **Spanish Blue** / CTI 6051
★★★★ **Uptown Conversation** / Emb. 521
★★★ **Where** / Prest. 7843
★★★ **Yellow and Green** / CTI 6064
Carter became known as the finest acoustic bassist in the Sixties, after his work with the legendary Miles Davis band that recorded the milestone album *Kind of Blue.* He has appeared as a session player on numerous records, and his taste, lyricism and rhythmic inventiveness have made him very influential on electric bassists but especially on keyboardists and percussionists who've worked with him. In this sense Carter had a profound influence on fusion stars like Herbie Hancock and Billy Cobham. His solo albums are examples of how vital small-ensemble jazz can sound without pandering to commercial tastes or avant-garde experimentation, just concen-

trating on superb playing, arrangements and song selection. *Uptown Conversation,* which features some electric bass playing by Carter and accompaniment from Hancock and Cobham, is among his best work. His CTI albums are especially noteworthy for avoiding the overarranged style of music that serves as the label's trademark.

Carter's CTI albums are some of the very few on that label not loaded with heavy string sections. He refuses to be accepted on grounds other than his playing, a stance of integrity that may have cost him some popularity but ensures a loyal following that can depend on his records not being clinkers. — J.S.

PHILIP CATHERINE
★★★★ **Nairam** / War. BS-2950
An accomplished instrumentalist in a number of different contexts, Catherine has worked with jazz saxophonist Dexter Gordon as well as fusion bands like Passport. He was also prominent in French violinist Jean-Luc Ponty's late-Sixties European band and is currently lead guitarist with the Dutch-based fusion group Focus. Catherine's first U.S. solo album, *Nairam,* which is compiled from his two European solo ventures, *September Man* and *Guitars,* is a stunning presentation of his compositional, soloing and accompaniment capabilities in a modified fusion context. The backup instrumentation, built around the Gerry Brown (drums)/John Lee (bass) rhythm section with which Catherine has done a number of sessions, is superb, and while there are occasional echoes of John McLaughlin's work with Miles Davis circa *Jack Johnson* and *Bitches Brew,* Catherine is obviously an original talent. — J.S.

DON CHERRY
★★★★★ **Complete Communion** / Blue N. 84226
★★ **Don Cherry** / Hori. SP-717
★★★★ **Gato Barbieri and Don Cherry** / Inner 1009
★★ **Hear and Now** / Atl. 18217
★★★★★ **Old and New Dreams** / Black S. 0013
★★★★ **Relativity Suite** / JCOA 1006
★★★★ **Where Is Brooklyn?** / Blue N. 84311
To a great extent, cornetist/pocket trumpeter Don Cherry is important because of his work with all of the Sixties' important saxophonists—Ornette Coleman, Sonny Rollins, Albert Ayler, Archie Shepp, John Coltrane—though his own bands have re-

inforced the spectrum of emotion contained within new music and the felicity of international influences.

While in Europe in 1965, Cherry assembled his best group—a quintet featuring Germany's Karl Berger on vibes and piano and a then-unknown Argentinian, Leandro "Gato" Barbieri, on tenor sax. Their recordings string playful themes together with solos that are free yet convey joy instead of the then prevalent anger. *Gato Barbieri and Don Cherry* is their first effort, a confident recital surpassed on *Complete Communion* through the use of Americans Henry Grimes and Ed Blackwell in the rhythm section. *Where Is Brooklyn?*, from 1966, is Cherry, Grimes and Blackwell with Pharoah Sanders in more discrete tracks and more biting performances.

Cherry's next American album, *Relativity Suite*, was made in 1973, after the trumpeter had traveled and studied in Africa, Asia and the more remote corners of Northern Europe. The piece is almost like an international travelogue, with lots of atmosphere and a few solo spots for Cherry, Carla Bley, Charlie Haden and Carlos Ward.

Later efforts by Cherry are a mixed bag of exotica, fusion and new-thing nostalgia. Both *Don Cherry* and *Hear and Now* attempt to cross over unsuccessfully; the former is defeated by electronic indulgence and poor playing on Cherry's part (except on "Malkauns"), while the latter sports poor material and the gloss one associates with producer Narada Michael Walden. Far superior is the Italian import *Old and New Dreams,* an Ornette Coleman alumni reunion collectively chaired by Cherry, Haden, Blackwell and Dewey Redman. — B.B.

CHARLIE CHRISTIAN

★★★★ Charley (sic) Christian—Charley Christian at Minton's / Saga 6919 (Import)
★★★★★ Solo Flight—The Genius of Charlie Christian / Col. G-30779

His recording career lasted only three years, but Charlie Christian (1919-1942) continues to be revered as the fountainhead of modern jazz guitar for first harnessing the newly electrified guitar to extended single-note solos characteristic for their melodic freshness and novel rhythmic ideas—ideas credited as a key element in the stylistic transition from swing to the bop movement of the postwar years.

Benny Goodman brought Christian from Oklahoma to New York in 1939, and virtually all of their recorded collaborations—both with the Goodman Sextet and Orchestra—are preserved on *Solo Flight.* Only two tracks—"Honeysuckle Rose" and the title tune—featuring Christian and the full orchestra exist, and both show his compact phrasing while confirming the definitive emergence of the guitar from the rhythm section. Christian was playing single-note lines as early as 1938, voicing them as a third part with trumpet and saxophone, and this ability was an integral part of his work with the sextet—which comprises most of the selections on this LP. A more forceful, experimental style can be found on three tracks credited to the "Charlie Christian Quintet," recorded live at a Minneapolis nightclub in 1940.

Charley Christian at Minton's comes from amateur recordist Jerry Newman's tapes of the legendary jams at Minton's and Monroe's in Harlem with Christian, Monk, Gillespie and Kenny Clarke. The recording quality is rough and the crowd boisterous, but these bop workshops, often guided by Christian's dramatic experiments in time, are of significant value. — J.C.C.

STANLEY CLARKE

★★★ Journey to Love / Nemp. 433
★★★ School Days / Nemp. 900
★★★★ Stanley Clarke / Nemp. 431

Stanley Clarke, the prodigiously talented young bassist who is coleader of Return to Forever along with Chick Corea in addition to fronting his own band, plays a pure hybrid of jazz rock because he is equally at home in either genre. His fuzz bass intro to "School Days" is a classic rock bass riff, and he pairs himself with electric guitarists Jeff Beck and John McLaughlin on *Journey to Love.* Yet his finest solo album is the more jazz-oriented *Children of Forever,* the deleted Polydor outing recorded with the original Latin-style Return to Forever. *Stanley Clarke,* the first for his new connections, is an all-star fusion session with vital contributions from ex-Lifetime drummer Tony Williams, ex-Mahavishnu keyboardist Jan Hammer and ex-Return to Forever guitarist Bill Conners. — J.S.

BILLY COBHAM

★★★ Crosswinds / Atl. 7300
★★ Funky Thide of Sings / Atl. 18149
★★ Life and Times / Atl. 18166
■ Live on Tour in Europe / Atl. 18194
★★★ Magic / Col. JC-34939
★★★ Shabazz / Atl. 18139

★★★★ **Spectrum** / Atl. 7268
★★ **Total Eclipse** / Atl. 18121
After serving a decade-long apprenticeship backing R&B bands and playing with Dreams and Miles Davis, drummer Billy Cobham's powerful early-Seventies propulsion of the Mahavishnu Orchestra enabled him to leave that band with superstar credentials, which were immediately justified by his first solo album, *Spectrum. Spectrum* eschewed Mahavishnu's cerebrations for a gut punch, and Cobham pushed late-rock guitarist Tommy Bolin to his finest moments as a soloist, getting a hit single, "Stratus," in the process.

Cobham then formed a band around soloists John Abercrombie (guitar), Randy Brecker (trumpet) and Michael Brecker (saxophone). Their three albums, *Crosswinds, Total Eclipse* and *Shabazz,* present them in top form, playing strong material with sublime fervor.

Cobham's next band, covering *Funky Thide, Life and Times* and *Live in Europe,* was an attempt at mid-Seventies disco funk that disappointed expectations generated by its stellar lineup (bassist Doug Rauch, keyboardist George Duke and guitarist John Scofield) and some inspired but all-too-brief moments of hot playing. As evidenced on its live album, the band's collective energy just didn't sustain each musician's chops, and Cobham's soloing, while still impressive, couldn't be as inventive as it once was.

Cobham retrenched for *Magic,* a shrewd move that speaks well of his judgment as a bandleader, and came up with an understated yet commercial session featuring instrumental support from keyboardist Joachim Kuhn, guitarist Pete Maunu, bassist Randy Jackson, percussionists Pete and Sheila Escovedo and clarinetist Alvin Batiste. — J.S.

ORNETTE COLEMAN
★★★ **Coleman Classics, Vol. 1** / IAI 37.38.52
★★★★ **Something Else!** / Contem. 7551
★★★★ **Tomorrow Is the Question!** / Contem. 7569
Coleman's particular genius, so centrally rooted to the blues continuum in one respect and yet so singularly eccentric, is really beyond a rating system. Perhaps two stars should be added to each of his albums as a mark of his consistent eloquence and undiminished importance.

The above albums are from his 1958-early 1959 Los Angeles period, when the alto saxophonist's conception of "free" jazz was still presented in group situations that stressed familiar chordal and structural formats. *Something Else!* is by a Coleman quintet including trumpeter Don Cherry and drummer Billy Higgins; the presence of a pianist (Walter Norris) ties the pieces further to the bop tradition. *Tomorrow,* without a keyboard, is closer to the breakthrough, and it's interesting to hear veteran rhythm players Percy Heath, Red Mitchell and Shelly Manne respond to the aharmonic flights of Coleman and Cherry. The IAI is newly released material from a 1958 club gig where pianist Paul Bley led Coleman's quartet.

★★★★★ **Change of the Century** / Atl. 1327
★★★★★ **Free Jazz** / Atl. 1364
★★★★★ **The Best of Ornette Coleman** / Atl. 1558
★★★★★ **The Shape of Jazz to Come** / Atl. 1317
★★★★★ **This Is Our Music** / Atl. 1353
★★★★★ **To Whom Who Keeps a Record** / Atl. (Japan) P-10085A
Coleman's quartet recordings on Atlantic, recorded between 1959 and 1961, are not compared lightly to Armstrong's Hot Fives and Sevens and Parker's Savoy and Dial quintets; their innovations in improvisation without chord changes, variable pitch, asymmetrical phrases and ensemble voicings achieved a freer and more natural jazz form which influenced several established masters (Rollins, Coltrane, McLean, to name three) as well as the generation that followed.

Atlantic's *Best of* anthology is a fine introduction to Coleman, since it collects his most accessible compositions: "Lonely Woman" (from *Shape of Jazz*), "Una Muy Bonita" and "Ramblin'" (from *Change of the Century*), "Blues Connotation" (from *This Is Our Music*), plus the excellent "C and D," currently unavailable elsewhere. Joining the leader's plastic alto are Cherry on pocket trumpet; Charlie Haden or Scott LaFaro on bass; Higgins or Ed Blackwell on drums.

These six musicians, plus Freddie Hubbard and Eric Dolphy, collectively improvised *Free Jazz,* a 36-minute performance with tremendous vitality and uncanny coherence. All play superbly, but Coleman's alto solo and the passage shared by the bassists are some of the avant-garde's most sublime moments.

★★★★★ **At the "Golden Circle" Stockholm, Vol. 1** / Blue N. 84224

★★★★ At the "Golden Circle" Stockholm,
Vol. 2 / Blue N. 84225
★★★ The Empty Foxhole / Blue N. 84246
Coleman's Blue Note albums from 1965 to
1966 reveal an even more directed lyricism
and, in the case of the *"Golden Circle"* vol-
umes, the spunky rhythm section of David
Izenson (bass) and Charles Moffett
(drums). On the minus side is Coleman's
self-taught trumpet and violin work, which
is moving in its ragged expressionism but
hardly on the level of his alto playing, and
(on *Foxhole*) the untutored drumming of
Coleman's ten-year-old son, Denardo.
★★★ Friends and Neighbors / Fly.
FDS-123
★★★★★ Science Fiction / Col. KC-31061
★★★★ Skies of America / Col. C-31562
The early Seventies found Coleman leading
one of his best groups, a quartet with Had-
en, Blackwell and Coleman's old Fort
Worth high school friend Dewey Redman
on tenor sax. The group made the informal
Friends at Coleman's Artists' House studio,
and participated in the fascinating retrospective *Science Fiction,* where they were
joined by early Coleman associates Cherry,
Higgins and Bobby Bradford (trumpet)
plus the Indian vocalist Asha Puthli, for a
multifaceted program of new Coleman
compositons.

Skies of America, performed by Coleman
with the London Symphony Orchestra, is
an extended composition based on Coleman's "harmelodic theory" of writing unison passages which do not transpose (i.e.,
instruments play the same pitch in different keys). The writing is fairly conventional by contemporary European standards, and there is unfortunately little
room for the composer's alto. (The two
Columbia albums are available as a double-record set.)
★★★★ Dancing in Your Head / Hori.
722
After a four-year recording hiatus, Coleman released his free fusion album, a ragged street jam congealed somewhere between Kingston and New Orleans (the
Bermuda Triangle?) with a backup quartet
of guitars, bass, drums and percussion
sounding like Denardo times five. The alto
playing, however, is still phenomenal, and
there is a brief trance piece taped with the
Master Musicians of Joujouka,
Morocco. — B.B.

JOHN COLTRANE / 1956-60
★★★ Bahia / Prest. 7353
★★★ Black Pearls / Prest. 24037 (includes

The Believer / Prest. 7292, and The
Black Pearls / Prest. 7316)
★★★★★ Blue Train / Blue N. 81577
★★★★★ Coltrane Jazz / Atl. 1354
★★★★ Countdown (with Wilbur Har-
den) / Savoy 2203
★★★ Dial Africa (with Wilbur Harden) /
Savoy 1110
★★★★★ First Trane / Prest. 7609
★★★★★ Giant Steps / Atl. 1311
★★★★★ John Coltrane / Prest.
24003
★★★ John Coltrane Plays for Lovers /
Prest. 7426
★★★ Kenny Burrell/John Coltrane /
Prest. 24059
★★★★★ Lush Life / Prest. 7581
★★★★ More Lasting than Bronze / Prest.
24014
★★★★★ The Art of John Coltrane / Atl.
2-313
★★★★★ The Best of John Coltrane / Atl.
1541
★★★ The Coltrane Legacy / Atl. 1553
★★★ The Last Trane / Prest. 7378
★★★ The Stardust Session / Prest. 24056
(includes Stardust / Prest. 7268, and The
Master / Prest. 7825)
★★★★★ Trane's Reign / Prest. 7746
★★★★ Trane Tracks / Trip 5001
★★★ Turning Point / Beth. 6024
★★★ Two Tenors / Prest. 7670 (also on
Elmo Hope, All-Star Sessions / Mile.
47037)
★★★ Wheelin' and Dealin' / Prest.
24069

JOHN COLTRANE / 1960-65
★★★ Africa/Brass / Imp. 6
★★★★ Africa/Brass, Vol. 2 / Imp.
9273
★★★★★ Afro-Blue Impressions / Pablo
26201 01

★★★★★ A Love Supreme / Imp. 77
★★★ Ballads / Imp. 32
★★★★ Coltrane / Imp. 21
★★★★ Coltrane Plays the Blues / Atl. 1382
★★★★★ Coltrane's Sound / Atl. 1419
★★★★ Crescent / Imp. 66
★★★ Feelin' Good / Imp. 9345
★★★★ First Meditations (For Quartet) / Imp. 9332
★★★★★ His Greatest Years, Vol. 1 / Imp. 9200
★★★★★ His Greatest Years, Vol. 2 / Imp. 9223
★★★★ His Greatest Years, Vol. 3 / Imp. 9278
★★★★★ Impressions / Imp. 42
★★★ John Coltrane with Johnny Hartman / Imp. 40
★★★★★ Live at Birdland / Imp. 50
★★★★★ Live at the Village Vanguard / Imp. 10
★★★★★ My Favorite Things / Atl. 1361
★★★★ Olé Coltrane / Atl. 1373
★★★ Selflessness / Imp. 9161
★★★★ Sun Ship / Imp. 9211
★★★★ The Gentle Side of John Coltrane / Imp. 9306
★★★★ The John Coltrane Quartet Plays / Imp. 85
★★★★ The Other Village Vanguard Tapes / Imp. 9325
★★★★ To the Beat of a Different Drummer / Imp. 9346
★★★★★ Transition / Imp. 9195

JOHN COLTRANE / 1965-67
★★★★ Ascension / Imp. 95
★★★★ Concert in Japan / Imp. 9246
★★★ Cosmic Music (with Alice Coltrane) / Imp. 9148
★★★★★ Expression / Imp. 9120
★★★★ Interstellar Space / Imp. 9277
★★★★ Kulu Sé Mama / Imp. 9106
★★★★★ Live at the Village Vanguard Again / Imp. 9124
★★★★★ Meditations / Imp. 9110
★★★ Om / Imp. 9140

Coltrane's extensive catalogue has been listed above in roughly chronological order. The three groupings represent albums under Coltrane's name made while he worked for Miles Davis and Thelonious Monk (1956-60); the era of the classic Coltrane quartet with McCoy Tyner, piano, Elvin Jones, drums, and eventually Jimmy Garrison, bass (1960-65); and the final "free" period with Garrison, Pharoah Sanders, tenor sax, Alice Coltrane, piano, and Rashied Ali, drums (1965-67). Records are ranked against each other internally, to emphasize the best recordings of each period (a *** Coltrane album thus may be worth **** or ***** generally); and the Atlantic and Impulse samplers are ranked for how well they represent the period covered.

For most of the first period covered above, Coltrane was under contract to Prestige Records, a label that (like several others at the time) recorded a fixed group of its artists in blowing sessions under rotating leadership. Some of the albums that now appear under Coltrane's name were actually jams loosely organized by one member of the band (often pianist Mal Waldron). Among the participants in these sessions were Donald Byrd, Jackie McLean, Freddie Hubbard, Red Garland and Paul Chambers. Among the best:

John Coltrane—two quartet sessions from 1957-58 with Garland, Chambers and drummer Art Taylor, all of whom had worked with Coltrane in the Miles Davis quintet. It was in this period that Coltrane developed what critic Ira Gitler called his "sheets of sound" approach—a harmonically intricate, oddly accented torrent of arpeggios delivered with superhuman intensity. Coltrane's starkly lyrical ballad approach also began to gain notice at this time.

Trane's Reign—the same quartet in a lesser-known but equally tight set.

Blue Train—a sextet album, celebrated for Coltrane's stirring tenor on two blues pieces, the presence of drummer Philly Joe Jones (a rare collaboration with Coltrane outside the Davis quintet) and "Moment's Notice," Coltrane's most challenging early composition. Lee Morgan is also present.

After moving to Atlantic in 1960, Coltrane summed up this era with two classic quartet albums. *Giant Steps,* the more celebrated, finds harmonic virtuosity at a peak on the title track, "Cousin Mary," "Spiral" and "Mr. P.C.," plus the first appearance of the beautiful "Naima." *Coltrane Jazz* features more standards and finds Coltrane experimenting with saxophone harmonics (producing several notes at once on the horn). Tommy Flanagan and Wynton Kelly sparkle on piano on each album.

In the second period, Coltrane's working quartet (with Steve Davis on bass) and the soprano sax were introduced on *My Favorite Things.* While the popularity of the title tune got the band off to a good start, equally impressive were the tenor solos on "Summertime" and "But Not for Me."

This same version of the quartet is heard on *Plays the Blues* and the well-programmed *Coltrane's Sound*. Both volumes of *Africa/Brass*, *Olé Coltrane*, *Live at the Village Vanguard*, *The Other Village Vanguard Tapes* and *Impressions* document the period between May and November 1961 when Eric Dolphy often collaborated with Coltrane (on *Olé*, Dolphy uses the pseudonym George Lane). This is also the time when Coltrane shifted to an emphasis on modal improvisation (a single scale or mode is used in place of chord sequences) and triple meter. On the *Africa/Brass* albums, Dolphy wrote background orchestrations for Coltrane's band, a project that sounds magnificent but never rises to its own potential. The best record of the Coltrane/Dolphy partnership is contained on the three collections from the Village Vanguard, particularly in the various takes of "Spiritual" and "India." Even more valuable from these live dates are two exhaustive tours de force for Coltrane's tenor and Elvin Jones, "Chasin' the Trane" (on *Live at the Village Vanguard*) and the title track on *Impressions*.

Over the next three years the quartet established itself as one of the premier groups in jazz history, becoming a major influence through its hypnotic modal ensemble style and the individual conceptions of the four individuals (Garrison joined in late 1961). *Afro-Blue Impressions*, a recently released European concert recording from the period, is one of the finest summaries of the group's repertoire and fever-pitch emotionalism.

Live at Birdland, similarly heated, contains such important performances as "Afro-Blue," "I Want to Talk about You" and the deeply moving "Alabama." *To the Beat of a Different Drummer* shows what happened when Jones was temporarily replaced in 1963 by Roy Haynes.

The masterpiece from the quartet's studio work is *A Love Supreme*, the first comprehensive statement of Coltrane's spiritual concerns, recorded in late 1964. Each man performs with eloquence and economy, and the album (along with *Giant Steps*) has formed the cornerstone of many Coltrane collections.

The remaining quartet albums, made in 1965, have a great deal of excellent music (the appropriately named *Transition* in particular), but by the time of *Sun Ship* and *First Meditations*, Coltrane was pushing toward greater harmonic and rhythmic freedom, a move which Tyner and Jones made reluctantly. The music is harsher, more unsettled, with hints that agreement is occasionally lacking in the rhythm section.

The final period produced the most tumultuous, unfettered music from a man never known for calm or restraint in his playing. Rashied Ali's loose, irregular percussion work was the key to this effort, while the railing presence of Pharoah Sanders allowed Coltrane to keep the energy constantly high at a time when his physical endurance began to fail.

The first four albums in this group (*Ascension, Kulu, Om, Meditations*) were actually recorded while Tyner and Jones were still in the band, but the presence of Sanders and other guests clearly puts them in the later period. *Ascension* was an avant-garde conclave for seven horns (including Marion Brown, Freddie Hubbard, Archie Shepp and John Tchicai); hailed as a landmark of energy music, it quickly evolves into a simple series of solos and is best appreciated for the writhing ensembles and the exposure it offered several young players. *Kulu Sé Mama* and *Om* are heavily spiritual and cacophonous, and strike this listener as Coltrane's least convincing efforts in the free genre.

Meditations, with Sanders, Tyner, Garrison, and Jones *and* Ali on drums, is a far more lasting realization of energy music, tempered as it is with a deep and accessible melodic strength. The same balance makes *Live at the Vanguard Again* such a coherent example of what many listeners dismiss as noise; both Coltrane and Sanders give a lesson in New Wave eloquence on "Naima" and "My Favorite Things." The band sounds strong on *Concert in Japan*, but (perhaps out of necessity) Sanders takes most of the solo space.

Coltrane's last recordings were made in February and March of 1967. *Interstellar Space*, four duets with Ali, are high-energy efforts in the style of the 1966 band, but *Expression* suggests something different. Aside from a negligible debut recording for Coltrane on flute, there are three brilliant free recitations for a quartet of Coltrane on tenor, Alice, Garrison and Ali. The sound of the tenor seems to have widened and deepened, and the melodic sweep subsumes the more abrasive aspects of the free style. Undoubtedly Coltrane was preparing to move on to yet another stage in his endless development, and the generous portion of music he left behind can only suggest what he took with him. — B.B.

CHICK COREA

★★★ **Inner Space / Atl. SD 2-305**

A two-record collection of everything pianist Chick Corea recorded for the Atlantic and Vortex labels in the late Sixties, with Joe Farrell, Woody Shaw, Steve Swallow, Hubert Laws, Ron Carter and others. This is a robust, aggressive Corea, still caught between the shadows of McCoy Tyner, Bill Evans and Horace Silver. While he was then prone to more complex harmonic pursuits, the Latin and classical impulses were also evident.

★★★ **Circle Paris—Concert / ECM/Poly. 1018/19 ST**

A collaborative effort with Anthony Braxton, David Holland and Barry Altschul, and as far into the free-jazz arena as Corea ever ventured. Some moments are impenetrably dense, others inexplicably evocative. This is music with teeth, but that doesn't mean it'll bite if you try to get close to it.

★★★★ **Circling In / Blue N. LA472-H2**

The definitive late-Sixties Corea collection, comprised of sessions United Artists saw unfit to release until 1975. Again, much of it is in the Circle spirit—breakneck, freeform excursions—while some tracks favor an intimate, abstract chamber-bop style.

★★★★★ **Piano Improvisations, Vols. 1 and 2 / ECM/Poly. 1014 and 1020**

Simply put, these two records represent the most wide-ranging and startling display of solo jazz piano since Art Tatum. It's like turning a tape recorder on in a man's mind, catching all of his fantasy and remorse, reveries and blues. Of all of Corea's albums, these wear the best with time, from the oblique cuts to the serene ones. One can hear intimations of major themes in his Return to Forever period. With the exception of two tracks, all selections are first take, flawless and spontaneously composed.

★★★★★ **Return to Forever / ECM/Poly. 1022**

The title, before it was a group. Although not released in the U.S. until 1975, this album was recorded three years earlier and marked Corea's first use of electric instruments since his tenure with Miles Davis and his first recorded attempts at songwriting, for Brazilian vocalist Flora Purim. Also Chick's first full-fledged flirtation with Latin music and sonata structures.

★★★★ **Light as a Feather, with Return to Forever / Poly. 5525**

Here, Corea blended the Latin flavor of the first Return to Forever with a curious blend of ballad sensitivities and rock dynamics. Several modern jazz classics reside within, including "You're Everything," "500 Miles High" and "Spain." Flora was given more room to scat and soar. Essential for its joyousness, flawed for its lengthy noodling.

★★★★★ **Hymn of the Seventh Galaxy, with Return to Forever / Poly. 5536**

With this 1973 outing, Chick forfeited Flora and Latin fantasies, and instead plugged in, turned up and joined the jazz-rock race. Not surprisingly, the results echoed the path previously charted by former Miles cohort John McLaughlin, with searing cross-levels of voracious synthesizers, lethal guitars and ear-numbing rhythm and tone clusters. Derivative but essential, a last bold lunge before fusion got funked.

★★★ **Where Have I Known You Before, with Return to Forever / Poly. 6509**

Amazing how subtle the shades are between novelty and cliché. *Where Have I Known You Before* reintroduced Corea's classical leanings, but neither he nor the band were sure how to offer them. Overweight with tiresome, aimless riffing, but noteworthy for sporadic glimpses of an exquisite acoustic leitmotif. Al DiMeola's first appearance.

★★ **No Mystery, with Return to Forever / Poly. 6512**

An apt title. No pleasure either. By this point (1975) the whole Return to Forever schtick seemed like a shuck. Gone were the graceful arching lines and fiery crossfire, and in their place resided a clobbery funk rhythm and fragmented riff phrasing.

★★★★ **The Leprechaun / Poly. 6062**

1976 was a banner year for Corea and his cohorts, and his own *The Leprechaun* was the most prodigious achievement of their combined efforts. For the first time, Chick touched all of his bases, from classical suites to rock grooves, from free-form improvisation to gentle vocalizations, and all with equal conviction and competence. A much needed reminder of Corea's all-encompassing composing and arranging abilities.

★★★★ **Romantic Warrior, with Return to Forever / Col. PC-34076**

The band's first for a new label, first without Corea's name in the forefront and their last as a quartet (unless a live album follows). Musically, it was a completely revivified, expanded approach. In place of improvisation, which translated to noodling before, Corea imposed a classical structure, complete with medieval motifs. A surprising milestone in a tired genre. — M.G.

LARRY CORYELL
★★★★ **Coryell** / Van. VSD-6547
★★★ **Lady Coryell** / Van. 6509
★★★ **Larry Coryell at the Village Gate** / Van. 6573

Though Larry Coryell is one of the most creative and accomplished modern electric guitarists, he has never been as popular as many less capable but better promoted musicians. Coryell came to New York in 1965 to play jazz and ended up as second string to legendary guitarist Gabor Szabo in Chico Hamilton's band. In less than a year Coryell began his recording career with Hamilton as Szabo's replacement, and by 1968 Coryell had a formidable reputation as a jazz soloist.

Lady Coryell is a tour-de-force debut with Coryell doing virtually all the playing, pinning high velocity runs with heavy-metal chord patterns. What the album loses through its psychedelic programing and Coryell's toneless singing is more than made up for by the freshness of the musical approach. *Coryell* is a better balanced effort where the guitarist is clearly a bandleader in firm control of his ideas. *Larry Coryell at the Village Gate* features Coryell live at the top of his rock form carrying a power trio.

★★★ **Barefoot Boy** / Fly. FD-10139
★★★ **Offering** / Van. 79319
★★★★ **The Real Great Escape** / Van. 79329

These albums, recorded between 1971 and 1973 with a band built around Coryell's old keyboard sidekick from high school rock bands, Mike Mandel, and saxophonist Steve Marcus, show a maturing Coryell less interested in soloing for its own sake than in a complete group sound with more harmonic variation. *Barefoot Boy* and *Offering* are almost traditional post-bop jazz albums until Coryell and Marcus duel with frenetic solos. This band reached its peak with *The Real Great Escape,* where Coryell comes closest to linking rock song structure and vocal dynamics with jazz execution.

★★★ **Aspects** / Ari. AL 4077
★★ **Basics** / Van. 79375
★★★★★ **Introducing the Eleventh House** / Van. 79342
★★★ **Planet End** / Van. 79367
★★★★ **Spaces** / Van. 79345
★★★ **The Essential Larry Coryell** / Van. 75/76
★★★★ **The Restful Mind** / Van. 79353

Spaces, recorded with guitarist John McLaughlin, keyboardist Chick Corea, bassist Miroslav Vitous and drummer Billy Cobham, features Coryell's most tasteful and subdued playing since his days with Chico Hamilton and Gary Burton. His next band was an electric music powerhouse. *Introducing the Eleventh House* is beautiful, intelligent music with guts and rock urgency. *The Restful Mind,* a mostly acoustic album recorded with Oregon, presents a dialogue between Coryell and Ralph Towner's brilliant guitar work that surpasses even the Coryell/McLaughlin duets on *Spaces. Essential Coryell* is a good best-of compilation from the Vanguard catalogue. *Planet End* consists of outtakes from the *Spaces* and *Eleventh House* sessions, while *Basics* are Vanguard's crudest and earliest outtakes, from around the time of the second album. *Aspects* traces Coryell's decline with the Eleventh House into well-performed but directionless music. — J.S.

TADD DAMERON
★★★★ **Strictly Bebop** / Cap. M-11059
★★★★ **The Arrangers' Touch** / Prest. 24049

Much of the modest recorded legacy of Tadd Dameron (1917–1965) is currently available under Fats Navarro's name, but the first great modern jazz arranger does get half of *The Arrangers' Touch* to display his 1953 and 1956 writing, with Clifford Brown and Philly Joe Jones featured on the earlier date. *Strictly Bebop,* a more representative sampler, has six 1949 orchestra tracks and the likes of Miles Davis, Dexter Gordon and Navarro to play the lean and lyrical charts. — B.B.

MILES DAVIS
★★★ **Agharta** / Col. PG-33967
★★★★★ **Big Fun** / Col. PG-32866

★★★★ Bitches Brew / Col. PG-26
★★★ ESP / Col. PC-9150
★★★★ Filles de Kilimanjaro / Col.
    PG-9750
★★★★ "Four" and More / Col. PC-9253
★★★ Get Up with It / Col. PG-33236
★★★★★ In a Silent Way / Col. PC-9875
★★★ Jack Johnson / Col. KC-30455
★★★★★ Kind of Blue / Col. PC-8163
★★★ Live-Evil / Col. CG-30954
★★★★ Miles Davis / Prest. 24001
★★★★ Miles in the Sky / Col. PC-9628
★★★★ Miles Smiles / Col. PC-9401
★★★★ Nefertiti / Col. PC-9594
★★★ On the Corner / Col. KC-31906
★★★★ Sorcerer / Col. PC-9532
★★★ Water Babies / Col. PC-34396
★★★★ Workin' and Steamin'! / Prest.
    24034

Miles Davis is widely conceded to be the father of modern jazz, not because he founded every major school of thought in the field since Charlie Parker—although his explorations as far back as the late Fifties set the stage for the Sixties' avant-garde explosion—but because he has attracted, tutored and spawned an unprecedented number of this last generation's jazz cognoscenti.

With his historic Newport appearance in 1955, and the formation of one of the most definitive quintets of all time (John Coltrane, Red Garland, Paul Chambers and Philly Joe Jones), Miles started to ride a crest of popularity that has only recently shown signs of dissipation. For anyone interested in learning of Davis' or Coltrane's germination, the Prestige twofers listed above are not only essential, but great fun. In either package, one will find the roots of three elements which were to characterize the Davis Sound for a generation and more: the lonely, muted, introspective trumpet tone (present here in the array of showtune ballads); the fast and furious neo-bop style; and a gradual movement away from traditional chord progressions and harmonics to a more spacious modal sound.

By the late Fifties the personnel of the quintet/sextet was in constant flux, and Miles fancied experimental settings. *Kind of Blue* (with Coltrane, Adderley, Chambers, James Cobb, Wynton Kelly and Bill Evans) was pivotal, the first jazz album to utilize modal principles in a wide-open improvisational framework. In 1964 Miles formed his second quintet of any significant duration, comprised of Ron Carter (bass), Tony Williams (drums), Herbie Hancock (piano) and Wayne Shorter

(tenor and soprano saxophone). With *"Four" and More*—the best live album of Miles' career—*ESP* and *Miles Smiles,* Miles forged a unique (albeit conservative) break from the modal freedom of *Kind of Blue* with the hard blues undercurrent of the mid-Fifties quintet with Coltrane et al. *Sorcerer* and *Nefertiti* inched closer to a new vision, a methodical mixture of elongated phrasing, cross-rhythms and a strange conception of still space.

Miles in the Sky (1968) introduced a heavy-handed, rock-derived emphasis on drums. It was also the first time Miles made use of electric instruments: piano and guitar (the latter played by George Benson, paving the way for a rapport with the rock audience). Anyone who had spent hours lost in the atonal reveries of the Airplane or Hendrix couldn't help but find something kindred in the loose-jointed rhythms and long solos that dominated Miles' late-Sixties music, particularly the masterful *Filles de Kilimanjaro.*

Like *Kind of Blue* eleven years before, *In a Silent Way* (1969) changed the whole spectrum of modern jazz. With its sparse instrumentation, metronomically even pulse, oblique solos and delicate rainfall motifs, it left the listener feeling suspended in space. The celebratory *Bitches Brew* followed, the definitive vision of jazz rock and Miles' greatest commercial success. *Jack Johnson,* the soundtrack for a never-released movie, was close to straight-ahead rock, with Miles' piercing horn nailed on top of Billy Cobham's explosive drums and John McLaughlin's roaring guitar. Where *Bitches Brew* seemed to have a new, inconceivable surprise at every turn, *Live-Evil* is an album of brilliant moments, linked together with aimless, soporific noodling. But its emphasis on a single-minded rhythm, predominant in places over the soloists, predated the current funk obsession in jazz.

On the Corner was a hard-funk polyrhythmic excursion. *Big Fun,* which includes a session from the same period, is the ideal sampler of "turning point" Miles material, from *Bitches Brew* to *On the Corner. Get Up with It,* released in 1974, was Miles' first studio release in three years, following a car accident and chronic physical problems that at times threatened to derail his career. A vastly underrated album, it is a strange pastiche of mournful movements, razor-sharp electric blues and the most joyfully lyrical playing Miles has tendered in a decade. *Agharta,* recorded live in Japan with Sonny Fortune on saxophones, is Davis' power-amp dream come true, perhaps a little too bombastic and jerky for most listeners. *Water Babies*—the first in an "archive" series of unreleased sessions—offers some brilliant outtakes from *Nefertiti* and a questionable side of pre-*Silent Way* work tracks, enlightening and welcome stuff, nevertheless, to anyone who has loved Miles in the last decade. — M.G.

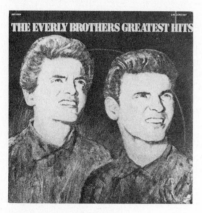

JACK DeJOHNETTE
★★ Complex / Mile. 9022
★★★★ Cosmic Chicken / Prest. 10094
★★★ Have You Heard? / Mile. 9029
★★★★ New Rags / ECM/Poly. 1-1103
★★★ Pictures / ECM/Poly. 1-1079
★★★ Sorcery / Prest. 10081
★★★ Untitled / ECM/Poly. 1-1074

DeJohnette pursues a style of drumming strongly rooted in R&B. His fluidity suggests Elvin Jones, but the beats do not roll inward toward the next phrase, as Jones' do, but shoot out in rock fashion.

You can trace the hard crack and confident grace to his work with Miles Davis, with whom DeJohnette began to play in 1970. It was then he began to make his own records, too. His light touch tapped a variety of tempos, a lesson learned from Tony Williams, co-drummer in Davis' band at the time. But through the years, DeJohnette strongly resists the urge to join the bionic metronomes (quadruple-time timekeepers such as Billy Cobham, Lenny White and Williams himself), revising his band's personnel to keep the concept clean.

He usually features some piano too, an instrument he studied for years and plays more than incidentally. — A.E.G.

AL DiMEOLA
★★★ Land of the Midnight Sun / Col. PC-34074

Guitarist Al DiMeola's shyness always seemed out of place in the context of the extroverted Return to Forever group, but his first solo album—made while still in Corea's employ—was an assertive, musically resilient surprise. For all of his rock artifice, DiMeola's sense of harmonics and melodicism is classically founded, as is his even style of attack. A fluid, celebratory fusion album that works within the pitfalls of that idiom's overworked clichés. — M.G.

ERIC DOLPHY
★★★ Copenhagen Concert / Prest. 24027
★★★ Dolphy in Europe, Vol. 2 / Prest. 7350
★★★★★ Eric Dolphy / Prest. 24008
★★★★★ Far Cry / Prest. 7747
★★★★ Here and There / Prest. 7382
★★★★★ Jitterbug Waltz / Douglas 6002
★★★★ Last Date / Lime. 86013 and Trip 5506
★★★★★ Magic / Prest. 24053
★★★★★ Out There / Prest. 7652
★★★★★ Out to Lunch / Blue N. 84163
★★★★★ Outward Bound / Prest. 7311
★★★ Status / Prest. 24070
★★★★ The Great Concert for Eric Dolphy / Prest. 34002
★★★★ Where? / Prest. 7843

Thanks to reissues, there is a healthy amount of Eric Dolphy (1928-1964) available—some of it in single and double album versions.

Outward Bound, a quintet with Freddie Hubbard and Jaki Byard, and *Out There,* an unusual quartet with Ron Carter's cello instead of the usual piano, are on *Eric Dolphy.* The first session, Dolphy's first as leader, thrust the alto saxophonist-bass clarinetist-flutist into the "new thing" controversy Ornette Coleman had created at the time (1960), but the conventional hard-bop format underlines that Dolphy could also be viewed as the most highly evolved sensibility still dealing with be-bop techniques.

From the same period come *Far Cry,* another quintet with trumpeter Booker Little and pianist Byard, and *Where?,* which is actually Ron Carter's debut as a leader. With Carter and drummer Roy Haynes in the rhythm section, *Far Cry* features one of Dolphy's best bands, plus such originals as "Miss Ann" and "Ode to Charlie Parker."

In July 1961 Dolphy played the Five Spot in New York with a cooperative quintet including Little, pianist Mal Waldron, bassist Richard Davis and drummer Roy Haynes. The three single volumes from that gig are now collected on *The Great Concert for Eric Dolphy,* which, given its long tracks, is uneven, but remains invaluable for the Dolphy and Little solos. Volume 1, if you just want a sample.

Two extra tracks from the Five Spot, plus other outtakes from the *Outward Bound* session and Dolphy's Copenhagen concerts of September 1961, are on *Here and There,* which contains the best bass-clarinet solo version of "God Bless the Child." The second volume of *Dolphy in Europe* is added to *Here and There* on the twofer *Status,* while Volumes 1 and 3 of *In Europe* comprise *Copenhagen Concert.* All of the European recordings present some very impressive Dolphy, but suffer from an unimaginative rhythm section.

Jitterbug Waltz, from 1963, is Dolphy's most varied twofer: one unaccompanied alto solo, three emotional duets with Richard Davis, three quintet tracks featuring Woody Shaw and Bobby Hutcherson, and two large ensemble pieces including the avant-garde mariachi of "Music Matador." A summation of Dolphy's roots.

Out to Lunch is well into the next phase and Dolphy's most impressive achievement. His compositions are now freer, the better to serve his always unfettered emotions, and they are performed by a dream group of Hubbard, Hutcherson, Davis and Tony Williams. From early 1964.

Shortly thereafter Dolphy went to Europe with a Charles Mingus band, where he died of natural but still clouded causes. *Last Date,* made in Holland with local players a month before he passed away, contains his flute tour de force on "You Don't Know What Love Is." Dolphy, like Coltrane, played with a passionate involvement that transcends his innovations and makes his music spellbinding for even the sometime jazz listener. Also hear him with Mingus, Coltrane, Coleman, Gunther Schuller, Andrew Hill, Oliver Nelson, Max Roach. — B.B.

URSZULA DUDZIAK
★★★ Urszula / Ari. 4065
The vocalist wife of violinist Michal Urbaniak is showcased here by her husband's production and band. Using her amazing range, she shrieks high, low and strikingly (there are no lyrics on the LP), and more extensively than on Urbaniak's records. However, at times the electric synthesized environment that surrounds her seems to be constricting, at least in comparison to her work on the out-of-print *Newborn*

Light. There, in duets with pianist Adam Makowicz, her yelps and moans achieve more nuance, and turn more tricks of timing. — M.R.

CHARLES EARLAND
★★★★ Black Drops / Prest. 10029
★★★ Black Talk / Prest. 10024
★ Great Pyramid / Mer. SRM-1-1113
★★★★ Intensity / Prest. 10041
★★★ Leaving This Planet / Prest. 66002
★ Odyssey / Mer. SRM-1-1049
During the spring and summer of 1970, Charles Earland's *Black Talk* album dominated jazz radio and even garnered uncharacteristic airplay on soul stations. Organist Earland put his stamp on pop songs like "More Today than Yesterday," developing an attractive, more spontaneous groove than the older B-3 players could muster. It was Earland who succeeded in updating the stale, heavy blues style of the Sixties organists by adding a furious bop approach and some snappy percussive flourishes. Though his pet licks were apparent from album to album, the appearance of sidemen like Lee Morgan, Jimmy Heath, Freddie Hubbard and Joe Henderson assured interesting moments.

The Mercury albums initiated a change in direction. Earland surrounded himself with synthesizers, electric piano and Arp string ensembles. Where once his songs carried titles like "Killer Joe" and "The Mighty Burner," *Odyssey* and *Great Pyramid* are replete with weighty appellations like "Intergalactic Love," "Cosmic Fever" and "Journey of the Soul." Earland layers the songs with his string Arp while playing electric piano over mild disco tracks. — J.MCE.

CLEVELAND EATON
★★ Half and Half / Gam. KZ-32077
★★ Instant Hip / Ova. 1703
Ex-Ramsey Lewis bassist tries his hand at becoming a Seventies jazz crossover artist but gets lost somewhere in the funk. — J.S.

EDWARD KENNEDY ("DUKE") ELLINGTON / Mono Recordings
★★★ A Drum Is a Woman / CSP JCL-951
★★★★★ Duke Ellington 1938 / Smithsonian R003 (Smithsonian albums available by mail only from Smithsonian, Box 10230, Des Moines, Iowa 50336)
★★★★★ Duke Ellington 1939 / Smithsonian R010

★★★ Greatest Hits / Col. CS-9629

★★★★ Hi-Fi Ellington Uptown / CSP CCL-830

★★★★ Hot in Harlem, Vol. 2 (1928-9) / MCA 2076

★★★★ Masterpieces / CSP JCL-825

★★★★★ Mood Indigo / Camd. ADL-2-0152

★★★★★ Music of Ellington / CSP JCL-558

★★★★★ Piano Reflections / Cap. M-11058

★★★★ Presents Ivie Anderson / Col. CG-32064

★★★★★ Rockin' in Rhythm, Vol. 3 (1929-31) / MCA 2077E

★★★★★ Such Sweet Thunder / CSP JCL-1033

★★★★ The Beginning (1926-8) / MCA 2075

★★★★★ The Bethlehem Years, Vol. 1 / Beth. 6013

★★★★★ The Carnegie Hall Concerts: January 1943 / Prest. 34004

★★★★★ The Carnegie Hall Concerts: December 1944 / Prest. 24073

★★★★★ The Carnegie Hall Concerts: January 1946 / Prest. 24074

★★★★★ The Carnegie Hall Concerts: December 1947 / Prest. 24075

★★★★★ The Ellington Era, Vol. 1 (1927-40) / Col. C3L-27

★★★★ The Golden Duke / Prest. 24029

★★★★ The World of Duke Ellington, Vol. 1 / Col. CS-32564

★★★ The World of Duke Ellington, Vol. 2 / Col. CS-33341

★★ The World of Duke Ellington, Vol. 3 / Col. CS-33961

★★★★★ This Is Duke Ellington / RCA VPM-6042

EDWARD KENNEDY ("DUKE")
ELLINGTON / Stereo Recordings

★★★★ Afro-Eurasian Eclipse / Fan. 9498

★★★ Best of Duke Ellington / Cap. SM-1602

★★★ Black, Brown and Beige (with Mahalia Jackson) / CPS JCS-8015

★★★★ Duke Ellington's Jazz Violin Session / Atl. 1688

★★★ Duke's Big 4 / Pablo 2310703

★★ Eastbourne / RCA APL1-1023

★★★ Ellingtonia Reevaluations: The Impulse Years, Vol. 1 / Imp. 9256

★★★ Ellingtonia Reevaluations: The Impulse Years, Vol. 2 / Imp. 9285

★★★ Ellington Indigos / Col. CS-8053

★★★ Greatest Hits / Rep. 6234

★★★ Jazz at the Plaza, Vol. 2 / Col. C-32471

★★★★ Jazz Party / CSP JCS-8127

★★★ Latin American Suite / Fan. 8419

★★★★ New Orleans Suite / Atl. 1580

★★★★★ Newport 1956 / Col. CS-8648

★★★★★ Pure Gold / RCA ANL1-2811

★★★★ Second Sacred Concert / Prest. 24045

★★★★ The Ellington Suites / Pablo 2310762

★★★ The Great Paris Concert / Atl. 2-304

★★★ The Intimate Ellington / Pablo 2310787

★★★ The Pianist / Fan. 9462

★★★ Yale Concert / Fan. 9433

EDWARD KENNEDY ("DUKE")
ELLINGTON / With Other Artists
Co-featured

★★★★ Duke Ellington and John Coltrane / Imp. 30

★★★★ Duke Ellington Meets Coleman Hawkins / Imp. 26

★★★★★ Echoes of an Era (with Louis Armstrong) / Rou. RE-108

★★★★★ First Time! (with Count Basie) / Col. CS-8515

★★★★ This One's for Blanton (with Ray Brown) / Pablo 2310721

Reviewing Duke Ellington's recording career in this limited space is a task comparable to a similar review of the collected works of Shakespeare—any attempt will hardly begin to convey the range of form, subject matter and emotion of such an invaluable treasury. Let me simply note that the rating system here might be called an "internal" one; that is, taking Ellington's greatest achievements as the (★★★★★) standard, the total works are ranked accordingly.

The Twenties and Thirties: During the

years between 1923 (when Ellington moved to New York from his native Washinton) and 1940, Duke Ellington built the most magnificent orchestra dedicated to the expression of one man's mind and soul in jazz history. Much of the secret was in the sidemen Duke attracted and used so very personally: Bubber Miley (1925–29), Cootie Williams (1929–40), Rex Stewart (1934–44), trumpets; Tricky Sam Nanton (1926–48) and Lawrence Brown (1932–51), trombones; Barney Bigard (1928–42), Johnny Hodges (1928–51), Ben Webster (1939–43), Harry Carney (1926–74), reeds; Jimmy Blanton (1939–41), bass; Sonny Greer (1923–51), drums; Ivie Anderson (1931–42), vocals; and Billy Strayhorn (1939–67), compositional collaborator. After citing the numerous key contributors, however, Ellington must be acknowledged for his ability to get so much out of performers (who almost never sounded so commanding on their own) and for his ability to draw the most direct yet strikingly original colors from standard Big Band instrumentation.

Ellington recorded for several small and large labels before World War II; the results are now scattered among Columbia, MCA and RCA and in various states of availability. MCA's material ends in 1931; of its three volumes, *Rockin' in Rhythm, Volume 3,* with some early classics and Ellington's first extended work ("Creole Rhapsody"), is the best. Columbia's three-album box *The Ellington Era, Volume 1* is an excellent overview of the period but hard to find, while the two Smithsonian albums, which focus on individual years and use Columbia-owned material exclusively, are available by mail only.

RCA owns some of the best Ellington from the early Thirties, plus *the best* Ellington by the best Ellington band (1940–42, after Webster, Blanton and Strayhorn had joined and before the wartime recording ban). Unfortunately RCA has not seen fit to reissue this material in any but the most cursory fashion, and it can only be sampled in bits and pieces on the Camden *Mood Indigo* and on *This Is Duke Ellington.* The bits and pieces are great, but just whet the appetite.

The Forties: The war took its toll on all Big Bands, though Ellington also had to fight a war of attrition that would have occurred anyway as sidemen left the band. Several key newcomers were attracted (Ray Nance, cornet and violin; Russell Procope and Jimmy Hamilton, reeds; Os-

car Pettiford, bass), but generally the Forties were a period of difficulty.

Few of these problems were evident when Ellington made his annual visit to Carnegie Hall, an opportunity to unveil new extended pieces as well as review old masters. Four Prestige collections from four of the concerts are, again, fine samplings of the band; especially recommended are the concerts from 1943 (with the complete *Black, Brown and Beige,* Ellington's magnum opus, and Ben Webster still around on tenor) and 1947 (*The Liberian Suite* and new compositions featuring piano). *The Golden Duke* has solid 1946 band performances, plus some Ellington-Strayhorn piano tracks from 1950, while the first two volumes of Columbia's *World of Duke Ellington* finds the band sliding its way into the Fifties.

The Fifties: Ellington absorbed what might have been a fatal blow in 1951, when Hodges, Brown and Greer left, and muddled on through a few years of indifferent performances. The best band work from the period is *Hi-Fi Ellington Uptown,* with good signs given by new tenor player Paul Gonsalves (1950–74). The 1953 *Piano Reflections* remains the best of Duke's rare keyboard albums.

By 1956 things began to turn around; there were fine new soloists (Clark Terry, trumpet; Britt Woodman, Quentin Jackson, trombones), the great Hodges had rejoined, and Ellington's compositional juices began flowing anew. *The Bethlehem Years,* from early 1956, is an excellent survey of earlier Ellingtonia, but it was the Newport album from the following summer, capped by Gonsalves' marathon tenor celebration on "Diminuendo and Crescendo in Blue," that put the band back on top with the public.

Of the work from the end of the decade, most of which has reappeared on Columbia Special Products, Ellington's Shakespearean suite *Such Sweet Thunder* is the finest example of his and the band's renewed capacities. *Jazz Party,* with folks like Jimmy Rushing and Dizzy Gillespie sitting in, is a lot of fun, and for the curious, the 1958 *Jazz at the Plaza* has Billie Holiday singing two tunes with the band.

The Sixties: At the top of the decade Ellington "met" several of his peers in the recording studio. The results were uniformly fascinating. Duke did some adventurous quartet blowing with Coltrane and featured Coleman Hawkins' tenor in front of a more Ducal ensemble (tracks from both of these albums are also available on Impulse's *Ellingtonia* sets, which collect Ellington compositions played by Duke and others). The Ellington/Armstrong encounter put Duke in the piano seat in Louis' sextet for an all-Ellington program (with alumnus Barney Bigard on clarinet)—an inspired approach that brings Ellington the small-band pianist to the fore. *First Time!* is a real powerhouse, with both Ellington's and Basie's full bands (one on each channel) wailing away.

The decade was also one of the orchestra's best, with old faces Cootie Williams and Lawrence Brown returning to the sections and several good albums of old and new material. *The Great Paris Concert,* from 1963, is the band's most inspired live work since Newport, while *Pure Gold* is another retrospective of similar quality done in a studio three years later. The best writing from the period (RCA's *Far East Suite*) is out of print, but the *Latin American* and *New Orleans* albums have exemplary music, and the latter features Hodges' final recordings. Pablo's *Ellington Suites* sandwiches the period (1969, 1971-72) with three lesser-known extended works. Atypical but fun is the *Violin Session,* a jam for Svend Asmussen, Stephane Grappelli and Ray Nance.

Ellington was often quoted to the effect that his *Sacred Concert* music was his greatest work, an opinion that at least this writer takes strong issue with. Currently only the second of three, which did have the most lasting music, is available.

The Seventies: musical and physical decline set in, beginning with the indifferent *Afro-Eurasian Eclipse* of 1971 and ending with the dreadful *Eastbourne* concert from shortly before Ellington's hospitalization (he died in 1974). There was also some small-band work on Pablo, of which *This One's for Blanton* stands out due to the bass work of Ray Brown. Yet even with this weak ending, and even with much of his work momentarily deleted, there is still more than enough magnificence left behind by the greatest composer America has produced. — B.B.

DON ELLIS
★★★★ Autumn / Col. CS-9721
★ Connection / Col. KC-31766
★★ Don Ellis at Fillmore / Col. CG-30243
★★★★★ Electric Bath / Col. CS-9585
★★★ Music from Other Galaxies and Planets / Atco 18227
★★★ New Ideas / Prest. 7607

★★★ Shock Treatment / Col. CS-9668
★★★★ Tears of Joy / Col. CG-30927
★★★ The New Don Ellis Band / Col. CS-9889

In his own way the innovative orchestra leader Don Ellis probably did as much to advance the conceptual possibilities of jazz rock as did John Coltrane or Miles Davis. Ellis, a fair trumpet player, writes spectacular, challenging arrangements that incorporate rock rhythmic and dynamic elements, and his charts on the landmark album *Electric Bath* undoubtedly influenced jazz-rock ensembles of the late Sixties such as Blood, Sweat and Tears, Chicago and Frank Zappa's various groups.

Blood, Sweat and Tears founder Al Kooper went on to produce *Autumn* for Ellis, which includes a live version of one of the more powerful tracks from *Electric Bath,* "Indian Lady."

Not all of Ellis' albums work, though. The live set from the Fillmore tries too hard to be space music and ends up stuck on Jupiter while *Connection* suffers from just the opposite impulse, an attempt to do an album of Big Band versions of current hits like "Jesus Christ Superstar," "Alone Again (Naturally)" and "Lean on Me." — J.S.

BILL EVANS
★★★★ New Jazz Conceptions / Riv. SMJ-6073M
★★★★★ Peace Piece and Other Pieces / Mile. 47024 (contains all material on Everybody Digs Bill Evans / Riv. 6090)

Evans' first album revealed a pianist with a uniquely introspective harmonic approach, a fine compositional sense (particularly on "Waltz for Debby"), and at the time, an attractively brittle feel for bop rhythm. The *Peace Piece* collection was made in

1958–59, when Evans was the pianist in Miles Davis' sextet, and benefits from the propulsive drumming of Philly Joe Jones.

★★★★★ Spring Leaves / Mile. 47034 (contains all material on Explorations / Riv. 6038)

★★★★★ The Village Vanguard Sessions / Mile. 47002 (contains all material on Waltz for Debby / Riv. 6118)

The trio Evans formed with bassist Scott La Faro and drummer Paul Motian in 1959 is one of the most influential groups in jazz history; they both not only redefined the interrelationship among the members of a piano trio, thanks to the free-ranging lines of La Faro and the subtle patterns of Motian, but also helped to spread the use of scalar rather than chordal improvisation (something Evans had tried in collaboration with George Russell as well as Miles Davis). Milestone's two two-fers represent the trio's total recorded output before La Faro was killed in a highway accident in 1961. Evans became less rhythmically aggressive and more quietly beautiful at this point.

★★★★ Alone / Verve V6-8792

★★★ Trio (Motian, Peacock), Duo (Hall) / Verve VE-2-2509

Most of Evans' work in the Sixties was done for Verve and is currently out of print, though we can hear him in solo, duo and trio settings from the period. By this time Evans had become a stylist and, while the music is always well crafted and romantically engaging, there is a sameness (albeit a very pretty sameness) that creates predictability, even when such talented players as guitarist Jim Hall and bassist Gary Peacock are involved.

★★★★ Living Time (with George Russell) / Col. KC-31490 (both this album and The Bill Evans Album are available together on CG-33672)

★★★ Montreux II / CTI 6004

★★★★ The Bill Evans Album / Col. C-30855

Evans entered the Seventies with bassist Eddie Gomez and drummer Marty Morrell in his trio, and the same old problem of finding new things to do within his well-established style. The Columbia albums are among the more notable of his recent efforts, especially *The Bill Evans Album* with its program of all-Evans compositions and mix of acoustic and Fender-Rhodes electric piano. *Living Time* is really George Russell's album, an exciting and radical use of a jazz orchestra that might hold to-

gether better if mounted around a more unfettered pianist.

★★★★ Intuition / Fan. 9475

★★★★★ Montreux III / Fan. 9510

★★★★ Quintessence / Fan. 9529

★★★ Since We Met / Fan. 9501

★★★★★ The Tokyo Concert / Fan. 9457

There have been few lapses in Evans' career—even the less interesting albums suffer from familiarity more than from any performance deficiencies—and his recent work is still rewarding if somewhat predictable. Both *Intuition* and *Montreux III* are duets with bassist Gomez, one of the most technically astounding bassists in the La Faro tradition, and *Quintessence* gathers a blue-ribbon quintet (Harold Land, Kenny Burrell, Ray Brown, Philly Joe Jones) for some mellow jamming. — B.B.

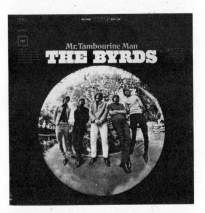

GIL EVANS

★★★ Big Stuff / Prest. 7756

★★★★★ Out of the Cool / Imp. 4

★★★★ Pacific Standard Time / Blue N. LA461-H2

★★★★ Svengali / Atl. SD-1643

★★★ The Gil Evans Orchestra Plays the Music of Jimi Hendrix / RCA CPL1-0667

★★★★ There Comes a Time / RCA APL1-1057

Although Gil Evans (b. 1912) had been arranging for Claude Thornhill and Miles Davis for nearly a decade, the 1957 recording *Big Stuff* was the first under his own name. Evans utilized his signature, unswerving lines for trumpet and sax sections, but granted soloists and percussionists a free reign. *Pacific Standard Time* is a valuable reissue of Evans' two late-Fifties albums, both attempts to orchestrate a bible of jazz standards. Evans' basic formula was to promote a soloist (Cannonball

Adderley or Johnny Coles in most cases) over a tightly checked orchestra, with the same style of seamless, lush undergrowth that characterized his haunting work with Miles. Shades of *Sketches of Spain* can be heard throughout *Out of the Cool,* the finest Evans album, although there's a quality of tension here missing from the Miles Davis classic. With its oddly punctuated counter-rhythm and lengthy Lydian chromatic blues statements, this album was ten years ahead of its time.

With *Svengali,* Gil Evans meets the rock age, which is much more interesting in concept than practice. Evans does nothing particularly innovative with the rock idiom, but rather transposes its dynamics and instrumentation—often embarrass-ingly—to the same concept at work in *Pacific Standard Time*: protruding solos with lush backgrounds. Evans was to have arranged for Jimi Hendrix, but the guitarist's sudden death iced the project. *Music of Jimi Hendrix* is a glimpse at that project, but it's not fully developed enough to give a real sense of what it should have been. The readings are perfunctory, lacking the sensuous, assaultive experience that Hendrix created. Evans only arranged two of the eight tracks. Japanese guitarist Ryo Kawasaki does provide some good moments, however.

There Comes a Time is Evans' first significant statement from the Seventies. Its scope ranges from tense, abstract blues and Evans' familiar Moorish obsessions to an elongated Tony Williams song and a swinging, revivified Jelly Roll Morton standard. Evans arranged and conducted the entire affair, and he gets the most from an impressive assembly of young musicians, including Tony Williams, David Sanborn, George Adams, Howard Johnson, Kawasaki, Hannibal Marvin Peterson and Lew Soloff. — M.G.

JOE FARRELL
★★★ Benson and Farrell / CTI 6069
★ Canned Funk / CTI 6053
★★★★ Moon Germs / CTI 6023
★★★ Outback / CTI 6014
★★★ Penny Arcade / CTI 6034
★★★ Song of the Wind / CTI 6067
★★★ Upon This Rock / CTI 6042
In the late Sixties, reedman Farrell played on small-group record dates led by Chick Corea and Elvin Jones. Their agenda was solid modal jazz: either lyrical, straight-ahead or nearly "free." Their LPs strongly influenced Farrell's first records as a

leader; *Song of the Wind, Outback* and *Moon Germs* are just as modal and they're also meatily composed and improvised. In addition they feature impressive personnel: pianists Corea and Herbie Hancock; bass-ists Stanley Clarke, David Holland and Buster Williams; drummers Jack DeJohn-ette and Airto; and guitarist John Mc-Laughlin. Their only fault, in fact, is their politeness; they lack the incisive ambiguities of a truly original product.

Such "politeness" is much more inappropriate when fused with a broader rock style. As a result, *Penny Arcade* is clumsily forced, and erratic; *Upon This Rock,* though more integrated, is not very distinctive; and *Canned Funk* is crude, even silly.

Benson and Farrell breaks back to the past a bit, featuring more lyrical, swinging Farrell soloing. (It even overshadows George Benson's usually contagious playing, which here seems obviously, lifelessly overdubbed.) However, the album makes too many commercial concessions to equal Farrell's best work. — M.R.

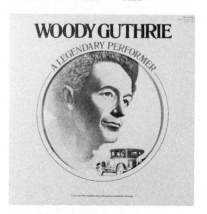

ELLA FITZGERALD
★★★ Ella and Duke at the Côte D'Azur / Verve 2-64072
★★★★ Ella and Louis / Verve 2-8811
★ Ella Fitzgerald with Gordon Jenkins' Orchestra and Chorus / Voc. VL-73797
★★★ Ella in Berlin: Mack the Knife / Verve MGVS-64041
★★★ Ella Sings Gershwin / MCA-215
★★ Memories / Cor. 20024
★★★★ The Best of Ella / MCA-2-4047
★★ The Best of Ella Fitzgerald / Verve V6-8720
★★★ The Best of Ella Fitzgerald, Vol. 2 / MCA 2-4016
★★★★ The Cole Porter Songbook / Verve VE-22511

★★★ **The History of Ella Fitzgerald /**
Verve 2 V6S-8817
The most perfect pop-jazz voice on record,
Fitzgerald's (b. 1918) technique was
matched by her serene impassivity. Guided
by musical form instead of by lyrics, she
brought an unparalleled sense of classicism
to everything she did—from scat to pop
ballads. Blessed with perfect pitch and perfect diction, she was mistress of the long-
lined narrative phrase. But if for some,
Fitzgerald was peerless, others found her
coolness boring.

The MCA albums catalogue her long career with Decca (from the late Thirties to
the mid-Fifties). But on Verve, the label
started by her manager, Norman Granz,
Fitzgerald hit her peak. The consistency of
the material was much higher, for her records here were conceived for history. On
Ella and Louis, she and Louis Armstrong
displayed an extraordinary yin-yang vocal
chemistry as they dueted on standard after
standard. Though Fitzgerald's graciousness
forbade wryness, *The Cole Porter Songbook*
remains a monument of sedate pop-jazz
that does the tunes proud. Fitzgerald's late-
Seventies records on Granz' RCA Custom
label, Pablo, show the voice in good repair
and the styling intact, in mostly small jazz
settings. — S.H.

SONNY FORTUNE
★★★★ **Awakening / A&M 704**
★★★ **Serengeti Minstrel / Atco 18225**
★★★★ **Waves of Dreams / A&M 711**
Fortune is a virtuoso saxophonist who also
plays flute and made quite a reputation for
himself as a sideman with McCoy Tyner
and Miles Davis before recording on his
own. His two A&M albums are magnificently conceived and recorded works in a
more traditional setting, with *Awakening*
earning a slight edge for the beautiful
ballad elegy to Duke Ellington and Cannonball Adderley, "For Duke and
Cannon." — J.S.

RONNIE FOSTER
★★★ **Cheshire Cat / Blue N.**
LA-425-G
★ **On the Avenue / Blue N. LA-261-G**
★ **Sweet Revival / Blue N. LA-098-G**
Foster is only an average jazz vocalist,
whose material is as toneless as a great
deal of his singing. The real interest here,
though, is George Benson's production,
and his backing vocals on *Cheshire Cat,*
which has the added advantage of guitarist
Joe Beck. (All three now deleted.) — D.M.

JAN GARBAREK
★★★★ **Belonging / ECM/Poly. 1050**
★★★ **Dansere / ECM/Poly. 1-1075**
★★★ **Dis / ECM/Poly. 1-1093**
★★★★ **Esoteric Circle / Ari. 1031**
★★★ **Luminescence / ECM/Poly. 1049**
★★★★ **Red Lanta / ECM/Poly. 1038**
★★★ **Triptykon / ECM/Poly. 1-1029**
★★★★ **Witchi-Tai-To / ECM/Poly. 1041**
Garbarek is a brilliant young Norwegian
saxophone theorist who studied the Lydian
Chromatic concept under the direction of
theorist/bandleader George Russell, under
whose auspices the challenging *Esoteric
Circle* was made. Garbarek's ECM/Polydor
work is among the best of the rigorous,
classically disciplined style carved out by
producer Manfred Eicher, and occasionally
he can sound a little too icy in this context,
but his collaborations with pianists Keith
Jarrett on *Belonging* and *Luminescence* and
Bobo Stenson on the beautiful *Witchi-Tai-
To* and *Dansere* show that he can be accessible as well as experimental. — J.S.

LUIS GASCA
★★★ **Born to Love You / Fan. 9461**
★★★ **Collage / Fan. 9504**
Here, the veteran Bay Area trumpeter,
with some good sidemen in tow (Joe and
Eddie Henderson, George Duke, Jack De-
Johnette, Patrice Rushen, Bobby Hutcher-
son), presents a selection of modal and
Latin-flavored tunes. The result is lyrical
or loping music; nice enough, but with a
relaxed sincerity that unfortunately borders
on corn. — M.R.

STAN GETZ
★★★ **Another World / Col. JG-35513**
★★★ **Best of—Two Worlds / Col.**
PC-33703
★★★★ **Captain Marvel / Col. PC-32706**
★★★★ **Diz and Getz / Verve 2-2521**
★★★ **Echoes of an Era—Basie and Getz**
and Vaughan Live at Birdland / Rou.
RE-126
★★★ **Echoes of an Era—Best of Stan**
Getz / Rou. RE-119
★★★ **Echoes of an Era—Johnny**
Smith-Stan Getz Years / Rou. RE-106
★★★ **Echoes of an Era—Stan Getz/Sonny**
Stitt / Rou. RE-123
★★★★★ **Focus / Verve 1-2528**
★★★★ **Jazz Samba / Verve 6-8432**
★★★ **Mixes / Main. 804**
★★★ **Opus de Bop / Savoy SJL-1105**
★★★ **Prestige Twofer Giants—Vol. 2 /**
Prest. PRP-2
★★★★ **Stan Getz / Prest. 24019**

★★★ Stan Getz Au Go Go / Verve 6-8600
★★ Stan Getz/Cal Tjader / Fan. 8348
★★★ Stan Getz Gold / Inner 1040-2
★★★ Stan Getz Greatest Hits / Prest. 7337
★★★★ Stan Getz/Joao Gilberto, Vol. 1 / Verve V6-8545
★★★★★ Stan Getz: The Chick Corea/Bill Evans Sessions / Verve 2-2510
★★★ The Peacocks / Col. JC-34873

Getz (b. 1927) is one of the few modern saxophonists to carve out a strong reputation without resorting to iconoclasm or self-conscious avant-garde posturing. He has remained a warm, romantic player throughout his over forty years of recording. His first major recognition came as part of the Woody Herman band in the late Forties, when he and Zoot Sims, Al Cohn and Serge Chaloff were nicknamed the "Four Brothers." Getz was the best of those players and soon went out on his own. His cool, relaxed style is influenced heavily by Lester Young and Charlie Parker, and even though he is known for his understated, breathy tone, Getz can blow surprisingly hot when the mood strikes him, and his accessible style is echoed in a lot of today's West Coast R&B session reed players.

Opus de Bop features Getz in small-combo bop sessions from the mid to late Forties and is a good representation of his early years. It wasn't until the Sixties, however, that he really began to take off. *Focus*, a brilliant 1962 collaboration with arranger Eddie Sauter, is an acknowledged classic and proof that plenty of experimentation was possible in a lyrical, understated context. Getz plays soaring, hypnotically rhythmic lines against the sweetly blocked-out string arrangements. A year later, Getz recorded an album of Brazilian tunes with guitarist Charlie Byrd. The record, *Jazz Samba*, started a bossa nova jazz craze when Antonio Carlos Jobim's "Desafinado" became a hit single. In the next few years Getz played with a variety of musicians. He produced the best samba records in the company of Jobim and guitarist Joao Gilberto, scoring a hit with "The Girl from Ipanema," for which he won four Grammy awards, and the *Getz/Gilberto* album in 1964. Rather than stay exclusively in that bag, Getz played with pianist Bill Evans, drummer Elvin Jones and bassists Ron Carter and Richard Davis (part of *Corea/Evans Sessions*); formed a touring band with vibraphonist Gary Burton, bassist Steve Swallow and drummer Roy

Haynes, a trio that went directly from playing with Getz to forming one of the first jazz-rock groups, the Gary Burton Quartet, with guitarist Larry Coryell; and recorded what may be his best album, *Sweet Rain*, with a quartet featuring the then-unknown pianist Chick Corea. That album is also included on the *Corea/Evans* set.

Getz was still making great records in the Seventies, reuniting with Corea for the fiery *Captain Marvel* and getting a Grammy nomination for his *Stan Getz Gold*, a live set recorded on his fiftieth birthday at a Copenhagen club he had opened twenty years before. — J.S.

JOHN BIRKS "DIZZY" GILLESPIE

★★★★ Afro-Cuban Jazz Moods (with Machito) / Pablo 2310771
★★★★★ And His Big Band / GNP 23E
★★★★ At the Salle Pleyel '48 / Prest. 7818E
★★★★★ Bahiana / Pablo 2625708
★★★★★ Big 4 / Pablo 2310719
★★★ Big 7 Montreux '75 / Pablo 2310749
★★★★ Carter, Gillespie, Inc. (with Benny Carter) / Pablo 2310781
★★★★ Composer's Concepts / Mer. 2-EM 410
★★★★ Dee Gee Days / Savoy 2209
★★★★ Diz and Getz (with Stan Getz) / Verve 2-2521
★★★★ Diz and Roy (with Roy Eldridge) / Verve 2524
★★★ Dizzy! / GNP 9028
★ Free Ride (with Lalo Schifrin) / Pablo 2310794
★★★★★ In the Beginning / Prest. 24030 (includes most of the selections on Big Bands 1942-6 / Phoenix 4 and Small Groups 1945-6 / Phoenix 2)
★★ Jam Montreux '77 / Pablo 2308211
★★★★ Oscar Peterson and Dizzy Gillespie / Pablo 2310740
★★★ Paris Concert / GNP 9006
★ Party / Pablo 2310784
★★★★ Something Old, Something New / Trip 5566
★★★ Swing Low, Sweet Cadillac / Imp. 9149
★★★★★ The Development of an American Artist / Smithsonian R004 (available by mail only from Smithsonian, Box 10230, Des Moines, Iowa 50336)
★★★ The Giant / Prest. 24047
★★★★ The Sonny Rollins/Sonny Stitt Sessions / Verve 2505
★★★ With Mitchell-Ruff Duo / Main. 325

Gillespie (b. 1917), one of the founding fathers of the modern era, good-time showman, be-bop personality, Big Band and small-combo leader, Afro-Cuban jazz sessionist and as spectacular as any musician who ever improvised on a trumpet, is at this writing fortunately still with us and much (although by no means all) of his five-decade career is represented in the catalogue.

One of the best ways to study the evolution of swing into be-bop is to study the Smithsonian album (which moves from 1940 sideman appearances with Cab Calloway through jam sessions at Harlem's Monroe's and 52nd St. combos to the classic 1946 recordings of "Confirmation" and "Round Midnight"). Several rare tracks are included, and the double album has been programed (for the sake of focus) minus any Gillespie–Charlie Parker collaborations.

Diz and Bird can be heard on *In the Beginning* in 1945 combo cuts ("Salt Peanuts," "Groovin' High," "Shaw 'Nuff," etc.), which quickly became the manifesto of a new musical generation. Also included are "Things to Come," "Our Delight," "Emanon" and five other tracks by Gillespie's late-Forties big band (the GNP *Big Band* and *At Salle Pleyel '48* have later live recordings by the band).

Gillespie was working with a combo and stressing novelty material by 1950 (*Dee Gee Days* exemplifies his music of the period); by 1953 he was affiliated with producer Norman Granz' Verve label, where he remained through 1961. The Verve years (a period that saw several interesting Gillespie projects, including a new orchestra that toured through 1956–57) are currently represented in reissue solely by encounters with other leaders. Recommended among these is the first session on *Diz and Getz* (a joyous date with Max Roach on drums) and the hard-blowing encounters, singly and together, with tenor giants Sonny Rollins and Sonny Stitt.

During the Sixties Gillespie led a strong quintet, featuring James Moody on reeds and pianist Kenny Barron, but his popularity waned as audiences turned their attention to more recent jazz and nonjazz styles. Few representations of the era remain available; of those (the Mercury, Trip and Impulse albums), *Something Old, Something New* is easily the best—the quintet does one side of be-bop venerables and one side of originals by Tom McIntosh (three of the new items are also on *Composer's Concepts*).

Popular interest in Gillespie has grown once again in recent years, at a time when

the trumpeter has made some of the best music of his life and Norman Granz (who now owns Pablo) has returned to produce records at a ridiculously prolific rate. The nine items released under Gillespie's full or partial leadership since 1975 include some dogs (particularly two embarrassing attempts at disco), but there are also two certified masterpieces: *Big 4*, a super-mellow quartet with Joe Pass (guitar), Ray Brown (bass) and Mickey Roker (drums); and *Bahiana*, a double album of stunning trumpet against a two-guitar rhythm section. Also notable are the meeting with composer/alto-sax elder statesman Benny Carter, the Afro-Cuban reunion with Machito's band and Chico O'Farrill's writing, and the Oscar Peterson duo album, which—despite the pianist's usual overenthusiasms—is one hell of a trumpet record. — B.B.

BENNY GOODMAN
★★★ All Time Greatest Hits / Col. PG-31547
★★ Benny Goodman and Giants of Swing / Prest. 7644
★★ Benny Goodman Live at Carnegie Hall / Lon. 2PS-918/9
★ Benny Goodman Plays / Cap. SM-706
■ Benny Goodman Plays Solid Gold Instrumental Hits / Col. PG-33405
★ Benny Goodman Presents Eddie Sauter Arrangements / CSP JGL-523
★★ Benny Goodman Presents Fletcher Henderson Arrangements / CSP JGL-524
★★★ Benny Goodman's Greatest Hits / Col. CS-9283
★ Benny Goodman Today / Lon. SPB-21
★★★★ Best of Benny Goodman / RCA AFL1-4005
★★★★★ Carnegie Hall Jazz Concert / Col. OSL-160

★★★★★ Complete Benny Goodman, Vol. 1 (1935) / RCA AXM2-5505
★★★★★ Complete Benny Goodman, Vol. 2 / RCA AXM2-5515
★★★★★ Complete Benny Goodman, Vol. 3 / RCA AXM2-5532
★★★★★ Complete Benny Goodman, Vol. 4 / RCA AXM2-5537
★★★★★ Complete Benny Goodman, Vol. 5 (1937-38) / RCA AXM2-5557
★ From Broadway to Paris / ABC X-773
★★ Great Benny Goodman / Col. CS-8643
★★ Hits of Benny Goodman / Cap. SM-1514
★ Jive Holiday / MCA 2-4018
★★★ King of Swing / Col. OSL-180
★★★★ Legendary Performers—Goodman / RCA CPL1-2470
★ On Stage (With Benny Goodman and His Septet) / Lon. BP-44182
★★★ Pure Gold / RCA ANL1-0973
★ The Benny Goodman Story / MCA 2-4055
★★★ This Is Benny Goodman / RCA VPM-6040

Clarinetist Benny Goodman (b. 1909) helped popularize a hotter, rhythmically complex jazz to white audiences who thought jazz had to be "cleaned up" before they could listen to it. His Thirties big bands and small groups were some of the best playing outfits of their time, featuring such instrumental stars as drummer Gene Krupa, guitarist Charlie Christian, pianist Teddy Wilson and vibraphonist Lionel Hampton (the latter two black performers made inroads to the white audience through Goodman's influence). Even some of the best Goodman sides might seem corny to most rock listeners because of their unabashed pop approach—in a sense, a lot of this is the kind of music rock & roll was invented to counteract. But in a very real sense rock & roll would not have been possible without it. The concept of swing was essential to this music, and this kind of danceability has continued through the rock era as a standard of hot playing. Goodman's most accessible moment to modern ears is undoubtedly the 1938 *Carnegie Hall Jazz Concert* on Columbia. There's plenty of unbridled energy on the record, and Gene Krupa's drum solo, featured on "Sing Sing Sing," is echoed strongly in a lot of Ginger Baker's playing with Cream, especially his solo spot, "Toad." This may not be the greatest aspect of rock—many would argue the opposite—but the influence is undeniable, and the effect apparently still works. — J.S.

JERRY GOODMAN AND JAN HAMMER
★★★ Like Children / Nemp. 430

Violinist Goodman and keyboardist Hammer recorded this engaging album fresh from their triumph as part of the Mahavishnu Orchestra. The atmosphere here is far more lighthearted than the intense pyrotechnics of their Mahavishnu work, and the fact that Hammer is a limited vocalist at best doesn't help things, but there are enough ideas at hand ("Country and Eastern Music" is a clever ploy) to make this a better than average fusion record. Hammer later had better luck with Jeff Beck. — J.S.

DEXTER GORDON
★★★★ Long Tall Dexter / Savoy 2211
★★★★ The Bethlehem Years / Beth. FCP-6008

Gordon (b. 1923) was not the only tenor saxophonist to reflect the dual influences of Lester Young and Charlie Parker in the Forties, but he was one of the first, and his mix (rhythmically charged and robustly inflected) became the primary influence on Sonny Rollins and John Coltrane.

Savoy's twofer has several of Gordon's influential 1945-47 sessions, with Bud Powell, Max Roach, Tadd Dameron, Art Blakey, J. J. Johnson and Fats Navarro among the personnel; there is also a touch of strident early R&B and a long jam from a California club. Drugs kept Gordon out of circulation for more than a decade, but he did make a couple of albums in the Fifties while he scuffled in Los Angeles. The Bethlehem set is a strong quartet outing.
★★★★★ A Swingin' Affair / Blue N. 84133
★★★★★ Dexter Calling / Blue N. 84083
★★★ Dexter Gordon / Blue N. LA393-H2
★★★★ Doin' All Right / Blue N. 84077
★★★★★ Go! / Blue N. 84112

In the span of one year (1961-62), Gordon returned to New York, signed with Blue Note, and reestablished himself as one of the crucial tenor stylists in jazz history. All of his work from the period is excellent, but the three quartet albums are the best— *Dexter Calling,* with Kenny Drew, Paul Chambers, Philly Joe Jones; *Go!* and *A Swingin' Affair,* with Sonny Clark, Butch Warren and Billy Higgins. *Go!* is his all-time masterpiece by consensus (Gordon included). The two-record reissue (LA393) gets low marks for its mundane choice of tunes.
★★★★ Blues Walk! / Black L. BL-309

★★★★ One Flight Up / Blue N. 84176
★★★★★ Our Man in Paris / Blue N.
84146
★★★★★ The Montmartre Collection,
Vol. 1 / Black L. BL-108
These albums are from Europe in the Sixties, where Gordon worked and lived after
his New York year. *Our Man* is a grand
reunion with Bud Powell and Kenny
Clarke, two other style-setting expatriates.
Both Black Lions were made at Copenha-
gen's Montmartre, a club in Gordon's
adopted hometown where he often played.
Volume 1 receives its high rating for the
power-packed blues jam on "Sonnymoon
for Two," one of the best recorded exam-
ples of what excitement Gordon can gener-
ate in a club.
★★★ Ca'Purange / Prest. 10051
★★★ Generation / Prest. 10069
★★★★ More Power! / Prest. 7680
★★★★ Tangerine / Prest. 10091
★★★★ The Jumpin' Blues / Prest. 10020
★★★★★ The Panther / Prest. 10030
★★★★ The Tower of Power / Prest. 7623
Prestige recorded Gordon whenever he vis-
ited New York between 1969 and '72, with
a host of first-class companions such as
James Moody, Thad Jones, Freddie Hub-
bard, Barry Harris and Stanley Clarke.
The best record of the series is *The Pan-
ther,* which uses the familiar quartet format
and has the benefit of Tommy Flanagan's
eloquent piano. The rest are all good, but
the excitement of the Blue Notes is often
missing.
★★★ Blues à la Suisse / Prest. 10079
★★★★ More Than You Know / Inner
2030
★★★★ Stable Mable / Inner 2040
★★★★ Swiss Nights / Inner 2050
★★★★ The Apartment / Inner 2025
Back to Europe and the present decade.
More Than You Know, an orchestral session
with occasionally overlush Palle Mikkel-
borg arrangements, has Gordon's debut on
soprano and his freest playing on "Ernie's
Tune." Otherwise these are quartet dates,
good in and of themselves but not as good
as *Go!.* I prefer *The Apartment,* which has
the best rhythm section.
★★★ Homecoming / Col. PG-34650
★★★★ Silver Blue / Xan. 137
★★★ Sophisticated Giant / Col. JC-34989
★★★ True Blue / Xan. 136
Gordon has made four albums in this
country since his triumphal Bicentennial
return—two jam sessions for Xanadu, the
live twofer *Homecoming* with the Woody
Shaw/Louis Hayes band and a small-or-

chestra album arranged by Slide Hampton.
Silver Blue is the best, pitting Gordon in a
side of tenor "battles" with Al Cohn that
includes their unaccompanied duet "On
the Trail." The Columbias have been disappointing—*Homecoming* for giving too
much space to Shaw and pianist Ronnie
Mathews and for often inappropriate material, and *Sophisticated* for the ordinary writing and low-intensity tenor solos. Yet Gordon remains an infectious swinger and,
when inspired, a first-class phrasemaker,
and his newfound popularity can only fore-
shadow more peaks ahead. — B.B.

CHARLIE HADEN
★★★★★ Closeness / Hori. SP-710
★★★★★ Liberation Music Orchestra /
Imp. AS-9183
Charlie Haden established a role for the
bass in nonchordal improvised music
through his work with Ornette Coleman
and his startling plucking and strumming
technique. Most of his career has been
spent with Coleman and Keith Jarrett, but
he has two excellent recordings of his own.
Liberation Music Orchestra is a 1969 musi-
cal and political statement touching on the
Spanish Civil War, Vietnam and the Chi-
cago convention, with a railing orchestra
containing Carla Bley (who arranged),
Don Cherry, Gato Barbieri and others.
Closeness, in contrast, joins the bassist with
Jarrett, Coleman, Alice Coltrane and Paul
Motian in four stunning duets. — B.B.

JERRY HAHN
★★★ Moses / Fan. 8006
Hahn is a jazz guitarist who understands
rock playing and mixes styles deftly. The
Midwest native has recorded in a variety of
groups, but this quartet with keyboardist
Merle Saunders, bassist Mel Graves and
drummer George Marsh is the only one remaining in print. Hahn's own writing on
this record is pretty ordinary but covers of
Donovan's "Sunshine Superman" and
Miles Davis' "All Blues" come off remarkably well. — J.S.

JIM HALL
★★★ Alone Together / Mile. 9045
★★★ Commitment / A&M 715
★★★★ Concierto / CTI 6060
★★★★ Jim Hall Live! / Hori. SP-705
★★★★ . . . Where Would I Be? / Mile.
9037
Lyrical invention, subtle swing and an un-
compromising dedication to jazz mark the
understated guitar of Jim Hall (b. 1930),

one of the instrument's greatest stylists. His albums, all of which were recorded in this decade, are consistent and never less than engaging.

. . . *Where Would I Be?* is a 1971 quartet with Airto Moreira on drums; Hall blows with calm assurance on a program heavily weighted with compositions by the guitarist and his wife. *Alone Together,* from the following year, is a live duo set with bassist Ron Carter. Both musicians are masters, but the consistently low-key mood detracts from the admittedly polished playing.

1975 brought two Hall albums. *Concierto* has the distinction of being one of the most substantial records ever cut according to the CTI formula. A stellar band (Carter, Chet Baker, Paul Desmond, Roland Hanna, Steve Gadd) blow politely with Hall on a few tracks, then expand beneficially on arranger Don Sebesky's reworking of "Concierto de Aranjuez." *Jim Hall Live!* was done in Toronto with just bass and drums; despite the overextended ballad mood on side one, the record has some of Hall's best work, especially on the faster tracks. The mood might be called guitarish Bill Evans (with whom hall has recorded several duets).

Commitment brought such simpatico players as Art Farmer and Tommy Flanagan into the studio with Hall, but a vocal track and another long Sebesky chart are unnecessary additions. — B.B.

JAN HAMMER
★★★★ **Like Children / Nemp. 430**
★★★ **Melodies / Nemp. 35003**
★★★★ **Oh, Yeah? / Nemp. 437**
★★★★ **The First Seven Days / Nemp. 432**
★★★ **Timeless / ECM 1047**
Jan Hammer became well known as John McLaughlin's multi-keyboardist in the

Mahavishnu Orchestra. His background was in free jazz of the New York school, as is amply demonstrated by his collaboration with John Abercrombie and Jack De-Johnette on 1974's sinewy *Timeless.* But his latent love was R&B, and Hammer came out of the closet for his series on Nemperor. The lyricism of his collaboration with Jerry Goodman (ex-violinist with Flock and Mahavishnu) on late 1974's *Like Children* and 1975's earth-hued *Seven Days* realized the sublimest meld of humanism with the new Electric Gestalt. For *Oh, Yeah?* (also the title of a 1962 Charlie Mingus album on Atlantic), he took along a talented young violinist named Steve Kindler (another ex-McLaughlin) plus drummer/lead singer Tony Smith (ex-Malo and Azteca) and bassist/vocalist Fernando Saunders in the rhythm battery. This has been his band ever since—it also backed up Jeff Beck on his 1976 tour. Trading concept for some mean blowing funk, *Oh, Yeah?* and *Melodies* leave behind the *musique-concrète,* digital sequencer, multi-track tape collage and sophistication of *Seven Days.* In fact, the sound has become closer to progressive R&B than Hammer's jazz roots over the years. — B.M.

HERBIE HANCOCK
★★★ **Herbie Hancock / Blue N. LA399-H2**
★★★ **The Best of Herbie Hancock / Blue N. 89907**
Hancock's career and his music have gone through some significant changes which reflect trends occurring throughout the jazz world. The above albums are both anthologies from his Blue Note years (1962–69) that contain material available on albums still in print. Neither album is representative of Hancock's true range.
★★★ **My Point of View / Blue N. 84126**
★★★★ **Takin' Off / Blue N. 84109**
Donald Byrd introduced Hancock to New York, and the young pianist/composer quickly revealed himself as someone who could write and play with taste, soul, daring, romanticism—whatever the situation called for. His first album did indeed take off, after his "Watermelon Man" became a pop hit in Mongo Santamaria's cover version. Dexter Gordon and Freddie Hubbard contributed to that first effort. The sequel, despite a couple of interesting tunes and more good sidemen (Byrd, Hank Mobley, Tony Williams) suffered from an excess of material tailored to the soul trade.
★★★★★ **Empyrean Isles / Blue N. 84175**

★★★★★ Maiden Voyage / Blue N. 84195
★★★ Succotash / Blue N. LA152-G
Hancock's work took a more experimental tack after he worked with Eric Dolphy briefly in 1962, and the forms used in his compositions became more harmonically and structurally diverse. His lyricism remained, however, nurtured no doubt by his association with Miles Davis, which began in 1963. *Succotash* has no horns and very loose compositions that the supporting players, with their heads still in bop, fail to energize. The other two, *Empyrean* and *Maiden,* are masterpieces of the modal period. Both have Hubbard, Williams and Ron Carter (the latter two were Hancock's mates in Davis' rhythm section), and George Coleman's tenor is added on *Maiden.* The music is occasionally blue or unbounded but always lean, intelligent and beautiful.

★★ Fat Albert Rotunda / War. 1834
★★★ Speak Like a Child / Blue N. 84279
★★★★ The Prisoner / Blue N. 84321
Speak, from 1968, finds Hancock employing a sextet with a front line of fluegelhorn, bass trombone and alto flute which produced impressionistic textures in a Gil Evans style. The piano solos are more attuned to mood than before, and the album is a bit too concerned with prettiness. Shortly after this album, Hancock left Davis and formed his own sextet, which utilized the distinctive three-horn blend to more robust effect. Johnny Coles (fluegelhorn) and Joe Henderson (tenor) were the prime soloists besides Hancock. *The Prisoner* is the better of this band's two albums, and the first of Hancock's to feature electric piano. *Fat Albert,* with music from a cartoon special, is tedious funk showing little indication of Hancock's later success in the genre.

★★★★ Crossings / War. B-2617
★★★ Mwandishi / War. 1898
★★★ Sextant / Col. C-32212
The 1970-73 Hancock band—with Eddie Henderson, trumpet; Julian Priester, trombones; Bennie Maupin, reeds; Buster Williams, basses; Billy Hart, drums; Patrick Gleeson, synthesizers—often tried to push in several directions at once. By turns free, jazz-rock, romantic and straight-ahead, it revealed and sometimes mastered a world of possibilities, but its recordings are often defeated by an excess of bass-line vamps or electronic overlays. *Crossings* is the best of the lot.

★★ "Death Wish" Soundtrack / Col. C-33199

★★★ Head Hunters / Col. PC-32731
★★ Man-Child / Col. PC-33812
★ Secrets / Col. PC-34280
★★★ Thrust / Col. PC-32965
Hancock moved to funk just in time to get in on the ground floor of disco, a trend his *Head Hunters* (and particularly the lead cut "Chameleon") was made for. The shift entailed Hancock's keeping Bennie Maupin as the only horn, doing all his own synthesizer work, hiring funk rhythm players like Paul Jackson, Harvey Mason and Bill Summers, and writing simpler compositions that stressed the beat instead of complex improvisations. *Head Hunters* was the first jazz album to be certified gold, so more of the same followed, and the formula quickly became stale.

★★★★★ The Quintet / Col. C2-34976
★★★★★ V.S.O.P / Col. PG-34688
Just when most jazz listeners had written Hancock off, the pianist looked over his shoulder and returned to his real strength. *V.S.O.P.* was done at a 1976 Newport retrospective concert and features two sides of what quickly became the Quintet (Hubbard, Wayne Shorter, Hancock, Carter, Williams), one side of the *Mwandishi* band and one side of the *Secrets* funk group. Hancock plays so much music on his electric grand piano he even salvages the tired licks of the final side.

The Quintet is more a collective effort than a Hancock album, with all five players contributing pieces and the pianist strictly acoustic (with one brief exception). Hancock's solos are much more reserved than on *V.S.O.P.,* but he comps marvelously and everyone else is very hot. — B.B.

JOHN HANDY
★ Carnival / Imp. AS-9324
★ Hard Work / Imp. ASD-9314
★★★ Live at the Monterey Jazz Festival / Col. CS-9262
★★★★ New View! / Col. CS-9497
Everything used to be high, loud and long from this California alto sax player. He was able to give his music a pop orientation (with the help of, first, guitarist Jerry Hahn and then Pat Martino and jazz violinist Mike White) without crass commercialism, and what he lacked in importance, he made up for with sheer stamina.

Then, eight years later, just when everyone was beginning to stop wondering about John Handy (he was teaching), he suddenly turned up on Impulse with a pair of albums, proving that underneath that sometimes hot high register was a flaccid, sloppy, lowest-common-denominator, lower register. — A.E.G.

EDDIE HARRIS
★★★★ Best of / Atco 1545
★★ Black Sax / Cres. 2-2073
★★ Cool Sax, Warm Heart / Col. CS-8968
★★ E.H. in the U.K. / Atco 1647
★★★ Exciting Eddie Harris / Kent 532
★★ Genius of Eddie Harris / Trad. 2067
★★ How Can You Live Like That / Atco 1698
★★★ Second Movement / Atco 1583
★★ Shades of Eddie Harris / Trad. X-5006
★★★★ Swiss Movement / Atco 1537
★★ That Is Why You're Overweight / Atco 3347

Though Harris first became known to the public through a 1960 ballad hit, a cover of the theme music for the film *Exodus,* his best work was recorded for Atlantic records later in his career. Like many other important jazz musicians, Harris has suffered from Atlantic's ruthless cutout policy, and much of his best work is now out of print.

Harris became one of the first jazz musicians to successfully adapt electronic effects to his horn with the 1968 album, *The Electrifying Eddie Harris,* which featured the space-funk classic "Listen Here." The album is now unavailable, but "Listen Here" is on the *Best of* collection.

Only the Atco records are truly representative of Harris, and aside from *Best of,* the only good ones left in print are the collaborations with keyboardist Les McCann, *Swiss Movement* and *Second Movement.* The later albums show Harris in search of another commercial formula, and to that end, reduced to singing, which usually spells disaster. Check for *Excursions* and the tremendous *Is It In* in cutout bins. — J.S.

COLEMAN HAWKINS
★★★ Battle of the Saxes / Trip 5527
★★★ Bean and the Boys / Prest. 7821
★★★ Blues Grooves / Prest. 7753
★★★ Classic Tenors / Fly. 10146
★★★ Coleman Hawkins / Ev. 252
★★★★ Coleman Hawkins and the Trumpet Kings / Trip 5515
★★★ Desafinado / Imp. 28
★★★★★ Duke Ellington Meets Coleman Hawkins / Imp. 26
★★★ Hawk Eyes / Prest. 7857
★★★★ Night Hawk / Prest. 7671
★★ Originals with Hawkins / Stin. 322
★★★★★ Sirius / Pablo 2310707
★★★ The Hawk in Holland / Cres. 9003
★★★★ Today and Now / Imp. 34
★★★ Very Saxy / Prest. 7790
★★★★ Wrapped Tight / Imp. 87

A contemporary of Louis Armstrong's, the young Hawkins (1904-1969) was influenced strongly by Armstrong's sharp, percussive style during his early days with the Fletcher Henderson band (1923), when Armstrong was also with that outfit. But Hawkins soon developed his own hard-hitting, full-throated tenor style, and is widely considered to be the first tenor saxophone soloist of note. He certainly had a lot to do with the tenor sax takeover of the soprano sax as the most popular jazz reed instrument. Hawkins in fact influenced every tenor player after him and carved out a style for the instrument that was to dominate jazz for almost twenty years, until Lester Young popularized a cooler, more relaxed approach. In that sense, the honking, guttural saxophones of Forties and Fifties R&B and rock bands may be traced back to Hawkins' influence, making him, however indirectly, a major contributor to rock & roll instrumental technique.

Hawkins became quickly acknowledged as the world's greatest tenor player during his stint with Henderson, which lasted until 1934. He recorded his most famous track, "Body and Soul," in 1939, setting an approach for reworking standard ballads that was to become the favorite format for jazz players jamming together when they weren't just playing blues progressions. A consummate musician with an open mind to experimentation, Hawkins embraced the small-combo be-bop era of the Forties when many of his contemporaries from the Big Band era disdained it. In almost every context he played, Hawkins managed to turn the convention into a statement of his playing's warm, rich personality.

Though Hawkins recorded many records, only a handful of his later recordings remain in print, but unlike many other musicians who seemed to grow tired with the passing years, Hawkins remained vital to the end. Aside from the attempt to cash in on the bossa nova craze, *Desafinado,* the Impulse sides sound particularly good, especially *Duke Ellington Meets Coleman Hawkins* and *Today and Now.* There is hardly a more moving record than *Sirius,* a recording of a concert filmed shortly before Hawkins' death in 1969. Even when ill health had enfeebled Hawkins, he still managed to express powerful music through his saxophone. — J.S.

EDDIE HENDERSON
★★★ Heritage / Blue N. LA636-G
★★★ Inside Out / Capri. CP-0122
★★★ Realization / Capri. CP-0118
★★★ Sunburst / Blue N. LA464-G

Trumpeter/fluegelhornist Henderson was first featured in Herbie Hancock's early-Seventies electric unit. Inspired and guided by Miles Davis' *Bitches Brew,* the band played angular riffs and solos over shifting patterns of ostinato rhythms. The experience also gave Henderson a conceptual framework (plus most of the personnel) for his first two Capricorn albums. Though a bit impenetrable at times, both LPs still manage to make the *Brew* formula, already incisive, more accessible.

But in 1975, after moving to Blue Note, Henderson rendered his music even more communicable; he moved into funk, and textural emphasis gave way to simpler structure. Yet he didn't lose his cerebral stance completely; *Heritage,* his best record, mixes danceable grooves with minor-key cutting-edge lyricism, plus Henderson's uncompromisingly linear style on electric horns. It's a nice blend of two worlds. — M.R.

FLETCHER HENDERSON
★★★★ Developing an American Orchestra 1923-1937 / Smithsonian R006 (Smithsonian album available by mail only from Smithsonian, Box 10230, Des Moines, Iowa 50336)
★★★★ The Complete Fletcher Henderson 1927-1936 / Blueb. AXM2-5507
★★★★ The Immortal Fletcher Henderson / Mile. 2005

Fletcher Henderson (1897–1952) led the first important Big Band in jazz history, featured an array of great soloists (Louis Armstrong, Coleman Hawkins, Roy Eldridge and Benny Carter for openers) and provided for the evolution of an approach to arranging (with contributions by Don Redman, Carter, brother Horace and Fletcher himself) that offered the foundation for the swing era.

Most of the great Henderson records owned by Columbia and MCA are currently out of print, leaving only two available collections on major-distribution labels. *The Immortal Fletcher Henderson* covers 1923-31, with a stress on the band's earliest recordings, while *The Complete Fletcher Henderson 1927-1936* works

through the swing period and is burdened with some deadly novelty vocals. The best of current Henderson collections is the Smithsonian's *Developing an American Orchestra 1923-1937,* a two-record summary of Henderson's musical and economic ups and downs. — B.B.

JON HENDRICKS
★★★ Tell Me the Truth / Ari. 4043

Scat-singing jazz master made his reputation with the vocal group Lambert, Hendricks and Ross. This reissued album, cut in the Fifties for Savoy, is not quite up to that group's brilliance, but is of interest, nonetheless, to fans of the genre. — D.M.

EARL "FATHA" HINES
★★★★ Another Monday Date / Prest. 324043
★★★ Earl "Fatha" Hines / Ev. 322
★★★ Earl Hines / Cres. 39010
★★★ Earl Hines All-Star Session / Trip 5807
★★★ Earl Hines and His All-Stars / Cres. 9042
★★★ Essential Earl "Fatha" Hines / Olym. 7125
★★★ Fatha / CSP JCS-9120
★★★ Grand Reunion / Trip 5557
★★★ Incomparable Earl "Fatha" Hines / Fan. 8381
★★★ Jazz Is His Old Lady and My Old Man / Cata. 7622
★★★★ Monday Date: 1928 / Mile. 32012

They call him "Fatha" because Earl Hines almost single-handedly carved out the standard vocabulary of jazz piano playing. After mastering the stride and ragtime piano techniques, Hines expanded the instrument's scope in a series of remarkable recordings with Louis Armstrong's Hot Five or Hot Seven in the late Twenties. Hines and Armstrong ran away from the other musicians who played with them—the rhythmic and melodic invention and their structural sense was too much for their fellow musicians to handle, so the two would end up accounting for most of the pyrotechnics on Armstrong's small-combo sessions. Hines' sound was often described as "hornlike" because of its staccato note clusters and piercing octave jumps—he and Armstrong obviously influenced each other as they played, and it took the rest of the jazz world ten years to catch up with them.

Hines went on to lead one of the hottest swing bands of the Thirties, based at Chicago's Grand Terrace Ballroom. The Hines organization became a training ground for Big Band jazz instrumentalists as he lost a succession of players to other, more successful groups. Later the group became known for such featured vocalists as Billy Eckstine and Sarah Vaughan. Like Coleman Hawkins, Hines was not afraid of change, and the early Forties band that featured Sarah Vaughan also included saxophonist Charlie Parker and trumpeter Dizzy Gillespie, two pioneers of the small-group be-bop revolution that marked the end of the Big Band era.

Hines remained a vibrant player on the later recordings, which feature him in small combos and on a delightful solo outing. *Another Monday Date* collects two fine Hines albums; one of Fats Waller tunes done with a quartet, the other a beautiful set of Hines solos. — J.S.

BILLIE HOLIDAY
★★★★★ **God Bless the Child** / Col. CG-30782
★★★★★ **Lady Day** / Col. CL-637
★★★★★ **The Billie Holiday Story, Vol. 1** / Col. PG-32121

★★★★★ **The Billie Holiday Story, Vol. 2** / Col. PG-32124
★★★★★ **The Billie Holiday Story, Vol. 3** / Col. PG-32127
★★★★ **The Original Recordings** / Col. C-32060

From teenage vocalist to celebrated nightclub attraction to ex-convict concert-hall amusement, Billie Holiday (1915-1959) was miscast throughout her life. During the early years of her career, a voice skillful enough to be featured on record with the most progressive jazz musicians of the day had no business residing in the body of so young a woman. Later, in her most fruitful years (the late Thirties), when club dates, concert tours and radio broadcasts attracted many, her records were restricted to the "race" labels, which distributed primarily to black neighborhoods. And although the hard drugs that put her in jail also took a toll on her voice, records from the years after her release from prison show there was still more reason to listen to her voice, midway between a moan and a sly reproach, than to gawk at this extremely beautiful, all-too-infamous woman of jazz.

Billie was blessed with an instinct for music as vigorous as it was untrained. She knew what she wanted to hear behind her and was fortunate to be teamed early in her career with pianist Teddy Wilson, with whom she recorded for Brunswick, Vocalion and Okeh from 1936 to 1942. All those Teddy Wilson dates are the bulk of Columbia's re-releases, and they are as much prized for the emboldening accompaniment as they are for Billie's tender nuances. Wilson's playing resembled Earl "Fatha" Hines' in its staccato riffs and lines suited more to a trumpet than to the piano; his style was the perfect match for Billie's blares, which were derived from Louis Armstrong's horn (the influence is most noticeable on the sessions from 1935 and 1936, Volumes 1 and 2 of the series).

Wilson hired men from Ellington's and Basie's bands, so he got the best: dozens of transitional musicians, including Roy Eldridge, Buster Bailey, Ben Webster and especially Lester Young on tenor sax, appearing again and again throughout the years to add one chorus or two of his taut tone and expansive ideas. Billie was often as unpredictable as the other musicians, and as continually rewarding.

The Columbia reissues exist in many overlapping forms. The two-volume, three-record sets called *The Golden Years* (not listed above) are the same as the three-volume, two-record sets dubbed *The Billie Holiday Story,* but neither compilation includes a number of important songs. *Lady Day* is a spirited supplement to the sets, a single-album feast of early recordings when Billie's voice was at its strongest—she sings from a point of wisdom, ripe with irony, turning Tin Pan Alley chestnuts into choice cuts.

The sides on *The Original Recordings* duplicate a few from *Lady Day*; most of the others can be found on Volume 2 of *The Billie Holiday Story.* The best two-record set is *God Bless the Child,* a collection that selects well from all three volumes of her recordings and adds about seven tunes, some of them gems not available on any other recording.

★★ **Lady in Satin / Col. CS-8048**
Lady in Satin presents the Lady overdressed. It's an album from the late Fifties, when most of Billie's punch was gone. She asked for the string arrangements, as Charlie Parker had also inadvisably done before her. At the time, jazz musicians thought strings brought them respectability.

★★★★ **Strange Fruit / Atl. SD-1614**
Billie recorded "Strange Fruit," a song about a black lynching in the South, for Commodore Records in 1939 when Vocalion wouldn't allow it. Her performance is surprisingly reserved, the music more consciously arranged to feature her than the songs recorded by Columbia (those were more like jam sessions), the lyrics all the more poignant for the straight rendition. "Fine and Mellow," the flip side of the original 78, was the big hit in Harlem. Most of the album was recorded five years later, when she had developed a dreamy delivery that reduced everything in range.

★★★ **The First Verve Sessions / Verve VE 2-2503**
By 1952-54, Billie knew what went over. Her vocal characteristics, still appealing, were more automatic than organic; she'd sustain the end of a word like "river," so that it would float along, dropping off into a trickle of air, or close off a syllable or two of "memories" to make the word sound far away. "Sing" frequently takes up two or three notes. Since Norman Granz was the producer, Oscar Peterson was the piano player, and the settings are marked by his dry musicality.

■ **A Day in the Life of Billie Holiday / Dif. DD1003**
This tape was never intended to be a record, but some greedy human insisted.

From a rehearsal very late in her career; not much left but the will to perform. — A.E.G.

DAVID HOLLAND
★★★★★ **Conference of the Birds / ECM/ Poly. 1027**
David Holland came to America from his native England with Miles Davis in 1968, and has proceeded to prove himself one of jazz' supreme bass players. *Conference of the Birds* features three frequent collaborators (Anthony Braxton, Sam Rivers, Barry Altschul) in a definitive 1972 statement of swinging free expression. — B.B.

FREDDIE HUBBARD
★ **Blue Spirit / Blue N. 84196**
★★★★★ **Breaking Point / Blue N. 84172**
★★★★★ **Freddie Hubbard / Blue N. LA356-H2**
★★★★★ **Goin' Up / Blue N. 84056**
★★★★★ **Hub-Tones / Blue N. 84115**
★★★★★ **Ready for Freddie / Blue N. 84085**
Arriving on the scene in the late Fifties and early Sixties, Freddie provided with regularity that component of Clifford Brown's trumpet playing that Lee Morgan sometimes disregarded: the fluency of motion, the agile gait. But then Lee developed fires that were a lot hotter than Hubbard's.

The two-record reissue *Freddie Hubbard* shows why he can be blamed for a lot of younger musicians sounding the same. The set contains selections from Freddie's first four albums for Blue Note, a few stray tracks from *Breaking Point* and the only really transcendent tune from *Blue Spirit.*

Lots of short, often unison, themes, then plenty of blowing in moody modes, makes *Goin' Up* a classic hard-bop session. And Hank Mobley, McCoy Tyner, Paul Chambers and Philly Joe Jones make it more than an all-star cast. But Freddie always had his choice of the Blue Note rotating roster; *Ready for Freddie* puts the attractive front line of Kiane Zawadi on euphonium and Wayne Shorter on tenor up against Coltrane's rhythm section. On *Hub-Tones,* he gets clear and courageous support from his frequent sideman James Spaulding, added to the shimmering chords of a fledgling Herbie Hancock.

Breaking Point is one of the early high points of Freddie's career, and still a pleasure because of the way each musician speaks with an independent voice. All but one composition are by the trumpeter, and he plotted them well. Each song demands something of the musicians in addition to containing its own appeal.

★ Backlash / Atl. 1477
★ First Light / CTI 6013
★ High Energy / Col. KC-33048
★★ Keep Your Soul Together / CTI 6036
★ Liquid Love / Col. PC-33556
★ Polar AC / CTI 6056
★★★★ Red Clay / CTI 6001
■ Windjammer / Col. PC-34166

The one Atlantic record of Freddie's still in the catalogue uses a soul groove for a substantial part of the album. Aside from being short on variety, Otis Ray Appleton, the drummer, doesn't really swing and he sure ain't funky. With him as guide, the jazz at times passes through a choking fog.

Red Clay became a classic, and for good reason: everybody plays great on it. Easily appealing, it is one good example of a sound very popular at CTI and with a lot of record buyers, but it started Freddie in a bad direction. *First Light,* for example, Freddie's Grammy-award-winning disc, contains a version of "Uncle Albert/Admiral Halsey" (with Don Sebesky's string arrangement) that manages to stay just this side of Muzak. Most everything else, however, is just the other side of real music. If only he didn't blow ballads prettier than anyone, there would be no reason to listen to this album more than once. From *Polar AC* on, it was a succession of fluegelhorn ballads, Freddie's characteristic, and safe, "tee-oo-whee!" in full force and songs where Freddie fluttered for his supper—all on some of the day's pop pablum and sophistifunk. — A.E.G.

ILLINOIS JACQUET
★★★ Blues: That's Me / Prest. 7731
★★★★ Bottoms Up / Prest. 7575
★★ How High the Moon / Prest. 24057
★★★ Message / Cadet 722
★★★ Soul Explosion / Prest. 7629
★★★ The King / Prest. 7597

Jacquet hails from Texas and cut his teeth playing in the hot combos of the Southwest in the Forties. He was featured tenor soloist in Lionel Hampton's band and later played with Count Basie before leading his own groups. Jacquet's solo on the Hampton band's 1943 side, "Flying Home," is regarded as a turning point between jazz and postwar R&B, characterized by honking volume and screeching high notes. Jacquet's sax style was highly influential on the early rock & rollers, who relied heavily on honking tenor solos before guitars took over. — J.S.

BOB JAMES
★ Bob James Four / CTI 7074
★ Explosions / ESP 1009
★ Heads / Col. JC-34896
★★ One / CTI 6043
★★ Three / CTI 6063

James began his recording career in 1965 with an avant-garde trio effort for ESP Disk called *Explosions,* which featured sound effect explosions mixed in with the playing. A statement about war, no doubt. A few years later James became the architect for Seventies Muzak jazz, helping define the CTI easy-listening style and later bringing the same ideas to Columbia. His efforts to commercialize jazz have been successful, but the records are unfortunately not much fun to listen to, although they always feature technically adept performances. Under his own name the James formula really suffers, although the results are remarkably similar to other albums he directs. Where the usual complaint is that James' style mutes the personality of the musician he's doctoring up, in his own case there's so little playing personality to begin with that the muting process is nowhere near as traumatic. — J.S.

KEITH JARRETT

★★★ **Arbour Zena** / ECM/Poly. 1070
★★★ **Backhand** / Imp. 9305
★★★ **Belonging** / ECM/Poly. 1050
★★★ **Birth** / Atl. 1612
★★★★ **Death and the Flower** / Imp. QC-9301
★★★ **Expectations** / Col. PG-31580
★★★★ **Facing You** / ECM/Poly. 1017
★★★★ **Fort Yawuh** / Imp. Q-9240
★★★ **Hymns-Spheres** / ECM/Poly. 2-1086
★★★ **In the Light** / ECM/Poly. 1033/4
★★★★ **Köln Concert** / ECM/Poly. 1064-65
★★★ **Luminessence** / ECM/Poly. 1049
★★ **Mourning of a Star** / Atl. 1596
★★★ **Mysteries** / Imp. 9315
★★ **Ruta and Daitya** / ECM/Poly. 1021
★★★★★ **Solo Concerts** / ECM/Poly. 1035-37
★★★★★ **Staircase** / ECM/Poly. 2-1090
★★ **Treasure Island** / Imp. Q-9274

Prodigiously gifted young jazz pianist and composer, ex-sideman with Miles Davis and Charles Lloyd, plays in virtually every contemporary style. Jarrett's late-Sixties Atlantic and Seventies Impulse albums feature him in ensemble with the cream of New York's avant-garde; his group work encompasses styles as diverse as Bill Evans lyricism and furious Ornette Coleman dissonance. In *Mourning* (1971), Jarrett reassembled the classic Ornette Coleman rhythm section of Charlie Haden (bass) and Paul Motian (drums), which, with the addition of saxophonist Dewey Redman on *Birth,* became the basic quartet on all the Impulse albums. The ensemble was augmented with guitarist Sam Brown for rock-oriented tunes and percussionist Guilherme Franco for Eastern exotica.

Jarrett's simultaneous career as an ECM "special projects" artist has been even more ambitious. *Facing You, Solo Concerts, Köln Concert* and *Staircase* feature extended free-form solo piano improvisations that blend European impressionism, gospel funk and LaMonte Young–Terry Riley–influenced trance music. *In the Light* collects eight orchestral and chamber works that favor an autumnal neoclassicism; *Hymns-Spheres* comprises pieces for organ. *Belonging, Luminessence* and *Arbour Zena* feature Norwegian saxophonist Jan Garbarek; the latter two have orchestral settings. Jarrett's expansiveness has been labeled

self-indulgent, and it's true that his "conservatory" pieces lack structural definition. But especially in his solo piano works, Jarrett's sheer outpouring of ideas, rendered with breathtaking physical resourcefulness, tends to override such criticisms. He's possibly the most important jazz pianist since Art Tatum, and certainly the most influential contemporary jazz keyboardist to rock players. — S.H.

EDDIE JEFFERSON

★★★★ **The Jazz Singer** / Inner 1016

Jefferson actually pioneered the scat-singing style made famous by King Pleasure and Lambert, Hendricks and Ross, but has never received credit for it. This posthumous 1977 release is from sessions made in 1959 and 1961 and includes an interesting version of Hank Crawford's "Sherry" that is very close to rock & roll, as well as "Moody's Mood for Love," to which Jefferson originally added lyrics for Pleasure. — D.M.

JAMES P. JOHNSON

★★★★ **Father of the Stride Piano** / Col. CL-1780
★★★★ **James P. Johnson 1921-1926** / Olym. 7132
★★★★ **James P. Johnson Piano Solos** / Folk. 2850
★★★★ **James P. Johnson Plays Fats Waller** / MCA 2-4112
★★★★ **New York Jazz** / Stin. 21
★★★★★ **Yamekraw** / Folk. 2842

Johnson (1891-1955) was one of the foremost practitioners of the stride piano style and a prolific composer of popular tunes. Johnson influenced Fats Waller, who in turn popularized many of Johnson's ideas. Other pianists, including Duke Ellington, learned a lot from Johnson. The albums available show Johnson's technical fluency and impeccable taste. He was also an experimenter, and his most ambitious work was *Yamekraw,* a rhapsody that was used as the soundtrack for a film short starring Bessie Smith. — J.S.

ELVIN JONES

★★★★ Dear John C. / Imp. 88
★★★ Heavy Sounds / Imp. 9160
★★★★ Illumination / Imp. 49
★★★ Jones Boys / Ev. 270
★★ Main Force / Van. 79372
★★★ New Agenda / Van. 79362
★★★ Night Dreamer / Blue N. 84173
★★★★ Oregon/Elvin Jones / Van. 79377
★★★ Outback / CTI 6014
★★★★ Puttin' It Together / Blue N. 84282
★★★★★ Reevaluations: Impulse Years / Imp. D-9283
★★★ Summit Meeting / Van. 79390
★★★ Time Capsule / Van. 79389
★★★★ Ultimate / Blue N. 84305

One of the most powerfully rhythmic drummers alive, Jones is a jazz virtuoso who has influenced all modern drummers, including R&B and jazz players. Jones played with Miles Davis and Sonny Rollins, but his work in the Sixties with John Coltrane earned him a secure place in music history, and his solo career, while not always consistent, features some fine moments. *Reevaluations* includes several outstanding tracks from the Coltrane days. While his fine Blue Note quintet albums with saxophonists George Coleman and Frank Foster are out of print, the trio sides for that label with saxophonist Joe Farrell and bassist Jimmy Garrison are quite good. Unfortunately Jones' recent recordings for Vanguard are not up to his fine standard, although the collaboration with Oregon is interesting. — J.S.

ROLAND KIRK

★★ Gifts and Messages / Trip 5572
★★★ Other Folk's Music / Atl. 1686
★★★ Rip, Rig and Panic / Trip 5592
★★★★ The Best of Rahsaan Roland Kirk / Atl. 1592
★★★ The Case of the Three-Sided Dream in Audio Color / Atl. 1674
★★★ The Return of the 5,000 Lb. Man / War. B-2918
★★★ We Free Kings / Trip 5541

Kirk's (1936-1977) most impressive characteristic was his resilience. A continual innovator on reed instruments of every imaginable type (the "miscellaneous" category in jazz polls was his own before the synthesizers and percussionists took over), he developed ways to play three instruments at once; to blow flute and sing simultaneously (which gave Jethro Tull's Ian Anderson the idea for the two licks he uses); to play, without stopping, from now until Tuesday, by employing a circular breathing technique; and to shift effortlessly from his most political original compositions to standards, jingles and a variety of unidentifiable, but vaguely recognizable, worn-out phrases which he retreads with his own brand of steely spikes. Late in the Seventies he fought back from a crippling stroke, at first playing with one hand until he regained his strength. All this from a man who had seen only dim light since childhood.

Kirk was at the same time a prankster, a storyteller and a professor of dynamism. He would fly through chord changes, his soul ruffled by some personal demon, then sound off in a hard-edged, bluesy ballad. He led his own bands for over fifteen years—his energy, logic and balls always racing somewhere ahead of the rhythm. — A.E.G.

JOHN KLEMMER

★★★ All the Children Cried / Cadet 326
★★ And We Were Lovers / Cadet 808
★★★ Arabesque / ABC 1068
★★ Barefoot Ballet / ABC D-950
★★★ Blowin' Gold / Cadet 321
★★★ Constant Throb / Imp. 9214
★★ Eruptions / Cadet 330
★★ Fresh Feathers / ABC 836
★★★ Intensity / Imp. Q-9244
★★ Involvement / Cadet 797
★ Lifestyle / ABC 1007
★★ Magic and Movement / Imp. Q-9269
★★ Magic Moments / Chess 2-401
★★ Touch / ABC 922
★★★ Waterfalls / Imp. Q-9220

This Chicago-based saxophonist/flautist studied under Stan Kenton and was featured soloist in Don Ellis' band before forming his own combo in the Sixties. On his first albums, recorded for Chess and Cadet, Klemmer was obviously influenced by John Coltrane, and made several attempts to incorporate social protest themes into the program of his music, all to little avail. Later, on his Impulse and ABC records, Klemmer went heavily into the use of Echoplex and other electronic effects on his saxophone. Some of these records sound interesting, but inevitably Klemmer's sound is just too gimmicky to hold up over repeated listenings. — J.S.

EARL KLUGH
★★★ **Earl Klugh** / Blue N. LA596-G
★★★ **Finger Painting** / Blue N. LA737-H
★★★ **Living inside Your Love** / Blue N.
  LA667-G

A strong melodic sense (frequently on covers of contemporary soul hits), plus the
first-rate percussion backing of Steve Gadd
and Ralph McDonald, has helped make
this Detroit-based guitarist one of the most
successful mainstream jazz guitarists of the
Seventies, both commercially and artistically. — D.M.

OLIVER LAKE
★★★★ **Bowie/Lake** / Sack. 2010
★★★★★ **Heavy Spirits** / Ari./Free 1008
★★★★★ **Holding Together** / Black S.
  0009
★★★ **Ntu: Point from Which Creation
  Begins** / Ari./Free 1024
★★★★ **Passing Through** / P.T. 4237

Oliver Lake has proven in a short time to
be the most interesting voice to emerge
from the St. Louis music collective, Black
Artists Group. A sample of BAG's scope
can be detected on *Ntu: Point from Which
Creation Begins,* a 1971 St. Louis production that manages to contain post-bop, acid
guitar, energy jazz and the adventures in
spontaneous form that the closely aligned
Association for the Advancement of Creative Music in Chicago first brought to national attention.

The best example of Lake the composer
and soloist (primarily on alto sax, though
he also uses soprano sax and flute) is
1975's *Heavy Spirits.* His commanding expressionism works equally well in the standard jazz quintet instrumentation, which is
enhanced by his irregular yet lyrical writing; a terse unaccompanied solo; and three
unique pieces for alto and three violins.
Trumpeter Olu Dara is impressive on the
quintet tracks.

New music fans should take the time to
seek out Lake's albums on foreign and private labels. *Passing Through,* his privately
produced album from a 1974 Paris solo
concert, has more variety and attention to
nuance than most unaccompanied ventures. In 1976 Lake led a quartet with the
innovative young guitarist Michael Gregory Jackson which tempered their wilder
moments with complex structures and abstract balladry; bassist Fred Hopkins and
drummer Paul Maddox complete the excellent group on the Italian *Holding Together.*
A Canadian duet concert with trombonist
Joseph Bowie has less shading but much

playing at the edge of current horn technique. — B.B.

LAMBERT, HENDRICKS AND ROSS
★★★ **Best of Lambert, Hendricks and
  Ross** / Col. C-32911
★★★ **Sing a Song of Basie** / Imper. 83
★★★ **Way Out Voices** / Odys.
  32-163-0292

Lambert, Hendricks and Ross took scat
singing to the next obvious stage: they
wrote lyrics to jazz tunes that didn't have
any (as well as performing a few jazz tunes
in bop style—e.g., their bizarre "Summertime"). For a time in the Fifties, this was
all the rage, especially since Jon Hendricks, Annie Ross and Dave Lambert had
such oddly listenable voices. More recently, Lambert, Hendricks and Ross have
proven a major influence on performers
like Bette Midler and Joni Mitchell, both
of whom have recorded their mental health
number, "Twisted."

Sing a Song of Basie was the group's first
effort, and features ten additional voices—a
concept put together by Lambert. The Columbia *Best of* is in fact a reissue of *The
Hottest New Group in Jazz,* which was what
critic Ralph J. Gleason was calling them; it
is in fact the best of their records, containing "Twisted" and their other well-known
song, "Cloudburst." — D.M.

GLORIA LYNNE
★ **Gloria Lynne** / Ev. 305
★ **I Don't Know How to Love Him** / ABC
  ASD9311

Gloria Lynne is a relatively minor jazz
singer with an unusually husky voice. She
has seen better days. The production on
both records is simultaneously garish and
cloddish, and it brings out the worst in
her—when she isn't drowned out by the
wah-wah effects and violins. — R.G.

RALPH MacDONALD
★★★★ **Sound of a Drum** / Mar. 2202
★★★★ **The Path** / Mar. 2210

After a long apprenticeship with Harry
Belafonte in the Sixties and Roberta Flack
in the early Seventies, MacDonald became
the Seventies' most prolific session percussionist. His solo outings have demonstrated
his shewdness and taste as a leader in as-
sembling excellent studio bands and providing commercial hooks for his records.
"Calypso Breakdown" and "Jam on the
Groove" from *Drum* have become popular
currency. *The Path* features MacDonald's
imaginative handling of synthesized drums

(syndrum), and that album's title track traces a musicological evolution of disco rhythms from African and Caribbean origins. — J.S.

CHUCK MANGIONE
★★★★ Alive / Mer. SRM-1-650
★★ Bellavia / A&M 4557
★★ Chase the Clouds Away / A&M 4518
★★★ Chuck Mangione Quartet / Mer. SRM-1-631
★★★ Encore / Mer. SRM-1-1050
★★ Feels So Good / A&M 4658
★★★★ Friends and Love / Mer. 2-800
★★★ Friends and Love (Highlights) / Mer. SRM-1-681
★★★ Jazz Brothers / Mile. 47042
★★★ Land of Make Believe / Mer. SRM-1-684
★★ Main Squeeze / A&M 4612
★★★ Together / Mer. SRM-2-7501

Trumpeter/fluegelhornist Chuck Mangione played in Art Blakey's band in the Sixties before leading his own group, the Jazz Brothers, with his brother Gap Mangione on keyboards. The *Friends and Love* live concert recording from 1970, a fine piece of multi-stylistic writing and direction in which Mangione combined his own band with the Rochester Philharmonic Orchestra, established his solo career, and led to a few similar projects. Mangione hit a commercial high point in collaboration with vocalist Esther Satterfield on "Land of Make Believe," which has since become a standard.

Mangione's quartet albums for Mercury are quite good, and feature Garry Niewood's excellent soprano-saxophone work as well as some fine playing by Mangione and consistently good session backing. *Alive,* with drummer Steve Gadd and bassist Tony Levin, is the best of the quartet records. Unfortunately, Mangione's later albums for A&M are exceedingly glib, so despite his musical taste and sense for commercial hooks, the records remain unrewarding. — J.S.

HERBIE MANN
★★★ Best of / Atco 1544
★★★ Best of / Prest. 7432
★★ Big Boss Man / Col. CS-1068
★★ Bird in a Silver Cage / Atco 18209
★★ Discotheque / Atco 1670
★★ Et Tu Flute / Verve 2V6-8821
★★★ Evolution of Mann / Atco 2-300
★★ Latin Mann / CSP JCS-9188
★★★ London Underground / Atco 1648

★★★★ Mann at the Village Gate / Atco 1380
★★ Mann in Sweden / Prest. 7659
★★★★ Memphis Underground / Atco 1522
★★ Reggae / Atco 1655
★★ Super Mann / Trip 5031
★★ Surprises / Atco 1682
★★★ Turtle Bay / Atco 1642
★★ With Flute to Boot / Sp. 4055

Mann (b. 1930) is a shrewd and accomplished bandleader who's been able to anticipate and cash in on musical fashions consistently for over two decades. His flute playing is almost always the least interesting aspect of his records, which are all carefully conceptualized around crack studio bands. During the Fifties and Sixties Mann organized an excellent Afro-Cuban combo and helped popularize that music by featuring top musicians in his group, especially great percussionists like Carlos "Potato" Valdes, Ray Barretto, Michael Olatunji, Ray Mantilla, Willie Bobo and Armando Peraza. Mann's records were always interesting during this period and a lot of people, including a number of rock musicians, were introduced to jazz through these records.

Unfortunately the only truly representative album from Mann's classic period which remains in print is *Mann at the Village Gate.* The rest of his older material is available only in compilations and shoddy repackagings. Check cutout bins for classics such as *Flautista, The Common Ground, Brazil Blues* and *Standing Ovation at Newport.*

Mann's late Sixties and Seventies attempts at contemporizing his material are less convincing, although at several points he locks into an exceptional R&B groove with the right supporting musicans. The best record from this period, *Memphis Underground,* is by far Mann's best-selling record and thus remains in print. Using guitarist Larry Coryell, vibraphonist Roy Ayers and a Memphis rhythm section, Mann put together a steamy groove that provided a link between jazz, R&B and some rock elements. The title track also became a hit single.

Mann's subsequent albums, often featuring the best studio musicians working out of New York, have been technically proficient and completely uninteresting. Titles like *Reggae* and *Discotheque* indicate the shallowness of Mann's attempts to stereotype these styles to his advantage, and it all ends up looking like he was casting around blindly, waiting for something to catch on.

One of the more interesting Seventies albums, *Push Push,* featured a guest appearance by Duane Allman on slide guitar, but that record is out of print. — J.S.

PAT MARTINO
★★★ **Consciousness / Muse 5039**
★★★ **Footprints / Muse 5096**
★★ **Joyous Lake / War. B-2977**
★★★★ **Live! / Muse 5026**
★★ **Starbright / War. B-2921**
★★★ **We'll Be Together Again / Muse 5090**

An excellent dark-toned jazz guitar player, Martino has also been a recording artist of such consistent quality it's hard for me to be critical. His five albums for Prestige (1967-72) start the skein; though all are out of print, they're worth looking for. On all those albums, Martino plays as much guitar—in long, supple, rich, lightning-fast lines—as is humanly possible. *Live!,* which is similar to the Prestige LPs, may be his best album in print. Its tunes are each over ten minutes long—giving the guitarist plenty of room to roll, regroup (usually by quoting from "The Flight of the Bumblebee"), and roll some more.

However, Martino's other Muse albums are really no less extensive, even though they show his slower, quieter and more conceptual side. *Consciousness* has a slight emphasis on Martino essaying solo ballads; *Footprints* is a varied tribute to Wes Montgomery's playing, and *Together Again* features soft duets with pianist Gil Goldstein.

After signing with Warner Brothers in 1976, Martino fit his oft-cooking, oft-somber nature into fusion. So even though *Starbright* is often as moody as *Baiyina* (out of print) and *Joyous Lake* sometimes soars like *Live!,* both newer albums use keyboard vamps aplenty, sometimes within a totally synthesized atmosphere. And both lose a star—because sometimes the bow to fusion seems too much like concession. — M.R.

HARVEY MASON
★★ **Earth Mover / Ari. 4096**
★★ **Funk in a Mason Jar / Ari. 4157**
★★ **Marching in the Street / Ari. 4054**

A top L.A. studio drummer, Mason was Herbie Hancock's pulse for the hit LP *Head Hunters.* His own albums are so-so. The first features many of Hancock's mid-Seventies bandmates playing Seventies mainstream, mildly electric jazz, instead of funk. Trouble is, they're joined by too many of Mason's studio buddies, who put an enervating gloss on everything. *Earth*

Mover's more commercial, eclectic (ranging from Blackbyrds-type stuff to a drum-keyboard duel with Jan Hammer) and energetic. — M.R.

BENNIE MAUPIN
★★★ **Slow Traffic to the Right / Mer. SRM 1-1148**
★★★★ **The Jewel in the Lotus / ECM/ Poly. 1043**

A sideman on many other LPs, including *Bitches Brew* and all of Herbie Hancock's electric sides, reedman Maupin's played ostinato funk and modal jazz with great emotion and facility. His *Jewel,* a 1974 release, is broodingly lyrical, an album of beautiful nuance; *Slow* is more commercial, but no less praiseworthy, setting steady grooves off against spacey soloing and melodies. Both albums feature Maupin's tunes and top sidemen. — M.R.

LES McCANN
★★ **Another Beginning / Atco 1666**
★★★ **Change, Change, Change / Imp. 9333**
★★ **Hustle to Survive / Atco. 1679**
★★ **Invitation to Openness / Atco 1603**
★★ **Layers / Atco 1646**
★★★ **Live at Montreux / Atco 2-312**
★★ **Live at Shelley's Manne Hole / Trip 5576**
★★★ **Live at the Bohemian Caverns, Washington, D.C. / Trip 5597**
★★ **Music Lets Me Be / Imp. 9329**
★★★ **Second Movement / Atco 1583**
★★★ **Stormy Monday / Cap. SM-1714**
★★★★ **Swiss Movement / Atco 1537**
★★ **The Man / A&M 4718**

Simplicity is the key word to use to describe McCann, used equally by his supporters and his critics. The sparseness and clap-along features of his hit "Compared to

What" have been reproduced numerous times, but never to the same effect. Almost his entire career can be seen as a footnote to that one cut and the album *Swiss Movement*.

Many of McCann's gospel and funk-based jazz ideas have been used far more successfully by Stanley Turrentine, Grover Washington, Donny Hathaway and Roberta Flack. On the now-deleted *Comment,* McCann's most interesting album, several luminaries-to-be cropped up—Flack (a discovery of his), Billy Cobham and Ashford and Simpson. Most of McCann's other albums tend to be either all instrumental or all vocal, but in both cases the result is awkward and uncomfortable. Individual cuts work—especially "Morning Song" on *Another Beginning* and "What's Goin' On" on *Invitation to Openness*—but these are exceptions in an unending stream of mediocre material and arrangements. — R.G.

JACK McDUFF

★★★ **Cookin' Together / Prest. 7325**
★★★ **George Benson/Jack McDuff /**
Prest. 24072
★ **Magnetic Feel / Cadet 60039**
★★ **Natural Thing / Cadet 812**
★★★★ **Rock Candy / Prest. 24013**

Like many of the big-name organists of the Sixties, Jack McDuff took up the instrument after Jimmy Smith's explosive ascendance. While Smith wowed audiences with his machine-gun assaults, McDuff favored sparser blues and gospel lines, giving his music a real country-soul flavor. McDuff's best work was on Prestige, where his material centered around blues, ballads and shuffles. With the advent of the synthesizer, the B-3 organ has become an anachronism and like many of the instrument's players, Jack McDuff has switched to the synthesizer on record, with predictably disastrous results. — J. MCE.

JIMMY McGRIFF

★★★ **Black and Blues / G.M. GM-2203**
★★★★ **Fly Dude / G.M. GM-509**
★★★★ **Flyin' Time / G.M. GM-4403 (reissue of GM-506 and GM-509)**
★★★★ **Giants of the Organ in Concert (with Richard "Groove" Holmes) / G.M. GM-3300**
★★ **Groove Grease / G.M. GM-503**
★★★★ **Supa Cookin' / G.M. GM-4409 (reissue of GM-520 and two sides of GM-3300)**

To make good jazz on the Hammond B-3, you play melody and improvisation on the organ's top keyboard while riding a contrapuntal bass line on the bottom one. The result: either the punchy bass just hovers behind, and snaps at, the lighter melody, or the upper-register, wailing melody contrasts with the rock-solid bass line. The formula may sound complex, but it's really classic in its simplicity, and Jimmy McGriff and a handful of other organists have it *down*.

A few of McGriff's records, in fact, are among the finest jazz organ LPs ever made. *Fly Dude,* featuring George Freeman on guitar and Ronald Arnold on tenor, is simple and cooking blues riffing off McGriff originals and a few jazz standards—an absolutely tight example of the genre save for one track, a commercialized atrocity called "Butterfly." McGriff's two collaborations with Richard "Groove" Holmes are almost as good; *In Concert,* recorded live at Boston's Paul's Mall, is especially stretched out and exciting. And *Black and Blues,* when it sticks to what its title suggests, is also nice 'n' basic.

Otherwise, the organist has had to "funk up" his art, ostensibly to avoid starving to death. Thing is, McGriff isn't musically sophisticated enough to commercialize compellingly. So the dismal cast of "Butterfly," something like a rabid Philly Dog, also marks many of his LPs, like *Groove Grease.*

Fans of McGriff may also know his earlier Solid State LPs. Though they contain a few nice moments, they're mostly too orchestrated and dated, and apparently heading out of print, anyway. — M.R.

JOHN McLAUGHLIN

★★★ **Apocalypse / Col. KC-32957**
★★★ **Between Nothingness and Eternity / Col. C-32766**
★★★★ **Birds of Fire / Col. PC-31996**
★★★ **Extrapolation / Poly. 1-6074**
★★★ **Handful of Beauty / Col. PC-34372**
★★★ **Inner Worlds / Col. PC-33908**
★★★ **Love, Devotion, Surrender / Col. PC-32034**
★★★ **Natural Elements / Col. JC-34980**
★★★ **Shakti / Col. PC-34162**
★★★★ **The Inner Mounting Flame / Col. PC-31067**
★★★ **Visions of the Emerald Beyond / Col. PC-33411**

John McLaughlin is among the most influential guitarists of the Seventies, but this is due less to his solo work, which has a sameness and lack of drive, than to his roles as leader of Mahavishnu Orchestra, the first popular jazz-rock fusion band, and as a sideman on Miles Davis' *In a Silent Way* and with Tony Williams' Lifetime.

McLaughlin was a staple figure on the traditional jazz scene in England from the early Sixties (the Polydor album is a relic of that era). But it was not until he joined Davis in 1969 and began to experiment with pulsating, heavily chorded electric guitar passages that he began to achieve an influential style. His first solo LP, 1971's *Devotion* (Douglas, deleted), was a post-Hendrix tour de force of guitar, with crashing accompaniment provided by Buddy Miles and Larry Young. This set the basic focus for his work with Williams' Lifetime (a band that was unfortunately never properly recorded) and with Mahavishnu Orchestra. On his own, perhaps due to his involvement with Eastern mysticism, McLaughlin's work is given to an introspective approach that is finally too bland to be as exhilarating as his work in various bands—the exceptions are *The Inner Mounting Flame, Birds of Fire* and *Love, Devotion, Surrender,* all of which are passionate. More recently, he has worked with fellow mystic Carlos Santana, who brings the heat of Latin salsa to the collaboration, and with Shakti, a band that attempts to fuse jazz rock with Indian devotional music, with similarly mixed results. — D.M.

THE BEST OF JOHN FAHEY

1959 ~ 1977

JACKIE McLEAN
★★★ Lights Out / Prest. 7757
★★ Strange Blues / Prest. 7500
★★★ Two Sides of Jackie McLean / Trip 2-5040E

Alto saxophonist McLean (b. 1932) recorded early and for a time quite often, thanks to encouragement from Bud Powell, Miles Davis and Charlie Parker; these albums (1955-57) reveal a clearly developed personality, particularly with the acid tone and vocalized inflections, often ignored amidst the tendency to label any alto player of the period a Parker imitator. The Trip album is notable for McLean's first session under his own name, with Donald Byrd and Mal Waldron, which contains his excellent composition "Little Melonae"; *Lights Out,* with Byrd again and the fine pianist Elmo Hope, is a typical blowing session of the era, built around "I Got Rhythm" chord changes and the blues; "Inding," however, has a more serpentine melodic line that would become known as "Quadrangle" during McLean's more adventurous period.

★★★★ Bluesnik / Blue N. 84067
★★★ 'Bout Soul / Blue N. 84284
★★★ Demon's Dance / Blue N. 84345
★★★★★ Destination Out / Blue N. 84165
★★★★ Jacknife / Blue N. 2-LA457-H2
★★★★★ Let Freedom Ring / Blue N. 84106
★★★★★ One Step Beyond / Blue N. 84137

Drug problems both active and passive (ex-offenders could not get a cabaret card, and thus could not work in New York nightclubs) limited McLean's activity in the Sixties. At decade's end he had stopped performing altogether, but his Blue Note albums (1962-67) contain his finest work. *Let Freedom Ring* is the breakthrough album, where McLean reconciles his bop roots with the newer influence of Ornette Coleman and the rest of what at the time was called "the new thing." As an example of compositional solo and group achievement, the album is a masterpiece.

One Step Beyond and *Destination Out* are equally essential, for McLean moves beyond the alto-plus-piano-trio format with an inspired quintet blend of his sax plus trombone (Grachan Moncur III, who shared composing duties), vibes (Bobby Hutcherson), bass and drums. *One Step,* the more fiery of the pair, is also the recording debut of drummer Tony Williams, whom McLean brought to New York from Boston at the age of seventeen. The other albums from this period have more standard formats and feature the premier modern mainstream trumpets of the era—Freddie Hubbard, Lee Morgan, Charles Tolliver and Woody Shaw.

★★★★ Antiquity (with Michael Carvin) / Inner 2028
★★★ Ghetto Baby / Inner 2013
★★★★ Live at Montmartre / Inner 2001
★★★ New York Calling / Inner 2023

★★★ Ode Super (with Gary Bartz) / Inner 2009
★★★ The Meeting (with Dexter Gordon) / Inner 2006
★★★★★ The Source (with Dexter Gordon) / Inner 2020

From 1972 to 1974, McLean renewed his recording career for the Danish Steeple-Chase label (the albums are now available on Inner City in the United States). The searing intensity and urgent rhythmic thrust are still present, particularly on side one of *Live at Montmartre* and *The Source,* with the altoist rising to the heady challenge of Dexter Gordon's tenor on the latter. *Antiquity,* a series of duets with percussionist Michael Carvin, is the imaginative album programmatically, while *New York Calling* documents the Cosmic Brotherhood, a young sextet McLean led that featured his son René on tenor and soprano sax and is particularly impresssive on the title piece. McLean now lives in Hartford, Connecticut, where he teaches and is deeply involved in Afro-American cultural activities.   — B.B.

PAT METHENY
★★★★ Bright Size Life / ECM/Poly. 1073
★★★ Watercolors / ECM/Poly. 1-1097

Pat Metheny (b. 1954) is the most refreshing guitarist to appear in recent years; with his full, warm tone, comprehensive yet unobtrusive technique and preference for direct melodicism and harmonic sophistication, he has returned to pre-jazz-rock verities in a contemporary context. His 1975 debut, *Bright Size Life,* benefits from the excellent support of Jaco Pastorius and Bob Moses, plus a well-balanced program. *Watercolors* was made shortly before Metheny left Gary Burton's quartet and covers much the same ground with less stimulat-

ing accompanists; the guitar playing remains convincing but doesn't deliver the expected step forward. Metheny is young, however, and will have much more to say.   — B.B.

CHARLES MINGUS
Bassist, composer, arranger, leader, author, sometimes pianist and vocalist Mingus (1922-1979) was one of the best-documented musicians in jazz with justification—he was one of the greatest. His relatively lesser known albums all bubbled over with intensity, his triumphs were sublime, and the following ratings are assigned with that in mind.
★★★★ Charles Mingus / Prest. 24010 (available singly as Chaz / Fan. 86002E and Quintet Plus Max Roach / Fan. 86009E)
★★★★ The Best of Charles Mingus / Atl. 1555
★★★★ Trio and Sextet / Trip X-5040

Mingus' first recordings as a leader show a rapid evolution toward greater power and cacophonous latitude for his sidemen with a constant personal stamp that uniquely drew on Ellington, black church music and modern European composers. The Trip album collects early (1954) compositions with great stress on the writing, European influences (the sextet features a cello) and early Thad Jones trumpet; the second half of the double album is a relaxed trio session from three years later with Hampton Hawes and Dannie Richmond (the latter also available as *Mingus Moods,* Trip 5017E). The Prestige twofer from 1955 is a looser though still carefully structured club recording with a quintet, revealing Mingus' sonic preference of the era (trombone and tenor sax, no trumpet). Max Roach drums on three of the tracks. *Best of* has the only available track by Mingus' excellent 1956 quintet with Jackie McLean on alto, J. R. Monterose on tenor and Mal Waldron on piano—the cataclysmic "Pithecanthropus Erectus."
★★★★★ Better Git It in Your Soul / Col. CG-30628 (contains Mingus Ah Um / Col. CS-8171)
★★★★★ Tijuana Moods / RCA APL1-0939
★★★★★ Wonderland / U. Artists 5637

In 1957, Mingus took a rhythm & blues tenor saxophonist named Dannie Richmond and, by his own account, taught him drums because he couldn't find another drummer besides Elvin Jones with whom he liked working. The Mingus/Richmond rhythm section, which has been intact with only occasional interruption ever since, ushered in the great Mingus era. Master-pieces from the 1957–59 period include "Haitian Fight Song" and "Wednesday Night Prayer Meeting," a bass and church-jazz tour de force respectively, on *Best of*; the whole of *Tijuana*, but especially "Ysa-bel's Table Dance"; the blowing tracks on *Wonderland* that pit John Handy's alto against Booker Ervin's tenor; and such var-ied gems from *Better Git It* as the title piece, the pensive Lester Young eulogy "Goodbye Pork Pie Hat," the pointedly evocative "Fables of Faubus," the abstract "Diane" and "Far Wells, Mill Valley," and such personal acknowledgements of sources as "Jelly Roll," "Open Letter to Duke," "Song with Orange" and "Self-Por-trait in Three Colors." Ervin, Richmond and trombonist Jimmy Knepper are in-valuable collaborators.

★★★★ **Mingus, Mingus, Mingus, Mingus, Mingus** / Imp. 54
★★★★★ **Mingus Revisited** / Trip 5513
★★★★★ **Stormy Weather** / Barn. 6015
★★★★★ **The Great Concert of Charles Mingus** / Prest. 34001
★★★★★ **Town Hall Concert** / Fan. JWS-9
★★★ **Town Hall Concert** / Solid St. 18024

Eric Dolphy worked with Mingus fre-quently between 1960 and the reed giant's death in 1964, and sparks flew at every en-counter. *Stormy Weather,* from early in the period and with the stunning quartet com-pleted by Richmond and trumpeter Ted Curson, contains several of their master-pieces (the version of "Original Faubus Fables," with lyrics, makes an interesting comparison with the more picturesque one done for Columbia the previous year). *Great Concert,* a three-record set, and the Fantasy *Town Hall* album feature the group that traveled to Europe, where Dol-phy died: Mingus, Dolphy, Richmond, Clifford Jordan on tenor, pianist Jaki Byard and trumpeter Johnny Coles. This is perhaps Mingus' best band.

Also, it was in this period Mingus began recording with expanded personnel: Dol-phy is heard on *Revisited,* the *Town Hall Concert* and the Impulse *Mingus, Mingus.* The Trip album, from 1960, is the most fas-cinating, as it features early Mingus or-chestrations such as the ambitious, quasi-classical "Half-Mast Inhibitions."

★★★★ **Mingus at Monterey** / Fan. JWS 1/2
★★★ **Mingus Plays Piano** / Imp. 60

★★★ **My Favorite Quintet** / Fan. JWS-5
★★★★★ **Right Now** / Fan. 86017
★★★★★ **The Black Saint and the Sinner Lady** / Imp. A-35

Mingus made equally important music without Dolphy during the Sixties, until his temporary withdrawal from the scene at the end of 1966. *Black Saint,* from 1962, is one of his most ambitious and best-real-ized works; an album-length exorcism of personal demons with a strong ten-piece band in which Charlie Mariano's alto stands out. While the 1965 Monterey Festi-val performance of "Meditations on Inte-grations" (also known as "Meditations on a Pair of Wire Cutters") has attained legend-ary status, I prefer the quartet version on *Right Now,* with tenor saxophonist Clifford Jordan outdoing himself.

★★★★★ **Changes One** / Atl. 1677
★★★★ **Changes Two** / Atl. 1678
★★★★★ **Charles Mingus and Friends in Concert** / Col. KG-31614
★★★★★ **Let My Children Hear Music** / Col. C-31039
★★★ **Mingus at Carnegie Hall** / Atl. 1667
★★★ **Mingus Moves** / Atl. 1653
★★★★ **Reincarnation of a Lovebird** / Prest. 24028
★★★ **Three or Four Shades of Blues** / Atco 1700

While Mingus was inconsistent in the Sev-enties, his best music of the period clearly ranked with the best of his career. This would include *Let My Children,* a wide-ranging orchestral recital, and the fertile *Changes* albums by a working quintet which included George Adams on tenor, Don Pullen on piano and of course Rich-mond. The loose *And Friends* record is rec-ommended for some of tenor saxophonist Gene Ammons' best recorded work. — B.B.

ROSCOE MITCHELL
★★★★★ **Congliptious** / Nessa 2
★★★★★ **Old/Quartet** / Nessa 5
★★★ **Roscoe Mitchell Quartet** / Sack. 2009
★★★★★ **Sound** / Del. DS-408
★★★★ **The Roscoe Mitchell Solo Saxophone Concerts** / Sack. 2006

Others will disagree, but I'd call Roscoe Mitchell the most important voice to emerge from Chicago's Association for the Advancement of Creative Musicians (AACM). As a composer, he developed the spontaneous group form that his Art En-semble (later called the Art Ensemble of Chicago) offered as an alternative to the endless blowout, and Mitchell's solo playing, primarily on alto sax, is among the most gripping experiences in the new music.

His 1966 debut, *Sound,* introduced the AACM to the world. Sololess performances, extended unaccompanied solos, sparing use of instruments and virtuoso performers (Lester Bowie, trumpet, and Malachi Favors, bass, would go on to collaborate with Mitchell in the Art Ensemble) abound.

Congliptious has a side of one solo piece each by Mitchell, Bowie and Favors, plus one of their best group performances, with drummer Robert Crowder added. Even better is *Old/Quartet,* recorded in 1967 before drummer Phillip Wilson left to join Paul Butterfield but only released in 1975. This is the best Mitchell sampler, with a solo, a free group form and homage to gutbucket funk.

Canada's Sackville label also has *The Roscoe Mitchell Solo Saxophone Concerts;* if you like such things, his tone and rhythm cut Braxton's. *Roscoe Mitchell Quartet* is only half quartet, and those pieces don't come off. Trombonist George Lewis duets with Mitchell and plays solo on the more interesting remainder of the album. — B.B.

MODERN JAZZ QUARTET

★★★★★ Best of the Modern Jazz Quartet / Atl. 1546
★★★★ Blues at Carnegie Hall / Atl. 1468
★★★ Blues on Bach / Atl. 1652
★★★★ Collaboration (with Laurindo Almeida) / Atl. 1429
★★★★★ European Concert / Atl. 2-603
★★★★★ Fontessa / Atl. 1231
★★★ In Memoriam / Li. Dav. 3001
★★★★ Last Concert / Atl. 2-909
★★★★★ Modern Jazz Quartet / Atl. 1265
★★★★★ Modern Jazz Quartet / Prest. 24005 (contains all material heard in Classics / Prest. 7425E; First Recordings / Prest. 7749E; MJQ Plays for Lovers / Prest. 7421E)
★★★★★ One Never Knows / Atl. 1284
★★★ Porgy and Bess / Atl. 1440
★★★★★ Pyramid / Atl. 1325
★★★★★ The Art of the Modern Jazz Quartet / Atl. 2-301
★★★ The Legendary Profile / Atl. 1623
★★★★ Third Stream Music / Atl. 1345

The MJQ began its life as the rhythm section of Dizzy Gillespie's 1946 big band, with pianist/composer John Lewis, vibraharpist Milt Jackson, bassist Ray Brown and drummer Kenny Clarke. The four worked and recorded together in various groups over the next five years; when they finally formed their cooperative band in 1952 under the musical direction of Lewis—and first used the name Modern Jazz Quartet—Brown had been replaced by another Gillespie alumnus, bassist Percy Heath.

The Prestige *Modern Jazz Quartet* twofer contains the band's 1952-55 work and highlights its most notable traits: the improvising prowess of Jackson on all types of material, but especially ballads ("Gershwin Medley," "Autumn in New York") and blues ("Ralph's New Blues"); Lewis' simple, optimistic piano, his conversational accompaniment, and compositions steeped in European counterpoint ("Concorde," "Vendome") as well as the blues, and such exquisite original forms as "Django"; and the superlative rhythm support of Heath, Clarke and drummer Connie Kay—the latter came on in 1955 to replace Clarke, who reportedly was uninterested in Lewis' baroque proclivities.

Kay's uncommonly subdued and sensitive drumming ushered in the MJQ's finest period, from 1956 to 60, when all of the above Atlantic albums with 1200 and 1300 catalogue numbers were recorded as well as the near-perfect *European Concert.* Among the quartet's greatest achievements are *Fontessa,* a well-balanced program with a fugue, a be-bop tune, three magnificent Jackson ballad solos, "Bluesology" and Lewis' lovely "Fontessa Suite"; *One Never Knows,* Lewis' film score for Roger Vadim's *No Sun in Venice,* with the joyous "Golden Striker"; and *Pyramid;* but it is the two-record *European Concert* that best summarizes the quiet power of the MJQ in fifteen of their most representative pieces.

Third Stream Music, also from 1960, finds Lewis in his most overt attempt to blend classical and jazz sources. Jimmy Giuffre's trio, a chamber quintet and a string quartet join the MJQ for five performances that, while modestly successful, serve as little more than an historic footnote to an unnaturally forced experiment. (Much of the great work from this period can be sampled in two Atlantic collections, *Best of* and the more comprehensive *Art of the MJQ.*)

After 1960, the MJQ became more and more predictable as Lewis produced fewer interesting compositions. The only albums from the decade still in print are the *Porgy and Bess* collection, a more spirited *Blues at Carnegie Hall* and some welcome variety in the form of *Collaboration* with acoustic guitarist Laurindo Almeida. This last has the best of three MJQ versions of the adagio from Rodrigo's *Concierto de Aranjuez* which Miles Davis recorded on *Sketches of Spain.*

Winding down to the disbanding of the group in late 1974 are albums where the strains of overfamiliarity become obvious. Lewis (as both writer and pianist) and Kay are both noticeably below their earlier peaks, and even the reliable Jackson can't shake the rut. A retreat to more classicism, in the form of Bach chorales and the orchestral *In Memoriam,* was a nonanswer to the problem of a group (and, more particularly, of a sensitivity embodied by John Lewis) that had outlived its time. But the MJQ went out wailing in a superb Carnegie Hall concert that carried the bite of a quarter-century's music-making. Several critics called *Last Concert* the MJQ's finest album, and while I don't feel it comes up to their earlier Atlantics, it definitely deserves its reputation as the final achievement in a career filled with much great music. — B.B.

THELONIOUS MONK
★★★★★ **The Complete Genius / Blue N. LA579-H2**
★★★ **Thelonious Monk / GNP 9008**
★★★★★ **Thelonious Monk / Prest. 24006**
That overworked term "genius" applies to pianist/composer Monk (b. 1917), a modern pioneer whose iconoclastic approach to complex harmony, space, rhythmic irregularity, melodic angularity and thematically centered improvisation created a thoroughly personal musical universe that inspired all of the most daring post-Parker musicians. Many of his recordings are cur-

rently available in more than one issue; the present list attempts to avoid duplication.

Complete Genius is all of his 1947-52 Blue Note work, with several classic compositions ("Round Midnight," "Criss Cross," "Misterioso," "Monk's Mood," etc.), and assists from Art Blakey, Milt Jackson, Max Roach, Kenny Dorham and Sahib Shibab. The Prestiger twofer summarizes his period with that label (1952-4), where he worked with trios and quintets. Tenor players Sonny Rollins and Frank Foster are impressive, and the Monk–Percy Heath–Art Blakey threesome is his perfect trio. The GNP, which is also available on Trip, is a solid solo effort.
★★★★★ **Brilliance / Mile. 47023**
★★★★ **In Person / Mile. 47033**
★★★★★ **Misterioso / Riv. 6119**
★★★★★ **Pure Monk / Trip X-5022**
★★★★★ **Thelonious in Action / Riv. 6102**
★★★★★ **Thelonious Monk and John Coltrane / Mile. 47011**
★★★★ **Thelonious Monk Meets Gerry Mulligan / Riv. 6107**
★★★ **Thelonious Monk Plays Duke Ellington / Riv. 6039-M**
★★★★ **The Unique Thelonious Monk / Riv. 6068M**
Monk's Riverside years, 1955-60, found the jazz public slowly catching up to his music. Of the top-rated albums above, *Pure Monk* collects all of his solo work from the period, easily his best unaccompanied performances; *Brilliance* features his two best quintet dates, one with Rollins and Roach featured, the other containing the inspired front line of Thad Jones' cornet and Charlie Rouse's tenor; *Monk/Coltrane* has the only tracks by the legendary 1957 Monk quartet with Coltrane, bassist Wilbur Ware and drummer Shadow Wilson, plus a quirky septet from the same year with Coltrane, Ware, Blakey and Coleman Hawkins; and *In Person* and *Misterioso* are live recordings by the underrated 1958 quartet of Johnny Griffin (tenor sax), Ahmed Abdul Malik (bass) and Roy Haynes (drums). *In Person* is also notable for the 1959 Town Hall concert by a large group playing Hall Overton arrangements of Monk pieces.
★★★★ **Criss-Cross / CSP JCS-8838**
★★★★ **It's Monk's Time / Col. CS-8984**
★★★★ **Misterioso / Col. CS-9216**
★★★ **Monk / Col. CS-9091**
★★★★ **Monk's Dream / CSP JCS-8765**
★★★ **Solo / Col. CS-9149**
★★★ **Straight No Chaser / Col. CS-9451**
★★★★ **Underground / Col. CS-9632**

★★★ **Who's Afraid of Big Bad Monk /**
Col. PG-32892
Monk's Columbia years, 1962–68, found
him primarily confined to the quartet format (with Rouse as horn soloist) and reworking his earlier triumphs in lesser versions. While the playing is consistently
good, the setting is predictable and both
Monk and especially Rouse occasionally
sound tired. *Who's Afraid* combines Monk's
two orchestral efforts of the time, a brilliant Philharmonic Hall concert and a ludicrous studio date with Oliver Nelson
charts.
★★★★ **Something in Blue / Black L. 152**
★★★★ **The Man I Love / Black L. 197**
While hardly the best Monk, these 1971
trios are valuable for reuniting the pianist
with his perfect accompanist, Art Blakey,
and demonstrating that the genius can still
play. — B.B.

WES MONTGOMERY
★★★★ **Beginnings / Blue N. LA531-H2**
★★★★ **Movin' / Mile. 47040**
★★★★★ **Small Group Recordings / Verve**
VE-2-2513
Belatedly discovered at the age of thirty-
four by Cannonball Adderley, Wes Montgomery (1925–1968) left his hometown of
Indianapolis for the West Coast and subsequently created a body of work that easily
established him as the most influential jazz
guitarist of the Fifties and Sixties. A thoroughly schooled player—he'd learned all of
Charlie Christian's solos note for note—
Montgomery immediately demonstrated a
fluid single-note style brilliantly interfaced
with a subtle use of chords. But Montgomery's signature sound was his phenomenal
octave technique (presumably developed
for a quieter sound so he wouldn't disturb
the neighbors when practicing), a device

first pioneered by Django Reinhardt.
Montgomery took this difficult-to-control
technique further than any other guitarist,
with the possible exception of George Benson, a modern apostle of Montgomery.
  Beginnings covers the late Indianapolis–early California period when Montgomery's style was rapidly solidifying. Although the Christian influence is still
strong on seminal tracks like "Bock to
Bock" and "Billie's Bounce," his dazzling
technique emerges on the instrumental
showpiece "Finger Pickin'," a recording
credited as having totally intimidated many
of Montgomery's contemporaries. Using
the competent if unspectacular talents of
his brothers Buddy (keyboards) and Monk
(bass) on most of these L.A. sessions,
Montgomery hits a high point in his collaboration with the underrated tenor sax
player Harold Land on tunes like "Old
Folks," "Leila," and "Wes' Tune." At this
point, Montgomery was concentrating on
his single note and chord work, and he
used octaves sparingly. As his records became more and more overproduced in the
latter part of his career, he would lean
more heavily on this effect.
  Small Group Recordings and *Movin'* preserve what is arguably Montgomery's most
focused work. The former captures a series
of stirring live performances at the old
Half Note with Montgomery sympathetically backed by the Wynton Kelly Trio.
His deep, warm tone—he played with his
thumb, not a pick—graces stunning versions of "Misty," "Portrait of Jennie" and
"Willow Weep for Me," songs that would
be massacred by saccharine orchestrations
on later Verve releases. His relaxed encounter with organist Jimmy Smith on side
four shows why the organ-guitar combo
was such a popular facet of the Fifties.
Movin' recaps Californian sessions with
producer Orrin Keepnews, in which Montgomery continues to refine his sound.
★★★ **Best of—Vol. 1 / Verve 6-8714**
★★★ **Bumpin' / Verve 6-8625**
★★ **Day in the Life / A&M 3001**
★★ **Down Here on the Ground / A&M**
3006
★★ **Greatest Hits / A&M 4247**
★★ **Return Engagement / Verve**
V3HB-8839
★★ **Road Song / A&M 3012**
In the waning stages of Montgomery's ten-
ure with Verve, Creed Taylor took charge
of his career and guided him in a pop
MOR direction that brought Wes a lot of
money and recognition while causing jazz

guitar enthusiasts untold pain. These recordings are not so much grouped together
for chronology as they are a representative
sampling of a downward trend in Montgomery's musical contribution. The late
Verve recordings and the A&M material
are characterized by a predominance of
cotton-soft octaves gently nudging up to
generally abysmal arrangements of chart
songs. The graphics of the A&M recordings are spectacular, but Montgomery
sounds weary and resigned. His tragic
death at the age of forty-three rendered the
question of his return to "straight jazz"
academic. — J.C.C.

Warren Zevon

LEE MORGAN
★★★ A-1 with Hank Mobley / Savoy
1104
★★★★ LeeWay / Blue N. 84034
★★★★ The Cooker / Blue N. 81-578
★★★ Two Sides of Lee Morgan / Trip
X-5003 (same as Lee Morgan / GNP
2-2074)
By 1956, trumpeter Morgan (1938-1972)
was taking featured solos in Dizzy Gillespie's Big Band and participating actively in
New York studio blowing sessions as
leader and sideman. The albums above
were made prior to 1961, when Morgan
temporarily dropped out and returned to
his native Philadelphia.
   Even at this early stage, Morgan's
brashly bright tone, crackling delivery, harmonic imagination and effective use of
smears, half-valving and other expressive
effects made him a major soloist. While his
albums are dismissed by some as merely
casual sessions, they are filled with swing
and passion, especially *The Cooker* (with
Pepper Adams, Bobby Timmons, Paul
Chambers, Philly Joe Jones) and *LeeWay*
(Jackie McLean, Timmons, Chambers, and

Morgan's employer, Art Blakey).
★★★★★ Cornbread / Blue N. 84222
★★★ Lee Morgan / Blue N. 84901
★★★★ Lee Morgan Memorial Album /
Blue N. LA224-G
★★★★ Live at the Lighthouse / Blue N.
89906
★★★★★ Search for the New Land / Blue
N. 84169
★★★★ The Gigolo / Blue N. 84212
★★★★ The Rumproller / Blue N. 84199
★★★★ The Sidewinder / Blue N. 84157
★★★ The Sixth Sense / Blue N. 84335
From his return in 1963 until the end of
his life (he was shot on a New York club
job by his long-time female companion),
Morgan continued to champion the post-
bop verities in work with all of the old ex-
citement plus added depth and eloquence.
Some of his albums may fail to reach their
potential, but all are satisfying. I would
single out *The Sidewinder,* Morgan's "comeback" album, with the title tune which was
his only commercial success; *Search for the
New Land,* with a sextet including Wayne
Shorter, Herbie Hancock and Billy Higgins, for its dramatic and far more substantial title piece; *Cornbread,* a hard-bop delight featuring McLean, Mobley and
Hancock, plus the exquisite "Ceora"; and
the intense Lighthouse double album with
Benny Maupin, Harold Mabern, Jymie
Merritt and Mickey Roker. Other live albums, not listed, may be bootlegs. — B.B.

JELLY ROLL MORTON
★★★★★ Jelly Roll Morton 1923-24 /
Mile. 47018
★★★★★ New Orleans Rhythm Kings /
Mile. 47020
★★★ Transcriptions for Orchestra / Col.
M-32587
One of the great disgraces in current jazz
discography is the unavailability in the
U.S. of the essential Red Hot Peppers recordings of Ferdinand Joseph La Menthe,
a.k.a. Jelly Roll Morton (1885-1941). The
virtual incarnation of New Orleans sporting life, and the subject of Alan Lomax's
biography *Mister Jelly Roll,* Morton
claimed to have invented jazz in 1902;
without question he was a brilliant pianist,
composer and arranger whose feeling for
improvisation, blues tonality and a more
relaxed, swinging sense of rhythm helped
move black music from ragtime and other
early sources to jazz.
   Jelly Roll Morton 1923-24, with all of his
early piano solos, is the best currently

available set (part of it is also available on Milestone 2003); he can also be heard with the *New Orleans Rhythm Kings,* the best white group from Morton's hometown. Some piano rolls from the Twenties are available on Biograph 1004Q and Trip 1; the out-of-print Red Hot Pepper material, a model of the traditional ensemble approach, is in the vaults of RCA, but can be obtained as an import on the Black and White label.

In *Transcriptions for Orchestra,* arranger/pianist Dick Hyman attempts to cash in on the Joplin craze by revamping Jelly for those who think any black composer who wrote before the Depression wrote only ragtime. — B.B.

ALPHONSE MOUZON
- **Funky Snakefoot / Blue N. LA222-G**
- **Mind Transplant / Blue N. LA398-G**
- **★★★ The Essence of Mystery / Blue N. LA059-F**
- **★★ The Man Incognito / Blue N. LA584-G**

Mouzon built up a reputation as a creative musician when he was McCoy Tyner's drummer in the early Seventies; then he moved on to play powerhouse fusion with Larry Coryell. But so far, a comparably notable solo artist he ain't. His debut LP, *Essence,* was pretty promising; a distinctive agenda of modal-tinged easy-listening jazz and catchy R&B, it featured some nice soprano sax from Buddy Terry and some respectably commercial vocals from Mouzon. Then began a two-album slide. *Incognito,* his fourth album, at least has searing George Duke synthesizer work and a couple of lyrical Mouzon charts. — M.R.

IDRIS MUHAMMAD
- **★★ Black Rhythm Revolution / Prest. 10005**
- **★★ Peace and Rhythm / Prest. 10036**
- **★★★ Power of Soul / Kudu 17**
- **★★ Turn This Mutha Out / Kudu 34**
- **★★ You Talk That Talk / Prest. 10019**

Versatile percussionist is generally more accomplished as a sideman than as a leader (check out his long drum duet with Ralph MacDonald on *The Path*), but does not disgrace himself on these efforts. *Power of Soul* is his most accessible and coherent session. — J.S.

MILTON NASCIMENTO
★★★★ Milton / A&M 4611

A strong, commercially minded 1977 American debut album from one of Brazil's most respected keyboardists and songwriters. Nascimento was featured on saxophonist Wayne Shorter's *Native Dancer* album, and here Shorter returns the favor, adding his graceful playing presence to the session. — J.S.

THEODORE "FATS" NAVARRO
- **★★★★ Fat Girl / Savoy SJL-2216**
- **★★★★ Fats Navarro Featured with the Tadd Dameron Band / Mile. 47041**
- **★★★★★ Prime Source / Blue N. LA507-H2**

Theodore "Fats" Navarro (1923–1950), whose long-lined and nearly impeccable middle-register approach offered the first successful modern trumpet alternative to Dizzy Gillespie, played some stunning music before heroin and tuberculosis took him out. His formative work (1946–47) is on *Fat Girl;* some of the earlier sessions, such as an all-star date with Kenny Dorham, Sonny Stitt, Bud Powell and Kenny Clarke, are ragged, but in the quintets with pianist/arranger Tadd Dameron, Navarro's poise and creativity are beyond reproach. *Fats Navarro Featured with the Tadd Dameron Band* contains the 1948 radio broadcast "air checks" from Manhattan's Royal Roost; besides Navarro, Dameron and Clarke there is the underrated early-bop tenor of Allen Eager. *Prime Source* is best overall, from 1947 to 1949, with more Dameron groups plus a Bud Powell quintet with young Sonny Rollins. — B.B.

Paul Simon. Still crazy after all these years.

HERBIE NICHOLS
★★★★★ The Third World / Blue N. LA485-HZ

Herbie Nichols (1919–1963) is one of the supreme jazz tragedies: a thoroughly original composer and pianist who received virtually no recognition in his lifetime. Over half of his complete output is on *The Third World,* twenty-two trio tracks (1955–56) of stark yet fluent, rhythmically challenging music, with Max Roach and Art Blakey sharing percussion duty. — B.B.

JOSEPH "KING" OLIVER

★★★★★ **Immortal King Oliver / Mile. 2006**

★★★★ **King Oliver Creole Jazz Band 1923 / Olym. 7133**

★★★★★ **King Oliver's Jazz Band—1923 / Smithsonian 2001 (Album available by mail only from Smithsonian, Box 10230, Des Moines, Iowa 50336)**

Louis Armstrong credits Joseph "King" Oliver (1885–1938) as his greatest (in fact, his only) influence. Oliver was recognized as the top cornet player of his era, which began before jazz groups started recording. He earned the nickname "King" from the great Dixieland bandleader Kid Ory, who used Oliver's piercing, emotive cornet as an integral part of his tight ensemble sound. Armstrong heard Oliver in New Orleans, but it wasn't until Oliver moved to Chicago in 1918 and called for Armstrong to join his Creole Jazz Band in 1922 that they began to work together.

From 1922 to 1924, Armstrong learned the ropes at Oliver's side and the two cornetists created the hottest sound of their time, accompanied by clarinetists Johnny Dodds and Jimmie Noone (on separate dates), trombonist Honoré Dutrey, pianist Lil Hardin (who later married Armstrong), drummer Baby Dodds and several different bassists. The 1923 recordings of the Creole Jazz Band are considered one of the finest examples of small ensemble playing in jazz history. The Olympic set suffers from poor reproduction, while the Milestone and Smithsonian sets cover Oliver comprehensively and with better than average reproduction quality. — J.S.

OREGON

★★★ **Distant Hills / Van. 79341**

★★★★ **In Concert / Van. 79358**

★★★ **Music of Another Present Era / Van. 79326**

★★ **Oregon/Elvin Jones/Together / Van. 79377**

★★★ **Winter Light / Van. 79350**

Oregon is not unlike its parent group, the Paul Winter Consort, in its use of Indian percussion and classical music compositional formalities to ground a jazzlike deployment of soloing. But Oregon differs from Winter and other transnationally uto-

pian outfits in the group's refusal to explore the "cultural significance" of its musical ecumenism with lyrics or orchestral program music. And that refusal leaves lots of space on their records to pursue the fresh ideas each of the members brought to the band originally.

With the rise to prominence in the mid-Seventies of guitarist Ralph Towner, Oregon's reputation grew as its three studio albums shifted colorations and compositional emphases from Indian/Western interplay back to jazz/modernist classical interface. *In Concert* serves as a marvelous summary of their music. Their collaboration with Elvin Jones provides lots of space for the shifts, dives and bass-cymbals playoffs Jones is famous for, but there isn't much fire—just a lot of technique. — B.T.

CHARLES ("YARDBIRD") PARKER

★★★★ **Apartment Jam / Zim 1006**

★★★★★ **Bird at the Roost / Savoy 1108**

★★★ **Bird with Strings Live / Col. JC-34832**

★★★★ **Charlie Parker / Prest. 24009**

★★★★ **Charlie Parker / War. 6B-3159 (6-record set) (also available in individual volumes as Charlie Parker on Dial / Spot. 101–106, and a two-record sampler, The Very Best of Bird / War. K-3198)**

★★★★★ **Charlie Parker, Vols. 1-5 / Arc. Folk 214, 232, 254, 295, 315**

★★★★★ **Echoes of an Era (with Dizzy Gillespie) / Rou. RE-105**

★★★★★ **Encores / Savoy 1107**

★★★★★ **First Recordings / Onyx 221**

★★★★★ **Giants of Jazz / Hall 617E**

★★★★★ **One Night in Birdland / Col. JG-34808**

★★★★ **Summit Meeting at Birdland / Col. JC-34831**

★★★★ Takin' Off / Hall 620E
★★★★★ The Savoy Recordings (Master Takes) / Savoy SJL-2201
★★★★ The Verve Years, 1948-50 / Verve 2-2501
★★★★ The Verve Years, 1950-51 / Verve 2-2512
★★★ The Verve Years, 1952-54 / Verve 2-2523

Charlie Parker (1920-1955) was the leading figure of the be-bop period, an unsurpassed alto saxophonist and one of the four or five greatest figures in jazz history; he was also a cult figure at a time when advances in recording and broadcast techniques allowed a lot of bootleg material to be captured and released. Thus ferreting out Parker's discography becomes akin to working out a crossword puzzle where some of the same clues apply to different boxes. This doesn't affect the music, of course, which is almost uniformly superb.

First Recordings has one side of Jay McShann's 1940 Kansas City band, with Parker's alto sax showing the unmistakable influence of Lester Young's tenor. There is also a 1942 Harlem jam tape on "Cherokee" that is like hearing the coming era in its embryo stage.

Between 1945 and 1948, Parker made most of his great recordings for Savoy and Dial. After Bird's death, both labels issued every available alternate take along with the originally issued master, and to compound the confusion the Dial material has also appeared on numerous other labels (of varying legality). The Savoy *Master Takes* twofer has the originals of "Now's the Time," "Ko-Do," "Donna Lee," "Parker's Mood" and others, with Miles Davis, Dizzy Gillespie, Bud Powell, John Lewis and Max Roach among the members of Parker's quintets. *Encores* samples the alternate takes, which besides having different alto solos often have better efforts by Miles Davis.

The Dial material is all over the place—it pops up on the Roulette and Hall of Fame albums as well as the Warner Bros. and Spotlites. The years of Parker's Dial affiliation, 1946 to 1947, were his most productive as far as recordings go, producing "Yardbird Suite," "Ornithology," "Night in Tunisia," "Bird of Paradise," "Relaxin' at Camarillo," "Klacto-veedseds-tene," "Out of Nowhere" and "Embraceable You," among other masterpieces. The Warner Bros. six-album set is complete but expensive and poorly annotated; their *Very Best* sampler also gives inadequate information

and includes seven alternate takes. The Spotlites (101-106) are the best bet—start with Volumes 1, 4, and 5. (The Roulette double LP is valuable for four incendiary Parker/Gillespie items from a mid-Forties Carnegie Hall concert.)

The "air check" recordings (taped from radio broadcasts) begin around 1948 and run through 1953. Much of this material is on the Archive of Folk volumes; they give virtually no information and occasionally overlap with the Columbia *One Night in Birdland,* but have superb music nonetheless. *One Night* features a model quintet, with Fats Navarro on trumpet, Bud Powell's piano and a drummer listed as Art Blakey (my ears say it may be Roy Haynes); *Summit Meeting,* with Dizzy, Powell and Haynes on one incredible side, is even better. No better manifestation of the Parker cult can be found than the Prestige Parker twofer—tapes from live concerts where the machine was turned off when Parker was not soloing.

Parker concluded his life under contract to producer Norman Granz, and the two often labored to find more marketable settings for Parker. Their efforts are now on three twofers titled *The Verve Years,* which, if below the high standards of the Savoy and Dial recordings, have much great music anyway: the best "with strings" session and a reunion with Dizzy and Thelonious Monk on Volume 1; the last great quintet sessions (with Miles or Red Rodney on trumpet) on Volume 2; and two agile quartet dates on Volume 3. The best Parker from his final years, however, is found on *The Greatest Jazz Concert Ever* (Prestige 24024), a 1953 Toronto meeting of Bird, Diz, Bud, Max Roach and Charles Mingus. — B.B.

HERMETO PASCOAL
★★★ Hermeto / Muse MR-5086
★★ Slaves Mass / War. B-2980
I haven't heard his Brazilian recordings, but on his American LPs, composer/arranger/multi-instrumentalist Pascoal throws too many ingredients into his musical stew. He loves his roots, complicated composition, sound effects, and angular jazz solos and voicings. Nice, even majestic in spots, but still spotty. — M.R.

JACO PASTORIUS
★★★★ Jaco Pastorius / Epic PE-33949
Exquisitely paced, strenuously orchestrated contemporary jazz; it's cerebral, but still composed accessibly enough to be pretty in

an obvious way. With a unique overtone-dominated style, Pastorius was the electric-bass phenomenon of 1976, the year he started recording with Weather Report. — M.R.

KING PLEASURE
★★★ **Golden Days** / Ev. 262
★★★★ **Original Moody's Mood** / **Prest. 7586**
★★★ **The Source** / Prest. 24017
Pleasure created a jazz craze when he began doing vocal versions of famous jazz solos in the Forties. (The style was pioneered by Eddie Jefferson, who wrote "Moody's Mood for Love," Pleasure's best-known improvisation.) The style was known as scat-singing, and, with Jefferson and the Lambert-Hendricks-Ross trio, Pleasure is its most famous exponent. It involves a lot of glossolalia that in fact heralds some of the less coherent tricks of recent rock singers. — D.M.

JIMMY PONDER
★★★ **Illusions** / Imp. D-9313
★★★ **While My Guitar Gently Weeps** / **Cadet 50048**
★★★ **White Room** / Imp. 9327
Talented young jazz guitarist has some good ideas and even covers rock tunes intelligently, especially on *While My Guitar Gently Weeps*. — J.S.

EARL "BUD" POWELL
★★★★ **Bouncing with Bud** / Del. DS-9406
★★★★ **Bud in Paris** / Xan. 102
★★★★ **Bud Powell Trio** / Fan. 86006
★★★★★ **Greatest Jazz Concert Ever** / **Prest. 24024**
★★ **Invisible Cage** / Black L. 153
★★★★ **Masters of the Modern Piano** / **Verve 2-2514**
★★★★★ **The Amazing Bud Powell, Vol. 1** / Blue N. 81503
★★★★★ **The Amazing Bud Powell, Vol. 2** / Blue N. 81504
★★★★★ **The Genius of Bud Powell** / **Verve 2-2506**
★★★ **The Scene Changes** / Blue N. 84009
★★ **Time Waits** / Blue N. 81598
★★ **Ups 'n' Downs** / Main. 385
Earl "Bud" Powell (1924–1966) was the premier pianist of the be-bop era, the most imitated man on his instrument, as well as one of the tragic casualties of an era overstocked with disaster.

Powell's recordings from the late Forties, after he had already been confined in a mental institution, are definitive be-bop.

The Amazing Bud Powell, Volume 1 features three takes of his classic "Un Poco Loco," in a trio that included drummer Max Roach, plus other famous Powell tunes performed by a quintet featuring Fats Navarro and the young Sonny Rollins. *The Genius of Bud Powell,* a double album of trios and unaccompanied solos, is also indispensable.

The first half of the Fifties saw Powell begin his decline, though he is still strong on *The Amazing . . . Volume 2,* much of which was done in 1953 and consists entirely of trios. *Bud Powell Trio,* with Mingus and Roach, is uncommonly dissonant Powell from the famous Massey Hall concert that also featured Charlie Parker and Dizzy Gillespie (available as a twofer on the *Greatest Jazz Concert Ever*). The Powell selections on *Masters of the Modern Piano,* from 1955, are his last consistently good American recordings.

Among his later work, *The Scene Changes,* made shortly before his 1959 departure for Paris, has some bright spots, but *Time Waits, Invisible Cage* and *Ups 'n' Downs* are more depressing than rewarding. His best later work is on the 1960 *Bud in Paris,* which has two duets with tenorman Johnny Griffin, and the 1962 *Bouncing with Bud,* which introduced the impressive Danish bassist Niels-Henning Orsted Pedersen, who was only fifteen at the time.

Powell played the piano with unmatched speed and intensity; his frenzied uptempo solos anticipate (emotionally if not through specific techniques) the avant-garde of the next decade. Besides his own best albums, Powell can be heard with Charlie Parker, Dexter Gordon, Fats Navarro and Sonny Stitt. — B.B.

BERNARD PURDIE
★★ **Delights of the Garden** / Casa. 7051
★★ **Purdie Good** / Prest. 10013
★★ **Shaft** / Prest. 10038
Purdie is an accomplished session drummer who apparently will never amount to much as a leader. His solo albums are banal and in desperate search of commercial hooks. — J.S.

DEWEY REDMAN
★★★★ **Coincide** / Imp. ASD-9300
★★★ **Look for the Black Star** / Ari./Free **1011**
★★★★★ **Old and New Dreams** / Black S. **0013**
★★★★ **The Ear of the Behearer** / Imp. **AS-9250**

514 / Django Reinhardt

His role of sideman with Ornette Coleman and Keith Jarrett has led many listeners to undervalue the strength of Dewey Redman, one of the finest contemporary tenor saxophonists. Limited recognition in this case has translated to limited albums under Redman's own name.

Look for the Black Star, from 1966, finds Redman formulating his talking-horn technique and adding Latin rhythms as well as more conventional free and modal touches. The album's greatest significance is its picture of the San Francisco jazz underground of the period.

Impulse recorded Redman to better effect in 1973-74, on *The Ear of the Behearer* and *Coincide.* Both use the same basic band (trumpeter Ted Daniel, bassist Sirone, drummer Eddie Moore), with cellist Jane Robertson a particularly valuable addition on the former. The weave of tenor and strings produces marvelous abstractions, while performances on Redman's secondary instruments (musette and zither) tend to be less interesting. Both albums find Redman equally commanding when he returns to his hard-cooking Texas roots, with "Qow" on *Coincide* a superior "inside" track.

Old and New Dreams, a collaboration with three other Ornette Coleman alumni, is a happy continuation of the Coleman tradition with compositions by participants Don Cherry and Charlie Haden as well as Redman. — B.B.

DJANGO REINHARDT
★★★★ Django 1935 / Cres. 9023
★★★★ Django 1935-39 / Cres. 9019
★★★ Django Reinhardt / Ev. 212
★★★ Django Reinhardt, Vol. 2 / Ev. 230
★★★ Django Reinhardt, Vol. 3 / Ev. 255
★★★ Django Reinhardt, Vol. 4 / Ev. 306
★★★ First Recordings / Prest. 7614
★★★★ Immortal Django Reinhardt / Cres. 9038
★★★★ Legendary Django Reinhardt / Cres. 9039
★★★ Parisian Swing / Cres. 9002
★★★★ QHCF/Reinhardt/Grappelli / Angel 36985
★★★ Quintet of Hot Club of France / Cres. 9001
★★ Swing It Lightly / Col. C-31479
Jean-Baptiste (Django) Reinhardt (1910-1953), a Belgian gypsy, developed the jazz guitar as lead instrument out of the romantic European tradition in the Thirties and Forties and continues to exert a powerful hold on young improvisational

guitarists, even though many jazz critics—especially in America where there is an understandable bias for Charlie Christian—hotly contest his credentials as a legitimate jazz musician.

Having lost the use of two fingers on his left hand in a fire, he created a technique to overcome this handicap, and in the process pioneered a dazzling single-note style that fairly shimmered with vibrato and a bright, sparkling tone. Improvising on contemporary standards with Stephane Grappelli (violin) and the Hot Club of France, Django would bring forth a flood of melodic ideas literally jumping over one another to get out of his guitar. Amid this torrent of notes, Reinhardt would effortlessly drop in frantic octave passages and hard-edged chord vamps to push the often-plodding Hot Club rhythm section along. On slower tunes, like his classic "Nuages," his melodic improvisations were simply uncanny. The tone and phrasing positively throbbed with feeling.

Most critics object to the Hot Club's "string heavy" sound and muddy rhythm sections, and even the most dedicated Reinhardt fan will grow weary of the slightly stodgy Hot Club style, but no one can deny the sheer emotional impact when Reinhardt digs into his Macaferri guitar to wrench out another stunning solo. It is really as pointless to criticize Reinhardt for playing too many notes as it would be to criticize Charlie Parker or John Coltrane for the same offense, since he exercised such an effortless control over his prodigious technique.

Of the existing discography in America, the Crescendo and Prestige LPs are probably the best available. Classic performances like "Mélodie du Crépuscule," "Minor Swing," "Place de Broukère," "Belleville," "Porto Cabello" and "September Song" can be found on a number of domestic and import albums. Hard-core Django aficionados like Peter Frampton favor the EMI-Pathé "Djangologies" import series—best for packaging and sound—but most of his work is readily available. — J.C.C.

REVOLUTIONARY ENSEMBLE
★★★★ Manhattan Cycles / India Navig. 1023
★★★★★ The People's Republic / Hori. 708
This trio, comprised of Leroy Jenkins on violin, Sirone (a.k.a. Norris Jones) on bass and trombone, and Jerome Cooper on

drums and piano, is the most exciting new music band of the Seventies. Their basic violin-bass-drums instrumentation is perfectly balanced and allows for maximum exploration without unnecessary assault. All three are demonic players, though each (especially the underrated Cooper) knows the value of restraint, and all three write intriguing material.

Manhattan Cycles, like two other recordings no longer listed in the catalogue, is a poorly recorded concert. The single composition performed (by trumpeter Leo Smith) sets the trio against prerecorded tape. Their Horizon album is well produced and nicely programed, though it lacks a bit of the fire heard on the concert albums.

Jenkins can also be heard on his own albums and with Anthony Braxton, Richard Abrams, Alice Coltrane and others. Sirone has recorded with Jenkins, Marion Brown, Dewey Redman, Roswell Rudd and Cecil Taylor; Cooper with Braxton and on the *Wildflowers* anthology. — B.B.

SAM RIVERS
★★★★ Contours / Blue N. 84206
★★★★ Fuchsia Swing Song / Blue N. 84184
★★★ Involution / Blue N. LA453-H2
After years of playing around Boston and the briefest of tours with Miles Davis, Rivers (who plays tenor sax, soprano sax and flute) finally got a record contract in 1965. Of his Blue Note work, *Fuchsia,* with fellow Boston iconoclasts Jaki Byard and Tony Williams, is the most intriguing mix of post-bop and freer strains; *Contours,* with Freddie Hubbard and Herbie Hancock, comes closest to being a conventional quintet; and *Involution* shows his awareness of Ayler and the ESP bands in perfor-

mances that perhaps try too hard to be "outside." Pianist Andrew Hill leads one of the bands on the last album.
★★★★ Crystals / Imp. ASD-9286
★★★★★ Dave Holland/Sam Rivers / IAI 37.38.43
★★★★ Hues / Imp. ASD-9302
★★★★★ Sam Rivers/Dave Holland, Vol. 2 / IAI 37.38.48
★★★ Sizzle / Imp. ASD-9316
★★★★★ Streams / Imp. ASD-9251
After several years of low-profile activity, Rivers returned in the Seventies with a fourth solo instrument (piano), an important New York music room of his own (Studio Rivbea), and an open-ended improvisational style that lets the ideas flow unfettered by rigid structure yet still finds many moments to swing straight out. Most notable among the above albums are *Streams,* from Montreux 1973, the only example of a complete standard Rivers performance (Cecile McBee, bass; Norman Connors, drums); *Crystals,* with his magnificent writing for a fourteen-piece band; and the first volume of his duets with bass master Holland, where Rivers plays tenor and soprano. *Sizzle,* sort of a free approach to crossover, is also special. At present, Rivers must be counted among the most daring and rewarding contemporary musicians. — B.B.

MAX ROACH
★★★★★ Clifford Brown and Max Roach at Basin Street / Trip 5511
★★★★★ Clifford Brown and Max Roach Inc. / Trip 5520
★★★ Drums Unlimited / Atl. 1467
★★★★ It's Time / Imp. 16
★★★ Jazz in 3/4 Time / Trip 5559
★★★ Max Roach on the Chicago Scene / Trip 5594
★★★★★ Max Roach + 4 / Trip 5522
★ Rich vs. Roach / Mer. 60133
★★★★ The Many Sides of Max / Trip 5599
★★★★ The Max Roach 4 Plays Charlie Parker / Trip 5574
Sometimes his rhythms sound so simple, you could teach a child to count to the beat. But it is those simple meters, crosscombined, that made him the most important drummer in jazz. He was first Dizzy Gillespie's, then (when Kenny Clarke left) Charlie Parker's associate, and with them he changed the drummer's product from pulse to propulsion. In the Fifties, his career paralleled those of Miles Davis and Art Blakey: he was quick to spot and

hire young musicians, including his ill-fated partner Clifford Brown, as well as Sonny Rollins, Booker Little (another trumpeter who died early) and George Coleman, a tenor player who worked with Miles in the Sixties and Mingus in the Seventies.

Harmonic advances were an inevitable dividend of Max's muscular, logical time-keeping, and his small band recordings paved the way in a style known as hard bop. With Clifford Brown, he established a special brotherhood that would never be duplicated. They could flex and bend, sing softly together, and swing out with what would have seemed to be terrible tempers had they not been constantly in control of their talents. Kenny Dorham was a fine replacement for Brownie, although the material the band performed with him never enabled the same personal stamp, with the exception of the Charlie Parker sides—Dorham had been a member of Mr. Parker's band, too.

From the late Fifties, Roach rarely used piano. On the Atlantic date, he tried other advances, including a few free-time compositions and features for solo percussion (Roach was leading an ensemble for that recording, which consisted mainly of Freddie Hubbard's working group). Even more significant an experiment was the Impulse LP, composed and orchestrated by Roach using a chorus throughout for spiritual-like chants. Only one piece included words. Later, Roach abandoned recording in favor of teaching children how to count (among other things) as a professor of music at the University of Massachusetts. — A.E.G.

SONNY ROLLINS
★★★★★ A Night at the Village Vanguard / Blue N. 81-581
★★★★ Alfie / Imp. 9111
★★★★ Contemporary Leaders / Contem. 7564
★★★ East Broadway Rundown / Imp. 9121
★★★★ Easy Living / Mile. 9080
★★★★ First Recordings / Prest. 7856
★★★★★ Freedom Suite Plus / Mile. 47007 (contains Freedom Suite / Riv. 6044M)
★★ Horn Culture / Mile. 9051
★★★★ Jazz Classics / Prest. 7433
★★★★★ More from the Vanguard / Blue N. LA474-H2
★★★★★ Newk's Time / Blue N. 84001
★★★ Nucleus / Mile. 9064
★★★ Plays for Bird / Prest. 7553E
★★★★ Pure Gold Jazz / RCA ANL1-2809

★★★★ Reevaluation: the Impulse Years / Imp. 9236
★★★★★ Saxophone Colossus and More / Prest. 24050 (contains Saxophone Colossus / Prest. 7326)
★★ Sonny Rollins / Arc. Folk 220E
★★★★ Sonny Rollins / Blue N. LA401-H
★★★ Sonny Rollins / Blue N. 81542
★★★★★ Sonny Rollins, Vol. 2 / Blue N. 81558
★★★★ Sonny Rollins / Prest. 24004
★★★★ Sonny Rollins' Next Album / Mile. 9042
★★★★ Sonny Rollins on Impulse / Imp. 91
★★★★★ Tenor Madness / Prest. 7657
★★★★ The Bridge / RCA AFL1-0859
★★★ The Cutting Edge / Mile. 9059
★ The Way I Feel / Mile. 9074
★★★★★ Three Giants / Prest. 7821
★★★★★ Way Out West / Contem. 7530
★★★★★ Worktime / Prest. 7750

There is a lot of Sonny Rollins currently available, as befits one of the great geniuses of jazz history. His career conveniently divides itself into eras, often based on the tenor saxophonist's own self-imposed retirements from active performing; and the albums listed above are easiest to deal with when divided into chronological bunches.

Getting It Together: sessions made under Rollins' name before his first sabbatical in 1955. *First Recordings,* from 1951 and 1953, finds his gruff tone, hard-driving rhythmic conception and sense of humor already well developed; the Modern Jazz Quartet backs him on four tracks, and "I Know" has Miles Davis on piano. *Jazz Classics* is a 1954 preview of the hard-bop era, with Kenny Dorham, Art Blakey and (on one stunning ballad) Thelonious Monk. Tracks from these albums are on the Prestige *Sonny Rollins* sampler.

New Star: Having gotten himself together in Chicago, Rollins joined the Max Roach/Clifford Brown Quintet at the end of 1955 and embarked on a brilliant series of albums for Prestige. *Saxophone Colossus* is the ultimate masterpiece, a quartet recital in which Rollins delivered his finest calypso composition ("St. Thomas") and his greatest achievement in thematically based improvisation ("Blue Seven"). Not far behind are *Worktime,* where Rollins and drummer Roach swing hard and fast; *Three Giants,* the Brown/Roach band under Sonny's name playing "Valse Hot" and "Pent-up House," two of the best Rollins compositions; and *Tenor Madness,* featuring Miles Davis' 1956 rhythm sections and the only recorded encounter between Rollins and John Coltrane.

1957 was perhaps Rollins' best year as a recording artist; his tone grew bolder, he began taking more harmonic chances, and often dispensed with piano in favor of the greater freedom offered by the tenor-bass-drums instrumentation. He also left Roach during 1957 and, after a brief stay with Miles Davis, established himself as a working bandleader. In the twelve months between March 1957 and 1958, he recorded three incredible trio records: *Way Out West,* with Ray Brown and Shelly Manne, is the most relaxed and melodic; *A Night at the Village Vanguard,* with Wilbur Ware and Elvin Jones, the clearest indication of Sonny's new and radical melodic-rhythmic ideas; and *Freedom Suite,* with Oscar Pettiford and Roach, an early example of extended improvisation-composition and the most finely balanced band.

In all of Rollins' records from this period, he develops further the concept known as thematic improvisation—using the starting melody as a thread which connects the disparate ideas and moods within a solo. Other essential examples of this approach, from 1957 through 1958, outside of the trio context are heard on *Sonny Rollins, Volume 2,* an all-star assemblage with piano by Horace Silver and Thelonious Monk (both appear on "Misterioso") and the quartet session *Newk's Time,* which is particularly well programed and has some of Philly Joe Jones' best drumming.

The Sixties: Rollins became disenchanted with the scene in 1959, when he was at the peak of his influence; he returned toward the end of 1961, after a jazz critic found him practicing on the Williamsburg Bridge. During the next three years, he recorded six albums for RCA, but only the first two are currently in American release (the French RCA reissues have been fairly easy to find on the East Coast, however). Both *The Bridge* and *Pure Gold Jazz* document the Rollins Quartet with guitarist Jim Hall, a quiet and intelligent player who was actually quite compatible with Rollins. *The Bridge* is best on the harder driving items, particularly the tricky "John S."; *Pure Gold Jazz* is a buoyant study in Latin rhythms, with two bossa novas by the quartet and two more bare-boned collaborations with percussionist Candido.

Before abandoning his recording career again in 1966, Rollins spent a year with Impulse and made three albums. *On Im-*

pulse is notable for the idea-filled solo on "Three Little Words" and the extremely boisterous "Hold 'Em Joe," and *Alfie* offers a rough-and-tumble reading of Rollins' score for the Michael Caine movie. Several critics praised *East Broadway Rundown,* where the Coltrane rhythm section of bassist Jimmy Garrison and Elvin Jones appear, but the title track (with Freddie Hubbard added) sounds like a strained attempt at something different and the funky "Blessing in Disguise" never really gets off the ground.

Back to Stay: Since his return to steady activity in 1972, Rollins has not made a great album. Part of the problem has been sidemen, though Sonny's recent efforts at crossover have also contributed to the drop in quality. Generally, though, there is at least something brilliant on each of his Milestone albums. *Next Album,* for instance, finds him deeply involved on "The Everywhere Calypso" and "Skylark," but the only true success on the sequel, *Horn Culture,* is the blues "Lover Man." *The Cutting Edge,* from Montreux 1974, gets off to a great start with the peppery title tune and the unaccompanied tenor soliloquy "To a Wild Rose," but ultimately winds down to the aridity of Rufus Harley's bagpipes. *Nucleus* is quasi-crossover with some comfortable funk (I dig the electronic groove on "Newkleus") and great straight-ahead Rollins tenor on "Azalea"; *The Way I Feel,* fusion all the way, is the most disappointing Rollins album ever recorded. Yet with *Easy Living,* Rollins proves that he can make pop material his own ("Isn't She Lovely") and still cook hard on straight jazz material ("Down the Line," "Easy Living"). At age fifty, Rollins seems to have a lot of great music left to play. — B.B.

PATRICE RUSHEN
★★ **Before the Dawn / Prest. 10098**
★★ **Prelusion / Prest. 10089**
★★★ **Shout It Out / Prest. P-10101**
Rushen, a jazz keyboardist/composer, made these LPs before she was turning twenty-three. On the first two, she writes well and with originality, within established modes. She plays acoustic and electric piano with great technical skill, but cops too much from Herbie Hancock. *Prelusion*'s aura is Seventies modal-mainstream jazz; it features Joe Henderson's angular tenor and makes only a few concessions to crossover. Somewhat less focused, *Before The Dawn* is also more

commercial; Hubert Laws is major guest soloist, and a couple of the tracks are dismally overproduced. Yet both records pale before the conceptual cohesion and panache of *Shout It Out.* Here, Rushen rigorously applies her composing, playing, even singing skills to a totally commercial product. — M.R.

GEORGE RUSSELL
★★★★★ Ezz-thetics / Riv. 6112
★★★★★ New York, N.Y. and Jazz in the
   Space Age / MCA 2-4017
★★★★★ Outer Thoughts / Mile. 47027

Russell (b. 1923) has played piano and percussion, but he is primarily important for his compositions and his *Lydian Chromatic Concept of Tonal Organization,* a theoretical study which predicted the shift from chord changes to scales or "modes" as the basis of jazz improvisation. His most influential recordings are from before his expatriation to Europe in 1964, especially in the years covered by the above albums (1958-61). MCA's double album joins two orchestral works, one a portrait of Manhattan, the other a more consciously far-out venture; soloists include John Coltrane, Art Farmer, Bill Evans and Paul Bley. *Outer Thoughts* samples the work of his various sextets, the best of which made *Ezz-thetics* and featured Don Ellis and Eric Dolphy.

★★★★ Electronic Sonata for Souls Loved
   by Nature / Strata-East 19761
★★★★ Listen to the Silence / Concept 002
★★★★ Othello Ballet Suite/Electric Organ Sonata No. 1 / Concept/Sonet 1409
★★★★★ The Essence of George Russell /
   Concept/Sonet 1411/12

Currently Russell teaches at Boston's New England Conservatory and works on the second volume of his *Lydian Concept.* These recordings represent ambitious com-positions from 1966 to 1971, recorded while he lived in Europe with responsive continental orchestras. *Essence* gives the best picture of his range, with a full band version of the Electronic Sonata (the album of that name is by a sextet). Also notable is the *Othello Ballet Suite,* with saxophonist Jan Garbarek as featured soloist, and *Listen to the Silence,* for electric/acoustic combo and chorus. — B.B.

TERJE RYPDAL
★★★ After the Rain / ECM/Poly. 1-1083
★★ Esoteric Circle / Ari. 1031
★★★ Odyssey / ECM/Poly. 1067/68
★★ What Comes After / ECM/Poly.
   1031
★★★ Whenever I Seem to Be Far Away /
   ECM/Poly. 1045

For all his talent, Norwegian guitarist Terje Rypdal veers dangerously close to sanctified cosmic trance music on some of his recorded work. His roots are rock & roll, but his rapid evolution into free jazz and studies of the Lydian Chromatic Concept of Tonal Organization with George Russell have led Rypdal into more abstract and reflective states, not readily accessible to most listeners.

Rypdal's ECM albums range from haunting melodic statements to long Mahavishnu-like passages over synthesizer textures (*Whenever I Seem to Be Far Away*), which a fan might call "stratosphere music." His most full-blooded work to date is on *Esoteric Circle* where his shadowy guitar provides the perfect counterpoint to Jan Garbarek's impassioned saxophone. — J.C.C.

DAVID SANBORN
★★★ Sanborn / War. 2957
★★★ Taking Off / War. 2873

On both these albums, oft-heard jazz-based studio altoist Sanborn (e.g., the sax break on James Taylor's cover of "How Sweet It Is") tried very hard to make music that's both commercial and good. Mostly, he succeeds. The composing has hooks without being condescending, and Sanborn's blowing, rooted in the classic R&B tradition, is still enough his own to be originally incisive. — M.R.

GUNTHER SCHULLER
★★ Country Dance / Col. M-33981
★★ Happy Feet: A Tribute to Paul Whiteman / GC 31043
★★★★★ Jazz Abstractions / Atl. 1365
★★ Road from Rags to Jazz / GC 31042

Besides his credits as a classical composer and conservatory president, Gunther Schuller has been actively involved at both ends of jazz' historical spectrum. Projects such as *Road from Rags to Jazz, Happy Feet: A Tribute to Paul Whiteman* and *Country Dance* re-create earlier musical forms with scholarly rigor. Much more important is *Jazz Abstractions,* from 1960, perhaps the best example of the melding of jazz and classical composition that Schuller dubbed Third Stream Music. The writing here, by Schuller and Jim Hall, is vibrant and challenging, particularly on the title piece and "Variations on a Theme by Thelonious Monk." Featured soloists Ornette Coleman, Eric Dolphy, Bill Evans, Scott LaFaro and Hall add immeasurably to the successful hybrid. — B.B.

DON SEBESKY
★★ Giant Box / CTI QX-6031/32
■ Rape of El Morro / CTI 6061
As house arranger for CTI, Sebesky is either the hero or villain of the slick, stylized Seventies jazz formularized by that label, depending on how you look at it. From this vantage point it looks pretty bad. — J.S.

SHAKTI
★★★ Handful of Beauty / Col. PC-34372
★★★ Natural Elements / Col. JC-34980
★★★ Shakti (with John McLaughlin) / Col. PC-34162
After the electronic blitz period of the Mahavishnu Orchestra died down, John McLaughlin gravitated to a collaboration with some of India's most gifted musicians. His acoustic style, first evinced on *My Goals Beyond,* was already highly evolved before he further refined it for Shakti.

Working with L. Shankar on violin and Zakir Hussain on tabla, McLaughlin uses an acoustic instrument redesigned to fit the needs of this music. The fretboard has been hollowed out like a sitar so that McLaughlin can bend notes and add vibrato in the Indian fashion, and the guitar has sympathetic strings across the soundboard.

Shakti, recorded live at Southampton College, introduces the group to an enthusiastic audience, and the long, ragalike compositions, both highly charged and softly reflective, serve as a contextual framework for McLaughlin, Shankar and Hussain to build their dizzying improvisations. One of the most heartfelt and intelligent syntheses of Eastern and Western music in many years. — J.C.C.

WOODY SHAW
★★★★ Blackstone Legacy / Contem. S-7626/28
★★★ Love Dance / Muse 5074
★★★ Song of Songs / Contem. 7632
★★★★ The Moontrane / Muse 5058
★★★ The Woody Shaw Concert Ensemble at the Berliner Jazztage / Muse 5139
Trumpeter Woody Shaw is the ideal leader for contemporary blowing sessions: he has good chops, can play outside without excess and inside without triviality, and he writes interesting tunes. The sessions made under his name vary according to the visiting roster.

Blackstone Legacy, a 1970 double album with Gary Bartz, Bennie Maupin, George Cables, Ron Carter, Clint Houston and Lenny White. Compositions by Shaw and Cables. The personnel tells the story.

Song of Songs, 1972, same setup but some less interesting players on reeds (Emanuel Boyd, Ramon Morris) and drums (Woodrow Theus II). With so much solo room, the soloists make the difference.

The Moontrane is back on the track. Good young players like Azar Lawrence, Steve Turre, Onaje Allen Gumbs and Victor Lewis, plus master bassists Buster Williams and Cecil McBee. Good variety from track to track, with four of the musicians contributing pieces. A 1974 date.

The following year's *Love Dance* is off the mark slightly. There isn't enough room for the interesting soloists (Rene McLean, Billy Harper, McBee), while the below-par piano of Joe Bonner is heard on each track. Again there are several players and friends contributing tunes.

The Woody Shaw Concert Ensemble at the Berliner Jazztage takes the same approach

with the quintet Shaw and drummer Louis
Hayes co-lead swollen to septet size. An
often bristling band, though below the level
of Shaw's *Blackstone* and *Moontrane*
groups. — B.B.

ARCHIE SHEPP
★★★★ Fire Music / Imp. A-86
★★★★★ Four for Trane / Imp. A-71
★★★ Kwanza / Imp. AS-9262
★★★★★ Mama Too Tight / Imp. 9134
★★★★ On This Night / Imp. A-97
★★★ The Magic of Ju-Ju / Imp. 9154
★★★ The Way Ahead / Imp. 9170

After being featured with Cecil Taylor in
1960 and John Coltrane in 1965, tenor
saxophonist Shepp became a leading figure
in the New York new-music scene of the
mid-Sixties. Often lost amidst the musical,
political and racial controversy surrounding Shepp is his superb playing, a mix of
asymmetrical melodies and exaggerated
tones that encompass much of the tenor's
past, and much romanticism, together with
the obvious avant-garde fury. As a com-
poser/arranger, Shepp has also displayed a
knack for utilizing small and large ensembles creatively in a loose style that suggests
the influence of Charles Mingus. In the
present decade, Shepp began featuring soprano sax and teaching at the University of
Massachusetts, played occasional piano, re-
cited his own poetry and wrote plays.

Impulse recorded Shepp throughout the
Sixties, with the earlier recordings making
the greatest impression. *Four for Trane*
gave important early exposure to trombonist Roswell Rudd and alto player John
Tchicai as well as Shepp in performances
of Coltrane tunes that now sound harmonically loose but rhythmically quite straightforward; still, the spirit and interaction of
the band is marvelous. *Fire Music* has more
interesting structures ("Hambone," "Los
Olvidados") and more good players (Ted
Curson, Marion Brown), plus the first of
many Shepp readings of an Ellington song.
On *Mama Too Tight*, from 1967, Shepp
borrows from James Brown on one track
and offers more shifting ensemble writing;
there is also a side-long quintet performance that captures Shepp's open-ended
railing combo style of the time. *The Magic
of Ju-Ju*, with a large percussion section,
begins Shepp's conscious incorporation of
African devices.

★★★ Archie Shepp and Philly Joe Jones /
  Fan. 86018
★★★ Attica Blues / Imp. AS-9222
★★★ Black Gypsy / Prest. 10034

★★★ Coral Rock / Prest. 10066
★★★ Doodlin' / Inner 1001

At decade's turn Shepp was recording extensively for a variety of European labels.
While the albums are often most interesting for their glimpse of the next generation
of innovators (Roscoe Mitchell, Anthony
Braxton), there is also a turn toward bop
and affiliations with older musicians like
Philly Joe Jones. *Coral Rock* and *Doodlin'*
feature Shepp the pianist. His 1972 orchestral effort for Impulse is often a hodgepodge of jazz soul, subadolescent vocalists
and political narrative, although there are
moments of true power and brief but sparkling saxophone solos by the leader.

★★★ A Sea of Faces / Black S. 0002
★★★ Montreux One / Ari./Free 1027
★★★ Montreux Two / Ari./Free 1034
★★★★ Steam / Inner 3002
★★★ There's a Trumpet in My Soul /
  Ari./Free 1016

Recent Shepp has been disappointing.
There's a Trumpet is among his most unimaginative large-group efforts, the Montreux volumes offer a bop program by a
band whose primary strength is not in the
bop genre, and the Black Saint has an excessive amount of vamp pieces. Only on
Steam, where Shepp enjoys the bare-bones
support of bassist Cameron Brown and
longtime associate Beaver Harris on
drums, does his virile imagination cut
through undimmed. — B.B.

WAYNE SHORTER
★★★★ Adam's Apple / Blue N. 84232
★★★★ Juju / Blue N. 84182
★★★★★ Native Dancer / Col. PC-33418
★★★★ Night Dreamer / Blue N. 84173
★★★★ Schizophrenia / Blue N. 84297
★★★ Shorter Moments / Trip X-5009
  (same as Wayne Shorter / GNP 2075)

★★★★★ **Speak No Evil / Blue N. 84194**
★★★★★ **Super Nova / Blue N. 84332**
★★★★★ **The All-Seeing Eye / Blue N. 84219**

Shorter is the most self-effacing great musician of the past twenty years. This stunning composer and saxophonist (first tenor, with soprano added in 1968) spent long stints as a sideman (with Art Blakey's Jazz Messengers, 1959-64, and Miles Davis, 1964-69) before forming the cooperative band Weather Report with Joe Zawinul and Miroslav Vitous (who was eventually replaced by Jaco Pastorius) in 1970. Albums under his own name are few and generally fine.

Shorter Moments, from the beginning of his Blakey tenure, features other good young players (Lee Morgan, Freddie Hubbard, Wynton Kelly, Paul Chambers) and nine Shorter originals, but is not up to his Jazz Messenger albums of the period. *Night Dreamer,* done four years later, gives a better picture of Shorter's personality; audible influences include the Blakey band (trumpeter Morgan is again present) and John Coltrane (in the McCoy Tyner-Reggie Workman-Elvin Jones rhythm section as much as in the tenor solos, which also show the effects of Sonny Rollins), as well as an airy, spacious feeling to the writing that is very much Shorter's own.

Juju, with the same rhythm section (all three had played together behind Coltrane) and no trumpet, almost seems like an attempt at minimalist Coltrane; even such scorchers as the title piece and "Yes or No" are marked by Shorter's characteristic economy. This leaner feeling is heightened in the excellent *Speak No Evil,* even with the presence of Hubbard's trumpet, by Miles Davis quintet colleagues Herbie Hancock and Ron Carter. Some of Shorter's finest writing is included—the ominous "Witch Hunt" and yearning "Infant Eyes" being most memorable.

While *The All-Seeing Eye,* an energy-laden septet session, hinted that Shorter was about to burst through to untempered avant-garde territory, the following *Adam's Apple* and *Schizophrenia* retreat to more tempered performances. On all three albums, Hancock and drummer Joe Chambers contribute greatly to Shorter's direct and meticulously conceived music. By 1968, when *Schizophrenia* was made, Shorter had developed a sensitivity on tenor that could only be matched by Stan Getz, one of his staunchest admirers.

The release of the 1969 *Super Nova,*

which followed hard on the heels of Miles Davis' *In a Silent Way* and *Bitches Brew* (both feature Shorter), heralded the jazz-rock era. To this writer's taste, *Super Nova* is the most interesting album of the three, the one with the most complex horn soloing (Shorter plays soprano sax throughout) and energetic accompaniment (including John McLaughlin and Sonny Sharrock's guitars, bassist Miroslav Vitous, Airto Moreira's percussion, and Jack DeJohnette and Chick Corea (!) on drums). Two Blue Note albums from the period in a similar vein, *Moto Grosso Feio* and *Odyssey of Iska,* are unfortunately out of print but also highly recommended.

Nothing came under Shorter's name until 1975 and *Native Dancer,* which is one of the classic recordings of the decade. This perfect meeting of America and Brazil is jointly formed by Shorter and singer/guitarist Milton Nascimento, who performs on five of his own tunes. Among numerous highlights are "Tarde," where Shorter's tenor solo reaches a depth of feeling akin to Miles Davis at his most intense; "Beauty and the Beast," infectious acoustic funk; "From the Lonely Afternoons," a wordless tour de force for Nascimento (and Shorter's latest reflections on Coltrane); and the absolutely exquisite Shorter composition "Diana." Reportedly Shorter began work on a new album in 1977; when it finally appears it should be a major event. — B.B.

HORACE SILVER
★★★★ **Best of Horace Silver / Blue. N. 84325**
★★★★★ **Blowin' the Blues Away / Blue N. 84017**
★★★★ **Cape Verdean Blues / Blue N. 84220**
★★★★ **Doin' the Thing / Blue N. 84076**
★★★★★ **Finger Poppin' / Blue N. 84008**
★★★★ **Horace Silver / Blue N. LA402-H**
★★★★★ **Horace Silver and the Jazz Messengers / Blue N. 81518**
★★★ **In Pursuit of the 27th Man / Blue N. LA054-G**
★★★ **Serenade to a Soul Sister / Blue N. 84277**
★★★ **Silver 'n' Percussion / Blue N. LA853-H**
★★ **Silver 'n' Voices / Blue N. LA708-G**
★★ **Silver 'n' Wood / Blue N. LA581-G**
★★★ **Silver's Serenade / Blue N. 84131**
★★★ **Silver's Blue / CSP JLA-16005**
★★★★ **Song for My Father / Blue N. 84185**

★ **That Healin' Feelin'** / Blue N. 84352
★★★★★ **The Stylings of Silver** / Blue N.
81562
★★★★ **The Trio Sides** / Blue N.
LA474-H2

In the course of a quarter-century with Blue Note (broken by a single Columbia Special Products album) pianist/composer Silver (b. 1928) has defined a quintet style that was the model of hard bop and funk (or what used to be known in the late Fifties as funk), perfected that style in a band that featured Blue Mitchell on trumpet and Junior Cook on tenor sax, then stuck with it while adding various accouterments with less than satisfying results.

Start with *The Trio Sides,* half of which were made in 1952-53, for a sense of Silver's brittle, bluesy, energetically personal amalgamation of Bud Powell, Thelonious Monk and earlier blues stylists. Then comes *Silver and the Messengers* in 1954-55, a cooperative band with Kenny Dorham, trumpet; Hank Mobley, tenor; Silver; Doug Watkins, bass; and Art Blakey, drums. In a program comprised mainly of Silver originals (including the popular "Doodlin' "), the Messengers hit upon the kind of bracing, punching modern style that Silver would carry with him when he left to form his own quintet in 1956.

Some of Silver's finest work from the next decade is either out of print or only available on sampler collections ("Senor Blues," for example, appears on *Best of,* while "Strollin' " and "Nica's Dream" are in the *Horace Silver* double album). Of four albums by early editions of his band, two are currently in print—*Silver's Blue,* a lesser effort, and *Stylings of Silver,* a typically varied program with the excellent front line of Mobley and trumpeter Art Farmer.

Finger Poppin', Blowin' the Blues Away, Doin' the Thing and *Silver's Serenade* are by the peerless 1959-63 quintet. Blue Mitchell and Junior Cook, though less famous than earlier Silver sidemen, shared a sense of lyrical economy perfectly suited to the often challenging compositions, bassist Gene Taylor was the soul of reliability, and drummer Louis Hayes (on the first two albums) never played with more taste (his replacement, Roy Brooks, is more of a basher). Silver was turning out memorable melodies that the ensemble delivered with audible joy, striking a spirit akin (as critic Martin Williams noted) to a later and smaller Basie band.

Of the four albums, *Finger Poppin'* and *Blowin' the Blues Away* are best; the latter has the rousing title tune and "Sister Sadie." *Doin' the Thing* was recorded at New York's Village Gate, and the title track on *Silver's Serenade* is perhaps Horace's most beautiful composition.

Mid-Sixties Silver quintets are heard on *Song for My Father, Cape Verdean Blues* (with J. J. Johnson making the band a sextet on some tracks) and *Serenade to a Soul Sister.* While the playing is generally good, and Silver had his biggest success with *Song for My Father,* the bands are not as tight and the writing begins to sound routine (Silver is also less successful with modal structures than the more boppish, heavily harmonic style of his earlier work). *Soul Sister* introduces electric piano to no particular effect, and features the horns of Stanley Turrentine and Charles Tolliver.

In 1970 Silver embarked on "The United States of Mind," a preachy, trendy series of vocal slogans; of three cloying albums that resulted from the project, only *That Healin' Feelin'* remains in print. *In Pursuit of the 27th Man* put Silver back in the instrumental business (with good help from the Brecker Brothers and vibist Dave Friedman); then another series began, the *Silver 'n'* sessions where his quintet is surrounded by various supporting ensembles (*Silver 'n' Brass,* the first and perhaps best in the series, is already deleted). The writing is good if familiar, with nice arranging touches except where voices are heard, and in trumpeter Tom Harrell, Silver has a soloist in the true spirit of his music. — B.B.

LONNIE LISTON SMITH AND THE COSMIC ECHOES

★★★ **Astral Traveling** / Fly. BXL1-0163
★★ **Cosmic Funk** / Fly. BXL1-0591
★★ **Expansions** / Fly. BXL1-0934
★★★★ **Reflections of a Golden Dream** /
Fly. BXL1-1460
★★★ **Renaissance** / RCA AFL1-1822
★★★ **Visions of a New World** / Fly.
BXL1-1196

On his first LP, *Astral Traveling,* Smith made acoustic, chordally limited, rhythmically ostinatoed, texture-laden music. But by Smith's fourth record, he'd given his work a funkier background, through mild electrification and an approach that owed more to R&B than to Coltrane. *Cosmic Funk* and *Expansions* evince this transition's growing pains, but Smith's next three albums, culminating in *Renaissance,* bring it to fruition. Currently, the keyboardist has a unified, original approach to fusion.

He writes tunes that rely on the whimsical beauty of certain minor-key chordal situations; beneath them chug vaguely danceable beats. There's something uniquely compelling about this juxtaposition, and it's enhanced by Smith's brother Donald, who sings stylishly yet poignantly in a cool, blissful near falsetto. — M.R.

JEREMY STEIG
★★ **Energy / Cap. SM-662**
★★ **Monium / Col. KC-32579**
★★ **Temple of Birth / Col. KC-33297**
★★★ **Wayfaring Stranger / Blue N. 84345**
In the late Sixties Steig formed one of the first jazz-rock outfits, Jeremy and the Satyrs, and has gone on to make additional albums featuring his flute playing in Western and Eastern rhythmic contexts. — J.S.

SUN RA
★★★★ **Sound of Joy / Del. DS-414**
★★★★ **Sun Song / Del. DS-411**
Most of the recorded work of composer/ arranger/multikeyboard artist Sun Ra (born Herman Blount and nicknamed "Sonny") is currently only available on his own exclusive Saturn label; the albums listed here are currently in the catalogue and thus fairly easy to obtain. Both Delmark records are from the 1956–57 period, when Sun Ra first organized the Arkestra that he continues to lead (with several original members, most notably tenor saxophonist John Gilmore) to this day. During this Chicago period Sun Ra had an intriguing boppish band that reflected such modern influences as Tadd Dameron and Charles Mingus as well as Sun Ra's former employer Fletcher Henderson; there are also a few visionary touches, particularly the leader's early use of electric keyboards.
★★★ **Cosmos / Inner 1020**
★★★ **Pictures of Infinity / Black L. 106**
★★★★ **Solo Piano, Vol. 1 / IAI 37.38.50**
Since leaving Chicago for New York and eventually Philadelphia, Sun Ra and his Arkestra have defined the potential for free-jazz Big Bands, while retaining touches of bop and earlier influences and a comprehensive outer space cum black nationalism mythology. The Arkestra's masterpieces (*The Magic City, Heliocentric Worlds of Sun Ra, Volume 1, Nothing Is*) are officially out of print, so the uneven Black Lion set is the best indication of the Arkestra's breadth. *Cosmos* stresses their "inside" tendencies in a 1976 session from their European tour. The solo album, with Sun Ra exclusively on acoustic piano, is one of his warmest and most restrained performances. For the best picture of this important innovator, search out the ESP and Impulse cutouts. — B.B.

GABOR SZABO
★ **Faces / Mer. SRM-1-1141**
★★ **Gabor Szabo: His Greatest Hits / Imp. 9204**
★★ **Mizrab / CTI 6026**
★ **Nightflight / Mer. SRM-1-1091**
★ **Rambler / CTI 6035**
★★ **The Drums / Imp. 9272**
★★ **Wind, Sky and Diamonds / Imp. 9151**
Hungarian guitarist Gabor Szabo (b. 1936) emigrated to America in 1956. Studying at Berklee School and playing with Chico Hamilton, he developed a thoughtful, supple style that reflected his background in Hungary. Playing with a variety of small groups, Szabo has incorporated a ton of exotic musical influences (Middle East, Indian, Oriental) to supplement his style.

But Szabo could also be described as an obsessive eclectic who has never really defined his approach on the guitar. His albums are characteristically Sixties in that they experiment to the point of dilution. His tone is rather thin and some of his production ideas and instrumental collaborations are heart-stopping in their awkwardness. *His Greatest Hits* is the only possible selection here, and even that recommendation is offered with great trepidation. — J.C.C.

ART TATUM
★★★★★ **Art Tatum / Cap. M-11028**
★★★★★ **God Is in the House / Onyx 205**
★★★★★ **Masterpieces / MCA 4019**
★★★★★ **Masterpieces, Vol. 2 (plus James P. Johnson) / MCA 4112**
★★★★ **Piano Starts Here / Col. CS-9655**

It is no exaggeration to label pianist Tatum (1910-1956), who had only partial vision in one eye, the greatest virtuoso ever to play jazz on any instrument. Beyond his unbelievable technique, Tatum had a supreme mastery of harmonic substitutions that inspired the modernists who came to prominence in the Forties.

The ratings assigned to the above albums, all made by Tatum in the Thirties and Forties, should be read as indicating the most essential of his performances. Volume 1 of *Masterpieces* is one of the essentials, covering the Thirties and early Forties and featuring Tatum solo, with his popular piano-guitar-bass trio, and in a small band with the great blues singer Joe Turner. Equally important is the recently unearthed *God Is in the House,* which contains privately made tapes of Tatum jamming in 1941 Harlem clubs; the closing tracks with trumpeter Frankie Newton achieve an amazing intensity. The Capitol album, perhaps the single best all-solo volume, is from the late Forties.

★★★★ **The Art Tatum Group Masterpieces / Pablo 2625706 (eight volumes)**
★★★★ **The Art Tatum Solo Masterpieces / Pablo 2625703 (thirteen volumes)**

Between 1953 and the year of his death, producer Norman Granz involved Tatum in these two mammoth projects that have been reissued in boxed sets and singly (six of the solo albums are still to come). Perhaps five-star ratings should be awarded for sheer effort, but Tatum was never the most accommodating band player, and his solos reveal that he often hit upon a routine (compare earlier versions). Few listeners will want the entire solo box, and should choose individual volumes according to one's preference for the songs included in each. Among the eight combo records, the session with tenor saxophonist Ben Webster is a true masterpiece of heart-on-sleeve emoting, and trumpeter Roy Eldridge is in a jousting mood. Lionel Hampton, Benny Carter, Buddy Rich, Jo Jones and Buddy DeFranco also appear. — B.B.

CECIL TAYLOR
★★★★ **In Transition / Blue N. LA458-H2**
★★★★ **Looking Ahead! / Contem. 7562**

Any understanding of post-Parker avantgarde jazz must be grounded in pianist/composer Cecil Taylor, the first player to successfully achieve a system of rhythmic energy, collectively shared by the others in his Units, which replaced the constant "time" (swing) common to all jazz through 1960.

In Transition, a double album, contains his first recordings (from 1956) with a quartet and a 1959 session for trio and quintet. Both dates suggest Monk in their percussiveness and angularity, though by the latter Taylor was giving clear indications of the rhythmic directions he would shortly pursue. "Carol/Three Points" is an early example of Taylor's declarative writing. *Looking Ahead!* is a 1958 quartet with a fine vibraphonist named Earl Griffith, and a particularly successful trio piece called "Of What."

(Other Taylor from this period, also highly recommended, is contained on the anthology *Masters of the Modern Piano,* Verve 2514, which has Taylor's 1957 Newport performance, and half of *Into the Hot,* Impulse A-9, three 1961 band tracks issued under Gil Evans' name.)

★★★★ **Cecil Taylor with the Jazz Composer's Orchestra / JCOA 1002**
★★★★★ **Conquistador / Blue N. 84260**
★★★★★ **Nefertiti, the Beautiful One Has Come / Ari./Free 1905**
★★★★ **The Great Concert of Cecil Taylor / Prest. 34003**
★★★★★ **Unit Structures / Blue N. 84237**

Nefertiti, made in a Copenhagen nightclub in 1962, is the breakthrough album, where the entire group feels Taylor's rhythmic passion for the first time. Jimmy Lyons on alto sax and Sunny Murray on drums complete the cataclysmic trio. Of the remaining Taylor recordings from the Sixties, *Unit Structures* is especially recommended for the variety of composition, the brilliant use Taylor makes of the septet (including three horns, two basses), and the inspired playing, especially from drummer Andrew Cyrille. *Conquistador,* by a sextet, is almost as good, though later performances fall into the trap of going on too long at one extreme dynamic level. The JCOA album is half of Michael Mantler's *Jazz Composer's Orchestra* box (JCOA 1001/2), available separately; here, an orchestra sets Taylor off on a railing solo. *Great Concert,* from Paris in 1969, is even more intense: three albums of high energy, with Lyons, Cyrille and Sam Rivers.

★★★★ **Indent / Ari./Free 1038**
★★★★ **Dark to Themselves / Inner 3001**
★★★★★ **Silent Tongues / Ari./Free 1005**
★★★★★ **Spring of Two Blue-J's / Unit Core 30551**

These albums, all from 1973 to 1976, are concert recordings, with the Arista/Freedoms being solo recitals. *Two Blue-J's* is recommended as the best introduction to Taylor—one side solo, the other with Lyons, Cyrille and the Revolutionary Ensemble's marvelous bassist Sirone. *Silent Tongues,* from Montreux 1974, is Taylor's most sustained and diverse solo work on record. *Dark* is the most recent (1976) and features a new group, with Lyons (remaining from the old Unit) and three exciting additions (Raphe Malik, trumpet; David Ware, tenor; Marc Edwards, drums). Taylor's performances could still stand editing, but there is no denying their power or the technical and emotional skill of the players. — B.B.

CHARLES TOLLIVER

★★★★ Paper Man / Ari./Free 1002
★★★ The Ringer / Ari./Free 1017

Tolliver, a strong trumpeter and composer in what is commonly called the post-bop style ("I feel, as Charlie Parker felt, that jazz is meant to swing and pretty notes be played" is the way he has put it), exemplifies the changes jazz recording has gone through in recent years. Had he arrived in New York in 1960, he would have cut several albums on one of the jazz labels; instead he arrived in the mid-Sixties, so his work was done for a European label and, eventually, his own Strata-East.

The Freedom albums are from 1968 and 1969, respectively. *Paper Man* is a true all-star quintet (Gary Bartz, Herbie Hancock, Ron Carter, Joe Chambers), but the leader's fine writing and the contained exuberance of his trumpet remain at the center of the session. *The Ringer* features the first edition of his Quartet Music Inc., with Stanley Cowell on piano.

★★★★★ Impact / Strata-East 19757
★★★★★ Live at Slugs', Vol. 1 / Strata-East 1972
★★★★★ Live at Slugs', Vol. 2 / Strata-East 19720
★★★ Live at the Loosdrecht Jazz Festival / Strata-East 19740/1
★★★ Live in Tokyo / Strata-East 19745
★★★★★ Music Inc. / Strata-East 1971

The best edition of the Music Inc. band, with Cowell, bassist Cecil McBee and drummer Jimmy Hopps, is heard on the two volumes recorded at Slugs' Saloon in 1970; the performances are lengthy, but the inspiration level remains generally high. *Loosdrecht* is a double album with the tight rhythm section of the infrequently heard John Hicks and Alvin Queen on piano and drums, plus bassist Reggie Workman.

The first and last Strata-East albums listed are orchestral versions of Tolliver's (and in the case of *Music Inc.,* Cowell's) music, and contain some of the most stirring large-ensemble work in the post-bop/modal idiom. *Music Inc.* is superior from the standpoint of compositional variety, while *Impact* makes room for neglected saxophone soloists Harold Vick, James Spaulding and George Coleman. — B.B.

RALPH TOWNER

★★★★ Diary / ECM/Poly. 1032
★★★★ Matchbook / ECM/Poly. 1056
★★★★ Sargasso Sea / ECM/Poly. 1080
★★★ Towner/Solstice / ECM/Poly. 1060

Ralph Towner plays twelve-string guitar, classical guitar and piano with equal brilliance. Generally, his music is quiet and introspective, with extraordinarily subtle shadings in terms of tone and dynamics. His technique is essentially classical but his background in jazz and his playing with Oregon have led him to a flexible compositional approach heightened by a startling sense of counterpoint and balance. He understands the use of space in improvisation and his compositions, although seemingly unstructured, are propelled by an inner logic.

His ECM/Polydor albums trace his already full solo career. *Diary,* aptly named, features Towner on all instruments and some of his best compositions, most notably the haunting "Icarus." "Images Unseen" recalls the Eastern influences that predominate in Oregon's music. *Matchbook* pairs Towner with the gifted Gary Burton on vibes, and their rapport is both instinctive and subtly complex. One of Towner's most successful collaborations to date is with John Abercrombie on *Sargasso Sea,* where Towner's rich twelve-string chording envelops Abercrombie's dry, stinging electric lead lines. — J.C.C.

McCOY TYNER

★★★★ Asante / Blue N. LA223–G
★★★★ Atlantis / Mile. 55002
★★★ Cosmos / Blue N. LA460–H2
★★★★★ Echoes of a Friend / Mile. 9055
★★★★★ Enlightenment / Mile. 55001
★★★★★ Expansions / Blue N. 84338
★★★★ Extensions / Blue N. LA006–F
★★★ Fly with the Wind / Mile. 9067
★★★ Focal Point / Mile. 9072
★★★ Inception / Imp. 18
★★★ Inner Voices / Mile. 9079

★★★★ "Live" at Newport / Imp. 48
★★★ Nights of Ballads and Blues / Imp.
39
★★★ Plays Ellington / Imp. 79
★★★★ Reaching 4th / Imp. 33
★★★★ Reevaluation: The Impulse Years /
Imp. 9235
★★★★★ Sahara / Mile. 9039
★★★★ Sama Layuca / Mile. 9056
★★★★ Song for My Lady / Mile. 9044
★★★★ Song of the New World / Mile.
9049
★★★★★ Supertrios / Mile. 55003
★★★ Tender Moments / Blue N. 84275
★★★ The Early Trios / Imp. 1A-9338/2
★★★ The Greeting / Mile. 9085
★★★★ The Real McCoy / Blue N. 84264
★★★★ Time for Tyner / Blue N. 84307
★★★★ Today and Tomorrow / Imp. 63
★★★★★ Trident / Mile. 9063

Record-company affiliations divide McCoy Tyner's recording career as a leader into three distinct and instructive phases. From 1962 to 1965, while still the pianist in John Coltrane's immortal quartet (with bassist Jimmy Garrison and drummer Elvin Jones), Tyner was under contract to Impulse, Coltrane's label. When he left the Coltrane group he also moved on to Blue Note, where he stayed for the next five years while his conception matured through several lean economic periods. By 1972, when he began his highly successful period with Milestone, his own playing had entered a new phase and he was leading the most powerful band working out of the middle-Coltrane tradition.

Tyner has stated that his Impulse albums were intended to present something different than what he did with Coltrane; that four of the six originally issued were trio albums liberally programed with pop standards suggests that the label was interested in developing its own more progressive entry for the piano-trio audience that supported Oscar Peterson, Erroll Garner, etc. The beneficial effect of horn players on Tyner's thick, darkly percussive style can be heard on *"Live" at Newport* and *Today and Tomorrow,* where trio tracks are mixed with larger combos (Clark Terry and Charlie Mariano are on the former, Thad Jones and John Gilmore on the latter).

Of the trio records, *Reaching 4th* has Tyner's strongest playing and the excellent support of Henry Grimes on bass and Roy Haynes' drums; *Inception,* however, also is notable for revealing that Tyner's now-familiar modal composition style was already taking shape on his debut album. All of his

Impulse work emphasizes his roots in the music of Bud Powell, Thelonious Monk and of course Coltrane. *Reevaluation,* a good sampler of the period, contains four tracks by Trane's band.

The Blue Note albums are marked by some excellent sideman appearances and Tyner's growing fascination with Afro-Asian music, a concern reflected in both his playing and writing. *The Real McCoy* begins the series with an excellent quartet (Joe Henderson, Ron Carter, Elvin Jones) and five characteristic tunes; *Tender Moments* is Tyner's first writing for more than three horns and features Lee Morgan; *Time for Tyner* is by trio and quartet, with vibist Bobby Hutcherson a perfect partner (especially on "African Village"). *Expansions,* made in 1968, is a fantastic session by Tyner's working quintet (Gary Bartz on alto, Woody Shaw, trumpet) plus two added starters from Miles Davis' band, Wayne Shorter and Ron Carter (on cello). The variety in the writing, excellent solos by the horns and the feisty drums of Freddie Waits make this album one of Tyner's best. The sequel *Extensions,* with Alice Coltrane's harp spelling Woody Shaw and Elvin Jones at the drums, isn't as strong, and the 1970 *Asante* is notable for the increased rhythmic interdependence in Tyner's two-handed solos and a rare glimpse of alto saxophonist Andrew White.

On *Sahara,* recorded slightly more than a year after *Asante* by Tyner's working quartet, everything finally falls together. Tyner now attacks the keyboard like a master African percussionist, building incredible solo swells and driving his Coltrane-derived horn soloists (Sonny Fortune here and on the next two albums) to unexpected heights. Alphonse Mouzon, who often deserves criticism for being too loud and unsympathetic, couldn't ask for a better setting to bash in.

A key to Tyner's success at Milestone is that he refuses to duplicate formats from one album to the next. Thus *Song for My Lady* has tracks by a septet (with Charles Tolliver, Michael White and Mtume added), *Echoes of a Friend* is a solo piano tour de force dedicated to Coltrane, and *Song of the New World* uses string or brass ensembles. By the time of Montreux 1973, where *Enlightenment* was recorded, Azar Lawrence was Tyner's saxophonist, and this two-record set remains the high-energy pinnacle of Tyner's working band recordings. (*Atlantis* was also done live the following year.)

If the limitations of Tyner's modal melodies become more apparent with the 1974 *Sama Layuca* (a nonet with Lawrence, Bartz, Hutcherson), there is still the invigorating strength of the music and the special delight of Tyner's piano. There is also an attempt to make Tyner's music more palatable to a nonjazz audience by adding strings (on the 1976 *Fly with the Wind*) and voices (*Inner Voices*, recorded in 1977); both albums are easy listening as far as Tyner goes, with a better rhythm section and horn soloists making *Inner Voices* preferable.

Tyner's real triumphs among his recent recordings are the trio albums *Trident* (with Ron Carter and Elvin Jones) and the two-record *Supertrios* (half Carter and Tony Williams, half Eddie Gomez and Jack DeJohnette). On these albums Tyner plays with masters on his own high level, a situation hard to sustain in his own working band. *The Greeting*, a live recording by his sextet from early 1978, is about what one would expect—hot, invigorating Afro-American music, but nothing that hasn't been done with more freshness and spirit on *Enlightenment* and *Sahara*. If Tyner has been in a holding pattern for the past few years, consolidating his ever-growing audience, we can take heart that his integrity is unsullied, his instrumental command and dedication to the improviser's art undimmed. — B.B.

MICHAL URBANIAK
★★★ Atma / Col. KC-33184
★★ Body English / Ari. 4086
★★★★ Fusion / Col. KC-32852
★★★ Fusion III / Col. PC-33582

Four colorful, contagious albums. Polish violinist Urbaniak's music sounds like Eastern European folk tunes gone sprightly fusion-funky. Full of rich synthesized touches and happy backbeat, his LPs also feature his wife, vocalist Urzula Dudziak; she sings as gutterally low as an electric bass, and as shriekingly high as Urbaniak's electric violin. It all adds up to persistently *musical* art. — M.R.

MIROSLAV VITOUS
★★★ Magical Shepherd / War. B-2925
★★★ Miroslav / Ari./Free 1040
★★★★★ Mountain in the Clouds / Atco 1622

Vitous arrived on the jazz scene from Czechoslovakia in the mid-Sixties and was immediately recognized as one of the best bass players available. After playing around with various leaders and working with Miles Davis and Herbie Mann, Vitous recorded his first solo album, *Infinite Search*. It was later rereleased with an additional track and called *Mountain in the Clouds*. This record features Vitous' virtuoso bass playing, Joe Henderson on tenor saxophone, John McLaughlin on guitar, Herbie Hancock on electric piano and Jack DeJohnette and Joe Chambers on drums. Vitous went on to help form Weather Report, but his solo career since then has been spotty. Looking for direction, he even started to play guitar, which was a big mistake. — J.S.

FATS WALLER
★★★★ Ain't Misbehavin' / RCA AFM1-1246
★★★★ Complete Fats Waller, Vol. 1 / RCA AXM2-5511
★★★ Fats Waller / Trip 5819
★★★ Fats Waller Legacy / Olym. 7106
★★★ Fats Waller on the Air / Trip 5808
★★★★ Fats Waller Piano Solos / RCA AXM2-5518
★★★ Fats Waller Plays Fats Waller / Ev. 319
★★★ Legend in His Lifetime / Trip X-5042

Waller (1904–1943) was a great stride-piano stylist and a very popular player, vocalist and songwriter. He served as an accompanist in the Twenties for Bessie Smith and other blues singers, then established himself as a composer and bandleader in the Thirties and early Forties before dying in 1943 at the age of forty-nine. His score for the Broadway show *Hot Chocolates* included his best-known song, "Ain't Misbehavin'." He also wrote "Honeysuckle Rose" and recorded great versions of any number of pop standards, one of which,

"I'm Gonna Sit Right Down and Write Myself a Letter," became his biggest hit. The RCA packages present Waller at his best. *Ain't Misbehavin'* has been in print for ages and holds up remarkably well. — J.S.

WEATHER REPORT
★★★★★ I Sing the Body Electric / Col. PC-31352
★★★ Weather Report / Col. PC-30661
Joe Zawinul (keyboards) and Wayne Shorter (saxophones) were well-known sidemen with Cannonball Adderley and Miles Davis, respectively, who had been prime movers in Davis' popular *In a Silent Way* and *Bitches Brew* albums; they formed Weather Report in 1971, with bassist Miroslav Vitous as original coleader, and have since released an album a year. The shifts in the band's music and personnel have charted both the pinnacles and pitfalls of jazz-rock "fusion" during the period.

The first album (30661), with Alphonse Mouzon and Airto Moreira on drums and percussion, was an extension of the style first forged on *Silent Way*—lots of ensemble mood, few solos (except on Shorter's "Eurydice," the album's most substantial piece) and an overall feeling of incompleteness. "Orange Lady," a lovely Zawinul melody that never goes anywhere, typifies the problems of the album.

I Sing the Body Electric features the first permanent touring version of the band, with Eric Gravatt on drums and Dom Um Romao on percussion. One side, recorded live in Tokyo, plus Zawinul's "Unknown Soldier" from the studio sessions, is the best recorded example of the kind of intensity Weather Report still generates in concert.
★★★★ Black Market / Col. PC-34099
★★★★★ Mysterious Traveller / Col. P-32494
★★★ Sweetnighter / Col. PC-32210
★★★★ Tale Spinnin' / Col. PC-33417
With *Sweetnighter* the band shows its intention to make a funkier music more directed to the rock audience, and while Zawinul's long pieces "Boogie Woogie Waltz" and "125th Street Congress" have the beat, they dissipate into a blue of electric jamming. From *Mysterious Traveller* forward there is a much keener awareness of studio technique, and a growing sense of how to integrate the various electronic keyboards on Zawinul's part; Vitous is replaced by the funkier electric bass of Alphonso Johnson and a string of players fill the percussion

chairs. *Mysterious Traveller* is the most successful album of this period but, excellent improvisations like "Cucumber Slumber" and "Blackthorn Rose" notwithstanding, there is energy missing in all of these works due to the contained percussion work and the overall technological veneer of the music. Most troublesome of all is the minimal presence of Shorter, one of the great contemporary musical minds, who has tended to play less and take a less central role in the recorded ensembles as time passes (in-person performances are fortunately different).
★★★★★ Heavy Weather / Col. PC-34418
Electric bassist Jaco Pastorius replaced Johnson in 1976 and quickly assumed coleader status with Shorter and Zawinul. Alejandro Acuna on drums and Manolo Badrena on percussion give the band a stable personnel, which recorded an album that manages to be both its most commercial and one of its most challenging. "Birdland," the hit from the record, shows the distance Zawinul has gone in his ability to use rock and studio techniques creatively, while "A Remark You Made" and "The Juggler" testify to his compositional range. Pastorius is simply the finest electric bassist around, and a multifaceted composer as well; and Shorter, ever pithier, contributes eloquent balladry on "Remark" and the infectious tune "Palladium." Like its namesake, Weather Report is always changing, occasionally frustrating and quite often right on target. — B.B.

EBERHARD WEBER
★★ Passengers / ECM/Poly. 1-1092
★★★ Ring / ECM/Poly. 1051
★★★★ The Colours of Chloe / ECM/ Poly. 1042
★★★★ The Following Morning / ECM/ Poly. 1-1084
★★★★ Yellow Fields / ECM/Poly. 1066
Weber is thirty-eight years old and has played cello for thirty-one years. His bass playing has been heard alongside Chick Corea, Jean-Luc Ponty, Wolfgang Dauner and Volker Kreigel, among other free jazzers. Europeans have been listening to his stuff for a long time and finally America has begun to catch up, due to Manfred Eicher's decision to turn him into the Leland Sklar of ECM's session scene. Eicher has sponsored Weber further by releasing his solo work, some of it brilliant, as on his tensile *Colours of Chloe*, released in 1974. Eicher has also teamed him with other ECM artists, such as Gary Burton on *Ring*

and *Passengers*. His bass playing is perhaps the most virtuosic in Germany, his cello is used with an expressionistic invention unrivaled in Europe and, though there is stiff competition from Martin Mull, Weber plays a mean ocarina. He brings out every drop of melancholy a cello can ring when he plays his fretless axe, creating the thousand spectacular voices of a singing-saw cello chorus (cello section shot through a Buchla synthesizer—along with heavy double-tracking, a trick he uses to great advantage). If America had more of Weber in its elevators, it'd be a better place to live. — B.M.

BEN WEBSTER
★ ★ ★ ★ ★ **Tenor Giants (with Coleman Hawkins) / Verve 2-2520**
One of the greatest tenor saxophonists of the classic jazz era and the master of gruff, raspy blues and breathy sensuality. Ben Webster's (1909–1973) important early work is scattered around; many of the most important performances, like the immortal Ellington band sides from 1940 to 1942, are now out of print, while Webster's mid-Forties combo work is spread over several Savoy and Onyx anthologies. *Tenor Giants* is from 1957 and 1959, to my mind his greatest period, and he can be heard outblowing his mentor Coleman Hawkins. Roy Eldridge, Budd Johnson (yes, a third tenor) and Oscar Peterson are among the other participants.
★ ★ ★ ★ ★ **Atmosphere for Lovers and Thieves / Black L. 111**
★ ★ ★ ★ **Duke's in Bed / Black L. 190**
★ ★ ★ ★ **Saturday Night at the Montmartre / Black L. 302**
★ ★ ★ ★ **See You at the Fair / Imp. 65**
Disinterest in his work at home led Webster to Europe in 1964, though the Impulse

disc shows he still was in noble form before he left. The Black Lions are all from 1965 and all fine, but *Atmosphere* contains probably the finest playing of Webster's European years.
★ ★ **At Work in Europe / Prest. 24031**
★ ★ ★ ★ **My Man / Inner 2008**
Although *At Work* is marred by a disjointed session employing two pianos, Webster's last recordings were generally high-quality affairs. *My Man,* made live in Copenhagen months before his death in 1973, captures him in a typically mellow mood and reminds American listeners what joys we missed when Webster chose Europe for his final home. — B.B.

RANDY WESTON
★ ★ ★ ★ **African Nite / Inner 1013**
★ ★ ★ **Berkshire Blues / Ari./Free 1026**
★ ★ ★ ★ **Blue Moses / CTI 6016**
★ ★ ★ **Blues / Trip 5033**
★ ★ ★ **Blues to Africa / Ari./Free 1014**
★ ★ ★ **Carnival / Ari./Free 1004**
★ ★ ★ **Get Happy / Riv. SMJ-6063M**
★ ★ ★ ★ ★ **Little Niles / Blue N. LA598-H2**
Randy Weston (b. 1926) has been an eloquent pianist and composer in the Duke Ellington-Thelonious Monk tradition for over two decades. His increasing interest in Africa led to his settling in Morocco for five years (1967–72). *Get Happy* has some of his first trio work, from 1955, with his strong touch and sense of dark harmonies and strategic silences already developed.

Little Niles is the finest Weston collection currently available. A 1958 sextet gives definitive readings of such memorable Weston compositions as the title track, "Pam's Waltz," and "Babe's Blues"; also included is a quintet with Kenny Dorham and Coleman Hawkins, adding such Weston staples as "High Fly" and "Where" in nightclub performances from 1959.

Weston spent the early Sixties with an excellent band that the record companies ignored. *Blues* represents a late addition of the group, after tenor saxophonist Booker Ervin had left. *Berkshire Blues,* produced in 1965 by Ellington, has one side of so-so trios by the band's rhythm section and a much more intriguing side of solo piano.

Recent years have brought Weston home and stepped up his recording activity. *Blue Moses* marked his return; there are the usual CTI lapses (electric piano, overdubbed orchestrations), but the basic combo tracks—with Freddie Hubbard, Grover Washington, Ron Carter and Billy Cobham—are among the label's most substantial. Weston has done all of his post-1973 recording in Europe, where his 1974 Arista/Freedom sessions were made. *Carnival,* a Montreux performance, has overextended quintet tracks (with Billy Harper and Don Moye) plus a heartfelt solo tribute to Ellington; *Blues to Africa* shows the more dramatic traces of his African experiences in eight piano solos.

African Nite is another solo set from a year later. Weston is exploring the keyboard with greater rhythmic freedom, yet his feeling for melody remains and several good new tunes are introduced. — B.B.

ANDREW WHITE
★★★★ **Collage / Andr. 14**
★★★★ **Passion Flower / Andr. 5**
★★★ **Seven Giant Steps for Coltrane /**
   Andr. 30
Washington, D.C.-based White is nothing if not unique. He has toured with Stevie Wonder and the Fifth Dimension on electric bass, recorded on that instrument plus English horn with Weather Report, transcribed 421 John Coltrane solos, arranged Coltrane's music for orchestra, and recorded as a saxophone soloist with McCoy Tyner (alto) and on thirty albums (alto and tenor) for his own label, Andrew's Music. White's album covers are uniformly gold print on white background, with, judging from those I have seen, a version of his composition "Theme" always included.

The White albums rated above are those which this writer has heard. Both *Passion Flower* and *Collage* are mid-Seventies quartets, with Steve Novosel on bass, and Blackbyrds Kevin Toney (piano) and Keith Killgo (drums) showing what they can do in a "straight-ahead" context. *Passion Flower* seems like a study of Coltrane's evolution, with White reflecting much of

the spectrum in tenor solos on his own blues lines. *Collage* stresses some interesting arranging ideas and tune choices (Wayne Shorter's "Contemplation," Coltrane's "Just for the Love," Les Baxter's "Dock at Papeete" [!]). *Seven Giant Steps,* containing seven live, unaccompanied alto solos, supposedly based on Coltrane's "Giant Steps," is a bit indulgent even for White. The records are available from 4830 S. Dakota Ave., N.E., Washington, D.C. 20017. — B.B.

LENNY WHITE
★★★ **Adventures of the Astral Pirates /**
   Elek. 6E-121
★★★ **Big City / Nemp. 441**
★★★ **Venusian Summer / Nemp. 435**
White is one of the better fusion drummers. His playing on the landmark *Hymn of the Seventh Galaxy* album with Chick Corea's Return to Forever gives better-known names like Billy Cobham a run for their money. But White suffers from the problem that seems to plague all fusion drummers when they try to record on their own—his albums are badly unfocused, trying to do a million different things at once and accomplishing none of them. Each of White's solo albums have moments that make them worthwhile, but none of them hold together for a full listening. — J.S.

TONY WILLIAMS
★★★★ **Believe It / Col. PC-33836**
★★★ **Million Dollar Legs / Col.**
   PC-34263
One of the few genuinely innovative post-Art Blakey jazz drummers, Tony Williams earned his reputation as the rhythmic mainspring for the mid-Sixties Miles Davis quintet that also included Herbie Hancock, Wayne Shorter and Ron Carter. Williams has been in the forefront of jazz-rock fusion since his collaboration with Jack Bruce, of Lifetime. His only in-print records are the two most recent efforts, both funk fusion delights featuring the guitar playing of ex-Soft Machine axeman Alan Holdsworth. — J.S.

LARRY YOUNG
★★★ **Groove Street / Prest. 7237**
★★★ **Larry Young's Fuel / Ari. 4051**
★★★ **Spaceball / Ari. 4072**
A wildly innovative keyboardist, Young (1940-1978) was noted for his virtuoso organ playing with Tony Williams, Jimi Hendrix and Miles Davis. He recorded a series of solo albums in the Sixties on Blue

Note and Prestige, most of which are unfortunately out of print. *Groove Street* is representative if not exemplary of this period. The two mid-Seventies recordings for Arista represent Young's attempt at a comeback in the disco-funk mold. The albums were neither commercial nor artistic successes, yet the force of Young's tremendous imagination keeps everything moving even at the worst moments. *Spaceball* especially is a triumph of musicianship over terrible ideas. Young's multi-keyboard pyrotechnics scale along interminable vamps with names like "Sticky Wicket." — J.S.

LESTER YOUNG
Lester Young (1909–1959), whom Billie Holiday dubbed the President (shortened to Pres or Prez), is one of the half-dozen greatest soloists in jazz history. He moved beyond Coleman Hawkins' domination of tenor sax style with his first recordings in 1936, producing a light tone and oblique melodic ideas that seemed to skim the music's harmonic surface. His swing, a strange blend of floating and stomping, was the most inexorable of the period, and nobody before or since has conveyed more soulful lyricism. Young's ideas led to be-bop, cool jazz and rhythm & blues—in other words, to every black music trend of the following decade. Rating his albums should be unnecessary, although the attempt has been made.
★★★★★ **The Lester Young Story, Vol. 1 / Col. JG-33502**
First in CBS' chronological series of every Young performance they own. This 1936–37 material has his debut, with a quintet from Count Basie's band (where Young worked until 1940), and his first transcendent collaborations with Teddy Wilson and Billie Holiday (Jo Jones, Benny Goodman and Buck Clayton also participate).
★★★★★ **Pres at His Very Best / Trip 5509**
From 1943 and 1944, before his emotionally damaging stay in the Army. His best quartet work, with Johnny Guarnieri, Slam Stewart and Sid Catlett; and a Basie septet featuring the Count, Clayton, Jones, Dickie Wells and Freddie Green.
★★★★★ **Classic Tenors / Fly. FD-10146**
Four tracks by a similar septet, same vintage, with Young's relevance to the R&B tenors especially evident. Also eight Coleman Hawkins titles from 1943.
★★★★★ **Pres/The Complete Savoy Recordings / Savoy L-2202**

Recorded just before entering the Army (with most of the Basie Band and combos featuring Cozy Cole and Basie), plus a side from 1949, less brilliant but still substantial Young.
★★★★★ **The Aladdin Sessions / Blue N. LA456-H2**
Quintets, sextets, septets from 1945 to 1948, with the scars of racial harassment and incarceration for possession of marijuana while in the service evident. The twenty-seven performances are still beautiful, in a kicking swing-to-bop style.
★★★★ **Lester Swings / Verve 2-2516**
Young is clearly a changed man in the 1950–51 quartets here, although the eight 1945 performances by the odd trio of Young, pianist Nat "King" Cole and drummer Buddy Rich are among the best postwar Pres.
★★★★★ **Bird and Pres: The 1946 Concerts / Verve VE 2-2518**
These Jazz at the Philharmonic tapes find Young lapsing into crowd-pleasing exhibitionism on the final side, but the company (Charlie Parker, Dizzy Gillespie, Coleman Hawkins) can't be beat.
★★★★★ **Pres Lives / Savoy SJL-1109**
Admittedly from 1950, but revealing for the aural picture of Young in a club blowing long and hard over his familiar mix of standards and blues.
★★★★★ **Pres and Teddy and Oscar / Verve 2-2502**
Teddy is Wilson, Oscar is Peterson, the collaborations are from 1956 and 1952 respectively. Young is changed, more predictable and sometimes too languid, but even in decline he was a master. His best from the Fifties.
★★★★ **Pres in Europe / Onyx ORI-218**
Privately recorded performances from 1956 and 1957. This supposedly defeated giant could still move mountains—hear "Lester's European Blues." He died in 1959 at the age of fifty. — B.B.

JOE ZAWINUL
★★★★ **Zawinul / Atco 1579**
This fine solo album by the master keyboardist who leads Weather Report includes an adaption of "In a Silent Way," which Zawinul wrote for one of Miles Davis' most innovative groups, and pairs Zawinul with another virtuoso keyboardist, Herbie Hancock. With Weather Report, Zawinul expanded his keyboard arsenal to an astounding array of synthesizers and related equipment, but here he uses only electric piano, to sublime effect. — J.S.

GOSPEL

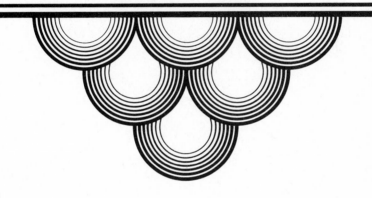

PROFESSOR ALEX BRADFORD
★★★★ **Best of Alex Bradford / Spec. 2133**
★★★ **He Lifted Me / Spec. 2143**
★★ **Obey His Will / Check. ACK 10092**
Combine Archie Brownlee with Alex
Bradford, add a horn section (and maybe
some strings), and you have a close approximation of the Atlantic-era Ray
Charles. Bradford, who began his career in
vaudeville, often expressed a desire to sing
pop à la Dionne and DeeDee Warwick
(whom he discovered) and LaVern Baker
(for whom he wrote Top Forty hits). His
idols include Petie Wheatstraw, Gatemouth
Moore and Eddie "Cleanhead" Vinson,
and a blues feel permeates all of Bradford's
best material. This is particularly true of
his imagery—check out his best-known
song, "Too Close to Heaven." Bradford
had an amazingly versatile voice that went
effortlessly from a deep moan to a high
shriek. *Best of* is essential to any basic gospel collection, but the other Specialty LP is
surprisingly strong. *Obey,* from late in his
career, is a fascinating, off-the-wall set of
pop-gospel, but it isn't always effective,
and Bradford's gravelly voice has become
weak and mannered.   — J.MO.

SHIRLEY CAESAR
★★ **First Lady / Road. LA744–R**
★★★★ **Shirley Caesar / Up. Fr. 189**
★★★★ **The Best of Shirley Caesar with
the Caravans / Savoy MG-14202**
Though young, Caesar reached her fame as
a note-bending preacher of gospel's old
school; she can also be the most mesmeriz-
ingly intense of modern singers. The Savoy
sides are crude and bluesy, her voice displaying astonishing power and range.
(Though the Caravans—also including Inez
Andrews and Albertina Walker—were one
of the most popular gospel groups, it's

mainly the sides with Caesar that are of interest to rock fans.)
   On her own, Caesar sang in a more old-
fashioned style; yet as a preacher, she also
rapped advice à la Millie Jackson and
showed abundant humor. These are her
Hob sides, some of which comprise the Up
Front compilation. *First Lady* is secular
songs with spiritual themes and proof that
the transition from gospel to soul isn't entirely natural: constricted by the style's
conventions, she is an undistinguished soul
singer.   — J.MO.

REVEREND JAMES CLEVELAND
★★★★ **Rev. James Cleveland and the An-
gelic Choir, Vol. 3: Peace Be Still / Sa-
voy 14076**
★★ **Rev. James Cleveland and the Angelic
Choir, Vol. 7 / Savoy 14171**
★★★ **Rev. James Cleveland and the
Southern California Community Choir /
Savoy 14235**
★★ **Rev. James Cleveland and the South-
ern California Community Choir: In the
Ghetto / Savoy 14322**
★★ **Rev. James Cleveland Presents the
Charles Fold Singers Recorded Live:
Jesus Is the Best Thing That Ever Hap-
pened to Me / Savoy 7005**
★★★ **Rev. James Cleveland with the An-
gelic Choir, Vol. 2 / Savoy 14063**
★★★★ **Rev. James Cleveland with the
Gospel All-Stars: Out on a Hill / Savoy
14045**
★★★ **Rev. James Cleveland with the
Greater Metropolitan Church of Christ
Choir: The Lord Is My Life / Savoy
14425**
★★ **Rev. James Cleveland with the South-
ern California Community Choir: Give It
to Me / Savoy 14412**
★ **Rev. James Cleveland with the Voices of**

Tabernacle: God Has Smiled on Me /
Savoy 14352
★ ★ ★ Songs of Dedication / Savoy 14125
★ ★ ★ This Sunday in Person: James
  Cleveland with the Angelic Gospel
  Choir / Savoy 14059

Many would argue that Cleveland took modern gospel music as far as it could go, that the only way a gospel artist could extend Cleveland's innovations would be to abandon some gospel conventions altogether (which, of course, is what eventually happened). Certainly, Cleveland has been influenced by such secular artists as Ray Charles, though not to the extent that he was shaped by gospel pioneers like Robert Martin. Cleveland's vocals are most conspicuously pop-tinged, though even his arrangements (and piano playing) showed he was quite aware of jazz. This was true *despite* the fact that Cleveland didn't stray from gospel for years. His voice, at its peak, was a sandpapery baritone that would have been an ideal blues vehicle.

Cleveland has recorded prolifically in a variety of settings; the albums listed above represent a cross section. The first, *Out on a Hill,* shows him to be a well-developed gospel singer, though his style is not quite as personal as it would become. Whatever technical niceties his voice lacks, he is a warm, robust and versatile singer, and some of his best compositions are here. The next two LPs, *This Sunday* and *Volume 2,* show him moving closer to his trademark sound, but the tempos are still a little too rigid; the vocals aren't quite there. (These LPs also mark the introduction of the teenage Billy Preston as Cleveland's organist, a position Preston maintained through several of Cleveland's most productive years. Preston's "sound effects" organ proved something of a gospel novelty.)

"Peace Be Still" (song and album) represents Cleveland's big breakthrough. It is an eighteenth-century madrigal that Cleveland arranges and sings like a perfect soul ballad. Tension builds and builds without release until the end; the choir answers him in traditional call-and-response, or embellishes his vocal lines. The entire album is a supreme example of slow gospel singing. (Cleveland sang slow ones almost exclusively, which may hinder some from hearing even his best albums all the way through.)

Songs of Dedication presents him without choir or group. It's just his voice and piano plus organ. Still, it's a satisfying album. However raucous his voice, Cleveland

sings with great taste, subtlety and conviction, and the high choral voices he usually used to set himself off are hardly missed.

By the time he began working with the Southern California Community Choir, Cleveland's voice had taken on even more resonance, but it had also mellowed (or faded, some might argue). Still, this was a hip, vibrant choir, and it worked well with Cleveland. About half the cuts were given over to other soloists, and they are usually at least as compelling as Cleveland himself. (In contrast, the Voices of Tabernacle is a thoroughly pedestrian choir.)

Of the four albums with this choir, the first is probably the best, owing to its ebullient feel and some of the freshest material Cleveland had cut in years. But the pairing also produced one of Cleveland's weakest albums. "In the Ghetto" is is an awkward stab at pop gospel, the stuttering bass of "When the Saints Go Marching In" an embarrassment. (The rest of the *Ghetto* LP is more typical gospel fare.)

For all its unevenness, the LP with the Church of Christ Choir is perhaps the most interesting pop-gospel fusion Cleveland has ever accomplished. And while his own voice has become rather ghostly, the album introduces an exciting new vocal soloist in the Reverend Isaac Whittmon. The album with the Fold Singers, like those with the Angelic Choir, benefits from being recorded live before an enthusiastic congregation, but the Folds themselves are an unnerving combination of the stately and the pointlessly hysterical. — J.MO.

DOROTHY LOVE COATES AND THE
GOSPEL HARMONETTES
★ ★ ★ ★ The Best of Dorothy Love Coates
  and the Original Gospel Harmonettes /
  Spec. 2134

★ ★ ★ **The Best of Dorothy Love Coates
and the Original Gospel Harmonettes,
Vol. 2 / Spec. 2141**
★ ★ **The Gospel Harmonettes / Savoy
MG-14050**

Dorothy Love Coates had a pleasingly raw
voice and a sassy style that was later
adapted by such soul singers as Aretha
Franklin and Millie Jackson. More importantly, she was one of the great writers of
gospel's golden era. Her imagery was rich
and vivid, sometimes even surreal; she often referred pointedly to social and political issues, a gospel taboo at the time.

The first Specialty album is a gem, featuring "You Better Run," which has the
feel of a jump blues à la Wynonie Harris,
and "Ninety-Nine and a Half," which Wilson Pickett later rewrote for a secular hit.
Volume 2, while hardly mediocre, suffers
slightly by comparison. The Harmonettes
broke up and regrouped several times; the
Savoy album is neither the best nor the
worst of their later work, but it is representative. Vocals are uncomfortably frayed,
and the semiclassical and operatic arrangements incongruous. — J.MO.

DIXIE HUMMINGBIRDS
★ ★ ★ **A Christian Testimonial / Pea. 100**
★ ★ ★ **Everyday Every Hour / Pea. 127**
★ ★ ★ ★ **In the Morning / Pea. 108**
★ ★ ★ **Prayer for Peace / Pea. 115**
★ ★ ★ ★ ★ **The Best of the Dixie Humming-
birds / Pea. 138**
★ ★ ★ **The Gentlemen of Song /
Pea. 153**
★ ★ ★ **Your Good Deeds / Pea. 144**

Long before Paul Simon introduced them
to a pop audience via "Loves Me Like a
Rock," the Hummingbirds were well
known on the black gospel circuit as one
of the best quartets, if not *the* best. Gos-

pel's vocabulary may be limited in words
and music, but no group exploited it more
fully than the 'Birds. Ira Tucker's lead vocals define the gospel style, and co-leader
James Walker is almost his equal. (Tucker's influence is apparent in such soul singers as Jackie Wilson, and he's coached
Bobby Bland, too.) The other 'Birds (baritone James Kavis, tenor Beachey Thompson, bass William Bobo) provide fine support, while guitarist Howard Carroll is the
most bracing in the field.

The 'Birds came along just as the jubilee
singing style, with its blue notes and emphasis on close harmonies, was fading. As
prime exponents of the modern quartet
style, with its bent notes, moaning and
more frenetic vocals, they were a major influence on soul music—especially Tucker,
who is also a top songwriter with a flair for
novelty songs ("Christian Automobile,"
covered by the Persuasions, and "Let's Go
Out to the Programs," for example).

Christian Testimonial is a good enough
introduction to their style. All emphasis is
on vocals, though Carroll slips easily into
jazzy guitar modes. The 'Birds are fairly
rural-sounding, and the instruments are recorded poorly enough that the singing
might as well be a cappella. The piano is
heard almost subliminally, as it is on most
of the group's early recordings. But *In the
Morning*, which appropriately begins with
the title song and ends with "This Evening," is the 'Birds at their absolute peak.
The scatting lead on "In the Morning" is
only one of several outstanding vocal efforts ("Bedside of a Neighbor," the moaning "This Evening" and the heavily syncopated "Jesus Walked the Water" are
others). Also of special interest are "My
Prayer," with its preaching vocal and orchestral arrangement, and "Let the Holy
Ghost Fall on Me," which has the feel of a
rock ballad. The rest of the 'Birds pre-pop
albums follow the mode of these two, and
show an enviable consistency in quality.
Best of is just what it says; this is one of the
most essential gospel albums in print.
★ ★ ★ **Live / Pea. 59231**
★ ★ **Thanks to Thee / Pea. 59217**
★ ★ ★ **We Love You Like a Rock /
Pea. 178**
★ ★ **Wonderful to Be Alive / Pea. 59226**

Like a Rock is their first excursion into
secular material and styles. It contains the
Simon song and Stevie Wonder's "Jesus
Children of America," on which Stevie
plays; there's still straight gospel material
here, though the secular songs are quite

good. Instrumentation runs from tuba to synthesizer, and one song even has a quasi-reggae beat. Other excursions into alien modes aren't quite as successful. The country instrumentation on *Thanks* is at first interesting (and also reaffirms the Hummingbirds' rural ties), but it's not very effective in the long run and the singing sounds like parody. *Wonderful* contains plenty of public-domain gospel material, but also a truly foolish novelty song; emphasis here is on lead singing rather than harmonies, and it sounds a bit tired. *Live,* with its mixture of previously unrecorded songs and 'Birds standards is a slight disappointment, as the singing is a little off—age must be catching up with them—but there are some superb performances here, and it's as atmospheric as a live gospel album should be. — J.MO.

FIVE BLIND BOYS
★★★ **Best of the Blind Boys, Vol. 2 / Pea. 188**
★★★ **Best of the Five Blind Boys / Pea. 139**
★★★ **Father, I Stretch My Hands to Thee / Pea. 113**
★★ **Precious Memories / Pea. 102**
★★★★ **The Original Five Blind Boys / Exo. 59**
Under Archie Brownlee, the Five Blind Boys were one of the first gospel groups to register in *Billboard*'s record-charts race. Judging from good-natured, uptempo shouters like "I'm a Soldier" and poppish ballads like "Oh Why," Brownlee should be considered one of the direct inspirations for rock & roll. Ray Charles' style was a distillation of Brownlee and Professor Alex Bradford; some twenty years after Brownlee cut "Where There's a Will There's a Way," Lonnie Mack had to change only a

few words to record his pop version. Sam Cooke's highly effective "yodel" also derives from Brownlee.

All the above-named songs are on the Exodus LP, a must for any basic gospel collection. The Peacock albums often invoke Brownlee's name, but he had died before they were cut. The two *Best of* albums are hence slightly misleading, in that they include many songs associated with Brownlee. But they aren't Brownlee's versions. They're cut with Henry Johnson singing lead for the *Memories* set, which was a Brownlee tribute. Still, Johnson matured into one of the more solid and versatile lead singers of the Sixties, and the group's arrangements made better use of rock and soul technique than did most gospel groups evolving along that course. So the Peacock sides aren't without interest. — J.MO.

THE EDWIN HAWKINS SINGERS
★★ **The Best of the Edwin Hawkins Singers / Bud. 5666-2**
Hawkins had an off-the-wall 1969 pop hit with "Oh Happy Day," which featured lead singer Dorothy Morrison over a surging, joyous choir. Then Morrison left and Hawkins began experimenting with pop, Vegas-like arrangements. Though mostly pedestrian, *Best* does contain a few exhilarating gospel cuts. — J.MO.

HIGHWAY QC'S
★★ **Be at Rest / Pea. 184**
★ **Stay with God / Savoy 14414**
The QC's once served as a sort of farm team for the Soul Stirrers: Sam Cooke, Johnnie Taylor and Willie Rogers all started here before moving up to that group. But apparently there are no readily available recordings of the group from that era. The Peacock album here has strangely cool and restrained lead vocals (Spencer Taylor is responsible), but the album may be of interest to fans of falsetto soul groups, since the QC's lean heavily in that direction. The Savoy set is a very uneasy fusion of soul and gospel. — J.MO.

MAHALIA JACKSON
Jackson is probably the best-known, and arguably the best, gospel singer in history, a path-breaker who drew from blueswomen Bessie Smith and Ma Rainey as well as from such influential gospel singers as Willie Mae Ford Smith and Roberta Martin.

With her pliable contralto, she preferred to sing slow hymns; they gave her plenty of room to stretch out, to repeat lines endlessly with the emphasis slightly different each time, to show off her full range of vocal slurs and bent notes. Because she did rely almost exclusively on slow hymns, her albums may appear sluggish to the casual listener; the trick is to listen for how many different things she could do with a group of songs so much alike.

What's most amazing is how effortless she makes it all sound. There's no sense of strain when Jackson reaches for a high note, as is often the case with gospel singers pushing their voices to the limit; she sounds relaxed even when she's shouting.

For our purposes, her career divides neatly into two periods. There are the Apollo sides (now on Kenwood) from the late Forties and early Fifties. These are pure gospel, usually just Jackson with her extraordinary pianist Mildred Falls and an unidentified organist, with background voices or maybe a guitar also added on occasion. Then there are the Columbia sides, beginning in 1954, with a full rhythm section; here she is sometimes saddled with an orchestra, pop tunes and all manner of other encumbrances.

★★★★★ Best of Mahalia Jackson / Ken. 500
★★★★ Christmas with Mahalia Jackson / Ken. 499
★★ God Answers Prayer / Ken. 508
★★★ How I Got Over / Col. C-34073
★★★ In the Upper Room / Ken. 474
★★★★ Just as I Am / Ken. 479
★★★ Mahalia! Mahalia! Mahalia! / Ken. 504
★★★★★ 1911–1972 / Ken. 506
★★★ Sing Out / Ken. 502
★★★★ World's Greatest Gospel Singer / Ken. 505

There is much duplication of material from album to album here. There are also several that might as well be called "best of," in addition to the one that has that title. For example, *Christmas,* despite its title, contains hardly any Christmas songs; it does have "Silent Night" plus many more of her best-known songs, all of which are also spread out amongst the other Kenwood LPs. It is an excellent introduction to Mahalia, but better still are *Best of* itself and *1911–1972*; the latter contains her original version of "Move On Up a Little Higher," which is said to have sold an astounding 2 million copies in the small gospel market, and such other favorites as "I'm On My Way to Canaan," "In the Upper Room" and "How I Got Over." These are the two essential Mahalia albums, and all but the hard-core fan would be well advised to stop right there.

Besides the title song, *Upper Room* features several more top early efforts ("City Called Heaven," "His Eye Is on the Sparrow," "Walking to Jerusalem"), but *Just as I Am* is superior. "Go Tell It on the Mountain" demonstrates her immaculate phrasing (as well as her peculiar, old-time New Orleans accent); there's also the title song, the wailing "Prayer Changes Things," and the haunting "What Then."

Of the rest, *Mahalia!* is unbeatable on side two, especially the bounce (another legacy of her New Orleans heritage) of "He Said He Would." *Sing Out,* which has what sounds like an overdubbed live audience on some cuts, seems to have been compiled with an eye to the folkie market; *God Answers Prayer* is another posthumous album, made up mostly of cuts best left in the can. Though released on Columbia, *How I Got Over* is listed here because it's closer to the Apollo sides in spirit and sometimes even chronologically. It's also a posthumous LP, made up of 1954 radio performances and a few songs from a 1963 TV show shot in a black church. Inexplicably, these are the only sides available of Mahalia cut before a black church congregation, though there are several live concert albums.

★★★ Great Gettin' Up Morning / Col. CS-8153
★★ A Mighty Fortress / Col. CS-9659
★★★ Bless This House / Col. CS-8761
★ Christmas with Mahalia / Col. CS-9727
★★ Garden of Prayer / Col. CS-9346
★★★ Mahalia Jackson: Greatest Hits / Col. CS-8804
★ I Believe / Col. CS-8349
★★★ In Concert / Col. CS-9490
★★ My Faith / Col. CS-9405
★★★ Right out of the Church / Col. CS-9813
★★ Sings America's Favorite Hymns / Col. CG-30744
★★ Sings the Best-Loved Hymns of Dr. Martin Luther King, Jr. / Col. CS-9686
★★ The Great Mahalia Jackson / Col. 31379
★ The Power and the Glory / Col. CS-8264
★ What the World Needs Now / Col. CS-9950

Here's where the going gets grimmer. There was always pressure on Mahalia to sing jazz especially, but also blues and pop. She resisted at first, but when she moved to Columbia in 1954, she compromised to some extent by doing such "mainstream" hymns as "Onward Christian Soldiers," "Rock of Ages," "The Old Rugged Cross," etc. By the end of her career, she had acquiesced, and was singing material like "Abraham, Martin and John," "Put a Little Love in Your Heart" and "What the World Needs Now."

Columbia recorded her some of the time with a rhythm section and background voices; often there were strings and even a full orchestra. *Power and Glory,* for example, features a full orchestra and choir directed by hackmeister Percy Faith (!), whose arrangements are so predictably bombastic that the album is barely listenable. Too often, Mahalia herself became just a pretty, operatic voice used to complement the arrangement.

Indeed, much of what made her great was stifled under Columbia in the interests of reaching a mass audience. Her unique sense of timing—the way she sang around the beat—suffered most. The piano style of Mildred Falls, who stayed with Mahalia to the end and is featured on many of these albums, was similarly ironed out.

Still, there is, to rework slightly the title of one of Mahalia's favorite songs, some wheat among the tares here; the following evaluations separate the two. The highs and lows are discussed; the in-betweens, which dominate her Columbia years, are not. Unfortunately, they tend to represent her output too well, being depressingly unmemorable in any way despite her voice.

A small group accompanies Mahalia on *Great Gettin' Up Morning,* and she is especially impressive on "How Great Thou Art." *Bless This House* also features a simple rhythm section, and while Mahalia is saddled with a "Summertime"/"Sometimes I Feel like a Motherless Child" medley, she pulls it off respectably; the bulk of the material is more fitting for her, especially "Standing Here Wondering Which Way to Go," "Trouble with This World" and "Precious Lord." *Greatest Hits* features re-recordings of some of her Apollo hits, plus newer songs; her singing has become perceptibly more stylized, but this will pass as an introduction to Mahalia for those who can't find the Kenwood albums. The *In*

Concert set shows that out of the studio, she retained many of her unique vocal characteristics; though her voice is a little frayed, "He Was Alone" is a superlative performance. *Right out of the Church* marks a return to the roots. With solid gospel material, a small rhythm section and some reasonably unobtrusive backup singers, Mahalia achieves the most vigorous album of the later stage of her career.

Musts to avoid, besides *Power and Glory:* *I Believe,* which is in a similar model and sounds like bad movie music; *Christmas,* which is a travesty of hokiness; and *What the World Needs Now,* which is mostly pop songs (some of which also appear on *The Great Mahalia Jackson,* a double album). — J.MO.

BLIND WILLIE JOHNSON
★★★★ Blues / Folk. 3585
★★★★ 1927–30 / Folk. RF-10
Excellent late-Twenties singer who specialized in religious songs and played knife guitar Hawaiian-style to accompany his moaning, chanting vocals. Johnson recorded a number of laments that would later become standards—"If I Had My Way," "Dark Was the Night and Cold the Ground," "Motherless Children," "Jesus Make Up My Dying Bed," "You're Gonna Need Somebody on Your Bond," "Keep Your Lamp Trimmed and Burning," "I Just Can't Keep from Crying" and "Let Your Light Shine on Me." These songs have been covered by rock groups from the Grateful Dead to Led Zeppelin, from Hot Tuna to Taj Mahal, indicating the breadth of Johnson's influence. — J.S.

THE ROBERTA MARTIN SINGERS
★★ God Is Still on the Throne / Savoy 14031
★★★ Grace / Savoy 14022
★★ He's Done Great Things for Me / Savoy 14119
★★★ Twelve Inspirational Songs / Savoy 14008
As a composer, arranger, pianist and singer, Roberta Martin is one of the founders and giants of modern gospel. Her influence extends down through later generations of gospel artists—the Rev. James Cleveland, most significantly—and on into soul music. One could easily build a case for Martin as an early model for Aretha Franklin—perhaps more so for her piano than her singing, but even vocally to some extent.

Yet the Martin Singers might not have much appeal for rock fans. This is partly because the style she pioneered got filtered through too many artists before it hit the soul field. True, many fine singers passed through her ranks—Myrtle Scott, Eugene Smith, Robert Anderson ("the Bing Crosby of gospel"), Norsalus McKissick, Bessie Folk, Willie Webb, Deloris Campbell and others. But they tend to be quite smooth, as Anderson's nickname implies, and perhaps as essential to the evolution of black nightclub singers as to soul singers. A gospel fanatic will want to hear Martin's work, but for most others she is primarily of historical interest—except, perhaps, for that thick, rich piano style. — J.MO.

THE MEDITATION SINGERS
★★★ **Change Is Gonna Come / Jewel 0048**
Though neither is apparent here, this gospel group spawned Laura Lee (whose mother is still its director) and Della Reese. An enjoyably modern group, they use arrangements that are decidedly nontraditional but still quite original and strangely compelling. — J.MO.

THE MIGHTY CLOUDS OF JOY
★★ **A Bright Side / Pea. 1212**
★★★ **Best of the Mighty Clouds of Joy / Pea. 183**
★★★ **Live! At the Apollo / Pea. 173**
★★ **Live at the Music Hall / Pea. 134**
★★ **Mighty Clouds of Joy Sing Songs of Rev. Julius Cheeks and the Nightingales / Pea. 163**
★★ **Presenting: The Untouchables / Pea. 151**
★★★ **The Best of the Mighty Clouds of Joy / Pea. 136**

The Mighty Clouds of Joy are one of the outstanding young, modern gospel quartets; they feature the lead voice of Joe Ligons rising out of a chorus of falsetto voices. Ligons also likes to preach à la the Rev. C. L. Franklin (Aretha's father), and if he sometimes sounds remarkably like Wilson Pickett, perhaps it's because he and Pickett both patterned themselves after Julius Cheeks of the Sensational Nightingales.

Yet the Clouds aren't always as sharp as they might seem from that description. Mainly, Ligons is an undisciplined singer who often screams for the sake of screaming. There are wonderful performances spread out over their albums—things like "We Think God Don't Care," from *Bright Side*, which sounds almost like a Sam and Dave ballad; "I Came to Jesus," from *Music Hall*; or Ligons' reading of "Burying Ground" on the Cheeks tribute album. But because of their inconsistencies, it's most advisable to stick with the two *Best of* LPs. There's little overlap in material between them, oddly enough; the earlier (136) might contain slightly better songs, but on the later (183), Ligons proves that as he grew, he did develop some subtlety and restraint. *Apollo* is the better of the two live albums because it offers more variety and a more exciting pace. Thanks in part to those high harmonies, the Mighty Clouds started sounding very much like the Impressions of the Curtis Mayfield era toward the end of the gospel phase of their career; and judging from the changes taking place in their arrangements, that's exactly what they were aiming for.
★★★ **It's Time / Dun. X-50177**
★★ **Kickin' / ABC ABCD-899**
★ **Truth Is the Power / ABC 986**
On paper, the Mighty Clouds' soul collaborations with Gamble and Huff look good. They could possibly have been another Harold Melvin and the Blue Notes featuring Theodore Pendergrass, given the similarities between Pendergrass and Ligons. But they came along with too little too late. They hooked up with the production team just as the Philly Sound was becoming mechanized and predictable. *It's Time* has a few flashy surprises, but by *Kickin'* the group is grunting through poorly chosen material like an "I've Got the Music in Me"/"Superstition" medley. On *Truth* they don't even have the benefit of the Philly producers, and they sound like just about any anonymous soul group. — J.MO.

THE PILGRIM TRAVELERS

★★★ **Best of the Pilgrim Travelers / Spec. 2121**

★★ **Best of the Pilgrim Travelers, Vol. 2 / Spec. 2140**

★★★ **Shake My Mother's Hand / Spec. 2147**

Lou Rawls sang briefly with the Pilgrim Travelers, and though he's not featured on these albums, it's easy to see how he fit into this gospel group. They could sound like a group of hollerin' field hands (listen to "Standing on the Highway" on the first album), but the Travelers favored cooler, urbane vocals; some of their harmonies even sound detached. They were one of the most popular quartets, though their featured singers (Kylo Turner and Keith Barber) didn't have styles as distinctively personal as the best leads. Besides "Standing on the Highway," *Best of* contains Turner's magnificent "Mother Bowed" and a novelty called "Jesus Hits like the Atom Bomb." The *Mother* album features "Peace of Mind" and "How Jesus Died" (rewritten by Ray Charles as "Lonely Avenue"). — J.MO.

THE SENSATIONAL NIGHTINGALES

★ **Almighty Hand / Pea. 59219**

★★★★ **Best of the Sensational Nightingales / Pea. 137**

★★★ **Glory Glory / Pea. 112**

★★★ **Heart and Soul / Pea. 154**

★★ **It's Gonna Rain Again / Pea. 175**

★★ **Prayed Too Late / Pea. 131**

★★★ **Songs of Praise / Pea. 101**

★★ **Travel On / Pea. 118**

★★ **You and I and Everyone / Pea. 177**

The Rev. Julius Cheeks, for years the mainstay of the Nightingales, was one of the wild men of gospel music, a tireless shouter and a flamboyant showman. He has had an ineradicable influence on soul music. Wilson Pickett modeled his singing after Cheeks in almost every respect, as the most cursory listening reveals. James Brown also picked up quite a few tips from Cheeks, particularly in his phrasing.

Unfortunately, Cheeks appears on none of these albums except on some of the *Best of* affair, which is chock full of such unvarnished gospel as "Burying Ground," "Standing at the Judgment" and "Prayed Too Late." Singing lead on the other albums are Herbert Robertson and Charles Johnson. But Cheeks' influence remained long after he himself left, especially on Robertson. (Johnson is a bit sweeter.) So the Nightingales continued to rate as one of the leading contemporary quartets through the Sixties. Perhaps they favored less feverishly paced material than before, but they could still cut loose when they wanted to.

They also remained very much the purists, which ultimately worked against them. While soul music absorbed their influence and then other gospel groups absorbed soul's influence, the Nightingales modernized only slightly, and in largely insignificant ways. Also, while they did later start to use some new instruments and arranging ideas, they continued to sing only religious material. If anything, they got slightly more country-sounding as the years passed. Aside from that, they lost Robertson and got less interesting. — J.MO.

THE SOUL STIRRERS

★★★★ **The Gospel Soul of Sam Cooke with the Soul Stirrers, Vol. 1 / Spec. 2116**

★★★ **The Gospel Soul of Sam Cooke with the Soul Stirrers, Vol. 2 / Spec. 2128**

★★★★ **The Original Soul Stirrers / Spec. 2137**

★★★★★ **The Soul Stirrers Featuring Sam Cooke / Spec. 2106**

The Soul Stirrers rose to gospel prominence with Rebert Harris as lead singer, but his successors included Sam Cooke and Johnnie Taylor. Under Harris, the group was the first to add a fifth member to the quartet lineup, so the lead singer could step out front and take solo lines while still keeping the four-part harmonies intact.

Cooke was gospel's first real sex symbol, and his work also pushed the group sound far enough toward pop that it wasn't exactly a shock when he left gospel for pop.

The Soul Stirrers Featuring Sam Cooke is the best of their albums because it demonstrates this process by including one of Cooke's gospel showcases ("Wonderful") and one of his leaning-toward-pop masterpieces (the desolate "Touch the Hem of His Garment"). But the album also contains a key Harris–Paul Foster lead ("By and By") and one of the best efforts ("The Love of God") by Taylor, who started out very much a Cooke imitator, just as Cooke began as a Harris imitator.

There's much overlap among the Specialty albums. Those interested solely in Cooke should check out both volumes of *Gospel Soul.* The first is slightly superior, due to the spectacular moaning of "Jesus Wash Away My Troubles" and the way Cooke builds and builds on "Peace in the Valley." His voice is already as sweet as it ever got on his pop sides, but the addition of a rough edge, and arrangements that really let him stretch out, lead some to argue that his gospel sides are his greatest achievements.
★★ **Best of the Soul Stirrers / Check. 10015**
★★ **Going Back to the Lord Again / Spec. 2150**
★★ **The Gospel Truth / Check. 10027**
Willie Rogers and Martin Jacox share leads on the Checker albums; while Rogers in particular shows great potential, both pale next to the earlier Specialty work. Richard Miles replaces Rogers on the later Specialty LP, and both the instrumentation and singing are a bit more modern (as is the material, such as a version of "Let It Be"). Finally, search for a copy of the out-of-print *Gospel Music, Volume 1/Soul Stirrers* (Imperial LM-94007). This is mostly a capella sides from the late Forties by the Harris-led group, and is a marvelous showcase for the relaxed but insistent style that first won the Soul Stirrers fame. — J.MO.

THE STAPLE SINGERS
★★★ **Great Day / Mile. 47028**
★★★ **Pray On / Epic 26237**
★★ **25th Day of December / Fan. 9442**
★★ **Use What You Got / Fan. 9423**
The Staple Singers allegedly sold out gospel music, but the truth is they were mostly outside the gospel mainstream from their inception. Their style had little to do with close-harmony jubilee or shouting quartet; instead, they harkened back to the days of the lone singer with untutored piano or guitar. Pops Staple's guitar playing

was redolent of both black and white country influences; Mavis' sexy contralto may have been an ideal gospel vehicle, but her phrasing and diction always showed considerable outside influence.

This batch of albums is from the early Sixties, their "folk-gospel" phase. They sang traditional hymns and spirituals—generally, but not strictly, Pops on the uptempo songs, Mavis on the slow ones—that were as well known to white people as to black. They also sang Bob Dylan and Woody Guthrie songs, as well as songs with religious themes that don't fit any particular definition. *Pray On* is the closest thing here to a traditional gospel album, but even it's not *that* close. *Great Day* offers both the most variety and the largest number of familiar songs. — J.MO.

THE SUPREME ANGELS
★★★★ **If I'm Too High / Nashb. 7072**
★★ **In Love with God / Nashb. 7165**
★★★ **Shame on You / Nashb. 7141**
★★★★★ **Supreme / Nashb. 7110**
This is probably the hippest and flashiest of the young, Seventies-style gospel groups. Lead singer Howard Hunt is very heavily influenced by Wilson Pickett (a blatant example of soul pointing the way for gospel, rather than vice versa); many of the group's arrangements rely on a relaxed, loping Jimmy Reed-type beat; the organ is jazzy; and guitarist Alfonso Dent sounds like he just stepped out of a South Side Chicago blues bar.

It's a virtual tossup between *Supreme* and *If I'm Too High,* with the nod going to *Supreme* because it offers a more interesting batch of songs, ranging from a truly inspired gospel version of "Lucky Old Sun" to a funereal "Precious Lord," a fine, slow vehicle for Hunt's improvisatory preaching and shouting style. The problem with the last album is that the Angels went too far with their soul leanings, so that the title song, which spotlights the high sweet lead of Gregory Kelly, is nothing but a soul ballad with religious lyrics. With its horns, strings and flute, it could be the Chi-Lites. But the arrangement, as with many cuts here, is soul at its most pedestrian. However, "You Can't Get to Heaven (By Living Like Hell)," with its crazed piano, is well worth hearing. — J.MO.

THE SWAN SILVERTONES
★★★★ **Love Lifted Me** / Spec. 2122
★★★ **My Rock** / Spec. 2148
★★★★ **The Swan Silvertones** / Exo. 58

Lead singer Claude Jeter's falsetto shriek is the touchstone for countless soul stylists, and when Al Green's voice runs up or down the scale or slides all around the beat, it is in blatant imitation of Jeter. The Swans also boasted the more modern "hard" singing of Solomon Womack; a classic screamer in Robert Crenshaw; and later, one of gospel's tightest arrangers in Paul Owens. *Rock* is only barely the lesser of the two Specialty albums; the title song is a Swans calling card, but so is "How I Got Over" from the *Love* LP, and the latter also contains "Glory to His Name" and a powerfully understated "I'm A-Rollin'." The Exodus sides are considered inferior, but are likely to be of more interest to rock fans, as they're in a modern "hard" style more similar to soul: especially "Mary Don't You Weep," with Louis Johnson building the lead and Jeter's falsetto filling in the spaces. — J.MO.

THE VIOLINAIRES
★★★ **Please Answer This Prayer** / Check. 2CK-10065
★★ **Stand By Me** / Check. 10011
★★ **The Fantastic Violinaires in Concert** / Check. 10053

Wilson Pickett is said to have sung briefly with the Violinaires, though if he recorded with them, it's undocumented. He's not on these albums, but the group is from Detroit, and shares stylistic similarities with Detroit soul singers. The background vocals on the live album's "My Mother Used to Hold Me," for example, instantly recall Pickett's "I Found a Love." This is one of the most modern-sounding gospel groups, all high-squealing voices and vocal arrangements full of background *oohs* and

ees. Through the Sixties, their progress paralleled soul as much as gospel. *Please* features modern instrumentation and vocals, and even songs that deal with such subjects as dope and Vietnam. It's fair to say that soul was at least as big an influence on them as they were on it. — J.MO.

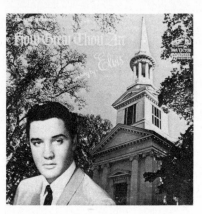

THE WARD SINGERS
★★ **I Feel the Holy Spirit** / Savoy MG-14026
★★★★ **Lord, Touch Me** / Savoy MG-14006
★★★ **Meeting Tonight** / Savoy MG-14015
★★★ **Packing Up** / Savoy MG-14020
★★★ **Surely God Is Able** / Savoy MG-14001
★★★ **That Old Landmark** / Savoy MG-14034

Founded by mother Gertrude Ward and perpetuated by daughter Clara, the Ward Singers are best known for the pop-gospel songs they've performed for white nightclub audiences from L.A. and Vegas to New York and Miami. Recordings of that era, primarily under the tutelage of Clara, aren't even considered here, for they are shameless self-exploitation, giving the white folks what they want to hear, whereas the earlier Ward groups were among the best and most moving gospel ever had to offer.

Clara's influence is everywhere in soul music; Aretha Franklin's first recordings were unabashed, exact copies of Clara's piano and singing. The group also had other lead singers that were easily Clara's equal, most notably the incandescent Marion Williams. The Wards were the first gospel group to utilize multiple lead singers, and one assumes that's because they simply had too many good voices to waste all but one on backgrounds and harmonies. (Others were Kitty Parham, Frances Steadman, Martha Bass, Willa Ward.) Mother Gertrude, Clara and Marion, in particular, all boasted range and pitch better heard than described, and their phrasing was dramatic even by gospel standards.

Touch Me is the album that best captures the group's overall scope and sense of dynamics, yet brilliant performances are scattered throughout the other albums. Williams' two best-loved songs ("Surely God Is Able" and "Packing Up") each head an LP, for example. And the *Meeting* album is a fascinating and well-thought-out document, with one side simulating an old campground meeting, the songs linked together by a theme chorus that weaves through the whole side. — J.MO.

ANTHOLOGIES, SOUNDTRACKS AND ORIGINAL CASTS

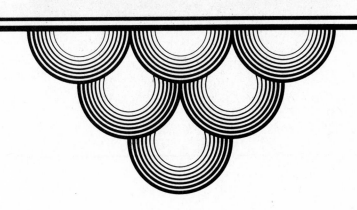

All the reviews in this section were written
by Dave Marsh.

★★★★★ Ain't That Good News / Spec.
115
*Artists include: Swan Silvertones; Original
Gospel Harmonettes; Five Blind Boys of Alabama; Sam Cooke and the Soul Stirrers;
Bessie Griffin; Chosen Gospel Singers; Meditation Singers; Pilgrim Travelers*
  Black gospel masterpieces—a legitimate
sacred *Best of* from vintage Fifties recordings, including Cooke's best religious number, "Touch the Hem of His Garment."

★★★★ All About Trains / RCA
ANL1-1052
Artists include: Hank Snow; Jimmie Rodgers
  As anyone who's ever toyed with a harmonica knows, there is something particularly musical about railroads. Here, two
important country artists sing songs with
rail themes—some of these are more-or-
less folk numbers, but all of them qualify
as excellent Americana and first-rate
C&W. Rodgers, of course, is better, but
what did you expect from the Singing
Brakeman? Sea chanteys?

★★★ All Platinum Gold / All Pl. 3016
*Artists include: Donnie Elbert; Retta Young;
Sylvia George Kerr; Brother to Brother; Moments; Hank Ballard; Chuck Jackson; What-
nauts; Linda Jones; Shirley and Company;
Derek Martin; Rim Shots*
  Spotty collection of Jersey soul and
disco that spans this decade's black pop
styles. Included are some inferior recent
items by Jackson and Ballard, which don't
match their early stuff, and a couple of recent, inspired one-shots: Elbert's bizarre
falsetto parody of Diana Ross on "Where
Did Our Love Go" and Shirley and Company's wildly kinky "Shame Shame

Shame," in which Shirley and friends drive
a Cadillac customized so completely it's
got a diamond in the back. The rest ranges
from perfunctory funk to ho-hum harmony.

★★ All This and World War II (Sound-
track) / 20th Cent. 2T-540
*Artists include: Ambrosia; Elton John; Leo
Sayer; Bee Gees; Bryan Ferry; Roy Wood;
Keith Moon; Rod Stewart; Four Seasons;
David Essex; Jeff Lynne; Helen Reddy; Lyn-
sey de Paul; Richard Cocciante; Frankie
Laine; Johnson Brothers; Status Quo; Henry
Gross; Frankie Valli; Tina Turner; Peter Gabriel; Will Malone/Lou Reizner; London
Symphony Orchestra*
  Soundtrack for a 1976 movie that coupled World War II battle footage with
Beatle songs. If that doesn't make sense,
you get the idea. Obviously there are some
terrific singers here, but there are also
some unaccountably silly ones, and the
material isn't necessarily well chosen for
even the best of them. There's little chance
that anyone who was properly matched—
say, Peter Gabriel to "Strawberry Fields
Forever"—would be able to survive the
glutinous London Symphony arrangements. Only Rod Stewart, who sticks in an
electric guitar on "Get Back," prevails.

★★★★ Duane Allman Anthology / Capri.
2CP-0108
*Artists include: Aretha Franklin; King Curtis;
John Paul Hammond; Boz Scaggs; Delaney
and Bonnie; Cowboy; Eric Clapton and
Duane Allman; Derek and the Dominos;
Hourglass; Wilson Pickett; Clarence Carter;
Duane Allman; Allman Brothers Band*
  Before he became a star with the Allman
Brothers Band, Duane Allman was a
heavyweight Muscle Shoals session guitar-
ist. This posthumously released album

gives a fair picture of his range—while the Franklin and Pickett sides have pop songs ("The Weight" and "Hey Jude" respectively) poorly suited to their styles, Derek and the Dominos' "Layla" and Boz Scaggs' "Loan Me a Dime" are not only the very best work of these artists, but are among Allman's greatest hits. The Allman Brothers tracks are better heard in the context of the band. The only genuine rarity is the Johnny Jenkins side (he was the singer for whom Otis Redding was originally chauffeur), the Clapton/Allman duet and the Duane Allman solo spot on "Goin' Down Slow."

★★★ **Duane Allman Anthology, Vol. 2 / Capri. 2CP-0139**
Artists include: Duane Allman; Aretha Franklin; King Curtis; Otis Rush; Ronnie Hawkins; Wilson Pickett; Arthur Conley; Hourglass; Lulu; Herbie Mann; Johnny Jenkins; Boz Scaggs; Sam Samudio; Delaney and Bonnie; Allman Brothers Band; Duck and the Bear
A spottier set than Volume 1. There isn't anything as grand as "Layla" here, though Johnny Jenkins' "Walk on Gilded Splinters" is fine funk and Aretha's "It Ain't Fair" is one of her best.

★★★★★ **American Graffiti (Soundtrack) / MCA 2-8001**
Artists include: Bobby Freeman; Bill Haley and the Comets; Flash Cadillac; Lee Dorsey; Crests; Buster Brown; Del Shannon; Platters; Fleetwoods; Tempos; Skyliners; Diamonds; Beach Boys; Monotones; Chuck Berry; Clovers; Johnny Burnette; Big Bopper; Five Satins; Regents; Silhouettes; Buddy Holly; Fats Domino; Mark Dinning; Cleftones; Buddy Knox; Heartbeats; Spaniels; Joey Dee and

the Starlighters; Sonny Til and the Orioles; Dell-Vikings; Booker T. and the MGs; Flamingos; Frankie Lymon
The music used in the 1974 hit film, which was mostly a series of fast-paced clichés about adolescence in the pre-Beatle Sixties. What made the movie work was the soundtrack, which had captured the beat and excitement of the era's radio. That means you have to sit through the Regents' "Barbara-Ann" and the Crests' "Sixteen Candles," which are almost insufferable, to get at gems like the Diamonds' "The Stroll" and "Little Darlin' " and the Dell-Vikings' "Come Go with Me." The big names (Berry, Holly, Domino, Beach Boys) are represented by the obligatory well-known hits. There isn't a true rarity in the bunch, but this is still one of the all-time party records and a fairly accurate picture of a 1963 golden oldies weekend.

★★★★ **American Graffiti, Vol. 2 / MCA 2-8008**
Artists include: Beach Boys; Dorados; Little Richard; Jerry Butler; Jody Reynolds; Everly Brothers; Ritchie Valens; Joe Jones; Jewel Akens; Chris Montez; Jimmy Reed; Toni Fisher; Bobby Helms; Harold Dorman; Ronnie Hawkins; Dorsey Burnette; Johnny Tillotson; Jimmie Rodgers; Lenny Welch; Teddy Bears; Wilbur Harrison; Kathy Young; Fendermen; Hollywood Argyles; Little Anthony and the Imperials; Olympics; Buddy Holly
Not a soundtrack—at least none of this is in the movie—but an extension of the boss beat weekend concept of Volume 1. There are fewer obligatory nods to big names here—the only superstars are Holly, the Beach Boys and the Everlys—which leaves room for at least a few things more obscure and harder to obtain on LP: Jody Reynolds' death classic "Endless Sleep," Harold Dorman's original "Mountain of Love," the Teddy Bears singing Phil Spector's first production of "To Know Him Is to Love Him" and the great "Western Movies" by the Olympics. While this isn't everything you'll want to hear by Ritchie Valens or Jerry Butler, it's certainly all you need from Dorsey Burnette, Jimmie Rodgers (the pop singer) and Lenny Welch. And though they have the wrong version of "The Big Hurt"—Timi Yuro (not to mention Elvis Presley) cuts Toni Fisher to *shreds*—who could be without the Hollywood Argyles' "Alley Oop"?

★★★ **American Hot Wax (Soundtrack) / A&M 6500**

Artists include: Big Beat Band; Delights; Professor LaPlano and the Planotones; Clark Otis; Chuck Berry; Chesterfields; Screamin' Jay Hawkins; Timmy and the Tulips; Jerry Lee Lewis; Jackie Wilson; Moonglows; Drifters; Mystics; Buddy Holly; Maurice Williams and the Zodiacs; Little Richard; Cadillacs; Elegants; Turbans; Bobby Darin; Frankie Ford; Spaniels

Soundtrack from the 1978 biography of pioneer DJ Alan Freed is like the movie: half of it is great. The problem is the first disc that includes cinematic groups rather than the real thing who fairly butcher the hits. The tracks by Berry, Hawkins and Lewis are acceptable live versions done for the film's climactic concert sequence; they're of interest mainly to collectors. But this does have some great stuff, beginning with Jackie Wilson, the Moonglows and the Drifters, and including the Mystics' "Hushabye," "Zoom" by the Cadillacs, the great Maurice Williams falsetto on "Stay," the rumbling "When You Dance" by the Turbans, Frankie Ford's raucous "Sea Cruise" and two enduring smooch classics—the sort Freed specialized in playing—"Goodnight It's Time to Go" by the Spaniels and the achingly lovely "Little Star" by the Elegants.

★★★★★ **Anthology of American Folk Music, Vol. 1: Ballads / Folk. FA-2951**

Artists include: Dick Justice; Nelstone's Hawaiians; Clarence Ashley; Coley Jones; Bill and Belle Reed; Buell Kazee; Chubby Parker and His Old Time Banjo; Uncle Eck Dunford; Burnett and Rutherford; Buster Carter and Preston Young; Carolina Tar Heels; G.B. Grayson; Kelly Harrell; Edward L. Crain; Furry Lewis; Carter Family; Williamson Brothers and Curry; Frank Hutchison; Charlie Poole with the North Carolina Ramblers; Mississippi John Hurt; William and Versey Smith; Bently Boys; Masked Marvel

The first two-disc, boxed, lavishly annotated set of Moe Asch's monumental tribute to the country's musical heritage. All of this is pre–World War II; most of it is pre-Depression. The remastering from old 78s occasionally leaves something to be desired, but this set, with its companion volumes, is the fundamental source of folk music preservation. The Poole, Hurt, Masked Marvel, Carolina Tar Heels and Clarence Ashley tracks are all vintage masterpieces.

★★★★★ **Anthology of American Folk Music, Vol. 2: Social Music / Folk. FA-2952**

Artists include: "Uncle Bunt" Stephens; J.W. Day (Jilson Setters); Prince Albert Hunt's Texas Ramblers; Delma Lachney and Blind Uncle Gaspard; Andrew and Jim Baxter; Eck Robertson and Family; Floyd Ming and His Pep-Steppers; Henry Thomas; Jim Jackson; Columbus Fruge; Joseph Falcon; Breaux Freres; Cincinnati Jug Band; Frank Cloutier and Victoria Cafe Orchestra; Reverend J.M. Gates; Alabama Sacred Harp Singers; Middle Georgia Singing Convention No. 1; Reverend Sister Mary Nelson; Memphis Sanctified Singers; Elders MacIntosh and Edwards Sanctified Singers; Reverend Moses Mason; Bascom Lumar Lunsford; Blind Willie Johnson; Carter Family; Ernest Phipps and His Holiness Singers; Reverend F.W. McGee; Reverend D.C. Rice and His Sanctified Congregation

Volume 2 of the masterful collection is devoted to the music Americans have listened to at parties, in churches and at dances. The church dominates, not only in quantity but in quality. Johnson's "John the Revelator" is amazing, on the gospel-blues side, but so is the Carters' country-gospel "Little Moses."

★★★★★ **Anthology of American Folk Music, Vol. 3: Songs / Folk. FA-2953**

Artists include: Clarence Ashley; Buell Kazee; Cannon's Jug Stompers; Didier Herbert; Rabbit Brown; "Dock" Boggs; Bascom Lumar Lunsford; Mr. and Mrs. Ernest V. Stoneman; Stoneman Family; Memphis Jug Band; Carter Family; Clemo Breaux and Joseph Falcon; Blind Lemon Jefferson; Sleepy John Estes; Ramblin' Thomas; Julius Daniels; Clemo Breaux with Joe Falcon and Ophy

Breaux; Uncle Dave Macon; Mississippi John Hurt; J. P. Nestor; Ken Maynard; Henry Thomas

The concluding volume of this exhaustive documentation of American folk styles may be the best listening of the three. Nearly every track here is winning, and some of it is absolutely essential to an understanding of the resources upon which rock & roll was built: listen to Rabbit Brown, for instance.

★★★★ **Anthology of the Banjo / Trad. 2077**
Artists include: Mason Williams; David Lindley; Joe Maphis; Erik Darling; Mike Seeger; Jim McGuinn; Billy Cheatwood

Good anthology of folk and country banjo styles that dates from the early Sixties folk revival. Rockers will be most curious about Jackson Browne sideman David Lindley, who shines on "Mad Mountain Medley," his only extant recording before his work with Kaleidoscope on the group's debut LP, and the track by McGuinn, made before he formed the Byrds or changed his name to Roger. Hilarious liner notes.

ANTHOLOGY OF THE BLUES (Series)
★★★ **Arkansas Blues / Kent 9007**
Artists include: Baby Face Turner; Drifting Slim; Sunny Blair; Robert Dudlow Taylor; James "Peck" Burtis; Junior Brooks
★★★ **Blues from the Deep South / Kent 9004**
Artists include: Pinetop Slim; Dixie Blues Boys; Leroy Simpson; Big Bill Dotson; Arkansas Johnny Todd; Mr. Harris and Arkansas Johnny Todd
★★★ **California Blues / Kent 9003**
Artists include: Johnny "Guitar" Watson; George Smith; James Reed; Walter Robertson; Johnny Fuller
★★★ **Detroit Blues / Kent 9006**
Artists include: John Lee Hooker; Eddie Kirkland; Eddie Burns; Sylvester Cotton
★★★★ **Memphis Blues / Kent 9002**
Artists include: Howlin' Wolf; Joe Hill Lewis; Walter Horton; Bobby Bland and Junior Parker; Bobby Bland; Willie Nix
★★★ **Mississippi Blues / Kent 9009**
Artists include: Boyd Gilmore; Houston Boines; Charley Booker
★★★★ **Texas Blues / Kent 9005**
Artists include: Little Son Jackson; Smokey Hogg; Jesse Thomas; Alexander Moore; Lowell Fulsom; Charlie Bradix
★★★ **West Coast Blues / Kent 9012**
Artists include: Mercy Dee; Jimmy Nelson;

Pee Wee Crayton; James Reed; Saunders King; J.W. Walker; Roy Hawkins

Excellently produced series, well annotated, gives a look at some of the second-level blues performers of each important region west of the Mississippi and up North. Probably of interest only to blues fanatics, however.

★★★ **Anthology of Folk Music, Vol. 1 / Sine 102**
Artists include: Pete Seeger; Odetta; Alan Lomax; Etta Baker; Ed McCurdy; David Hammond; Italian Brass Band; Leadbelly; Woody Guthrie; Josh White; Lightnin' Hopkins; Clancy Brothers and Tommy Makem; Sonny Terry and Brownie McGhee; Glenn Yarbrough; Glen Campbell; John Lee Hooker; Mississippi State Penitentiary

A much more erratic sampling of American traditional music. Some of the names are well known and important—Seeger, Guthrie, Leadbelly, Hopkins, Terry and McGhee, Hooker—but some of them are atrocious performers, particularly Yarbrough and Campbell. Not bad but decidedly inferior to the Folkways' anthology of American folk-music sets. Five discs.

★★★★ **Anthology of Folk Music, Vol. 2 / Sine 126**
Artists include: Judy Collins; Theodore Bikel; Will Holt; Dillards; Oscar Brand; Ed McCurdy; Odetta; Mason Williams; Glen Campbell; A.L. Lloyd; John Jacob Niles; Clancy Brothers and Tommy Makem; Ewan MacColl; Mary O'Hara; Mississippi State Penitentiary; Woody Guthrie and Cisco Houston; Pete Seeger; Lightnin' Hopkins; Sonny Terry and Brownie McGhee; John Lee Hooker; Hoyt Axton; Leadbelly; Josh White; Limeliters; Eric Weisberg and Marshall Brickman; The Band

The same flaws as Volume 1 in this set pertain to this four-disc followup. And some of the artistic inclusions are unaccountable: the Band's "Up on Cripple Creek" and "Rag Mama Rag" are *not* folk music.

★★ **Anthology of the 12-String Guitar /**
Trad. 2071
Artists include: Glen Campbell; Mason Williams; Bob Gibson; James McGuinn; Howard Roberts; Joe Maphis; Billy Strange
Passable country and folk guitar instrumentals. All that might be of interest to nonguitarists are the McGuinn (he's now Roger, late of the Byrds) and Maphis selections.

★ **Award Winners / RCA AHL1-2262**
Artists include: Charley Pride; Chet Atkins; Ronnie Milsap; Dave and Sugar; Dolly Parton; Jim Ed Brown and Helen Cornelius; Atkins String Company; Nashville Brass and Danny Davis; Chet Atkins and Les Paul; Dickey Lee
Impoverished collection of Seventies country-pop hits. All that saves this from the trash bin is Atkins' duet with Paul, and that one is available on an LP of similar duets.

★★★ **Bang and Shout Super Hits / Bang**
220
Artists include: Van Morrison; Neil Diamond; Strangeloves; Donald Height; Erma Franklin; McCoys; Derek; Freddie Scott; Jackie Moore; Jerry O
Relics of pop-rock (and pop-soul) past. The Morrison track, "Brown Eyed Girl," is pure genius; the McCoys and Strangeloves are ancestral punk rock; Diamond was at his best on Bang and "Cherry Cherry" was his best there. But most importantly, this

record has Erma Franklin (Aretha's sister) doing the original "Piece of My Heart," which will make you forget Janis Joplin's strident version P.D.Q. (Scott and Moore are interesting, but very minor, soul performers.)

★★★★ **Barefoot Rock and You Got Me /**
Duke X-72
Artists include: Junior Parker; Bobby Bland
Two of the best modern R&B singers split a disc, one side each, just as they once shared a band. Bland is a better singer, in a way, but Parker is tons more challenging, both to his band and his listeners. This will make anyone a fine introduction to either man (or both).

■ **Beatlemania (Original Broadway Cast) /**
Ari. 8501
There are twenty-two Beatle-composed songs here, performed by the puppets from the stage show that enjoyed a long run on Broadway. This horrible piece of garbage is the best evidence that the Beatles didn't make it on haircuts alone—and that some record companies are utterly shameless. Get the plague first.

★★★ **Bebop Singers / Prest. 7828**
Artists include: Annie Ross; Eddie Jefferson; Joe Carroll
Jefferson and Ross are two of the best jazz singers of the past thirty years. For anyone interested in vocal experiments and scat singing, this should prove of value. The highlight is Ross' "Twisted."

★★★ **Beserkely Chartbusters / Beserk.**
PZ-34751
Artists include: Earth Quake; Greg Kihn; Jonathan Richman; Rubinoos
Mostly this sampler from the original American New Wave label is flaccid. Kihn, Earth Quake and the Rubinoos have a very tame idea of what rocking out means. But Jonathan Richman reaches his peak with this album's "New Teller," "Government Center" and the grand "Road Runner." The latter is so sick it has to be heard to be believed.

★★ **Best of the Blues / Sine 103**
Artists include: Jimmy Witherspoon and Groove Holmes; Jimmy Witherspoon; Lightnin' Hopkins; Ray Charles; John Lee Hooker; Sonny Terry and Brownie McGhee; Big Joe Williams; Leadbelly; Josh White; Big Bill Broonzy; Jimmy Reed; Memphis Slim; Otis Spann

An unfocused collection of blues styles. Some good tracks—particularly the Leadbelly, Hooker and Spann numbers—but not enough cohesion. Better overviews of the genre are available.

★★ Best of the Blues, Vol. 2 / Sine 124
Artists include: Sonny Terry and Brownie McGhee; Bessie Smith; Louis Armstrong; King Oliver; Leadbelly; Fats Waller; Big Joe Williams; Jimmy Witherspoon and Richard "Groove" Holmes; Lightnin' Hopkins; Cisco Houston; Johnny Hammond; John Lee Hooker; Gary Davis; Junior Wells; Otis Spann; James Cotton; Otis Rush

Again blues without definition: what links King Oliver and Fats Waller with James Cotton and John Lee Hooker, much less what connects Otis Spann and Johnny Hammond, is mysterious except to collectors who already have this stuff in more reasonable formats.

★★★ Best of Burt Bacharach / Trip X-3503
Artists include: Dionne Warwick; Dusty Springfield; Timi Yuro; Jerry Butler; Bobby Vinton; Jackie DeShannon; Shirelles; Chuck Jackson; B.J. Thomas; Gene Pitney; Tommy Hunt; Buddy Greco

Bacharach, with partner Hal David, was one of the most formidable pop songwriters of the Sixties. This isn't quite his greatest hits, because if it were, it would be a Dionne Warwick LP with guest appearances by Presley, DeShannon and the Shirelles. But it gives a good picture of the kind of romantic material Bacharach and David wrote, and the sort of artists for whom they wrote it. Highlights: Shirelles' "Baby It's You," Jackson's "Any Day Now," Pitney's "The Man Who Shot Liberty Valance," from the great John Ford

film, and Warwick's "Anyone Who Had a Heart," "Walk On By," "Alfie" and "Do You Know the Way to San Jose." Bacharach not only co-wrote but co-produced all of the Warwick tracks with David.

★★★★ Best of the Chicago Blues / Van. VSD-1/2
Artists include: Jimmy Cotton; Junior Wells; Otis Spann; Buddy Guy; J.B. Hutto; Homesick James; Walter Horton; Johnny Young

Collection of mostly West Side Chicago blues recorded by Sam Charters in the Sixties. Spann and Wells are in top form; the rest aren't bad.

★ Best of a Great Year, Vol. 3 / RCA CPL2-0449
Artists include: Eddy Arnold; Chet Atkins; Bobby Bare; Skeeter Davis; Jim Ed Brown; George Hamilton IV; Johnny Bush; Floyd Cramer; Nashville Brass and Danny Davis; Waylon Jennings; Dickey Lee; Dolly Parton; Kenny Price; Jerry Reed; Jim Reeves; Johnny Russell; Charlie Rich; Connie Smith; Hank Snow; Nat Stuckey; Porter Wagoner; Dottie West; Dolly Parton and Porter Wagoner; Norro Wilson

Four sides of C&W banality and corn relieved intermittently by the simple competence of Rich, Jennings, Reeves and Parton, who keep better company elsewhere.

★★★ Big Bad Boss Beat / Orig. Sound 8871
Artists include: Champs; Dee Dee Sharp; B. Bumble and the Stingers; Sandy Nelson; Preston Epps; Ernie Fields; Gary "U.S." Bonds; Bill Doggett; Revels

Early Sixties rock, mostly instrumental. Rolling Stone contributor Langdon Winner played piano on "Church Key" by the Revels, but in that kind of company what stands out is the classic outer-space recordings of Bonds: "Quarter to Three" and "New Orleans" will set your pacemaker aflutter. The Champs' "Tequila" isn't bad, and Preston Epps' "Bongo Bongo Bongo" and "Bongo Rock" make him the Perez Prado of rock & roll. This should get a bonus star for its title, unquestionably the product of inspiration.

■ Big Dance Records in the Big Apple / Ari. ST-50011
Artists include: Alexander's Disco Time Band; Polly Brown; Atlanta Disco Band; Jackie Robinson; Pretty Maid Company; Charlie Calello

Wretched dance disc.

★★ **The Bitter End Years / Rox. 300**
Artists include: Peter, Paul and Mary; Lime-liters; Tom Paxton; Pete Seeger; Judy Collins; Phil Ochs; Everly Brothers; Simon Sisters; Tom Rush; Josh White; Theodore Bikel; Jerry Jeff Walker; John Denver; Melanie; Arlo Guthrie; John Prine; James Taylor; Bette Midler; John Sebastian; Isley Brothers; Dion; Van Morrison; Curtis Mayfield; Lily Tomlin; Robert Klein; Joan Rivers; David Steinberg; Woody Allen; David Frye

For a dozen years or more, the Bitter End was New York's chief new artist showcase. At first it specialized in folk, then folk rock, but in the end it was open to all. Apparently, a tape recorder was running full time but caught little that was exceptional. Van Morrison, Dion, Prine, and maybe Midler are worth hearing. So are some of the rest—but elsewhere.

★★★ **Blue Collar (Soundtrack) / MCA 3034**
Jack Nitzsche's track for director/screenwriter Paul Schrader's film about Detroit auto workers. This makes it for two reasons: the inclusion of Howlin' Wolf's "Wang Dang Doodle," and Captain Beefheart's reworked "I'm a Man," here called "Hard Workin' Man."

★★★★ **Bluegrass for Collectors / RCA APM1-0568**
Artists include: J. E. Mainer and the Mountaineers; Bill Monroe and the Bluegrass Boys; Charlie Monroe and the Kentucky Pardners; Riley Puckett; Gid Tanner and the Skillet Lickers

Fine collection of classic pre-World War II bluegrass, highlighted by the Monroe Brothers and Gid Tanner.

★★★★ **Blues at Newport—1963 / Van. 79145**
Artists include: Brownee McGhee and Sonny Terry; Mississippi John Hurt; John Hammond; Reverend Gary Davis; John Lee Hooker; Dave Van Ronk

Fine set from one of the early Sixties festivals that helped so much in publicizing the rediscovered bluesmen like Hurt. Hurt, in fact, *owns* this set, with his wonderful "Candy Man," "Trouble I've Had It All My Days" and "Frankie." McGhee and Terry, Davis and white popularizers Hammond and Van Ronk rise admirably to the occasion, as does Hooker, although he is clearly at his best with an electric band, which the purism of the Newport committee would not allow.

★★ **Blues from Big Bill's Copa Cabana / Chess 1533**
Artists include: Muddy Waters; Buddy Guy; Sonny Boy Williamson; Howlin' Wolf; Muddy Waters; Willie Dixon and Buddy Guy

A Sixties session from Chicago blues disc jockey Big Bill Hill's nightclub. Nothing really exceptional here, although the Dixon, Waters, Guy trio is a rarity.

★★★★ **Blues Project / Elek. 7264**
Artists include: Dave Van Ronk; John Koerner; Ian Buchanan; Geoff Muldaur; Mark Spoelstra; Danny Kalb; Dave Ray; Eric Von Schmidt

Early Sixties collection of young folk-blues guitarists. The outstanding performers here are Koerner, Van Ronk and Ray. Danny Kalb would later perform in a band called the Blues Project. And Ian Buchanan turns in a nice song called "Winding Boy," though he dropped from sight immediately afterward. This record is legendary because Bob Dylan plays under a pseudonym on one track—we'll let you figure out which song, and what name. It won't take long.

★ **Bound for Glory (Soundtrack) / U. Artists LA695-H**
Only Hollywood would make a Woody Guthrie biography starring the TV master of kung fu, David Carradine. Well, David's not as good as Bruce Lee was at martial arts, he can't act as well as his father, and while he may not be much worse at singing than his brother, Keith, he isn't much better. Stick with Arlo Guthrie and his old man.

★★★ **Breakout: Top 40 Hits of Today / Col. D-32519**
Artists include: Mott the Hoople; Ten Years After; Andy Pratt; Hollies; Looking Glass; Edgar Winter Group; Argent; Dr. Hook and the Medicine Show; Chi Coltrane; Loggins and Messina; Loudon Wainwright III

Surprisingly solid collection of 1973 hits, highlighted by Andy Pratt's now rare near-miss, "Avenging Annie". Mott, the Hollies, Winter and Looking Glass turn in good pop efforts (Mott's is a lot better than good, and the rest is innocuous with the exception of Chi Coltrane's, which is atrocious).

★★★★ **Brunswick's Greatest Hits / Bruns. 754186**
Artists include: Chi-Lites; Artistics; Barbara Acklin; Jackie Wilson; Young-Holt Unlim-

ited; Lost Generation; Tyrone Davis; Little Richard

Vintage soul from the label that did so much to bring you the second payola scandal of 1973-76. The Wilson and Chi-Lites sides are triumphal, the Davis is tougher than it first appears, and Little Richard is mediocre compared to his Specialty stuff, although "Baby Don't You Tear My Clothes" is a great reworking of a Beatles idea. Only Young-Holt and Lost Generation are lousy.

■ **Bye Bye Birdie / RCA LSO-1081**
This 1963 LP featuring Dick Van Dyke, Ann-Margret and Bobby Rydell (Paul Lynde's absent, fortunately for him, unhappily for us) is offered as evidence that Robert Stigwood did not invent the insipid rock musical, but was only extrapolating from a long, ignoble tradition.

★★★ **Cadence Classics, Vol. 1 / Barn. 4000**
Artists include: Everly Brothers; Johnny Tillotson; Chordettes; Eddie Hodges; Link Wray
This is mostly banal pop, although the Everly Brothers songs are strong—especially "Bye Bye Love"—and Link Wray's lone contribution is his best song, "The Rumble," an instrumental that still cooks.

★★ **Cadence Classics, Vol. 2 / Barn. 4001**
Artists include: Chordettes; Everly Brothers; Eddie Hodges; Johnny Tillotson; Charlie McCoy; Link Wray
Buy an Everly Brothers anthology instead. This time, not even Link Wray saves the set.

★★ **Cadence Classics, Vol. 3 / Barn. 4002**
Artists include: Everly Brothers; Chordettes; Marion Marlowe; Lenny Welch; Don Shirley Trio; Johnny Tillotson; Archie Bleyer; Julius La Rosa; Bill Hayes
Whaddya want this for? Julius La Rosa? Buy the Everly Brothers alone and you'll feel better about it.

★★★★ **Car Wash (Soundtrack) / MCA 2-8010**
1976 discofied soundtrack was one of the year's best-selling albums, thanks to Rose Royce's title track. The song made that group a hit, although nothing of the rest of Rose Royce's music, or the background score, or the Pointer Sisters' art-deco funk matches up to it. The movie, naturally, was mediocre.

★★★★★ **Chicago Blues Anthology / Chess 2-60012**
Artists include: Robert Nighthawk; Johnny Shines; Memphis Slim; Jimmy Rogers; Willie Mabon; Floyd Jones; Elmore James; Big Bill Broonzy and Washboard Sam; Big Boy Spires; John Brim; Otis Rush; J. B. Lenoir; Eddie Boyd; Buddy Guy
First-rate compilation of Chicago blues tracks, most of some importance, recorded from 1949 to 1964 by the city's chief blues label. Broonzy and Washboard Sam are near the end of the line, but Lenoir, Elmore James and Shines are at the peak of their abilities. Superb notes by Pete Welding. An excellent source for anyone interested in Chicago blues beyond Waters/Wolf/Williamson/Walter.

★★★★ **Concert for Bangla Desh / Apple STCX-3385**
Artists include: Ravi Shankar and Ali Akbar Khan and Alla Rakah; George Harrison; Billy Preston; Ringo Starr; George Harrison and Leon Russell; George Harrison and Eric Clapton; Leon Russell; Leon Russell and Don Preston; Bob Dylan
The Big Event of 1972, recorded live at Madison Square Garden, proceeds supposedly to UNICEF. But the only music that's really happening is Dylan's—he hadn't been onstage for a long time, and really puts out. "Just Like a Woman" is an utter revelation, the best version he's ever done of it, and his other numbers (which range from "Blowin' in the Wind" and "Mr. Tambourine Man" to the unlikely "It Takes a Lot to Laugh It Takes a Train to Cry") aren't far behind. Aside from Dylan, the highlight is George Harrison and Eric Clapton's reprise of their Beatles' duet on "While My Guitar Gently Weeps."

★★ **Country Boy and Country Girl / RCA AHL1-1244**

Artists include: Jim Reeves and Dottie West; Bobby Bare and Skeeter Davis; Hank Snow and Anita Carter; Bobby Bare, Norma Jean and Lynn Anderson; Jimmy Dean and Dottie West; Waylon Jennings and Anita Carter; Archie Campbell and Linda Mann; Connie Smith and Nat Stuckey; Dottie West and Don Gibson

This volume of duets is far from the best of that odd C&W subgenre, probably because George Jones, the best duet singer in country, never recorded for RCA.

★ **Country Chart Busters, Vol. 1 / Col. KC-32720**

Artists include: Earl Scruggs; Tanya Tucker; Lynn Anderson; Freddy Weller; Barbara Fairchild; Johnny Cash; Sonny James; Bob Luman; Carl Smith; Jody Miller; Johnny Paycheck

Mediocre assembly of Columbia's country artists. The best items are Cash's "Oney" and Tanya Tucker's splendidly weird "Bloody Red and Going Down."

★ **Country Chart Busters, Vol. 2 / Col. KC-32718**

Artists include: Tammy Wynette; Tanya Tucker; Jody Miller; Charlie McCoy; Ray Price; Sonny James; Freddy Weller; Lynn Anderson; Johnny Cash; Earl Scruggs; Johnny Duncan

Another grab bag of CBS country performers. Anything here worth having—only Wynette's "D-I-V-O-R-C-E"—is available with more interesting companions elsewhere.

★ **Country Chart Busters, Vol. 3 / Col. KC-32721**

Artists include: Lynn Anderson; Barbara Fairchild; Carl Smith; Tanya Tucker; Sonny James; Freddy Weller; Charlie Rich; Ray Price; David Houston; George Jones; Tammy Wynette

Another lousy grab bag.

★ **Country Chart Busters, Vol. 4 / Col. KC-32723**

Artists include: Charlie McCoy; George Jones; George Jones and Tammy Wynette; Tommy Cash; Bob Luman; Johnny Cash; Johnny Duncan; Barbara Fairchild; Stonewall Jackson; Mac Davis

When they get to Mac Davis on one of these anthologies, you *know* they're scraping the bottom of the barrel.

★ **Country Chart Busters, Vol. 5 / Col. KC-32724**

Artists include: Charlie Rich; Johnny Paycheck; Jody Miller; Tammy Wynette; Freddy Weller; Sonny James; David Houston; Lynn Anderson; Connie Smith; Barbara Mandrell

The final installment in Columbia's exploration of the rube potential of the C&W audience is just as dismal as the first four.

★★ **Country 45s / Epic BG-33357**

Artists include: George Jones; Johnny Paycheck; Charlie Rich; Tanya Tucker; Tammy Wynette; David Houston; David Houston and Barbara Mandrell; Barbara Mandrell; Freddy Weller; Jody Miller; Sandy Posey; Johnny Duncan

Decent selection of Seventies C&W hits. Producer Billy Sherrill, with his fondness for big, bland arrangements, did too many of these for our taste, but Jones, Wynette, Rich and Tucker all perform respectably. Wynette's "Stand by Your Man" is a true masterpiece, but it's available in better company elsewhere. Freddy Weller ought to lay off the Chuck Berry songs. "Promised Land" is a message whose irony he seems unable to appreciate.

★★★ **Country Hits of the Fifties / Cap. SM-885**

Artists include: Tennessee Ernie Ford; Jean Shepard; Ferlin Husky; Hank Thompson; Freddie Hart; Sonny James; Faron Young; Jean Shepard and Ferlin Husky; Skeets McDonald; Tommy Collins

Nice assemblage of Fifties C&W hits. Ford's "Sixteen Tons" is a kind of rockabilly, and Thompson's "The Wild Side of Life" might be. James' "Young Love" was the most familiar pop hit of this bunch.

★★★ **Country Hits of the Forties / Cap. SM-884**
Artists include: Tex Williams; Tennessee Ernie Ford; Margaret Whiting and Jimmy Wakely; Merle Travis; Tex Ritter; Jimmie Davis; Al Dexter; Jimmy Wakely; Leon Payne; Jack Payne; Jack Guthrie

Solid set of country hits from the post–World War II era. Ritter, Ford and Davis are all significant C&W grandfathers (though none of these songs, except perhaps Ford's "Mule Train," are among their best) and Jimmie Davis, who sings "You Are My Sunshine," went on to become governor of Alabama, a process George Wallace is unlikely to reverse.

★★ **Country Hits of the Sixties / Cap. SM-886**
Artists include: Glen Campbell; Wanda Jackson; Wynn Stewart; Faron Young; Buck Owens; Tex Ritter; Merle Haggard; Roy Clark; Sonny James; Ferlin Husky

So-so collection, inferior to the Forties and Fifties volumes of the series. The highlights are Haggard's "Today I Started Loving You Again" and Faron Young's "Hello Walls." Tex Ritter's "I Dreamed of a Hillbilly Heaven" is a kitsch classic.

★ **Country Love, Vol. 2 / Col. CG-32010**
Artists include: Patti Page; Ray Price; Tommy Cash; Statler Brothers; Judy Lynn; Tammy Wynette; Charlie Rich; Lynn Anderson; Sammi Smith; Stonewall Jackson; Carl Smith; Marty Robbins; Sonny James; Arlene Harden; Barbara Mandrell; Johnny Cash; Jody Miller; David Houston; Nashville Strings; Carl Perkins

Utterly undistinguished package of Columbia's country roster.

★ **Country Love, Vol. 3 / Col. CG-32725**
Artists include: Arlene Harden; Barbara Mandrell; Lynn Anderson; Marty Robbins; Charlie McCoy; Tammy Wynette and George Jones; Tammy Wynette; David Houston; George Jones; David Houston and Barbara Mandrell; Jody Miller; Charlie Rich; Johnny Paycheck; Ray Price; Connie Smith; Freddy Weller; Barbara Fairchild; Johnny Cash and June Carter; Sonny James; Tanya Tucker

Columbia raids its catalogue without rhyme or reason. Symptom: Barbara Mandrell's "Treat Him Right" is included both here and on Volume 2 of the series. Wasn't *anybody* paying attention?

★★★★ **Country Music and Bluegrass at Newport—1963 / Van. 79146**
Artists include: Jim and Jesse; Morris Brothers; Clint Howard and Doc Watson; Clarence Ashley; Clint Howard; Mac Wiseman; New Lost City Ramblers; Tom Logan; Doc Watson

Good selection of genre favorites as performed at the influential folk festival in its peak year. Infectious and fun.

★★★ **Country's Greatest Hits / Col. CG-9**
Artists include: Johnny Cash; George Morgan; Billy Walker; Jimmy Dean; Carl Smith; Marty Robbins; Little Jimmy Dickens; Roy Acuff; Johnny Horton; Carl Perkins; Ray Price; Lefty Firzzell; Claude King; Lonzo and Oscar; Charlie Walker; Tommy Collins; Stonewall Jackson; Statler Brothers; Flatt and Scruggs; Johnny Cash and June Carter

A spotty set, but one with highlights: Cash's "I Walk the Line," Price's "Release Me," Horton's "North to Alaska," Acuff's "Wabash Cannonball" and Robbins' "El Paso." Perkins, however, is represented by a remake of "Blue Suede Shoes" that pales next to his spectacular Sun original.

★★ **Dark Muddy Bottom Blues / Spec. 2149**
Artists include: John Lee Hooker; Pinebluff Pete; Big Joe Williams; Lightnin' Hopkins; Clarence London; Country Jim

Fifties blues from Texas and the West Coast, primarily. Highlights are Hooker, Hopkins and Williams; the others are extremely minor.

★★★ **Death Wish (Soundtrack) / Col. C-33199**
Herbie Hancock effectively scored this 1975 film about Central Park vigilantism. It's the usual jazz-rock fusion blend.

★★ **A Decade of Gold (1955-1965) / Era 602**
Artists include: Gogi Grant; Teddy Bears; Castells; Donnie Brooks; Dorsey Burnette; Art and Dotty Todd; Jewel Akens; Dave Dudley; Chris Montez; Castaways; Hollywood Argyles; Pastel Six; Larry Verne; Fendermen

Lightweight rock with a few exceptions on the positive side: Teddy Bears' "To Know Him Is to Love Him" is Phil Spector's earliest production; the Castaways' "Liar Liar" is a terrific 1965 Minnesota one-shot; the Hollywood Argyles' "Alley Oop," the Fendermen's "Muleskinner Blues" and Dave Dudley's "Six Days on the Road" are all memorable novelties.

★★★ **Dells vs. Dramatics / Cadet 60027**
Artists include: Dells; Dramatics; Dells and Dramatics

Two top-flight soul groups combine with surprising effectiveness. Each group is represented by four tracks, and they join forces on "Love Is Missing from Our Lives" and "I'm in Love."

★★ **Disco Express / RCA APL1-1402**
Artists include: Tymes; Faith, Hope and Charity; Bill Harris; Charles Drain; Blood Hollins; Zulema; Brothers; Destiny; Choice Four

Seventies dance-party album has some decent tracks—Faith, Hope and Charity's "To Each His Own," Charles Drain's "What You Don't Know"—but not enough.

★ **Disco Funk / RCA ANL1-1118**
Artists include: Brother Soul; Con-Funk-Shun; Lillian Hale; Hudson County; Madeira; People; T.C.B.; Third Time Around

Bottom-of-the-barrel Seventies dance music, each performance interchangeable with a dozen other rhythm machines.

★★★ **Dr. Demento's Delights / War. B-2855**
Artists include: Allan Sherman; Possum; R. Crumb and His Cheap Suit Serenaders; Spike Jones and His City Slickers; Doodles Weaver; Napoleon XIV; Holy Modal Rounders; Ben Gay and the Silly Savages; Harry "The Hipster" Gibson; Jim Kweskin Jug Band; Jef Jaisun

Pop and rock oddities compiled and annotated by well-known discophile Barrett Hansen. Too crazy for mass consumption, and definitely not approved by the Vinyl Conservation Society, but the Rounders' "Boobs a Lot," Napoleon XIV's widely banned "They're Coming to Take Me Away, Ha Ha" and Kweskin's "If You're a Viper" are worth it for those with a penchant for the truly silly.

★★★★ **Doo Wop / Spec. 2114**
Artists include: Chimes; Monitors; Larry Williams; Vernon Green and the Phantoms; Jesse and Marvin; Marvin and Johnny; Four Flames; Roddy Jackson; Roy Montrell; King Perry and the Pied Pipers; Bob "Froggy" Landers; Rene Hall Band; Joe Lutcher

Oldies comedy from the Fifties. These really were hits—some of them—and John Lennon immortalized Larry Williams' "Bad Boy" on *Beatles VI*. Strictly for laughs but a good time, graphically well presented.

■ **Doonesbury's Jimmy Thudpucker (and the Walden West Rhythm Section Greatest Hits) / Wind. BXL1-2589**
From the 1977 Christmas special. Thudpucker is supposed to be Garry Trudeau's fantasy of a union between John Denver and Bob Dylan, and unfortunately he lives up to the synthesis. B-o-r-i-n-g.

★★★ **Drop Down Mama / Chess 411**
Artists include: Johnny Shines; Robert Nighthawk; Big Boy Spires; Honey Boy Edwards; Floyd Jones; Claude Smith

Second-echelon Chicago blues performers. Shines' "So Glad I Found You" and "Joliet Blues," Nighthawk's venerable "Sweet Black Angel" and Jones' "Dark Road" are standouts. A nice complement to Chess' *Chicago Blues Anthology*.

★ **Dueling Banjos from *Deliverance* (Soundtrack) / War. B-2683**
From the 1972 John Boorman film that was supposed to take star Burt Reynolds and poet/author James Dickey into the artistic big time. Instead, the only hit this produced was Eric Weisberg's title track and some other banjo numbers that are much less exciting.

★★★★★ **Echoes of a Rock Era: The Early Years / Rou. 111**
Artists include: Sonny Til and the Orioles; Faye Adams; Bo Diddley; Penguins; Cadillacs; Moonglows; Chuck Berry; Nutmegs; Jesse Belvin; Heartbeats; Frankie Lymon; Crows; Chuck Willis; Fleetwoods; Jimmie Rodgers; Buddy Knox; Rays

Excellent Fifties anthology, drawing from a variety of sources—Chess (Berry's "Roll Over Beethoven" and "Maybellene," Diddley's "Bo Diddley," "Sincerely" by the Moonglows), Atlantic ("Gee" by the Crows and Chuck Willis' "C. C. Rider"), West Coast harmony groups (Penguins' "Earth Angel"), gospel R&B (Til's "Crying in the Chapel") and Southwestern rockabilly (Knox' "Party Doll"). Only the Jimmie Rodgers tracks are truly weak, and while there's nothing really obscure, the presentation is very attractive.

★★★★ Echoes of a Rock Era: The Groups, Vol. 1 / Rou. RE-114
Artists include: Crows; Harptones

Two prime Fifties vocal groups from the East Coast, doo-wopping to their—and your—hearts' content. Lush and soulful, if a bit primitive. The Crows are best remembered for "Gee," the Harptones for "Sunday Kind of Love." Not as good for general interest as the survey LPs in the series, but fine for aficionados of street-corner soul.

★★★★ Echoes of a Rock Era: The Groups, Vol. 2 / Rou. RE-115
Artists include: Heartbeats; Shep and the Limelites

Seminal New York group harmony from the Fifties. The general survey LPs in this series are great starter sets for rock fans; these are for collectors. The Heartbeats' best song was "A Thousand Miles Away," but the group's brooding wistfulness sustains its sides. Shep and the Limelites came up with the unsettling ballad "Daddy's Home," contributing a haunted quality that pervades the group's material here.

★★★★ Echoes of a Rock Era: The Later Years / Rou. 113
Artists include: Maxine Brown; Carla Thomas; Shirelles; Chubby Checker; Cleftones; Silhouettes; Lee Dorsey; Bobby Lewis; King Curtis; Mary Wells; Ben E. King; Little Eva; Dave "Baby" Cortez; Joey Dee and the Starliters; Essex; Joe Henderson; Lou Christie

Final volume of this fine survey gives a nice look at rock just before the Beatles: Motown is represented with Mary Wells' "My Guy," Atlantic with Ben E. King's "Don't Play That Song" and King Curtis' great "Soul Twist," Stax with Carla Thomas' "Gee Whiz," girl groups by the Shirelles' "Baby It's You" and "Dedicated to the One I Love," New Orleans by Lee

Dorsey's "Ya Ya," one-shot pop by Little Eva's immortal "The Locomotion," and so forth. Some froth (Cleftones, Lou Christie) but general excellence.

★★★★★ Echoes of a Rock Era: The Middle Years / Rou. 112
Artists include: Monotones; Silhouettes; Dee Clark; Chantels; Jimmie Rodgers; Little Anthony and the Imperials; Coasters; Flamingos; Wilbur Harrison; Johnny and the Hurricanes; Crests; Fiestas; Billy Bland; Maurice Williams and the Zodiacs; Joe Jones; Maxine Brown; Dovels; Joey Dee and the Starliters

Rock and R&B from about 1958 to around 1962—the latter part of the harmony group era (Monotones' "Book of Love," Coasters' "Poison Ivy" and "Charley Brown," the Chantels' "Maybe" and Maurice Williams' "Stay" are all masterpieces of that genre) to the beginning of the twist (Joey Dee and the Starliters' "Peppermint Twist" is perhaps the best of the dance-craze discs). The only clinkers are Jimmie Rodgers (the pop one, of course) and the Crests, whose "Sixteen Candles" is teen exploitation music, not rock. Attractively packaged.

★★★★★ Eighteen King Size Country Hits / Col. CS-9468
Artists include: Cowboy Copas; Moon Mullican; Grandpa Jones; Carlisle Brothers; Bonnie Lou; William Raney; Joe Osborne; Hawkshaw Hawkins; Delmore Brothers; D. Reno and R. Smiley; Clarence Moody; Stanley Brothers; J. Cardwell; Pop Eckler

Excellent sampler of C&W sides made for King, the Cincinnati-based label that made most of its impact in the Forties and Fifties. Well annotated by Sire Records owner, Seymour Stein, and highlighted by the bluegrass of the Delmore and Stanley Brothers, and the honky-tonk singing of Cowboy Copas and Hawkshaw Hawkins.

Even better is the companion volume, *Eighteen King Size Rhythm and Blues Hits,* released at the same time but now deleted. It features profoundly important material by James Brown, Little Willie John and Hank Ballard, among others, with ample commentary, again by Stein. Seek out both.

★★ **England's Greatest Hit Makers / Lon. PS-430**
Artists include: Rolling Stones; Kathy Kirby; Them; Tom Jones; Unit Four Plus Two; Bern Elliott; Mike Leander Orchestra; Bachelors; Lulu and the Lovers; Zombies; Johnny Howard Band; Billy Fury; Applejacks; Dave Berry
Your Anglophilia has to run pretty deep to want this collection of dated English pop from the mid-Sixties. The Stones' track is the obscure but easily available, "Surprise Surprise"; Them checks in with "Little Girl"; the Zombies with "Nothing's Changed." Aside from those, the most interesting item here is Unit Four Plus Two's "Woman from Liberia," which is hardly as good as their hit, "Concrete and Clay." In context, this is rot, and instructive to anyone who believes the British Invasion was all gold—but it isn't worth more than a couple of bucks, for any purpose.

■ **Evita (Original Cast) / MCA 2-1103**
The best thing about this 1976 "rock" opera, based on the life of Evita Peron, the Argentine Rasputin, and written by the *Jesus Christ Superstar* team of Andrew Lloyd Webber and Timothy Rice, is the

reappearance on record of former Manfred Mann lead singer, Paul Jones. Unfortunately, Jones has lost his touch, a problem exacerbated by the surroundings: wooden singing, horrid songwriting and a stupid concept. The play was a hit in London, so this may enjoy a revival. It's up to *you* to prevent it.

★★★★ **FM (Soundtrack) / MCA 2-12000**
Artists include: Jimmy Buffett; Doobie Brothers; Eagles; Dan Fogelberg; Foreigner; Billy Joel; Randy Meisner; Steve Miller; Tom Petty and the Heartbreakers; Queen; Linda Ronstadt; Boz Scaggs; Bob Seger; Steely Dan; James Taylor; Joe Walsh
Had it not been released in 1978—the year of *Saturday Night Fever*—this soundtrack from the flop movie about rock radio might have been regarded as a true phenomenon, since it spent a fair share of time in the Top Ten. Even so, this is a peculiarly flawed picture of what goes on in rock in the late Seventies.

The bias toward California rock is extreme, symbolized by the inclusion of two Linda Ronstadt cover versions, "Tumbling Dice" and "Poor Poor Pitiful Me," both of them demonstrably inferior to the Rolling Stones and Warren Zevon originals. There is also a bent toward lightweight pop of all kinds (thus, Billy Joel's "Just the Way You Are"), and a complete underrating and underestimation of hard rock: why Foreigner's "Cold as Ice" formula crap and Queen's contemptible neofascist chant "We Will Rock You" rather than the Who and Lynyrd Skynyrd, two acts who actually record for MCA?

Producer Irving Azoff, who manages the Eagles, Steely Dan, Buffett, Meisner, Scaggs, Fogelberg and Walsh, seems to have let his taste dictate the contents. Especially given Steely Dan's otherwise unavailable title track, this could have been the new *Woodstock,* a comprehensive overview of a contemporary moment in rock. Instead, that place goes to *Saturday Night Fever,* which at least accurately reflects the energy and scope of disco.

★★★ **John Fahey, Leo Kottke and Peter Lang / Tak. 1040**
Sampler of Takoma's three most prominent folk-blues-based guitarists. Fahey is a genius, but Kottke and Lang are only slightly his inferiors. All of this is pleasant, although every one of them is better when given more space to stretch out.

★★★ Fantasy Blues Two-Fer Giants / Fan. FP-4

Artists include: Jimmy Witherspoon; Lightnin' Hopkins; Reverend Gary Davis; Furry Lewis; Memphis Slim; John Lee Hooker; Jesse Fuller; Sonny Terry and Brownie McGhee; Tom Rush; Dave Van Ronk; Holy Modal Rounders

Interesting collection that's not really blues at all but a sampling of the best blues and folk from Prestige albums, which Fantasy now owns and reissues. The last three artists—Rush, Van Ronk and the Rounders—are all white folkies who depart, in various ways, from black blues tradition. The first nine are all for the real bluesman, though, and while this isn't anyone's best work, these Fifties and Sixties recordings have a certain vitality and make a nice introduction to mostly country (only Hooker and Witherspoon are electric or band artists) blues.

★★★★ A Fistful of Dollars (Soundtrack) / RCA LSO-1135

This outstanding score by Ennio Morricone is interesting to rock fans because the Italian composer uses electric guitar to create effects more deadly than most rock musicians. Morricone's influence has seeped into several young electric guitarists since this picture appeared in the late Sixties. (The film is Clint Eastwood's second cosmic Western with director Sergio Leone.)

★★★★ Fourteen Golden Recordings from the Vaults of Duke Records, Vol. 1 / ABC X-784

Artists include: Bobby "Blue" Bland; Johnny Ace; Casuals; Willie Mae Thornton; O.V. Wright; Junior Parker; Torros; Clarence "Gatemouth" Brown; Rob Roys; Roy Head; Joe Hinton

Fine sampler of R&B from the Texas-based Duke label. Most of these are minor R&B hits from the Fifties and Sixties. Bland's "There Ain't Nothing You Can Do" and "Further Up the Road" are among his best, Head's "Treat Her Right" and Hinton's "Funny" take the R&B-country fusion beyond rockabilly, Ace's "Pledging My Love" is a genre masterpiece. There's some surprisingly good group vocalizing—the Casuals' "So Tough," "Dance with Me" by the Torros—a peculiar black-consciousness item by Wright ("Ace of Spades") and, of course, Thornton's "Hound Dog," which is where Elvis learned it. Annotation is only adequate, which is all that holds this back.

★★★★ Fourteen Golden Recordings from the Vaults of Vee Jay Records / ABC X-785

Artists include: Dells; Gene Chandler; Betty Everett and Jerry Butler; Dee Clark; Gladys Knight and the Pips; Jimmy Reed; Jerry Butler; John Lee Hooker; Betty Everett; Eddie Harris

Interesting collection of hits from the formidable Chicago label, one of the few black-owned ones of the Fifties and Sixties. "Duke of Earl," by Chandler, is a classic rock mystery: who is the Duke and why? The Everett/Butler duet on "Let It Be Me," Butler's own "He Will Break Your Heart" and Gladys Knight's "Every Beat of My Heart" are transitional records between R&B and soul of some importance, while Reed and Hooker's blues are both well known because they were so easily adapted to rock & roll by the British bands, particularly the Animals.

★★★★★ Alan Freed's Memory Lane / Rou. 42041

Artists include: Dells; Jerry Butler; Flamingos; Crests; Sonny Til and the Orioles; Jacks; Five Satins; Moonglows; Teen Queens; Rays; Little Anthony and the Imperials; Robert and Johnny; Mello Kings; Jesse Belvin

The fact that this is a fine collection of slow dance R&B ballads is secondary to the fact that it's narrated by Freed, giving those who missed the first great rock disc jockey's radio shows a chance to hear him. Freed probably isn't at the peak of his form—this album and its nonnarrative companion, *Alan Freed's Top 15*, were made for George Goldner's End label after Freed's career had been destroyed in the payola witch hunt. But it's still a thrill to hear the voice that started it all, and if none of these tracks are obscure—well, maybe the Jacks' "Why Don't You Write Me"—that's a tribute to the prescience of his (and Goldner's) taste.

★★★★ Alan Freed's Top 15 / Rou. 42042

Artists include: Wilbur Harrison; Buster Brown; Etta James; Santo and Johnny; Nutmegs; Spaniels; Dee Clark; Shirelles; Lee Dorsey; Silhouettes; Faye Adams; Charlie and Ray; Cadillacs; Rivileers; Edna McGriff

Not as exceptional as *Alan Freed's Memory Lane*—he doesn't narrate it—but this LP has more diversity. And, presuming he really picked the cuts, the album confirms the excellence of the great DJ's taste. You can imagine, with awe, that this is what the music on his shows sounded like, and be overwhelmed by its scope: "Kansas City" by Harrison and "Fanny Mae" by Brown are hard rockers, while the beautiful "Shake a Hand" by Faye Adams is a barely secular gospel derivative.

★ Fritz the Cat (Soundtrack) / Fan. 9406
Artists include: Bo Diddley; Billie Holiday; Alice Stuart; Jim Post; Merl Saunders; Cal Tjader; Bernard Purdie

Very spotty record, from Ralph Bakshi's animated feature based on R. Crumb's horny cartoon feline. Diddley and Holiday are overwhelmed by the trio of West Coast mediocrities, who noodle aimlessly over the rest of the disc.

★★★ From the Historic Vaults of Duke Peacock / ABC X-789
Artists include: Bobby Bland; Johnny Ace; Junior Parker; John Roberts; Lamp Sisters; Ernie K-Doe; Paulette Parker; Clarence and Calvin; O. V. Wright; Jeanette Williams; Roy Head; Willie Mae Thornton; Insights

Much more spotty than its companion volume, *14 Golden Recordings,* this set nonetheless gives a pretty good picture of the actual Duke release pattern. The Lamp Sisters' "Today Will Be Yesterday, Tomorrow" is a nice R&B oddity, but the Bland and Parker selections are poor, and the rest is simple middle-level R&B, without much distinction.

★★★★★ From Spirituals to Swing / Van. VSD-47/48
Artists include: Benny Goodman Sextet; Count Basie; Helen Humes; Hot Lips Page; Kansas City Six; James P. Johnson; New Orleans Feetwarmers; Golden Gate Quartet; Sonny Terry; Joe Turner and Pete Johnson;

Pete Johnson; Meade Lux Lewis; Albert Ammons; Big Bill Broonzy; Sonny Terry and Bull City Red; Mitchell's Christian Singers; Ida Cox

John Hammond's memorable 1936 Carnegie Hall concert delivers just what it promises: spirituals, swing and everything in-between, including blues, ragtime, hot New Orleans jazz—the works. Probably of value only to historians and collectors—the recordings are not great—but a nice perspective on the development of black American music, nonetheless.

★★★ Golden Hits from the Gang at Bang / Bang 215
Artists include: Neil Diamond; McCoys; Strangeloves; Exciters

Anthology of mid-Sixties hits that range from Diamond's formula pop-rock ("Cherry Cherry" and "Solitary Man") to the Exciters' pop-soul and primordial punk rock (Strangeloves with "I Want Candy" and "Cara-lin," and the McCoys with "Hang on Sloopy" and "Fever"). Worth having for the latter.

★★★ Get Down and Boogie / Casa. 7042
Artists include: Donna Summer; Giorgio; Parliament; Roberta Kelly; Smoke

Mixed bag of recent funk and disco material. Summer is the contemporary siren of the dance floor and "Love to Love Ya Baby" is the first indication of how and why: this is her best and most sultry moan and groan. Parliament's "Give Up the Funk" is probably the most accessible kind of music that leader George Clinton makes. But the rest of this is just the modern-dance formula, done without much distinction, unless you like Giorgio's Muzak-inspired "Nights in White Satin."

■ **Godspell (Original Cast) / Ari. 4001**
■ **Godspell (Soundtrack) / Ari. 4005**
One of Broadway's lamer attempts to go counterculture, with a musical based on St. Matthew's gospel. In language the authors would pretend to understand, somebody's going to earn an awful lot of bad karma for these electrified recyclings of Rodgers and Hart. Don't mess with the Kid.

★★★★ **Golden Age of Rhythm and Blues / Chess 2CH-50030**
Artists include: Bluejays; Coronets; El-Rays; Moonglows; Moonlighters; Orchids; Flamingos; Five Notes; Ravens; Quintones; Tornadoes; Students; Sentimentals; Lee Andrews and the Hearts; Monotones; Pastels; Revels; Sonics; Miracles
Chess Records is thought of as a blues label, but it also produced some of the dreamiest doo-wop of the Fifties. These harmony groups are mostly Chicago based (the big exception is the Miracles, whose "Bad Girl" was done before Berry Gordy dreamed up Motown). Unfortunately, given the inclusion of so many obscure groups, this collection is not annotated, but the best of it—"Bad Girl," the Moonglows' "Sincerely," Lee Andrews and the Hearts' "Teardrops," the Flamingos' "I'll Be Home" and "The Vow," and particularly "I'm So Young" by the Students—is downright essential.

★★★★ **Golden Soul (in Aid of the World's Refugees) / Atl. 18198**
Artists include: Otis Redding; Ray Charles; Roberta Flack; Wilson Pickett; King Curtis; Ben E. King; Drifters; Sam and Dave; Spinners; Percy Sledge; Joe Tex; Aretha Franklin
This album's proceeds go to UNICEF, and it is an interesting, if limited, look at the development of Atlantic's version of soul from Charles' "What'd I Say" (1955) to Flack's "Feel Like Makin' Love" (1974). What happens in between is the story of R&B's development into soul and the ability of the music to surpass nomenclature barriers. Everything here represents the artist at the height of his/her powers. Unfortunately, there is no annotation. Ideally, one should look for the eight-volume *History of Rhythm and Blues* (now deleted), which tells Atlantic's story in much more detail. Failing that, however, this has to do.

★★ **Golden Summer / U. Artists LA627-H2**
Artists include: Beach Boys; Marketts; Fantastic Baggys; Jan and Dean; Surfaris; Frog-

men; Frankie Avalon; Dick Dale and the Deltones; Trashmen; Tradewinds; Jack Nitzsche; Annette Funicello; Routers; Ventures
A concept collection gone wrong. Inferior Beach Boys selections (where's "Surfin' USA"?), some poor covers ("Pipeline" by the Ventures, when the hit version by the Chantays is far, far superior), and some pure nonsense: Annette and Frankie carry the concept too far. In fact, the best stuff here is *not* about surfing: Nitzsche's "Lonely Surfer," the Tradewinds' "New York's a Lonely Town" and the Trashmen's gibberish masterpiece, "Surfin' Bird," are among the truest ancestors of the punk rock of the Ramones and Sex Pistols.

★★★ **The Good, the Bad and the Ugly (Soundtrack) / U. Artists 5172**
From the 1968 Sergio Leone film starring Clint Eastwood. Hugo Montenegro parlayed the theme song into a pop hit. But composer Ennio Morricone's arrangement is tougher, more electric; it could pass for a kind of post-Hendrix rock. Still, this is the least exciting of Morricone's Leone scores.

★★★ **Good Old Country Gospel / RCA LSP-4778**
Artists include: Chet Atkins; Floyd Cramer; Jim Reeves; Skeeter Davis; Dolly Parton; Porter Wagoner and the Blackwood Brothers; Connie Smith; Dottie West
A rather skimpy assortment, of which the Wagoner track with the Blackwood Brothers is most worthwhile. Hearing the other singers here do hymns is like watching the most outrageous Saturday night reveler arrive for church next morning: his contrition may be suspect, but not his faith. It's a shame there isn't at least one selection here, though, from Elvis Presley's three wonderful gospel LPs.

★★★★ **Gospel at Its Best / Pea. 59200**
Artists include: Dixie Hummingbirds; Inez Andrews; Sensational Nightingales; Pilgrim Travelers; Jackson Southernaires; Mighty Clouds of Joy; Loving Sisters; Biblical Gospel Singers; Five Blind Boys; Williams Brothers
A fine collection of Fifties and Sixties gospel music, which might make a nice supplement to Columbia's *The Gospel Sound* sets. The Hummingbirds, Nightingales, Pilgrim Travelers, Blind Boys and Mighty Clouds are all among the most important groups in the genre.

★★★★★ **The Gospel Sound, Vol. 1 / Col. CG-31086**
Artists include: Blind Willie Johnson; Reverend J.M. Gates; Arizona Dranes; Golden Gate Jubilee Quartet; Mahalia Jackson; Mitchell's Christian Singers; Abyssinian Baptist Choir; Dixie Hummingbirds; Dorothy Love Coates; Staple Singers; Angelic Gospel Singers and the Dixie Hummingbirds; Marion Williams

A splendid double-disc gospel compilation with material spanning the era from Johnson's 1927 "Motherless Children" and "If I Had My Way" to Coates' 1968 "Strange Man." The annotation is by Tony Heilbut, the best critic in the field. This is part of Columbia's John Hammond Collection, and is packaged and chosen with that venerable gentleman's usual perspicacity. These two volumes are perhaps *the* fundamental overview of black gospel styles.

★★★★★ **The Gospel Sound, Vol. 2 / Col. CG-311595**
Artists include: Blind Willie Johnson; Eddie Head and Family; Marion Williams; Arizona Dranes; Golden Gate Jubilee Quartet; Mahalia Jackson; Reverend J. M. Gates; Dorothy Love Coates and the Gospel Harmonettes; Pilgrim Travelers; Staple Singers; Bessie Griffin; Mitchell's Christian Singers; R. Harris and the Christian Singers

The second lovely volume of black gospel music, presented as part of Columbia's John Hammond Collection and annotated by Tony Heilbut. Fundamental for anyone with an interest in America's black musical heritage.

★★ **The Graduate (Soundtrack) / Col. JS-3180**
This album made Simon and Garfunkel huge stars in 1968, but it's too skimpy on Paul Simon songs—"Mrs. Robinson" and "Sounds of Silence" as well as the inevitable "Scarborough Fair" and a couple of others—while the set is filled out with the usual background music. This album doesn't hold up much better than the Mike Nichols–directed period picture it is derived from.

■ **Grease (Original Cast) / MGM SE-34**
★ **Grease (Soundtrack) / RSO 2-4002**
The Broadway show is concrete evidence that that medium ought to be legally barred from any association with rock & roll, or the Fifties. Dumb, obvious and boring. The film version is a different matter: John Travolta might have been a great greaser, if he'd been able to avoid the travesty of his surroundings. While any movie with an affection for Sandra Dee and Fabian is a movie we can do without, this is slightly redeemed by the presence of "You're the One That I Want," a 1978 hit in which Travolta and Newton-John capture a sliver of the sound and innocent spirit of the era. A smart guy would save himself a lot of dough by springing for the single and forgetting about this dud.

★★★★★ **Great Bluesmen / Van. 25/26**
Artists include: Homesick James; John Lee Hooker; Sleepy John Estes; Muddy Waters; Jesse Fuller; Reverend Gary Davis; Mance Lipscomb; Mississippi John Hurt; Junior Wells; Johnny Shines; Son House; Sonny Terry; Joe Turner and Pete Johnson; Brownie McGhee and Sonny Terry; Otis Spann; Big Bill Broonzy; Lightnin' Hopkins; Johnny Young; James Cotton; Jimmy Rushing; Skip James; J. B. Hutto; Fred McDowell; Ida Cox; Robert Pete Williams; Otis Rush

The full scope of blues: delta stylists like Hurt and House, to relatively sophisticated Kansas City performers (Rushing, Turner, Johnson) and a good deal of Chicago material—Waters, Cotton, Spann, James, Rush, Hutto, Young. Also some eccentrics and transitional figures: Broonzy, Fuller, Hooker, Lipscomb, Davis, Estes. Perfunctorily annotated, but nonetheless, this is a comprehensive blues perspective, although little of it (perhaps only Hurt's "Moanin' the Blues") is definitive.

★★★★ **Great Bluesmen at Newport / Van. VSD-77/78**
Artists include: Robert Pete Williams; Sonny Terry and Brownie McGhee; John Lee Hooker; Son House; Skip James; Sleepy John Estes; Willie Doss; Mississippi Fred

McDowell; Mississippi John Hurt; Reverend Gary Davis; Lightnin' Hopkins; Dock Reese

Fine selection of live, mostly delta-based folk-blues artists, from the 1963 and 1964 Newport Folk Festivals, at which nearly all the major rediscovered bluesmen appeared. Those shows were occasions, and often, the performances reflect it. The annotation, unfortunately, is completely inadequate, and Estes, for instance, is clearly well past his prime.

★★★★★ **Great Golden Gospel Hits, Vol. 1 / Savoy 14069**
Artists include: James Cleveland; Gospel Harmonettes; Roberta Martin Singers; Imperial Gospel Singers; Ward Singers; Davis Sisters; Five Blind Boys; Gospel Clefs; Caravans; Alex Bradford; Staple Singers; Gay Sisters

A fine representation of black religious music, from the label that has done the most to preserve its treasures. These tracks range from the late Forties through the Sixties, and feature a great many of this music's biggest names. Dilettantes and beginners will get more from Columbia's *Gospel Sound* as an overview, but those interested in the continuing breadth and vitality of gospel as a musical genre should investigate this, and its companion volumes.

★★★★★ **Great Golden Gospel Hits, Vol. 2 / Savoy 14104**
Artists include: James Cleveland; Caravans; Gospel Harmonettes; Rosie Wallace; Dorothy Norwood; Gospel Clefs; Southwestern Michigan Choir; Reverend Charles Watkins; Roberta Martin Singers; Five Blind Boys; Robert Anderson; Raspberry Singers

The second excellent collection in Savoy's series.

★★★★★ **Great Golden Gospel Hits, Vol. 3 / Savoy 14165**
Artists include: James Cleveland; Reverend Cleophus Robinson; Dr. C. J. Johnson; Banks Brothers; Jesse Dixon; Dorothy Norwood; Southwestern Michigan Choir; Caravans; Gospel Wonders; Vill Moss; D. Barrett; Angelic Choir

Collection sustains its quality through the third set in Savoy's series.

★★★ **Great Golden Gospel Hits, Vol. 4 / Savoy 14262**
Artists include: James Cleveland; Dorothy Norwood; Jesse Dixon; Davis Sisters; Rosetta Tharpe; Roberta Martin Singers; Angelic

Choir; James Herndon; Caravans; Voices of Tabernacle; Hulah Gene and Carolyne; Bill Moss

The concluding volume of Savoy's gospel collection has fewer big names than the others but is still a fine selection.

★★ **Great Moments at the Grand Ole Opry / RCA CPL2-1904**
Artists include: Minnie Pearl; Connie Smith; Sonny James; Chet Atkins; Bobby Bare; Hank Snow; Don Gibson; Dolly Parton; Jim Reeves; Porter Wagoner; Johnny Russell and Archie Campbell; Ronnie Milsap; Billy Walker; Dottie West; Jim Ed Brown

Doesn't deliver on the title's promise. These are mostly average tracks from a group of average singers, with a handful of exceptions: Parton, Reeves, Wagoner and Bare, who turn in interesting versions of predictable songs.

★★★ **Great Soul Hits / Bruns. 754129**
Artists include: Jackie Wilson; Young-Holt Unlimited; Barbara Acklin; Artistics; Gene Chandler; Big Maybelle

A collection of Brunswick's R&B successes. Wilson's "Doggin' Around" and "Lonely Teardrops" are masterful, Acklin's "Love Makes a Woman" and the Artistics' "I'm Gonna Miss You" acceptable soul, Young-Holt and Chandler's sides undistinguished, while Big Maybelle's "Candy" and "The Trouble I've Seen" are tough blues, a bit out of place in such company.

★★ **Greatest Country and Western Hits / Col. CS-8881**
Artists include: Jimmy Dean; Marion Worth; Marty Robbins; Ray Price; Flatt and Scruggs; Johnny Cash; Carl Smith; Claude King; Lefty Frizzell; Carl Butler; Stonewall Jackson; Little Jimmy Dickens

Undistinguished selection of Columbia's big country hits is hardly anybody's greatest: Cash's "Ring of Fire" might be his, but how can anyone stand the insufferable *Beverly Hillbillies* TV theme, "Ballad of Jed Clampett," assigned to Flatt and Scruggs? Jimmy Dean's "Big Bad John" and Claude King's "Wolverton Mountain" are both country-pop novelties that haven't dated well. Forget about this.

★★★★ **Greatest Folksingers of the Sixties / Van. VSD-17/18**
Artists include: Ian and Sylvia; Rooftop Singers; Buffy Sainte-Marie; Joan Baez; Cisco Houston; Country Joe and the Fish; Odetta; Richard and Mimi Fariña; Phil Ochs; Eric Andersen; Jim Kweskin and the Jug Band; Doc Watson; John Hammond; Jack Elliott; Mississippi John Hurt; Judy Collins and Theodore Bikel; Weavers; Bob Gibson and Hamilton Camp; Tom Paxton; José Feliciano; Staple Singers; Joan Baez and Bob Gibson; Flatt and Scruggs; Bob Dylan and friends; Peggy Seeger and Ewan MacColl; Paul Butterfield Blues Band; Chamber Brothers; New Lost City Ramblers; Tommy Makem; Oscar Brand and Jean Ritchie; Pete Seeger
The definition of "folk music" here is so broad that it encompasses everything from a purist like Pete Seeger to a Puerto Rican pop singer like José Feliciano; renegades like Bob Dylan and Country Joe and the Fish and traditionalists like Watson, Brand and Ritchie; ancient bluesmen like Hurt, bluegrass traditionalists like Flatt and Scruggs, modern white bluesmen like Hammond and Butterfield, and old-timey revivalists like the Ramblers.
Still, during the scattered decade that was the Sixties, the term "folk" had just about that many applications. The music

here is representative of the various permutations of what folk fans found themselves exposed to in those years. The Dylan track, by the way, is a version of "Blowin' in the Wind" recorded at the 1963 Newport Folk Festival, the same place where Dylan would be attacked two years later for going electric. Nothing else here is terribly obscure, and the lack of notes hurts.

★★★★ **Greatest Gospel Gems, Vol. 1 / Spec. 2144**
Artists include: Sam Cooke and the Soul Stirrers; Brother Joe May; Pilgrim Travelers; Five Blind Boys; Alex Bradford; Dorothy Love Coates and the Gospel Harmonettes; Swan Silvertones; Robert Anderson; Chosen Gospel Singers; Wynona Carr; Soul Stirrers
The first of two excellent compilations of Specialty's Fifties gospel recordings.

★★★★ **Greatest Gospel Gems, Vol. 2 / Spec. 2145**
Artists include: Alex Bradford; Johnnie Taylor and the Soul Stirrers; Sam Cooke and the Soul Stirrers; Meditation Singers; Pilgrim Travelers; Brother Joe May; Five Blind Boys; Brother Joe May and the Pilgrim Travelers; Swan Silvertones; Reverend James Cleveland; Dorothy Love Coates and the Gospel Harmonettes
Second Specialty gospel compilation is especially interesting because it features gospel recordings by no less than three future soul singers: Cooke, of course; Johnny Taylor, who replaced Cooke in the Soul Stirrers and went on to record "Who's Makin' Love" and "Disco Lady"; and Laura Lee, famous now for "Women's Love Rights," but much earlier a member of the Motown-based Meditation Singers.

★★★ **Greatest Hits from England / Par. 71010**
Artists include: Fortunes; Tom Jones; Them; Moody Blues; Hedgehoppers Anonymous; Los Bravos; Unit Four Plus Two; Jonathan King; Zombies; Kathy Kirby; Noel Harrison; Nashville Teens
Oddly enough, this 1966 collection is a pretty good presentation of the second wave of the British Invasion, and far superior to London's *England's Hit Makers,* which is a kind of companion volume. There's nothing by the Stones here, but that's made up for by the gaggle of punk-prototype hits that are included: Them's "Gloria," "Go Now" by the Moody Blues, Los Bravos' odd "Black Is Black," the

Zombies' "She's Not There" and especially the most raunchy of them all, "Tobacco Road" by the Nashville Teens. Although a good deal of the rest is sentimental pop, Jonathan King's "Everyone's Gone to the Moon" is at least futuristic sentimentality and Tom Jones' "It's Not Unusual" is the bluesiest item he has ever recorded.

★★ Greatest Songs of Woody Guthrie / Van. VSD-35/36

Artists include: Woody Guthrie; Cisco Houston; Weavers; Odetta; Country Joe McDonald; Jack Elliott; Woody Guthrie and Cisco Houston; Babysitters; Jim Kweskin; Joan Baez

This could have been a magnificent set. Guthrie ranks with Hank Williams, Jimmie Rodgers and the Carter Family as a pre-rock songwriter of enormous imagination, vitality and humanity. At times, in fact, this set can't help living up to its hero's legend: particularly on his own numbers ("This Land Is Your Land," "Hard Traveling," three others), but also on Elliott's "Talking Fish Blues" and "1913 Massacre," and Kweskin's "Buffalo Skinners." The others treat Guthrie too much as a national monument to get at the spirit of roughneck fun and the utter lack of pious sanctimoniousness that lies at the heart of his musical vision—a problem epitomized by Joan Baez' reading of the outlaw ballad "Pretty Boy Floyd."

★★ Guitar Album / Poly. PD2-3008

Artists include: Eric Clapton; Roy Buchanan; Rory Gallagher; T. Bone Walker; Ellen McIlwaine; Stone the Crows; Link Wray; John McLaughlin; Area Code 615

Right players, but mostly the wrong songs. This scattershot collection features Buchanan and Gallagher at their best (Bu-

chanan's "The Messiah Will Come Again" is the highlight of his solo career), Clapton with some good material ("Slunky," "Let It Rain," "Have You Ever Loved a Woman") from his Derek and the Dominos period. Wray and McLaughlin have done better elsewhere, Stone the Crows produced "Maggie Bell" but not much noteworthy guitar, and McIlwaine's eccentric approach doesn't make sufficient sense in this limited slot.

★ Guitar Greats / Ev. 243

Artists include: Glen Campbell; Dick Rosmini; Joe Maphis; Billy Strange; Fred Gerlach; Jim Helms; Tommy Tedesco; Joe Maphis and James McGuinn; James McGuinn; Mason Williams

Only players will be interested in this set of tunes by Sixties folk and country sidemen, the best known of whom today are McGuinn, Campbell and Maphis. The others are forgotten, not necessarily regrettably.

★ Guitar Players / Main. 410

Artists include: Amboy Dukes; Jay Berliner; David T. Walker and Arthur Wright; Lightnin' Hopkins; Brownie McGhee; Jim Raney; David Spinoza; Jack Wilkins

All that saves this collection from the trash bin is the Amboy Dukes' "Baby Please Don't Go," which was Ted Nugent's pro debut and a punk-rock prototype, and the Hopkins and McGhee blues tracks. The rest, including well-known sessionman Spinoza's "Thank You," is the sort of tepid jazz-funk Mainstream makes its speciality.

■ Hair (Original Broadway Cast) / RCA LSO-1150
■ Hair (Original Cast) / RCA ANL1-0986
■ Hair (Soundtrack) / RCA LBL2-3274

What the squares thought the Sixties were about. If you must hear "Aquarius," you'll be a lot better off with the Fifth Dimension's version, which was a hit.

★★★ Happy Trails / U. Artists LA766-J2

Artists include: Roy Rogers; Billie Jo Spears; Slim Whitman; Dave Dudley; Willie Nelson; Crystal Gayle; Bob Wills and the Texas Playboys; Johnny Darrell; Jean Shepherd; Bobby Goldsboro; George Jones; Walter Brennan; Del Reeves; Warren Smith; Freddy Fender; Patsy Cline; Bob Wills and Tommy Duncan

Solid country sampler. Nelson's "Funny How Time Slips Away" and "Night Life" are two of his first compositions, and two of his best; Wills' "San Antonio Rose" is immortal. Jones' "She Thinks I Still Care" ranks with his best, too, and Fender's "Wasted Days and Wasted Nights" is the only really remarkable thing his long career has produced. But perhaps this album's strongest inclusion is Dudley's one-shot hit, "Six Days on the Road."

★★★★★ **The Harder They Come (Soundtrack) / Is. 9202**
Artists include: Jimmy Cliff; Scotty; Melodians; Toots and the Maytals; Slickers; Desmond Dekker
The greatest reggae sampler, and the soundtrack to the Jamaican outlaw picture that had tremendous impact on college crowds in the Northeast and in San Francisco, where the reggae cult began to bloom. Cliff's title song, "You Can Get It If You Really Want," "Many Rivers to Cross" and "Sitting in Limbo" are the strongest, purest reggae he's ever done. The Maytals' "Pressure Drop" and "Sweet and Dandy" are treasures. The other songs, while done by obscure artists, are up to the standard of the above: the Melodians' "Rivers of Babylon" is particularly haunting. But the song that says it all—catches Jamaican politics and the culture that nurtures reggae and the sensibility of the film—is the Slickers' "Johnny Too Bad," a virtual anthem of Third World rebellion. This album isn't platinum, or even gold, but it is as influential as anything released in the Seventies: witness the Rolling Stones, Patti Smith and the Clash, among others. A must.

★ **Heavy Traffic (Soundtrack) / Fan. 9436**
Track to Ralph Bakshi's second animated feature (followup to *Fritz the Cat*) features silly versions of "Scarborough Fair," none of them by Simon and Garfunkel.

★★★★★ **Jimi Hendrix and Otis Redding Live at the Monterey International Pop Festival / Rep. 2029**
Great performances by two now-deceased immortals, caught at the festival at which both made their national breakthroughs. Otis is at his raving best on one side, while on the other, Hendrix gives what may have been his greatest show ever: the versions of "Wild Thing" and "Like a Rolling Stone" are everything they should, and could, have been. A lot more than just a memory here.

★ **Here Comes Some Soul from Otis Redding and Joe Curtis / Als. 5082**
A cheat: on the cover, Redding's billing is about three times as large as Curtis'. And while Curtis is a fair journeyman soul man himself, this isn't his best work—much less Redding's.

★★ **History of Bell U.K. (1970-1975) / Ari. 4112**
Artists include: Hello; Glitter Band; Gary Glitter; Showaddywaddy; Bay City Rollers; Linda Lewis; Pearls; Drifters; Barry Blue; Slik
British hit singles from the kind of power pop labels over there. Unfortunately, aside from sweet-voiced Linda Lewis, whose "It's in His Kiss" is superior to any of her American releases, this is pretty tame stuff. These Drifters are a long way from the originals and unless the ersatz excitement of the Rollers' "Keep on Dancing" is your idea of high energy, there's mighty thin pickings in this batch for anyone but a terminal Anglophile.

★★★ **History of British Blues / Sire 2-3701**
Artists include: Cyril Davies Rhythm and Blues All-Stars; Alexis Korner Blues Inc.; Spencer Davis R&B Quartet; Yardbirds; Graham Bond Organization; Downliners Sect; John Mayall's Bluesbreakers; Aynsley Dunbar Retaliation; Fleetwood Mac; Savoy Brown; Duster Bennett; Chicken Shack; T.S. McPhee; Jo Ann Kelly; John Lee's Groundhogs; Gordon Smith; Christine Perfect; Key Largo; Climax Blues Band; Jellybread; Mike Vernon
First-rate assembly of British interpretations of blues. In the Sixties, some of these were names to contend with, and some of them still are, though not necessarily the

same ones. Current Fleetwood Mac fans won't recognize that group, which was playing straight-ahead Chicago-style blues on "Homework" or even Christine McVie, who works under her maiden name, Christine Perfect, on "Crazy 'bout You Baby" and with Chicken Shack on "It's Okay with Me Baby."

Davies and Korner are important because it was their bands from which the Rolling Stones, among others, sprang. The Yardbirds, represented by "Baby What's Wrong," were at their bluesiest with the original guitarist, Eric Clapton. So was John Mayall, when Clapton was in his Bluesbreakers. McPhee founded the Groundhogs, while Savoy and Climax went on to Seventies success in the States. Downliners Sect has undergone something of a revival in the punk era, while Mike Vernon, to move to the opposite pole of the album's concern, is more noteworthy for the bluesmen he recorded than for his own performances.

★★★★ History of British Rock, Vol. 1 / Sire 2-3703
Artists include: Kinks; Dave Clark Five; Bee Gees; Manfred Mann; Donovan; Mungo Jerry; Rod Stewart; Troggs; Gerry and the Pacemakers; Peter and Gordon; Walker Brothers; Searchers; Wayne Fontana; Uriah Heep; Hollies; Small Faces; Billy J. Kramer; Mindbenders; Silkie; Vanity Fare; Dusty Springfield; Freddy and the Dreamers; Cliff Richard; Honeycombs; Swinging Blue Jeans; Merseys; Status Quo; Pretty Things

While no anthology that omits the Rolling Stones and Beatles can claim to be a definitive look at British rock in the Sixties and early Seventies, this two-disc set does a commendable job of surveying both top-rank artists (Kinks, Manfred Mann, Rod

Stewart, Small Faces, Hollies) and some significant minor ones. If Dave Clark Five and Mungo Jerry are remembered only by fanatics and trivia buffs, the Troggs' "Wild Thing" and "Needles and Pins" by the Searchers are worth remembering for their energy, excitement and influence (particularly on punk and New Wave rock, but also on heavy-metal and California harmony groups). The best of Sire's trio of historical investigations.

★★★★ History of British Rock, Vol. 2 / Sire H-3705
Artists include: Beatles; Peter and Gordon; Billy J. Kramer and the Dakotas; Cilla Black; Dave Clark Five; Searchers; Gerry and the Pacemakers; Kinks; Sandie Shaw; Donovan; Rod Stewart; Hollies; Chad and Jeremy; Manfred Mann; Troggs; Dusty Springfield; Van Morrison; Tremeloes; Small Faces; Cream; Who; Badfinger; Bee Gees; Elton John; Deep Purple; Julie Driscoll/ Brian Auger Trinity; Arthur Brown; Thunderclap Newman

More Sixties period pieces. The Beatles' track is a bad one, the version of "Ain't She Sweet" from the Tony Sheridan period in Germany—while a great many of the Merseybeat artists who originally followed the Beatles out of Liverpool and London today sound very weak: Kramer and the Dakotas, Black, Gerry and the Pacemakers, Chad and Jeremy, and Peter and Gordon (who are even represented by their best songs) all suffer from this. And a bit of the selection is more pop than rock—that applies to the Bee Gees and Elton John, but more especially to the Tremeloes and the Donovan track.

Yet there are still some gems here: Manfred Mann's "Mighty Quinn," a great Dylan version; the Kinks' "All Day and All of the Night," Cream's "Sunshine of Your Love" and the Who's "Call Me Lightning," all magnificently powerful; and some lost obscurities, particularly "Fire" by Brown and Thunderclap Newman's exhilarating "Something in the Air."

★★★★ History of British Rock, Vol. 3 / Sire H-3712
Artists include: Searchers; Beatles; Animals, featuring Eric Burdon; Gerry and the Pacemakers; Kinks; Troggs; Donovan; Them; Olivia Newton-John; Dusty Springfield; Manfred Mann; Peter and Gordon; Badfinger; Elton John; Derek and the Dominos; David Bowie; Billy J. Kramer and the Dakotas; Unit Four Plus Two; Zombies; Dave Clark Five; Mat-

thew's Southern Comfort; Python Lee Jackson; Chris Farlowe; Cream; Deep Purple; Mary Hopkin; Bee Gees

The final set in Sire's series ends disappointingly—still no Rolling Stones, and weak choices from the Beatles, John, the Animals and Deep Purple—but with some encouraging and interesting material nonetheless. Newton-John doesn't belong here; neither does Hopkin. And while Kramer and the Dakotas as well as Gerry and the Pacemakers are certainly overrepresented, Cream's "Anyone for Tennis" is sufficiently obscure to be treasured, while Them's "Here Comes the Night," the Zombies' "She's Not There" and Farlowe's "Out of Time" are well worth having. Chances are this is for collectors more than casual fans, but the Sire series is still a fine adjunct to a collection with any pretensions to being comprehensive, even if no volume is strong enough to single out.

★ **Hits of the Mersey Era / Cap. / EMI M 11690**
Artists include: Gerry and the Pacemakers; Billy J. Kramer and the Dakotas; Swinging Blue Jeans; Cilla Black; Freddie and the Dreamers; Hollies

Aside from the Hollies, this is fluff—and "Stay" isn't a particularly good Hollies track. All of these groups were influenced by the Beatles, but they were among the first to pull the rock side of that foursome into the background in favor of conventional show-business song values. The Blue Jeans' "Hippy Hippy Shake" is almost worth the time, although more because amateurish enthusiasm dates better than pop warbling. Everying that's here and worthwhile is included, among more interesting company, on Sire's three-volume *History of British Rock,* anyhow.

★★ **Hustle Hits / De-Lite 2019**
Artists include: Gary Toms Empire; Crown Heights Affair; Kool and the Gang; Kay Gees; Zakariah; Yambu

The hustle is the only new dance *step* introduced by the Seventies' disco movement; it's a kind of easy-to-learn tango, but more licentious. This is fine stuff for it, or more free-form movement, particularly Kool and the Gang's tracks ("Spirit of the Boogie," "Mother Earth"), although how easy it is to adapt conventional pop songs to the beat is indicated by Zakariah's "Girl from Ipanema" and Yambu's "Sunny," the latter a reworking of the great Bobby Hebb hit.

★ **In Concert / RCA CPL2-1014**
Artists include: Charley Pride; Dolly Parton; Ronnie Milsap; Dolly Parton and Ronnie Milsap; Jerry Reed; Chet Atkins; Jerry Reed and Chet Atkins

Miserable collection of RCA's country artists in performance. The highlights are all Parton's.

★★ **In the Heat of the Night (Soundtrack) / U. Artists LA290-G**
Quincy Jones' score is notable principally for Ray Charles' singing on the title song. The rest is unobtrusive background music, including the other vocals (a second by Charles, and one each from Gil Bernal and Glen Campbell).

■ **Jesus Christ Superstar (Original Broadway Cast) / MCA 5000**
★ **Jesus Christ Superstar (Original London Cast) / MCA 2-10000**
★★ **Jesus Christ Superstar (Soundtrack) / MCA 2-11000**
Broadway cast LP is only the highlights of the Andrew Webber–Timothy Rice score. The other two are complete, and the consistent element is Yvonne Elliman, who turns in a good performance (as Mary Magdalene) singing "I Don't Know How to Love Him." The soundtrack has the advantage of Murray Head's version of "Superstar," the Judas soliloquy. But mostly this is a sappy hippie's version of St. Matthew's Gospel, which ought to be equally odious to true believers of all faiths, if only for the musical pablum it offers as a substitute for conviction.

★★★ **Jewels, Vol. 1 / SSS 24**
Artists include: Tommy James; Ad Libs; Peggy Scott and Jo Jo Benson; Jerry Lee Lewis; Rugbys; Shangri-Las; Bill Justis;

Alive and Kickin'; Dixie Cups; Jelly Beans; Three Degrees; Carl Perkins

Good collection, but compiled without rhyme or reason. Perkins' "Blue Suede Shoes" and Lewis' "Whole Lotta Shakin' Goin' On" are the only masterpieces, but the girl-group hits—"Boy from New York City" (Ad Libs), "Leader of the Pack" (by the hallowed Shangri-Las, toughest broads in the universe), "Chapel of Love" (Dixie Cups) and "I Wanna Love Him So Bad" (Jelly Beans)—are all worth hearing again. Not so the Three Degrees' "Maybe," which pales next to the Chantels' original.

★ **Jewels, Vol. 2 / SSS 25**
Artists include: Billy Hemmons and Clay's Composite; Betty La Vette; Gloria Taylor; Johnny Adams; Wilbert Harrison; Big John Hamilton; George Perkins and the Silver Stars; Peggy Scott and Jo Jo Benson; Calvin Leavy; Hank Ballard; Mickey Murray

Ringers all. There isn't a song here worth doing more than once that someone else hasn't done better. Hearing the immensely talented Ballard wasted on Kristofferson's "Sunday Mornin' Comin' Down" moves me to tears for all the wrong reasons.

★★★★ **Johnny Otis Show Live at Monterey / Epic BG-30473**
Artists include: Johnny Otis; Esther Phillips; Eddie Vinson; Big Joe Turner; Ivory Joe Hunter; Roy Milton; Gene Conners; Roy Brown; Shuggie Otis; Margie Evans; Pee Wee Crayton; Delmar Evans

Otis was one of the Fifties' leading talent scouts and impresarios as well as an R&B band leader of some repute, although "Willie and the Hand Jive," a reworking of the "Bo Diddley" riff, is his only well-remembered hit. This is a recording of a 1970 appearance that featured his revue of that period: Phillips, Brown, Milton, Hunter and Turner are all primordial soul shouters, who retained a good deal of their performance acumen well past their prime. (Only Phillips and Turner have accomplished much since then, though.) This is also probably the best presentation on record of Shuggie Otis, a fine blues guitarist. Good set for parties attended by pop music historians.

■ **Joseph and the Amazing Technicolor Dreamcoat (Original Cast) / MCA 399**
A rock "cantata" by Andrew Lloyd Webber and Timothy Rice, the pair who brought you *Jesus Christ Superstar* and *Evi-*

ta. This one's from the Old Testament, which makes the wrath one feels at such an undisguised artistic ripoff in keeping with the period. More in keeping than the music or lyrics, anyway.

★★ **Joyride (Soundtrack) / U. Artists LA784-H**
Half this record is dominated by old-time Hollywood arranger Jimmie Haskell, but it also includes six songs by Electric Light Orchestra, including the hit "Tightrope." But none of it is sufficiently outstanding to be of interest to anyone except a hard-core ELO follower.

★★★★ **The Last Waltz (Soundtrack) / War. 3WS-3146**
Artists include: Band; Ronnie Hawkins; Neil Young; Joni Mitchell; Neil Diamond; Dr. John; Paul Butterfield; Muddy Waters; Eric Clapton; Bobby Charles; Van Morrison; Bob Dylan

The soundtrack from Martin Scorsese's troubling cinematic obituary filmed at the Band's final performance on Thanksgiving, 1976, at Winterland in San Francisco. This was a sort of last gasp for rock's old guard, and it is the oldest players, with a couple of exceptions, who come off best. The Band runs through its old repertoire with less gusto than it has sometimes shown, but Muddy Waters comes up with as grand a version of his classic "Mannish Boy" as he has ever done. Dr. John's "Such a Night" and Ronnie Hawkins' "Who Do You Love" are also lively. No one is embarrassing—though this show was mostly about past glory, you'd never know it from the heart Van Morrison puts into "Tura Lura Lura" or Neil Young's soul-searching "Helpless." And for one moment, the Band comes completely to life, when drummer

Levon Helm duets on "Mystery Train" with Paul Butterfield. Eerie, sometimes nerve-wracking as this is, it might work for anyone but old fogeys. In some weird way, this is a small triumph, in keeping with the ostentatious understatement of the Band's career.

★★★ Laurie Golden Goodies / Laur. 2041
Artists include: Music Explosion; Chiffons; Gary "U.S." Bonds; Royal Guardsmen; Jarmels; Dion and the Belmonts; Mystics; Gerry and the Pacemakers
Good selection of hits. The Chiffons' "He's So Fine" and Dion's "Runaround Sue" and "Teenager in Love" are well-known early Sixties masterworks. The Mystics' lovely "Hushabye," and the Jarmels' "A Little Bit of Soap" aren't but ought to be. The best stuff of all is a kind of outer-space rock & soul music perfected by U.S. Bonds on "Quarter to Three" and "New Orleans," two of the most poorly recorded and most exciting of all post-Presley, pre-Beatles hits. The Royal Guardsmen's "Snoopy vs. the Red Baron" records ought to be buried, though. Unannotated.

★★★ Let's Clean Up the Ghetto / Phil. JZ-34659
Artists include: Lou Rawls; Philadelphia International All-Stars; Dee Dee Sharp Gamble; Teddy Pendergrass; Three Degrees; O'Jays; Billy Paul; Archie Bell and the Drells; Intruders; Harold Melvin and the Blue Notes
Producers Kenneth Gamble and Leon Huff gathered together the leading lights of their record company to make this LP; the profits (if there have been any) to go to "Community Development Programs" (their capitals). The All-Stars are an assemblage of the artists listed, and they

aren't bad on the title track. But unfortunately, with the exception of the Blue Notes' interpretation of Fred Neil's "Everybody's Talkin'," the material isn't adequate. Only Sharp, the Three Degrees and the Intruders fare well, probably because they get songs from their albums, rather than newly recorded social consciousness songs done especially for this project.

★★★ Let's Do It Again (Soundtrack) / Cur. 5005
One of Curtis Mayfield's better blaxploitation film tracks, principally because it features the Staple Singers, who got a hit from the title track. Not as superb as *Superfly* (one of the best soundtracks ever made in any genre), but a decent example of Seventies black genre music.

★★★ Like 'Er Red Hot / Duke X-73
Artists include: Bobby "Blue" Bland; Clarence "Gatemouth" Brown; Little Jr. Parker; Paul Perryman; Johnny Ace; Casuals; Rob Roys; Ernie Harris; Torros; Willie Mae Thornton
Good collection from the Texas soul and blues label, but not as solid as ABC's reissue compilations, *From the Vaults of Duke/Peacock*. Only Perryman is unrepresented there. Still if you can't find the others, this will more than do you: Bland's "Farther Up the Road," Parker's "Next Time You See Me" and Ace's "Pledging My Time" are among the greatest R&B made in the Fifties and Sixties—tough, committed music. And Thornton (usually referred to as "Big Mama") contributes a version of "Hound Dog" from which, of course, Elvis Presley modeled his.

■ Lipstick (Soundtrack) / Atl. 18178
The movie was supposed to make Margaux Hemingway, the model, a star, but left her still a model. The soundtrack was supposed to make French synthesizer-rocker Michel Polnareff a household name in rock circles, but left him a laughingstock. Drivel.

★★ Live and Let Die (Soundtrack) / U. Artists LA100-G
Wings got a hit single from Paul McCartney's title song to this James Bond film, which would put them right up there with Carly Simon and Shirley Bassey—except that "Live and Let Die" actually has exciting passages. The rest of the score is John Barry's usual decent pop-jazz.

★ **Live at Bill Graham's Fillmore West /
Col. CS-9893**
*Artists include: Nick Gravenites; Mike
Bloomfield; Bob Jones; Taj Mahal*
Beware the album that headlines the impresario, and old rock epigram ought to
read. Unlike John Hammond Sr., Graham
is no philanthropist. As well intentioned as
this set may once have been, it is now
grossly outdated (like *Live at CBGB's*, for
that matter). Bloomfield's "Oh Mama" is
an exercise in wretched excess, and the
Gravenites and Mahal tracks are below
their usual standards. Nobody we've met
remembers Jones, which his "Love Got
Me" deserves.

★★ **Live at CBGB's / Atl. SD2-508**
*Artists include: Tuff Darts; Shirts; Mink De-
Ville; Laughing Dogs; Miamis; Sun; Stuart's
Hammer; Manster*
An odd reflection of New York's so-
called New Wave, circa winter 1976-77.
None of the scene's big stars are here—that
means Patti Smith, Television, the Ramones and Talking Heads, in case you're
wondering what big star means in this context. But Mink DeVille has made a pair of
good rock and soul albums, and the Darts
and Shirts both landed record deals, although the resulting albums weren't much.
But this LP is already a period piece; what
it will seem like five years from now is
barely imaginable.

★★ **Live Jam / Cap. SVBB-3392**
*Artists include: John Lennon and Yoko Ono/
Plastic Ono Band; John Lennon and Yoko
Ono with Frank Zappa and the Mothers of
Invention*
An eccentric pairing from an early Sev-
enties Fillmore East gig. Not nearly as ex-
citing as Lennon's Plastic Ono set from
Toronto, but a lot more experimental. Not
the Beatle reunion of your dreams, though,
is it? Well, neither is *Concert for Bangla
Desh*. Or *Wings over America*, for that mat-
ter.

★★★ **Looking for Mr. Goodbar (Soundtrack) / Col. JS-35029**
*Artists include: Thelma Houston; Commo-
dores; O'Jays; Donna Summer; Diana Ross;
Bill Withers; Boz Scaggs; Marlene Shaw*
A rather creepy film, this movie about a
good Irish Catholic girl who screws around
and doesn't fall in love in a discothèque
setting, nevertheless offers a hell of a dance
record as its soundtrack. The Commodores' "Machine Gun" and O'Jays' "Back-
stabbers" are their very best songs, and
both Ross' "Love Hangover" and Scaggs'
"Low Down" are top-notch. The rest is
only so-so, but the groove is galvanizing.

★★★ **Mackintosh and T.J. (Soundtrack) /
RCA APL1-1520**
*Artists include; Waylon Jennings; Johnny
Gimble; Willie Nelson; Ralph Mooney; Waylors*
Waylon Jennings provides most of the
music for this late-Seventies modern cow-
boy-trucker flick. His "All Around Cowboy" and "Bob Wills Is Still the King,"
Mooney's "Crazy Arms" and Nelson's
"Stay a Little Longer" are the right honky-
tonk for the occasion, loose and easy. Still,
the set is too unfocused to achieve much.

★★★ **Memphis Country / Sun 120**
*Artists include: Johnny Cash; Jerry Lee Lew-
is; Charlie Rich; David Houston; Jack Clem-
ent; Carl Perkins; Barbara Pittman; Dale
Wheeler; Conway Twitty; Warren Smith;
Roy Orbison; Texas Bill*
Straight country from the great rocka-
billy home label. Lewis' "You Win Again,"
Cash's original "I Walk the Line" and
Rich's "Sittin' and Thinkin' " are all
among their best work, but Perkins, Orbi-
son and Twitty are better on rockers.
Clement's "Ten Years" is worth hearing,
too, though.

★ **Midnight Cowboy (Soundtrack) / U.
Artists 5198**
John Barry scored most of this early Seventies statement on New York lowlife. The
exception is Nilsson's "Everybody's
Talkin'," which made the Fred Neil song a
Top Ten hit; Nilsson has a couple of other
tracks, too, but that's all that anyone would
want to hear.

★★★★ **More American Graffiti / MCA
2-8007**
*Artists include: Chantels; Bill Haley and the
Comets; Larry Williams; Coasters; Betty Ev-
erett; Dion and the Belmonts; Little Richard;
Brenda Lee; Cadillacs; Gene Chandler;
Buddy Holly and the Crickets; Danleers;
Lloyd Price; Crows; Carl Dobkins; Tune
Weavers; Carole King; Little Eva; Kingsmen;
Jerry Butler; Dubs; Shirelles*
Third and final volume of MCA's dou-
ble-disc oldies compilation again has little
or nothing to do with the George Lucas
flick. But the collection's a good one, with-
out anything terribly obscure but with a
few hard-to-find gems (King's "It Might As

Well Rain Until September," the Kingsmen's "Louie Louie," which misses most collections, and "Could This Be Magic" by the Dubs), plenty of Holly and Little Richard, and few, if any, ringers.

★★★★★ **Motown Story** / **Mo. M9-726**
Artists include: Barrett Strong; Marvellettes; Marvin Gaye; Smokey Robinson and the Miracles; Stevie Wonder; Martha and the Vandellas; Diana Ross and the Supremes; Mary Wells; Temptations; Four Tops; Junior Walker and the All-Stars; Gladys Knight and the Pips; Jimmy Ruffin; Marvin Gaye and Tammi Terrell; Supremes and Temptations; Jackson Five; Originals; Supremes
Five-record documentary history of the great black pop label. Nearly every major hit the label has ever had is included, and all of its major artists—Gaye, Robinson and the Miracles, Ross and the Supremes, Jackson Five, Four Tops, Wonder, Knight and the Pips, Temptations, Martha and the Vandellas. But the narrative introductions to each song are intrusive for less than scholarly listening, even though some convey interesting information (Robinson on how he came to write "I Second That Emotion"; Levi Stubbs of the Four Tops on why he didn't understand the lyric of "Reach Out I'll Be There"). Still, there is so much essential music here that the package rates top ranking anyway. Insufficient liner notes, probably because the real annotation is in the grooves.

★ **Music from** *Outlaw Blues* / **Cap. ST-11691**
Artists include: Steve Fromholz; Peter Fonda; Peter Fonda and Susan St. James; Charles Bernstein; Hoyt Axton
Almost all wrong. Fromholz and Axton deliver their usual journeyman country-

rock performances; but what business has Fonda got singing, much less doing duets with St. James? Bernstein's tracks are background score. As big a mess as the picture.

★ **Nashville (Soundtrack)** / **ABC D-893**
Robert Altman's country music film suffered, among other things, from the lack of an adequate score. Richard Baskin's C&W pastiche can't fill out the movie—or the disc—sufficiently to hold interest. Only Keith Carradine's stud posturing, "I'm Easy," has adequate melodic and lyrical interest to work away from the action.

★★ **Ned Kelly (Soundtrack)** / **U. Artists LA300-G**
Artists include: Kris Kristofferson; Waylon Jennings; Mick Jagger; Tom Ghent
Jagger starred in this film biography about an infamous Australian outlaw. His singing isn't much (one song, "Wild Colonial Boy"), nor is Ghent's, but Jennings offers the title track and a bit more, while Kristofferson comes up with three passable tunes. This is for hard-core Stones fans only, though why *Ned Kelly* is still in print and the far superior Jagger score of *Performance* is deleted is beyond the reckoning of any humans except Warner Bros. accounts.

★★★ **New and Old Sounds** / **U. Artists LA808-H**
Artists include: Bob Marley; Meditation; Dillinger; Delroy Wilson; Ken Boothe; Dobby Dobson; Burning Spear; Heptones; Jackie Mittoo
Selection of vintage reggae tracks. Marley's "One Love" is among his earliest recordings, as are the Heptones' "In the Groove" and "Pretty Looks Isn't All." Burning Spear's tracks don't compare with the group's later recordings, but Boothe's "This Is the Time" is one of his most solid.

★★★★★ **New Orleans Jazz and Heritage Festival** / **Is. 9424**
Artists include: Allen Toussaint; Lee Dorsey; Ernie K-Doe; Robert Parker; Irma Thomas; Earl King; Lightnin' Hopkins; Professor Longhair
This sure ain't jazz. In fact, it is the cream of the city's rhythm & blues tradition, which definitely falls into the Heritage category. Toussaint has never sounded better than he does in this live, open-air context, as he plays for his neighbors. His "Shoorah Shoorah" and "Play Something

Sweet" are particularly free and effective here.

Dorsey, K-Doe, Thomas, King and Longhair have sounded better but not much. Each is represented by his or her most famous song—K-Doe's "Mother-in-Law," Dorsey's "Holy Cow" and "Workin' in a Coal Mine," Parker's "Barefootin'," Thomas' "I Done My Part" and King's "Trick Bag" lead up to Longhair's "Tipitina" and "Mardi Gras in New Orleans." There is still great pleasure and power to be found in these songs, although all of the originals were cut before the advent of the Beatles.

The only ringer is Hopkins, who is actually a Houston bluesman. But he contributes "Baby Please Don't Go" and "Mojo Hand" like a good country neighbor, so the historical inaccuracy is more than excusable.

★★★ **Newport Broadside / Van. 79144**
Artists include: Jim Garland; Ed McCurdy; Phil Ochs; Peter La Farge; Joan Baez and Bob Dylan; Pete Seeger and Bob Dylan; Tom Paxton; Sam Hinton; Bob Davenport; Freedom Singers

Political folksinging (so-called topical songwriting) from the 1963 folk festival. Much of this has now dated, particularly the songs by doctrinaire writers like Paxton and Ochs. Dylan's duet on "With God on Our Side" is historically interesting but his alliance with the sanctimonious Pete Seeger on the rare "Ye Playboys and Playgirls" is slightly embarrassing today. But it is mostly the Dylan performances that lend this set much interest now.

★★★★ **Newport Folk Festival '63 (Evening Concert) / Van. 79148**
Artists include: Ian and Sylvia; Freedom Singers; Joan Baez; Bob Dylan; Sam Hinton; Mississippi John Hurt; Jack Elliott; Rooftop Singers

Surprisingly, in almost two decades, this set has not dated much. It helps that the political rhetoric and pious folklore mongering (that walked hand in hand) have been kept to a minimum here. Hurt's "C. C. Rider," "Stagolee," "Coffee Blues" and "Spikedriver Blues" give a sense of what magic his rediscovery and appearance here must have been, while Dylan's "Blowin' in the Wind" is so overwhelming to the crowd that the rejection of his rock & roll by a similar audience a couple of years later is unimaginable. The rest isn't

up to par, although Elliott's "Diamond Joe" isn't bad.

★★★ **Newport Folk Festival '64 (Evening Concerts) / Van. 79184**
Artists include: Pete Seeger; Sleepy John Estes; Buffy Sainte-Marie; José Feliciano; Rodrigues Brothers; Phil Ochs; Frank Proffitt; Jim Kweskin and the Jug Band

This isn't nearly as exciting as the 1963 set, not only because Dylan is missing but because there isn't any other performer who can match Hurt's brilliant appearance. Estes' "Corinna" is moving, Proffitt's "Tom Dooley" takes the song back from the Kingston Trio into the tradition where it belongs, and Kweskin's Maria Muldaur feature, "I'm a Woman" is good fun. But Seeger and Ochs are doctrinaire, and have not dated well, and the appearance of Feliciano is inexplicable at such a purist gathering.

NEWPORT FOLK MUSIC FESTIVAL 1959-1960
★★★ **Volume 1 / Folk. 2431**
Artists include: O.J. Abbott; Willie Thomas and Butch Cage; Pat Clancy; Mike Seeger; Pete Seeger; Alan Mills; Frank Hamilton
★★★ **Volume 2 / Folk. 2432**
Artists include: Brownie McGhee and Sonny Terry; New Lost City Ramblers; Frank Warner; Fleming Brown; Guy Carawan; John Greenway

Before the big folk revival boom of the Sixties, Newport was much more traditionally oriented than its later topical politics would indicate. The outstanding performers here are not as well known as those on the other Newport sets released by Vanguard, but "I'm a Stranger Here" by Hamilton on Volume 1 and Volume 2's "Asheville Junction" by Warner as well as Guy Carawan's moving "We Shall Overcome" are all worth hearing.

★★ 9-30-55 (Soundtrack) / MCA 2313
This film, based on a young man's James Dean fanaticism, is pre-rock & roll in its music orientation. It contains "In the Jailhouse Now" by Webb Pierce and Kitty Wells' "Making Believe," both strong country standards, a Leonard Rosenman score that isn't much, plus narration by Richard Thomas that is good enough to belie his role as John-Boy in TV's *The Waltons.* Interesting for trivia fans.

★★★★★ Nuggets / Sire-H 3716
Artists include: Standells; Electric Prunes; Strangeloves; Knickerbockers; Vagrants; Mouse; Shadows of Knight; Blues Project; Seeds; Remains; Barbarians; Castaways; Magicians; 13th Floor Elevators; Count Five; Leaves; Michael and the Messengers; Cryan Shames; Blues Magoos; Amboy Dukes; Chocolate Watch Band; Mojo Men; 3rd Rail; Sagittarius; Nazz; Premiers; Magic Mushrooms
Probably the most delightful unpretentious collection of mid-Sixties artifacts imaginable, thanks to the compilation and witty annotation by critic/historian Lenny Kaye, who now plays guitar for Patti Smith's group. These are somewhat bluesy, somewhat psychedelic, always amateurish, and for the most part, utterly unself-conscious in their naiveté. Anyone who doesn't understand the nostalgia of certain old-timers for that golden age of rock blossoming into art needs to hear this, and anyone who does comprehend that feeling needs to own it.

There are stars here before their time (Ted Nugent in the Amboy Dukes; Leslie West in the Vagrants; Todd Rundgren in the Nazz). There are local legends: the Dukes in Detroit, the Shadows of Knight in Chicago, Nazz in Philly, Vagrants and Blues Project in New York, the Barbarians and Remains in Boston, Mouse (and the Traps) and the Elevators in Texas. But most of all, these are witty three-minute attempts at hit singles, often with a bizarre cast: "Moulty" is the story of how the Barbarians' hook-handed drummer got that way. "Lies" by the Knickerbockers is the most perfect copying of the Beatles ever done; you could say the same thing about Mouse's "Public Execution" and Bob Dylan. "Psychotic Reaction" by Count Five is

a great jumbling of the Yardbirds' "I'm a Man" extrapolation; the Leaves' "Hey Joe" and the Seeds' "Pushin' Too Hard" are folk rock that manages to get raunchy.

There is a great deal of distorted blues and high school stud posturing—"Dirty Water" by the Standells, the Vagrants' "Respect," "No Time like the Right Time" by the Blues Project, and the Blues Magoos' "Tobacco Road," for instance. Anyone who remembers can't resist these songs; anyone who has forgotten will blush in disbelief; those who never knew don't know what they're missing.

★★★★ Old Time Music at Newport— 1963 / Van. 79147
Artists include: Doc Watson; Clarence Ashley; Jenes Cottrell; Dock Boggs; Maybelle Carter; Dorsey Ashley; Clinton Howard; Fred Price and Doc Watson
Nice selection of mountain music from early Sixties folk festival marks the reblossoming of Appalachian music. Carter's "Storms Are on the Ocean" is a wonder, and the final Ashley-Howard-Price-Watson quartet features versions of "The Intoxicated Rat," "Wreck on the Highway" and "Weaveroom Blues" that capture the essential community feeling of the genre.

★★ Old N' Golden / Jamie 3031
Artists include: Fantastic Johnny C; Tommy McLain; Barbara Lynn; Barbara Mason; James Boys; Volcanoes; Sunny and the Sunglows; Crispian St. Peters; Cliff Nobles and Company; Brenda and the Tabulations; Showstoppers; Dale and Grace; Della Humphrey; Helene Smith; Duane Eddy; Kit Kats
Random assortment of old rock and R&B hits has a few, but not quite enough, rarities to make it worthwhile: Johnny C's

"Boogaloo Down Broadway," the Show-
stoppers' "Ain't Nothin' but a House
Party," Eddy's "Rebel Rouser" and Dale
and Grace's "I'm Leaving It Up to You"
are about the best of this spotty lot.

★★ **The Oldies / Doo. 855**
*Artists include: Penguins; Souvenirs; Pearls;
Calvanes; Pipes; Romancers; Silks; Medal-
lions; Meadowlarks; Crescendos*
An assortment of *very* minor doo-wop
artists. Even the Penguins, the best-known
group here, are represented not by "Earth
Angel," their greatest hit, but by the more
obscure (but not bad) "Please Mr. Junk-
man." Cultists only.

★★★ **Oldies But Goodies, Vol. 1 / Orig.
Sound 8850**
*Artists include: Five Satins; Penguins; Teen
Queens; Mello Tones; Don Julian; Medal-
lions; Shirley and Lee; Cadets; Sonny
Knight; Jaguars; Etta James; Oscar McLollie*
Leadoff volume of Original Sound's im-
pressive oldies series (unannotated, of
course) comes up with more than its share
of winners: "In the Still the Night" (Five
Satins), "Earth Angel" (Penguins), "Let the
Good Times Roll" (Shirley and Lee),
"Stranded in the Jungle" (Cadets) and
"Dance with Me Henry" (Etta James).
More R&B oriented than rock & roll,
though "Stranded" is so riotous that it
qualifies in both directions.

★★★ **Oldies But Goodies, Vol. 2 / Orig.
Sound 8852**
*Artists include: Clovers; Heartbeats; Jesse
Belvin; Crows; Velvetones; Nutmegs; Charts;
Joe Turner; Peppermint Harris; Tony Allen;
Turbans; Faye Adams*
The best tracks here include Turner's
"Shake Rattle and Roll," a cornerstone of
R&B's evolution into a sound attractive to
whites; Adams' gospel-like "Shake a
Hand"; "Devil or Angel" by the Clovers
and "Gee" by the Crows, two of Atlantic's
best early group records; "Story Untold"
by the Nutmegs, "1,000 Miles Away" by
the Heartbeats, "When You Dance" by the
Turbans and "Good Night My Love" by
Belvin, all swell R&B hits.

★★★★ **Oldies But Goodies, Vol. 3 / Orig.
Sound 8853**
*Artists include: Dell-Vikings; Frankie Ford;
Little Anthony and the Imperials; Flamingos;
Little Richard; Dells; Preston Epps; El Dora-
dos; Huey Smith; Shields; Jerry Butler; Gene
and Eunice*

The quality here is unassailable; if there
were adequate (or any) liner notes in this
series, it would be a five-star disc. "Come
Go with Me" by the Dell-Vikings, the Imperials' lush "Two People in the World,"
"Lovers Never Say Goodbye" by the Flamingos and the Dells' "Oh What a Night"
are the best sort of group rhythm & blues.
Butler's "For Your Precious Love" is a
masterpiece of solo crooning. Smith's
pounding "Don't You Just Know It,"
Ford's honking "Sea Cruise" and Richard's
shouted "Long Tall Sally" are among the
greatest hits of New Orleans rock and
R&B. For weirder tastes, too, there is Preston Epps with the decidedly mortal
"Bongo Rock." Put this set in a time capsule and you'll probably confuse people
three hundred years from now. But you'll
also exhilarate them.

★★★★ **Oldies But Goodies, Vol. 4 / Orig.
Sound 8854**
*Artists include: Gloria Mann; Rays; Five
Satins; Six Teens; Mickey and Sylvia; Dubs;
Chantels; Jerry Lee Lewis; Sandy Nelson;
Norman Fox and the Rob Roys; Barrett
Strong; Carl Perkins*
This album comes as close to the modern era as anything in Original Sound's series by including Strong's "Money," the
first Motown hit. Alongside "Blue Suede
Shoes" by Perkins and Lewis' "Whole Lotta Shakin' Goin' On," this is perhaps the
hardest-driving set in the Original Sound
series. Not that frontier material is neglected: the Satins' "To the Aisle" and
"Could This Be Magic" by the Dubs are
drippingly romantic. Nelson's "Teen Beat"
drum tour de force has dated, but Mickey
and Sylvia's salacious R&B novelty, "Love
Is Strange," has not.

★★★★ **Oldies But Goodies, Vol. 5 / Orig.
Sound 8855**
*Artists include: Elegants; Rosie and the Origi-
nals; Skyliners; Paradons; Dominoes; Maurice Williams; Shep and the Limelites; Channels; Hollywood Argyles; Bobby Day; Preston
Epps; Jewels*
Mostly obscure, mostly beautiful. The
Elegants' "Little Star" is an achingly pure
group vocal; "Angel Baby" by Rosie and
the Originals is a profoundly silly one. The
Skyliners' "Since I Don't Have You" is a
teenager's dream, while the Dominoes'
"Sixty Minute Man" is his fantasy. Some
of these simply transcend themselves:
"Stay" by Maurice Williams is a reckless
lover's plea; "Daddy's Home" by Shep and

the Limelites is a tortured step toward adulthood; "Hearts of Stone" by the Jewels adds that fitting touch of adolescent self-pity. Not that there is no silliness here: if the Argyles' "Alley Oop" doesn't satisfy you, check Preston Epps, who returns (he was last seen in Volume 3) with "Bongo Bongo Bongo." Huh?

★★★★ **Oldies But Goodies, Vol. 6 / Orig. Sound 8856**
Artists include: Gary "U.S." Bonds; Fireflies; Bill Doggett; Dion; Safaris; Skyliners; Gene Chandler; Dee Dee Sharp; Little Caesar and the Romans; Dee Clark; Gladys Knight and the Pips

This album contains Little Caesar's ode to such things, "Those Oldies but Goodies (Remind Me of You)." As if to demonstrate why that's so, it also features Bonds' "Quarter to Three," a space sound from the past, Doggett's primitive instrumental "Honky Tonk," Chandler's mysterious "Duke of Earl" (who is this man and what does he want?), Sharp's dance hit "Mashed Potato Time," Dee Clark's "Raindrops" and the debut appearance of Knight and the Pips, on the ballad "With Every Beat of My Heart."

★★★ **Oldies But Goodies, Vol. 7 / Orig. Sound 8857**
Artists include: Tommy Edwards; Gary "U.S." Bonds; Mark Dinning; Paris Sisters; Ritchie Valens; Chimes; Jerry Butler; Jimmy Jones; Champs; Dion; Barbara George; B. Bumble and the Stingers

This set contains more of the teen-exploitation music (Edwards, Dinning, Paris Sisters, Jones, even B. Bumble) than is usual in the Original Sound series. But it also has some memorable moments: "New Orleans" by Bonds, "I Know" by George,

"Tequila" by the Champs, Dion's "Run-around Sue" and Butler's "He Will Break Your Heart." Best of all, it has Valens' heartbreaking "Donna," which makes you wonder what he might have achieved if he hadn't decided to board a certain airplane back in 1959.

★★★★ **Oldies But Goodies, Vol. 8 / Orig. Sound 8858**
Artists include: Dixie Cups; Terry Stafford; Bobby Darin; Ritchie Valens; Inez Foxx; Troy Shondell; Dale and Grace; Carla Thomas; Blue Jays; Coasters; Ernie Fields; Ernie Freeman

Nice blend of the obvious and the obscure. Dixie Cups' "Chapel of Love" is a good New Orleans girl-group hit, Darin's "Splish Splash" is one of Atlantic's first white rock records, Carla Thomas' "Gee Whiz" one of Stax' first hit productions, the Coasters' "Searchin' " an immortal. On the ballad side, there's Stafford's "Suspicion," which Elvis elevated to an anthem of paranoia; Shondell's "This Time" and the soaring "Lover's Island" by the Blue Jays. For pure fun, this has "La Bamba," Valens' reworking of a Mexican folk melody, and Foxx's "Mockingbird," a similar restructuring of a Yankee folk song.

★★★ **Oldies But Goodies, Vol. 9 / Orig. Sound 8859**
Artists include: Timi Yuro; Casinos; Esther Phillips; Don and Juan; Cathy Jean and the Roommates; J. Frank Wilson; Bobby Day; Del Shannon; Bobby Fuller; Castaways; Jewel Akens; Bobby Bland

One of the series' weaker sets. Aside from Bland's "Turn On Your Lovelight," Shannon's "Runaway," Fuller's "I Fought the Law," the Castaways' "Liar Liar" and "What's Your Name" by Don and Juan, most of these are dispensable or worse: do you want to hear J. Frank Wilson's morbid "Last Kiss" ever again?

★★★★ **Oldies But Goodies, Vol. 10 / Orig. Sound 8860**
Artists include: Righteous Brothers; Frankie Avalon; Shirelles; Tune Weavers; Duprees; Johnny Ace; Chuck Berry; Isley Brothers; Fats Domino; Bo Diddley; Sam the Sham and the Pharaohs; Olympics

Another solid set. Domino, Isleys, Berry, Diddley and Shirelles tracks are the more or less obvious sort. So is "You've Lost That Lovin' Feelin' " by the Righteous Brothers, but it's too good not to merit special mention. Less well known but still charming are "You Belong to Me" by the Duprees, Ace's "Pledging My Love" and two grandly silly novelties, "Hully Gully" by the Olympics and Sam the Sham's "Wooly Bully." Big drawback: Frankie Avalon's "Venus," which deserves to be napalmed.

★★★★ **Oldies But Goodies, Vol. 11 /
Orig. Sound 8861**
Artists include: Righteous Brothers; Little Anthony and the Imperials; Bobby Hebb; Mary Wells; Classics IV; Harvey and the Moonglows; Little Richard; Kingsmen; Diamonds; Chuck Berry; Angels; Soul Survivors

Perhaps the best set in the series: diverse, unusual, exciting. "Soul and Inspiration" is one of the Righteous Brothers' best, while "Goin' Out of My Head" *is* Little Anthony's best. Hebb's "Sunny" is a marvelous ballad, and Wells' "My Guy" one of the all-time Motown standards. Richard's "Tutti Frutti" and "Maybellene" by Berry are definitive examples of their music. The Moonglows' "Ten Commandments of Love" is a perfect doo-wop choice, while the Classics IV's "Traces" shows what happened to that sound in the Sixties. The Angels' "My Boyfriend's Back" is probably the most blustering of the girl-group hits. But the heart and soul of rock is captured exquisitely by such minor gems as the incoherent "Little Darlin' " (Diamonds), the raunchy "Louie Louie" (Kingsmen) and the unlikely but pungent "Expressway to Your Heart" (Soul Survivors), the latter being the oddest record Gamble and Huff ever made.

★★★★ **Oldies But Goodies, Vol. 12 /
Orig. Sound 8862**
Artists include: Everly Brothers; Delfonics; Lenny Welch; Ruby and the Romantics;

James and Bobby Purify; Impressions; Box Tops; Chuck Berry; Jerry Lee Lewis; Little Richard; Fontella Bass; Contours

Continues the pattern of the best LPs in the series: some rock & roll (Berry, Lewis, Richard), a big ballad (Welch's "Since I Fell for You"), a lot of mainstream soul (Impressions, Purify Brothers, Bass, Contours, Delfonics). This works even better than most, maybe because the kind of Sixties soul it includes—Bass' "Rescue Me," the Contours' wild "Do You Love Me," Purify Brothers' "I'm Your Puppet"—is less often anthologized than the Fifties R&B earlier discs in the series rely upon. And the girl-group number, Ruby and the Romantics' "Our Day Will Come," is one of the few in that genre that's truly erotic.

★★★★ **Oldies But Goodies, Vol. 14 /
Orig. Sound 8864**
Artists include: Platters; Dionne Warwick; Crests; Brenda Lee; Lloyd Price; Dinah Washington; Bill Haley and the Comets; Martha and the Vandellas; Chiffons; Wilson Pickett; McCoys; Shirelles

Hardly a miss in the bunch. This is, of course, really the thirteenth volume in the previously available series—maybe someone at Original Sound is superstitious. But whatever the number, there's barely a miss in a group including "Smoke Gets in Your Eyes" (Platters), "Don't Make Me Over" (Warwick), "I'm Sorry" (Lee), "Sixteen Candles" (Crests—a little wimpy, but it's the only one), "Just Because" (Price), "Unforgettable" (Washington), Haley's "Rock around the Clock," the Vandellas' "Dancing in the Street" (an anthem), the Chiffons' "He's So Fine" (possibly the best girl-group hit of all), "Funky Broadway" (Pickett), "Hang on Sloopy" (McCoys) and "Will You Still Love Me Tomorrow" (Shirelles). If this set had been pieced together with a shred more scholarship—if it had notes, I mean—this, like the other four-star LPs in the series, would rate a full five.

★★★★ **Once Upon a Time in the West
(Soundtrack) / RCA LSP-4736**
Sergio Leone's fourth and final Western is a kind of cosmic Marxist view of life and death. Supposedly country rocker Gary Stewart's favorite album, this is composer Ennio Morricone at the height of his powers. He uses electric guitars in a way that slashes and bleeds, his orchestra is percussive in a manner akin to recent rock, and the evocative power of his compositions is

alternately chilling and exultant. Leone's best film; Morricone's best score.

★★ One Flew Over the Cuckoo's Nest (Soundtrack) / Fan. 9500
Passable score by Jack Nitszche has too few electronic elements to qualify as rock, although the presence of the legendary Lonely Surfer and Spector arranger lends it some interest.

★★★ Original Golden Hits of the Great Groups / SSS 32
Artists include: Ad Libs; Jelly Beans; Dixie Cups; Shangri-Las; Butterflys; Tradewinds
But for the inclusion of the Tradewinds' "New York's a Lonely Town," this would be a decent sampler of girl-group records. The final track throws the focus off, not that the producers care. In this incoherent context, the two Shangri-Las songs— "Leader of the Pack" and "Remember (Walking in the Sand)"—and the Dixie Cups' set—"People Say," "Chapel of Love"—stand out.

STEREO

ORIGINAL GOLDEN HITS-VOLUME 2

★★★★ Original Memphis Rock and Roll / Sun 116
Artists include; Carl Perkins; Carl Mann; Bill Justice; Carl McVoy; Warren Smith; Jerry Lee Lewis; Roy Orbison; Charlie Rich; Billy Lee Riley
The only American Sun collection (in England, there are a dozen or more). The obvious items are here—Orbison's "Ooby Dooby" and Rich's "Lonely Weekends" to go with Lewis' "Whole Lotta Shakin' Goin' On" and "Great Balls of Fire" as well as Perkins' "Honey Don't" and "Blue Suede Shoes." But with a couple of exceptions (Riley's raucous "Red Hot" and Mann's "Mona Lisa"), the rest is pretty poorly chosen.

★★ Original New York Rock and Roll / SSS 6
Artists include: Tradewinds; Evie Sands; Dixie Cups; Alvin Robinson; Ad Libs; Jelly Beans; Shangri-Las
Weak selection of tracks from the old Shadow Morton production company, Red Bird Records. Shangri-Las' "Leader of the Pack" and the odd, snowbound surfer song, "New York's a Lonely Town" by the Tradewinds, are the best things here. But they're available in better company elsewhere. (Charly Records, the British label, has a pair of Red Bird collections that are much much better chosen and presented.)

★★ Original Rock and Roll / Power. 251
Artists include: Carl Perkins; Jimmy Clanton; Ad Libs; Roy Orbison
Poorly packaged sampler. Only Clanton's "Just a Dream" is mildly obscure. Everything else is easily available elsewhere.

★★ Original Rock and Roll, Vol. 2 / Power. 294
Artists include: Platters; Boyd Bennett; Coasters; Bobby Lewis; Bill Doggett
Another poorly packaged compilation— nothing special here.

★★★★ Original Rock Oldies—Golden Hits, Vol. 1 / Spec. 2129
Artists include: Little Richard; Larry Williams; Lloyd Price; Monotones; Sam Cooke; Johnnie and Joe; Arthur Lee Maye and the Crowns; Chimes; Tony Allen and the Champs; Don and Dewey
First-rate collection of the label's Fifties hits, beautifully packaged. Richard's "Rip It Up" and "Long Tall Sally," Price's "Lawdy Miss Clawdy" and the Monotones' "Book of Love" are the best-known selections, but the other tracks are fine and Sam Cooke's very early pop single, "I'll Come Running Back to You," is a must for his fans.

★★★★ Original Rock Oldies—Golden Hits, Vol. 2 / Spec. 2130
Artists include: Little Richard; Tommy Tucker; Larry Williams; Tony Allen and the Champs; Don and Dewey; Clifton Chenier; Johnny Fuller; Chimes; Lloyd Price; Sam Cooke
Not as stellar as the first set, but still solid. Richard is represented by "Good Golly Miss Molly" and "Lucille," Price by the less well-known "Baby Please Come Home," Don and Dewey by "Justine,"

Cooke by another early pop ballad, "Forever." But the highlight is one of the most outrageous hits ever made, Tommy Tucker's "High-Heeled Sneakers," an invitation to transvestism (I guess).

★★ Original Surfin' Hits / Cres. 84
Artists include: Sentinals; Rhythm Kings; Soul Kings; Jim Waller and the Deltas; Bob Vaught and the Renegaids; Dave Myers and the Surftones; Breakers

Very minor surf music. You have to still love *Gidget* movies and lust in your heart after Annette Funicello to have any desire to hear these.

★★ Patty (Soundtrack) / Stang 1027
Blaxpoitation flick about you-know-who and the SLA. A couple of nice songs from the Moments and Chuck Jackson can't make this more than passable, however.

★ Phantom of the Paradise (Soundtrack) / A&M 3653
Brian De Palma's rock version of *The Phantom of the Opera* was cinematically brilliant, but burdened with a stupefying Paul Williams score that rendered everything around it false. Here, all you get is Williams' stupefaction, a miserable prospect; there is a kind of hatred for hard rock here that emerges as soured contempt. A competent performance by Jeffrey Commanor on a couple of oldies pastiches is all that keeps this one from biting the bullet.

★★★★ Philadelphia Classics / Phil. PZG-34940
Artists include: MFSB; MFSB and Three Degrees; Three Degrees; O'Jays; Harold Melvin and the Blue Notes; Intruders

Good (though hardly sufficiently extensive) survey of producers Gamble and Huff's Seventies output. "TSOP" by MFSB and the Three Degrees, "Love Train" by the O'Jays," "Bad Luck" by the Blue Notes and the Intruders' "I'll Always Love My Mama" are the highlights.

★★★ Pick Hits of the Radio Good Guys, Vol. 1 / Laur. 2021
Artists include: Chiffons; Demensions; Gary "U.S." Bonds; Passions; Dion; Randy and the Rainbows; Jarmels; Tokens; Mystics

A spotty mid-Sixties period piece, before the disc jockey became such a figure of calculated hipness that his (or her) personality evaporated altogether. This is AM music, and some of it (Bonds' two songs, the Mystics' "Hushabye," the Jarmels' "A Lit-

tle Bit of Soap" and, of course, Dion and the Chiffons) is the best kind of Top Forty sound. Some of it isn't too good and all of it is available in better-produced packages, though the cover is quaint.

★★ Porgy and Bess / RCA CPL2-1831
A great idea: get Ray Charles to sing the male lead of Gershwin's great operetta. It went wrong when Cleo Laine, a white British jazz singer with a stilted demeanor, was picked to play Bess. With Sarah Vaughan, Ella Fitzgerald and, to pick randomly but more wisely, Aretha Franklin, still living, that's like asking Helen Reddy to play Superfly's girlfriend. For Charles fanatics only.

★★★★ Precious Lord (Great Gospel Songs of Thomas A. Dorsey) / Col. CG-32151
Artists include: Marion Williams; Alex Bradford; Sallie Martin; Dixie Hummingbirds; R. H. Harris; Bessie Griffin; Delois B. Campbell

Dorsey was the greatest of the black gospel composers and this is a grand testament to the fact. Williams shines on "Take My Hand Precious Lord," "What Could I Do?" and three others; other important songs include "Hide Me in Thy Bosom," "Peace in the Valley," "Never Turn Back," "If You See My Savior," "Old Ship of Zion" and "My Desire." A nice supplement to Columbia's *Gospel Sound* collections.

★ The Progressives / Col. CG-31574
Artists include: Weather Report; Soft Machine; Charles Mingus; Don Ellis; Paul Winter; Maynard Ferguson; John McLaughlin Mahavishnu Orchestra; Walter Carlos; Bill Evans; Ornette Coleman; Albert Dailey; Keith Jarrett

Beware the record-company assessment of the avant-garde. I'd like someone to explain just what Don Ellis and John McLaughlin ultimately have in common, much less Paul Winter and Charles Mingus. Some good progressive stuff here, but if you're aware enough to tell the difference, you don't need this sampler. If you're not, it will only mislead you.

★★★ Pure Soul / Kent 517
Artists include: B. B. King; Lowell Fulsom; Elmore James; Little Richard; Vernon and Jewell; Z. Z. Hill

Pure nothing but still a pretty decent compilation. King, Fulsom and James play pretty much straight blues: King's "Eyesight to the Blind," a Sonny Boy Williamson song, Fulsom's "Black Nights" and James' "Dust My Blues" are all worth hearing. Richard and Hill, Vernon and Jewell are R&B (the former more properly rock & roll) artists. Nothing exceptional from them, unfortunately.

★★★ Ramblin' On My Mind (Train and Travel Blues) / Mile. 3002
Artists include: Johnny Young; Carl Hodges; Leroy Dallas; Jimmy Brewer; Honeyboy Edwards; Big Joe Williams; Connie Williams; Dr. Isaiah Ross; John Lee Granderson; Bill Jackson; Elijah Brown; W. B. "Piano Bill" Bryson

Thematically organized anthology of minor blues performers. Has its moments.

★★ Rancho Deluxe (Soundtrack) / U. Artists LA466-G
Modern cowboy flick for which country hippie Jimmy Buffett provided six songs, none of them terribly memorable. Fodder for the Buffett clique and no one else. So laid-back it doesn't have to prove it.

★★ Raw Blues / Lon. PS-543
A hodgepodge of the label's blues repertoire: British performers like John Mayall and Eric Clapton plus some minor work by Otis Spann and Champion Jack Dupree. Nothing special here that isn't more accessible in a better format somewhere else.

★★ Redneck Mothers / RCA APL1-2438
Artists include: Johnny Russell; Gary Stewart; Willie Nelson; Steve Young; Bobby Bare; Tennessee Pulleybone; Jerry Reed; Vernon Oxford

Country music for anthropologists. RCA apparently couldn't make up its mind about whether to fill this set out with more outlaw performers like Stewart, Nelson and Young or attempt to force a few of its more mainstream C&W artists like Bare and Reed into the mix, in hope of country-rock crossover. Aside from "Renegade Picker" and "Tobacco Road" by Young, Stewart's "Honky Tonkin' " and Bare's "Up Against the Wall, Redneck Mother" (an outrageous hillbilly exploitation tune), slim pickin's around here.

★★★ Reggae Spectacular / A&M 3529
Artists include: Jimmy Cliff; Blue Haze; Bob and Marcia; Glen and Dave; Harry J. and the Allstars

Pretty minor reggae, except Cliff's. And most of his tracks are better presented on *The Harder They Come* soundtrack, or his own LPs.

★★★ Remember How Great, Vol. 1 / Rou. 42027
Artists include: Heartbeats; Frankie Lymon; Flamingos; Fiesta; Monotones; Chuck Berry; Little Anthony and the Imperials; Lee Dorsey; Lee Anderson and the Hearts; Robert and Johnny; Etta James; Chantels

Predictable assortment of Fifties hits, from hard rock (Berry) to doo-wop (Heartbeats, Monotones). Always nice to hear Lymon and Dorsey, but you can do better than this.

★★★ Remember How Great, Vol. 2 / Rou. 42028
Artists include: Moonglows; Frankie Lymon; Maurice Williams and the Zodiacs; Five Satins; Shirley and Lee; Coasters; Sonny Til; Billy Bland; Penguins; Bobby Freeman; Cadillacs

Decent but predictable Fifties assortment.

★★★ Remember How Great, Vol. 3 / Rou. 42029
Artists include: Joe Jones; Silhouettes; Edsels; Wilbur Harrison; Don and Dee Dee Ford; Chantels; Coasters; Harptones; Drifters; Crests; Jerry Butler; Bo Diddley

Another decent selection, this one with a few fairly obscure items: Don and Dee Dee Ford's "I Need Your Lovin' " is as pounding as any rock ever made, and the Harptones' "Sunday Kind of Love" is as smooth as good R&B gets.

★★★ Remember How Great, Vol. 4 / Rou. 42031
Artists include: Spaniels; Nutmegs; Flamingos; Mello Kings; Chantels; Dreamlovers; Little Anthony and the Imperials; Willows; Ben E. King; Dave "Baby" Cortez; Moonglows

A little more coherent than the other volumes in the series, because it focuses on groups, except for King's grand "Don't Play That Song" and Cortez's awful "Happy Organ." The rest is solid enough but unexceptional. Chantels' "He's Gone" is a good one that doesn't pop up often.

★★★ Remember How Great, Vol. 5 / Rou. 42032
Artists include: Cleftones; Bobbettes; Chuck Berry; Ben E. King; King Curtis; Tempos;

Ray Barretto; Dubs; Rays; Buddy Knox; Essex; Gloria Mann

A few more oddities than the other volumes in the series, but still nothing truly exceptional. Worth noting are Barretto's "Watusi," to this day the only substantial salsa hit of the rock era, and the Essex's "Easier Said Than Done."

■ **Rock and Roll: Evolution or Revolution? / Laur. 2044**
Given this kind of documentary, is there anyone out there who can't answer the question. Positive proof that the Sixties weren't entirely golden.

"The Best of Bobby Bland"

★★★ **Rock and Roll Festival, Vol. 1 / Kent 544**
Artists include: Little Richard; Joe Houston; Etta James; B. B. King; Ike and Tina Turner; Cadettes; Ikettes; Jacks; Elmore James; Shirley Gunter and the Queens; Teen Queens; Oscar McLollie; Marvin and Johnny; Jessie Belvin

Most of the more familiar names here are represented by their most familiar tracks. James' and King's tracks, in fact, are their signature songs, "Dust My Blues" and "Rock Me Baby" respectively. Worth noting: "Cherry Pie" by Marvin and Johnny, "Convicted" by McLollie and "Oop Shoop" by Gunter. Good set with a smattering of the unusual.

★★★ **Rock and Roll Show / Gusto 0002**
Artists include: Bill Doggett; Chuck Berry; Sammy Turner; Jerry Lee Lewis; Moonglows; Billy Ward and the Dominoes; Screamin' Jay Hawkins; Coasters; Frankie Ford

Nothing terribly rare here, but Berry and Lewis are well represented (two tracks each of their original hits), and the Moonglows, Ford, Coasters, Hawkins and Dom-

inoes tracks are all their best. Only Doggett's "Honky Tonk" and "Lavender Blue" by Turner seem minor.

★ **Rock Guitar Greats, Vol. 1 / Sp. 4042**
Artists include: Jimi Hendrix; Eric Clapton; Jimmy Page; Sonny Boy Williamson; Jeff Beck

It will come as news to Williamson's admirers that the master blues harpist is a guitar great as well. But this sleazy ripoff, which contains the most mediocre material done by each performer, is hardly the place to find out about it. Williamson is actually represented on some tracks cut with Clapton's Yardbirds in England. The rest are outtakes that should have stayed that way.

★ **Rock Guitar Greats, Vol. 2 / Sp. 4601**
Artists include: Eric Clapton; Jeff Beck; Rory Gallagher; Stevie Winwood; Jimi Hendrix; Jimmy Page and Sonny Boy Williamson; Ron Wood and the Faces

More outtakes from diverse sources. Wood's "Collibosher" with the Faces may have been the worst thing they ever recorded; Beck's "New York City Blues" is the Yardbirds retitled and so forth. The Hendrix selection is a real atrocity.

★★★ **Rock-O-Rama, Vol. 1 / Abkco 4222**
Artists include: Chubby Checker; Tymes; Orlons; Bobby Rydell; Dee Dee Sharp; Question Mark and the Mysterians; Charlie Gracie; Terry Knight and the Pack; Dovells; Rays

Erratic collection from the Cameo-Parkway label, which Abkco owner Allen Klein now controls. This ranges from Rydell's dismal teen-idol schlock to Checker's twist hits, the minor girl-group dance hits of the Orlons and Sharp to such punk classics as Question Mark's "96 Tears," and Dovells' boisterous "You Can't Sit Down." Not bad, altogether.

★★ **Rock-O-Rama, Vol. 2 / Abkco 4223**
Artists include: Bobby Rydell; Dovells; Tymes; Orlons; Dee Dee Sharp; Chubby Checker; Zacherle; Candy and the Kisses; Charlie Gracie; Question Mark and the Mysterians; Don Covay; Jo Ann Campbell

Much weaker than Volume 1 of this series and equally uneven. The good Dovells, Question Mark and Checker tracks appear on the other set; Rydell contributes even more limp work. Highlight: Zacherle's "Dinner with Drac," which is better than "Monster Mash." Lowlife: Campbell's "The Girl from Wolverton Mountain," a truly horrid novelty.

★ **Rock Vocal Greats / Sp. 4062**
*Artists include: Jimi Hendrix; Jeff Beck and
the Yardbirds; Animals, featuring Eric Burdon; Jack Bruce/Ginger Baker/Dick Heck-
stal; Gregg and Duane Allman; Rod Stewart;
Stevie Winwood and the Spencer Davis
Group; Rory Gallagher*
　Some great names make some lousy music. Beck isn't even the vocalist on his
track. Hendrix, Animals, Allmans and
Stewart are all shown at their very worst.

★★ **Rocky (Soundtrack) / U. Artists
LA-693-G**
Included mostly because soundtrack composer Bill Conti's theme song, "Gonna Fly
Now," became a catchy 1977 hit. But nothing much but mush for the rest of it. The
story is a good rock-star-type fable, though.
Might have made an interesting Elvis vehicle—there was a guy who could take a
punch.

★ **Roots of Rock / Ev. 296**
Artists include: Jimi Hendrix; Little Richard
　Mediocre assortment of re-recorded
Richard tracks and Hendrix halfway hu-
miliating himself doing "Lawdy Miss
Clawdy." Forget it.

★★★★★ **The Roots of Rock and Roll /
Savoy 2221**
*Artists include: Wild Bill Moore; Paul Wil-
liams; Hal Singer; "Big Jay" McNeely; Sam
Price; Johnny Otis; Nappy Brown; Huey "Piano" Smith; Varetta Dillard; Big Maybelle;
Ravens; Clarence Palmer and the Jive Bombers; Luther Bond and the Emeralds*
　Wonderful selection of late-Forties and
early-Fifties R&B hits shows the development of R&B styles toward something
identifiable as rock & roll. (Smith's "You
Make Me Cry" and Maybelle's "Candy"

are very close to rock, indeed.) There is an
accent on sax performers here—McNeely,
Moore and Price are some of the best
honkers of the era. Williams' "The Hucklebuck" kicked off an early rock-style dance
fad, the Ravens was one of the seminal vocal groups of the period (inspiring a variety
of other groups to name themselves after
birds), and Moore's "We're Gonna Rock,
We're Gonna Roll" is one of rock's earlier
anthems. Excellent annotation.

★★★ **Roxy London WC2 (Jan.-April
1977) / EMI SHSP-4069**
*Artists include: Johnny Moped; Eater; X-Ray
Spex; Buzzcocks; Slaughter and the Dogs;
Unwanted; Wire; Adverts*
　Selection of live tracks from the London
punk club that only existed during the period indicated. Some of the genre's best
groups—X-Ray Spex, Buzzcocks, Wire,
Adverts—are represented, although everyone else is generally unworthy of vinyl.
Check X-Ray's "Oh, Bondage, Up Yours"
for a kick.

★★★ **Rural Blues / Fan. 24716**
*Artists include: Robert Pete Williams; Snooks
Eaglin*
　Selection of tracks, originally done for
Prestige, by two minor country bluesmen.
Interesting for blues fans.

★★ **Saturday Night Disco / De-Lite
DSR-9508**
*Artists include: Made in U.S.A.; Crown
Heights Affair; Kool and the Gang; Kay Gees*
　Saturday Night Fever cash-in attempt.
Kool's "Open Sesame" is a hot track, but
the rest is nothing special.

★★★★★ **Saturday Night Fever (Soundtrack) / RSO 2-4001**
*Artists include: Bee Gees; Yvonne Elliman;
Walter Murphy; Tavares; David Shire; Kool
and the Gang; Ralph McDonald; K.C. and
the Sunshine Band; MFSB; Trammps*
　This set sold about 15 million copies in
1977 and 1978, so chances are you've heard
of it, at least. Truth to tell, it dispels a lot
of foolish notions about disco: this is a
fabulous pop album, with great warmth,
and very little of it is mechanistic (with the
exception of David Shire's background music, and even that's atmospheric enough to
work). Most of the best moments belong to
the Bee Gees—"Stayin' Alive" would be a
classic in any idiom—but the Trammps'
"Disco Inferno" is the single most propulsive track here. Does for the Seventies

what *Woodstock* did for the Sixties: defines
an era's taste, and celebrates it.

■ **Sgt. Pepper's Lonely Hearts Club Band
(Soundtrack) / RSO 2-4100**
*Artists include: Peter Framptom; Aerosmith;
Steve Martin; Bee Gees; George Burns; Earth
Wind and Fire; Billy Preston; Alice Cooper;
Sandy Fariña; Paul Nicholas; Frankie Howard; Dianne Steinberg; Stargard*
    An utter travesty. The discovery, on
screen, that there is no plot (except a kind
of parboiled cross between *Magical Mystery
Tour* and *Yellow Submarine*), that absolutely no one in the picture can act (*especially* not Frampton and the Bee Gees) and
that the special-effects crew apparently
worked with two tons of dry ice and a box
of Scotch tape pales next to the musical
travesty perpetrated on the Beatles' most
influential work. (Not all of the music
comes from *Sgt. Pepper,* of course.) Aerosmith ("Come Together") and Earth Wind
and Fire ("Got to Get You into My Life")
turn in passable performances, but that's
no excuse for being involved with this holocaust. Two million people bought this album, which proves that P.T. Barnum was
right and that euthanasia may have untapped possibilities. Easily the worst album
of any notoriety in this book.

★ **Sheba, Baby (Soundtrack) / Bud. 5634**
Van McCoy score for mediocre blaxploitation flick features a few tracks by Barbara
Mason and Monk Higgins, none of which
rises to the level of listenability.

★★★ **Six Pak, Vol. 1 / Lone 4600**
*Artists include: Willie Nelson; Ray Wylie
Hubbard; Cooder Browne; Don Bowman;
Steve Fromholz; Geezinslaw Brothers*
    Collection of so-called outlaw country
artists fares better at the hands of Nelson's
Lone Star label than through a big corporation: these guys now seem like friends
rather than freaks. The highlights, in addition to Willie's two songs, are Hubbard's
"Up Against the Wall, Redneck Mother"
and Fromholz' "Heroes" and "Fool's
Gold," although Don Bowman's "Willon
and Waylee" will give country-outlaw ini-
tiates a smile.

★★ **Sixteen Rock Guitar Greats / Trip
TOP-16-27**
*Artists include: Jimi Hendrix; Jeff Beck;
Yardbirds; Rory Gallagher; Ron Wood and
the Faces; Spencer Davis Group; Lonnie*

*Mack; Big Bill Broonzy; Elmore James; Ar-
thur "Big Boy" Crudup; Canned Heat; Jimmy Page and Sonny Boy Williamson*
    Sometimes dire, sometimes excellent
sampler of tracks from a variety of performers not all of whom—Crudup, James
and Broonzy, for instance—are rockers.
The Page and Williamson, Wood and
Faces, and unfortunately, Hendrix tracks
are poor. The Yardbirds—from the Eric
Clapton era—are strong, Gallagher is his
usual rollicking self, and the Spencer Davis
version of "Dimples" is one of vocalist
Stevie Winwood's finest moments, though
it has nothing to do with guitar playing.

★★ **Sixteen Rock Vocal Greats / Trip
TOP-16-30**
*Artists include: Rod Stewart; Long John Bal-
dry; Spencer Davis Group; Yardbirds; Rory
Gallagher; Jimi Hendrix; Brian Auger;
Cream; Liverpool Roadrunners; James Taylor; Animals*
    A few gems, much dross. Stewart's
tracks are wretched; Baldry may be the
most overrated of all the obscure English
singers; the Davis tracks pop up on almost
every Trip and Springboard anthology, a
distinction of which their mild virtues are
hardly worthy; Taylor's work is from his
pre-Apple career. The Animals, Yardbirds,
Cream and Gallagher aren't bad, Auger is
acceptable, and Hendrix gets a halfway decent treatment, thanks to the inclusion of
his "Red House" blues.

★ **Skateboard (Soundtrack) / RCA
ABL1-2769**
Exploitation film about the skateboard
craze that infected late Seventies' teenagers
produces exploitation music aimed at same
market, only less effectively.

★ **Smokey and the Bandit (Soundtrack) / MCA 2099**
This Burt Reynolds film produced a score with some barely passable Jerry Reed and Bill Justis country songs and a lot of incidental CB dialogue.

★★★ **Sorcerer (Soundtrack) / MCA 2277**
Tangerine Dream's score for William Friedkin's film *noir* mistake is much more affecting on the screen, but serviceable on disc for fans of electronic improvisations.

★★★★ **Soul Years / Atl. SD2-504**
Artists include: LaVern Baker; Booker T. and the MGs; Ray Charles; Drifters; Aretha Franklin; Clovers; Coasters; Otis Redding; Spinners; Brook Benton; Bobbettes; Ruth Brown; Solomon Burke; Clarence Carter; Chords; Wilson Pickett; King Floyd; Ivory Joe Hunter; Sam and Dave; "Stick" McGee; Percy Sledge; Joe Tex; Joe Turner; Chuck Willis; Betty Wright

While this hardly makes up for the deletion of the great eight-volume *History of Rhythm and Blues,* which was superbly chosen and annotated, it's a nice two-disc overview of Atlantic's progress as this country's foremost (with Motown, anyway) black music label. It covers the Fifties in much detail—highlights include Willis' "C. C. Rider," Turner's ground-breaking "Shake, Rattle and Roll," Baker's "Tweedle Dee," "Money Honey" from the first Drifters, "Yakety Yak" by the Coasters. "One Mint Julep" by the Clovers, "Sh-Boom" by the Chords, and Hunter's "Since I Met You Baby," among others of that period, are also included. Its Sixties representatives are even more stellar: Franklin's "Respect" and "Natural Woman," Redding's "Dock of the Bay," the MGs' "Green Onions," Pickett's "In the Midnight Hour," "When a Man Loves a Woman" by Sledge, and Burke's "Just out of Reach," among others. The Seventies performances are more limited but still solid: King Floyd's "Groove Me," Wright's "Clean Up Woman" and the Spinners' "I'll Be Around."

Best of all, a chance to hear Ray Charles' "What'd I Say" and "I Got a Woman," which did more to popularize secular-gospel fusion than any other hits of the Fifties, and the Drifters' "There Goes My Baby," which introduced strings into R&B, paving the way for its development into soul music, and gave the wonderful Ben E. King his start.

A good set, lacking only organization (the sequence is scattered) and annotation to make it perfect.

★★★ **Southbound / Van. 79213**
Artists include: John Pilla; Merle Watson and Doc Watson; Doc Watson
Good album of old-timey guitar playing. Doc Watson is the best there is at it, and Pilla is his protégé, Merle is his son.

★★★ **South's Greatest Hits, Vol. 1 / Capri. 0187**
Artists include: Allman Brothers Band; Charlie Daniels; Elvin Bishop; Outlaws; Marshall Tucker Band; Gregg Allman; Atlanta Rhythm Section; Lynyrd Skynyrd; Amazing Rhythm Aces; Dr. John; Wet Willie
Showcases a variety of post–Allman Brothers Southern rock performers. There are some fine songs here—notably Dr. John's "Right Place Wrong Time," Wet Willie's "Keep on Smilin'," Skynyrd's "Sweet Home Alabama," "Ramblin' Man" by the Allmans and Bishop's "Fooled Around and Fell in Love," though the latter is a pop hit without much regional feeling. The groove is generally steady and easy, but somehow, one can't help feeling that these performances are all shown to better advantage in the context of their original LPs.

★★★ **South's Greatest Hits, Vol. 2 / Capri. 0209**
Artists include: Marshall Tucker Band; Atlanta Rhythm Section; Charlie Daniels Band; Outlaws; Allman Brothers Band; Elvin Bishop Sea Level; Stillwater; Wet Willie
Second set in series lacks anything as strong as Lynyrd Skynyrd's "Sweet Home Alabama" from the first, but does nicely

with Tucker's "Heard It in a Love Song," Atlantic Rhythm Section's "So In to You," Allmans' "Jessica" and Willie's "Street Corner Serenade." But the Outlaws are dreadful and Daniels isn't much better—neither is Stillwater, for that matter. Of the additions and more recent groups here, only Sea Level indicates that there is much life left in the Southern hard-rock genre.

★★ **Souvenirs of Music City, U.S.A. / Plant. 506**
Artists include: Jeannie C. Riley; Charlie Rich; Jimmy C. Newman; Hank Locklin; Leroy Van Dyke; Gordon Terry; James O'Gwynn; Rita Remington; Roy Orbison; David Allan Coe; Willie Nelson; Carl Perkins; Johnny Cash; Ray Pillow; Rex Allen Jr.; Sleepy LaBeef; George Jones; Little David Wilkins; Carl Belew; David Houston
A hodgepodge. The only sizable country hit here is Riley's "Harper Valley P.T.A." The Rich, Orbison, Perkins, Cash and LaBeef tracks are from Sun Records, but only LaBeef's "Black Land Farmer" is moderately rare, and the others are better heard on Sun anthologies. Nelson, Jones and Coe are at least interesting, but most of the rest is mediocre.

★★★ **Spirituals to Swing (John Hammond's Thirtieth Anniversary Concert—1967) / Col. CG-30776**
Artists include: George Benson; Marion Williams; Count Basie; Joe Turner; Cafe Society Band; Joe Turner and Pete Johnson; John Handy; Big Mama Thornton
Obviously, this thirtieth-anniversary show can't hope to compete artistically with the music produced at Hammond's ground-breaking 1937 concert, which brought black American music to Carnegie Hall and highbrow America for what amounted to the first time. But it has its fair share of good moments—especially from Williams, Basie and Turner.

★ **Spy Who Loved Me (Soundtrack) / U. Artists LA774-H**
This Marvin Hamlisch score is bone-dull except for Carly Simon's theme-song hit, "Nobody Does It Better," which is heard to better advantage on her album.

★ **Stardiscs / Lon. BP-704-5**
Artists include: Larry Page Orch; André Gagnon; John Miles; Hodges, James and Smith; Al Green; Olympic Runners; Bloodstone; Nature Zone; Steve Bender
With exception of Al Green's "Full of

Fire," this is all dross. Even Miles and Bloodstone aren't up to their best tricks here.

★ **Star Wars (Soundtrack) / 20th Cent. 2T-541**
John Williams' score, discofied by a couple of artists, made some commercial inroads in 1977, yet nothing like the ones made by the movie. Title theme isn't bad, but the rest is dispensable.

★★ **The Story of Star Wars / 20th Cent. 550**
Dialogue, music and sound effects from the film. More interesting than the score alone, but strictly for cultists, nonetheless.

★★ **Steppin' Out (Disco's Greatest Hits) / Poly. PD2-9007**
Artists include: Chakachas; Isaac Hayes; Bionic Boogie; Roy Ayers; Don Ray; Gloria Gaynor; Fatback Band; Kongas; Joe Simon; Trax; Crystal Grass
Doesn't live up to the subtitle. Gaynor's "Never Can Say Goodbye," which is as propulsive as any disco music ever made, and Simon's sweet-tempered "I Need You, You Need Me" are the best of a pretty dull assortment.

★★ **Steppin' Out / Mid. Int. BKL1-2423**
Artists include: Silver Convention; Carol Douglas; Touch of Class; Liquid Pleasure; Andrea True Connection
Passable disco sampler. "Fly Robin Fly" by Silver Convention is about the best of it, although former porno starlet True's "More More More" has its own fascination.

★★★★★ **Story of the Blues / Col. CG-30008**
Artists include: Fra-Fra Tribesmen; Mississippi John Hurt; Blind Willie McTell; Leadbelly; Blind Lemon Jefferson; Charley Patton; Texas Alexander; Peg Leg Boy Fuller and Sonny Terry; Brownie McGhee; Joe Williams and Sonny Boy Williamson; Big Bill Broonzy; Joe Turner and Pete Johnson; Otis Spann; Elmore James; Johnny Shines; Barbecue Bob and Laughing Charley; Henry Williams and Eddie Anthony; Mississippi Jook Band; Memphis Jug Band; Bessie Smith; Lillian Glinn; Bertha Hill; Butterbeans and Susie; Leroy Carr and Scrapper Blackwell; Faber Smith and Jimmy Yancey; Peetie Wheatstraw; Casey Bill and Black Bob; Bo Carter; Robert Johnson; Bukka White; Memphis Minnie

Fantastic assortment of pre–World War II blues. Includes all the major figures: Johnson, Patton, Bessie Smith, James (who stretches toward Chicago-style city blues of the postwar era), Broonzy, McGhee and Terry, Hurt, Leadbelly, Jefferson. Plus an assortment of band tracks, piano blues—nearly every style of blues imagined so far is represented here. Recommended; well annotated.

★★★ Sunday Down South / Sun 119
Artists include: Johnny Cash; Jerry Lee Lewis

Two rockabillies remember their religious roots. Hymns for be-bop backsliders, or something like that. Don't step on my patent-leather Easter shoes? Good stuff anyhow.

★★ Super Groups / Pick. 166
Artists include: Mighty Clouds of Joy; Jackson Southernaires; Dixie Hummingbirds; Highway Q.C.'s; Sensational Nightingales

Poorly packaged set nonetheless contains some fine music from several male groups that are among the biggest names in black gospel.

★★★ Super Hits, Vol. 1 / Atl. 501
Artists include: Percy Sledge; Sam and Dave; Wilson Pickett; Young Rascals; Joe Tex; Booker T. and the MGs; Barbara Lewis; Aretha Franklin; Eddie Floyd; Mar Keys

All that's left of Atlantic's old five-volume series of its R&B pop crossover hits. Not a bad song in the bunch; also nothing rare, and silly notes. You can get this stuff—most of it, anyhow—in better condition on this label's *The Soul Years.*

★★★ Super Oldies of the Fifties, Vol. 1 / Trip TOP-50-1
Artists include: Little Anthony and the Imperials; Crows; Five Satins; Danleers; Chantels; Cadillacs; Dubs; El Dorados; Lloyd Price; Mystics; Little Richard; Lee Andrews and the Hearts; Bobby Freeman; Jimmy Clanton; Jesters; Johnnie and Joe; Penguins; Sonny Til and the Orioles; Ritchie Valens; Harptones

Decent oldies set, unannotated, with no surprises except possibly Freeman's "Do You Want a Dance," a Sixties record.

★★★ Super Oldies of the Fifties, Vol. 2 / Trip TOP-50-2
Artists include: Flamingos; Frankie Lymon; Sam Cooke; Teen Queens; Heartbeats; Monotones; Wilbur Harrison; Shirelles; Lloyd Price; Charts; Olympics; Dion; Little Richard; Dave "Baby" Cortez; Dee Clark; Bobby Day; Spaniels; Ritchie Valens; Frankie Ford; Dubs

No real surprises here, but some nice oddities: the Spaniels' "Stormy Weather," a beautiful ballad; the somewhat hilarious "Western Movies" by the Olympics; Price's "Stagger Lee," rather than the usually anthologized "Lawdy Miss Clawdy."

★★★★ Super Oldies of the Fifties, Vol. 3 / Trip TOP-50-3
Artists include: Platters; Diamonds; Crests; Little Richard; Scarlets; Harptones; Jerry Lee Lewis; Five Satins; Channels; Willows; Crew Cuts; Lloyd Price; Spacemen; Eugene Church; Lee Andrews and the Hearts; Continentals

Some relative rarities here, highlighted by Price's "I'm Gonna Get Married" and Lee Andrews and the Hearts' "Try the Impossible." But beware "Sh-Boom," by the Crew Cuts; it is a white cover version of the infinitely superior black original done by the Chords.

★★★ Super Oldies of the Fifties, Vol. 4 / Trip TOP-50-4
Artists include: Moonglows; Platters; Tune Weavers; Crests; Jerry Lee Lewis; Little Richard; Kodaks; El Dorados; Spaniels; Paragons; Harptones; Jacks; Wailers; Channels; Marvin and Johnny; Eternals; Velvets; Donnie Owens

Good one for doo-wop aficionados, with the tracks from the Moonglows, Spaniels, El Dorados, Harptones, Jacks and Paragons. Also for anarchists, with Little Richard performing not only his own hit, "Lucille," but also Larry Williams' "Short Fat Fanny." "Rockin' in the Jungle" by the Eternals is a cute spinoff from the Cadets' "Stranded in the Jungle."

★★ **Super Oldies of the Fifties, Vol. 5 / Trip TOP-50-5**
Artists include: Platters; Channels; Tommy Edwards; Shirley and Lee; Diamonds; Anita Bryant; Jack Scott; Cadillacs; Fire Flies; Shepherd Sisters; Phil Phillips; Champs; Jerry Wallace; Johnny Preston; Jerry Butler; Paul Evans; Thomas Wayne; Johnny and the Hurricanes; Tony Bellus; Della Reese

Bad pop singers (Bryant) and silly novelties like Evans' "Seven Little Girls (Sittin' in the Back Seat)," Preston's "Running Bear." Little good stuff: Diamonds do the "Stroll," Platters have "Smoke Gets in Your Eyes," Butler "For Your Precious Love," which launched his career, and that of the Impressions. Plus two hot instrumentals, "Red River Rock" by Johnny and the Hurricanes and "Tequila" by the Champs. Still, too spotty for comfort.

★★★ **Super Oldies of the Fifties, Vol. 6 / Trip TOP-50-6**
Artists include: Crests; Platters; Three Friends; Moonglows; Dell-Vikings; Little Richard; Spaniels; Teen Chords; Faye Adams; Jerry Lee Lewis; Starlights; Cadillacs; Continentals; Jimmy Reed; Lloyd Price; Sam Cooke; Huey "Piano" Smith

Odds and ends in this erratic collection. The better sides include: Price's "Where Were You on Our Wedding Day," Reed's "Honest I Do," "Only Sixteen" by Cooke, "Rockin' Pneumonia and the Boogie Woogie Flu" by Smith, Little Richard's three tracks, the Dell-Vikings' "Come Go with Me," Lewis' hilarious (but intense) "High School Confidential" and the Platters' "My Prayer." Not to mention "Secret Love" by the Moonglows. But some of this is bubblegum light—two songs by the Crests is enough to give you cavities, fluoride or no fluoride.

★★★★ **Super Oldies of the Fifties, Vol. 7 / Trip TOP-50-7**
Artists include: Big Bopper; Channels; Cadets; Platters; Crests; Diamonds; Jack Scott; Little Richard; Magnificents; Collegians; Paragons; Cadillacs; Moonglows; Jesters; Dells; Jesse Belvin; Etta James; Lloyd Price; Flamingos

No set that includes "Chantilly Lace" (Bopper), "Stranded in the Jungle" (Cadets), two by Little Richard, "Oh What a Night" (Moonglows) and "Goodnight My Love" (Belvin) can be dismissed out of hand. Especially when it finishes with the Flamingos' "I'll Be Home."

★★ **Super Oldies of the Fifties, Vol. 8 / Trip TOP-50-8**
Artists include: Fleetwoods; Fats Domino; Santo and Johnny; Eddie Cochran; Clovers; Bill Haley and the Comets; Frankie Avalon; Penguins; Teen Queens; Bill Doggett; Falcons; Fabian; Five Satins; Jimmy Clanton; Dubs; Mickey and Sylvia

Heavily padded: the Five Satins' "In the Still of the Night" and Clanton's "Just a Dream" appear on Volume 1 of the series, and there's just no excuse for remembering Fabian and Frankie Avalon, unless you like to torture yourself. Three tracks by Haley seems excessive, too. Highlight: "Love Is Strange" by Mickey and Sylvia, a grand track rarely anthologized.

★★★ **Super Oldies of the Sixties, Vol. 1 / Trip TOP-60-1**
Artists include: Shirelles; Kingsmen; Jive Five; Dion; Chantels; Kathy Young; Shells; Angels; Cascades; Gene Chandler; Dave "Baby" Cortez; Del Shannon; Ron Holden; Rosie and the Originals; Troy Shondell; Frankie Avalon; Les Cooper; Little Caesar and the Romans

Decent selection of pre-Beatles Sixties hits includes some girl groups (Shirelles, Angels, Chantels), some doo-wop and assorted New York–style harmony (Jive Five, Dion, Rosie and the Originals), some teen-exploitation music (Avalon, Shondell, Cortez) and some oddball gems: "Louie Louie," the raunch rock classic by the Kingsmen; "Duke of Earl," Gene Chandler's mysterious lament-tribute; Shannon's "Runaway"; and Little Caesar's anthemic (if nasal) "Those Oldies but Goodies."

★★★ **Super Oldies of the Sixties, Vol. 2 / Trip TOP-60-2**
Artists include: Shep and the Limelites; Capris; Dale and Grace; Lee Dorsey; Chiffons;

Dee Clark; Blue Jays; Dionne Warwick;
Harold Dorman; Paul Evans; Joe Jones;
Anita Bryant; Paul Peterson; Shirelles;
James Darren; Fendermen; Sam Cooke;
Freddie Scott; Dovells

A good sampler, among other things, for
those who think that rock between the
time Presley entered the army and the
Beatles entered the American charts was
all wimps and no successes. In fact, as
shown by Dorsey's "Ya Ya," the Chiffons'
"He's So Fine," Harold Dorman's wild
"Mountain of Love," Scott's "Hey Girl"
and the Fendermen's "Muleskinner Blues,"
this was a fertile era, particularly for black
performers: Cooke's "Wonderful World"
has become a standard, for instance. But
the impression that there was a great deal
of bathetic pop (Anita Bryant) and purely
exploitive teen-market music (Peterson,
Darren) isn't altogether wrong. A bag as
mixed as the era it draws upon.

★★★★ **Super Oldies of the Sixties, Vol.**
3 / Trip TOP-60-3
Artists include: Chuck Jackson; Barbara
Lynn; Jerry Butler; Ike and Tina Turner;
Shirelles; Wilson Pickett; Jimmy Hughes;
Maxine Brown; Joe Henderson; Gladys
Knight and the Pips; Dionne Warwick; Mon-
go Santamaria; Patti LaBelle and the Blue-
belles; Betty Harris; King Curtis

This amounts to a survey of black musi-
cal styles of the early (pre-Beatle) Sixties.
Jackson (represented by "Any Day Now"),
Butler ("He Will Break Your Heart,"
"Moon River"), Brown ("All in My
Mind," "Funny") and Warwick ("Don't
Make Me Over") were crooners—ballad
singers who brought a world of emotion to
pop ballads that no white singers had done,
and yet conveyed the songs conventionally
enough to enjoy substantial white pop appeal. Pickett ("If You Need Me"), Ike and
Tina ("It's Gonna Work Out Fine," "Poor
Fool"), Harris ("Cry to Me") even Lynn
("You'll Lose a Good Thing") are tougher,
more directly black in their approach. Curtis ("Soul Twist") and Santamaria ("Watermelon Man") contribute two of the era's
funkiest instrumentals. Nice set.

★★★ **Super Oldies of the Sixties, Vol. 4 /**
Trip TOP-60-4
Artists include: Bobby Lewis; Randy and the
Rainbows; Dion; Del Shannon; Terry Staf-
ford; Jimmy Charles; Don and Juan; Bar-
bara George; Trashmen; Volumes; Shirelles;
Paragons; Beach Boys; Cathy Jean and the
Roommates; Dixie Cups; Don Gardner and

Dee Dee Ford; Dual; Inez Foxx; Angels;
Chris Kenner

In addition to the usual teen-exploitation
music, R&B one-shots, girl groups and
wild novelties, this set begins to get into
the kind of heavily produced (Shannon)
but somehow more authentic (Beach Boys)
music that paved the way for the Beatles
and the British Invasion. Still, the highlight
of the set is a nonsense song, the Trashmen's "Surfin' Bird," which proves that all
great art knows where the garbage dump
lies.

FANTASY 8093

★★★ **Super Oldies of the Sixties, Vol. 5 /**
Trip TOP-60-5
Artists include: Toys; Little Eva; B. J.
Thomas; Happenings; Beach Boys; Turtles;
Robert Parker; Chad and Jeremy; Shelley
Fabares; Dionne Warwick; Mitch Ryder and
the Detroit Wheels; Gerry and the Pacemak-
ers; Betty Everett; Raindrops; Cookies; Clas-
sics; Shirelles; Shangri-Las; Dobie Gray

A nice sampling of hits from the period
immediately before and just after the emergence of the Beatles. The British selections
(Pacemakers, Chad and Jeremy) are the
weakest of the bunch; Fabares' "Johnny
Angel" is pure pubescent exploitation. But
there are a number of indications of the
way in which Phil Spector's Wall of Sound
approach was beginning to have an effect
(Toys, Happenings, Thomas, even Little
Eva); a different sort of resonance appears
in the girl-group sides (Shangri-Las, Shirelles) that indicates that performers, writers
and producers were beginning to see themselves as camp. The R&B selections are
few but strong—Parker's "Barefootin' " is
the best. Plus two tracks from the best
blue-eyed soul group in the land—at least
until the advent of the Righteous Brothers
and the Young Rascals—Mitch Ryder and

the Detroit Wheels. The Beach Boys ("Surfer Girl") move into a ballad style, and the Turtles ("It Ain't Me Babe") signify the arrival of Bob Dylan, folk rock and bohemian California as factors in rock.

★★★★ **Super Oldies of the Sixties, Vol. 6 / Trip TOP-60-6**
Artists include: Percy Sledge; Sam and Dave; Don Covay; Bobby Freeman; Otis Redding; Capitols; Slim Harpo; Dionne Warwick; Brenton Wood; Joe Jeffrey Group; James Brown; Jerry Butler and Betty Everett; Esquires; B. B. King; Packers; Alvin Cash; Tommy Tucker; Meters; Maxine Brown

A diversity of mid-Sixties soul music. Atlantic and Stax are well represented by Redding, Sam and Dave, Sledge, Cash and Covay (whose "Mercy Mercy" might be an outline for Mick Jagger's vocal style). King's "Rock Me Baby" is a definitive version of his blues style. Butler and Everett continue a version of doo-wop tradition, while Warwick takes black balladry into mainstream pop. In a way, though, the most fascinating numbers here are the wildest: Freeman's "C'mon and Swim" was produced by Sly Stone and is unlike most dance discs of the period in its unleashed ferocity, Tucker's "High-Heeled Sneakers" is utterly bizarre, Harpo's "Scratch My Back" has sexual connotations that it's hard to believe were permissible fifteen years ago and the Meters' "Cissy Strut" is virtually a schematic diagram of the fundamental New Orleans rhythm pattern.

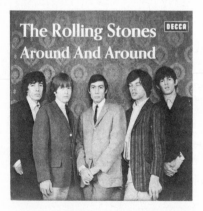

★★★ **Super Oldies of the Sixties, Vol. 7 / Trip TOP-60-7**
Artists include: J. Frank Wilson; Soul Survivors; Shangri-Las; Gerry and the Pacemak-

ers; Chad and Jeremy; Dionne Warwick; Happenings; Dixie Cups; B. J. Thomas; Turtles; Royal Guardsmen; Jackie Lee; Beach Boys; Ad Libs; Jelly Beans

Despite some good last-gasp girl-group selections (Shangri-Las, Dixie Cups, Ad Libs, Jelly Beans), most of this is too wimpy to be listenable today. Gerry and the Pacemakers and Chad and Jeremy were among the least consequential British groups, the Beach Boys' "Surfin' " is the dullest of that group's teen-craze discs, and the Happenings, Wilson and the Royal Guardsmen explicit rock without contributing anything to it. But Lee's dance record, "The Duck," is nice, as are Warwick's two ballads, and the Soul Survivors' "Expressway to Your Heart" is a fine hunk of period soul music.

★★★ **Super Oldies of the Sixties, Vol. 8 / Trip TOP-60-8**
Artists include: Turtles; B. J. Thomas; Tommy James; Dionne Warwick; Brenton Wood; Deon Jackson; John Fred and the Playboy Band; Mitch Ryder and the Detroit Wheels; Toussaint McCall; Happenings; Aaron Neville; Chiffons; Forum; Leaves; Bobby Fuller Four; Seeds; Count Five

Mixed bag. There is some fine hard rock here: Fuller's "I Fought the Law," "Psychotic Reaction" by Count Five, "Hey Joe" by the Leaves and "Pushin' Too Hard" by the Seeds are all minor but strong. Ryder's tracks are powerful white R&B. Jackson and Wood contribute nice black pop hits, while Fred's "Judy in Disguise (With Glasses)" is a great *Sgt. Pepper* takeoff. Too much of the rest is too pop, insufficiently rocking not to have dated.

★★ **Super Oldies of the Sixties, Vol. 9 / Trip TOP-60-9**
Artists include: Duprees; Crests; Dionne Warwick; Roommates; Beach Boys; Chimes; Janie Grant; Embers; Jan and Dean; Champs; Premiers; Tradewinds; B. J. Thomas; Raindrops; Johnny Crawford; Evie Sands; Jerry Wallace; Chad and Jeremy; Jack Scott

This is mostly very minor, and often it's awful (Sands, Crests, Roommates, Crawford, Chad and Jeremy, Wallace). Scott's "What in the World's Come over You" is an odd rockabilly ballad, "Surfin' USA" is one of the Beach Boys' best (although "Heart and Soul" is probably Jan and Dean's worst) and aside from that, there's not a lot here.

★★ **Super Oldies of the Sixties, Vol. 10 / Trip TOP-60-10**
Artists include: Lesley Gore; Dickey Lee; Duprees; Leroy Van Dyke; Vogues; Cowsills; Flares; Every Mother's Son; B. J. Thomas; Cannibal and the Headhunters; Jay and the Techniques; Dionne Warwick; Roger Miller; Sam the Sham and the Pharaohs; Gentrys; Shangri-Las

Weak pop set, little rock or soul. Big exception is Cannibal and the Headhunters' "Land of 1000 Dances." Jay and the Techniques have a continually listenable pop-soul item, "Apples Peaches Pumpkin Pie," and Warwick is her usual fine self. "Wooly Bully" (Sam the Sham) is a genuine weirdo, but like Gore's "It's My Party," it is more memorable than playable, today. Which is still an improvement over most of the rest of what is here.

★★★ **Super Oldies of the Sixties, Vol. 11 / Trip TOP-60-11**
Artists include: Nat Kendricks and the Swans; Billy Preston; Patti LaBelle and the Bluebelles; John Lee Hooker; Wilson Pickett; Manhattans; Baby Washington; Ike and Tina Turner; Gene Chandler; Lloyd Price; Jimmy Reed; Jennell Hawkins; Joe Simon; Gladys Knight and the Pips; Jimi Hendrix; Chantels

Decent soul collection from the period, with some blues (Reed, Hooker) additions. The songs by Preston and Hendrix are not the sort of thing that would be remembered but for the success those two enjoyed in later years.

★★★ **Super Oldies of the Sixties, Vol. 12 / Trip TOP-60-12**
Artists include: Angels; Lesley Gore; Platters; Bobby Hebb; B. J. Thomas; Mark Dinning; Standells; Left Banke; Cowsills; Knickerbockers; Stan Getz/Astrud Gilberto; Duprees; Crests; Dionne Warwick; David Rose; Friend and Lover; Jerry Butler; Johnny Crawford; Rochell and the Candles

Mediocre. For every "Dirty Water" by the Standells, there's Getz and Gilberto; for every "Walk Away Renee" by the Left Banke, there's the rank pop instrumental of David Rose. Nice stuff by Butler, Gore (even), Hebb dragged down by silliness of much of the rest.

★★ **Super Oldies of the Sixties, Vol. 13 / Trip TOP-60-13**
Artists include: Bobby Goldsboro; Exciters; Cher; Dennis Yost and Classics IV; Bob Lind; Animals; Jackie De Shannon; Johnny Burnette; Buddy Knox; Buckinghams; Rivingtons; Bobby Vee; Little Anthony and the Imperials; Dick and Dee Dee; Jay and the Americans; Turtles; Ventures; Capris

Mixed bag: for every lushly romantic ballad like the Capris' "There's a Moon Out Tonight," there's a lushly stupid pop song like Goldsboro's "Honey." Despite the Animals, De Shannon, and the inspired insipidity of "Bird's the Word" by the Rivingtons, there's not much here that you can't get in better company elsewhere.

★★★ **Super Oldies of the Sixties, Vol. 14 / Trip TOP-60-14**
Artists include: Little Anthony and the Imperials; Gene McDaniels; Jay and the Americans; Johnny Burnette; Bobby Goldsboro; Jackie De Shannon; Rivieras; Timi Yuro; Cher; C.O.D.s; Bobby Vee; Dennis Yost and the Classics IV; Sugarloaf; Animals; Rivingtons; Fabian; Frankie Avalon; Ernie K. Doe

Final volume of the set epitomizes its virtues (good rock and R&B tracks by Burnette, Anthony and the Imperials, Animals, Rivingtons and K. Doe) and imperfections (the teen-idol muck of Fabian, Avalon and Cher, the sentimental pop of Goldsboro, the wretched "Michael" by the C.O.D.s).

★★★★ **Super Super Blues Band / Check. 3010**
Artists include: Muddy Waters; Howlin' Wolf; Bo Diddley

Three of the Chess stable's best combine on their classics: Waters' "Long Distance Call," Wolf's "Spoonful" and "Red Rooster," Diddley's "Diddley Daddy."

★★★ **Swamp Blues / Ex. 8015-16**
Artists include: Clarence Edwards; Whispering Smith; Henry Gray; Silas Hogan; Arthur "Guitar" Kelly

Excello was always the oddest, funkiest, most down-home of blues labels, and this collection shows why. It's not just the crudity of the music—which seems lost between plantation sounds of Mississippi and Muddy Waters' breakthrough up north—but also their themes: Arthur Kelly's "No. 10 at the Station and No. 12 Is on the Road," which must be the most long-winded restatement of the mystery-train theme, for instance. Consistently intriguing.

★★ **Tell Me That You Love Me Junie Moon (Soundtrack) / Col. OS-3540**
Folk idealogue Seeger and Pacific Gas and Electric, a minor San Francisco group,

provide the background music for Otto
Preminger's improbable and sentimental
story of three misfit losers, one facially dis-
figured, one an epileptic, one a wheelchair-
bound homosexual. If you can figure out
the cinematic combination, you can probably fathom the musical one.

★★★★ **Texas Country / U. Artists
LA574-H2**
*Artists include: Willie Nelson; Freddy
Fender; Asleep at the Wheel; Bob Wills and
the Texas Playboys*
  A fine set, without much depth, but a
good representation of the artists included.
Nelson and Wills made good music,
though not their best, for United Artists—
both are represented, however, by a selection of their best-known titles. Fender, by
far the most minor figure here, has four
sides, of which only the anthology-peren-
nial, "Wasted Days and Wasted Nights,"
amounts to much. But Asleep at the
Wheel's five songs are from the group's
first album, and it may be the best music
they have ever made, particularly the versions of "Take Me Back to Tulsa" and
"Cherokee Boogie." Good set.

★★★★ **This Is How It All Began, Vol. 1 /
Spec. 2117**
*Artists include: Chosen Gospel Singers; Soul
Stirrers; Mercy Dee; Alex Bradford; John
Lee Hooker; Frankie Lee Sims; Roy Milton;
Percy Mayfield; Joe Liggins; Four Flames;
Jimmy Liggins; Camille Howard; Swan Sil-
vertones*
  Fine selection of gospel, blues and R&B
sounds influential on the development of
modern rock and soul.

★★★★ **This Is How It All Began, Vol. 2 /
Spec. 2118**
*Artists include: Lloyd Price; Guitar Slim;
Jesse Belvin and Marvin Phillips; Tony Allen
and the Champs; Little Richard; Larry Wil-
liams; Sam Cooke; Art Neville; Jerry Byrne;
Don and Dewey*
  Fine album of early rock and soul per-
formances, includes early secular singing
from Cooke, two Richard hits, a pair of
Williams novelties, Price's "Lawdy Miss
Clawdy," and other solid L.A. and New
Orleans sides.

★★★★ **This Is Reggae Music, Vol. 1 / Is.
9251**
*Artists include: Zap Pow; Wailers; Jimmy
Cliff; Lorna Bennett; Joe Higgs; Heptones;
Maytals; Owen Gray*

While it's hardly as fundamental as *The
Harder They Come,* this sampler offers
some fine reggae, including the Wailers' "I
Shot the Sheriff" and "Concrete Jungle,"
the Heptones' "Book of Rules" and the
Maytals' "Funky Kingston" and "Louie
Louie."

★★★ **This Is Reggae Music, Vol. 2 / Is.
9327**
*Artists include: George Dekker; Peacemakers;
Scotty and Lorna Bennett; Rudie Mowatt;
Third World; Augustus Pablo; Heptones; Ar-
thur Louis; Desi Young; Burning Spear*
  Collection of minor reggae tracks none-
theless includes the outstanding "Marcus
Garvey" by Burning Spear, Arthur Louis'
odd cover of Dylan's "Knocking on Heav-
en's Door" and the Heptones' "Country
Boy."

★★★★ **This Is Reggae Music, Vol. 3 / Is.
9391**
*Artists include: Junior Murvin; Lee Perry;
Max Romeo; Justin Hines and the Dominoes;
Aswad; Jah Lion; Burning Spear; Prince
Jazzbo and the Upsetters; Peter Tosh; Bunny
Wailer*
  Fine collection of Jamaican hits includes
Murvin's "Police and Thieves," Romeo's
"War in a Babylon," Burning Spear's
"Man in the Hills," "Rastaman" by Wailer
and "No Sympathy" by Tosh—all impor-
tant reggae artists and/or songs.

★★★ **To Mother / Spec. 2152**
*Artists include: Pilgrim Travelers; Alex Brad-
ford; Five Blind Boys; Detroiters; Soul Stirrers; Bessie Griffin; Swan Silvertones*
  Tributes to Mom and her faith in God
from a number of gospel's leading lights.

★ **Tommy (Soundtrack) / Poly.
9502**
Before Robert Stigwood butchered *Sgt.
Pepper,* he did the same for the Who's rock
opera *Tommy,* although with considerably
more justification: Roger Daltrey, the
Who's vocalist, starred (albeit with Ann-
Margret, the *doyenne* of Elvis flicks), and
composer Pete Townshend added some
new incidental music. But while Townshend's increased use of synthesizer on the
soundtrack is interesting, most of the vocals are not: Ann-Margret, Jack Nicholson
and Oliver Reed don't have an octave of
range among them; Elton John's version of
"Pinball Wizard" is feeble next to the
original; and Tina Turner's "Acid Queen"
is a screeching parody of the Who's, and of

her own soul-slut persona. No excuse for this while you can still obtain the original.

★ Twenty Golden Souvenirs (Of Music City) / Plant. 533

Artists include: Johnny Cash; Jerry Lee Lewis; Charlie Rich; Leroy Van Dyke; Jimmy C. Newman; Hank Locklin; Charlie Walker; John Wesley Ryles; Willie Nelson; Dave Dudley; David Allan Coe; Jeannie C. Riley; James O'Gwynn; Murry Kellum; Gordon Terry; Paul Martin; Rufus Thibodeaux; Rex Allen Jr.; Jimmie Davis; Rita Remington

Even the best-known performers here are represented by minor examples of their work. The others are minor, indeed.

★ Twenty Great Hits / Plant. 521

Artists include: Jimmy C. Newman; David Allan Coe; Rex Allen Jr; Eddie Burns; James O'Gwynn; John Wesley Ryles; Linda Martell; Tennessee Guitars; Robbie Harden; Ruby Wright; Sleepy LaBeef; Ray Pillow; Debbie Lori Kaye; Harlow Wilcox; Little David Wilkins; Jeannie C. Riley; Dee Mullins; Maxine Brown; Tokyo Matsu; Leroy Van Dyke

Very minor country collection.

★★ Twenty Great Country Hits / RCA CPL2-1286

Artists include: Chet Atkins; Bobby Bare; Jim Ed Brown; Jessi Colter; Floyd Cramer; Nashville Brass; Waylon Jennings; Ronnie Milsap; Dolly Parton; Jerry Reed; Charlie Rich; Jim Reeves; Johnny Russell; Hank Snow; Gary Stewart; Porter Wagoner; Porter Wagoner and Dolly Parton; Billy Walker; Dottie West

Scattershot collection of RCA's acts. Bare, Jennings, Reed, Rich and Stewart are represented by excellent examples of their work. Others aren't.

★★★ Twenty Greatest Rhythm and Blues Hits / Kent 527

Artists include: B. B. King; Jimmy Witherspoon; Roosevelt Sykes; Elmore James; Jimmy McCracklin; Pee Wee Crayton; Howlin' Wolf; S. King; Smokey Hogg; Lowell Fulsom; Lightnin' Hopkins; Roscoe Gordon; John Lee Hooker; Jimmy Nelson; Junior Beasley

Fine collection of mostly twelve-bar blues artists. King is particularly well represented with three tracks, including his momentous "Sweet Sixteen," while Hooker chips in with "Boogie Chillen," and James with the inevitable "Dust My Blues" and "Standing at the Crossroads."

★★ Twenty Super Rhythm and Blues Hits / Kent 530

Artists include: B. B. King; Etta James; Ikettes; Joe Houston; Lowell Fulsom; Pee Wee Crayton; Young Jessie; Jimmy Witherspoon; Cadets; John Lee Hooker; Ike and Tina Turner; Jacks; Johnny "Guitar" Watson

Good selection includes everything from novelties like "Stranded in the Jungle" (Cadets) to doo-wop like "Why Don't You Write Me?" (Jacks) and straight twelve-bar blues (King).

★★★ Underground Blues / Kent 535

Artists include: Elmore James; B. B. King; Howlin' Wolf; Jimmy Reed; Lightnin' Hopkins; John Lee Hooker

By "underground" Kent presumably means artists who were influential upon the white rock-blues groups of the Sixties, and this is a representative sampling of names, if not always of repertoire. (James and King are not given their best songs; Wolf's and Hooker's are perhaps overfamiliar.) Good introduction to the originals that may be familiar in versions by the Animals, Stones, and so forth.

★★★ Urban Blues / Fan. 24717

Artists include: Roosevelt Sykes; Little Brother Montgomery

Two blues pianists, not necessarily major ones, on a set of songs originally recorded for Prestige. Title is a bit misleading, since this hardly gives a sampling of the full range of urban blues styles. Nice music anyway.

★★ Volunteer Jam / Capri. 0172

Artists include: Charlie Daniels Band; Marshall Tucker Band

Live set of minor Southern rockers is hardly the cream of the genre.

596 / Anthologies and Soundtracks

★★ **Walnut Valley Spring Thing / Tak. 1054**

Artists include: John Hartford; Tut Taylor and Don Humphreys; New Grass Revival; Merle Travis; Cathy Barton; Hutchison Brothers

Live recordings from the bluegrass festival. Highlight is Travis, working out on some of his best songs—"Smoke That Cigarette," "Dark as a Dungeon," "White Heat."

★ **Welcome to L.A. (Soundtrack) / U. Artists LA703-H**

Score from confused picture about Hollywood scene is less than worthy. Keith Carradine is a lot less comfortable with these Richard Baskin songs than with the ones in *Nashville,* and Baskin's own singing is expendable, to be charitable.

★★ **West Side Story (Original Cast) / Col. JS-32603**
★★★ **West Side Story (Soundtrack) / Col. JS-2070**

This is a fairly successful attempt to exploit the rock ambiance of the Fifties. None of the tunes—written by Leonard Bernstein, after all—is a rocker, but the "Jet Song" has entered the rock consciousness (as a takeoff point for Alice Cooper parodies, if nothing else) and "Somewhere" is a great ballad, although it lacked an "inside" interpretation until Tom Waits did his. These songs were influential, in their way, in making juvenile delinquency (thus, rock) a subject matter fit for middlebrows.

★ **White Mansions / A&M 6004**

Artists include: Jessi Colter; Waylon Jennings; John Dillon; Steve Cash; Waylon Jennings and Jessi Colter; John Dillon and Jessi Colter; Steve Cash, John Dillon and Waylon Jennings; Voices of Deliverance

Genuinely horrid attempt to tell the story of the Civil War from the South's perspective; written by an Englishman, this manages to misinterpret the politics of the era, and repeats every social cliché about the period. It gets one star because Jennings sings a few of the songs as though he means business.

★★★ **The Wiz (Original Cast) / Atl. 18137**
★ **The Wiz (Soundtrack) / MCA 2-14000**

In making the original-cast album of the black Broadway revival of *The Wizard of Oz,* producer Jerry Wexler circumvented many problems by adding a soul rhythm section. The result is that the intensity of the performances transcends the stagy phrasing. Stephanie Mills, who plays Dorothy, is the chief offender in the latter regard; Tasha Thomas and Dee Dee Bridgewater turn in convincing performances that show both as musicians as much as actresses.

The soundtrack had many advantages; recorded with top-flight studio musicians, its stars are musical ones first: Diana Ross, Michael Jackson, and the pair together. But it never jells because the arrangements are precisely as flatulent as the Broadway ones Wexler eschewed. As disastrous on the turntable as it was on the screen.

★ **World of Country Giants / Col. CG-30893**

Artists include: Marty Robbins; Ray Price; Johnny Horton; Tommy Cash; Tammy Wynette; Johnny Cash; David Houston; Carl Smith; Stonewall Jackson; Bob Luman; Lynn Anderson; Freddy Weller; Jody Miller; Carl Perkins; Jerry Reed; David Rogers; Sammi Smith; Johnny Duncan

Country names at their worst. Chief (almost only) exception is Johnny Cash's version of Dylan's "Don't Think Twice, It's All Right."

■ **You Light Up My Life (Soundtrack) / Ari. 4159**

Spawned Debby Boone's career with the title song. But this doesn't even have the hit version. Symptomatic of how much rock has *not* changed pop music.

Five-Star Records

Ain't That Good News / Specialty
Allman Brothers Band / **Allman Brothers Band at Fillmore East** / Capricorn
American Graffiti (Soundtrack) / MCA
Anthology of American Folk Music, Vol. 1: Ballads / Folkways
Anthology of American Folk Music, Vol. 2: Social Music / Folkways
Anthology of American Folk Music, Vol. 3: Songs / Folkways
Atlanta Rhythm Section / **A Rock and Roll Alternative** / Polydor
Average White Band / **AWB** / Atlantic
The Band / **Music from Big Pink** / Capitol
The Band / **Rock of Ages** / Capitol
The Band / **The Band** / Capitol
The Beach Boys / **All Summer Long/California Girls** / Capitol
The Beach Boys / **Endless Summer** / Capitol
The Beatles / **Abbey Road** / Capitol
The Beatles / **Help!** / Capitol
The Beatles / **Hey Jude** / Capitol
The Beatles / **Live at the Hollywood Bowl** / Capitol
The Beatles / **Meet the Beatles!** / Capitol
The Beatles / **Revolver** / Capitol
The Beatles / **Rubber Soul** / Capitol
The Beatles / **Something New** / Capitol
The Beatles / **The Beatles** / Capitol
The Beatles / **The Beatles/1962–1966** / Capitol
The Beatles / **The Beatles/1967–1970** / Capitol
The Beatles / **The Beatles' Second Album** / Capitol
The Beatles / **The Early Beatles** / Capitol
The Beatles / **Yesterday . . . and Today** / Capitol
Captain Beefheart and His Magic Band / **Trout Mask Replica** / Reprise
Chuck Berry / **Chuck Berry's Golden Decade** / Chess
Chuck Berry / **Chuck Berry's Golden Decade, Vol. 2** / Chess
Bobby "Blue" Bland / **The Best of Bobby Bland** / Duke
Bobby "Blue" Bland / **The Best of Bobby Bland, Vol. 2** / Duke
Bobby "Blue" Bland / **Two Steps from the Blues** / Duke
Blood, Sweat and Tears / **Child Is Father to the Man** / Columbia
The Bonzo Dog Band / **The History of the Bonzos** / United Artists
James Brown / **Soul Classics, Vol. 1** / Polydor
Jackson Browne / **Running on Empty** / Asylum
Jackson Browne / **The Pretender** / Asylum
Buffalo Springfield / **Buffalo Springfield** / Atco
Buffalo Springfield / **Buffalo Springfield Again** / Atco
Solomon Burke / **The Best of Solomon Burke** / Atlantic
Burning Spear / **Marcus Garvey** / Island
Jerry Butler / **The Best of Jerry Butler** / Mercury
The Byrds / **Byrds' Greatest Hits** / Columbia
The Byrds / **Mr. Tambourine Man** / Columbia
The Byrds / **Sweetheart of the Rodeo** / Columbia
The Byrds / **Turn! Turn! Turn!** / Columbia
The Byrds / **Younger Than Yesterday** / Columbia
John Cage / **Indeterminacy** / Folkways
The Carter Family / **Happiest Days of All** / Camden
The Carter Family / **Lonesome Pine Special** / Camden
The Carter Family / **More Golden Gems from the Original Carter Family** / Camden

The Carter Family / **The Original and Great Carter Family** / Camden

Johnny Cash / **Johnny Cash at Folsom Prison** / Columbia

Johnny Cash / **Johnny Cash: The Legend** / Sun

Ray Charles / **Ray Charles Live** / Atlantic

Ray Charles / **The Greatest Ray Charles** / Atlantic

Cheap Trick / **Live at Budokan** / Epic

Clifton Chenier / **Bogalusa Boogie** / Arhoolie

Chicago Blues Anthology / Chess

The Chi-Lites / **Give More Power to the People** / Brunswick

Joe Cocker / **Joe Cocker!** / A&M

Judy Collins / **Who Knows Where the Time Goes** / Elektra

Ry Cooder / **Paradise and Lunch** / Reprise

Sam Cooke / **The Best of Sam Cooke** / RCA

Sam Cooke / **The Gospel Soul of Sam Cooke** / Specialty

Alice Cooper / **Alice Cooper's Greatest Hits** / Warner Bros.

Creedence Clearwater Revival / **Chronicle** / Fantasy

Creedence Clearwater Revival / **Green River** / Fantasy

Creedence Clearwater Revival / **Willy and the Poor Boys** / Fantasy

Derek and the Dominos / **Layla** / RSO

Bo Diddley / **Got My Own Bag of Tricks** / Chess

Dion / **Everything You Always Wanted to Hear by Dion and the Belmonts** / Laurie

Dr. John / **Gris-Gris** / Atco

Dr. John / **Gumbo** / Atco

Fats Domino / **Fats Domino** / United Artists

The Doors / **L.A. Woman** / Elektra

The Doors / **Strange Days** / Elektra

The Doors / **The Doors** / Elektra

The Doors / **13** / Elektra

Dyke and the Blazers / **Dyke's Greatest Hits** / Original Sound

Bob Dylan / **Blonde on Blonde** / Columbia

Bob Dylan / **Bob Dylan** / Columbia

Bob Dylan / **Bob Dylan's Greatest Hits, Vol. 2** / Columbia

Bob Dylan / **Bringing It All Back Home** / Columbia

Bob Dylan / **Highway 61 Revisited** / Columbia

Bob Dylan / **John Wesley Harding** / Columbia

Bob Dylan / **The Basement Tapes** / Columbia

Bob Dylan / **The Freewheelin' Bob Dylan** / Columbia

Earth, Wind and Fire / **Gratitude** / Columbia

Echoes of a Rock Era: The Early Years / Roulette

Echoes of a Rock Era: The Middle Years / Roulette

Dave Edmunds / **Dave Edmunds and Love Sculpture—The Classic Tracks—1968/1972** / One Up/EMI (Import)

Eighteen King Size Country Hits / Columbia

Brian Eno / **Another Green World** / Island

The Everly Brothers / **The Everly Brothers' Greatest Hits** / Barnaby

John Fahey / **Best of John Fahey (1959-1977)** / Takoma

John Fahey / **Blind Joe Death** / Takoma

Fairport Convention / **Fairport Convention** / A&M

Fairport Convention / **Unhalfbricking** / A&M

Firesign Theatre / **Don't Crush That Dwarf, Hand Me the Pliers** / Columbia

Firesign Theatre / **Everything You Know Is Wrong** / Columbia

Firesign Theatre / **Forward into the Past** / Columbia

Firesign Theatre / **How Can You Be in Two Places at Once When You're Not Anywhere at All?** / Columbia

The Four Tops / **Anthology** / Motown

Aretha Franklin / **Amazing Grace** / Atlantic

Aretha Franklin / **Aretha's Gold** / Atlantic

Aretha Franklin / **Aretha's Greatest Hits** / Atlantic

Aretha Franklin / **I Never Loved a Man (The Way I Love You)** / Atlantic

Aretha Franklin / **Young, Gifted and Black** / Atlantic

Alan Freed's Memory Lane / Roulette

From Spirituals to Swing / Vanguard

Marvin Gaye / **Anthology** / Motown

Marvin Gaye / **Let's Get It On** / Tamla

Marvin Gaye / **What's Going On** / Tamla

Mickey Gilley / **Mickey Gilley's Greatest Hits, Vol. 1** / Playboy

The Gospel Sound, Vol. 1 / Columbia

The Gospel Sound, Vol. 2 / Columbia

Great Bluesmen / Vanguard

Great Golden Gospel Hits, Vol. 1 / Savoy

Great Golden Gospel Hits, Vol. 2 / Savoy

Great Golden Gospel Hits, Vol. 3 / Savoy

Al Green / **Call Me** / Hi (Cream)

Al Green / **Let's Stay Together** / Hi (Cream)

Al Green / **Greatest Hits** / Hi (Cream)

Guess Who / **Best of the Guess Who** / RCA

Arlo Guthrie / **Amigo** / Reprise

Woody Guthrie / **A Legendary Performer** / RCA

Woody Guthrie / **Dust Bowl Ballads** / Folkways

Woody Guthrie / **This Land Is Your Land** / Folkways

Woody Guthrie / **Woody Guthrie: Library of Congress Recordings** / Elektra

Merle Haggard / **Songs I'll Always Sing** / Capitol

Merle Haggard / **The Best of the Best of Merle Haggard** / Capitol

Tom T. Hall / **Tom T. Hall's Greatest Hits** / Mercury

George Harrison / **All Things Must Pass** / Apple

Jimi Hendrix / **Are You Experienced?** / Reprise

Jimi Hendrix / **Axis: Bold as Love** / Reprise

Jimi Hendrix and Otis Redding / **Jimi Hendrix and Otis Redding Live at the Monterey International Pop Festival** / Reprise

The Hollies / **Greatest Hits** / Epic

Buddy Holly / **Buddy Holly** / MCA (Import)

Buddy Holly / **Buddy Holly—Legend** / MCA (Import)

Buddy Holly / **The "Chirping" Crickets** / MCA (Import)

The Impressions / **Impressions 16 Greatest Hits** / ABC

The Impressions / **Vintage Years—The Impressions featuring Jerry Butler and Curtis Mayfield** / Sire

The Jackson 5 / **Anthology** / Motown

The Jackson 5 / **Greatest Hits** / Motown

Etta James / **Peaches** / Chess

The Jefferson Airplane / **Volunteers** / RCA

The Jefferson Starship / **Red Octopus** / Grunt

Jethro Tull / **Living in the Past** / Chrysalis

Elton John / **Greatest Hits** / MCA

George Jones / **Double Gold George Jones** / Musicor

George Jones / **The Battle** / Epic

Spike Jones / **Spike Jones Is Murdering the Classics** / RCA

Louis Jordan / **Louis Jordan's Greatest Hits** / MCA

Louis Jordan / **The Best of Louis Jordan** / MCA

Carole King / **Tapestry** / Ode

The Kinks / **Greatest Hits!** / Reprise

The Kinks / **Lola Versus Powerman and the Moneygoround** / Reprise

The Kinks / **Something Else** / Reprise

The Kinks / **The Kinks Are the Village Green Preservation Society** / Reprise

Kool and the Gang / **Kool and the Gang Spin Their Top Hits** / De-Lite

Leo Kottke / **Greenhouse** / Capitol

Leo Kottke / **My Feet Are Smiling** / Capitol

Leadbelly / **Leadbelly's Last Sessions, Vol. 1** / Folkways

Leadbelly / **Leadbelly's Last Sessions, Vol. 2** / Folkways

Led Zeppelin / **Untitled** / Atlantic

John Lennon / **John Lennon/Plastic Ono Band** / Apple

Jerry Lee Lewis / **Best of Jerry Lee Lewis** / Smash

Jerry Lee Lewis / **Jerry Lee Lewis' Original Golden Hits, Vol. 1** / Sun

Jerry Lee Lewis / **Jerry Lee Lewis' Original Golden Hits, Vol. 2** / Sun

Jerry Lee Lewis / **Jerry Lee Lewis' Original Golden Hits, Vol. 3** / Sun

Jerry Lee Lewis / **Monsters** / Sun

Little Richard / **Little Richard's Grooviest 17 Original Hits** / Specialty

Little Richard / **The Fabulous Little Richard** / Specialty

Little Richard / **Well Alright!** / Specialty

Love / **Forever Changes** / Elektra

The Lovin' Spoonful / **Best of the Lovin' Spoonful** / Kama Sutra

Loretta Lynn / **Loretta Lynn's Greatest Hits** / MCA

Martha and the Vandellas / **Anthology** / Motown

Marvelettes / **Anthology** / Motown

John Mayall / **Bluesbreakers** / London LC-50009

John Mayall / **Bluesbreakers** / London PS-492

Paul McCartney and Wings / **Band on the Run** / Apple

Harold Melvin and the Blue Notes / **To Be True** / Philadelphia International

The Meters / **Rejuvenation** / Reprise

Joni Mitchell / **Blue** / Reprise

Joni Mitchell / **Court and Spark** / Asylum

Moby Grape / **Moby Grape** / Columbia

Bill Monroe / **Bean Blossom** / MCA

Van Morrison / **Astral Weeks** / Warner Bros.

Van Morrison / **Moondance** / Warner Bros.

The Mothers of Invention/Frank Zappa / **We're Only in It for the Money** / Verve

The Mothers of Invention/Frank Zappa / **Uncle Meat** / Bizarre

Motown Story / Motown

Mott the Hoople / **Mott** / Columbia

The Move / **The Best of the Move** / A&M

Ricky Nelson / **Legendary Master Series** / United Artists

Willie Nelson / **Red Headed Stranger** /
Columbia
Randy Newman / **Sail Away** / Reprise
Randy Newman / **Twelve Songs** / Reprise
Thunderclap Newman / **Hollywood
Dream** / MCA
New Orleans Jazz and Heritage Festival /
Island
Nuggets / Sire
The O'Jays / **Back Stabbers** / Philadelphia
International
Roy Orbison / **All-Time Greatest Hits** /
Monument
Graham Parker / **Heat Treatment** / Mer-
cury
Graham Parker / **Howlin' Wind** / Mercury
Dolly Parton / **The Best of Dolly Parton** /
RCA APL1-1117
Dolly Parton / **The Best of Dolly Parton** /
RCA LSP-4449
Carl Perkins / **Blue Suede Shoes** / Sun
The Persuasions / **Chirpin'** / Elektra
Wilson Pickett / **The Best of Wilson Pick-
ett** / Atlantic
Wilson Pickett / **Wilson Pickett's Greatest
Hits** / Atlantic
Pink Floyd / **Dark Side of the Moon** /
Harvest
Poco / **Pickin' Up the Pieces** / Epic
Elvis Presley / **A Date with Elvis** / RCA
Elvis Presley / **C'mon Everybody** / Camden
Elvis Presley / **Elvis** / RCA AFL1-2011
Elvis Presley / **Elvis** / RCA AFM1-4088
Elvis Presley / **Elvis' Golden Records,
Vol. 1** / RCA
Elvis Presley / **Elvis' Golden Records,
Vol. 2** / RCA
Elvis Presley / **Elvis' Golden Records,
Vol. 3** / RCA
Elvis Presley / **Elvis' Golden Records,
Vol. 4** / RCA
Elvis Presley / **Elvis Presley** / RCA
Elvis Presley / **For LP Fans Only** / RCA
Elvis Presley / **From Elvis in Memphis** /
RCA
Elvis Presley / **He Touched Me** / RCA
Elvis Presley / **His Hand in Mine** / RCA
Elvis Presley / **How Great Thou Art** /
RCA
Elvis Presley / **Sun Sessions** / RCA
Elvis Presley / **That's the Way It Is** / RCA
Elvis Presley / **World Wide Fifty Gold
Award Hits, Vol. 1** / RCA
Procol Harum / **A Salty Dog** / A&M
Procol Harum / **A Whiter Shade of Pale** /
A&M
The Rascals / **The Rascals' Greatest Hits/
Time-Peace** / Atlantic
Otis Redding / **History of Otis Redding** /
Atco

Otis Redding / **Otis Redding Live in Eu-
rope** / Atco
Otis Redding / **The Best of Otis Redding** /
Atco
Otis Redding / **The Immortal Otis Red-
ding** / Atco
Lou Reed / **Rock 'n' Roll Animal** / RCA
Lou Reed / **Street Hassle** / Arista
Charlie Rich / **The Fabulous Charlie
Rich** / Epic
The Righteous Brothers / **The Righteous
Brothers' Greatest Hits, Vol. 1** / Verve
Smokey Robinson and the Miracles / **An-
thology** / Motown
Smokey Robinson and the Miracles /
Greatest Hits, Vol. 2 / Tamla
Jimmie Rodgers / **Best of the Legendary
Jimmie Rodgers** / RCA
Jimmie Rodgers / **Country Music Hall of
Fame: Jimmie Rodgers** / RCA
The Rolling Stones / **Aftermath** / London
The Rolling Stones / **Around and Around** /
Decca (Import)
The Rolling Stones / **Beggar's Banquet** /
London
The Rolling Stones / **Big Hits (High Tide
and Green Grass)** / London
The Rolling Stones / **More Hot Rocks
(Big Hits and Fazed Cookies)** / London
The Rolling Stones / **The Rolling Stones,
Now!** / London
Linda Ronstadt / **Heart Like a Wheel** /
Capitol
The Roots of Rock and Roll / Savoy
Roxy Music / **Siren** / Atco
Rufus / **Rufusized** / ABC
Todd Rundgren / **Something/Anything** /
Bearsville
Tom Rush / **The Circle Game** / Elektra
Doug Sahm / **Together After Five** / Smash
Sam and Dave / **The Best of Sam and
Dave** / Atlantic
Saturday Night Fever (Soundtrack) / RSO
Bob Seger / **Night Moves** / Capitol
The Shirelles / **The Shirelles Sing Their
Very Best** / Springboard
Simon and Garfunkel / **Simon and Gar-
funkel's Greatest Hits** / Columbia
Paul Simon / **Paul Simon** / Columbia
Paul Simon / **Still Crazy After All These
Years** / Columbia
Paul Simon / **There Goes Rhymin' Simon** /
Columbia
Frank Sinatra / **September of My Years** /
Reprise
Frank Sinatra / **What Is This Thing Called
Love?** / Capitol
Sly and the Family Stone / **Greatest Hits** /
Epic
Sly and the Family Stone / **Stand!** / Epic

Sly and the Family Stone / **There's a Riot Goin' On** / Epic

Soft Machine / **Third** / Columbia

Phil Spector / **Phil Spector's Christmas LP** / Spector

Phil Spector / **Phil Spector's Greatest Hits** / Spector

Spinners / **Pick of the Litter** / Atlantic

Spinners / **Spinners** / Atlantic

Bruce Springsteen / **Born to Run** / Columbia

Bruce Springsteen / **Darkness on the Edge of Town** / Columbia

Ringo Starr / **Ringo** / Capitol

Rod Stewart / **Every Picture Tells a Story** / Mercury

Story of the Blues / Columbia

Barbra Streisand / **Barbra Streisand's Greatest Hits** / Columbia

The Supremes / **Anthology: Diana Ross and the Supremes** / Motown

Billy Swan / **Billy Swan** / Columbia

James Taylor / **Sweet Baby James** / Warner Bros.

The Harder They Come (Soundtrack) / Island

Toots and the Maytals / **Funky Kingston** / Island

Peter Townshend / **Rough Mix** / MCA

Traffic / **Traffic** / United Artists

Merle Travis / **The Best of Merle Travis** / Capitol

Ike and Tina Turner / **River Deep—Mountain High** / A&M

The Velvet Underground / **Loaded** / Cotillion

The Velvet Underground / **1969 Velvet Underground Live** / Mercury

The Velvet Underground / **The Velvet Underground and Nico** / Verve

Porter Wagoner / **The Best of Porter Wagoner** / RCA

Bob Marley and the Wailers / **Live** / Island

Junior Walker and the All Stars / **Anthology** / Motown

Dionne Warwick / **Dionne Warwick: More Greatest Hits** / Springboard

The Weavers / **The Weavers at Carnegie Hall** / Vanguard

The Who / **Meaty, Beaty, Big and Bouncy** / MCA

The Who / **The Who Sing My Generation** / MCA

The Who / **Who's Next** / MCA

Hank Williams Sr. / **24 Greatest Hits, Vol. 2** / MGM

Hank Williams Sr. / **24 of Hank Williams' Greatest Hits** / MGM

Bob Wills and His Texas Playboys / **Bob Wills Anthology** / Columbia

Stevie Wonder / **Innervisions** / Tamla

Stevie Wonder / **Looking Back** / Motown

Stevie Wonder / **Music of My Mind** / Tamla

Stevie Wonder / **Songs in the Key of Life** / Tamla

Stevie Wonder / **Talking Book** / Tamla

Tammy Wynette / **Tammy's Greatest Hits** / Epic

The Yardbirds / **The Yardbirds Great Hits** / Epic

The Yardbirds / **Yardbirds Favorites** / Epic

Yes / **Close to the Edge** / Atlantic

Yes / **The Yes Album** / Atlantic

Neil Young / **Decade** / Reprise

Neil Young / **Everybody Knows This Is Nowhere** / Reprise

Neil Young / **Tonight's the Night** / Reprise

Warren Zevon / **Warren Zevon** / Asylum

Glossary

A&R Man: A&R originally stood for artist and repertoire, and the A&R man's responsibilities, in the early rock era, involved matching performer and material. More recently, that role has devolved to the record producers—the first of whom were A&R men, anyway. In the contemporary record business, persons known as A&R men are now concerned almost exclusively with talent acquisition and the logistics of record release, only rarely playing any creative role.

A Cappella: Literally, voices singing without instrumental accompaniment. A common approach in gospel music, a capella R&B music enjoyed an East Coast vogue during 1964-66, partly as a reaction to the rise of the Beatles (whom most R&B fans didn't like) and partly because of the discovery of some practice tapes by the Nutmegs. The Nutmegs records, issued on the Times Square label by Slim Rose, sold only a few thousand copies, but inspired many of the kids who'd been harmonizing in subways and hallways throughout the urban Northeast ("looking for an echo," in the words of the Persuasions' song). Some a cappella was overpolished, but some of it was grand, with pure soaring voices. Today, the genre is the almost exclusive province of one group, the Persuasions.

Acid Rock: Music of the psychedelic era, often intended to mimic (or replicate) in some fashion the psychedelic drug experience. Examples of acid-rock performers include the early Grateful Dead and the early Pink Floyd. Applied to mid- to late-Seventies music, acid rock is almost always a sign of diminished faculties. All songs that refer to drugs are *not* acid rock; the term implies a specific sensibility of the late-Sixties period. No longer a particu-larly useful term (except in odd instances), for which one can be thankful or remorseful at whim.

Ad Lib: To improvise, especially vocally.

Arrangement: Setting out, usually but not always in writing, the particular manner of playing a given tune: i.e., as regards tempo, voicing of individual instruments, solos, etc. Unwritten arrangements are sometimes called "head arrangements" or "heads."

Art Rock: Rock is a pop music, and notions of art didn't enter the picture until the mid-Sixties (with the advent of Bob Dylan's lyrics and the more baroque works of the Beatles). Art rock generally refers, however, to late Sixties and Seventies forms based upon principles derived from European classical or avant-garde forms. The implication is of high seriousness, often bordering upon or lapsing into pomposity and pretentiousness. Examples of art-rock performers include Emerson, Lake and Palmer; King Crimson; Brian Eno and perhaps Roxy Music, among many others.

Art Song: Any ambitious pop song, but more usually such songs that appropriate stylistic elements or devices from European classical music. The kind of ambition is crucial: a folk- or rock-based songwriter (e.g., Jackson Browne) is less likely to find his work labeled "art song" than a pop-based one (e.g., Eric Carmen).

A Side: The hit (or most heavily promoted) side of a single.

Automatic Drum Machine: Mechanical percussion device, used in situations (like pure one-man solo work or disco) where a human drummer is unavailable or insufficiently precise. The automatic drum machine—the most popular brand was once made by the Putney Company, and Putney is another way of referring to the automatic drum machine—has one great advantage over human drummers: the tempo is never varied—set it and forget it. This is also its great disadvantage.

Axe: Musical instrument, most often applied to a guitar or horn.

B-3: The most common variety of electric organ used in rock. It is made by the Hammond Organ Company; Model B-3 is its official designation.

Ballad: Originally, an ancient song that told a story, with a long succession of verses and a repeated melody; later, any narrative song. But today, in pop music at least, most slow or midtempo love songs are called "ballads," and non-narrative singers from Frank Sinatra to Billy Joel are sometimes thought of as balladeers.

Baroque: Elaborate, heavily arranged. Borrowed from classical music, where the baroque period stretched from the mid-seventeenth to early-eighteenth century, and includes, among others, the works of J. S. Bach. Used to describe any overly ornate arrangement.

Barrelhouse: Rough and unruly blues piano playing, from the New Orleans brothels (barrelhouses) where it was supposedly first performed. Usually associated with a diving beat, so that any heated piano interlude may sometimes be referred to as "barrelhousing."

Beat: 1. Rhythm. 2. Fifties bohemians (as beatniks). 3. In English slang, the music of the northern groups who followed the Beatles out of Liverpool, etc. Our British Invasion is called, in Britain, the Beat Era.

Bent Notes: In guitar playing, notes shaped by literally bending a string, along the fret, creating a kind of quarter-tone effect. Bent notes are a common blues device.

Big Band: A large (fourteen to twenty pieces) jazz band of the swing era (from 1935 to 1950). Prominent Big Band leaders included Duke Ellington, Count Basie and Benny Goodman, among a host of others. The rise of R&B coincided with the fall

from grace of swing and the end of the Big Band Era.

Biz: Business—as, for instance, "show biz," "music biz."

Blowing Session: A jam session.

Bluebeat: West Indian pop idiom, the precursor to reggae. In America, only one bluebeat hit enjoyed substantial success, Millie Small's "My Boy Lollipop." But such reggae stars as Toots and the Maytals originally played bluebeat in the Sixties. *See also* Reggae.

Bluegrass: Traditional country music form, derived from "old-timey." Bluegrass (the name comes from the Kentucky/Virginia bluegrass region where many of the performers got their start) is string-band music in which the guitar is generally absent; the lead instrument is usually banjo, fiddle or sometimes mandolin. The best-known contemporary bluegrass performers are Bill Monroe, Lester Flatt and Earl Scruggs.

Blues: Almost every dictionary and reference work available defines blues as a slow, melancholy musical expression. This is in fact grossly inaccurate and misleading. Blues is a basic form of black American musical expression that originated in the South among rural blacks as a twelve-bar form derived from field hollers and perhaps latent Africanisms. But since the Twenties, when the blues reached urban America, it has become an enormously diverse form, ranging from the acoustic (and admittedly sometimes mournful) country blues of Mississippi John Hurt to the excitable Texas electric guitar and brass section blues of T-Bone Walker (primarily a Texas and Southwestern American expression) to the roaring, electrified Chicago style pioneered by Muddy Waters and Howlin' Wolf. Blues can be as sophisticated as Jimmy Rushing's singing with Count Basie, as earthy as Leadbelly or Blind Lemon Jefferson's work, as "pop" as Bobby "Blue" Bland or B. B. King's sessions with sophisticated uptown arrangements.

In the sense that blues is a matter of emotional content, blues themes are more closely linked with the resiliency and passion of black culture than its more somber, defeatist aspects. Rock & roll is inconceivable without blues as a part of its base, as is jazz. Neither is particularly melancholy—both draw much of their exuberance from blues. Emotionally and musically, blues is a wellspring of American music, arguably the first important native style.

Boogie: This term descended to rock from the jazz form "boogie-woogie," through such recordings as John Lee Hooker's "Boogie Chillen." Hooker's relaxed, insistent groove is seemingly the sourcepoint for the dozens of rock groups (so-called boogie bands) that play debased forms of blues and rhythm and blues.

As a verb, "to boogie" means a sedate swinging of the hips while standing in place, usually in front of a bandstand. Only white people boogie any more, and then only outdated Caucasians—everyone else is at the discothèque doing real dancing. In any event, thinking of what "boogie" has come to represent as a form of dancing is like thinking of a weekend pickup game in the park as the World Series.

Boogie-Woogie: In jazz, music (most often piano music) played eight to the bar, with left-hand bass supporting right-hand improvisation. The style was shaped in clubs and dance halls, emerging in 1928 with "Pine Top's Boogie-Woogie" by Pine Top Smith and enjoying a substantial national vogue in the late Thirties when Pete Johnson and Joe Turner brought it to New York City. Other notable boogie-woogie performers include pianists Meade Lux Lewis, Cripple Clarence Lofton and Albert Ammons. Boogie-woogie was transferred to guitar by Albert Smith with "'Guitar Boogie" after World War II and was even adapted to country music by the Delmore Brothers, among others. It was this incarnation of the form that was picked up by rock bands.

Bop: Originally be-bop. The style of jazz founded post–World War II by Charlie Parker and Dizzy Gillespie, among others. The form is characterized by triadal chords with the first and third notes played an octave below the second. In general, bop features soloing based around melodies (many taken from pop songs). It is generally performed by small groups, reflective of the club atmosphere in which it was born, and its period development as a reaction to the big swing bands of the Forties.

Bottleneck Guitar: *See* Slide Guitar.

Bottom: Bass response on a record.

Brass Pop: Pop songs centered around brass instruments (most often, trumpets). Pioneered by so-called jazz-rock groups like Chicago and Blood, Sweat and Tears, brass pop lacks the essential warmth of rock and R&B horn music, which balances the shrillness of trumpets with the mellower tones of saxophones. As a result, brass pop has never been a genre much admired among rock aficionados.

Break: A solo passage, or a move away from the dominant structure of a song. A vocal number might have an instrumental break that isn't truly a solo passage—for instance, a string break or horn break. Most often however, the break is a solo: guitar break, drum break, etc.

Bridge: 1. In songwriting, a passage (sometimes involving a key change) used to link together two parts of a tune, usually two verses. Phil Spector, Bruce Springsteen and Bob Seger have recently popularized the use of multiple bridges in pop songs. **2.** In guitars and some other string instruments, the piece of wood that holds the strings off the belly of the instrument and transmits their vibrations to the soundbox.

British Blues Revival: A phenomenon of the middle Sixties, when a variety of English performers began to explore the American form, some (John Mayall's Bluesbreakers, the early Fleetwood Mac) with almost slavish devotion, others extrapolating rock excesses to blues form (Cream the most prominent in this regard). In general, blues in this context meant twelve-bar country or Chicago blues, but how far afield the British interpretations ranged depended on the performer's imagination, drug-use pattern, good taste (or lack of it) and depth of knowledge of the Real Thing. While it wasn't always emotionally satisfying, the British Blues Revival did provide an opening for young white Americans to learn about blues, and some of the artists who emerged from British blues—most notably Eric Clapton—went on to achieve stylistic identity of their own.

British Invasion: The period, beginning in 1964 with the arrival of the Beatles, during which British rock dominated the charts. The era can be considered to have ended by about 1966, when there was a momentary lull in U.K. new arrivals in the States. Those few months produced, however, a carload lot of bands, including the Beatles, Rolling Stones, Who, Kinks, Manfred Mann, Animals, Yardbirds, Gerry and the Pacemakers, Freddy and the Dreamers, Herman's Hermits and even lesser lights. This is arguably the golden age of the Sixties, although even nostalgists would have to admit that the attendant hysteria and commerical trappings mark the British Invasion movement as a marketing phenomenon at least as much as a pop or rock renaissance.

B Side: The alternate, nonhit side of a single record. Also known as the flip side.

Bubblegum: Bubblegum (nasal vocal, heavy beat, moronic lyrics) was the commerical trend of 1968–69. Pioneered by the production team Kastenatz-Katz, and performed by such groups as 1910 Fruitgum Company and the Ohio Express, who never performed outside the studio and were in fact merely aggregations of studio musicians pulled together for specific record sessions. Geared as it was to the least common denominator of the pop market, Bubblegum earned the quick derision of the "progressive" rock faction, and soon anything insufficiently hip in manner or sound was likely to be tagged "bubblegum." It is this meaning that survives today, although the form is now recognized as a breeding ground for production talent and recording experimentation.

C&W: Abbreviation for country & western. *See* Country.

Cajun: Literally, Louisianans of French-Canadian descent. The term is a corruption of "Acadian"; French Canada was known as Acadia until the British conquest, when many French-Canadian settlers moved themselves to settle in Louisiana, which was a French colony until Jefferson bought it from Napoleon.

Cajuns have retained their cultural identity, and their version of rock & roll has many French—and some black—elements. (When performed by blacks, Cajun music is known as zydeco, an offshoot of the blues popularized recently by the accordionist Clifton Chenier.) Cajun music is sung in a French-American patois that's unintelligible to the uninitiated; its accents tend to be lilting and sonorous. Doug Kershaw is a Cajun, although he doesn't play Cajun music any more.

Charts: 1. Musical arrangements—string charts, horn charts, etc.—probably because they are written on staff paper, which resembles graph or chart paper. **2.** The trade paper or radio station listings of the current week's most popular or best-selling songs. Arranged numerically so that No. 1 is top of the charts, the ideal place to be.

Chicago Blues: Chicago blues is a direct outgrowth of delta blues. It was chiefly developed after World War II by musicians from the delta regions of Mississippi, Louisiana and Arkansas who came north for jobs during the war years. It is both an attempt to retain some sense of rural tradition and a response by people steeped in that tradition to their encounters with urban living. While Chicago blues kept some stylistic elements of delta blues, it discarded and deemphasized others. While the resulting form is less lyrical, it is more powerful, accenting heavy beat, incorporating drums and electric guitars and bass. The chief difference between Chicago and delta styles is that the former is band music, usually including guitar, bass, drums, harmonica and/or piano, and the latter is solo- or duo-oriented. Key Chicago bluesmen include Muddy Waters, Howlin' Wolf, both Sonny Boy Williamsons and Little Walter, among a host of others. The influence of Chicago blues on modern rock has been enormous, indicated by the fact that the current rock group lineup is derived from the basic Chicago setup.

Chops: Skill. From slang expression for lips ("busted right in the chops"), and thus a synonym for embouchure among hornmen. Essentially jazz usage, occasionally applied to rock, as a guitarist with "great chops."

Chromatic Scale: Intervals outside the standard, or diatonic, scale are incorporated in the chromatic one, which is ordered by semitones rather than full ones. Chromatic pieces are extensively modulated. There is also a much larger version of the common harmonica, called a chromatic harp, which permits playing these intervals.

Concept Album: Literally, any album unified by a theme, whether instrumental, compositional, narrative or lyric. Most often, the latter applies, though some of the most famous concept albums—especially the Beatles' *Sgt. Pepper's Lonely Hearts Club Band*—are linked by a concept that is exclusively musical. Pete Townshend's extended narrative works *Tommy* and *Quadrophenia,* the so-called rock operas, are certainly concept albums, but no more so than *The Who Sell Out,* in which the songs are not narratively tied together but the tracks are unified by inserting radio commercial parodies between them. And, at least arguably, *The Who by Numbers* is a concept album, linked together by Townshend's continual brooding on the plight of the aging rockers. This does not mean that an album of love songs is necessarily a concept album, however; some overriding and self-conscious attempt to link such songs together is usually implied. It is fair to say, however, that most "classic" rock albums since *Sgt. Pepper* are unified in some such fashion and that the LP-as-art-form is inevitably conceptual.

Cool: Jazz idiom devised on West Coast in Fifties, notable for a much softer approach than the dominant jazz of the time, bop. Cool was developed principally by white, college-educated musicians, and never was very "cool" (in the slang sense) among jazz insiders on the East Coast. The great exception, though, was Miles Davis, who made some exquisite recordings in the style in the early Fifties.

Country: More specifically, country & western, but generally abbreviated to just the former. Country is the music of rural Southern and Southwestern America, arguably founded by the late-Twenties recordings of the Carter Family and Jimmie Rodgers. It bears some relationship to blues—the repertoire shares common folk antecedents, and certain musical elements are common to both—but country tends to be a music of resignation (particularly social resignation) rather than the release that is the staple of blues. In the last twenty years, country has become an appendage of pop and has lost much of its stylistic identity in the process of homogenization.

Country Rock: Hybrid of rock beat and country accents. Rockabilly—the style of rock & roll Elvis Presley sang—had specific country elements, but country rock was really founded as a hybrid genre in the late Sixties by such albums as the Byrds' *Sweetheart of the Rodeo.* Sometimes the reference is as much to visual style—long hair

and so forth—as to sound: the background of the performers also plays a part. The Flying Burrito Brothers, in Gram Parsons' tenure with them, played almost straight country music, but the hirsute band members, some of whom had rock bands in the shadows of their past, made it a country-rock group. Generally, as with most hypenated rock forms, country rock has not been terribly successful artistically; the Burritos and the later incarnations of the Byrds were probably the best at it, although by now nearly everyone from the Beatles and Rolling Stones to Elvis Costello and Bruce Springsteen has written or performed some country-rock material.

Cover Versions: A cover version is, broadly, any recording of a song by a performer other than the original *or* a version of a song performed by a singer other than the writer. Linda Ronstadt is a cover artist because she does not write her own material; her Buddy Holly interpretations are covers, regardless of whether Holly wrote the songs. More narrowly, a cover is a carbon copy of another's performance, a practice that was rampant in the Fifties, when white singers (Pat Boone, the Crew-Cuts, etc.) made exact imitations of R&B hits for the white market, thereby usurping sales and airplay of the originals. In the Fifties, this generally meant taking the overt sexuality out of song, though not all covers crossed racial or stylistic lines: Elvis Presley covered Carl Perkins' original of "Blue Suede Shoes," for instance, without emasculating it. The latter kind of cover is still a common practice in reggae and European pop; the last major cover version in America was Stories' cover of "Brother Louie," originally done by the biracial English group Hot Chocolate.

Cut: 1. To record (cut an album, cut a hit, etc.). **2.** An individual track on an LP (the opening cut, etc.). **3.** For one musician to show up another—in freeform jams, such rivalries often develop. They are called cutting sessions.

Cutout: *See* Deleted.

Date: A recording session (e.g., recording date).

Deleted: In record industry parlance, a disc which is no longer in a company's catalogue. Equivalent of the publishing industry's "remaindered." Generally, records that fail to sell at all or do not sell a certain minimum number of copies in a specific period (one year, say) are deleted, or cut out.

Delta Blues: Blues from the Mississippi River delta region, which stretches from just south of Memphis to northern Louisiana and takes in the principal cotton-growing areas of Mississippi and Arkansas. Many of the greatest bluesmen—Robert Johnson, Charley Patton, Muddy Waters, Howlin' Wolf, Son House, both Sonny Boy Williamsons—were of delta origin. In part, the notion of blues as a music of oppression comes from its association with this region, which is probably the most racist in America. However, delta blues has a wide emotional range, and in the hands of a master like Mississippi John Hurt, for instance, can move from liltingly lyrical dance tunes to bad-man ballads. All rural blues is not delta blues, although the greatest rural blues did emerge from the delta.

Demo: A tape or disc made for demonstration purposes, as when a songwriter makes a skeletal arrangement of his tune in hopes of attracting a singer to it. Sometimes, such a tape or record when made by a performer in hopes of obtaining a recording contract.

Detroit Sound: 1. In R&B and soul, Motown's sound, which fused adult black music with teenage concerns and became a dominant Sixties pop expression. **2.** In rock, the later hard rock of such groups as MC5, the Stooges, Grand Funk Railroad and Ted Nugent. The hard rock of Detroit played a major role in shaping both punk and heavy metal, with its heavy emphasis on industralized beat and walls of electronic sound.

Disco: An abbreviation of the word discothèque. The term refers either to a dance hall (discos enjoyed a brief pre-Beatles Sixties vogue, when the Twist was the rage), or in the Seventies, to records designed to be played in discothèques. A dominant pop form in the late Seventies.

Dixieland: Name given to the New Orleans jazz style of pre-World War I vintage, but applies only to its later embellishments and (mostly) corruptions, not to real "hot jazz" itself.

Dobro: Basically, a guitar with raised strings that came into popular use in country and folk music after 1930. Dobros also have a special resonator cone, and the combination of the resonator and raised strings gives it something of the sound of a Hawaiian guitar. The word comes from the name of the people who developed it, the Dopera brothers. Its inventor, John Dopera, was a Czechoslovakian-American; *dobro* means "good" in the Czech language. Used in both folk rock and country rock for special effects.

Doo-Wop: Term applied to a style of black R&B vocal groups in the Fifties, who often based their harmonies around simple, repeated phrases like "doo-wop." The term does not properly apply to any nonsense-syllable singing, but only to the kind of ornately arranged vocal choruses popularized by the so-called street-corner groups, who worked out their moody sounds on the street corners of New York, Philadelphia, etc. Classic doo-wop singles include "Gee" by the Crows, "Sh-Boom" by the Chords and the Penguins' "Earth Angel."

Double: A performer who plays more than one instrument in a group is said to double. Thus a trumpet player might double on clarinet, and so forth.

Double-Track: To record, usually in synch, the same part more than once (on two tracks of the tape). Thus double-tracked voice, double-tracked guitar. A common studio device.

Downbeat: First beat of a measure. Also the preeminent American jazz magazine since the Forties.

Dub: 1. To record additional instruments (or voices) on a previously taped song. This is known as overdubbing, and is done at a different time than, and sometimes in a different place from, the recording of the so-called basic track. Most rock songs are pieced together in this fashion, although the recent trend is to avoid overdubs where possible. **2.** A test pressing of a record. **3.** In reggae, instrumental backing tracks over which vocalists known as DJs chant their own improvised, stream-of-consciousness palaver.

Dulcimer: A dulcimer is properly a European stringed instrument in which the strings are struck with hammers. In American folk and country (rarely in rock), the name is given to an instrument with three or four (sometimes up to six) strings, which are plucked, and a long, hollow fret block extending the length of the instrument, which serves as part of the sound box. This is the Appalachian or mountain dulcimer, which is of Scandinavian or American hill origin, depending on which expert you consult. It is used in rock, if at all, almost only in folk rock; properly it is termed a zither.

Echo: Adding distancing reverberation to a sound, especially a recording. In the studio, this is usually done through the use of an echo chamber, which may be a room or a mechanical device. Echo is an important feature of many kinds of rock, particularly rockabilly and the Phil Spector Wall of Sound approach.

Echoplex: Foot-pedal device for guitars, which adds echo through the amplifier.

Electronic Music: Not merely music played by electric instruments, but avant-garde music in which composers work with sounds artifically produced (through synthesizers, tone generators, etc.). Rock has incorporated many electronic innovations, and a few groups that are ostensibly rock bands (because of their audience) might more properly be thought of as electronic ensembles. This is especially true of German acts such as Kraftwerk and Tangerine Dream.

Engineer: The person responsible for running the tape machines in a recording studio, and for making certain that the instruments are properly miked and (when more than one is played simultaneously) balanced.

English Invasion: *See* British Invasion.

English Music Hall: An English institution that more or less parallels American vaudeville, although it has more ancient origins and lasted a bit longer. Like vaudeville, music hall had a variety format, but its values have in some sense descended to certain modern rockers, especially the Kinks' Ray Davies, whose *Village Green Preservation Society* is the kind of quaint look at England that music hall favored. More than anything, however, it is the sense of humor in English rock that is derived from the music-hall tradition.

EP: Extended play record, usually a disc seven inches in diameter that plays at 33 rather than 45. EPs have not been a common recording form in this country since the Sixties, but in Europe they are still often issued.

Fender: Electric guitar developed by Leo Fender (founder of the Fender Musical Instrument Company) which comes in two basic models, the Telecaster and the Stratocaster. Also, the electric bass Fender developed. All three are widely popular among rock musicians.

Festivals: Day-long (sometimes multi-day) outdoor rock concerts. Woodstock was a rock festival, as was Altamont. Popularized in the Sixties, festivals always feature some stars abetted by a variety of supporting acts. For logistical and security reasons, festivals have grown increasingly rare as the Seventies have waned, and the term is also used loosely to describe single-day outdoor stadium events of any kind.

Fiddle: In folk or country music, a violin. In pop, "violin" if used in an orchestral-style arrangement, "fiddle" in more rustic contexts.

Figure: Any short musical phrase, usually one that is repeated and recognizable.

Fill: Brief instrumental figures inserted between lines or verses (guitar fill, piano fill, etc.).

Finger-Pick: To play guitar using the fingers, rather than any object, to pluck the strings.

Flat Pick: 1. The typical flat, triangular pick used to pluck the strings of a guitar. Most rock is played using such picks. 2. Playing guitar using a flat pick.

Flip Side: *See* B Side.

Folk Music, Folk Song: Essentially, music that is part of oral rather than written musical tradition (though since the eighteenth century most Anglo-American folk tunes, in most or all of their variations, have been collected by musicologists and transcribed). Because they are transmitted orally, folk songs generally exist in a variety of versions; generally they are developed in a musically "primitive"—or musically preliterate—society, and it is essential that the songs have enjoyed, at some time, wide popularity, though all pop songs aren't folk songs.

Folk songs in America, however, have also come to include the often topical compositions of certain rustic performers, such as Woody Guthrie or Leadbelly, even when of recent vintage and written origin. Bob Dylan was at first considered a folksinger, and it is common to refer to anyone who seems to follow in the tradition of such performers as a folkie.

Folk Revival: The folk revival began around 1958; it was centered, oddly enough, around college campuses and large cities, the places least likely to produce authentic folk music. The movement was at least as much social and political—with intimate connections to the antiwar and civil rights movements—as it was musical, and reflected not only the growing leftism that boomed in the Sixties but also some of the "back to nature" philosophy that would characterize the next decade's thinking.

The Kingston Trio kicked the revival off in '58 with their hit "Tom Dooley," a traditional gallows ballad. For the next several years, until Bob Dylan splintered the movement by going electric, there was a widespread upheaval of interest in old songs and forgotten performers. Although such pop performers as Harry Belafonte, the Kingston Trio and the Limeliters, among others, prospered, the folk revivalists were also responsible for unearthing a remarkable number of legendary and obscure bluesmen, country singers and the like. Among those who found themselves with rejuvenated careers thanks to the folk revival were Muddy Waters, Mississippi John Hurt and a score of other bluesmen, Elizabeth Cotten, Mother Maybelle Carter, Dock Boggs, and Roscoe Holcomb. The folk revival also developed writers and interpreters of its own, including (besides Dylan) Pete Seeger, Joan Baez, Judy Collins, Dave Van Ronk, Ramblin' Jack Elliott and the New Lost City Ramblers. While a kind of arch-conservatism prevailed—electric instruments were out, ruled inauthentic by the folk tastemakers— such elitism cannot deny the important steps the folk revival took toward the Sixties folk-rock explosion.

Folk Rock: Originally, rock derived from folk sources, though this meant rock that reflected the bohemian leftism of the folk

revival from the beginning, and that always included original songs much more than those in the traditional repertoire. (The Byrds' "Turn! Turn! Turn!"—based on Ecclesiastes, with a melody by Pete Seeger— is almost the only folk song that became a major folk-rock hit.) The first folk-rock hits came about in 1965, when Bob Dylan released his first electric album, *Bringing It All Back Home*; the Byrds quickly scored a hit single with "Mr. Tambourine Man," a song from Dylan's disc, and the boom was on. Other prominent folk-rock performers included the Lovin' Spoonful, Buffalo Springfield, the original (pre-Grace Slick) Jefferson Airplane, the Turtles and Barry McGuire.

Folk rock was the first genre to give rock lyrical respectability (not to say intelligence, which had been creeping in for years). The songs themselves rarely used folk devices beyond an occasional banjo lick or cribbed melody. Often the songs were topical or "protest" oriented, which means that even something as meretricious as McGuire's "Eve of Destruction" fits the fad. Today, folk rock survives principally as an influence on the singer/songwriters of the Seventies and as an indirect ancestor of country rock.

45: A 45 record, usually seven inches in diameter and with only one song on each side. *See* Single.

Free Jazz: The modal, superficially unstructured modern jazz that succeeded bop, beginning in the late Fifties with such albums as Ornette Coleman's *Free Jazz*. Free jazz pays much less attention to conventional song structure than does any other native American music.

Fret: The fixed pieces of wood or metal on the neck of a guitar or other stringed instrument. The player presses down at the frets to shorten the length of the string and raise the pitch. Fretted instruments do not include violins, although they do include the banjo, lute, mandolin and viola.

Front Man: Usually, the singer (who stands in front of the band onstage), but sometimes the leader or visual centerpiece of the group, regardless of musical role. Front men are said to front a group or band.

Funk: Originally, as the adverb "funky," descriptive of low-life sights, sounds and smells. Later, the pejorative connotation was lost, and *funky* became a (mostly black) synonym for "authentic." Rock has adopted the latter meaning. *Funk* also connotes music that is played soulfully, with mellow, syncopated rhythm arrangements, or more recently, any black percussion-based instrumental music of sufficient complexity.

Fusion: *See* Jazz Rock.

Gibson: Guitar maker famous for its two electric models, the SG and the Les Paul, the latter developed by the musician it is named for. Early Les Paul models, from the Fifties, are now treasured collector's items, especially by blues musicians, for their deep resonance and wonderful tone.

Gig: A job, specifically a job in a band or at a particular club, concert hall or other venue.

Girl Groups: Though the term now seems somewhat sexist, "girl groups" is actually the most fitting way to describe the attitude and approach of the female vocal groups of the Sixties, whose lingering charm is based precisely upon their encapsulation of purely adolescent fantasies. The first girl-group hit was "Will You Love Me Tomorrow" by the Shirelles (1960), which set the pattern for the teasing moralism that then extended to a variety of other acts (Shangri-Las, Crystals, Ronettes, Angels, Dixie Cups), almost all of them individually faceless and collectively irresistible. Phil Spector was probably the greatest creator of girl-group hits, and his airy yet foreboding Wall of Sound is characteristic of the musical and moral tensions of the genre. One of the most charmingly innocent rock & roll styles.

Gospel: For the purposes of this volume, black American religious music, descended from the spiritual but transferred (as was blues) to an urban context. Mostly, gospel music arose from the upsurge of fundamentalist sanctified churchgoing in such black communities, even in the pre-Depression years, although the genre came to full flower a bit later. Gospel includes a wide variety of musical styles, notably the spiritual blues of Blind Willie Johnson and Reverend Gary Davis, the call-and-response techniques of many of the groups of the late Forties and Fifties and the more

rugged male and female harmonies of the post–World War II groups. As R&B evolved into soul, its gospel roots became ever more prominent, and most of the best-known black singers of that decade had spent at least some time in gospel groups before turning to secular material. (Sam Cooke and Aretha Franklin, among others, were full-fledged gospel stars before crossing over.)

Grease: Lowdown, down to earth, relating to street life or sounds as an insider. Reflective both of the roots of R&B in rib joints, etc., that served greasy foods, and of rock's original creators, who were presumed to have greasy hair or fingernails (depending on whether they doubled as mechanics).

Groove: 1. The channel a record player stylus travels in decoding the sound from vinyl. **2.** More importantly, capturing and keeping a strong sense of rhythmic flow—particularly important in black-oriented music, especially soul and R&B. These days, one might warn, only squares use "groove" as a verb.

Gutbucket: The sort of R&B that might have been played in a cheap saloon; gutbuckets were the kind of dives (featuring both gambling and liquor) in which such music got its start, the musicians playing for contributions from the customers.

Hard Rock: Rock played with driving, forceful rhythm. The phrase came into use only after soft rock, such as singer/songwriter music, came into vogue in the late Sixties/early Seventies. Now generally regarded as encompassing most blues-based rock and such offshoots as heavy metal and punk.

Harmonium: Small portable organ (usually electrified in rock). Originally used to accompany hymns; now extensively used in folk rock.

Harp: Harmonica (from mouth harp). Also various combined forms: blues harp, for instance.

Hawaiian Guitar: Steel guitar. Tuned differently from a standard (or Spanish) guitar, and played with a metal bar ("steel"), which by sliding along the strings allows for playing the variable intervals characteristic of the instrument.

Heavy Metal: Heavily, sluggishly rhythmic rock of the late Sixties and early Seventies that relied heavily on technology and very little on technique. The classic heavy metal bands were Grand Funk Railroad, Blue Oyster Cult, Black Sabbath and, oddly, the early Led Zeppelin. All distorted the blues through heavy amplification, screaming vocals and rhythms of absolutely no subtlety. Presumed to appeal primarily—almost exclusively—to working-class young men, and heavily associated with downer (barbituates, etc.) use. The term was coined by critic Lester Bangs from certain passages in Burroughs' *Naked Lunch*.

Hit: Commercially successful record.

Honky-Tonk: A cheap saloon or roadhouse, usually featuring gambling, drinking and dancing, common in the South. Specifically, the music—usually country & western—played in such joints. Great honky-tonk singers include George Jones and Lefty Frizzell.

Hook: The part of a song that grabs the listener's ear. In the record industry, it is the highest sort of accolade to say that a composer's songs have "hooks," which indicate their commercial potential.

Hootenanny: A concert, often informal, of folk songs—the campus folk craze of the early Sixties was built around such events.

Improvise: To perform spontaneously; to play music without any written arrangement. This may mean creating a tune ad hoc or (especially in jazz) extemporizing upon the melody line or chord changes of a given tune.

Instrumental: Music without the human voice—that is, played exclusively by instruments. In rock and pop, these divide neatly into dance and mood pieces. Bill Doggett's 1957 "Honky Tonk" was one of the first rock instrumentals, and while there has never been a craze for nonvocal rock, the success of Johnny and the Hurricanes, Sandy Nelson, Duane Eddy, the Ventures and others through the Sixties indicates the continuing vitality of the concept. Far fewer pure instrumentals have been recorded in the Seventies rock field, although many performers use voice as a kind of dehumanized horn (particularly European avant-gardists like Kraftwerk and Brian Eno).

Jacket: The cover of a record album.

Jam or Jam Session: Informal, improvised performances. Jazz phrase adopted, in the Sixties, by rockers.

Jazz: Term used throughout this century to describe black American music built around improvisation; sometimes also applied to related forms of dance music. Originally characterized by syncopation and strongly reiterated rhythm, but no longer formally limited—some jazz is modal in conception, some electronic, some traditional, with the result that some of the less traditional players now reject the term.

Jazz Rock: Although rock developed (partially) from rhythm & blues, which had been derived (partially) from jazz, this process had reversed itself by the mid-Sixties, when jazz performers began to become interested in the innovations of rock and soul music. Such performers as Gary Burton and Miles Davis began to utilize rock-style instrumentation—electrified guitars and keyboards, for example—while many young British horn players, who had apprenticed in rock groups, began to turn back toward their first love, jazz. The result was an improvisatory electrified form—now often called "fusion"—that uses little of rock's thematic or emotional structure but a great deal of its technology.

Jazz rock is also used to describe the brass-oriented pop bands, such as Blood, Sweat and Tears and Chicago, who first made their appearance in the late Sixties. But this sort of music finally lacks both emotional conviction and any sense of instrumental challenge, which means that it qualifies as neither jazz nor rock.

Jig: Irish folk dance tune, usually performed in 6/8 time.

Jug Band: A group, usually playing folk-style material, featuring a jug as one of the instruments. (The jug, empty, is played by blowing air over its mouth.) Developed by blacks in the rural South during the ragtime era, the jug was just a novelty—the central instruments were actually banjo, guitar, kazoo, harmonica and sometimes washboard or mandolin. Notable jug bands have included Gus Cannon and the Jug Stompers, and in the Sixties folk revival, the Jim Kweskin Jug Band.

Juke Joint: *See* Juking.

Juking: Southern slang for cruising road-houses in search of liquor and women (as, for example, in Lynyrd Skynyrd's "Down South Juking"). The original connotation of the word "juke" is sexual—the act itself or a sleazy brothel where sex was a sweaty commodity; the word was then transferred to the sort of R&B associated with such joints.

Jump Blues: Swing blues played with a fast, heavily accented rhythm, often by combos smaller than the popular swing orchestras of the Forties. Important transitional step in the rise of R&B.

Junkanoo: New Orleans rhythm & blues horn sound.

Keyboard: Instruments played by pushing down keys (e.g., piano, organ, etc.). The keyboard player in rock is also generally the musician who plays such exotica as synthesizers, Mellotrons and the like.

Lament: Any grief-struck song, but especially one that grieves over death. Also, the bagpipe pieces played at clan funerals in Scotland, though none of these are included here.

L.A. Sound: Until the mid-Sixties, Los Angeles did not have a specific recording style, as music centers like Nashville, Detroit or Memphis did. Although a great many early rock and R&B hits were released by the city's dozens of record labels, taken together they did not conform to a regional identity, as even New York rhythm & blues records tended to do. But, perhaps influenced by its movie and TV showbiz environment, L.A. did begin to develop a slick, craftsmanlike recording style later in the Sixties, first with the surf music of the Beach Boys, Jan and Dean, and others, and later with a pack of session players, many of whom had come originally from such country-influenced areas as Arkansas, Texas and Oklahoma (for example, Glen Campbell, Leon Russell and David Gates of Bread).

Lou Adler, a producer/entrepreneur, combined these styles in a version of folk rock that resulted in the hit single "Eve of Destruction" by Barry McGuire and in the Mamas and the Papas, a major group. Essentially, Adler added a very facile pop approach to the rougher-sounding folk rock developed in the East, using strings and horns where appropriate. Los Angeles also produced a more authentic folk-rock style, highlighted by the Buffalo Springfield and the Byrds. The city's synthesis of folk, rock and country approaches with mainstream pop became most prominent in the Seventies, when it contributed country rock (in the form of later incarnations of the Byrds, as well as such bands as the Flying Burrito Brothers), the major impetus to the singer/songwriter movement (including such central figures as Randy Newman, Jackson Browne and the transplanted Canadians Joni Mitchell and Neil Young), and such completely studio-contrived approaches as the Eagles' and Fleetwood Mac's.

Lay Down: As in the expression "to lay down tracks," to record in the studio.

Les Paul Guitar: *See* Gibson.

Lick: A break, riff or short instrumental phrase, usually introduced between melodic phrases. Most commonly used, at least in rock, to refer to guitarists' hot licks.

Liner Notes: Annotation appearing on the sleeve (or liner) of a record.

Lip Synch: *See* Synch.

Live: Recorded in onstage performance *or* recorded in the studio, without an audience, but also without using overdubs—that is, all in one performance, rather than spliced together from several. A live album is almost always of the former set, but "recorded live" may mean either.

Liverpool Sound: This northern English port city produced not only the Beatles but a whole gang of beat groups in the early Sixties (350 of them, according to a 1962 survey). Liverpool groups mostly played Anglicized R&B, as did groups in London, Manchester, Birmingham and elsewhere, but the Liverpool bands generally had a brighter, lighter veneer to their approach. Among the groups that followed the Beatles out of Liverpool were the Searchers, the Merseybeats, Ian and the Zodiacs, the Swinging Blue Jeans, Gerry and the Pacemakers, Billy J. Kramer and the Dakotas, and Cilla Black. The phenomenon, known as Merseybeat (because the Mersey River runs through Liverpool), was a short-lived craze, and by 1965 the Liverpool scene was dead and only the Beatles survived it.

LP: Literally means long-playing. But designates the twelve-inch, 33⅓ rpm album, as opposed to the seven-inch single.

Lyric: 1. The words to be sung with a song. **2.** A short poem or song that expresses the writer's feelings.

Madrigal: Contrapuntal composition for several voices for secular use, from the sixteenth and seventeenth centuries. Instruments in madrigals are used only to double the vocal parts. Some English folk-rock application.

Mandolin: Plucked string instrument, much smaller than a guitar, commonly used in country rock and folk rock as well as their precursors.

Marimba: Large, deeper-toned xylophone, played with soft-headed sticks rather than mallets. Latin American but of African origin.

Master: After music is recorded and mixed, it is then "mastered": that is, a copy is made from which the various reproducing parts (for LP, tape, etc.) can then be created. Because independent producers usually stop at this stage, a purchase of an independently made record is sometimes called a master purchase.

Melisma: A group of notes sung to a single syllable; used commonly in blues and thus brought into play by gospel, R&B and soul singers ever since. Al Green is a notable example of a singer whose style is based on melisma.

Memphis Sound: In the Fifties, thanks to Sam Phillips and Sun Records, Memphis became a key Southern recording center, producing a variety of blues and country recordings and serving as the site (appropriate to its central location) of the Elvis Presley-led rockabilly boom. In 1958, former Sun session bassist Bill Black moved to Hi Records, and the city's second important label was born, recording a similar mix of rhythm & blues and C&W. The next year, Stax, arguably the most important R&B label of the Sixties, was formed.

Memphis had been an important town for black field recording as early as the Twenties, of course. But its real importance stems from these three labels, which gave us, in additon to Presley, Jerry Lee Lewis, Roy Orbison, Charlie Rich, Johnny Cash, Howlin' Wolf, Al Green, Ann Peebles, Sam and Dave, Otis Redding, Rufus and Carla Thomas, Johnnie Taylor, Eddie Floyd, William Bell, Booker T. and the MGs, Isaac Hayes and several others. As a rock and R&B recording center, Memphis ranks with Nashville, L.A. and New York—even some outside soul singers, such as Aretha Franklin and Wilson Pickett, recorded there, thanks to Stax' close association with Atlantic. But since the demise of Stax in the early Seventies, the city has fallen on hard times. Only Hi, under Willie Mitchell's direction, continues to be a factor in contemporary record-making, and that thanks mostly to two artists, Green and Peebles.

Merseybeat: *See* Liverpool Sound.

Miami Sound: Miami's recording business is situated around two studios, Criteria, used for pop, rock and disco productions, and TK, a complex formed by the distributor Henry Stone that concentrates most exclusively on disco and black music. Criteria has been used by many top names—Aretha Franklin, Crosby, Stills and Nash, Dr. John, James Brown, the Bee Gees—while TK focuses on Stone's own roster of acts, the best known being KC and the Sunshine Band and Betty Wright.

Mike: 1. Microphone. **2.** As a verb, "to mike" means to record using a microphone to catch the sound of an amplifier, for instance, rather than sending the electronic signal directly to the tape. (The latter method is called "direct.") In performance, drums are miked—that is, microphones are placed around the kit to ensure that all of the sound reaches the public address system and that a proper balance is achieved. Sometimes it works.

Mix: After a recording is made, the producer and engineer work on balancing the various sounds, playing some up and deemphasizing others; the process is called mixing. It comes into play only on recordings with two or more tracks.

Modal: A system of ordering the notes of a scale, but most often not meaning the conventional European major and minor modes. In modal music (as practiced by many jazz modernists and such rock bands as the Grateful Dead), the kind of scale is linked with its pitch—as opposed to the

Western key system, in which scales are relative and apply at any pitch. After being driven out of European classical forms in the sixteenth century, modal systems survived mostly in folk music until their revival by the free jazz players of the late Fifties and early Sixties.

Mono: Monaural sound—that is, recorded sound which emanates from one source rather than two (which is stereo) or four (quadraphonic).

MOR: Middle of the Road—that is, music that straddles the midstream of pop taste. Applied to rock- or R&B-based music, this is almost always pejorative, implying extreme conservatism and blandness.

Motown: Berry Gordy created Motown records (originally Tamla, a subsidiary that survives, along with several others) in 1960, as a vehicle for his own songs and productions. After Smokey Robinson and the Miracles, the Supremes (with Diana Ross), Marvin Gaye, the Temptations, Mary Wells, the Four Tops and Martha and the Vandellas, among others, produced major Sixties hit records, Motown was established as the country's highest-profile black corporation. Based in Detroit (thus the name), Motown combined the gospel intensity of R&B with a pop surface and teen lyrics that lived up to its motto: The Sound of Young America. Motown's Sixties records are among the best dance and party (not to mention radio) music ever made, as machine-tooled as a Cadillac and just as powerful.

In the Seventies, after Gordy moved the company to Los Angeles and into film production as well as record-making, the company has lost some of its singularity and a great deal of its commerciality. Only Stevie Wonder, Gay and Ross remain from the vaunted Sixties stable of talent, although such new black bands as the Commodores continue the label's tradition of heavy profit-making.

Multitracked: Technique of recording the same vocal or instrumental part more than once (on more than one segment, or track, of the tape) to achieve a breadth of sound not otherwise possible. Guitars and voices are among the most commonly multitracked parts.

Muscle Shoals Sound: This small Alabama town became a recording center in 1961

when Rick Hall, a former Memphis sessionman and songwriter, opened Fame Studios in Florence (which is served by the Muscle Shoals airport). Oddly, the sessionmen who created this fundamental Southern R&B style were almost all white. They include keyboard players Spooner Oldham and Barry Beckett; guitarists Jimmy Johnson, Pete Carr, and for a time, Duane Allman; David Hood on bass and the remarkable Roger Hawkins on drums.

The identity of this rhythm section is less stylized than those in Memphis or New Orleans, though the band's feel for slow ballads tends to be very churchy (e.g., Percy Sledge's "When a Man Loves a Woman"). Among the wide variety of artists who have recorded in Muscle Shoals are Wilson Pickett, Sledge, Aretha Franklin, Bob Seger, Rod Stewart, Arthur Conley, Etta James, Irma Thomas, Ronnie Hawkins, Otis Rush and Cher.

Mute: Any contrivance that reduces the volume of an instrument, or one that modifies its tone; on bowed instruments, a pronged damper placed at the bridge; on horns, an object placed in the bell. Using the soft pedal of a piano or muffling a drum is also in effect a mute.

Nashville Sound: Often called "Music City U.S.A.," Nashville is the principal C&W recording center; only Los Angeles can compete with it. This developed about 1925, when local radio station WSM, with a signal that could be heard throughout the South, began broadcasting the Grand Ole Opry; WSM attracted most of country's major performers to Nashville. But the first record label in Nashville wasn't established until 1945, which coincides with country's rise in the marketplace. By the early Fifties, all of the major labels had offices there.

A distinctive Nashville sound, as a C&W variant, developed in response to the rockabilly pouring out of Memphis and the Southwest. This forced the Nashville sessionmen to adapt, using electric guitars and drums, both previously forbidden. The fiddle and banjo simultaneously declined in use. By the late Fifties, the studio players organized around Chet Atkins had become famous as the most slick and professional in the world. By 1963, Nashville was producing half the recordings made in the United States.

When first Bob Dylan (for *Blonde on Blonde* and *Nashville Skyline*) and then the

Byrds went to Nashville to record in the late Sixties, Nashville also became a pop music center. In response, country productions were splintered into pop and rock factions, the pop too bland and the rock too aggressive to fit in with traditional C&W conceptions. Not until the mid-Seventies, when Waylon Jennings and Willie Nelson inaugurated the so-called outlaw movement, did country rediscover its roots—and then the records were often made outside Nashville. The Seventies country sound involves heavy use of strings as well as steel guitar and extensive application of vocal choruses, so that most country records are more like old-fashioned pop than the pop records of New York and L.A. are.

New Orleans Sound: New Orleans rhythm & blues played a major role in Fifties rock, with such prominent performers as Little Richard and Fats Domino emerging from the city, and many other classics—including some Ray Charles songs—were recorded at Cosimo Matassa's studio.

New Orleans R&B is perhaps rhythm & blues's most stylized form, characterized by a heavily accented rhythm section (which borrows much from the "second line" of the city's jazz style), light piano and horns (often punctuated by baritone sax), and strong lead guitar and vocal. Through the artists above and such others as Ernie K-Doe, Irma Thomas, Robert Parker, Professor Longhair, Frogman Henry, Smiley Lewis, Frankie Ford and Lee Dorsey, New Orleans R&B set a pattern for developments in both soul and rock in the Sixties. But by 1963 the New Orleans scene was finished; both performers and the city's many record labels (Minit, Ace, AFO) had left for California. A healthy studio scene thrived for only a few more years before it too was spent. Today, the only prominent New Orleans R&B players are the Meters, Allen Toussaint and Mac Rebennack, now called Dr. John. Others—notably Lee Dorsey and Professor Longhair—record sporadically.

Newport Festivals: Folk festivals held in July in Newport, Rhode Island, off and on through the Sixties. At the late Fifties through about 1965 festivals, many important folk writer/performers, bluesmen and old-timey rediscoveries were introduced. But the festivals ended after booking hard-rock acts in the late Sixties, which resulted in near riots and an unsavory crowd that upset the wealthy local community. Not to be confused with the Newport Jazz Festival, which continues to be held—in New York.

New Wave: Term adopted by the bands (or applied to them) that arose in the New York and London street scenes in the late Seventies, playing unpolished but highly energetic and emotionally explosive rock. Patti Smith and the Ramones were the key figures in New York, the Sex Pistols and the Clash in London. New Wave represents a return to the emotional (and political) roots of early rock, but not to its technical or musical ones. The term encompasses punk rock, but is not synonymous with it, a principal difference being the degree of collaboration between some New Wave artists and European art-rock stylists (e.g., Talking Heads and Brian Eno).

New York Sound: Major record companies were always based in Manhattan, but in the Forties many new "independent" labels came into being, designed to record specialty music (rhythm & blues, gospel, jazz). By the Fifties, such companies as Atlantic, the longest-lived, had etched out a significant segment of the overall pop marketplace for themselves, with an array of variants on R&B in response to Southern rock. There were group records (the Drifters), solo vocalists (Clyde McPhatter, Ray Charles), doo-wop one-shots (which might include the Drifters but also many lesser-knowns like the Harptones) and even some attempts at white rock (Bobby Darin).

In the Sixties, New York did not develop much of a local rock scene, but R&B recording continued to proliferate, though it was nothing to match the doo-wop street-corner harmony gangs of the Fifties. The Greenwich Village scene did produce the folk revival movement and Bob Dylan (a Minnesota transplant) as well as some early psychedelic bands, such as Blues Project, the Lovin' Spoonful and the Fugs. But this did not constitute a scene with a specific style. Nor did the white rhythm & blues of the Young Rascals, although they spawned many imitators.

In the Seventies, following the New York Dolls, a local scene did develop, known in America as New Wave and in England as punk. Patti Smith, the Ramones, Talking Heads and Television are among its spearheads.

But for the most part, New York recording in the Seventies has been characterized by the development of disco music, which has, in any case, made its greatest technical strides in the studios of Philadelphia, Miami and Munich, Germany.

Noodling: Playing aimlessly.

Novelty: Literally, records that do not conform to any known genre or pattern of past successes. In rock, this term is often given to odd comic efforts, such as Dick Goodman and Bill Buchanan's "Flying Saucer," Sheb Wooley's "Purple People Eater" or Zacherle's "Dinner with Drac."

Off Beat: The beat not accented—in straight 4/4 time, the second and fourth beats. Syncopation is accenting the off beat, giving a sound odd (the term's alternate meaning) to European-trained ears.

Orchestration: Literally, arranging for an orchestra, but in pop, more often meaning an arrangement that includes strings.

Ostinato: Persistently repeated rhythm or figure—ostinato bass is a dominant characteristic in jazz rock, for instance.

Outlaw: The country music, somewhat influenced by rock but more directly traditional, developed by Willie Nelson and Waylon Jennings, among others, in the Seventies. Originally called outlaw because it represented a rebellion against the pop conventions Nashville had created, the music is now (and perhaps more properly) called progressive country, an elastic term that includes some performers (Kris Kristofferson) who are as much rock- and folk-oriented as country, as well as doggedly anti-Nashville, tradition-rooted players like Tompall Glaser and Gary Stewart.

Outtake: A performance left out of a release. This may be an alternate version of a song officially presented, or different material altogether. Sometimes outtakes are released much later, either by a record company exploiting an artist's death, or by a company that no longer has recording rights to the artist.

Overdub: To record over a previously done track—e.g., adding voices to a previously recorded rhythm bed. *See* Dub.

Pastiche: Directly composing in another's style—or sometimes, creating a style by

amassing a variety of elements from a number of sources. A long and fairly honorable mode of creation in rock.

Philadelphia Sound: In the late Fifties and early Sixties, Philadelphia symbolized anti-rock, with its pantheon of teen idols (Fabian, Frankie Avalon, et al.) promoted to Dick Clark's *American Bandstand,* originally broadcast from that city. But the city's large black population always made it an R&B hot spot, and the one prominent local label, Cameo-Parkway, was responsible for some excellent dance records, notably Chubby Checker's series of twist hits.

In the late Sixties, producers Kenneth Gamble and Leon Huff began working with a variety of soul groups (e.g., the Intruders), first on their own Gamble Records and later as staff producers for Atlantic (where they did Wilson Pickett and Archie Bell and the Drells). After making a remarkable series of soul hits with Chicago-based Jerry Butler, Gamble and Huff formed their own company, Philadelphia International Records, and in the Seventies, this has been the stylistic equivalent of Motown in the Sixties, with such enormously popular and imaginative artists as the O'Jays, Harold Melvin and the Blue Notes, Theodore Pendergrass and a number of others. Philadelphia International also became a major production complex, making records for outside artists at the Sigma Sound studios, with a staff of writers and producers much similar to Motown's heyday. The Philly sound is now ornate and heavily rhythmic (everything verges on disco, though it is closer to pop than the Munich-style recordings of Donna Summer, for instance).

Gamble and Huff's only peer in Philadelphia was Thom Bell, whose work with the Delfonics paralleled their early work and whose later records with the Spinners parallels their contemporary productions. But Bell has now relocated in Seattle, though he still sometimes records in Philly.

Pick: A plectrum.

Pick-up: Device on an electric instrument that picks up vibration (usually of a string, sometimes of a reed), converts it to an electrical signal, and transmits it to an amplifier, which reconverts it to a sonic vibration again. Because different pick-ups have different characteristics of resonance, etc., electric guitars especially are often fitted with multiple pick-ups, with a toggle switch allowing the player to suggest which effect he wishes to use.

Plectrum: Device that plucks the strings of an instrument.

Polyrhythm: Several rhythms performed simultaneously, as in bands with several percussionists.

Power Trio: Any blues-based rock played by a trio, usually at excessive length and with leaden rhythm. The approach was popularized by Cream, became a marketplace phenomenon with Grand Funk Railroad, and in between spawned dozens of wooden imitators, most of them among the worst things that happened to rock in the late Sixties and early Seventies.

Prepared Piano: A piano in which various strings are doctored—by damping them or tuning them differently from the rest—for specific tonal effect. Process pioneered by John Cage, sometimes adopted by rock avant-gardists.

Producer: *See* A&R Man.

Progressive Country: *See* Outlaw.

Progressive Rock: Rock oriented to European classical methods, or to technological experimentalism, is sometimes referred to as progressive, though if this be progressive, Little Richard is Mona Lisa. Important progressive rock groups include King Crimson, Roxy Music, Yes, Emerson, Lake and Palmer, and most of the better-known European bands (Focus, Tangerine Dream, etc.).

Psychedelic: *See* Acid Rock.

Pub Rock: Late Sixties-early Seventies English phenomenon in which several interesting, creative rock groups (most notably Ducks Delux and Brinsley Schwarz) played in pubs (English barrooms) because of their lack of success in more established rock venues. While such bands did not have a genuinely common musical base, all were less interested in theatrics and "progressivism" than their big-time British compatriots. Pub rock is one of the seminal forces that later helped create the British arm of New Wave (but not punk).

Punk Rock: 1. In America, in the middle Sixties, the (often amateurish) response to the British Invasion, as performed by grass-roots groups with more desire than skill—typical punk rock of the period included "Psychotic Reaction" by Count Five and "Dirty Water" by the Standells. So-called because the performers were usually aggressive and uncouth. **2.** In England, in the Seventies (somewhat in America, though with less success), music forming the left wing of the New Wave, characterized by relentless guitar attack, abrasive vocals and funkless rhythm. Most Seventies punk is derived from such American bands as the Stooges, MC5 and New York Dolls, who were heir to, but not part of, the first punk movement. Notable punk acts include the Sex Pistols and Clash in the U.K. and the Ramones in America.

Quadraphonic, Quad: Recording system in which sound emanates from four separate channels—usually left front, right front, left rear, right rear. Claimed to produce a more natural, concert hall-style effect, but in reality more artificial than either monaural or stereophonic reproduction.

Race Music: Pre-World War II term for black music, be it jazz, R&B or blues.

R&B: Abbreviation for rhythm & blues.

Reggae: Jamaican music derived from R&B and soul through the variants bluebeat and ska. Characterized by an odd rhythm pattern of false starts and straight-ahead beats, a uniquely mobile bass pattern, and odd guitar and vocal effects, some as smooth as Smokey Robinson, some as raspy as James Brown (the difference is epitomized by hearing Toots and the Maytals back to back with, say, Peter Tosh or the Wailers). There is also often an emphasis in the lyrics on the back-to-Africa millenarianism of the Rastafarians, who belong to a Jamaican religious cult. Because so many Jamaicans live in England, reggae is a kind of pop music there and has been widely adopted by rock superstars (Rolling Stones, Eric Clapton, the Clash), although in America it remains a minor cult style.

Rhythm & Blues: The black popular music of the late Forties and Fifties. Rhythm & blues adapted swing rhythm and horn charts, blues vocal technique and some elements of gospel into a uniquely urban popular music; much of this was later transmitted to rock & roll. Rhythm & blues was regionally stylized (*see* New Orleans Sound, New York Sound, etc.) and intensely emotive but without the high seriousness of purpose that its contemporary jazz idiom, be-bop, displayed. As a result, it was looked down upon by sophisticates, although the continuing vitality of the honking saxophone, the moaning or wailing vocalist and the supercharged rhythm section belies the charges of frivolity originally leveled against it. Rhythm & blues was contemporaneous with rock & roll, and some artists (Fats Domino, for instance) overlap both genres; similarly, there is some overlap with soul, which further heightened the gospel elements (Ray Charles was perhaps the key transitional figure here).

Riff: A repeated musical figure, especially on guitar. Also used as a verb to describe the playing of such figures.

Roadhouse: *See* Juking.

Rockabilly: The country-influenced rock style of the Fifties, as exemplified by Elvis Presley and Buddy Holly. Derived from the juke-joint country music of the South, it was almost exclusively the domain of Southerners, whose knowledge of country string-band instrumentation merged with their exposure to black rhythm concepts. There was pre-Presley rockabilly of a sort—wild, black-influenced country dance music—but it was not quite rock & roll until Elvis emerged. Occasional noises are made about a rockabilly revival, but these are not to be taken seriously until John Fogerty re-forms Creedence Clearwater Revival.

Rock & Roll: Twenty-five years after Elvis Presley first recorded, rock & roll is still without adequate definition. Detractors will claim that innovators they particularly appreciate were actually R&B or country singers, while purists sometimes maintain that it was all over by 1957, but the continuing use of the term demands a more philosophical definition, although stating it precisely is like entering a minefield. Rock & roll isn't just what rock fans, a notoriously eclectic group, say it is, but it also isn't restricted to any particular geographical, ethnic or musicological group; great rock & roll has been made by blacks and whites, Northerners and Southerners, men and women, Americans, Englishmen and Jamaicans, although rarely by Europeans, Latin Americans (*pace* Ritchie Valens), old

men (*pace* Muddy Waters) or TV stars. It is susceptible only to subjective and usually emotional definition, and next time you want to start a bar fight, try to limit it further. We're not pacifists, but we're not idiots either. This will have to serve.

Rock Opera: Concept first introduced by Pete Townshend to explain such extended narrative works as "A Quick One While He's Away" and *Tommy.* But rock opera finally is closer to operetta in both conception and structure, and except for Townshend's work (*Tommy* and *Quadrophenia*), rock operas (e.g., *Jesus Christ Superstar*) are rarely recognizable musically as rock at all.

SG: Guitar—*see* Gibson.

San Francisco Sound: Although it had always provided a hospitable atmosphere to jazz and other bohemian artists, San Francisco did not become a rock center until the mid-Sixties, as a result of the city's also becoming the center of the hippie movement. In late 1966 and early 1967, the burgeoning psychedelic dances at the Fillmore and Avalon ballrooms spewed out an array of talent that included Janis Joplin, the Jefferson Airplane, Grateful Dead, Steve Miller Band (featuring Boz Scaggs), Quicksilver Messenger Service, Country Joe and the Fish, and half a dozen more.

San Francisco rock, however, owed little to the rockabilly of Elvis Presley or the rhythm & blues of urban blacks in the East. Instead, it insisted on eclecticism and experimentalism, taking more of its form and ideology from jazz and folk music than from rock & roll. In this respect, although the bands above were obviously influenced visually and socially by the British beat bands, they can hardly be said to be rock at all (with the exception of Joplin and Miller). Oddly, the Sixties San Francisco figures whose legacy has proved most substantial were not connected to the hippie Fillmore circuit: Sly Stone, a local DJ and record producer (who had worked with Grace Slick before she joined the Airplane and produced some hits for the local Autumn label), revolutionized soul music; Creedence Clearwater Revival, led by John Fogerty, represented what amounted to a rejection of hippie musical values, pounding out a series of concise, energized three-minute singles very much in the rockabilly/R&B tradition. Ironically, all of the surviving San Francisco groups—the Dead and the Airplane, especially—now have abandoned eclectic experimentalism for pop-rock music far more formulaic than Sly's or Creedence's.

Scat Singing: Wordless vocalizing to the melody of a song, often in imitation of a famous jazz solo. Many jazz singers have claimed to be the originators of scat singing (or, more simply, scatting), but the most important scat singers are probably Eddie Jefferson, Louis Armstrong, King Pleasure and the vocal trio Lambert, Hendricks and Ross. Yoko Ono can be called a scat vocalist only at the risk of looking foolish, however.

Schlock: Literally, garbage, trash. But there is good trash and bad trash in rock (and in all pop culture). "96 Tears" is superlative schlock; "Mandy" by Barry Manilow is *mere* schlock.

Score: An arrangement that shows all the various parts each instrument or voice is to play. As a verb, meaning to write such an arrangement.

Session: A recording date.

Sessionman: A musician whose principal or exclusive role is playing at record dates, rather than being a member of an individual performance group. But some groups—e.g., Booker T. and the MGs, the Section—are composed of sessionmen.

Set: A group's concert repertoire on a given night.

78: Seven-inch records that revolve at 78 rpm and that preceded the single and LP of the present. Only the earliest rock appeared originally on 78s, although most blues and jazz and much R&B did.

Side: 1. Used to distinguish one surface of a record from another (on LPs, side one, side two; on 45s, A side, B side). **2.** Also, any record—musicians' argot, mostly dated. **3.** Rarely, an individual band, or track, on an LP.

Singer/Songwriter: A performer who both sings and writes, usually one whose musical base is closer to soft-rock pop or folk music, and who might, if performing in one of these genres, be able to do all of his or her material completely solo—with just an acoustic guitar or piano, for instance. As-

sociated with a confessional variety of personal lyric writing, the classic singer/songwriters include Joni Mitchell, Jackson Browne, James Taylor—but not, say, Pete Townshend, Paul McCartney or other similar writer/performers, because their songs are written so that rock band accompaniment and/or orchestration is implicitly necessary.

Single: Seven-inch record that revolves at 45 rpm and usually contains only one song on each side. *See* 45, EP.

Sitar: Five-foot-long Indian stringed instrument, held similarly to a guitar but usually played sitting down because of its size. About four feet of the instrument consists of a rectangular, fretted neck; the remainder is a bowl-shaped sound box. Sitars may have as many as thirty-five strings, seven main ones playing the melody with the remainder providing accompaniment. Its use in rock was pioneered by Beatle George Harrison in his early Oriental period, and the sitar's association with Indian classical culture made it a necessary adjunct to the more mystically inclined psychedelic bands.

Sit In: Not a demonstration. Sitting in means to play with, usually in the studio, as in "recorded with X sitting in on piano." Or, in an informal jamming situation.

Skiffle: Craze in England, circa 1956-58, contemporaneous with rock 'n' roll and the folk revival movement in the U.S. Skiffle instrumentation was similar to jug-band lineups—washboards proliferated—but with a rhythm inherited from trad or Dixieland jazz. Lonnie Donegan's "Rock Island Line" was the best-known skiffle hit, but the ease with which skiffle bands could be formed (just a guitar, a washboard and some sort of jury-rigged bass sufficed) and the simplicity of playing it made it a performance music for amateurs as well as pros. Indeed, John Lennon's first band, the Quarrymen, was a skiffle group.

Slide Guitar: Guitar played using a bottleneck, metal bar or other device that fits over the finger and is slid across the frets to create a multitonal effect somewhat similar to (and perhaps inspired by) Hawaiian slack key guitar. Common blues device often adapted by rock bands.

Smash: A big hit.

Soft Rock: If this seems a contradiction in terms, you're on the right track. Soft rock is a Seventies creation, some sort of merger between rock and pop that encompasses singer/songwriter music like Jackson Browne's, creative pop writing like Randy Newman's, and pop with a vague rock beat, such as the songs of Elton John or the Bee Gees. But this doesn't mean just ballad singing: Elvis Presley wasn't doing soft rock with "Are You Lonesome Tonight?" although Buddy Holly may have predicted the genre with fluff like "Raining in My Heart."

Soul: In black slang, soul is a quality of heart, of funkiness, an ineffable feeling that some have and others don't, a matter of spirit and sensibility. Musically it is possible to be much more precise: soul developed in the late Fifties out of what had been known as rhythm & blues. The principal differences were ones of technical sophistication, although the original transformation had to do with a willingness to break the taboo against adapting gospel songs to secular contexts.

This wasn't merely a matter of reworking elements of religious style into a pop form—which jazz and blues and R&B in particular had always done. In soul, many hits were simply rewritten gospel numbers: Ray Charles' "What'd I Say," "Hallelujah I Love Her So" and "Lonely Avenue" were erotic rewrites of hymns of praise to God. Also Ben E. King's "Stand By Me," which didn't change even the title of its source song. After Charles' initial adaptations of gospel, a number of gospel singers converted their music to more carnal imagery—most notably Sam Cooke, though nearly every famous soul singer of the Sixties had some church music in his background.

Equally important, however, was the additional sophistication of soul arrangements. The most revolutionary moment, perhaps, came in 1959 with the Drifters' "There Goes My Baby," to which producers Jerry Leiber and Mike Stoller added strings. The result was closer to pop, at least on the surface, than R&B had ever been, but it was really neither. The new sound quickly became "soul," which was adopted from the black jargon. In the studios of Atlantic, Stax and Motown records, among others, the genre became an art form, setting a style for Aretha Franklin, Sam and Dave, Otis Redding, Wilson Pickett and dozens more. In Chicago, Curtis

Mayfield's Impressions and former Impression Jerry Butler were the major artists. Shortly soul was everywhere, although as the list of artists associated with it implies, it was a very elastic term. Not until first Sly Stone, and then Jimi Hendrix, appeared to challenge its conventions did the genre show any sign of flagging, and even then, what has replaced it has done so only slowly.

Space Rock: Any science-fiction-oriented rock, but also (and especially) records such as Pink Floyd's *A Saucerful of Secrets,* which attempt to create a kind of aerospace program music.

Spiritual: Folk song (usually black) of religious orientation. *See* Gospel.

Staccato: Short notes played or sung rapidly.

Stax Sound: *See* Memphis Sound.

Steel Guitar: There are three types of steel guitar: **1.** the Hawaiian steel guitar, which is defined elsewhere; **2.** the pedal steel guitar, which adapted the slack key found in Hawaiian guitar for American country music purposes; **3.** the national steel guitar, which (unlike the other two) is shaped like a regular guitar, is held in the hand rather than floor-mounted, and has a metal resonator, which gives a sound somewhat closer to slide guitar than Hawaiian.

Stratocaster: *See* Fender.

Stride: Jazz piano style, popular from the mid-Thirties to the early Forties, characterized by single bass notes on the first and third beats and chords on the second and fourth. Associated with James P. Johnson, Joe Turner and Pete Johnson, among many others.

String Band: Band composed completely of stringed instruments, though not usually of more than one in the violin/fiddle family: usually, guitar, mandolin, fiddle, banjo and upright bass, although other combinations are conceivable.

Strings: Literally, any stringed instrument (or the strings themselves). More usually, the term refers to violin-family orchestrations on pop records; string arrangements, for instance, don't include guitars, although guitars have strings.

Surf Music: A basically Southern California trend, surf music began with such hits as the 1961 "Stick Shift" by the Duals (there was an overlapping with hot-rod subject matter), which had what later came to be identified as the surf sound: strong, trebly guitar lines and firm rock rhythms. Dick Dale's staccato guitar was actually program music for surfers, designed to simulate the feel of riding the waves.

But Brian Wilson and the Beach Boys made the local phenomenon a national craze. The earlier bands above were instrumental; Wilson grafted their sound to the vocal ideas of Jan and Dean ("Baby Talk," 1959), the other major group of the genre, for a series of classic hits in the pre- and post-Beatle early Sixties. The songs were a tribute to California youth and sun worship, with lyrics that depicted in detail a life of cars, girls, the beach and irresponsibility. There was an utter absence of rebellion, which has led some to claim that surf music made rock & roll safe for middle-class ears. The trend died out in 1966, just as psychedelia, which made older concepts of fun seem frivolous, was about to burst in. History may judge, however, that the earlier frivolity was more substantial than the drug-induced naiveté that succeeded it.

Swamp Rock: Somewhat artificial term applied (notably by producer Jerry Wexler) to rock records such as those of John Fogerty's Creedence Clearwater Revival and the Louisiana country-rock singer Tony Joe White, which sounded down-home in the late Sixties, whether they authentically emerged from the Louisiana bayous (the source of the term) or not. White did, Fogerty didn't, but history will surely judge Fogerty's "artificial" work superior.

Swing: Jazz style evolved by the big bands of the late Twenties and throughout the Thirties, and which became a national dance craze, particularly among teens, in the early Forties. Usually played by very large groups. Trumpets, saxophones, drums and piano are featured quite prominently (other instruments are used mostly for rhythm and ensemble passages). The groups often improvised upon standards, although such composers as Duke Ellington, Count Basie and Fletcher Henderson created a considerable body of original swing tunes (many of which now qualify as standards).

The fad died out after World War II, and the advent of be-bop did much to further erode swing's base. But the term survives as an ultimate accolade for playing that is free, natural and rhythmically soulful, as in "Charlie Watts makes the Rolling Stones swing," or "Led Zeppelin's problem is that it just doesn't swing."

Synch: To mime the words of a song—usually on a TV show, sometimes in films—to a prerecorded track.

Take: In the studio, one performance of a song. Takes are numbered consecutively, so that a first take is the initial time a song is played through; second take, third take, etc., represent successive attempts to get it right.

Tape Loop: Literally, a loop of tape constructed so that it repeats endlessly. Used for various effects, including lengthening disco songs by extending instrumental breaks.

Telecaster: *See* Fender.

Tenor: Usually, saying someone is on tenor means he is playing tenor saxophone (as opposed to the other saxes—alto, soprano and baritone). Sometimes, but rarely, it refers to the natural upper male vocal range.

Tex-Mex Sound: Applied to Latin-inflected rock and country styles developed in Texas, near Mexican border regions. Buddy Holly's music has sometimes been included, although it displays very little Latin influence. Sir Douglas (Doug Sahm) is more aptly characterized in this way, as is the Chicano country singer Freddy Fender. Many minor artists throughout the Southwest have some Tex-Mex influences.

Theremin: Upright electronic instrument that produces tones based on the movement of the human hand around it. Developed in Russia in the Twenties and enjoyed occasional use among Sixties psychedelic bands, who liked toying with its one-note, five-octave range and various colorations.

Tin Pan Alley: Old-time music publishers. By extension, the pre-rock music industry itself.

Trad Jazz: British term for traditional New Orleans jazz, or its corruption (the latter is called Dixieland in the U.S.).

Played by relatively small groups, patterned after the World War I New Orleans groups of King Oliver, etc. Trad jazz bands led by Chris Barber, Ken Colyer, Mick Mullian and others contributed such figures as Alexis Korner and Lonnie Donegan to the early British skiffle and R&B scene. It was associated with bohemian culture and left politics, but the rise of British rock was also a reaction to its purism, and to the fact that, with the success of Acker Bilk, Colyer's saxophonist, the genre had merged with the pop mainstream.

Trades: The three music-industry magazines (*Cash Box, Billboard* and *Record World*) that publish the charts of record sales and airplay popularity. Also applied to various tip sheets for radio programmers, designed to spotlight future hits. *See* Charts.

Tremolo: Rapid fluctuation in volume (sometimes, misapplied to mean rapid fluctuation in pitch—but that is really vibrato). Some electric guitars come equipped with a tremolo bar, a lever that can be activated to produce the effect.

Trill: Rapid alternation, vocally or instrumentally, between the note and the note above it.

Twelve-String Guitar: Guitar with twelve, rather than the usual six, strings. Each pair is tuned an octave apart, which produces a full, ringing effect. Leadbelly was the first to promote the use of the instrument, which has been used in rock bands only occasionally—most successfully by Roger (né Jim) McGuinn of the Byrds, on the group's early folk-rock records.

Upbeat: (From the motion of the symphonic conductor's baton) The beat preceding the main, or accented beat. *See* Downbeat.

Vamp: Improvised instrumental accompaniment or introduction.

Wall of Sound: Pop production style, devised by Phil Spector, in which the individual articulation of each instrument is deliberately obscured to create a massed effect.

Western Swing: Country music influenced by jazz, as played by Texas-Oklahoma string bands of the Thirties through the Fifties. Under the influence of Bob Wills and some others, such groups added horn sections and created what is also known as hillbilly jazz. Most groups had fiddlers, steel guitarists, horns, regular guitarists, voices, banjos and upright bass. In addition to traditional fiddle music, the Western swing repertoire encompassed jazz and pop standards and even some blues. This was of course primarily dance music, and it enjoyed wide popularity throughout the Southwest. The genre had a wide influence on country music in general, opening it to newer sources of inspiration, although today few groups (the exceptions are the remnants of Wills' Texas Playboys and the country-rock band Asleep at the Wheel) actually play it.

Selected Bibliography

The Age of Rock: Sounds of the American Cultural Revolution, Vols. 1 and 2, edited by Jonathan Eisen (Random House, 1969, 1970; pbk., Vintage)
Separating the wheat from the chaff here is arduous, but there are thoughtful, provocative essays in each of these books. Much of it is simply schoolboy silly, of course, but something like Tom Smucker's "The Politics of Rock" in Volume 2 or Jon Landau's Motown essay in the first book is worth the strain.

Any Old Way You Choose It: Rock and Other Pop Music, 1967-1973 by Robert Christgau (Penguin Books, 1973)
The *Newsday, Esquire* and *Village Voice* critic with a wide range of essays on the whole spectrum of rock and soul. Christgau is sometimes wrong-headed (at Monterey, Jimi Hendrix was *unimpressive?*), sometimes prophetic (Christgau was on to Al Green before anybody else, even his record company), but he is always—*always*—provocative.

Apple to the Core by Peter McCabe and Robert D. Schonfield (Pocket Books, 1976)
Nice job of reporting on the rise and fall of Apple, and (necessarily) the disintegration of the Beatles. One of the better inside jobs on the music business.

The Beach Boys and the California Myth by David Leaf (Grosset & Dunlap, 1978; pbk., Today Press, 1978)
Scarifying history of Brian Wilson as Hollywood pop music savant, and his psychological destruction at the hands of family, friends and the local pill pushers. The California myth is conspicuous in its absence. Fantastic photographs and other graphics, including posters of early gigs.

Well reported, acceptably written, but the perspective is definitly not for skeptics.

The Beatles: An Illustrated Record by Roy Carr and Tony Tyler (Harmony, 1978)
Slick presentation seems to have been done mostly for the graphics, which are great. But Carr is perhaps the most reliable journalist on any of the British music weeklies, and his long-time familiarity with the scene and access to information gives the book a sharp sense of detail.

The Beatles: The Authorized Biography, rev. ed., by Hunter Davies (McGraw-Hill, 1978)
The basic facts, with a great deal of fudging about their sex lives, money—even their art. Unsatisfying because it's so cleaned up, but still more detailed than anything else available.

Black Music by Imamu Amiri Baraka (LeRoi Jones) (Morrow, 1967)
Sequel to *Blues People,* but by now the insight has been heavily altered by what's becoming doctrinaire ideology.

Black Music of Two Worlds by John Storm Roberts (Morrow, 1974)
A classic musicological/sociological analysis of black music, in black nations (Africa, the Caribbean) and white (principally England and America). Scholarly but definitely readable, this little-known work is actually one of the best publications about popular music of this decade.

Blues People: Negro Music in White America by Imamu Amiri Baraka (LeRoi Jones) (Morrow, 1963)
Provocative essays on jazz in the early Sixties by the poet/dramatist who has since

become an ideological musician of a sort himself.

Catalyst: The Sun Records Story by Colin Escott and Martin Hawkins (Aquarius Books, 1975)

Available only in England, this survey of the company that produced Elvis Presley, Jerry Lee Lewis, Carl Perkins, Roy Orbison, Charlie Rich and Johnny Cash (among others) isn't as well written as it ought to be, but it does have all the facts and is well organized.

Chicago Breakdown by Mike Rowe (Drake, 1975)

Exhaustive chronicle of Chicago blues scene contains definitive commentary on each of the city's blues record companies, no matter how obscure, and interviews with many of the great and minor players in the scene. It also has some of the most arresting illustrations available in any music book: how about the second Sonny Boy Williamson's death certificate, in which cause of death is listed as "murder." Out of print.

Clive: Inside the Record Business by Clive Davis and James Willwerth (Morrow, 1975; pbk., Ballantine, 1976)

Egocentric though this may be, it's also an instructive example of how the record business worked from the mid-Sixties until about 1972, as the independent labels were absorbed by conglomerates and business continued to boom without a new Beatles. Although much of it merely represents conventional corporate wisdom, such information has rarely been presented in such readable fashion.

Conversations with Eric Clapton by Steve Turner (Abacus, 1976)

Good question-and-answer session with Clapton on his career and heroin addiction and treatment. Not printed in the United States.

Country Music, U.S.A.: A Fifty-Year History by Bill C. Malone (University of Texas Press, 1968; pbk., University of Texas Press, 1971)

First-rate study of the genre.

Country Music: White Man's Blues by John Grissim (Paperback Library, 1970)

A good survey of Nashville circa the turn of the decade. Waylon Jennings and Willie Nelson, among others, have seen to it that this one is now seriously dated, however.

Country: The Biggest Music in America by Nick Tosches (Stein & Day, 1977)

Not for facts but for fun. Tosches is one of the most hilarious writers who has ever commented on American pop, and one of the most salacious: his material on Jerry Lee Lewis alone is enough scare off the faint-hearted. But beneath his eccentricity, Tosches has tapped into a stream of perversity and psychic sickness that must be one of the sources of country's continuing vitality. Breaks every one of Nashville's social taboos, with as much panache as Presley and Lewis did its musical ones.

A Decade of the "Who": An Authorized History in Music, Paintings, Words and Photographs by Peter Townshend (Omnibus/Music Sales, 1977)

Except for a lovely piece by Steve Turner about Pete Meaden, the group's first manager, this is overpriced (at $9.95) and under-annotated. Pete Townshend's few comments about his songs are mostly for guitarists only, and the graphics were dated before publication.

The Deejays by Arnold Passman (Macmillian, 1971)

This survey of disc jockeys spends too much time on the development of radio from a diverse medium into a platter-spinning one, but has some decent information on Alan Freed, Dick Clark, Tom Donahue and other key rock figures. Out of print.

Diary of a Rock and Roll Star by Ian Hunter (Panther, 1974)

Mott the Hoople's lead singer kept this journal on a 1972 tour of America, right after the group scored its only hit, "All the Young Dudes." His fascination with his own success can't keep away the seeds of doubt about its permanence. This is stardom, anyway, without champagne and first-class suites. Instead, you get bus rides, missed airplane connections, mangled sound systems and the real-life grief. Not printed in the United States.

The Drifters by Bill Millar (Collier Books/ Macmillan, 1972)

Really, this is a history of rhythm & blues in the Fifties by a fanatic Englishman who writes more passionately than well. Analysis of the music is only so-so, but the depth of knowledge of the genre is thorough.

Bob Dylan: An Intimate Biography by Anthony Scaduto (Grosset & Dunlap, 1971; pbk., Signet Books/New American Library, 1973)
There's a wealth of information on Dylan's early years here, and a decent interview with the post-*John Wesley Harding* Dylan at the end. But the middle years of the man's improbable career—when he made his greatest music on albums like *Blonde on Blonde*—are unaccountably skimpy, tossed off in a few pages. Flawed but essential for an understanding of one of rock's key figures.

Bob Dylan: A Retrospective, edited by Craig McGregor (Morrow, 1972)
Good selection of writing about Dylan. Includes Paul Nelson on Newport '65, Nat Hentoff's *Playboy* interview, Jon Landau on *John Wesley Harding* and Robert Christgau's *Tarantula* essay.

Elvis by Jerry Hopkins (Simon & Schuster, 1971; pbk., Warner Books, 1972)
This could use an update, but it's still the best biography of the King of Rock & Roll. No big revelations, but a good job of reporting and a smoothly written text as well.

Elvis: What Happened? by Red West, Sonny West and Dave Hebler, as told to Steve Dunleavy (Ballantine, 1977)
Purportedly the inside story as told by his bodyguards. You couldn't call this book reliable, but it opened the door to aspects of Preseley's life that no one else had the courage to do. The fact that he died only a few days after its publication makes it more fascinating. (He'd read it.) To be enjoyed, but not trusted.

The Encyclopedia of Folk, Country and Western Music by Irwin Stambler and Grelun Landon (St. Martin's Press, 1969)
Nicely presented survey of country and folk performers. The biographies often seem written by a record-company publicist (which is Landon's job), but there is a wealth of information here (especially on country performers) that is difficult to find anywhere else. Out of print.

The Encyclopedia of Rock and Roll, Vols. 1-3, edited by Phil Hardy and Dave Laing (Panther, 1976)
An excellent staff, including critics Greil Marcus, Charlie Gillett and Simon Frith, assembled this lengthy collection of short, fact-crammed essays on notable and obscure figures and styles of the past two decades. Especially strong on British rock and its roots. Not available in the United States.

Feel Like Going Home: Portraits in Blues and Rock 'n' Roll by Peter Guralnick (Fusin Book/Sunrise Book/Dutton, 1971)
Meticulous profiles of key figures in blues and rock and roll, including Muddy Waters, Howlin' Wolf, Jerry Lee Lewis and Charlie Rich. The essay on Rich is one of the best insights into the middle-level star's failures and delusions available anywhere.

The Festival Song Book, photographs by David Gahr, text by Paul Nelson and Tony Glover (Music Sales, 1974)
Gahr was the chief photographic chronicler of the folk revival, Nelson the most astute critic it developed, Glover a fringe figure as both critic and musician (one-third of Koerner, Ray and Glover). The pictures are solid; the Nelson piece is as intense as all his best writing, exploring the rock/folk festival as a social phenomenon that didn't quite work out; and Glover's "Addendum" is nothing less than hilarious in his best deadpan manner. There's also a collection of songs in the back, in case you need something to sing while you're looking at the pictures. Out of print.

The Gospel Sound: Good News and Bad Times by Tony Heilbut (Simon & Schuster, 1971)
Wonderful study of gospel in this century, with massive biographical detail on important performers and composers. Marred only by a rather hysterical anti-pop attitude, this is a definitive study of a neglected genre.

Hardening Rock by Bruce Chipman (Little, Brown, 1972)
Mostly a photo book, but what pictures! Odd, unlikely shots, not so much of rock stars—though there are enough of those— but of the whole panoply of teen culture from the Fifties through the early Seventies. The bulk of the text consists of song lyrics, from something as dumb as "Norman" to something as profound as "Who Do You Love"; those two happen to be back to back, the kind of juxtaposition that makes this volume (now out of print) one of the few photo books to capture the energy of rock.

Buddy Holly by Dave Laing (Collier Books/Macmillan, 1972)
Not as well researched as Jon Goldrosen's book, but in some ways a more interesting artistic analysis.

Buddy Holly: His Life and Music by Jon Goldrosen (Bowling Green University Press, 1975; pbk., Quick Fox/Music Sales, 1979)
Excellent study of the Fifties star, much initimate detail and a fine analysis of the records. Avoids some of the dead-rock-star hagiography of other Holly writing.

Honkers and Shouters: The Golden Years of Rhythm and Blues by Arnold Shaw (Macmillan, 1978; pbk., Collier Books/ Macmillan, 1978)
Shaw has some trouble getting his facts straight, and his analysis of rock & roll is incredibly wrongheaded, but his biographies of blues, R&B and related performers and his interviews with a great many of the business and associated figures makes this 600-odd-page volume indispensable.

The Illustrated Elvis Presley by W. A. Harbinson (Today Press/Madison Square Press/Grosset & Dunlap, 1976)
Originally published by the British Presley fan club, this is much more noteworthy for its excellent photos than for its somewhat fawning, poorly written text. Still, one of the better Elvis efforts.

The Illustrated Encyclopedia of Rock by Nick Logan and Bob Woffinden of New Musical Express (Harmony, 1977)
This is a comprehensive volume, but it is full of errors. Stronger on British artists; includes lots of obscure ones. Good discographies.

It's Too Late to Stop Now: A Rock & Roll Journal by Jon Landau (Straight Arrow, 1972; pbk., Simon & Schuster, 1972)
Fine selection of pieces by one of rock's premier critics (now a well-regarded record producer). Landau was almost single-handedly responsible for transplanting the ideas of auteur film criticism to rock, and if the merger was ultimately doomed, it was nonetheless audacious. The concluding essays, especially the title piece and "Confessions of an Aging Rock Critic," are good theoretically, but it is Landau's writing on Otis Redding, Bob Dylan and other artists that holds up best.

The Jefferson Airplane and the San Francisco Sound by Ralph J. Gleason (Ballantine, 1969)
Gleason loved rock, but his most interesting insights were about almost every other kind of American music. The book includes Gleason's journalism on the early San Francisco dance concerts, and the freshness of the moment still jumps off the page. Out of print.

Lennon Remembers: The Rolling Stone Interviews by Jann Wenner (Popular Library, 1971)
These are the famous interviews in which Lennon denounced the Beatles (after first signifying that they were indeed all through with one another), and began his short-lived espousal of primal therapy and radical politics. One of the most soul-searching question-and-answer sessions in the history of journalism.

The Making of Superstars: The Artists and Executives of the Rock Music World by Robert Stephen Spitz (Anchor Press/ Doubleday, 1978)
Interviews with a host of music-business personalities. Often loses focus, but is worthwhile if only for agent Frank Barsalona's wonderful anecdote about his first encounter with the Who.

Making Tracks by Charlie Gillett (Sunrise Books/Dutton, 1974)
Excellent history of Atlantic Records. Traces the rise of an independent label and its stars and executives from obscurity to prominence and absorption by a multimedia conglomerate (in this case, Warner Communications). Gillett also uses the Atlantic story to delve into the history of the independent label boom of the Fifties, which had so much to do with creating rock & roll and blues. An interesting sequel to *The Sound of the City.* Out of print.

Midnight Special: The Legend of Leadbelly by Richard M. Garvin and Edmond G. Addeo (Bernard Geis, 1971)
Good biography of the Texas twelve-string guitarist, felon and songster.

Mystery Train: Images of America in Rock 'n' Roll Music by Greil Marcus (Dutton, 1976)
A superb study of rock—beginning actually with the country blues of Robert Johnson—this concludes with the definitive piece on Elvis, "Presliad," after cogent dis-

cussions of Sly Stone, Randy Newman and the Band. A work of scholarship and passion, *Mystery Train* is the first book to fit rock into the currents of traditional American culture and thought.

A New Dictionary of Music by Arthur Jacobs (Penguin, 1958)
Fine guide to terms and styles, written from a classical music vantage point. Not much pop or rock argot, unfortunately, but as ultimately indispensable for a critic as a rhyming dictionary is for a songwriter.

1988: The New Wave Punk Rock Explosion by Caroline Coon (Hawthorn, 1978)
The best yet on the scene that turned rock around in the past couple of years. The bug-eyed shot of Johnny Rotten on the cover says it all—or so you think until you get inside. Remarkable illustrations, good writing and an insider's analysis.

Out of His Head: The Sound of Phil Spector by Richard Williams (Dutton, 1972)
Not the best thing ever written about Spector—the nod goes to Nik Cohn's essays on him—but certainly the most comprehensive. Biographically well-informed, an excellent discography (which could use an update now), breezily written, and an analysis that, while it lacks Cohn's accurate outrage, is still substantial. Out of print.

Record Hits: The British Top Fifty by Clive Solomon (Omnibus, 1977)
Every British Top Fifty hit from 1954 to 1976, listed by artist and cross-referenced by title. A necessary supplement to Joel Whitburn's *Record Research*. Not printed in the United States.

Revolt into Style by George Melly (Anchor Books/Doubleday, 1971)
Mod and its commercialization, and the way of all such things in modern Britain. Good insight into what set up the conditions for the English rock boom. Out of print.

Rock Almanac: Top Twenty American and British Singles and Albums of the Fifties, Sixties, and Seventies, edited by Stephen Nugent and Charlie Gillett (Anchor Books/Doubleday, 1978)
This is an attempt to create an American equivalent of the British *Rock File* series. But it was published four years after it was compiled. Finally the comparisons of British and American Top Twenty charts are only a curiosity, and the book's greatest value is Paul Gambaccini's essay on British and American pop radio practices.

Rock and Roll Will Stand, edited by Greil Marcus (Beacon, 1969)
Late-Sixties collection of San Francisco Area rock writing, not enough of it by Marcus, is dated but engaging as one of the saner tomes of that deranged place and time. Out of print.

Rock File, Vols. 1, 2, 3, and 4, edited by Charlie Gillett and (for Vols. 2 and 4) Simon Frith (Panther, 1972, 1974, 1975, 1976)
Interesting attempt to provide a kind of hipster's yearbook to the British music scene. (*Rock Almanac* is a disastrous attempt to do the same for the States.) Much information on and discussion of British record charts, and some good essays as well. Not printed in the United States.

Rock Folk by Michael Lydon (Dial, 1971; Delta Books/Dell, 1973)
Good set of profiles of music figures, black and white. Sometimes gets a bit arch, but generally well-reported.

Rock from the Beginning by Nik Cohn (Stein & Day, 1969)
The best-written, wittiest rock history. Must be taken as frivolously as it's intended—unlike Gillett's scholarship, which won him a master's degree from Columbia University, Cohn's is entirely of the street. So if he thinks that Bob Dylan is fairly useless and that the Rolling Stones should have died in a plane crash at thirty, that's just part of the sport. This has the rhythm, the energy and the commitment of the music itself.

Rock On: The Illustrated Encyclopedia of Rock 'n' Roll, Vols. 1 and 2, by Norm N. Nite (Crowell, 1974; Vol. 2, pbk., Popular Library, 1977)
The bare facts, poorly written and without any sense of artistic or commercial proportion. A botched job.

The Rolling Stone Illustrated History of Rock & Roll, edited by Jim Miller (Rolling Stone Press/Random House, 1976)
The best-looking, best-edited study of the music. Fantastic pictures, excellent writing. All that mars it are omissions. Fine discographies, as well.

The Rolling Stone Interviews, Vol. 1 (Paperback Library, 1971) and Vol. 2 (Warner Books, 1973)
The best of *Rolling Stone,* in a way, has always been its detailed question-and-answer sessions with important rock creators. Volume 1 is the better of these two—if only for Jann Wenner's seminal discussion with Pete Townshend, in which the Who guitarist first sketched out the concept for *Tommy*—but both have a storehouse of facts and memorabilia.

The Rolling Stone Record Review, Vols. 1 and 2 (Pocket Books, 1971, 1974)
Haphazard selection of old *Rolling Stone* reviews, interesting more as curios of the late Sixties and early Seventies than as criticism. Though there is very good work here—especially the sections on rock oldies in Volume 1, which is now out of print.

The Rolling Stone Rock and Roll Reader, edited by Ben Fong-Torres (Bantam, 1974)
An ambitious sampler of *Rolling Stone* news items, feature profiles and reportage from the first eight years. The selection has more to do with what was good about rock than what was essential about *Rolling Stone,* so that some pieces of little literary merit are included. Still, mostly readable and in its way a nice history of a specific rock era. Out of print.

The Rolling Stones: An Unauthorized Biography in Words, Photographs and Music, edited by David Dalton (Amesco, 1972)
Fine selection of critical pieces, reportage, the standard photos and most of the group's songs in piano arrangement. Out of print.

The Rolling Stones: Our Own Story, rev. ed., as told to Pete Goodman (Bantam, 1970)
Even better than Brian Epstein's *Cellarful of Noise,* possibly because the Stones weren't so overprotective of their image. Cheap, exploitative and inaccurate—a wonderful testimony to the sense of humor of a great rock band. Out of print.

Roxon's Rock Encyclopedia, revised by Ed Naha (Universal Library/Grosset & Dunlap, 1978)
Lillian Roxon, the Australian journalist who first compiled this tome, had enough verve to make what was never much more

than a rewrite of record-company biographies (with all the attendant inaccuracies) seem essential or at least fun. Naha, a better writer, is too smart-alecky for his own good, and his revision curdles Roxon's innocence into naiveté of the cynical.

The Sociology of Rock by Simon Frith (Constable, 1978)
A provocative study by a leftist college professor who is arguably one of the three best rock critics England has produced (the others are Nik Cohn and either Charlie Gillett or Richard Williams). The analysis is more pertinent to Britain than America, at least in terms of detail, but if a revised American edition is published (as seems likely), this will stand as the best on the relationship of rock to contemporary youth and big business. Not available in the United States.

Song and Dance Man: The Art of Bob Dylan by Michael Gray (Dutton, 1972)
Heavy literary textual analysis of Bob Dylan's songs. Said to be readable by those who can get through such things. Out of print.

The Soul Book by Ian Hoare et al., edited by Simon Frith (Delta/Dell, 1976)
Good selection of critical historical essays on soul movements and genres, although somewhat odd to American eyes and ears, because it is written by white Englishmen (with one exception). Intelligent, if sometimes naive.

The Sound of Philadelphia by Tony Commings (Methuen, 1975)
Typically, the only full-length study of Philly soul, from Chubby Checker to the O'Jays, has never been published in the United States. Commings is one of the best soul critics in the U.K., and the text is well informed, although marred by hyperbole. Good photos. Not available in the United States.

The Sound of the City: The Rise of Rock and Roll by Charlie Gillett (Outerbridge & Dienstrey/Dutton, 1970)
The most thorough and scholarly history of the music, although far from the breeziest read. Gillett is fantastic on detail—his analysis of various regional styles, his assessment of minor artists are, if not invariably incontestable, a treasure trove of data. And *The Sound of the City* provides

the most straightforward exposition of early rock 'n' roll as the creation of independent entrepeneurs looking for chinks in the armor of major corporations. Out of print.

Star-Making Machinery: The Odyssey of an Album by Geoffrey Stokes (Bobbs-Merrill, 1976)
The best study of the American music industry and how it works. Stokes spent several months studying Commander Cody and His Lost Planet Airmen as they made an album and watched it fail in the marketplace. Stokes sees the musician essentially as a worker for giant media corporations, powerless, in the end, to do much to affect the sale of his work—a proposition his reporting makes utterly convincing.

The Story of Rock, 2nd ed., by Carl Belz (Oxford University Press, 1972; pbk., Colophon Books/Harper & Row, 1972)
Overrated middlebrow history.

S.T.P.: A Journey through America with the Rolling Stones by Robert Greenfield (Dutton, 1974)
Greenfield covered the 1972 Stones tour of the States for *Rolling Stone*, but his book is better than his dispatches. Perhaps the best tome on the perils of stardom, especially for nonstars who get too close. Out of print.

Twilight of the Gods: The Beatles in Retrospect by Wilfred Mellers (Viking Press, 1974)
A musicologist defends the Beatles. Unnecessary as hell, but twice that funny.

Urban Blues by Charles Keil (University of Chicago Press, 1966)
With the exception of Rowe, Keil has done the best survey of urban black music as it developed out of rural resources. A fundamental study that has dated very little.

What's That Sound? The Contemporary Music Scene from the Pages of Rolling Stone, edited by Ben Fong-Torres (Rolling Stone Press/Anchor Books/Doubleday, 1976)
Good selection of *Rolling Stone* features, smartly written, smartly chosen.